A Clinical Introduction to Psychosis

A Clinical Introduction to Psychosis

Foundations for Clinical Psychologists and Neuropsychologists

Edited by

Johanna C. Badcock

Georgie Paulik

ELSEVIER

ACADEMIC PRESS

An imprint of Elsevier

Academic Press is an imprint of Elsevier
125 London Wall, London EC2Y 5AS, United Kingdom
525 B Street, Suite 1650, San Diego, CA 92101, United States
50 Hampshire Street, 5th Floor, Cambridge, MA 02139, United States
The Boulevard, Langford Lane, Kidlington, Oxford OX5 1GB, United Kingdom

Library of Congress Cataloging-in-Publication Data
A catalog record for this book is available from the Library of Congress

British Library Cataloguing-in-Publication Data
A catalogue record for this book is available from the British Library

ISBN 978-0-12-815012-2

For information on all Academic Press publications visit our website at https://www.elsevier.com/books-and-journals

Publisher: Nikki Levy
Acquisition Editor: Nikki Levy
Editorial Project Manager: Timothy Bennett
Production Project Manager: Bharatwaj Varatharajan
Cover Designer: Christian J. Bilbow

Typeset by SPi Global, India

Dedication

For David, Ben, and Anna (JCB).

For Rohan, Ruby, and Hector (GP).

Contents

Section 5 • New Directions in Research and Practice

Contributors

Mario Alvarez-Jimenez Centre for Youth Mental Health, University of Melbourne, Melbourne; Orygen, The National Centre of Excellence in Youth Mental Health, Parkville, VIC, Australia

Lisa Andermann Mount Sinai Hospital; Equity, Gender and Populations Division, Department of Psychiatry, University of Toronto, Toronto, ON, Canada

Alexandra Andrea Department of Psychology, University of Maryland, College Park, MD, United States

Johanna C. Badcock School of Psychological Science, University of Western Australia, Crawley, WA, Australia

Amanda L. Baker School of Medicine and Public Health, University of Newcastle, Newcastle, NSW, Australia

Vaughan Bell Psychological Interventions Clinic for Outpatients with Psychosis, South London and Maudsley NHS Foundation Trust; Research Department of Clinical, Educational and Health Psychology, University College London, London, United Kingdom

Imogen H. Bell Centre for Mental Health, School of Health Sciences, Swinburne University of Technology, Hawthorn; Alfred Health, Melbourne, VIC, Australia

Katherine Berry Division of Psychology and Mental Health, School of Health Sciences, University of Manchester; Greater Manchester Mental Health Foundation Trust, Manchester Academic Health Sciences Centre, Manchester, United Kingdom

Jone Bjornestad Department of Social Studies, Faculty of Social Sciences, University of Stavanger, Stavanger, Norway

Jack J. Blanchard Department of Psychology, University of Maryland, College Park, MD, United States

Alex S. Cohen Department of Psychology, Louisiana State University, Baton Rouge, LA, United States

Patrick W. Corrigan Illinois Institute of Technology, Lewis College of Human Sciences, Chicago, IL, United States

Jan Cosgrave Perelman School of Medicine, University of Pennsylvania, Philadelphia, PA; Nuffield Department of Clinical Neurosciences, Sleep and Circadian Neuroscience Institute, University of Oxford, Oxford; Department of Clinical, Educational and Health Psychology, University College London, London, United Kingdom

Clair de la Lune Western Australia, Australia

Alexandra M.J. Denham School of Medicine and Public Health, University of Newcastle, Newcastle, NSW, Australia

Lyn Ellett Department of Psychology, Royal Holloway University of London, Egham, United Kingdom

Brita Elvevåg Department of Clinical Medicine, UiT The Arctic University of Norway; Norwegian Centre for eHealth Research, University Hospital of North Norway, Tromsø, Norway

Taylor L. Fedechko Department of Psychology, Louisiana State University, Baton Rouge, LA, United States

Hamish Fibbins Keeping the Body in Mind Program, South Eastern Sydney Local Health District; School of Psychiatry, University of New South Wales, Sydney, NSW, Australia

Joseph Firth NICM Health Research Institute, University of Western Sydney, Sydney, NSW; Centre for Youth Mental Health, University of Melbourne, Melbourne, VIC, Australia; Division of Psychology and Mental Health, University of Manchester, Manchester, United Kingdom

Kenneth P. Fung Equity, Gender and Populations Division, Department of Psychiatry, University of Toronto; Toronto Western Hospital, Toronto, ON, Canada

Philippa Anne Garety Department of Psychology, King's College London, Institute of Psychiatry, Psychology & Neuroscience; South London and Maudsley NHS Foundation Trust, London, United Kingdom

Jesse Gates Orygen, The National Centre of Excellence in Youth Mental Health, Parkville; La Trobe University, Melbourne, VIC, Australia

Philip Gehrman Perelman School of Medicine, University of Pennsylvania, Philadelphia, PA, United States

Evie Glasshouse School of Psychology and Exercise Science, Murdoch University, Murdoch, WA, Australia

César González-Blanch University Hospital Marqués de Valdecilla-IDIVAL, Santander, Spain

Gillian Haddock Division of Psychology and Mental Health, School of Health Sciences, University of Manchester; Greater Manchester Mental Health Foundation Trust, Manchester Academic Health Sciences Centre, Manchester, United Kingdom

Jay A. Hamm Eskenazi Health Midtown Community Mental Health, Indianapolis; Purdue University, College of Pharmacy, West Lafayette, IN, United States

Amy Hardy Department of Psychology, Institute of Psychiatry, Psychology and Neuroscience, King's College London; South London and Maudsley NHS Foundation Trust, London, United Kingdom

Anthony Harris Discipline of Psychiatry, Sydney Medical School, University of Sydney; Brain Dynamics Centre, The Westmead Institute for Medical Research, Sydney, NSW, Australia

Mark Hayward University of Sussex, Brighton; Sussex Partnership NHS Foundation Trust, Worthing, United Kingdom

Terje B. Holmlund Department of Clinical Medicine, UiT The Arctic University of Norway, Tromsø, Norway

Clara S. Humpston Institute of Psychiatry, Psychology and Neuroscience, King's College London, London, United Kingdom

Megan Ichinose Department of Psychology, Vanderbilt University, Nashville, TN, United States

Louise Isham Oxford Cognitive Approaches to Psychosis (O-CAP), University of Oxford; Oxford Cognitive Therapy Centre, Oxford Health NHS Foundation Trust, Oxford, United Kingdom

Srividya N. Iyer Department of Psychiatry; Division of Social & Transcultural Psychiatry, McGill University; Prevention and Early Intervention Program for Psychosis, Douglas Mental Health University Institute; ACCESS Open Minds (Pan-Canadian Youth Mental Health Research Network), Montreal, QC; Frayme, Youth Mental Health-Focused Knowledge Translation Network, Ottawa, ON, Canada

Henry J. Jackson School of Psychological Sciences, University of Melbourne, Melbourne, VIC, Australia

G. Eric Jarvis Department of Psychiatry; Division of Social & Transcultural Psychiatry, McGill University; Cultural Consultation Service & Culture and Mental Health Research Unit of the Jewish General Hospital, Montreal, QC, Canada

Louise Johns Oxford Health NHS Foundation Trust; Department of Psychiatry, University of Oxford, Oxford, United Kingdom

Rebecca Kelly Psychological Interventions Clinic for Outpatients with Psychosis, South London and Maudsley NHS Foundation Trust, London, United Kingdom

Eóin Killackey Orygen, The National Centre of Excellence in Youth Mental Health, Parkville; Centre for Youth Mental Health, The University of Melbourne, Melbourne, VIC, Australia

Jessica Kingston Department of Psychology, Royal Holloway University of London, Egham, United Kingdom

Elizabeth A. Klingaman Department of Psychiatry, University of Maryland School of Medicine, Baltimore; US Department of Veterans Affairs, VISN 5 Capitol Health Care Network, Linthicum, MD, United States

Ann M. Kring Department of Psychology, University of California, Berkeley, CA, United States

Oscar Lederman Keeping the Body in Mind Program, South Eastern Sydney Local Health District; School of Medical Sciences, University of New South Wales, Sydney, NSW, Australia

Bethany L. Leonhardt Indiana University School of Medicine, Department of Psychiatry; Eskenazi Health Midtown Community Mental Health, Indianapolis, IN, United States

Michelle H. Lim Centre for Mental Health, School of Health Sciences; Iverson Health Innovation Research Institute, Swinburne University of Technology, Hawthorn, VIC, Australia

Paul H. Lysaker Indiana University School of Medicine, Department of Psychiatry; Roudebush Veteran Affairs Medical Center, Indianapolis, IN, United States

Rachel Manser Oxford Cognitive Therapy Centre, Oxford Health NHS Foundation Trust, Oxford, United Kingdom

Kristen McCarter School of Medicine and Public Health, University of Newcastle, Newcastle, NSW, Australia

Alice Medalia College of Physicians and Surgeons, Columbia University Irving Medical Center, New York, NY, United States

Kim T. Mueser Center for Psychiatric Rehabilitation, Departments of Occupational Therapy, Psychological and Brain Sciences, and Psychiatry, Boston University, Boston, MA, United States

Katherine Nieweglowski Illinois Institute of Technology, Lewis College of Human Sciences, Chicago, IL, United States

Deysi Paniagua Illinois Institute of Technology, Lewis College of Human Sciences, Chicago, IL, United States

Sohee Park Department of Psychology, Vanderbilt University, Nashville, TN, United States

Georgie Paulik Perth Voices Clinic, Murdoch; University of Western Australia, Perth, WA, Australia

Amy E. Pinkham School of Behavioral and Brain Sciences, The University of Texas at Dallas, Richardson, TX, United States

Sonja Pohlman School of Medicine and Public Health, University of Newcastle, Newcastle, NSW, Australia

Sang Qin Illinois Institute of Technology, Lewis College of Human Sciences, Chicago, IL, United States

Simon Rice Centre for Youth Mental Health, University of Melbourne, Melbourne; Orygen, The National Centre of Excellence in Youth Mental Health, Parkville, VIC, Australia

Simon Rosenbaum School of Psychiatry, University of New South Wales, Sydney; Black Dog Institute, Randwick, NSW, Australia

Mar Rus-Calafell Department of Psychiatry, Oxford University; Oxford Health NHS Foundation Trust, Oxford, United Kingdom

Olga Santesteban-Echarri Hotchkiss Brain Institute, Mathison Centre for Mental Health Research & Education, University of Calgary, Calgary, AB, Canada

Alice Saperstein College of Physicians and Surgeons, Columbia University Irving Medical Center, New York, NY, United States

Christina Savage Department of Psychology, University of Maryland, College Park, MD, United States

LeeAnn Shan Department of Psychology, University of Maryland, College Park, MD, United States

Bryony Sheaves Oxford Cognitive Approaches to Psychosis, Department of Psychiatry; Nuffield Department of Clinical Neurosciences, Sleep and Circadian Neuroscience Institute, University of Oxford; Oxford Health NHS Foundation Trust, Oxford, United Kingdom

Christopher Shoulder Psychological Interventions Clinic for Outpatients with Psychosis, South London and Maudsley NHS Foundation Trust, London, United Kingdom

Helen J Stain School of Social and Health Sciences, Leeds Trinity University, Horsforth, United Kingdom; TIPS—Network for Clinical Research in Psychosis, Stavanger University Hospital, Stavanger, Norway

Shuichi Suetani Metro South Mental Health and Addiction Services, Brisbane; Queensland Centre for Mental Health Research, The Park Centre for Mental Health, Wacol; Queensland Brain Institute, The University of Queensland, St Lucia, QLD, Australia

Neil Thomas Centre for Mental Health, School of Health Sciences, Swinburne University of Technology, Hawthorn; Alfred Health, Melbourne, VIC, Australia

Irene van de Giessen Director of Non-Profit Organization, Foundation for Recovery Talent, Koudekerke, The Netherlands

David van den Berg Parnassia Psychiatric Institute, The Hague; VU University, Amsterdam, The Netherlands

Catherine van Zelst Department of Psychiatry and Neuropsychology, User Research Centre, Maastricht University, Maastricht; Institute for Mental Health Care Eindhoven (GGzE); Mental Health First Aid (MHFA), Eindhoven, The Netherlands

Felicity Waite Oxford Cognitive Approaches to Psychosis, Department of Psychiatry, University of Oxford; Oxford Health NHS Foundation Trust, Oxford, United Kingdom

Thomas Ward Department of Psychology, King's College London, Institute of Psychiatry, Psychology & Neuroscience; South London and Maudsley NHS Foundation Trust, London, United Kingdom

Lauren Weittenhiller Department of Psychology, University of California, Berkeley, CA, United States

Preface

This book shows you—the clinical psychologists and neuropsychologists of the future—how much you have to offer to help people with psychosis recover. In brief, it aims to give psychologists an introduction to current thinking on the nature of psychotic symptoms and their impact in everyday life; how specific psychotic disorders, such as schizophrenia, develop; and the vast array of skills that psychologists bring to the assessment and treatment of people with psychotic experiences.

In recent years, research and clinical practice on psychotic symptoms has come a long way. As a result, neither the public perception of psychosis (as someone with hallucinations and delusions) nor the clinical conception of psychotic illness (as unrelenting disorders with poor prognosis) is in line with the current evidence base. For example, people with schizophrenia report a broad array of changes in thought, emotion, and behaviour, and the majority experience complete or partial recovery over time. In fact, the emphasis on symptoms is gradually widening as new evidence shows the importance of impaired cognition, motivation, and social functioning in the development of schizophrenia and in the onset of individual psychotic symptoms across diagnostic boundaries. Indeed, for patients with psychotic symptoms, their goals for treatment often focus on other problems—such as loneliness, depression, and sleep disturbance—rather than symptom control alone. Yet, people with psychotic symptoms rarely receive the psychological services that they need. As a consequence, both the general competencies, and the specific skill-set, of clinical psychologists and neuropsychologists are in high demand. Since the former are covered in many excellent texts already, they will not be tackled here. Rather, the intention of this book is to introduce you, the professional psychologists of the future, to some of the specific skills and evidence relevant to this area of practice and encourage you to see the enormous opportunities you have to make a real difference in the lives of people with psychosis.

The target audience of this book is graduate students in professional training programs for clinical and neuropsychology, but it may also be of interest to advanced undergraduates and experienced clinicians undertaking ongoing professional development in the area of psychosis.

Editors' Notes

The editors and contributors to this text have tried to ensure that the information and resource suggestions provided are accurate and in keeping with general professional and ethical standards for psychologists at the time of publication.

However, clinical practice guidelines and regulatory frameworks vary between countries and are routinely updated, whilst the psychological research evidence base continues to change. Furthermore, the best care for clients and their families must be guided by individual circumstances and context. Consequently, practitioners must not rely solely on the content of the material in this textbook to guide their work. Similarly, it is the responsibility of the reader to make their own decisions regarding the currency, reliability, and correctness of information in suggested external websites and materials.

We also acknowledge the wide range of terms used to refer to people who see a psychologist (e.g. clients, patients, consumers) and to the experience of psychosis (i.e. psychotic disorders or individual symptoms of psychosis). Such terms carry explicit and implicit baggage that may subtly, or not so subtly, bias our attention, thinking, and decision making. As clinicians and researchers, it pays to revisit our language use from time to time to ensure it is serving us well. The editors and contributors to this text have made every effort to use language that is both respectful and scientifically accurate.

Acknowledgements

We would like to express our gratitude to the following people who have helped in many and varied ways in the development of this book. To my parents (JCB), Margaret and Peter, who gave me a love of learning. To my mother (GP), Debbie, for teaching me about compassion for self and others, and to Jo Badcock, for being my untiring mentor. To other mentors, friends, and colleagues who have inspired, challenged, and encouraged us as clinicians and researchers: Pat Michie, Vera Morgan, Melanie Clark, Romola Bucks, and Jackie Curtis. To Susie Hincks, Keith Wilson, Maria Halphen, Nev Jones, Greg Ralls, Lyn Mahboub, and Evie Glasshouse whose advocacy for people with psychosis, or hearing voices, has motivated our efforts. To our clients and students—past, current, and future—for everything you have taught me. Finally, to Dennis McGonagle, Tim Bennett, Nikki Levy, and all the staff at Elsevier without whose assistance this textbook would not have seen the light of day.

SECTION 1
The Basics

CHAPTER 1
What Is Psychosis?

Part One: Lived Experience Perspectives

When you talk, you are only repeating what you already know. But if you listen, you may learn something new

Dalai Lama

Past, Present, and Future

Clair de la Lune
Western Australia, Australia

I am a 56-year-old woman who 'lost' most of her twenties to undiagnosed mental illness. My family and friends didn't understand what was going on with me and awareness of mental illness in Australia was not as advanced in the 1980s as it is today. I was finally diagnosed with a mild form of schizophrenia when I was 28 years of age.

I grew up on a sheep farm in the South-West of Western Australia, enjoying country life and my ponies. I graduated from school, then worked on the farm and had various other jobs for some years. At age 21, I went to university to study English and found my studies challenging—writing properly constructed essays was difficult and I was confused by this as I was able to write well at school. I began feeling depressed and then my parents separated, so I left university after 1 year. I then had two jobs as a nanny, but it was becoming obvious that something was not right with me.

Then the illness really began to manifest itself as I lacked motivation, became withdrawn and uncommunicative, was often rude and abrupt and displayed a lack of self-care. I usually went to bed at about three or four o'clock in the morning and slept in until two or three in the afternoon—such sleep patterns are common symptoms of mental illness. Symptoms such as paranoia and delusions becoming more pronounced as I began perceiving things differently. I believed the television and radio were sending me personal messages through

A Clinical Introduction to Psychosis. https://doi.org/10.1016/B978-0-12-815012-2.00001-8

their songs and advertisements—mostly not very nice messages although some could be positive and gave me brief respite from my usual 'down' state of mind. I didn't trust my family and occasionally thought people were trying to 'get me'. I remember waiting at a bus stop when some young men drove by and one of them yelled out at me 'He's going to shoot you!' That was how I heard it anyway, which added to my already growing fears. Unlike many people diagnosed with schizophrenia, I did not hear voices, which is indicative of how symptoms of mental illness are unique to the individual.

I was frightened to go out during the day so often ventured out at night, sometimes not knowing where I was—a dangerous way of living for a young woman. During this period, I went missing—I met someone at a bar and stayed with them for three weeks without informing anyone where I was. I was no longer aware of social obligations such as letting people know where I was. After going missing, I was referred to a psychiatrist who I saw unwillingly as I didn't think there was anything wrong with me. The psychiatrist thought I may have schizo-effective disorder or a schizoid personality and he offered me medication, which I refused. In retrospect, I wish I had taken some medication then despite the side effects such as weight gain.

Finally, my mother described my symptoms to a consultant psychiatrist she met and he thought I may have schizophrenia and sent a nurse around to see me. I wasn't pleasant to the nurse, so then the psychiatrist himself came to see me. Sometime after that visit, two young policemen came to my flat. They told me they were taking me to a psychiatric hospital. I didn't think I was sick (thinking this way when mentally ill is known as 'lack of insight'—I don't like this term as I think this symptom is simply another manifestation of your different perception and is not a lack of anything—semantics!), so I refused to go. They were insistent and packed a bag for me, so I went with them to the nurse's car and was given a police escort to hospital, feeling confused about what was happening to me.

When first given medication in hospital, I would put the tablet under my tongue and spit it out in the bathroom. This is common behaviour and the nurses soon gave me a liquid medication instead. Within a few days I responded to the medication and my mother noticed quite a dramatic change in me. We had dinner together and had our first proper conversation in years. I spent 5 weeks in hospital and was released when I consented to having two injections in the buttocks. I continued to have injections of medication every 2 weeks for some years until I started taking an antipsychotic pill every day. On release, I was put on a disability pension, saw a psychiatrist regularly as an outpatient, and began the slow return to 'normal' life—something I think I am still doing after all these years. I remember seeing a woman with schizophrenia interviewed on television once, talking about how she felt her personality was 'shattered' by her illness which I think is a good description. I tried to 'become me' again and due to the unusual experiences and altered brain chemistry I think it unlikely anyone would be the same person as before.

Today I am on a daily low dose of aripiprazole and although I have had a couple of hiccups along the way, I haven't been treated again in a psychiatric hospital.

I have worked part-time looking after children and cared for my grandmother for a couple of years. I now do some mental illness advocacy and have spoken at universities, schools and a couple of Rotary Mental Health Forums as I believe educating and humanising the experience will help to foster understanding and contribute to reducing the stigma so often associated with mental illness. I contributed to a book called *FASCInATE* (Fremantle Arts Centre Press, 2017), which had poetry and prose written by people with mental illness about their experiences, under the guidance of a literary tutor. Although this project was not meant to be therapeutic, the act of writing and talking about our experiences was rather cathartic. The book was published and distributed throughout high schools in Western Australia in 2006 to educate young people about mental illness.

I believe that scientific research into the brain and mental illness will one day lead us to better treatments and outcomes for people with mental illness so I participate in, and advocate for, schizophrenia research. I also promote the involvement of people with lived experience of mental illness in scientific research, not just as participants but as partners, as they can give a unique perspective and create a sense of urgency.

The approach to psychiatric treatment in 1989, when I was diagnosed, was less holistic than today. Psychotic illnesses are complex diseases, often requiring different modes of care and I believe psychology is an important part of this. I wish I had been referred to a psychologist after I was first treated, to deal with the consequences of my illness both past, present, and future. Stigma, and consequent self-stigma, is an issue for people with mental illness as is the guilt associated with out-of-character things you may have done when you are sick. When responding well to treatment, there may be guilt associated with realising what family and friends have gone through as a result of your illness. Many people experience grief at their loss of capacity and life expectations, and there is also the loneliness associated with living with a mental illness. These issues need to be addressed. When I was eventually referred to a psychologist to deal with issues arising from my illness, I felt a sense of relief as I was listened to, and my experience and feelings were validated.

When in psychosis, a person's perception may be altered. What a well person may think is a reasonable statement, comment, etc. may be perceived very differently by someone in psychosis. Your words may have a different and very impactful meaning (frightening, prescient, etc.) for them. What seems irrational to you is real and rational to them and a calm and nonjudgemental response is so important. I have found over the years that some people often 'see you as your illness' and forget that the illness is a part of my life but I am not my illness—I am more than that. Sometimes I feel like saying 'I was once like you – schizophrenia-free – mental illness was not a part of my life'. I also dislike being called 'a schizophrenic' (the media tend to use this term with all its negative connotations); this, once again, indicates to me that I am only my illness. I prefer—I suffer from schizophrenia, I live with schizophrenia, or I have schizophrenia.

Some of the compassionate and inspirational people I have been privileged to meet because of my illness include psychiatrists, nurses, psychologists, social workers, occupational therapists, scientific researchers and, of course, my brave fellow sufferers. These people have given me hope and renewed my faith in humanity. My experience of schizophrenia has been very challenging, but I have learnt about empathy and tolerance and what it is to be truly human.

Reference

Fremantle Arts Centre Press (2017). *FASCInATE: Friends of Alma Street Centre Inspiring Action Towards Equity*. North Fremantle, WA: Fremantle Arts Centre Press.

My Hidden Superpower

Evie Glasshouse
School of Psychology and Exercise Science, Murdoch University, Murdoch, WA, Australia

When we think of someone hearing voices, we generally think of the worst-case scenario; the raving lunatic on the street corner or the serial killer in the horror film. This image of the 'crazy voices in your head' is so prevalent that I did not even recognise that *I* was a voice hearer until my later life: simply because my experience was not what I had seen in the movies.

I have been hearing voices for as long as I can remember. The best way I can describe my experience is to imagine having a radio switched on in the corner of your room 24/7. Most of the time, the sound is set just below the threshold of hearing: you can make out that there is talking, but you have to focus to make out the words. However, in times of stress, this radio gets turned up automatically: making it very hard to concentrate or focus on anything else. I am fortunate as my voices are mostly pleasant, but some activities can be hampered by having what seems like an auditorium of people in your head, all talking at once!

My voices likely originated as a coping mechanism from my childhood experiences. I was left alone for extended periods of time, and so, desperate for human interaction, I imagined people to play with instead. Over time, I began to carry these made-up people around with me inside my head wherever I went, like my own personal advisory committee. I was never lonely or bored, because I always had someone to talk to. However, this only served to isolate me further from my peers as I was labelled 'the weird kid'. I was withdrawn and depressed, which likely only made me rely on my voices more, further isolating myself. It was a vicious cycle.

My breaking point with my voices was when I was 25. I had just broken up with my partner of 11 years and was in the middle of my final year of my university degree. While for me it is normal to hear voices daily, I heard a voice that was particularly loud and clear. This voice seemed to belong to an individual person, rather than my other voices which I considered a part of myself. This voice told me in an ominous tone, 'I have seen what happens next, and you're not going to like it'. The experience rattled me so much that I immediately checked myself into my local emergency mental health clinic.

At the clinic, I was asked concerning questions. 'Do the voices tell you to hurt people? Do they tell you to hurt yourself?' For my voices, this was unthinkable. My primary concern was that this new voice experience was abnormal for me and indicated something was very wrong. Nevertheless, as I was in no immediate danger, I was discharged with some antipsychotics and no further follow-up. I felt lost and terrified—was I going to end up like the people in the movies? I was the right age for the onset of mental illness, and this thought was crippling. What if I could never be normal again?

Luckily for me, I searched up a psychology clinic, which specialised in voice hearing. After an intensive course of cognitive behavioural therapy, I realised that my voices were trying to help me, not harm me. Discovering the link between my childhood experiences and my voices was crucial to my personal acceptance that what I was hearing wasn't 'bad' or 'good', it just is something that happens. Managing my anxiety and depression in turn helped my voices become more manageable.

When I get a chance to speak about my voices, people always ask if I have found a way to get rid of them. But I consider my voices an integral part of me, and I would feel very lonely without their presence. I wouldn't be the person I am today without growing up with these unusual experiences.

I believe that the view that voices are something to 'fix' should be shifted towards asking what voices may represent instead, and helping an individual see their voices in a positive or helpful light. For me, my voices becoming more frequent or louder are a warning signal that I am not coping with daily stress—and this helps me focus on making the changes I need to in order to feel better. This may not be true for every voice hearer, but this may serve to reduce the stigma for people like me who hear unusual things. Reassurance that you are not crazy for hearing voices is very comforting and changing from the concept that voices are an illness may help individuals who do hear voices to feel safe to seek the help they require.

While my personal journey certainly is not finished, I now live comfortably with my daily voice experience. They are very helpful when I practice presentations or helping me outline a new idea for a novel: who can say that they have a personal cheerleading team in their heads? I view my voices as my secret superpower rather than a hindrance, and I would hope that other voice hearers can one day feel the same about their own experiences too.

I am now embarking on my postgraduate degree working in the cognitive neuropsychology field, where I am aiming to find brain areas, which generate a voice hearing experience in some individuals and not others. Without my voice hearing experience, I likely would not be pursuing this line of research. A few years ago, I thought I was doomed to be a victim of worsening mental illness, but now it motivates me to help others who have similar experiences.

My take-home message to future clinicians who hope to work with voice hearers in the future would be to try to see the experience of hearing voices as more than a symptom needing to be cured. Not all voices are bad or mean, nor need to be removed entirely from an individual's life. To the voice hearer, I hope that experiences such as mine help to reduce the stigma we have for our unusual experiences, which make us the unique person we are today.

Part Two: Current Conceptualisation of Psychosis—Clinical and Research Perspectives

Clara S. Humpston*, and Henry J. Jackson†
*Institute of Psychiatry, Psychology and Neuroscience, King's College London, London, United Kingdom, †School of Psychological Sciences, University of Melbourne, Melbourne, VIC, Australia

Key Learning Objectives

- To learn about current conceptualisations of psychosis.
- To critically evaluate categorical and dimensional approaches to diagnosis.
- To introduce clinical practice guidelines in the management of psychotic disorders.
- To appreciate strengths and limitations of staging models of psychosis.
- To understand ways to improve communication with people with psychosis.

INTRODUCTION

'Psychosis' is a generic term that refers to distortions and impairments of thought, feeling, and behaviour leading to a loss of contact with consensual reality. It is signified by delusions, hallucinations, thought disorder, grossly disorganised or abnormal motor behaviour, and negative symptoms (APA, 2013). The term can be confusing as it is used to refer to both diagnostic categories and to individual symptoms (experiences) with variable levels of severity, duration, and clinical significance. At the categorical level, schizophrenia-spectrum disorders include schizophrenia, schizophreniform disorder, schizoaffective disorder, delusional disorder, brief psychotic disorder, substance/medication-induced

Usage of the term 'psychosis' is highly variable and the subject of ongoing debate.

psychotic disorder, and schizotypal (personality) disorder, psychotic disorder due to another medical condition, catatonia, and other specified and unspecified schizophrenia spectrum and other psychotic disorders (APA, 2013; WHO, 2018). Schizophrenia has received various narrower and broader definitions over time. It is the psychotic disorder that attracts most attention and one reason may be that it is the most common; for example, the lifetime prevalence of schizophrenia is about 0.9%, compared to 0.3% for schizoaffective disorder (Perälä et al., 2007). Nevertheless, one should not neglect the other schizophrenia-spectrum disorders as the terms 'psychotic disorder' and 'schizophrenia' are not equivalent. Importantly, psychotic symptoms can be found in a range of other disorders, although not as a defining feature, most notably in mood disorders (major depression and bipolar disorder), substance-related and addictive disorders, posttraumatic stress disorder, borderline personality disorder, and neurocognitive disorders (e.g. Alzheimer's disease). At the symptom level, psychotic symptoms and psychotic-like symptoms are also found in the general population and people with these experiences may or may not require care.

This chapter, and indeed this book, is concerned with current conceptualisations of psychosis, with a particular emphasis on the schizophrenia spectrum disorders. It is important to recognise the contributions of seminal figures in the field, including Emil Kraepelin, credited with the *dementia praecox* concept; Eugen Bleuler, who redefined *dementia praecox* as schizophrenia; and Kurt Schneider who identified 11 first-rank symptoms, presumed characteristic of schizophrenia. Current classificatory systems for schizophrenia and related disorders have their roots in this early work (see Additional Reading), but have evolved over time in an effort to improve reliability, validity, and clinical utility.

Over the last 30–40 years various psychological disciplines, including clinical, experimental, and neuro-psychologists, have made important contributions as clinicians and researchers working with people with psychotic disorders and symptoms to understand their experiences. Furthermore, they have developed and evaluated a wide range of assessments, treatments, interventions and services, thus contributing to a deeper understanding of these disorders.

MULTIPLE CONCEPTUALISATIONS OF PSYCHOSIS

The purpose of this section is to briefly introduce four different perspectives on psychosis: the neurobiological, phenomenological, cognitive, and socio-developmental accounts. Each provides a different level of explanation; yet there is considerable overlap. Consequently, it is important to take an integrative approach (the theme of Chapter 2), both in research and clinical practice.

A Neurobiological View of Psychosis

Schizophrenia and related psychotic disorders have long been conceptualised as neurobiological or 'brain' illnesses, involving changes in genetic, molecular, cellular, and circuitry function. Indeed, there has been a vigorous and ongoing debate about the fundamental nature of schizophrenia: 'Is it a classical organically based biomedical disorder with clean boundaries due to the effects of a single etiologic agent, or is it the severe end of a spectrum of syndromes that aggregate together in families?' (Kendler, 2015, p. 11). For example, early genetic models rested on the assumption of a single gene for schizophrenia, whilst later proposals have favoured a polygenic model (Gottesman & Shields, 1972; Kendler, 2015). Increasing evidence suggests that the risk of schizophrenia is more likely continuous and polygenic (International Schizophrenia Consortium, 2009)—involving a large number of common single-nucleotide polymorphisms (SNPs), each having a very small effect, with a smaller contribution from rare copy number and single-nucleotide variants (Purcell et al., 2014).

Single-nucleotide polymorphisms are variations of a single nucleotide (building blocks of DNA) that occur at specific locations within a genome.

Measures of brain structure and function provide important insights into the underlying mechanisms of psychotic disorders. A comprehensive review of this literature is beyond the scope of this chapter; however, recent advances may have important implications for clinical practice. For example, new strategies are currently being trialled to identify distinct subgroups—or biotypes—of people with psychosis sharing more similar characteristics, using biomarkers and genetics (e.g. Tamminga et al., 2017), with the aim of designing more individually tailored treatments.

Biotypes represent more biologically similar subgroups of psychosis than traditional diagnostic categories.

Nonetheless, neurobiological models of schizophrenia clearly recognise that the emergence of psychotic symptoms involves an interplay between genetic vulnerability and exposure to (environmental or psychosocial) stressors (Howes, McCutcheon, Owen, & Murray, 2017). However, phenomenology is often only acknowledged superficially in these accounts, at least when viewed from a philosophical perspective, which is considered next.

Phenomenology is the study of consciousness and the objects of direct experience.

Phenomenological Perspective and Self-Disturbance Model of Psychosis

In stark contrast to neurobiological conceptualisations, phenomenological perspectives on psychosis emphasise a basic disturbance of one's minimal self (Nelson, Parnas, & Sass, 2014).

The minimal self is the most basic sense of having experiences that are one's own.

The self-disturbance model (or *ipseity* disturbance, Latin *ipse*—self or itself) is deeply embedded in the phenomenological tradition and continental philosophy and is a concept that may appear alien to many trainees in clinical or neuropsychology and psychiatry. Likewise, the idea of *minimal self* (as opposed to narrative self) is unfamiliar to many. In fact, it has been described as a disappearing heritage of modern psychiatry (Parnas, 2011) since self-disturbances featured in DSM-III as a part of the descriptions of schizophrenia, but less so since then. According to this view, these symptoms often involve a permeation or destruction of one's *ego boundary*, i.e. the ability to differentiate and demarcate between self and other, the internal and the external 'worlds'. Bleuler classically reported patients complaining of being only 'reflections of themselves', or having 'lost

Narrative self: the sense that we have of ourselves as having an evolving story through past and future.

their individual self' (for examples see Henriksen & Parnas, 2012). Though now given less prominence in diagnosis, prototypical 'first-rank' symptoms involve severe disruptions of the ownership and agency of thought (thought insertion, withdrawal, broadcast, etc.) and of action/volition (passivity phenomena, 'made' actions). Without an intact sense of agency and ownership, a fragmentation of the minimal self is perhaps an unsurprising end result.

Agency: the sense that mental events and behaviours, such as actions and thoughts, originate from oneself, i.e. one is the agent and has first-person experience.

Ownership: the sense that one is physically responsible ('owns') for the mental events one initiates.

The **minimal self** is viewed as being severely affected in schizophrenia-spectrum psychoses.

Sass and Parnas (2003) proposed a model of self- or *ipseity*-disturbance consisting of three integral factors, all of which contribute to a disordered selfhood considered an essential feature of schizophrenia spectrum disorders. The first is termed hyperreflexivity, which refers to an exaggerated self-consciousness where normally tacit and nonvolitional processes, such as inner thought, become a focus of intense attention and scrutiny. In other words, what is tacit becomes explicit. A second complementary process, termed diminished self-affection (unrelated to 'affection' in an emotional sense), refers to a decreased feeling of existence as a subject of self-awareness or an agent of thoughts and actions. The final factor, disturbed 'grip' or 'hold', refers to fundamental distortions in one's relations to external reality and how one experiences external stimuli, accompanied by alterations in the 'reality-status' of the world. Such self-disorders are thought to bear some degree of specificity to schizophrenia-spectrum psychoses, rather than bipolar disorder or other psychological disorders, and have significant predictive validity for transitioning to psychosis from nonspecific prodromal phases (e.g. Nelson, Thompson, & Yung, 2012). Nevertheless, their overlap with nonpsychotic syndromes remains a topic of debate, for example with depersonalisation–derealisation.

Hyperreflexivity refers to an exaggerated self-consciousness.

Diminished self-affection involves a decreased feeling of existence as a subject of self-awareness.

The self-disturbance model is not a widely adopted clinical approach at present; however, assessing disturbances in the sense of minimal self in those at clinical high risk or in the first episode of psychosis could provide improved specificity for diagnosis (in turn, affecting prognosis and treatment), and is therefore a topic of much research and debate (Sass, Borda, Madeira, Pienkos, & Nelson, 2018).

Cognitive Approaches to Psychosis

Cognitive approaches to psychosis emphasise the role of cognitive, social, and emotional processes in the onset and persistence of psychotic symptoms. According to these models, it is the interpretation and meaning given to events and experiences, i.e. appraisals, that play a critical role in the transition from anomalous thoughts and experiences to psychotic symptoms (Chadwick & Birchwood, 1994; Garety, Kuipers, Fowler, Freeman, & Bebbington, 2001). Thus, individuals who have psychotic experiences that are appraised as positive and helpful are unlikely to seek treatment. According to this view, psychosis exists on a continuum with 'normal' experiences in the general population.

Appraisals refer to the emotional–motivational significance given to stimuli and drives emotional responses.

Whilst the details of specific cognitive models vary, they all provide a psychological description of subjective experiences, which serves as bridge between the phenomenological experience and the associated neurobiology (Garety et al., 2001). For example, Garety and colleagues proposed two 'proximal routes' to the development of positive symptoms in schizophrenia, namely one combining cognitive and affective disturbances and the other via affective disturbances alone (Garety et al., 2001). The authors argued that in individuals vulnerable to psychotic experiences, there is often a triggering event that leads to distortions of cognitive processes, which may involve the sense that something inexplicable is going on in the earlier phases of psychosis (e.g. delusional mood), to the alienation and externalisation of self-generated actions and thoughts in full-blown psychosis (e.g. thought insertion).

Not surprisingly, such experiences are highly salient and sometimes very distressing, leading to high levels of emotional arousal. The individual therefore is likely to embark on a natural search for meaning in order to find explanations (and thus possible resolution) for such experiences, which is susceptible to conscious and unconscious cognitive biases. Indeed, recent research has found that the way in which an individual appraises psychotic experiences differs in people with and without a need for care (Peters et al., 2017). A tendency to appraise psychotic experiences as external, threatening/paranoid, and negative often paves ways to the persistence of psychosis and may also be related to the corresponding neurobiology of threat processing (Underwood, Kumari, & Peters, 2016), whereas individuals not distressed by their psychotic experiences have more positive, less hostile appraisals.

Emotions have also been argued to have a direct effect on the formation and maintenance of delusions and hallucinations, without a primary cognitive underpinning (Freeman & Garety, 2003). Recent longitudinal evidence, for example, has shown that baseline levels of anxiety and depression predict persistence of paranoia two years later, whilst baseline delusions did not predict later negative affect (Fowler et al., 2012). These findings suggest that negative affect isn't simply a consequence of paranoid thinking, rather it plays a direct, causal role in the experience of this symptom (Hartley, Barrowclough, & Haddock, 2013). However, a potentially more realistic possibility is that both direct and indirect pathways link negative affect to paranoia (e.g. So et al., 2018). From the lens of the cognitive model, therefore, psychosis is viewed in terms of how we think and feel, much like other psychological problems and, importantly, it identifies underlying causal mechanisms that can be targeted in therapy.

Socio-Developmental Perspectives on Psychosis

Lastly, according to the socio-developmental view, a full understanding of the question 'What is psychosis?' can only be gained by incorporating a focus on early life events, social environment, and the subsequent development of an individual's psychological world and mental wellbeing. Again this psychosocial perspective may potentially link neurobiology, cognition, and personal narratives of psychosis. For example, adverse life events, particularly childhood trauma, frequently trigger the formation of unhealthy coping mechanisms and aberrant cognitive appraisals (e.g. Reininghaus et al., 2016) when evaluating self and others (an obvious example may be blaming oneself for the abuse one suffered, viewing oneself as bad or others as hostile). Whilst highly aroused, emotional states may simultaneously construct a 'nonself' dissociative barrier to the trauma, alter the function of key neurotransmitters involved in psychosis such as glutamate and dopamine (Howes & Nour, 2016), and damage the brain's cortical structure via neurotoxic effects (Habets, Marcelis, Gronenschild, Drukker, & van Os, 2011).

Furthermore, social adversity is not limited to childhood abuse. Cultural, political, and demographical factors (e.g. Bourque, van der Ven, Fusar-Poli, & Malla, 2012), including immigrant and/or minority ethnic status, along with the discrimination and poverty one may experience as a result, can all predispose vulnerable individuals to similar unhealthy behaviours such as cannabis use, abusive relationships, and poor mental health in general. In turn, these behaviours may bias the individual's cognitive appraisal style to perceive the outside world and other people as antagonistic. As a consequence, the socio-developmental perspective on psychosis highlights the need for clinicians to move beyond a focus on *intra*individual factors relevant to psychotic symptoms, to a fuller appreciation of the person in their developmental and social context (Howes & Murray, 2014).

Social adversity is a well-established risk factor for psychosis.

DIAGNOSING PSYCHOSIS

Categorical Approaches: A Brief Introduction

Categorical approaches to diagnosing schizophrenia spectrum and other psychotic disorders (termed schizophrenia spectrum for short) are based on the concept that the signs and symptoms of these disorders correlate in a meaningful and reliable pattern (i.e. a syndrome), and can be distinguished from other syndromes (see Box 1.1 for a brief recap on terms and definitions).

Clinical and neuropsychologists worldwide use two established categorical systems for classifying schizophrenia spectrum disorders, namely the *Diagnostic and Statistical Manual of Mental Disorders* (5th Edition; APA, 2013) and the *International Classification of Diseases* (ICD, 11th Edition; WHO, 2018, https://icd.who.int/browse11/l-m/en). Full details on the symptoms and diagnostic criteria for schizophrenia spectrum disorders are provided in these sources, so they will not be reproduced here. From a descriptive psychopathological perspective, *traditionally* psychotic symptoms include those that are termed positive symptoms and those that are termed negative symptoms (Andreasen, 1982, 1984; Oyebode, 2014; Sims, 1988). ICD-11 has now included anomalous self-experiences. However, there is disputation about a simple grouping of symptoms into two categories, discussed in more detail in the section on Dimensional approaches below (see, e.g. Blanchard & Cohen, 2006).

Positive symptoms include hallucinations, delusions, positive thought disorder, and bizarre behaviour.

Negative symptoms include affective flattening or blunting, alogia, avolition-apathy, asociality, and inattention.

Despite attempts to harmonise the diagnoses in DSM-5 (APA, 2013) and ICD11 (WHO, 2018; see Biedermann & Fleischhacker, 2016), one can see that some disorders appear in both nosologies whilst others don't. Moreover, where the diagnostic labels are identical, the criteria sets used to reach a diagnosis differ across

Box 1.1 A Recap on Terms and Definitions

Categories: refer to groups of signs and symptoms that share some similar features.

Convergent validity: is demonstrated when the signs or symptoms of a category are highly correlated.

Classical category: to meet the category, *all* specified criteria (signs and symptoms) must be present.

Divergent validity: is demonstrated when signs and symptoms that are not supposed to be related to the category of interest are unrelated to that category.

Polythetic category: to meet the category, a certain number of symptoms or signs from a given list is sufficient (e.g. any five of eight), though none is essential.

Quasi-polythetic category: to meet this criteria, firstly a person must have one or two specified criteria (signs and symptoms), but then can have a certain number of other specified criteria. This system is adopted in the DSM-5 approach to diagnosing schizophrenia spectrum and other psychotic disorders.

Signs: what the clinician directly observes, e.g. thought disorder, gait disturbance or flattened affect

Symptoms: what the patient reports, e.g. a delusion or hallucination

the two systems. Potentially, this could lead to a patient being described with a specific psychotic disorder in ICD and another type of psychotic disorder in DSM. Additionally, various disorders listed under the schizophrenia-spectrum in both the DSM-5 and ICD-11 differ according to duration of symptoms, configuration of symptoms, the presence or absence of mood symptoms, and the influences of legal and illegal substances.

ADVANTAGES OF CATEGORICAL SYSTEMS

In general, the advantages of categorical systems are that they lend themselves to efficient communication between clinicians and are consistent with the kind of practice found in other medical disciplines. They also are helpful in epidemiological studies in determining population prevalence and incidence rates, and health service provision. They also allow the examination of etiological factors, factors maintaining the conditions, and factors associated with the syndrome, e.g. age of onset, gender ratio, and course. Further, they lend themselves to tests of interrater and test–retest reliability as well as convergent and divergent validity (Jackson & McGorry, 2009).

PROBLEMS AND PITFALLS WITH CATEGORIES (AND DIAGNOSTIC SYSTEMS)

Many criticisms have been made of the categorical approach embedded in the two official nosologies of ICD-11 and DSM-5. For example, Frances (2014) asserted that the descriptive psychopathological approach has overreached itself by increasingly pathologising aspects of normal experience. Insel and colleagues (e.g. Cuthbert & Insel, 2013) have also argued for the limitations of the descriptive psychopathological approach and instead proposed a reverse engineering approach by identifying potential biological markers and then linking these to signs and symptoms—a bottom-up approach known as the NIMH Research Domain Criteria (RDoC). Others reject nosological systems entirely and would rather deal with the person in an *idiographic* fashion—that is, deal with the symptoms or complaints that a specific person presents with, without regard for diagnostic labelling or concern for any biological processes (Cooke & Kinderman, 2018).

Idiographic methods focus on the unique experiences and life history of each individual.

Specifically, if we turn to the categorisation of psychotic disorders, many issues have been raised. Tandon (2016) succinctly summarises these as: …'a) unclear boundaries *between* disorders (e.g. between psychotic bipolar disorder, schizoaffective disorder and schizophrenia); b) enormous unexplained clinical heterogeneity *within* individual psychotic disorders; c) the frequent co-occurrence of mood and psychotic symptoms; and d) poorly described relationships between subclinical psychotic phenomena in the general population and defined psychotic disorders.' (p. 133) (see also Tandon, Nasrallah, & Keshavan, 2009). Finally, the diagnosis of a specific psychotic disorder may change with subsequent episodes, which is not due to different diagnostic practices of individual clinicians but a changing clinical picture or presentation. Such change is also less likely to occur with a diagnosis of schizophrenia but more likely to be the case with other psychotic disorders, such as delusional disorder (see Fusar-Poli et al., 2016).

Dimensional Approaches: A Brief Introduction

There are a number of approaches to dimensionality of mental disorder. First, if we turn to psychopathology per se, Caspi et al. (2014) identified three higher-order factors for mental disorders (Internalising, Externalising, and Thought Disorder) along with a broad, general (transdiagnostic) psychopathology dimension, termed 'p' (much like the idea that general intelligence or 'g' comprises multiple, specific components). Similarly, Markon (2010) identified four broad superordinate dimensions of psychopathology: Internalising, Externalising, Thought Disorder, and Pathological Introversion. Finally, the Hierarchical Taxonomy of Psychopathology (HiTOP) Consortium (Krueger et al., 2018) is developing an empirical and quantitative classification of psychopathology based on dimensions rather than categories. HiTOP proposes a complex multi-level model ranging from (i) Super Spectra (higher-order dimensions) through to (vi) Symptoms (e.g. signs and symptoms) as an alternative to traditional, categorical taxonomies, though the system is not (yet) ready for use in clinical practice.

Dimensions: capture meaningful variation in symptom severity, e.g. a continuum of negative symptoms ranging from 'not present' to 'present and severe'.

As regards to psychosis per se, factor analysis has often been employed to ascertain the latent structure of symptoms underlying the schizophrenia spectrum. In reviewing factor analytic studies of psychosis rating scales, Fulford et al. (2014) found that, in general, there were three to five factors, which did not differ across patients with recent-onset or chronic schizophrenia. These scales were typically the Scale for the Assessment of Negative Symptoms (SANS; Andreasen, 1983), the Scale for the Assessment of Positive Symptoms (SAPS; Andreasen, 1984), the Brief Psychiatric Rating Scale (BPRS; Overall & Gorham, 1962), and the Positive and Negative Syndrome Scale (PANSS; Kay, Fiszbein, & Opler, 1987). Of note, Blanchard and Cohen (2006) confirmed the presence of three to five factors for psychosis but found negative symptoms to be the one constant factor across studies. Although psychometrically untested, Barch et al. (2013) proposed five symptom domains for dimensional assessment of psychosis (these being hallucinations, delusions, disorganised speech, abnormal psychomotor behaviour, and negative symptoms) plus three other domains (mania, depression, and cognition) that can be applied to all psychotic disorders and have been incorporated into Section III Assessment Measures in DSM-5 (APA, 2013, pp. 742–744).

A second approach to dimensionality has been to ascertain the structure of psychosis within a general population and then compare that structure across psychosis and 'normal' populations. This is the so-called continuum model of psychosis. For example, using data from a very large study of adults in the general community in United States, Shevlin, McElroy, Bentall, Reininghaus, and Murphy (2017) found a general psychosis factor that was uncorrelated with five secondary, specific factors, labelled: positive symptoms, negative symptoms, disorganisation, mania, and depression. The similarity in these findings with those previously reported in patients supports the idea of a continuum between clinical and subclinical psychotic experiences.

Van Os and colleagues adduce further evidence for a continuum model (Guloksuz & van Os, 2018). They argue that schizophrenia is heterogeneous; that the concept of 'schizophrenia' has become reified and is considered to be a disorder of severe symptoms, severe dysfunction, and poor outcome; that it is seen as the hallmark of the psychotic disorder spectrum and attracts the most attention. They further argue that an overfocus on clinical samples has ignored the fact that within the general community there is a range of people with various *degrees* of subthreshold psychotic disorders/symptoms (referring not only to positive symptoms, but also to negative and disorganised symptoms); that these symptoms are intermingled with nonpsychotic symptoms, especially affective (both manic and depressive) symptoms; and, that the psychotic symptoms are often transient. Van Os and colleagues (Guloksuz & van Os, 2018; van Os & Guloksuz, 2017) highlight that many individuals identified as being at ultra high-risk (UHR) for psychosis present with anxiety and mood disorders, though a relatively small number, progress to a first episode of psychosis. Consequently, they argue that these individuals should not be seen through the 'schizoprism' lens (i.e. schizophrenia spectrum disorders) but treated for their depression, anxiety, and substance misuse disorder/symptoms. McGorry, Hartmann, Spooner, and Nelson (2018) reject this position, stating that UHR states are for psychosis generally, not specifically for schizophrenia.

Another line of evidence supporting a continuum model of psychosis comes from cross-sectional studies showing that people in the community may have delusions or hallucinations and be convinced of their veracity but are not distressed by them and lead productive lives (see seminal papers about delusions by Peters, Day, McKenna, & Orbach, 1999; van Os, Linscott, Myin-Germeys, Delespaul, & Krabbendam, 2009; and a review of voice hearers by Beavan, Read, & Cartwright, 2011). These findings provide further support for: (i) the notion of a continuum between normality and psychosis and, (ii) the necessity to consider the multidimensionality of delusional beliefs and hallucinatory experiences.

Finally, a recent alternative to both categorical and dimensional models is the network approach to psychopathology. In this approach, a condition like schizophrenia is construed as arising from the interactions or connectivity (i.e. a causal network) amongst the signs and symptoms of the disorder, not from an underlying disease entity (e.g. Wigman, de Vos, Wichers, van Os, & Bartels-Velthuis, 2017). Although Guloksuz, Pries, and van Os (2017) evaluate this network approach as promising, they also point out a number of pitfalls, including the (lack of) stability and reproducibility of findings.

ADVANTAGES AND DISADVANTAGES OF DIMENSIONAL/CONTINUUM APPROACHES

Factor analysis allows for the identification of a small number of factors (dimensions) and how strongly or weakly each sign and symptom loads on those factors. It allows for the identification of symptom profiles and how a person could score higher or lower on each factor. The most important prospect for clinicians is the possibility of creating new measures that comprehensively cover the whole span of signs and symptoms within the schizophrenia spectrum. Conversely, there is the opportunity to develop improved measurement of specific symptom groupings. For example, Blanchard and Cohen (2006) identified two subfactors within the structure of negative symptoms, namely diminished expression and anhedonia–asociality, which has driven the development of new and more precise tools for the assessment of these negative symptom dimensions (see Chapter 7). Tandon (2016) argues that clinicians could use dimensional measures to assess a patient's treatment progress over time, and such measures will have important and direct applications in research.

The limitations of factor analysis can be listed as follows: the type of symptom measures used (i.e. their breadth or narrowness of scope); the type of factor analysis and factor solution chosen; the nature of the sample selected (i.e. the narrowness or breadth of people with specific psychotic disorders examined); the phase of illness (chronic or acute), and the time frame measured by a scale (see, amongst others, Peralta & Cuesta, 2001; Blanchard & Cohen, 2006). Moreover, cross-sectional factor analytic studies assume stability of signs and symptoms (see, e.g. Shevlin et al., 2017). Finally, patients with affective psychosis, psychotic disorder due to another medical condition or substance misuse (intoxication and withdrawal) have typically been omitted from factor analytic studies—though these are all conditions where psychotic phenomena can occur.

van Bork, Epskamp, Rhemtulla, Borsoom, and van der Mass (2017) caution against acceptance of general factor modelling (e.g. the *p* factor of Caspi et al.,

2014), arguing against overreliance on fit indices in nearly equivalent factorial models and in deciding the optimal factor structure. They state that sampling differences can lead to different theories about the nature of a general factor and that the *p* factor in one study is not necessarily the same *p* factor in another study. Furthermore, where one has positive correlations amongst symptoms, mathematically this will lead inevitably to some form of a general factor to fit the data. Theoretical interpretation of the meaning of factors is needed but so too is consideration and application of alternative models, e.g. network models, as the true underlying model may not be a factor model at all. In fact, it could be a class or admixture (class and dimensions) model.

Additional Considerations

DIAGNOSING PSYCHOSIS ACROSS CULTURES

Culture refers to 'systems of knowledge, concepts, rules, practices that are learned and transmitted across generations' (APA, 2013).

Culture refers to the customary beliefs, attitudes, values, goals and practices and social norms, of a racial, religious, or social group. It affects both the *form* (the type of symptoms) and the *content* (themes, beliefs, subjective experience) of psychotic symptoms, so there are differences in the prevalence of symptoms and the nature of their content across cultures and within subcultures (e.g. Badcock, Clarke, & Morgan, 2018; Campbell et al., 2017; Jones & Luhrmann, 2016; Laroi et al., 2014). In fact, some would argue that what is viewed as psychosis or disorder in Western cultures may not be considered as pathological by another culture (see Kalra, Bhugra, & Shah, 2012).

Jablensky et al. (1992) conducted the WHO collaborative study across 12 research centres in 10 countries. This seminal study showed that patients with schizophrenia living in developing nations have a better course, outcome, prognosis, and recovery than those in developed nations. Some possible reasons for this are better support and better acceptance or tolerance of (or less stigmatising attitudes towards) 'odd' (deviant) behaviour in these cultures. From a clinician perspective, understanding a person's explanatory model of psychosis is critical, in that one needs to understand the person's views about the onset, causes, and course of symptoms, its impact on the person, and what that person considers to be effective treatment (see Box 1.2 with Kleinman, Eisenberg, and Good's (1978) original eight questions concerning explanatory beliefs). In this way, the clinician can understand, and take into account, the patient's perspective and then assess the distance/commonality between their own perspective and that of their patient. Lloyd et al. (1998) developed a slightly more elaborated version of the explanatory model as created by Kleinman et al., 1978, termed the Short Explanatory Model Interview (SEMI). Although intended for use with patients with common mental disorders, the SEMI has also been used with patients with psychosis (e.g. Joy, Manoranjtham, Samuel, & Jacob, 2017 ; McCabe & Priebe, 2004). One emerging issue to note from this literature is that people may have multiple and seemingly contradictory explanatory models of their illness (Asher, Fekadu, & Hanlon, 2018).

Box 1.2 Eight Explanatory Model Questions

1. What do you think has caused your problem?
2. Why do you think it started when it did?
3. What do you think your problem does to you? How does it work?
4. How severe is your problem? Will it have a short or long course?
5. What kind of treatment do you think you should receive?
6. What are the most important results you hope to receive from this treatment?
7. What are the chief problems your problem has caused for you?
8. What do you fear most about your problem?

From Kleinman, A., Eisenberg, L., & Good, B. (1978). Culture, illness, and care: Clinical lessons from anthropologic and cross-cultural research. *Annals of Internal Medicine, 88*, 251–258. The word 'sickness' has been replaced by the word 'problem'.

Various clinical practice guidelines (see Table 1.1 for a brief overview of selected examples) and psychological society codes of ethics outline similar and common recommendations for the management of people with schizophrenia and related disorders, including a focus on cultural competencies. Distilled they are: that clinicians who are inexperienced should seek advice and supervision from those who are transculturally informed; the need for culturally sensitive assessment; the importance of understanding the explanatory models of the person (and their family and community); the need for psycho-education as to aetiology and treatment options, treatment expectations and adherence issues, and the need to involve working with community member organisations.

Regarding the two major nosologies of ICD and DSM, Paniagua (2018) compared the ICD-10 and DSM-5 on cultural variables. He found ICD-10 to be 'mute regarding the need to consider such variables in this context of diagnosing people with mental disorders, whereas the DSM-5 does alert mental health practitioners that they should not make a diagnosis in this context without considering the cultural variables potentially affecting the assessment and diagnosis of such disorders.' (p. 1). The release notes for ICD-11 schizophrenia now state that: 'The categories in this grouping should not be used to classify the expression of ideas, beliefs, or behaviours that are culturally sanctioned'. https://icd.who.int/browse11/l-m/en#/http%3a%2f%2fid.who.int%2ficd%2fentity%2f405565289. A more detailed consideration of culture and psychosis is given in Chapter 4.

PSYCHOSIS AS A TRANSDIAGNOSTIC PHENOMENON

Psychotic symptoms are by no means only limited to patients diagnosed with schizophrenia. Given the difference in the prevalence of psychotic-like experiences in the general population (approximately 5%–10%; McGrath et al., 2015) compared to that of schizophrenia (approximately 1%), it is not surprising that many if not most people with psychotic-like symptoms will *not* be

Table 1.1 An Overview of Clinical Practice Guidelines for Schizophrenia and Related Disorders[a]

Australia and New Zealand: RANZCP clinical practice guidelines
Source: Galletly et al. (2016) https://www.ncbi.nlm.nih.gov/pubmed/27106681
Objectives: Provides recommendations on clinical management and best-practice principles for *all* health professionals working with people with schizophrenia and related disorders in Australia and New Zealand. The recommendations were developed by expert consensus, based on the quality of current evidence. The guidelines cover the management of ultra-high-risk syndromes, first-episode psychoses and prolonged psychoses, including psychoses associated with substance use; they do *not* cover childhood schizophrenia or persistent delusional disorder. The guidelines take a holistic, recovery-oriented approach, addressing all aspects of the care of people with schizophrenia and related disorders, including correct diagnosis and symptom relief, optimal recovery of social function and physical health, and emphasis on the need for shared decision making. The need for cultural awareness is also stressed throughout.

Highlights:

- Cognitive Behaviour Therapy (CBT) is the preferred psychological intervention, reflecting the high level of evidence in published intervention studies.
- The need for family interventions, lifestyle interventions for prevention of weight gain, vocational recovery services, and interventions for tobacco use is underscored.
- Provision of neuropsychological assessment and cognitive remediation is recommended where cognitive problems are affecting recovery and function.
- For patients with persistent/unremitting illness, psychosocial interventions are recommended along with a recovery plan, including regular contact with general practitioners and partnerships with other mental health services.

Issues for psychologists:

- Recovery focus: Need for team approach, e.g. housing, engage with vocational services.
- Expert pharmacotherapy and review from psychiatrists and not general practitioners.
- Need for detailed assessment concerning symptoms, history formulation, and treatment plan.
- Family involvement is encouraged where possible

The **United Kingdom**—National Institute for Clinical Excellence (NICE) guidelines
Source: https://www.nice.org.uk/guidance/cg178
Objectives: This guideline represents the gold standard in the treatment and management of schizophrenia-spectrum psychoses in adults (18 years and older) with onset before 60 years. The psychotic disorders covered by this guideline include schizophrenia, schizoaffective disorder, schizophreniform disorder, and delusional disorder. Other disorders that may have psychotic features (e.g. major affective disorders) are covered by other NICE guidelines. In addition, there is a separate guideline on the treatment and management of psychotic disorders in children and adolescents. This guideline provides detailed recommendations from the prodromal or at-risk mental state to treatment-resistant and refractory episodes of schizophrenia and is very comprehensive in its coverage of best practice in pharmacological, psychological, and social approaches (e.g. assistance with employment and housing issues).

Table 1.1 An Overview of Clinical Practice Guidelines for Schizophrenia and Related Disorders[a]—cont'd

Highlights:

- More emphasis has been put on the use of psychological interventions for the prevention of transitioning to frank psychosis in at-risk individuals.
- Primary-care (general) practitioners should refer individuals who are distressed, have a decline in social functioning and risk factors for psychosis to be assessed 'without delay' by a consultant psychiatrist or a trained specialist.
- Individual cognitive behavioural therapy with or without family intervention is the first-line intervention recommended, as well as other psychological interventions for anxiety, emerging personality disorders, or substance misuse.
- Antipsychotics should *not* be offered as prophylactic measures nor started in primary care, but instead should be initiated by secondary mental health services.
- Early intervention services are recommended to follow up individuals whose psychosis-like experiences lead to significant distress for up to 3 years, and may be extended if the person has not improved or recovered after a first episode.
- For subsequent acute episodes of established schizophrenia, crisis resolution and home treatment teams should be the only point from where all other acute services in the community and the hospital (where necessary) are referred.
- Oral antipsychotics as well as CBT for psychosis are the first-line interventions for an acute episode, exacerbation, or recurrence of schizophrenia.
- Social skills training, adherence therapy, counselling, and supportive psychotherapies are *not* recommended as routine interventions.
- Due to the potential compounding of side effects, polypharmacy (the use of two or more antipsychotics) is not recommended.

Issues for psychologists:

- Similar to other guidelines, the need for a team-based approach is highlighted.
- People at ultra-high risk frequently meet full criteria for other disorders, e.g. depression and anxiety and these disorders or syndromes deserve treatment in their own right, e.g. CBT (see NICE guidelines on major depression for example).

United States, National Institute of Mental Health and the Agency for Healthcare Research and Quality—The Schizophrenia Patient Outcomes Research Team (PORT) treatment recommendations
Source: https://www.ncbi.nlm.nih.gov/pubmed/19955388
Objectives: Over the last 26 years, the PORT treatment recommendations have been updated twice to reflect the more recent advances in the management of schizophrenia-spectrum psychoses, including findings from the Clinical Antipsychotic Trials of Intervention Effectiveness and the Cost Utility of the Latest Antipsychotic Drugs in Schizophrenia Study. Treatment recommendations for schizophrenia covered by this guideline range from first-episode psychosis to more chronic stages and from the perspectives of both psychopharmacological and psychosocial interventions. There is also a separate statement on the latter (https://www.ncbi.nlm.nih.gov/pubmed/19955389). It is important to note that the PORT guidelines do not cover the prodromal or ultra-high clinical risk stages of psychosis.

Continued

Table 1.1 An Overview of Clinical Practice Guidelines for Schizophrenia and Related Disorders[a]—cont'd

Highlights:

- For first-episode psychosis, antipsychotics other than clozapine and olanzapine should be first-line treatment, with lower doses than those used in multiple episodes.
- For multiepisode schizophrenia responsive to treatment, each antipsychotic drug needs to be trialled for 2–6 weeks before switching.
- In cases of treatment-resistance, clozapine should be offered after 2 adequate trials of other antipsychotics; trial of clozapine should be at least 8 weeks to achieve a plasma level of 350 ng/mL. Clozapine is also recommended for persistent hostility, violence, or suicidal behaviours.
- For acute agitation, oral or intramuscular antipsychotic alone or with rapid-acting benzodiazepine should be used.
- Low-frequency (1 Hz) repetitive transcranial magnetic stimulation (rTMS) over the left temporoparietal cortex is recommended for treating persistent and treatment-resistant auditory hallucinations.
- Psychosocial treatment recommendations include Assertive Community Treatment, supported employment, and skills training for social and independent living.
- Cognitive Behavioural Therapy for psychosis is recommended in a group or individual setting for a duration of 4–9 months.

Issues for psychologists:

- An urgent need for a team-based approach, especially with those who have a chronic course.
- Assessment of ultra-high risk may still be an issue in individuals presenting with attenuated psychotic symptoms who are help seeking.

[a]Professional psychologists are required to be familiar with the clinical practice guidelines relevant to their location and keep informed with any updates.

diagnosed with schizophrenia or even other schizophrenia-spectrum psychoses (e.g. schizoaffective disorder). Instead, they are more likely to be diagnosed with common mental disorders such as depression (unipolar or bipolar) or anxiety, or borderline personality disorder—especially in people who report hallucinations along with affective instability. However, the presence of psychotic symptoms even in the context of the more common disorders predicts greater symptom severity, poorer treatment response, and worse functioning (Varghese et al., 2009; Yung et al., 2005). Therefore, it is still crucial to identify and manage psychotic experiences even in nonpsychotic disorder help-seeking populations.

Conclusions on Diagnosis

Whilst characterising schizophrenia spectrum disorders as dimensions or categories is highly contested, it seems unlikely that in the near-to-medium future we will be able to dispense completely with categorical diagnostic systems such as

ICD or DSM. We should consider diagnoses or syndromes as fuzzy *descriptive* prototypes: with repeated episodes the patient is likely to show a more consistent picture.

In support of a categorical view, McGorry et al., 2018, Kendler (2018), and Tyrer (2018) take a pragmatic approach emphasising utility; they argue that ultimately clinicians need to dichotomise people's problems whether the condition is dimensional or not (for commentaries see Jablensky, 2018; Tandon, 2016; Reed, 2018; Wittchen & Beesdo-Baum, 2018; Zachar, 2018). For example, blood pressure, temperature, and intelligence are all dimensional, but categories are formed in selecting people on the basis of cut-points for treatment or entry into services. Categories are also important for legal/medical purposes, e.g. insurance claims and for decisions in forensic psychiatry.

A diagnostic system has *utility* if it helps with treatment planning, prediction of course and outcomes, and identifying biological or social correlates.

Interestingly, Guloksuz and van Os (2018) also acknowledge the current problem of the utility of dimensional measures in clinical practice given clinical decisions are often dichotomous. With regard to the HiTOP model, Krueger et al. (2018) accept the 'possibility that there are meaningful thresholds, beyond which social and occupational dysfunction becomes increasingly likely' (p. 285). Finally, Caspi et al. (2014) acknowledge that it remains to be seen whether 'p' is 'merely a statistical reductio ad absurdum or is it real and meaningful' (p. 132).

Finally, it is important to understand that the structure of psychopathology is not the same as a diagnostic nosology—they are two very different things. Clinicians work from a 'bottom-up' approach. They are interested in the patient's presenting problem (signs and symptoms), the persistence of those signs and symptoms and their impact on the patient's functioning, but they are also concerned with what other signs and symptoms that patient has, as well as what they don't have. Differential diagnosis is critical in excluding other conditions, e.g. a person with dementia may have psychotic phenomena as may people with substance-induced psychoses. Adhering to a nosology and the ability to make a correct and timely diagnosis can prevent serious consequences in the right context, such as professional neglect.

CLINICAL STAGING MODEL OF PSYCHOSIS

One prominent criticism of the current diagnostic system in psychiatry is the lack of biological disease markers to fully support the claim that mental disorders are, after all, no more than brain disorders. Although the role played by biological processes such as genetics and brain structure cannot be denied, the strength of evidence is not yet sufficient for definitive or clinically useful (e.g. diagnostic, staging, prognostic, or theranostic) biomarkers (for a review, see Prata, Mechelli, & Kapur, 2014; also Levine, Rabinowitz, Uher, & Kapur, 2015 for treatment response markers). As such, there is no clear analogy between the diagnostic tests used in general medicine and psychiatric diagnoses. More recently, however, inspired by staging models in oncology, the clinical staging model of psychosis and severe mood disorders (McGorry, Hickie, Yung, Pantelis, &

Jackson, 2006; Wood, Yung, McGorry, & Pantelis, 2011) draws striking parallels with diseases encountered in other branches of medicine.

According to this heuristic model, the psychotic disorder spectrum has four main clinical stages, some with subcomponents (see Table 1.2). Each stage has recommended intervention strategies for its target population and may be linked to indicative biological and endophenotypic markers. For example, pathological changes in the brain's structure and function should be more severe in the later stages than they would otherwise be (if any) in the earlier stages, although in the current model no new markers are defined after a first episode of psychosis (i.e. progression into a fully disordered state).

Despite its advantages in guiding treatment (see Box 1.3), predicting outcome, and potential to integrate biological, social, and psychological aspects of mental disorder, the staging model has also attracted a number of controversies and criticisms. The model was first developed as a heuristic, but recent efforts to operationalise it have revealed difficulties in determining where the precise cut-point is once an individual gets past the first episode stage and into Stage 3 with its various substages. The consensus is that this determination is difficult and that although far from satisfactory, operationalising the number, length, and severity of episodes is an obvious way forward. Significant heterogeneity is therefore

Table 1.2 Clinical Staging Model for Psychotic Disorders

Clinical stage	Definition	Target population and preferred interventions
0	Increased risk of psychotic disorder; no current symptoms	First-degree teenage relatives of patients; psychoeducation, family education, and brief cognitive skills training
1a	Mild, nonspecific symptoms, including neurocognitive deficits, mild functional change or decline	Screening and referrals of teenage populations by school counsellor or primary care; formal psychoeducation, formal CBT, active substance abuse reduction
1b	Ultra-high risk; moderate but subthreshold symptoms, with moderate cognitive and/or functional decline to qualify caseness (GAF < 70)	Referral by educational, welfare agencies, primary care or emergency departments; formal psychoeducation, formal CBT, active substance abuse reduction, low-dose atypical antipsychotics, antidepressants, or mood stabilisers
2	First episode psychosis; full threshold disorder with moderate-to-severe symptoms	Referral by primary care, emergency departments, welfare, specialist care, drug and alcohol services; formal psychoeducation, formal CBT, active substance abuse reduction, low-dose atypical antipsychotics, antidepressants or mood stabilisers, vocational rehabilitation

Table 1.2 Clinical Staging Model for Psychotic Disorders—cont'd

Clinical stage	Definition	Target population and preferred interventions
3a	Incomplete remission from first episode; could be 'fast-tracked' to Stage 4	Primary and specialist care services; interventions same as Stage 2 but additional emphasis on medical and psychosocial strategies to achieve full remission
3b	Recurrence or relapse of psychotic disorder, which stabilises after treatment; GAF, residual symptoms, neurocognition below those of first episode	Primary and specialist care services; interventions same as Stage 3a but additional emphasis on relapse prevention and early warning signs
3c	Multiple relapses, worsening in clinical course and clear impact on functioning	Specialist care services; interventions same as Stage 3b but with emphasis on long-term stabilisation
4	Severe, persistent/resistant, or unremitting illness as judged on symptoms, neurocognition, or functional disability criteria	Specialised care services; interventions same as Stage 3c but with emphasis on clozapine and other tertiary treatments, ongoing disability management

Source: Adapted from McGorry, P. D., Hickie, I. B., Yung, A. R., Pantelis, C., & Jackson, H. J. (2006). Clinical staging of psychiatric disorders: a heuristic framework for choosing earlier, safer and more effective interventions. *Australian and New Zealand Journal of Psychiatry, 40*(8), 616–622.

Box 1.3 Key Advantages of the Clinical Staging Model

(1) Improves potential for intervening at the earliest possible stage and preventing the illness from progressing to later stages
(2) Strengthens capacity to offer treatments in earlier stages that are both more effective and less harmful than those used in later stages (i.e. with less side effects but equivalent or superior effectiveness)
(3) May improve prognostic estimates (though early intervention may change progression and prognosis)
(4) Highlights the importance of early intervention services in the detection and management of subclinical psychotic experiences.

expected not only within, but also across the Stage 3 substages, and the following data support this observation.

Attempts to validate the staging model have yielded inconsistent results, which may largely arise because of the difference in patient- and clinician-oriented perspectives. For example, following retrospective allocation of patients with schizophrenia-spectrum disorder to clinical stages, Tedja, Velthorst, van Tricht, de Haan & Colleagues (2017) found that the clearest distinction between stages involved worse symptoms and daily functioning in the first episode stage (Stage 2) and last stage of persistent/severe illness (Stage 4)—compared to intermediate stages, suggesting that the precision and prognostic validity of intermediate stages is limited. In a more recent study (Berendsen et al., 2018), the findings (i.e. differences in symptom severity, number of psychotic episodes, work and daily activities, etc.) confirmed the distinction between early and late (chronic) stages and generally supported the construct validity of the staging model. Nevertheless, other works cast doubt on the viability of a universal (or transdiagnostic) staging model (Duffy, Malhi, & Grof, 2017), in particular with regard to the definition of 'recovery'. Some also challenge the model's utility by highlighting perceived pessimism in prognosis and its potential detrimental impact on patients (Baumann, Marion-Veyron, Bardy, Solida, & Conus, 2015), which may result from a rigid staging model (though the original authors of the staging model did admit fluidity and flexibility between stages). In fact, an alternative staging model was proposed by Andresen, Oades, and Caputi (2003) well before the formal introduction of the clinically focused staging model, grounded in the psychological processes of recovery from psychotic illness.

RECOMMENDATIONS ON COMMUNICATING A DIAGNOSIS OF PSYCHOSIS TO PATIENTS

Effective communication is critical in mental health (Priebe et al., 2011), but especially so when clinicians are faced with the difficult task of informing patients with schizophrenia spectrum disorders of their diagnosis (Ditton-Phare et al., 2015; McCabe & Priebe, 2004). Ditton-Phare et al. (2015) reported that less than 50% of psychiatrists explicitly informed patients of their diagnosis of schizophrenia and about 40% of patients received insufficient information about their diagnosis. Reasons put forward by psychiatrists for the full or partial omission of diagnostic details were diagnostic uncertainty, patient distress and stigma, lack of mental health resources, and time constraints (see also Outram, Harris, Kelly, Cohen, et al., 2015). On the other hand, patients and carers preferred a named diagnosis and saw the benefits as outweighing the negatives of receiving a diagnosis (see also Loughland, Cheng, et al., 2015; Luderer & Bocker, 1993).

Milton and Mullan (2014a) identified and reviewed 14, mostly descriptive studies, relating to the communication of the diagnosis of schizophrenia-spectrum disorders from the patient's perspective. Key themes identified were: preferences towards disclosure, diagnostic terminology, health professional training, stigma-related issues, and the use of diagnostic models. Specific qualitative studies have identified varying numbers and types of themes regarding client's information needs and preferences, highlighting the complexities and challenges of giving and receiving a diagnosis (e.g. Loughland, Cheng, et al., 2015 ; Milton & Mullan, 2015).

The needs and perspective of family caregivers are also important, as many patients live with or close to their caregivers (Onwumere, Shiers, & Chew-Graham, 2016). Outram, Harris, Kelly, Bylund, et al. (2015) using qualitative analysis of interviews with family caregivers of patients with schizophrenia found '...long and difficult pathways to being given a diagnosis, high unmet needs for information, exclusion from the medical care process and problematic communication and general interactions with mental health clinicians.' (p. 10).

Whilst qualitative thematic studies have been limited to small samples and found a variety of themes relating to the process of communicating a diagnosis, a number of common issues are also apparent, reflecting concerns of patients and families/caregivers alike. In particular, there is a strong preference for shared decision-making in people with schizophrenia (Byrne, Davies, & Morrison, 2010; McCabe & Priebe, 2008; Outram, Harris, Kelly, Bylund, et al., 2015), pointing to the need for a better understanding of the barriers and facilitators to its attainment. For example, Farrelly et al. (2015) and Milton, Mullan, and Hunt (2016) have reported on clinician-reported barriers to communication and shared decision-making in mental health care (see Box 1.4).

Communication Models

Milton and Mullan (2014b) conducted a systematic review of the literature and concluded that there was a need for communication protocols for communicating a mental health diagnosis. In Australia, Ditton-Phare and colleagues have developed a communication skills package specifically for communicating diagnostic information to patients and their families (Ditton-Phare et al., 2015; Ditton-Phare, Sandu, Kelly, Kissane, & Loughland, 2016). This program, named ComPsych CST, was derived from the Comskil Training Program (Memorial Sloan Kettering Cancer Center, New York; see Links to Resources) and consists of an introductory lecture with exemplary demonstration videos, modular booklets for trainees, facilitated small group in vitro role plays with an actor playing the part of a patient, feedback, and peer discussion.

In their Cochrane reviews, Farooq, Johal, Ziff, and Naeem (2017) found no randomised controlled trials that assessed the effects of strategies for communicating the diagnosis of schizophrenia and related disorders, whilst Papageorgiou, Loke, and Fromage (2017) identified one pilot cluster-randomised controlled trial by McCabe et al. (2016); this essentially focussed on clinicians' efforts (via self-repair) to establish shared understanding during sessions with patients. Both patients and clinicians who received training rated the therapeutic relationship as being significantly more positive at 5-month follow-up. However, Papageorgiou et al. (2017) also highlighted the weaknesses with this study, notably the small sample size and its pilot nature.

Self-repair refers to a clinician's ongoing reworking of their speech to make it more understandable and acceptable to the listener

In a study of 30 psychiatry trainees, using a pretest/posttest design, Ditton-Phare et al. (2016) found that following training communication skills increased for *agenda setting* while *questioning skills* decreased. Similarly, Loughland, Kelly, et al. (2015) conducted a preliminary study of the first two modules of the CompPsych program with 38 junior medical officers. At posttest, communication skills were reported to be improved with regard to conveying prognostic information for patients.

Box 1.4 Selected Barriers to Clinician Communication and Shared Decision-Making (SDM)

Barrier or challenge	Example
1. Ambivalence about care planning[a]	■ Clinician belief that service users did not value or use care plans developed in routine care ■ Clinician belief that routine care planning was designed to meet the needs of mental health services
2. Clinician perceptions that they were already doing SDM[a]	■ Strong commitment by clinicians to the idea of joint care planning but clear that many clinicians did not realise this ideal ■ Clinicians failed to take into account the power differential between them and the service user
3. Concerns regarding the clinical 'appropriateness of service users' choices[a]	■ Clinicians concerned that service users would make choices they considered not in the service users' best interest, e.g. treatment refusal
4. Limited 'availability of service users' choices[a]	■ Clinician concern that service users would request treatments or services that clinicians could not provide
5. Stigma, diagnosis, and risk factors[b]	■ More complex disorders are more difficult to discuss ■ Discussion of diagnosis may interfere with therapeutic alliance ■ Problem with accuracy of diagnoses
6. Service structure[b]	■ Difficulty arranging follow-up sessions ■ Insufficient time for full discussions ■ Interruptions in workplace
7. Individual circumstances[b]	■ Individual is culturally and linguistically diverse from me ■ The person being unwell at the time of the conversation ■ The individual does not want diagnostic information

[a]From Farrelly et al. (2015).
[b]From Milton, Mullan, MacCann, and Hunt (2018).

In sum, the extant evidence for communication skills training (CST) is sparse and seemingly still in its infancy. We could find no communication skills training programs for schizophrenia/severe mental illness specifically for clinical or neuro-psychologists. From a clinical perspective, and integrating information from the existing manuals and guidelines, contextualisation and timing are critical to the effective communication of a diagnosis of psychosis (see Milton et al., 2016) and need to take into account the current mental state of the patient. It is necessary for the therapist to provide the patient with the most up-to-date evidence-based information about diagnosis, aetiology, and treatment. Furthermore, patients and caregivers should be encouraged to ask questions and not be passive recipients of information, whilst negative stereotypical beliefs held by patients and carers should be dispelled. Indeed, the importance of maintaining an optimistic, hopeful but realistic approach is backed up by data and stated in management and treatment guidelines for schizophrenia and related disorders (see Table 1.1). Finally, Milton et al. (2018) conclude that clinicians should be aware of how their own stigmatising beliefs and background affect their communication—a topic covered more extensively in Chapter 3.

CONCLUSION—THE WAY FORWARD

It is perhaps not at all surprising that because of the sheer heterogeneity and complexity involved in the conceptualisation, diagnosis, and treatment of psychotic disorders, that controversies are inevitable when it comes to the question—'what is psychosis?' A prominent example of such controversy concerns the role of traumatic life events in the pathogenesis of psychotic symptoms, especially auditory-verbal hallucinations. In a recently published metaanalysis, Bailey et al. (2018), found that despite statistically significant correlations between childhood trauma and auditory-verbal hallucinations, the variance explained by trauma was very small (approximately 4%). This finding runs counter to the dominant role of trauma in many of the newer models of voice-hearing and suggests that the relationship between the two is perhaps far more nuanced than previously thought. Moreover, it serves a useful reminder of the need for trainee psychologists—and established mental health professionals from all disciplines—to keep their beliefs, assumptions, and clinical practice updated by the best available evidence on psychosis.

ADDITIONAL READING

Hamilton, M. (ed.) (1976). *Fish's schizophrenia* (2nd ed.). Bristol: John Wright & Sons.

Millon, T. (2004). *Masters of the mind: Exploring the story of mental illness from ancient times to the new millennium.* New Jersey: Wiley.

Shorter, E. (1997). *A history of psychiatry: From the era of the asylum to the age of Prozac.* New York, NY: John Wiley & Sons, Inc.

LINKS TO RESOURCES FOR PATIENTS, FAMILIES, CARERS, AND CLINICIANS

- NICE guidelines on communication and shred decision making https://www.nice.org.uk/guidance/cg136.
- Royal College of Psychiatrists fact sheet for caregivers https://www.rcpsych.ac.uk/healthinformation/informationforcarers/severementalillness.aspx.

- Clinical guidelines for early psychosis https://www.orygen.org.au/Education-Training/Resources-Training/Resources/Free/Clinical-Practice/Australian-Clinical-Guidelines-for-Early-Psychosis.
- Orygen Tip Sheet on helping someone with psychosis https://www.orygen.org.au/Education-Training/Resources-Training/Resources/Free/Fact-Sheets/helping-psychosis-yp/helping-someone-psychosis-factsheet?ext=.
- Information about Comskil: Communication Skills Training Program & Research Laboratory https://www.mskcc.org/departments/psychiatry-behavioral-sciences/communication-skills-research.
- Information about Tempo Training (to improve communication with patients with psychosis https://medicine.exeter.ac.uk/tempo/trainingmanual/.

References

American Psychiatric Association. (2013). *Diagnostic and statistical manual of mental disorders (DSM5)*. Washington, DC: American Psychiatric Association.

Andreasen, N. C. (1982). Negative symptoms in schizophrenia definition and reliability. *Archives of General Psychiatry, 39*, 784–788.

Andreasen, N. C. (1983). *Scale for the assessment of negative symptoms*. Iowa City: University of Iowa Press.

Andreasen, N. C. (1984). *Scale for the assessment of positive symptoms*. Iowa City: University of Iowa Press.

Andresen, R., Oades, L., & Caputi, P. (2003). The experience of recovery from schizophrenia: Towards an empirically validated stage model. *Australian & New Zealand Journal of Psychiatry, 37*(5), 586–594.

Asher, L., Fekadu, A., & Hanlon, C. (2018). Global mental health and schizophrenia. *Current Opinion in Psychiatry, 31*, 193–199. https://doi.org/10.1097/YCO.0000000000000404.

Badcock, J. C., Clarke, M., & Morgan, V. A. (2018). Hallucinations in indigenous and non-indigenous Australians: Findings from the second Australian national survey of psychosis. *Schizophrenia Research, 197*, 581–582.

Bailey, T., Alvarez-Jimenez, M., Garcia-Sanchez, A. M., Hulbert, C., Barlow, E., & Bendall, S. (2018). Childhood trauma is associated with severity of hallucinations and delusions in psychotic disorders: A systematic review and meta-analysis. *Schizophrenia Bulletin*. https://doi.org/10.1093/schbul/sbx161.

Barch, D. M., Bustillo, J., Gaebel, W., Gur, R., Heckers, S., Malaspina, D., et al. (2013). Logic and justification for dimensional assessment of symptoms and related clinical phenomena in psychosis: Relevance to DSM-5. *Schizophrenia Research, 150*, 15–20.

Baumann, P. S., Marion-Veyron, R., Bardy, S., Solida, A., & Conus, P. (2015). Beyond clinical staging of psychiatric disorders. *The Lancet Psychiatry, 2*(10), e27.

Beavan, V., Read, J., & Cartwright, C. (2011). The prevalence of voice-hearers in the general population: A literature review. *Journal of Mental Health, 20*, 281–292. https://doi.org/10.3109/09638237.2011.562262.

Berendsen, S., van der Paardt, J., van Bruggen, M., Nusselder, H., Jalink, M., Peen, J., et al. (2018). Exploring construct validity of clinical staging in schizophrenia spectrum disorders in an acute psychiatric ward. *Clinical Schizophrenia & Related Psychoses*. https://doi.org/10.3371/CSRP.BEPA.061518.

Biedermann, F., & Fleischhacker, W. W. (2016). Psychotic disorders in DSM-5 and ICD-11. *CNS Spectrums, 21*(Special Issue 4), 349–354. https://doi.org/10.1017/S1092852916000316.

Blanchard, J. J., & Cohen, A. S. (2006). The structure of negative symptoms within schizophrenia: Implications for assessment. *Schizophrenia Bulletin, 32*, 238–245. https://doi.org/10.1093/schbul/sbj013.

Bourque, F., van der Ven, E., Fusar-Poli, P., & Malla, A. (2012). Immigration, social environment and onset of psychotic disorders. *Current Pharmaceutical Design, 18*(4), 518–526.

Byrne, R., Davies, L., & Morrison, A. P. (2010). Priorities and preferences for the outcomes of treatment of psychosis: A service user perspective. *Psychosis, 2*(3), 210–217. https://doi.org/10.1080/17522430903456913.

Campbell, M. M., Sibeko, G., Mall, S., Baldinger, A., Nagdee, M., Susser, E., et al. (2017). The content of delusions in a sample of South African Xhosa people with schizophrenia. *BMC Psychiatry, 17*. [Article number 41]. https://doi.org/10.1186/s12888-017-1196-3.

Caspi, A., Houts, R. M., Belsky, D. W., Goldman-Mellor, S. J., Harrington, H., Israel, S., et al. (2014). The p factor: One general factor in the structure of psychiatric disorders. *Clinical Psychological Science, 2*, 119–137. https://doi.org/10.1177/2167702613497473.

Chadwick, P., & Birchwood, M. (1994). The omnipotence of voices. A cognitive approach to auditory hallucinations. *British Journal of Psychiatry, 164*(2), 190–201.

Cooke, A., & Kinderman, P. (2018). "But what about real mental illnesses?" Alternatives to the disease model approach to "schizophrenia". *Journal of Humanistic Psychology, 58*(1), 47–71. [Part 2: Special issue]. https://doi.org/10.1177/0022167817745621.

Cuthbert, B. N., & Insel, T. R. (2013). Toward the future of psychiatric diagnosis: The seven pillars of RDoC. *BMC Medicine, 11*. [Article number 126]. https://doi.org/10.1186/1741-7015-11-126.

Ditton-Phare, P., Halpin, S., Sandu, H., Kelly, B., Vamos, M., Outram, S., et al. (2015). Communication skills in psychiatry training. *Australasian Psychiatry, 23*, 429–431. https://doi.org/10.1177/103985621559006.

Ditton-Phare, P., Sandu, H., Kelly, B., Kissane, D., & Loughland, C. (2016). Pilot evaluation of a communication skills program for psychiatry residents using standardised patient assessment. *Academic Psychiatry, 40*, 768–775.

Duffy, A., Malhi, G. S., & Grof, P. (2017). Do the trajectories of bipolar disorder and schizophrenia follow a universal staging model? *The Canadian Journal of Psychiatry, 62*(2), 115–122.

Farooq, S., Johal, R. K., Ziff, C., & Naeem, F. (2017). Different communication strategies for disclosing a diagnosis of schizophrenia and related disorders. *Cochrane Data Base of Systematic Reviews*, (10). Article number CD011707. https://doi.org/10.1002/14651858.CD011707.pub2.

Farrelly, S., Lester, H., Rose, D., Birchwood, M., Marshall, M., Waheed, W., et al. (2015). Barriers to shared decision-making in mental health care: qualitative study of the Joint Crisis Plan for psychosis. *Health Expectations, 19*, 448–458. https://doi.org/10.1111/hex.12368.

Fowler, D., Hodgekins, J., Garety, P., Freeman, D., Kuipers, E., Dunn, G., et al. (2012). Negative cognition, depressed mood, and paranoia: a longitudinal pathway analysis using structural equation modeling. *Schizophrenia Bulletin, 38*(5), 1063–1073.

Frances, A. (2014). ICD, DSM and the Tower of Babel. *Australian and New Zealand Journal of Psychiatry, 48*(4), 371–377.

Freeman, D., & Garety, P. A. (2003). Connecting neurosis and psychosis: The direct influence of emotion on delusions and hallucinations. *Behaviour Research and Therapy, 41*(8), 923–947.

Fulford, D., Pearson, R., Stuart, B. K., Fisher, M., Mathalon, D. H., Vonogradov, S., et al. (2014). Symptom assessment in early psychosis: The use of well-established rating scales in clinical high-risk and recent-onset populations. *Psychiatry Research, 220*(3), 1077–1083.

Fusar-Poli, P., Cappucciati, M., Rutigliano, G., Heslin, M., Stahl, D., Brittenden, Z., et al. (2016). Diagnostic stability of ICD/DSM first episode psychosis diagnoses: Meta-analysis. *Schizophrenia Bulletin, 42*(6), 1395–1406. https://doi.org/10.1093/schbul/sbw020.

Galletly, C., Castle, D., Dark, F., Humberstone, V., Jablensky, A., Killackey, E., et al. (2016). Royal Australian and New Zealand College of Psychiatrists clinical practice guidelines for the management of schizophrenia and related disorders. *Australian and New Zealand Journal of Psychiatry, 50* (5), 1–117.

Garety, P. A., Kuipers, E., Fowler, D., Freeman, D., & Bebbington, P. E. (2001). A cognitive model of the positive symptoms of psychosis. *Psychological Medicine, 31*(2), 189–195.

Gottesman, I. I., & Shields, J. (1972). A polygenic theory of schizophrenia. *International Journal of Mental Health, 1*(1–2), 107–115.

Guloksuz, S., Pries, L. K., & van Os, J. (2017). Application of network methods for understanding mental disorders: pitfalls and promise. *Psychological Medicine, 47*, 2743–2752. https://doi.org/10.1017/S0033291717001350.

Guloksuz, S., & van Os, J. (2018). The slow death of the concept of schizophrenia and the painful birth of the psychosis spectrum. *Psychological Medicine, 48*, 229–244. https://doi.org/10.1017/S0033291717001775.

Habets, P., Marcelis, M., Gronenschild, E., Drukker, M., & van Os, J. (2011). Reduced cortical thickness as an outcome of differential sensitivity to environmental risks in schizophrenia. *Biological Psychiatry, 69*(5), 487–494.

Hartley, S., Barrowclough, C., & Haddock, G. (2013). Anxiety and depression in psychosis: a systematic review of associations with positive psychotic symptoms. *Acta Psychiatrica Scandinavica, 128*(5), 327–346.

Henriksen, M. G., & Parnas, J. (2012). Clinical manifestations of self-disorders and the Gestalt of schizophrenia. *Schizophrenia Bulletin, 38*(4), 657–660.

Howes, O. D., McCutcheon, R., Owen, M. J., & Murray, R. M. (2017). The role of genes, stress, and dopamine in the development of schizophrenia. *Biological Psychiatry, 81*(1), 9–20.

Howes, O. D., & Murray, R. M. (2014). Schizophrenia: an integrated sociodevelopmental-cognitive model. *Lancet, 383*(9929), 1677–1687. https://doi.org/10.1016/S0140-6736(13)62036-X.

Howes, O. D., & Nour, M. M. (2016). Dopamine and the aberrant salience hypothesis of schizophrenia. *World Psychiatry, 15*(1), 3–4.

International Schizophrenia Consortium. (2009). Common polygenic variation contributes to risk of schizophrenia and bipolar disorder. *Nature, 460*(7256), 748–752.

Jablensky, A. (2018). The dialectic of quantity and quality in psychopathology. [Commentary]. *World Psychiatry, 18*, 300–301. https://doi.org/10.1002/wps.20562.

Jablensky, A., Sartorius, N., Ernberg, G., Anker, M., Korten, A., Cooper, J. E., et al. (1992). Schizophrenia: manifestations, incidence and course in different cultures. A World Health Organization ten-country study. *Psychological Medicine, Monograph Supplement, 20*, 1–97.

Jackson, H. J., & McGorry, P. D. (2009). Psychiatric diagnoses: Purposes, limitations and alternative approach. In S. J. Wood, N. B. Allen, & C. Pantelis (Eds.), *The neuropsychology of mental illness* (pp. 178–192). New York: Cambridge University Press.

Jones, N., & Luhrmann, T. M. (2016). Beyond the sensory: Findings from an in-depth analysis of the phenomenology of "auditory hallucinations" in schizophrenia. *Psychosis, 8*, 191–202.

Joy, D. S., Manoranjtham, S. D., Samuel, P., & Jacob, K. S. (2017). Explanatory models and distress in primary caregivers of patients with acute psychotic presentations: A study from South India. *International Journal of Social Psychiatry, 63*, 563–568.

Kalra, G., Bhugra, D., & Shah, N. (2012). Cultural aspects of schizophrenia. *International Review of Psychiatry, 24*, 441–449.

Kay, S. R., Fiszbein, A., & Opler, L. A. (1987). The Positive and Negative Syndrome Scale (PANSS) for schizophrenia. *Schizophrenia Bulletin, 113*, 261–276.

Kendler, K. S. (2015). A joint history of the nature of genetic variation and the nature of schizophrenia. *Molecular Psychiatry, 20*(1), 77–83.

Kendler, K. S. (2018). Classification of psychopathology: Conceptual and historical background. [Editorial]. *World Psychiatry, 17*, 241–242. https://doi.org/10.1002/wps.20549.

Kleinman, A., Eisenberg, L., & Good, B. (1978). Clinical lessons from anthropologic and cross-cultural research. *Annals of Internal Medicine, 88*, 251–258.

Krueger, R. F., et al. (2018). Progress in achieving quantitative classification of psychopathology. *World Psychiatry, 17*, 282–293.

Laroi, F., Luhrmann, T. M., Bell, V., Christian, W. A., Jr., Deshpande, S., Fernyhough, C., et al. (2014). Culture and hallucinations: Overview and future directions. *Schizophrenia Bulletin, 40*(Suppl. 4), S213–S220. https://doi.org/10.1093/schbul/sbu012.

Levine, S. Z., Rabinowitz, J., Uher, R., & Kapur, S. (2015). Biomarkers of treatment outcome in schizophrenia: Defining a benchmark for clinical significance. *European Neuropsychopharmacology, 25*(10), 1578–1585.

Lloyd, K. R., Jacob, K. S., Patel, L., St Louis, L., Bhugra, D., & Mann, A. H. (1998). The development of the Short Explanatory Model Interview (SEMI) and its use among primary-care attenders with common mental disorders. *Psychological Medicine, 28*, 1231–1237.

Loughland, C., Cheng, K., Harris, G., Kelly, B., Cohen, M., Sandhu, H., et al. (2015). Communication of a schizophrenia diagnosis: A qualitative study of patients' perspectives. *International Journal of Social Psychiatry, 61*, 729–734.

Loughland, C., Kelly, B., Ditton-Phare, P., Sandhu, H., Vamos, M., Outram, S., et al. (2015). Improving clinician competency in communication about schizophrenia: A pilot educational program for psychiatry trainees. *Academic Psychiatry, 39*, 160–164. https://doi.org/10.1007/s40596-014-0195-7.

Luderer, H. J., & Bocker, F. M. (1993). Clinician information habits, patients knowledge of diagnoses and etiologic concepts in 4 different clinical samples. *Acta Psychiatrica Scandinavica, 88*, 266–272. https://doi.org/10.1111/j.1600-0447.1993.tb03455.x.

Markon, K. E. (2010). Modeling psychopathology structure: a symptom-level analysis of Axis I and II disorders. *Psychological Medicine, 40*, 273–288.

McCabe, R., John, P., Dooley, J., Healey, P., Cushing, A., Kingdon, D., et al. (2016). Training to enhance psychiatrist communication with patients with psychosis (TEMPO): Cluster randomised controlled trial. *British Journal of Psychiatry, 209*, 517–524. https://doi.org/10.1192/bjp.bp.115.179499.

McCabe, R., & Priebe, S. (2004). Explanatory models of illness in schizophrenia: Comparison of four ethnic groups. *British Journal of Psychiatry, 185*, 25–30.

McCabe, R., & Priebe, S. (2008). Communication and psychosis: It's good to talk, but how? *British Journal of Psychiatry, 192*, 404–405. https://doi.org/10.1192/bjp.bp.107.048678.

McGorry, P. D., Hartmann, R. A., Spooner, R., & Nelson, B. (2018). Beyond the "at risk mental state" concept: Transitioning to transdiagnostic psychiatry. *World Psychiatry, 17*, 133–142.

McGorry, P. D., Hickie, I. B., Yung, A. R., Pantelis, C., & Jackson, H. J. (2006). Clinical staging of psychiatric disorders: a heuristic framework for choosing earlier, safer and more effective interventions. *Australian and New Zealand Journal of Psychiatry, 40*(8), 616–622.

McGrath, J. J., Saha, S., Al-Hamzawi, A., Alonso, J., Bromet, E. J., Bruffaerts, R., et al. (2015). Psychotic experiences in the general population: A cross-national analysis based on 31 261 respondents from 18 countries. *JAMA Psychiatry, 72*(7), 697–705.

Milton, A. C., Mullan, B., & Hunt, C. (2016). Information giving challenges and support strategies at the time of a mental health diagnosis: Qualitative views from Australian health professionals. *Social Psychiatry and Psychiatric Epidemiology, 51*, 735–746. https://doi.org/10.1007/s00127-016-1187-6.

Milton, A. C., Mullan, B., MacCann, C., & Hunt, C. (2018). An evaluation of communication barriers and facilitators at the time of a mental health diagnosis: A survey of mental health professional practices. *Epidemiology and Psychiatric Sciences, 27*, 357–368. https://doi.org/10.1017/S2045796016001153.

Milton, A. C., & Mullan, B. A. (2014a). Diagnosis telling in people with psychosis. *Current Opinion in Psychiatry, 27*, 302–307.

Milton, A. C., & Mullan, B. A. (2014b). Communication of a mental health diagnosis: A systematic review synthesis and narrative review. *Journal of Mental Health, 23*, 261–270. https://doi.org/10.3109/09638237.2014.951474.

Milton, A. C., & Mullan, B. A. (2015). A qualitative exploration of service user's information needs and preferences when receiving a serious mental health diagnosis. *Community Mental Health Journal, 51*, 459–466. https://doi.org/10.1007/s10597-014-9761-4.

Nelson, B., Parnas, J., & Sass, L. A. (2014). Disturbance of minimal self (ipseity) in schizophrenia: Clarification and current status. *Schizophrenia Bulletin, 40*(3), 479–482.

Nelson, B., Thompson, A., & Yung, A. R. (2012). Basic self-disturbance predicts psychosis onset in the ultra high risk for psychosis "prodromal" population. *Schizophrenia Bulletin, 38*(6), 1277–1287.

Onwumere, J., Shiers, D., & Chew-Graham, C. (August, 2016). [Editorials]. Understanding the needs of carers of people with psychosis in primary care. *British Journal of General Practice*, 400–401.

Outram, S., Harris, G., Kelly, B., Bylund, C. L., Cohen, M., Landa, Y., et al. (2015). We didn't have a clue': Family caregivers'experiences of the communication of a diagnosis of schizophrenia. *International Journal of Social Psychiatry, 61*, 10–16. https://doi.org/10.1077/0020764014535751.

Outram, S., Harris, G., Kelly, B., Cohen, M., Bylund, C. L., Landa, Y., et al. (2015). Contextual barriers to discussing a schizophrenia diagnosis with patients and families: Need for leadership and teamwork training in psychiatry. *Academic Psychiatry, 39*, 174–180. https://doi.org/10.1007/s40596-014-0226-4.

Overall, J. E., & Gorham, D. R. (1962). The Brief Psychiatric Rating Scale (BPRS). *Psychological Reports, 10*, 799–812.

Oyebode, F. (2014). *Sims' symptoms in the mind: Textbook of descriptive psychopathology* (5th ed.). Philadelphia, PA: Saunders Ltd.

Paniagua, F. A. (2018). ICD-10 versus DSM-5 on cultural issues. *Sage Open*, (January–March, 1–14). https://doi.org/10.1177/2158244018756165.

Papageorgiou, A., Loke, Y. K., & Fromage, M. (2017). Communication skills training for mental health professionals working with people with severe mental illness. *Cochrane Data Base of Systematic Reviews*, (6) [Article number CD010006],

Parnas, J. (2011). A disappearing heritage: the clinical core of schizophrenia. *Schizophrenia Bulletin, 37*(6), 1121–1130.

Perälä, J., Suvisaari, J., Saarni, S. I., Kuoppasalmi, K., Isometsä, E., Pirkola, S., et al. (2007). Lifetime prevalence of psychotic and bipolar I disorders in a general population. *Archives of General Psychiatry, 64*, 19–28.

Peralta, V., & Cuesta, M. J. (2001). How many and which are the psychopathological dimensions in schizophrenia? Issues influencing their ascertainment. *Schizophrenia Research, 49*, 269–285.

Peters, E., Day, S., McKenna, J., & Orbach, G. (1999). Delusional ideation in religious and psychotic populations. *British Journal of Clinical Psychology, 38*(1), 83–96.

Peters, E., Ward, T., Jackson, M., Woodruff, P., Morgan, C., McGuire, P., et al. (2017). Clinical relevance of appraisals of persistent psychotic experiences in people with and without a need for care: an experimental study. *Lancet Psychiatry, 4*(12), 927–936.

Prata, D., Mechelli, A., & Kapur, S. (2014). Clinically meaningful biomarkers for psychosis: a systematic and quantitative review. *Neuroscience & Biobehavioral Reviews, 45*, 134–141.

Priebe, S., Dimic, S., Wildgrube, C., Jankovic, J., Cushing, A., & McCabe, R. (2011). Good communication in psychiatry—A conceptual review. *European Psychiatry, 26*, 403–407. https://doi.org/10.1016/j.erupsy.2010.07.010.

Purcell, S. M., Moran, J. L., Fromer, M., Ruderfer, D., Solovieff, N., Roussos, P., et al. (2014). A polygenic burden of rare disruptive mutations in schizophrenia. *Nature, 506*(7487), 185–190.

Reed, G. M. (2018). HiTOP must meet the use requirements of the ICD before it can aspire to replace it. [Commentaries]. *World Psychiatry, 17*, 296–298. https://doi.org/10.1002/wps.20560.

Reininghaus, U., Gayer-Anderson, C., Valmaggia, L., Kempton, M. J., Calem, M., Onyejiaka, A., et al. (2016). Psychological processes underlying the association between childhood trauma and psychosis in daily life: An experience sampling study. *Psychological Medicine, 46*(13), 2799–2813.

Sass, L., Borda, J. P., Madeira, L., Pienkos, E., & Nelson, B. (2018). Varieties of self disorder: A bio-*pheno*-social model of schizophrenia. *Schizophrenia Bulletin*. https://doi.org/10.1093/schbul/sby001.

Sass, L. A., & Parnas, J. (2003). Schizophrenia, consciousness, and the self. *Schizophrenia Bulletin, 29*(3), 427–444.

Shevlin, M., McElroy, E., Bentall, R. P., Reininghaus, U., & Murphy, J. (2017). The psychosis continuum: Testing a bifactor model of psychosis in a general population sample. *Schizophrenia Bulletin, 43*(1), 133–141.

Sims, A. (1988). *Symptoms in the mind. An introduction to descriptive psychopathology*. London: Balliere Tindall.

So, S. H. W., Chau, A. K., Peters, E. R., Swendsen, J., Garety, P. A., & Kapur, S. (2018). Moment-to-moment associations between negative affect, aberrant salience, and paranoia. *Cognitive Neuropsychiatry, 23*(5), 299–306.

Tamminga, C. A., Pearlson, G. D., Stan, A. D., Gibbons, R. D., Padmanabhan, J., Keshavan, M., et al. (2017). Strategies for advancing disease definition using biomarkers and genetics: The bipolar and schizophrenia network for intermediate phenotypes. *Biological Psychiatry: Cognitive Neuroscience and Neuroimaging, 2*(1), 20–27.

Tandon, R. (2016). Conceptualising psychotic disorders: don't throw the baby out with the bathwater. *World Psychiatry, 15*, 133–134.

Tandon, R., Nasrallah, H. A., & Keshavan, M. S. (2009). Schizophrenia, "just the facts" 4. Clinical features and conceptualization. *Schizophrenia Research, 110*, 1–23. https://doi.org/10.1016/j.schres.2009.03.005.

Tedja, A., Velthorst, E., van Tricht, M., de Haan, L., & GROUP. (2017). Preliminary validation of a clinical staging model in schizophrenia and related disorders. *Clinical Schizophrenia & Related Psychoses*. https://doi.org/10.3371/CSRP.ATEV.071317.

Tyrer, P. (2018). Dimensions fit the data, but can clinicians fit the dimensions? [Commentaries]. *World Psychiatry, 17*, 295–296. https://doi.org/10.1002/wps.20559.

Underwood, R., Kumari, V., & Peters, E. (2016). Cognitive and neural models of threat appraisal in psychosis: a theoretical integration. *Psychiatry Research, 239*, 131–138.

van Bork, R., Epskamp, S., Rhemtulla, M., Borsboom, D., & van der Maas, H. L. J. (2017). What is the p-factor of psychopathology? Some risks of general factor modelling. *Theory & Psychology, 27*, 759–773. https://doi.org/10.1177/0959354317737185.

van Os, J., & Guloksuz, S. (2017). A critique of the "ultra high risk" and "transition" paradigm. *World Psychiatry, 16*, 200–206.

van Os, J., Linscott, R. J., Myin-Germeys, I., Delespaul, P., & Krabbendam, L. (2009). A systematic review and meta-analysis of the psychosis continuum: Evidence for a psychosis proneness-persistence-impairment model of psychotic disorder. *Psychological Medicine, 39*, 179–195.

Varghese, D., Scott, J., Welham, J., Bor, W., Najman, J., O'callaghan, M., et al. (2009). Psychotic-like experiences in major depression and anxiety disorders: a population-based survey in young adults. *Schizophrenia Bulletin, 37*(2), 389–393.

Wigman, J. T. W., de Vos, S., Wichers, M., van Os, J., & Bartels-Velthuis, A. A. (2017). A transdiagnostic framework approach to psychosis. *Schizophrenia Bulletin, 43*, 122–123.

Wittchen, H.-U., & Beesdo-Baum, K. (2018). "Throwing out the baby with the bathwater"? Conceptual and methodological limitations of the HiTOP approach. *World Psychiatry, 17*, 298–299. https://doi.org/10.1002/wps.20561.

Wood, S. J., Yung, A. R., McGorry, P. D., & Pantelis, C. (2011). Neuroimaging and treatment evidence for clinical staging in psychotic disorders: From the at-risk mental state to chronic schizophrenia. *Biological Psychiatry, 70*(7), 619–625.

World Health Organization (WHO). (2018). *International statistical classification of diseases and related health problems* (11th ed.). Geneva: WHO.

Yung, A. R., Buckby, J. A., Cotton, S. M., Cosgrave, E. M., Killackey, E. J., Stanford, C., et al. (2005). Psychotic-like experiences in nonpsychotic help-seekers: Associations with distress, depression, and disability. *Schizophrenia Bulletin, 32*(2), 352–359.

Zachar, P. (2018). Quantitative classification as (re-) descriptive psychopathology. [Commentaries]. *World Psychiatry, 17*, 294–295. https://doi.org/10.1002/wps.20558.

Definition of Key Terms

Agency The sense that mental events and behaviours. such as actions and thoughts, originate from oneself, i.e. one is the agent and has first-person experience.

Appraisals The emotional–motivational significance given to stimuli and drive emotional responses.

Diminished self-affection Involves a decreased feeling of existence as a subject of self-awareness.

Hyperreflexivity An exaggerated self-consciousness

Minimal self Refers to the most basic sense of having experiences that are one's own.

Narrative self The sense that we have of ourselves as having an evolving story through past and future.

Ownership The sense that one is physically responsible ('owns') for the mental events one initiates.

Phenomenology The study of consciousness and the objects of direct experience.

Single-nucleotide polymorphisms Variations of a single nucleotide (building blocks of DNA) that occur at specific locations within a genome.

CHAPTER 2

Models of Schizophrenia. A Selective Review of Genetic, Neuropharmacological, Cognitive, and Social Approaches

Megan Ichinose, Sohee Park
Department of Psychology, Vanderbilt University, Nashville, TN, United States

Key Learning Objectives

- Identify the role of genetic and environmental factors in the development of psychotic disorders (i.e. schizophrenia).
- Describe the major neurochemical hypotheses of schizophrenia.
- Describe major cognitive models that characterise symptoms of schizophrenia.
- Describe key social factors that may underlie and contribute to symptoms associated with schizophrenia.

INTRODUCTION

As Clara Kean describes in her first person account (2009; see Box 2.1), her distraught experience of psychosis is about disconnection. Not only does she feel unable to communicate with her doctor, she is disconnected from herself. From the perspective of individuals with schizophrenia, phenomenological, subjective experiences form the backbone of the illness (for a series of first-person accounts, see *Schizophrenia Bulletin*). On the other hand, to the clinician or research scientist who does not have personal access to these lived-in experiences, the disease process is defined by observed behaviour (symptoms). It follows then, that the first step towards successful outcome and recovery for complex neuropsychiatric conditions such as schizophrenia should involve bridging the chasm between the subjective illness experiences and the objectively defined disease.

A Clinical Introduction to Psychosis. https://doi.org/10.1016/B978-0-12-815012-2.00002-X

Box 2.1 First Person Account

I was simply sectioned again, detached from my real self, observing what was being done to me in a third-person perspective. When I said this to my psychiatrist after being rescued from the top of a multistory car park, he dismissed my comment by saying that "you certainly communicate your distress clearly." It was not even my own distress—I was totally separated from myself, not knowing what action I was taking, let alone considering how to "communicate" to others. I was unaware of myself, and my psychiatrist was unaware of me. What he chose to see was nothing but the symptoms alone.

Kean (2009, p. 1034)

Indeed, the past two decades have seen a resurgence in research integrating biology with phenomenology to explain the self-experiences of those with schizophrenia (e.g. Nelson & Sass, 2017; Wong & Van Tol, 2003). Thus, neurobiological and psychological models of schizophrenia can help translate between the subjective phenomenology and the observed behaviours. Such models not only guide ongoing research on the aetiology and treatment of schizophrenia, they importantly guide clinicians when providing psychoeducation to patients, formulating cases, and planning treatment. In this chapter, a selective review of genetic, pharmacological, cognitive and social approaches is presented to elucidate the core nature of schizophrenia. These models are derived from decades of progress in neuroscience, genetics, psychological sciences, and psychiatry that have dramatically transformed the field of schizophrenia research.

GENETIC CONTRIBUTIONS TO SCHIZOPHRENIA

Early evidence for the genetic basis of schizophrenia came from family, twin and adoption studies, which indicated that the risk for schizophrenia steadily increased with genetic closeness (see Gottesman & Shields, 1976). These conclusions have since been bolstered by national family and metaanalytic twin studies that estimate heritability of schizophrenia to be as high as 60%–80% (Lichtenstein et al., 2006, 2009; Sullivan, Kendler, & Neale, 2003). While heritability estimates may conflate shared environmental and genetic risk factors, the importance of genetic contributions is observed in the much greater concordance rate for monozygotic twins for schizophrenia than that for the dizygotic twins or full siblings (for reviews, see Cardno & Gottesman, 2000, Kendler, 1983). Furthermore, the prevalence rate for psychosis is elevated in biological children of individuals with schizophrenia even if they were adopted in infancy (Tienari et al., 2000, 2003). Conversely, growing up with an adoptive parent with schizophrenia does not seem to increase the risk for schizophrenia in biological children of nonschizophrenic parents.

While the heritability evidence may emphasise the genetic contributions to schizophrenia, shared environmental factors cannot be ignored. For instance, the approximate concordance rate for monozygotic twins is far below what would be expected if schizophrenia was conferred entirely or even mostly via shared genetic material (i.e. 100%). Rather, there seems to be a significant gene–environment interaction, such that both genetic liability and environmental factors contribute to psychosis risk (for a review, see van Os, Rutten, & Poulton, 2008). One elegant example of such an interaction is that for adopted children of biological mothers with schizophrenia, only adverse adoptive-family environment predicts schizophrenia (Tienari et al., 2004).

A complex variety of interactions between genes and environmental factors contribute to psychotic disorders.

Evidence for the influence of environmental factors on the development of psychosis is also overwhelmingly significant (see Howes & Murray, 2014). Birth complications, prenatal insults (e.g. viral infection), pregnancy complications (e.g. foetal hypoxia), and other early adverse events have been shown to increase the risk for schizophrenia as well as other psychiatric disorders (Brown, 2011). In addition, childhood trauma (Gibson, Alloy, & Ellman, 2016), migration (Cantor-Graae & Selten, 2005), chronic stress, and other social environmental factors are heavily implicated in the increased risk for psychosis, possibly via alterations in the dopamine system (Selten, Booij, Buwalda, & Meyer-Lindenberg, 2017). In sum, Gottesman and Shields's (1976) classic diathesis–stress model of gene–environment interaction and more recent, schizophrenia-specific iterations (see Pruessner, Cullen, Aas, & Walker, 2017) remain a foundational framework for understanding the emergence of schizophrenia as the final outcome of multiple genetic and environmental factors across developmental stages (Pruessner et al., 2017). More recently, sophisticated genomic technology has been applied to very large samples to elucidate the underlying genetic basis of schizophrenia, which involves rare, common, and de novo risk alleles distributed across very large number of genes.

A number of environmental factors throughout development confer substantial risk for schizophrenia.

Contributions of Rare CNVs

Much of the genetic risk for schizophrenia may be inherited, but de novo genetic mutations (mutations or genetic alterations arising for the first time in a family member) have also been found to contribute. For example, the rate of de novo copy number variant (CNV) mutations is significantly higher in those with schizophrenia as compared to control groups (Kirov et al., 2012; Xu et al., 2008). Analyses of rare CNVs involving large databases have found associations at 11–15 loci since the first discovery of a deletion at 22q11.2 (see Rees et al., 2014). While these CNVs increase the risk of developing schizophrenia (odds ratios between 2 and 50), it is important to note that these mutations are rare among those who are diagnosed with schizophrenia. Thus, the contribution of the rare CNVs such as the deletion at 22q11.2 to the total genetic liability for schizophrenia seems relatively weak. However, these rare CNVs in schizophrenia are implicated in neurobiological factors that are highly relevant to psychosis, such as the NMDA receptors (NMDAR) found at excitatory synapses, and the metabotropic glutamate receptor 5 (mGluR5) components of the post synaptic density (e.g. Kirov et al., 2012). Lastly, there is a considerable overlap across multiple neuropsychiatric conditions. Schizophrenia-associated CNVs are also associated with increased risk for other neuropsychiatric disorders (e.g. Prader–Willi syndrome, autism spectrum disorder, epilepsy, attention-deficit hyperactivity disorder) (Sebat, Levy, & McCarthy, 2009).

Single-Nucleotide Polymorphisms (SNPs)

Genome-wide association studies have helped identify *many* common risk variants spanning the genome that are associated with schizophrenia.

Genome-wide association studies (GWAS) of single-nucleotide polymorphisms (SNPs) suggest that genetic risk of schizophrenia is conferred by a large number of alleles at over 100 loci (Ripke et al., 2014). Such identified alleles also include several common alleles associated with schizophrenia. These SNPs are collectively estimated to account for about a third (and possibly up to half) of the variation in schizophrenia genetic liability. Although the effects of individual alleles on the risk are weak, there are promising leads. According to the work by the Schizophrenia Working Group of the Psychiatric Genomics Consortium (see Giegling et al., 2017), the most significant allelic association is found on the extended major histocompatibility complex (MHC) on the short arm of chromosome 6. Interestingly, MHCs play an important role in the immune system, which suggests a potential link between schizophrenia risk and abnormal immune system functioning. In addition, genome-wide significant associations for schizophrenia risk have been found for the dopamine receptor D2 gene. Again, it is important to note that both abnormal immune system functioning and dopamine receptors are implicated in a wide range of neuropsychiatric conditions (e.g. bipolar disorder, major depressive disorder, attention deficit hyperactivity disorder, and autism spectrum disorder). Thus, it is best to think of genetic mutations that are hypothesised to be implicated in schizophrenia as converging on common biological pathways that impair calcium signalling, alter postsynaptic density and synaptic plasticity, and influence epigenetic regulations. Of note, variations in these genetic risk factors have also been used to identify subtypes of schizophrenia, which may not only help characterise one's predominant symptoms (e.g. Hallmayer et al., 2005; Zai, Robbins, Sahakian, & Kennedy, 2017), but also inform one's response to certain medications (e.g. Blasi et al., 2015) and therapeutic interventions (Panizzutti, Hamilton, & Vinogradov, 2013).

Summary

Genetics of schizophrenia and related conditions are still poorly understood. Combined effects of multiple genetic changes, each with a small effect, and their complex interaction with environmental challenges such as prenatal infections or childhood trauma increase the risk of developing schizophrenia. Although there is an increased familial risk, the inheritance pattern is not known, and it is important to note that most biological relatives of people with schizophrenia do not develop psychosis. Recent findings indicate that prenatal complications interact with genetic risk for schizophrenia such that high-risk individuals with verified prenatal complication history were four to five times more likely to develop schizophrenia than those with similar genetic risks without prenatal complications (Ursini et al., 2018).

PHARMACOLOGICAL MODELS

Leading explanations of schizophrenia neurobiology have largely been driven by research on the effects of psychotropic drugs that modulate psychosis and the related perceptual and cognitive experiences associated with schizophrenia. The hypothesised actions of such drugs have thus prompted neurochemical models of schizophrenia based on the potential breakdown or amplification of these pharmacological mechanisms. Of note, the complex and heterogeneous symptom profile that accompanies schizophrenia, including positive, negative, and cognitive symptoms, is often poorly accounted for by a singular molecular explanation. Indeed, schizophrenia has been examined via a wide range of drug models implicating a number of neurotransmitter systems, including dopamine, glutamate, gamma-aminobutyric acid (GABA), cannabinoid, serotonin, cholinergic, and kappa opioids (for a review, see Steeds, Carhart-Harris, & Stone, 2015). Thus, the more common strategy has been to identify common final pathways that account for the pathophysiology of schizophrenia symptoms across multiple levels of pharmacological, imaging, genetic, and behavioural findings (Coyle, 2006). In this section, we focus on two prominent models that continue to guide and organise research pertaining to the biological underpinnings of schizophrenia: (1) the dopaminergic drug model and (2) glutamatergic drug model.

Psychotic symptoms have been associated with imbalances in multiple neurotransmitter systems.

Dopamine System

The dopamine (DA) hypothesis is one of the major persistent neurochemical models of schizophrenia symptomology. Its initial conceptualisation stemmed from the remedial effects of antipsychotics (DA antagonists) on the characteristic positive symptoms of schizophrenia. With the discovery that the clinical effectiveness of antipsychotics was related to their capacity to block DA D2 receptors (Creese, Burt, & Snyder, 1976; Seeman & Lee, 1975; Seeman, Lee, Chau-Wong, & Wong, 1976), the classic DA hypothesis held that an increase in DA availability or hyperactive DA transmission primarily accounted for the disorder (Creese et al., 1976). This early hypothesis was further bolstered by evidence that psychostimulant drugs known to enhance DA transmission (e.g. amphetamine) induced psychosis in those without schizophrenia (Lieberman, Kane, & Alvir, 1987). However, the unidirectional dysregulation of DA was called into question given inconsistent evidence that individuals with schizophrenia exhibited changes in D2/D3 receptor availability (Howes et al., 2012) and the unclear relation between DA dysregulation and negative and cognitive symptoms.

An important extension to this original hypothesis came from positron emission tomography (PET) and single-photon emission computed tomography (SPECT) imaging studies showing that the direction of abnormal DA transmission in schizophrenia may vary according to brain region and DA receptor type, such that both high and low DA activity could co-occur in schizophrenia (Davis, Kahn, Ko, & Davidson, 1991). For example, such work found D2 receptor concentration in medication naïve, first-episode patients to be elevated in subcortical regions (e.g. Kessler et al., 2009; Weinberger & Laruelle, 2002) but reduced in the cingulate cortex (Buchsbaum et al., 2006; Suhara et al., 2002) and midbrain (Kessler et al., 2009). D1 receptor binding, on the other hand, has been found to be reduced in frontotemporal regions (Abi-Dargham & Moore, 2003; Hirvonen et al., 2006). Some hypothesise a cortical/subcortical DA imbalance (Abi-Dargham & Moore, 2003), which purports hypoactivity of mesocortical DA projections to prefrontal cortex (PFC) and hyperactivity of subcortical mesolimbic DA pathways. The former has been associated with the positive symptoms of schizophrenia and is a target of antipsychotic medications, while the latter has been associated with negative and cognitive symptoms (i.e. working memory dysfunction), which in this model are understandably untreated by DA antagonists.

A growing body of molecular imaging studies provides indirect measures of DA synthesis in patients with schizophrenia, offering further clarification of DA's involvement in the pathophysiology of this condition. Such work points to increased DA synthesis capacity, DA release, and baseline synaptic DA concentrations in those with schizophrenia (Howes et al., 2012; Lyon et al., 2009). Summarised in Howes and Murray (2014), these molecular imaging studies support presynaptic DA dysregulation as the primary source of DA dysfunction in schizophrenia. Furthermore, presynaptic DA dysfunction seems to track the worsening of the disorder and general severity of psychotic symptoms (Howes et al., 2011), suggesting that DA dysregulation has a direct role to play in disease state and progression.

Evidence shows that dopamine synthesis capacity is increased in the prodromal phase of schizophrenia.

Importantly, Howes and Murray (2014) also place the evidence of presynaptic DA disturbance within the broader context of neurodevelopment. For instance, the impact of known developmental risk factors for schizophrenia such as neonatal insults (e.g. hypoxia), social isolation, and stress, sensitises the DA system in both animals and humans (see Howes & Murray, 2014). Such developmental insults lead to sustained changes in the DA system, manifested as an increase in DA synthesis capacity in response to physical and psychosocial stress. This pattern of DA change has been characterised as DA sensitisation, in which the chemical response is amplified after repeated stimulation of the system across time. Thus, DA dysregulation in schizophrenia may arise via gene–environment interactions between known environmental risk factors and various DA-related (e.g. COMT) and neurodevelopmental genes (e.g. *disc1*), resulting in DA sensitisation following repeated exposure to life stressors.

Despite robust evidence of dopaminergic involvement in schizophrenia neurochemistry, current D2 receptor blocking antipsychotics remain problematic in the comprehensive treatment of the disorder. First, they have a modest effect on the debilitating negative symptoms and cognitive deficits accompanying schizophrenia (Buckley & Stahl, 2007; Erhart, Marder, & Carpenter, 2006). Second, approximately one-third of patients show a limited response to dopaminergic antipsychotics (Meltzer, 1997). Such individuals who experience this incomplete recovery may not exhibit the same changes in presynaptic DA transmission as is typically associated with schizophrenia (Demjaha et al., 2014; Demjaha, Murray, McGuire, Kapur, & Howes, 2012). Alternatively, this group may exhibit more glutamatergic abnormalities (Demjaha et al., 2012), which brings us to the second major drug model in schizophrenia.

Glutamate System

Similar to the DA hypothesis, the prevalence of the glutamate model in schizophrenia arose through a series of pharmacological studies demonstrating the immediate perceptual and behavioural effects of psychotropic drugs impacting glutamatergic neurotransmission. In particular, drugs such as phencyclidine (PCP), dizocilpine (MK-801), and ketamine induce many of the positive, negative, and cognitive disturbances associated with schizophrenia in healthy adults, thus mimicking a wider range of symptoms than alternative pharmacological models (Javitt & Zukin, 1991; Krystal et al., 1994; Tsai & Coyle, 2002). Such drugs work by noncompetitively blocking *N*-methyl-D-aspartate (NMDA)-type glutamate receptors—sites of excitatory neurotransmission located extensively throughout the brain. The prevailing glutamatergic model of schizophrenia thus implicates NMDA receptor *hypofunction*, which results in downstream changes in glutamatergic activity that alter the excitatory–inhibitory balance of cortical neurotransmission (for reviews, see Howes, McCutcheon, & Stone, 2015; Moghaddam & Javitt, 2012). Pharmacological infusion studies have importantly demonstrated that subanaesthetic doses of NMDA-receptor antagonists such as ketamine yield a schizophrenia-like pattern of cognitive deficits, with both areas of deficient and preserved function (Krystal et al., 1994). Given the centrality of cognitive impairment in schizophrenia, such work has been particularly influential in identifying and testing potential glutamate system targets for treatment.

Glutamate is the primary excitatory neurotransmitter in the brain and central nervous system.

The glutamate model of schizophrenia implicates reduced function of key glutamate receptors (NMDA receptors).

In addition to infusion studies, the NMDA receptor hypofunction model has been bolstered by a range of genetic and brain imaging findings (Howes et al., 2015). For instance, several proposed candidate risk genes for schizophrenia directly affect glutamatergic neurotransmission (e.g. GRM3, G-72). Because NMDA receptors are mainly localised at postsynaptic dendrites, positive associations between schizophrenia and genes involved in NMDA receptor expression and function (e.g. NR1, NR2B) suggest disruption at the postsynaptic level of neurotransmission. However, research also supports abnormal presynaptic glutamatergic activity in schizophrenia (for a review, see Moghaddam & Javitt, 2012). Findings from animal and human imaging studies suggest that NMDA receptor antagonists actually increase presynaptic glutamate activity at some non-NMDA receptors (e.g. AMPA receptors) in prefrontal cortex (PFC). One explanation for this activity increase may be the downstream effects of

NMDA receptor antagonists on inhibitory GABA neurons (Homayoun & Moghaddam, 2007). In cortical regions where excitatory pyramidal cell activity is stabilised by GABAergic feedback, NMDA receptor antagonists may reduce the overall inhibitory impact of GABA, resulting in the disinhibition and destabilisation of key cortical networks supporting cognition, particularly executive functions like working memory (Homayoun & Moghaddam, 2007). The unfocused, nontarget related increase in neural activity in schizophrenia may reflect heightened internal neural 'noise', which distorts a given perceptual or memory signal and interferes with efficient information processing (Krystal et al., 2017; Murray et al., 2012). Interestingly, computational models of cortical networks incorporating NMDA receptor hypofunction produce the same pattern of behavioural deficits on cognitive tasks (i.e. working memory impairment) as observed in schizophrenia (Murray et al., 2012; Starc et al., 2017), further pointing to primary dysfunction in NMDA receptors.

Such cortical destabilisation due to abnormal glutamatergic and GABAergic transmission has also been described more broadly as a cortical excitatory/inhibitory (E/I) imbalance (e.g. Insel, 2010; Kehrer, Maziashvili, Dugladze, & Gloveli, 2008). In addition to providing a potential mechanism for the cognitive deficits associated with schizophrenia, the E/I imbalance has also been hypothesised to underlie positive symptoms, such as hallucinations and delusions (Jardri et al., 2016). The E/I imbalance is again thought to be primarily driven by inhibitory failure, with evidence of irregularities at both glutamate and GABA circuits (Gao & Penzes, 2015). Of note, the E/I imbalance has also been used to characterise other neuropsychiatric conditions with overlapping perceptual and social phenotypes, particularly autism spectrum disorder (Foss-Feig et al., 2017; Gao & Penzes, 2015).

The glutamate model of schizophrenia predicts widespread cortical dysfunction given the extensive presence of NMDA receptors throughout the cortex.

Finally, given the widespread distribution of NDMA receptors throughout the brain, the NMDA receptor hypofunction model of schizophrenia implicates more global cortical and subcortical disruption than that of the dopaminergic model, which points to primary disturbance at a selective set of brain regions (e.g. dorsolateral PFC, striatum) based on DA projection sites (Moghaddam & Javitt, 2012). Glutamatergic models may thus help explain findings of abnormal perception and behaviour related to both primary sensory and higher-order cortical regions. For instance, administration of ketamine results in a similar disruption to electrophysiological indices of auditory cortex function commonly observed in schizophrenia (Javitt, 2000). A widespread disruption in cortical communication also reflects current neuroimaging evidence of more global versus isolated abnormalities in functional and structural connectivity in schizophrenia (Pettersson-Yeo, Allen, Benetti, McGuire, & Mechelli, 2011; Uhlhaas & Singer, 2010).

While growing evidence points to glutamatergic dysfunction in schizophrenia, it is important to note that glutamate and DA systems interact in the brain on a number of different levels, making it difficult to attribute the effects of NMDA receptor antagonists to purely glutamatergic abnormalities. Thus, the most complete explanation of schizophrenia symptomology may come from a combination or integration of the NMDA hypofunction and presynaptic DA dysfunction models (Howes et al., 2015). Some propose that DA dysfunction in schizophrenia is secondary to disrupted glutamatergic activity (McGuire, Howes, Stone, & Fusar-Poli, 2008), as DA neurons are partly regulated by glutamatergic projections. Indeed, NMDA receptor antagonists have been shown to increase DA release in humans, though this may only occur when the DA system is already challenged or sensitised (e.g. following amphetamine administration) (Howes et al., 2015).

Summary

Robust evidence points to presynaptic DA disturbance in schizophrenia that is present at the onset of illness and related to illness conversion. DA antagonists also improve positive symptoms for a substantial portion of patients. However, the current dopaminergic account fails to clearly explain negative and cognitive symptoms or the pathophysiological mechanism for the roughly one-third of patients who fail to show a therapeutic response to dopaminergic antipsychotics. The glutamate hypothesis involving NMDA receptor hypofunction appears to better accommodate these aspects of the disorder, though it remains to be seen whether the glutamatergic model will lead to significant advances in treatment. Importantly, the two hypotheses are not mutually exclusive (see Howes et al., 2015 for an integrated model). As DA and glutamate interact extensively throughout the brain, developmental insults to either may cause downstream effects to one or both systems, and a combination of both may best account for the heterogeneous symptom profile associated with schizophrenia.

The clinical symptoms of schizophrenia may be best accounted for by a combination of presynaptic dopamine dysfunction and glutamate system changes via NMDA receptor hypofunction.

COGNITIVE MODELS OF SCHIZOPHRENIA

Cognitive impairments are prevalent throughout the course of schizophrenia and contribute significantly to poor functional outcome (e.g. Green, Kern, & Heaton, 2004). While there is extensive evidence of pervasive cognitive deficits across a range of performance measures (e.g. Gold & Dickinson, 2013; Schaefer, Giangrande, Weinberger, & Dickinson, 2013), the largest effect sizes are demonstrated for memory and processing speed (see Schaefer et al., 2013). Importantly, these cognitive impairments are not solely a manifestation of amorphous generalised deficit or simply the consequences of clinical symptoms or medication effects. Cognitive impairments in schizophrenia are likely to be closer to disease pathophysiology than the surface manifestation of psychotic symptoms and thus, can be more precisely targeted for intervention (Lencz et al., 2006). Although it is relatively easy to demonstrate the existence of cognitive deficits, the origins of these problems have not yet been clearly identified. Given the robust link between cognitive deficits and functional outcome, elucidating the core mechanistic components that underlie these problems is of utmost importance for developing effective treatments. Powerful cognitive models of working memory, context processing, and cognitive control have contributed significantly towards our understanding of the neural mechanisms underlying schizophrenia and have opened up new approaches to seek treatment targets. The breadth of work in this area precludes a comprehensive review in this chapter; instead, a summary of select influential cognitive models is described.

Representational Guidance of Behaviour and the Working Memory Hypothesis

Working memory is a limited-capacity, active short-term memory system that maintains information to guide and control behaviour. This capacity to encode, generate, and maintain mental representations form the basic building block of abstract thought that allows us to use stored representations to generate predictions and plan for future goals. In the early 1990s, Patricia Goldman-Rakic, who transformed our understanding of the neural basis of mental representation, hypothesised that 'a defect in working memory—the ability to guide behavior by representations—may be the fundamental impairment leading to schizophrenic thought disorder' (Goldman-Rakic, 1994). According to this hypothesis, deficits of executive or cognitive control, which includes distractibility, perseveration, and failure to inhibit irrelevant responses, may reflect an inability to utilise working memory to guide behaviour adaptively. These impairments may arise from abnormal regulation of various prefrontal circuits that are engaged in holding information 'on line' while updating past and current information moment to moment.

Metaanalytic studies support this hypothesis and indicate that stable and reliable working memory deficits are found in individuals with schizophrenia across diverse paradigms, methods, and techniques (e.g. Lee & Park, 2005; Park & Gooding, 2014). Moreover, those at risk for schizophrenia (e.g. unaffected first-degree relatives) also show working memory deficits. In individuals with schizophrenia, the working memory deficit is permanent and stable even when their clinical symptoms are largely in remission. Such persistent and trait-like nature of the working memory deficit in the schizophrenia-spectrum suggests that it may be an endophenotypic marker, and hence a potential aid to discovering the genetic basis of schizophrenia. Moreover, working memory deficit predicts functional outcome better than do clinical symptoms and is associated with poor social functioning in schizophrenia. Not surprisingly, working memory impairment has become a major therapeutic target for pharmacological and behavioural treatment strategies. Thus, it is important to specify the origins and consequences of this deficit.

Working memory deficits are present in schizophrenia, even when positive symptoms subside.

When components of working memory deficits are examined closely, encoding and maintenance problems seem specific to the schizophrenia-spectrum and do not necessarily extend to bipolar disorder (Mayer & Park, 2012). Individuals with schizophrenia seem to be affected by poor encoding processes that may originate from reduced fidelity or quality of sensory input ('bottom-up' processes) as well as those that require more 'top-down' control that involve attention. Difficulties with encoding could lead to either having no memory or 'false memory' of the past. In addition to encoding difficulties, individuals with schizophrenia may be impaired in maintaining encoded information over time to guide behaviour. Interestingly, even though individuals with schizophrenia experience difficulties in encoding and maintaining memory traces, they show pockets of intact or enhanced mental imagery ability. For example, individuals with schizophrenia show no deficits in their capacity to rotate, transform, and manipulate mental imagery (Matthews, Collins, Thakkar, & Park, 2014). Such intact manipulation of mental representations alongside impaired encoding of the representation itself may stem from a lack of functional coordination between the prefrontal and parietal cortical systems (e.g. Deserno, Sterzer, Wüstenberg, Heinz, & Schlagenhauf, 2012). Abnormal parietal activity is associated with reduced working memory capacity (Kim et al., 2003), excessive mental imagery (Ganis, Thompson, & Kosslyn, 2004), and anomalous multisensory experiences (Blanke & Arzy, 2005; Ionta et al., 2011) that are central to schizophrenia, such as weakened sense of bodily self. The parietal cortex reaches maturity during late adolescence, the period that overlaps with the premorbid and prodromal stages of schizophrenia and offers an optimal window for targeted intervention. In sum, working memory deficit in schizophrenia, first reported in the early 1990s, is now broadly accepted as a core feature and endophenotypic marker of schizophrenia (for a review, see Park & Gooding, 2014). It is also a useful behavioural tool for probing the pathophysiology of this disorder and remains a critical target for treatment (see Arnsten, 2011).

Stored Regularities, Context, and Predictions

Integrating learning theory based on animal studies with human cognitive models of attention, Jeffery Gray and David Hemsley (1991) developed a comprehensive framework for understanding schizophrenia. The basic problem in schizophrenia was proposed to be 'a weakening of the influences of stored memories of regularities of previous input on current perception' (Gray, Feldon, Rawlins, Hemsley, & Smith, 1991). In other words, cognitive deficits and symptoms of schizophrenia may arise when 'stored regularities' are not integrated with the current sensory input and ongoing motor programs, or when the spatiotemporal context fails to activate appropriate context from memory. Internal representations are also central to Hemsley's updated (2005) model, though the emphasis is placed on the importance of long-term memory and activation of appropriate, contextual information from stored regularities to guide current and future behaviour. Neuroanatomically, this model highlights the role of abnormal hippocampal structure and function in cognitive deficits and clinical symptoms of schizophrenia (for a review, see Harrison, 2004). The hippocampus receives inputs from the prefrontal cortex (PFC), which represents goals or 'predictions'. Hippocampal regions are thought to perform a comparative function to detect potential discrepancy between predicted goals and the current input. When a significant discrepancy is detected, recursive networks are activated to resolve the detected conflict. However, weakened contextual influence

Problems with learning and long-term memory are common in schizophrenia and linked to hippocampal dysfunction.

or access to stored regularities can derail this process and disrupt adaptive behaviour. Contextual disturbance that depend on stored regularities are also associated with the NMDA receptor hypofunction that implicates sensory and perceptual information processing. Therefore, it is apparent that both top-down, contextual influences and bottom-up, sensory information processing contribute to the cognitive deficits of schizophrenia.

Hemsley's (2005) conceptualisation of schizophrenia has since been expanded and reframed within the past decade into computational models that focus on Bayesian inference and predictive coding (see Corlett, Honey, & Fletcher, 2016). In this reincarnation, feed-forward and feedback neural processing represent bottom-up sensory input and top-down prior knowledge, respectively, which are integrated according to Bayes' theorem of learning. As a result, the brain is able to form a hierarchical representation of the environment, from low-level sensory features to high-level goals. The brain constructs a model of the internal and external environment and continuously refines it by reducing the discrepancy between what is predicted versus what is observed through computational learning (Rao & Ballard, 1999). An imbalance between the top-down and the bottom-up processes could lead to misperception or false perception. For example, excessive weighting of top-down processes (i.e. predictions or prior beliefs) against sensory inputs could lead to experiencing things that are not there (i.e. hallucinations) (e.g. Fletcher & Frith, 2009; Horga, Schatz, Abi-Dargham, & Peterson, 2014).

Strong evidence supports the important role of context processing and long-term memory deficits with associated hippocampal and frontal cortical abnormalities in schizophrenia. Episodic memory is conceptualised as long-term memory for one's own past experiences, including temporally dated information and spatiotemporal relations. Therefore, episodic memory links one's past, present, and future to generate a continuous sense of self across time and context. Individuals with schizophrenia demonstrate deficits in episodic memory that seem to arise from problems during encoding, retrieval, and a general failure of strategy. If past experiences cannot be stored or accessed, generation or activation of appropriate context for the task at hand becomes difficult. Context processing has been most often tested with a family of continuous performance task (CPT-AXE) paradigms that require participants to maintain a sequence of events in order to make appropriate responses. Context processing deficits are reliably observed in individuals with schizophrenia and their healthy first-degree relatives, and these deficits are associated with dorsolateral PFC abnormalities. With respect to Bayesian models, aberrant prediction error-driven associative learning has been linked to delusion formation and maintenance in schizophrenia.

Executive Functions: Response Monitoring and Control of Action

Cognitive control refers to the diverse cognitive abilities involved in the adjustment of perceptual selection and action in a way that supports flexible, context-dependent behaviour. It is largely subserved by PFC and its coordination with sensory and motor brain regions. More specifically, dorsolateral PFC is involved in maintaining the context, or rules, and using this context to influence future behaviour via its impact on lower brain regions. The anterior cingulate cortex, on the other hand, is involved in performance monitoring and signalling to the PFC when greater cognitive control over lower brain regions is needed. Cognitive control is impaired in the schizophrenia spectrum and is linked to functional outcome (see Lesh, Niendam, Minzenberg, & Carter, 2011 for a comprehensive review).

Cognitive control is thought to regulate a wide range of cognitive functions, including attention and memory. Therefore, impaired cognitive control and associated dysfunctions in prefrontal cortical recruitment may lie at the heart of the cognitive deficits of schizophrenia (Carter et al., 1998; Ragland et al., 2009). Individuals with schizophrenia have consistently been shown to have profound cognitive control impairments. Note that cognitive control itself is a multifaceted construct (Miyake et al., 2000) and can be further divided into proactive and reactive control (Braver, 2012). Proactive control refers to maintaining goal-relevant information to prepare for future action, whereas reactive control refers to activating control processes in response to an event to guide behaviour. To date, there is stronger evidence for impairments in proactive control compared to reactive control in schizophrenia (Lesh et al., 2013), though reactive control impairments have also been reported (Thakkar, Schall, Logan, & Park, 2011, 2015).

Impairments in cognitive control in schizophrenia are manifested in separable cognitive and behavioural response inhibition and performance monitoring deficits, which have been most extensively investigated in the psychosis spectrum (Badcock & Hugdahl, 2014). Response inhibition is a form of cognitive control, defined as the ability to deliberately inhibit actions (Rabbitt, 1997). Patients with schizophrenia and their unaffected relatives appear to perform poorly on tasks that rely on response inhibition. Both anterior cingulate and prefrontal cortices have been implicated in response to inhibition deficits of schizophrenia (Kerns et al., 2005). These response inhibition impairments may be related to impulsivity-related behaviours in schizophrenia (e.g. substance abuse).

Performance or response monitoring involves the ability to evaluate actions and use feedback signalling success or failure to guide future performance. Performance monitoring is often indexed by error detection on a cognitive task and subsequent reaction time (RT) adjustments; after an error had been made, the RT on the subsequent trial is often lengthened (see Thakkar et al., 2011). Error monitoring is associated with the integrity of the anterior cingulate, which is purported to be the generator of the error-related negativity (ERN), an event-related potential that occurs approximately 80–180 ms following an error. ERN has been shown to be reduced in schizophrenia and associated with patients' negative symptoms (Foti et al., 2016), but ERN abnormalities also seem to be responsive to intervention (Reinhart, Zhu, Park, & Woodman, 2015).

The cognitive models discussed thus far tend to best account for the persistent and often debilitating cognitive deficits that often accompany schizophrenia. However, as noted earlier, failures in contextual representation, predictive coding mechanisms, and long-term memory may also contribute to a cognitive interpretation of delusions and hallucinations. Additional cognitive models have been proposed to directly account for positive symptoms, with a particular emphasis on the role of cognitive appraisal and emotional response for contributing to the development and maintenance of psychosis (e.g. Freeman, Garety, Kuipers, Fowler, & Bebbington, 2002; Garety, Bebbington, Fowler, Freeman, & Kuipers, 2007; Garety & Freeman, 1999; Garety, Kuipers, Fowler, Freeman, & Bebbington, 2001). For instance, Garety et al. (2001) point to specific biases in reasoning and information processing, preexisting beliefs about oneself and others, and emotional changes in response to an anomalous experience (e.g. a hallucination) that contribute to psychosis. More specifically, this group has found evidence of a 'jumping to conclusions' cognitive style and externalising attributional bias, which, along with a negative emotional state (anxiety, depression), can make anomalous experiences much more distressing, ultimately forming a delusional belief (Garety & Freeman, 1999). Given the prominent role of cognitive style and emotional response in this model, it has spurred an important line of research on the therapeutic treatment of psychosis with cognitive behavioural therapy, tailored to address the specific attributional errors and schematic beliefs associated with psychosis (cognitive behavioural therapy for psychosis, CBTp) (Beck & Rector, 2005; Garety, Fowler, & Kuipers, 2000; Kuipers et al., 2006).

Summary

Cognitive impairments are core features of schizophrenia. Though no single model can completely account for the wide range of cognitive and perceptual abnormalities observed in schizophrenia, each cognitive model is suited to elucidate specific deficits. Overall, there are significant difficulties with representational guidance or control of behaviour as well as the encoding and maintenance of the internal representation itself, leading to practical difficulties with daily functions and the phenomenological experience of a fragmented internal landscape. At the symptom level, such deficits in maintaining stable internal perceptual and cognitive representations of the world and oneself may contribute to characteristic cognitive styles or attributions, resulting in aberrant beliefs and contributing to the emotionally charged quality of delusions and hallucinations.

SOCIAL ENVIRONMENTAL APPROACH: SOCIAL DISCONNECTION, SOCIAL DEFEAT, AND SOCIAL ISOLATION

Social withdrawal and social impairments are additional core features of schizophrenia, present from the prodromal stage and predictive of poor functional outcome (Green et al., 2008). Social impairments are closely related to negative symptoms such as anhedonia and asociality, and positive symptoms such as delusions, but it is unclear whether psychosis precedes social problems or if social withdrawal leads to psychosis. It is likely that both play an interactive role during the premorbid stages of illness; psychotic symptoms do impair social functioning, but it is also likely that the impact of social isolation and withdrawal brings about psychotic experiences. There is solid evidence to indicate that biological and psychological consequences of long-term exposure to stress from social isolation or exclusion may be a major risk factor for psychosis, which likely exacerbates psychotic symptoms in those who are diagnosed with schizophrenia (Hoffman, 2007; Selten, van der Ven, Rutten, & Cantor-Graae, 2013).

The association of social disconnection with psychotic symptoms may be understood within the framework of the Social Deafferentation (Hoffman, 2007) and the Social Defeat (Selten et al., 2013) Hypotheses. In both cases, the detrimental impact of social disconnection through isolation, exclusion, or defeat is eventually expressed in psychotic symptoms. For example, prior to first onset of auditory hallucinations, over 70% of respondents in a large survey-based study experienced social isolation (Hoffman, Varanko, Gilmore, & Mishara, 2008). In fact, impairments in social activity associated with pervasive social isolation can be observed up to 15 years before the first episode of schizophrenia (Velthorst et al., 2016). But how does social isolation lead to hallucinations and delusions? Hoffman's Social Deafferentation Hypothesis (2007) postulates that social isolation for a vulnerable individual has similar consequences as the cortical reorganisation that occurs after limb amputation (e.g. Phantom Limb syndrome), except that in the case of social isolation, 'amputation' is not physical but psychological. If one is cut off from society, resulting in a drastic loss of social input to the brain, compensatory hyperactivity of the brain regions associated with social information processing triggers hallucinations and delusions that are highly social in nature. Within this framework, social hallucinations and delusions represent the isolated brain's solution to this adverse condition. Once delusions take hold, it is of course much more difficult to make social connections, thus beginning a downward spiral towards worsened social functioning.

Chronic social isolation may increase risk (and exacerbate) psychosis through compensatory hyperactivity of social brain networks.

In a similar vein, the Social Defeat hypothesis (Selten et al., 2013) strongly implicates the adverse effects of chronic social exclusion in psychosis. Social defeat in this context is conceptualised as a subordinate (defeated) position in society, or an outcast status. Major risk factors for development of schizophrenia within the Social Defeat framework include migration, disadvantaged status, urban upbringing, and trauma, all of which involve forms of exclusion (Selten et al., 2013, 2017). Chronic social defeat is experienced routinely by outsiders, and indeed there is a significant increase in the incidence of schizophrenia among immigrants (e.g. Moroccan-Dutch in the Netherlands) or those who belong to a disadvantaged minority group (e.g. Afro-Caribbeans in the United Kingdom or the Inuit in Denmark). In addition to urban upbringing, childhood trauma and disability also contribute to social defeat. Animal studies have shown that the result of long-term outcome repeated social defeat is the sensitisation of the mesolimbic dopamine system (Selten et al., 2013), which increases the risk for schizophrenia.

Exclusion from society (i.e. 'social defeat') via status and/or culture may increase risk of psychosis, potentially through changes in dopamine system function.

Summary

Social Defeat and Social Deafferentation hypotheses of schizophrenia emphasise the detrimental impact of disconnection, exclusion, and isolation that lead to neural and psychological changes over time in vulnerable individuals. It is important to note that in both cases, the *subjective experience* of social defeat or social deafferentation seems to be crucial. Individual differences in need for affiliation, availability of social support, trauma history, substance use, dopamine receptor polymorphisms, and other factors also interact with the experienced social defeat or exclusion. Lastly, considering the fact that social isolation and loneliness result in poor mental and physical health (Cacioppo, Grippo, London, Goossens, & Cacioppo, 2015), it is important to address the epidemic of loneliness among people with psychosis (Badcock et al., 2015). According to the Australian National Survey of Psychosis, up to 80% of individuals diagnosed with psychosis reported feeling lonely in the past year (Stain et al., 2012). Thus, available social support and vulnerability to isolation must remain at the forefront of consideration throughout case conceptualisation and treatment planning.

INTEGRATIVE SUMMARY AND CLINICAL IMPLICATIONS

Vast progress made in genetics, neuroscience, and psychological sciences in recent decades allows us to chip away at the aetiology of schizophrenia. In this chapter, a selective review of neuropharmacological, cognitive, and social models of schizophrenia was introduced. This summary by no means covers the rich and flourishing literature in each one of these domains, but rather is meant to provide a brief, directed overview and starting point for appreciating the complex and multifaceted models of schizophrenia aetiology and symptom generation. Importantly, these approaches can be integrated within a developmental framework (see Fig. 2.1), which indicates the potential points at which different intervention strategies can be deployed. For instance, recent integrative models (Howes & Murray, 2014; Pruessner et al., 2017) emphasise how the complex interactions between genetic and environmental risk factors during development (e.g. early life adversity) negatively impact one's vulnerability to *future* life stressors via various pathways (i.e. dysregulation of one's stress response, dopaminergic transmission). Accordingly, treatment considerations must also include how to best reduce stress and increase resiliency towards stress in this population (Pruessner et al., 2017).

For the clinician, the challenge becomes integrating these foundational models to best conceptualise and treat the individual client in front of you, with their own specific biological and environmental risk factors, life stressors, symptomology, and ideas of treatment and recovery. Given the breadth of these models, which perhaps best account for different aspects of psychosis (e.g. cognitive deficits, positive symptoms, biological risk factors), case conceptualisation may then necessitate multiple assessment and treatment targets as well as ongoing

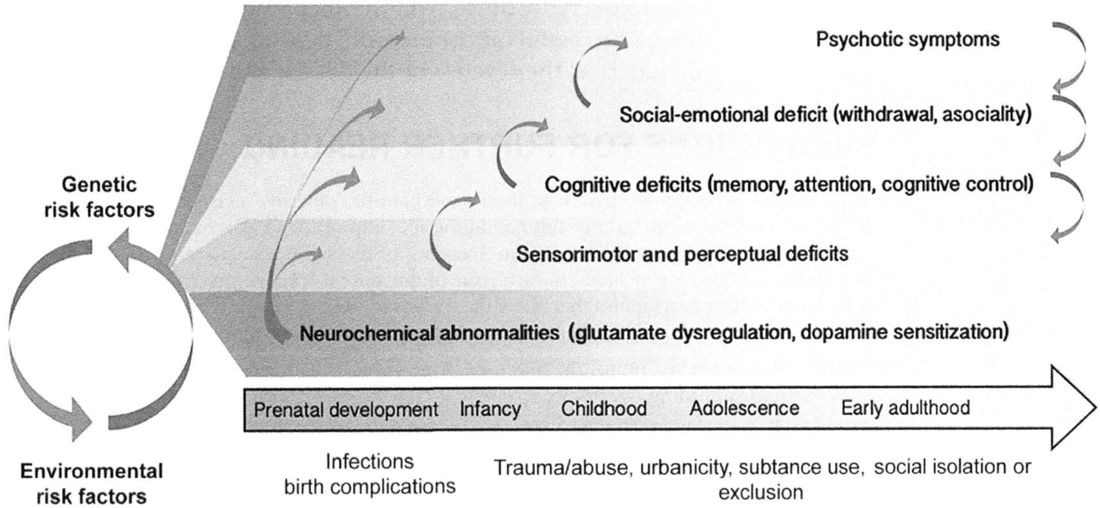

FIG. 2.1
Risk factors and potential intervention strategies within a developmental framework.

re-evaluation to determine an intervention's efficacy. These models also provide psychoeducational tools for dispelling the stigma associated with having or treating schizophrenia and psychosis. The latter is particularly important given evidence that internalised stigma of having a mental illness relates to negative recovery outcomes (Yanos, Roe, Markus, & Lysaker, 2008). Stigma is critically influenced by the causal explanations a client attributes to their disorder, which may change over time according to one's social, personal, and cultural experiences (McCabe & Priebe, 2004). More recent evidence suggests that the type of causal explanation (biological, psychosocial, spiritual) may also differentially influence treatment-related behaviours, such as medication adherence and engagement in therapy (Carter, Read, Pyle, & Morrison, 2017). Thus, the way in which a clinician conceptualises and communicates how the disorder develops and is maintained seems to play a significant role in a client's outcome.

Lastly, given the fairly consistent incidence of schizophrenia across the globe, it is possible that schizophrenia emerged during the early stages of human evolutionary history. Although schizophrenia itself is associated with reduced fecundity, the steady incidence across time hints at potential advantages of the schizophrenia spectrum in milder expressions (Crow, 2000; Huxley, Mayr, Osmond, & Hoffer, 1964). Indeed, there is empirical evidence to indicate increased creativity in those who share latent liability for psychosis (Barrantes-Vidal & Kaufman, 2014; Folley & Park, 2005). Thus, the 'schizophrenia paradox' (Huxley et al., 1964) poses a practically important clinical and research question: is a complete cure the only 'good' outcome of clinical and research efforts? Managing clinical symptoms and improving cognitive and social functioning with the support of available therapies may be sufficient first step towards alleviating the suffering and promoting the recovery of those who are diagnosed with schizophrenia. However, the ultimate successful outcome would depend as much on the society around these individuals as the severity of the disease process.

SUGGESTIONS FOR FURTHER READING

In this chapter, we approach psychosis from a mechanistic, 'objective' perspective, but without the 'subjective' or 'lived-in' account of this condition, it is impossible to arrive at an understanding. It is, therefore, essential to read 'First-Person Accounts' or biographies in concert with this textbook. First-person accounts are included in each issue of the journal *Schizophrenia Bulletin*. There are also numerous excellent biographies that allow the readers to step into the internal world of psychosis.

Saks, E. R. (2007). *The center cannot hold: My journey through madness*. New York, NY: Hyperion.

Schiller, L., & Bennett, A. (1996). *The quiet room: A journey out of the torment of madness*. New York, NY: Grand Central Publishing.

Cockburn, P., & Cockburn, H. (2011). *Henry's demons: Living with schizophrenia, a father and son's story*. New York, NY: Simon & Schuster.

QUIZ QUESTIONS

1. Which of the following statements about cognitive deficits in schizophrenia is NOT true?
   (a) Cognitive impairments in schizophrenia include deficits of episodic memory deficits, cognitive control, and response inhibition.
   (b) Abnormal hippocampal function and structure are involved in memory deficits of schizophrenia.
   (c) Working memory deficits predict functional outcome.
   (d) One unifying model of context processing can accurately account for cognitive impairments in schizophrenia.
2. Which of the following statement describes the Social Defeat Hypothesis of schizophrenia?
   (a) Social cognition is a multidimensional construct that includes areas of ability (e.g. emotion recognition) as well as bias (e.g. hostility bias).
   (b) Chronic experience of being excluded from the majority group leads to an increased sensitisation of the mesolimbic dopamine system, thereby increasing the risk for psychosis.
   (c) Social isolation for a vulnerable individual has similar consequences as the cortical reorganisation that occurs after limb amputation.
   (d) Anhedonia protects against loneliness in schizophrenia.
3. Which of the following statements about copy number variants (CNVs) is true?
   (a) Schizophrenia-associated CNVs are also associated with decreased risk for autism spectrum disorder.
   (b) CNVs involve substitutions of one nucleotide at a specific location in the genome.
   (c) Deletion at 22q11.2 is frequently found in individuals with schizophrenia.
   (d) The rate of de novo CNV mutations is significantly elevated in individuals with schizophrenia as compared to control groups.

4. Which of the following statements provide evidence for the involvement of the glutamate system in schizophrenia?
   (a) NMDA receptor hyperfunction leads to positive symptoms.
   (b) Phencyclidine and ketamine can induce major depression in individuals with schizophrenia.
   (c) Subanaesthetic doses of NMDA-receptor antagonists such as ketamine given to healthy participants yield a pattern of cognitive deficits that are observed in individuals with schizophrenia.
   (d) Dopamine dysfunction in schizophrenia is secondary to disrupted glutamatergic activity.

ANSWERS TO QUIZ QUESTIONS:

1. (d)
2. (b)
3. (d)
4. (c)

References

Abi-Dargham, A., & Moore, H. (2003). Prefrontal DA transmission at D1 receptors and the pathology of schizophrenia. *The Neuroscientist, 9*(5), 404–416.

Arnsten, A. F. (2011). Prefrontal cortical network connections: Key site of vulnerability in stress and schizophrenia. *International Journal of Developmental Neuroscience, 29*(3), 215–223.

Badcock, J. C., & Hugdahl, K. (2014). A synthesis of evidence on inhibitory control and auditory hallucinations based on the Research Domain Criteria (RDoC) framework. *Frontiers in Human Neuroscience, 8*, 180.

Badcock, J. C., Shah, S., Mackinnon, A., Stain, H. J., Galletly, C., Jablensky, A., et al. (2015). Loneliness in psychotic disorders and its association with cognitive function and symptom profile. *Schizophrenia Research, 169*(1–3), 268–273.

Barrantes-Vidal, N., & Kaufman, J. C. (2014). Creativity and the spectrum of affective and schizophrenic psychoses. In J. C. Kaufman (Ed.), *Creativity and mental illness* (pp. 169–204). Storrs, CT: Cambridge University Press.

Beck, A. T., & Rector, N. A. (2005). Cognitive approaches to schizophrenia: Theory and therapy. *Annual Review of Clinical Psychology, 1*, 577–606.

Blanke, O., & Arzy, S. (2005). The out-of-body experience: Disturbed self-processing at the temporoparietal junction. *The Neuroscientist, 11*(1), 16–24.

Blasi, G., Selvaggi, P., Fazio, L., Antonucci, L. A., Taurisano, P., Masellis, R., et al. (2015). Variation in dopamine D2 and serotonin 5-HT2A receptor genes is associated with working memory processing and response to treatment with antipsychotics. *Neuropsychopharmacology, 40*(7), 1600–1608.

Braver, T. S. (2012). The variable nature of cognitive control: A dual mechanisms framework. *Trends in Cognitive Sciences, 16*(2), 106–113.

Brown, A. S. (2011). The environment and susceptibility to schizophrenia. *Progress in Neurobiology, 93*(1), 23–58.

Buchsbaum, M. S., Friedman, J., Buchsbaum, B. R., Chu, K. W., Hazlett, E. A., Newmark, R., et al. (2006). Diffusion tensor imaging in schizophrenia. *Biological Psychiatry, 60*(11), 1181–1187.

Buckley, P. F., & Stahl, S. M. (2007). Pharmacological treatment of negative symptoms of schizophrenia: Therapeutic opportunity or Cul-de-sac? *Acta Psychiatrica Scandinavica, 115*(2), 93–100.

Cacioppo, S., Grippo, A. J., London, S., Goossens, L., & Cacioppo, J. T. (2015). Loneliness: Clinical import and interventions. *Perspectives on Psychological Science, 10*(2), 238–249.

Cantor-Graae, E., & Selten, J. P. (2005). Schizophrenia and migration: A meta-analysis and review. *American Journal of Psychiatry, 162*(1), 12–24.

Cardno, A. G., & Gottesman, I. I. (2000). Twin studies of schizophrenia: From bow-and-arrow concordances to star wars Mx and functional genomics. *American Journal of Medical Genetics, 97*(1), 12–17.

Carter, C. S., Braver, T. S., Barch, D. M., Botvinick, M. M., Noll, D., & Cohen, J. D. (1998). Anterior cingulate cortex, error detection, and the online monitoring of performance. *Science, 280*(5364), 747–749.

Carter, L., Read, J., Pyle, M., & Morrison, A. P. (2017). The impact of causal explanations on outcome in people experiencing psychosis: A systematic review. *Clinical Psychology & Psychotherapy, 24*(2), 332–347.

Corlett, P. R., Honey, G. D., & Fletcher, P. C. (2016). Prediction error, ketamine and psychosis: An updated model. *Journal of Psychopharmacology, 30*(11), 1145–1155.

Coyle, J. T. (2006). Glutamate and schizophrenia: Beyond the dopamine hypothesis. *Cellular and Molecular Neurobiology, 26*(4–6), 363–382.

Creese, I., Burt, D. R., & Snyder, S. H. (1976). Dopamine receptor binding predicts clinical and pharmacological potencies of anti-schizophrenic drugs. *Science, 192*(4238), 481–483.

Crow, T. J. (2000). Schizophrenia as the price that Homo sapiens pays for language: A resolution of the central paradox in the origin of the species. *Brain Research Reviews, 31*(2–3), 118–129.

Davis, K. L., Kahn, R. S., Ko, G., & Davidson, M. (1991). Dopamine in schizophrenia: A review and reconceptualization. *The American Journal of Psychiatry, 148*(11), 1474–1486.

Demjaha, A., Egerton, A., Murray, R. M., Kapur, S., Howes, O. D., Stone, J. M., et al. (2014). Antipsychotic treatment resistance in schizophrenia associated with elevated glutamate levels but normal dopamine function. *Biological Psychiatry, 75*(5), e11–e13.

Demjaha, A., Murray, R. M., McGuire, P. K., Kapur, S., & Howes, O. D. (2012). Dopamine synthesis capacity in patients with treatment-resistant schizophrenia. *American Journal of Psychiatry, 169*(11), 1203–1210.

Deserno, L., Sterzer, P., Wüstenberg, T., Heinz, A., & Schlagenhauf, F. (2012). Reduced prefrontal-parietal effective connectivity and working memory deficits in schizophrenia. *Journal of Neuroscience, 32*(1), 12–20.

Erhart, S. M., Marder, S. R., & Carpenter, W. T. (2006). Treatment of schizophrenia negative symptoms: Future prospects. *Schizophrenia Bulletin, 32*(2), 234–237.

Fletcher, P. C., & Frith, C. D. (2009). Perceiving is believing: A Bayesian approach to explaining the positive symptoms of schizophrenia. *Nature Reviews Neuroscience, 10*(1), 48–58.

Folley, B. S., & Park, S. (2005). Verbal creativity and schizotypal personality in relation to prefrontal hemispheric laterality: A behavioral and near-infrared optical imaging study. *Schizophrenia Research, 80*(2–3), 271–282.

Foss-Feig, J. H., Adkinson, B. D., Ji, J. L., Yang, G., Srihari, V. H., McPartland, J. C., et al. (2017). Searching for cross-diagnostic convergence: Neural mechanisms governing excitation and inhibition balance in schizophrenia and autism spectrum disorders. *Biological Psychiatry, 81*(10), 848–861.

Foti, D., Perlman, G., Hajcak, G., Mohanty, A., Jackson, F., & Kotov, R. (2016). Impaired error processing in late-phase psychosis: Four-year stability and relationships with negative symptoms. *Schizophrenia Research, 176*(2–3), 520–526.

Freeman, D., Garety, P. A., Kuipers, E., Fowler, D., & Bebbington, P. E. (2002). A cognitive model of persecutory delusions. *British Journal of Clinical Psychology, 41*(4), 331–347.

Ganis, G., Thompson, W. L., & Kosslyn, S. M. (2004). Brain areas underlying visual mental imagery and visual perception: An fMRI study. *Cognitive Brain Research, 20*(2), 226–241.

Gao, R., & Penzes, P. (2015). Common mechanisms of excitatory and inhibitory imbalance in schizophrenia and autism spectrum disorders. *Current Molecular Medicine, 15*(2), 146–167.

Garety, P. A., Bebbington, P., Fowler, D., Freeman, D., & Kuipers, E. (2007). Implications for neurobiological research of cognitive models of psychosis: A theoretical paper. *Psychological Medicine, 37*(10), 1377–1391.

Garety, P. A., & Freeman, D. (1999). Cognitive approaches to delusions: A critical review of theories and evidence. *British Journal of Clinical Psychology, 38*(2), 113–154.

Garety, P. A., Fowler, D., & Kuipers, E. (2000). Cognitive-behavioral therapy for medication-resistant symptoms. *Schizophrenia Bulletin, 26*(1), 73–86.

Garety, P. A., Kuipers, E., Fowler, D., Freeman, D., & Bebbington, P. E. (2001). A cognitive model of the positive symptoms of psychosis. *Psychological Medicine, 31*(2), 189–195.

Gibson, L. E., Alloy, L. B., & Ellman, L. M. (2016). Trauma and the psychosis spectrum: A review of symptom specificity and explanatory mechanisms. *Clinical Psychology Review, 49*, 92–105.

Giegling, I., Hosak, L., Mössner, R., Serretti, A., Bellivier, F., Claes, S., et al. (2017). Genetics of schizophrenia: A consensus paper of the WFSBP Task Force on Genetics. *The World Journal of Biological Psychiatry, 18*(7), 492–505.

Gold, J. M., & Dickinson, D. (2013). "Generalized cognitive deficit" in schizophrenia: Overused or underappreciated? *Schizophrenia Bulletin, 39*(2), 263–265.

Goldman-Rakic, P. S. (1994). Working memory dysfunction in schizophrenia. *The Journal of Neuropsychiatry and Clinical Neurosciences, 6*(4), 348–357.

Gottesman, I. I., & Shields, J. (1976). A critical review of recent adoption, twin, and family studies of schizophrenia: Behavioral genetics perspectives. *Schizophrenia Bulletin, 2*(3), 360–401.

Gray, J. A., Feldon, J., Rawlins, J. N. P., Hemsley, D. R., & Smith, A. D. (1991). The neuropsychology of schizophrenia. *Behavioral and Brain Sciences, 14*(1), 1–20.

Green, M. F., Kern, R. S., & Heaton, R. K. (2004). Longitudinal studies of cognition and functional outcome in schizophrenia: Implications for MATRICS. *Schizophrenia Research, 72*(1), 41–51.

Green, M. F., Penn, D. L., Bentall, R., Carpenter, W. T., Gaebel, W., Gur, R. C., et al. (2008). Social cognition in schizophrenia: An NIMH workshop on definitions, assessment, and research opportunities. *Schizophrenia Bulletin, 34*(6), 1211–1220.

Hallmayer, J. F., Kalaydjieva, L., Badcock, J., Dragovic, M., Howell, S., Michie, P. T., et al. (2005). Genetic evidence for a distinct subtype of schizophrenia characterized by pervasive cognitive deficit. *American Journal of Human Genetics, 77*(3), 468–476.

Harrison, P. J. (2004). The hippocampus in schizophrenia: A review of the neuropathological evidence and its pathophysiological implications. *Psychopharmacology, 174*(1), 151–162.

Hemsley, D. R. (2005). The development of a cognitive model of schizophrenia: Placing it in context. *Neuroscience & Biobehavioral Reviews, 29*(6), 977–988.

Hirvonen, J., van Erp, T. G., Huttunen, J., Aalto, S., Någren, K., Huttunen, M., et al. (2006). Brain dopamine D1 receptors in twins discordant for schizophrenia. *American Journal of Psychiatry, 163*(10), 1747–1753.

Hoffman, R. E. (2007). A social deafferentation hypothesis for induction of active schizophrenia. *Schizophrenia Bulletin, 33*(5), 1066–1070.

Hoffman, R. E., Varanko, M., Gilmore, J., & Mishara, A. L. (2008). Experiential features used by patients with schizophrenia to differentiate 'voices' from ordinary verbal thought. *Psychological Medicine, 38*(8), 1167–1176.

Homayoun, H., & Moghaddam, B. (2007). NMDA receptor hypofunction produces opposite effects on prefrontal cortex interneurons and pyramidal neurons. *Journal of Neuroscience, 27*(43), 11496–11500.

Horga, G., Schatz, K. C., Abi-Dargham, A., & Peterson, B. S. (2014). Deficits in predictive coding underlie hallucinations in schizophrenia. *Journal of Neuroscience, 34*(24), 8072–8082.

Howes, O. D., Bose, S., Turkheimer, F., Valli, I., Egerton, A., Stahl, D., et al. (2011). Progressive increase in striatal dopamine synthesis capacity as patients develop psychosis: A PET study. *Molecular Psychiatry, 16*(9), 885–886.

Howes, O. D., Kambeitz, J., Kim, E., Stahl, D., Slifstein, M., Abi-Dargham, A., et al. (2012). The nature of dopamine dysfunction in schizophrenia and what this means for treatment: Meta-analysis of imaging studies. *Archives of General Psychiatry, 69*(8), 776–786.

Howes, O. D., McCutcheon, R., & Stone, J. (2015). Glutamate and dopamine in schizophrenia: An update for the 21st century. *Journal of Psychopharmacology, 29*(2), 97–115.

Howes, O. D., & Murray, R. M. (2014). Schizophrenia: An integrated sociodevelopmental-cognitive model. *The Lancet, 383*(9929), 1677–1687.

Huxley, J., Mayr, E., Osmond, H., & Hoffer, A. (1964). Schizophrenia as a genetic morphism. *Nature, 204*(4955), 220–221.

Insel, T. R. (2010). Rethinking schizophrenia. *Nature, 468*(7321), 187–193.

Ionta, S., Heydrich, L., Lenggenhager, B., Mouthon, M., Fornari, E., Chapuis, D., et al. (2011). Multisensory mechanisms in temporo-parietal cortex support self-location and first-person perspective. *Neuron, 70*(2), 363–374.

Jardri, R., Hugdahl, K., Hughes, M., Brunelin, J., Waters, F., Alderson-Day, B., ... Debbané, M. (2016). Are hallucinations due to an imbalance between excitatory and inhibitory influences on the brain? *Schizophrenia bulletin, 42*(5), 1124–1134.

Javitt, D. C. (2000). Intracortical mechanisms of mismatch negativity dysfunction in schizophrenia. *Audiology and Neurotology, 5*(3–4), 207–215.

Javitt, D. C., & Zukin, S. R. (1991). Recent advances in the phencyclidine model of schizophrenia. *The American Journal of Psychiatry, 148*(10), 1301–1308.

Kean, C. (2009). Silencing the self: Schizophrenia as a self-disturbance. *Schizophrenia Bulletin, 35*(6), 1034–1036.

Kehrer, C., Maziashvili, N., Dugladze, T., & Gloveli, T. (2008). Altered excitatory-inhibitory balance in the NMDA-hypofunction model of schizophrenia. *Frontiers in Molecular Neuroscience, 1*, 6.

Kendler, K. S. (1983). Overview: A current perspective on twin studies of schizophrenia. *The American Journal of Psychiatry, 140*(11), 1413–1425.

Kerns, J. G., Cohen, J. D., MacDonald, A. W., III, Johnson, M. K., Stenger, V. A., Aizenstein, H., et al. (2005). Decreased conflict-and error-related activity in the anterior cingulate cortex in subjects with schizophrenia. *American Journal of Psychiatry, 162*(10), 1833–1839.

Kessler, R. M., Woodward, N. D., Riccardi, P., Li, R., Ansari, M. S., Anderson, S., et al. (2009). Dopamine D2 receptor levels in striatum, thalamus, substantia nigra, limbic regions, and cortex in schizophrenic subjects. *Biological Psychiatry, 65*(12), 1024–1031.

Kim, J. J., Kwon, J. S., Park, H. J., Youn, T., Kang, D. H., Kim, M. S., ... Lee, M. C. (2003). Functional disconnection between the prefrontal and parietal cortices during working memory processing in schizophrenia: A [15O] H2O PET study. *American Journal of Psychiatry, 160*(5), 919–923.

Kirov, G., Pocklington, A. J., Holmans, P., Ivanov, D., Ikeda, M., Ruderfer, D., et al. (2012). De novo CNV analysis implicates specific abnormalities of postsynaptic signalling complexes in the pathogenesis of schizophrenia. *Molecular Psychiatry, 17*(2), 142–153.

Krystal, J. H., Anticevic, A., Yang, G. J., Dragoi, G., Driesen, N. R., Wang, X. J., et al. (2017). Impaired tuning of neural ensembles and the pathophysiology of schizophrenia: A translational and computational neuroscience perspective. *Biological Psychiatry, 81*(10), 874–885.

Krystal, J. H., Karper, L. P., Seibyl, J. P., Freeman, G. K., Delaney, R., Bremner, J. D., et al. (1994). Subanesthetic effects of the noncompetitive NMDA antagonist, ketamine, in humans: Psychotomimetic, perceptual, cognitive, and neuroendocrine responses. *Archives of General Psychiatry, 51*(3), 199–214.

Kuipers, E., Garety, P., Fowler, D., Freeman, D., Dunn, G., & Bebbington, P. (2006). Cognitive, emotional, and social processes in psychosis: Refining cognitive behavioral therapy for persistent positive symptoms. *Schizophrenia Bulletin, 32*(S1), S24–S31.

Lee, J., & Park, S. (2005). Working memory impairments in schizophrenia: A meta-analysis. *Journal of Abnormal Psychology, 114*(4), 599–611.

Lencz, T., Smith, C. W., McLaughlin, D., Auther, A., Nakayama, E., Hovey, L., et al. (2006). Generalized and specific neurocognitive deficits in prodromal schizophrenia. *Biological Psychiatry, 59*(9), 863–871.

Lesh, T. A., Niendam, T. A., Minzenberg, M. J., & Carter, C. S. (2011). Cognitive control deficits in schizophrenia: Mechanisms and meaning. *Neuropsychopharmacology, 36*(1), 316–338.

Lesh, T. A., Westphal, A. J., Niendam, T. A., Yoon, J. H., Minzenberg, M. J., Ragland, J. D., et al. (2013). Proactive and reactive cognitive control and dorsolateral prefrontal cortex dysfunction in first episode schizophrenia. *NeuroImage: Clinical, 2*, 590–599.

Lichtenstein, P., Björk, C., Hultman, C. M., Scolnick, E., Sklar, P., & Sullivan, P. F. (2006). Recurrence risks for schizophrenia in a Swedish national cohort. *Psychological Medicine, 36*(10), 1417–1425.

Lichtenstein, P., Yip, B. H., Björk, C., Pawitan, Y., Cannon, T. D., Sullivan, P. F., et al. (2009). Common genetic determinants of schizophrenia and bipolar disorder in Swedish families: A population-based study. *The Lancet, 373*(9659), 234–239.

Lieberman, J. A., Kane, J. M., & Alvir, J. (1987). Provocative tests with psychostimulant drugs in schizophrenia. *Psychopharmacology, 91*, 415–433.

Lyon, G. J., Abi-Dargham, A., Moore, H., Lieberman, J. A., Javitch, J. A., & Sulzer, D. (2009). Presynaptic regulation of dopamine transmission in schizophrenia. *Schizophrenia Bulletin, 37*(1), 108–117.

Matthews, N. L., Collins, K. P., Thakkar, K. N., & Park, S. (2014). Visuospatial imagery and working memory in schizophrenia. *Cognitive Neuropsychiatry, 19*(1), 17–35.

Mayer, J. S., & Park, S. (2012). Working memory encoding and false memory in schizophrenia and bipolar disorder in a spatial delayed response task. *Journal of Abnormal Psychology, 121*(3), 784–794.

McCabe, R., & Priebe, S. (2004). Explanatory models of illness in schizophrenia: Comparison of four ethnic groups. *The British Journal of Psychiatry, 185*(1), 25–30.

McGuire, P., Howes, O. D., Stone, J., & Fusar-Poli, P. (2008). Functional neuroimaging in schizophrenia: Diagnosis and drug discovery. *Trends in Pharmacological Sciences, 29*(2), 91–98.

Meltzer, H. Y. (1997). Treatment-resistant schizophrenia-the role of clozapine. *Current Medical Research and Opinion, 14*(1), 1–20.

Miyake, A., Friedman, N. P., Emerson, M. J., Witzki, A. H., Howerter, A., & Wager, T. D. (2000). The unity and diversity of executive functions and their contributions to complex "frontal lobe" tasks: A latent variable analysis. *Cognitive Psychology, 41*(1), 49–100.

Moghaddam, B., & Javitt, D. (2012). From revolution to evolution: The glutamate hypothesis of schizophrenia and its implication for treatment. *Neuropsychopharmacology, 37*(1), 4–15.

Murray, J. D., Anticevic, A., Gancsos, M., Ichinose, M., Corlett, P. R., Krystal, J. H., et al. (2012). Linking microcircuit dysfunction to cognitive impairment: Effects of disinhibition associated with schizophrenia in a cortical working memory model. *Cerebral Cortex, 24*(4), 859–872.

Nelson, B., & Sass, L. A. (2017). Towards integrating phenomenology and neurocognition: Possible neurocognitive correlates of basic self-disturbance in schizophrenia. *Current Problems of Psychiatry, 18*(3), 184–200.

Panizzutti, R., Hamilton, S. P., & Vinogradov, S. (2013). Genetic correlate of cognitive training response in schizophrenia. *Neuropharmacology, 64*(1), 264–267.

Park, S., & Gooding, D. C. (2014). Working memory impairment as an endophenotypic marker of a schizophrenia diathesis. *Schizophrenia Research: Cognition, 1*, 127–136.

Pettersson-Yeo, W., Allen, P., Benetti, S., McGuire, P., & Mechelli, A. (2011). Dysconnectivity in schizophrenia: Where are we now? *Neuroscience & Biobehavioral Reviews, 35*(5), 1110–1124.

Pruessner, M., Cullen, A. E., Aas, M., & Walker, E. F. (2017). The neural diathesis-stress model of schizophrenia revisited: An update on recent findings considering illness stage and neurobiological and methodological complexities. *Neuroscience & Biobehavioral Reviews, 73*, 191–218.

Rabbitt, P. (1997). The Alan Welford memorial lecture ageing and human skill: A 40th anniversary. *Ergonomics, 40*(10), 962–981.

Ragland, J. D., Laird, A. R., Ranganath, C., Blumenfeld, R. S., Gonzales, S. M., & Glahn, D. C. (2009). Prefrontal activation deficits during episodic memory in schizophrenia. *American Journal of Psychiatry, 166*(8), 863–874.

Rao, R. P., & Ballard, D. H. (1999). Predictive coding in the visual cortex: A functional interpretation of some extra-classical receptive-field effects. *Nature Neuroscience, 2*(1), 79.

Rees, E., Walters, J. T., Georgieva, L., Isles, A. R., Chambert, K. D., Richards, A. L., et al. (2014). Analysis of copy number variations at 15 schizophrenia-associated loci. *The British Journal of Psychiatry, 204*(2), 108–114.

Reinhart, R. M., Zhu, J., Park, S., & Woodman, G. F. (2015). Medial–frontal stimulation enhances learning in schizophrenia by restoring prediction error signaling. *Journal of Neuroscience, 35*(35), 12232–12240.

Ripke, S., Neale, B. M., Corvin, A., Walters, J. T., Farh, K. H., Holmans, P. A., et al. (2014). Biological insights from 108 schizophrenia-associated genetic loci. *Nature, 511*(7510), 421–427.

Schaefer, J., Giangrande, E., Weinberger, D. R., & Dickinson, D. (2013). The global cognitive impairment in schizophrenia: Consistent over decades and around the world. *Schizophrenia Research, 150*(1), 42–50.

Sebat, J., Levy, D. L., & McCarthy, S. E. (2009). Rare structural variants in schizophrenia: One disorder, multiple mutations; one mutation, multiple disorders. *Trends in Genetics, 25*(12), 528–535.

Seeman, P., & Lee, T. (1975). Antipsychotic drugs: Direct correlation between clinical potency and presynaptic action on dopamine neurons. *Science, 188*(4194), 1217–1219.

Seeman, P., Lee, T., Chau-Wong, M., & Wong, K. (1976). Antipsychotic drug doses and neuroleptic/dopamine receptors. *Nature, 261*(5562), 717–719.

Selten, J. P., Booij, J., Buwalda, B., & Meyer-Lindenberg, A. (2017). Biological mechanisms whereby social exclusion may contribute to the etiology of psychosis: A narrative review. *Schizophrenia Bulletin, 43*(2), 287–292.

Selten, J. P., van der Ven, E., Rutten, B. P., & Cantor-Graae, E. (2013). The social defeat hypothesis of schizophrenia: An update. *Schizophrenia Bulletin, 39*(6), 1180–1186.

Stain, H. J., Galletly, C. A., Clark, S., Wilson, J., Killen, E. A., Anthes, L., et al. (2012). Understanding the social costs of psychosis: The experience of adults affected by psychosis identified within the second Australian National Survey of Psychosis. *Australian & New Zealand Journal of Psychiatry, 46*(9), 879–889.

Starc, M., Murray, J. D., Santamauro, N., Savic, A., Diehl, C., Cho, Y. T., et al. (2017). Schizophrenia is associated with a pattern of spatial working memory deficits consistent with cortical disinhibition. *Schizophrenia Research, 181*, 107–116.

Steeds, H., Carhart-Harris, R. L., & Stone, J. M. (2015). Drug models of schizophrenia. *Therapeutic Advances in Psychopharmacology, 5*(1), 43–58.

Suhara, T., Okubo, Y., Yasuno, F., Sudo, Y., Inoue, M., Ichimiya, T., et al. (2002). Decreased dopamine D2 receptor binding in the anterior cingulate cortex in schizophrenia. *Archives of General Psychiatry, 59*(1), 25–30.

Sullivan, P. F., Kendler, K. S., & Neale, M. C. (2003). Schizophrenia as a complex trait: Evidence from a meta-analysis of twin studies. *Archives of General Psychiatry, 60*(12), 1187–1192.

Thakkar, K. N., Schall, J. D., Logan, G. D., & Park, S. (2011). Response inhibition and response monitoring in a saccadic countermanding task in schizophrenia. *Biological Psychiatry, 69*(1), 55–62.

Thakkar, K. N., Schall, J. D., Logan, G. D., & Park, S. (2015). Response inhibition and response monitoring in a saccadic double-step task in schizophrenia. *Brain and Cognition, 95*, 90–98.

Tienari, P., Wynne, L. C., Läksy, K., Moring, J., Nieminen, P., Sorri, A., et al. (2003). Genetic boundaries of the schizophrenia spectrum: Evidence from the Finnish Adoptive Family Study of Schizophrenia. *American Journal of Psychiatry, 160*(9), 1587–1594.

Tienari, P., Wynne, L. C., Moring, J., Laksy, K., Nieminen, P., Sorri, A., et al. (2000). Finnish adoptive family study: Sample selection and adoptee DSM-III-R diagnoses. *Acta Psychiatrica Scandinavica, 101*(6), 433–443.

Tienari, P., Wynne, L. C., Sorri, A., Lahti, I., Läksy, K., Moring, J., et al. (2004). Genotype-environment interaction in schizophrenia-spectrum disorder: Long-term follow-up study of Finnish adoptees. *British Journal of Psychiatry, 184*, 216–222.

Tsai, G., & Coyle, J. T. (2002). Glutamatergic mechanisms in schizophrenia. *Annual Review of Pharmacology and Toxicology, 42*(1), 165–179.

Uhlhaas, P. J., & Singer, W. (2010). Abnormal neural oscillations and synchrony in schizophrenia. *Nature Reviews Neuroscience, 11*(2), 100–113.

Ursini, G., Punzi, G., Chen, Q., Marenco, S., Robinson, J. F., Porcelli, A., et al. (2018). Convergence of placenta biology and genetic risk for schizophrenia. *Nature Medicine, 24*(6), 792–801.

van Os, J., Rutten, B. P. F., & Poulton, R. (2008). Gene-environment interactions in schizophrenia: Review of epidemiological findings and future directions. *Schizophrenia Bulletin, 34*(6), 1066–1082. https://doi.org/10.1093/schbul/sbn117.

Velthorst, E., Fett, A. K. J., Reichenberg, A., Perlman, G., van Os, J., Bromet, E. J., et al. (2016). The 20-year longitudinal trajectories of social functioning in individuals with psychotic disorders. *American Journal of Psychiatry, 174*(11), 1075–1085.

Weinberger, D. R., & Laruelle, M. (2002). Neurochemical and neuropharmacological imaging in schizophrenia. In K. L. Davis, D. Charney, J. T. Coyle, & C. Nemeroff (Eds.), *Neuropsychopharmacology: The fifth generation of progress* (pp. 833–855). New York, NY: Lippincott Williams and Wilkins.

Wong, A. H. C., & Van Tol, H. H. (2003). Schizophrenia: From phenomenology to neurobiology. *Neuroscience & Biobehavioral Reviews, 27*(3), 269–306.

Xu, B., Roos, J. L., Levy, S., Van Rensburg, E. J., Gogos, J. A., & Karayiorgou, M. (2008). Strong association of de novo copy number mutations with sporadic schizophrenia. *Nature Genetics, 40*(7), 880–885.

Yanos, P. T., Roe, D., Markus, K., & Lysaker, P. H. (2008). Pathways between internalized stigma and outcomes related to recovery in schizophrenia spectrum disorders. *Psychiatric Services, 59*(12), 1437–1442.

Zai, G., Robbins, T. W., Sahakian, B. J., & Kennedy, J. L. (2017). A review of molecular genetic studies of neurocognitive deficits in schizophrenia. *Neuroscience & Biobehavioral Reviews, 72*, 50–67.

Definition of Key Terms

Diathesis-stress model Psychological theory that disorders develop from a genetic or biological predisposition for that illness (diathesis) combined with stressful life or environmental conditions, which play a precipitating or facilitating role.

De novo mutation A genetic alteration that is present for the first time in one family member as a result of a variant in a germ cell (egg or sperm) of one of the parents, or a variant that arises in the fertilised egg itself during early embryogenesis.

Copy number variant (CNV) Refers to the genetic trait involving the number of copies of a particular gene present in the genome of an individual. Copy number variants account for a significant proportion of the genetic variation between individuals.

Genome-wide association study (GWAS) A method that surveys the entire genome for genetic polymorphisms (variations) that occur more frequently in cases (e.g. some disorder) than in controls.

Single-nucleotide polymorphism (SNP) A type of genetic polymorphism involving variation of a single base pair at a specific location in the genome. DNA sequence variations can occur when a single nucleotide in the genome sequence is altered.

Major histocompatibility complex (MHC) Group of genes that code for proteins found on the surfaces of cells that help the immune system recognise foreign (nonself) substances. MHC proteins are found in all higher vertebrates.

Working memory Active short-term memory that supports representational guidance of behaviour.

Cognitive control The set of cognitive abilities/processes, which allow information processing and behaviour to vary according to one's current goals, also thought of as 'executive control'.

Dopamine A neurotransmitter involved in cognition, emotion, and movement.

Glutamate A neurotransmitter widely distributed throughout the brain and central nervous system whose primary role is to excite (increase firing of) nearby neurons. As the main excitatory neurotransmitter, it is critical to nearly all aspects of information processing.

Gamma-aminobutyric acid (GABA) A neurotransmitter widely distributed throughout the cortex whose primary role is to inhibit nearby neuronal activity. It is involved in many cortical functions, including visual processing, emotion regulation, learning and memory, and motor control.

NMDA receptor A type of glutamate receptor distributed throughout the cortex that plays a key role in learning, memory, and synaptic plasticity.

Excitatory/inhibitory (E/I) balance The relative contributions of excitatory and inhibitory synaptic inputs that maintains neuronal activity of a circuit within a safe and narrow range.

Bayesian inference A statistical method in which prior information is used to update predictions (hypotheses) and estimate the probability of some event, based on Bayes' theorem of learning (a mathematical formula for determining the likelihood of an event based on the prior occurrence of the event—its *conditional probability*).

Predictive coding Neural processing by which the brain predicts incoming sensorimotor input based on previous experience to facilitate appropriate reactions.

Jumping to conclusions bias A reasoning style in which one accepts a hypothesis based on insufficient (or less) evidence.

CHAPTER 3

Understanding the Impact of Mental Health Stigma and the Role of Clinicians as Allies

Katherine Nieweglowski, Sang Qin, Deysi Paniagua, Patrick W. Corrigan
Illinois Institute of Technology, Lewis College of Human Sciences, Chicago, IL, United States

Key Learning Objectives

- Clinicians will learn what it means to be an ally and how to stand *WITH* people with mental illness in the fight to end stigma.
- Public stigma and self-stigma of people with psychosis will be described.
- Three social-cognitive constructs of stigma are defined: stereotypes, prejudice, and discrimination.
- Affirming attitudes and behaviours are described as key ways for clinicians to replace prejudice and discrimination in treatment.
- The efficacy of protest, education, and contact strategies is reviewed as approaches to combat public stigma and self-stigma.
- Disclosure is identified as a key factor for people with lived experience when leading antistigma efforts.

INTRODUCTION

Stigma is a complex construct that negatively affects many minorities and outgroups. Racism, for example, leads to discrimination against people of colour, and the stigma of AIDS leads to discrimination towards people with the disease. The stigma of mental illness is in the same category of importance and will be the focus of this chapter with examples specific to people with psychosis. This involves a discussion of the different forms of stigma affecting people with mental illness such as public stigma and self-stigma. We expand on this discussion by considering how clinicians unintentionally worsen the stigma of mental illness. We then review strategies to combat public and self-stigma, including protest, education, and contact approaches. Clinicians who are the intended audience

Stigma comprises stereotypes, prejudice, and discrimination that discredit people with mental illness.

Public Stigma refers to how the general population views and treats people with mental illness.

Self-Stigma occurs when individuals internalise public stigma of mental illness into their self-concepts.

A Clinical Introduction to Psychosis. https://doi.org/10.1016/B978-0-12-815012-2.00003-1

Box 3.1 Lived Experience

A *person with lived experience* is someone who has personally faced the disabling effects of mental illness. Clinicians with lived experience should share the driver's seat when it comes to antistigma efforts. Sitting in the driver's seat means acting as a leader and using one's personal experiences with mental illness to provide feedback on the needs and barriers experienced by people in the community. Clinicians without lived experience are allies. Clinicians with lived experience have a unique role if they choose to disclose their mental illness.

Ally is a person that provides support and stands *WITH* people with mental illness in the fight to end stigma.

of this book should read this chapter through the lens of an Ally. An ally is a person who provides support and stands *WITH* people with mental illness in the fight to end stigma. People with Lived Experience themselves need to sit in the driver's seat and lead antistigma efforts (see Box 3.1). Clinicians are responsible for endorsing affirming attitudes and behaviours whilst taking the backseat as supporters (Corrigan, 2018).

CASE STUDY 3.1: WHAT DOES IT MEAN TO BE AN ALLY?

Lisa is a third-year clinical psychology student at a private university in Chicago who just started her practicum training at a treatment centre for young adults with first-episode psychosis. Her brother, Matthew, was diagnosed with schizophrenia during his sophomore year of college whilst Lisa was still in high school. Matthew sought treatment for his symptoms at a place just like the one in which Lisa is now training. In fact, his journey to recovery has been Lisa's primary inspiration for pursuing a career as a clinician.

When Lisa first realised that she wanted to become a clinician and help people like her brother, she thought she knew exactly what to do. As she started learning more about schizophrenia, she made assumptions about Matthew's experiences. She told her parents not to bring up school so that it wouldn't stress him out; she made sure his friends didn't overwhelm him with invitations; and she castigated other family members if they said something stigmatising about her brother's condition. One day Matthew had to confront Lisa. He said that he knew her heart was in the right place, but that she had to let him take control of his own recovery. Just because he had schizophrenia did not mean that he could not speak up for himself.

As a family member of a person with psychosis, Lisa now stands in solidarity *WITH* her brother. She has learned from her earlier efforts and understands that it is important for Matthew to speak directly to others about his needs and experiences in order to bring about change. As a service provider, Lisa encourages people with mental illness to take the driver's seat in the fight to end stigma. She knows that the fight cannot be won without persons with lived experience like her brother at the forefront. Lisa gladly takes the backseat as a family member and clinician without lived experience.

UNDERSTANDING STIGMA

Sociologist Erving Goffman (1963) laid out the groundwork for the concept of stigma, identifying three types that result from: (1) being part of a marginalised group (e.g. race, religion); (2) having physical defects (i.e. deformities of the body, physical disability); and (3) having marred character traits (e.g. mental illness, substance use disorder). Link and Phelan (2001) built on his work and organised stigma into social psychological constructs that are observed through interactions between labelled differences and discrimination. Persons with noticeable differences (i.e. skin colour) are viewed as having undesirable attributes. They are then separated from the 'norm' thus becoming victims of rejection, segregation, and other forms of discrimination (Link, Yang, Phelan, & Collins, 2004). Stigmatised groups, such as people with mental illness, also find themselves at a disadvantage because of their perceived differences. Consequently, it is difficult for them to access social, economic, and political resources. In turn, this reinforces their devalued social identities and leads to poor quality of life.

Stereotypes are the negative beliefs about people with mental illness.

Prejudice is the negative emotional reaction that occurs as a result of the stereotype.

Discrimination is the negative behavioural reaction exhibited towards people with mental illness.

Stigma is also understood through a social cognitive model characterised by stereotypes, prejudice, and discrimination (Link & Phelan, 2001; see Table 3.1). Stereotypes are the negative beliefs about people with mental illness ('People with psychosis are dangerous'.). Prejudice is the negative emotional reaction that occurs as a result of the stereotype ('I feel afraid to be around people with psychosis'.); and Discrimination is the negative behavioural reaction exhibited towards people with mental illness ('I avoid people with psychosis in the community or in the workplace'.).

Implicit stigma occurs when people are not fully aware that their beliefs about a certain group contribute to their behaviours.

Explicit stigma occurs when people have conscious knowledge of their beliefs and how they contribute to their behaviours.

Negative attitudes and behaviours may be the result of either implicit or explicit stigma (Brener, Grenville, von Hippel, & Wilson, 2013; Sheehan, Nieweglowski, & Corrigan, 2017). Implicit stigma occurs when people are not fully aware that their beliefs about a certain group contribute to their behaviours. For example, family members may limit their loved one's financial autonomy because they have an unconscious belief that individuals cannot be independent because of their mental illness. Explicit stigma, on the other hand, occurs when people have conscious knowledge of a stereotype and are aware that their endorsement of this stereotype contributes to their behaviours. In this case, family members are aware that their decision to control finances is a result of their belief that people with mental illness are not able to be independent.

In the next sections, we focus on explicit stigma and provide an overview of the stereotypes of people with mental illness (i.e. psychosis) and how explicit knowledge and agreement with these stereotypes generates prejudice and discrimination. We also examine throughout how clinicians may play a role in exacerbating the negative effects of stigma.

Stereotypes

Common stereotypes of mental illness include dangerousness, unpredictability, and incompetence (Pescosolido, Monahan, Link, Stueve, & Kikuzawa, 1999). A systematic review on attitudes towards mental illness demonstrated that older females endorsed more positive beliefs whilst younger males reported the most negative stereotypes (Parcesepe & Cabassa, 2013). People who endorse these stereotypes may say things like, 'these mentally ill people cannot work and are

Table 3.1 **Conceptualising Stigma Matrix**

	Public stigma	Self-stigma	Label avoidance
Stereotypes Negative beliefs that the public holds about people with mental illness and psychosis.	People with psychosis are *dangerous* and *unpredictable*.	People with psychosis are *incompetent*.	People with psychosis are *psycho*.
Prejudice Affective responses, or emotional reactions, that result from stereotypes.	I feel *afraid* to be around people with psychosis.	I am a person with psychosis and therefore ashamed. Who would want to hire me?	I have psychosis and I'm ashamed to be seen as *psycho*.
Discrimination Behavioural responses that result from the stereotype and prejudice interaction.	I *avoid* people with psychosis in the community or in the workplace.	I think 'Why Try' and stop looking for a job.	I don't seek treatment for psychosis for fear that I will be treated negatively by my providers.

drains on society' or, even worse, 'this crazy person will go on a shooting rampage if we're not careful'. Despite efforts to correct these negative beliefs, misconceptions about mental illness remain prevalent among the general public (Angermeyer & Dietrich, 2006). Some stereotypes are especially common for serious mental illnesses. People with schizophrenia, for example, are believed to be the most dangerous and unpredictable: they are seen as more capable of violence, aggressive behaviours, and self-harm (Angermeyer & Dietrich, 2006).

Stereotypes endorsed by clinicians may also vary across diagnoses as certain disorders are seen as more detrimental than others. People with psychosis are viewed by providers as most difficult to communicate with, most distinct from others, and less likely to recover (Björkman, Angelman, & Jönsson, 2008). What is even more surprising is that healthcare professionals (e.g. psychiatrists, nurses, psychologists) sometimes uphold more negative stereotypes than the general public. One study comparing attitudes of mental health professionals revealed that psychiatrists, followed by nurses and other providers (i.e. social workers, vocational counsellors), reported more negative stereotypes towards individuals with severe mental illness than the average person (Nordt, Rössler, & Lauber, 2006). Clinicians also play a large role in promoting incompetence, the belief that people with psychosis are incapable of making their own healthcare decisions (Hamilton, Heaven, Thomson, Wilson, & Exley, 2016; Knaak, Mantler, & Szeto, 2017). This can result in stigmatising attitudes such as Authoritarianism ('others should make health decisions for them') and Benevolence ('people with mental illness need to be protected and cared for like children') (Holmes, Corrigan, Williams, Canar, & Kubiak, 1999). Nevertheless, having knowledge of stereotypes related to mental illness does not automatically set the stage for discrimination. Whilst clinicians may be aware of stereotypes, they may choose to disagree with them. Those who agree with stereotypes about

Authoritarianism suggests that people with mental illness are incapable of making their own decisions; so others should make their decisions for them.

Benevolence suggests that people with mental illness need to be protected and cared for.

people with mental illness generate prejudice or negative emotions. Prejudice bridges the interaction between stereotypes and discrimination (Corrigan & Watson, 2002).

PUBLIC STIGMA

Now that we have reviewed stereotypes of mental illness, prejudice and discrimination can be understood according to three types of stigma: public stigma, self-stigma, and label avoidance (see Table 3.1). First, we discuss public stigma. Public Stigma refers to how the general population views and treats people with mental illness. Prejudice and discrimination occur when the public agrees with the stereotypes thus leading to negative emotions and behaviours. Clinicians are responsible for enacting these stigmatising responses within healthcare settings.

Label Avoidance occurs when the individual decides not to engage in care seeking due to awareness of stigma related to one's mental illness.

Prejudice and Discrimination

Common prejudice exhibited towards people with mental illness includes fear and anger (Corrigan & Watson, 2002; Link et al., 2004). Individuals agree with the stereotype ('I agree that people with psychosis are dangerous...') leading to emotional reactions ('...therefore, I am afraid of them'). Prejudice such as anger can increase discrimination through social rejection ('I will not be friends with them'). Discrimination also manifests itself as restriction of opportunities to pursue life goals (i.e. education, employment, independent living, intimate relationships, wellness, etc.). Landlords may avoid renting or leasing apartments to people with psychosis who are viewed as dangerous, and employers might avoid hiring them (Corrigan, 2005). Cultural differences (described in more detail in Chapter 4) may also play a role in the way people discriminate against individuals with mental illness. This is evident among different racial groups in the United States. For example, African Americans and Asians perceive people with mental illness as more dangerous than European Americans leading to greater endorsement of segregation (Rao, Feinglass, & Corrigan, 2007). Similar behaviours have been found among healthcare providers (Lauber, Anthony, Ajdacic-Gross, & Rössler, 2004; Nordt et al., 2006). Clinicians who endorse negative stereotypes and prejudice may agree with overmedication and coercive treatment behaviours (Arboleda-Flórez, 2005; Arboleda-Flórez & Stuart, 2012; MacNeela, Scott, Treacy, Hyde, & O'Mahony, 2012).

Historically, people with psychiatric disorders were segregated from their community resulting in involuntary admission to 'mental institutions', removal of social connections, and isolation. These practices violated individuals' freedom and strengthened public misconceptions about their ability to make healthcare decisions, engage in self-care, and live independently (Arboleda-Flórez, 2005). One type of coercion that may remain today is imposing psychiatric medications as 'quick fixes' for people with psychosis (Pescosolido, Perry, Martin, McLeod, & Jensen, 2007; Spence, 2013). This practice diminishes autonomy and exacerbates discrimination in healthcare settings (Levy, Celen-Demirtas,

Surguladze, & Sweeney, 2014; Novak & Švab, 2009). Other subtle forms of discrimination include reluctance to release people in recovery into their communities and an unwillingness to develop therapeutic rapport (Corrigan, Watson, Warpinski, & Gracia, 2004; MacNeela et al., 2012).

Clinicians specialising in physical health concerns have been found to lack skills required to care for people with comorbid mental illnesses (Zolnierek, 2009). Signs of physical illness may be misattributed to mental health diagnoses, which can delay proper treatment (Thornicroft, Rose, & Kassam, 2007). Stigma of mental illness endorsed by some healthcare providers may determine whether people qualify for adequate healthcare. Clinicians need to be mindful of how health and treatment outcomes of people with mental illness are impacted by discrimination in healthcare settings.

SELF-STIGMA

As can be seen in Table 3.1, self-stigma occurs when individuals internalise the public stigma of mental illness into their own self-concepts (Bathje & Pryor, 2011). The process of internalisation happens in four progressively worsening stages: awareness, agreement, application, and harm; see Fig. 3.1. First, people are *aware* of the stereotype ('The public believes people with psychosis are unpredictable.'). Second, they *agree* with that stereotype ('I think that people with psychosis are unpredictable.'). Third, they *apply* that stigma or stereotype into their own identities ('I see myself as unpredictable because I have psychosis.'). Fourth, this application causes harm, which is the ultimate consequence of self-stigma ('I currently respect myself less because I am unpredictable.') (Corrigan & Calabrese, 2005; Corrigan, Watson, & Barr, 2006).

Self-stigma results in harmful consequences for the well-being and recovery of people with psychosis. Research shows that individuals with psychosis who have higher self-stigma experience more symptoms (i.e. hallucinations and delusions)

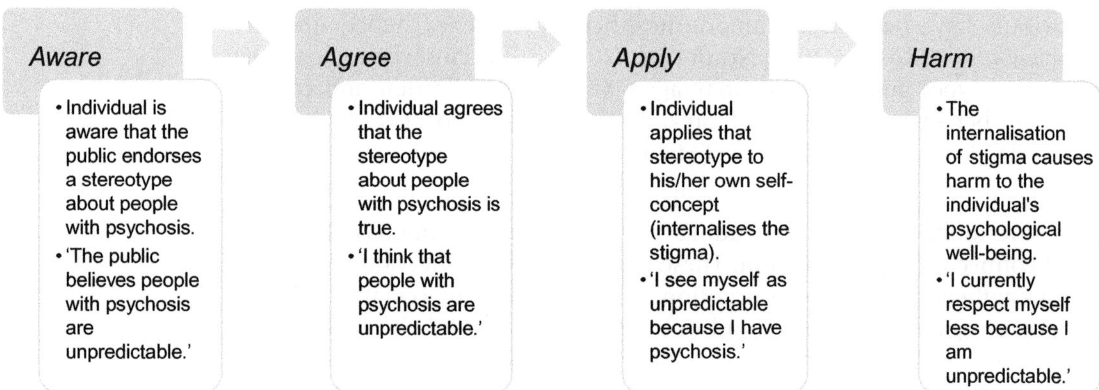

FIG. 3.1
Four-step process of self-stigma.

(Cavelti, Rüsch, & Vauth, 2014; Ho et al., 2018), higher suicide risk (Yanos, Roe, West, Smith, & Lysaker, 2012), impaired social and vocational functioning (Yanos, Lysaker, & Roe, 2010; Yanos, Roe, & Lysaker, 2010), and lower quality of life (Drapalski et al., 2013). Alienation and shame are some of the most harmful consequences of self-stigma (Gerlinger et al., 2013). Greater loneliness can decrease social networks and worsen interpersonal skills (Chrostek, Grygiel, Anczewska, Wciórka, & Świtaj, 2016).

Diminished self-esteem may also cause the individual to feel less empowered to make positive life choices that can facilitate recovery or promote treatment adherence (Fung, Tsang, & Corrigan, 2008). This can lead to what is known as the 'Why Try' effect (Corrigan, Larson, & Rüsch, 2009). Individuals start to feel as if they are not worthy or not capable of achieving certain life goals. For example, those who internalise the idea that people with psychosis are unable to work may not engage in job seeking ('Why try to get a job? I am not capable of performing well. I am not worthy of having a good job.') (Corrigan et al., 2009). The 'Why Try' effect can also impact interpersonal relationships ('Why try to make friends? I am not capable of being a good friend. I am not worthy of having good friends.'), treatment seeking ('Why try to go to counseling? I'll never get better. I am not worthy of recovery.'), and starting a family ('Why try to have children? I am not stable enough to be a good parent. I am not worthy of starting a family.').

'Why Try' effect occurs when individuals feel incapable or unworthy of accomplishing their goals.

LABEL AVOIDANCE

As outlined in Table 3.1, another consequence of self-stigma is Label Avoidance—when individuals decide not to engage in care seeking due to awareness of stigma related to their mental illness (Ben-Zeev, Young, & Corrigan, 2010). Labels prompt stereotypes about a condition and place individuals in a specific category (e.g. mentally ill, psychotic), thus causing them to expect negative public treatment (Kroska & Harkness, 2006; Link, 1987). Most people with psychosis hide or conceal their diagnosis because they do not want to be hurt by that label (Harangozo et al., 2014). This may cause them to avoid seeking services (Ben-Zeev et al., 2010), stop taking medications (Jenkins & Carpenter-Song, 2009), or even drop out of treatment completely (Kessler et al., 2001).

Label avoidance may be exacerbated by visibility of the condition and symptoms (Nieweglowski & Corrigan, 2017). People who have more overt symptoms of psychosis, such as hallucinations and delusions, are more quickly labelled and placed into the 'mentally ill' or 'psychotic' group. For example, people who are responding to auditory hallucinations on the bus may be labelled as 'crazy'. This can cause them to be more readily discriminated against and rejected. More visible symptoms result in more perceived public stigma, which leads to stereotype agreement and, ultimately, self-stigma (Ho et al., 2018). However, visible symptoms and labels may also make it easier for people to seek help because symptoms of psychosis are more apparent. This is known as the Labelling Paradox (Perry, 2011). Diagnosis may facilitate treatment by helping

Labelling Paradox occurs when visible symptoms of mental illness make it easier for people to seek help.

determine effective treatment plans, medications, and psychotherapeutic interventions. Nonetheless, diagnosis is a type of label that facilitates the internalisation of stigma (Lai, Hong, & Chee, 2001). Clinicians should be mindful of how labels affect the self-evaluation of people with mental illness in addition to their own biases. People with mental illness may discontinue treatment if they perceive that they are or will be treated negatively because of their diagnosis (Kessler et al., 2001).

Effects of Familiarity

Familiarity refers to the level of intimacy and experience that one has with people with mental illness.

Level of familiarity may influence the impact of stigma by clinicians in treatment settings. Familiarity here is the intimacy and experience that one has with people with mental illness (see Box 3.2). It may vary from having an acquaintance to sharing an intimate relationship with someone with mental illness. Existing research largely describes an inverse relationship between familiarity and public stigma (Corrigan & Nieweglowski, 2019). That is, the more familiar a person is with a mental illness, the less likely that person is to engage in stigmatising attitudes and behaviours (Adewuya & Makanjuola, 2008; Angermeyer, Holzinger, & Matschinger, 2009). However, some studies demonstrate that familiarity can also be positively correlated with stigma (Corrigan et al., 2005; Wolkenstein & Meyer, 2009) leading to a U-shaped relationship (Corrigan & Nieweglowski, 2019): Stigma is inversely correlated with familiarity when the relationship is less intimate (i.e. acquaintance, co-worker), but the correlation becomes positive as the relationship becomes closer (i.e. parents, healthcare providers).

Perceived Responsibility is the recognised duty of others to take care of people with mental illness.

This model supports previous findings that show clinicians pose a higher level of stigma than other groups (Nordt et al., 2006). Despite higher levels of familiarity in treatment relationships, clinicians may endorse negative stereotypes of people with mental illness and discriminate against them due to a perceived responsibility for their welfare. The formation of this U-shaped relationship between familiarity and stigma can be explained by the perceived responsibility that healthcare providers feel towards the well-being of persons with mental illness (Corrigan & Nieweglowski, 2019). Perceived Responsibility refers to the recognised duty of others, such as parents and clinicians, to take care of people with mental illness. Clinicians who endorse benevolence stereotypes may perceive themselves as being responsible for protecting and making 'wise' decisions on behalf of people with mental illness. As a result, these unintended consequences can undermine the person's autonomy and their ability to recover.

CASE STUDY 3.2: IS LISA TOO FAMILIAR WITH MENTAL ILLNESS?

Lisa's familiarity with mental illness is key to being an ally in the fight to end stigma. First, Lisa is a sister. She has observed her brother's recovery journey and struggles along the way. This has led her to have a better understanding about the negative impacts of stigma. Second, Lisa is a rehabilitation counsellor. She possesses advanced knowledge about symptoms, medications, and other effective strategies.

As a counsellor, Lisa has the perceived responsibility to make what she believes are the best treatment decisions for her clients. She sometimes finds herself becoming impatient with people she is serving when they want to quickly discontinue medications due to side effects. However, Lisa now recognises that perceived responsibility is causing her to view her clients as incompetent and engage in coercive practices. Although this is coming from a place of care, Lisa recognises that she needs to encourage self-determination and respect the autonomy of her clients in their treatment decisions. Lisa's goal as an ally is to make sure that her familiarity with mental illness does not cause her to stigmatise and push persons with lived experience into the backseat.

AFFIRMING ATTITUDES AND BEHAVIOURS

Clinicians who adopt affirming attitudes and behaviours will help stigma change be successful. Affirming attitudes for people with mental illness include recovery, self-determination, and empowerment (Corrigan, 2018). Recovery encompasses hope and achievement ('People with mental illness *can* and *do* get better'.). Regardless of symptoms, people with psychosis have aspirations for their careers, relationships, and independent living. Clinicians as allies endorse the idea that people are able to recover and accomplish these goals. Self-determination happens when people with psychosis feel *able* to decide for themselves what their personal aspirations are and how they are going to achieve them (Corrigan & Kosyluk, 2013). Self-determination promotes empowerment, the obverse of self-stigma. People who are empowered have increased self-esteem, are optimistic about their goals, actively participate in their communities, and use righteous anger to facilitate change (Rogers, Chamberlin, Ellison, & Crean, 1997). Clinicians must mirror these feelings of empowerment in order to support people with mental illness.

Recovery is a process that involves notions of hope and achievement.

Self-determination occurs when people with mental illness feel able to choose and accomplish their goals.

Empowerment is the obverse of self-stigma involving increased self-esteem and optimism.

Affirming attitudes must lead to affirmative actions or behaviours. Reasonable accommodation as outlined in the Americans with Disabilities Act (ADA) is one example of affirmative actions that tear down stigma and promote idea of recovery and self-determination (ADA, 1990). According to the ADA, employees with disabilities cannot be discriminated against (i.e. not hired, terminated) if they are able to perform the essential functions of the job with

Reasonable accommodation: an adjustment made to an environment to make it more accessible and functional for people with disabilities.

Box 3.2 Familiarity With Mental Illness and Stigma

The lowest possible level of familiarity is having no experience with mental illness. Level of familiarity increases when the relationship intimacy increases (i.e. acquaintance, co-worker, friend, family member, parent, provider). The highest possible level of familiarity is personally experiencing psychiatric symptoms or having lived experience. This is even higher than being a parent or provider because the individual can describe firsthand the negative effects of mental illness. Remember, a person who has lived experience can serve as a leader in antistigma efforts. This includes clinicians who have lived experience because they have a higher level of familiarity than their fellow providers.

reasonable accommodations. Reasonable accommodations, such as job coaches, modified work schedules, and quiet work places, replace unjust attitudes by encouraging and allowing individuals with mental illness and other disabilities to pursue employment goals and achieve a sense of recovery in related aspects of life (Carling, 1993). Another example is The Fair Housing Act, which requires landlords to provide reasonable accommodations so that individuals with disabilities can accomplish independent living goals (Schonfeld, 1997).

Nevertheless, affirming attitudes and behaviours alone are not enough to change stigma. Stigma change requires evidence-based strategies that demonstrate lasting results in real-world settings. We continue here by discussing specific strategies to combat public and self-stigma.

STRATEGIES TO COMBAT PUBLIC STIGMA

Protest is a strategy to target negative representations of mental illness and seek to stop them.

Education challenges inaccurate assumptions of mental illness replacing myths with facts.

Contact refers to strategic interactions between community members and persons with lived experience who are willing to disclose.

Three common strategies are frequently applied to combat the effects of public stigma (Corrigan & Kosyluk, 2014). (1) Protests target negative representations and misconceptions of mental illness and seek to stop them. (2) Education challenges inaccurate assumptions about mental illness by replacing myths with facts. (3) Contact involves strategic interactions between persons with lived experience who are willing to disclose and members of the community. Examples and implications of each approach are thoroughly reviewed in the next section. Table 3.2 summarises the strengths and limitations of each approach.

Protest

The efficacy of protests is evident in many historical arenas: Gandhi's Salt March against the British in India (Weber, 2002), and the March on Washington led by Dr. Martin Luther King, Jr., against racism and economic inequality (King, Carson, Carson, & Armstrong, 1992) are two. Despite these examples, research has shown only partial benefits generated by protest efforts (Ottati, Bodenhausen, & Newman, 2005; Wenzlaff & Wegner, 2000). Protests are largely based on suppressing prejudice and negative viewpoints, which may have undesired effects (Macrae, Bodenhausen, Milne, & Jetten, 1994) such as stirring up 'rebound' effects (Corrigan & Shapiro, 2010). If protests call for the public to stop endorsing stereotypical messages about people with mental illness, oftentimes negative attributes re-appear in people's minds at a stronger rate. For example, when protesters call for an end to associating mass shootings with history of psychiatric diagnosis, they may inadvertently strengthen these associations rather than mitigating them. This may also explain why messages such as 'Don't Discriminate' sometimes backfire and cause people to discriminate even more (Paluck & Green, 2009). Although a few studies argue that protests are effective in removing detrimental messages and addressing the misrepresentation of mental illness in the media (Corbière, Samson,

Villotti, & Pelletier, 2012; Wahl, 1995), findings are largely mixed. Research should seek to better understand the effectiveness of this strategy (Corrigan, Morris, Michaels, Rafacz, & Rüsch, 2012).

Education

Education approaches combat stigma by providing accurate information about mental illness that challenge stigmatising attitudes and misconceptions. Education can be carried out in various ways (e.g. books, webpages, news media, training programs, etc.) with many leading to positive outcomes (Corrigan et al., 2012). One example is Mental Health First Aid (MHFA). MHFA is a mental health literacy program developed in Australia by Kitchener and Jorm (2006) that is used worldwide and teaches community members first-aid skills designed for helping people who may be experiencing mental health or substance use-related crises. Trainees receive an 8-hour-long MHFA course that teaches them to identify symptoms of a crisis and intervene properly. A metaanalysis examining MHFA effectiveness found people who received MHFA training presented an increase of mental literacy and a decrease of negative attitudes (Hadlaczky, Hökby, Mkrchian, Carli, & Wasserman, 2014). However, not all education approaches have this desired effect. An example of this is the use of hallucination simulations. Participants listen to audio, which replicates the feeling of an auditory hallucination. Research has found that this approach leads to an increase in negative attitudes towards people with psychosis and an increased desire for social distance (Brown, 2010; Kalyanaraman, Penn, Ivory, & Judge, 2010; McEnteggart, Barnes-Holmes, & Adekuoroye, 2016). As a cost-effective approach, education is suitable for reaching larger audiences; however, information and materials delivered through education approaches should be cautiously selected in order to avoid reinforcing stigmatising messages.

BIOGENETIC VERSUS BIOPSYCHOSOCIAL PERSPECTIVE

The Biogenetic Perspective of mental illness defines mental illness as a biological, medical disorder (Angermeyer, Holzinger, Carta, & Schomerus, 2011). Schizophrenia, for example, is framed as a brain disease with a fundamental genetic vulnerability (Haslam & Kvaale, 2015). Attributing mental illness to physiological causes (e.g. imbalance of neurotransmitters) aims to reduce the stigma. It implies that persons have limited control over their mental illness; thus, they are less likely to be blamed for it (Schlier, Schmick, & Lincoln, 2014). However, this perspective induces a pessimistic prognosis of mental illnesses that prevents recovery (Crisp, Gelder, Goddard, & Meltrzer, 2005; Luty, Umoh, Sessay, & Sarkhel, 2007). Thus, the public believes people with mental illness will not recover.

Biogenetic Perspective describes mental illness as a biological, medical disorder.

A systematic review on public attitudes of mental illness showed that there has been a verifiable increase in the biological understanding of mental illness and treatment acceptance (i.e. people with mental illness have a brain disorder with genetic aetiology) (Schomerus et al., 2012). Nevertheless, minimal effects on

Table 3.2 **Public Stigma Reduction Strategies**

	Protest	Education	Contact
Strengths	Protests stop the endorsement of negative beliefs and misrepresentations about mental illness in the media.	Education approaches replace myths with factual information about mental illness.	Contact exposes the public to people with mental illness who are in recovery which diminishes stigmatising attitudes and behaviours.
Limitations	Protests sometimes stir up rebound effects by suppressing stigma instead of eliminating it.	Education approaches sometimes deliver materials and information that unintentionally reinforce stigmatising messages.	Persons with lived experience must be willing to disclose and be open about their mental illness to make contact effective.

stigma reduction were found. In fact, stigmatising attitudes, such as desired social distance and perceived threat, seemed to increase for schizophrenia. Additional evidence suggests the biogenetic perspective is responsible for aggravating prejudice and discrimination (Carter, Read, Pyle, & Morrison, 2019; Read, Haslam, Sayce, & Davies, 2006; Schlier et al., 2014). A review on its effectiveness in reducing stigma of psychosis concluded that negative stereotypes were reinforced and social acceptance decreased (Read et al., 2006). The lasting influences of the biogenetic perspective also reflect the dominance of the medical model of disability, which focuses on symptoms that need to be cured or managed. Providers should be aware of how their knowledge and clinical training may affect attitudes and influence their treatment practices. Focusing on strengths and fostering hope in treatment may promote greater service outcomes (Corrigan, 2018).

Biopsychosocial Perspective describes mental illness as a result of psychological, social, environmental, and biological factors.

The Biopsychosocial Perspective introduces psychological (e.g. stress, personality, coping habits) and social environmental factors (e.g. culture, social support, healthcare system) to the understanding of mental illness (Lincoln, Arens, Berger, & Rief, 2008). Biopsychosocial factors incorporate recent life stressors and adversity in upbringing in addition to biological factors (e.g. inherited genetic vulnerability). Contrary to the biogenetic perspective, psychosocial viewpoints are more effective in reducing endorsement of negative stereotypes (i.e. dangerousness, unpredictability) towards people with psychosis (Carter et al., 2019; Lee et al., 2014). Lower desire for social distance is also observed when individuals receive a biopsychosocial explanation of psychosis (Lee et al., 2014).

People who are less likely to endorse the medical model of disability preferred the biopsychosocial explanation. In fact, individuals who support the biopsychosocial perspective tend to promote the benefits of psychotherapeutic treatment (Read et al., 2006). Thus, clinicians must incorporate psychosocial factors of mental illness into their education and training to develop more autonomous and empowering treatment plans.

Contact

Contact originated from the idea that those who have more exposure with people with mental illness are less likely to execute stigmatising attitudes and behaviours (Corrigan & Penn, 1999). In general, contact has yielded more positive results on stigma change than education and protest approaches (Corrigan et al., 2012; Corrigan, Michaels, & Morris, 2015). Healthcare professionals who have more contact with individuals with mental illness (i.e. providers in somatic units) endorsed less negative stereotypes (Björkman et al., 2008). Yet contact is limited as it requires openness from people with lived experience and may pose risks such as more vulnerability to public stigma.

A successful contact intervention is more likely to take place when people (1) interact with each other as peers, (2) work towards a common goal, and (3) have face-to-face contact (Corrigan, 2017; Corrigan et al., 2015). Peers come from similar backgrounds and have equal levels of social status. They can be people with or without lived experience. In treatment settings, clinicians (who may not have lived experience) and people with lived experience can act as peers through shared decision making. Shared decision making promotes self-determination for persons with mental illness and encourages input on an equal basis (Adams, Drake, & Wolford, 2007; Charles, Gafni, & Whelan, 1997).

Peers are people who come from similar backgrounds and have equal levels of social status.

STRATEGIES TO COMBAT SELF-STIGMA

Strategies to combat self-stigma can also be divided into education and contact approaches (Corrigan & Rao, 2012; Yanos, Lucksted, Drapalski, Roe, & Lysaker, 2015). Education approaches here are more commonly referred to as psychoeducation. Psychoeducation as applied to stigma is a method of counselling used to teach people about the stigma related to their mental illness and how it may affect their well-being. Knowledge of stigma helps people take control of their lives by understanding how negative attitudes and behaviours are internalised. Research has shown that psychoeducation approaches have led to decreased self-stigma in people with psychosis (Uchino, Maeda, & Uchimara, 2012). However, one study demonstrated that, although self-stigma was reduced, there were no significant changes in empowerment or perceived discrimination (Štrkalj-Ivezić, Sesar, & Mužinić, 2017). This suggests that psychoeducational approaches alone do not target all aspects of self-stigma and may not have lasting effects.

Psychoeducation teaches people about mental illness stigma and how it affects their well-being.

Cognitive therapy is often combined with psychoeducation to combat self-stigma. It helps clients restructure distressing thoughts that are self-stigmatising; this is done through reviewing evidence and evaluating symptoms and behaviours more positively (e.g., 'I am not lazy; sometimes my medications just make me tired') (Garety, Fowler, & Kuipers, 2000; Mittal, Sullivan, Chekuri, Allee, & Corrigan, 2012; Wood, Burke, Byrne, & Morrison, 2016). Designated programs utilising these cognitive restructuring strategies include Healthy Self-Concept (McCay et al., 2006, 2007), Self-Stigma Reduction Program (Fung, Tsang, & Cheung, 2011), and Ending Self-Stigma (Lucksted et al., 2011).

Randomised controlled trials on the first two programs have demonstrated a decrease in self-stigma and an increase in hopefulness (Fung et al., 2011; McCay et al., 2007).

An additional approach to self-stigma change, called Narrative Enhancement and Cognitive Therapy (NECT), combines cognitive restructuring and psychoeducation with narrative strategies meant to promote positive self-reflection of mental health experiences (Yanos, Roe, & Lysaker, 2011). Participants in NECT interventions are asked to write or tell stories about their experiences with mental illness and how they view themselves. This allows other participants in the group to help them identify and challenge cognitive distortions to achieve a sense of empowerment. Although an RCT failed to yield significant results (Yanos et al., 2012), a quasiexperiment exhibited reduced self-stigma and improved self-esteem, hope, and quality of life (Roe et al., 2014).

Contact strategies for changing self-stigma, such as peer interactions and mutual support, require the person to 'identify' with some aspect of lived experience. In mental health, this seems contrary to avoiding the negative consequences of 'psychotic' or 'mentally ill' labels. Assuming the 'sick patient' role or deciding to identify with the illness results in pessimistic attitudes (Lally, 1989; Thompson, 1988; Yanos, Roe, & Lysaker, 2010). However, this depends on insight and whether the individual perceives the stigma as legitimate. Higher perceived public stigma along with self-stigma is associated with higher depression in individuals with psychosis (Kao et al., 2016; Rossi et al., 2017). Identifying with the illness and having more insight does not automatically lead to more depressive symptoms; rather, it is the perceived legitimacy of the stigma that harms emotional health (Rüsch et al., 2009; Rüsch, Lieb, Bohus, & Corrigan, 2006).

Disclosure is the action of telling others about one's mental illness and journey to recovery.

If identifying with the illness has a potentially positive impact, then disclosure may yield beneficial changes to health and self-stigma. Disclosure is the action of telling others about one's mental illness and recovery journey. Honest Open Proud (HOP) is a standardised peer support program that is meant to help people challenge the self-stigma of mental illness by deciding whether or not to disclose (Corrigan, Sokol, & Rüsch, 2013). Here peers are others with lived experience of mental illness only. HOP is divided into three lessons: (1) Learn the pros and cons of disclosure; (2) Review the different ways to disclose; and (3) Determine how to tell one's recovery story. Implementation of HOP has led to immediate positive effects for combatting self-stigma (Corrigan et al., 2015; Mulfinger et al., 2018; Rüsch et al., 2014).

CONCLUSION

Stigma is understood through a social cognitive framework, which crosses structures with types. The most prevalent stereotype for people with psychosis is that they are dangerous. Both clinicians and the general public may experience an emotional response, or prejudice, towards people with mental illness as a result of agreeing with the stereotype. One emotion here would be fear. Finally, those who accept negative stereotypes of psychosis may exhibit negative behaviour or discrimination in response to this fear. This may include avoiding people with psychosis or segregating them from the rest of society. Clinicians may believe that people with lived experience of psychosis are incapable of making their own healthcare decisions.

Education and contact approaches have been outlined as strategies to combat both public and self-stigma. Contact seems to produce more long-term effects compared to education. However, clinicians may experience perceived responsibility for the well-being of people with psychosis. This may result in viewing their clients as incompetent or in practicing coercive treatment behaviours. Individuals with lived experience who have achieved recovery need to be open to disclosure for contact to be effective. Additionally, clinicians need to support people with psychosis by displaying affirming attitudes related to recovery and self-determination during treatment and mirror feelings of empowerment. With clinicians serving as allies, it is ultimately up to people with mental illness to sit in the driver's seat and lead efforts in the fight to end stigma.

QUIZ QUESTIONS

1. This chapter suggests clinicians must act as allies when supporting people with lived experience in the fight to end stigma. Which of the following describes an ally?
   (a) Clinicians who singlehandedly do what they feel is right and in the best interest of persons with mental illness.
   (b) Clinicians that take the back seat when it comes to leading stigma change efforts by standing alongside people with lived experience.
   (c) Clinicians who take the lead in efforts to change stigma even if they do not have lived experience.
2. Public stigma is manifested in different ways. Please select the option that does NOT represent public stigma.
   (a) People with psychosis are unpredictable and capable of violent behaviours.
   (b) People with psychosis are incompetent and not able to make their own healthcare decisions.
   (c) People with psychosis avoid seeking help and treatment services because they want to conceal their diagnosis.
3. Self-stigma occurs when individuals internalise the public stigma of mental illness. Which of the following is not a consequence of self-stigma?
   (a) People with psychosis consciously avoid the mental illness label due to awareness of stigma related to that condition.
   (b) People presenting overt symptoms of psychosis are quickly labelled as being 'mentally ill' and 'psychotic'.
   (c) People with psychosis give up on finding a job because they don't think they are capable of performing well.

4. Which of following situations demonstrates discrimination in clinical treatment?
   (a) The clinician tells his/her patients that they need to take a specific medication despite side effects.
   (b) The clinician recommends a specific medication to his/her patients.
   (c) The clinician helps his/her patient make healthcare decisions.

ANSWERS TO QUIZ QUESTIONS:

1. (b)
2. (c)
3. (b)
4. (a)

SELF-DIRECTED LEARNING SUGGESTIONS

1. Read *The Stigma Effect* by Patrick W. Corrigan. This book expands on the concepts described in this chapter and is written from three perspectives: person with lived experience, clinician, and researcher.
2. Read Chapter 3, Structures and Types of Stigma, in *The Stigma of Mental Illness-End of Story?* co-authored by Lindsay Sheehan and Katherine Nieweglowski. It dives deeper into the different types of stigma and expands on the social psychological constructs described in the current chapter.
3. Read *Stigma of Disease and Disability* edited by Patrick W. Corrigan. This book includes detailed chapters on the stigma of mental illness and other conditions (i.e. substance use disorders, physical disability, intellectual disability, cancer, Alzheimer's Disease, etc.).

References

Adams, J. R., Drake, R. E., & Wolford, G. L. (2007). Shared decision-making preferences of people with severe mental illness. *Psychiatric Services, 58*(9), 1219–1221.

Adewuya, A. O., & Makanjuola, R. O. (2008). Social distance towards people with mental illness in southwestern Nigeria. *Australian and New Zealand Journal of Psychiatry, 42*(5), 389–395.

Americans With Disabilities Act of 1990. (1990). *Pub. L. No. 101-336, 104 Stat. 328.*

Angermeyer, M. C., & Dietrich, S. (2006). Public beliefs about and attitudes towards people with mental illness: A review of population studies. *Acta Psychiatrica Scandinavica, 113*(3), 163–179.

Angermeyer, M. C., Holzinger, A., Carta, M. G., & Schomerus, G. (2011). Biogenetic explanations and public acceptance of mental illness: Systematic review of population studies. *The British Journal of Psychiatry, 199*(5), 367–372.

Angermeyer, M. C., Holzinger, A., & Matschinger, H. (2009). Mental health literacy and attitude towards people with mental illness: A trend analysis based on population surveys in the eastern part of Germany. *European Psychiatry, 24*(4), 225–232.

Arboleda-Flórez, J. (2005). Stigma and discrimination: An overview. *World Psychiatry, 4*(1), 8–10.

Arboleda-Flórez, J., & Stuart, H. (2012). From sin to science: Fighting the stigmatization of mental illnesses. *The Canadian Journal of Psychiatry, 57*(8), 457–463.

Bathje, G., & Pryor, J. (2011). The relationships of public and self-stigma to seeking mental health services. *Journal of Mental Health Counseling, 33*(2), 161–176.

Ben-Zeev, D., Young, M. A., & Corrigan, P. W. (2010). DSM-V and the stigma of mental illness. *Journal of Mental Health, 19*(4), 318–327.

Björkman, T., Angelman, T., & Jönsson, M. (2008). Attitudes towards people with mental illness: A cross-sectional study among nursing staff in psychiatric and somatic care. *Scandinavian Journal of Caring Services, 22*(2), 170–177.

Brener, L., Grenville, R., von Hippel, C., & Wilson, H. (2013). Implicit attitudes, emotions, and helping intentions of mental health workers toward their clients. *Journal of Nervous and Mental Disease, 201*, 460–463.

Brown, S. A. (2010). Implementing a brief hallucination simulation as a mental illness stigma reduction strategy. *Community Mental Health Journal, 46*(5), 500–504.

Carling, P. J. (1993). Reasonable accommodations in the workplace for individuals with psychiatric disabilities. *Consulting Psychology Journal: Practice and Research, 45*(2), 46–62.

Carter, L., Read, J., Pyle, M., & Morrison, A. P. (2019). Are causal beliefs associated with stigma? A test of the impact of biogenetic versus psychosocial explanations on stigma and internalized stigma in people experiencing psychosis. *Stigma and Health, 4*(2), 170–178.

Cavelti, M., Rüsch, N., & Vauth, R. (2014). Is living with psychosis demoralizing? Insight, self-stigma, and clinical outcome among people with schizophrenia across 1 year. *The Journal of Nervous and Mental Disease, 202*(7), 521–529.

Charles, C., Gafni, A., & Whelan, T. (1997). Shared decision-making in the medical encounter: What does it mean? (or it takes at least two to tango). *Social Science & Medicine, 44*(5), 681–692.

Chrostek, A., Grygiel, P., Anczewska, M., Wciórka, J., & Świtaj, P. (2016). The intensity and correlates of the feelings of loneliness in people with psychosis. *Comprehensive Psychiatry, 70*, 190–199.

Corbière, M., Samson, E., Villotti, P., & Pelletier, J. F. (2012). Strategies to fight stigma toward people with mental disorders: Perspectives from different stakeholders. *The Scientific World Journal, 2012*.

Corrigan, P. W., Lurie, B. D., Goldman, H. H., Slopen, N., Medasani, K., & Phelan, S. (2005). How adolescents perceive the stigma of mental illness and alcohol abuse. *Psychiatric Services, 56*(5), 544–550.

Corrigan, P., Michaels, P. J., & Morris, S. (2015). Do the effects of antistigma programs persist over time? Findings from a meta-analysis. *Psychiatric Services, 66*(5), 543–546.

Corrigan, P. W. (Ed.), (2005). *On the stigma of mental illness: Practical strategies for research and social change*. Washington, DC: American Psychological Association.

Corrigan, P. W. (2017). Making the most of contact to erase stigma. *Clinical Psychology: Science and Practice, 24*(3), 324–326.

Corrigan, P. W. (2018). *The stigma effect*. New York, NY: Columbia University Press.

Corrigan, P. W., & Calabrese, J. D. (2005). Strategies for assessing and diminishing self-stigma. In P. W. Corrigan (Ed.), *On the stigma of mental illness: Practical strategies for research and social change* (pp. 239–256). Washington, DC: American Psychological Association.

Corrigan, P. W., & Kosyluk, K. A. (2013). Erasing the stigma: Where science meets advocacy. *Basic and Applied Social Psychology, 35*(1), 131–140.

Corrigan, P. W., & Kosyluk, K. A. (2014). Mental illness stigma: Types, constructs, and vehicles for change. In P. W. Corrigan (Ed.), *The stigma of disease and disability: Understanding causes and overcoming injustices* (pp. 35–56). Washington, DC: American Psychological Association.

Corrigan, P. W., Larson, J. E., & Rüsch, N. (2009). Self-stigma and the "why try" effect: Impact on life goals and evidence-based practices. *World Psychiatry, 8*(2), 75–81.

Corrigan, P. W., Morris, S. B., Michaels, P. J., Rafacz, J. D., & Rüsch, N. (2012). Challenging the public stigma of mental illness: A meta-analysis of outcome studies. *Psychiatric Services, 63*(10), 963–973.

Corrigan, P. W., & Nieweglowski, K. (2019). How does familiarity impact the public stigma of behavioral health conditions? *Clinical Psychology Review, 70*, 40–50.

Corrigan, P. W., & Penn, D. L. (1999). Lessons from social psychology on discrediting psychiatric stigma. *American Psychologist, 54*(9), 765.

Corrigan, P. W., & Rao, D. (2012). On the self-stigma of mental illness: Stages, disclosure, and strategies for change. *The Canadian Journal of Psychiatry, 57*(8), 464–469.

Corrigan, P. W., & Shapiro, J. R. (2010). Measuring the impact of programs that challenge the public stigma of mental illness. *Clinical Psychology Review, 30*(8), 907–922.

Corrigan, P. W., Sokol, K. A., & Rüsch, N. (2013). The impact of self-stigma and mutual help programs on the quality of life of people with serious mental illnesses. *Community Mental Health Journal, 49*(1), 1–6.

Corrigan, P. W., & Watson, A. C. (2002). The paradox of self-stigma and mental illness. *Clinical Psychology: Science and Practice, 9*(1), 35–53.

Corrigan, P. W., Watson, A. C., & Barr, L. (2006). The self-stigma of mental illness: Implications for self-esteem and self-efficacy. *Journal of Social and Clinical Psychology, 25*(8), 875–884.

Corrigan, P. W., Watson, A. C., Warpinski, A. C., & Gracia, G. (2004). Stigmatizing attitudes about mental illness and allocation of resources to mental health services. *Community Mental Health Journal, 40*(4), 297–307.

Crisp, A., Gelder, M., Goddard, E., & Meltrzer, H. (2005). Stigmatization of people with mental illnesses: A follow-up study within the Changing Minds campaign of the Royal College of psychiatrists. *World Psychiatry, 4*(2), 106–113.

Drapalski, A. L., Lucksted, A., Perrin, P. B., Aakre, J. M., Brown, C. H., DeForge, B. R., et al. (2013). A model of internalized stigma and its effects on people with mental illness. *Psychiatric Services, 64*(3), 264–269.

Fung, K. M., Tsang, H. W., & Cheung, W. M. (2011). Randomized controlled trial of the self-stigma reduction program among individuals with schizophrenia. *Psychiatry Research, 189*(2), 208–214.

Fung, K. M., Tsang, H. W., & Corrigan, P. W. (2008). Self-stigma of people with schizophrenia as predictor of their adherence to psychosocial treatment. *Psychiatric Rehabilitation Journal, 32*(2), 95–104.

Garety, P. A., Fowler, D., & Kuipers, E. (2000). Cognitive-behavioral therapy for medication-resistant symptoms. *Schizophrenia Bulletin, 26*(1), 73–86.

Gerlinger, G., Hauser, M., De Hert, M., Lacluyse, K., Wampers, M., & Correll, C. U. (2013). Personal stigma in schizophrenia spectrum disorders: A systematic review of prevalence rates, correlates, impact and interventions. *World Psychiatry, 12*(2), 155–164.

Goffman, E. (1963). *Stigma: Notes on the management of spoiled identity.* New York, NY: Simon and Schuster, Inc.

Hadlaczky, G., Hökby, S., Mkrchian, A., Carli, Y., & Wasserman, D. (2014). Mental Health First Aid is an effective public health intervention for improving knowledge, attitudes, and behavior: A meta-analysis. *International Review of Psychiatry, 26*(4), 467–475.

Hamilton, D. W., Heaven, B., Thomson, R. G., Wilson, J. A., & Exley, C. (2016). Multidisciplinary team decision-making in cancer and the absent patient: A qualitative study. *BMJ Open, 6*(7).

Harangozo, J., Reneses, B., Brohan, E., Sebes, J., Csukly, G., Lopez-Ibor, J. J., et al. (2014). Stigma and discrimination against people with schizophrenia related to medical services. *International Journal of Social Psychiatry, 60*(4), 359–366.

Haslam, N., & Kvaale, E. P. (2015). Biogenetic explanation of mental disorder. *Current Directions in Psychological Science, 24*(5), 399–404.

Ho, R., Chang, W., Kwong, V., Lau, E., Chan, G., Jim, O., et al. (2018). Prediction of self-stigma in early psychosis: 3-Year follow up of the randomized-controlled trial on extended early intervention. *Schizophrenia Research, 195*, 463–468.

Holmes, E. P., Corrigan, P. W., Williams, P., Canar, J., & Kubiak, M. A. (1999). Changing attitudes about schizophrenia. *Schizophrenia Bulletin, 25*(3), 447–456.

Jenkins, J. H., & Carpenter-Song, E. A. (2009). Awareness of stigma among persons with schizophrenia. *The Journal of Nervous and Mental Disease, 197*(7), 520–529.

Kalyanaraman, S. S., Penn, D. L., Ivory, J. D., & Judge, A. (2010). The virtual doppelganger: Effects of a virtual reality simulator on perceptions of schizophrenia. *The Journal of Nervous and Mental Disease, 198*(6), 437–443.

Kao, Y. C., Lien, Y. J., Chang, H. A., Wang, S. C., Tzeng, N. S., & Loh, C. H. (2016). Evidence for the indirect effects of perceived public stigma on psychosocial outcomes: The mediating role of self-stigma. *Psychiatry Research, 240*, 187–195.

Kessler, R. C., Berglund, P. A., Bruce, M. L., Koch, J. R., Laska, E. M., Leaf, P. J., et al. (2001). The prevalence and correlates of untreated serious mental illness. *Health Services Research, 36* (6 Pt 1), 987.

King, M. L., Carson, C., Carson, S., & Armstrong, T. H. (1992). *The papers of Martin Luther King, Jr., volume VI: Advocate of the social gospel, September 1948 March 1963. Vol. 6*. Univ of California Press.

Kitchener, B. A., & Jorm, A. F. (2006). Mental health first aid training: Review of evaluation studies. *Australian and New Zealand Journal of Psychiatry, 40*, 6–8.

Knaak, S., Mantler, E., & Szeto, A. (2017). Mental illness-related stigma in healthcare: Barriers to access and care and evidence-based solutions. *Healthcare Management Forum, 30*(2), 111–116.

Kroska, A., & Harkness, S. K. (2006). Stigma sentiments and self-meanings: Exploring the modified labeling theory of mental illness. *Social Psychology Quarterly, 69*(4), 325–348.

Lai, Y. M., Hong, C. P. H., & Chee, C. Y. (2001). Stigma of mental illness. *Singapore Medical Journal, 42*(3), 111–114.

Lally, S. J. (1989). Does being in Here mean there is something wrong with me? *Schizophrenia Bulletin, 15*(2), 253–265.

Lauber, C., Anthony, M., Ajdacic-Gross, V., & Rössler, W. (2004). What about psychiatrists' attitude to mentally ill people? *European Psychiatry, 19*(7), 423–427.

Lee, A. A., Laurent, S. M., Wykes, T. L., Andren, K. A. K., Bourassa, K. A., & McKibbin, C. L. (2014). Genetic attributions and mental illness diagnosis: Effects on perceptions of danger, social distance, and real helping decisions. *Social Psychiatry and Psychiatric Epidemiology, 49*(5), 781–789.

Levy, B., Celen-Demirtas, S., Surguladze, T., & Sweeney, K. K. (2014). Stigma and discrimination: A socio-cultural etiology of mental illness. *The Humanistic Psychologist, 42*(2), 199–214.

Lincoln, T. M., Arens, E., Berger, C., & Rief, W. (2008). Can antistigma campaigns be improved? A test of the impact of biogenetic vs psychosocial causal explanation on implicit and explicit attitudes to schizophrenia. *Schizophrenia Bulletin, 34*(5), 984–994.

Link, B., & Phelan, J. (2001). Conceptualizing stigma. *Annual Review of Sociology, 27*(1), 363–385.

Link, B., Yang, L., Phelan, J., & Collins, P. (2004). Measuring mental illness stigma. *Schizophrenia Bulletin, 30*(3), 511–541.

Link, B. G. (1987). Understanding labeling effects in the area of mental disorders: An assessment of the effects of expectations of rejection. *American Sociological Review, 52*(1), 96–112.

Lucksted, A., Drapalski, A., Calmes, C., Forbes, C., DeForge, B., & Boyd, J. (2011). Ending self-stigma: Pilot evaluation of a new intervention to reduce internalized stigma among people with mental illnesses. *Psychiatric Rehabilitation Journal, 35*(1), 51.

Luty, J., Umoh, O., Sessay, M., & Sarkhel, A. (2007). Effectiveness of Changing Minds campaign factsheets in reducing stigmatized attitudes towards mental illness. *Psychiatric Bulletin, 31*(10), 377–381.

MacNeela, P., Scott, P. A., Treacy, M., Hyde, A., & O'Mahony, R. (2012). A risk to himself: Attitudes toward psychiatric patients and choice of psychosocial strategies among nurses in medical-surgical units. *Research in Nursing and Health, 35*(2), 200–213.

Macrae, C. N., Bodenhausen, G. V., Milne, A. B., & Jetten, J. (1994). Out of mind but back in sight: Stereotypes on the rebound. *Journal of Personality and Social Psychology, 67*(5), 808.

McCay, E., Beanlands, H., Leszcz, M., Goering, P., Seeman, M. V., Ryan, K., et al. (2006). A group intervention to promote healthy self-concepts and guide recovery in first episode schizophrenia: A pilot study. *Psychiatric Rehabilitation Journal, 30*(2), 105.

McCay, E., Beanlands, H., Zipursky, R., Roy, P., Leszcz, M., Landeen, J., et al. (2007). A randomised controlled trial of a group intervention to reduce engulfment and self-stigmatisation in first episode schizophrenia. *Australian e-journal for the Advancement of Mental Health, 6*(3), 212–220.

McEnteggart, C., Barnes-Holmes, Y., & Adekuoroye, F. (2016). The effects of a voice hearing simulation on implicit fear of voices. *Journal of Contextual Behavioral Science, 5*(3), 154–159.

Mittal, D., Sullivan, G., Chekuri, L., Allee, E., & Corrigan, P. W. (2012). Empirical studies of self-stigma reduction strategies: A critical review of the literature. *Psychiatric Services, 63*(10), 974–981.

Mulfinger, N., Müller, S., Böge, I., Sakar, V., Corrigan, P. W., Evans-Lacko, S., et al. (2018). Honest, open, proud for adolescents with mental illness: Pilot randomized controlled trial. *Journal of Child Psychology and Psychiatry, 59*(6), 684–691.

Nieweglowski, K., & Corrigan, P. W. (2017). *Stigma and health.* Oxford Research Encyclopedia of Psychology. Retrieved from: *http://psychology.oxfordre.com/view/10.1093/acrefore/9780190236557.001.0001/acrefore-9780190236557-e-83.*

Nordt, C., Rössler, W., & Lauber, C. (2006). Attitudes of mental health professionals toward people with schizophrenia and major depression. *Schizophrenia Bulletin, 32*(4), 709–714.

Novak, L., & Švab, V. (2009). Antipsychotics side effects' influence on stigma of mental illness: Focus group study results. *Psychiatria Danubina, 21*(1), 99–102.

Ottati, V., Bodenhausen, G. V., & Newman, L. S. (2005). Social psychological models of mental illness stigma. In P. W. Corrigan (Ed.), *On the stigma of mental illness: Practical strategies for research and social change* (pp. 99–128). Washington, DC: American Psychological Association.

Paluck, E. L., & Green, D. P. (2009). Prejudice reduction: What works? A review and assessment of research and practice. *Annual Review of Psychology, 60*, 339–367.

Parcesepe, A. M., & Cabassa, L. J. (2013). Public stigma of mental illness in the United States: A systematic literature review. *Administration and Policy in Mental Health and Mental Health Services Research, 40*(5), 384–399.

Perry, B. L. (2011). The labeling paradox: Stigma, the sick role, and social networks in mental illness. *Journal of Health and Social Behavior, 52*(4), 460–477.

Pescosolido, B. A., Monahan, J., Link, B. G., Stueve, A., & Kikuzawa, S. (1999). The public's view of the competence, dangerousness, and need for legal coercion of persons with mental health problems. *American Journal of Public Health, 89*(9), 1339–1345.

Pescosolido, B. A., Perry, M. L., Martin, J. K., McLeod, J. D., & Jensen, P. S. (2007). Stigmatizing attitudes and beliefs about treatment and psychiatric medications for children with mental illness. *Psychiatric Services, 58*(5), 613–618.

Rao, D., Feinglass, J., & Corrigan, P. (2007). Racial and ethnic disparities in mental illness stigma. *The Journal of Nervous and Mental Disease, 195*(12), 1020–1023.

Read, J., Haslam, N., Sayce, L., & Davies, E. (2006). Prejudice and schizophrenia: A review of the 'mental illness is an illness like any other' approach. *Acta Psychiatrica Scandinavica, 114*(5), 308–318.

Roe, D., Hasson-Ohayon, I., Mashiach-Eizenberg, M., Derhy, O., Lysaker, P. H., & Yanos, P. T. (2014). Narrative enhancement and cognitive therapy (NECT) effectiveness: A quasi-experimental study. *Journal of Clinical Psychology, 70*(4), 303–312.

Rogers, E. S., Chamberlin, J., Ellison, M. L., & Crean, T. (1997). A consumer-constructed scale to measure empowerment among users of mental health services. *Psychiatric Services, 48*(8), 1042–1047.

Rossi, A., Galderisi, S., Rocca, P., Bertolino, A., Rucci, P., Gibertoni, D., et al. (2017). Personal resources and depression in schizophrenia: The role of self-esteem, resilience and internalized stigma. *Psychiatry Research, 256*, 359–364.

Rüsch, N., Abbruzzese, E., Hagedorn, E., Hartenhauer, D., Kaufmann, I., Curschellas, J., et al. (2014). Efficacy of coming out proud to reduce stigma's impact among people with mental illness: Pilot randomised controlled trial. *The British Journal of Psychiatry, 204*(5), 391–397.

Rüsch, N., Corrigan, P. W., Powell, K., Rajah, A., Olschewski, M., Wilkniss, S., et al. (2009). A stress-coping model of mental illness stigma: II. Emotional stress responses, coping behavior and outcome. *Schizophrenia Research, 110*(1–3), 65–71.

Rüsch, N., Lieb, K., Bohus, M., & Corrigan, P. W. (2006). Self-stigma, empowerment, and perceived legitimacy of discrimination among women with mental illness. *Psychiatric Services, 57*(3), 399–402.

Schlier, B., Schmick, S., & Lincoln, T. M. (2014). No matter of etiology: Biogenetic, psychosocial and vulnerability-stress causal explanations fail to improve attitudes towards schizophrenia. *Psychiatry Research, 215*(3), 753–759.

Schomerus, G., Schwahn, C., Holzinger, A., Corrigan, P. W., Grabe, H. J., Carta, M., et al. (2012). Evolution of public attitudes of mental illness: A systematic review and meta-analysis. *Acta Psychiatrica Scandinavica, 2012*, 440–452.

Schonfeld, R. L. (1997). Reasonable accommodation under the federal fair housing amendments act. *Fordham Urban Law Journal, 25*, 413–441.

Sheehan, L., Nieweglowski, K., & Corrigan, P. W. (2017). Structures and types of stigma. In W. Gaebel, W. Rössler, & N. Sartorius (Eds.), *The stigma of mental illness—End of story?* (pp. 43–66). Switzerland: Springer International Publishing.

Spence, D. (2013). Are antidepressants overprescribed? Yes. *BMJ, 346*, f191.

Štrkalj-Ivezić, S., Sesar, M. A., & Mužinić, L. (2017). Effects of a group psychoeducation program on self-stigma, empowerment and perceived discrimination of persons with schizophrenia. *Psychiatria Danubina, 29*(1), 66–73.

Thompson, E. H., Jr. (1988). Variation in the self-concept of young adult chronic patients: Chronicity reconsidered. *Psychiatric Services, 39*, 771–775. https://doi.org/10.1176/ps.39.7.771.

Thornicroft, G., Rose, D., & Kassam, A. (2007). Discrimination in health care against people with mental illness. *International Review of Psychiatry, 19*(2), 113–122.

Uchino, T., Maeda, M., & Uchimara, N. (2012). Psychoeducation may reduce self-stigma of people with schizophrenia and schizoaffective disorder. *The Kurume Medical Journal, 59*(1.2), 25–31.

Wahl, O. F. (1995). *Media madness: Public images of mental illness.* New Brunswick, NJ: Rutgers University Press.

Weber, T. (2002). Gandhian nonviolence and the salt march. *Social Alternatives, 21*(2), 46.

Wenzlaff, R. M., & Wegner, D. M. (2000). Thought suppression. *Annual Review of Psychology, 51*(1), 59–91.

Wolkenstein, L., & Meyer, T. D. (2009). What factors influence attitudes towards people with current depression and current mania? *International Journal of Social Psychiatry, 55*(2), 124–140.

Wood, L., Burke, E. M., Byrne, R., & Morrison, A. (2016). Examining service user experiences of a cognitive therapy intervention for self-stigma in psychosis. *Psychosis, 8*(3), 238–249.

Yanos, P. T., Lucksted, A., Drapalski, A. L., Roe, D., & Lysaker, P. (2015). Interventions targeting mental health self-stigma: A review and comparison. *Psychiatric Rehabilitation Journal, 38*(2), 171.

Yanos, P. T., Lysaker, P. H., & Roe, D. (2010). Internalized stigma as a barrier to improvement in vocational functioning among people with schizophrenia-spectrum disorders. *Psychiatry Research, 178*(1), 211–213.

Yanos, P. T., Roe, D., & Lysaker, P. H. (2010). The impact of illness identity on recovery from severe mental illness. *American Journal of Psychiatric Rehabilitation, 13*(2), 73–93.

Yanos, P. T., Roe, D., & Lysaker, P. H. (2011). Narrative enhancement and cognitive therapy: A new group-based treatment for internalized stigma among persons with severe mental illness. *International Journal of Group Psychotherapy, 61*(4), 576–595.

Yanos, P. T., Roe, D., West, M. L., Smith, S. M., & Lysaker, P. H. (2012). Group-based treatment for internalized stigma among persons with severe mental illness: Findings from a randomized controlled trial. *Psychological Services, 9*(3), 248.

Zolnierek, C. D. (2009). Non-psychiatric hospitalization of people with mental illness: Systematic review. *Journal of Advanced Nursing, 65*(8), 1570–1583.

Definition of Key Terms

Ally A person that provides support and stands *WITH* people with mental illness in the fight to end stigma.

Authoritarianism Suggests that people with mental illness are incapable of making their own decisions; therefore, others should make their decisions for them.

Benevolence Suggests that people with mental illness need to be protected and cared for.

Biogenetic Perspective Describes mental illness as a biological, medical disorder.

Biopsychosocial Perspective Describes mental illness as a result of psychological, social environmental, and biological factors.

Contact Strategic interactions between community members and persons with lived experience who are willing to disclose.

Disclosure The action of telling others about one's mental illness and journey to recovery.

Discrimination Negative behavioural reactions exhibited towards people with mental illness.

Education Challenges inaccurate assumptions of mental illness replacing myths with facts.

Empowerment The obverse of self-stigma involving increased self-esteem and optimism.

Explicit stigma When people have conscious knowledge of their beliefs and how they contribute to their behaviours.

Familiarity The level of intimacy and experience that one has with people with mental illness.

Implicit stigma Occurs when people are not fully aware that their beliefs about a certain group contribute to their behaviours.

Label Avoidance Deciding not to engage in care-seeking due to awareness of stigma related to one's mental illness.

Labelling Paradox Occurs when visible symptoms of mental illness make it easier for people to seek help.

People with Lived Experience Those who have personally faced the disabling effects of mental illness.

Perceived Responsibility Recognised duty of others to take care of people with mental illness.

Peers People who come from similar backgrounds and have equal levels of social status.

Prejudice Negative emotional reactions that occur as a result of agreeing with stereotypes.

Protest Target negative representations of mental illness and seek to stop them.

Psychoeducation Teaches people about mental illness stigma and how it affects their well-being.

Public Stigma How the general population views and treats people with mental illness.

Reasonable accommodation An adjustment made to an environment to make it more accessible and functional for people with disabilities.

Recovery A process that involves notions of hope and achievement.

Self-Determination Occurs when people with mental illness feel able to choose and accomplish their goals.

Self-Stigma Occurs when individuals internalise public stigma of mental illness into their self-concepts.

Stereotypes Negative beliefs about people with mental illness.

'Why Try' Effect Occurs when individuals feel incapable or unworthy of accomplishing their goals.

CHAPTER 4

Culture and Psychosis in Clinical Practice

G. Eric Jarvis[*,†,‡], **Srividya N. Iyer**[*,†,§,¶,||], **Lisa Andermann**[#,**], **Kenneth P. Fung**[**,††]

[*]Department of Psychiatry, McGill University, Montreal, QC, Canada, [†]Division of Social & Transcultural Psychiatry, McGill University, Montreal, QC, Canada, [‡]Cultural Consultation Service & Culture and Mental Health Research Unit of the Jewish General Hospital, Montreal, QC, Canada, [§]Prevention and Early Intervention Program for Psychosis, Douglas Mental Health University Institute, Montreal, QC, Canada, [¶]ACCESS Open Minds (Pan-Canadian Youth Mental Health Research Network), Montreal, QC, Canada, [||]Frayme, Youth Mental Health-Focused Knowledge Translation Network, Ottawa, ON, Canada, [#]Mount Sinai Hospital, Toronto, ON, Canada, [**]Equity, Gender and Populations Division, Department of Psychiatry, University of Toronto, Toronto, ON, Canada, [††]Toronto Western Hospital, Toronto, ON, Canada

Key Learning Objectives

- To recognise the limits of standard diagnostic tools in identifying psychotic disorders in culturally diverse clientele.
- To understand that, for social and cultural reasons, recovery from psychosis may be better in poor than in wealthy countries.
- To introduce ways of evaluating and treating psychosis in a culturally sensitive manner.
- To highlight resources for culturally informed interventions.

INTRODUCTION

Many believe psychotic disorders, including schizophrenia, to derive mostly from biology independent of sociocultural influences (Marsella, 1988). Despite twin concordance of 50% for schizophrenia and developmental biology as key to the onset, course, and outcome of psychotic disorders, substantial evidence shows that culture and society also influence psychosis—perhaps as much as biogenetic factors. Cultural influence manifests in a number of practical ways: clients from linguistically and culturally diverse backgrounds access mental

Culture refers to 'systems of knowledge, concepts, rules, practices that are learned and transmitted across generations' (APA, 2013).

A Clinical Introduction to Psychosis. https://doi.org/10.1016/B978-0-12-815012-2.00004-3

health services less often; and when they do seek help they are often misunderstood and receive treatment based on stereotypes of their culture of origin rather than the mental health problems they may be facing. Recognising the problem, professional associations have added working with culture sections to official guidelines and training programs have begun to include cultural diversity as part of competency-based curricula. Despite these advances, few culturally adapted materials, such as diagnostic surveys and treatment protocols have been culturally adapted either to specific populations or more generally. This chapter reviews the interplay between culture and psychosis by discussing the history of schizophrenia; the cultural shaping of its onset, diagnosis, symptoms, course, and outcomes; the suitability of various diagnostic tools for diverse populations; the utility of the Outline for Cultural Formulation (OCF) and the Cultural Formulation Interview (CFI) in fostering cultural sensitivity; and the availability of culturally informed interventions and resources. Readers will discover that psychosis is a culturally embedded condition whose proper treatment warrants due regard to culture. Enabling cultural awareness and competence in clinicians will expedite recovery from psychosis.

PSYCHOSIS IN HISTORICAL CONTEXT

Schizophrenia and psychosis gained recognition in Western Europe and North America in the 19th century amidst rapid industrialisation and culture change and spread globally over the 20th century. Cases fitting modern criteria for schizophrenia rarely appear before 1800. Debate continues on whether changing sociobiological circumstances or improved recognition drove the post-1800 proliferation of well-defined cases (Altschuler, 2001; Evans, McGrath, & Milns, 2003; Hare, 1988; Higgins & Kose, 2007).

Kahlbaum and Hecker (c. 1871) offered the first clinical description of schizophrenia as a distinct disease (Shorter, 1997, p. 104). Earlier, auditory hallucinations and religious delusions were accepted across Europe. For instance, Joan of Arc (d. 1431) was revered as an inspired leader with intense religious visions (Jenkins, 2011). Today, her experiences likely would be deemed symptoms of psychosis and devalued as such. Instead of being a war leader, Joan of Arc would likely be relegated to a psychiatric facility for the treatment of delusions.

Thus, dominant sociocultural narratives evolve over time and in large part determine what may be considered noteworthy, aberrant, or acceptable. In the modern rational era, psychotic symptoms of irrationality, disorganisation, and lack of productivity run counter to the values of industrialisation and therefore are of concern. Nonetheless, clients are at different points in the continuum between traditional and modern perspectives. Determining where the client, family, or community lies along this continuum is an important part of cross-cultural assessment and care.

THE CULTURAL SHAPING OF PSYCHOSIS

This section reviews how aspects of culture shape and influence the clinical components of psychosis beginning with diagnosis and reported rates; continuing with attributed aetiology, common symptoms and insight; and ending with treatment, outcome, stigma, and recovery. In addition to the cultures of client and family, professional cultures need to be acknowledged by clinicians so that care may be negotiated rather than imposed.

Diagnosis and Reported Rates of Psychosis

The first task for many clinicians will be to establish the presence or absence of psychosis in the patients they see. This can be challenging in cross-culture situations due to unfamiliarity with the languages, behavioural norms, and beliefs of clients from diverse backgrounds. For example, exotic colonial portrayals of the disorder in Africa emphasised atypical symptoms called *bouffée délirante* (in French Africa) and confused, amorphous psychoses by the British (German, 1972). Such portrayals emphasised how Africans were especially prone to psychosis, especially when encountering European civilisation (Carothers, 1972). Dilemmas in the diagnosis of psychosis persist and may be compared and contrasted in countries with influential mental health communities, namely the United Kingdom, the United States, and France.

Historically, psychoses have ranked just after neurological diseases (i.e. relatively high) in the importance of biology over culture or environment (Marsella, 1988); and a consensus that schizophrenia occurred at much the same rate worldwide has endured for decades: The Determinants of Outcome of Severe Mental Disorders (DOSMeD) study reported similar incidence rates for schizophrenia (0.7–1.4/10,000) in several countries (Jablensky et al., 1992) (see Table 4.1).

Over the last 30 years, numerous British-led studies challenged these notions, finding many times higher rates of psychosis among immigrants than in native Europeans. Factors like discrimination and social disadvantage were presumed to account for these differences (Harrison, Owens, Holton, Neilson, & Boot, 1988; Harrison et al., 1989; Kirkbride et al., 2006; Fearon et al., 2006; Jongsma et al., 2018). In the United Kingdom specifically, these rates have been assumed to be true differences, and not a consequence of misdiagnosis. Examining the social determinants of mental health in marginalised communities is important. Dismissing misdiagnosis or assuming that minorities and immigrants might have an inherent predisposition to psychosis may create new problems. Critiques of these assumptions exist (Fernando, 1995, 1998; Ferns et al., 2010; Hickling, McKenzie, Mullen, & Murray, 1999; Zandi et al., 2008, 2010; Zandi, Havenaar, Laan, Kahn, & van den Brink, 2016), but have remained relatively neglected in the United Kingdom.

Current evidence challenges the prevailing view that symptom expression and rates of psychotic illness are similar across cultures.

By contrast, in the United States, reported rates of psychosis in African Americans have fluctuated over the last 200 years—lower-than-average rates in the slave-owning South; higher-than-average rates after emancipation; and rates comparable to white Americans since the civil rights movement. These variations have been linked to how evolving political agendas stereotyped African Americans (Jarvis, 2008). For example, Metzl (2009) noted that some African Americans were misdiagnosed with schizophrenia in the context of the civil rights

Table 4.1 Epidemiologic Studies of Psychotic Disorders

	IPSS (Leff, Sartorius, Jablensky, Korten, & Ernberg, 1992)	DOSMeD (Jablensky et al., 1992)	ISoS (Hopper, Harrison, & Wanderling, 2007)	EU-GEI (Jongsma et al., 2018)
Full name	International Pilot Study of Schizophrenia	Determinants of Outcome of Severe Mental Disorders	International Study of Schizophrenia	European Network of National Schizophrenia Networks Studying Gene–Environment Interactions
Years	1973	1992	2000, 2007	2010–2015
Data sources	1202 Patients in 9 countries: Colombia, Czechoslovakia, Denmark, India, Nigeria, China, U.S.S.R., United Kingdom, and United States	12 Sites in 10 countries: One each in Denmark, Colombia, Ireland, Nigeria, U.S.S.R., Japan, United Kingdom, and Czechoslovakia; two each in United States and India	Pooled data from the IPSS, DOSMeD and RAPyD (Reduction and Assessment of Psychiatric Disability)	17 Catchment areas in 6 countries: England, France, Italy, Netherlands, Spain, Brazil
Study type	Hospital-based, prevalence	Prospective, longitudinal incidence	Analysis of pooled data	Treated incidence
Principal findings	Better outcomes in developing countries	Similar schizophrenia incidence across sites; better outcomes in developing countries	Confirmed previous WHO study findings	Varying rates of psychosis incidence across sites
Limitations	Not an incidence study	Developed vs. developing world dichotomy; category fallacy; PSE and its reliance on first-rank symptoms	Assessment of social functioning must be understood in local context and meanings	Crude ethnic variables (Susser & Martínez-Alés, 2018); difficulties collecting ethnic data in France

movement. Hence, in the United States misdiagnosis has assumed an important position with respect to minorities and psychosis. Gara et al. (2012) found that African Americans were significantly likelier than whites to be diagnosed with schizophrenia, even after controlling for covariates and the presence of serious affective disorder. The authors concluded that clinicians tended to overvalue psychotic symptoms in African Americans due to the idioms of distress that

African Americans used to describe their experiences, their general language use, and cultural mistrust and healthy paranoia.

In the third country of comparison, France, where ethno-racial categorisation is prohibited, nothing is known about intergroup variance in the incidence of psychosis. France's 'choice of ignorance' (Simon, 2008), has intensified since WWII, and has been justified as a bulwark against identity-based abuses like the Holocaust. Despite blindness to ethnicity by researchers and census statisticians, clinician case notes may include ethnic and cultural material in addition to allusions to ethnocultural characteristics. For example, a 'sensitive residential environment' may be code for an immigrant suburb; and a person's communicating abilities may refer to a foreign accent (Larchanché, 2010). Thus, in France, the clinical diagnosis of psychosis is complicated by an avoidance of ethnicity- and religion-related issues that may result in unwitting clinician bias.

Country comparisons highlight how local professional cultures influence the diagnosis of psychosis in immigrant minorities and how data is interpreted, misused or ignored in various contexts. Consequently, psychosis diagnoses must be made cautiously and the personal/professional cultures of the clinician/researcher must be taken into account at all stages. Culture is less something that dwells in the client as a negotiated space that emerges during the clinical encounter.

Attributed Aetiology

Attributed causes and origins of psychosis also vary by setting and culture. For example, in India, Nigeria and Trinidad, the INTREPID study (Cohen et al., 2016) found that psychosis was ascribed to supernatural; psychological and social (thinking too much, family problems); biological (heritability, brain injury); and substance-related causes. Among supernatural schema, black magic was favoured in India, spells in Nigeria, and curses in Trinidad. In Australia, the mental health issues of Aboriginal and Torres Strait Islanders, as for other Indigenous peoples, are linked to a relationship to land and culture, and physical, emotional, spiritual and social factors (AIPA, 2014). The supernatural forces to which people attribute psychosis are grounded in, but not limited to, local histories and cultures. In Europe and North America, too, patients of diverse backgrounds may tacitly endorse alternate aetiologies, only to be silenced by the dominance of biomedical theories. Biomedical hegemony is a serious problem if it impedes therapeutic dialogue about alternate health beliefs. Attributed aetiology may vary even among professional cultures. Jarvis, Bhat, Jurcik, Spigonardo, and Whitley (2014) found that the American Journal of Psychiatry tends to publish biomedical explanations of psychosis whereas the British Journal of Psychiatry shows a relative preference for psychosocial theories, differences stemming from local traditions.

Common Symptoms

Symptoms of psychosis are culturally mediated. Studies have reported hallucinations in 0.6%–84% of the general population (median of 13.2%) (Beavan,

Read, & Cartwright, 2011; Larøi et al., 2014). Delusion-like beliefs, too, may be widespread (Pechey & Halligan, 2011). Delusional beliefs may be secular (being infested by parasites, being exceptionally gifted, etc.) or religious/spiritual (reincarnation, communicating with spirits, etc.). Their content is influenced by cultural paradigms. The negative views of hallucinations and delusions in Euro-American culture may suppress their reporting (Al-Issa, 1995). Clinicians must interpret reported hallucinations and delusions within cultural contexts before concluding that they constitute signs of psychosis. Bizarre, unpleasant or horrific experiences are likelier indicative of psychoses. Brief, uplifting experiences (especially in the context of grief or trauma) that are neither secretive nor cultural outliers are less likely to be pathological. Time spent to understand psychotic symptoms in cultural context is worth the extra effort. It is crucial, though, not to assume that a client is the same as others of their linguistic, religious or historical tradition. Evaluating the presence of psychotic symptoms must be a culturally informed but person-centred process (see Vignette #1, Box 4.1).

Developing a culturally appropriate understanding of your client takes time.

Developing a culturally appropriate understanding of your client takes time. When working with interpreters, allow a 2-hour intake interview. Invite family members to participate if they haven't initially. Take the time to inquire about the family understanding of the client's symptoms. What kinds of treatments would they expect to be helpful? Patiently gathering information will pay dividends over the long-term.

Insight

Illness insight, or the capacity to recognise that one is ill, is often compromised in patients with psychotic disorders (White, Bebbington, Pearson, Johnson, & Ellis, 2000). However, the traditional view of illness insight as the degree to which

Box 4.1 Vignette #1[a]

A 25-year-old Haitian refugee claimant explained that she was chosen in childhood by a "loa" (spirit) to become the family spiritual leader. She realized this through a vision in which people performed a night song. She regretted not having chosen to "sit the spirit," who was a trickster being wooed by her brothers. She doubted her own chosen status and thought her older brother was better prepared for the role. While she desired stronger faith to accept the loa and usher in peace and prosperity (Voodoo worldview), she also felt the need to work hard to get things for herself (Protestant worldview).

Comment: Given this narrative and the presence of insomnia, agitation, erratic decision-making and socio-occupational decline, such a person could easily have been prematurely or erroneously diagnosed with psychosis. However, a psychosis diagnosis is withheld when the culture broker says, 'That's what we talk about all the time in Haiti'. This case illustrates the complexities of cross-cultural diagnosis and symptom interpretation, especially among patients negotiating hybrid identities (Voodoo-African and Protestant-European, in this case).

[a]Details have been systematically disguised to protect client confidentiality.

patients agree with clinicians' explanations of psychosis origins and treatment recommendations is limited and limiting. Just as hybrid identities (see Vignette #1) are normal, it is also common for individuals to have hybrid explanations for mental symptoms. Insight is thus a sociocultural process that may or may not include explanations of psychosis, recognition of symptoms, or acceptance of treatments consonant with that of caregivers (Kirmayer, Corin, & Jarvis, 2004). In fact, some individuals with poor insight by professional standards may benefit from reduced stigma and access to comforting traditional therapies by espousing nonpsychological accounts of their distress.

Treatment and Outcome

Clients with psychotic symptoms who do not accept that they have a mental illness may be difficult to engage in interventions of any kind. Part of this reluctance may be due to the inequities in treatment that have been noted among cultural groups in the United States, the United Kingdom, Australia, Canada, and several low and middle-income countries (LMICs). Ethnocultural minorities underutilise mental health services (McKenzie, Hansson, Tuck, & Lurie, 2010); access services via more difficult pathways, e.g. police (Anderson, Flora, Archie, Morgan, & McKenzie, 2014; Anderson, Fuhrer, & Malla, 2010; Jarvis, Kirmayer, Jarvis, & Whitley, 2005; Morgan et al., 2017) or after longer delays (Anderson, Fuhrer, Schmitz, & Malla, 2013); are likelier to drop-out (Rathod & Turkington, 2005) and be dissatisfied with their care (Boydell et al., 2012; Whitley, Wang, Fleury, Liu, & Caron, 2017); and have inferior access to therapy (Bhui et al., 2003). In LMICs, where services and service providers are scarce (WHO Atlas, 2015), 80%–90% of persons with serious mental illnesses remain untreated (Patel et al., 2016; Wang et al., 2005). Minority patients may feel unwelcome or misunderstood by mainstream mental health services, which may create a negative feedback loop of low expectations, dissatisfaction, and perceived discrimination.

As a discipline, ethnopsychopharmacology draws attention to the problematic racial categories used to classify responses to medications and highlights cultural attitudes to medication and side effects, and how ethnic foods and traditional medicines can affect the metabolism of medications (Chen, Chen, & Lin, 2008; Ninnemann, 2012). While nonphysician mental health professionals may never prescribe medications, they are in a unique position to explore cultural and ethno-social factors that influence attitudes towards prescription medications and traditional remedies. Listening to these concerns may counteract baseline distrust of mental health interventions and open opportunities for dialogue and negotiation.

More generally regarding schizophrenia and outcome, World Health Organization (WHO) studies over the last four decades (see Table 4.1) have repeatedly found that patients with treated schizophrenia fare better in developing than in advanced countries (Hopper et al., 2007; Jablensky et al., 1992; Leff et al., 1992). This implies that the outcomes of psychosis depend at least in part on sociocultural factors. Unfortunately, the protective effect of hailing from a

Epidemiology studies suggest that outcomes of schizophrenia in developing societies are better than in wealthy societies.

developing country does not survive migration to Western countries: as already discussed, for instance, Afro-Caribbeans with psychosis experience worse outcomes in the United Kingdom than their native-born counterparts.

Stigma

Critiquing the DOSMeD findings, Cohen, Patel, Thara, and Gureje (2008) found variation in the patterns and course of schizophrenia in non-Western countries. In many traditional societies, stigma undermined recovery and wellbeing. Traditional extended families have been thought to afford protection to individuals with severe mental disorders. However, studies from India (Thara, Kamath, & Kumar, 2003), Nigeria (Gureje, Lasebikan, Ephraim-Oluwanuga, Olley, & Kola, 2005), and Ethiopia (Shibre et al., 2001) suggest that stigma within families contributes to patients' marital, familial, and social conflict. More recently, the INDIGO study found high rates of experienced discrimination (>75%) across 27 countries, including among 732 participants with schizophrenia (Lasalvia et al., 2013; Thornicroft et al., 2009). There was significant intra- and intercountry variation in experienced, but not anticipated, discrimination (Lasalvia et al., 2015).

Recovery

Patterns of illness in clients with psychotic disorders tend to be worse for some ethnic minorities, such as Black Africans and Black Caribbeans in the United Kingdom, but the categories that define outcome and recovery mostly include clinical and social factors, and service use (Ajnakina et al., 2017; Morgan et al., 2017). None have been culturally adapted. Whitley (2016) drew attention to this problem and examined definitions, barriers, and facilitators of recovery in Euro- and Caribbean-Canadian participants. God and religion were important elements of recovery among Caribbean-Canadians, but not for Euro-Canadians. Apart from this finding few other differences emerged. Cross-cultural recovery concepts need urgent research attention.

Culture and society shape psychotic disorders at all levels, from diagnosis through treatment and recovery. Unfortunately, the research literature for many domains is in its infancy. Quantitative and qualitative investigations need to refine definitions of symptoms and disorder, investigate cultural explanations of distress and insight concepts, evaluate traditional therapies, and adapt medical and psychological interventions. In general, listening to patients and their families, while recognising the limits of mental health perspectives, will encourage a culturally appropriate approach to psychosis.

LOST IN TRANSLATION: LACK OF CULTURALLY ADAPTED ASSESSMENTS

Diagnostic tools commonly used to identify clients with psychotic disorders include the Present State Examination (PSE) and its successor, the Schedules for Clinical Assessment in Neuropsychiatry (SCAN); the Comprehensive

Assessment of Symptoms and History (CASH); the Diagnostic Interview Schedule (DIS); and the Diagnostic Interview for Genetic Studies (DIGS) (see Table 4.2). Despite having been translated into various languages, these unquestionably valuable instruments have not been validated across cultural settings and risk perpetuating the category fallacy (see Definition of Terms and Kleinman, 1977, 1988). Many large-scale studies (e.g. DOSMeD, AESOP, Coid et al., 2008, etc.) of psychoses in and across several cultural contexts have used the PSE and SCAN, despite concerns having been voiced over the last 50 years.

Most diagnostic tools have not been validated for different cultural settings despite being translated into various languages.

The PSE relies upon the interviewer's clinical judgement (Kendell, Everett, Cooper, Sartorius, & David, 1968) and forces raters to endorse the presence or absence of symptoms (like delusions), regardless of their severity (Robins et al., 1981). Because research, like any human activity, is never done in a cultural vacuum, interviewers may systematically rate diverse patients according to the expectations and legacies of their own scientific cultures. Thus, the scope for clinical judgement in the SCAN and PSE risks inaccurate diagnosis of psychotic disorders in some minority groups.

In contrast, the DIS and its successor, the Composite International Diagnostic Interview (CIDI), may flatten rates of psychosis in minorities. The DIS minimises the role of clinical judgement by requiring raters (often lay interviewers) to ask specified probes and input responses into a computer that generates the final diagnosis. Unlike the PSE, reported symptoms that do not reach clinical significance are not recorded. Such automation may reduce the influence of dominant scientific paradigms and perceptions about minorities. Notably, the DIS-generated African American-to-white American schizophrenia prevalence ratio of 2:1 (Keith, 1991) was flattened compared to corresponding PSE- or SCAN-generated minority-to-majority prevalence ratios of 5–10:1 in the United Kingdom (Fearon et al., 2006; Harrison et al., 1988, 1989) and elsewhere (Jongsma et al., 2018).

In the Netherlands, researchers used the CASH to establish high rates of psychosis among immigrants, particularly Moroccans (Selten et al., 2001). Critiquing these findings, Zandi et al. (2010) reported that the first-contact incidence of schizophrenia among Moroccan immigrants was not higher than among the native-born Dutch when a culture-sensitive version of the CASH was applied (risk ratios of 7.8 and 1.5 for the standard and culture-sensitive diagnostic interviews, respectively). Hallucinations and dissociative possession states were rejected as symptoms of psychosis for lack of certainty of their significance. The lack of a Berber word for depression and its widespread stigmatisation minimised the identification of depression among Moroccans. Recently, Zandi et al. (2016) found that the culturally sensitive CASH identified significantly more mania symptoms and fewer delusions among Moroccan immigrants who, using the CASH, were overdiagnosed with schizophrenia.

Scales for specific aspects of psychosis have also been adapted for cross-national or cross-cultural use (e.g. E.U.-wide EPSILON study,

Table 4.2 **Comparison of Select Diagnostic Tools**

	PSE/SCAN	DIS/CIDI	CASH	DIGS
Piloting team	Wing, Birley, Cooper, Graham, and Isaacs (1967) and Wing et al. (1990)	Robins, Helzer, Croughan, and Ratcliff (1981) and WHO (1990)	Andreasen, Flaum, and Arndt (1992)	Nurnberger et al. (1994)
Country	UK/WHO	USA/WHO	USA	USA/NIMH Genetics Initiative
Used by	US–UK diagnostic project, WHO studies, UK studies, some EU-GEI sites	The Epidemiologic Catchment Area (ECA) study	Dutch studies, including the Dutch EU-GEI 2018 site	Gara et al. (2012); France in the EU-GEI 2018
Translations	35+ (Wing, Sartorius, & Üstün, 1998)	At least 16 (Wittchen, 1994)	Arabic, Berber (Zandi et al., 2008)	At least 4
Methodology	Examiner report of symptom presence and severity	Respondent self-report and standardised questions	Semistructured interview of experiences and their phenomenology	Structured interview that generates diagnoses
Limitations	Room for rater judgement creates risk for misattributed diagnosis	Minimal clinical judgement or rater initiative	Focus on reliability rather than validity	Not easily used by lay interviewers or with disorganised subjects
Cross-cultural validation	Taiwan (Cheng et al., 2001); Thailand (Paholpak et al., 2011)	Unclear	Moroccans and Berbers in Netherlands (Zandi et al., 2008)	France, India, Korea, and Croatia (Deshpande et al., 1998; Joo et al., 2004; Kralj et al., 2017; Preisig, Fenton, Matthey, Berney, & Ferrero, 1999)

van Wijngaarden et al., 2003; functional outcome measures in an 8-country, 31-site study, Velligan et al., 2010; a psychosis knowledge scale for British African-Caribbeans, Degnan et al., 2018; and translations of the Calgary Depression Scale, Sarró et al., 2004). Another example of culturally adapted assessment comes from Australia (Balaratnasingam, Anderson, Janca, & Lee, 2015) in which the authors developed assessment tools specifically for Aboriginals and Torres Strait Islanders. These adaptions required attention to literal and conceptual equivalence in translation; and face, content, criterion, and construct validity in varied contexts (Bhui et al., 2003). However, it remains difficult to ascertain whether differences observed using adapted scales are real or attributable to sample characteristics, cultural characteristics, or instrument bias.

The solution to these problems lies in taking the time and effort to adapt standardised instruments to the cultural groups being studied. The WHO (2018) has published guidelines available online, with the following steps: forward translation, expert panel back-translation, pretesting and cognitive interviewing, and production of the final linguistically and culturally adapted version. Although some instruments have been linguistically translated (see Table 4.2), this is not enough. Zandi et al. (2008) discussed how they adapted the CASH to Moroccan culture (see p. 246) after linguistic translation of items via interpreters. The first step was to conduct focus groups to review the appropriateness of CASH items for use with Moroccan patients. Specifically, the focus groups, consisting of mental health professionals with experience working with Moroccan patients, evaluated potentially false-positive symptoms, such as hallucinations; affective symptoms; and dissociative phenomena. Problems noted by the focus groups were, for example, that Moroccan patients may hear voices when they develop fever, do not have a specific word for depression in Moroccan Arabic (Darija) or Berber, and possession and trance states with religious connotations. These cultural issues may predispose Moroccan patients to excessive psychosis and fewer affective diagnoses. In addition, focus groups prepared guidelines to negotiate taboo subjects and facilitate open discussion of sensitive material. Clinical information was gathered from families whenever possible and a cultural formulation by attending clinicians was part of the diagnostic procedure. Zandi et al. (2010) found that many psychosis diagnoses identified by the standard CASH were re-diagnosed by the culture sensitive CASH as mood disorders. Adeponle, Thombs, Groleau, Jarvis, and Kirmayer (2012) had similar results when cultural formulation was applied to referrals with intake diagnoses of psychosis. Clearly these procedures take time and resources, but without careful attention to cultural adaptation for the groups being assessed, diagnostic bias will remain unexamined.

Linguistic translation does *not* equal cultural validation.

FILLING IN THE GAPS: FOSTERING CLINICAL CULTURAL COMPETENCE

With gaps in the cultural adaptation of diagnostic and treatment tools, clinicians must learn to work directly with culturally diverse clientele. Important issues arise around stigma; cross-cultural communications; the experience and self-reporting of symptoms; clinician and client understanding of psychotic illness; and adapting clinical work to situational contexts. In psychosis, as interpretation of events may become distorted and insight may be impaired, history from family members is often an important part of standard clinical assessment. Further, in cross-cultural contexts, history from families, cultural communities, or cultural consultants can help contextualise whether the presenting symptoms lie within cultural norms or are bizarre enough to warrant consideration of a psychosis diagnosis.

Families, carers, and cultural consultants can provide valuable information towards a culturally appropriate diagnosis, formulation, and collaborative treatment plan.

To start with, generic cultural competence assessments should include the attitudes, knowledge, and skills needed for effective cross-cultural therapeutic

The Outline for Cultural Formulation is a framework to organise culturally relevant information.

The Cultural Formulation Interview is a practical tool to guide cultural assessments and can be flexibly used by any clinician.

encounters (Andermann & Lo, 2006; Fung & Lo, 2012; Lo & Fung, 2003). The Outline for Cultural Formulation (OCF) in DSM-4-TR (APA, 2000) and DSM-5 (APA, 2013) is a useful tool informing assessment, formulation, and treatment. The DSM-5 introduces the 16-question Cultural Formulation Interview (CFI) that helps generate content for the OCF domains during assessment. Although the DSM has been immensely influential in developing the OCF and CFI, evidence for effectiveness remains sparse. Lewis-Fernandez et al. (2017) studied the feasibility, acceptability, and clinical utility of the CFI and found reasonable outcomes on all domains. Adeponle et al. (2012) used the OCF to revise intake diagnoses of psychosis in almost one-half of their culturally diverse clientele. And other approaches do exist. Groen, Richters, Laban, and Devillé (2016) piloted the Brief Cultural Interview in the Netherlands to reduce the time required to conduct a culturally competent evaluation. Programs teaching cultural competence have borrowed from the work of Stanley Sue (2006), who highlights general aspects of cultural competence like scientific mindedness and dynamic sizing. Barriers to implementing cultural competence tools, like the OCF and CFI, include the time it takes to complete evaluations, lack of clinician interest or awareness, clinical severity of patients precluding in depth interviews, lack of access to cultural consultants and good interpreters, reliance on templates and standardised questions (as in the CFI), and difficulty mastering specific cultural skills and knowledge. Aggarwal, Nicasio, DeSilva, Boiler, and Lewis-Fernandez (2013) acknowledged that the OCF and CFI are far from perfect, and require ongoing evaluation in various settings, but nonetheless are widely available and implemented by mental health practitioners around the world.

The first OCF domain, the patient's cultural identity, comprises ethnicity, language, and degree of acculturation. Other aspects of cultural identities include gender, religion, profession, and familial roles and relationships. These provide the basic building blocks with which to understand clients from diverse backgrounds.

The second OCF domain pertains to explanatory models and how patients and families understand the illness. These can be explored using Kleinman's questions (Kleinman, Eisenberg, & Good, 1978) (see Box 4.3) or the CFI (APA, 2013). Patients experiencing psychotic symptoms may endorse explanations that make sense to them culturally (e.g. possessions or hexes), but that may be unfamiliar or bizarre to the clinician. The explanation may be culturally acceptable but still of delusional intensity. A cultural interpreter or family member can help distinguish culturally normative beliefs from delusional ones. Such distinctions may include considerations of illness course, severity, functional impact, and accompanying symptoms like disorganised thoughts and behaviour. Discussions with patients and family members may reveal explanatory models that conflict with those of the medical team.

An assessment of psychosocial stressors comprises the third OCF domain, especially with respect to aspects of culture that predispose to vulnerability to psychosis or resilience. Immigrants and refugees have been reported to have elevated rates of psychosis (Kirkbride & Hollander, 2015) due to acculturative stress, racial discrimination, structural inequities, and higher rates of unemployment and poverty (Fung & Guzder, 2018); while living in ethnic enclaves (i.e. high ethnic density) may be protective (Bécares, Dewey, & Das-Munshi, 2017). Engaging cultural communities may facilitate recovery for some clients except when the source of distress (e.g. stigma) originates from the community of origin (Li, Wong, Cain, & Fung, 2016). For refugees and immigrants with trauma histories, posttraumatic symptoms like dissociation and flashbacks may be mistaken for psychotic symptoms. Trauma can also co-exist with psychosis, an illness that increases vulnerability to abuse and unsafe conditions like poverty, addiction, and homelessness. The relationship between trauma and psychosis is complex (Stevens, Spencer, & Turkington, 2017). These psychosocial factors need careful assessment when evaluating clients of diverse backgrounds.

The fourth OCF domain, applying a culture lens to the clinician–patient relationship, goes beyond concerns with transference and countertransference to consider power differences arising from the cultural backgrounds of clinicians and patients (Fung & Lo, 2017). For some individuals, particularly those who describe psychotic experiences using subtle cultural references, ethnically matched clinicians or culture brokers may be helpful. For others, especially in small communities, stigma and confidentiality concerns may paradoxically impede therapeutic relationships in ethnically matched clinician–patient pairs; hence, client's preference and availability of such resources need to be taken into account.

Ethnic match between clinician and client *may* improve trust, effective communication, interpretation of symptoms, and negotiation of treatment plans.

In longer-term therapeutic relationships, OCF domains should be assessed repeatedly (Fung & Lo, 2012). Culturally competent assessment and formulation may further be tailored to clinical contexts according to a three-tiered model (Fung & Lo, 2017): (i) Focused assessment of symptoms, stressors, and supports in emergency departments; (ii) In ambulatory or inpatient settings, assessment using a grid that intersects bio-psycho-socio-spiritual factors with predisposing–precipitating–perpetuating–protecting factors, with culture being considered in every cell; and (iii) In long-term/ongoing care settings, the DSM-5 CFI and supplementary modules should be used to conduct more elaborate culturally competent assessments (Lo & Fung, 2003).

The scenario in Box 4.2 highlights the complexities of identifying psychotic symptoms in cultural context.

CULTURALLY INFORMED INTERVENTIONS AND RESOURCES

Culturally informed interventions have evolved in various parts of the world to fill local needs. Typically, when clinics see large numbers of a given ethnic community, they may adapt services accordingly. Cultural consultation and ethnocultural assertive community treatment are examples of approaches that

Box 4.2 Vignette #2[a]

A 75-year-old Chinese man in Toronto was referred for cultural consultation after having killed a friend. He had immigrated to Canada about 20 years ago. Over the past 10 years, he had begun developing psychotic symptoms after retiring from manual labor. He periodically complained about hearing "dirty stuff" (污糟嘢) from ghosts. Despite not believing in it, his family hired a female shaman (神婆) in China to conduct a ritual called "hit little man" (打小人). They did so only to appease the patient, who felt better for a while. His delusions were reinforced by perceptions of being sat upon by ghosts as he slept (俾鬼責), which may have been due to sleep paralysis. Over the years, numerous family doctors had made no diagnoses, attributing his experiences to superstition. A year earlier, doctors repairing his fractured leg had noted that he had attributed a fall to being pushed by a ghost, but had not sought psychiatric consultation.

Comment: Assisting the psychiatrist of Chinese origin, an interpreter carefully preserved cultural nuance in interpreting from one Chinese dialect to another. The interpreter revealed that in rural China, where the client had grown up with little education, it was common to blame ghosts when livestock went missing. The family had ascribed the man's psychotic symptoms, an 'accidental' overdose, and increasing forgetfulness to the sort of 'old age confusion' that they had seen in their village. A forensic psychiatric assessment was conducted only after voices had allegedly 'forced' him to push an elderly friend who died from the resultant injuries. While his lack of education made cognitive assessments difficult, cognitive impairment and long-standing psychotic symptoms were confirmed, which he minimised. The client was ultimately diagnosed with late-onset schizophrenia and Alzheimer's disease and began receiving antipsychotic treatment after he and his family learned about the illness and its treatment.

[a] Details have been systematically disguised to protect client confidentiality.

provide culturally informed models of care. More generally, Arthur Kleinman advocated a patient-centred approach to understand how clients from diverse origins understand their concerns (Kleinman et al., 1978) (see Box 4.3 for sample questions). Cultural humility, and linguistic and cultural interpreters are tools that clinicians may use when working with diverse clientele. This section concludes with tips for clinicians and a list of resources.

Culturally Adapted Interventions

Several metaanalyses have concluded that culturally adapted psychological/psychosocial interventions are more efficacious than a one-size-fits-all approach (Benish, Quintana, & Wampold, 2011; Griner & Smith, 2006; Hall, Ibaraki, Huang, Marti, & Stice, 2016). Some psychosocial interventions for psychosis have been culturally adapted and evaluated in select populations, mostly in Asia. These evaluations (about 46 studies) have found that adaptations have beneficial impacts (Degnan et al., 2018; Maura & de Mamani, 2017), with the degree of adaptation appearing correlated with symptom reduction

Box 4.3 Sample Questions to Explore Clients' Understanding of Their Concerns

1. Can you please describe what your main concern is and how you have been affected by it?
2. Do you or others in your cultural community have a name for this concern?
3. Help me understand more about the concern involved—what caused it, what makes it worse, and what makes it better?
4. How serious is it? How long do you expect it to last?
5. How do you or others in your cultural community usually address this concern?
6. Who should be involved and what kinds of interventions or treatments would be helpful?
7. Do you have any other worries about this concern?

(Degnan et al., 2018). Typically, adaptations have involved translation; the use of specific phrases and metaphors; logistical modifications (e.g. duration, location, etc.); and regard for religion/spirituality, family factors, culture-specific communication styles (e.g. respect versus assertiveness), and cultural beliefs about attributions, symptoms and help seeking.

Notable adaptations include those of cognitive behavioural therapy for psychosis for Pakistan (Naeem et al., 2015) and for British South Asian and African-Caribbean immigrants (Rathod, Kingdon, Phiri, & Gobbi, 2010; Rathod et al., 2013); skills training for Latino Americans (Kopelowicz, Liberman, & Wallace, 2003; Valencia et al., 2010); and psychoeducation for Korean Americans (Shin & Lukens, 2002). Culturally adapted family interventions have shown promise among British Afro-Caribbeans (Edge et al., 2016); persons in China and Asian Americans (Bae & Kung, 2000; Chien & Wong, 2007; Kung, Tseng, Wang, Hsu, & Chen, 2012); and Spanish-speaking immigrants in America (Barrio & Yamada, 2010; Kopelowicz et al., 2012; López et al., 2009; Patterson et al., 2005; Weisman, Duarte, Koneru, & Wasserman, 2006). The few interventions adapted for Black patients have generally yielded greater benefits than usual treatment (Agara & Onibi, 2007; Asmal, Mall, Emsley, Chiliza, & Swartz, 2014; Baker, Stokes-Thompson, Davis, Gonzo, & Hishinuma, 1999; Pooe et al., 2010). Despite some limitations (Degnan et al., 2018; Helms, 2015; Maura & de Mamani, 2017), research on culturally adapted interventions has shown that they are useful for members of ethnocultural communities and should therefore be offered whenever possible.

Edge et al. (2016) attempt a culturally adapted family intervention for African-Caribbeans diagnosed with schizophrenia. Their efforts highlight some common pitfalls in this line of work. The study assigns people from the Caribbean into one group as though family structures, beliefs, and values are the same among all peoples of the Caribbean. This problem undermines the study from beginning to end: What does African-Caribbean mean? And to whom will the findings apply? The authors do not consider these concerns, so answers are not available.

Balaratnasingam et al. (2015) offer a procedure for adapting interventions to cultural minorities. The first phase involves consulting with key informants to establish local concepts of psychosis and translating them into common language. A glossary of terms contains the results of these efforts and informs the language of the first version of the intervention. A second stage seeks input from mental health clinicians working locally to inform whether questions and concepts are meaningful and appropriate. The second version of the intervention comes from this process. When the second draft is piloted on clients, results are compared to clinical ratings, diagnosis, or outcome. The procedure is time consuming and demanding, but should be reproduced for each group to be considered in cultural context. It is important not to apply culturally adapted material from one group to another even if both are 'Asian', 'African', 'White', or other generalised category.

The Cultural Consultation Service offers in depth mental health evaluation of immigrants and refugees.

Cultural consultation is an approach that gives due regard to the role of culture in the diagnosis and treatment of individuals and families in local context. In a multicultural neighbourhood of Montreal, the Cultural Consultation Service (CCS) began in 1999 to help clinicians evaluate language, ethnicity, migration, and religion-related issues that arise in the diagnosis and treatment of immigrants and refugees with mental health problems (Kirmayer, Groleau, Guzder, Blake, & Jarvis, 2003). Many CCS consultations are for patients with established or suspected psychosis. The CCS employs linguistic and cultural interpreters (brokers) and a person-centred approach founded on principles of cultural safety and humility (Kirmayer, Rousseau, Jarvis, & Guzder, 2015). Cultural safety refers to recognising power imbalances in the clinical encounter and creating a safe space where patients with historical legacies of trauma can openly discuss their problems (Williams, 1999). Cultural humility refers to a clinician recognising the limits of their cultural knowledge; and therefore seeking inputs from patients, families, community members, and interpreters; and modifying standard mental health practices accordingly (Tervalon & Murray-Garcia, 1998).

Cultural humility refers to clinicians' awareness of, and willingness to overcome, the limits of their cultural expertise.

Toronto's Mount Sinai Hospital Ethnocultural Assertive Community Treatment Team (EACTT) serves around 100 Asian, South Asian, and Afro-Caribbean patients with severe mental illness. This team of bilingual and bicultural social workers, nurses, occupational therapists, and psychiatrists provides medication monitoring and community-based, recovery-focused psychosocial treatment (e.g. storytelling/exercise groups, family psychoeducation) (Yang et al., 2005) and has incorporated the CFI into its standard psychiatric assessment. Whereas the CCS is a consultation service, the EACTT provides ongoing care.

Working with linguistic interpreters. The first step towards a culturally informed intervention is to assess the client's linguistic capacities and provide relevant translation services, or at least offer the option. Doing so tells a client that their language and culture are valued. Many patients are relieved to recount their stories in their mother tongue, sometimes for the first time. A few patients may prefer no interpreter for reasons of confidentiality (Leanza, Miklavcic, Boivin, & Rosenberg, 2014). Some psychotic patients may present with temporarily decreased language fluency. In such cases, working with an interpreter becomes even more crucial. To maximise engagement, confidentiality and the interpreter's role should be carefully explained to clients, especially those who are paranoid. Interpreters should not correct patients' disordered thoughts.

Working with culture brokers. When linguistic interpreters alone cannot clarify some complaints and narratives, culture brokers can bridge the gap between clients and clinicians. Culture brokers may be linguistic interpreters with additional skills, or they may be professionals (clinicians or social scientists) with expertise in a given culture or society. They provide advice to the treating team about issues relevant to diagnosis, understanding symptoms, and treatment options (Miklavcic & LeBlanc, 2014).

The example in Box 4.4 underscores the dilemma of when to diagnose psychosis and how a culture broker may offer essential clinical input.

Culturally adapted interventions and programs are few and far between. They have not assumed a standardised format, but represent local efforts to improve mental health services for clients and their families. One exception may the Cultural Consultation Service in Montreal. The CCS model has been exported to several sites, mostly in Europe and North America. The CCS initiated the International Consortium for Cultural Consultation (ICCC) to monitor the progress of and improve networking among various participating clinics.

Tips for integrating cultural considerations. Psychosis can be difficult to understand and treat in cultural context. Clinicians may find the following rules of thumb helpful as supplements to local clinical practice guidelines.

(1) *Determine the need for an interpreter*. Inquiring about language proficiency before a first appointment is important. Employing family members or clinic staff as interpreters should be avoided. As interpreters, family members may want to portray loved ones favourably, thereby unintentionally obscuring the presence of symptoms like thought disorder; or they may not divulge sensitive material like abuse or loss of religious faith. Even professional interpreters may have difficulty translating when psychotic patients become vague or incoherent.

(2) *Allow extra time for linguistically or culturally diverse patients*. Appointments are sometimes kept short to minimise logistical burdens and maximise healthcare provider income. In the long run, however, longer appointments can prevent the dissatisfaction and errors caused by too-rapid consultations. Scheduling extra time for first meetings (up to 2 h if interpreters are involved) helps improve treatment adherence, family engagement, and assessments of risks.

(3) *Identify priorities*. Migrants and refugees with psychosis face urgent practical problems whose resolution may need attention before standard

Box 4.4 Vignette #3[a]

A 40-year-old from Guinea in West Africa was referred for evaluation of psychosis. He had lived mostly in a shelter for five years, resisting efforts to find him housing and employment. He seemed content to sleep on a mat by night and store away his meager possessions by day. He always carried a well-worn Bible and said he was "obeying God's commandments" as best he could. He explained that since being "touched" at the age of nine years, he had felt God guiding and speaking to him continuously. He reassured evaluators that the Lord would provide and show him the next steps to take. Meanwhile, living on practically nothing (which, to him, was a virtue) allowed him to send most of his welfare allowance to his family in Guinea. He appeared remarkably tranquil, given his destitution.

Comment: The cultural interpreter explained that the patient's condition (i.e. no home, few possessions) was consistent with the lives of the poor in many African societies. A diagnosis of mild psychotic disorder was deferred in favour of a cultural formulation that noted his rural origins, low education, religious worldview, and imperative to provide for his family. Recommendations were practical and included helping the man obtain legal status in Canada (to which he was entitled), linking him to a supportive religious community, and bettering his connections to family in Africa. Medication and medical follow-up were not indicated.

[a]Details have been systematically disguised to protect client confidentiality.

treatments. Such urgent matters can include asylum hearings, finding legal counsel, procuring healthcare coverage, finding shelter, and securing a work permit.

(4) *Cultivate cultural humility*. Clinicians may be tempted to assert the supremacy of mental health professional models in assessing and treating psychosis. Forcibly fitting everyone into the neat rubrics of professional categories amounts to a denial of diversity. Gently exploring ethno-specific beliefs about psychosis will improve the therapeutic alliance with clients and families. Traditional therapies should be respectfully discussed. A curious attitude towards religious beliefs and practices can identify valuable community supports. With cultural humility, worldviews should be negotiated rather than conquered, and appropriate treatments proffered rather than imposed.

(5) *Adopt a flexible approach*. Immigrants and refugees may unwittingly seek help or conduct themselves in ways that are improper in their new country. Examples include missing or arriving late to appointments; misunderstanding the purpose of consultations; changing personal information in asylum claim documents; forgetting medical insurance and other important papers; bringing children to evaluations; rejecting interpreters and insisting on speaking broken English; and concealing key information. These challenges will be resolved as the clinician adopts a patient, flexible attitude.

(6) *Be self-reflective*. Clinician biases, assumptions, and prejudices rooted in majority cultures negatively impact patient outcomes. Clinicians can minimise this risk by adopting an attitude of reflexivity, facilitated by dialogue or supervision. Some reflective questions for clinicians are listed in Box 4.5.
(7) *Engage families*. Promoting family involvement will facilitate positive outcomes in psychosis. Family culture is the immediate context for the patient's symptoms. Families offer support and are key allies of the treating team. Interventions targeted to educate families should be culturally adapted rather than standardised for general populations and should include discussion of how religion and spirituality, racism, migration, and cultural interventions interact with psychosis. In this way, patients and families will grow together through the experience of psychosis and will find solutions acceptable to their beliefs and values.
(8) *Consider alternatives to a psychosis diagnosis*. When in doubt, clinicians should start with a diagnosis of mood disorder with psychotic features to counteract the known tendency of overdiagnosing schizophrenia in minority clients. Alternative diagnoses to rule out include PTSD, dissociation, and culturally normative short-lived religious experiences.

These tips are not in order of importance nor are they mutually exclusive. In fact, all will likely come into play over the course of clinical work with clients from diverse backgrounds with psychosis. The important thing to remember for any clinician is to sit back, relax, and develop genuine curiosity about the client sitting before you. Listen carefully to their experiences and explanations. Spend time to make sure they understand that your evaluation will be confidential. Accept the input of the linguistic interpreter and culture broker. Make sure the

Box 4.5 Reflective Questions for Clinicians

1. Has the clinical team offered to conduct the evaluation in the client's mother tongue?
2. Have principles of cultural humility and safety been part of the clinical meeting?
3. Has the clinic been set up in a way to be friendly to culturally diverse clientele? Are signs written in more than one language? Are the religious traditions of cultural communities respected? Are gender norms honoured to the degree possible?
4. Has the clinical team asked what is most at stake for the client?
5. Has the client's migration history been evaluated, including histories of trauma, gender-based violence, and persecution?
6. Has the clinical team engaged the client's family?
7. Have the client's religious beliefs and practices (or lack thereof) been addressed?
8. Have proposed interventions been negotiated with the client, family, and with a leader of the religious community (when appropriate)?
9. Have traditional health beliefs and practices been discussed with the client (when appropriate)?
10. Has the team sought cultural consultation for difficulties in the evaluation or treatment of the client?

client is comfortable with those in attendance, including the interpreter. Invite family members into the consultation. Take breaks if the client becomes overwhelmed. Seek additional help if you don't understand something or are not sure how to proceed.

Resources

A growing number of online resources can help keep clinicians abreast of current issues in culture and psychosis and equip them with information to guide the cultural assessment and treatment of clients with psychosis (see URLs in the Additional Resources list).

CONCLUSION

There is significant interplay between culture and psychotic disorders like schizophrenia. Culture influences psychoses via historical legacies, diagnostic conventions, symptom expression, and patterns of course and outcome. The main concern in this chapter has been that mainstream theories, practices, and interventions cannot suffice for assessing and treating psychosis in diverse patients. Clinicians must sometimes set aside what they have learned to enter the perspective of the clients they are treating. Doing so lets them build trust and understanding; engage families and communities; incorporate religious beliefs and practices into treatment; and be duly cautious of the perils of cross-cultural diagnosis. Clinicians must acknowledge their limitations and the roles that their institutions play in fashioning responses to diversity. Engendering cultural awareness can awaken clinicians and encourage those with psychosis towards recovery.

ADDITIONAL RESOURCES

Center for Society, Health, and Medicine. Retrieved from https://research.shanghai.nyu.edu/cshm. Produces podcasts with an international perspective, although not specifically about psychosis.

Center of Excellence for Cultural Competence. Retrieved from https://nyculturalcompetence.org/. Provides a variety of helps for consumers from the U.S. perspective.

Multicultural Mental Health Resource Centre. Retrieved from http://www.multiculturalmentalhealth.ca/. Provides helps for consumers, services available, clinical tools, policy, training resources, although mostly geared to the Canadian context. The site provides a large number of training videos and podcasts, some of which specifically treat psychosis and schizophrenia.

Orygen, the National Centre of Excellence in Youth Mental Health. Retrieved from https://www.orygen.org.au/Education-Training/Resources-Training/Resources/Free/Clinical-Practice/Working-with-cultural-diversity-in-early-psychosis/Working-with-cultural-diversity-in-early-psychosis?ext=. Provides tips for working with culture in early psychosis in an Australian context.

RADAR Films. Retrieved from https://www.radarmentalhealth.com/films. Highlights first-person accounts of individuals living with severe mental disorders in a variety of circumstances, some of which are created and directed by the sufferers themselves.

Social Psychology Network. Retrieved from https://www.socialpsychology.org/cultural.htm. Many cultural psychology resources are available at this website, although the content is not about psychosis specifically.

Society for the Psychological Study of Culture, Ethnicity, and Race. Retrieved from http://division45.org/resources/teaching-resources/. Is a division of the American Psychological Association (APA) and promotes the study of ethnicity and culture in psychology. Division 45, as it is called, provides online resources, such as teaching resources, webinars, and guidelines.

Society for the Study of Psychiatry and Culture. Retrieved from https://psychiatryandculture.org/webinars/. Promotes cultural psychiatry mainly from a North American perspective. A webinar series covers topics in culture and mental health, although only members can access the recorded webinars. Anyone may register for the live webinars.

References

Adeponle, A. B., Thombs, B. D., Groleau, D., Jarvis, E., & Kirmayer, L. J. (2012). Using the cultural formulation to resolve uncertainty in diagnoses of psychosis in ethnoculturally diverse patients. *Psychiatric Services, 63*(2), 147–153.

Agara, A. J., & Onibi, O. E. (2007). Effects of group psychoeducation (GPE) on compliance with scheduled clinic appointments in a neuro-psychiatric hospital in Southwest Nigeria: A randomised control trial (RCT). *Annals of the Academy of Medicine, Singapore, 36*, 272.

Aggarwal, N. K., Nicasio, A. V., DeSilva, R., Boiler, M., & Lewis-Fernandez, R. (2013). Barriers to implementing the DSM-5 cultural formulation interview: A qualitative study. *Culture, Medicine and Psychiatry, 37*, 505–533.

AIPA (Australian Indigenous Psychologists Association). (2014). *Cultural competence workshops.* Retrieved July 27, 2018 from: http://www.indigenouspsychology.com.au/workshop/about-the-workshops/.

Ajnakina, O., Lally, J., Di Forti, M., Kolliakou, A., Gardner-Sood, P., Lopez-Morinigo, J., et al. (2017). Patterns of illness and care over the 5 years following onset of psychosis in different ethnic groups; the GAP-5 study. *Social Psychiatry and Psychiatric Epidemiology, 52*, 1101–1111.

Al-Issa, I. (1995). The illusion of reality or the reality of illusion: Hallucinations and culture. *The British Journal of Psychiatry, 166*(3), 368–373.

Altschuler, E. L. (2001). One of the oldest cases of schizophrenia in Gogol's Diary of a Madman. *BMJ: British Medical Journal, 323*(7327), 1475.

Andermann, L. F., & Lo, H.-T. T. (2006). Cultural competence in psychiatric assessment. In *Psychiatric clinical skills* (pp. 21–28): Elsevier.

Anderson, K., Flora, N., Archie, S., Morgan, C., & McKenzie, K. (2014). A meta-analysis of ethnic differences in pathways to care at the first episode of psychosis. *Acta Psychiatrica Scandinavica, 130*(4), 257–268.

Anderson, K., Fuhrer, R., & Malla, A. (2010). The pathways to mental health care of first-episode psychosis patients: A systematic review. *Psychological Medicine, 40*(10), 1585–1597.

Anderson, K. K., Fuhrer, R., Schmitz, N., & Malla, A. K. (2013). Determinants of negative pathways to care and their impact on service disengagement in first-episode psychosis. *Social Psychiatry and Psychiatric Epidemiology, 48*(1), 125–136.

Andreasen, N. C., Flaum, M., & Arndt, S. (1992). The Comprehensive Assessment of Symptoms and History (CASH): An instrument for assessing diagnosis and psychopathology. *Archives of General Psychiatry, 49*(8), 615–623.

APA. (2000). *Diagnostic and statistical manual of mental disorders, fourth edition: DSM-IV-TR®*. American Psychiatric Association.

APA. (2013). *Diagnostic and statistical manual of mental disorders (DSM-5®)*. American Psychiatric Association.

Asmal, L., Mall, S., Emsley, R., Chiliza, B., & Swartz, L. (2014). Towards a treatment model for family therapy for schizophrenia in an urban African setting: Results from a qualitative study. *International Journal of Social Psychiatry, 60*, 315–320.

Bae, S.-W., & Kung, W. W.-M. (2000). Family intervention for Asian Americans with a schizophrenic patient in the family. *American Journal of Orthopsychiatry, 70*, 532.

Baker, F. M., Stokes-Thompson, J., Davis, O. A., Gonzo, R., & Hishinuma, E. S. (1999). Two-year outcomes of psychosocial rehabilitation of black patients with chronic mental illness. *Psychiatric Services, 50*, 535–539.

Balaratnasingam, S., Anderson, L., Janca, A., & Lee, J. (2015). Towards culturally appropriate assessment of Aboriginal and Torres Strait Islander social and emotional well-being. *Australasian Psychiatry, 23*(6), 626–629.

Barrio, C., & Yamada, A.-M. (2010). Culturally based intervention development: The case of Latino families dealing with schizophrenia. *Research on Social Work Practice, 20*, 483–492.

Beavan, V., Read, J., & Cartwright, C. (2011). The prevalence of voice-hearers in the general population: A literature review. *Journal of Mental Health, 20*(3), 281–292.

Bécares, L., Dewey, M. E., & Das-Munshi, J. (2017). Ethnic density effects for adult mental health: Systematic review and meta-analysis of international studies. *Psychological Medicine*, 1–19.

Benish, S. G., Quintana, S., & Wampold, B. E. (2011). Culturally adapted psychotherapy and the legitimacy of myth: A direct-comparison meta-analysis. *Journal of Counseling Psychology, 58*, 279–289. https://doi.org/10.1037/a0023626.

Bhui, K., Stansfeld, S., Hull, S., Priebe, S., Mole, F., & Feder, G. (2003). Ethnic variations in pathways to and use of specialist mental health services in the UK: Systematic review. *British Journal of Psychiatry, 182*, 105–116.

Boydell, J., Morgan, C., Dutta, R., Jones, B., Alemseged, F., Dazzan, P., et al. (2012). Satisfaction with inpatient treatment for first-episode psychosis among different ethnic groups: A report from the UK AeSOP study. *International Journal of Social Psychiatry, 58*, 98–105.

Carothers, J. C. (1972). *The mind of man in Africa*. London: Tom Stacey Ltd.

Chen, C.-H., Chen, C.-Y., & Lin, K.-M. (2008). Ethnopsychopharmacology. *International Review of Psychiatry, 20*(5), 452–459.

Cheng, A., Tien, A., Chang, C., Brugha, T., Cooper, J., Lee, C., et al. (2001). Cross-cultural implementation of a Chinese version of the Schedules for Clinical Assessment in Neuropsychiatry (SCAN) in Taiwan. *The British Journal of Psychiatry, 178*(6), 567–572.

Chien, W. T., & Wong, K.-F. (2007). A family psychoeducation group program for Chinese people with schizophrenia in Hong Kong. *Psychiatric Services, 58*, 1003–1006.

Cohen, A., Padmavati, R., Hibben, M., Oyewusi, S., John, S., Esan, O., et al. (2016). Concepts of madness in diverse settings: A qualitative study from the INTREPID project. *BMC Psychiatry, 16*(1), 388.

Cohen, A., Patel, V., Thara, R., & Gureje, O. (2008). Questioning an axiom: Better prognosis for schizophrenia in the developing world? *Schizophrenia Bulletin, 34*(2), 229–244.

Coid, J. W., Kirkbride, J. B., Barker, D., Cowden, F., Stamps, R., Yang, M., et al. (2008). Raised incidence rates of all psychoses among migrant groups: Findings from the East London first episode psychosis study. *Archives of General Psychiatry, 65*(11), 1250–1258.

Degnan, A., Baker, S., Edge, D., Nottidge, W., Noke, M., Press, C. J., et al. (2018). The nature and efficacy of culturally-adapted psychosocial interventions for schizophrenia: A systematic review and meta-analysis. *Psychological Medicine, 48*, 714–727. https://doi.org/10.1017/S0033291717002264.

Deshpande, S. N., Mathur, M. N., Das, S. K., Bhatia, T., Sharma, S., & Nimgaonkar, V. L. (1998). A hindi version of the diagnostic interview for genetic studies. *Schizophrenia Bulletin, 24*(3), 489.

Edge, D., Degnan, A., Cotterill, S., Berry, K., Drake, R., Baker, J., et al. (2016). Culturally-adapted Family Intervention (CaFI) for African-Caribbeans diagnosed with schizophrenia and their families: A feasibility study protocol of implementation and acceptability. *Pilot and Feasibility Studies, 2*, 39.

Evans, K., McGrath, J., & Milns, R. (2003). Searching for schizophrenia in ancient Greek and Roman literature: A systematic review. *Acta Psychiatrica Scandinavica, 107*(5), 323–330.

Fearon, P., Kirkbride, J. B., Morgan, C., Dazzan, P., Morgan, K., Lloyd, T., et al. (2006). Incidence of schizophrenia and other psychoses in ethnic minority groups: Results from the MRC AESOP Study. *Psychological Medicine, 36*(11), 1541–1550.

Fernando, S. (1995). Psychotic illness in ethnic groups. Study did not deal with "category fallacy". *BMJ: British Medical Journal, 310*(6975), 331.

Fernando, S. (1998). Studies into issues of 'race' and culture in psychiatry carry far reaching social implications and so the methodology used in them, as well as their presentation in journals, should be approached with caution and sensitivity. *Psychological Medicine, 28*(2), 495–497 [To the Editor].

Ferns, P., Barker, P., Beresford, P., Blackman, P. S., Bracken, P., Christie, Y., et al. (2010). Poor research or an attack on black people? Open letter. *The Guardian*. (February 3). Retrieved from: https://www.theguardian.com/society/2010/feb/03/mental-health-bme-schizophrenia-letter.

Fung, K., & Lo, T. (2012). Culturally competent practice and management of mental health in primary care. In *Collaborative mental health*. Toronto, Canada: Centre for Addiction and Mental Health.

Fung, K., & Lo, T. (2017). An integrative clinical approach to cultural competent psychotherapy. *Journal of Contemporary Psychotherapy, 47*(2), 65–73.

Fung, K. P., & Guzder, J. (2018). Canadian immigrant mental health. In D. Moussaoui, D. Bhugra, & A. Ventriglio (Eds.), *Mental health and illness in migration. Mental health and illness worldwide*. Singapore: Springer.

Gara, M. A., Vega, W. A., Arndt, S., Escamilla, M., Fleck, D. E., Lawson, W. B., et al. (2012). Influence of patient race and ethnicity on clinical assessment in patients with affective disorders. *Archives of General Psychiatry, 69*(6), 593–600.

German, G. A. (1972). Aspects of clinical psychiatry in sub-Saharan Africa. *The British Journal of Psychiatry, 121*(564), 461–479.

Griner, D., & Smith, T. B. (2006). Culturally adapted mental health intervention: A meta-analytic review. *Psychotherapy: Theory, Research, Practice, Training, 43*, 531–548. https://doi.org/10.1037/0033-3204.43.4.531.

Groen, S. P. N., Richters, C. J., Laban, C. J., & Devillé, W. L. J. M. (2016). Implementation of the cultural formulation through a newly developed brief cultural interview: Pilot data from the Netherlands. *Transcultural Psychiatry, 54*(1), 3–22.

Gureje, O., Lasebikan, V. O., Ephraim-Oluwanuga, O., Olley, B. O., & Kola, L. (2005). Community study of knowledge of and attitude to mental illness in Nigeria. *The British Journal of Psychiatry, 186*(5), 436–441.

Hall, G. C. N., Ibaraki, A. Y., Huang, E. R., Marti, C. N., & Stice, E. (2016). A meta-analysis of cultural adaptations of psychological interventions. *Behavior Therapy, 47*, 993–1014. https://doi.org/10.1016/j.beth.2016.09.005.

Hare, E. (1988). Schizophrenia as a recent disease. *The British Journal of Psychiatry, 153*(4), 521–531.

Harrison, G., Holton, A., Neilson, D., Owens, D., Boot, D., & Cooper, J. (1989). Severe mental disorder in Afro-Caribbean patients: Some social, demographic and service factors. *Psychological Medicine, 19*(3), 683–696.

Harrison, G., Owens, D., Holton, A., Neilson, D., & Boot, D. (1988). A prospective study of severe mental disorder in Afro-Caribbean patients. *Psychological Medicine, 18*(3), 643–657.

Helms, J. E. (2015). An examination of the evidence in culturally adapted evidence-based or empirically supported interventions. *Transcultural Psychiatry, 52*, 174–197.

Hickling, F., McKenzie, K., Mullen, R., & Murray, R. (1999). A Jamaican psychiatrist evaluates diagnoses at a London psychiatric hospital. *The British Journal of Psychiatry, 175*(3), 283–285.

Higgins, E. S., & Kose, S. (2007). Absence of schizophrenia in a 15th-century Islamic medical textbook. *The American Journal of Psychiatry, 164*(7), 1120. author reply 1120-1121. https://doi.org/10.1176/ajp.2007.164.7.1120a.

Hopper, K., Harrison, G., & Wanderling, J. (2007). An overview of course and outcome in ISoS. In *Recovery from schizophrenia: An international perspective; a report from the WHO collaborative project, the international study of schizophrenia* (pp. 23–38).

Jablensky, A., Sartorius, N., Ernberg, G., Anker, M., Korten, A., Cooper, J. E., et al. (1992). Schizophrenia: Manifestations, incidence and course in different cultures a World Health Organization Ten-Country Study. *Psychological Medicine Monograph Supplement, 20*, 1–97.

Jarvis, G. E. (2008). Changing psychiatric perception of African Americans with psychosis. *European Journal of American Culture, 27*(3), 227–252.

Jarvis, G. E., Bhat, V., Jurcik, T., Spigonardo, V., & Whitley, R. (2014). Transatlantic variation in the attributed etiology of psychosis. *International Journal of Social Psychiatry, 61*(6), 577–582.

Jarvis, G. E., Kirmayer, L. J., Jarvis, G. K., & Whitley, R. (2005). The role of Afro-Canadian status in police or ambulance referral to emergency psychiatric services. *Psychiatric Services, 56*(6), 705–710.

Jenkins, C. (2011). *A brief history of France.* Philadelphia: Running Press.

Jongsma, H. E., Gayer-Anderson, C., Lasalvia, A., Quattrone, D., Mulè, A., Szöke, A., et al. (2018). Treated incidence of psychotic disorders in the multinational EU-GEI study. *JAMA Psychiatry, 75*(1), 36–46.

Joo, E.-J., Joo, Y.-H., Hong, J.-P., Hwang, S., Maeng, S.-J., Han, J.-H., et al. (2004). Korean version of the diagnostic interview for genetic studies: Validity and reliability. *Comprehensive Psychiatry, 45* (3), 225–229.

Keith, S. J. (1991). Schizophrenic disorders. In L. N. Robins, & D. A. Regier (Eds.), *Psychiatric disorders in America: The epidemiologic catchment area study.* New York: The Free Press.

Kendell, R., Everett, B., Cooper, J., Sartorius, N., & David, M. (1968). The reliability of the "present state examination". *Social Psychiatry, 3*(3), 123–129.

Kirkbride, J. B., Fearon, P., Morgan, C., Dazzan, P., Morgan, K., Tarrant, J., et al. (2006). Heterogeneity in incidence rates of schizophrenia and other psychotic syndromes: Findings from the 3-center AeSOP study. *Archives of General Psychiatry, 63*(3), 250–258.

Kirkbride, J. B., & Hollander, A.-C. (2015). Migration and risk of psychosis in the Canadian context. *Canadian Medical Association Journal, 187*(9), 637–638.

Kirmayer, L. J., Corin, E., & Jarvis, G. E. (2004). Inside knowledge: Cultural constructions of insight in psychosis. In *Insight and psychosis* (pp. 197–229). New York: Oxford University Press Inc.

Kirmayer, L. J., Groleau, D., Guzder, J., Blake, C., & Jarvis, E. (2003). Cultural consultation: A model of mental health service for multicultural societies. *The Canadian Journal of Psychiatry, 48*(3), 145–153.

Kirmayer, L. J., Rousseau, C., Jarvis, G. E., & Guzder, J. (2015). The cultural context of clinical assessment. In A. Tasman, J. Kay, J. A. Lieberman, M. B. First, & M. B. Riba (Eds.), *Psychiatry* (4th ed., pp. 56–70). New York: John Wiley & Sons.

Kleinman, A. (1988). *Rethinking psychiatry: From cultural category to personal experience.* New York: The Free Press.

Kleinman, A., Eisenberg, L., & Good, B. (1978). Culture, illness, and care: Clinical lessons from anthropologic and cross-cultural research. *Annals of Internal Medicine, 88*(2), 251–258.

Kleinman, A. M. (1977). Depression, somatization and the "new cross-cultural psychiatry". *Social Science & Medicine (1967), 11*(1), 3–9.

Kopelowicz, A., Liberman, R. P., & Wallace, C. J. (2003). Psychiatric rehabilitation for schizophrenia. *International Journal of Psychology and Psychological Therapy, 3*(2), 283–298.

Kopelowicz, A., Zarate, R., Wallace, C. J., Liberman, R. P., Lopez, S. R., & Mintz, J. (2012). The ability of multifamily groups to improve treatment adherence in Mexican Americans with schizophrenia. *Archives of General Psychiatry, 69*, 265–273. https://doi.org/10.1001/archgenpsychiatry.2011.135.

Kralj, Ž., Dedic, M., Kovacevic, A., Malicki, M., Dedic, J., Pelivan, M., et al. (2017). Diagnostic interview for genetic studies: Validity and reliability of the Croatian version. *Psychiatric Genetics, 27*(1), 17–22.

Kung, W. W., Tseng, Y. F., Wang, Y., Hsu, P. C., & Chen, D. (2012). Pilot study of ethnically sensitive family Psychoeducation for Chinese-American patients with schizophrenia. *Social Work in Mental Health, 10*, 384–408. https://doi.org/10.1080/15332985.2012.678570.

Larchanché, S. (2010). *Cultural anxieties and institutional regulation: "Specialized" mental healthcare and "immigrant suffering" in Paris, France* [Dissertation manuscript].Paris: Washington University in St. Louis and EHESS

Larøi, F., Luhrmann, T. M., Bell, V., Christian, W. A., Jr., Deshpande, S., Fernyhough, C., et al. (2014). Culture and hallucinations: Overview and future directions. *Schizophrenia Bulletin, 40*(Suppl. 4), S213–S220.

Lasalvia, A., Van Bortel, T., Bonetto, C., Jayaram, G., Van Weeghel, J., Zoppei, S., et al. (2015). Cross-national variations in reported discrimination among people treated for major depression worldwide: The ASPEN/INDIGO international study. *The British Journal of Psychiatry, 207*, 507–514.

Lasalvia, A., Zoppei, S., Van Bortel, T., Bonetto, C., Cristofalo, D., Wahlbeck, K., et al. (2013). Global pattern of experienced and anticipated discrimination reported by people with major depressive disorder: A cross-sectional survey. *The Lancet, 381*, 55–62.

Leanza, Y., Miklavcic, A., Boivin, I., & Rosenberg, E. (2014). Working with interpreters. In L. J. Kirmayer, J. Guzder, & C. Rousseau (Eds.), *Cultural consultation: Encountering the other in mental health care* (pp. 89–114). New York: Springer.

Leff, J., Sartorius, N., Jablensky, A., Korten, A., & Ernberg, G. (1992). The international pilot study of schizophrenia: Five-year follow-up findings. *Psychological Medicine, 22*(1), 131–145.

Lewis-Fernandez, R., et al. (2017). Feasibility, acceptability and clinical utility of the Cultural Formulation Interview: Mixed-methods results from the DSM-5 international field trial. *The British Journal of Psychiatry, 210*(4), 290–297. https://doi.org/10.1192/bjp.bp.116.193862.

Li, A. T.-W., Wong, J. P.-H., Cain, R., & Fung, K. P.-L. (2016). Engaging African-Caribbean, Asian, and Latino community leaders to address HIV stigma in Toronto. *International Journal of Migration, Health and Social Care, 12*(4), 288–300.

Lo, H.-T., & Fung, K. P. (2003). Culturally competent psychotherapy. *The Canadian Journal of Psychiatry, 48*(3), 161–170.

López, S. R., Lara, M., Kopelowicz, A., Solano, S., Foncerrada, H., & Aguilera, A. (2009). La CLAve to increase psychosis literacy of Spanish-speaking community residents and family caregivers. *Journal of Consulting and Clinical Psychology, 77*, 763.

Marsella, A. J. (1988). Cross-cultural research on severe mental disorders: Issues and findings. *Acta Psychiatrica Scandinavica, 78*(S344), 7–22.

Maura, J., & de Mamani, A. W. (2017). Culturally adapted psychosocial interventions for schizophrenia: A review. *Cognitive and Behavioral Practice, 24*, 445–458. https://doi.org/10.1016/j.cbpra.2017.01.004.

McKenzie, K., Hansson, E., Tuck, A., & Lurie, S. (2010). *Improving mental health services for immigrant, refugee, ethno-cultural and racialized groups.* Canadian Issues (p. 65).

Metzl, J. (2009). *The protest psychosis: How schizophrenia became a black disease.* Boston: Beacon Press.

Miklavcic, A., & LeBlanc, M. N. (2014). Culture brokers, clinically applied ethnography, and cultural mediation. In L. J. Kirmayer, J. Guzder, & C. Rousseau (Eds.), *Cultural consultation: Encountering the other in mental health care* (pp. 115–137). New York: Springer.

Morgan, C., Fearon, P., Lappin, J., Heslin, M., Donoghue, K., Lomas, B., et al. (2017). Ethnicity and long-term course and outcome of psychotic disorders in a UK sample: The ÆSOP-10 study. *The British Journal of Psychiatry, 211*, 88–94.

Naeem, F., Saeed, S., Irfan, M., Kiran, T., Mehmood, N., Gul, M., et al. (2015). Brief culturally adapted CBT for psychosis (CaCBTp): A randomized controlled trial from a low income country. *Schizophrenia Research, 164*, 143–148. https://doi.org/10.1016/j.schres.2015.02.015.

Ninnemann, K. M. (2012). Variability in the efficacy of psychopharmaceuticals: Contributions from pharmacogenomics, ethnopsychopharmacology, and psychological and psychiatric anthropologies. *Culture, Medicine, and Psychiatry, 36*(1), 10–25.

Nurnberger, J. I., Blehar, M. C., Kaufmann, C. A., York-Cooler, C., Simpson, S. G., Harkavy-Friedman, J., et al. (1994). Diagnostic interview for genetic studies: Rationale, unique features, and training. *Archives of General Psychiatry, 51*(11), 849–859.

Paholpak, S., Krisanaprakornkit, T., Piyavhatkul, N., Arunpongpaisal, S., Rangseekajee, P., Pajanasoontorn, N., et al. (2011). Validity and reliability study of the Thai version of WHO Schedules for Clinical Assessment in Neuropsychiatry version 2.1. *Journal of the Medical Association of Thailand, 93*(4), 497.

Patel, V., Xiao, S., Chen, H., Hanna, F., Jotheeswaran, A. T., Luo, D., et al. (2016). The magnitude of and health system responses to the mental health treatment gap in adults in India and China. *The Lancet, 388*, 3074–3084.

Patterson, T. L., Bucardo, J., McKibbin, C. L., Mausbach, B. T., Moore, D., Barrio, C., et al. (2005). Development and pilot testing of a new psychosocial intervention for older latinos with chronic psychosis. *Schizophrenia Bulletin, 31*, 922–930.

Pechey, R., & Halligan, P. (2011). The prevalence of delusion-like beliefs relative to sociocultural beliefs in the general population. *Psychopathology, 44*(2), 106–115.

Pooe, J. M., Sokudela, B., Roos, J. L., Motlana, L. M., Dlamini, N., & Snyman, M. (2010). Testing the effectiveness of existing psycho-educational material (The Alliance Programme) for patients suffering from schizophrenia in the South African context. *African Journal of Psychiatry, 13*, 302–308.

Preisig, M., Fenton, B. T., Matthey, M.-L., Berney, A., & Ferrero, F. (1999). Diagnostic interview for genetic studies (DIGS): Inter-rater and test-retest reliability of the French version. *European Archives of Psychiatry and Clinical Neuroscience, 249*(4), 174–179.

Rathod, S., Kingdon, D., Phiri, P., & Gobbi, M. (2010). Developing culturally sensitive cognitive behaviour therapy for psychosis for ethnic minority patients by exploration and incorporation of service users' and health professionals' views and opinions. *Behavioural and Cognitive Psychotherapy, 38*, 511–533. https://doi.org/10.1017/S1352465810000378.

Rathod, S., Phiri, P., Harris, S., Underwood, C., Thagadur, M., Padmanabi, U., et al. (2013). Cognitive behaviour therapy for psychosis can be adapted for minority ethnic groups: A randomised controlled trial. *Schizophrenia Research, 143*, 319–326. https://doi.org/10.1016/j.schres.2012.11.007.

Rathod, S., & Turkington, D. (2005). Cognitive-behaviour therapy for schizophrenia: A review. *Current Opinion in Psychiatry, 18*(2), 159–163.

Robins, L. N., Helzer, J. E., Croughan, J., & Ratcliff, K. S. (1981). National Institute of Mental Health Diagnostic Interview Schedule. Its history, characteristics, and validity. *Archives of General Psychiatry, 38*(4), 381–389.

Sarró, S., Dueñas, R. M., Ramı´rez, N., Arranz, B., Martı´nez, R., Sánchez, J. M., et al. (2004). Cross-cultural adaptation and validation of the Spanish version of the Calgary Depression Scale for Schizophrenia. *Schizophrenia Research, 68*, 349–356.

Selten, J.-P., Veen, N., Feller, W., Blom, J. D., Kahn, R., Schols, D., et al. (2001). Incidence of psychotic disorders in immigrant groups to The Netherlands. *The British Journal of Psychiatry, 178*(4), 367–372.

Shibre, T., Negash, A., Kullgren, G., Kebede, D., Alem, A., Fekadu, A., et al. (2001). Perception of stigma among family members of individuals with schizophrenia and major affective disorders in rural Ethiopia. *Social Psychiatry and Psychiatric Epidemiology, 36*(6), 299–303.

Shin, S.-K., & Lukens, E. P. (2002). Effects of psychoeducation for Korean Americans with chronic mental illness. *Psychiatric Services, 53*, 1125–1131. https://doi.org/10.1176/appi.ps.53.9.1125.

Shorter, E. (1997). *A history of psychiatry: From the era of the asylum to the age of Prozac*. New York: Wiley and Sons.

Simon, P. (2008). The choice of ignorance: The debate on ethnic and racial statistics in France. *French Politics, Culture & Society, 26*(1), 7–31.

Stevens, L. H., Spencer, H. M., & Turkington, D. (2017). Identifying four subgroups of trauma in psychosis: Vulnerability, psychopathology, and treatment. *Frontiers in Psychiatry, 8*, 21.

Sue, S. (2006). Cultural competency: From philosophy to research and practice. *Journal of Community Psychology, 34*(2), 237–245.

Susser, E., & Martínez-Alés, G. (2018). Putting psychosis into sociocultural context: An international study in 17 locations. *JAMA Psychiatry, 75*(1), 9–10.

Tervalon, M., & Murray-Garcia, J. (1998). Cultural humility versus cultural competence: A critical distinction in defining physician training outcomes in multicultural education. *Journal of Health Care for the Poor and Underserved, 9*(2), 117–125.

Thara, R., Kamath, S., & Kumar, S. (2003). Women with schizophrenia and broken marriages-doubly disadvantaged? Part I: Patient perspective. *International Journal of Social Psychiatry, 49*(3), 225–232.

Thornicroft, G., Brohan, E., Rose, D., Sartorius, N., Leese, M., & Group, I. S (2009). Global pattern of experienced and anticipated discrimination against people with schizophrenia: A cross-sectional survey. *The Lancet, 373*, 408–415.

Valencia, M., Rascon, M. L., Juarez, F., Escamilla, R., Saracco, R., & Liberman, R. P. (2010). Application in Mexico of psychosocial rehabilitation with schizophrenia patients. *Psychiatry: Interpersonal and Biological Processes, 73*, 248–263. https://doi.org/10.1521/psyc.2010.73.3.248.

van Wijngaarden, B., Schene, A., Koeter, M., Becker, T., Knapp, M., Knudsen, H. C., et al. (2003). People with schizophrenia in five countries: Conceptual similarities and intercultural differences in family caregiving. *Schizophrenia Bulletin, 29*, 573.

Velligan, D. I., Rubin, M., Fredrick, M. M., Mintz, J., Nuechterlein, K. H., Schooler, N. R., et al. (2010). The cultural adaptability of intermediate measures of functional outcome in schizophrenia. *Schizophrenia Bulletin, 38*, 630–641.

Wang, P. S., Wang, P. S., Lane, M., Lane, M., Olfson, M., Olfson, M., et al. (2005). Twelve-month use of mental health services in the United States. *Archives of General Psychiatry, 62*, 629–640.

Weisman, A., Duarte, E., Koneru, V., & Wasserman, S. (2006). The development of a culturally informed, family-focused treatment for schizophrenia. *Family Process, 45*, 171–186.

White, R., Bebbington, P., Pearson, J., Johnson, S., & Ellis, D. (2000). The social context of insight in schizophrenia. *Social Psychiatry and Psychiatric Epidemiology, 35*(11), 500–507.

Whitley, R. (2016). Ethno-racial variation in recovery from severe mental illness: A qualitative comparison. *The Canadian Journal of Psychiatry, 6*(16), 340–347.

Whitley, R., Wang, J., Fleury, M.-J., Liu, A., & Caron, J. (2017). Mental health status, health care utilisation, and service satisfaction among immigrants in Montreal: An epidemiological comparison. *The Canadian Journal of Psychiatry, 62*, 570–579.

WHO. (1990). *Composite International Diagnostic Interview (CIDI): (a) CIDI interview (version 1.0); (b) CIDI user manual; (c) CIDI training manual; (d) CIDI computer programs*. Geneva: World Health Organization.

WHO. (2015). *Mental health atlas 2014*. Geneva: World Health Organization.

Williams, R. (1999). Cultural safety—What does it mean for our work practice? *Australian and New Zealand Journal of Public Health, 23*(2), 213–214. https://doi.org/10.1111/j.1467-842X.1999.tb01240.x.

Wing, J. K., Babor, T. T., Brugha, T. T., Burke, J., Cooper, J. E., Giel, R., et al. (1990). Scan: Schedules for clinical assessment in neuropsychiatry. *Archives of General Psychiatry, 47*(6), 589–593. https://doi.org/10.1001/archpsyc.1990.01810180089012.

Wing, J. K., Birley, J. L., Cooper, J. E., Graham, P., & Isaacs, A. D. (1967). Reliability of a procedure for measuring and classifying "present psychiatric state". *The British Journal of Psychiatry, 113*(498), 499–515.

Wing, J. K., Sartorius, N., & Üstün, T. B. (1998). *Diagnosis and clinical measurement in psychiatry: A reference manual for SCAN.* Cambridge University Press.

Wittchen, H.-U. (1994). Reliability and validity studies of the WHO-Composite International Diagnostic Interview (CIDI): A critical review. *Journal of Psychiatric Research, 28*(1), 57–84.

World Health Organization. (2018). *Process of translation and adaptation of instruments.* Retrieved August 8, 2018 from: http://www.who.int/substance_abuse/research_tools/translation/en/#.

Yang, J., Law, S., Chow, W., Andermann, L., Steinberg, R., & Sadavoy, J. (2005). Best practices: Assertive community treatment for persons with severe and persistent mental illness in ethnic minority groups. *Psychiatric Services, 56*(9), 1053–1055.

Zandi, T., Havenaar, J., Smits, M., Limburg-Okken, A., Van Es, H., Cahn, W., et al. (2010). First contact incidence of psychotic disorders among native Dutch and Moroccan immigrants in the Netherlands: Influence of diagnostic bias. *Schizophrenia Research, 119*(1), 27–33.

Zandi, T., Havenaar, J. M., Laan, W., Kahn, R. S., & van den Brink, W. (2016). Effects of a culturally sensitive assessment on symptom profiles in native Dutch and Moroccan patients with a first psychosis referral. *Transcultural Psychiatry, 53*(1), 45–59.

Zandi, T., Havenaar, J. M., Limburg-Okken, A. G., Van Es, H., Sidali, S., Kadri, N., et al. (2008). The need for culture sensitive diagnostic procedures. *Social Psychiatry and Psychiatric Epidemiology, 43*(3), 244–250.

Definition of Key Terms

Category fallacy The application of diagnostic categories from one culture onto a sample of deviant behaviour from another. Diagnostic categories are cultural categories and as such are not culture free.

Cultural competence Attitudes, skills, and knowledge that permit effective clinical evaluation and treatment of clients from diverse backgrounds.

Cultural consultation Clinical assessment of how ethnicity, gender, class, language, migration, religion, and history influence the expression of distress.

Cultural formulation A heuristic framework for organising cultural clinical material, such as the Outline for Cultural Formulation proposed in the DSM-IV and DSM-5. Typical aspects include identity, explanations of distress, cultural stressors and resilience factors, the clinician–client relationship, and an overall synthesis.

Cultural humility In the clinical encounter, acknowledging the limits of Euro-American mental health paradigms and focusing on what can be learned from diverse perspectives.

Cultural safety In the clinical encounter, acknowledging the power differences that exist between the clinician and client—not just by virtue of their roles in the therapy, but also due to historical legacies of oppression and marginalisation that may be of relevance.

Culture The taken for granted; the evolving social environment; shared values, beliefs, attitudes, and expectations; the sacred and taboo—all that informs the world of human relations and is handed down from one generation to the next.

Cultural broker A person who bridges two cultures, often the professional culture of the clinician with the culture of the client, family, or community.

CHAPTER 5

The Recovery Model and Psychosis

Bethany L. Leonhardt[*,†], **Jay A. Hamm**[†,‡], **Paul H. Lysaker**[*,§]
[*]Indiana University School of Medicine, Department of Psychiatry, Indianapolis, IN, United States, [†]Eskenazi Health Midtown Community Mental Health, Indianapolis, IN, United States, [‡]Purdue University, College of Pharmacy, West Lafayette, IN, United States, [§]Roudebush Veteran Affairs Medical Center, Indianapolis, IN, United States

Key Learning Objectives

- Identify the tenets of the recovery movement and understand the historical context from which they emerge.
- Understand ways to implement interventions that promote recovery for persons with psychosis.
- Identify how five central components of recovery-oriented practice are related to ethical practice for psychologists.

INTRODUCTION

Recovery is the desired and achievable outcome for persons with serious mental illnesses, including psychosis. Yet it remains a topic fraught with controversy, posing challenges that must be dealt with by psychologists and other mental health professionals at both theoretical and practical levels. There are many reasons for the current controversy, including stigma, historical context, and political issues within mental healthcare. In this chapter, we seek to make the concept of recovery available to inform the practice of clinical and neuropsychologists. To do so, we review the history of the recovery movement and explore a range of definitions of recovery. We then discuss the tenets of the recovery model and the evidence supporting it, including first-person accounts, quantitative, and qualitative research. Finally, we discuss recovery-oriented practice and factors that could either hinder or promote recovery. To illustrate and concretise the

Recovery: the desired and achievable outcome for people with psychosis.

A Clinical Introduction to Psychosis. https://doi.org/10.1016/B978-0-12-815012-2.00005-5

implications of these concepts for clinical and neuropsychologists, we offer two case examples of individuals we have encountered in our respective clinical settings who were able to move towards self-directed recovery.

HISTORICAL VIEWS AND EMERGENCE OF THE RECOVERY MOVEMENT

Pessimistic views of outcome from serious mental illnesses date back to the early definitions of these conditions. Throughout history, an incomplete understanding of mental illness and recovery has been linked with a chequered history of iatrogenic and often inhumane treatments offered to, or forced upon, individuals with psychosis. Over the last two centuries, mainstream treatments for people diagnosed with serious mental illnesses have included a long list of interventions that resulted in harm, demoralisation, and undermined movements towards independence. A nonexhaustive list of such interventions includes emetics (medicine, rotator machines), hydrotherapies (simulated drowning, forced baths, wet wraps), shock therapies (metrazol, insulin coma, electroconvulsive), psychosurgery (e.g. lobotomy, leucotomy), and various means of control and incarceration (Hinshaw, 2017; Whitaker, 2002). This list highlights a long history of frequent shifts wherein mainstream treatment practices were later eliminated and viewed as inhumane. Often, however, these treatments were given without consent and rarely were patient preferences considered. It is not surprising that ideas about the possibility for recovery were uncommon given that what was accepted as treatment could hardly improve mental health. It is thus possible that views of outcome and the treatments offered became caught up in a recursive loop, with pessimism about the capabilities of these persons leading to forced interventions that demoralised or physically harmed individuals, making good outcomes even less possible.

This is not to suggest the history of treatment of mental illness involved uniform inhumanity or cruelty. Within the history of the treatment of serious mental illnesses such as psychosis were multiple individuals and group reform movements; for instance the parallel efforts of the Tukes and Pinel known as Moral Treatment, social reform efforts by Dix, early written first-person accounts of recovery from serious mental illness (Beers, 1908; Frame, 1860), as well as a number of early 20th century psychotherapists who argued for the possibilities of therapy as a way to support meaningful recovery in psychosis (King, Viney, & Woody, 2009).

Despite these early attempts at reform, by the late 1900s, serious mental illness remained linked with a quite pessimistic outlook. In perhaps the most prominent and influential example of this, Kraepelin's 'dementia praecox', characterised psychotic disorders as early forms of dementia, expected to follow a chronic, deteriorating course. Within these early models, individuals who appeared to get better were believed to have been misdiagnosed as it was accepted that poor prognosis was a defining feature of disorder. Recovery was thus not considered a viable possibility, and clinical efforts were focused on management and attempts to slow progression of illness.

Partially motivated by desire to challenge the conventional pessimism, Bleuler offered a reformulation of dementia praecox and introduced the term 'schizophrenia' in the early 1900s. Bleuler, who had lived and worked closely with patients experiencing psychosis, emphasised the heterogeneity of outcomes that he witnessed. Despite Bleuler's more optimistic casting of outcomes, the pessimistic prognosis associated with psychosis has been an enduring feature of lay and professional perspectives, despite findings from multiple levels of evidence supporting Bleuler's views.

Evidence of variability in outcomes challenges the pessimistic prognosis previously associated with psychosis.

Consistent with Bleuler's observations, empirical research has repeatedly found broad variability of outcomes, suggesting that many, if not most, persons who experience psychosis can become well (e.g. Carpenter & Strauss, 1991; Ciompi, 1980; Harding, Brooks, Ashikaga, et al., 1987). In addition to epidemiological findings, a grassroots movement that gained increased visibility in the 1980s and 1990s began to challenge the idea that individuals with serious mental illness could at best achieve stability or avoid negative outcomes such as hospitalisation and incarceration. This movement, known as the recovery movement, argued for a broader and more individualised understanding of what recovery in mental health means and called for substantial reform to mental health services. Early on, guiding these efforts Anthony (1993) described recovery as: "*...a deeply personal, unique process of changing one's attitudes, values, feelings, goals, skills, and/or roles... It is a way of living a satisfying, hopeful, and contributing life even with the limitations caused by illness.*" (p. 527). By the early 2000s, the findings from the recovery movement had gained more professional and political influence, with many guidelines for mental health treatment, including the core tenets of the recovery movement. The broad shifts in guidelines towards the expectation that professional services embrace recovery appears a major success for the recovery movement; though like any paradigm shift, recovery approaches continue to face a number of barriers for more complete implementation in routine clinical practice and in the public imagination.

One such barrier is the persistence of stigma of mental illness or widely held societally based beliefs regarding mental illnesses, and schizophrenia in particular (Yanos, 2018). The persistent stigma includes unsupported and pessimistic views of recovery, as well as associated beliefs about competence, dangerousness, and social acceptance. As explored in more detail earlier in this book (see Chapter 3), mental health professionals, including psychologists, are not immune to stigmatising views about people with mental illness and tend to reflect the same views as the lay public, including that psychosis, more than other mental health diagnoses, is associated with dangerousness and incompetence (Smith, Mittal, Chekuri, Han, & Sullivan, 2017). These stigmatising views appear to be a direct barrier to successful implementation of recovery model in practice settings explored and are likely reinforced by the availability bias or 'the clinician's illusion' (Cohen & Cohen, 1984), in which clinician views are shaped

Stigmatising views about psychosis can pose a barrier to recovery-oriented practice.

Availability bias: the tendency to let examples that come easily to mind influence decision making.

by having more contact with more severely ill individuals. While clinicians are more likely to see individuals during their time of greatest need, they often have less contact with individuals who recover quickly or who never enter the mental health system at all, making the group that clinicians encounter in daily practice unrepresentative of the diverse outcomes individuals diagnosed with psychosis experience. Clinicians are thus at risk of generalising their experiences with the most severely ill individuals to all people experiencing psychosis, reinforcing beliefs that psychosis has an enduring, deteriorating course (Cohen & Cohen, 1984).

An additional barrier to complete implementation of recovery approaches in practice stems from the diverse and sometimes contradictory ways in which 'recovery' has been conceptualised as well as ongoing efforts to more clearly articulate and find consensus on what constitutes 'recovery-oriented practice'. To address these important considerations, we will next explore the ways in which the term recovery has been operationalised and review the related evidence.

MULTIPLE DEFINITIONS OF RECOVERY

Objective and Subjective Definitions of Recovery

Prior to the recovery movement, the term recovery was used to describe clinical outcomes, usually synonymous with symptom remission. With the recovery movement, there was a paradigm shift that moved from *recovery from* a disease state to *recovery in*, or the process of reclaiming one's life and living a satisfying life regardless of symptom remission (Davidson & Roe, 2007). Although instances of clinical recovery as an outcome have been found in early texts, the use of the term recovery as process can be seen to parallel the tradition within the substance abuse field to describe the ongoing process by which individuals attempt to combat addiction.

One of the challenges for clinical and neuropsychologists trying to practice within the recovery model is the inconsistent operationalisation of the term recovery (Leonhardt et al., 2017). Specifically, some have used the term recovery to refer to clinical outcomes (also called clinical recovery or objective recovery; Silverstein & Bellack, 2004). Examples of these include studies that refer to recovery as a matter of symptom remission (Kane, 2013) or the attainment of levels of psychosocial role functioning such as working or attending school for a varying period of time. In these studies, recovery involves the measurable achievement of objective states determined by others for amounts of time, which may differ from study to study. From this perspective then, a person would be said to be recovered after they no longer experienced significant levels of symptoms and or had attained some form of recognised role function including participating in one's larger community.

Objective recovery is defined in relation to measureable clinical outcomes, e.g. symptom remission, defined by others.

By contrast, others have referred to recovery as a primarily subjective phenomenon (also called subjective recovery or personal recovery; Lysaker, Hamm, Hasson-Ohayon, Pattison, & Leonhardt, 2018). Examples of these include

Subjective recovery is defined by the self, based on personally valued goals and preferences.

studies that refer to recovery as a matter of attaining a personally defined acceptable quality of life or recapturing a rich and full sense of self. In these studies, recovery involves in part a judgement made by the person diagnosed with the condition regarding how they and their life are progressing. Subjective recovery poses the additional challenge of trying to operationalise a process that is unique to each individual. However, through qualitative studies and meetings that involved many types of stakeholders in the recovery movement, several core elements of personal recovery have been identified. The Substance Abuse and Mental Health Services Administration (SAMHSA, 2012) in the USA has offered one such list of core principles, which includes self-direction, holistic approaches, individualised, empowerment, nonlinear paths, strengths-based, peer support, respect, responsibility, and hope. Of note, consistent with the fact that objective and subjective domains of recovery are conceptually distinct, empirical research has suggested that they may exist independently (Jorgensen et al., 2015).

Views of Recovery Internationally

While recovery has been conceptualised in parallel ways, which differ according to whether objective or subjective phenomena are its defining features, a broader understanding of recovery calls for consideration of larger societal and cultural contexts. The views of recovery in Westernised countries tend to be similar and evoke similar principles to the guidelines mentioned earlier in this chapter from SAMHSA (Gopal & Henderson, 2015); however, it is important to note that the definition of recovery may change in different cultural contexts, and should be reflective of the values of society as well as that of the individual (Greenberg, Kalian, & Witzum, 2010; Noordsy et al., 2002). Recent work has explored subjective recovery in eastern and collectivist cultures (Ng et al., 2008; Tse, Cheung, Kan, Ng, & Yau, 2012) and emphasised the importance of understanding how some of the values of recovery fit within the surrounding culture and offer individualised care. For example, individuals living in the USA might value independent living highly, whereas an individual living in India may not find this as desirable an option and value interdependence instead, as it is common for family members to live together (Gopal & Henderson, 2015). Thus, recovery must be personal and culturally informed to match the unique needs of the individual.

ONGOING RESEARCH ON RECOVERY

Since it has been recognised that older pessimistic appraisals of outcome in psychosis were a matter of expectation rather than fact, research on recovery has grown exponentially. This also poses a challenge to clinical and neuropsychologists, as this work is truly multimodal and includes first-person accounts, qualitative and qualitative work and requires integration of information from these multiple sources. It is important to integrate multiple sources of information to eliminate any potential bias and offer an in-depth view of the evidence for recovery.

Beginning with first-person accounts of mental illness, rooted in a centuries-old tradition of individuals writing about their experiences of psychosis and recovery (Hornstein, 2009), these involve descriptions of persons' personal experiences of the challenges and successes they have faced with psychosis. These accounts render the experience of psychosis recognisable within the continuum of human experience. As such, they humanise medicalised perspectives on psychosis, reduce stigma, inform practice, offer outcome data, and advocate for the rights of individuals experiencing psychosis.

First person accounts go beyond listing symptoms and offer a picture of a unique person with a unique experience, living with and responding to the challenges of psychosis. They allow for a sense of what hospitalisation may be like, what it is like to be treated by healthcare professionals, and what kinds of things constitute success and wellness. These offer clinicians a counterpoint to the clinician's illusion (Cohen & Cohen, 1984) and other enduring pessimism about the potential outcomes for individuals experiencing serious mental illness (Greenberg et al., 2010). While they defy being collapsed into a few bullet points, these stories tell us that for recovery to be possible, persons diagnosed with psychosis have to make sense of the things they face in their own ways, according to their own unique background and perspective (Hornstein, 2009). Recovery also requires that persons take charge of their own recovery (Deegan, 2002). Across reports, we see that an essential component is becoming in charge of one's own life and rejecting a sense of self based on passivity or identification with disability (e.g. Korsbek, 2016; Saks, 2007).

First-person evidence suggests that recovery is often linked to a sense of being in charge of one's own life.

Qualitative research on recovery, in parallel, has largely focused on describing the process of recovery through content and thematic analyses of interviews with individuals experiencing psychosis and qualitatively analysing these interviews. Largely, qualitative analyses of interviews about the process of recovery with consumers identify social connection, sense of agency, personal meaning making of mental health experiences, hope, and sense of self (Connell, Schweitzer, & King, 2015; Cotton & Loewenthal, 2015; Leamy, Bird, Le Boutilier, Williams, & Slade, 2011). Leamy et al. (2011) have synthesised these concepts in their CHIME model: Connectedness to others; Hope and optimism; Identity; Meaning; and Empowerment. In an exploration of the principles set forth by SAMHSA, Ellison, Belanger, Niles, Evans, and Bauer (2018) conducted a thematic analysis of the recovery components that emerged across 67 different reviews of the concept and found that the four components of recovery with the most concordance were person-centred, empowerment, purpose, and hope. McCarthy-Jones, Marriott, Knowles, Rowse, and Thompson (2013) conducted a metasynthesis of qualitative studies of the first-person experience of psychosis and reported a pattern across studies of broad losses in sense of self, relationships, and life direction. These findings have appeared consistently in different countries (Jose et al., 2015) and emphasise how cross culturally, recovery is a nonlinear process and the essential process of making meaning of one's experiences to establish agency, hope, and a sense of oneself as more than a mental patient (Yarborough, Yarborough, Janoff, & Green, 2016).

Sense of agency involves feeling in control of making decisions in one's own life; having self-direction.

Finally, one arm of qualitative research on recovery has explored the incidence of objective aspects of recovery. As we have summarised elsewhere (Leonhardt et al., 2017), in early psychosis studies, with follow up that ranged from 6 months to 10 years, reported symptom remission was achieved for 37%–91.4% of the samples, functional recovery was achieved for 29%–58%, and 14%–29.5% achieved a period of both symptom remission and functional recovery. For individuals with more prolonged psychosis, with follow-up periods ranging from cross sectional to 20 years, symptom remission was achieved in 37%–89% of the samples, functional recovery in 21%–53% of the sample, and 13%–27% experienced both symptom remission and functional recovery for some period of time (Leonhardt et al., 2017). The data are summarised in Fig. 5.1.

We provide the data to illustrate the point that many, if not most, individuals experiencing psychosis will achieve some level of objective recovery, challenging the myth that a deteriorating course of psychosis is inevitable. Importantly, this research also has limitations, as the ranges of outcomes are wide and likely a result of different study methods. The range of outcomes and variety of study methods makes comparing across studies difficult as well as posing challenges to translate these findings into particular clinical contexts.

A second arm of qualitative research has been simultaneously devoted to developing ways to quantify some of the more subjective elements of recovery. Reviews of these instruments (Cavelti, Kvrgic, Beck, Kossowsky, & Vauth, 2012; Law, Morrison, & Byrne, 2012) have concluded that while a gold standard has not yet been created, there are several self-report instruments with acceptable psychometric qualities and consumer input that appear to measure subjective recovery. These include the Recovery Assessment Scale (RAS; Corrigan, Giffort,

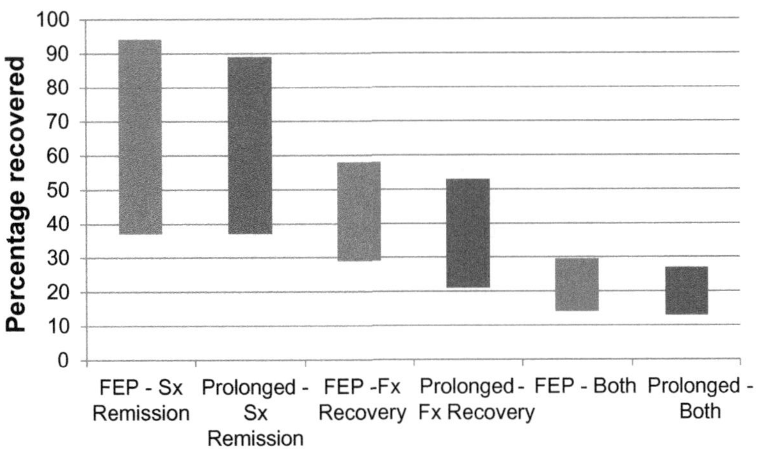

FIG. 5.1

Rates of objective recovery for FEP and prolonged psychosis samples. Note: *FEP*, First episode psychosis; *Sx*, Symptom remission; *Fx*, Functional recovery; *Both*, symptom and functional recovery.

Rashid, Leary, & Okeke, 1999)—that measures five domains of subjective recovery: personal confidence and hope, goal and success orientation, willingness to ask for help, connection with others, and not feeling dominated by symptoms—the Recovery Process Inventory (RPI; Jerrell, Cousins, & Roberts, 2006), Mental Health Recovery Measure (MHRM; Campbell-Orde, Chamberlin, Carpenter, & Leff, 2005), and Stages of Recovery Inventory (STORI; Andresen, Caputi, & Oades, 2006). Many of these assessments are freely available for use in studies and clinics. Cross sectional studies using these instruments have found intriguing evidence that subjective recovery is influenced by depressive symptoms (Jorgensen et al., 2015), social support, and attachment security (Gumley, Taylor, Schwannauer, & MacBeth, 2014; Stumbo, Yarborough, Paulson, & Green, 2015; Topor, Borg, di Girolomo, & Davidson, 2011). In a recent review and thematic analysis, Soundy et al. (2015) note that positive recovery outcomes are promoted by the ability to adjust to experiencing psychosis, responding to the illness, and social support. Conversely, they found that negative social interactions, internal barriers, and hopelessness tended to hinder recovery outcomes. These findings help to understand what may hinder or promote subjective recovery, and offer important clinical considerations.

RECOVERY-ORIENTED PRACTICE

As we have so far reviewed, pessimistic views of outcome in psychosis have been challenged by the recovery movement and its attendant research base. While the concept of recovery remains complex and yet to be fully articulated, there are clear implications for the practice of clinical and neuropsychologists. The overarching value of these implications is that recovery-oriented practice is not a matter of delivering a specific intervention. To be explicit, what determines whether an intervention is recovery oriented is as much the conditions under which it is delivered as is it content of that intervention. Recovery-oriented practice could be implemented from a cognitive behavioural, humanistic, psychodynamic, or rehabilitative framework. What we suggest makes an intervention truly a recovery-oriented practice has to do with how the recovering person is approached during the interventions and how they are positioned to either move towards or away from recovery.

For the sake of clarity, we have divided these conditions into six different components, though each clearly overlaps some with the others. To frame each component, we will discuss how they are not only essential for wellness but also for ethical practice as required by the principles of the American Psychological Association's ethical code (APA, 2016), and equivalent professional practice guidelines internationally. Specifically, these six components relate to Principles A and E, presented in Box 5.1.

(1) Psychologists Must Acknowledge and Reject Stigma

For any intervention to be recovery oriented, we suggest that it must first acknowledge and reject stigma. As long as individuals diagnosed with psychosis

Box 5.1 Ethical Principles for Psychologists[a]

Principle A, Beneficence and Nonmaleficence states, "Psychologists strive to benefit those with whom they work and take care to do no harm... psychologists seek to safeguard the welfare and rights of those with whom they interact professionally and other affected persons ... Because psychologists' scientific and professional judgments and actions may affect the lives of others, they are alert to and guard against personal, financial, social, organizational, or political factors that might lead to misuse of their influence...".

Principle E, Respect for Persons' Rights and Dignity states, "Psychologists respect the dignity and worth of all people, and the rights of individuals to privacy, confidentiality, and self-determination. Psychologists are aware that special safeguards may be necessary to protect the rights and welfare of persons or communities whose vulnerabilities impair autonomous decision making. Psychologists are aware of and respect cultural, individual, and role differences, including those based on age, gender ... and consider these factors when working with members of such groups. Psychologists try to eliminate the effect on their work of biases based on those factors, and they do not knowingly participate in or condone activities of others based upon such prejudices."

[a]American Psychological Association's ethical code (APA, 2016).

accept stigma, clearly there cannot be a full movement towards recovery. However, this is not merely a matter that is left up to the patient to accept or reject. We suggest that the APA's ethical principles A and E both require that psychologists remain vigilant and on guard against joining explicitly or tacitly stigmatising beliefs which work against recovery. Principle A warns against doing harm by virtue of the influence of psychologists. The opinions of a psychologist can carry great weight for recovering persons, and any implicit or explicit behaviour on the part of the psychologist that suggests the patient is incompetent or dangerous would work against health. It may incline persons with psychosis to accept the negative images of themselves prevalent in social discourse (e.g. see themselves as unstable and dangerous). It may also put in place self-fulfilling prophecies of failure (Firmin et al., 2018; Lysaker, Davis, Warman, Strasburger, & Beattie, 2007), and negate any chance of achieving a more complex understanding of themselves that is necessary to move towards personal recovery. Similarly, Principle E calls for the promotion of autonomy and again, stigmatising beliefs on the part of the psychologist here would work against autonomy and pose an ethical dilemma.

Recovery-oriented practice: requires acknowledging and changing stigmatising views about people with psychosis.

Psychologists must, therefore, be aware of their own stigmatising views, including not only negative beliefs but also covert stigma that might be found in seemingly benign interventions in which, for instance, psychologists expect significantly less competency of the consumer than they do of others or of themselves. Stigma may appear in psychologists' attitudes when they are less interested in consumers' own understanding of life events and are more concerned that consumers accept that they are experiencing a disorder or illness. Stigma may also present when psychologists are unwilling to share difficult or negative feedback, seeing the consumer as in part a child who cannot 'handle the truth'.

(2) Recovery Is Possible

Recovery-oriented practice: means accepting that individuals experiencing psychosis can recover.

Continuing to think about the influence of psychologists noted in Principle A, a second essential component of recovery-oriented practice is the acceptance that individuals experiencing psychosis can and do recover. Here we refer not to an acceptance of this as an abstract thought, but that the unique individual the psychologist is consulting with is someone who can recover. This can be complicated, however, by any number of factors. Trying to understand the experience of another person who is in the midst of acute psychosis or in a highly dysregulated state can be frightening and confusing for psychologists. It can be difficult to think when in the company of someone actively experiencing the world as fragmented, and efforts geared towards understanding become more difficult when added to a history of pessimism about the course of psychosis and the human tendency to interpret the states of others as enduring traits. Well-meaning psychologists can still be tempted to believe that a specific person in this situation can at best resolve acute problems and achieve something called 'stability', and come to think that the specific person in front of him/her as genuinely unable to recover. This is likely further reinforced in institutions in which staff at all levels only talk about 'stability', rather than growth that could be expected.

Likewise, consumers who have been indoctrinated to think of themselves as helpless or who have come to feel comfortable with the sick role and potentially terrified of giving it up can also complicate acknowledgement of potential for recovery in the person sitting before them. Given pressures in the moment and the pressures that persist within larger institutional structures, it is easy to see how clinicians can routinely lose sight that recovery is *always* possible, and that it may look differently for different persons. Thus, for psychologists to truly adopt this belief, they must tolerate their own anxiety, be flexible, and know that the path to recovery is not always clear. This component may hinder recovery if the psychologist does not manage their own certainty of what is possible for an individual and comes to embrace the notion that recovery is not possible for a particular individual or population. Additionally, it is important not to adopt an overly optimistic view that may not be shared by the consumer, or may be neglectful of the real difficulties an individual faces (Stuart, Tansey, & Quayle, 2017). As in the first component of recovery-oriented practice, we call to mind Principle E requires we promote autonomy, and psychologists thus have an ethical obligation to not lose sight that recovery is possible.

Recovery-oriented practice: has an ethical foundation, which endorses that recovery is possible.

(3) Recovery Is Self-Directed

Recovery-oriented practice: requires awareness that recovery is best promoted when primarily directed by the consumer.

The third component that defines a recovery-oriented practice is awareness that recovery occurs when primarily directed by the consumer (Davidson & Roe, 2007; Deegan, 2002; Hamm, Buck, Leonhardt, Luther, & Lysaker, 2017). An individual is moving towards recovery when they are an active participant in making decisions about the unique life at hand rather than as a passive recipient of care. For psychologists, we see the same threats to carrying out this component as in the first, including psychologists being required to tolerate and attempt to understand persons who may be in the midst of acute psychosis, pervasively demoralised, cacophonous, barren, or in a highly dysregulated state. Such states can provoke anxiety and the immediate sense that the psychologist must take charge of this person in this circumstance. This is not to say that there will never come a time in which a psychologist must take action, as crises can emerge, and firm action is needed (e.g. acute risk for self-harm). Those states are also likely reinforced by institutional factors, including heightened concern over safety, or consumers who may be demoralised or have decided they should reject agency and resist taking charge of their own path. However, recovery may be hindered if the psychologist fails to establish, or loses along the way, the idea that a unique individual can get to a place of directing personal recovery. This involves what can be called 'the dignity of risk', in that it allows individuals to make choices for their own lives about what matters to them and what paths to pursue (Ragins & Pollack, 2013). If psychologists fail to establish this component in their practice, they will likely play into iatrogenic factors of mental health care that reinforce to consumers that they are not capable of making choices about their own lives (Bentall, 1990). It is not uncommon for many who experience psychosis and other forms of serious mental illness to be forced or coerced into treatment at times. These experiences can often be quite painful and at times traumatic for consumers, and to support self-direction in recovery, it is important for psychologists to attend to these factors and experiences when assisting persons towards recovery. Again, this seems a requirement of Principle E and any efforts, which hinder it, would be prohibited by Principle A.

(4) Nonhierarchical Relationship

The fourth component of a recovery-oriented practice concerns the relationship, and can be seen as flowing directly from Principles A and E. It posits that the consumer-psychologist relationship must be nonhierarchical, which is essential if psychologists are to genuinely assist persons in directing their own recovery. Again, in real practice, this is not always very simple and may be challenged by many factors, including that some consumers have been socialised by exposure to the mental health system, and perhaps by messages embedded in our larger social discourse, to see clinicians as more powerful and knowing than they are. It is not uncommon to encounter consumers relating stories in which they ignored medical advice, experienced something undesirable, and then decided as a result that they no longer trust their own judgement. Psychologists also possess power through expertise, the fact that they are paid, appointments are generally in the psychologist's office, and the potential to hospitalise consumers against their will. We do not dispute that there is a power differential inherent in clinical practice, but we argue that psychologists must seek to be thought of, first and foremost, as a consultant who offers reflection and challenges that may be accepted or rejected by the consumer. There must be constant negotiation about the working alliance and the role of each within it

(Hasson-Ohayon, Kravetz, & Lysaker, 2016). Importantly, having a nonhierarchical relationship does not require that psychologists give up or deny their expertise, but that the psychologist-consumer relationship reflects a dialogue. This seems naturally to be a condition of Principles A and E.

Recovery-oriented practice: initiates a nonhierarchical relationship between psychologist and consumer.

(5) The Experience of Psychosis Can Be Understood

The fifth component of a recovery-oriented practice requires that psychologists see the consumer as a whole person and as psychotic experiences are on the continuum of human experience and thus are able to be understood (Leonhardt, Hamm, Fogley, Buck, & Lysaker, 2015). This principle is essential to assist consumers in making meaning of psychotic experiences, which are often confusing and emotionally laden but also ripe with personal meaning, as consumers navigate the path to recovery. Symptoms will likely occur within the course of treatment and psychologists must resist treating consumers' unusual thoughts and experiences as something to be removed or snuffed out and instead regard such experiences as potentially meaningful, including the content of delusions, and that such symptoms are likely connected to the path of recovery for the individual. This is consistent with research that finds that symptoms emerge from clear factors, including emotional distress and vulnerability (Belanger, Leonhardt, George, Firmin, & Lysaker, 2017; Hamm, Buck, & Lysaker, 2015; Leonhardt et al., 2017; Searles, 1965). Given that psychotic experiences are tied to factors such as emotional distress and vulnerability, psychologists who do not treat such experiences as potentially meaningful and deserving of exploration risk stigmatising and 'othering' the consumer, suggesting to the consumer that they are somehow damaged, defective, or otherwise unlike their fellow humans, which clearly does not support the spirit of recovery.

Concerning the ethical requirements of this condition, we suggest that again it is the influence of the psychologist noted in Principle A, which should be monitored to ensure that it is not employed in a manner than diminishes the humanity of the consumer.

(6) Greater Levels of Awareness Are Linked With Greater Pain

In recovery-oriented practice, psychologists need to be aware that pain often accompanies the process of recovery.

Finally, we suggest that recovery-oriented practice requires that the psychologist be aware that pain often accompanies the process of recovery and anticipate that different kinds of pain are likely to emerge. As persons form an increasingly complex sense of themselves and their lives, it can lead to deep distress in several different ways, including a sense of loss of past identities and the pain of forming new aspects of identity (Buck et al., 2013; Degen & Nasper, 1996). Overall, we believe understanding the emergence of pain positions psychologists to anticipate the need to foster an atmosphere allowing for consumers to feel safe experiencing and discussing pain in session (Liotti & Gilbert, 2011). Psychologists must be attentive to affective disturbances in consumers and be willing to actively assist them to manage painful affects by naming and discussing these affects as they emerge. The atmosphere of the therapeutic relationship needs to be such that both the psychologist and consumer can accept the consumer's pain without alarm, and with the expectation that pain can be understood and endured in the context of a compassionate exchange with others. Without being attuned to the likelihood of the emergence of grief and loss along the path to recovery, psychologists may invalidate consumers' experiences, or be overly focused on new gains the individual is making, without attending to the complex nature of what recovery truly entails. This is a requirement of Principle A, which calls for responsible attention to be paid to the negative consequences, which come from any intervention.

Limitations

Of note, there are some limitations important to consider related to the concept of recovery-oriented practice. As mentioned earlier, recovery-oriented practice is flexible, and much of what determines whether an intervention or mode of treatment is recovery-oriented is if it supports the tenets of the recovery movement. As such, there are many types of practices that can fit under this umbrella (or not, depending on how the individual provider is approaching it). This level of flexibility poses challenges to assessing whether particular treatments are recovery oriented, as there is much variability. Thus, it can be difficult to assess the efficacy of recovery-oriented treatments unless studies are designed to evaluate whether the treatment was offered in a way that is consistent with the recovery model. Additionally, parameters of efficacy would need to be redefined, as traditional models of evaluating the efficacy of treatments often focus on symptoms and psychosocial functioning, and as we have detailed earlier, a recovery-oriented approach focuses instead on helping a unique individual live a personally meaningful life. Thus, the paradigm for evaluating efficacy of treatment would need to be redefined when evaluating recovery-oriented treatment. Future research is needed to develop tools to make these aims possible.

While little exists in the literature about negative consequences of recovery-oriented treatment, it is always possible that any treatment could offer negative or side effects. If health means taking risks, some of those risks may not lead to what persons want or expect. Certainly some consumers, especially those who may identify with a sick role, may not desire to have agency or to direct their own care, and may instead be more comfortable being offered prescriptive treatment. Such instances must be handled sensitively and with respect to the individual consumer. Consistent with basic principles of person-centred care and shared decision making, we view these instances as additional opportunities to invite dialogue and reflection about ambivalence towards a more self-directed stance, as well as potential difficulties or grief associated with relinquishing a familiar social role. As with any treatment, individual differences and preferences must be considered when making decisions about care.

Case Examples

The case examples in Boxes 5.2 and 5.3 are offered to provide clinical illustrations of how the aforementioned components were important in the individual

Box 5.2 Case Example: Lola

Lola was a young woman seen in an early psychosis clinic at a community mental health center. Lola had experienced her first episode of psychosis when she was in high school. Her youth, along with her family's involvement in her treatment, her disposition to be agreeable to others, and provider paternalism resulted in difficulty with shared decision making in her care. With her family and medical professional's urging, she took medication but did not share her preference to have it reduced or discontinued, as she found that the medication impeded her ability to think clearly and made her feel she was losing an essential part of herself, as she has always been quite bright and was an excellent student. She also had a tendency to avoid interpersonal interactions in which she felt a disagreement was possible. For example, she once quit a job she described that she enjoyed after the schedule was changed to be inconsistent with what she had agreed to, but never approached her supervisor to discuss her concerns and see if the schedule could be changed so she could maintain her employment.

Lola engaged in psychotherapy and began to explore different aspects of her identity, including her emerging desire to be an independent adult (she was approaching her early twenties) and her desire to have children while not taking medication that she was told by her prescriber she would need for the rest of her life. Her therapist succeeded in creating and maintaining a nonhierarchical relationship in which her self-directed desires to be independent could be explored, and through this dialogue Lola decided to be more open with her prescriber about her preferences to decrease and eventually stop her antipsychotic. Shared decision making was truly enacted at this point and a plan was made to taper her medication and eventually stop it entirely. Lola has since found a job that she enjoys, is actively dating, is involved with a cultural community that is important to her, and has a strong social support network. She also describes that she is more able to share her opinions without fear of how others will regard her and describes that she feels more in charge of her mental healthcare.

Box 5.3 Case Example: Marie

Marie was a woman in her early 40s, who had received a range of serious mental illness diagnoses (bipolar disorder, schizoaffective disorder, schizophrenia) and had been heavily involved in outpatient community mental health services since her mid-20s. For much of this time, Marie maintained a passive and cooperative stance in services, meeting with staff multiple times per week for various supportive interventions (assistance managing her money, nursing help to prefill medication boxes, home-based support to help with basic maintenance and interactions with her landlord). She heard distressing voices that were intertwined with persecutory delusions, had few friends outside of other clients at the clinic, and had been unemployed for approximately 15 years. She appeared to have high levels of internalised stigma and generally could be seen as inhabiting a sick role.

Marie was a clear example of someone who was largely 'stable' (i.e. independent housing, many years since last hospitalisation, supported by professionals and government benefits). Both Marie and some of her past providers had largely accepted her ongoing level of dysfunction and had limited hope of any additional major changes this many years into her psychiatric difficulties. However, after referral to psychotherapy and supported employment services, she demonstrated a number of gradual shifts towards a more self-directed stance and made significant strides over a four-year period towards improving her quality of life. For one, consistent with the principle noted here regarding the emergence of pain, she was slowly able to acknowledge and express intense anger, sadness, and embarrassment, albeit initially in an amorphous, disorganised manner.

After some time, and in the context of a consultative therapeutic relationship aimed at developing understanding of the pain, she was able to disclose and reflect upon extensive childhood trauma history, a number of interpersonal losses. She found a job at a large retail store, made some friends in the community, found a romantic partner (and

Box 5.3 Case Example: Marie—cont'd

had a painful break-up), and slowly established a clearer account of her life, improved sense of self-efficacy and hope. She applies fewer stigmatising ideas about mental illness to herself. She also made marked gains in independently managing her life, taking over control of her finances for the first time in a decade and learning how to manage her medicine independently without supportive nursing services.

Marie continues to struggle with the impact of multiple traumas on her ability to form trusting relationships with others, occasionally expresses grandiose or paranoid ideas, and continues hearing voices. However, she has formed a clearer personal understanding of the voices, and notes that more often than not now the content of the voices is companionate or flattering. She reports generally positive appraisals of her work functioning by her boss, and notes that despite persistent loneliness the current period represents the most satisfied she has ever been with her life.

recovery of consumers seen by the authors in their clinical settings. Each of the psychologists in these case examples utilised Metacognitive Reflection and Insight Therapy (MERIT; Lysaker & Klion, 2017), a recovery-oriented psychotherapy that includes these six components as core values of the approach. These cases are based on real individuals and have been systematically disguised to protect their confidentiality.

CONCLUSION

Recovery from psychosis is possible, but poses challenges to psychologists and other mental health professionals at both theoretical and practical levels. In order for the reality of recovery to be fully recognised and supported by accompanying recovery-oriented interventions, several adjustments to traditional practice and theory seem important to uphold. At the theoretical level, psychologists and other mental health professionals need to recognise that beyond a collection of symptoms, psychosis often reflects a life that has been interrupted. Adopting recovery-oriented practices that reflect this more holistic conceptualisation requires psychologists to move away from solving problems for consumers and instead offer interventions that promote self-direction in recovery. Promoting recovery can be challenging work, and requires a balance between viewing an individual solely as a cluster of symptoms at one end, and not attending to symptoms entirely, possibly not acknowledging the profound pain that often accompanies psychosis at the other end. Serious mental illness, a category psychosis is included in, by definition, means that unique human beings are struggling to find ways to meet their needs in the world as they encounter medicalised criteria that describe impairment in work, relationships, and carrying out daily life. In our supervision of psychologists, we have found that they often struggle to find balance between engaging with the consumer beyond their symptoms and addressing these impairments in various domains of life. In this regard, recovery-oriented care can be quite challenging and involves a stance in which psychologists acknowledge that people can recover and must be at the helm of directing this recovery. Our view is that this is usually accomplished when psychologists resist making decisions for consumers, as well as telling them, through some prescriptive decree, how to acquire health (Hamm, Buck, Vohs, Westerlund, & Lysaker, 2016). Recovery-oriented practice often instead finds psychologists striving to assist persons to develop improved sense of agency through genuine encounters with them. This may involve being challenging at times, or being supportive and warm, or any other host of interventions, but ultimately requires that the psychologist takes a position of trying to promote reflectivity within the individual with serious mental illness to figure out what it is that they want in life and then how to go about doing that. To have agency, an individual must be able to make sense of their own experiences and what a meaningful life means to them. Only then they can figure out how to carry out those goals and respond to the hurdles that are in the way. But first, and fundamentally, persons with psychosis have to see themselves as agents, and recovery-oriented care indicates that psychologists find ways to facilitate this.

The two case examples, while different in many ways, demonstrate the importance of managing the two types of challenges discussed here. Both individuals experienced a period of significant distress and disability, and all were able to some degree to recapture a sense of agency and pursue self-directed recovery. The psychologists in these cases promoted recovery by knowing the consumers beyond their symptoms, helping them to make sense of what had happened in their unique lives and to decide what they would like to do about it. Of note, none of these recovery stories involved inherent opposition to professional intervention; quite the contrary, both significantly benefited from a range of interventions. Though for each of them there were deeply personal concerns that had to be addressed in order to recapture a sense of self, in none of the examples were symptoms seen as irrelevant or ignored by the professionals involved. Understanding recovery is not to negate the difficulties symptoms or skills deficits might pose—rather it is not to reduce the person down to these or assume that they should be the primary focus of intervention. In the two examples here, self-directed recovery was an outgrowth of improved capacity to engage in meaning making, and symptoms for both became more manageable after strides in improved reflective abilities.

References

American Psychological Association. (2016). Revision of ethical standard 3.04 of the "Ethical Principles of Psychologists and Code of Conduct" (2002, as amended 2010). *American Psychologist, 71*, 900.

Andresen, R., Caputi, P., & Oades, L. (2006). Stages of recovery instrument: development of a measure of recovery from serious mental illness. *Australian and New Zealand Journal of Psychiatry, 40* (11 – 12), 972–980.

Anthony, W. A. (1993). Recovery from mental illness: the guiding vision of the mental health service system in the 1990s. *Psychosocial Rehabilitation Journal, 16*(4), 11–23.

Beers, C. (1908). *A mind that found itself.* New York, NY: Longmans, Green.

Belanger, E. A., Leonhardt, B. L., George, S. E., Firmin, R., & Lysaker, P. H. (2017). Negative symptoms and therapeutic connection: a qualitative analysis in a single case study with a patient with first episode psychosis. *Journal of Psychotherapy Integration.* https://doi.org/10.1037/int0000107.

Bentall, R. P. (1990). *Reconstructing schizophrenia.* London, England: Routledge.

Buck, K. D., Roe, D., Yanos, P. T., Buck, B., Fogely, R., Grant, M., et al. (2013). Challenges to assisting with the recovery of personal identity and wellness for persons with serious mental illness: Considerations for mental health professionals. *Psychosis, 5*(2), 134–143.

Campbell-Orde, T., Chamberlin, J., Carpenter, J., & Leff, S. (2005). *Measuring the promise: A compendium of recovery measures. Vol. II.* Cambridge, MA: Human Services Research Institute.

Carpenter, W. T., & Strauss, J. S. (1991). The prediction of outcome in schizophrenia IV: eleven year follow up of the Washington IPSS cohort. *Journal of Nervous and Mental Disease, 179,* 517–525.

Cavelti, M., Kvrgic, S., Beck, E. M., Kossowsky, J., & Vauth, R. (2012). Assessing recovery from schizophrenia as an individual process: a review of self-report instruments. *European Psychiatry, 27,* 19–32.

Ciompi, L. (1980). The natural history of schizophrenia in the long term. *British Journal of Psychiatry, 136,* 413–420.

Cohen, P., & Cohen, J. (1984). The clinician's illusion. *Archives of General Psychiatry, 41,* 1178–1182.

Connell, M., Schweitzer, R., & King, R. (2015). Recovery from first-episode psychosis and recovering self: a qualitative study. *Psychiatric Rehabilitation Journal, 38*(4), 359–364.

Corrigan, P. W., Giffort, D., Rashid, F., Leary, M., & Okeke, I. (1999). Recovery as a psychological construct. *Community Mental Health Journal, 35*(3), 231–239.

Cotton, T., & Loewenthal, D. (2015). Personal vs. medical meanings in breakdown, treatment, and recovery from 'schizophrenia'. In D. Loewenthal (Ed.), *Critical psychotherapy, psychoanalysis and counseling: Implications for practice, Part III* (pp. 77–92). Basingstoke, UK: Palgrave Macmillan.

Davidson, L., & Roe, D. (2007). Recovery from vs recovery in serious mental illness: one strategy for lessening confusion plaguing recovery. *Journal of Mental Health, 16*(4), 459–470.

Deegan, P. E. (2002). Recovery as a self-directed process of healing and transformation. *Occupational Therapy in Mental Health, 17,* 5–21. https://doi.org/10.1300/J004v17n03_02.

Degen, K., & Nasper, E. D. (1996). *Developments in clinical psychiatry. Return from madness: Psychotherapy with people taking the new antipsychotic medications and emerging from severe, lifelong, and disabling schizophrenia.* Lanham, MD, US: Jason Aronson.

Ellison, M. L., Belanger, L. K., Niles, B. L., Evans, L. C., & Bauer, M. S. (2018). Explication and definition of mental health recovery: a systematic review. *Administrative Policy in Mental Health and Mental Health Research, 45*(1), 91–102. https://doi.org/10.1007/s10488-016-0767-9.

Firmin, R., Lysaker, P. H., Luther, L., Yanos, P. T., Leonhardt, B. L., Breier, A., et al. (2018). Internalized stigma in adults with early phase vs prolonged psychosis. *Early Intervention in Psychiatry,* 1–7.

Frame, J. (1860). *The philosophy of insanity. By a late inmate of the Glasgow asylum for lunatics at Gartnavel.* Edinburgh/London/Glasgow: MacLachlan & Stewart/Holston & Wright/William Love.

Gopal, S., & Henderson, A. R. (2015). Trans-cultural study of recovery from severe enduring mental illness in Chennai, India and Perth, Western Australia. *Journal of Psychosocial. Rehabilitation and Mental Health, 2,* 51. https://doi.org/10.1007/s40737-015-0031-8.

Greenberg, D., Kalian, M., & Witzum, E. (2010). Value-sensitive psychiatric rehabilitation. *Transcultural Psychiatry, 47*(4), 629–646.

Gumley, A., Taylor, H. E., Schwannauer, M., & MacBeth, A. (2014). A systematic review of attachment and psychosis: measurement, construct validity, and outcomes. *Acta Psychiatrica Scandanavica, 129*(4), 257–274.

Hamm, J. A., Buck, B., & Lysaker, P. H. (2015). Reconciling the ipseity-disturbance model with the presence of painful affect in schizophrenia. *Philosophy, Psychiatry, & Psychology, 22*(3), 197–208.

Hamm, J. A., Buck, K. D., Leonhardt, B., Luther, L., & Lysaker, P. H. (2017). Self-directed recovery: attending to patients' agendas in psychotherapy. *Journal of Psychotherapy Integration, 28*(2), 188–201. https://doi.org/10.1037/int0000070.

Hamm, J. A., Buck, K. D., Vohs, J., Westerlund, R., & Lysaker, P. H. (2016). Interpersonal stance and dialogue in psychotherapy for schizophrenia: a supervisory approach. *The Clinical Supervisor, 35*(1), 42–62.

Harding, C. M., Brooks, G. W., Ashikaga, T., et al. (1987). The Vermont longitudinal study of persons with severe mental illness I: methodology, study sample, and overall status 32 years later. *American Journal of Psychiatry, 144*, 718–726.

Hasson-Ohayon, I., Kravetz, S., & Lysaker, P. H. (2016). Special challenges of psychotherapy with persons with psychosis: intersubjective metacognitive model of agreement and shared meaning. *Clinical Psychology and Psychotherapy, 24*(2), 428–440.

Hinshaw, S. (2017). *Another kind of madness*. New York, NY: St Martin's Press.

Hornstein, G. A. (2009). *Agnes' jacket: A psychologist's search for the meanings of madness*. New York, NY: Gildan Media, LLC.

Jerrell, J. M., Cousins, V. C., & Roberts, K. M. (2006). Psychometrics of the recovery process inventory. *Journal of Behavioral Health Services Research, 33*(4), 464–473.

Jorgensen, R., Zoffmann, V., Munk-Jorgensen, P., Buck, K., Jensen, S. O., Hasson, I., et al. (2015). Relationships over time of subjective and objective elements of recovery in persons with schizophrenia. *Psychiatry Research, 228*, 14–19.

Jose, D., Ramachandra, Lalitha, K., Gandhi, S., Desai, G., & Nagarajaiah (2015). Consumer perspectives on the concept of recovery in schizophrenia: a systematic review. *Asian Journal of Psychiatry, 14*, 13–18.

Kane, J. M. (2013). Improving patient outcomes in schizophrenia: achieving remission, preventing relapse, and measuring success. *Journal of Clinical Psychiatry, 74*(9). https://doi.org/10.4088/JCP.12117tx1c.

King, D. B., Viney, W., & Woody, W. D. (2009). *A history of psychology: Ideas and context*. New York, NY: Pearson Education, Inc.

Korsbek, L. (2016). Corecovery: Mental health recovery in a dynamic interplay between humans in a relationship. *American Journal of Psychiatric Rehabilitation, 19*(3), 196–205.

Law, H., Morrison, A., Byrne, R., & Hodson, E. (2012). Recovery from psychosis: a user informed review of self-report instruments for measuring recovery. *Journal of Mental Health, 21*(2), 192–207.

Leamy, M., Bird, V., Le Boutilier, C., Williams, J., & Slade, L. (2011). Conceptual framework for personal recovery in mental health: systematic review and narrative synthesis. *British Journal of Psychiatry, 199*(6). https://doi.org/10.1192/bjp.bp.110.083733.

Leonhardt, B. L., Hamm, J. A., Fogley, R. L., Buck, K. D., & Lysaker, P. H. (2015). Allowing for psychosis to be approachable and understandable as a human experience: a role for the humanities in psychotherapy supervision. *American Journal of Psychotherapy, 69*(1), 35–51.

Leonhardt, B. L., Huling, K., Hamm, J. A., Roe, D., Hasson-Ohayon, I., McLeod, H., et al. (2017). Recovery and serious mental illness: a review of current clinical and research paradigms and future directions. *Expert Review of Neurotherapeutics, 17*(11), 1117–1130.

Liotti, G., & Gilbert, P. (2011). Mentalizing, motivation, and social mentalities. *Psychology and Psychotherapy: Theory, Research, and Practice, 84*(1), 9–25.

Lysaker, P. H., Davis, L. W., Warman, D. M., Strasburger, A., & Beattie, N. (2007). Stigma, social function, and symptoms in schizophrenia and schizoaffective disorder: associations across 6 months. *Psychiatry Research, 149*(1–3), 89–95.

Lysaker, P. H., Hamm, J. A., Hasson-Ohayon, I., Pattison, M. L., & Leonhardt, B. L. (2018). Promoting recovery from severe mental illness: Implications from research on metacognition and metacognitive reflection and insight therapy. *World Journal of Psychiatry, 8*(1), 1–11.

Lysaker, P. H., & Klion, R. (2017). *Recovery, meaning making, and severe mental illness: A comprehensive guide to metacognitive and reflection insight therapy*. New York, NY: Routledge.

McCarthy-Jones, S., Marriott, M., Knowles, R., Rowse, G., & Thompson, A. R. (2013). What is psychosis? A meta-synthesis of inductive qualitative studies exploring the experience of psychosis. *Psychosis, 5*(1), 1–16.

Ng, R. M. K., Pearson, V., Lam, M., Law, C. W., Chiu, C. P. Y., & Chen, E. Y. H. (2008). What does recovery from schizophrenia mean? Perceptions of long-term patients. *International Journal of Social Psychiatry, 54*(2), 118–130.

Noordsy, D., Torrey, W., Mueser, K., Mead, S., O'keefe, C., & Fox, L. (2002). Recovery from severe mental illness: an intrapersonal and functional outcome definition. *International Review of Psychiatry, 14*, 318–326.

Ragins, M., & Pollack, D. (2013). Recovery and community mental health. In K. Yeager, et al. (Eds.), *Modern community mental health: An interdisciplinary approach* (pp. 385–404). New York, NY: Oxford University Press.

Saks, E. (2007). *The center cannot hold*. New York, NY: Hyperion Books.

Searles, H. (1965). *Collected papers on schizophrenia and related subjects*. New York, NY: International Universities Press.

Silverstein, S. M., & Bellack, A. S. (2004). A scientific agenda for the concept of recovery as it applies to schizophrenia. *Clinical Psychology Review, 28*, 1108–1124.

Smith, J. D., Mittal, D., Chekuri, L., Han, X., & Sullivan, G. (2017). A comparison of provider attitudes toward serious mental illness across different health care disciplines. *Stigma and Health, 2* (4), 327–337. https://doi.org/10.1037/sah0000064.

Soundy, A., Stubbs, B., Roskell, C., Williams, S. E., Fox, A., & Vancampfort, D. (2015). Identifying the facilitators and processes which influence recovery in individuals with schizophrenia: a systematic review and thematic synthesis. *Journal of Mental Health, 24*(2), 103–110. https://doi.org/10.3109/09638237.2014.998811.

Stuart, S. R., Tansey, L., & Quayle, E. (2017). What we talk about when we talk about recovery: a systematic review and best-fit framework synthesis of qualitative literature. *Journal of Mental Health, 26*(3), 291–304. https://doi.org/10.1080/09638237.2016.1222056.

Stumbo, S. P., Yarborough, B. J. H., Paulson, R. I., & Green, C. A. (2015). The impact of adverse child and adult experiences on recovery from serious mental illness. *Psychiatric Rehabilitation Journal, 38*(4), 320–327.

Substance Abuse and Mental Health Services Administration (SAMHSA). (2012). *SAMHSA's working definition of recovery*. Retrieved from: https://store.samhsa.gov/product/SAMHSA-s-Working-Definition-of-Recovery/PEP12-RECDEF.

Topor, A., Borg, M., di Girolomo, S., & Davidson, L. (2011). Not just an individual journey: social aspects of recovery. *International Journal of Social Psychiatry, 57*(1), 90–99.

Tse, S., Cheung, E., Kan, A., Ng, R., & Yau, S. (2012). Recovery in Hong Kong: service user participation in mental health services. *International Review of Psychiatry, 24*(1), 40–47.

Whitaker, R. (2002). *Mad in America: Bad science, bad medicine, and the enduring mistreatment of the mentally ill*. New York, NY: Perseus Publishing.

Yanos, P. T. (2018). *Written off: Mental health stigma and the loss of human potential*. Cambridge, UK: Cambridge University Press.

Yarborough, B. H., Yarborough, M. T., Janoff, S. L., & Green, C. A. (2016). Getting by, getting back, and getting on: matching mental health services to consumers' recovery goals. *Psychiatric Rehabilitation Journal, 39*(2), 97–104.

Definition of Key Terms

Agency Feeling in control of making decisions in one's own life; self-direction.

Objective recovery Measureable clinical outcomes, e.g. symptom remission, defined by others.

Recovery-oriented practice Clinical practice that utilises shared decision making and embraces core concepts of the recovery movement, rejecting paternalism and promoting agency within the consumer.

Subjective recovery A process, defined by the self, based on personally valued goals and preferences.

SECTION 2
Assessment

CHAPTER 6

Assessment in Psychosis

Rebecca Kelly*, Christopher Shoulder*, Vaughan Bell*,†
*Psychological Interventions Clinic for Outpatients with Psychosis, South London and Maudsley NHS Foundation Trust, London, United Kingdom, †Research Department of Clinical, Educational and Health Psychology, University College London, London, United Kingdom

Key Learning Objectives

This chapter will help the reader to:

- Appreciate how to maximise the acceptability and helpfulness of the assessment process for the client.
- Identify why you need to carry out an assessment and what form it will take.
- Understand what information you need to gather.
- Identify which assessment tools might help, and their advantages and disadvantages.

INTRODUCTION

Completing a sensitive, engaging, and ultimately helpful assessment with someone experiencing psychosis is an essential part of providing high-quality clinical care but can be challenging for both the psychologist and the patient. For the patient, an assessment may be an anxiety-provoking initial meeting with mental health services when feeling distressed or disoriented, or, perhaps, may feel like one of a long line of encounters with yet another professional where they're asked to recount their 'story'. For the psychologist, working with someone who may be struggling with paranoia, or who does not share seemingly widespread assumptions about the nature of what could be happening to them, or who may have had traumatic experiences during previous contact with mental health services, may mean the person needs a different approach than for people with other mental health problems.

Psychological assessment must be adapted to the needs of the individual and the context.

Importantly, there are no guidelines that apply to all contexts because assessment is essentially a process of better understanding the situation with regard to what the clinician and service can offer and this will vary greatly depending on the needs of the person and the resources available. Assessing someone who has presented to a hospital emergency department after the sudden onset of

A Clinical Introduction to Psychosis. https://doi.org/10.1016/B978-0-12-815012-2.00006-7

hallucinated voices is markedly different to assessing someone with long-term experience of psychosis who has experienced a recent increase in paranoid thinking that is interfering with their work.

This chapter is written with perhaps the most common context for clinical and neuropsychologists in mind: assessing someone as part of consideration or participation in a course of collaborative psychological therapy. However, all assessments involve both interpersonal and technical aspects and we hope this chapter will contain useful advice and recommendations that apply widely.

PREPARING FOR THE ASSESSMENT

Perhaps the most important step occurs before the assessor and the person being assessed have met and involves clarifying the purpose and potential outcomes of the assessment. This is not only to guide the process of assessment but also to ensure that the person being assessed can discuss what's involved and what the consequences might be, to allow them to give informed consent regarding their participation.

Common reasons for assessments might include:

- To determine the needs and perspective of the person being assessed
- For diagnostic purposes
- To ascertain or confirm need for care
- For informing specific treatments that might be offered, including which treatment services and which particular medications or therapies might be appropriate
- In order to provide tailored, formulation-based psychological therapy (e.g. CBT)
- For research purposes
- For statutory purposes, for example medico-legal, for insurance, and for reports for court or forensic purposes.

Therefore, it's important to clarify the purpose or referral question related to the assessment, what information is needed, and what form the assessment will take (single session or many, free-form discussion or structured tests, and so on). For any kind of assessment, there is a need to consider what information is needed and for whom, and to balance the need for information with the potential impact on the person being assessed.

ASSUMPTIONS AND EXPECTATIONS

Clear communication about the assessment process can help to build trust between client and clinician.

Assessment is a routine part of most clinical roles, but it is easy to underestimate how it can be a major and potentially stressful event for patients. Assumptions about the purpose and implications of an assessment can vary wildly, even when clinicians think the reason for the assessment is clear. Similarly, past negative experiences of working with professionals or the effect of paranoia during the

Box 6.1 First-Person Perspective

"I had lots of expectations of my first clinical assessment. All negative. I found the prospect of retelling my story for what seemed like the hundredth time exhausting and distressing. Repeating it served only to compound how I felt about myself, my life, and the terrifying psychotic incidents I was experiencing.

Over a period of around twenty years, I had received no effective therapy. Even before the assessment had begun, I was already sure nothing would come of it, like all the rest.

Answering the questions, again, was very wearing; draining, in fact, going over old ground, trying to remember more things to add that I felt were important, while having to dredge up and recount all the things I wanted to be rid of again. I was angry too; angry at having to explain everything again. I was angry at the content of what I had to describe."

assessment may raise doubts about the true intentions of the psychologist (see example in Box 6.1). Transparency as far as possible is key, and this involves not only being transparent about the declared aspects of the assessment but also explicitly addressing common assumptions about the process.

One of the most important initial steps in an assessment is to be clear about who you are, what you do, and explicitly ask about why the person believes they have been referred to the assessment and what they understand about the purpose and potential outcomes. It is important to ensure that the client has a clear idea of what the assessment will entail, e.g. how long it will last, what topics will be covered, whether they need to provide a spontaneous description of their difficulties or just respond to questions as they are posed, whether they need to provide detail or simply select a number or response from a list of options. Similarly, many people will not be familiar with what psychologists do and how they differ from other professionals and so being clear about this may help people choose what they want to discuss with you (see Box 6.2).

It is also worth noting how the process of assessment can be misperceived in seemingly subtle but potentially important ways. People with psychosis often have a lot of experience of people telling them they are mistaken about their strongly held beliefs, ideas, or concerns, and may expect the same from this new encounter. With the best of intentions, family members, friends, or professionals may hope that a meeting with a psychologist is a chance for a professional to finally 'get them to accept they are mistaken' and the person being assessed might attend the session assuming that this is one of the intentions behind the meeting. This should never be the focus of an assessment and, with this in mind, it is important that a psychological assessment is nonjudgemental. The psychologist can make this explicit but also needs to be aware of how their personal reactions during the meeting could reinforce this perception. This approach can provide space for the person to express concerns that may have always been responded to with contradiction until now.

Box 6.2 First-Person Perspective

"Directly after the assessment, there were several distinct and contradictory emotions coursing through me. I was anxious and a bit panicky in case I hadn't said enough. I still felt scared that I couldn't be 'fixed'. There was a feeling of relief too. I was out of there and could breathe again. Things slowed down somewhat in my head.

There were times during the assessment when I felt very apprehensive and suspicious. However, thinking about the experience later, I felt that the psychologist had made a genuine effort to be more empathic and attentive to me, than in any of the many 'proper' therapy sessions I'd previously had elsewhere. This had been the first time that anybody had explained to me the purpose of CBT and what it aimed to address. The psychologist had taken time to tell me about the clinic I would be seen in and its holistic approach to therapy. She had given me the space to ask any questions I may have had, though I couldn't think of any to ask at that moment. At the time all this was happening, I was too involved in the moment to appreciate what a gentle grilling I'd had. It had been such a different experience to the previous, fruitless encounters with mental health professionals. In fact it had been my first assessment ever."

Engagement is a broad concept, and involves putting the person at ease and gaining their trust.

Adopting an open-minded, curious, and conversational approach and exploring concerns as important to the person (regardless of how they might differ from your own or others) is an approach that works when discussing any deeply held beliefs and important experiences and is equally as useful when discussing experiences associated with psychosis. Engagement is a critical part of therapy, and for therapy to be effective it has been argued that therapists need to ensure that they are adhering to key values and principles, namely offering hope, adopting a recovery-focused perspective, listening to and supporting the person, and validating and supporting them in the process of making sense of distressing experiences (Brabban, Byrne, Longden, & Morrison, 2017). In an assessment context, this involves active listening and empathy, being aware of emotional state and distress, using the person's own language to describe their experiences; and validating that their experiences are real and important to them, however unusual or unlikely they might seem.

People with psychosis have typically experienced high levels of social victimisation, trauma (Varese et al., 2012; see also Chapter 10) and may have experienced being treated or detained against their will and so may be understandably wary about engaging in a conversation about their experiences with someone perceived, potentially correctly, as having more power and influence than them. Given this potential power imbalance, the process of assessment itself has the potential to be highly distressing given that it may involve asking about past experiences of trauma and victimisation, which may be difficult to recount but which the person feels compelled to describe.

Importantly, this situation does not necessarily involve the psychologist intentionally imposing demands on the person to discuss sensitive issues against their will, because the demands are implicit in the context. This means it is easy to

Box 6.3 Key Tips for Assessing Trauma in Psychosis

1. Ensure you gain consent to discuss past experiences or trauma history
2. Approach the assessment of past experiences of psychosis as you might approach an assessment of prior trauma.
3. Ensure the person has adequate support and that any worsening of symptoms or risk will be monitored by their care team if the person does describe traumatic experiences during an assessment.

assume that these demands are not present, or any distress arising from the assessment can be understood as entirely detached from the context. Although it might seem useful to gather as much information as possible, including on these important issues, the person doing the assessment needs to be mindful of these risks. It is often also useful to ask clients if there are certain topics they would *not* feel comfortable discussing or agree a way they can signal if they are finding the assessment overwhelming or distressing and need to stop or take a break (a metaphorical 'panic button', e.g. Johns, Jolley, Keen, & Peters, 2014). Further key tips are highlighted in Box 6.3.

CLINICAL SYMPTOMS AND WIDER ANOMALOUS EXPERIENCES

In clinical terms, psychosis is fundamentally characterised by the presence of delusions (Gilleen & David, 2005) with hallucinations, particularly hallucinated voices, being a common co-occurrence. Delusions are often grouped into themes that include paranoid or persecutory, grandiose, somatic and erotomanic with many specific subtypes discussed in the literature to varying degrees (delusions of parasitosis, misidentification delusions, and so on). Additional groupings include passivity delusions (delusions of being controlled by external forces) and thought interference delusions (thought broadcasting, echo, insertion, and withdrawal) with these latter two having been given particular significance as part of the 'first-rank symptoms' of schizophrenia in some diagnostic symptoms (Nordgaard, Arnfred, Handest, & Parnas, 2007), although in the DSM 5 the special place of first-rank symptoms has been removed (Tandon et al., 2013). Delusions may also be classified as being mood congruent or incongruent, depending on whether the theme reflects the mood states of co-existing depression or mania.

Accompanying symptoms vary in terms of their inclusion in definitions of psychosis, but diagnostically, diagnostic criteria for psychotic disorders can also include thought disorder, typically manifesting as speech communication problems, and negative symptoms that include alterations to motivation and emotional reactivity, poverty of speech, and social withdrawal. Alterations to movement related to catatonia and changes to personality are often considered to be present in more severe presentations.

It is important to note that individual symptoms of psychosis, for example auditory hallucinations, can occur in other clinical groups and in nonclinical populations (e.g. Waters, Blom, Jardri, Hugdahl, & Sommer, 2018). In nonclinical populations, such phenomena might be termed psychotic-like experiences or unusual experiences. Such experiences are not always associated with distress or need for care (Peters et al., 2016).

Anomalous experiences in psychosis vary widely, extending beyond the simple classifications in diagnostic manuals.

First-person reports (for an example, see Box 6.4) and phenomenological analysis include a vast array of additional changes to subjective experience that can include pervasive feelings of meaningfulness, alterations to the experience of intersubjectivity (Van Duppen, 2017), and the experience of interaction with social agents (Bell, Mills, Modinos, & Wilkinson, 2017).

Because of this, anomalous experiences are often difficult to put into words, potentially because it could be the first time the person has attempted to describe their unusual experiences to someone else. It's therefore critical to allow time and space for the person to articulate their own difficulties in their own way. For example, experiences like dissociation and depersonalisation or intrusive trauma memories can be common in individuals experiencing psychosis and are not easily classified into symptom categories, not least as the person might find it difficult to put them into words at all (see the example in Box 6.5).

Other aspects of psychosis can also present additional challenges to the person feeling secure in describing their experiences—most notably paranoia or critical and commanding voices. There can often be fears about the potential consequences of disclosing thoughts and experiences, including fears relating to the delusion (e.g. "you're part of the plot against me or will pass this information on to the people following me"—see example in Box 6.6). People who hear voices might hear voices urging them not to tell anyone about the voices, or to withhold certain information, or telling them that they're not worthy of

Box 6.4 First-Person Perspective

"The assessment was a rollercoaster ride. There were many layers of thoughts all happening at the same time for me. I had worked myself up into a highly emotionally aroused state before arriving for the assessment. I remember trying to hold it together and to look and sound 'reasonable' to the psychologist. All the while my brain was racing, leaping from one disparate thought to another. I was thinking about so many different things at once, because, even though I wasn't convinced any good would come of the assessment, I didn't want to leave one minute detail out about how I was feeling... I kept going off at tangents, talking about things I hadn't been asked about, panicking, in case I missed out even the smallest thing I thought significant. My thoughts were very disorganised and therefore so were my answers."

Box 6.5 First-Person Perspective

"I felt frustrated and angry at myself for not being able to adequately describe the dissociative episodes and all the horror that came with them. This was what I wanted to explain most, because it was the most terrifying experience for me."

Box 6.6 First-Person Perspective

"Even though my mouth and brain were running away with me, I felt concerned that the psychologist might tell the 'authorities' about me and that they would use what I had told her against me. I didn't know who the 'authorities' were exactly, or how they would use the information I'd given her. I just knew that they might."

the help. Individuals might be highly vigilant for signs that confirm their fears and concerns, and highly perceptive and sensitive to the assessors choice of wording, body language, and other details. As noted, considering and prioritising engagement and putting the person at ease is key, but it can also be helpful to ask explicitly if there is anything the person might need to know or check with you in order to feel comfortable proceeding with the assessment.

PERSONAL UNDERSTANDING

One of the main ways that formulation for psychological therapy differs from diagnostic classification is that it incorporates the person's subjective understanding and 'mental model' of the situation to a far greater degree (see Chapter 14). A psychological therapy assessment should specifically focus on the person's own understanding of how these experiences started, are caused, and the impact they see on their own life. Understanding the personal meanings associated with these experiences is key in this process and may involve far more than a simple explanation of causes. This also requires understanding how the person sees their experiences in terms of the social context in which they live. Someone may believe, for example, both that they have been blessed with special powers and understand that others treat them as if they are 'mad'. Understanding this tension and its relationship to the person's beliefs about spirituality, for example, could be key in understanding what the person feels is most important and distressing about their situation.

COGNITIVE AND COMMUNICATION DIFFICULTIES

Difficulties with concentration, memory, and problem solving can represent challenges in terms of the person being able to communicate with the assessor, understand and respond to questions and stay on topic, recall and answer long

Reading difficulties are common in people diagnosed with schizophrenia, and need to be considered in assessment.

multiple-choice questions or manage highly structured interviews. Individuals diagnosed with schizophrenia-spectrum disorders also frequently have difficulty with reading (e.g. Whitford, O'Driscoll, & Titone, 2018). Given these issues, it is important to be flexible with how structured and how long the assessment session is, to offer breaks, to keep questions brief and simple if possible, to provide prompts and summaries or their own copies of questionnaires or response scales to help keep the person on track, and to check in with the person regularly about their understanding and how they are finding the assessment process.

RISK AND SAFETY

Assessment of risk is a common procedure in mental health and many of the same principles apply when working with someone with psychosis than someone without. Currently no scales reliably categorise risk in psychiatry either in relation to self-harm and suicide (Chan et al., 2016) or violence to others (Singh, Fazel, Gueorguieva, & Buchanan, 2014), meaning that risk assessment is best conducted as an assessment of risk and needs specific to the individual. When specifically considering psychosis, a similar picture emerges. For example, psychotic symptoms are statistically associated with risk at the population level, but the association is not strong enough to indicate that the simple presence of symptoms necessarily increases risk for any one individual (Coid, Ullrich, Bebbington, Fazel, & Keers, 2016).

Victimisation rates for people with psychosis are higher than the general population.

In terms of individual presentation, it is always worth noting that violence from others is a significantly greater risk for people with psychosis than the risk of violence towards others, contrary to common stereotypes (e.g. de Vries et al., 2018). Similarly, psychosis can also place the person at risk of self-neglect and exploitation making safeguarding a high priority during risk assessment.

Command hallucinations and delusions that are acted on should be the subject of special attention, particularly when they increase the chances of increased vulnerability, or the individual putting themselves or others in risky situations. Both history of abuse, substance use, distress, past compliance, and beliefs about compliance have been identified as predictors of compliance with command hallucinations (Dugré, Guay, & Dumais, 2018). Similarly, delusions that involve specific content and which the person acts on should be evaluated in terms of their content and in terms of the likelihood of leading to danger and harm to the patient or to others.

COMMON SCALES IN THE ASSESSMENT OF PSYCHOSIS

There are hundreds of scales that have been designed to measure aspects of psychosis for different contexts or with different emphases. Here we present some of the most widely used for the assessment of psychosis.

Interview-Based Psychosis Symptom Measures

POSITIVE AND NEGATIVE SYNDROME SCALE (PANSS)

The PANSS (Kay, Fiszbein, & Opler, 1987) is a 30-item interview-based scale that includes sections dedicated to positive symptoms, negative symptoms, and general psychopathology, which, despite its name, measures additional symptoms commonly associated with psychosis. Ratings are based on patient interview and additional corroborative information from carers and professionals and measures symptoms of psychosis over the past week. Each item has a brief symptom description followed by a 1–7 scale to rate severity, conceptualised as impact on functioning, with each severity rating having a symptom specific description. The PANSS requires rater training to achieve acceptable interrating reliability (Cohen's kappa above 0.6; Müller & Wetzel, 1998) but shows a high degree of interrater reliability when used by suitably trained individuals. Because of its complexity, it tends to be used for clinical outcome studies rather than in routine clinical assessment. It also aims for 'breadth' rather than 'depth' and includes only a single item to rate delusions and a single item for hallucinations, meaning it does not distinguish between subtypes of these experiences.

Formal rater training helps ensure assessments are reliable and standardised.

SCALE FOR THE ASSESSMENT OF POSITIVE SYMPTOMS (SAPS)

The SAPS (Andreasen, 1984) is a 34-item interview-based scale that also draws on other sources of corroborative information. It includes sections on hallucinations, delusions, bizarre behaviour, and positive formal thought disorder, with each section including items that covers a broad range of phenomena within the category. For example, in the hallucinations section, it includes specific ratings for auditory hallucinations, voices commenting, voices conversing, somatic or tactile hallucinations, olfactory hallucinations and visual hallucinations as well as a global severity rating. Each item has a detailed description and is scored on a 0–5 severity scale that largely reflects symptom frequency and intensity. The SAPS is perhaps the most widely used scale in research studies and shows a high degree of interrater reliability even in cross-cultural settings (Andreasen, Flaum, Arndt, Alliger, & Swayze, 1991) although is time consuming and therefore not ideal for clinical assessments. The SAPS has consistently been found to have good interrater reliability in the original and follow-up studies (Norman, Malla, Cortese, & Diaz, 1996).

SCALE FOR THE ASSESSMENT OF NEGATIVE SYMPTOMS (SANS)

The SANS (Andreasen, 1983) was designed as a complement to the SAPS and follows a similar format having five sections (affective flattening or blunting, alogia, avolition—apathy, anhedonia—a sociality, and attention), each of which includes several specific items and a global severity scale. Severity is rated on a 0–5 scale with information gathered from clinical interview and other corroborative sources. The SANS typically has lower interrater reliability than the SAPS, although it still remains acceptable when tested across sites (Mueser, Sayers, Schooler, Mance, & Haas, 1994).

PSYCHOTIC SYMPTOM RATINGS SCALES (PSYRATS)

The PSYRATS (Haddock, McCarron, Tarrier, & Faragher, 1999) includes two distinct scales—the delusions scale and the auditory hallucinations scale, each of which can be used entirely separately and both of which rate the symptoms over the last week. The delusions scale has six items that rate amount of preoccupation with delusions, duration of preoccupation with delusions, conviction, amount of distress, intensity of distress, disruption to life caused by beliefs, each on a 0–4 scale from not present to maximum severity. Both versions of the PSYRATS show excellent interrater reliability for all items (all intraclass correlation coefficients above 0.75). The auditory hallucinations scale includes 11 items that measure frequency, duration, location, loudness, beliefs regarding the origin of voices, amount of negative content of voices, degree of negative content, amount of distress, intensity of distress, disruption to life caused by voices, and controllability of voices also on a 0–4 scale of the same format. Notably, these items measure not only symptom severity but also several additional characteristics, including metacognitive evaluations, distress, and impact. These scales are conducted as semistructured interviews and are relatively brief, meaning they are more feasible for routine clinical work, although the scale is also widely used for research and clinical trials.

STRUCTURED INTERVIEW FOR PSYCHOSIS-RISK SYNDROMES/SCALE OF PRODROMAL SYMPTOMS

The Structured Interview for Psychosis-Risk Syndromes (SIPS; Miller et al., 2002) is an extensive in-depth structured interview that aims to identify people at high risk of developing psychosis. It was originally called the Structured Interview for Prodromal Syndrome but was renamed in 2009 to better describe its focus on prospectively identifying people at risk of developing psychosis. The SIPS is a broad measure that includes the Scale of Prodromal Symptoms (SOPS), a specific measure of psychosis-like symptoms, along with the DSM criteria for schizotypal personality disorder, an assessment of family background and the Global Assessment of Functioning—a widely used scale used to measure the social, occupational, and psychological impact of mental health problems. The SIPS can be used as complete assessment or the SOPS can be used independently. The SOPS covers four symptom scales: positive symptoms, negative symptoms, disorganisation symptoms, and what it calls 'general symptoms' that include sleep disturbance, alterations to mood, motor disturbances, and impaired tolerance to stress. Symptoms are recorded, as present, absent or where no information is available to decide, and interview as well as corroborative information can be used to complete the scale. When a symptom is recorded as present, the rater records description, onset, duration and frequency, along with degree of distress, degree of interference with life, and degree of conviction/meaning. The symptom scales are then given an overall severity score from 0 (absent) to 6 (extreme).

The risk syndrome is defined by the person being assessed experiencing at least one positive symptom four times per week for a month, or one full psychotic symptom for at least one day if the symptom is severe. Notably the SIPS/SOPS is an in-depth and time-consuming assessment that is best suited to research or comprehensive assessments for early intervention services.

DSM-5 CLINICIAN-RATED DIMENSIONS OF PSYCHOSIS SYMPTOM SEVERITY

The Clinician-Rated Dimensions of Psychosis Symptom Severity is a brief scale that has been included in the DSM-5 as an 'emerging measure' for further study rather than as part of its core diagnostic criteria. It includes 8 items that rate hallucinations, delusions, disorganised speech, abnormal psychomotor behaviour, negative symptoms, impaired cognition, depression, and mania on severity scale of 0 (not present) to 4 (severe) with individual description for each score on each symptom to aid assessment. Although included in the DSM-5, it has currently been subject to little research, meaning it should be treated as experimental until better investigated.

Self-Report Psychosis Symptom Measures

Psychosis involves delusions and hallucinations and agreement about the extent to which these are unrealistic will differ considerably between individuals. By definition, if you believe something you do not recognise it as false, meaning self-reporting of delusions would seem to be an impossible task. Self-report scales in the assessment of psychosis therefore largely rely on reported experiences or beliefs of certain types and themes, which can be reported descriptively regardless of how they are understood, or involve measuring appraisals related to psychotic experiences.

PETERS ET AL. DELUSIONS INVENTORY (PDI)

The PDI was originally published as a 40-item version (Peters, Joseph, & Garety, 1999), but the 21-item version is the most commonly used (Peters, Joseph, Day, & Garety, 2004). The questionnaire includes a series of items describing common delusion-like ideas to which the respondent can answer 'yes' or 'no'. If they respond 'yes', they are asked to rate the item in terms of how distressing it is, how preoccupying it is, and how strongly they believe it. Each of these is rated on a 1–5 scale with description given for each scale's end points. The scale can be completed relatively briefly, in 5–10 min, and is widely used in research but can also be a useful clinical measure for helping to determine the points of distress across a range of common, potentially delusional concerns.

LAUNAY-SLADE HALLUCINATIONS SCALE (LSHS)

The LSHS is one of the most widely used scales in research and has been frequently modified by researchers wanting to highlight specific aspects of the hallucinatory experience, meaning there are several validated versions in circulation. The initial version was a 12-item scale that involved yes/no responding (Launay & Slade, 1981) but was subsequently modified to include a 5-point Likert scale response to allow each item to be rated on frequency of occurrence (Bentall & Slade, 1985). A subsequent version expanded the items to 24 and included additional questions on auditory and visual hallucinations, vividness of mental imagery, and day dreams (Morrison et al., 2002). Subsequent versions have included additional questions on hallucinations in other sensory modalities (Larøi et al., 2004; Larøi & Van der Linden, 2005). In all versions, the Launay Slade has the advantage of being brief although lacks any distress or functioning based measure and tends towards including items most associated with hallucinatory experience associated with psychiatric disorders.

CARDIFF ANOMALOUS PERCEPTIONS SCALE (CAPS)

The CAPS (Bell, Halligan, & Ellis, 2005) is a 32-item scale focused on measuring hallucinations and related perceptual distortions and follows the same response format as the Peters et al. Delusions inventory, in that it includes specific questions that require a yes/no answer to indicate the presence or absence of experiences, and asks the respondent to rate each experience on three scales measuring distress, intrusiveness, and frequency if they indicate the experience is present. The CAPS contains items that ask about hallucinatory experiences common in psychiatry (hallucinated voices, visual hallucinations, etc.) but also includes items that ask about wider anomalous perceptual experiences such as changes in sensory intensity, being flooded with sensory information and time distortion. It also aims to take differing levels of insight into account when asking about hallucinatory experience. However, as with the Peters et al. Delusions Inventory, the conditional rating of dimensions can make this scale more difficult to complete for people who are cognitively impaired or have reduced concentration.

SCALES MEASURING PARANOID IDEATION

Several scales are available to measure paranoid thinking. The oldest and probably most widely used is the Paranoia Scale (Fenigstein & Vanable, 1992), which is a 20-item scale, which includes classically persecutory ideas of believing others intend harm as well as items relating to psychosis-like experiences (mind influenced by others), negative views of others, and social disaffection. The Green et al. Paranoid Thoughts Scale (GPTS; Green et al., 2008) consists of two parts (A and B) each with 16 items describing paranoia-related experiences. It asks respondents to rate each item on how much the person has felt each experience over the past month. Part A describes experiences of social reference and Part B describes ideas of being persecuted by others. Part B can be administered independently if a shorter scale specifically focused on persecutory ideation is needed. The Persecutory Ideation Questionnaire (PIQ; McKay, Langdon, & Coltheart, 2006) is a brief 10-item questionnaire that focuses on persecutory ideation but aims to include common experiences in paranoia such as conspiracy, ideas of reference, and harassment and asks respondents to rate each item on a scale of 0 (very untrue) to 4 (very true). The Paranoia/Suspiciousness

Questionnaire (PSQ; Rawlings & Freeman, 1996) is a 47-item questionnaire that requires 'yes/no' answers and aims to cover a wide range of paranoid thoughts and related experiences with subscales measuring interpersonal suspiciousness and hostility, negative mood and withdrawal, anger and impulsiveness, mistrust and wariness, and perceived hardship and resentment.

Scales Measuring Appraisals of Psychotic Symptoms

There is a large body of evidence to show that appraisals or evaluations of psychotic symptoms partly mediate the distress and disability arising from them. Several scales have been developed that measure aspects of these appraisals.

Evidence shows that the way psychotic experiences are appraised is key to the distress felt.

BELIEFS ABOUT VOICES QUESTIONNAIRE

Typically used in its revised version (BAVQ-R; Chadwick, Lees, & Birchwood, 2000) this scale is a 35-item questionnaire that measures how people understand and respond to their voices. It was inspired by evidence that beliefs about the identity, power, and purpose of hallucinated voices mediate their impact on functioning and distress and that complying with command hallucinations relates to beliefs about consequences. A recent factor analysis supported a 29-item version, with items loading onto 3 separate factors: persecutory beliefs, resistance, and engagement (Strauss et al., 2018).

BELIEFS ABOUT PARANOIA SCALE

The beliefs about paranoia scale are a 31-item questionnaire (Morrison et al., 2005) that also exists as an 18-item short form (Gumley, Gillan, Morrison, & Schwannauer, 2011). Both versions measure negative beliefs about paranoia (e.g. 'my paranoia distresses me'), beliefs about paranoia as a survival strategy (e.g. 'my paranoia protects me', and normalising beliefs (e.g. 'most people feel paranoid sometimes') with the original 31-item questionnaire also measuring positive beliefs about paranoia (e.g. 'Life would be dull if it wasn't for my paranoia').

VOICE POWER DIFFERENTIAL SCALE

This scale, created by Birchwood, Meaden, Trower, Gilbert, and Plaistow (2000), measures the perceived power difference in the relationship between the hallucinated voice and the voice hearer, on the basis of evidence that the perceived dominance and power of the voice has an impact on distress and compliance with command hallucinations. The voice power differential scale is a 7-item scale that asks whether the voice hearer feel more or less powerful, strong, confident, able to harm each other, superior, knowledgeable and whether the voice respects the voice hearer more than vice versa. Each item is rated on a 1–5 scale, and each point on the scale has a specific description. Birchwood et al. (2000) reported the scale had an internal reliability of 0.80 using Cohen's Kappa and re-test reliability 0.77.

Scales Measuring Insight

SCHEDULE FOR THE ASSESSMENT OF INSIGHT (SAI)

The SAI is most commonly used in its most recent form the Schedule for the Assessment of Insight-Expanded version (SAI-E; Kemp & David, 1997), which is an 11-item interview that measures symptom relabeling, illness awareness, and adherence to treatment. 'Symptom relabeling' items assess two components that include awareness and explanation of the most prominent psychotic symptom. Items are scored on a scale of 0 (complete lack of awareness) to 4 (full awareness). Interrater reliability for the SAI-E is high with trained raters (Intraclass correlations between 0.92 and 0.98; Morgan et al., 2010).

BIRCHWOOD INSIGHT SCALE (BIS)

The BIS (Birchwood et al., 1994) is a widely used 8-item self-report scale that includes subscales that measure relabeling symptoms (2 items), awareness of illness (2 items), and need for treatment (4 items). The scale shows good internal reliability (Cronbach's alpha of 0.75) and generally acceptable test-retest reliability with relabeling symptoms dropping slightly below a correlation cut-off of 0.7 in the original validation study.

VAGUS INSIGHT INTO PSYCHOSIS SCALE

The VAGUS insight into psychosis scale (Gerretsen et al., 2014) has both clinician-rated (VAGUS-CR) and self-report (VAGUS-SR) versions with the clinician-rated version, including 5 items, and the self-report scale, including 10 items. Each measures four domains of insight: general illness awareness, symptom attribution, awareness of need for treatment, and awareness of negative consequences. The validation study reported that the clinician-rated version had good interrater reliability (all intraclass correlation coefficients above 0.8) with the self-report version showing good internal reliability (alpha of 0.773). Both versions were strongly correlated with one another and other scales of insight in psychosis.

Scales Measuring Psychosis-Related Experiences

OXFORD LIVERPOOL INVENTORY OF EXPERIENCES (O-LIFE SCALE)

The O-LIFE is one of the most widely used measures of schizotypy—a concept that represents personality traits and experiences assumed to be on a continuum with schizophrenia. The O-LIFE is available in its original 150-item version (Mason, Claridge, & Jackson, 1995) and in a 33-item short form (Mason, Linney, & Claridge, 2005). Both include four subscales aiming to reflect different symptom groups of schizophrenia: unusual experiences, cognitive disorganisation, introvertive anhedonia, and impulsive nonconformity.

SENSED PRESENCE QUESTIONNAIRE (SENPQ)

The SenPQ (Barnby & Bell, 2017) is a 16-item questionnaire that measures the experience of sensed presence—the 'feeling or sense that another entity, individual or being is present despite no clear sensory or perceptual evidence'. The experience of sensed presence is reported across the general population but has also been reported in people with psychotic disorder and is an early sign of psychosis in Parkinson's disease. The SenPQ has good internal reliability (0.95) and shows good validity in the general population but has not as yet been tested in patients with psychosis.

CONCLUSION

The process of assessment is both a personal one, designed as a humane approach to evaluating an individual's need in light of available help, and a technical one, that involves selecting, which measures are needed and/or appropriate given the focus and complexity of assessment. It is worth noting that the issues are broader than are described here, both in terms of working sensitively with people who may be experiencing psychosis and in terms of the range of assessments available. With this in mind, it is perhaps also worth mentioning the most important tool we have not yet mentioned here—supervision. Clinical supervision is usually thought of as a method for ensuring quality of care during clinical intervention, but it is equally as important for assessments and no assessments should be completed without access to a more experienced supervisor who can advise on the many challenges that assessment can bring.

SELF-DIRECTED READING

For a wide-ranging overview of issues and measures used in the assessment of psychosis: Waters, F., & Stephane, M. (Eds.). (2014). *The assessment of psychosis: A reference book and rating scales for research and practice.* Routledge.

For a thorough introduction to a person-centred approach to working with people with psychosis: Chadwick, P. (2006). *Person-based cognitive therapy for distressing psychosis.* John Wiley & Sons.

For a helpful guide to personal and therapeutic qualities that can greatly assist the assessment process: Brabban, A., Byrne, R., Longden, E., & Morrison, A. P. (2017). The importance of human relationships, ethics and recovery-orientated values in the delivery of CBT for people with psychosis. *Psychosis, 9*(2), 157–166.

For a first person account of experiences of therapy assessment and the therapy relationship: Sen, D. (2017). What stays unsaid in therapeutic relationships. *Psychosis, 9*(1), 90–94.

QUIZ QUESTIONS

1. Why should the assessor clearly explain what the assessment will involve?
2. What issues might require adaptation of the assessment process?

3. What risk issues should the assessor focus on during an assessment: (a) the risk of the person perpetrating violence, (b) the risk of the person causing harm to themselves, (c) the person being harmed by others?
4. True or False: Auditory hallucinations are a hallmark of psychotic disorder and therefore would not be present in other clinical groups.

ANSWERS TO QUIZ QUESTIONS:

1. To put the person at ease and to start to gain their trust
2. The person's particular needs, anxiety levels, past experiences of assessments, paranoia, current distress, current positive or negative symptoms, reading ability, and a wide range of other issues!
3. All of the these, with consideration of the fact that the risk of the person experiencing a violent attack by others is higher than the risk of the person perpetrating a violent attack.
4. False

References

Andreasen, N., Flaum, M., Arndt, S., Alliger, R., & Swayze, V. W. (1991). Positive and negative symptoms: assessment and validity. In *Negative versus positive schizophrenia* (pp. 28–51). Berlin, Heidelberg: Springer.

Andreasen, N. C. (1983). *The scale for the assessment of negative symptoms (SANS)*. Iowa City: University of Iowa.

Andreasen, N. C. (1984). *Scale for the assessment of positive symptoms (SAPS)*. Iowa City: University of Iowa.

Barnby, J. M., & Bell, V. (2017). The Sensed Presence Questionnaire (SenPQ): initial psychometric validation of a measure of the "Sensed Presence" experience. *PeerJ*, *5*, e3149.

Bell, V., Halligan, P. W., & Ellis, H. D. (2005). The Cardiff Anomalous Perceptions Scale (CAPS): a new validated measure of anomalous perceptual experience. *Schizophrenia Bulletin*, *32*(2), 366–377.

Bell, V., Mills, K. L., Modinos, G., & Wilkinson, S. (2017). Rethinking social cognition in light of psychosis: reciprocal implications for cognition and psychopathology. *Clinical Psychological Science*, *5*(3), 537–550.

Bentall, R. P., & Slade, P. D. (1985). Reliability of a scale measuring disposition towards hallucination: a brief report. *Personality and Individual Differences*, *6*(4), 527–529.

Birchwood, M., Meaden, A., Trower, P., Gilbert, P., & Plaistow, J. (2000). The power and omnipotence of voices: subordination and entrapment by voices and significant others. *Psychological Medicine*, *30*(2), 337–344.

Birchwood, M., Smith, J., Drury, V., Healy, J., Macmillan, F., & Slade, M. (1994). A self-report insight scale for psychosis: reliability, validity and sensitivity to change. *Acta Psychiatrica Scandinavica*, *89* (1), 62–67.

Brabban, A., Byrne, R., Longden, E., & Morrison, A. P. (2017). The importance of human relationships, ethics and recovery-orientated values in the delivery of CBT for people with psychosis. *Psychosis*, *9*(2), 157–166.

Chadwick, P., Lees, S., & Birchwood, M. A. X. (2000). The revised beliefs about voices questionnaire (BAVQ-R). *The British Journal of Psychiatry*, *177*(3), 229–232.

Chan, M. K., Bhatti, H., Meader, N., Stockton, S., Evans, J., O'connor, R. C., et al. (2016). Predicting suicide following self-harm: systematic review of risk factors and risk scales. *The British Journal of Psychiatry*, *209*(4), 277–283.

Coid, J. W., Ullrich, S., Bebbington, P., Fazel, S., & Keers, R. (2016). Paranoid ideation and violence: meta-analysis of individual subject data of 7 population surveys. *Schizophrenia Bulletin, 42*(4), 907–915.

de Vries, B., van Busschbach, J. T., van der Stouwe, E. C. D., Aleman, A., van Dijk, J. J. M., Lysaker, P. H., et al. (2018). Prevalence rate and risk factors of victimization in adult patients with a psychotic disorder: a systematic review and meta-analysis. *Schizophrenia Bulletin, 45*(1), 114–126.

Dugré, J. R., Guay, J. P., & Dumais, A. (2018). Risk factors of compliance with self-harm command hallucinations in individuals with affective and non-affective psychosis. *Schizophrenia Research, 195*, 115–121.

Fenigstein, A., & Vanable, P. A. (1992). Paranoia and self-consciousness. *Journal of Personality and Social Psychology, 62*(1), 129.

Gerretsen, P., Remington, G., Borlido, C., Quilty, L., Hassan, S., Polsinelli, G., et al. (2014). The VAGUS insight into psychosis scale–self-report and clinician-rated versions. *Psychiatry Research, 220*(3), 1084–1089.

Gilleen, J., & David, A. S. (2005). The cognitive neuropsychiatry of delusions: from psychopathology to neuropsychology and back again. *Psychological Medicine, 35*(1), 5–12.

Green, C. E. L., Freeman, D., Kuipers, E., Bebbington, P., Fowler, D., Dunn, G., et al. (2008). Measuring ideas of persecution and social reference: the Green et al. Paranoid Thought Scales (GPTS). *Psychological Medicine, 38*(1), 101–111.

Gumley, A. I., Gillan, K., Morrison, A. P., & Schwannauer, M. (2011). The development and validation of the Beliefs About Paranoia Scale (Short Form). *Behavioural and Cognitive Psychotherapy, 39* (1), 35–53.

Haddock, G., McCarron, J., Tarrier, N., & Faragher, E. B. (1999). Scales to measure dimensions of hallucinations and delusions: the psychotic symptom rating scales (PSYRATS). *Psychological Medicine, 29*(4), 879–889.

Johns, L., Jolley, S., Keen, N., & Peters, E. (2014). *CBT with people with psychosis. How to become a more effective CBT therapist* (pp. 191–207).

Kay, S. R., Fiszbein, A., & Opler, L. A. (1987). The positive and negative syndrome scale (PANSS) for schizophrenia. *Schizophrenia Bulletin, 13*(2), 261–276.

Kemp, R., & David, A. (1997). Insight and compliance. In B. Blackwell (Ed.), *Treatment compliance and the therapeutic alliance* (pp. 61–84). Australia: Harwood Academic Publishers. Wisconsin.

Mason, O., Claridge, G., & Jackson, M. (1995). New scales for the assessment of schizotypy. *Personality and Individual Differences, 18*(1), 7–13.

Mason, O., Linney, Y., & Claridge, G. (2005). Short scales for measuring schizotypy. *Schizophrenia Research, 78*(2–3), 293–296.

McKay, R., Langdon, R., & Coltheart, M. (2006). The persecutory ideation questionnaire. *The Journal of Nervous and Mental Disease, 194*(8), 628–631.

Miller, T. J., McGlashan, T. H., Rosen, J. L., Somjee, L., Markovich, P. J., Stein, K., et al. (2002). Prospective diagnosis of the initial prodrome for schizophrenia based on the structured interview for prodromal syndromes: preliminary evidence of interrater reliability and predictive validity. *American Journal of Psychiatry, 159*(5), 863–865.

Morgan, K. D., Dazzan, P., Morgan, C., Lappin, J., Hutchinson, G., Suckling, J., et al. (2010). Insight, grey matter and cognitive function in first-onset psychosis. *The British Journal of Psychiatry, 197*(2), 141–148.

Morrison, A. P., Gumley, A. I., Schwannauer, M., Campbell, M., Gleeson, A., Griffin, E., et al. (2005). The beliefs about paranoia scale: preliminary validation of a metacognitive approach to conceptualizing paranoia. *Behavioural and Cognitive Psychotherapy, 33*(2), 153–164.

Mueser, K. T., Sayers, S. L., Schooler, N. R., Mance, R. M., & Haas, G. L. (1994). A multisite investigation of the reliability of the scale for the assessment of negative symptoms. *American Journal of Psychiatry, 151*(10), 1453–1462.

Müller, M. J., & Wetzel, H. (1998). Improvement of inter-rater reliability of PANSS items and subscales by a standardized rater training. *Acta Psychiatrica Scandinavica, 98*(2), 135–139.

Nordgaard, J., Arnfred, S. M., Handest, P., & Parnas, J. (2007). The diagnostic status of first-rank symptoms. *Schizophrenia Bulletin, 34*(1), 137–154.

Norman, R. M., Malla, A. K., Cortese, L., & Diaz, F. (1996). A study of the interrelationship between and comparative interrater reliability of the SAPS, SANS and PANSS. *Schizophrenia Research, 19* (1), 73–85.

Peters, E., Joseph, S., Day, S., & Garety, P. (2004). Measuring delusional ideation: the 21-item Peters et al. Delusions Inventory (PDI). *Schizophrenia Bulletin, 30*(4), 1005–1022.

Peters, E., Ward, T., Jackson, M., Morgan, C., Charalambides, M., McGuire, P., et al. (2016). Clinical, socio-demographic and psychological characteristics in individuals with persistent psychotic experiences with and without a "need for care" *World Psychiatry, 15*(1), 41–52.

Peters, E. R., Joseph, S. A., & Garety, P. A. (1999). Measurement of delusional ideation in the normal population: introducing the PDI (Peters et al. Delusions Inventory). *Schizophrenia Bulletin, 25*(3), 553–576.

Rawlings, D., & Freeman, J. L. (1996). A questionnaire for the measurement of paranoia/suspiciousness. *British Journal of Clinical Psychology, 35*(3), 451–461.

Singh, J. P., Fazel, S., Gueorguieva, R., & Buchanan, A. (2014). Rates of violence in patients classified as high risk by structured risk assessment instruments. *The British Journal of Psychiatry, 204*(3), 180–187.

Strauss, C., Hugdahl, K., Waters, F., Hayward, M., Bless, J. J., Falkenberg, L. E., et al. (2018). The beliefs about voices questionnaire – revised: a factor structure from 450 participants. *Psychiatry Research, 259*, 95–103.

Tandon, R., Gaebel, W., Barch, D. M., Bustillo, J., Gur, R. E., Heckers, S., et al. (2013). Definition and description of schizophrenia in the DSM-5. *Schizophrenia Research, 150*(1), 3–10.

Van Duppen, Z. (2017). The intersubjective dimension of schizophrenia. *Philosophy, Psychiatry, & Psychology, 24*(4), 399–418.

Varese, F., Smeets, F., Drukker, M., Lieverse, R., Lataster, T., Viechtbauer, W., et al. (2012). Childhood adversities increase the risk of psychosis: a meta-analysis of patient-control, prospective-and cross-sectional cohort studies. *Schizophrenia Bulletin, 38*(4), 661–671.

Waters, F., Blom, J. D., Jardri, R., Hugdahl, K., & Sommer, I. E. C. (2018). Auditory hallucinations, not necessarily a hallmark of psychotic disorder. *Psychological Medicine, 48*, 529–536.

Whitford, W., O'Driscoll, G. A., & Titone, D. (2018). Reading deficits in schizophrenia and their relationship to developmental dyslexia: a review. *Schizophrenia Research, 193*, 11–22.

Definition of Key Terms

Engagement Encompasses the development of the therapist–client bond, specific therapeutic procedures and activities that the therapist utilises, as well as the extent to which the client actively participates in the assessment or therapy process.

Psychological formulation A hypothesis or collection of hypotheses about the causes, precipitants and maintaining influences of a person's difficulties and distress, which may be used to inform treatment.

Scale In the sense used in this chapter, a scale is a formalised and typically standardised questionnaire or interview used to measure the presence of certain experiences or characteristics.

CHAPTER 7

Negative Symptoms and Their Assessment in Schizophrenia and Related Disorders

Jack J. Blanchard*, LeeAnn Shan*, Alexandra Andrea*, Christina Savage*, Ann M. Kring†, Lauren Weittenhiller†
*Department of Psychology, University of Maryland, College Park, MD, United States, †Department of Psychology, University of California, Berkeley, CA, United States

Key Learning Objectives

- To understand the definition and clinical significance of negative symptoms.
- Learn about the development of negative symptom interviews and the limitations of these instruments.
- Become familiar with next-generation negative symptom scales and the latest research on their similarities and differences.
- Learn about general guidelines and suggestions to incorporate in clinical practice when assessing negative symptoms.
- Gain an understanding of approaches other that interviews that might be used for negative symptom assessment.

INTRODUCTION: NEGATIVE SYMPTOMS DEFINED

Negative symptoms can best be defined as a decrease in subjective experiences and behaviours that are normally present in a person from the same culture (Blanchard, Kring, Horan, & Gur, 2011). Kirkpatrick, Fenton, Carpenter Jr. and Marder (2006) established a consensus regarding what domains comprise negative symptoms in order to guide future scale development. These domains included anhedonia (diminished pleasure experienced from range of activities such as social, recreational, school, and work activities), asociality (decreased motivation and desire to be in affiliative relationships), avolition (diminished

Anhedonia refers to the diminished experience of pleasure.

Asociality refers to a diminished motivation and desire for affiliative interactions and relationships.

Avolition is defined as decreased motivation to achieve goals in different contexts (e.g. social, academic, work).

A Clinical Introduction to Psychosis. https://doi.org/10.1016/B978-0-12-815012-2.00007-9

Blunted affect refers to diminished expressive behaviour, including fewer facial expressions and gestures.

Alogia refers to diminished speech production characterised by very brief answers and lack of elaboration.

motivation for goal-oriented pursuits, including recreational, academic, or occupational), blunted affect (diminished facial expression or expressive gestures and reduced vocal intonation), and alogia (reduced speech output) (see a case example, in Box 7.1).

In the case described in Box 7.1, Terry evidences a lack of engagement with and disinterest in his roommates. Relatedly he is not interested or motivated to establish new friendships, preferring to self-isolate. Even with family relationships, Terry does not report any affiliative feelings towards his sister and his limited interest in her seems to be more financially motivated. In terms of occupational motivation and pleasure, Terry is clearly not engaging in much goal-directed behaviour and reports a lack of motivation for obtaining employment. All of these characteristics are consistent with deficits in motivation and behaviour in both social and occupational spheres—aspects of negative symptoms. Notably, some of Terry's expressive behaviour (smiles, gestures) appear to be in normal limits and suggests that he may not have an elevation in the negative symptom of blunted affect. This later observation highlights the fact that individuals can experience elevations in one domain of negative symptoms (e.g. motivation and behaviour), while the other domain in not necessarily symptomatic (e.g. expressive behaviour). The two main domains of negative symptoms will be fully described now.

CLINICAL IMPORTANCE

Negative symptoms have been shown to be of clinical importance for a variety of reasons. First, negative symptoms are not merely correlates of other symptom domains such as positive symptoms (delusions, hallucinations, thought disorder) or depression. Rather, negative symptoms emerge as a distinct symptom factor that is largely separate from other symptoms (e.g. Blanchard et al., 2017; Kring, Gur, Blanchard, Horan, & Reise, 2013; see review by Blanchard & Cohen, 2006). These results emphasise the importance of including negative symptoms in any clinical evaluation.

Negative symptoms are clinically informative: being significantly associated with poorer social functioning and quality of life.

In addition to the statistical separation from other symptoms, negative symptoms are highly informative regarding overall functioning. Negative symptoms have been repeatedly found to be associated with poorer clinician-rated social functioning (e.g. Blanchard et al., 2017; Kalin et al., 2015; Kring et al., 2013; Rocca et al., 2014; Ventura et al., 2015) and are associated with poorer self-reported quality of life (Blanchard et al., 2017; Eack & Newhill, 2007; Edgar et al., 2014; Lysaker & Davis, 2004). Negative symptoms may also contribute to family burden and conflict (Perlick et al., 2006; Weisman, Nuechterlein, Goldstein, & Snyder, 2000). Finally, in young adults at clinical high risk, negative symptoms appear to manifest in the prodrome (i.e. the period during which symptoms and other difficulties may emerge, but diagnostic criteria are not met) of the illness, often precede attenuated positive symptoms (Pelletier-Baldelli, Strauss, Visser, & Mittal, 2017; Velthorst et al., 2009), and may

Box 7.1 Case Example: 'Terry'[a]

Terry is a 35-year-old black male diagnosed with schizophrenia, who has been attending an outpatient psychiatric program for the past 15years. Terry presents as relaxed and approachable in his demeanour—smiling, making eye contact, and occasionally gesturing with his hands as he speaks. Although Terry responds when spoken to, his answers are typically quite brief and he rarely if ever initiates any conversations.

Terry's treatment has been going well, although he hears voices 'occasionally', and sometimes will demonstrate odd behavior (i.e. giggling to himself or wearing several layers of clothing in the summer). He currently resides in a residential group home, which he shares with seven other men. Although Terry has frequent contact with other housemates (e.g. during meals or when sitting in the same community room), upon more detailed questioning it is clear that these contacts are brief and passive in nature (someone asking him for a cigarette) and he indicates that he does not consider his housemates as friends. When asked if he would like to have friends, Terry notes that he is not really interested in having friends and describes himself as content to be alone. Terry's sister calls on a weekly basis (he never initiates the call to her) but Terry confides that he does not feel close to his sister and only looks forward to these calls so that he can ask for money. When asked if being part of a family is important to him, Terry says that he could take it or leave it.

Though Terry has attended vocational rehabilitation groups recommended by his therapist, he has not taken any steps to look for job openings and notes that he really does not miss having a job as he does not feel that being employed is particular enjoyable and he has no particular interest in making the effort to get a new job. When asked about future plans, Terry shrugs and says, 'I'll be doing the same thing I did last week'.

[a]Hypothetical case.

contribute to the transition to psychosis and poor functional outcomes (Addington et al., 2016; Lencz, Smith, Auther, Correll, & Cornblatt, 2004; Meyer et al., 2014; Piskulic et al., 2012).

Despite the clinical importance of negative symptoms, we have made only modest progress in treating these symptoms. Current medications appear to only partially reduce the severity of negative symptoms (Leucht, Pitschel-Walz, Abraham, & Kissling, 1999; Montgomery et al., 2004; Murphy, Chung, Park, & McGorry, 2006; Remington et al., 2016). No medication has received approval from the United Sates Food and Drug Administration (FDA) with an indication for negative symptoms (Laughren & Levin, 2006). Psychotherapeutic approaches to negative symptoms have yielded mixed results with social skills training showing some modest promise (e.g. Elis, Caponigro, & Kring, 2013; Granholm, Holden, Link, & McQuaid, 2014; see metaanalysis by Turner, van der Gaag, Karyotaki, & Cuijpers, 2014). Longitudinal research on the course of negative symptoms has found these symptoms to be relatively stable across the lifespan (Möller et al., 2010). Though fewer studies have focused specifically on negative symptoms in late adulthood, negative symptom severity among geriatric patients with schizophrenia has been found to be increased at one-year follow-up (Harvey et al., 1996), or remain unchanged

Long-term follow-up studies suggest that negative symptoms are relatively stable over the course of illness.

(McGurk et al., 2000). Because of limited treatment success (Aleman et al., 2017), it is critical that continued research examine the causes and interventions for these symptoms.

CLINICAL INTERVIEW ASSESSMENTS

First-wave measures of negative symptoms have a number of weaknesses, including problematic item content and questionable construct validity.

First-wave measures. Given the prevalence, stability, and clinical significance of negative symptoms, it is important to be able to reliably assess these symptoms in both research and clinical settings. A variety of negative symptom clinical interviews have been developed to assess the severity of negative symptoms (for more detailed reviews, see Blanchard et al., 2011; Lincoln, Dollfus, & Lyne, 2017). The first wave of instruments came in the 1980s and included the Scale for the Assessment of Negative Symptoms (SANS; Andreasen, 1984), the Positive and Negative Syndrome Scale (PANSS; Kay, Fiszbein, & Opfer, 1987), and the Negative Symptom Assessment (NSA; Alphs, Summerfelt, Lann, & Muller, 1989). These scales share many features including their broad assessment of the five domains described earlier.

The development of these scales marked an important milestone as researchers and clinicians for the first time could reliably assess and quantify the severity of negative symptoms and explore the associations between these symptoms and other symptom domains, as well as how negative symptoms were related to functioning and outcome. The subsequent decades of research clearly established the clinical importance of negative symptoms and, as reviewed earlier, their impact on functioning and outcomes. However, these measures were not without problems and limitations (not unusual with the first-generation instruments). By reviewing these measurement difficulties, it is also intended to convey the clinical issues that need to be considered in assessing negative symptoms regardless of the instrument selected.

One problem with these earlier instruments concerns their item content, which in some cases does not reflect our current understanding of the negative symptom construct. For example, the SANS includes ratings of *'attention'* while the PANSS rates *'abstract thinking'* and *'stereotyped thinking'*. These cognitive items are not conceptually consistent with current definitions of negative symptoms and potentially conflate negative symptoms with cognitive ability (e.g. Farreny, Usall, Cuevas-Esteban, Ochoa, & Brebion, 2018). Studies examining the factor structure of these items have found that such cognitive items do not load on a negative symptom factor (Sayers, Curran, & Mueser, 1996; White, Harvey, Opler, & Lindenmayer, 1997). Further, cognitive impairment appears to be distinct from negative symptoms (Couture, Granholm, & Fish, 2011; Harvey, Koren, Reichenberg, & Bowie, 2006) and cognitive ability and negative symptoms have differential associations with disability (e.g. Strassnig et al., 2015).

A further difficulty with measures such as the SANS and NSA is that some items may include content that is not conceptually related to the central features of the symptom being rated. As summarised by Blanchard et al. (2011), this includes ratings of the SANS item 'anhedonia–asociality', which can reflect frequency of social contact and social activity, decreased interest, decreased pleasure, and, problematically, hostility. Thus, a high score on this item could reflect changes in pleasure and social drive but could also be influenced by conflictual social relations—a characteristic that does not represent the prevailing understanding of anhedonia-asociality. Similarly, the NSA includes a rating of reduced emotional range that reflects diminished pleasure (anhedonia) but is also defined as reflecting a *lack of negative emotional experience*, including anxiety or sadness. Diminished negative affect is again not consistent with how negative symptoms are presently defined. Such an item could lead to an unusual circumstance in which an individual who is not anxious or sad is actually rated more pathologically to reflect a reduction in emotional range. This could also yield an odd outcome in the case that a treatment induces greater anxiety or sadness—such a treatment would be seen as 'improving' this symptom as the person would be viewed as having more emotional range.

It is challenging to identify the best way to assess core negative symptom constructs that involve internal or experiential states (e.g. pleasure, affiliative desire, motivation). We have previously noted (Blanchard et al., 2011) that with the PANSS, items such as 'emotional withdrawal', 'poor rapport', and 'passive/apathetic social withdrawal' are conceptually defined in terms of internal states, including interest, affect, empathy, and closeness; however, within the PANSS, these are rated exclusively based on observation of behaviour during the interview and reports of social behaviour and functioning from care workers or family. Thus, ratings that should be informed by deficits in the experience of emotion, interest, and feelings of empathy and closeness do not consider patient reports but instead rely on observer ratings of social success and functioning. Such reliance on behavioural indicators can be problematic as social success may reflect factors unrelated to experiential deficits in hedonic experience, affiliative drive, or motivation and instead reflect unrelated barriers to social functioning, including poor behavioural social skills (Bellack, Sayers, Mueser, & Bennett, 1994), lack of opportunity, neighbourhood deprivation, and economic issues such as limited occupational choices because of disability payments. It is certainly true that negative symptoms can contribute to both skills deficits and diminished subjective affiliative responses (Blanchard, Park, Catalano, & Bennett, 2015) but relying exclusively on fallible behavioural indicators can lead to an inaccurate appraisal of symptoms that are at their core intended to reflect internal experiential deficits.

The reliance of first-generation assessments on purely behavioural indicators of negative symptoms may result in a more limited understanding of their internal, experiential aspects.

Next-generation measures. Two instruments have been developed in order to address the above concerns and provide enhanced measurement of negative symptoms: The Clinical Assessment Interview for Negative Symptoms (CAINS; Blanchard et al., 2011; Horan, Kring, Gur, Reise, & Blanchard, 2011; Kring et al., 2013) and the Brief Negative Symptom Scale (BNSS; Kirkpatrick et al., 2011; Strauss et al., 2012; Strauss et al., 2012). Table 7.1 summarises

Table 7.1 Comparing Next Generation Clinical Interviews of Negative Symptoms

Measure	CAINS	BNSS
Number of items	13	13
Administration time	15–30 min	10–15 min
Time frame	Past week and next week	Past week and near future
Rating Scale	0–4	0–6
Informant Source	Client	Client
Life Domains Assessed	Social; Education/ Vocation; Recreation	Not considered separately
Types of experience assessed	Not considered separately	Internal experience; behaviour
Symptom Domains Assessed	Motivation and Pleasure; Expression	Motivation and Pleasure; Distress; Expression
Frequency of Activity Assessment Method	Precise count of activities	Global consideration of behaviour

Note: *CAINS*, Clinical Assessment Interview for Negative Symptoms; *BNSS*, Brief Negative Symptom Scale.

the features of these two measures. The CAINS and BNSS emerged from an investigative group that was involved with the 2006 National Institute of Mental Health (NIMH) consensus meeting on negative symptoms (Kirkpatrick et al., 2006). Two teams addressed the development of the next-generation negative symptom scales with somewhat different strategies (Blanchard et al., 2011). The BNSS sought to develop an instrument that was brief and quick to administer that could be developed and deployed for use in a rapid manner. The initial BNSS 13-item set was established and after initial psychometric testing (Kirkpatrick et al., 2011) was deployed and examined in subsequent studies (Strauss, Hong, et al., 2012; Strauss, Keller, et al., 2012). The BNSS takes approximately 15 min to complete.

The CAINS development was supported by an NIMH grant, involved four academic research centres, and adopted a strategy that would ensure inclusiveness and breadth in early developmental tests of the scale. Based on a feasibility study (Forbes et al., 2010), a longer beta-version of the CAINS (23-items; Horan et al., 2011) was initially developed with the expectation that this longer scale would be exposed to a data-driven iterative process to psychometrically refine the scale, including revising and trimming items (steps that no other negative symptom instrument had followed). Based on preliminary findings (Horan et al., 2011), the CAINS was revised to 16-items and the revised item set was examined in a large-scale multisite study yielding a final edited version of 13-items (Kring et al., 2013). The CAINS was subsequently examined by an independent investigative team in a multisite study of over 500 participants and its psychometric properties replicated and extended (Blanchard et al., 2017). It is estimated that the CAINS takes approximately 15–30 min to complete.

Despite their different approaches to scale development, the CAINS and BNSS have a number of similarities. The CAINS and BNSS rely exclusively on results and observations during the interview and do not require informants to complete the assessments. Each is 13-items and both sought to assess the consensus domains of negative symptoms (anhedonia, asociality, amotivation, blunted or flat affect, and alogia) and both yield separate scores reflecting Motivation and Pleasure (MAP) and Expressivity (EXP). Both scales consider behaviour and self-reports of internal experience and each scale attempts to obtain assessments in the moment as well as of expected or anticipated pleasure. Overall both the CAINS and BNSS show good internal consistency, rater agreement, test–retest reliability, as well as convergent and discriminant validity. A direct comparison of the CAINS and BNSS (Strauss & Gold, 2016) demonstrated similar psychometric properties across the measures and moderate-to-high correspondence on amotivation, asociality, blunted affect, and alogia items. Translations of the CAINS are available to enhance international studies, including versions in Czech, French, Spanish, Mandarin, Cantonese, Korean, Polish, Greek, Swedish, Lithuanian, and German (e.g. Chan et al., 2015; Engel, Fritzsche, & Lincoln, 2014; Jang et al., 2016; Valiente-Gómez et al., 2015; Xie et al., 2018). Similarly, the BNSS has been translated into Spanish, Italian, and Turkish (Mané et al., 2014; Merlotti, Mucci, Bucci, Nardi, & Galderisi, 2014; Mucci et al., 2015; Nazli et al., 2016).

Differences do emerge, however, when looking closer at the BNSS and CAINS. Strauss and Gold (2016) found lower cross-measurement correlations were achieved between the CAINS and BNSS items tapping anhedonia, and this may reflect the different definitions of these items (with the CAINS examining frequency of pleasure and the BNSS also assessing intensity) and how they are assessed (the CAINS devotes separate items to assess pleasure from social, work, and recreational sources, while the BNSS assess these in a combined manner and adds physical experiences). Further, the BNSS has been found to be more strongly correlated with measures of cognitive ability than the CAINS (Strauss & Gold, 2016); weak correlations between the CAINS and cognitive assessments have been previously reported (e.g. Blanchard et al., 2017; Kring et al., 2013). There are different perspectives on such a finding with some such as Strauss (Strauss & Gold, 2016) seeing a relation with cognition as a demonstration of convergent validity. However, other research supports the view that cognitive functioning is a related but distinct domain (Couture et al., 2011; Harvey et al., 2006; Strassnig et al., 2015) and that too much common variance might raise concerns about the negative symptom scale being contaminated by cognitive ability rather than tapping constructs such as affiliation, pleasure, and motivation. Future research will need to examine this issue and further evaluate whether the two scales are truly differentially influenced by various domains of cognitive functioning. A final difference is that the BNSS includes an item on lack of 'distress'. As described earlier with the NSA's item on reduced emotional range, the BNSS 'distress' item is not consistent with definitions of negative symptoms, appears inconsistent with research findings (e.g. Horan & Blanchard, 2003), and risks pathologising healthy behaviour when an individual may not experience negative affect to certain events (and again interventions that increase depression or anxiety would oddly be seen as *improving* this symptom). The psychometric data from the BNSS show that this item does not clearly load on either MAP or EXP factor and is reported as a separate single-item score (Kirkpatrick et al., 2011; Strauss & Gold, 2016).

GENERAL CONSIDERATIONS

Two main domains of negative symptoms are (i) deficits in motivation and pleasure, and (ii) diminished expressivity.

Assessing two domains of negative symptoms. As noted earlier, the CAINS and BNSS yield scores reflecting motivation and pleasure deficits and diminished expression. These scores are consistent with factor analyses of these scales (e.g. Blanchard et al., 2017; Kring et al., 2013), and this same bifactor structure has been found in studies of other symptom scales (Liemburg et al., 2013; Messinger et al., 2011; Mueser, Sayers, Schooler, Mance, & Haas, 1994; Peralta & Cuesta, 1995; Strauss, Hong, et al., 2012; for a review see Blanchard & Cohen, 2006; also see Foussias & Remington, 2010). Thus, a replicable finding is that negative symptoms are composed of two distinct, though modestly correlated, facets reflecting experiential and expressive deficits. This finding has important assessment implications in that deficits in one domain should not be used to infer deficits in the other.

In examining the two negative symptom domains, research has demonstrated that these facets have differential correlates. Motivation and pleasure deficits appear to be more robustly related to functional impairment than expressive deficits (e.g. Kalin et al., 2015; Rocca et al., 2014). Studies of the CAINS have found that although both subscales are related to functional impairment, the motivation and pleasure domain is more strongly related to social functioning (Blanchard et al., 2017; Kring et al., 2013; but see Strauss and Gold (2016) for a failure to find this differential association in either the CAINS or BNSS). Another differential correlate has to do with self-reported quality of life. Motivation and pleasure rated on the CAINS is significantly related to poorer quality of life, while the expressive domain was not related to this patient-reported outcome (Blanchard et al., 2017).

The findings demonstrate the advantages of using measures of negative symptoms that provide separate ratings of motivation and pleasure and expressivity (Rocca et al., 2014). As noted by Blanchard et al. (2017), negative symptom measures that were designed to only offer a single aggregate negative symptom score (like the NSA-4 and PANSS) are problematic in not being able to detect differential correlates or treatment effects across these two distinct facets of negative symptoms. One could try to develop subscale scores for the NSA-4, but this would result in each such subscale score being based on only two items tapping expression and two items tapping motivation and pleasure—raising concerns about the adequacy of such an assessment. PANSS items have been used to generate subscale scores for the two negative symptom facets (e.g. Liemburg et al., 2013; Stiekema et al., 2016), but each of these approaches has included PANSS negative symptom items that are not conceptually related to negative symptoms (e.g. active social avoidance that reflects fear, hostility or distrust) and are typically excluded in other factor work on the PANSS (Wallwork, Fortgang, Hashimoto, Weinberger, & Dickinson, 2012). When such items are excluded, like the NSA-4, the PANSS yields only two items tapping the motivation and pleasure domain.

Measures of depression and negative symptoms tend to be weakly correlated, suggesting they need to be considered separately in clinical assessments.

Relations with other (nonnegative) symptoms. Since the early development of negative symptom measures, a fundamental question has been to what extent are these unique and independent of other symptoms of the illness, including psychotic symptoms, depression, or anxiety. Psychotic symptoms such as paranoia (Freeman, 2016) may lead to social withdrawal and isolation that appear similar to asociality and social anhedonia. Research examining the association between negative and positive symptoms have yielded variable findings but modest positive correlations (typically *r*'s less than .35) have been found between broad indices of positive symptoms and facets of negative symptoms on different scales (Blanchard et al., 2017; Kring et al., 2013; Strauss & Gold, 2016). This suggests that positive symptoms may be associated with negative symptoms regardless of rating scale used, but that the contribution is typically limited, with approximately 12% of the variance in negative symptoms accounted for by positive symptoms.

A defining feature of depression is anhedonia (Blanchard, Horan, & Brown, 2001) and depression can be associated with social withdrawal and isolation—thus raising the possibility that negative symptoms may in part be influenced by depression. However, research has shown that negative symptoms (across a variety of different scales) are often not significantly or only weakly associated with clinical ratings of depression (e.g. Blanchard et al., 2017; Kring et al., 2013; Strauss & Gold, 2016). Thus, in most cases, negative symptom ratings do not seem to reflect co-occurring depression.

Although the findings are somewhat reassuring, it is important for clinicians to be aware of other symptoms such as paranoia or depression and how these may have an impact on functioning and responding to a negative symptom assessment (Carpenter Jr., Heinrichs, & Wagman, 1988). Just how to handle the presence of other symptoms is not clearly addressed in most negative symptom interviews (but see later regarding the deficit syndrome). The BNSS manual provides no instructions on how other symptoms might be considered. The CAINS manual suggests that raters may find it useful to conduct other symptom interviews prior to the CAINS to allow for a better understanding of the individual's full symptom presentation and how other symptoms may be relevant to consider when interpreting responses and making ratings of negative symptoms. The CAINS also notes that delusional beliefs (e.g. the false belief that a television actor is actually a personal friend) are not rateable with regard to social motivation and functioning. The CAINS does direct interviewers to explore with a participant why they may not be engaging in behaviour or why they are not interested and motivated. This may provide some direction for a rater to parse apart the possible influence of nonnegative symptoms but just how to disentangle different symptoms is left to the user to determine. Again, the correlational findings with other symptoms would suggest that this may not be a major issue, but clinically this remains a concern and interviewers should at least conduct a full symptom evaluation to best understand the possible role of nonnegative symptoms in rating deficits in motivation and pleasure and diminished expressivity.

Ratings of negative symptoms as primary or secondary (e.g. assessing deficit syndrome) can be challenging and problematic in typical clinical settings.

One approach to dealing with the contribution of other symptoms to negative symptoms was suggested by Carpenter and colleagues who proposed the concept of the deficit syndrome (Carpenter Jr. et al., 1988; Kirkpatrick, Buchanan, Ross, & Carpenter Jr., 2001). The deficit syndrome concept seeks to differentiate 'true' or primary negative symptoms from those that are transient in their presentation and secondary to other symptoms such as positive symptoms, depression, anxiety, medication side effects, and other factors. However, making such a differentiation is not readily achieved as we illustrate later. The Schedule for the Deficit Syndrome (SDS; Kirkpatrick, Buchanan, McKenney, Alphs, & Carpenter, 1989) was developed to assess the deficit syndrome. Items on the SDS include some but not all of the consensus negative symptom domains. Diminished expression can be captured by the SDS item restricted affect; diminished motivation and pleasure can be partially captured by SDS items curbing of interests, diminished sense of purpose, and diminished social drive. Two other SDS items, poverty of speech and diminished emotional range, do not clearly map onto a consensus negative symptom domain. To meet criteria for the deficit syndrome, at least two SDS items must be present for at least the preceding twelve months, and not be deemed to be secondary to other factors, including positive symptoms, depression, anxiety, and drug effects.

There are several challenges posed in using the SDS. First, like older negative symptom measures, it does not fully assess the consensus negative symptom domains and it includes other domains that are not part of the negative symptoms. Second, the requirement to determine stability of symptoms over a one-year period is difficult when clinicians may not have access to such longitudinal data. Third, determining the contribution of other nonnegative symptoms is also challenging as one would need to document that negative symptoms covary with or follow exacerbations of other symptoms (again, data that may not be available in many research or clinical settings). Fourth, even when richer clinical histories are available, it may be difficult to determine the temporal relationship between symptoms and thus the proper categorisation of participants. Reflecting this challenge, in the original report on the deficit syndrome, almost a quarter of the sample were placed in an uncertain group that did not clearly fit in either a deficit or nondeficit category (Carpenter Jr. et al., 1988). Finally, the deficit syndrome yields a categorical determination that does not reflect severity on a dimension and the single grouping into a deficit category does not address the bifactor structure found in negative symptoms (though the individual SDS symptoms can yield similar factor structure; Kimhy et al., 2006) and may miss the important differential associations found between the experiential and expressive domains.

Perhaps most critically, in attempting to differentiate primary and secondary negative symptoms, there is sometimes a simplistic approach to viewing the presence of any other symptoms such as elevated paranoia or depression as somehow causally responsible for negative symptoms. Indeed, as reviewed earlier, the association with depression is typically quite weak and the relationship between negative symptoms and positive symptoms is modest—thus, simple elevations in other symptom domains are not grounds for concluding that they must underlie negative symptoms. Further, as noted by Blanchard et al. (2017), it is possible that positive symptoms may be secondary to negative symptoms. Negative symptoms may give rise to social environments that contribute to vulnerability for the development or exacerbation of positive symptoms (Jolley et al., 2014; Saha, Scott, Varghese, & McGrath, 2012) or depression. Clinical high-risk studies have shown that negative symptom may contribute to the development or exacerbation of psychotic symptoms (Addington et al., 2016; Lencz et al., 2004; Meyer et al., 2014; Piskulic et al., 2012). The point is that in conducting clinical assessments consideration should be given to all symptom domains and care should be taken in determining how symptoms may be causally related.

Cultural considerations. Culture has been acknowledged as an important consideration in any clinical assessment (e.g. Sue & Sue, 1987; Tseng & Streltzer, 2013; Westermeyer, 1987), and culturally adapted psychosocial interventions are being examined for schizophrenia (Degnan et al., 2017). The availability of translated versions of negative symptom scales has shown that the general properties of these scales are replicable cross-culturally (e.g. Xie et al., 2018). However, we know little about the role of race or culture in the experience and assessment of negative symptoms. Typically, studies of negative symptom scales do not examine the role of race and culture or, when examined, this is simply at the level of racial group differences in symptom severity (Blanchard et al., 2017; Kring et al., 2013). Kring et al. (2013) reported that White individuals were rated higher on the CAINS expression scale compared to African Americans. Blanchard et al. (2017) examined differences in African American and White individuals with schizophrenia and found that African-American participants had higher CAINS MAP scores than did white participants, but there were no racial differences in the CAINS EXP nor were there racial differences in overall negative symptom scores on the NSA-4 or PANSS. These limited and variable findings clearly indicate the need for additional study, including research on how cultural factors beyond broad racial categories may influence the rating of negative symptoms.

We have a limited understanding of how culture and gender influence the experience of negative symptoms.

Regarding gender differences in negative symptoms, some studies have found that men at ultra-high risk for developing psychosis and men diagnosed with schizophrenia exhibit more severe negative symptoms than do their female counterparts (Galderisi, Bucci, Üçok, & Peuskens, 2012; Gur, Petty, Turetsky, & Gur, 1996; Willhite et al., 2008). However, other studies have found no gender differences in negative symptoms (e.g. Blanchard et al., 2017; Kring et al., 2013). It is important to note that prior research has typically focused on mean group differences in negative symptoms, and few of these studies have looked at whether there may be potential differential correlates of negative symptoms in men and women. Overall, as with the role of race and ethnicity, additional research is necessary to explore the relationship between gender and negative symptoms.

SELF-REPORT ASSESSMENT

Not all individuals with psychosis have negative symptoms that warrant clinical attention and some estimates are that approximately 30% to 40% have elevated negative symptoms (Blanchard, Horan, & Collins, 2005). Thus, a screening mechanism to identify those that could benefit from a more in-depth clinical interview might be time efficient and cost effective. Blanchard and colleagues have developed a 15-item self-report scale that focuses on the motivation and pleasure domain of negative symptoms, the CAINS Motivation, and Pleasure Scale-Self-Report (MAPS-SR; Llerena et al., 2013; Park et al., 2012). Preliminary research indicated that a scale attempting to obtain self-reported expressive deficits had poor internal consistency and weak relations with interview ratings (Park et al., 2012).

The CAINS MAP-SR includes items assessing anhedonia, asociality, and avolition/motivation. Anhedonia is assessed with 6 items tapping experienced (intensity and frequency) pleasure across social, physical, and recreational/vocational events as well as expected pleasure in these domains. An example anhedonia item: '*Looking ahead to being with other people in the next few weeks, how much pleasure do you expect you will experience from being with others?*' (rated from 0, 'No pleasure' to 4, 'Extreme pleasure'). Asociality is measured with 3 items assessing the importance of relationships (family, friends, and romantic) and the preference for being with others versus being alone. An example asociality item: '*When it comes to close relationships with your family members, how important have these relationships been to you over the past week?*' (rated from 0, 'Not at all important to me' to 4, 'Extremely important to me'). Avolition is assessed with 6 items that ask about how much the individual wanted, or was motivated, to do various activities in the past week and how much effort they have made to actually do them. An example avolition item: '*In the past week how much effort have you made to do things at work or school? (If you are not working or going to school, how much effort have you made to look for a job or go to school.)*' (rated from 0, 'No effort' to 4, 'Very much effort').

Results from four studies have indicated encouraging convergence between the CAINS MAP-SR and clinician-rated CAINS MAP (Engel & Lincoln, 2016; Engel & Lincoln, 2017; Kim et al., 2016; Llerena et al., 2013). Llerena et al. (2013) reported robust correlations across methods and found that the CAINS MAP-SR was unrelated to positive symptoms or depression (though symptoms of agitation-mania were related to the self-report scale). The CAINS MAP-SR was also highly correlated with other self-report measures tapping social anhedonia and social affiliation and the CAINS MAP-SR was also correlated with clinician-rated social network relationships. Engel and Lincoln (2016) examined the degree of agreement between a German-language version of the clinician-rated MAP symptoms and self-reported symptoms based on the CAINS MAP-SR (Llerena et al., 2013). Convergence with the clinician-rated CAINS-MAP was similar to that of Llerena et al. (2013) with no correlation with positive symptoms but a moderate correlation with self-reported depression. Engel and Lincoln (2017) further examined the performance of the CAINS MAP-SR in patients and healthy participants, and again the two forms of the MAP were highly correlated across the two groups. Examination of disparities across the two forms of assessment suggested that clinical participants tended to have lower self-reported symptoms compared to those rated by the clinician. The authors caution that discrepancies can occur across methods, suggesting that the self-report questionnaire might be used to complement rather than replace interview assessments. Should discrepancies arise across the two methods, this can serve as the basis of clinical discussion to determine how the patient may perceive their experiences differently from the clinician and whether the differing views can be resolved. Finally, a Korean version of the CAINS MAP-SR (Kim et al., 2016) has obtained similar findings with strong cross-method correlations.

Dollfus, Mach, and Morello (2016) developed a 20-item self-report scale (Self-Evaluation of Negative Symptoms; SENS) with the intent to tap each of the five domains of negative symptoms. Four items tap each domain of social withdrawal (I prefer to be alone in my corner), avolition (I find it difficult to meet the objectives I set myself), anhedonia (When I imagine doing one thing or another, I don't feel any particular pleasure in the idea), and alogia (I don't have as much to talk about as most people). A fifth domain refers to 'diminished emotional range' ('There are many happy or sad things in life but I don't feel concerned by them.'). Interestingly, the factor analysis indicated a bivariate structure but alogia loaded on a single factor with anhedonia and amotivation while the diminished emotional range was a separate factor (Dollfus et al., 2016). Thus, the factor structure appears to raise concerns about the rationale of including diminished emotional range within an assessment of negative symptoms (consistent with the points we raised above regarding the PANSS and BNSS and this type of item). The correlation between the SENS interview-based negative symptoms was encouraging; however, the SENS was also strongly correlated with depression, suggesting that it may be more influenced by negative mood than the CAINS MAP-SR.

Although self-report measures of negative symptoms may be useful in clinical and research settings, this approach has limitations. A key issue is that there are no established normative scores or cutoffs for what might denote clinically significant problems. However, self-report measures could be used to help inform clinical assessment and the need for more in-depth clinician-rated symptom evaluation. Although self-report scales could potentially be used to track ongoing symptom severity, there are currently limited longitudinal data regarding the scales temporal stability with no data on the scales' sensitivity to clinical improvement in treatment.

LABORATORY ASSESSMENT

Another means to assess negative symptoms can be the use of laboratory paradigms (Kring & Elis, 2013). These paradigms typically involve presenting emotionally evocative stimuli (e.g. pictures, films, foods, smells) and assessing outward expressions, reports of emotional experience, brain activation, and/or bodily responses (e.g. heart rate).

One of the most well-replicated findings using such paradigms is that people with schizophrenia are much less expressive (both facially and vocally) than people without schizophrenia in response to a variety of emotional situations and stimuli and using different methods to measure expression, including observational coding systems and acoustical analyses of speech (Kring & Elis, 2013). These findings map onto the negative symptom domain of diminished expression.

The external validity of laboratory assessments of negative symptoms is not yet established, and the time and equipment needed currently limit their clinical utility.

Laboratory assessments to assess diminished motivation and pleasure have yielded more mixed findings, perhaps reflecting the nature of the tasks (Kring & Barch, 2014). For example, tasks designed to assess effort expenditure have been used as a proxy for assessing motivation. Performance on these tasks does not always clearly map onto the negative symptom domain of avolition, likely because diminished motivation in actual life is much more complex than performance on a laboratory task.

Indeed, a limitation and challenge for laboratory assessments of negative symptoms is the linkage to not only negative symptoms but also day-to-day behaviour. In addition, laboratory assessments can be more time consuming than clinical assessments and require specialised equipment and space that may not be readily available to all who want to assess negative symptoms. Nevertheless, they can provide 'real time' assessments of the behaviour and experiences that comprise negative symptoms and they do not require accurate recall as clinical interviews and self-report measures do.

FUTURE DIRECTIONS

Ecological momentary assessment. Indeed, the use of interviews or questionnaires in clinical assessment is potentially prone to error as we rely on individuals' retrospective recall of past behaviour and experiences. The passage of time and such individual characteristics as current mood state or memory difficulties may all undermine the validity of such assessments. Ecological momentary assessment (EMA) involves the periodic assessment of ongoing daily experience (Shiffman, Stone, & Hufford, 2008) and can rely on the completion of brief paper questionnaires (prompted by watch alarms or text messages) or the completion of surveys on smartphones. With the widespread adoption of smartphones, EMA is remarkably easy to employ with a variety of software applications now available. EMA has been used in an enormous range of clinical disorders, including schizophrenia and other psychotic disorders (Gard et al., 2014; Gaudiano, Moitra, Ellenberg, & Armey, 2015; Granholm et al., 2007; Granholm, Holden, Link, McQuaid, & Jeste, 2013; Myin-Germeys, Birchwood, & Kwapil, 2011; Oorschot, Kwapil, Delespaul, & Myin-Germeys, 2009). A recent innovative study (Moran, Culbreth, & Barch, 2017) examined the potential use of smartphone-based EMA in assessing motivation and pleasure negative symptoms in schizophrenia (Moran et al., 2017). Their EMA assessment was modelled after the CAINS MAP scale items and assessed activity (e.g. *'What are you doing right now?'*), pleasure (e.g. *'How much are you enjoying X?'*), and interest (e.g. *'How interested are you in X?'*). Participants completed the EMA assessment four times each day over seven days. Results indicated that EMA-rated MAP symptoms were significantly correlated with clinician-rated CAINS MAP scores as well as the self-report MAP-SR. Working memory impairments appeared to diminish the strength of the relationship between clinical-rated negative symptoms and those obtained from EMA. The EMA-based assessments of motivation and pleasure negative symptoms were related to laboratory tasks assessing effort-based decision making, but this relationship did not emerge between clinician-rated symptoms and laboratory tasks. The authors conclude that EMA's use of multiple in-the-moment measurements across each day and aggregated over several days may provide a more sensitive measure of motivation and pleasure than do cross-sectional clinical interviews. Practical constraints do remain, including the lack of easily available applications that are ready to deploy in applied clinical settings and the challenges posed by analysis of the multiple data points generated by EMA may make this approach of limited use in nonresearch settings. In any case, overall the results of Moran et al. (2017) are very promising and suggest the possible use of EMA in assessing motivation and pleasure negative symptoms (Fig. 7.1).

Transdiagnostic and prodrome considerations. It is perhaps important to note that the preceding review has focused primarily on existing negative symptom assessments originally developed for adults formally diagnosed with psychosis. However, negative symptoms are a transdiagnostic feature, and research has shown that negative symptom domains such as anhedonia and asociality exist across other diagnostic groups, including those with nonschizophrenia-spectrum disorders (Kaiser, Heekeren, & Simon, 2011) and individuals at clinical high risk for psychosis (Devoe, Peterson, & Addington, 2017). Regarding the latter, the development of new scales such as the Prodromal Inventory of Negative Symptoms (PINS) have attempted to address more attenuated forms of negative symptomatology within a subclinical population (Pelletier-Baldelli

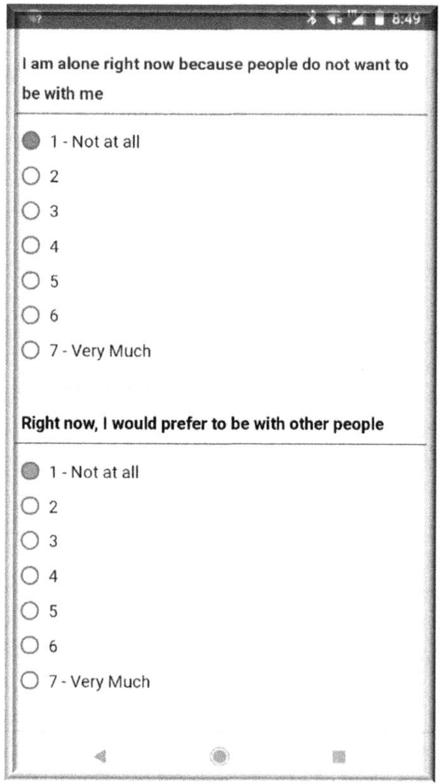

FIG. 7.1
Example of EMA survey questions presented on a smartphone.

et al., 2017). Nevertheless, empirical questions remain about the dimensional nature of negative symptoms, and future research on the prevalence and clinical meaningfulness of these symptoms among other psychiatric disorders is warranted.

FURTHER READING

Barch, D. M., Gold, J. M., & Kring, A. M. (2017). Paradigms for assessing hedonic processing and motivation in humans: Relevance to understanding negative symptoms in psychopathology. *Schizophrenia Bulletin, 43*(4), 701–705. http://doi:10.1093/schbul/sbx063

Blanchard, J. J., Bradshaw, K. R., Garcia, C. P., Nasrallah, H. A., Harvey, P. D., & Casey, D. (2017). Examining the reliability and validity of the clinical assessment interview for negative symptoms within the management of schizophrenia in clinical practice (MOSAIC) multisite national study. *Schizophrenia Research, 185*, 137–143.

Lincoln, T. M., Dollfus, S., & Lyne, J. (2017). Current developments and challenges in the assessment of negative symptoms. *Schizophrenia Research, 186*, 8–18. doi:10.1016/j.schres.2016.02.035

Website for accessing CAINS training: https://www.med.upenn.edu/bbl/cainsvideos.html

Website for accessing BNSS training: https://ugacanlab.com/resources

References

Addington, D. E., Norman, R., Bond, G. R., Sale, T., Melton, R., McKenzie, E., et al. (2016). Development and testing of the First-Episode Psychosis Services Fidelity Scale. *Psychiatric Services, 67*(9), 1023–1025. https://doi.org/10.1176/appi.ps.201500398.

Aleman, A., Lincoln, T. M., Bruggeman, R., Melle, I., Arends, J., Arango, C., et al. (2017). Treatment of negative symptoms: where do we stand, and where do we go? *Schizophrenia Research, 186*, 55–62. https://doi.org/10.1016/j.schres.2016.05.015.

Alphs, L. D., Summerfelt, A., Lann, H., & Muller, R. J. (1989). The negative symptom assessment: a new instrument to assess negative symptoms of schizophrenia. *Psychopharmacological Bulletin, 25*(2), 159–163.

Andreasen, N. C. (1984). *The Scale for the assessment of Positive Symptoms (SAPS)*. Iowa City, Iowa: The University of Iowa.

Bellack, A. S., Sayers, M., Mueser, K. T., & Bennett, M. (1994). Evaluation of social problem solving in schizophrenia. *Journal of Abnormal Psychology, 103*(2), 371–378.

Blanchard, J. J., Bradshaw, K. R., Garcia, C. P., Nasrallah, H. A., Harvey, P. D., Casey, D., et al. (2017). Examining the reliability and validity of the clinical assessment interview for negative symptoms within the management of schizophrenia in clinical practice (MOSAIC) multisite national study. *Schizophrenia Research, 185*, 137–143. https://doi.org/10.1016/j.schres.2017.01.011.

Blanchard, J. J., & Cohen, A. S. (2006). The structure of negative symptoms within schizophrenia: Implications for assessment. *Schizophrenia Bulletin, 32*(2), 238–245. https://doi.org/10.1093/schbul/sbj013.

Blanchard, J. J., Horan, W. P., & Collins, L. M. (2005). Examining the latent structure of negative symptoms: is there a distinct subtype of negative symptom schizophrenia? *Schizophrenia Research, 77*(2–3), 151–165. https://doi.org/10.1016/j.schres.2005.03.022.

Blanchard, J. J., Kring, A. M., Horan, W. P., & Gur, R. (2011). Toward the next generation of negative symptom assessments: the Collaboration to Advance Negative Symptom Assessment in Schizophrenia. *Schizophrenia Bulletin, 37*(2), 291–299. https://doi.org/10.1093/schbul/sbq104.

Blanchard, J. J., Park, S. G., Catalano, L. T., & Bennett, M. E. (2015). Social affiliation and negative symptoms in schizophrenia: examining the role of behavioral skills and subjective responding. *Schizophrenia Research, 168*(1–2), 491–497. https://doi.org/10.1016/j.schres.2015.07.019.

Blanchard, J. L., Horan, W. P., & Brown, S. A. (2001). Diagnostic differences in social anhedonia: a longitudinal study of schizophrenia and major depressive disorder. *Journal of Abnormal Psychology, 110*(3), 363–371. https://doi.org/10.1037/0021-843X.110.3.363.

Carpenter, W. T., Jr., Heinrichs, D. W., & Wagman, A. M. (1988). Deficit and nondeficit forms of schizophrenia: the concept. *American Journal of Psychiatry, 145*(5), 578–583. https://doi.org/10.1176/ajp.145.5.578.

Chan, R. C. K., Shi, C., Lui, S. S. Y., Ho, K. K. Y., Hung, K. S. Y., Lam, J. W. S., et al. (2015). Validation of the Chinese version of the Clinical Assessment Interview for Negative Symptoms (CAINS): a preliminary report. *Frontiers in Psychology, 6*(7). https://doi.org/10.3389/fpsyg.2015.00007.

Couture, S. M., Granholm, E. L., & Fish, S. C. (2011). A path model investigation of neurocognition, theory of mind, social competence, negative symptoms and real-world functioning in schizophrenia. *Schizophrenia Research, 125*(2–3), 152–160. https://doi.org/10.1016/j.schres.2010.09.020.

Degnan, A., Baker, S., Edge, D., Nottidge, W., Noke, M., Press, C. J., et al. (2017). The nature and efficacy of culturally-adapted psychosocial interventions for schizophrenia: a systematic review and meta-analysis. *Psychological Medicine, 48*(5), 714–727. https://doi.org/10.1017/S0033291717002264.

Devoe, D. J., Peterson, A., & Addington, J. (2017). Negative symptom interventions in youth at risk of psychosis: a systematic review and network meta-analysis. *Schizophrenia Bulletin, 44*(2), 463. https://doi.org/10.1093/schbul/sbx139.

Dollfus, S., Mach, C., & Morello, R. (2016). Self-evaluation of negative symptoms: a novel tool to assess negative symptoms. *Schizophrenia Bulletin, 42*(3), 571–578. https://doi.org/10.1093/schbul/sbv161.

Eack, S. M., & Newhill, C. E. (2007). Psychiatric symptoms and quality of life in schizophrenia: a meta-analysis. *Schizophrenia Bulletin, 33*(5), 1225–1237. https://doi.org/10.1093/schbul/sbl071.

Edgar, C. J., Blaettler, T., Bugarski-Kirola, D., Le Scouiller, S., Garibaldi, G. M., & Marder, S. R. (2014). Reliability, validity and ability to detect change of the PANSS negative symptom factor score in outpatients with schizophrenia on select antipsychotics and with prominent negative or disorganized thought symptoms. *Psychiatry Research, 218*(1–2), 219–224. https://doi.org/10.1016/j.psychres.2014.04.009.

Elis, O., Caponigro, J. M., & Kring, A. M. (2013). Psychosocial treatments for negative symptoms in schizophrenia: current practices and future directions. *Clinical Psychology Review, 33*(8), 914–928. https://doi.org/10.1016/j.cpr.2013.07.001.

Engel, M., Fritzsche, A., & Lincoln, T. M. (2014). Validation of the German version of the Clinical Assessment Interview for Negative Symptoms (CAINS). *Psychiatry Research, 220*(1–2), 659–663. https://doi.org/10.1016/j.psychres.2014.07.070.

Engel, M., & Lincoln, T. M. (2016). Motivation and Pleasure Scale-Self-Report (MAP-SR): validation of the German version of a self-report measure for screening negative symptoms in schizophrenia. *Comprehensive Psychiatry, 65*, 110–115. https://doi.org/10.1016/j.comppsych.2015.11.001.

Engel, M., & Lincoln, T. M. (2017). Concordance of self- and observer-rated motivation and pleasure in patients with negative symptoms and healthy controls. *Psychiatry Research, 247*, 1–5. https://doi.org/10.1016/j.psychres.2016.11.013.

Farreny, A., Usall, J., Cuevas-Esteban, J., Ochoa, S., & Brebion, G. (2018). Amendment of traditional assessment measures for the negative symptoms of schizophrenia. *European Psychiatry, 49*, 50–55. https://doi.org/10.1016/j.eurpsy.2017.11.003.

Forbes, C., Blanchard, J. J., Bennett, M., Horan, W. P., Kring, A., & Gur, R. (2010). Initial development and preliminary validation of a new negative symptom measure: the Clinical Assessment Interview for Negative Symptoms (CAINS). *Schizophrenia Research, 124*(1–3), 36–42. https://doi.org/10.1016/j.schres.2010.08.039.

Foussias, G., & Remington, G. (2010). Negative symptoms in schizophrenia: avolition and Occam's razor. *Schizophrenia Bulletin, 36*(2), 359–369. https://doi.org/10.1093/schbul/sbn094.

Freeman, D. (2016). Persecutory delusions: a cognitive perspective on understanding and treatment. *Lancet Psychiatry, 3*(7), 685–692. https://doi.org/10.1016/s2215-0366(16)00066-3.

Galderisi, S., Bucci, P., Üçok, A., & Peuskens, J. (2012). No gender differences in social outcome in patients suffering from schizophrenia. *European Psychiatry, 27*(6), 406–408. https://doi.org/10.1016/j.eurpsy.2011.01.011.

Gard, D. E., Sanchez, A. H., Cooper, K., Fisher, M., Garrett, C., & Vinogradov, S. (2014). Do people with schizophrenia have difficulty anticipating pleasure, engaging in effortful behavior, or both? *Journal of Abnormal Psychology, 123*(4), 771–782. https://doi.org/10.1037/abn0000005.

Gaudiano, B. A., Moitra, E., Ellenberg, S., & Armey, M. F. (2015). The promises and challenges of ecological momentary assessment in schizophrenia: development of an initial experimental protocol. *Healthcare (Basel), 3*(3), 556–573. https://doi.org/10.3390/healthcare3030556.

Granholm, E., Holden, J., Link, P. C., & McQuaid, J. R. (2014). Randomized clinical trial of cognitive behavioral social skills training for schizophrenia: improvement in functioning and experiential negative symptoms. *Journal of Consulting and Clinical Psychology, 82*(6), 1173–1185. https://doi.org/10.1037/a0037098.

Granholm, E., Holden, J., Link, P. C., McQuaid, J. R., & Jeste, D. V. (2013). Randomized controlled trial of cognitive behavioral social skills training for older consumers with schizophrenia: defeatist performance attitudes and functional outcome. *The American Journal of Geriatric Psychiatry, 21*(3), 251–262. https://doi.org/10.1016/j.jagp.2012.10.014.

Granholm, E., McQuaid, J. R., McClure, F. S., Link, P. C., Perivoliotis, D., Gottlieb, J. D., et al. (2007). Randomized controlled trial of cognitive behavioral social skills training for older people with schizophrenia: 12-month follow-up. *The Journal of Clinical Psychiatry, 68*(5), 730–737. https://doi.org/10.4088/JCP.v68n0510.

Gur, R. E., Petty, R. G., Turetsky, B. I., & Gur, R. C. (1996). Schizophrenia throughout life: sex differences in severity and profile of symptoms. *Schizophrenia Research, 21*(1), 1–12.

Harvey, P. D., Koren, D., Reichenberg, A., & Bowie, C. R. (2006). Negative symptoms and cognitive deficits: what is the nature of their relationship? *Schizophrenia Bulletin, 32*(2), 250–258. https://doi.org/10.1093/schbul/sbj011.

Harvey, P. D., Lombardi, J., Leibman, M., White, L., Parella, M., Powchik, P., et al. (1996). Cognitive impairment and negative symptoms in geriatric chronic schizophrenic patients: a follow-up study. *Schizophrenia Research, 22*(3), 223–231.

Horan, W. P., & Blanchard, J. J. (2003). Neurocognitive, social, and emotional dysfunction in deficit syndrome schizophrenia. *Schizophrenia Research, 65*(2–3), 125–137.

Horan, W. P., Kring, A. M., Gur, R. E., Reise, S. P., & Blanchard, J. J. (2011). Development and psychometric validation of the Clinical Assessment Interview for Negative Symptoms (CAINS). *Schizophrenia Research, 132*(2–3), 140–145. https://doi.org/10.1016/j.schres.2011.06.030.

Jang, S.-K., Choi, H.-I., Park, S., Jaekal, E., Lee, G.-Y., Cho, Y. I., et al. (2016). A two-factor model better explains heterogeneity in negative symptoms: evidence from the Positive and Negative Syndrome Scale. *Frontiers in Psychology, 7*.

Jolley, S., Ferner, H., Bebbington, P., Garety, P., Dunn, G., Freeman, D., et al. (2014). Delusional belief flexibility and informal caregiving relationships in psychosis: a potential cognitive route for the protective effect of social support. *Epidemiology and Psychiatric Sciences, 23*(4), 389–397. https://doi.org/10.1017/S2045796013000553.

Kaiser, S., Heekeren, K., & Simon, J. J. (2011). The negative symptoms of schizophrenia: category or continuum? *Psychopathology, 44*, 345–353. https://doi.org/10.1159/000325912.

Kalin, M., Kaplan, S., Gould, F., Pinkham, A. E., Penn, D. L., & Harvey, P. D. (2015). Social cognition, social competence, negative symptoms and social outcomes: inter-relationships in people with schizophrenia. *Journal of Psychiatric Research, 68*, 254–260. https://doi.org/10.1016/j.jpsychires.2015.07.008.

Kay, S. R., Fiszbein, A., & Opfer, L. A. (1987). The Positive and Negative Syndrome Scale (PANSS) for Schizophrenia. *Schizophrenia Bulletin, 13*(2), 261–276. https://doi.org/10.1093/schbul/13.2.261.

Kim, J.-S., Jang, S.-K., Park, S.-C., Yi, J.-S., Park, J.-K., Lee, J. S., et al. (2016). Measuring negative symptoms in patients with schizophrenia: reliability and validity of the Korean version of the Motivation and Pleasure Scale-Self-Report. *Neuropsychiatric Disease and Treatment, 12*, 1167–1172.

Kimhy, D., Delespaul, P., Corcoran, C., Ahn, H., Yale, S., & Malaspina, D. (2006). Computerized experience sampling method (ESMc): assessing feasibility and validity among individuals with schizophrenia. *Journal of Psychiatric Research, 40*(3), 221–230. https://doi.org/10.1016/j.jpsychires.2005.09.007.

Kirkpatrick, B., Buchanan, R. W., McKenney, P. D., Alphs, L. D., & Carpenter, W. T. (1989). The Schedule for the Deficit Syndrome: an instrument for research in schizophrenia. *Psychiatry Research, 30*(2), 119–123. https://doi.org/10.1016/0165-1781(89)90153-4.

Kirkpatrick, B., Buchanan, R. W., Ross, D. E., & Carpenter, W. T. , Jr. (2001). A separate disease within the syndrome of schizophrenia. *Archives of General Psychiatry, 58*(2), 165–171. https://doi.org/10.1001/archpsyc.58.2.165.

Kirkpatrick, B., Fenton, W. S., Carpenter, W. T., Jr., & Marder, S. R. (2006). The NIMH-MATRICS consensus statement on negative symptoms. *Schizophrenia Bulletin, 32*(2), 214–219. https://doi.org/10.1093/schbul/sbj053.

Kirkpatrick, B., Strauss, G. P., Nguyen, L., Fischer, B. A., Daniel, D. G., Cienfuegos, A., et al. (2011). The Brief Negative Symptom Scale: psychometric properties. *Schizophrenia Bulletin, 37*(2), 300–305. https://doi.org/10.1093/schbul/sbq059.

Kring, A. M., & Barch, D. M. (2014). The motivation and pleasure dimension of negative symptoms: neural substrates and behavioral outputs. *European Neuropsychopharmacology, 24*(5), 725–736. https://doi.org/10.1016/j.euroneuro.2013.06.007.

Kring, A. M., & Elis, O. (2013). Emotion deficits in people with schizophrenia. *Annual Review of Clinical Psychology, 9*, 409–433. https://doi.org/10.1146/annurev-clinpsy-050212-185538.

Kring, A. M., Gur, R. E., Blanchard, J. J., Horan, W. P., & Reise, S. P. (2013). The Clinical Assessment Interview for Negative Symptoms (CAINS): final development and validation. *The American Journal of Psychiatry, 170*(2), 165–172. https://doi.org/10.1176/appi.ajp.2012.12010109.

Laughren, T., & Levin, R. (2006). Food and Drug Administration perspective on negative symptoms in schizophrenia as a target for a drug treatment claim. *Schizophrenia Bulletin, 32*(2), 220–222. https://doi.org/10.1093/schbul/sbi039.

Lencz, T., Smith, C. W., Auther, A., Correll, C. U., & Cornblatt, B. (2004). Nonspecific and attenuated negative symptoms in patients at clinical high-risk for schizophrenia. *Schizophrenia Research, 68*(1), 37–48. https://doi.org/10.1016/S0920-9964(03)00214-7.

Leucht, S., Pitschel-Walz, G., Abraham, D., & Kissling, W. (1999). Efficacy and extrapyramidal side-effects of the new antipsychotics olanzapine, quetiapine, risperidone, and sertindole compared to conventional antipsychotics and placebo. A meta-analysis of randomized controlled trials. *Schizophrenia Research, 35*(1), 51–68. https://doi.org/10.1016/S0920-9964(98)00105-4.

Liemburg, E., Castelein, S., Stewart, R., van der Gaag, M., Aleman, A., & Knegtering, H. (2013). Two subdomains of negative symptoms in psychotic disorders: established and confirmed in two large cohorts. *Journal of Psychiatric Research, 47*(6), 718–725. https://doi.org/10.1016/j.jpsychires.2013.01.024.

Lincoln, T. M., Dollfus, S., & Lyne, J. (2017). Current developments and challenges in the assessment of negative symptoms. *Schizophrenia Research, 186*, 8–18. https://doi.org/10.1016/j.schres.2016.02.035.

Llerena, K., Park, S. G., McCarthy, J. M., Couture, S. M., Bennett, M. E., & Blanchard, J. J. (2013). The Motivation and Pleasure Scale–Self-Report (MAP-SR): reliability and validity of a self-report measure of negative symptoms. *Comprehensive Psychiatry, 54*(5), 568–574. https://doi.org/10.1016/j.comppsych.2012.12.001.

Lysaker, P. H., & Davis, L. W. (2004). Social function in schizophrenia and schizoaffective disorder: associations with personality, symptoms and neurocognition. *Health and Quality of Life Outcomes, 2*, 15. https://doi.org/10.1186/1477-7525-2-15.

Mané, A., Garcia-Rizo, C., Garcia-Portilla, M. P., Berge, D., Sugranyes, G., Garcia-Alvarez, L., et al. (2014). Spanish adaptation and validation of the Brief Negative Symptoms Scale. *Comprehensive Psychiatry, 55*(7), 1726–1729. https://doi.org/10.1016/j.comppsych.2014.05.024.

McGurk, S. R., Moriarty, P. J., Harvey, P. D., Parrella, M., White, L., & Davis, K. L. (2000). The longitudinal relationship of clinical symptoms, cognitive functioning, and adaptive life in geriatric schizophrenia. *Schizophrenia Research, 42*(1), 47–55.

Merlotti, E., Mucci, A., Bucci, P., Nardi, A., & Galderisi, S. (2014). Italian version of the 'Brief Negative Symptom Scale'. *Journal of Psychopathology, 20*(2), 199–215.

Messinger, J. W., Trémeau, F., Antonius, D., Mendelsohn, E., Prudent, V., Stanford, A. D., et al. (2011). Avolition and expressive deficits capture negative symptom phenomenology: implications for DSM-5 and schizophrenia research. *Clinical Psychology Review, 31*(1), 161–168. https://doi.org/10.1016/j.cpr.2010.09.002.

Meyer, E. C., Carrión, R. E., Cornblatt, B. A., Addington, J., Cadenhead, K. S., Cannon, T. D., et al. (2014). The relationship of neurocognition and negative symptoms to social and role functioning over time in individuals at clinical high risk in the first phase of the North American prodrome longitudinal study. *Schizophrenia Bulletin, 40*(6), 1452–1461. https://doi.org/10.1093/schbul/sbt235.

Möller, H. J., Jäger, M., Riedel, M., Obermeier, M., Strauss, A., & Bottlender, R. (2010). The Munich 15-year follow-up study (MUFUSSAD) on first-hospitalized patients with schizophrenic or affective disorders: comparison of psychopathological and psychosocial course and outcome and prediction of chronicity. *European Archives of Psychiatry and Clinical Neuroscience, 260*(5), 367–384. https://doi.org/10.1007/s00406-010-0117-y.

Montgomery, J., Winterbottom, E., Jessani, M., Kohegyi, E., Fulmer, J., Seamonds, B., et al. (2004). Prevalence of hyperprolactinemia in schizophrenia: association with typical and atypical antipsychotic treatment. *The Journal of Clinical Psychiatry, 65*(11), 1491–1498. https://doi.org/10.4088/JCP.v65n1108.

Moran, E. K., Culbreth, A. J., & Barch, D. M. (2017). Ecological momentary assessment of negative symptoms in schizophrenia: relationships to effort-based decision making and reinforcement learning. *Journal of Abnormal Psychology, 126*(1), 96–105. https://doi.org/10.1037/abn000024010.1037/abn0000240.supp [Supplemental].

Mucci, A., Galderisi, S., Merlotti, E., Rossi, A., Rocca, P., Bucci, P., et al. (2015). The Brief Negative Symptom Scale (BNSS): independent validation in a large sample of Italian patients with schizophrenia. *European Psychiatry, 30*(5), 641–647. https://doi.org/10.1016/j.eurpsy.2015.01.014.

Mueser, K. T., Sayers, S. L., Schooler, N. R., Mance, R. M., & Haas, G. L. (1994). A multisite investigation of the reliability of the Scale for the Assessment of Negative Symptoms. *The American Journal of Psychiatry, 151*(10), 1453–1462. https://doi.org/10.1176/ajp.151.10.1453.

Murphy, B. P., Chung, Y.-C., Park, T.-W., & McGorry, P. D. (2006). Pharmacological treatment of primary negative symptoms in schizophrenia: a systematic review. *Schizophrenia Research, 88*(1–3), 5–25. https://doi.org/10.1016/j.schres.2006.07.002.

Myin-Germeys, I., Birchwood, M., & Kwapil, T. (2011). From environment to therapy in psychosis: a real-world momentary assessment approach. *Schizophrenia Bulletin, 37*(2), 244–247. https://doi.org/10.1093/schbul/sbq164.

Nazli, I. P., Ergül, C., Aydemir, Ö., Chandhoke, S., Üçok, A., & Gönül, A. S. (2016). Validation of Turkish version of brief negative symptom scale. *International Journal of Psychiatry in Clinical Practice, 20*(4), 265–271. https://doi.org/10.1080/13651501.2016.1207086.

Oorschot, M., Kwapil, T., Delespaul, P., & Myin-Germeys, I. (2009). Momentary assessment research in psychosis. *Psychological Assessment, 21*(4), 498–505. https://doi.org/10.1037/a0017077.

Park, S. G., Llerena, K., McCarthy, J. M., Couture, S. M., Bennett, M. E., & Blanchard, J. J. (2012). Screening for negative symptoms: preliminary results from the self-report version of the Clinical Assessment Interview for Negative Symptoms. *Schizophrenia Research, 135*(1–3), 139–143. https://doi.org/10.1016/j.schres.2011.12.007.

Pelletier-Baldelli, A., Strauss, G. P., Visser, K. H., & Mittal, V. A. (2017). Initial development and preliminary psychometric properties of the Prodromal Inventory of Negative Symptoms (PINS). *Schizophrenia Research, 189*, 43–49. https://doi.org/10.1016/j.schres.2017.01.055.

Peralta, V., & Cuesta, M. J. (1995). Negative symptoms in schizophrenia: a confirmatory factor analysis of competing models. *The American Journal of Psychiatry, 152*(10), 1450–1457. https://doi.org/10.1176/ajp.152.10.1450.

Perlick, D. A., Rosenheck, R. A., Kaczynski, R., Swartz, M. S., Cañive, J. M., & Lieberman, J. A. (2006). Components and correlates of family burden in schizophrenia. *Psychiatric Services, 57*(8), 1117–1125. https://doi.org/10.1176/appi.ps.57.8.1117.

Piskulic, D., Addington, J., Cadenhead, K. S., Cannon, T. D., Cornblatt, B. A., Heinssen, R., et al. (2012). Negative symptoms in individuals at clinical high risk of psychosis. *Psychiatry Research, 196*(2–3), 220–224. https://doi.org/10.1016/j.psychres.2012.02.018.

Remington, G., Foussias, G., Fervaha, G., Agid, O., Takeuchi, H., Lee, J., et al. (2016). Treating negative symptoms in schizophrenia: an update. *Current Treatment Options in Psychiatry, 3*, 133–150.

Rocca, P., Montemagni, C., Zappia, S., Piterà, R., Sigaudo, M., & Bogetto, F. (2014). Negative symptoms and everyday functioning in schizophrenia: a cross-sectional study in a real world-setting. *Psychiatry Research, 218*(3), 284–289. https://doi.org/10.1016/j.psychres.2014.04.018.

Saha, S., Scott, J., Varghese, D., & McGrath, J. (2012). Social support and delusional-like experiences: a nationwide population-based study. *Epidemiology and Psychiatric Sciences, 21*(2), 203–212. https://doi.org/10.1017/S2045796011000862.

Sayers, S. L., Curran, P. J., & Mueser, K. T. (1996). Factor structure and construct validity of the Scale for the Assessment of Negative Symptoms. *Psychological Assessment, 8*(3), 269–280. https://doi.org/10.1037/1040-3590.8.3.269.

Shiffman, S., Stone, A. A., & Hufford, M. R. (2008). Ecological momentary assessment. *Annual Review of Clinical Psychology, 4*, 1–32. https://doi.org/10.1146/annurev.clinpsy.3.022806.091415.

Stiekema, A. P. M., Liemburg, E. J., van der Meer, L., Castelein, S., Stewart, R., van Weeghel, J., et al. (2016). Confirmatory factor analysis and differential relationships of the two subdomains of negative symptoms in chronically ill psychotic patients. *PLoS One, 11*(2). https://doi.org/10.1371/journal.pone.0149785.

Strassnig, M. T., Raykov, T., O'Gorman, C., Bowie, C. R., Sabbag, S., Durand, D., et al. (2015). Determinants of different aspects of everyday outcome in schizophrenia: the roles of negative symptoms, cognition, and functional capacity. *Schizophrenia Research, 165*(1), 76–82. https://doi.org/10.1016/j.schres.2015.03.033.

Strauss, G. P., & Gold, J. M. (2016). A psychometric comparison of the Clinical Assessment Interview for Negative Symptoms and the Brief Negative Symptom Scale. *Schizophrenia Bulletin, 42*(6), 1384–1394. https://doi.org/10.1093/schbul/sbw046.

Strauss, G. P., Hong, L. E., Gold, J. M., Buchanan, R. W., McMahon, R. P., Keller, W. R., et al. (2012). Factor structure of the Brief Negative Symptom Scale. *Schizophrenia Research, 142*(1–3), 96–98. https://doi.org/10.1016/j.schres.2012.09.007.

Strauss, G. P., Keller, W. R., Buchanan, R. W., Gold, J. M., Fischer, B. A., McMahon, R. P., et al. (2012). Next-generation negative symptom assessment for clinical trials: Validation of the Brief Negative Symptom Scale. *Schizophrenia Research, 142*(1–3), 88–92. https://doi.org/10.1016/j.schres.2012.10.012.

Sue, D., & Sue, S. (1987). Cultural factors in the clinical assessment of Asian Americans. *Journal of Consulting and Clinical Psychology, 55*(4), 479–487. https://doi.org/10.1037/0022-006x.55.4.479.

Tseng, W. S., & Streltzer, J. (2013). *Culture and psychopathology: A guide to clinical assessment.* New York: Routledge.

Turner, D. T., van der Gaag, M., Karyotaki, E., & Cuijpers, P. (2014). Psychological interventions for psychosis: A meta-analysis of comparative outcome studies. *The American Journal of Psychiatry, 171* (5), 523–538. https://doi.org/10.1176/appi.ajp.2013.13081159.

Valiente-Gómez, A., Mezquida, G., Romaguera, A., Vilardebò, I., Andrés, H., Granados, B., et al. (2015). Validation of the Spanish version of the Clinical Assessment for Negative Symptoms (CAINS). *Schizophrenia Research, 166*(1–3), 104–109. https://doi.org/10.1016/j.schres.2015.06.006.

Velthorst, E., Nieman, D. H., Becker, H. E., van de Fliert, R., Dingemans, P. M., Klassenn, R., et al. (2009). Baseline differences in clinical symptomatology between ultra high risk subjects with and without a transition to psychosis. *Schizophrenia Research, 109*, 60–65. https://doi.org/10.1016/j.schres.2009.02.002.

Ventura, J., Subotnik, K. L., Gitlin, M. J., Gretchen-Doorly, D., Ered, A., Villa, K. F., et al. (2015). Negative symptoms and functioning during the first year after a recent onset of schizophrenia and 8 years later. *Schizophrenia Research, 161*(2–3), 407–413. https://doi.org/10.1016/j.schres.2014.10.043.

Wallwork, R. S., Fortgang, R., Hashimoto, R., Weinberger, D. R., & Dickinson, D. (2012). Searching for a consensus five-factor model of the Positive and Negative Syndrome Scale for schizophrenia. *Schizophrenia Research, 137*(1–3), 246–250. https://doi.org/10.1016/j.schres.2012.01.031.

Weisman, A. G., Nuechterlein, K. H., Goldstein, M. J., & Snyder, K. S. (2000). Controllability perceptions and reactions to symptoms of schizophrenia: a within-family comparison of relatives with high and low expressed emotion. *Journal of Abnormal Psychology, 109*(1), 167–171. https://doi.org/10.1037/0021-843X.109.1.167.

Westermeyer, J. (1987). Cultural factors in clinical assessment. *Journal of Consulting and Clinical Psychology, 55*(4), 471–478. https://doi.org/10.1037/0022-006X.55.4.471.

White, L., Harvey, P. D., Opler, L., & Lindenmayer, J. P. (1997). Empirical assessment of the factorial structure of clinical symptoms in schizophrenia. A multisite, multimodel evaluation of the factorial structure of the Positive and Negative Syndrome Scale. The PANSS Study Group. *Psychopathology, 30*(5), 263–274. https://doi.org/10.1159/000285058.

Willhite, R. K., Niendam, T. A., Bearden, C. E., Zinberg, J., O'Brien, M. P., & Cannon, T. D. (2008). Gender differences in symptoms, functioning and social support in patients at ultra-high risk for developing a psychotic disorder. *Schizophrenia Research, 104*(1–3), 237–245. https://doi.org/10.1016/j.schres.2008.05.019.

Xie, D. J., Shi, H. S., Lui, S. S. Y., Shi, C., Li, Y., Ho, K. K. Y., et al. (2018). Cross cultural validation and extension of the clinical assessment interview for negative symptoms (CAINS) in the Chinese context: evidence from a spectrum perspective. *Schizophrenia Bulletin*. https://doi.org/10.1093/schbul/sby013.

Definition of Key Terms

Alogia Diminished speech production characterised by very brief answers and lack of elaboration.

Anhedonia The diminished capacity to experience of pleasure across varied activities.

Asociality A diminished motivation and desire for affiliative interactions and relationships.

Avolition Decreased motivation to engage in goal-directed behaviour. This can occur in different contexts, including motivation for social relationships or academic and occupational achievement.

Blunted affect Diminished expressive behaviour, including fewer facial expressions and gestures.

Negative symptoms A decrease in subjective experiences and behaviours that are normally present in a person from the same culture.

CHAPTER 8

Assessing Cognition and Social Cognition in Schizophrenia & Related Disorders

Amy E. Pinkham*, **Johanna C. Badcock**†
* School of Behavioral and Brain Sciences, The University of Texas at Dallas, Richardson, TX, United States, † School of Psychological Science, University of Western Australia, Crawley, WA, Australia

Key Learning Objectives

- To introduce key issues and domains of assessment in social cognition and basic cognition
- To learn about ongoing debates on the specificity, profile, and course of cognitive impairments
- To introduce some common tools to assess cognitive abilities and biases, and consider their psychometric properties
- To appreciate the challenges and opportunities when assessing cognition

ASSESSING SOCIAL COGNITION

Introduction

Social cognition broadly refers to how individuals understand and use social information. While some debate exists as to what is included under the term social cognition, this wide-ranging construct is often conceptualised as consisting of four core domains: emotion processing, social processing, mentalising, and attribution style/bias (see Box 8.1 for more detailed definitions and examples) (Pinkham et al., 2014). These domains reflect the idea that social cognition includes both *ability* (i.e. whether one is able to get the correct answer) and *bias* (i.e. the tendency to respond in certain ways) (Roberts & Pinkham, 2013; Walss-Bass, Fernandes, Roberts, Service, & Velligan, 2013).

Social cognition refers to how we perceive, encode, and apply information about other people and social situations.

A Clinical Introduction to Psychosis. https://doi.org/10.1016/B978-0-12-815012-2.00008-0

Box 8.1 Core Domains of Social Cognition

Emotion Processing: Perceiving and using emotions. Lower perceptual levels include recognising emotion from faces or voices, and higher levels include managing and regulating emotion (Green et al., 2008).

Example: knowing that a smile typically indicates happiness or that thinking about positive things typically leads to positive mood.

Social Perception: Decoding and interpreting social cues in others (Penn, Ritchie, Francis, Combs, & Martin, 2002; Sergi & Green, 2003). It includes knowledge of social rules and how these rules influence others' behaviours (Corrigan & Green, 1993).

Example: Understanding that when you are meeting someone new, an outstretched hand is an invitation to shake hands.

Mentalising or Theory of Mind: The ability to represent the mental states of others, including the inference of intentions, dispositions, and/or beliefs (Frith, 1992; Penn, Addington, & Pinkham, 2006).

Example: Inferring that someone who comments about how delicious your cookies look may actually be asking you to share them.

Attributional Style/Bias: The way in which individuals explain the causes, or make sense, of social events or interactions (Green et al., 2008; Penn et al., 2006).

Example: Concluding that your friend must be mad at you when he/she does not respond immediately to a text or call.

A now well-established body of literature demonstrates that individuals with psychosis show impairments across each of the four domains noted here (Savla, Vella, Armstrong, Penn, & Twamley, 2013). Difficulties in emotion processing and mentalising tend to be the most pronounced, but it is currently unclear whether this is due to these being the most well-studied domains, or if we may learn of more uniform impairments as the field progresses and as measurement improves. More importantly, however, social cognitive deficits show a strong connection to real-world outcomes like community and social functioning (Couture, Penn, & Roberts, 2006). As illustrated in the case example (see Box 8.2), social cognitive impairments can make it much harder to maintain relationships as well as employment. Fortunately, improving social cognition via treatment leads to better social outcomes, including social adjustment, social functioning, social relationships, and social skills (Fiszdon, 2013; Kurtz & Richardson, 2012). Thus, social cognition represents a viable target for efforts to improve quality of life for individuals with psychosis.

For individuals with schizophrenia, social cognitive difficulties are a primary contributor to poor social functioning and lower quality of life.

A common question raised about social cognition is whether it differs from other, basic cognitive skills like attention and memory. Several pieces of evidence, including correlational studies (Ventura, Wood, & Hellemann, 2011), factor analyses (Sergi et al., 2007), and differential deficit designs (Pinkham et al., 2014), all support the idea that social cognition is largely independent from other cognitive abilities. It is therefore important to keep in mind that even cognitively intact individuals may still show difficulties in social cognition and that assessment of cognitive dysfunction in psychosis should include assessments of both social and basic forms of cognition.

Box 8.2 Client Example: Arjun[a]

Profile: Male, aged 25 years.

Cultural and religious identity: Born in India, Sikh.

Education & employment: Completed high school. Not employed or in training.

Current status: Arjun lives at home with his parents and a younger sister. He was diagnosed with schizophrenia 6 years ago (aged 19) after a gradual decline in social functioning and school performance, and increasingly odd ideas and behaviour.

Personal & clinical history: The family migrated from India when Arjun was thirteen years old. After moving to Australia, he found it difficult to 'fit in' and was often bullied by class mates. Although Arjun aimed to attend university, his grades in the end of school exams were poor and he did not qualify. Previously, Arjun had difficulties concentrating in class, reading and memorising notes, and organising his homework. He also had a lot of trouble sleeping, which made things worse. He became increasingly demotivated about achieving his career goals, and his self-esteem was low. At this point, he developed the belief that someone was trying to harm him and was tracking his activity with wireless sensors. He had only one friend and spent much of his time alone playing video games.

Arjun was admitted to hospital after an episode of psychosis during which he heard 'voices' telling him he was useless and his speech was disorganised. He was treated with a second-generation antipsychotic. Although his 'voices' have receded, they have not completely gone. He is not receiving psychological therapy.

Arjun would like to be employed so that he can be more independent. He has tried several part-time jobs but struggles in interactions with co-workers because he finds it difficult to understand what they may be thinking or feeling. Eventually he would like to achieve his goal of going to university.

[a] Composite patient profile.

Factors That Affect Social Cognitive Abilities

Social cognitive impairments are seen widely across psychiatric and neurological illnesses and are even included as core diagnostic criteria for some disorders such as autism spectrum disorder and behavioural-variant frontotemporal dementia (Henry, von Hippel, Molenberghs, Lee, & Sachdev, 2016; Kennedy & Adolphs, 2012). While deficits in social cognition do not yet contribute to diagnoses of psychotic disorder, there is some evidence that such deficits may be more characteristic of psychosis than other disorders. For example, emotion recognition deficits are evident in schizophrenia spectrum illnesses even when compared to individuals with depression (Weniger, Lange, Ruther, & Irle, 2004) and bipolar disorder (Emre Bora & Pantelis, 2016), and there is growing evidence that social cognitive impairment may exist on a continuum of increasing severity from psychotic bipolar disorder to schizoaffective disorder to schizophrenia (Ruocco et al., 2014). Diagnosis may therefore provide some clues as to the likelihood of social cognitive impairment, but new estimates indicate that as many as 1/3 of individuals with schizophrenia may show normative levels of social cognitive performance (Hajduk, Harvey, Penn, & Pinkham, 2018). For this reason, the current evidence does not support using diagnosis as a rationale for foregoing formal assessment.

In addition to diagnosis, the type of symptoms an individual is currently experiencing also impacts social cognitive functioning. Within the domain of emotion recognition, active paranoid ideation is associated with incorrectly perceiving neutral facial expressions as angry (Pinkham, Brensinger, Kohler, Gur, & Gur, 2011), and prominent negative (Sachs, Steger-Wuchse, Kryspin-Exner, Gur, & Katschnig, 2004) and disorganised symptoms (Ventura, Wood, Jimenez, & Hellemann, 2013) are linked to poorer emotion recognition abilities. More prominent hostile attributional biases are also related to increased paranoia (Pinkham, Harvey, & Penn, 2016), and similar relationships exists for mentalising. Undermentalising, or the failure to infer the intentions of others, is most likely in individuals with primarily negative symptoms, whereas overmentalising (i.e. making too many inferences about the mental states of others) is associated with the experience of positive symptoms (Fretland et al., 2015; Montag et al., 2011).

Undermentalising refers to being less able to perceive and infer the intentions or beliefs of others.

Overmentalising involves overattributing intentions to others, or to nonintentional stimuli.

Social cognitive impairments in psychosis appear to be impacted by diagnosis, current symptoms, and perhaps, duration of illness.

Unlike diagnosis and symptoms, which have marked impacts on social cognition, the role of duration of illness is less clear. Emotion processing impairments are evident early in the course of psychosis, including the prodromal phase (Kohler et al., 2014) and the initial psychotic episode (Barkl, Lah, Harris, & Williams, 2014). The same is true for mentalising and social perception (Barbato et al., 2015; Bora & Pantelis, 2013). Additionally, both cross-sectional (Comparelli et al., 2013) and longitudinal studies (Horan et al., 2012; Piskulic et al., 2016) demonstrate that social cognitive impairment is largely stable across time. However, a recent metaanalysis shows that effect sizes for social cognitive impairment in the prodromal phase are about half the magnitude of those seen for chronic patients (Lee, Hong, Shin, & Kwon, 2015). Thus, debate remains about whether these are truly stable impairments or if there may be a degenerative process that continues after illness onset. Nevertheless, the presence of such impairments at all stages of illness underscores the importance of testing for impairment regardless of how long an individual has shown signs of illness.

Measurement of Social Cognitive Abilities

COMMON TOOLS

In beginning this section, it is important to note that social cognition is a relatively new construct, particularly when compared to neurocognition, and that until recently, there has been no consensus on which measures best index a social cognitive domain. As a result, many researchers who investigate social cognition have created their own customised measures to address specific hypotheses. While this has yielded hundreds of instruments for assessing social cognition, it also results in two major caveats that must be considered. First, social cognitive measures tend to be poorly validated and are clearly less well developed than their traditional cognitive counterparts. Indeed, the vast majority of social cognitive measures either have no reported psychometric data or tend to show substandard psychometric properties. Second, most assessments of social cognition are not standardised and lack normative data. This means that while you will be able to derive a score for a particular client, it will be much harder to determine whether that score constitutes impairment. To help in this regard, mean scores and standard deviation for a group of healthy individuals are provided for each task listed in Table 8.1. These values can be used as rough benchmarks for levels of performance that would be consistent with intact abilities—whilst their psychometric properties are further evaluated (see Box 8.3).

In the sections that follow, we highlight the current recommendations from the field in regard to assessing social cognition. The recommendations included here are based on the results of the multiphase Social Cognition Psychometric Evaluation (SCOPE) study, which identified the best existing measures of social cognition and systematically evaluated their psychometric properties (Pinkham et al., 2018; Pinkham, Penn, et al., 2014; Pinkham, Penn, et al., 2016). Efforts were made to validate tasks from each of the four domains of social cognition; however, no measures of social perception were recommended for use. Thus, we focus on the domains of emotion processing and mentalising, but you should keep in mind the evolving nature of this area and the likelihood that new tasks, for these domains and the others, will be introduced as our understanding of social cognition matures.

For emotion processing, two tasks of emotion recognition, the Penn Emotion Recognition Test (ER-40) (Kohler et al., 2003) and the Bell Lysaker Emotion Recognition Task (BLERT) (Bryson, Bell, & Lysaker, 1997), showed good reliability and validity. Both tasks require examinees to identify the emotion being expressed by a stimulus individual, but the ER-40 uses static photos of racially diverse faces (see Fig. 8.1 for an example item), whereas the BLERT uses video clips that provide dynamic displays of emotion, including prosodic speech. One could argue that the BLERT has better ecological validity because it utilises videos, but the same Caucasian male actor is used for all stimuli, which may render the task less appropriate for use with non-Caucasian individuals (Pinkham, Kelsven, Kouros, Harvey, & Penn, 2017).

For the domain of mentalising, the Hinting Task (Corcoran, Mercer, & Frith, 1995) was identified as the top performing measure. This task examines the ability to infer the true intent of indirect speech. Short vignettes are read aloud in which one character drops a hint to the other, and the examinee must identify what the character truly meant. Each item is scored in real time, with opportunities for additional prompts if an initial answer does not earn full credit. This makes administration of the task more challenging, but detailed manuals are available to guide scoring decisions. The Awareness of Social Inferences Test,

Table 8.1 Common Tools to Assess Social Cognition

Test or battery	Domain(s) assessed	Mode of testing	Time	User information	Psychometric properties
Objective assessments					
Penn Emotion Recognition Test	Emotion processing	Computerised	3–4 min	Available from developers. See https://penncnp.med.upenn.edu/request.pl	Psychometric properties (see Pinkham, Harvey, & Penn, 2018) *Healthy M* = 32.94 (3.19)*
Bell Lysaker Emotion Recognition Task	Emotion processing	Videos played via computer, scoring via paper & pencil	6–8 min	Available from first author upon request.	Psychometric properties (see Pinkham et al., 2018) *Healthy M* = 15.92 (2.70)*
Hinting Task	Mentalising	Paper and pencil	5–7 min	Available from first author upon request. Revised scoring criteria from Dr. A. Pinkham (amy.pinkham@utdallas.edu)	Psychometric properties (see Pinkham et al., 2018) *Healthy M* = 15.38 (2.68)*
The Awareness of Social Inferences Test, Part III	Mentalising	Videos played via computer, scoring via paper & pencil	Full test: 30–45 min Part III only: 17–19 min	Available from the Australasian Society for the Study of Brain Impairment. See https://assbi.com.au/Assessments-to-Buy	Psychometric properties (see Pinkham et al., 2018 and manual) *Healthy M* = 50.57 (6.80)*
Subjective assessments					
Observable Social Cognition: A Rating Scale	Emotion processing Mentalising Attributional style Cognitive rigidity Jumping to conclusions	Semistructured interview with client or informant-based questionnaire	15–20 min	Available from authors on request.	Psychometric properties (see Healey et al., 2015)

Social Cognitive Biases					
Ambiguous Intentions Hostility Questionnaire	Hostility Bias (HB) Aggression Bias (AB) Blaming (BS)	Paper and pencil	5–7 min	Available from first author upon request.	Psychometric Properties (see Pinkham, Penn, Green, & Harvey, 2016) *Healthy M (SD)***: HB: 1.99 (0.60) AB: 1.83 (0.26) BS: 7.02 (2.31)
The Intentional Bias Task	Personalising Bias	Computer administered	5–6 min	Available from authors upon request.	Psychometric Properties (see Pinkham et al., 2018) *Healthy M)* = 0.40 (0.15)

* Means, M (SD) for healthy individuals are taken from Pinkham et al. (2018), which included a sample of 154 individuals who were free of psychiatric diagnoses.

** Means, (SD), for healthy individuals are taken from Pinkham, Penn, et al. (2016), which included a sample of 104 individuals who were free of psychiatric diagnoses.

Box 8.3 Characteristics of Good Psychological Tests

Psychometric properties: quantifiable metrics that relate to the statistical strength or weakness of a standardised assessment tool. The term generally refers to a measure's reliability and validity.

Reliability: the extent to which a measure is consistent in assessing the construct of interest. Reliability can refer to internal consistency (how items relate to one another), alternate form reliability (how different versions of the same measure relate to one another), interrater reliability (the rate of agreement between individuals evaluating the same information), or test-retest reliability (consistency across time).

Validity: the extent to which a measure captures the domain of interest. Validity includes the degree to which the content of the items on the measure adequately reflects the construct of interest, how well the measure correlates with measures assessing the same construct, and how well it relates to important outcomes (e.g. does a high score on a measure of depression predict risk for suicide). To paraphrase Yates (1966)—if a test can identify only those clients whose cognitive dysfunction is obvious, then the test serves no useful purpose, since it confirms what needs no confirmation.

Utility: the extent to which a measure is useful and practical for clinical applications. This includes considerations of practice effects, as well as floor and ceiling effects, all of which should be minimal. It can also include aspects of practicality (e.g. is the task easy to administer and score in a timely manner) and tolerability (e.g. do clients like the test or hate it).

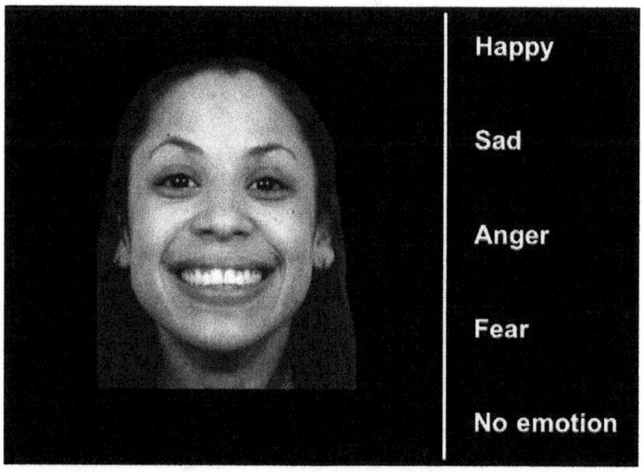

FIG. 8.1
An example item from the Penn Emotion Recognition (ER40) test. (Participants view 40 photos, like the one shown here, and must choose which emotion they believe the person is expressing. Photos can be viewed for as long as the participant would like, and the task is indexed as the total number of stimuli correctly identified.) Reproduced with permission of Sasson, N. J., Pinkham, A. E., Richard, J., Hughett, P., Gur, R. E., & Gur, R. C. (2010). Controlling for response biases clarifies sex and age differences in facial affect recognition. *Journal of Nonverbal Behavior, 34*(4), 207–221, *from Springer Nature.*

Part III (TASIT) (McDonald, Flanagan, Rollins, & Kinch, 2003), is also a viable option for assessing mentalising ability. While its psychometric properties were not as strong as the Hinting task, it does offer several advantages, including an alternate form and normative data. The TASIT is also available commercially, whereas the other tasks must be obtained by contacting the test developers.

As a final note on assessing social cognitive ability, stage of illness appears to be an important consideration when choosing the best assessment tools. Evaluation of the SCOPE tasks in a sample of individuals within the first five years of psychotic illness demonstrated that only the Hinting task showed strong psychometric properties (Ludwig, Pinkham, Harvey, Kelsven, & Penn, 2017). BLERT was not recommended for use with this population due to a failure to differentiate psychosis from nonpsychosis, and the ER-40 showed inadequate test-retest reliability. This study had a relatively small sample of early psychosis individuals and more work is clearly needed, but these findings do emphasise the need to carefully consider client characteristics when selecting assessment tools and interpreting the resulting data.

ALTERNATIVE METHODS OF ASSESSING SOCIAL COGNITIVE ABILITIES

At present, only one alternative to performance-based measures is available for the assessment of social cognition. The Observable Social Cognition: A Rating Scale (OSCARS; Healey et al., 2015) is an 8-item measure that can be administered either as a semistructured interview or as an informant-based questionnaire. Items broadly assess all domains of social cognition and comprise a question regarding abilities or typical behaviours within a given domain. Example behaviours reflecting impairment are provided and used to determine the level of difficulty. The OSCARS has been reported to be reliable, but some caution is warranted because of relatively limited evidence of convergent validity (i.e. correlations with performance-based tasks). The psychometric properties of the OSCARS when completed by an informant have also not yet been established; thus, while it is hoped that further development will improve the OSCARS, it is recommend that this assessment be used only as a supplement to other performance-based tasks and not in isolation.

Measurement of Social Cognitive Biases

COMMON TOOLS

Current work addressing attributional style in people with psychotic disorders has focused on two primary biases: the personalising bias (e.g. my friend did not meet me at the coffee shop today because she does not want to be friends anymore) and the hostility bias (e.g. my friend did not meet me at the coffee shop today because she wanted to hurt my feelings). Both are linked to more severe persecutory delusions in psychosis (Buck et al., 2017; Mehl et al., 2014), and in a direct comparison of individuals with schizophrenia who were either high or low in paranoia, paranoid patients showed a greater hostility bias than nonparanoid patients (Pinkham, Harvey, & Penn, 2016). While this may suggest that the bias is specific to paranoia, this has not yet been conclusively demonstrated, and it is likely that these biases are better viewed as existing along a continuum. Thus, assessing these biases will likely aid your case conceptualisation even if paranoia is not prominent. Additionally, as the tendency to make

Personalising Bias refers to the tendency to attribute negative social events or outcomes to other people rather than situational factors.

Hostility Bias involves the tendency to infer hostile intent in the behaviours of others.

hostile attributions is highly related to the likelihood of engaging in aggressive or violent acts (Harris, Oakley, & Picchioni, 2014) and is among the best predictors of social functioning (Lahera et al., 2015), the assessment of attributional style seems all the more important.

Unfortunately, psychometrically sound assessments of attributional style have been elusive. This may be due in part to the limited number of available measures, but there are two current measures that appear promising and that are likely to be of clinical value. The first is the Ambiguous Intentions Hostility Questionnaire (AIHQ; Combs, Penn, Wicher, & Waldheter, 2007), which targets the hostility bias. Clients are asked to read short descriptions of hypothetical, negative situations, to imagine the scenario happening to them, and to respond to questions about why the scenario occurred, how they would feel about it, and how they would react. Both open-ended questions and rating scales are used, and responses to the open-ended questions require trained coders, which can make the assessment burdensome. However, recent studies demonstrate that the rated items can stand alone and are more psychometrically sound than the measure as a whole (Buck et al., 2017). These items also show significant correlations with hostility and suspicious symptoms and with functional outcomes like interpersonal conflict (Buck, Pinkham, Harvey, & Penn, 2016). Thus, assessing the hostility bias might aid you in predicting the likelihood of future symptom exacerbations and/or interpersonal difficulty.

The second measure is newer than the AIHQ but also shows promise for predicting functional outcomes. The Intentional Bias Task (IBT; Rosset, 2008) taps into the personalising bias and assesses the tendency to attribute intentionality to the actions of others. Examinees read 24 brief descriptions of actions (e.g. 'He broke the window') and indicate whether that action occurred 'on purpose' or 'by accident'. The IBT can be scored in various ways (see Buck et al., 2018), but the most straightforward is simply to calculate the percentage of items designated as occurring on purpose, with higher scores indicating greater bias. Recent research demonstrates that this index of bias predicts hostility, role functioning, functional capacity, and real-world functional outcome independent of the influence of social cognitive skill (Buck et al., 2018; Pinkham et al., 2018). These findings are particularly important because they underscore the added utility of examining both social cognitive ability and bias in clinical practice.

ALTERNATIVE METHODS OF ASSESSING SOCIAL COGNITIVE BIAS

Given the relative paucity of social cognitive attributional-style measures, it is not surprising that alternatives to performance-based measures are not currently available. The previously mentioned OSCARS does however include an item related to attributional style, and it is possible that future work will develop a self-report or informant-based measure that is specific to this domain. As noted previously, the assessment of social cognition is relatively nascent and rapidly evolving. We expect many improvements in the coming years and encourage you to continue to seek opportunities for continued education regarding appropriate assessment tools. We acknowledge that doing so may be somewhat difficult given the lack of formal resources promoting social cognitive assessment; however, we hope that the momentum currently bolstering this area will continue and will follow a similar course to that seen in assessing basic domains of cognition, which has yielded excellent tools and coalesced resources for assessment—which we turn to next.

ASSESSING BASIC COGNITION

Introduction

A vast and ever-growing body of research provides consistent evidence of difficulties across the major, basic domains of cognition (such as memory, executive functioning, attention, language, sensory and motor functions) in people with psychotic disorders (Schaefer, Giangrande, Weinberger, & Dickinson, 2013). These include both *deficits* (i.e. a reduction or loss) and *biases* (systematic deviations) in information processing. Cognitive testing is typically conducted on a core set of domains (memory, attention, reasoning/problem solving, and speed of processing; see Box 8.4) and current cognitive ability is indexed with reference to age, sex and education-adjusted norms, and in terms of decline (or not) from the person's own premorbid level of functioning.

Cognitive deficits: a reduction or loss in basic perceptual and cognitive processes compared to the norm.

Cognitive bias: a systematic deviation from the norm in perceptual and cognitive processes.

For individuals with schizophrenia, a pattern of compromised or 'generalised' poorer performance across all, or most, cognitive domains, is common (think back to Arjun in Box 8.2 for an example of a client who struggles with both memory and attention difficulties). However, it is important to note that individual differences in performance are considerable. Thus, whilst the cognitive deficits observed are often around 1.0–2.5 standard deviations below the norm, many studies now show a substantial subgroup of people with psychosis with relatively spared or near normal cognitive abilities (e.g. Chiang, Ni, Tsai, & Lin, 2016). Other evidence suggests that approximately 98% of people with schizophrenia have a current level of cognition functioning that falls below the level predicted by premorbid estimates (Keefe, Eesley, & Poe, 2005). Yet, new research shows a subgroup of patients with schizophrenia with verbal memory functioning in the normal range, and no evidence of decline from premorbid ability levels (Heinrichs, Parlar, & Pinnock, 2017). Such findings challenge the idea that cognitive impairment is a 'hallmark' or core feature of schizophrenia, and remain an area of much debate.

Deficits, strengths, and biases in cognition are clinically relevant. Specifically, they contribute to the evolution of symptoms (e.g. Badcock & Hugdahl, 2012; Beck & Rector, 2005; Marder & Galderisi, 2017), influence the skills required for social, vocational, and educational functioning, and predict important outcomes in everyday life, such as the ability to live and work independently (e.g. Santesteban-Echarri et al., 2017, and see Box 8.2 for an example). Accordingly, the Diagnostic and Statistical Manual of Mental Disorders, fifth edition (DSM 5),

Box 8.4 Core Domains of Basic Cognition

Memory: The ability to accurately encode, store, and retrieve information. Episodic long-term memory is often severely impaired in schizophrenia, especially for information that requires organisation at encoding, when relationships between items must be recalled, and when retrieval is tested with recall rather than recognition tasks.

Common tests: verbal list learning and recall, visual/figural learning and recall.

Example: difficulty remembering the content of a lecture you have just attended or struggling to recall the new route you recently learned to walk to the clinic.

Attention: The ability to focus and concentrate on tasks in a sustained way.

Common tests: continuous performance tests; measures of attention bias.

Example: struggling to maintain focus on a task at work when co-workers keep chatting, or difficulty following a TV show at home because your mind constantly wanders.

Reasoning: The capacity to apply logical thinking, comprehend relationships, and make practical judgements on how best to approach and solve problems.

Common tests: Mazes tests; self-report measures of data gathering and reasoning biases.

Example: being unable to figure out what to do when you have locked yourself out of your home; having difficulty adapting your plans for dinner when your guests are early and you have forgotten an important ingredient.

Speed of information processing: The speed with which individuals encode, process, and retrieve information (in different modalities) is often markedly impaired in schizophrenia, but may be intact in individuals at high risk who do not go on to develop a psychotic disorder.

Common tests: digit symbol coding; trail making, category fluency.

Example: being unable to keep pace with conversations or daily activities, because your ability to think, remember, and act is too slow.

states that '*Many individuals with psychotic disorders have impairments in a range of cognitive domains that predict functional status*' (American Psychiatric Association, 2013). Similarly, severity rating of cognitive impairment is included in the eleventh revision of the International Classification of Diseases (ICD-11) ensuring that more attention is given to the assessment and impact of cognition on functional outcome.

Given this evidence, difficulties and strengths in cognitive functioning need to be considered when developing a case formulation with your client, incorporating both objective and subjective perspectives. The lived experience of cognitive impairment tends to receive less attention than formal neuropsychological testing, and can provide important insights into how clients understand and manage these difficulties (Wood, Cupitt, & Lavender, 2015). However, standardised measures of patients' knowledge, perceived impact, and responses to cognitive dysfunction are still in development (Welch et al., 2017).

Factors That Affect Cognitive Abilities

Though often described as a 'core' feature of schizophrenia, cognitive deficits were not included as a diagnostic criterion for schizophrenia, or any other psychotic disorder, in DSM 5. This decision reflects the available evidence that cognitive impairment does not (yet) aid in the diagnosis of psychotic disorders. In particular, the profile of deficits observed across major cognitive domains does not reliably discriminate schizophrenia and related disorders from either bipolar disorder or major depressive disorder with psychosis (Emre Bora & Pantelis, 2015; Jimenez-Lopez et al., 2017). However, the *severity* of impairment does appear to increase along a continuum from bipolar disorder to schizophrenia and schizoaffective (depressive subtype), which is not explained by differences in medication use or current symptoms (e.g. Lynham et al., 2017). Similarly, recent metaanalyses suggest that (some) biases in cognition may not help in differential diagnosis of psychotic disorders, though they may be related to symptom severity (McLean, Mattiske, & Balzan, 2017).

From a developmental perspective, a substantial body of evidence shows that deficits in cognition arise well before a formal diagnosis of schizophrenia has been made (e.g. Mollon & Reichenberg, 2018). These findings include problems in verbal learning, poor school performance, and an average premorbid intelligence quotient (IQ) deficit of around 8 points in children and adolescents who go on to develop schizophrenia (think again about Arjun in Box 8.2). The specificity, test profile, and course of premorbid cognitive functioning in schizophrenia compared to other psychotic disorders are all topics of active research and debate (e.g. Hochberger et al., 2017). Recent evidence from longitudinal studies suggests that after illness-onset individuals with schizophrenia experience further decline in IQ (Meier, Caspi, Reichenberg, et al., 2014), but thereafter (up to 65 years) cognitive impairment may remain relatively stable. This nonprogressive nature of cognitive impairment in schizophrenia therefore stands in contrast with the progressive cognitive decline typically observed in Alzheimer's disease. However, since cognitive deficits clearly precede the onset of schizophrenia and occur throughout all phases of illness, they are included in clinical staging models of schizophrenia and need to be taken into account when planning treatment.

People with schizophrenia often experienced subtle cognitive deficits during childhood.

The specificity, profile, and course of cognitive functioning in schizophrenia spectrum disorders is still under investigation.

Measurement of Basic Cognitive Abilities

COMMON TOOLS AND BATTERIES

The cognitive deficits associated with schizophrenia, and other psychotic disorders, are multifaceted, with severity typically 1–2 standard deviations below normal. As a consequence, assessment of cognitive strengths and difficulties in people with, or at increased risk for, psychotic disorders is a core competency for clinical and neuropsychologists. A wide range of tools is available for the assessment of cognition in people with psychotic disorders, including brief screening instruments to more extensive batteries covering multiple cognitive domains (see selected examples in Table 8.2). In 2008, the National Institute of Mental Health began the Measurement and Treatment Research to Improve Cognition in Schizophrenia (MATRICS) initiative (http://www.matricsinc.org/). It resulted in the MATRICS Consensus Cognitive Battery (MCCB) to encourage a more standardised approach to the assessment of key domains of cognition in schizophrenia and related disorders. The domains identified were speed of processing, attention/vigilance, working memory, verbal learning, visual learning, reasoning and problem solving, and social cognition. The MCCB exhibits sound psychometric properties and small practice effects, and is the US Food and Drug Administration gold standard outcome measure for the assessment of cognitive treatment effects in clinical trials of schizophrenia (Georgiades et al., 2017).

Whilst the MCCB primarily uses paper and pencil tests, others are based entirely on computerised administration and scoring. The latter include more extensive assessment tools, such as the Cambridge Automated Neuropsychological Test Battery (CANTAB-Schizophrenia), along with briefer options providing reliable but rapid cognitive screening, such as the tablet-based Brief Assessment of Cognition in Schizophrenia (BAC App; Atkins et al., 2017) and the CogState Schizophrenia Battery (Maruff et al., 2009). These—and other well-validated batteries—provide clinicians with a wealth of options to assess the nature and magnitude of cognitive impairments—and strengths—in your clients. Computerised assessment of cognition may offer a number of advantages over traditional paper and pencil neurocognitive batteries, such as more standardised delivery of task stimuli and instructions, higher efficiency of data collection, and lower rates of scoring errors. However, automated assessment has also been linked with increased rates of missing data and prior experience with digital technologies may influence task performance. Furthermore, standardised batteries may not capture all cognitive abilities relevant to your client. For example, people with schizophrenia exhibit a wide range of language problems, from the level of phonology to pragmatics and expressed in the form of abnormal speech perception, production, and linguistic content (Murphy & Benítez-Burraco, 2016). Test batteries such as the MCCB noted here do not include a formal, systematic assessment of these language abilities. Overall, these strengths and weaknesses serve a useful reminder that the suitability of these tools for individual clients needs to be continually evaluated, and that the clinician-client relationship plays an important role in the process of cognitive testing.

ALTERNATIVE METHODS OF ASSESSING COGNITIVE ABILITY

DSM 5 now includes a dimensional assessment of cognitive impairment within its new rating instrument, the Clinician-Rated Dimensions of Psychosis Symptom Severity (CRDPSS; American Psychiatric Association, 2013; Section III, Emerging Measures and Models). The aim of the CRDPSS is to help provide a more individualised approach to treatment planning and highlight the potential need for treatment specifically targeting cognitive deficits (see Chapter 17). This new assessment tool requires the clinician to make a judgement on the severity of cognitive impairment as experienced by the individual over the past seven days, with anchored ratings made on a five point scale (0 = Not present; 4 = present and severe). Of note, diagnosis can be made without the use of the severity specifier, which implies that use of the tool is not considered essential. The advantages of the CRDPSS include its brevity, suitability for monitoring treatment

Table 8.2 Common Tools to Assess Basic Cognition

Test or battery	Domain(s) assessed	Mode of testing	Time	User information	Psychometric qualities
Objective Assessments					
MATRICS Consensus Cognitive Battery	Processing speed, Attention, Working Memory, Verbal Learning, Visual Learning, Reasoning & Social Cognition	6 Paper & pencil tests, 1 via Computer; Computerised scoring program.	60–90 min	User qualifications apply. Available from www.matricsinc.org	Psychometric properties (see Georgiades et al., 2017).
CANTAB, Schizophrenia Test Battery	Working memory, Episodic memory, Executive function, Emotion recognition, Cognitive flexibility, Processing speed, Sustained attention	Computerised	~60 min	Available from www.cambridgecognition.com	Reviewed in Barnett et al. (2010)
Brief Assessment of Cognition in Schizophrenia-App	Working Memory, Verbal Memory, Executive Function, Verbal Fluency, Processing Speed, Motor Function	Computerised	30 min	Designed for use by a variety of testers. Available from www.neurocogtrials.com	Validation of tablet-based assessment (see Atkins et al., 2017)
CogState Brief Battery (Cognigram)	Psychomotor function, Attention, Working Memory, Learning	Computerised	12–15 min	Available from: www.cogstate.com	Construct and criterion validity (Maruff et al., 2009)
Subjective Assessments					
Clinician-Rated Dimensions of Psychosis	Single dimension of cognitive impairment	Clinician rated		Available from American Psychiatric Association	Psychometric properties not yet published.

Continued

Table 8.2 Common Tools to Assess Basic Cognition—cont'd

Test or battery	Domain(s) assessed	Mode of testing	Time	User information	Psychometric qualities
Symptom Severity				www.psychiatry.org/dsm5	
Cognitive Assessment Interview	Working Memory, Attention, Verbal Learning, Reasoning and Problem Solving, Speed of Processing, Social Cognition.	Clinician interview of patients and informants, 10 items	~15 min per interview	Manual and rating form available from the author (Dr. J. Ventura) upon request.	Development, reliability, validity and sensitivity to change (Ventura et al., 2010; Ventura, Subotnik, Ered, Hellemann, & Nuechterlein, 2016)
Schizophrenia Cognition Rating Scale	Attention,Memory, Working Memory, Language, Problem Solving, Motor Skills, Reasoning, Social Cognition	Clinician interview of patients and informants, 20 items, rated on a 4-point scale.	~15 min per interview	See Keefe et al. (2015). Available from: www.neurocogtrials.com	Development, reliability, validity and treatment sensitivity (Keefe et al., 2015)
Measure of Insight into Cognition Self-Rated.	Attention, Memory, Executive functioning	Self-rated, 12 items, rated on a frequency scale 0–3	~5 min	Copyrighted. Available from the first author (Prof A. Medalia) upon request.	Internal consistency, test-retest reliability, test specificity and validity (Medalia, Thysen, & Freilich, 2008)
Cognitive biases					
Cognitive Biases Questionnaire for Psychosis	Jumping to Conclusions, Intentionalising, Catastrophising, Emotional Reasoning, Dichotomous Thinking	Self-report. 30 vignettes, forced choice response format		Public domain	Development, reliability, concurrent & construct validity. (Peters et al., 2014). Cross-cultural validation in Japan (Ishikawa et al., 2017)
Davos Assessment of	Jumping to Conclusions, Belief Inflexibility, Selective	Self-report. 42 items, 7 point rating scale		Public domain	Development, reliability, criterion validity & norms (van

Cognitive Biases Scale	Attention to Threat, External Attribution				der Gaag et al., 2013) Reliability & validity (Bastiaens et al., 2013)
Dysfunctional Attitudes Scale	Defeatist performance beliefs (DPB); Need for approval beliefs (NFA)	Self-rated. DPB = 15-items NFA = 10-items	5–10 min	Public domain. DPB items in Grant and Beck (2009)	Development (Weissman, 1978). Internal consistency and criterion validity (Horan et al., 2010)
The Beck Cognitive Insight Scale	Self Certainty Scale, Self Reflectiveness Scale	Self-report. 15-items	5 min	Public domain	Development, reliability & validity (Beck, Baruch, Balter, Steer, & Warman, 2004). Qualitative review (Riggs, Grant, Perivoliotis, & Beck, 2012)

progress, and potential for adoption in electronic medical records. However, a standardised approach to using the CRDPSS is lacking. For example, the range of cognitive (and social cognitive) domains considered by clinicians when deriving a single rating of cognitive impairment may vary between individuals, and over time. Furthermore, no evidence on the psychometric properties of this tool is currently available.

Other methods for screening cognitive impairment in people with—or at high risk for—psychotic disorders include semistructured clinical interviews and self-report measures (see examples in Table 8.2). Such tools have often been designed with a greater emphasis on 'real world' competencies that may compliment (but not substitute for) objective neuropsychological assessment. As clinicians you therefore need to critically analyse the strengths and weaknesses of these instruments. For example, the Schizophrenia Cognition Rating Scale (SCoRS; Keefe, Poe, Walker, Kang, & Harvey, 2006) and the Cognitive Assessment Interview (Ventura et al., 2010) are interview-based measures of cognition that exhibit good reliability, validity, and sensitivity to change (Keefe et al., 2015; Ventura et al., 2016). However, the need for informants who know a client well may limit the practicality of these measures in clinical practice. In addition, the reliability and sensitivity of these tools may vary as a function of rater training (Keefe et al., 2015) and stage of illness (Sanchez-Torres et al., 2016).

Several self-report scales have been developed to assess subjective cognitive dysfunction in schizophrenia. However, people with psychotic disorders often have problems with various forms of self-assessment, including difficulties self-assessing basic cognition. As a consequence, client reports often do not correlate with objective assessments of cognitive performance. Incomplete or absent awareness of cognitive difficulties—or lack of cognitive insight—undermines the utility of self-report measures when assessing people with psychotic disorders (Burton, Harvey, Patterson, & Twamley, 2016). For example, a tendency to overestimate one's actual cognitive ability could mean that potential benefits from trying cognitive remediation would be missed. However, self-assessment can be clinically useful during case formulation discussions about cognition, regardless of whether performance is objectively good or bad. For example, '*Those with poor performance could be helped to attempt to match their aspirations to accomplishments and improve over time. Good performers could have their functioning bolstered by recognising their competence*' (Harvey & Pinkham, 2016; p. 53).

Measurement of Cognitive Bias

COMMON ASSESSMENT TOOLS

There are numerous cognitive biases associated with psychotic disorders, including deviations or selective processing in attention, interpretation, judgement, decision making, and reasoning. Such biases may be applied to various types of information; consequently, the boundaries between social and nonsocial cognitive biases are not always clear-cut. Furthermore, the relationship of these biases to one another and to deficits in basic and social cognition is still poorly understood and the focus of much ongoing research. Cognitive models of psychosis propose that information processing biases play a key role in the formation and maintenance of particular symptoms, and provide the focus for cognitive-behavioural interventions. To illustrate just a few, research evidence shows that the tendency towards jumping to conclusions (gather too little information) and belief inflexibility (have high conviction in thoughts and low consideration of alternative ideas)—sometimes characterised as *'fast-thinking'* biases—are consistently associated with paranoia (McLean et al., 2017). Similarly, externalising biases (the tendency to attribute internally generated events to external sources) are linked to hallucinatory experiences (Brookwell, Bentall, & Varese, 2013), whilst an inclination to negative (e.g. defeatist) performance beliefs and expectations is associated with elevated levels of negative (especially motivation/pleasure) symptoms in people with schizophrenia (Grant & Beck, 2009). The latter are typically assessed by subjective reports, whilst the former have been measured with a variety of objective experimental tasks (see Table 8.2).

Jumping to conclusions bias involves the tendency to gather too little information before making a decision.

Belief inflexibility refers to a high conviction in thoughts and low consideration of alternative ideas.

Externalising biases involve the tendency to attribute internally generated events to external sources.

Translating experimental research paradigms of cognitive bias into standardised tools for routine clinical practice has proven challenging. To take just one example, the jumping to conclusions bias is most commonly measured with the beads task. Individuals are shown two jars of coloured beads, in different ratios. The jars are hidden from view and individual beads are drawn consecutively from one jar. The participants' task is to decide from which jar the beads are being drawn. Metaanalyses provide robust evidence that people with delusions and psychosis make this decision on the basis of less information (i.e. with fewer draws) (McLean et al., 2017). However, there are numerous variants of the beads task, with different stimulus types, ratios, valence, instructions, and mode of presentation. In addition, both the reliability and interpretability of the beads task have been subject of criticism, which is inspiring new task variants to overcome these limitations. In short, there currently appears to be no 'gold-standard' version of this tool to assess fast-thinking biases in the clinic. However, on a more positive note, a range of new psychological therapies aimed at ameliorating reasoning (and other) biases has recently emerged. These metacognitive therapies are showing encouraging results. As such, routine pre- and posttreatment assessment of cognitive biases is increasingly being incorporated into these therapies in order to assess their efficacy (Schneider et al., 2016).

ALTERNATIVE METHODS OF ASSESSING COGNITIVE BIAS

Self-report measures of cognitive bias in psychosis are widely used in research, but scales suitable for clinical practice have only recently been developed and are, therefore, still being evaluated. Some offer the advantage of assessing multiple cognitive and social cognitive biases concurrently. For example, the

Cognitive Biases Questionnaire for Psychosis (CBQp: Peters et al., 2014) assesses jumping to conclusions, intentionalising, catastrophising, dichotomous thinking, and emotional reasoning biases. Initial evidence suggests it has good reliability and concurrent validity. One weakness is that individual biases are highly correlated; so, the CBQp may index a general thinking bias rather than distinct cognitive biases. In addition, CBQp scales are poorly correlated with experimental measures of each construct, raising doubts about the validity of subjective methods to assess cognitive bias (Bastiaens, Claes, Smits, Vanwalleghem, & De Hert, 2018).

Subjective and objective methods of assessing cognitive bias are often poorly correlated.

The Davos Assessment of Cognitive Biases Scale (DACOBS; van der Gaag et al., 2013) was designed to measure four cognitive biases (jumping to conclusions, belief inflexibility, selective attention to threat, and external attribution) believed to be specific to the positive symptoms of psychosis. Recent evidence suggests that these biases are in fact equally present in patients with psychotic and non-psychotic disorders (Bastiaens et al., 2018). Such findings could indicate that the suite of biases covered in the DACOBS are necessary but not sufficient for the development of psychosis.

Dysfunctional beliefs and expectancies are also considered important in the development and maintenance of negative symptoms of psychosis (see Beck & Rector, 2005). A systematic review of the evidence suggests a significant, though small, association between '*defeatist performance beliefs*' (e.g. 'If you cannot do something well, there is little point in doing it at all') and worse negative symptoms and functional outcomes in people with schizophrenia (Campellone, Sanchez, & Kring, 2016). Defined as overgeneralised negative thoughts about one's ability to successfully perform goal-directed behaviour, such beliefs can contribute to reduced interest and motivation to persist with social and employment opportunities (Reddy et al., 2017). Interventions targeting negative beliefs and expectancies could therefore help to improve everyday functioning and recovery in people with negative symptoms.

Defeatist performance beliefs are defined as overgeneralised negative thoughts about one's ability to successfully perform goal-directed behaviour.

One of the most widely used measures of cognitive bias in psychosis is the Beck Cognitive Insight Scale (BCIS; Beck & Rector, 2005). It provides measures of biases in self-certainty and self-reflectiveness, which are combined in a composite index of '*cognitive insight*' (see critique in Van Camp, Sabbe, & Oldenburg, 2017). Importantly, changes in cognitive insight appear to precede changes in neuropsychological performance, which suggests that improving cognitive insight could bolster cognitive functioning (Bredemeier, Beck, & Grant, 2018). However, higher cognitive insight may also be linked to higher levels of depression and lower levels of self-reported quality of life (Lysaker, Pattison, Leonhardt, Phelps, & Vohs, 2018). Case conceptualisation with your clients will therefore benefit from careful consideration of the complexity of these effects.

Cognitive insight refers to a lack of awareness of, and ability to re-evaluate and correct, distorted thoughts and beliefs.

Self certainty refers to the degree of confidence or certainty in one's (mis) interpretations.

Self reflectiveness refers to the capacity for self-awareness and willingness to re-evaluate one's thoughts and beliefs.

COMMON ASSESSMENT CHALLENGES AND OPPORTUNITIES

Detailed consideration of the principles and best practice in the use of psychological tests is covered elsewhere (see Self-directed Reading), so will not be discussed here. Rather, we conclude by highlighting some of the practical challenges and opportunities when assessing people with psychotic symptoms and disorders.

Challenge 1: When to test. To ensure the best interests of your clients, assessment of social and basic cognition must be sensitive to the broader clinical and personal context. In Australia, for example, clinical practice guidelines for the management of schizophrenia and related disorders state that *'cognitive assessment should take place as part of the initial assessment (once acute symptoms have settled) and before and after specific interventions'* (Galletly et al., 2016; p. 50). A systematic approach to assessment allows you to evaluate changes in performance following an intervention and judge whether therapy is on track.

Challenge 2: Selecting tests. Test selection should consider if measures are appropriate in length, content and purpose; have suitable norms available; have adequate psychometric properties, and meet the needs of culturally and linguistically diverse clients with psychosis. Lengthy testing can be a considerable challenge, so a balance must be struck between adequate assessment for differential diagnosis and treatment planning, and client/clinician burden. Also be aware that selecting adequate tests for the assessment of social cognition may be more challenging than identifying appropriate assessments for basic cognition, since there is no current gold-standard social cognitive battery. However, given the functional relevance of social cognition, this challenge should not deter you from attempting to assess these abilities and biases in your clients.

Challenge 3: Interpreting test performance. Both clinical experience and an emerging evidence base suggest that a large range of factors can influence your client's performance on cognitive tests, including high levels of stress, lack of motivation, defeatist performance beliefs, disrupted sleep, medication or drug effects, cultural similarity to the examiner, sensory impairments, and reading difficulties. Clinicians face the challenging task of taking these factors into account when interpreting the reasons for any performance deficits observed. These observations are also encouraging a more fundamental reconsideration of the contribution of cognition as a 'core' feature of psychosis (Beck, Himelstein, Bredemeier, Silverstein, & Grant, 2018).

Challenge 4: Benefiting from the latest developments. One of the practical challenges that you face as clinical and neuropsychologists is how to keep up to date with the literature. Fortunately, online resources are beginning to provide ready access to reliable, high-quality evidence summaries (see Resource Links below) to help you with your ongoing professional development.

Challenge 5: Taking the client and carer's perspective. Negative attitudes and behaviours of clinicians (e.g. all people with schizophrenia are incompetent, so why bother with assessment) can deter client engagement with services and impede recovery. Reflecting on your client's viewpoint helps you to appreciate the need to develop skills and practices that facilitate stigma reduction (Knaak, Mantler, & Szeto, 2017). Finally, clients, their relatives, and other carers may not associate cognitive or social cognitive difficulties with psychosis or know that these skills can be remediated. Consequently, offering psychoeducation provides a valuable opportunity to increase knowledge, correct myths, and improve outcomes as part of an integrated treatment plan to improve cognitive functioning.

QUIZ QUESTIONS

1. Which of the following statements is inaccurate (select 1 answer only):
   (a) Social cognition is a multidimensional construct that includes areas of ability (e.g. emotion recognition) as well as bias (e.g. hostility bias).
   (b) Social cognition has limited impact on day-to-day function and therefore assessment should only consider social cognition if time allows.
   (c) Assessment of social cognition should be viewed as an evolving area that should see significant improvement and innovation over the next several years.
   (d) The nature of social cognitive impairments appears to be impacted by diagnosis and the type of symptoms one experiences.
2. Psychometrically sound and well-validated tasks are currently available for assessing which of the following domains of social cognition (select all that apply):
   (a) Emotion processing
   (b) Social perception
   (c) Mentalising
   (d) Attributional style
3. Assessing basic cognition in people with psychosis has which of the following benefits (select 1 answer only):
   (a) It provides a profile of strengths and weaknesses to guide appropriate interventions
   (b) It can identify individuals whose cognitive ability is within the normal range
   (c) It can establish the degree of cognitive deficit/ability, which varies across different psychotic disorders and stage of illness
   (d) It can provide baseline level of performance for comparison posttreatment, to help judge whether cognitive remediation is on track
   (e) All of the above
4. Cognitive test performance of people with psychosis can be influenced by which of the following factors? (select all that apply):
   (a) The degree of training and experience of the examiner

(b) The intrinsic motivation and expectations of the client
(c) Lack of suitable norms to fit the client's age, gender, or culture
(d) Inappropriate test selection

ANSWERS TO QUIZ QUESTIONS:

1. (b)
2. (a) and (c)
3. (e)
4. (a), (b), (c), and (d)

SELF-DIRECTED READING

Harvey, P. D. (Ed.) (2013). *Cognitive Impairment in Schizophrenia: Characteristics, Assessment and Treatment.* GB: Cambridge University Press.

Lezak, Howieson, Bigler and Tranel (2012). *Neuropsychological Assessment* 5th ed. Oxford: Oxford University Press, Inc.

Roberts, D. L., & Penn, D. L. (Eds.). (2013). *Social Cognition in Schizophrenia. From Evidence to Treatment.* US: Oxford University Press Inc.

LINKS TO RESOURCES

American Psychological Society: Testing and Assessment. http://www.apa.org/science/programs/testing/index.aspx

Clinician-Rated Dimensions of Psychosis Symptom Severity, available at www.psychiatry.org/dsm5

Neuroscience Research Australia (NeuRA) Virtual library on bipolar disorder https://www.neura.edu.au/discovery-portal/bipolar-disorder-library/

Research Australia (NeuRA) Virtual library on schizophrenia https://library.neura.edu.au/

The Australian Psychological Society: Position Statement on Psychological Tests and Testing. https://www.psychology.org.au/getmedia/77b78f6e-3f52-4e08-92ba-529419c9b574/APS-position-statement-on-tests-and-testing.pdf.pdf

The British Psychological Society: Psychological Testing Centre https://ptc.bps.org.uk/

References

American Psychiatric Association. (2013). *Diagnostic and Statistical Manual of Mental Disorders: DSM 5.* Washington, DC: American Psychiatric Pub Incorporated.

Atkins, A. S., Tseng, T., Vaughan, A., Twamley, E. W., Harvey, P., Patterson, T., et al. (2017). Validation of the tablet-administered Brief Assessment of Cognition (BAC App). *Schizophrenia Research, 181*, 100–106. https://doi.org/10.1016/j.schres.2016.10.010.

Badcock, J. C., & Hugdahl, K. (2012). Cognitive mechanisms of auditory verbal hallucinations in psychotic and non-psychotic groups. *Neuroscience and Biobehavioral Reviews, 36*(1), 431–438. https://doi.org/10.1016/j.neubiorev.2011.07.010.

Barbato, M., Liu, L., Cadenhead, K. S., Cannon, T. D., Cornblatt, B. A., McGlashan, T. H., et al. (2015). Theory of mind, emotion recognition and social perception in individuals at clinical high risk for psychosis: Findings from the NAPLS-2 cohort. *Schizophrenia Research: Cognition, 2*(3), 133–139.

Barkl, S. J., Lah, S., Harris, A. W., & Williams, L. M. (2014). Facial emotion identification in early-onset and first-episode psychosis: A systematic review with meta-analysis. *Schizophrenia Research, 159*(1), 62–69.

Barnett, J. H., Robbins, T. W., Leeson, V. C., Sahakian, B. J., Joyce, E. M., & Blackwell, A. D. (2010). Assessing cognitive function in clinical trials of schizophrenia. *Neuroscience & Biobehavioral Reviews, 34*(8), 1161–1177.

Bastiaens, T., Claes, L., Smits, D., De Wachter, D., van der Gaag, M., & De Hert, M. (2013). The Cognitive Biases Questionnaire for Psychosis (CBQ-P) and the Davos Assessment of Cognitive Biases (DACOBS): Validation in a Flemish sample of psychotic patients and healthy controls. *Schizophrenia Research, 147*(2–3), 310–314. https://doi.org/10.1016/j.schres.2013.04.037.

Bastiaens, T., Claes, L., Smits, D., Vanwalleghem, D., & De Hert, M. (2018). Self-reported cognitive biases are equally present in patients diagnosed with psychotic versus nonpsychotic disorders. *Journal of Nervous and Mental Disease, 206*(2), 122–129. https://doi.org/10.1097/nmd.0000000000000763.

Beck, A. T., Baruch, E., Balter, J. M., Steer, R. A., & Warman, D. M. (2004). A new instrument for measuring insight: The Beck Cognitive Insight Scale. *Schizophrenia Research, 68*(2–3), 319–329. https://doi.org/10.1016/S0920-9964(03)00189-0.

Beck, A. T., Himelstein, R., Bredemeier, K., Silverstein, S. M., & Grant, P. (2018). What accounts for poor functioning in people with schizophrenia: A re-evaluation of the contributions of neurocognitive v. attitudinal and motivational factors. *Psychological Medicine*, 1–10. https://doi.org/10.1017/s0033291718000442.

Beck, A. T., & Rector, N. A. (2005). Cognitive approaches to schizophrenia: Theory and therapy. *Annual Review of Clinical Psychology, 1*, 577–606. https://doi.org/10.1146/annurev.clinpsy.1.102803.144205.

Bora, E., & Pantelis, C. (2013). Theory of mind impairments in first-episode psychosis, individuals at ultra-high risk for psychosis and in first-degree relatives of schizophrenia: Systematic review and meta-analysis. *Schizophrenia Research, 144*(1), 31–36.

Bora, E., & Pantelis, C. (2015). Meta-analysis of cognitive impairment in first-episode bipolar disorder: Comparison with first-episode schizophrenia and healthy controls. *Schizophrenia Bulletin, 41*(5), 1095–1104. https://doi.org/10.1093/schbul/sbu198.

Bora, E., & Pantelis, C. (2016). Social cognition in schizophrenia in comparison to bipolar disorder: A meta-analysis. *Schizophrenia Research, 175*(1), 72–78.

Bredemeier, K., Beck, A. T., & Grant, P. M. (2018). Exploring the temporal relationship between cognitive insight and neurocognition in schizophrenia: A prospective analysis. *Clinical Psychological Science, 6*(1), 76–89. https://doi.org/10.1177/2167702617734019.

Brookwell, M. L., Bentall, R. P., & Varese, F. (2013). Externalizing biases and hallucinations in source-monitoring, self-monitoring and signal detection studies: A meta-analytic review. *Psychological Medicine, 43*(12), 2465–2475. https://doi.org/10.1017/S0033291712002760.

Bryson, G., Bell, M., & Lysaker, P. (1997). Affect recognition in schizophrenia: A function of global impairment or a specific cognitive deficit. *Psychiatry Research, 71*(2), 105–113.

Buck, B. E., Hester, N. R., Pinkham, A. E., Harvey, P. D., Jarskog, F., & Penn, D. L. (2018). The bias toward intentionality in schizophrenia: Automaticity, context, and relationships to symptoms and functioning. *Journal of Abnormal Psychology, 127*(5), 503–512.

Buck, B. E., Iwanski, C., Healey, K. M., Green, M. F., Horan, W. P., Kern, R. S., et al. (2017). Improving measurement of attributional style in schizophrenia; a psychometric evaluation of the Ambiguous Intentions Hostility Questionnaire (AIHQ). *Journal of Psychiatric Research.*

Buck, B. E., Pinkham, A. E., Harvey, P. D., & Penn, D. L. (2016). Revisiting the validity of measures of social cognitive bias in schizophrenia: Additional results from the Social Cognition Psychometric Evaluation (SCOPE) study. *British Journal of Clinical Psychology, 55*(4), 441–454. https://doi.org/10.1111/bjc.12113.

Burton, C. Z., Harvey, P. D., Patterson, T. L., & Twamley, E. W. (2016). Neurocognitive insight and objective cognitive functioning in schizophrenia. *Schizophrenia Research, 171*(1–3), 131–136. https://doi.org/10.1016/j.schres.2016.01.021.

Campellone, T. R., Sanchez, A. H., & Kring, A. M. (2016). Defeatist performance beliefs, negative symptoms, and functional outcome in schizophrenia: A meta-analytic review. *Schizophrenia Bulletin, 42*(6), 1343–1352. https://doi.org/10.1093/schbul/sbw026.

Chiang, S. K., Ni, C. H., Tsai, C. P., & Lin, K. C. (2016). Validation of the cognitively normal range and below normal range subtypes in chronically hospitalized patients with schizophrenia. *Schizophrenia Research: Cognition, 5*, 28–34. https://doi.org/10.1016/j.scog.2016.06.002.

Combs, D. R., Penn, D. L., Wicher, M., & Waldheter, E. (2007). The Ambiguous Intentions Hostility Questionnaire (AIHQ): A new measure for evaluating hostile social-cognitive biases in paranoia. *Cognitive Neuropsychiatry, 12*(2), 128–143. https://doi.org/10.1080/13546800600787854.

Comparelli, A., Corigliano, V., De Carolis, A., Mancinelli, I., Trovini, G., Ottavi, G., et al. (2013). Emotion recognition impairment is present early and is stable throughout the course of schizophrenia. *Schizophrenia Research, 143*(1), 65–69.

Corcoran, R., Mercer, G., & Frith, C. D. (1995). Schizophrenia, symptomatology and social inference: Investigating "theory of mind" in people with schizophrenia. *Schizophrenia Research, 17* (1), 5–13.

Corrigan, P. W., & Green, M. F. (1993). Schizophrenic patients' sensitivity to social cues: The role of abstraction. *American Journal of Psychiatry, 150*(4), 589–594.

Couture, S. M., Penn, D. L., & Roberts, D. L. (2006). The functional significance of social cognition in schizophrenia: A review. *Schizophrenia Bulletin, 32*(1), S44–SS63. https://doi.org/10.1093/schbul/sbl029.

Fiszdon, J. M. (2013). Introduction to social cognitive treatment approaches for schizophrenia. In D. L. Roberts, & D. L. Penn (Eds.), *Social cognition in schizophrenia* (pp. 285–310). New York, NY: Oxford University Press.

Fretland, R. A., Andersson, S., Sundet, K., Andreassen, O. A., Melle, I., & Vaskinn, A. (2015). Theory of mind in schizophrenia: Error types and associations with symptoms. *Schizophrenia Research, 162*(1), 42–46.

Frith, C. D. (1992). *The cognitive neuropsychology of schizophrenia.* Psychology Press.

Galletly, C., Castle, D., Dark, F., Humberstone, V., Jablensky, A., Killackey, E., et al. (2016). Royal Australian and New Zealand College of Psychiatrists clinical practice guidelines for the management of schizophrenia and related disorders. *Australian and New Zealand Journal of Psychiatry, 50* (5), 410–472. https://doi.org/10.1177/0004867416641195.

Georgiades, A., Davis, V. G., Atkins, A. S., Khan, A., Walker, T. W., Loebel, A., et al. (2017). Psychometric characteristics of the MATRICS consensus cognitive battery in a large pooled cohort of stable schizophrenia patients. *Schizophrenia Research, 190*, 172–179. https://doi.org/10.1016/j.schres.2017.03.040.

Grant, P. M., & Beck, A. T. (2009). Defeatist beliefs as a mediator of cognitive impairment, negative symptoms, and functioning in schizophrenia. *Schizophrenia Bulletin, 35*(4), 798–806. https://doi.org/10.1093/schbul/sbn008.

Green, M. F., Penn, D. L., Bentall, R., Carpenter, W. T., Gaebel, W., Gur, R. C., et al. (2008). Social cognition in schizophrenia: An NIMH workshop on definitions, assessment, and research opportunities. *Schizophrenia Bulletin, 34*(6), 1211–1220. https://doi.org/10.1093/schbul/sbm145.

Hajduk, M., Harvey, P., Penn, D. L., & Pinkham, A. E. (2018). Social cognitive impairments in individuals with schizophrenia vary in severity. *Journal of Psychiatric Research, 104*, 65–71.

Harris, S. T., Oakley, C., & Picchioni, M. M. (2014). A systematic review of the association between attributional bias/interpersonal style, and violence in schizophrenia/psychosis. *Aggression and Violent Behavior, 19*(3), 235–241.

Harvey, P. D., & Pinkham, A. (2016). Impaired self-assessment in schizophrenia: Why patients misjudge their cognition and functioning. *Current Psychiatry, 14*(4), 53–59.

Healey, K. M., Combs, D. R., Gibson, C. M., Keefe, R. S., Roberts, D. L., & Penn, D. L. (2015). Observable social cognition – A rating scale: An interview-based assessment for schizophrenia. *Cognitive Neuropsychiatry, 20*(3), 198–221.

Heinrichs, R. W., Parlar, M., & Pinnock, F. (2017). Normal-range verbal-declarative memory in schizophrenia. *Neuropsychology, 31*(7), 778–786. https://doi.org/10.1037/neu0000365.

Henry, J. D., von Hippel, W., Molenberghs, P., Lee, T., & Sachdev, P. S. (2016). Clinical assessment of social cognitive function in neurological disorders. *Nature Reviews Neurology, 12*(1), 28–39. https://doi.org/10.1038/nrneurol.2015.229.

Hochberger, W. C., Combs, T., Reilly, J. L., Bishop, J. R., Keefe, R. S. E., Clementz, B. A., et al. (2017). Deviation from expected cognitive ability across psychotic disorders. *Schizophrenia Research, 192*, 300–307. https://doi.org/10.1016/j.schres.2017.05.019.

Horan, W. P., Green, M. F., DeGroot, M., Fiske, A., Hellemann, G., Kee, K., et al. (2012). Social cognition in schizophrenia, part 2: 12-month stability and prediction of functional outcome in first-episode patients. *Schizophrenia Bulletin, 38*(4), 865–872.

Horan, W. P., Rassovsky, Y., Kern, R. S., Lee, J., Wynn, J. K., & Green, M. F. (2010). Further support for the role of dysfunctional attitudes in models of real-world functioning in schizophrenia. *Journal of Psychiatric Research, 44*(8), 499–505.

Ishikawa, R., Ishigaki, T., Kikuchi, A., Matsumoto, K., Kobayashi, S., Morishige, S., et al. (2017). Cross-cultural validation of the cognitive biases questionnaire for psychosis in Japan and examination of the relationships between cognitive biases and schizophrenia symptoms. *Cognitive Therapy and Research, 41*(2), 313–323.

Jimenez-Lopez, E., Aparicio, A. I., Sanchez-Morla, E. M., Rodriguez-Jimenez, R., Vieta, E., & Santos, J. L. (2017). Neurocognition in patients with psychotic and non-psychotic bipolar I disorder. A comparative study with individuals with schizophrenia. *Journal of Affective Disorders, 222*, 169–176. https://doi.org/10.1016/j.jad.2017.07.014.

Keefe, R. S., Davis, V. G., Spagnola, N. B., Hilt, D., Dgetluck, N., Ruse, S., et al. (2015). Reliability, validity and treatment sensitivity of the Schizophrenia Cognition Rating Scale. *European Neuropsychopharmacology, 25*(2), 176–184. https://doi.org/10.1016/j.euroneuro.2014.06.009.

Keefe, R. S., Eesley, C. S., & Poe, M. (2005). Defining a cognitive function decrement in schizophrenia. *Biological Psychiatry, 57*(6), 688–691. https://doi.org/10.1016/j.biopsych.2005.01.003.

Keefe, R. S., Poe, M., Walker, T. M., Kang, J. W., & Harvey, P. D. (2006). The schizophrenia cognition rating scale: An interview-based assessment and its relationship to cognition, real-world functioning, and functional capacity. *American Journal of Psychiatry, 163*(3), 426–432. https://doi.org/10.1176/appi.ajp.163.3.426.

Kennedy, D. P., & Adolphs, R. (2012). The social brain in psychiatric and neurological disorders. *Trends in Cognitive Sciences, 16*(11), 559–572. https://doi.org/10.1016/j.tics.2012.09.006.

Knaak, S., Mantler, E., & Szeto, A. (2017). Mental illness-related stigma in healthcare: Barriers to access and care and evidence-based solutions. *Healthcare Management Forum, 30*(2), 111–116. https://doi.org/10.1177/0840470416679413.

Kohler, C. G., Richard, J. A., Brensinger, C. M., Borgmann-Winter, K. E., Conroy, C. G., Moberg, P. J., et al. (2014). Facial emotion perception differs in young persons at genetic and clinical high-risk for psychosis. *Psychiatry Research, 216*(2), 206–212.

Kohler, C. G., Turner, T. H., Bilker, W. B., Brensinger, C. M., Siegel, S. J., Kanes, S. J., et al. (2003). Facial emotion recognition in schizophrenia: Intensity effects and error pattern. *American Journal of Psychiatry, 160*(10), 1768–1774.

Kurtz, M. M., & Richardson, C. L. (2012). Social cognitive training for schizophrenia: A meta-analytic investigation of controlled research. *Schizophrenia Bulletin, 38*(5), 1092–1104. https://doi.org/10.1093/schbul/sbr036.

Lahera, G., Herrera, S., Reinares, M., Benito, A., Rullas, M., González-Cases, J., et al. (2015). Hostile attributions in bipolar disorder and schizophrenia contribute to poor social functioning. *Acta Psychiatrica Scandinavica, 131*(6), 472–482.

Lee, T. Y., Hong, S. B., Shin, N. Y., & Kwon, J. S. (2015). Social cognitive functioning in prodromal psychosis: A meta-analysis. *Schizophrenia Research, 164*(1), 28–34.

Ludwig, K. A., Pinkham, A. E., Harvey, P. D., Kelsven, S., & Penn, D. L. (2017). Social cognition psychometric evaluation (SCOPE) in people with early psychosis: A preliminary study. *Schizophrenia Research, 190*, 136–143. https://doi.org/10.1016/j.schres.2017.03.001.

Lynham, A. J., Hubbard, L., Tansey, K. E., Hamshere, M. L., Legge, S. E., Owen, M. J., et al. (2017). Examining cognition across the bipolar/schizophrenia diagnostic spectrum. *European Neuropsychopharmacology, 27*, S726–S727. https://doi.org/10.1016/s0924-977x(17)31336-6.

Lysaker, P. H., Pattison, M. L., Leonhardt, B. L., Phelps, S., & Vohs, J. L. (2018). Insight in schizophrenia spectrum disorders: Relationship with behavior, mood and perceived quality of life, underlying causes and emerging treatments. *World Psychiatry, 17*(1), 12–23. https://doi.org/10.1002/wps.20508.

Marder, S. R., & Galderisi, S. (2017). The current conceptualization of negative symptoms in schizophrenia. *World Psychiatry, 16*(1), 14–24. https://doi.org/10.1002/wps.20385.

Maruff, P., Thomas, E., Cysique, L., Brew, B., Collie, A., Snyder, P., et al. (2009). Validity of the CogState brief battery: Relationship to standardized tests and sensitivity to cognitive impairment in mild traumatic brain injury, schizophrenia, and AIDS dementia complex. *Archives of Clinical Neuropsychology, 24*(2), 165–178. https://doi.org/10.1093/arclin/acp010.

McDonald, S., Flanagan, S., Rollins, J., & Kinch, J. (2003). TASIT: A new clinical tool for assessing social perception after traumatic brain injury. *Journal of Head Trauma and Rehabilitation, 18*(3), 219–238.

McLean, B. F., Mattiske, J. K., & Balzan, R. P. (2017). Association of the Jumping to conclusions and evidence integration biases with delusions in psychosis: A detailed meta-analysis. *Schizophrenia Bulletin, 43*(2), 344–354.

Medalia, A., Thysen, J., & Freilich, B. (2008). Do people with schizophrenia who have objective cognitive impairment identify cognitive deficits on a self report measure? *Schizophrenia Research, 105* (1), 156–164. https://doi.org/10.1016/j.schres.2008.07.007.

Mehl, S., Landsberg, M. W., Schmidt, A.-C., Cabanis, M., Bechdolf, A., Herrlich, J., et al. (2014). Why do bad things happen to me? Attributional style, depressed mood, and persecutory delusions in patients with schizophrenia. *Schizophrenia Bulletin, 40*(6), 1338–1346.

Meier, M. H., Caspi, A., Reichenberg, A., et al. (2014). Neuropsychological decline in schizophrenia from the premorbid to the postonset period: Evidence from a population-representative longitudinal study. *American Journal of Psychiatry, 171*(1), 91–101.

Mollon, J., & Reichenberg, A. (2018). Cognitive development prior to onset of psychosis. *Psychological Medicine, 48*(3), 392–403. https://doi.org/10.1017/s0033291717001970.

Montag, C., Dziobek, I., Richter, I. S., Neuhaus, K., Lehmann, A., Sylla, R., et al. (2011). Different aspects of theory of mind in paranoid schizophrenia: Evidence from a video-based assessment. *Psychiatry Research, 186*(2), 203–209.

Murphy, E., & Benítez-Burraco, A. (2016). Bridging the gap between genes and language deficits in schizophrenia: An oscillopathic approach. *Frontiers in Human Neuroscience, 10*, 422. https://doi.org/10.3389/fnhum.2016.00422.

Penn, D. L., Addington, J., & Pinkham, A. E. (2006). Social cognitive impairments. In J. A. Lieberman, T. S. Stroup, & D. O. Perkins (Eds.), *A textbook of schizophrenia*. Washington: American Psychiatry Press.

Penn, D. L., Ritchie, M., Francis, J., Combs, D., & Martin, J. (2002). Social perception in schizophrenia: The role of context. *Psychiatry Research, 109*(2), 149–159.

Peters, E. R., Moritz, S., Schwannauer, M., Wiseman, Z., Greenwood, K. E., Scott, J., et al. (2014). Cognitive biases questionnaire for psychosis. *Schizophrenia Bulletin, 40*(2), 300–313. https://doi.org/10.1093/schbul/sbs199.

Pinkham, A. E., Brensinger, C., Kohler, C., Gur, R. E., & Gur, R. C. (2011). Actively paranoid patients with schizophrenia over attribute anger to neutral faces. *Schizophrenia Research, 125*(2–3), 174–178.

Pinkham, A. E., Harvey, P. D., & Penn, D. L. (2016). Paranoid individuals with schizophrenia show greater social cognitive bias and worse social functioning than non-paranoid individuals with schizophrenia. *Schizophrenia Research: Cognition, 3*, 33–38.

Pinkham, A. E., Harvey, P. D., & Penn, D. L. (2018). Social cognition psychometric evaluation: Results of the final validation study. *Schizophrenia Bulletin, 44*(4), 737–748. https://doi.org/10.1093/schbul/sbx117.

Pinkham, A. E., Kelsven, S., Kouros, C., Harvey, P. D., & Penn, D. L. (2017). The effect of age, race, and sex on social cognitive performance in individuals with schizophrenia. *The Journal of Nervous and Mental Disease, 205*(5), 346–352. https://doi.org/10.1097/NMD.0000000000000654.

Pinkham, A. E., Penn, D. L., Green, M. F., Buck, B. E., Healey, K., & Harvey, P. D. (2014). The social cognition psychometric evaluation study: Results of the expert survey and RAND panel. *Schizophrenia Bulletin, 40*(4), 813–823. https://doi.org/10.1093/schbul/sbt081.

Pinkham, A. E., Penn, D. L., Green, M. F., & Harvey, P. D. (2016). Social cognition psychometric evaluation: Results of the initial psychometric study. *Schizophrenia Bulletin, 42*(2), 494–504. https://doi.org/10.1093/schbul/sbv056.

Pinkham, A. E., Sasson, N. J., Kelsven, S., Simpson, C. E., Healey, K., & Kohler, C. (2014). An intact threat superiority effect for nonsocial but not social stimuli in schizophrenia. *Journal of Abnormal Psychology, 123*(1), 168.

Piskulic, D., Liu, L., Cadenhead, K. S., Cannon, T. D., Cornblatt, B. A., McGlashan, T. H., et al. (2016). Social cognition over time in individuals at clinical high risk for psychosis: Findings from the NAPLS-2 cohort. *Schizophrenia Research, 171*(1), 176–181.

Reddy, L. F., Horan, W. P., Barch, D. M., Buchanan, R. W., Gold, J. M., Marder, S. R., et al. (2017). Understanding the association between negative symptoms and performance on effort-based decision-making tasks: The importance of defeatist performance beliefs. *Schizophrenia Bulletin*, sbx156. https://doi.org/10.1093/schbul/sbx156.

Riggs, S. E., Grant, P. M., Perivoliotis, D., & Beck, A. T. (2012). Assessment of cognitive insight: A qualitative review. *Schizophrenia Bulletin, 38*(2), 338–350. https://doi.org/10.1093/schbul/sbq085.

Roberts, D. L., & Pinkham, A. E. (2013). The future of social cognition in schizophrenia: Implications for the normative literature. In D. L. Roberts, & D. L. Penn (Eds.), *Social cognition in schizophrenia* (pp. 401–414). New York: Oxford University Press.

Rosset, E. (2008). It's no accident: Our bias for intentional explanations. *Cognition, 108*(3), 771–780.

Ruocco, A. C., Reilly, J. L., Rubin, L. H., Daros, A. R., Gershon, E. S., Tamminga, C. A., et al. (2014). Emotion recognition deficits in schizophrenia-spectrum disorders and psychotic bipolar disorder: Findings from the Bipolar-Schizophrenia Network on Intermediate Phenotypes (B-SNIP) study. *Schizophrenia Research, 158*(1–3), 105–112. https://doi.org/10.1016/j.schres.2014.07.001.

Sachs, G., Steger-Wuchse, D., Kryspin-Exner, I., Gur, R. C., & Katschnig, H. (2004). Facial recognition deficits and cognition in schizophrenia. *Schizophrenia Research, 68*(1), 27–35.

Sanchez-Torres, A. M., Elosua, M. R., Lorente-Omenaca, R., Moreno-Izco, L., Peralta, V., & Cuesta, M. J. (2016). The cognitive assessment interview: A comparative study in first episode and chronic patients with psychosis. *Schizophrenia Research, 178*(1–3), 80–85. https://doi.org/10.1016/j.schres.2016.08.028.

Santesteban-Echarri, O., Paino, M., Rice, S., González-Blanch, C., McGorry, P., Gleeson, J., et al. (2017). Predictors of functional recovery in first-episode psychosis: A systematic review and meta-analysis of longitudinal studies. *Clinical Psychology Review, 58*, 59–75. https://doi.org/10.1016/j.cpr.2017.09.007.

Savla, G. N., Vella, L., Armstrong, C. C., Penn, D. L., & Twamley, E. W. (2013). Deficits in domains of social cognition in schizophrenia: A meta-analysis of the empirical evidence. *Schizophrenia Bulletin, 39*(5), 979–992. https://doi.org/10.1093/schbul/sbs080.

Schaefer, J., Giangrande, E., Weinberger, D. R., & Dickinson, D. (2013). The global cognitive impairment in schizophrenia: Consistent over decades and around the world. *Schizophrenia Research, 150*(1), 42–50. https://doi.org/10.1016/j.schres.2013.07.009.

Schneider, B. C., Brüne, M., Bohn, F., Veckenstedt, R., Kolbeck, K., Krieger, E., et al. (2016). Investigating the efficacy of an individualized metacognitive therapy program (MCT+) for psychosis: Study protocol of a multi-center randomized controlled trial. *BMC Psychiatry, 16*(1), 51. https://doi.org/10.1186/s12888-016-0756-2.

Sergi, M. J., & Green, M. F. (2003). Social perception and early visual processing in schizophrenia. *Schizophrenia Research, 59*(2–3), 233–241.

Sergi, M. J., Rassovsky, Y., Widmark, C., Reist, C., Erhart, S., Braff, D. L., et al. (2007). Social cognition in schizophrenia: Relationships with neurocognition and negative symptoms. *Schizophrenia Research, 90*(1–3), 316–324.

Van Camp, L. S. C., Sabbe, B. G. C., & Oldenburg, J. F. E. (2017). Cognitive insight: A systematic review. *Clinical Psychology Review, 55*, 12–24. https://doi.org/10.1016/j.cpr.2017.04.011.

van der Gaag, M., Schutz, C., Ten Napel, A., Landa, Y., Delespaul, P., Bak, M., et al. (2013). Development of the Davos assessment of cognitive biases scale (DACOBS). *Schizophrenia Research, 144* (1–3), 63–71. https://doi.org/10.1016/j.schres.2012.12.010.

Ventura, J., Reise, S. P., Keefe, R. S., Baade, L. E., Gold, J. M., Green, M. F., et al. (2010). The Cognitive Assessment Interview (CAI): Development and validation of an empirically derived, brief interview-based measure of cognition. *Schizophrenia Research, 121*(1–3), 24–31. https://doi.org/10.1016/j.schres.2010.04.016.

Ventura, J., Subotnik, K. L., Ered, A., Hellemann, G. S., & Nuechterlein, K. H. (2016). Cognitive Assessment Interview (CAI): Validity as a co-primary measure of cognition across phases of schizophrenia. *Schizophrenia Research, 172*(1–3), 137–142. https://doi.org/10.1016/j.schres.2016.01.028.

Ventura, J., Wood, R. C., & Hellemann, G. S. (2011). Symptom domains and neurocognitive functioning can help differentiate social cognitive processes in schizophrenia: A meta-analysis. *Schizophrenia Bulletin, 39*(1), 102–111.

Ventura, J., Wood, R. C., Jimenez, A. M., & Hellemann, G. S. (2013). Neurocognition and symptoms identify links between facial recognition and emotion processing in schizophrenia: Meta-analytic findings. *Schizophrenia Research, 151*(1–3), 78–84. https://doi.org/10.1016/j.schres.2013.10.015.

Walss-Bass, C., Fernandes, J. M., Roberts, D. L., Service, H., & Velligan, D. (2013). Differential correlations between plasma oxytocin and social cognitive capacity and bias in schizophrenia. *Schizophrenia Research, 147*(2–3), 387–392. https://doi.org/10.1016/j.schres.2013.04.003.

Weissman, A. (1978). *Dysfunctional attitudes scale: A validation study*. Philadelphia, PA: University of Pennsylvania.

Welch, L. C., Trudeau, J. J., Silverstein, S. M., Sand, M., Henderson, D. C., & Rosen, R. C. (2017). Initial development of a patient-reported outcome measure of experience with cognitive impairment associated with schizophrenia. *Patient Related Outcome Measures, 8*, 71–81. https://doi.org/10.2147/PROM.S123266.

Weniger, G., Lange, C., Ruther, E., & Irle, E. (2004). Differential impairments of facial affect recognition in schizophrenia subtypes and major depression. *Psychiatry Research, 128*(2), 135–146.

Wood, H., Cupitt, C., & Lavender, T. (2015). The experience of cognitive impairment in people with psychosis. *Clinical Psychology & Psychotherapy, 22*(3), 193–207. https://doi.org/10.1002/cpp.1878.

Definition of Key Terms

Attribution style The tendency to explain the causes of events in a certain way.

Cognitive bias A systematic deviation from the norm in perceptual and cognitive processes.

Cognitive deficits A reduction or loss in basic perceptual and cognitive processes compared to the norm.

Emotion processing Perceiving and using emotions.

Mentalising Inferring the thoughts and intentions of others.

Social cognition Perceiving, encoding, and applying information about other people and social situations.

Social perception Decoding and interpreting social cues in others.

CHAPTER 9

Assessing Social Functioning Across the Life Course of Psychosis

Helen J Stain*,†, Jone Bjornestad‡

*School of Social and Health Sciences, Leeds Trinity University, Horsforth, United Kingdom, †TIPS—Network for Clinical Research in Psychosis, Stavanger University Hospital, Stavanger, Norway, ‡Department of Social Studies, Faculty of Social Sciences, University of Stavanger, Stavanger, Norway

Key Learning Objectives

- To learn about social functioning and how it is affected across the course of psychosis.
- To understand the domains that should be included in a measure of social functioning.
- To appreciate the indicators of a robust measure of social functioning in psychosis.

INTRODUCTION

Social functioning impairment is a core component of psychotic disorders and thus measures of social functioning are crucial for clinical assessment, prognosis, and outcome in psychosis (as illustrated in the example in Box 9.1) (van Os, Kenis, & Rutten, 2010). Persistent and severe social deficits were integral to the initial identification of schizophrenia as a disorder that was derived by clinical observations of adults with schizophrenia (Kraepelin, 1919/1971). A recent Australian national survey found that more than one-third of adults with psychosis rated social functioning issues as their greatest challenge for the future (Stain et al., 2012) and this is echoed in other populations (Balaji et al., 2012). Long-term deficits in social functioning have been linked to negative symptoms in psychosis such as social withdrawal, apathy, and avolition (Kirkpatrick, Fenton, Carpenter, & Marder, 2006; Marder & Galderisi, 2017) as well as impaired social cognitive functioning such as mentalisation and theory of mind (MacBeth & Gumley, 2008; van Os et al., 2010; Zipursky, 2014). Negative symptoms are defined as an absence or reduction of behaviours that are normally present in the general population. The negative symptoms of schizophrenia include social withdrawal, diminished affective

A Clinical Introduction to Psychosis. https://doi.org/10.1016/B978-0-12-815012-2.00009-2

Box 9.1 Client Example

I still had three arenas—school, organised workout, girlfriend—which I focused on. I said to myself:

> "okay, no matter how it goes, I must continue to concentrate on these three arenas." These arenas made me ignore my difficult situation... The three arenas made me think: "focus now, now I have to stand up, now I must go to the gym, now I have to go to school, you cannot sit up all night and mope, now you need to concentrate. Tomorrow is a new day, you'll have to get up again then."

So these three arenas have somehow made me work (Bjornestad, 2017).

While social deficits are common in psychosis, these also occur, although milder and more fluctuating, in ultra high risk (UHR) for psychosis populations.

response, lack of interest, poor social drive, and decreased sense of purpose or goal-directed activity. Early conceptualisations of schizophrenia posited negative symptoms as the core or defining features, while positive symptoms such as hallucinations or delusions were secondary features of the disorder (Jablensky, 2010). Compared to positive symptoms, negative symptoms are more difficult to treat (Chang et al., 2011) and are better predictors of current and future socio-occupational functioning (Milev, Ho, Arndt, & Andreasen, 2005).

Negative symptoms are behaviours or functions that are absent such as loss of drive (avolition). Although associations have been found between impaired social functioning and positive symptoms such as delusions and bizarre behaviour (Kundu, Sinha, Paul, & Desarkar, 2013), negative symptoms have been shown to have a greater impact on long-term outcomes. While social deficits are common in psychosis, these also occur, although milder and more fluctuating, in ultra high risk (UHR) for psychosis populations (Fusar-Poli et al., 2013, 2015; McHugh et al., 2017). Following a first psychotic episode, around 20% of individuals with schizophrenia achieve full recovery defined as long-term stable improvement in both symptoms and functioning, including social functioning (Jaaskelainen et al., 2013; Morgan et al., 2014). However, most interventions only have marginal effects on functioning (Robinson, Woerner, McMeniman, Mendelowitz, & Bilder, 2004; Wykes, Steel, Everitt, & Tarrier, 2008), and individuals achieving symptomatic recovery often continue to experience social and functional problems (Oorschot et al., 2012).

Social functioning is a reliable predictor of recovery for psychosis.

Difficulties in social functioning are common in people with, or at high risk for, psychosis. Social functioning is a reliable predictor of recovery for psychosis (Bjornestad, 2017; MacBeth & Gumley, 2008; Norman, MacDougall, Manchanda, & Harricharan, 2018). Individuals with schizophrenia who have poor premorbid social functioning are likely to display worse social adjustment throughout the course of the disorder compared to individuals whose premorbid social functioning is more intact (Hafner et al., 2003; Pogue-Geile & Harrow, 1985). In enduring psychosis, some people experience a loss of desire for social interaction, yet often without the prominent subjective discomfort seen in other psychiatric conditions, such as depression (Santini, Koyanagi, Tyrovolas,

Mason, & Haro, 2015). If severe and long lasting, then this lack of social desire is regarded as a negative symptom of psychosis, termed asociality, and contributes to the maintenance of poor social role functioning (Marder & Galderisi, 2017).

A systematic review of birth cohort, case–control, and familial high-risk studies found greater social impairment in children and adolescents who go on to develop schizophrenia than in healthy controls (Tarbox & Pogue-Geile, 2008). The review concluded that for children around age 7–8 years in the general population, poor social functioning was a moderately sensitive predictor of schizophrenia onset in adolescence. However, for familial high-risk (HR) children, social functioning was a predictor of schizophrenia onset in adolescence at the earlier age of 5–6 years. Thus research suggests that social functioning is a predictor of the illness itself and also a predictor of outcome or recovery for individuals with psychosis.

DEFINING SOCIAL FUNCTIONING

Social functioning refers to how people live and function in a given societal context (Priebe, 2007) and has been defined as the capacity of a person to fulfil different societal roles. Social functioning is measured using objective indicators such as the amount of social contacts, and whether the person has a partner, and subjective indicators, such as feelings and thoughts about the social situation and the performance of social roles (Brissos, Molodynski, Dias, & Figueira, 2011; Kakela et al., 2014; Priebe, 2007). Social functioning defines an individual's interactions with their environment and the ability to fulfil their role within such environments as work, social activities, and relationships with partners and family. In psychiatry, social functioning has been defined as 'the level at which an individual functions in his or her social context, such function ranging between self preservation and basic living skills to the relationship with others in society' (Tyrer & Casey, 1993; p. 8).

Social functioning is the level at which an individual functions in his or her social context.

MEASURING SOCIAL FUNCTIONING

The diagnostic criteria for many mental disorders, including psychosis, require a significant impairment in social, occupational, or other important areas of functioning (American Psychiatric Association, 2013). For schizophrenia, Criterion B of the Diagnostic and Statistical Manual of Mental Disorders (DSM5) requires a marked decline in functioning in one or more areas such as work, interpersonal relations, or self-care as compared to the level of functioning prior to onset (American Psychiatric Association, 2013). While the DSM5 has abandoned the multiaxial approach to diagnosis, previous versions included an axis for the assessment of functioning. This axis included three unidimensional scales, namely the Global Assessment of Functioning (GAF) scale, the Social and Occupational Functioning Scale (SOFAS), and the Global Assessment of Relational Functioning (GARF) scale. These scales are commonly used in clinical practice due to the link with the DSM criteria. However, there is a lack of criteria for rating these scales, thus making it difficult to train raters and resulting in high variability between raters (Priebe, 2007).

A multidimensional approach to the measurement of social functioning includes behavioural and affective indicators of social functioning (Priebe, 2007) similar to the objective versus subjective approach to social functioning. Behavioural indicators represent objective measures of social functioning such as social network size, frequency of social activities, and frequency of perceived social support (Priebe, 2007). Affective indicators reflect more subjective measures of interpersonal and socio-emotional functioning such as loneliness, affiliation, and perceived social disability (Priebe, 2007). However, indicators such as loneliness and perceived social functioning ability do not fully capture the person's satisfaction with their social functioning, and thus clinicians may also consider life satisfaction measures in conjunction.

Social functioning measures are primarily observer rated (often as an interview format), although some are also available as self-report versions (e.g. Social Functioning Scale) and take on average 20 (e.g. Strauss-Carpenter Level of Role Functioning scale) to 60 min (e.g. Social Adjustment Scale) to complete (Bjornestad et al., 2019). Most of the measures use a Likert response format and assess traditional forms of social functioning such as face-to-face or telephone contact with friends and family. Systematic reviews consistently report poor-to-moderate psychometric properties of measures of social functioning in psychosis (Burns & Patrick, 2007; Priebe, 2007). Construct validity is particularly weak, service user involvement is rare, both in the preparatory phases and in the development of measure instruments and adequate theoretical frameworks are typically lacking (Box 9.2).

Service user involvement in the development and evaluation of measures is critical.

SOCIAL FUNCTIONING IN A CHANGING SOCIAL CONTEXT

Social media platforms are web-based virtual communities that allow users to maintain both online and offline interactions (Kuss & Griffiths, 2011). Since the advent of Facebook in 2004, social media has become increasingly important in the establishment and maintenance of social relationships among the general population (Duggan & Maeve, 2015; Valmaggia, 2017). Globally, approximately 2.5 billion people have a registered social media profile and the number of people using social media is expected to grow by an additional 500 million over the next 4 years (Statista, 2017). The Internet has become an influential source of mental health information for people with psychosis (Villani & Kovess-Masfety, 2017), and thus social media and digital devices have been utilised to support mental healthcare (Batra et al., 2017; Naslund et al., 2017) and de-stigmatisation campaigns (Ladea, Bran, & Marcel Claudiu, 2016). Particularly for the youngest age group with psychosis and UHR, there has already been developed social media based interventions targeted on psychological, functional, and social recovery (Alvarez-Jimenez et al., 2017; Alverez & Thomas,

Box 9.2 Psychometric Properties of Measures

Validity

Validity is the degree to which a measure accurately measures the attribute or ability proposed. There are several types of validity:

Predictive validity (criterion oriented validation)—the degree to which scores on the measure are associated with scores on another measure taken at a **later** date.
Concurrent validity (criterion oriented validation))—the degree to which scores on the measure are associated with scores on another measure taken at the **same** time.
Content validity—the degree to which the items of the measure match the objectives/focus of the measure.
Construct validity—the degree to which the measure measures the attribute or ability claimed to be the focus of the measure.
Discriminant validity—the degree to which scores on two measures claiming NOT to measure the same construct are unrelated.
Convergent validity—the degree to which scores on two measures claiming to measure the same construct are related (correlated).
Ecological validity—the degree to which a measure predicts behaviour in the real world.

Reliability

Reliability is the degree to which the same score will be produced across test occasions and raters.

Test–retest reliability—the degree to which scores at one time match scores at a later date.
Interrater reliability—the degree to which two different raters produce the same scores on the measure.
Internal consistency (reliability)—the degree to which each of the items of a measure relate to the core attribute being measured.

2017). These new technologies may have the potential of solving some of the current problems we see with single-point, retrospective assessment of social functioning with the available measures.

Currently, however, capturing dimensions of social activity on social media is mostly absent both in the conceptualisation and measurement of social functioning (Bjornestad et al., 2019; Burns & Patrick, 2007). This shortcoming of not including social media social activity is likely to reflect the period during which existing inventories were developed. Most inventories were created before the launch of the Internet in 1992, and only a few have been developed or revised since the advent of Facebook in 2004 (Bjornestad et al., 2019). Failure to capture social activity on social media may result in an underestimate of social functioning for people with psychosis. The age range of high-frequency social media users (88% of people between 18 and 29 years; Duggan & Maeve, 2015) correlates strongly with the typical ages of the prodrome or onset of psychosis (Fonseca-Pedrero, Gooding, Ortuno-Sierra, & Paino, 2016; Fusar-Poli et al., 2015). Therefore, as individuals with psychosis appear to use social media platforms both as frequently as the general population and as individuals with other mental health conditions (Alvarez-Jimenez et al., 2014; Firth & Torous, 2015; Highton-Williamson, Priebe, & Giacco, 2015), including social media interactions, may enhance our understanding of social functioning for individuals with psychosis. Compared to offline communications, social media may be more suited to the needs of persons with psychosis, particularly during periods of exacerbations of symptoms such as higher anxiety levels. Social media may allow people with psychosis to maintain social contacts at times when their illness prevents them from attending school or work and thus limits face to face interactions (Peters et al., 2016). Thus, social media platforms may play a significant role in the opportunity for social interactions and hold preventive and therapeutic value for individuals with psychosis.

MEASURES OF SOCIAL FUNCTIONING

A recent systematic review of social functioning measures for psychosis and UHR for psychosis (Bjornestad et al., 2019) identified 58 measures (Bjornestad et al., 2019) (see Table 9.1 for a selection of relevant measures). The three most frequently used measures were the Social Functioning Scale, Quality of Life Scale, and World Health Organisation Quality of Life-BREF scale. However, it is important to note that frequency of use does not necessarily equate to the ratings of psychometric properties of the measures. This frequency of use may arise from ease of availability of some measures, brevity of measures, and perceived lack of

Table 9.1 Selected Social Functioning Measures With Psychometric Properties

Measure	Reference	Description	Validity	Reliability[a]
Disability Assessment Schedule—II (DAS-II)	WHO (1988)	Observer rated 12, 36, or 97 items, scoring based on all available information (e.g. patient's written records or data from informants) 6 Domains: Understanding and communicating, getting around, self care, getting along with others, household and work activities, participation in society Several versions: DAS, DAS_II-sv, SDSS, WHO-DAS, DAS-M	Moderate concurrent validity (1)	Good internal consistency (1) Excellent test retest reliability (1)
First Episode Social Functioning Scale (FESFS)	Lecomte et al. (2014)	Self report 34 Items, 4-point Likert response format 9 Domains: independent living skills, interacting with people in different contexts, social	Good convergent validity (2) Good discriminant validity (2)	Good sensitivity to change (2)

Table 9.1 Selected Social Functioning Measures With Psychometric Properties—cont'd

Measure	Reference	Description	Validity	Reliability
		activities, intimacy, friendships, family relations, work, and school Perceived ability and actual behaviour rated for each item		
Global Functioning—Social (GF-S)	Cornblatt et al. (2007)	Observer rated 7 Probe questions, 10-point Likert response format Assesses levels of social contact and friendships outside of the family	Good construct validity (3)	Good interrater reliability (3)
Health of the Nation Outcome Scale (HoNOS)	Wing, Curtis, and Beevor (1996)	Observer rated 12 Items, 4-point Likert point response format Aggression, self-harm, drug and alcohol use, cognitive problems, physical illness and disability, hallucinations and delusions, depression, other symptoms, social relationships, activities of daily living, residential environment, and day-time activity	Good concurrent validity (4) Good discriminant validity (4)	Poor-good interrater reliability(4) Poor-acceptable test retest reliability (4)
Personal and Social Performance (PSP)	Morosini, Magliano, Brambilla, Ugolini, and Pioli (2000)	Observer rated Single-item, 100-point response format (score determined by domain score range) 4 Domains (6-point response format per domain): socially useful activities, personal and social relationships, self-care, disturbing and aggressive behaviours	Good construct validity (5)	Good interrater reliability (5) Excellent test retest reliability (5)
Social Behaviour Scale (SBS)	Wykes and Sturt (1986)	Observer rated 21 Items, 5-point Likert response format 6 Domains: Occupation, behavioural problems, personal self care, leisure activities, performance and expectations, communication skills	Good discriminant validity (6) Good concurrent validity (6)	Good interrater reliability (7) Good inter informant reliability (7) Good test retest reliability (7)
Social Functioning Scale (SFS)	Birchwood, Smith, Cochrane,	Self-report or observer 79 Items, 4-point Likert response format	Good construct validity (8)	Good interrater reliability (8)

Continued

Table 9.1 Selected Social Functioning Measures With Psychometric Properties—cont'd

Measure	Reference	Description	Validity	Reliability
	Wetton, and Copestake (1990)	7 Domains: social engagement, interpersonal behaviour, prosocial activities, recreation, independence—competence, independence—performance, employment/occupation	Good discriminant validity (8) Good convergent validity (8)	
Quality-of-life scales with social functioning dimension				
Manchester Short Assessment of Quality of Life (MANSA)	Priebe, Huxley, Knight, and Evans (1999)	Observer-rated clinical interview 25 Items, 7-point Likert response format 12 Domains with 3 subscales: stable personal patient details, personal details that may change over time (e.g. education), questions that must be asked at each assessment, including both objective and subjective items concerning quality of life and social life	Good concurrent validity (9)	Good internal consistency (10)
Quality of Life Interview (QoLI)	Lehman (1983)	Observer-rated semi-structured interview 143 Items (brief versions: 33 or 78 items) 8 Domains: accommodation, family, social relations, leisure, safety, finances, physical and mental health	Good construct validity	Good-acceptable internal consistency (11) Poor-good test retest-reliability (11)
Quality of Life Scale (QLS)	Heinrichs, Hanlon, and Carpenter (1984)	Observer-rated semi-structured interview 21 Items, 7-point Likert response format 4 Domains: intrapsychic foundations, interpersonal relations, instrumental role, common objects and activities	Poor-to-good convergent validity (12)	Excellent interrater reliability (12)
World Health Organisation Quality of Life—BREF (WHOQoL-BREF)	The WHO QoL Group (1998)	Self-report 268 Items, 5-point Likert response format 4 Domains: physical, psychological, social, environmental	Poor-to-moderate construct validity (13)	Good internal consistency (13)

See Bjornestad et al. 2019) for full list of measures.

[a]*Reliability*: 1: perfect reliability, $\geq$0.9: excellent reliability, $\geq$0.8 < 0.9: good reliability, $\geq$0.7 < 0.8: acceptable reliability, $\geq$0.6 < 0.7: questionable reliability, $\geq$0.5 < 0.6: poor reliability, <0.5: unacceptable reliability, 0: no reliability.

need for training in administration of the measures or lack of understanding of psychometric properties. Several measures (e.g. Social Adjustment Scale II, Global Functioning-Social Scale, Global Functioning-Role Scale) had been used to assess social functioning in UHR populations. Although developed for young people (e.g. Cornblatt et al., GF-S), none of these measures were exclusively used in UHR for psychosis populations.

The review identified 41 social functioning measures and 17 quality-of-life measures that included an assessment of social functioning. Most measures assessed behaviours related to traditional forms of social functioning, such as face-to-face or telephone contact with friends and family. There was wide variability in the extent to which measures assessed social functioning characteristics, ranging from the First Episode Social Functioning Scale (FESFS) with nine subscales, to those that had only a few items (e.g. part of a single subscale) of social functioning. The quality-of-life measures primarily focussed on subjective evaluations of general life domains rather than social functioning.

Online social activity was largely absent, including for the newer measures. The only measure that included an assessment of social activity on social media was the First Episode Social Functioning Scale (FESFS) (Bjornestad et al., 2019). The FESFS was developed in 2014 and is administered as observer rated or self-report, with each item rating frequency of behaviour and perceived individual ability (Lecomte et al., 2014). The FESFS comprises 34 items across nine subscales of social functioning and the item language was chosen for face validity with the target population (e.g. 'hanging out with buddies', 'chatting on the net'). Two items from the subscales of 'Friends and activities' and 'Living skills' address social media activity explicitly. Scale validation was based on the self-report version only. The validation sample was 203 people, average age of 24.5 years, diagnosed with a schizophrenia spectrum psychotic disorder and with an average of 12.7 years of education. The nine subscales showed good internal consistency (the degree to which each of the items of a measure relate to the core attribute being measured), ranging from acceptable to good. Good convergent validity (the degree to which two measures that claim to measure the same construct are related) and discriminant validity (the degree to which two measures that claim to measure different constructs are not related), as well as good sensitivity to change were also demonstrated. Three subscales correlated negatively with negative symptoms. While the FESFS assesses behaviour and ability as well as including contemporary forms of social functioning such as online activity, it does have limitations. The average age of 24.5 years for the validation sample is relatively high for early psychosis and UHR populations. The validation of the work and education subscales is limited by the small proportion of the validation sample engaged in work or education. Test–retest reliability for the measure has not been conducted and neither factorial structure nor construct validity has been confirmed. Furthermore, the FESFS has limited cross-validation (Wang et al., 2013) (as opposed to the PSP or the SFS), which implies uncertainty regarding robustness and usability.

UTILITY OF SOCIAL FUNCTIONING MEASURES IN CLINICAL PRACTICE

In choosing any psychological measurement tool, it is important to consider the psychometric properties of validity and reliability. From the included measures in the review of social functioning measures for psychosis, 55% had been validated in samples of individuals with psychosis. While there were more data available for reliability (53 measures) than validity (47 measures), a lack of information prevented a comprehensive evaluation of the psychometric properties of most measures examined in the review (Bjornestad et al., 2019). Construct validity was particularly poorly reported for the measures. When psychometric properties were reported, measures showed overall good validity and reliability for the assessment of offline or face-to-face social functioning. The Social Functioning Scale (SFS), Groningen Social Disability Schedule (GSDS), and the Health of the Nation Outcomes Scale (HoNOS) are examples of measures with comprehensive reporting of this type of social functioning (Bjornestad et al., 2019). Although the developers of the FESFS endeavoured to incorporate offline social activity in that scale, more exploration and development is required to achieve valid and reliable assessment of these types of activities.

Benefits of Assessment in Clinical Practice

It is notable that the first measures of social functioning in psychosis were developed with chronic inpatients (e.g. Interview Schedule for Social Interactions). However, there is now an emphasis on early intervention and quality of life in the treatment for younger individuals in the early psychosis stage (as opposed to chronic inpatients) (Fusar-Poli, McGorry, & Kane, 2017), and these measures do not capture the current social context of activity on social media. While measures such as the SFS and the HoNOS show good reliability and validity, there remains a lack of ecological validity such that assessment of social functioning fails to fully reflect real-world functioning. For example, failing to assess social media activity may lead to an underestimation or overestimation of the social functioning of young people with psychosis. Moreover, the core negative symptom of social withdrawal may manifest differently in a social media context compared to an offline context.

Ignoring online social functioning threatens the ecological validity of measures.

ENSURING ECOLOGICAL VALIDITY: SERVICE USER INVOLVEMENT

In most contemporary healthcare systems, service user involvement is highly prioritised and valued (Wykes, 2014). The systematic inclusion of service user communities in the evaluation and development of measures is likely to enhance the validity of the measures. For example, the ecological validity of measures must be maintained by modifying measures to reflect the current context of social functioning such as capturing activity on social media. The current conceptualisation of social functioning is not sensitive to societal changes and changes in interactions of people with psychosis. It is essential that revisions be made to measures to include an assessment of social activity on social media platforms in order to accurately assess social functioning in psychosis.

SUMMARY

Social functioning impairment is considered a core factor in psychosis. Hence, valid operationalisation of social functioning is critical for comprehensive scientific and clinical assessments. Social functioning occurs both offline and online. Particularly for young people, including the main target group for psychosis, social media use is an integrated part of social functioning. Current measures do not assess online social functioning, thus leaving researchers, clinicians, carers, and other stakeholders with a severe blind spot and limiting the validity of current methods of social functioning assessment. Finally, we suggest a new framework that allows for measures to be adapted to changing societal contexts through inclusion of the voices of service users. It is important that not only do clinicians and researchers hear the voices of service users but that we provide opportunity for those voices to connect with each other. The following quote from a service user echoes the findings from the Australian National Survey of Psychosis that social functioning issues are their greatest challenge for the future (Stain et al., 2012) (Box 9.3).

Box 9.3 Client Example

We talked about everything. Gave each other advice. The important thing is to open up to friends and speak out. That has helped me a lot. There has been a lot of support from them. They have helped me get started on the path that led me to where I am now. The person I am today, I´ve built up through other people. I´ve found myself, what I like, and what I don´t. I know who I am and what I'm comfortable with.

Bjornestad (2017)

QUIZ QUESTIONS

1. How are social functioning measures evaluated?
2. Does frequency of use or popularity of a social functioning measure indicate it is an appropriate measure?
3. What are the different stages of psychosis that should be considered when choosing a social functioning measure?
4. Describe the debate around the assessment of online social functioning.
5. What is ecological validity and why is it important in assessing social functioning in psychosis?

ANSWERS TO QUIZ QUESTIONS:

1. The psychometric properties of validity and reliability provide an indication of the strength and accuracy of a measure. For example, construct validity assesses the degree to which a measure assesses the attribute (in this case social functioning) claimed by the measure. Test–retest reliability reports the degree to which consistent scores will be attained over different assessment occasions.
2. No, it is important to check the psychometric properties of the measures as these measures may be in frequent use due to ease of access to the measure, brevity of the measure, the high frequency of use of the measure in the literature, perceived lack of a need for training in the administration of the measure, or a lack of understanding of psychometrics.
3. The three stages related to the selection of social functioning measures are the ultra high risk for psychosis stage, first-episode psychosis stage, and established psychosis stage.
4. The response should include the importance and prevalence of online social activity, the relevance of this to UHR and FEP young people, and potential challenges in developing such measures.
5. Ecological validity is the degree to which a measure reflects that behaviour in the real world. The response should include a discussion of the need for psychological assessments to be valid and reliable as well as being generalisable to everyday settings.

RECOMMENDED READINGS

1. **Psychometric properties**

   Ayearst, L. E., & Bagby, R. M. (2010). Evaluating the psychometric properties of psychological measures. In M. M. Antony & D. H. Barlow (Eds.), *Handbook of assessment and treatment planning for psychological disorders* (pp. 23–61). New York, NY: Guilford Press.

2. **Online social functioning**

   Alvarez-Jimenez, M., Gleeson, J. F., Bendall, S., Penn, D. L., Yung, A. R., Ryan, R. M., ... Nelson, B. (2018) Enhancing social functioning in young people at Ultra High Risk (UHR) for psychosis: A pilot study of a novel strengths and mindfulness-based online social therapy. *Schizophrenia Research, 202*, 369–377. https://doi.org/10.1016/j.schres.2018.07.022.

3. **Service user involvement**

   Omeni, E., Barnes, M., MacDonald, D., Crawford, M., & Rose, D. (2014). Service user involvement: Impact and participation: A survey of service user and staff perspectives. *BMC Health Services Research, 14*, 491. https://doi.org/10.1186/s12913-014-0491-7.

   Gordon, J., Franklin, S. & Eltringham, S. A. (2018). Service user reflections on the impact of involvement in research. *Research Involvement and Engagement, 4*, 11. https://doi.org/10.1186/s40900-018-0095-1.

   Gibbons, C. J., Bee, P. E., Walker, L., Price, O., & Lovell, K. (2014). Service user- and carer-reported measures of involvement in mental health care planning: Methodological quality and acceptability to users. *Frontiers in Psychiatry, 5*, 178. https://doi.org/10.3389/fpsyt.2014.00178.

4. **Importance of social functioning in managing psychosis**

   Burns, T., Patrick, D. (2007). Social functioning as an outcome measure in schizophrenia studies. *Acta psychiatrica Scandinavica, 116*(6), 403–418.

   Sarkar, S., Hillner, K., & Velligan, D. I. (2015). Conceptualization and treatment of negative symptoms in schizophrenia. *World journal of psychiatry, 5*(4), 352–361. https://doi.org/10.5498/wjp.v5.i4.352.

References

Alvarez-Jimenez, M., Alcazar-Corcoles, M., Gonzalez-Blanch, C., Bendall, S., McGorry, P., & Gleeson, J. (2014). Online, social media and mobile technologies for psychosis treatment: A systematic review on novel user-led interventions. *Schizophrenia Research, 156*(1), 96–106.

Alvarez-Jimenez, M., Gleeson, J., Bendall, S., Rice, S., D'Alfonso, S., Eleftheriadis, D., et al. (2017). Momentum: A novel online social media, mindfulness, and strengths-based intervention to promote functional recovery in ultra high risk (UHR) patients. *Schizophrenia Bulletin, 43*(Suppl. 1), S206–S207.

Alverez, M., & Thomas, N. (2017). Innovations in technology-based treatments and management for pyschosis—Moderated online social therapy (Horyzons) and self-management and recovery technology. *Australian and New Zealand Journal of Psychiatry, 51*(1 Suppl. 1), 50. https://doi.org/10.1177/0004867417702054.

American Psychiatric Association. (2013). *Diagnostic and statistical manual of mental disorders* (5th ed.). Washington, DC: American Psychiatric Association.

Balaji, M., Chatterjee, S., Brennan, B., Rangaswamy, T., Thornicroft, G., & Patel, V. (2012). Outcomes that matter: A qualitative study with persons with schizophrenia and their primary caregivers in India. *Asian Journal of Psychiatry, 5*(3), 258–265. https://doi.org/10.1016/j.ajp.2012.06.002.

Batra, S., Baker, R. A., Wang, T., Forma, F., DiBiasi, F., & Peters-Strickland, T. (2017). Digital health technology for use in patients with serious mental illness: A systematic review of the literature. *Medical Devices (Auckland, NZ), 10*, 237–251. https://doi.org/10.2147/MDER.S144158.

Birchwood, M., Smith, J., Cochrane, R., Wetton, S., & Copestake, S. (1990). The Social Functioning Scale: The development and validation of a new scale of social adjustment for use in family intervention programmes with schizophrenic patients. *British Journal of Psychiatry, 157*, 853–859.

Bjornestad, J. (2017). *Factors facilitating recovery in first episode psychosis: A multi method approach.* Doctor of Philosophy Stavanger, Norway: University of Stavanger. Thesis UiS No. 367.

Bjornestad, J., Hegelstad, W. T. V., Berg, H., Davidson, L., Joa, I., Johannessen, J. O., et al. (2019). Social media and social functioning in psychosis: A systematic review. *Journal of Medical Internet Research, 21*(6)(2019). https://www.jmir.org/2019/6/e13957.

Brissos, S., Molodynski, A., Dias, V. V., & Figueira, M. L. (2011). The importance of measuring psychosocial functioning in schizophrenia. *Annals of General Psychiatry, 10*, 18. https://doi.org/10.1186/1744-859x-10-18.

Burns, T., & Patrick, D. (2007). Social functioning as an outcome measure in schizophrenia studies. *Acta Psychiatrica Scandinavica, 116*(6), 403–418. https://doi.org/10.1111/j.1600-0447.2007.01108.x.

Chang, W., Hui, C., Tang, J., Wong, G., Lam, M., Chan, S., et al. (2011). Persistent negative symptoms in first-episode schizophrenia: A prospective three-year follow-up study. *Schizophrenia Research, 133*(1–3), 22–28.

Cornblatt, B. A., Auther, A. M., Niendam, T., et al. (2007). Preliminary findings for two new measures of social and role functioning in the prodromal phase of schizophrenia. *Schizophrenia Bulletin, 33*, 688–702.

Duggan, & Maeve (2015). *Messaging and social media.* Retrieved from: http://www.pewinternet.org/2015/08/19/mobile-messaging-and-social-media-2015/Mobile.

Firth, J., & Torous, J. (2015). Smartphone apps for schizophrenia: A systematic review. *JMIR mHealth and uHealth, 3*(4), e102. https://doi.org/10.2196/mhealth.4930.

Fonseca-Pedrero, E., Gooding, D. C., Ortuno-Sierra, J., & Paino, M. (2016). Assessing self-reported clinical high risk symptoms in community-derived adolescents: A psychometric evaluation of the Prodromal Questionnaire-Brief. *Comprehensive Psychiatry, 66*, 201–208. https://doi.org/10.1016/j.comppsych.2016.01.013.

Fusar-Poli, P., Borgwardt, S., Bechdolf, A., Addington, J., Riecher-Rössler, A., Schultze-Lutter, F., et al. (2013). The psychosis high-risk state: A comprehensive state-of-the-art review. *JAMA Psychiatry, 70*(1), 107–120.

Fusar-Poli, P., McGorry, P. D., & Kane, J. M. (2017). Improving outcomes of first-episode psychosis: An overview. *World Psychiatry, 16*(3), 251–265. https://doi.org/10.1002/wps.20446.

Fusar-Poli, P., Rocchetti, M., Sardella, A., Avila, A., Brandizzi, M., Caverzasi, E., et al. (2015). Disorder, not just state of risk: Meta-analysis of functioning and quality of life in people at high risk of psychosis. *The British Journal of Psychiatry, 207*(3), 198–206. https://doi.org/10.1192/bjp.bp.114.157115.

Hafner, H., Maurer, K., Loffler, W., an der Heiden, W., Hambrecht, M., & Schultze-Lutter, F. (2003). Modeling the early course of schizophrenia. *Schizophrenia Bulletin, 29*(2), 325–340.

Heinrichs, D. W., Hanlon, T. E., & Carpenter, W. T. (1984). The Quality of Life Scale: An instrument for rating the schizophrenic deficit syndrome. *Schizophrenia Bulletin, 10*(3), 388–398.

Highton-Williamson, E., Priebe, S., & Giacco, D. (2015). Online social networking in people with psychosis: A systematic review. *The International Journal of Social Psychiatry, 61*(1), 92–101. https://doi.org/10.1177/0020764014556392.

Jaaskelainen, E., Juola, P., Hirvonen, N., McGrath, J. J., Saha, S., Isohanni, M., et al. (2013). A systematic review and meta-analysis of recovery in schizophrenia. *Schizophrenia Bulletin, 39*(6), 1296–1306. https://doi.org/10.1093/schbul/sbs130.

Jablensky, A. (2010). The diagnostic concept of schizophrenia: Its history, evolution, and future prospects. *Dialogues in Clinical Neuroscience, 12*(3), 271–287.

Kakela, J., Panula, J., Oinas, E., Hirvonen, N., Jaaskelainen, E., & Miettunen, J. (2014). Family history of psychosis and social, occupational and global outcome in schizophrenia: A meta-analysis. *Acta Psychiatrica Scandinavica, 130*(4), 269–278. https://doi.org/10.1111/acps.12317.

Kirkpatrick, B., Fenton, W. S., Carpenter, W. T., Jr., & Marder, S. R. (2006). The NIMH-MATRICS consensus statement on negative symptoms. *Schizophrenia Bulletin, 32*(2), 214–219. https://doi.org/10.1093/schbul/sbj053.

Kraepelin, E. (1919/1971). *Dementia praecox and paraphrenia.* Huntington, New York: Robert E. Krieger Publishing Co. Inc.

Kundu, P., Sinha, V., Paul, S., & Desarkar, P. (2013). Current social functioning in adult-onset schizophrenia and its relation with positive symptoms. *Industrial Psychiatry Journal, 22*(1), 65–68.

Kuss, D. J., & Griffiths, M. D. (2011). Online social networking and addiction—A review of the psychological literature. *International Journal of Environmental Research and Public Health, 8*(9), 3528–3552. https://doi.org/10.3390/ijerph8093528.

Ladea, M., Bran, M., & Marcel Claudiu, S. (2016). Online destigmatization of schizophrenia: A Romanian experience. *European Psychiatry, 33(Suppl.)*, S276. https://doi.org/10.1016/j.eurpsy.2016.01.736.

Lecomte, T., Corbiere, M., Ehmann, T., Addington, J., Abdel-Baki, A., & Macewan, B. (2014). Development and preliminary validation of the First Episode Social Functioning Scale for early psychosis. *Psychiatry Research, 216*(3), 412–417.

Lehman, A. F. (1983). The well-being of chronic mental patients: Assessing their quality of life. *Archives of General Psychiatry, 40*, 369–373.

MacBeth, A., & Gumley, A. (2008). Premorbid adjustment, symptom development and quality of life in first episode psychosis: A systematic review and critical reappraisal. *Acta Psychiatrica Scandinavica, 117*(2), 85–99. https://doi.org/10.1111/j.1600-0447.2007.01134.x.

Marder, S. R., & Galderisi, S. (2017). The current conceptualization of negative symptoms in schizophrenia. *World Psychiatry, 16*(1), 14–24. https://doi.org/10.1002/wps.20385.

McHugh, M. J., McGorry, P., Yuen, H., Hickie, I., Thompson, A., de Haan, L., et al. (2017). The ultra-high-risk for psychosis groups: Evidence to maintain the status quo. *Schizophrenia Research 195*, 543–548.

Milev, P., Ho, B., Arndt, S., & Andreasen, N. (2005). Predictive values of neurocognition and negative symptoms on functional outcome in schizophrenia: A longitudinal first-episode study with 7-year follow-up. *American Journal of Psychiatry, 162*(3), 495–506.

Morgan, C., Lappin, J., Heslin, M., Donoghue, K., Lomas, B., Reininghaus, U., et al. (2014). Reappraising the long-term course and outcome of psychotic disorders: The AESOP-10 study. *Psychological Medicine, 44*(13), 2713–2726. https://doi.org/10.1017/s0033291714000282.

Morosini, P. L., Magliano, L., Brambilla, L., Ugolini, S., & Pioli, R. (2000). Development, reliability and acceptability of a new version of the DSM-IV Social and Occupational Functioning Assessment Scale (SOFAS) to assess routine social functioning. *Acta Psychiatrica Scandinavica, 101*, 323–329.

Naslund, J. A., Aschbrenner, K. A., McHugo, G. J., Unutzer, J., Marsch, L. A., & Bartels, S. J. (2017). Exploring opportunities to support mental health care using social media: A survey of social media users with mental illness. *Early Intervention in Psychiatry, 20*. https://doi.org/10.1111/eip.12496.

Norman, R. M., MacDougall, A., Manchanda, R., & Harricharan, R. (2018). An examination of components of recovery after five years of treatment in an early intervention program for psychosis. *Schizophrenia Research, 195*, 469–474.

Oorschot, M., Lataster, T., Thewissen, V., Lardinois, M., van Os, J., Delespaul, P. A., et al. (2012). Symptomatic remission in psychosis and real-life functioning. *The British Journal of Psychiatry, 201*(3), 215–220. https://doi.org/10.1192/bjp.bp.111.104414.

Peters, E., Ward, T., Jackson, M., Morgan, C., Charalambides, M., McGuire, P., et al. (2016). Clinical, socio-demographic and psychological characteristics in individuals with persistent psychotic experiences with and without a "need for care". *World Psychiatry, 15*(1), 41–52. https://doi.org/10.1002/wps.20301.

Pogue-Geile, M. F., & Harrow, M. (1985). Negative symptoms in schizophrenia: Their longitudinal course and prognostic importance. *Schizophrenia Bulletin, 11*(3), 427–439.

Priebe, S. (2007). Social outcomes in schizophrenia. *The British Journal of Psychiatry. Supplement, 50*, s15–s20.

Priebe, S., Huxley, P., Knight, S., & Evans, S. (1999). Application and results of the Manchester Short Assessment of Quality of Life (MANSA). *International Journal of Social Psychiatry, 45*(1), 7–12.

Robinson, D. G., Woerner, M. G., McMeniman, M., Mendelowitz, A., & Bilder, R. M. (2004). Symptomatic and functional recovery from a first episode of schizophrenia or schizoaffective disorder. *The American Journal of Psychiatry, 161*(3), 473–479. https://doi.org/10.1176/appi.ajp.161.3.473.

Santini, Z. I., Koyanagi, A., Tyrovolas, S., Mason, C., & Haro, J. M. (2015). The association between social relationships and depression: A systematic review. *Journal of Affective Disorders, 175*, 53–65. https://doi.org/10.1016/j.jad.2014.12.049.

Stain, H. J., Galletly, C. A., Clark, S., Wilson, J., Killen, E. A., Anthes, L., et al. (2012). Understanding the social costs of psychosis: The experience of adults affected by psychosis identified within the second Australian national survey of psychosis. *The Australian and New Zealand Journal of Psychiatry, 46*(9), 879–889.

Statista. (2017). *The statistics portal. Most famous social network sites worldwide.* https://www.statista.com/statistics/272014/global-social-networks-ranked-by-number-of-users/.

Tarbox, S. I., & Pogue-Geile, M. F. (2008). Development of social functioning in preschizophrenia children and adolescents: A systematic review. *Psychological Bulletin, 134*(4), 561–583. https://doi.org/10.1037/0033-2909.34.4.561.

The WHO QoL Group (1998). Development of the World Health Organization WHO QoL-BREF quality of life assessment. *Psychological Medicine, 28*(3), 551–558. https://doi.org/10.1017/s0033291798006667.

Tyrer, P., & Casey, P. (1993). *Social function in psychiatry: The hidden axis of classification exposed.* Petersfield, England: Wrightson Biomedical Publishing.

Valmaggia, L. (2017). The use of virtual reality in psychosis research and treatment. *World Psychiatry, 16*(3), 246–247. https://doi.org/10.1002/wps.20443.

van Os, J., Kenis, G., & Rutten, B. P. (2010). The environment and schizophrenia. *Nature, 468*(7321), 203–212. https://doi.org/10.1038/nature09563.

Villani, M., & Kovess-Masfety, V. (2017). How do people experiencing schizophrenia spectrum disorders or other psychotic disorders use the internet to get information on their mental health? Literature review and recommendations. *JMIR Mental Health, 4*(1), e1. https://doi.org/10.2196/mental.5946.

Wang, Y., Yeh, Y.-h., Tsang, S.-m., Liu, W.-h., Shi, H.-s., Li, Z., et al. (2013). Social functioning in Chinese college students with and without schizotypal personality traits: An exploratory study of the Chinese version of the first episode social functioning scale. *PLoS One, 8*(5).

WHO (World Health Organization) (1988). *WHO psychiatric disability assessment schedule (WHO/DAS): With a guide to its use.* Geneva, CH: WHO.

Wing, J., Curtis, R., & Beevor, A. (1996). *Health of the nation outcome scales: Glossary for HoNOS:* (pp. 1–14). Royal College of Psychiatrists.

Wykes, T. (2014). Great expectations for participatory research: What have we achieved in the last ten years? *World Psychiatry,* (1), 24–27.

Wykes, T., Steel, C., Everitt, B., & Tarrier, N. (2008). Cognitive behavior therapy for schizophrenia: Effect sizes, clinical models, and methodological rigor. *Schizophrenia Bulletin, 34*(3), 523–537. https://doi.org/10.1093/schbul/sbm114.

Wykes, T., & Sturt, E. (1986). The measurement of social behaviour in psychiatric patients: An assessment of the reliability and validity of the SBS schedule. *British Journal of Psychiatry, 148,* 1–11.

Zipursky, R. B. (2014). Why are the outcomes in patients with schizophrenia so poor? *The Journal of Clinical Psychiatry, 75*(Suppl. 2), 20–24. https://doi.org/10.4088/JCP.13065su1.05.

Definition of Key Terms

Psychosis a serious mental illness (such as schizophrenia) characterised by impaired or lost contact with reality, often with hallucinations or delusions.

Schizophrenia symptoms of schizophrenia spectrum disorders include hallucinations, delusions, disorganised thinking, grossly disorganised or abnormal motor behaviour, and negative symptoms.

Social media Social media is a computer-based technology that facilitates the sharing of ideas and information and the building of virtual networks and communities.

Social functioning the level at which an individual functions in his or her social context, such function ranging between self preservation and basic living skills to the relationship with others in society.

Measure An instrument, often a questionnaire, designed to measure a person's attributes, functioning, or behaviour.

Assessment a process of testing that uses a combination of techniques to help arrive at an hypotheses about a person and their behaviour, personality, and capabilities.

Systematic review is an appraisal and synthesis of primary research papers using a rigorous and clearly documented methodology in both the search strategy and the selection of studies. This minimises bias in the results. The clear documentation of the process and the decisions made allow the review to be reproduced and updated.

CHAPTER 10

Trauma, Posttraumatic Stress, and Psychosis

Amy Hardy*[,†], Irene van de Giessen[‡], David van den Berg[§,¶]
*Department of Psychology, Institute of Psychiatry, Psychology and Neuroscience, King's College London, London, United Kingdom, [†]South London and Maudsley NHS Foundation Trust, London, United Kingdom, [‡]Director of Non-Profit Organization, Foundation for Recovery Talent, Koudekerke, The Netherlands, [§]Parnassia Psychiatric Institute, The Hague, The Netherlands, [¶]VU University, Amsterdam, The Netherlands

Key Learning Objectives

After reading the chapter, we hope that you will be able to:

- Summarise the nature of trauma, posttraumatic stress, and trauma-related psychotic symptoms.
- Understand the psychological factors that may contribute to the development and maintenance of posttraumatic stress in psychosis.
- Be able to formulate a person's difficulties within a trauma-focused cognitive-behavioural model of posttraumatic stress in psychosis.

INTRODUCTION: TRAUMA AND POSTTRAUMATIC STRESS IN PSYCHOSIS

Influential models of psychosis have historically focused on biomedical factors. This started to shift in the 1960s, with Brown and Birley' seminal finding that people were more likely to experience psychosis if they had experienced stressful life events (Brown & Birley, 1968). Later studies highlighted that trauma, particularly childhood victimisation, may have a role in shaping psychotic experiences. More recent, methodologically robust research appears to indicate that traumatic events play a casual role in psychosis, at least for a subgroup of people. Understanding the mechanisms by which trauma can impact on psychotic experiences is necessary for effective assessment, formulation, and intervention. In this chapter, we will describe the main problems people can experience and what research tells us about the psychological factors that may contribute to them. We will conclude by outlining a

Trauma: any event(s) that a person interprets as a significant physical or psychological threat to the self.

A Clinical Introduction to Psychosis. https://doi.org/10.1016/B978-0-12-815012-2.00010-9

trauma-focused cognitive-behavioural model of psychosis, illustrated by an example formulation. This model and formulation will be revisited in Chapter 19, when we describe our phased approach for trauma-focused cognitive-behavioural therapy for psychosis.

WHAT IS TRAUMA?

Establishing the prevalence of trauma in psychosis is dependent on the definition of trauma used. Trauma definitions have been subject to much debate and vary over time and culture (see Friedman, Resick, Bryant, & Brewin, 2011, for further discussion of the area). A key controversy relates to whether to define trauma according to objective attributes and/or subjective reactions. There has been a tendency to characterise traumas as events that involve a serious threat to the physical integrity of the self, with previous DSM-IV criteria for Posttraumatic Stress Disorder (PTSD; APA, 1994) also requiring that this physical threat is accompanied by a subjective reaction of fear, horror, and helplessness. However, these definitions of trauma are problematic as they do not incorporate psychologically threatening events, such as emotional abuse and neglect, or allow for other common trauma-related emotions such as shame. In relation to people with psychosis, they would also exclude subjectively threatening events such as hearing a voices saying 'I am going to kill you'. This is problematic given that subjective experiences can have a comparable experiential impact to if they were externally generated events (Fornells-Ambrojo, Gracie, Brewin, & Hardy, 2016).

Due to these concerns, the traumatic event criterion of PTSD in ICD-11 (WHO, 2018) allows for the events to be subjectively defined, and in DSM 5 (APA, 2013) the types of trauma have been broadened to include, for example, sexual violence. In line with ICD 11, our position is to adopt a pragmatic definition, which specifies that trauma is 'any event(s) that a person interprets as representing a significant physical or psychological threat to the self'. This definition merges both objective and subjective attributes and so allows for the inclusion of events that may not be conceptualised as objectively traumatic, but which nonetheless are currently traumatising for the person. This definition ensures personally relevant traumas are not missed in clinical practice. As we will see at the end of the chapter, thorough assessment of traumas involves first identifying the events that people have experienced, and then evaluating which of those represent a current traumatic threat.

How Common Is Trauma in Psychosis?

Before considering the prevalence of trauma in psychosis, it is important to highlight that traumatic events are common in the general population. In a large epidemiological survey of 24 countries, 70.4% of people reported trauma (Kessler et al., 2017). However, rates vary by trauma type, with nonvictimisation more prevalent than interpersonal, victimisation events (e.g. 14% of the sample reported sexual violence). Despite trauma being a frequent occurrence, there appears to be a particularly high prevalence of multiple victimisation traumas

Victimisation traumas include physical, emotional, and sexual abuse, and physical and emotional neglect.

in psychosis, both during childhood and adulthood, including psychosis-related events (e.g. hearing a voice saying 'I'll kill you', involuntary admission to hospital and physical restraint) (de Vries et al., 2018; Matheson, Shepherd, Pinchbeck, Laurens, & Carr, 2013; Steel, Doukani, & Hardy, 2017). de Vries et al. (2018) conducted a systematic review of victimisation and report that the median prevalence rate for any victimisation event was 19%–20%, with rates being four to six times higher than in the general population. Victimisation traumas include physical, emotional, and sexual abuse, and physical and emotional neglect (see Box 10.1 for a description of Janet's trauma history, who is a fictional person based on Amy and David's therapy experiences). The findings in relation to victimisation appear to be consistent across a range of assessment methods (interviews, self-report questionnaires, and case note reviews) and populations (ultra-high risk, first-episode, and persistent psychosis). Investigating psychosis-related traumas, Steel et al. (2017) report that 50.3% and 63.6% of a sample of 163 people with schizophrenia-spectrum diagnoses disclosed traumas associated with psychiatric treatment and psychosis, respectively. Whilst there has been debate over the reliability of trauma reports in people with psychosis, it appears that assessments in this group are as reliable as in the general population (Fisher et al., 2011). Nonetheless, it is important to note that trauma reports are somewhat unreliable across all groups, given that memory retrieval is dependent on context. People seem to be more likely to recall trauma if they are experiencing mental health difficulties, and less likely to disclose previously reported trauma if they are not experiencing problems (Colman et al., 2016; Newbury et al., 2018).

HOW DOES TRAUMA IMPACT ON MENTAL HEALTH?

Research indicates that resilience and recovery are the most frequent outcomes after traumatic events, followed by chronic and delayed onset trajectories (Galatzer-Levy, Huang, & Bonanno, 2018). Experiencing problems in the immediate aftermath of trauma is therefore fairly typical, as people attempt to adapt to what has happened. The impact of trauma on mental health appears to be moderated by pre- and posttraumatic psychological (e.g. coping style) and contextual (e.g. social support) factors. This means we need to look beyond discrete events to understand what contributes to the resolution or maintenance of problems. Trauma is associated with a range of mental health difficulties, and in people with PTSD, diagnostic comorbidity and symptomatic overlap is common. For example, 50% of people with a diagnosis of PTSD also meet criteria

Box 10.1 Janet's Past Context

Janet is a 52-year-old woman, who grew up with her mother and father. Her father sexually and physically abused her during her childhood and her mum had severe mental health problems. The family struggled financially, and Janet was often dirty and hungry. She was bullied at school. She had no friends or other family. She always felt too ashamed and scared to tell anyone what was happening, and thought people did not want to know.

for major depressive disorder. Substance use, anxiety disorders, emotionally unstable personality disorder, and antisocial personality disorder are other common co-morbid problems, together with physical health problems such as diabetes and medically unexplained symptoms (Flory & Yehuda, 2015; Sareen, 2014).

Re-experiencing occurs when traumatic memories intrude into conscious awareness suddenly, without intent.

Hyperarousal denotes the heightened levels of anxiety and altered arousal response.

Avoidance is the cognitive or behavioural effort to avoid triggers of traumatic memories and associated bodily responses.

This overlap has led to considerable debate about the boundaries of the diagnosis of PTSD, leading to revisions of its criterion in the diagnostic manuals. In DSM 5 (APA, 2013), the symptom clusters are broader, with four specified (i.e. re-experiencing, hyperarousal, avoidance, and negative cognitions and mood) alongside a dissociative subtype. This expansion of symptom types from DSM IV (APA, 1994) means there are now 636,120 ways to meet diagnostic criteria for PTSD (Galatzer-Levy & Bryant, 2013). In contrast, in ICD 11 (WHO, 2018), the symptom criteria for PTSD have been restricted to those most characteristic of PTSD (re-experiencing, avoidance, and hyperarousal) with a new diagnostic category of complex PTSD (cPTSD), which encompasses the PTSD criteria together with 'disturbances of identity' symptoms relating to self-concept, interpersonal relating, and disruptions in emotion regulation. Therefore, both the ICD-11 and DSM 5 criteria now incorporate a broader impact of trauma on mental health than was specified in previous diagnostic definitions. However, the cPTSD diagnosis is subject to much debate with some arguing it represents severe PTSD and does not necessitate a separate category (Brewin et al., 2017). The inclusion of cPTSD will support research comparing cPTSD, PTSD, and other trauma-related mental health difficulties, to establish if cPTSD is indeed a useful concept.

PTSD in Psychosis

Given the elevated rates of trauma in psychosis, unsurprisingly, rates of PTSD in psychosis are also increased relative to the general population. Reported prevalence rates for PTSD vary depending on the sample and assessment measure used (Barbano et al., 2019). However, a meta-analysis identified that 12.4% of the people with psychosis meet criteria for posttraumatic stress disorder, compared to 1.4% in the general population (Achim et al., 2011; Kessler et al., 2017). This was confirmed in a large Dutch study that found that approximately one in six people in care for a schizophrenia-spectrum diagnosis currently meet criteria for PTSD (de Bont et al., 2015). It should also be noted that a larger proportion of people will experience PTSD symptoms that do not meet a diagnostic threshold but are nonetheless of clinical significance. The presence of comorbid PTSD is associated with more severe psychiatric symptoms, lower levels of social functioning, and more suicide attempts (Lysaker & Larocco, 2008; Seow et al., 2016). Traumatised people with psychosis also have poorer service engagement and treatment adherence, they use higher doses of psychotropic medications, while they benefit less of antipsychotic medication (Hassan & De Luca, 2015; Schneeberger, Muenzenmaier, Castille, Battaglia, & Link, 2014). Providing effective support to people with PTSD and psychosis is therefore a priority to minimise the significant impact of these difficulties on individuals, healthcare services, and society.

Trauma-Related Psychosis

Despite higher prevalence of trauma and PTSD in psychosis, robustly demonstrating causal relationships between trauma and psychosis is challenging, although there are a number of empirical indications of causality (Hill, 1965). These include demonstration of trauma preceding the onset of psychosis; the replication of identified associations between trauma and symptoms; the presence of a dose–response relationship; the resolution of traumatic sequelae resulting in improvements in psychosis; and the specificity of associations between trauma and symptom types, based on the premise that certain types of trauma may be particularly potent in provoking specific symptoms due to their impact on particular mechanisms (van Winkel, van Nierop, Myin-Germeys, & van Os, 2013).

In support of trauma playing a casual role in psychotic experiences, a meta-analysis by Varese et al. (2012) including 80,000 participants with diagnosed psychosis and from nonclinical samples found that psychosis was associated with odds of being 2.8 times more likely to have experienced childhood victimisation, in methodologically robust case–control, prospective, and epidemiological studies. The majority of studies investigating severity identified a dose–response effect. It was estimated that if the trauma had not occurred in the population there would be a 33% reduction in the occurrence of psychosis. This striking figure has clear implications for public policy, and the importance of preventative interventions and early intervention across society.

Studies also point to traumatic resolution being associated with the reduction of psychosis. Kelleher et al. (2013) studied 2232 adolescents and found that when bullying ceased, psychotic-like experiences also remitted. In a clinical sample, van den Berg et al. (2015) found that trauma-focused therapies targeting PTSD were also effective in reducing paranoia, although not voice hearing (see Chapter 19 for further details). A recent meta-analysis investigating the specificity of relationships between trauma type and psychotic symptoms in people with diagnosed psychosis found that sexual abuse was more strongly related to hallucinations than neglect, and had a smaller effect on delusions, and neglect but not sexual abuse was associated with negative symptoms (Bailey et al., 2018). This suggests sexual abuse and neglect may have a differential impact on the psychological processes that contribute to voices and negative symptoms, respectively. There are also indications that trauma is associated with the persistence of psychosis (Trotta, Murray, & Fisher, 2015), and several studies report associations between the content of traumas and psychosis (Corstens & Longden, 2013; Hardy et al., 2005). Thematic associations in content appear to be most common (e.g. when a person who has been controlled in an abusive relationship has intrusive, controlling, and derogatory voices), although direct, content associations are also found (e.g. when a voice who is identified as the

Thematic associations are where the content of trauma is evident (but not exactly replicated) in delusions or hallucinations.

Direct associations are where the content of the trauma is directly played out in delusions or hallucinations.

perpetrator of a violent assault replays exactly what they said during the trauma). Being diagnosed with PTSD also increases the odds of being diagnosed with psychosis in the following year more than 20-fold (Okkels, Trabjerg, Arendt, & Pedersen, 2017). Finally, psychotic experiences also occur in other mental health problems associated with trauma, including PTSD, dissociative disorders, personality disorder, bipolar affective disorder, and depression (Brewin & Patel, 2010; Kelleher & DeVylder, 2017; Okkels et al., 2017; Palmier-Claus, Berry, Bucci, Mansell, & Varese, 2016; Schroeder, Fisher, & Schafer, 2013).

POSTTRAUMATIC STRESS IN PSYCHOSIS: A PROBLEM-FOCUSED APPROACH

As we have seen, rates of trauma and PTSD are elevated in people with psychosis compared to the general population, and research indicates there are causal relations between trauma and psychosis, at least for a subgroup of people. The diagnostic and phenomenological overlap between symptoms of PTSD and psychosis, together with limitations of psychosis-related diagnoses outlined elsewhere in the book, leads us to recommend that categorical conceptualisations of PTSD and psychosis may not be valid and clinically useful. Instead, we recommend adopting a symptom or problem-specific approach. In keeping with this, rather than focusing on comorbid PTSD and psychosis, we use the term posttraumatic stress in psychosis (PTSp), to support our problem-specific approach to formulation and therapy. This allows us to understand and intervene with any trauma-related difficulty, regardless of whether a person meets certain diagnostic criteria or where they are on the psychosis spectrum. In Box 10.2, Irene explains the impact of traumatic experiences on her life, eloquently drawing attention to the limitations of a categorical, diagnostic approach, and the need to understanding the psychosocial processes contributing psychosis. We will now outline the most common symptoms of PTSD and psychosis, illustrated by descriptions of Janet's difficulties. For each symptom, we briefly examine what research tells us about the psychological processes that may contribute to its development and maintenance. This will give us clues as to how processes and symptoms interact, to support us in developing a trauma-focused cognitive-behavioural model of posttraumatic stress in psychosis.

Posttraumatic stress in psychosis (PTSp) is a transdiagnostic approach to posttraumatic stress difficulties in people with psychosis.

PTSD: Re-experiencing Symptoms

Re-experiencing symptoms are considered the hallmark symptoms of PTSD, with their defining feature being involuntary memories that are accompanied by a sense of occurring in the 'here and now' so the person feels 'as if' aspects of what happened (e.g. thoughts, feelings, sensations, perceptions) are occurring again. This gives rise to another key characteristic of PTSD, experiencing a sense of current threat in relation to a past event. Re-experiencing can happen during the day or manifest as nightmares (which may have more thematic instead of direct links to the trauma memory). The 'here and now' quality of re-experiencing can vary in severity, from mild, fleeting intrusions to more severe dissociative

Box 10.2 Irene's Story

As a baby, I was totally dependent on my mother to survive, but there was too little time, energy, and love to give me what I unconditionally needed as a child. I became insecure, restless, experienced emptiness. The message that actually I should not have been there, was pretty clear to me. I was a burden. I considered myself a stupid child when my father was angry and hit me. Of course he had the right to do so. It was me who had been in his way and I should have known that. A pestering mother I understood all too well, having a child like me was a true punishment. Sexual abuse I also understood. I was a very attractive girl and in that situation it was not at all easy to control your feelings. A mother of a child that was not allowed to play with me, I could also understand. I could not even be a friend to myself. The teacher who called me retarded because I spoke with an accent, I understood him. Of course I was retarded. I understood why I did not belong. I could see the meaning of everything.

Nothing was left but to develop a strategy of survival in an attempt yet to fill my needs. My main strategy became to cut the connection with my emotions. Unaware I kept continuing this behaviour in adulthood and in so doing fed the jungle of emotions in a dark cavern of my mind. Somewhat later I started self-harm. In my view, it was a rather effective way of coping with what I had lived through. Then I discovered that I could throw up. That gave me a sense of control. Discovering that I could fast was even greater. Fasting I transcended my body and all human needs. I felt really powerful. This was one of the ways I could keep some control in a world that was indescribably harsh and in which I could meet violence any moment.

Eventually I ended up in a foster home. There the strategy of survival I had set up no longer functioned adequately. The crisis I was in gave me a strong sense of helplessness and confusion. Everything I had learned so far had become obsolete. Penetrating emotions such as fear, grief, and anger came to the fore. My psychiatrist did not discover that the paranoia I suffered was explainable through a total loss of confidence in other people. For I had little experience with really secure circumstances and had few possibilities to avoid being maltreated or abused. The norms and values that weighed on my personality I partly internalised and so formed my conscience, my shame and my sense of guilt. This became my critical inner voice. The voice wishing all kinds of terrible things for me, the psychiatrist might also have interpreted as a reaction to the maltreatment I had suffered. Possibly as the echo of the voice of the person who abused me, instead of seeing it as a symptom of schizophrenia.

flashbacks, where people can experience minutes or hours of reliving the trauma as though it is occurring again. The intrusive nature of re-experiencing symptoms is due to direct retrieval of trauma memories by stimuli associated with trauma, meaning that people understandably experience them as uncontrollable. Triggers can be external or internal. For example, following a terrifying sexual assault, re-experiencing symptoms may occur in the form of physical pain, thoughts of being killed and intense fear, triggered by seeing men with a similar physical appearance to the attacker or when experiencing anxiety. Over time, these triggers may start to generalise as other stimuli become associated with the intrusive trauma memories, such that any man, or any person, triggers re-experiencing.

Autobiographical memory: our memory for our past experiences, consisting of sensory-perceptual, contextual, and meaning-based information.

Re-experiencing happens because of the way trauma impacts on the encoding and retrieval of autobiographical memory. To make sense of why trauma memories can intrude as re-experiencing symptoms, it is first necessary to understand theories of how autobiographical memories are stored and retrieved. In a memory of an everyday event, the information is organised into a network with three levels (Conway & Pleydell-Pearce, 2000; Prebble, Addis, & Tippett, 2013). The lowest level, the sensory-perceptual level, consists of the things that are experienced during the events (i.e. sights, sounds, smells, tastes, sensations, and automatic thoughts). The second, or contextual, level is how the sensory-perceptual experiences are organised in time and place, which helps us tell a coherent, clear story about when and where things happened. The highest, or meaning, level comprises the meanings about the event. These meanings can be event categories (which consist of event types, e.g. 'travelling to work' or life periods, e.g. 'my time at school') as well as schematic beliefs (e.g. 'I am a competent person').

The hierarchical organisation of memories in these levels is important in ensuring memories are only retrieved voluntarily when we choose to, and to guard us from a constant bombardment by involuntary intrusions. A memory of a specific event can usually only be recalled if a voluntary retrieval attempt first accesses the relevant category and/or belief (e.g. what happened at work yesterday or the idea that 'I am loveable'). This then searches through the events related to the specified category and beliefs, until it identifies the contextual level of the target event, which in turn leads to the reconstruction of the associated sensory-perceptual level and the recall of an event memory.

The strong emotions experienced during traumatic events can impact the way in which these memories are encoded. Evidence-based theoretical accounts suggest there are two main ways this can happen (Brewin, Gregory, Lipton, & Burgess, 2010). First, the sensory-perceptual level can get stored in more detail than usual, at the expense of the contextual level. This is because our brains have evolved to process sensory-perceptual information in detail when experiencing threat, as it helps us to act quickly to protect ourselves. To get safe, it is more important to focus on what we are experiencing (e.g. seeing a car speeding towards us and feeling fear) than on the context of what is happening (e.g. the temporal and spatial sequence of what is happening) or on what it means (e.g. that accidents can happen). The consequence is that the memory is stored in an incomplete way; the sensory-perceptual level is very vivid and detailed, with the contextual level impaired. This means it may be difficult for the person to clearly tell the contextual story (narrative) of what happened, or they may tell the story but be unaware that some contextual parts are missing. The memory may therefore be distorted and not a fair reflection of all that happened. Also, because the sensory-perceptual level is not sufficiently embedded below a contextual level, the incomplete memory may have a low threshold for being triggered by associated stimuli. As a result, the memory may involuntarily intrude in the present, which makes the person feel as if the trauma, or parts of the trauma, is actually happening again. This can provide a helpful function as it provides an opportunity to make sense of and integrate the trauma after the threat has passed, which can be useful in the future (e.g. learning to avoid dangerous situations). However, if the intrusions are too overwhelming for the person to tolerate and engage with (see section on 'PTSD: Survival Strategies and Emotion Regulation'), then they will not be processed and persist. As described in Box 10.3, it seems that Janet's nightmares,

Box 10.3 Janet's Intrusive Traumatic Memories

Janet often experiences flashbacks to her dad raping her that make her feel like she is back there. These include visual images of what was happening, together with the physical sensations, smells, sounds, and the emotions she experienced at the time. She also has nightmares of being raped and attacked. Reminders of the past, such as seeing children, always leave her feeling like she did back then. Janet reports memories of being bullied popping into her mind. She says these feel more like past memories than her recollections of sexual abuse, although these bullying memories are still very vivid and distressing. Janet explains that she was always terrified during the sexual assaults, and was not really aware of what was going on. She talks about how the bullying was very difficult too, but she did not feel as scared and was more able to make sense of what was happening at the time.

flashbacks, and emotional and physiological intrusions relating to being abused by her dad reflect the retrieval of this type of memory.

A second way memory encoding can be impacted during emotional events is when the sensory-perceptual level again gets encoded in more detail, but without any disruption to the contextual level. This means that when the memory is retrieved, it is recalled with a coherent, contextual story (and is therefore experienced as a past event), but the sensations and emotions attached to the event will be more vivid than in other memories. This type of vivid memory, also known as 'flashbulb' memory, is characteristic of emotionally intense, but not completely overwhelming, events. There is an ongoing debate about whether these types of memories should be included in the PTSD criteria for re-experiencing, as they occur in other difficulties such as depression and social anxiety (Brewin et al., 2017). In ICD 11, they have been excluded from the symptom criteria but are still included in DSM 5. Being aware of the distinction between re-experiencing and intrusive memories has potential implications for therapy planning, as we will discuss in Chapter 19. For Janet, it seems that her vivid memories of being bullied that are not associated with a sense of re-experiencing reflect this memory type.

PTSD: Negative Beliefs and Mood

As we described earlier, beliefs are encoded at the highest level of autobiographical memory, based on the contextual and sensory-perceptual information associated with events. The sensory-perceptual encoding of traumatic events in memory will therefore influence the nature of beliefs (Box 10.4). For example, vivid feelings of shame in a trauma memory may lead to negative judgements about the self at the meaning level. Further, beliefs that are not a fair reflection of the actual events are thought to be particularly likely to form when the contextual level is incomplete, such as someone believing they should have stopped an assault as they are not fully aware of the context of what happened and how powerless they actually were at the time. Beliefs can reflect ideas about the world and self, or 'life stories', and also include metacognitive beliefs (or beliefs about

Box 10.4 Janet's Negative Beliefs and Emotions

Janet reports believing that the abuse was her fault, that she is a bad and weak person, and that others will harm her. She also thinks that she cannot control her traumatic memories. These beliefs, together with her re-experiencing symptoms, contribute to her feeling scared, sad, ashamed, and guilty. Janet describes how she has always viewed herself and others in this way, because of how she was treated in the past.

internal experiences). Looking at the description of Janet's negative beliefs and mood in Box 10.3, it is clear that her beliefs about herself and others have been influenced by her memories of abuse and bullying, which both contribute to distressing emotions. Importantly, her beliefs are likely to maintain the sensory-perceptual and contextual levels of her traumatic memories in their current, unhelpful form, so that they continue to intrude. This is because they reinforce her biased recollections about what happened, and so prevent further elaboration about the actual events and hinder the development of more helpful beliefs.

PTSD: Survival Strategies and Emotion Regulation

Emotional regulation: the regulation of emotion through cognitive, behavioural, and interpersonal strategies.

Traumatic events are inherently threatening and give rise to difficult emotions. Our nature is to automatically engage in strategies to survive trauma and manage these emotions. However, these strategies can become habitual ways of managing emotions, or emotional regulation, which can have unintended, unhelpful consequences and manifest as PTSD symptoms. There are two main ways in which stress is regulated (Schauer & Elbert, 2010):

- First, hyperaroused fight and flight responses (linked to sympathetic nervous system activation), such as fear, active avoidance, anger, or being on guard. In line with this, Box 10.5 describes how Janet coped with her abuse and bullying by always being on guard and actively keeping her distance from others.
- Second, hypoaroused flag and faint responses (linked to parasympathetic nervous system activation), such as passive avoidance, dissociative detachment, or tonic immobility. Janet also appears to have engaged in this type

Box 10.5 Janet's Survival Strategies and Emotional Regulation

Janet describes how she tries to cope with her difficulties by not going outside, drinking alcohol to numb herself from the pain, and pushing away memories and thoughts. She almost always feels on guard, and at times can feel spacey and dissociated. These coping strategies mirror how she tried to survive her traumatic experiences. She withdrew as she did not feel safe around others, and even when by herself she was always alert and on the look out for danger. When her father assaulted her, she would 'go outside' of herself and would not be fully aware of what was happening.

of strategy by dissociation or 'going outside of herself' during the abuse and withdrawing from life.

Dissociation: processes that involve the disruption of usually integrated cognitive functions.

As we can see from Janet's difficulties outlined in Box 10.5, survival strategies and ways of managing emotions can occur on different levels, whether cognitive (e.g. internal avoidance and dissociation), behavioural (e.g. alcohol use and not going outside), or interpersonal (e.g. avoidant relating). The coping strategies in themselves may lead to secondary problems, such as being on guard leading to problems concentrating, irritability, and tension. People may oscillate between different strategies, potentially giving rise to emotional instability. As with Janet's beliefs, her ways of managing her emotions are likely to maintain her traumatic memories in their current form, as she reacts to them with avoidance, dissociation, or hyperarousal, which prevents them from becoming more contextualised and associated with helpful beliefs.

Trauma-Related Psychosis: Voices and Other Hallucinatory Experiences

The psychological processes that have been described as contributing to Janet's PTSD symptoms (i.e. trauma-related memories, beliefs, and emotion regulation strategies) may cause or shape her hallucinatory experiences described in Box 10.6 in three ways. First, negative traumatic beliefs and emotions can influence the content of voices, such that the voices mirror interactions with others in the past or negative beliefs associated with the trauma memories. These types of voices are sometimes regarded to be based on inner speech that is attributed externally (McCarthy-Jones et al., 2014). Second, emotion regulation difficulties may contribute to hallucinatory experiences (Hardy et al., 2016; McCarthy-Jones et al., 2014) via sympathetic hyperarousal and associated hypervigilance to danger. This can result in a reduced threshold for detecting threats in the environment, leading to selective attention to danger such as perceiving background sounds as derogatory voices. Similarly, dissociative detachment linked to parasympathetic hypoarousal may give rise to hallucinatory experiences due to its detrimental impact on information processing, which can lead to distortions in the perception of sensory stimuli.

Finally, it is plausible that trauma memories may lead to hallucinations through a similar process as re-experiencing symptoms. However, in the case of trauma

Box 10.6 Janet's Hallucinatory Experiences

Janet often hears a voice telling her she is bad, and has the taste of semen in her mouth. She believes both of these experiences are caused by the devil wanting to punish her. She explains that these experiences started after she left home and escaped the abuse. She found them very confusing at the time, but soon realised they were happening because she is indeed a bad and weak person. Janet explains how she has tried to cope with them by pushing them away and having her guard up for protection, but neither seem to help.

memory–related hallucinatory experiences, it is suggested that the contextual level of memory encoding may be even more disrupted, such that when the sensory-perceptual information intrudes, it is not experienced with any autonoetic awareness of recollecting a past event. As a result, the intrusive sensory elements of the memory are experienced as a perception in the here and now (e.g. a voice talking). This may be more likely in some people with a sensitivity to experiencing psychosis, as research suggests they have particular difficulties with contextual integration, also known as the 'catastrophic interaction hypothesis' (Fowler et al., 2006; Steel, Fowler, & Holmes, 2005). In Janet's case, it may be that some aspects of the abuse she experienced were encoded in detail at the sensory-perceptual level with a severely fragmented contextual level, such that the taste of semen is actually a re-experiencing of trauma that she does not recognise as connected to what happened in the past.

Trauma-Related Psychosis: Paranoia

Paranoia, or persecutory delusions, as described in Box 10.7, commonly arise as a result of people's trauma-related beliefs and survival strategies. This is supported by findings implicating the role of schemas, social defeat, insecure attachments, and interpersonal sensitivity in psychosis (Bentall et al., 2014; Hardy et al., 2016; Meisel, Garety, Stahl, & Valmaggia, 2018). Janet's views of herself and others increase the likelihood of her interpreting current experiences, such as others glancing at her, as a sign that they intend to cause her harm. This is then exacerbated by her threat-related attentional and reasoning biases, which are an understandable attempt to feel safer but actually perpetuate her perceptions of danger. These processes reflect how beliefs and information processing styles are conceptualised within the seminal cognitive-behavioural models of paranoia (Freeman, 2016; Garety, Kuipers, Fowler, Freeman, & Bebbington, 2001).

Trauma-Related Psychosis: Experiential and Expressive Negative Symptoms

Recent conceptualisations of negative symptoms draw a distinction between expressive (i.e. blunted affect and alogia, or impaired content of thought) and experiential symptoms (i.e. low motivation, anhedonia, and social withdrawal) (Kirkpatrick, 2014; also see Chapter 7). From a psychological perspective, negative symptoms have been relatively less researched, and our understanding of

Box 10.7 Janet's Paranoia

Janet describes how she is sure that other people want to get her. She says she knows this because when she is around others, they look at her in a negative way as if everyone knows she is bad and weak. Janet says she is always on the look out for signs of danger when she is outside, and uses her gut instinct to know when she is at risk of harm. She often avoids going outside as it does not feel safe.

the mechanisms underlying them needs further development. Nonetheless, in relation to trauma and psychosis, the overlap between the avoidance and numbing symptoms of PTSD and negative symptoms has been noted, suggesting they may share common mechanisms. It has also been proposed they may, for some people, represent a shutting down or withdrawal response to the psychologically overwhelming trauma of psychosis (Stampfer, 1990). The plausibility of a link between the impact of traumatic events and negative symptoms is also supported by the emphasis in cognitive-behavioural models of negative symptoms on self-defeatist and self-efficacy beliefs, which could relate to beliefs encoded in memory during or after traumatic events (Grant & Beck, 2009). As Box 10.8 illustrates, the negative symptoms that Janet experiences are interlinked with her posttraumatic survival strategies and ways of regulating her emotions and are understandable attempts to keep herself safe and manage threat, which paradoxically have a detrimental impact on her wellbeing. These problems are likely to play a role in maintaining her difficulties, as they present an obstacle to change.

BLURRED BOUNDARIES: POSTTRAUMATIC STRESS IN PSYCHOSIS

So far, we described the symptoms of PTSD and psychosis. Consistent with our proposed conceptualisation of PTSp, you will have noticed that there is a marked overlap between posttraumatic stress and psychosis and the boundaries between them are blurred. From a phenomenological perspective, re-experiencing symptoms of PTSD can be difficult to distinguish from intrusive hallucinatory experiences and thoughts in psychosis, such as threatening voices, scary visions, physical pains, and thoughts about being harmed. One distinction is that re-experiencing is experienced as a memory and attributed to past trauma, whereas hallucinations are not. However, as illustrated by Janet's hallucinatory tastes of semen, in practice this distinction is less clear-cut, particularly when flashbacks are more severe or when people recognise their hallucinations as relating to past events. It is even more problematic differentiating hyperarousal, avoidance, negative emotions and beliefs in psychosis and posttraumatic stress. Further, disruptions to self-concept, relationships, and emotional regulation that comprise the additional features of cPTSD are also often experienced by people with psychosis. In terms of mechanisms, Janet's description of her problems highlights that event

Box 10.8 Janet's Negative Symptoms

Janet's difficulties with going outside and being around others mean that she rarely spends time with other people. She finds it very difficult to motivate herself to do any activities involving social contact and anticipates that she will not enjoy them. When she is around others, she finds it difficult to express herself. She can often struggle to take care of herself as she feels so overwhelmed by her problems.

memories, beliefs, emotions, and emotion regulation strategies play a role in both PTSD and psychosis. Her PTSD symptoms appear to shape her experience of voice hearing, paranoia, and experiential negative symptoms, suggesting that trauma-focused therapies targeting her posttraumatic stress problems may also reduce the severity of her trauma-related psychosis. However, the relationships between specific trauma-related processes and problems in the context of psychosis require further investigation, and it is possible that distinct subtypes of PTSp will emerge. There have not yet been any sophisticated prospective studies of the interplay between these factors, and relationships identified at the group level may not translate individual situations. A transdiagnostic, network analytic approach, examining potential causal systems of interacting symptoms, seems a promising way forward (Isvoranu et al., 2017; Isvoranu, Borsboom, van Os, & Guloksuz, 2016; Looijesetijn, Dirk Blom, Aleman, Hoek, & Goekoop, 2015).

A TRAUMA-FOCUSED COGNITIVE-BEHAVIOURAL MODEL OF PTSp

If our aim is to improve the support we provide to people with PTSp, how can we use existing theoretical models to understand their difficulties and guide intervention? We view traditional cognitive-behavioural models of psychosis as trauma-informed, given that, as highlighted in our symptom descriptions, they emphasise the role of life events in shaping beliefs, appraisals, and coping responses (Garety et al., 2001; Morrison, 2001). Indeed, these models are often sufficient for understanding and intervening, depending on the nature of a person's PTSp difficulties. However, they do not consider the role of memory in problems, and so we need to draw on the cognitive models of PTSD to inform how we can target distressing memories in therapy (Brewin et al., 2010; Ehlers & Wild, 2015). Given the phenomenological and mechanistic overlaps between PTSD and psychosis, our approach has therefore been to integrate their respective theoretical models to make sense of PTSp. Fig. 10.1 shows Janet's difficulties formulated within our trauma-focused cognitive-behavioural model, which is based on a theoretically informed framework of PTSp (Hardy, 2017). The model is a heuristic for conceptualising how the key psychological mechanisms we have described contribute to common trauma-related difficulties in people presenting with posttraumatic stress and psychosis, and in doing so cuts across categorical diagnostic boundaries. Please note that the aim is to provide a concise guide for understanding PTSp, and so it does not comprehensively reflect the complexity of people's problems or resilience factors in real life. The central premise is that past experiences stored in event memories interact with beliefs, survival strategies, and emotion regulation to create a vulnerability for having problematic experiences, explanations, and responses in the present, which then maintain each other.

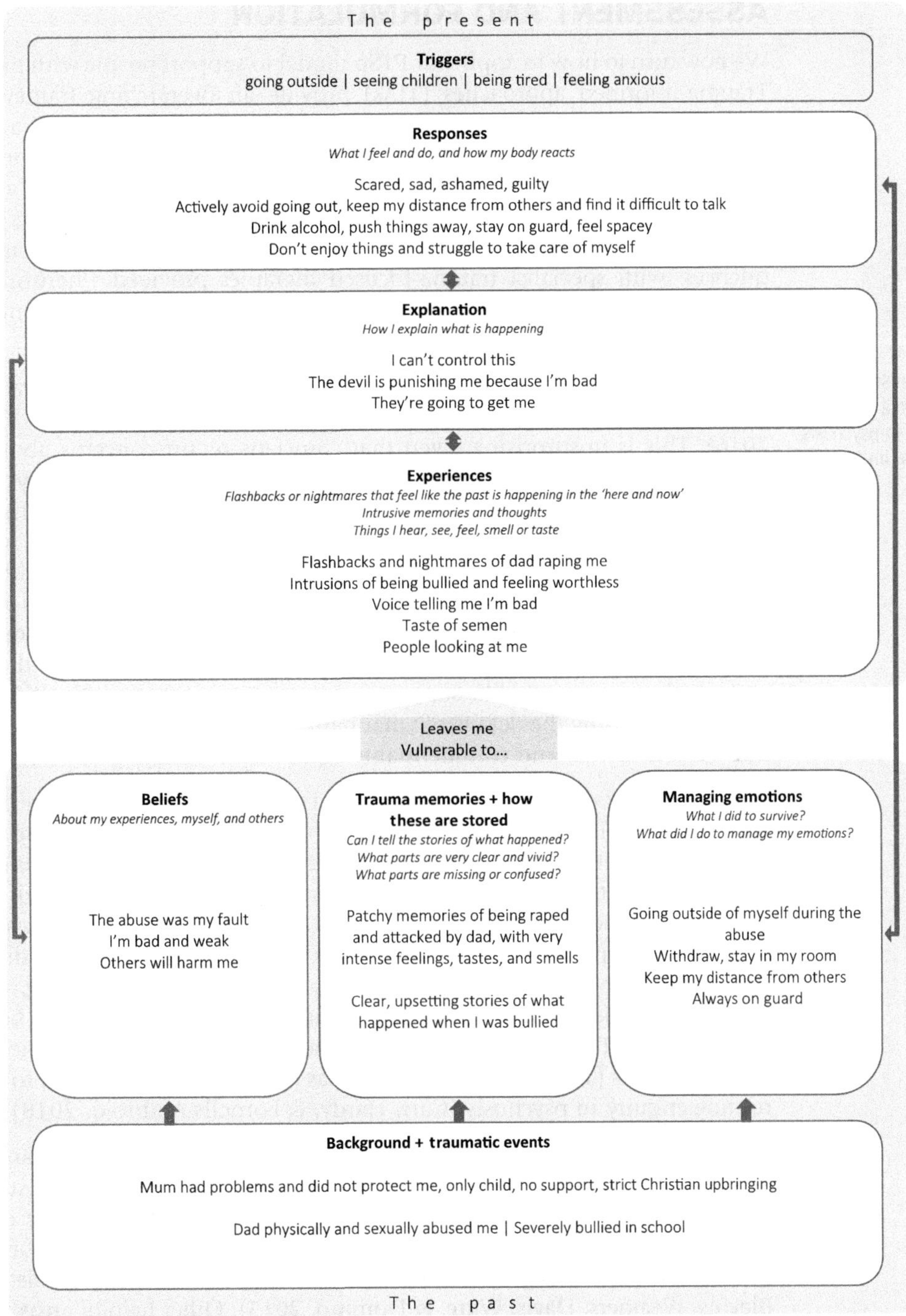

FIG. 10.1
Trauma-focused cognitive-behavioural model of posttraumatic stress in psychosis.

ASSESSMENT AND FORMULATION

We now turn to how to apply our PTSp model to support people with psychosis. Trauma-informed approaches (TIAs) provide an overarching framework for practice in this area (Sweeney & Taggart, 2018). TIAs encompass a systems approach to service delivery, whereby mental health services adopt a broad definition of trauma and its potential impact, alongside a person-centred approach to care that accommodates trauma-related needs and prevents further re-traumatisation. This includes sensitive enquiry about trauma and its consequences, with specialist trauma-focused therapies provided where indicated. For the remainder of the chapter, we will focus on assessment and formulation. Our trauma-focused therapy framework is outlined in Chapter 19.

Routine, sensitive enquiry about trauma and abuse in psychosis needs to be improved.

Evidence suggests that routine screening of trauma and posttraumatic stress responses is rare in frontline services (Brooker, Tocque, Brown, & Kennedy, 2016). This is unsurprising given that clinicians report concerns about when and how to ask. The timing of assessments should be informed by whether the person has capacity to give informed consent, and if there are risk issues or crises that need to be prioritised. If the person is able to engage in the informed consent process, then a brief rationale for asking about trauma should be provided (e.g. trauma is common and can continue to have an impact, and so asking about trauma and its effects can support recovery). It should also be emphasised that the focus will be on how any traumas are currently impacting on the person and whether they would like support for posttraumatic stress difficulties, not (at this stage) eliciting the details of what happened. Risk and safeguarding should also be considered, and confidentiality agreed before starting the assessment.

We advise therapists to use standardised checklists for initial enquiry. This reduces the likelihood of missing important events, and can be a more normalising and containing approach to disclosure than being asked questions during a clinician-led interview. However, checklists should be administered flexibly, according to client needs and preferences. Checklists also help to ensure that behaviourally specific, neutral language is used, which can support disclosure (e.g. asking about 'unwanted sexual contact, which includes talking, looking, touching, and penetration' instead of enquiring whether a person has been 'sexually abused'). There are a number of measures available, including The Trauma and Life Events (TALE) checklist, which has recently been developed to support routine enquiry in psychosis (Carr, Hardy, & Fornells-Ambrojo, 2018).

Informed by the PTSp model, interview questions and questionnaires can be used to explore the person's current difficulties and how these relate to past vulnerability factors. The trauma assessment supports the identification of the currently most distressing event(s), which can then be used to as the anchor for a PTSD assessment (e.g. using the Posttraumatic Stress Disorder Checklist (PCL); Blevins, Weathers, Davis, Witte, & Domino, 2015). Other helpful areas to assess include psychosis (the Psychotic SYmptom RAting Scales, PSYRATS; Haddock, McCarron, Tarrier, & Faragher, 1999); beliefs (the Posttraumatic Cognitions

Inventory, PTCI; Foa, Ehlers, Clark, Tolin, & Orsillo, 1999) and the Brief Core Schema Scales, BCSS; Fowler et al., 2006); and emotional regulation (Brief Version of the Difficulties in Emotion Regulation Scale, DERS-16; Bjureberg et al., 2016).

Following assessment, a collaborative shared formulation can be developed exploring potential links between beliefs, emotion regulation, and event memories formed in the past on the one hand, and experiences, explanations, and responses in the present on the other. Complexity is the norm in working with trauma in psychosis, which presents challenge for assessment and formulation. People generally have experienced multiple types of adversities and present with a range of posttraumatic stress and psychotic symptoms. Subsequently, there are many ways in which these factors can be associated or interact with each other. Moreover, although associations are sometimes very clear, they are always probabilistic. We can never be sure that a psychotic symptom was caused solely by the impact of a certain traumatic event or chain of events. There are always interactions between someone's current and past context. Therefore, all we can do is collaboratively develop a shared understanding of what happened, what processes are involved, and how this is influencing the person. We believe that it is extremely useful to develop these formulations to guide treatment planning, but we should always keep in mind that they are models and be transparent about this when working with people (see Chapter 14 for more on Case Formulations). Further, formulation should be adapted to the person's preferences, abilities, and goals.

CONCLUSIONS

We hope that this chapter helps to improve your understanding of the potential impact of trauma on PTSp, and the psychological processes that may give rise to and maintain problems. Improving mental healthcare for people with these difficulties is an urgent priority, given that it is still relatively rare for trauma-related symptoms to be assessed and treated in people with psychosis, and clinician anxieties about working with this group are common (de Bont et al., 2015; van den Berg et al., 2015). The formulation model outlined here provides a foundation for intervention, and we will describe our phased approach to trauma-focused therapy for psychosis in Chapter 19.

Acknowledgements

We are grateful to Dr. Rachel Brand and Dr. Neil Thomas for their comments on an earlier version of this chapter.

References

Achim, A. M., Maziade, M., Raymond, E., Olivier, D., Mérette, C., & Roy, M. A. (2011). How prevalent are anxiety disorders in schizophrenia? A meta-analysis and critical review on a significant association. *Schizophrenia Bulletin*, *37*(4), 811–821.

American Psychiatric Association (APA). (1994). Diagnostic and statistical manual of mental disorders, 3rd ed. Washington, DC: American Psychiatric Association.

American Psychiatric Association (APA). (2013). *Diagnostic and statistical manual of mental disorders* (5th ed.). Washington, DC: American Psychiatric Association.

Bailey, T., Alvarez-Jimenez, M., Garcia-Sanchez, A. M., Hulbert, C., Barlow, E., & Bendall, S. (2018). Childhood trauma is associated with severity of hallucinations and delusions in psychotic disorders: A systematic review and meta-analysis. *Schizophrenia Bulletin, 44*(5), 1111–1122.

Barbano, A., Van der Mei, W., Bryant, R., Delahanty, D., DeRoon-Cassini, T., Matsuoka, Y., & Shalev, A. (2019). Clinical implications of the proposed ICD-11 PTSD diagnostic criteria. *Psychological Medicine, 49*(3), 483–490. https://doi.org/10.1017/S0033291718001101.

Bentall, R., de Sousa, P., Varese, F., Wickham, S., Sitko, K., Haarmans, M., et al. (2014). From adversity to psychosis: Pathways and mechanisms from specific adversities to specific symptoms. *Social Psychiatry and Psychiatric Epidemiology, 49*, 1011–1022.

Bjureberg, J., Ljótsson, B., Tull, M. T., Hedman, E., Sahlin, H., Lundh, L. G., et al. (2016). Development and validation of a brief version of the difficulties in emotion regulation scale: The DERS-16. *Journal of Psychopathology and Behaviour Assessment, 38*(2), 284–296.

Blevins, C. A., Weathers, F. W., Davis, M. T., Witte, T. K., & Domino, J. L. (2015). The Posttraumatic Stress Disorder Checklist for DSM-5 (PCL-5): Development and initial psychometric evaluation. *Journal of Traumatic Stress, 28*(6), 489–498. https://doi.org/10.1002/jts.22059.

Brewin, C. R., Cloitre, M., Hyland, P., Shevlin, M., Maercker, A., Bryant, R. A., et al. (2017). A review of current evidence regarding the ICD-11 proposals for diagnosing PTSD and complex PTSD. *Clinical Psychology Review, 58*, 1–15.

Brewin, C. R., Gregory, J. D., Lipton, M., & Burgess, N. (2010). Intrusive images in psychological disorders: Characteristics, neural mechanisms, and treatment implications. *Psychological Review, 117*(1), 210–232.

Brewin, C. R., & Patel, T. (2010). Auditory pseudohallucinations in United Kingdom war veterans and civilians with posttraumatic stress disorder. *Journal of Clinical Psychiatry, 71*, 419–425.

Brooker, C., Tocque, K., Brown, M., & Kennedy, A. (2016). Sexual violence and abuse and the care programme approach. *British Journal of Psychiatry, 209*(5), 359–360. https://doi.org/10.1192/bjp.bp.116.186122.

Brown, G. W., & Birley, J. L. (1968). Crises and life changes and the onset of schizophrenia. *Journal of Health and Social Behaviour, 9*, 203–214.

Carr, S., Hardy, A., & Fornells-Ambrojo, M. (2018). The Trauma and Life Events (TALE) checklist: development of a tool for improving routine screening in people with psychosis. *European Journal of Psychotraumatology, 9*(1), 1512265.

Colman, I., Kingsbury, M., Garad, Y., Zeng, Y., Naicker, K., Patten, S., et al. (2016). Consistency in adult reporting of adverse childhood experiences. *Psychological Medicine, 46*(3), 543–549.

Conway, M. A., & Pleydell-Pearce, C. W. (2000). The construction of autobiographical memories in the self-memory system. *Psychological Review, 107*, 261–288.

Corstens, D., & Longden, E. (2013). The origins of voices: Links between life history and voice hearing in a survey of 100 cases. *Psychosis, 5*(3), 270–285.

de Bont, P. A., van den Berg, D. P., van der Vleugel, B. M., de Roos, C., de Jongh, A., van der Gaag, M., et al. (2015). Predictive validity of the trauma screening questionnaire in detecting post-traumatic stress disorder in patients with psychotic disorders. *British Journal of Psychiatry, 206*(5), 408–416.

de Vries, B., van Busschbach, J. T., van der Stouwe, E. C. D., Aleman, A., van Dijk, J. J. M., Lysaker, P. H., et al. (2018). Prevalence rate and risk factors of victimization in adult patients with a psychotic disorder: A systematic review and meta-analysis. *Schizophrenia Bulletin, 43*(Suppl. 1), S206.

Ehlers, A., & Wild, J. (2015). Cognitive therapy for PTSD: Updating memories and meanings of trauma. In U. Schnyder, & M. Cloitre (Eds.), *Evidence based treatments for trauma-related psychological disorders* (pp. 161–187). Cham, Switzerland: Springer.

Fisher, H. L., Craig, T. K., Fearon, P., Morgan, K., Dazzan, P., Lappin, J., et al. (2011). Reliability and comparability of psychosis patients' retrospective reports of childhood abuse. *Schizophrenia Bulletin, 37*, 546–553. https://doi.org/10.1093/schbul/sbp103.

Flory, J. D., & Yehuda, R. (2015). Comorbidity between post-traumatic stress disorder and major depressive disorder: Alternative explanations and treatment considerations. *Dialogues in Clinical Neuroscience, 17*(2), 141–150.

Foa, E. B., Ehlers, A., Clark, D. M., Tolin, D. F., & Orsillo, S. M. (1999). The Posttraumatic Cognitions Inventory (PTCI): Development and validation. *Psychological Assessment, 11*(3), 303–314.

Fornells-Ambrojo, M., Gracie, A., Brewin, C. R., & Hardy, A. (2016). Narrowing the focus on the assessment of psychosis-related PTSD: A methodologically orientated systematic review. *European Journal of Psychotraumatology, 7*(1), 32095.

Fowler, D., Freeman, D., Steel, C., Hardy, A., Smith, B., Hackman, C., et al. (2006). The catastrophic interaction hypothesis: How do stress, trauma, emotion and information processing abnormalities lead to psychosis? In W. Larkin, & A. P. Morrison (Eds.), *Trauma and psychosis: New directions for theory and therapy* (pp. 101–134). Hove: Routledge.

Freeman, D. (2016). Persecutory delusions: A cognitive perspective on understanding and treatment. *Lancet Psychiatry, 3*(7), 685–692.

Friedman, M. J., Resick, P. A., Bryant, R. A., & Brewin, C. R. (2011). Considering PTSD for DSM-5. *Depression and Anxiety, 28*, 750–769.

Galatzer-Levy, I. R., & Bryant, R. A. (2013). 636,120 ways to have post-traumatic stress disorder. *Perspectives on Psychological Science, 8*(6), 651–662.

Galatzer-Levy, I. R., Huang, S. H., & Bonanno, G. A. (2018). Trajectories of resilience and dysfunction following potential trauma: A review and statistical evaluation. *Clinical Psychology Review, 63*, 41–55.

Garety, P. A., Kuipers, E., Fowler, D., Freeman, D., & Bebbington, P. E. (2001). A cognitive model of the positive symptoms of psychosis. *Psychological Medicine, 31*(2), 189–195.

Grant, P. M., & Beck, A. T. (2009). Defeatist beliefs as a mediator of cognitive impairment, negative symptoms, and functioning in schizophrenia. *Schizophrenia Bulletin, 35*(4), 798–806.

Haddock, G., McCarron, J., Tarrier, N., & Faragher, E. B. (1999). Scales to measure dimensions of hallucinations and delusions: the psychotic symptom rating scales (PSYRATS). *Psychological Medicine, 29*(4), 879–889.

Hardy, A. (2017). Pathways from trauma to psychotic experiences: A theoretically informed model of posttraumatic stress in psychosis. *Frontiers in Psychology*, 8697.

Hardy, A., Emsley, R., Freeman, D., Bebbington, P., Garety, P. A., Kuipers, E. E., et al. (2016). Psychological mechanisms mediating effects between trauma and psychotic symptoms: The role of affect regulation, intrusive trauma memory, beliefs, and depression. *Schizophrenia Bulletin, 42 Suppl.*, S34–S43.

Hardy, A., Fowler, D., Freeman, D., Smith, B., Steel, C., Evans, J., et al. (2005). Trauma and hallucinatory experience in psychosis. *Journal of Nervous and Mental Disease, 193*(8), 501–507.

Hassan, A. N., & De Luca, V. (2015). The effect of lifetime adversities on resistance to antipsychotic treatment in schizophrenia patients. *Schizophrenia Research, 161*, 496–500.

Hill, A. B. (1965). The environment and disease: Association or causation? *Proceedings of the Royal Society of Medicine, 58*, 295–300.

Isvoranu, A. M., Borsboom, D., van Os, J., & Guloksuz, S. (2016). A network approach to environmental impact in psychotic disorders: Brief theoretical framework. *Schizophrenia Bulletin, 42*, 870–873.

Isvoranu, A. M., van Borkulo, C. D., Boyette, L. L., Wigman, J. T. W., Vinkers, C. H., Borsboom, D., et al. (2017). A network approach to psychosis: Pathways between childhood trauma and psychotic symptoms. *Schizophrenia Bulletin, 43*, 187–196.

Kelleher, I., & DeVylder, J. E. (2017). Hallucinations in borderline personality disorder and common mental disorders. *British Journal of Psychiatry, 210*, 230–231.

Kelleher, I., Keeley, H., Corcoran, P., Ramsay, H., Wasserman, C., Carli, V., et al. (2013). Childhood trauma and psychosis in a prospective cohort study: Cause, effect, and directionality. *The American Journal of Psychiatry, 170*(7), 734–741. https://doi.org/10.1176/appi.ajp.2012.12091169.

Kessler, R. C., Aguilar-Gaxiola, S., Alonso, J., Benjet, C., Bromet, E. J., Cardoso, G., et al. (2017). Trauma and PTSD in the WHO World Mental Health Surveys. *European Journal of Psychotraumatology, 8*(Suppl. 5).

Kirkpatrick, B. (2014). Progress in the study of negative symptoms. *Schizophrenia Bulletin, 40*(Suppl. 2), S101–S106.

Looijesetijn, J., Dirk Blom, J., Aleman, A., Hoek, H. W., & Goekoop, R. (2015). An integrated network model of psychotic symptoms. *Neuroscience and Biobehavioural Reviews, 59*, 238–250.

Lysaker, P. H., & Larocco, V. A. (2008). The prevalence and correlates of trauma-related symptoms in schizophrenia-spectrum disorder. *Comprehensive Psychiatry, 49*, 330–334.

Matheson, S. L., Shepherd, A. M., Pinchbeck, R. M., Laurens, K. R., & Carr, V. J. (2013). Childhood adversity in schizophrenia: A systematic meta-analysis. *Psychological Medicine, 43*(2), 225–238.

McCarthy-Jones, S., Thomas, N., Strauss, C., Dodgson, G., Jones, N., Woods, A., et al. (2014). Better than mermaids and stray dogs? Subtyping auditory verbal hallucinations and its implications for research and practice. *Schizophrenia Bulletin, 40* Suppl. 4. S275–S284.

Meisel, S., Garety, P., Stahl, D., & Valmaggia, L. (2018). Interpersonal processes in paranoia: A systematic review. *Psychological Medicine, 48*(14), 1–14.

Morrison, A. P. (2001). The interpretation of intrusions in psychosis: An integrative approach to hallucinations and delusions. *Behavioural and Cognitive Psychotherapy, 29*, 257–276.

Newbury, J. B., Arseneault, L., Moffitt, T. E., Caspi, A., Danese, A., Baldwin, J. R., et al. (2018). Measuring childhood maltreatment to predict early-adult psychopathology: Comparison of prospective informant-reports and retrospective self-reports. *Journal of Psychiatric Research, 96*, 57–64. https://doi.org/10.1016/j.jpsychires.2017.09.020. Epub 2017 Sep 21.

Okkels, N., Trabjerg, B., Arendt, M., & Pedersen, C. B. (2017). Traumatic stress disorders and risk of subsequent schizophrenia spectrum disorder or bipolar disorder: A nationwide cohort study. *Schizophrenia Bulletin, 43*(1), 180–186.

Palmier-Claus, J. E., Berry, K., Bucci, S., Mansell, W., & Varese, F. (2016). Relationship between childhood adversity and bipolar affective disorder: Systematic review and meta-analysis. *British Journal of Psychiatry, 209*, 454–459.

Prebble, S. C., Addis, D. R., & Tippett, L. J. (2013). Autobiographical memory and sense of self. *Psychological Bulletin, 139*, 815–840.

Sareen, J. (2014). Posttraumatic stress disorder in adults: Impact, comorbidity, risk factors, and treatment. *Canadian Journal of Psychiatry Revue Canadienne de Psychiatrie, 59*(9), 460–467.

Schauer, M., & Elbert, T. (2010). Dissociation following traumatic stress: Etiology and treatment. *Zeitschrift für Psychologie, 218*, 109–127.

Schneeberger, A. R., Muenzenmaier, K., Castille, D., Battaglia, J., & Link, B. (2014). Use to psychotropic medication groups in people with severe mental illness and stressful childhood experiences. *Journal of Trauma and Dissociation, 15*, 494–511.

Schroeder, K., Fisher, H. L., & Schafer, I. (2013). Psychotic symptoms in patients with borderline personality disorder: Prevalence and clinical management. *Current Opinion in Psychiatry, 26*, 113–119.

Seow, L. S., Ong, C., Mahesh, M. V., Sagayadevan, V., Shafie, S., Chong, S. A., et al. (2016). A systematic review on comorbid post-traumatic stress disorder in schizophrenia. *Schizophrenia Research, 176*, 441–451.

Stampfer, H. G. (1990). "Negative symptoms": A cumulative stress disorder? *Australian and New Zealand Journal of Psychiatry, 24*, 516–528. https://doi.org/10.3109/00048679009062908.

Steel, C., Doukani, A., & Hardy, A. (2017). The PCL as a brief screen for posttraumatic stress disorder within schizophrenia. *International Journal of Psychiatry and Clinical Practice*, (2), 1–3.

Steel, C., Fowler, D., & Holmes, E. A. (2005). Traumatic intrusions in psychosis: An information processing account. *Behavioural and Cognitive Psychotherapy, 33*, 139–152.

Sweeney, A., & Taggart, D. (2018). (Mis)understanding trauma-informed approaches in mental health. *Journal of Mental Health, 27*(5), 383–387.

Trotta, A., Murray, R. M., & Fisher, H. L. (2015). The impact of childhood adversity on the persistence of psychotic symptoms: A systematic review and meta-analysis. *Psychological Medicine, 45*(12), 2481–2498.

van den Berg, D. P., de Bont, P. A., van der Vleugel, B. M., de Roos, C., de Jongh, A., Van Minnen, A., et al. (2015). Prolonged exposure vs eye movement desensitization and reprocessing vs waiting list for posttraumatic stress disorder in patients with a psychotic disorder: A randomized clinical trial. *JAMA Psychiatry, 72*(3), 259–267.

van Winkel, R., van Nierop, M., Myin-Germeys, I., & van Os, J. (2013). Childhood trauma as a cause of psychosis: Linking genes, psychology, and biology. *Canadian Journal of Psychiatry, 58*(1), 44–51.

Varese, F., Smeets, F., Drukker, M., Lieverse, R., Lataster, T., Viechtbauer, W., et al. (2012). Childhood adversities increase the risk of psychosis: A meta-analysis of patient-control, prospective- and cross-sectional cohort studies. *Schizophrenia Bulletin, 38*(4), 661–671.

World Health Organisation (WHO). (2018). *International classification of diseases, version 11.*

Definition of Key Terms

Autobiographical memory Our memory for our past experiences, consisting of sensory-perceptual, contextual, and meaning-based information. Arousal and safety behaviours associated with traumatic events can lead to the development and maintenance of intrusive memories, flashbacks, and anomalous experiences.

Emotional regulation The processes by which emotions are managed. These include cognitive, behavioural, and interpersonal strategies, influenced by reflective awareness and beliefs.

Posttraumatic stress in psychosis The range of posttraumatic stress difficulties that people with psychosis may experience following trauma, reflecting a transdiagnostic approach.

Trauma Trauma can be defined as any event(s) that a person interprets as representing a significant physical or psychological threat to the self, including those that they witness in others.

CHAPTER 11

Effectively Assessing Sleep and Circadian Rhythms in Psychosis

Jan Cosgrave*[,†,‡], Elizabeth A. Klingaman[§,¶], Philip Gehrman*

*Perelman School of Medicine, University of Pennsylvania, Philadelphia, PA, United States, [†]Nuffield Department of Clinical Neurosciences, Sleep and Circadian Neuroscience Institute, University of Oxford, Oxford, United Kingdom, [‡]Department of Clinical, Educational and Health Psychology, University College London, London, United Kingdom, [§]Department of Psychiatry, University of Maryland School of Medicine, Baltimore, MD, United States, [¶]US Department of Veterans Affairs, VISN 5 Capitol Health Care Network, Linthicum, MD, United States

Key Learning Objectives

- To understand the two-process model of sleep, the function of the suprachiasmatic nucleus and how it responds to light
- To be familiar with how sleep and circadian rhythm disturbances can occur and be a pervasive problem across a number of different mental health disorders (not just psychosis), and how this may impact assessment
- To identify the most common sleep disorders in psychosis and familiarise yourself with how to assess them
- To be aware of differential diagnoses when it comes to assessing sleep in people with psychosis

INTRODUCTION

Emil Kraepelin, one of modern psychiatry's core founders, first documented the relationship between abnormal sleep patterns and mental health in his first textbook in 1883 (Kraepelin, 2007). Previously, recognition of sleep and circadian rhythm disruption (SCRD) in psychiatric disease was limited to the context of secondary factors such as side-effects of medication (Wirz-Justice, Haug, & Cajochen, 2001), abnormal light exposure (Wirz-Justice, 2006), abnormal social timing (Grandin, Alloy, & Abramson, 2006) and pain (Smith, Perlis, Smith, Giles, & Carmody, 2000). However, the identification of common mechanistic pathways

A Clinical Introduction to Psychosis. https://doi.org/10.1016/B978-0-12-815012-2.00011-0

(including hypothalamic pituitary axis dysregulation; autonomic nervous system dysfunction; overlapping genetic risk & emotional dysregulation) between SCRD and psychiatric disease has led researchers to question whether SCRD could be more causally implemented in mental health problems (Wulff, Gatti, Wettstein, & Foster, 2010). This evidence has very important implications for how we conceptualise and assess SCRD in the context of serious mental illness.

As research into SCRD in mental health has become more prolific, several accounts of SCRD have been cited as comorbidities in a host of psychiatric disorders (Table 11.1). Changes in sleep behaviour are now listed as key diagnostic criteria for a number of affective disorders (including seasonal affective disorder, major depressive disorder, bipolar disorder) and are considered a transdiagnostic factor for the development and maintenance of psychiatric disease (Harvey, Murray, Chandler, & Soehner, 2011; Wulff et al., 2010). It is important to recognise that while certain psychiatric disorders have stronger associations with specific sleep phenotypes (e.g. posttraumatic stress disorder with fragmented sleep, daytime naps, and hyposomnia—too little sleep), schizophrenia is associated with all of the listed sleep phenotypes. Hence, it is imperative to comprehensively assess SCRD in schizophrenia.

Table 11.1 Sleep Wake Phenotypes Found to Be Associated With Different Psychiatric Disorders

Sleep phenotype	Explanation of sleep phenotype	Related disorder
Delayed sleep phase	When your bedtime is considerably later than the normative times for that age group and is usually in the early hours of the morning (e.g. 3–4 a.m.)	Schizophrenia Obsessive compulsive disorders Seasonal affective disorder Bipolar disorder
Non-24-h sleep phase	This is when your sleep–wake cycle is not following a 24-h rhythm (which humans have evolved to do). This usually looks as though someone is going to bed later and later each night before eventually going around the clock. This is different from delayed sleep phase (DSP) as you are not going to bed at the same time each night (whereas usually in DSP you are)	Schizophrenia
Irregular sleep–wake cycle	Extremely variable or erratic sleep–wake timings	Schizophrenia (48 h cycle)
Fragmented sleep with daytime naps	Experiencing disrupted sleep at night and using naps during the day to compensate	Schizophrenia Posttraumatic stress disorder Unipolar depression
Hypersomnia	Having an elongated sleep period every night (and struggling without it), usually around 10–14 h	Bipolar disorder (depressive phase) Unipolar depression Schizophrenia

Continued

Table 11.1 **Sleep Wake Phenotypes Found to Be Associated With Different Psychiatric Disorders—cont'd**

Sleep phenotype	Explanation of sleep phenotype	Related disorder
Insomnia	Disruption of night-time sleep with excessive day-time sleepiness	Schizophrenia Chronic insomnia Posttraumatic stress disorder Alcoholism Bipolar disorder (both depressive and manic phases) Unipolar depression Autism Generalised anxiety disorder

Adapted from Wulff, K., Porcheret, K., Cussans, E., & Foster, R. G. (2009). Sleep and circadian rhythm disturbances: multiple genes and multiple phenotypes. *Current Opinion in Genetics & Development*, *19*(3), 237–246. http://doi.org/10.1016/j.gde.2009.03.007.

THE BASIC PRINCIPLES OF SLEEP—INTRODUCING THE TWO-PROCESS MODEL

Before understanding how sleep can go wrong for people with psychosis, it is important to grasp the fundamental processes governing sleep and circadian rhythms. It is also important to acknowledge that sleep is a pervasive process, essential for many bodily functions including mood regulation, emotional processing, and learning and memory (Walker, 2009): it is the end product of interactions among several neural circuits, neurotransmitters, and hormones; none of which are exclusive to sleep's production. It is thus imperative to acknowledge sleep and circadian rhythms as holistic bodily processes, all of which may be related to the experience of poor mental health (Foster et al., 2013).

Sleep regulation is controlled by two independent processes: Process S and Process C.

Sleep regulation is governed by two independent (but interrelated) processes: a homeostatic mechanism, which is determined by accumulative sleep debt (Process S), and the circadian system that coordinates sleep initiation during the biological night and wakefulness in the morning independent of sleep–wake behaviours (Process C). This is known as the two-process model of sleep regulation and was first championed by Borbély (1982). A schematic representation of the two-process model is displayed in Fig. 11.1.

Circadian processes recur naturally, with a period of roughly 24 h.

The term 'circadian' refers to an endogenous rhythmic biological process that repeats itself approximately every 24 h, even in the absence of external time cues (circa and diem are Latin for 'about a day'). The circadian process (Process C) in the Two-Process Model represents the temporal configuration that governs regulatory mechanisms of adaptive behaviours, including feeding, reproduction,

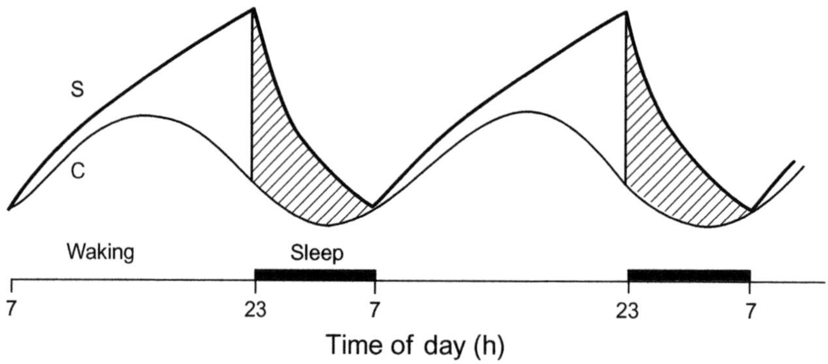

FIG. 11.1
Schematic representation of the Two-Process Model of Sleep Regulation. The *upper line* represents Process S or the sleep drive. Sleep pressure is low upon awakening and progressively increases as a function of time awake throughout the day, peaking around bedtime (in this diagram 11 p.m.) and then dissipating during sleep. Process C *[the lower line]* coordinates the timing of sleep and wake. When sleep pressure peaks, Process C initiates sleep; when sleep pressure falls, Process C initiates wake. Adapted from Daan, S., Beersma, D. G., & Borbély, A. A. (1984). Timing of human sleep: Recovery process gated by a circadian pacemaker. *American Journal of Physiology—Regulatory, Integrative and Comparative Physiology, 246*(2), R161–R183.

and sleep–wake cycles. These precisely coordinated temporal patterns are self-regulating and oscillate with a period of around 24 h (Crowley, Acebo, & Carskadon, 2007). The 'period' of the rhythm refers to the time needed to complete one full oscillation (Grandin et al., 2006). These rhythms originate from the suprachiasmatic nucleus (SCN), which is more commonly known as the 'biological' or 'master' clock, and is found in the anterior hypothalamus.

Process S is understood to be reasonably autonomous from circadian timing. Put simply, Process S can be described as an increasing propensity or need for sleep, also known as sleep pressure, as a result of time awake. The pressure dissipates as one sleeps and restarts the following morning upon wakefulness (Crowley et al., 2007).

THE SUPRACHIASMATIC NUCLEUS

The suprachiasmatic nucleus sits directly above the optic chiasm and generates circadian rhythms.

Process C's generator (the SCN) is a small region of the hypothalamus containing just 10,000 bilateral nuclei (Takahashi, Hong, Ko, & McDearmon, 2008). It receives photic or light information collected by photoreceptor cells in the retina via the retinohypothalamic tract (RHT). The retina comprises not only rods and cones but also intrinsically photosensitive retinal ganglion cells (ipRGCs), which possess a photopigment called 'melanopsin', rendering them particularly sensitive to short wavelength blue light. Although rods and cones themselves are thought to also be involved in the communication made to the SCN, the ipRGCs are sufficient, as animals and humans who are visually blind are still able to follow the light–dark cycle (Freedman et al., 1999). Thus, light perceived in the retina acts as a neural signal to the SCN, and is transmitted via the RHT (Fig. 11.2).

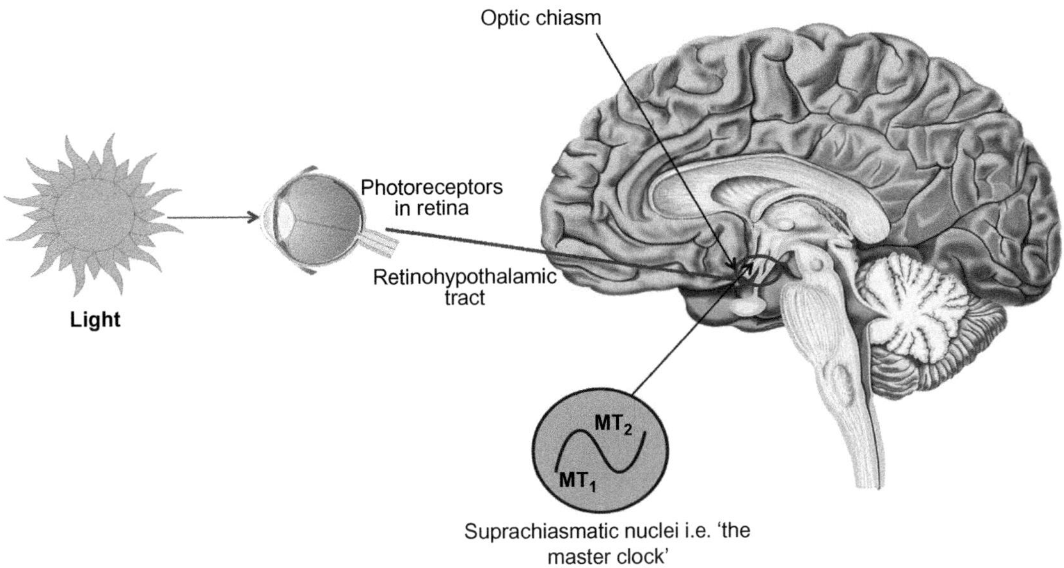

FIG. 11.2
How light entrains the biological clock.

Box 11.1 Rhythmicity in the Suprachiasmatic Nucleus (SCN)

The term *free running* refers to the SCN's rhythmicity in the absence of external time cues. It usually presents as a progressive delay in sleep resulting in someone going 'around the clock', i.e. at some points they are going to bed during the day and waking up at night. However, the vast majority of people are considered 'entrained' to external cues or 'zeitgebers'. Light is our most potent zeitgeber, but several nonphotic zeitgebers can also influence the rhythmic signals from the SCN, including mealtimes, clocks, and exercise.

While it is impossible in humans to directly measure the output of the SCN, a measurement by proxy can be obtained via the 24-h rhythms of physiological processes the SCN governs, including core body temperature, melatonin, and cortisol synthesis (see Box 11.1).

INDIVIDUAL DIFFERENCES IN CIRCADIAN TIMING

It is generally thought that most people have a period (the time taken to complete one full oscillation) of around 24 h, but there is also evidence to suggest that the period of the biological clock may be subject to interindividual variability. Under laboratory conditions, the clock period has been found to range from 23.89 to 24.40 h (Wright, Hughes, Kronauer, Dijk, & Czeisler, 2001).

The timing of an individual's activity and sleep across the day defines their chronotype.

Subtle changes in the period length can give rise to substantial differences in behaviour, particularly in the timing of the sleep–wake cycle. These differences allow us to discern between individuals who may identify as early (or 'larks'), late (or 'owls'), and intermediate types. The global term for such categorisations is 'chronotype' (Roenneberg et al., 2007).

The self-reported preferred timing of the sleep–wake rhythm is one of the most frequently used markers of chronotype (Roenneberg et al., 2007). The misalignment between the endogenous internal timing of the clock (that gives rise to chronotype/preferred sleep timing) and external timing (e.g. shift working patterns, socialising) is thought to impact a number of different variables, including mood and cognitive performance (Biss & Hasher, 2012). Chronotype itself is impacted by a number of demographic variables, including age, gender, and genetic profile (Clarisse, Le Floc'h, Kindelberger, & Feunteun, 2010). Several genetic polymorphisms are also associated with different chronotypes (Archer et al., 2010), as are different psychiatric disorders including psychosis (Wulff et al., 2010).

THE ARCHITECTURE OF SLEEP

The process of sleep itself is both structured and rhythmic. It can be categorised into two genres: rapid-eye movement (REM) sleep, and nonrapid eye movement (NREM) sleep. NREM sleep is further divided into three stages on the basis of electroencephalographic (EEG) changes. Typically, NREM and REM sleep occur in alternating cycles with each full cycle normally lasting between 90 and 120 min. Generally, a healthy young adult should spend approximately 70%–90% of their total sleep time (approximately 5–10 h) in NREM stages; stage N1 accounting for 3%–5% of total sleep time, stage N2 for 50%–60%, and stage N3 for 10%–20% (Benbadis, 2006). Stage N1 is observed immediately after the onset of sleep and is categorised by slow rolling eye movements (SREM). Stage N2 sleep is determined by the presence of specific wave types called sleep spindles (short bursts of high frequency between 12 and 14 Hz) and K-complexes and predominantly lies in the theta band (6–7 Hz). Stage N3, or slow wave sleep (SWS), is characterised by delta activity (Benbadis, 2006). REM sleep is characterised by rapid eye movements and temporary motor paralysis (Hobson, 2009). It is also considered the most active wake-like sleep stage. Conversely, SWS is considered to be the deepest and most restorative sleep stage, and shows the strongest relationship to how we report subjective sleep quality (Åkerstedt, Hume, Minors, & Waterhouse, 1997).

Sleep pressure builds the longer you have been awake, then dissipates when you sleep.

Slow wave sleep (SWS; stage N3) and slow wave activity (SWA, power in the 0.75–4.5 Hz range) are considered a physiological hallmark of homeostatic sleep pressure (Process S). As such, SWA is high during the first half of the sleep period when sleep pressure is at its peak, and then declines exponentially across the repeated episodes of nonrapid eye movement (NREM) sleep (Crowley et al., 2007).

SLEEP AND CIRCADIAN RHYTHM DISRUPTION

By now, you (the reader) will hopefully have grown to appreciate the intricacy of the sleep–wake system. This intricacy makes it vulnerable to disruption. Sleep and circadian rhythm disruption refers to interference in Process C and/or Process S. Social timing, such as staying out late with friends and having a lie in on the weekend, impacts both the availability and duration of sleep (Foster et al., 2013; see example in Box 11.2).

While this is an example of everyday sleep disruption, it is not an overly problematic form of SCRD. SCRD encompasses much further-reaching sleep complaints. These include more extreme forms of circadian misalignment, such as advanced/delayed cycles, bidian cycles (having a cycle length of 50h), non-24h cycle lengths, highly irregular and fragmented sleep patterns, hyposomnia or insomnia complaints (see later), shift work disorders, hypersomnia, and parasomnias (nightmares, sleep paralysis, sleep hallucinations, etc.; Koffel & Watson, 2009). Please refer to Fig. 11.3 for a schematic overview of different sleep phenotypes. As such, it is perhaps unsurprising that perturbations to the sleep–wake system can have extensive ramifications on physical and mental health (Fig. 11.3; taken from Wulff et al., 2010). This is why it is essential for clinical psychologists to conceptualise sleep and sleep disorders/disruptions holistically.

SLEEP, CIRCADIAN RHYTHMS, AND PSYCHOSIS

Having covered Processes C and S, the structure and architecture of sleep, the master clock in the brain and how all of these processes can be disturbed, we can now start to examine what happens in SCRD in people with psychosis more carefully.

Evidence is now accruing that sleep and circadian rhythm disruption (SCRD) is an important feature of psychosis. A study by Cohrs (2008) highlighted that between 30% and 80% of people with a diagnosis of schizophrenia report sleep disturbances. More recent research into the frequency of patients meeting criteria for a variety of different sleep disorders in early psychosis indicated a prevalence

Box 11.2 Social Jet Lag

Often we use alarm clocks to meet work obligations, drink caffeine to compensate for a truncated sleep period, and then in turn use sleep-promoting medication in the evening to correct for the stimulants taken during the day. This can easily become a habitual cycle. To consecutively repeat this vicious cycle often means we need to compensate on the weekends by having a 'lie in' in the mornings (Foster et al., 2013). This constant misalignment is referred to as 'social jet lag' (Roenneberg, Wirz-Justice, & Merrow, 2003) and is one of many ways we can compromise the sleep–wake regulatory systems and experience sleep and circadian rhythm disruption (SCRD; Foster et al., 2013).

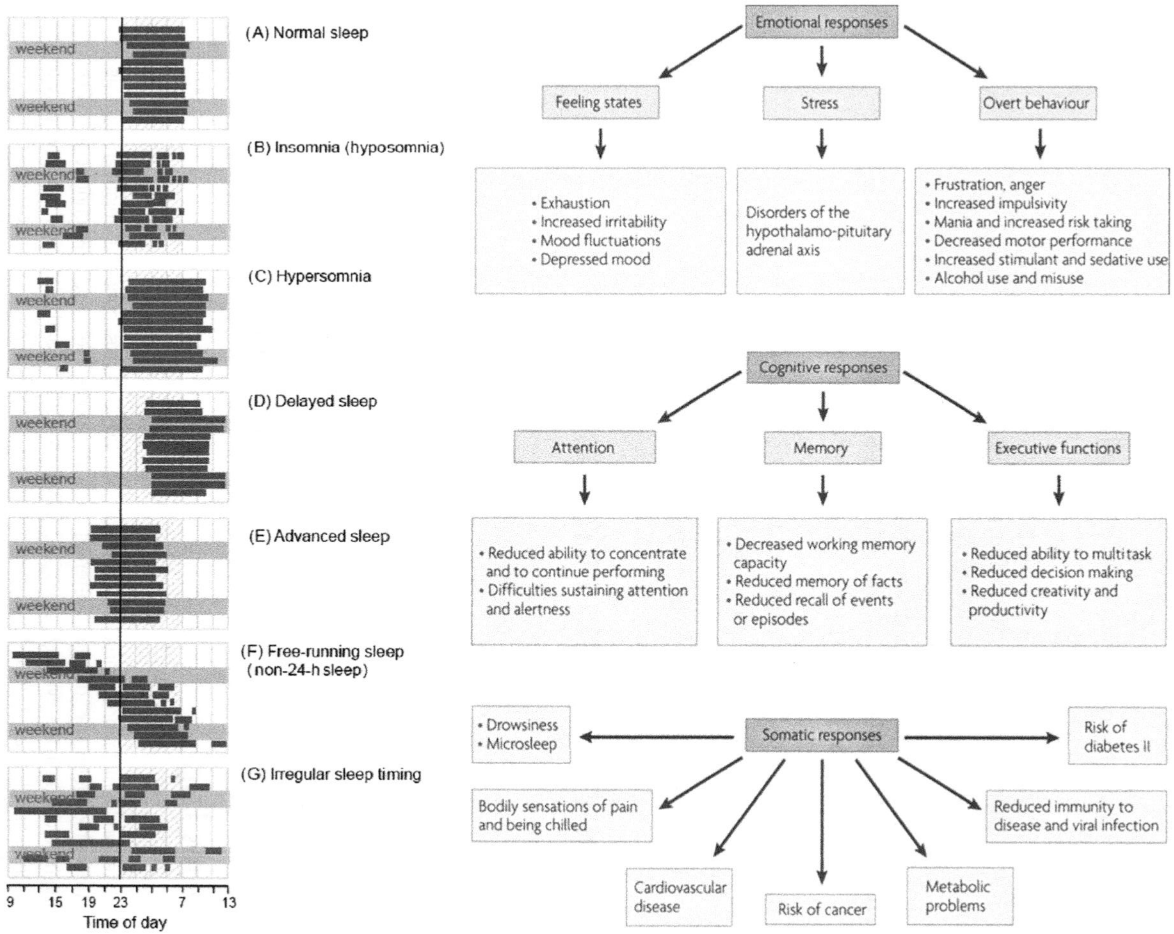

FIG. 11.3

Normal and abnormal sleep, and consequences of sleep and circadian disruption. On the left-hand side, normal sleep (A) is compared to abnormal sleep patterns (B–G). In order for a sleep patterning or phenotype to be classified as abnormal, it must be such that the individual reports it as distressing and impactful upon their wellbeing/ability to go about daily obligations. Individuals with insomnia (or hyposomnia) have reduced sleep, as opposed to those with hypersomnia who show excessive sleep. Some SCRD phenotypes can be thought of as pathological extremes of morning or evening chronotypes (e.g. delayed (D), advanced (E) and non-24 h (or free-running) sleep phase types. Irregular sleep–wake cycles (G) lack any kind of clear temporal structure; this is different from insomnia (B), as insomnia is typified by the repeated disruption of nocturnal sleep with excessive daytime sleepiness. Irregular sleep, hyposomnia, and hypersomnia are thought to arise from a complex interaction between Processes C and S, whereas advanced and delayed cycles are primarily arise from Process C–related problems. However, all of these phenotypes fall under the umbrella of SCRD. On the right-hand side, the ramifications of reduced sleep duration and circadian desynchrony (SCRD) on emotional, cognitive, and somatic responses are displayed. From Wulff, K., Gatti, S., Wettstein, J. G., & Foster, R. G. (2010). Sleep and circadian rhythm disruption in psychiatric and neurodegenerative disease. *Nature Reviews. Neuroscience*, *11*(8), 589–599. http://doi.org/10.1038/nrn2868.

of 80% (with insomnia and nightmares highlighted as the most common). Comorbidity among sleep disorders is also reported to be high with an average 3.3 disorders per patient. Those who report a sleep disorder also reported significantly higher scores on psychotic experiences (paranoia, hallucinations, and cognitive disorganisation), depression, anxiety and lower on wellbeing. Furthermore, it is estimated that only 53.1% of the sleep disorders were discussed with a clinician and only a quarter of those reported received treatment (Reeve, Sheaves, & Freeman, 2018), as such SCRD remains both prevalent and under recognised in psychosis (Box 11.3).

People with psychotic disorders often experience more than 1 type of comorbid sleep problem.

Outside of symptomatology, SCRD is also associated with several important clinical outcomes, including relapse (Waters & Manoach, 2012), poorer coping (Ritsner et al., 2004) higher distress (Hofstetter, Lysaker, & Mayeda, 2005), increased frequency of depressive disorders (Palmese et al., 2011), and completed suicide (Pompili et al., 2009). Thus, it is essential for clinical psychologists to comprehensively and holistically assess sleep and circadian rhythms within the context of psychosis.

More recently, it has been debated that SCRD may represent a risk factor for, or may in fact directly contribute to, the development and persistence of psychotic experiences. This is evidenced by the omnipresence of poor sleep across the core phases of the disorder, including the prodrome (with an estimated prevalence of 70%–100%) (Yung & McGorry, 1997), acute (Kupfer, Wyatt, Scott, & Snyder, 1970), chronic,

SCRD is arguably a risk factor for, or causally related to, the onset and persistence of psychosis.

Box 11.3 Arousal and Hyperarousal in SCRD

One of the key mechanisms thought to underpin SCRD (and particularly insomnia, the most common disorder in SCRD) is physiological hyperarousal. To understand this, we have to understand the basic structure of the stress axis, which is divided into two branches: the hypothalamic–pituitary adrenal axis (HPA; which is best known in psychology for the production of cortisol), and the autonomic nervous system (ANS). Within the ANS, there are the sympathetic and parasympathetic nervous systems. Colloquially, they are known as the 'fight or flight' or 'rest and digest' systems, respectively.

Taken together the stress axis is responsible for a number of psychological (e.g. emotional processing) and physiological processes (e.g. endocrine and cardiovascular activation) processes, to maintain physiological homeostasis or balance. Regulation of the stress axis is under circadian control (i.e. it follows a 24-h rhythm; for example cortisol has a very distinct 24-h rhythm) and is heavily influenced by sleep (e.g. both sleep architecture and quality have a profound effect on cardiovascular functioning). Other examples include elevated resting heart rate (HR) and lowered heart rate variability (HRV), which are frequently cited physiological hallmarks of hyperarousal. High HR and low HRV have been cited in several serious mental illnesses (including psychosis) and are influenced by both sleep and circadian rhythms. As such, hyperarousal and dysregulation of the stress axis represent one of the possible common mechanistic pathways that mediate the relationship between SCRD and serious mental illness.

and residual phases (Waters et al., 2011). There are now two comprehensive systematic reviews examining the evidence to date in support of this relationship (Davies, Haddock, Yung, Mulligan, & Kyle, 2016; Reeve, Sheaves, & Freeman, 2015). Furthermore, there is also evidence that there may be a shared genetic and environmental lineage underlying psychotic experiences and SCRD (Taylor, Gregory, Freeman, & Ronald, 2015).

Interestingly, the disturbance observed in the prodromal phase equates to what is observed when the person has transitioned to their first episode of psychosis: extended sleep onset latency, difficulties with sleep continuity, and circadian timing abnormalities (Castro et al., 2015; Zanini et al., 2013). Circadian disruption (lower daily activity, fragmented sleep patterning/desynchronisation from the light–dark cycle) at baseline predicted increased psychotic symptom severity and psychosocial impairment at a 1-year follow-up in a cohort at clinically high-risk for psychosis (when compared to healthy controls; Lunsford-Avery et al., 2017). The authors concluded that circadian rhythm disturbance might signify a potential vulnerability marker for the emergence of psychosis. However, a major limitation of these findings is that the relationships stated are largely reliant on pairwise correlational analyses. Longitudinal research may 1 day show that interventions to stabilise sleep–wake rhythms offer promise in early intervention services. Until then, it behoves psychologists to become proficient in identifying and monitoring SCRD in those most vulnerable to its negative effects.

SPECIFIC SLEEP DISORDERS COMMONLY RECOGNISED WITHIN PSYCHOSIS AND HOW TO ASSESS THEM

Building on the reader's understanding of sleep and circadian rhythms, and how they are impacted in psychosis, the next section describes specifically which sleep disorders most often present in psychosis, their prevalence, and how to assess them, alongside some case studies to help combat differential diagnoses in SCRD. It may be worth repeating that patients with psychosis meet criteria (based on subjective report) for an average 3.3 sleep disorders, highlighting that comorbidity in sleep disturbances is very common in this group.

Insomnia Disorder

DIAGNOSIS

Insomnia has a strong impact on cognition, mood, behaviour, and quality of life.

Insomnia is the most prevalent sleep disorder. An estimated 25% of adults report dissatisfaction with their sleep, and approximately 10%–15% report insomnia symptoms allied with daytime impairment, with 6%–10% meeting the criteria for insomnia disorder (Buysse, 2008). This renders insomnia one of the most common complaints in primary care (Aikens & Rouse, 2005). At a chronic level, the burden of insomnia to the individual is great, with reduced quality of life, cognitive impairments, and an increased risk of accidents occurring at home, work, and while driving, as well as an increased risk of other psychiatric and medical health disorders (Morin & Benca, 2012).

Insomnia is characterised as either the complaint of persistent discontent with subjective quality or duration of sleep, difficulties initiating or maintaining sleep, or the impression that the sleep obtained is nonrestorative. In order to meet the definition of insomnia, these subjective complaints of sleep must coincide with reports of daytime distress or dysfunction and must be present for at least 3 nights per week for a minimum period of 3 months (American Psychiatric Association, 2013). The prevalence of insomnia in psychosis varies depending on the sample. A study by Palmese and colleagues highlighted 44% of outpatients ($n = 175$) receiving treatment for schizophrenia reported scores within the moderate-to-severe clinical range using the Insomnia Severity Index (ISI; Palmese et al., 2011; Morin, Belleville, Bélanger, & Ivers, 2011). Again using the ISI, another study by Freeman, Pugh, Vorontsova, and Southgate (2009) reported the rate to be as high as 54% with a sample of 300 people who reported current persecutory delusions or a clinical diagnosis of schizophrenia (Freeman et al., 2009). The authors also found a further 30% scoring at the subthreshold level for insomnia. More recent papers include a study published in 2018, which reported a 22.6% prevalence rate of clinical insomnia in a sample of people with first-episode psychosis in an Early Intervention Service in Singapore (Subramaniam et al., 2018). Furthermore, in a Chinese population with a diagnosis of schizophrenia, insomnia prevalence was reported to be 28.9%. The authors also reported that only 53.3% of persons who met criteria were receiving treatment, indicating that insomnia is a frequently overlooked problem in schizophrenia (Hou et al., 2017).

Clinicians often do not ask about sleep problems in people with psychosis.

Assessment

Recent diagnostic guidelines for insomnia in DSM-5 permit the diagnosis of insomnia as a primary condition alongside other psychiatric diagnoses (American Psychiatric Association, 2013). This change acknowledges a consensus that insomnia merits treatment in its own right and can be treated concurrently with other diagnoses, including psychotic disorders (American Psychiatric Association, 2013). Insomnia is best assessed by taking a comprehensive sleep history and asking the client to complete a sleep diary for 1–2 weeks (Cunnington, Junge, & Fernando, 2013). Alongside this, certain questionnaires can be helpful in the assessment of insomnia (see Table 11.2).

Assessment Tools

Sleep History A sleep history is essential to understand the nature of premorbid baseline sleep. This is imperative for effective case conceptualisation and formulation and the creation of treatment goals (Cunnington et al., 2013). A clinician must therefore ask what a person's usual sleep routine looked like before the onset of insomnia. From there, it is important to understand how the person's sleep has changed since the onset of insomnia. This comprises asking for the person's description of their current typical sleep pattern over the past week

Table 11.2 An Overview of Commonly Used Sleep Questionnaires for the Assessment of Insomnia and Chronotype in Psychosis

Questionnaire	Description
Insomnia	
The Insomnia Severity Index (ISI)	The ISI is a brief questionnaire devised to measure both the night-time and day-time elements of insomnia. The ISI ranges from 0 to 28, with scores of 10 and above considered optimal for detecting insomnia in community samples (Morin et al., 2011). A score of 15 or above it the clinical cut off for insomnia. It shows good psychometric properties for use in both clients and healthy controls (Backhaus, Junghanns, & Hohagen, 2004; Carpenter & Andrykowski, 1998; Morin et al., 2011)
Pittsburgh Sleep Quality Index (PSQI)	The PSQI measures subjective sleep quality over the previous month, yielding a score ranging from 0 to 21, with higher scores representing poorer quality sleep. The standardised cut-off score for poor sleep quality is 5 (Buysse, Reynolds III, Monk, Berman, & Kupfer, 1989). The PSQI is widely used in both clinical and nonclinical populations and has demonstrated good psychometric properties (Backhaus, Junghanns, Broocks, Riemann, & Hohagen, 2002; Carpenter & Andrykowski, 1998)
Short Form Sleep Condition Indicator (SCI)	The SCI comprises just two items: (1) 'thinking about a typical night in the last month, how many nights a week do you have a problem with your sleep?' and (2) 'thinking about the past month, to what extent has poor sleep troubled you in general?'. Possible responses to the first question are '0–1', '2', '3', '4', and '5–7'; these are scored 4, 3, 2, 1, and 0, respectively. Possible responses to the second question are 'not at all', 'a little', 'somewhat', 'much', and 'very much'; these are also scored 4, 3, 2, 1, and 0, respectively. The scores from these two questions are added to give the SCI score: the lower the score, the more aggressive the insomnia complaint. The SCI has demonstrated good psychometric properties (Espie et al., 2014)
Chronotype	
Morning-Eveningness Questionnaire (MEQ)	The most commonly used assessment of chronotype is the Horne-Östberg Morningness-Eveningness Questionnaire (MEQ; Horne & Ostberg, 1976). The MEQ assesses subjective daily preferences and results in a score along a morningness-eveningness axis, with the lowest score (16) being extreme Eveningness type, and the highest score (86) being extreme Morningness type. These preferences are based on when people prefer to be active or to rest. The MEQ does not differentiate between work days and free days
Munich Chronotype Questionnaire (MCTQ)	The MCTQ contains simple questions about sleep timing, such as bedtime, time to get ready for sleep, sleep latency, time of wake-up, and time to get up (or time in bed after wake-up). These are asked separately for work and free days, and respondents are asked to judge their sleep habits over the last 2 weeks. The questionnaire response produces a time-based variable, the mid-sleep phase on free days (MSF), which correlates well with the period of the circadian clock. The MSF is then corrected for sleep deficits accumulated

Continued

Table 11.2 An Overview of Commonly Used Sleep Questionnaires for the Assessment of Insomnia and Chronotype in Psychosis—cont'd

Questionnaire	Description
	during the work-week (Roenneberg et al., 2007). MSFsc (Mid-Sleep Phase on Free days Corrected for the Sleep Deficit accumulated during the work week) provides a quantitative measure of chronotype as a continuous, time-based variable (Allebrandt & Roenneberg, 2008), with larger values indicating a later mid-sleep point. The continuous distribution of MSFsc, with extreme early and late types on either end, is population specific. The MCTQ-assessed information allows the calculation of 'social jetlag', defined as the discrepancy between social and endogenous time (absolute difference in hours between the uncorrected MSF and mid-sleep on work days; (Wittmann, Dinich, Merrow, & Roenneberg, 2009)

(or a typical recent week if the last week was atypical). As such, a clinician should enquire about the habitual bedtime, time taken to fall asleep, the frequency and duration of awakenings, and at what time they wake up. Furthermore, the clinician should assess any patterns in the insomnia—are there instances or periods where their sleep is restored to baseline? Was there a triggering event or did the symptoms just suddenly appear? Further examining this narrative—was the onset connected with a stressful event or trauma, or the experience of anxiety or depression? How long has the sleep disturbance been present? It is also helpful to examine contributing or exacerbating factors (lifestyle or otherwise) that may influence the sleep disturbance. These include questions about caffeine, exercise, alcohol consumption, shift work, television and/or pets in the room, safety concerns, and nicotine use. Are there any daytime consequences of the poor sleep? These could consist of irritability, low mood, cognitive dysfunction such as memory loss, fatigue, or low energy. Finally, it is important to determine the person's cognitions, beliefs, and worries about sleep—clues for this can often be found in the way they describe their sleep (both the language and emotion). This enquiry can help in more targeted formulations, which may include behavioural and calming techniques to support a more restful sleep (Cunnington et al., 2013).

Sleep Diary and Questionnaires It is common for a person with insomnia to miscalculate the level of sleep disturbance. As such, a 1–2 week sleep diary can be a helpful means of gaining a more accurate insight into their sleep as opposed to just taking an oral account of their sleep history (Cunnington et al., 2013). A sleep diary should include a number of pivotal metrics, including nightly bedtime, sleep onset latency (the amount of time it takes to get to sleep), wakefulness after initial sleep onset (wake after sleep onset, WASO), total sleep time (TST), time spent in bed (TIB), wake up time, and a subjective rating of the quality of sleep, which should reflect an overall assessment of nightly sleep (Carney et al., 2012). From this, sleep efficiency can be calculated (ratio of TST to time in bed × 100%). The consensus sleep diary is an expert consensus

Many people with insomnia misperceive their sleep timing or duration.

standardised sleep diary that is free and widely used in sleep research (Carney et al., 2012). Other metrics not usually in the standardised sleep diary are the use of sleeping medication and caffeine consumption. It is generally thought that a sleep diary of 1–2 weeks is sufficient for the assessment of insomnia (Cunnington et al., 2013).

DIFFERENTIAL DIAGNOSES

As mentioned earlier, sleep is governed by both Processes C and S. Insomnia treatment largely relies on manipulating the homeostatic drive or Process S. It is therefore essential when assessing insomnia in psychosis to be able to examine possible differential diagnoses (as sleep disturbances are notoriously heterogeneous in psychosis; Wulff, Dijk, Middleton, Foster, & Joyce, 2012). This allows the clinician to be certain it is not Process C or other common comorbidities that can appear as an insomnia complaint. Examples of these include depression, anxiety, chronic medical conditions, which can incur sleep disturbance (e.g. chronic pain; Dragioti, Bernfort, Larsson, Gerdle, & Levin, 2018), or other sleep disorders or experiences (e.g. if a person cannot sleep as a result of nightmares or night terrors).

Distinguishing the person's chronotype can be an important factor to verify that Process C is not the primary culprit of the sleep disturbance and therefore helps exclude circadian rhythm disorders. Earlier in the chapter, we discussed the difference between 'owls' and 'larks'. An extreme night 'owl' may well be diagnosed with delayed sleep phase disorder (DSPD), which is a variant of the biological clock that means a person is inclined to go to sleep much later (usually long after midnight). Someone with DSPD will usually sleep well throughout the night if permitted to go to bed late and will awaken much later than those without DSPD. Naturally, this sleep cycle is at odds with regular school and work schedules that can incur sleep disturbances (trying to go to bed earlier but not feeling tired; feeling chronically sleep deprived from a late bedtime but early awakening; Cunnington et al., 2013). DSPD and other circadian disruptions mentioned previously in the chapter (fragmented/non-24-h cycles) require the use of actigraphy (described Section 'Circadian Rhythm Disorders'). It would be unusual to recommend an overnight sleep study or polysomnography (PSG) for diagnosing insomnia, but it is pertinent in diagnosing several adjacent sleep disorders, which can generally present as sleep disturbances (including obstructive sleep apnea, sleep-related movements disorders, parasomnias, or treatment-resistant insomnia; (Cunnington et al., 2013).

Circadian Rhythm Disorders

BACKGROUND

To date, the actual prevalence of circadian disruption still remains elusive in research—yet this really is crucial for the effective conceptualisation, recognition, and treatment of SCRD in schizophrenia (Cosgrave, Wulff, & Gehrman, 2018). This is also why it is essential for clinical psychologists to be aware of and be able to recognise circadian rhythm disturbances and how they differ from a complaint of insomnia. Based on the work by Wulff et al. (2012), half of a small sample of people with psychosis ($n=20$) presented with circadian rhythm abnormalities. Generally, this is when the sleep–wake cycle is misaligned with the environmental light–dark cycle and it can include an advanced or delayed sleep cycle (going to bed very early or late), a non-24-h period (when the sleep–wake cycle is longer or shorter than that of a 24-h period), free-running (when sleep gets progressively later each day, eventually circling the clock; see Box 11.1), and highly irregular/fragmented sleep patterns (when it is difficult to see any discernible pattern in the sleep–wake cycle; (Wulff et al., 2012). The only other psychiatric disorder reported to display such a heterogeneous display of sleep and circadian rhythm phenotypes is bipolar disorder (Bradley et al., 2017; see Box 11.4), which is now considered to lie on the same axis as schizophrenia (Craddock & Owen, 2010).

ASSESSMENT

Actigraphy and sleep diaries can aid in effective diagnoses of circadian rhythm disorders (Morgenthaler et al., 2007). An actigraph is a wrist-worn device that measures wrist movement over a number of days or weeks. This permits more longitudinal assessments of an individual's sleep–wake cycle. These devices are often fitted with light sensors, which provide additional information about the duration and timing of light exposure throughout the day. Often the actigraphy data are examined in conjunction with the sleep diary to gain a more comprehensive picture of the sleep–wake cycle (Cosgrave, Haines, et al., 2018). Similar to a sleep diary, an actigraph can be used to calculate a number of useful sleep metrics, including sleep onset, sleep offset, sleep period (time between sleep onset and sleep offset, including WASO), sleep fragmentation (an index

Actigraphy is a reliable, noninvasive method of monitoring rest and activity.

Box 11.4 Sleep and Circadian Rhythm Disorders in Bipolar Disorder

Goals and methods: A seminal piece of work by Bradley et al. (2017) examined the prevalence (and extent) of sleep and circadian rhythm disruption in bipolar disorder. Forty-six patients with bipolar disorder (BD) and forty-two controls undertook a comprehensive sleep and circadian rhythm assessment with polysomnography, accelerometry, sleep questionnaires, and melatonin level sampling.

Outcomes: The authors found that 50% of the patients with BD had abnormal sleep. 52% of those with sleep disturbances displayed circadian rhythm disturbances (delayed/advanced sleep phase, irregular sleep–wake phase or non-24-h sleep disorder) and 29% had obstructive sleep apnea. They also mentioned considerable overlap between sleep and circadian rhythm phenotypes. This makes bipolar disorder the only other psychiatric disorder (outside schizophrenia) to date to display such heterogeneous and profound SCRD and should therefore be considered when assessing clients with a diagnosis of BD with psychotic features.

derived from the frequency and intensity of physical movement during the sleep period), sleep onset latency (SOL; the amount of time between bedtime and sleep onset), wake after sleep onset (WASO; the amount of time spent above a predefined activity threshold), total sleep time (TST; time between sleep onset and final wake time, excluding WASO), sleep efficiency (% of time in bed spent asleep excluding sleep onset latency), and variability in sleep onset and sleep duration (measured by their standard deviations). An actigraph should help inform all of the sleep patterns described in Fig. 11.3. In the author's experience of recruiting in an early intervention service for psychosis in both England and America, the use of actigraphy and sleep diaries for multiple consecutive nights is well tolerated among people with psychosis (see learning point in Box 11.5). When assessing circadian rhythm disorders, an adequate duration of observation is crucial to discern the true nature of the circadian dysfunction. For instance, a delayed phase can be witnessed using a week of actigraphy, but more complex patterns (free-running, non-24-h rhythms) often require 2–3 weeks for clarity. This is because people will entrain to a normal pattern for 2–3 days but then begin to slip into unusual rhythms or patterns, which they themselves may be unaware of.

The examples in Boxes 11.6 and 11.9 illustrate how accurate assessment of sleep can assist clients and clinicians to gain a full understanding of the type and impact of sleep.

Obstructive Sleep Apnea

BACKGROUND

Obstructive sleep apnea (OSA) is the most prevalent type of sleep apnea whereby the upper airway is either partially or completely blocked by soft tissue found in the back of the throat. This causes epochs of reduced breathing called 'apneas', which usually last around 20–40 s. *OSA* is a very serious sleep disorder but can often go unnoticed by the individual as they are unaware of the difficulty breathing while asleep (American Academy of Sleep Medicine, 2005).

Box 11.5 Administering Actigraphy Watches in Clients With Paranoia or Persecutory Ideas

When administering the actigraph, it may be pertinent to comprehensively examine the presence of any persecutory ideas/paranoid ideation for clients with psychosis. In our clinical experience, it has happened that participants have deconstructed and or tampered with an actigraph watch due to undisclosed paranoia. If you are already aware that a client may be experiencing paranoia or persecutory ideas, it is advisable to give a clear description or information sheet, outlining what the watch can and can't do, which usually results in a high uptake and compliance.

Box 11.6 Hypothetical Client Example: 'James'

Thinking of a hypothetical example—let's imagine 'James' is a 25-year-old male diagnosed with schizophrenia with paranoid features. He is being treated in an early intervention service (in the community) and so this is his first episode. He was referred for having sleeping difficulties and poor concentration. Of note, pinpointing habitual sleep and wake times was incredibly difficult for James (who describes that when he goes to bed he could sleep through the night). This usually precludes a diagnosis of insomnia. However, let's say that James reports high daytime dysfunction due to sleep disturbances. Examples of high daytime dysfunction would be decreased concentration during the day or cognitive impairment, excessive daytime sleepiness (such as falling asleep unintentionally in the appointment or during the day generally), memory loss, poorer quality of life or ability to cope, increased irritability, or even fatigue-related accidents. Let's say James was struggling to stay awake in appointments and had poor short-term memory. This should make a clinician worry about sleep apnea, but we will say in James's case that sleep apnea has been ruled out (with an appropriate assessment of overnight polysomnography).

A psychologist at this point would want to conduct a full sleep history, including when the sleep-related impairments began. Considering James says he sleeps through the night, you would need to consider whether he thought that his sleep was much better than it actually was. Sleep overestimation is reported to be more prevalent in schizophrenia than among people without (Bian et al., 2016). Following that, you would also want to consider sleep timing, especially because in this case James is struggling to give a habitual bedtime—why might that be? Could this be a circadian related concern?

Ideally, James would be asked if he could keep a sleep diary and wear an actigraph to provide further insight. Cases matching these symptoms in the past have been found to display unusual sleep timings, which can be a marker of problems with Process C, and can go unnoticed by the patient.

A case similar to James was found to be able to wear the watch for 10 days and the actigraphy highlighted that they could entrain to a normal sleep routine for 2–3 days, but then would continually delay their bedtime until they were going to bed during the day and sleep during the night. When daytime sleeping, they would feel lonely and isolated and would stay awake all night in order to 'reset the clock'. As they were delaying going to bed so quickly, periodic nights of total sleep deprivation were quite frequent. Combined with a highly variable bedtime, this was considered during case formulation as a likely explanation for the marked daytime dysfunction.

In this scenario, you would also want to refer the client for a more comprehensive sleep assessment in a sleep clinic. While issues with circadian timing (like free-running or non-24 h cycles) or highly irregular and fragmented sleep patterns (this would be suspected to be free-running but is still unclear with only 10 days of actigraphy) could be helped with behavioural treatment, referral to the sleep clinic was warranted for more specialised assessment and treatment (e.g. to rule out the possibility of traumatic brain injury, in differential diagnosis, for example).

A review on OSA in schizophrenia highlighted prevalence rates up to 52%. It is therefore essential that clinical psychologists think about this when examining sleep disturbances in schizophrenia (Myles et al., 2016). A study by Winkelman (2001) including 364 people who were referred to a sleep clinic from a psychiatric inpatient hospital found that those with schizophrenia had higher rates of OSA compared to other psychiatric disorders. It was also reported that when present, OSA was in the severe range (Winkelman, 2001). Risk factors for OSA were being older, male, and having a higher BMI, paralleling risk factors found in the general population. Winkelman (2001) also reported that

Obstructive sleep apnea is common in people with schizophrenia.

antipsychotic use for 6 months prior to hospitalisation both additionally and independently increased the risk for OSA. This could mean that even given the known side effect of decreased metabolic rate in antipsychotics (thus increasing BMI; De Hert, Detraux, van Winkel, Yu, & Correll, 2012), there is an independent, increased risk for OSA in schizophrenia (Boufidis et al., 2003), again reiterating the importance of ruling out OSA as an underlying cause for sleep disturbances in psychosis.

DIAGNOSIS AND ASSESSMENT

Not dissimilar to insomnia, obstructive sleep apnea should include a comprehensive sleep history. The focus should be on specific sleep parameters such as snoring and daytime sleepiness, observed apneas, gasping or shortness of breath (e.g. do you find yourself gasping for air/short of breath while asleep?), choking, sleep fragmentation, an obesity assessment, retrognathia (where the lower jaw sits significantly behind the upper jaw often appearing as severe overbite) or hypertension. Endorsing some of these items should provoke a broader sleep history and a physical examination when necessary (Klingaman, Palmer-Bacon, Bennett, & Rowland, 2015). Objective testing is required to confirm the presence of sleep apnea; this can be done either at home or in-laboratory with full polysomnography or more limited monitoring of respiration and airflow (Epstein et al., 2009). Generally, the presence of OSA is defined as a respiratory disturbance index (apneas or hypopneas) greater than 10 events per hour (Winkelman, 2001). If you suspect a client has sleep apnea, brief screening tools can give an indication of the need for objective testing of OSA. These include the STOP-BANG Sleep Apnea Questionnaire (Chung, Abdullah, & Liao, 2016) or the Berlin Questionnaire for Sleep Apnea (Netzer, Stoohs, Netzer, Clark, & Strohl, 1999) both of which are free online, quick, sensitive, and easy to administer.

Restless Leg Syndrome

Restless leg syndrome is characterised by uncomfortable sensations in the legs, usually accompanied by an overwhelming urge to move or stretch the legs in order to relieve the sensations. Quite often, these experiences are worse in the evening/at night and when at rest especially when lying or sitting (American Academy of Sleep Medicine, 2005).

Restless leg syndrome (RLS) is an important and prevalent comorbidity among people with psychosis. Estimates of prevalence in RLS in psychosis (21.4%) are double the prevalence in the normal population (Kang et al., 2007). RLS is of particular interest in psychosis, as akathisia and RLS can be a side effect of antipsychotics (see Box 11.7). Simple questions about leg discomfort, the need to move or stretch the legs to alleviate this sensation, and discomfort worsening at night or in the evening can give a preliminary indication for RLS.

Box 11.7 Akathisia vs Tardive Dyskinesia

These terms are often used in the context of treatment for psychosis as they are side effects of antipsychotics (also known as neuroleptic drugs). Akathisia is primarily based upon subjective report and is characterised by a desire to be in constant movement, which often means the patient finds it difficult to sit still as they are continually compelled to move. Tardive dyskinesia is the presence of an involuntary movement (or parkinsonism, but not to be confused with Parkinson's disease). It is characterised by repeated purposeless movements—typically involving the lips, tongue, or cheeks, but sometimes also legs or arms (Munetz & Cornes, 1983).

Parasomnias (Nightmares; Sleep Paralysis; Night Terrors)

Parasomnias are a broad group of sleep disorders that are characterised by undesirable motor, sensory, or behavioural experiences that can happen upon entering sleep, during sleep itself, or during an arousal from sleep (American Academy of Sleep Medicine, 2005). Common examples include nightmare disorder, sleep terrors, sleep paralysis (where a person when awakening or falling asleep has consciousness but is unable to move or speak yet may hear, see, or feel things that are not there), sleep walking, and sleep-related eating disorders (Waters, Moretto, & Dang-Vu, 2017). It has been reported that these experiences are considerably elevated in psychosis and can lead to serious dysfunction due to the sleep disruption incurred, the potential risk to self or others (in cases of sleep walking and REM behavioural disorder), and the emotional burden given that several of these experiences (like sleep paralysis or terrors) can be terrifying (Waters et al., 2017). The term parasomnia is broad, so a comprehensive overview in this chapter is not possible. However, the references within the key reading do provide a comprehensive overview.

Parasomnias: a group of sleep disorders linked by abnormal behaviours, emotions, and dreams during sleep.

Parasomnias are reported to be considerably higher in psychosis compared to the 'normal' population. A study by Gangdev, Dua, and Desjardins (2015) found sleep paralysis to be present in 15% of outpatients with a diagnosis of a schizophrenia-spectrum disorder (Gangdev et al., 2015; see example in Box 11.8). This is approximately double that of those without a psychiatric diagnosis (7.6% lifetime prevalence; Ohayon & Guilleminault, 2006). Sleep paralysis can often be neglected in psychosis, as the hypnagogic and hypnopompic hallucinations commonly experienced during the paralysis are often discounted as psychiatric symptoms (Waters et al., 2017; see Box 11.9).

Outside of sleep paralysis, frequent nightmares occur in 9%–55% of people with schizophrenia (Li et al., 2016; Sheaves, Onwumere, Keen, Stahl, & Kuipers, 2015). This can be very important for case conceptualisation and formulation as the treatments for nightmares and insomnia differ substantially. An overview of psychological approaches to treatment of distressing nightmares is provided in Chapter 20 (this volume).

Box 11.8 Hypothetical Client Example: 'Ray'

Again thinking of another hypothetical example—let's imagine 'Ray' is referred for psychological assessment and is recovering from his first episode of psychosis. In this scenario, Ray is presenting with very severe sleep disturbances as a result of sleep paralysis. As a result, Ray was terrified to sleep because of the visions they would get at night (common examples of which may be ghosts or demonic presences in the bedroom). They were nervous to disclose these experiences for fear that the clinical team would readmit them to hospital. This is not uncommon given that hypnogogic and hypnopompic hallucinations are often misinterpreted as psychiatric symptoms and not a byproduct of a sleep disorder.

In a situation like this, Ray should be asked to describe the experiences in the assessment with opening questions like—'do these experiences occur only at night?', 'is it usually around the time that you are falling asleep or waking up?', 'do the things you see influence how you think during the day at all?', 'do they ever appear during the day?', 'do you feel a pressure on your chest while this is happening or is it difficult to move?'. Prefacing the interview as a sleep assessment can be really helpful in these cases in order to destigmatise some of these experiences and help to put the client more at ease to share their experiences freely.

If the client endorses experiences like having difficulty moving in bed when these things happened, as the assessing psychologist you can then explain that this may not be psychosis, but rather, a sleep condition called sleep paralysis. In sleep paralysis, the body is a bit slower to shake off the effects of REM sleep (the stage where a lot of us dream), or doesn't go into full REM straight away. In cases like these, we would also encourage the client that they shouldn't be worried about telling the psychiatrist about them but rather just to be sure to describe them within the context of sleep (and to mention the difficulty moving). In cases similar to Ray, we would also encourage you to discuss this with the psychiatrist directly. Often with parasomnias (like sleep paralysis), it can be helpful to get a referral for a sleep clinic to confirm the presence of parasomnias, which can really help the client feel validated and destigmatised in their experience as well as offering the optimal treatment options.

Box 11.9 Hypnagogia

The term 'hypnagogia' refers to any transitory perceptual experiences that take place during the shift from wake to sleep (hypnagogic hallucinations) and for sleep to wake (hypnopompic hallucinations). They are spontaneous, contain variable emotional content, and are experienced in up to 70% of the population. 86% of hypnagogia are visual (e.g. flashing lights, shapes, geometric patterns but also people and faces, which are often highly detailed and colourful). Auditory experiences are less common (somewhere between 8% and 34% of hypnagogia) and can be voices or other sounds (e.g. phone or doorbell). Hypnagogia can also manifest as somatic experiences (approx. 25%–44%), which can include bodily distortions or the sense of a presence in the room.

Importantly, these are _not_ psychiatric symptoms but instead are related to an intrusion of REM sleep to the wake state. It has been estimated that about 75% of hypnagogia are associated with sleep paralysis, and sleep paralysis itself has a lifetime prevalence of approximately 30%. Sleep paralysis is also very prevalent in narcolepsy; a sleep disorder characterised by excessive sleepiness and sleep attacks (Santomauro & French, 2009; Waters et al., 2016).

CLOSING REMARKS

This chapter was designed to give a broad overview of sleep disturbances and disorders in psychosis, how to recognise and assess them, and how to combat differential diagnoses. Our goal remains to be person-focused when designing case conceptualisations and formulations, which in the context of sleep disturbances requires asking not just about bed time or sleep quality but taking a detailed and holistic account of sleep history to ensure that you have an accurate summary of the problem at hand. Sleep disorders are as far and wide-ranging a disorder category as any other category of disorders in mental health and should be treated as such to ensure optimal outcomes for clients.

QUIZ QUESTIONS

1. Insomnia would be considered a disruption to …
   (a) Process C
   (b) Process S
   (c) The biological clock
2. A client says that they are seeing and hearing things upon awakening and going to sleep, and this is a recent change. As a psychologist, I would think they are:
   (a) Relapsing
   (b) Experiencing hypnagogia
   (c) Both A and B
3. I have a client who says that they cannot get to sleep early and so they stay up until 4 a.m. and play computer games every night. Do I think …
   (a) They have delayed sleep-phase syndrome
   (b) That they have poor sleep hygiene
   (c) I need to examine what their sleep is like without the computer gaming
4. Which of the following are <u>all</u> examples of how sleep and circadian disruption may causally relate to serious mental illness.
   (a) Medication, genetics, and HPA axis dysregulation
   (b) Genetics, HPA axis dysregulation, and emotional dysregulation
   (c) Medication, emotional dysregulation, and genetics

ANSWERS TO QUIZ QUESTIONS:

1. Answer: (b)

   Process S—since insomnia is characterised as a complaint of poor sleep quality. However, there are certain things a client might be doing that are more related to Process C (or the biological clock) but are contributing to the experience of insomnia. Examples might be unusual eating times or exposure to artificial light at different times. This is why, as a psychologist, you should always ask questions that relate to both Processes C and S in a sleep assessment. These include variability in bedtimes, daytime sleeping or napping, chronically late or early bedtimes, meal times, and other every day routines or habits.

2. Answer: (b)

   Seeing and hearing things upon awakening and going to sleep are not in and of themselves symptoms of psychosis: they are examples of hypnagogia, but they do come with considerable distress. However, sudden changes in sleep–wake rhythms are considered important indicators of relapse in psychosis, so you should be cautious if a client suddenly starts experiencing big changes at night. It would be important to determine if these were accompanied by shifts in their daytime thinking, how they attribute these experiences, and if these experiences are happening at any other time outside the sleep period. You also may want to examine the presence of paralysis, any medication changes or changes in drug/alcohol use, which could have precipitated the change.

3. Answer: (c)

   There are a couple of important things here. First, all adolescents go through a delay in their sleep period, which is a normal part of developmental biology. If your client is an adolescent, this could be contributing as to why they find it hard to go to sleep early. However, the problem with computer games is they often have a lot of bright light (our most potent zeitgeber) and are highly arousing. It is therefore hard to know what your client's sleep would be like without these confounding variables (arousal and light) on Processes C and S. You should therefore ask about sleep prior to when they started video gaming. If this is several years ago and they have since come into adolescence, you might want to ask them to stop gaming a couple of hours before bedtime alongside other good sleep hygiene advice to see if that impacts the problem. If it doesn't, they might have DSPD; if it does, it is likely the environment that is delaying their sleep phase.

4. Answer: (b)

   Medication is variable, which influences both sleep and circadian rhythms and mental health, but it is not a fundamental mechanism that links the two things together. However, medication interactions are always something you would want to rule out when examining sleep and circadian disruption in psychosis. The other three examples are mechanisms that could causally link both mental illness and sleep and circadian rhythm disruption together.

KEY READING

Review of mechanisms underpinning the relationship between sleep and circadian rhythms in serious mental illness:

Wulff, K., Gatti, S., Wettstein, J. G., & Foster, R. G. (2010). Sleep and circadian rhythm disruption in psychiatric and neurodegenerative disease. *Nature Reviews Neuroscience, 11*(8), 589.

The original paper investigating sleep and circadian rhythm disruption in schizophrenia:

Wulff, K., Dijk, D. J., Middleton, B., Foster, R. G., & Joyce, E. M. (2012). Sleep and circadian rhythm disruption in schizophrenia. *The British Journal of Psychiatry, 200*(4), 308–316.

Recent research replicating the above paper in bipolar disorder:

Bradley, A. J., Webb-Mitchell, R., Hazu, A., Slater, N., Middleton, B., Gallagher, P., McAllister-Williams, H. & Anderson, K. N. (2017). Sleep and circadian rhythm disturbance in bipolar disorder. *Psychological Medicine, 47*(9), 1678–1689.

A review of parasomnias:

Waters, F., Moretto, U., & Dang-Vu, T. T. (2017). Psychiatric illness and parasomnias: A systematic review. *Current Psychiatry Reports, 19*(7), 37.

A brief review of how to assess sleep in schizophrenia:

Klingaman, E. A., Palmer-Bacon, J., Bennett, M. E., & Rowland, L. M. (2015). Sleep disorders among people with schizophrenia: emerging research. *Current Psychiatry Reports,* 17(10), 79.

A general overview of where the research is to date:

Cosgrave, J., Wulff, K., & Gehrman, P. (2018). Sleep, circadian rhythms, and schizophrenia: where we are and where we need to go. *Current Opinion in Psychiatry, 31*(3), 176–182.

Acknowledgements

The lead author (Jan Cosgrave) is supported by the NIHR Oxford Health Biomedical Research Centre, The Fulbright Commission (Ireland) and the Oxford Health Small Research Committee which support her work into understanding the importance of sleep and circadian rhythms in psychosis.

References

Aikens, J. E., & Rouse, M. E. (2005). Help-seeking for insomnia among adult patients in primary care. *Journal of the American Board of Family Practice, 18*(4), 257–261. https://doi.org/10.3122/jabfm.18.4.257.

Åkerstedt, T., Hume, K., Minors, D., & Waterhouse, J. (1997). Good sleep—Its timing and physiological sleep characteristics. *Journal of Sleep Research, 6*(4), 221–229. https://doi.org/10.1111/j.1365-2869.1997.00221.x.

Allebrandt, K. V., & Roenneberg, T. (2008). The search for circadian clock components in humans: New perspectives for association studies. *Brazilian Journal of Medical and Biological Research, 41*(8), 716–721. https://doi.org/10.1590/S0100-879X2008000800013.

American Academy of Sleep Medicine. (2005). *International classification of sleep disorders. Diagnostic and coding manual*: (pp. 51–55). Rochester, MN: American Academy of Sleep Medicine.

American Psychiatric Association. (2013). *Diagnostic and statistical manual of mental disorders (DSM-5®)*. American Psychiatric Pub.

Archer, S. N., Carpen, J. D., Gibson, M., Lim, G. H., Johnston, J. D., Skene, D. J., et al. (2010). Polymorphism in the PER3 promoter associates with diurnal preference and delayed sleep phase disorder. *Sleep, 33*, 695–701.

Backhaus, J., Junghanns, K., Broocks, A., Riemann, D., & Hohagen, F. (2002). Test–retest reliability and validity of the Pittsburgh Sleep Quality Index in primary insomnia. *Journal of Psychosomatic Research, 53*(3), 737–740. https://doi.org/10.1016/S0022-3999(02)00330-6.

Backhaus, J., Junghanns, K., & Hohagen, F. (2004). Sleep disturbances are correlated with decreased morning awakening salivary cortisol. *Psychoneuroendocrinology, 29*(9), 1184–1191. https://doi.org/10.1016/j.psyneuen.2004.01.010.

Benbadis, S. R. (2006). Introduction to sleep electroencephalography. In *Sleep: A comprehensive handbook*. Wiley.

Bian, Y., Wang, Z. X., Le Han, X., Chen, L., Zhu, Y., & Wu, C. J. (2016). Sleep state misperception in schizophrenia: Are negative symptoms at work? *Comprehensive Psychiatry, 67*, 33–38.

Biss, R. K., & Hasher, L. (2012). Happy as a lark: Morning-type younger and older adults are higher in positive affect. *Emotion, 12*(3), 437–441. https://doi.org/10.1037/a0027071.

Borbély, A. A. (1982). A two process model of sleep regulation. *Human Neurobiology 1*, 195–204.

Boufidis, S., Kosmidis, M. H., Bozikas, V. P., Daskalopoulou-Vlahoyianni, E., Pitsavas, S., & Karavatos, A. (2003). Treatment outcome of obstructive sleep apnea syndrome in a patient with schizophrenia: Case report. *International Journal of Psychiatry in Medicine, 33*(3), 305–310.

Bradley, A. J., Webb-Mitchell, R., Hazu, A., Slater, N., Middleton, B., Gallagher, P., et al. (2017). Sleep and circadian rhythm disturbance in bipolar disorder. *Psychological Medicine, 47*, 1–12.

Buysse, D. J. (2008). Chronic insomnia. *American Journal of Psychiatry 165*, 678–686.

Buysse, D. J., Reynolds, C. F., III, Monk, T. H., Berman, S. R., & Kupfer, D. J. (1989). The Pittsburgh sleep quality index: A new instrument for psychiatric practice and research. *Psychiatry Research, 28*(2), 193–213. https://doi.org/10.1016/0165-1781(89)90047-4.

Carney, C. E., Buysse, D. J., Ancoli-Israel, S., Edinger, J. D., Krystal, A. D., Lichstein, K. L., et al. (2012). The consensus sleep diary: Standardizing prospective sleep self-monitoring. *Sleep, 35*(2), 287. https://doi.org/10.5665/sleep.1642.

Carpenter, J. S., & Andrykowski, M. A. (1998). Psychometric evaluation of the Pittsburgh sleep quality index. *Journal of Psychosomatic Research, 45*(1), 5–13. https://doi.org/10.1016/S0022-3999(97)00298-5.

Castro, J., Zanini, M., Gonçalves, B. D. S. B., Coelho, F. M. S., Bressan, R., Bittencourt, L., et al. (2015). Circadian rest–activity rhythm in individuals at risk for psychosis and bipolar disorder. *Schizophrenia Research, 168*(1–2), 50–55. https://doi.org/10.1016/j.schres.2015.07.024.

Chung, F., Abdullah, H. R., & Liao, P. (2016). STOP-Bang questionnaire: A practical approach to screen for obstructive sleep apnea. *Chest, 149*(3), 631–638.

Clarisse, R., Le Floc'h, N., Kindelberger, C., & Feunteun, P. (2010). Daily rhythmicity of attention in morning vs. evening type adolescents at boarding school under different psychosocial testing conditions. *Chronobiology International, 27*(4), 826–841. https://doi.org/10.3109/07420521003794051.

Cohrs, S. (2008). Sleep disturbances in patients with schizophrenia. *CNS Drugs, 22*(11), 939–962. https://doi.org/10.2165/00023210-200822110-00004.

Cosgrave, J., Haines, R., van Heugten-van der Kloet, D., Purple, R., Porcheret, K., Foster, R., et al. (2018). The interaction between subclinical psychotic experiences, insomnia and objective measures of sleep. *Schizophrenia Research, 193*, 204–208.

Cosgrave, J., Wulff, K., & Gehrman, P. (2018). Sleep, circadian rhythms, and schizophrenia: Where we are and where we need to go. *Current Opinion in Psychiatry, 31*(3), 176–182. https://doi.org/10.1097/YCO.0000000000000419.

Craddock, N., & Owen, M. J. (2010). The Kraepelinian dichotomy–going, going … but still not gone. *British Journal of Psychiatry, 196*(2), 92–95.

Crowley, S. J., Acebo, C., & Carskadon, M. A. (2007). Sleep, circadian rhythms, and delayed phase in adolescence. *Sleep Medicine, 8*(6), 602–612. https://doi.org/10.1016/j.sleep.2006.12.002.

Cunnington, D., Junge, M. F., & Fernando, A. T. (2013). Insomnia: Prevalence, consequences and effective treatment. *Medical Journal of Australia, 199*(8), S36–S40.

Davies, G., Haddock, G., Yung, A. R., Mulligan, L. D., & Kyle, S. D. (2016). A systematic review of the nature and correlates of sleep disturbance in early psychosis. *Sleep Medicine Reviews*. https://doi.org/10.1016/j.smrv.2016.01.001.

De Hert, M., Detraux, J., van Winkel, R., Yu, W., & Correll, C. U. (2012). Metabolic and cardiovascular adverse effects associated with antipsychotic drugs. *Nature Reviews Endocrinology, 8*(2), 114.

Dragioti, E., Bernfort, L., Larsson, B., Gerdle, B., & Levin, L.-Å. (2018). Association of insomnia severity with well-being, quality of life and health care costs: A cross-sectional study in older adults with chronic pain (PainS65+). *European Journal of Pain, 22*(2), 414–425.

Epstein, L. J., Kristo, D., Strollo, P. J., Friedman, N., Malhotra, A., Patil, S. P., et al. (2009). Clinical guideline for the evaluation, management and long-term care of obstructive sleep apnea in adults. *Journal of Clinical Sleep Medicine, 5*(03), 263–276.

Espie, C. A., Kyle, S. D., Hames, P., Gardani, M., Fleming, L., & Cape, J. (2014). The sleep condition indicator: A clinical screening tool to evaluate insomnia disorder. *BMJ Open, 4*(3), e004183. https://doi.org/10.1136/bmjopen-2013-004183.

Foster, R. G., Peirson, S. N., Wulff, K., Winnebeck, E., Vetter, C., & Roenneberg, T. (2013). Sleep and circadian rhythm disruption in social jetlag and mental illness. *Progress in Molecular Biology and Translational Science, 119*, 325–346.

Freedman, M. S., Lucas, R. J., Soni, B., von Schantz, M., Muñoz, M., David-Gray, Z., et al. (1999). Regulation of mammalian circadian behavior by non-rod, non-cone, ocular photoreceptors. *Science, 284*(5413), 502–504. https://doi.org/10.1126/science.284.5413.502.

Freeman, D., Pugh, K., Vorontsova, N., & Southgate, L. (2009). Insomnia and paranoia. *Schizophrenia Research, 108*(1–3), 280–284. https://doi.org/10.1016/j.schres.2008.12.001.

Gangdev, P., Dua, V., & Desjardins, N. (2015). Isolated sleep paralysis and hypnic hallucinations in schizophrenia. *Indian Journal of Psychiatry, 57*(4), 383.

Grandin, L. D., Alloy, L. B., & Abramson, L. Y. (2006). The social zeitgeber theory, circadian rhythms, and mood disorders: Review and evaluation. *Clinical Psychology Review, 26*(6), 679–694. https://doi.org/10.1016/j.cpr.2006.07.001.

Harvey, A. G., Murray, G., Chandler, R. A., & Soehner, A. (2011). Sleep disturbance as transdiagnostic: Consideration of neurobiological mechanisms. *Clinical Psychology Review, 31*(2), 225–235. https://doi.org/10.1016/j.cpr.2010.04.003.

Hobson, J. A. (2009). REM sleep and dreaming: Towards a theory of protoconsciousness. *Nature Reviews. Neuroscience, 10*(11), 803–813. https://doi.org/10.1038/nrn2716.

Hofstetter, J. R., Lysaker, P. H., & Mayeda, A. R. (2005). Quality of sleep in patients with schizophrenia is associated with quality of life and coping. *BMC Psychiatry, 5*(1), 165. https://doi.org/10.1186/1471-244X-5-13.

Horne, J. A., & Ostberg, O. (1976). A self-assessment questionnaire to determine morningness-eveningness in human circadian rhythms. *International Journal of Chronobiology, 4*(2), 97–110.

Hou, C. L., Li, Y., Cai, M. Y., Ma, X. R., Zang, Y., Jia, F. J., et al. (2017). Prevalence of insomnia and clinical and quality of life correlates in Chinese patients with schizophrenia treated in primary care. *Perspectives in Psychiatric Care, 53*(2), 80–86.

Kang, S.-G., Lee, H.-J., Jung, S. W., Cho, S. N., Han, C., Kim, Y.-K., et al. (2007). Characteristics and clinical correlates of restless legs syndrome in schizophrenia. *Progress in Neuro-Psychopharmacology and Biological Psychiatry, 31*(5), 1078–1083.

Klingaman, E. A., Palmer-Bacon, J., Bennett, M. E., & Rowland, L. M. (2015). Sleep disorders among people with schizophrenia: Emerging research. *Current Psychiatry Reports, 17*(10), 79.

Koffel, E., & Watson, D. (2009). Unusual sleep experiences, dissociation, and schizotypy: Evidence for a common domain. *Clinical Psychology Review, 29*(6), 548–559. https://doi.org/10.1016/j.cpr.2009.06.004.

Kraepelin, E. (2007). *Compendium der Psychiatrie: zum Gebrauch für Studierende und Ärzte*. VDM Publishing.

Kupfer, D. J., Wyatt, R. J., Scott, J., & Snyder, F. (1970). Sleep disturbance in acute schizophrenic patients. *American Journal of Psychiatry, 126*(9), 1213–1223. https://doi.org/10.1176/ajp.126.9.1213.

Li, S. X., Lam, S. P., Zhang, J., Yu, M. W. M., Chan, J. W. Y., Chan, C. S. Y., et al. (2016). Sleep disturbances and suicide risk in an 8-year longitudinal study of schizophrenia-spectrum disorders. *Sleep, 39*(6), 1275–1282. https://doi.org/10.5665/sleep.5852.

Lunsford-Avery, J. R., Gonçalves, B. D. S. B., Brietzke, E., Bressan, R. A., Gadelha, A., Auerbach, R. P., et al. (2017). Adolescents at clinical-high risk for psychosis: Circadian rhythm disturbances predict worsened prognosis at 1-year follow-up. *Schizophrenia Research*. https://doi.org/10.1016/j.schres.2017.01.051.

Morgenthaler, T. I., Lee-Chiong, T., Alessi, C., Friedman, L., Aurora, R. N., Boehlecke, B., et al. (2007). Practice parameters for the clinical evaluation and treatment of circadian rhythm sleep disorders. *Sleep: Journal of Sleep and Sleep Disorders Research, 30*(11), 1445–1459.

Morin, C. M., Belleville, G., Bélanger, L., & Ivers, H. (2011). The Insomnia Severity index: Psychometric indicators to detect insomnia cases and evaluate treatment response. *Sleep 34*, 601–608.

Morin, C. M., & Benca, R. (2012). Chronic insomnia. *The Lancet, 379*(9821), 1129–1141. https://doi.org/10.1016/S0140-6736(11)60750-2.

Munetz, M. R., & Cornes, C. L. (1983). Distinguishing akathisia and tardive dyskinesia: A review of the literature. *Journal of Clinical Psychopharmacology, 3*(6), 343–350.

Myles, H., Myles, N., Antic, N. A., Adams, R., Chandratilleke, M., Liu, D., et al. (2016). Obstructive sleep apnea and schizophrenia: A systematic review to inform clinical practice. *Schizophrenia Research, 170*(1), 222–225.

Netzer, N. C., Stoohs, R. A., Netzer, C. M., Clark, K., & Strohl, K. P. (1999). Using the Berlin Questionnaire to identify patients at risk for the sleep apnea syndrome. *Annals of Internal Medicine, 131*(7), 485–491.

Ohayon, M. M., & Guilleminault, C. (2006). Epidemiology of sleep disorders. In *Sleep: A comprehensive handbook* (p. 73). Wiley.

Palmese, L. B., DeGeorge, P. C., Ratliff, J. C., Srihari, V. H., Wexler, B. E., Krystal, A. D., et al. (2011). Insomnia is frequent in schizophrenia and associated with night eating and obesity. *Schizophrenia Research, 133*(1–3), 238–243. https://doi.org/10.1016/j.schres.2011.07.030.

Pompili, M., Lester, D., Grispini, A., Innamorati, M., Calandro, F., Iliceto, P., et al. (2009). Completed suicide in schizophrenia: Evidence from a case-control study. *Psychiatry Research, 167*(3), 251–257. https://doi.org/10.1016/j.psychres.2008.03.018.

Reeve, S., Sheaves, B., & Freeman, D. (2015). The role of sleep dysfunction in the occurrence of delusions and hallucinations: A systematic review. *Clinical Psychology Review, 42*(C), 96–115. https://doi.org/10.1016/j.cpr.2015.09.001.

Reeve, S., Sheaves, B., & Freeman, D. (2018). Sleep disorders in early psychosis: Incidence, severity, and association with clinical symptoms. *Schizophrenia Bulletin 45*, 287–295.

Ritsner, M., Gibel, A., Perelroyzen, G., Kurs, R., Jabarin, M., & Ratner, Y. (2004). Quality of life outcomes of risperidone, olanzapine, and typical antipsychotics among schizophrenia patients treated in routine clinical practice: A naturalistic comparative study. *Journal of Clinical Psychopharmacology, 24*(6), 582–591.

Roenneberg, T., Kuehnle, T., Juda, M., Kantermann, T., Allebrandt, K., Gordijn, M., et al. (2007). Epidemiology of the human circadian clock. *Sleep Medicine Reviews, 11*(6), 429–438. https://doi.org/10.1016/j.smrv.2007.07.005.

Roenneberg, T., Wirz-Justice, A., & Merrow, M. (2003). Life between clocks: Daily temporal patterns of human chronotypes. *Journal of Biological Rhythms, 18*(1), 80–90. https://doi.org/10.1177/0748730402239679.

Santomauro, J., & French, C. C. (2009). Terror in the night. *The Psychologist 22*, 672–675.

Sheaves, B., Onwumere, J., Keen, N., Stahl, D., & Kuipers, E. (2015). Nightmares in patients with psychosis: The relation with sleep, psychotic, affective, and cognitive symptoms. *Canadian Journal of Psychiatry. Revue Canadienne de Psychiatrie, 60*(8), 354–361.

Smith, M. T., Perlis, M. L., Smith, M. S., Giles, D. E., & Carmody, T. P. (2000). Sleep quality and presleep arousal in chronic pain. *Journal of Behavioral Medicine, 23*(1), 1–13. https://doi.org/10.1023/A:1005444719169.

Subramaniam, M., Abdin, E., Shahwan, S., Satghare, P., Vaingankar, J. A., Rama Sendren, J., et al. (2018). Prevalence, correlates and outcomes of insomnia in patients with first episode psychosis from a tertiary psychiatric institution in Singapore. *General Hospital Psychiatry, 51*, 15–21.

Takahashi, J. S., Hong, H.-K., Ko, C. H., & McDearmon, E. L. (2008). The genetics of mammalian circadian order and disorder: Implications for physiology and disease. *Nature Reviews Genetics, 9*(10), 764–775. https://doi.org/10.1038/nrg2430.

Taylor, M. J., Gregory, A. M., Freeman, D., & Ronald, A. (2015). Do sleep disturbances and psychotic-like experiences in adolescence share genetic and environmental influences? *Journal of Abnormal Psychology, 124*(3), 674–684. https://doi.org/10.1037/abn0000057.

Walker, M. P. (2009). The role of sleep in cognition and emotion. *Annals of the New York Academy of Sciences, 1156*(1), 168–197. https://doi.org/10.1111/j.1749-6632.2009.04416.x.

Waters, F., Blom, J. D., Dang-Vu, T. T., Cheyne, A. J., Alderson-Day, B., Woodruff, P., et al. (2016). What is the link between hallucinations, dreams, and hypnagogic–hypnopompic experiences? *Schizophrenia Bulletin, 42*(5), 1098–1109.

Waters, F., & Manoach, D. S. (2012). Sleep dysfunctions in schizophrenia: A practical review. *Open Journal of Psychiatry, 2012*(04), 384–392. https://doi.org/10.4236/ojpsych.2012.224054.

Waters, F., Moretto, U., & Dang-Vu, T. T. (2017). Psychiatric illness and parasomnias: A systematic review. *Current Psychiatry Reports, 19*(7), 37.

Waters, F., Sinclair, C., Rock, D., Jablensky, A., Foster, R. G., & Wulff, K. (2011). Daily variations in sleep–wake patterns and severity of psychopathology: A pilot study in community-dwelling individuals with chronic schizophrenia. *Psychiatry Research, 187*(1–2), 304–306. https://doi.org/10.1016/j.psychres.2011.01.006.

Winkelman, J. W. (2001). Schizophrenia, obesity, and obstructive sleep apnea. *Journal of Clinical Psychiatry, 62*(1), 8–11.

Wirz-Justice, A. (2006). Biological rhythm disturbances in mood disorders. *International Clinical Psychopharmacology, 21*(Supplement 1), S11–S15. https://doi.org/10.1097/01.yic.0000195660.37267.cf.

Wirz-Justice, A., Haug, H.-J., & Cajochen, C. (2001). Disturbed circadian rest-activity cycles in schizophrenia patients: An effect of drugs? *Schizophrenia Bulletin, 27*(3), 497–502. https://doi.org/10.1093/oxfordjournals.schbul.a006890.

Wittmann, M., Dinich, J., Merrow, M., & Roenneberg, T. (2009). Social jetlag: Misalignment of biological and social time. *Chronobiology International, 23*(1–2), 497–509. https://doi.org/10.1080/07420520500545979.

Wright, K. P., Hughes, R. J., Kronauer, R. E., Dijk, D. J., & Czeisler, C. A. (2001). Intrinsic near-24-h pacemaker period determines limits of circadian entrainment to a weak synchronizer in humans. *Proceedings of the National Academy of Sciences, 98*(24), 14027–14032.

Wulff, K., Dijk, D. J., Middleton, B., Foster, R. G., & Joyce, E. M. (2012). Sleep and circadian rhythm disruption in schizophrenia. *British Journal of Psychiatry, 200*(4), 308–316. https://doi.org/10.1192/bjp.bp.111.096321.

Wulff, K., Gatti, S., Wettstein, J. G., & Foster, R. G. (2010). Sleep and circadian rhythm disruption in psychiatric and neurodegenerative disease. *Nature Reviews. Neuroscience, 11*(8), 589–599. https://doi.org/10.1038/nrn2868.

Yung, A. R., & McGorry, P. D. (1997). Is pre-psychotic intervention realistic in schizophrenia and related disorders? *Australian and New Zealand Journal of Psychiatry, 31*(6), 799–805. https://doi.org/10.3109/00048679709065502.

Zanini, M., Castro, J., Coelho, F. M., Bittencourt, L., Bressan, R. A., Tufik, S., et al. (2013). Do sleep abnormalities and misaligned sleep/circadian rhythm patterns represent early clinical characteristics for developing psychosis in high risk populations? *Neuroscience and Biobehavioral Reviews, 37*(10), 2631–2637. https://doi.org/10.1016/j.neubiorev.2013.08.012.

Definition of Key Terms

Advanced sleep phase A variant of the biological clock that means a person is inclined to go to sleep much earlier. This is much rarer than delayed sleep phase disorder (DSPD).

Circadian rhythms Comes from the Latin 'circa' and 'diem' meaning about a day. This refers to any biological rhythm that repeats itself every ~24 h. The focus of this chapter is the sleep–wake cycle.

Delayed sleep phase A variant of the biological clock that means a person is inclined to go to sleep much later (usually long after midnight). This can be transitory or can form a sleep disorder called delayed sleep-phase disorder (DSPD).

Entrainment This refers to the process of a person responding to the external cues (or zeitgebers) given to the clock. The vast majority of people are considered 'entrained'. However, if your clock wasn't responding to those cues (e.g. in blind people who may not perceive light), you would most likely be 'free-running', i.e. the clock is running on its own time and not taking into account your environment (light-dark cycle, meal times, exercise, etc.)

Free running Refers to the biological clock's rhythmicity in the absence of any external time cues (like light). As most people have a period of just over 24 h, free running usually presents as a progressive delay in someone's sleep period.

Hypnagogia This term is refers to any transitory perceptual experiences that take place during the shift from wake to sleep (hypnagogic hallucinations) and for sleep to wake (hypnopompic hallucinations).

Insomnia The most common sleep disorder. Insomnia is characterised as either the complaint of persistent discontent with subjective quality or duration of sleep, difficulties initiating or maintaining sleep, or the impression that the sleep obtained is nonrestorative.

Obstructive sleep apnea Obstructive sleep apnea (OSA) is the most prevalent type of sleep apnea whereby the upper airway is either partially or completely blocked by soft tissue found in the back of the throat. This causes epochs of reduced breathing called 'apneas', which usually last around 20–40 s.

Parasomnia Parasomnias are a broad group of sleep disorders that are characterised by undesirable motor, sensory, or behavioural that can happen upon entering sleep, during sleep itself, or during an arousal from sleep. Common examples include nightmare disorder, sleep terrors, sleep paralysis, sleep walking, and sleep-related eating disorders.

Phenotype When describing the origins of behaviour, you have both genotypes and phenotypes. A genotype is the set of genes responsible for a specific trait. Conversely, a phenotype is the expression of the trait, which can be the person's (or organism's) appearance, development, or behaviour.

Restless leg syndrome A sleep disorder characterised by uncomfortable sensations in the legs, which is usually accompanied by an overwhelming urge to move or stretch the legs in order to relieve the sensations.

Social jet lag Refers to the misalignment of sleep–wake timing as a result of social exploits. Usually this manifests as going to and getting out of bed much later on the weekend (a form of jet lag in and of itself).

Suprachiasmatic nucleus A small part of the brain, which is most commonly known as the 'biological', or 'master' clock, which is responsible for the generation of biological rhythms in humans (and many other species).

Zeitgeber Refers to any signal that the biological clock uses for entrainment. These can be photic (i.e. light) or nonphotic (e.g. meal times, exercise, alarm clocks).

CHAPTER 12

Benefits, Assessment, and Preferences of Physical Activity in Psychosis

Shuichi Suetani*,†,‡, Joseph Firth§,¶,‖

*Metro South Mental Health and Addiction Services, Brisbane, QLD, Australia, †Queensland Centre for Mental Health Research, The Park Centre for Mental Health, Wacol, QLD, Australia, ‡Queensland Brain Institute, The University of Queensland, St Lucia, QLD, Australia, §NICM Health Research Institute, University of Western Sydney, Sydney, NSW, Australia, ¶Division of Psychology and Mental Health, University of Manchester, Manchester, United Kingdom, ‖Centre for Youth Mental Health, University of Melbourne, Melbourne, VIC, Australia

Key Learning Objectives

- To understand how physical inactivity may contribute towards the physical health inequalities in people with psychosis
- To appreciate both the benefits and barriers towards increasing physical activity in people with psychosis
- To gain insight into the development and evaluation of physical activity interventions for people with psychosis

INTRODUCTION

It has been estimated that people with psychosis lose approximately 15 years of potential life to the illness (Hjorthoj, Sturup, McGrath, & Nordentoft, 2017). The majority of this reduced life expectancy is due to preventable cardio-metabolic diseases such as ischaemic heart disease and diabetes mellitus (Olfson, Gerhard, Huang, Crystal, & Stroup, 2015). Cardio-metabolic risk status for people with psychosis has been well described in the Survey of High Impact Psychosis, or the SHIP, study from Australia. With data from over 1800 people living with psychosis, the Survey of High Impact Psychosis study found that: (i) three-quarters of participants were either overweight or obese with more than 80% having central abdominal obesity, (ii) two-thirds of participants were

A Clinical Introduction to Psychosis. https://doi.org/10.1016/B978-0-12-815012-2.00012-2

Box 12.1 Metabolic Syndrome

The metabolic syndrome is a cluster of risk factors comprising:

- **Elevated waist circumference:** Cut-offs vary by gender and ethnicity
- **Elevated triglyceride concentration** *(or drug treatment for elevated triglycerides)*: ≥1.7 mmol/L
- **Reduced high-density lipid concentration** *(or drug treatment for reduced HDL-C)*: <1.0 mmol/L in men, <1.3 mmol/L in women
- **Elevated blood pressure** *(or drug treatment for hypertension)*: ≥130 systolic or ≥85 diastolic
- **Elevated fasting glucose concentration** *(or drug treatment for elevated glucose)*: >5.5 mmol/L

Prior to 2009, there was considerable controversy about the many definitions of metabolic syndrome. Following a meeting of several major national and international organisations, a joint statement was released in an attempt to provide unifying criteria. Based on this attempt to harmonise existing definitions, the presence of three or more of the risk factors is now considered diagnostic of the metabolic syndrome (Alberti et al., 2009). The metabolic syndrome is considered indicative of increased risk of cardiovascular diseases, and associated elevation in mortality rate, but remains an active area of debate.

current cigarette smokers, and (iii) more than half the people in the study met the criteria for metabolic syndrome (see Box 12.1; Galletly et al., 2012). There is now a general acknowledgment among professionals involved in the care of people with psychosis regarding the importance of physical health and associated lifestyle modifications (Suetani, Scott, & McGrath, 2017). In particular, physical activity is increasingly recognised as a safe, cost-effective, and efficacious intervention to reduce cardio-metabolic risk factors in this vulnerable patient cohort (Suetani, Rosenbaum, Scott, Curtis, & Ward, 2016; Vancampfort et al., 2010).

The main challenge we now face in the field is translating the efficacy of physical activity interventions seen in research into effectiveness among our patients in everyday clinical practice (Bartels, 2015; Lederman et al., 2017). To understand physical activity better, we need to know how good it is, how we can measure it, and how we can implement it among our patients. Accordingly, we have divided this chapter into three main sections. In the first section, we briefly describe the magnitude of the benefit of physical activity in people living with psychosis. In the second section, we outline what we know about motivation factors and preferences for physical activity in people with psychosis. Finally, in the third section, we describe physical activity can be measured and assessed, and strengths and limitations of various physical activity measurement tools.

BENEFITS OF PHYSICAL ACTIVITY FOR PEOPLE LIVING WITH PSYCHOSIS

Physical activity is most commonly defined as 'any bodily movement produced by skeletal muscles that results in energy expenditure'. (Caspersen, Powell, &

Christenson, 1985). Physical activity can be either structured (e.g. *exercise*) or incidental (e.g. occupational and transport related).

Exercise is a subtype of physical activity that is planned, repetitive, and structured, and has a specific intention of improving or maintaining fitness.

In the general population, there is a large body of evidence to indicate beneficial effects of physical activity in reducing mortality (Leitzmann et al., 2007), particularly by its effect on reducing the magnitude of cardio-metabolic morbidities (Lee et al., 2012). Even though the World Health Organisation recommends at least 150 min of moderate-intensity aerobic physical activity per week for adults aged 18–64 to improve cardiorespiratory fitness and reduce risks of chronic physical conditions and depression, the evidence is accumulating that *any* physical activity is better than *no* physical activity (see Box 12.2). For example, a very large study ($n=661{,}137$) that examined combined data from six population-based cohorts from the United States and Europe demonstrated a comparable benefit of physical activity in those who met, or exceeded the recommended physical activity level. Of note, even those who did not meet the recommended physical activity level showed a lesser yet statistically significant reduction in mortality with a hazard ratio of 0.80 with 95% confidence interval of 0.78 and 0.82 compared to those who engaged in no physical activity at all (Arem et al., 2015) (see Box 12.3, for a reminder on how hazard ratios are calculated). In addition, a large ($n=204{,}542$) Australian prospective study (Gebel et al., 2015) with a mean follow up of 6.5 years also showed the beneficial effect of physical activity, even at the level *below* the recommended amount (hazard ratio = 0.66: 95% confidence interval: 0.61–0.71) compared to those who engaged in no physical activity at all. The magnitudes of benefits were, however, larger for those who met or exceeded the recommendation, especially those who engaged in vigorous physical activity.

Box 12.2 Intensity of Physical Activity

The intensity of physical activity can be expressed in terms of

Metabolic Equivalent of Task, or, **MET**.

One MET is defined as the energy cost of sitting at rest, and equivalent to a caloric consumption of 1 kcal/kg/h. It is estimated that compared with sitting quietly, a person's caloric consumption is three to six times higher when engaged in moderate physical activity (3–5.9 METs) and six times or higher when engaged in vigorous physical activity (>6 METs) (WHO, 2010).

Box 12.3 Hazard Ratios

A hazard ratio is an estimate of the ratio of the hazard rates (e.g. mortality rates) between one group (e.g. those who met the physical activity recommendation) and comparison group/s (e.g. those who did not) over the entire study duration.

The **hazard rate** is the rate of participants experiencing the event of interest (e.g. death) over a shorter time interval within each of the groups examined in the study.

Furthermore, a recent study consisting of 63,591 older adults (mean age of 58.6) demonstrated that compared with the inactive participants, the hazard ratio for all-cause mortality was 0.70 (95% confidence interval, 0.60–0.82) in what they called the 'weekend warrior' participants—that is, those reporting more than 150 min in moderate-intensity or 75 min in vigorous-intensity activities from one or two sessions per week. This benefit was comparable to those who were engaged in regular physical activity over the week (hazard ratio = 0.65: 95% confidence interval, 0.58–0.73). Once again, even those who did not meet the recommended amount demonstrated comparable benefit (hazard ratio = 0.66: 95% confidence interval, 0.62–0.72) from physical activity (O'Donovan, Lee, Hamer, & Stamatakis, 2017). Even though these studies were limited by the use of subjective measures (i.e. self-report questionnaires) to assess physical activity levels, the consistency of the findings indicates the robustness of the evidence.

Many people with psychotic disorders are missing out on the well-known benefits gained from physical activity.

Among people living with psychosis, the Survey of High Impact Psychosis study in Australia estimated that nearly 50% of people with psychosis were engaged in insufficient level of physical activity (Suetani, Waterreus, et al., 2016). Likewise, in a cohort of 450 community patients with psychosis in the United Kingdom, 44% were engaged in insufficient levels of physical activity (Gardner-Sood et al., 2015). Further, a meta-analysis consisting of 35 studies with 3453 people estimated that people with psychosis engaged in 80.4 min of light-intensity physical activity, 16.2 min of moderate-intensity physical activity, and only 1.1 min of vigorous-intensity physical activity per day, with over 40% of them not meeting the recommended 150 min of moderate physical activity per week (Stubbs et al., 2016). The same review found that in comparison to the general population, people with psychosis engaged in significantly less moderate-intensity physical activity (14.2 min less per day) and vigorous-intensity physical activity (3.4 min less per day). It is important to note, however, these studies were limited by relying on self-reported physical activity engagement using different questionnaires. As discussed later in the chapter, the way physical activity engagements are measured in population studies remains a major weakness of the current evidence base in this field.

There is a growing research evidence base for the benefits of physical activity for cardiovascular functioning in people with schizophrenia. Using data from 20 studies with 695 participants, a systematic review by Firth, Cotter, Elliott, French, and Yung (2015) found that even though physical activity interventions had no significant effect on body mass index, or, BMI (see Box 12.4), they led to improvement in measures of physical fitness, as well as reducing both positive and negative symptoms of schizophrenia. The study also found that the benefits of physical activity were prominent in those who were engaged in around 90 min or more per week of moderate/vigorous physical activity.

Furthermore, several systematic reviews have demonstrated a wide range of benefits of physical activity interventions for people with psychosis beyond cardiovascular functioning. Dauwan, Begemann, Heringa, and Sommer (2016) examined 29 studies consisting of 1109 individuals to find that physical activity interventions can improve quality of life in addition to clinical symptoms of

Box 12.4 Body Mass Index

Body mass index (BMI) is a commonly used indicator of anthropometric height to weight characteristics in adults. It allows individuals to be categorised into different groups according to their nutritional status. The body mass index is calculated as an individual's weight in kilograms divided by the square of the individual's height in metres (kg/m^2). The body mass index is categorised as follows:

- Less than 18.5 kg/m^2: underweight
- Between 18.5 and 24.9 kg/m^2: normal weight
- Between 25.0 and 29.9 kg/m^2: overweight
- More than 30.0 kg/m^2: obese

schizophrenia. This review utilised Hedges' g to estimate effect sizes of included studies. Physical activity interventions had significant benefit on quality of life (Hedges' $g=0.55$: 95% confidence interval, 0.35–0.76), the effect size comparable to the benefits seen in clinical symptoms total psychiatric symptoms (Hedges' $g=0.39$: 95% confidence interval, 0.19–0.58), positive symptoms (Hedges' $g=0.49$: 95% confidence interval, 0.14–0.50), negative symptoms (Hedges' $g=0.49$: 95% confidence interval, 0.31–0.67), and depression (Hedges' $g=0.71$: 95% confidence interval, 0.33–1.09). This review also examined cognition in four subdomains (working memory, long-term memory, processing speed, and attention and executive functioning) to find no significant benefit of physical activity interventions on cognitive function. In contrast, another systematic review by Firth, Stubbs, Rosenbaum, et al. (2017) specifically examined effects of physical activity interventions on cognitive functioning. Using ten studies consisting of 385 participants with schizophrenia, the review found that physical activity interventions significantly improved global cognition (Hedges' $g=0.33$: 95% confidence interval, 0.13–0.53), as well the subdomains of working memory, social cognition, and attention/vigilance but no benefit was found in processing speed, verbal memory, visual memory, and reasoning and problem solving.

Hedges' *g* estimates the effect size for the difference between means of two distinct samples. As a rough rule, Hedges' *g* of 0.2, 0.5, and 0.8 represent small, medium, and large effect, respectively.

Another systematic review explored the impact of physical activity on brain volume (Firth, Cotter, Carney, & Yung, 2017). The authors identified five studies that examined the relationship between physical activity engagement and brain volume in people with schizophrenia. All five studies examined hippocampus volume; two studies reporting increase in hippocampus volume while three found no change. Two of the three studies that found no change in hippocampus volume demonstrated increases in volumes of other regions of the brain (left anterior lobe in one and total cerebral volume in another). In addition, the only one study that found no association between physical activity and brain volumes was limited by its very small sample number (only five participants in the study). Combined with the existing evidence indicating positive association between physical activity and increased brain volumes in other populations, the review proposed that simulation of neurogenesis may be one of the pro-cognitive mechanisms of physical activity in people with schizophrenia (Firth, Cotter, et al., 2017).

Cardiorespiratory fitness is the ability of the circulatory, respiratory, and muscular systems to supply oxygen during sustained physical activity.

Related to physical activity, a similar yet distinct concept of cardiorespiratory fitness is gaining much interest currently. Cardiorespiratory function is defined as the ability of the circulatory, respiratory, and muscular systems to supply oxygen during sustained physical activity (Caspersen et al., 1985). People with psychosis have significantly reduced cardiorespiratory function compared to the general population, and physical activity interventions with higher intensity or frequency are associated with greater improvement in cardiorespiratory function (Vancampfort, Rosenbaum, et al., 2017). These findings suggest that cardiorespiratory function in people with psychosis may be independently associated with the increased cardiovascular mortality rate, thus making it another potential treatment target. Another important measure of fitness that is related to cardiorespiratory fitness is muscular strength. Reduced muscular strength is associated with increased mortality rate in the general population (Leong et al., 2015; Ortega, Silventoinen, Tynelius, & Rasmussen, 2012). Maximal isometric handgrip is an easy-to-measure proxy assessment of muscular strength in clinical settings (Firth et al., 2018). While there have been few studies that explored the clinical implication of handgrip strength in people with psychosis, a recent large cross-sectional study found that maximal isometric handgrip strength was associated with visual memory and reaction time, but not prospective memory, number memory, or reasoning, in people with schizophrenia (Firth et al., 2018). Thus, there is a growing interest in how this brief assessment can be incorporated into future research and clinical practice for people with psychosis.

However, the research to date has only established these relationships in older adults, and the generalisability to other populations is unknown. In particular, there is an absence of research examining the relationships between muscular strength and health outcomes in psychiatric populations.

Over the last several years, a few notable intervention studies have explored the efficacy of physical activity treatment in people with severe mental disorders. The Achieving Healthy Lifestyles in Psychiatric Rehabilitation (ACHIEVE) trial was a randomised control study of 18 months' duration. The study consisted of 291 overweight/obese participants with severe mental disorders with more than half (58%) of participants having a diagnosis of schizophrenia (Daumit et al., 2013). The intervention group received both individual and group physical activity and nutritional counselling, as well as on-site physical activity sessions. The control group received standard nutrition and physical activity information at baseline with general health classes offered quarterly. At the completion of the study, the mean weight loss for the intervention group was 3.4 kg compared to 0.3 kg in the control group. Similarly, 37.8% of people in the intervention group lost 5% or more of their initial weight, compared to 22.7% in the control group ($P=0.009$). Another randomised controlled trial from the United States, the STRIDE trial, included 200 participants with severe mental disorders with an initial body mass index of over 27 (i.e. in the overweight range) (Green et al., 2015). Almost all, 98%, of the participants had a diagnosis of either schizophrenia or affective psychosis/bipolar disorder. The intervention in the STRIDE trial consisted of two 6-month phases. The first 6 months—or the active phase—consisted of two 1-h group meetings covering topics, including nutrition, physical activity, and lifestyle changes as well as a 20-min physical activity session. The participants then moved on to the maintenance phase for another 6 months. During this second phase, or the maintenance phase, participants engaged in monthly group meetings and individual monthly contacts from intervention group facilitators. At the completion of the active phase, participants in the intervention group lost an average of 4.4 kg more than those in the control group. At the completion of the maintenance phase, those in the intervention group lost an average of 2.6 kg more than those in the control group. Additionally, the intervention group also had a significant decline in their fasting glucose level, while those in the control group did not. It is important to acknowledge, however, that most of the weight loss in the intervention group occurred in the first six months. There was no statistically significant difference in the weight loss between the groups in the maintenance phase. Finally, the In SHAPE study compared the In SHAPE fitness program with a free fitness club membership and education (which acted as control) (Bartels et al., 2013). The study included 133 participants with severe mental disorders with a body mass index greater than 25, with just over 40% of the participants having a diagnosis of schizophrenia. People in the intervention group received weekly supervised training session at a gym with a qualified fitness trainer. After 12 months, 40% of the participants in the intervention group achieved a clinically meaningful improvement in fitness as defined by an improvement of more than 50 m in the 6-min walk test—twice that of the control group (20%). There was, however, no significant difference between the groups in terms of clinically meaningful weight loss (weight loss of more than 5% of the initial weight). When the study was replicated at a larger scale ($n=200$) a couple of years later, 51% of the participants in the intervention group achieved clinically meaningful improvement in either fitness or weight loss, compared to only 38% in the control group (Bartels et al., 2015). Furthermore, the benefit appeared to be sustained 6 months after the completion of the study, with 48% of people in intervention group still maintaining the improvement. More recently, the same group was able to further implement the In SHAPE intervention in multiple community mental health centres within a naturalistic setting (Bartels et al., 2018).

Outside of the United States, the Keeping the Body in Mind (KBIM) Program in Sydney, Australia, provides a pragmatic example of how lifestyle interventions with an emphasis on physical activity can be integrated within a public mental health service setting. KBIM began with the implementation of routine metabolic screening in a first-episode psychosis service, gradually evolving over a number of years to incorporate a range of interventions to reduce the cardio-metabolic risk profile of people with psychosis. Located within a public community mental health centre, an in-house gym was built with an exercise physiologist working one-on-one with patients to prescribe and supervise individualised exercise programs. This led to a multidisciplinary KBIM mental health team consisting of a senior nurse, a dietician, an exercise physiologist, and a peer-support worker, with medical input from both psychiatrists and an endocrinologist. An evaluation of the KBIM program showed that those who engaged in the KBIM intervention (a 12-week program of individual sessions with members of the KBIM team and the opportunity to participate in weekly sports groups) experienced significantly less weight gain (1.8 kg) compared to those in the standard care group (who gained an average of 7.8 kg) (Curtis et al., 2016).

In sum, the current body of research evidence indicates that physical activity interventions are feasible in clinical practice, and can greatly improve both psychiatric symptoms and physical parameters in people living with psychosis.

INFLUENCING FACTORS AND PREFERENCES OF PHYSICAL ACTIVITY IN PEOPLE LIVING WITH PSYCHOSIS

To enable translation of the efficacy demonstrated in experimental studies into effectiveness in clinical practice, recognising and addressing factors influencing physical activity, and patient preferences of physical activity engagement, are critical (see Box 12.5, for a lived experience perspective).

A comprehensive systematic review (Vancampfort et al., 2012) found factors such as the presence of negative symptoms, and cardio-metabolic comorbidities such as metabolic syndrome and obesity to be strongly associated with low physical activity status in people with psychosis. To a lesser degree, factors such as medication side effects, lack of knowledge regarding cardio-metabolic risk profile, low self-efficacy and physical self-perception, unhealthy eating habits, and social isolation were also found to be associated with low physical activity status. Further, using the data from the Survey of High Impact Psychosis study, Suetani, Waterreus, et al. (2016) found that factors such as older age, employment/

Box 12.5 A Lived Experience Perspective

'Miguel's' experience (described in Noordsy, Burgess, Hardy, Yudofsky, & Ballon, 2018)

Miguel had been actively involved in team sports whilst at school. He experienced signs of early psychosis, at age 16, and initial treatment led to weight gain and lethargy. Following further evaluation at an early psychosis program, Miguel was given a diagnosis of schizophreniform disorder.

Miguel's initial treatment plan included regular physical exercise (alongside cognitive-behavioural therapy for psychosis and medication) which he enjoyed, and led to improvements in mood, relaxation, and symptoms. Importantly, Noordsy and colleagues note that 'Both the patient and his family agreed that he felt his best during exercise, and his family committed to support him in regular participation' (Noordsy et al., 2018, p. 209).

educational nonparticipation, and loneliness were associated with low physical activity status in people with psychosis. Having a better understanding of these correlates will assist us in understanding the underlying mechanisms behind physical activity as a behaviour and help us optimise the physical activity treatment implementation. For example, the findings from these studies suggest that people with psychosis who are older, heavier, and have less social support may be particularly vulnerable to having lower physical activity status, and thus need to be specifically targeted for physical activity interventions.

Another systematic review demonstrated that, much like the general population, many people with psychosis considered things like weight loss, improved mood, and reduced stress as major motivating factors to engage in physical activity (Firth et al., 2016). At the same time, related factors such as low mood and high level of stress, as well as lack of social support, were seen as major barriers to physical activity engagement by people with psychosis. Further, a systematic review and meta-analysis that included data from 19 randomised controlled trials consisting of 594 individuals with psychosis found that those that were supervised by qualified physical activity professionals had statistically significantly reduced dropout rates from the studies (Vancampfort et al., 2016).

Factors motivating engagement in physical activity vary between individuals, and may include stress reduction, mood regulation, and weight loss.

In an Australian study examining physical activity preferences among 142 community dwelling participants with mental illness (with 45% reporting psychotic disorders), Chapman et al. found that walking was the most preferred type of physical activity (83%). Most participants reported that they preferred activities that are done close to home (84%) and are part of a healthy lifestyle program (76%), with the most preferred source of support being exercise instructor guiding them through each exercise session (71%) (Chapman, Fraser, Brown, & Burton, 2016). Likewise, another cross-sectional study from England examined 120 participants with mental illness (43.3% diagnosed with psychotic disorders) to find that the majority of participants (90%) preferred exercising at home, with walking being the most preferred type of exercise (70%). Despite their preference for exercising at home, less than half (48%) of participants reported that they would exercise more at home compared to at the gym, and more than half (58%) reported that having an instructor would help increase their exercise level (Ussher, Stanbury, Cheeseman, & Faulkner, 2007). More recently, a study conducted in Canada (Subramaniapillai et al., 2016) explored physical activity preference of 173 people with diagnoses of schizophrenia (65.3%) or bipolar disorder (34.7%). They found that participants preferred outdoors (52.0%) or gym (48.6%) over home (37.0%), and moderate intensity physical activity (61.3%) over high (27.7%) or low (22.5%) intensity. The most preferred type of activity was walking (59.5%). Of note, a majority (67.6%) wanted to incorporate strength or resistance training to their physical activity routines. Combined together, the current limited evidence suggest that walking is the most preferred type of physical activity among people with mental illness, and having an exercise instructor was also commonly considered to be beneficial. This is, however, an area that needs further exploration, particularly among those with psychotic disorders specifically.

Considering motivations and preferences for physical activity will assist when developing a case formulation with your clients.

In their overview, Lederman et al. (2017) examined potentially useful strategies in achieving sustainable physical activity intervention implementation based on some successful examples in Australia. They identified that most successful physical activity interventions for people with psychosis included components such as an early intervention approach, including prevention when possible, routine metabolic monitoring, multidisciplinary team approach including patient and carer involvement, the use of behavioural change strategies, as well as programs being both individualised and supervised. They also argued that for sustainable implementation of physical activity interventions to occur within mental health services, factors such as creating cultural changes within the mental health services (i.e. acknowledgement that physical wellbeing of our patients is as important as their mental health), building capacity among staff members to allow for facilitation of physical activity interventions, and developing formalised collaboration with community organisations, are essential.

Combined together, current research evidence suggest that future physical activity interventions for people with psychosis should address weight loss/attenuation, or prevention of weight gain when possible, in a socially supportive manner, with consideration given for individual patient preferences for types and settings of exercise, and should be supervised by physical activity professionals to maximise engagement and minimise dropouts. Moreover, existing studies have also identified particular vulnerable subpopulation within people with psychosis—those who are obese, with prominent negative symptoms, and little social support—the same cohort of people who are traditionally difficult to recruit into physical activity intervention studies. Thus, there remains an urgent need to design and conduct pragmatic studies that can help us understand how to understand those who are hardest to engage with, yet likely to benefit most from, physical activity interventions.

ASSESSMENT OF PHYSICAL ACTIVITY IN PEOPLE LIVING WITH PSYCHOSIS

How best to measure physical activity in people with psychotic disorders is still being actively investigated, with new tools currently in development.

Despite the established benefit of physical activity in people with psychosis, how best to measure physical activity status remains unestablished, both in research and clinical settings. Physical activity is defined as 'any bodily movement produced by skeletal muscles that requires energy expenditure' (Caspersen et al., 1985).

As such bodily movement is embedded in everyday life, often unstructured, and varies from minute to minute in both intensity and duration, measuring and assessing physical activity is inherently complex and difficult (Knowles, 2017). This is an important consideration especially in research, as imprecise measurements may lead to misleading conclusions. Currently, the measurement tools for physical activity can essentially be divided into two broad types: either objective or subjective measures. Objective physical activity measurement tools include doubly labelled water, accelerometers, and pedometers.

Subjective physical activity measurement tools include log books, structured interviews, and self-report questionnaires. In determining usefulness of each measurement tool, there are many factors that need to be considered (Dowd et al., 2018). One needs to be certain of the accuracy of the measurement tools—this may include methodological concepts such as validity (*are we measuring what we are intending to measure?*), reliability (*does the measurement tool produce consistent results regardless of who is administering it or when it is being administered?*), and sensitivity (*does the measurement tool capture changes over time adequately?*). Further, the practicality of measurement tools is also important. The measurement tool needs to be feasible in implementation, acceptable to the participants, and tolerated in terms of discomfort and potential side effects. Thus, most appropriate physical activity measurement tool is likely to be different depending on the setting and participants, as well as the intention behind measurement.

Measurement of physical activity must be practical: tools need to be feasible, acceptable, well tolerated by patients, and appropriate to the clinical setting.

The gold standard measurement tools for physical activity energy expenditure during free-living conditions remains doubly labelled water assessment (Klein et al., 1984). Briefly, in this assessment, participants have to consume a dose of doubly labelled water containing $H_2^{18}O$ and H_2O isotopes on day one. Subsequently, daily urine samples are collected for 10–14 days. The difference in the elimination rates of the two isotopes from the body is equivalent to the rate of carbon dioxide production, which can be converted to the average daily energy expenditure. One study from Brisbane, Queensland in Australia (Sharpe, Stedman, Byrne, Wishart, & Hills, 2006), examined the physical activity level of eight men with schizophrenia who were on long-term clozapine treatment in a residential mental health facility using the doubly labelled water assessment. While their findings confirmed that the participants were much less physically active compared to the population average, the study also highlighted practical difficulties of using this method widely in clinical research. For example, only eight out of 43 people approached for the study agreed to participate, and the cost and availability of doubly labelled water also limited the recruitment.

Other objective measurement tools have been used more widely in people with psychotic disorders. Pedometers are much more cost effective and seem more feasible compared to doubly labelled water, but there may be difficulties associated with recording of daily step logs (Kane, Lee, Sereika, & Brar, 2012). Further, compared to other objective measures, the range of information that pedometers gather is limited (i.e. step counts) and they do not allow for exploration of other aspects of physical activity such as domain, intensity, and diurnal variation. With the rapid advancement in technology, decreasing costs and increasing availability, accelerometers and similar devices are being used more commonly in research studies both in the general population (Dohrn, Sjostrom, Kwak, Oja, & Hagstromer, 2017; Huberty, Ehlers, Kurka, Ainsworth, & Buman, 2015) and in people with psychosis (Bueno-Antequera, Oviedo-Caro, & Munguia-Izquierdo, 2017; Petzold et al., 2017). For example, Bueno-Antequera and colleagues examined physical activity using a SenseWear Pro3 Armband (BodyMedia Inc., Pittsburgh, PA, United States). In this study, participants were required to wear the SenseWear on their left arm triceps muscle for 9 consecutive days, 24 h per day, except when showering or swimming. Forty-three participants with psychosis from outpatient settings in Spain were able to complete the 9 days monitoring to be included in the study (Bueno-Antequera et al., 2017). Likewise, 84 participants were recruited from outpatient settings in Germany to measure physical activity using ActiGraph GT1M accelerometers (ActiGraph, Pensacola, FL, United States). The participants in this study wore the accelerometers on average for around 13 h per day, with the average number of valid days (defined as meeting the minimal wear requirement of 10 h per day) of 5.9 out of seven requested (Petzold et al., 2017).

Murakami et al. (2016) recently compared estimation of energy expenditure between a wide range of wearable objective devices and doubly labelled water. While the study consisted of only 19 healthy adults, it found that all wearable devices examined (including those used in research like Garmin Vivofit and ActiGraph GT3X) *underestimated* the daily total energy expenditure by 69–590 kcal per day compared to doubly labelled water. The authors postulated that the underestimation may be due to periods of not wearing the devices during the measurement period. Future studies examining the relationship with a larger number of participants, and those with psychosis, would be useful in further determining the validity of wearable objective physical activity measurement devices.

Even though objective measurements may have more favourable features in terms of validity, reliability, and sensitivity compared to subjective measurements, this needs to be weighed against practical issues such as feasibility, acceptability, and tolerability, especially if the study requires the participants to wear these devices for a considerable amount of time. People with psychosis may also have additional challenges such as positive symptoms of the illness influencing the adherence with wearing the watches, especially in acute psychotic phases as many persecutory delusions consist of fear of being monitored. Negative and cognitive symptoms of the illness may also lead to lower motivation or forgetting to put the devices back on. Self-report questionnaires, on the other hand, are much less resource intensive both from the participants' and researchers' points of view. While there are many self-report questionnaires designed to assess physical activity status, the International Physical Activity Questionnaire or, IPAQ, remains one of the most widely validated and used research tools in population studies (Craig et al., 2003; Lee, Macfarlane, Lam, & Stewart, 2011). The International Physical Activity Questionnaire asks for self-report on the frequency, intensity (sitting, walking, moderate, vigorous) and duration of activity over the past seven days in four different domains (job-related physical activity, transport-related physical activity, domestic and gardening activities, and leisure-time physical activity). The International Physical Activity Questionnaire short form consists of seven items covering all domains of physical activity within generic intensity-specific items (e.g. vigorous activities are defined as any activity that 'take hard physical effort and make you breathe much harder than normal', moderate physical activity is any activity that make you breathe 'somewhat harder than normal'). The International Physical Activity Questionnaire long form, on the other hand, consists of 27 items that examines domain-specific activity for each intensity-specific category (Bauman et al., 2009). Faulkner, Cohn, and Remington (2006) assessed the test-retest reliability and validity compared to accelerometer of the International Physical Activity Questionnaire short-form among 35 patients with psychosis. The study reported reliability of $\rho = 0.68$ based on Spearman's correlation, and validity of $\rho = 0.37$, suggesting that the International Physical Activity Questionnaire has acceptable reliability but limited validity. These findings were comparable to the reliability and validity found in the general population ($\rho = 0.76$ and $\rho = 0.30$ respectively (Craig et al., 2003)). A more recent study (Duncan, Arbour-Nicitopoulos, Subramanieapillai, Remington, & Faulkner, 2017) expanded on this by examining the reliability of the International Physical Activity Questionnaire over a longer time period, and assessing validity with a larger sample number. Among 130 people with psychosis enrolled, 113 participants completed the study. The test-retest reliability in this study was found to be $\rho = 0.47$, suggesting that the International Physical Activity Questionnaire may not be as reliable in this particular cohort. The validity, however, was once again found to be comparable at $\rho = 0.30$. These studies illustrate the limitations of psychometric properties of self-report physical activity measurement tools, but these limitations appear largely comparable to those seen in the general population.

Spearman's correlation coefficient, rho (ρ) measures strength of association between the rankings of two variables. Spearman's ρ of 1 and -1 indicate a perfect positive and a perfect negative correlation respectively.

A recent study (Vancampfort, De Hert, et al., 2017) consisting of only 19 patients with first-episode psychosis examined the validity of International Physical Activity Questionnaire with the Sensewear Armband. The study found that there was no significant correlation between the self-reported mean time (minutes per day) spent in activity based on the International Physical Activity Questionnaire and that recorded with the Sensewear Armband, for either moderate physical activity (correlation: 0.29, $P = 0.23$) or vigorous physical activity (correlation: -0.11, $P = 0.66$). They also found that the International Physical Activity Questionnaire overestimated moderate physical activity by 35% and vigorous physical activity by 54%. Based on their findings, the authors recommended using the International Physical Activity Questionnaire with caution in this population. Given the small number of participants, however, the study may have been underpowered, thus contributing to the null results. At a much larger scale, Firth, Stubbs, Vancampfort, et al. (2017) utilised the dataset from the United Kingdom Biobank to compare physical activity status as measured by the International Physical Activity Questionnaire with that measured by accelerometer (Axivity AX3 wrist-worn triaxial accelerator) among people with psychosis ($n = 1078$) and those without ($n = 450{,}549$). Of note, the study demonstrated that even though there was no difference in physical activity status reported by the International Physical Activity Questionnaire in people with psychosis and the general population, accelerometer data showed that people with psychosis engaged in significantly less physical activity.

These recent findings demonstrating the impreciseness of self-report measures compared to objective measures have some important implications in interpreting results from research studies. For instance, in a study that examined the effects of different physical activity measurement tools on the relationship between physical activity status and cardio-metabolic factors in the general population (Celis-Morales et al., 2012), the authors found that the International Physical Activity Questionnaire underestimated the strength of many risk factors examined, suggesting that the International Physical Activity Questionnaire was not accurate enough to find significant associations between physical activity and cardio-metabolic risk factors that accelerometers were able to identify. Similarly, even though Suetani, Saha, et al. (2017) found no significant cross-sectional association between physical activity and depression among 8841 people using a self-report physical activity questionnaire in Australia, a smaller ($n=2862$) cohort study from the Netherlands observed strong cross-sectional association between higher levels of physical activity and reduced odds of depression (Vallance et al., 2011). These conflicting findings raise the possibility that self-reported physical activity may not be precise enough to find potentially significant associations between physical activity and mental disorders.

There remains an urgent need for researchers in this field to explore an appropriate and consistent tool to measure physical activity status in both research and clinical settings. Further, given how quickly the technology is advancing, it is likely that most measurement devices that are used at the baseline data collection today will be out of date by the follow-up point in longitudinal studies with long durations. Thus, subjective physical activity measurement tools will be likely to retain an important role in the future. Currently, Rosenbaum, Ward, and International Working Group (2016) and an international working group are in the process of validating the Simple Physical Activity Questionnaire, or SIMPAQ. The Simple Physical Activity Questionnaire is a five-item self-report questionnaire specifically designed to capture physical activity status in people with mental disorders in clinical settings. The questionnaire is available in many different languages (see www.simpaq.org). Such questionnaires may be able to better strike the balance between the methodological robustness and practicality needed for people with mental disorders, and improve the preciseness of self-reported physical activity status.

Another variable that is being increasingly used in people with psychosis in combination with physical activity status measurements is measurement of cardiorespiratory fitness. There have been a few studies to suggest that people with psychosis have significantly reduced cardiorespiratory fitness compared to the general population, which may be independently associated with the increased cardiovascular mortality rate (Vancampfort, Rosenbaum, et al., 2017). In terms of symptoms, lower cardiorespiratory fitness has been associated with a higher level of negative symptoms in some cross-sectional studies (Vancampfort, Rosenbaum, Probst, et al., 2015). The 'gold standard' measure for cardiorespiratory fitness is VO_2 max (Ross et al., 2016). Testing VO_2 max, however, requires the participant to undergo a graded exercise test using either a treadmill or a cycle ergometer while wearing a VO_2 mask to measure ventilation as well as oxygen and carbon dioxide concentration of the inhaled and exhaled air. VO_2 max is defined as the point where oxygen consumption plateaus in spite of an increase in workload. The utility of the VO_2 max testing is somewhat limited in clinical settings due to the availability of, and the discomfort associated with, the equipment required. On the other hand, proxy measures of cardiorespiratory fitness such as the 6-min walk test can be conducted among people with psychosis without much difficulty. In essence, the test measures the distance covered over a time of 6 min to estimate the submaximal level of functional exercise capacity. Participants are asked to walk as far as possible, at a self-determined pace, within the 6-min period. The test only requires a long flat, straight, hard surfaced, enclosed corridor of at least 30 m, a pulse oximeter, and a stop watch (Laboratories, 2002). Using such proxy measures of cardiorespiratory fitness, the understanding of the importance of cardiorespiratory fitness in people with mental disorders is growing (Vancampfort, Rosenbaum, Probst, et al., 2015; Vancampfort, Rosenbaum, Ward, & Stubbs, 2015). Therefore, measures of cardiorespiratory fitness may represent a suitable modifiable risk factor worth monitoring in both research and clinical practice in the near future.

CONCLUSION

People living with psychosis suffer from disproportionally higher rates of mortality and morbidity compared to those without. Current research evidence indicates short-term benefits of physical activity interventions for both physical and psychological well-being of people with psychosis. The next critical step in this field is to translate the existing research evidence into sustainable implementation in our day-to-day practice to improve physical activity status for people with psychosis. To achieve this, we need to continue asking difficult research and clinical questions, like *how do we engage people who are hardest to engage* and *how do we accurately assess, monitor and evaluate physical activity status in different settings*?

QUIZ QUESTIONS

1. Which of the following is a subjective method of measuring physical activity?
   (a) Double-labelled water method
   (b) Accelerometry
   (c) The SIMPAQ
   (d) Pedometers
2. Self-reported physical activity measures in people with psychosis generally seem to:
   (a) Overestimate actual physical activity
   (b) Underestimate actual physical activity
   (c) Accurately measure actual physical activity
   (d) Have no relationship with actual physical activity
3. Which of the following factors in people with psychosis reduces their likelihood of engaging in PA?
   (a) Obesity

(b) Young age
(c) Social support
(d) All of the above

4. Along with the benefits for physical health, top-tier evidence from meta-analyses of randomised controlled trials have demonstrated that exercise interventions for schizophrenia also improve:
(a) Quality of life
(b) Psychiatric symptoms
(c) Cognitive functioning
(d) All of the above

ANSWERS TO QUIZ QUESTIONS:

1. (c)
2. (a)
3. (a)
4. (d)

SELF-DIRECTED LEARNING

Firth, J., Carney, R., Elliott, R., French, P., McPhee, J. S., McIntyre, R., & Yung, A. R. (2016). Exercise as an intervention for first-episode psychosis: A feasibility study. *Early Intervention in Psychiatry, 12* (3), 307–315.

Firth, J., Stubbs, B., Vancampfort, D., Ward, P. B., Schuch, F. B., Rosenbaum, S., Sarris, J., & Yung, A. R. (2017). The validity and value of self-reported physical activity and accelerometry in people with schizophrenia: A population-scale study of the UK Biobank. *Schizophrenia Bulletin*. doi: https://doi.org/10.1093/schbul/sbx149.

Korman, N. H., Shah, S. H., Suetani, S. U., et al. Evaluating the feasibility of a pilot exercise intervention implemented within a residential rehabilitation unit for people with severe mental illness: GO HEART. *Frontiers in Psychiatry, 9*, 343.

Yung, A. R., & Firth, J. (2016). How should physical exercise be used in schizophrenia treatment? *Expert Review of Neurotherapeutics, 17* (3), 213–214.

References

Alberti, K. G., Eckel, R. H., Grundy, S. M., Zimmet, P. Z., Cleeman, J. I., Donato, K. A., et al. (2009). Harmonizing the metabolic syndrome: A joint interim statement of the International Diabetes Federation Task Force on Epidemiology and Prevention; National Heart, Lung, and Blood Institute; American Heart Association; World Heart Federation; International Atherosclerosis Society; and International Association for the Study of Obesity. *Circulation, 120*(16), 1640–1645. https://doi.org/10.1161/CIRCULATIONAHA.109.192644.

Arem, H., Moore, S. C., Patel, A., Hartge, P., Berrington de Gonzalez, A., Visvanathan, K., et al. (2015). Leisure time physical activity and mortality: A detailed pooled analysis of the dose-response relationship. *JAMA Internal Medicine, 175*(6), 959–967. https://doi.org/10.1001/jamainternmed.2015.0533.

ATS Committee on Proficiency Standards for Clinical Pulmonary Function Laboratories. (2002). ATS statement: Guidelines for the six-minute walk test. *American Journal of Respiratory and Critical Care Medicine, 166*(1), 111–117. https://doi.org/10.1164/ajrccm.166.1.at1102.

Bartels, S. J. (2015). Can behavioral health organizations change health behaviors? The STRIDE study and lifestyle interventions for obesity in serious mental illness. *The American Journal of Psychiatry, 172*(1), 9–11. https://doi.org/10.1176/appi.ajp.2014.14101246.

Bartels, S. J., Aschbrenner, K. A., Pratt, S. I., Naslund, J. A., Scherer, E. A., Zubkoff, L., et al. (2018). Implementation of a lifestyle intervention for people with serious mental illness in State-Funded Mental Health Centers. *Psychiatric Services*. https://doi.org/10.1176/appi.ps.201700368.

Bartels, S. J., Pratt, S. I., Aschbrenner, K. A., Barre, L. K., Jue, K., Wolfe, R. S., et al. (2013). Clinically significant improved fitness and weight loss among overweight persons with serious mental illness. *Psychiatric Services, 64*(8), 729–736. https://doi.org/10.1176/appi.ps.003622012.

Bartels, S. J., Pratt, S. I., Aschbrenner, K. A., Barre, L. K., Naslund, J. A., Wolfe, R., et al. (2015). Pragmatic replication trial of health promotion coaching for obesity in serious mental illness and maintenance of outcomes. *American Journal of Psychiatry, 172*(4), 344–352. https://doi.org/10.1176/appi.ajp.2014.14030357.

Bauman, A., Ainsworth, B. E., Bull, F., Craig, C. L., Hagstromer, M., Sallis, J. F., et al. (2009). Progress and pitfalls in the use of the International Physical Activity Questionnaire (IPAQ) for adult physical activity surveillance. *Journal of Physical Activity & Health, 6*(Suppl. 1), S5–S8.

Bueno-Antequera, J., Oviedo-Caro, M. A., & Munguia-Izquierdo, D. (2017). Sedentary behaviour, physical activity, cardiorespiratory fitness and cardiometabolic risk in psychosis: The PsychiActive project. *Schizophrenia Research*. https://doi.org/10.1016/j.schres.2017.10.012.

Caspersen, C. J., Powell, K. E., & Christenson, G. M. (1985). Physical activity, exercise, and physical fitness: Definitions and distinctions for health-related research. *Public Health Reports, 100*(2), 126–131.

Celis-Morales, C. A., Perez-Bravo, F., Ibanez, L., Salas, C., Bailey, M. E., & Gill, J. M. (2012). Objective vs. self-reported physical activity and sedentary time: Effects of measurement method on relationships with risk biomarkers. *PLoS One, 7*(5), e36345. https://doi.org/10.1371/journal.pone.0036345.

Chapman, J. J., Fraser, S. J., Brown, W. J., & Burton, N. W. (2016). Physical activity preferences, motivators, barriers and attitudes of adults with mental illness. *Journal of Mental Health, 25*(5), 448–454. https://doi.org/10.3109/09638237.2016.1167847.

Craig, C. L., Marshall, A. L., Sjostrom, M., Bauman, A. E., Booth, M. L., Ainsworth, B. E., et al. (2003). International physical activity questionnaire: 12-country reliability and validity. *Medicine and Science in Sports and Exercise, 35*(8), 1381–1395. https://doi.org/10.1249/01.mss.0000078924.61453.fb.

Curtis, J., Watkins, A., Rosenbaum, S., Teasdale, S., Kalucy, M., Samaras, K., et al. (2016). Evaluating an individualized lifestyle and life skills intervention to prevent antipsychotic-induced weight gain in first-episode psychosis. *Early Intervention in Psychiatry, 10*(3), 267–276. https://doi.org/10.1111/eip.12230.

Daumit, G. L., Dickerson, F. B., Wang, N. Y., Dalcin, A., Jerome, G. J., Anderson, C. A., et al. (2013). A behavioral weight-loss intervention in persons with serious mental illness. *New England Journal of Medicine, 368*(17), 1594–1602. https://doi.org/10.1056/NEJMoa1214530.

Dauwan, M., Begemann, M. J., Heringa, S. M., & Sommer, I. E. (2016). Exercise improves clinical symptoms, quality of life, global functioning, and depression in schizophrenia: A systematic review and meta-analysis. *Schizophrenia Bulletin, 42*(3), 588–599. https://doi.org/10.1093/schbul/sbv164.

Dohrn, I. M., Sjostrom, M., Kwak, L., Oja, P., & Hagstromer, M. (2017). Accelerometer-measured sedentary time and physical activity—a 15 year follow-up of mortality in a Swedish population-based cohort. *Journal of Science and Medicine in Sport*. https://doi.org/10.1016/j.jsams.2017.10.035.

Dowd, K. P., Szeklicki, R., Minetto, M. A., Murphy, M. H., Polito, A., Ghigo, E., et al. (2018). A systematic literature review of reviews on techniques for physical activity measurement in adults: A DEDIPAC study. *International Journal of Behavioral Nutrition and Physical Activity, 15*(1), 15. https://doi.org/10.1186/s12966-017-0636-2.

Duncan, M. J., Arbour-Nicitopoulos, K., Subramanieapillai, M., Remington, G., & Faulkner, G. (2017). Revisiting the International Physical Activity Questionnaire (IPAQ): Assessing physical activity among individuals with schizophrenia. *Schizophrenia Research, 179*, 2–7. https://doi.org/10.1016/j.schres.2016.09.010.

Faulkner, G., Cohn, T., & Remington, G. (2006). Validation of a physical activity assessment tool for individuals with schizophrenia. *Schizophrenia Research, 82*(2–3), 225–231. https://doi.org/10.1016/j.schres.2005.10.020.

Firth, J., Cotter, J., Carney, R., & Yung, A. R. (2017). The pro-cognitive mechanisms of physical exercise in people with schizophrenia. *British Journal of Pharmacology, 174*(19), 3161–3172. https://doi.org/10.1111/bph.13772.

Firth, J., Cotter, J., Elliott, R., French, P., & Yung, A. R. (2015). A systematic review and meta-analysis of exercise interventions in schizophrenia patients. *Psychological Medicine*, 1–19. https://doi.org/10.1017/S0033291714003110.

Firth, J., Rosenbaum, S., Stubbs, B., Gorczynski, P., Yung, A. R., & Vancampfort, D. (2016). Motivating factors and barriers towards exercise in severe mental illness: A systematic review and meta-analysis. *Psychological Medicine, 46*(14), 2869–2881. https://doi.org/10.1017/S0033291716001732.

Firth, J., Stubbs, B., Rosenbaum, S., Vancampfort, D., Malchow, B., Schuch, F., et al. (2017). Aerobic exercise improves cognitive functioning in people with schizophrenia: A systematic review and meta-analysis. *Schizophrenia Bulletin, 43*(3), 546–556. https://doi.org/10.1093/schbul/sbw115.

Firth, J., Stubbs, B., Vancampfort, D., Firth, J. A., Large, M., Rosenbaum, S., et al. (2018). Grip strength is associated with cognitive performance in schizophrenia and the general population: A UK Biobank study of 476559 participants. *Schizophrenia Bulletin, 44*(4), 728–736. https://doi.org/10.1093/schbul/sby034.

Firth, J., Stubbs, B., Vancampfort, D., Schuch, F. B., Rosenbaum, S., Ward, P. B., et al. (2017). The validity and value of self-reported physical activity and accelerometry in people with schizophrenia: A population-scale study of the UK Biobank. *Schizophrenia Bulletin*. https://doi.org/10.1093/schbul/sbx149.

Galletly, C. A., Foley, D. L., Waterreus, A., Watts, G. F., Castle, D. J., McGrath, J. J., et al. (2012). Cardiometabolic risk factors in people with psychotic disorders: The second Australian national survey of psychosis. *Australian and New Zealand Journal of Psychiatry, 46*(8), 753–761. https://doi.org/10.1177/0004867412453089.

Gardner-Sood, P., Lally, J., Smith, S., Atakan, Z., Ismail, K., Greenwood, K. E., et al. (2015). Cardiovascular risk factors and metabolic syndrome in people with established psychotic illnesses: Baseline data from the IMPaCT randomized controlled trial. *Psychological Medicine*, 1–11. https://doi.org/10.1017/S0033291715000562.

Gebel, K., Ding, D., Chey, T., Stamatakis, E., Brown, W. J., & Bauman, A. E. (2015). Effect of moderate to vigorous physical activity on all-cause mortality in middle-aged and older Australians. *JAMA Internal Medicine, 175*(6), 970–977. https://doi.org/10.1001/jamainternmed.2015.0541.

Green, C. A., Yarborough, B. J., Leo, M. C., Yarborough, M. T., Stumbo, S. P., Janoff, S. L., et al. (2015). The STRIDE weight loss and lifestyle intervention for individuals taking antipsychotic medications: A randomized trial. *American Journal of Psychiatry, 172*(1), 71–81. https://doi.org/10.1176/appi.ajp.2014.14020173.

Hjorthoj, C., Sturup, A. E., McGrath, J. J., & Nordentoft, M. (2017). Years of potential life lost and life expectancy in schizophrenia: A systematic review and meta-analysis. *Lancet Psychiatry*. https://doi.org/10.1016/S2215-0366(17)30078-0.

Huberty, J., Ehlers, D. K., Kurka, J., Ainsworth, B., & Buman, M. (2015). Feasibility of three wearable sensors for 24 hour monitoring in middle-aged women. *BMC Womens Health, 15*, 55. https://doi.org/10.1186/s12905-015-0212-3.

Kane, I., Lee, H., Sereika, S., & Brar, J. (2012). Feasibility of pedometers for adults with schizophrenia: Pilot study. *Journal of Psychiatric and Mental Health Nursing, 19*(1), 8–14. https://doi.org/10.1111/j.1365-2850.2011.01747.x.

Klein, P. D., James, W. P., Wong, W. W., Irving, C. S., Murgatroyd, P. R., Cabrera, M., et al. (1984). Calorimetric validation of the doubly-labelled water method for determination of energy expenditure in man. *Human Nutrition. Clinical Nutrition, 38*(2), 95–106.

Knowles, G. (2017). Physical activity and mental health: Commentary on Suetani et al. 2016: Common mental disorders and recent physical activity status: Findings from a National Community Survey. *Social Psychiatry and Psychiatric Epidemiology, 52*(7), 803–805. https://doi.org/10.1007/s00127-017-1399-4.

Lederman, O., Suetani, S., Stanton, R., Chapman, J., Korman, N., Rosenbaum, S., et al. (2017). Embedding exercise interventions as routine mental health care: Implementation strategies in residential, inpatient and community settings. *Australasian Psychiatry, 25*(5), 451–455. https://doi.org/10.1177/1039856217711054.

Lee, P. H., Macfarlane, D. J., Lam, T. H., & Stewart, S. M. (2011). Validity of the International Physical Activity Questionnaire Short Form (IPAQ-SF): A systematic review. *International Journal of Behavioral Nutrition and Physical Activity, 8*, 115. https://doi.org/10.1186/1479-5868-8-115.

Lee, I. M., Shiroma, E. J., Lobelo, F., Puska, P., Blair, S. N., Katzmarzyk, P. T., et al. (2012). Effect of physical inactivity on major non-communicable diseases worldwide: An analysis of burden of disease and life expectancy. *Lancet, 380*(9838), 219–229. https://doi.org/10.1016/S0140-6736(12)61031-9.

Leitzmann, M. F., Park, Y., Blair, A., Ballard-Barbash, R., Mouw, T., Hollenbeck, A. R., et al. (2007). Physical activity recommendations and decreased risk of mortality. *Archives of Internal Medicine, 167*(22), 2453–2460. https://doi.org/10.1001/archinte.167.22.2453.

Leong, D. P., Teo, K. K., Rangarajan, S., Lopez-Jaramillo, P., Avezum, A., Jr., Orlandini, A., et al. (2015). Prognostic value of grip strength: Findings from the Prospective Urban Rural Epidemiology (PURE) study. *Lancet, 386*(9990), 266–273. https://doi.org/10.1016/S0140-6736(14)62000-6.

Murakami, H., Kawakami, R., Nakae, S., Nakata, Y., Ishikawa-Takata, K., Tanaka, S., et al. (2016). Accuracy of wearable devices for estimating total energy expenditure: Comparison with metabolic chamber and doubly labeled water method. *JAMA Internal Medicine, 176*(5), 702–703. https://doi.org/10.1001/jamainternmed.2016.0152.

Noordsy, D.L., Burgess, J. D., Hardy, K. V., Yudofsky, L. M. & Ballon, J. S. (2018). Therapeutic potential of physical exercise in early psychosis. American Journal of Psychiatry, 175(3), 209-214. https://doi.org/10.1176/appi.ajp.2017.17060716

O'Donovan, G., Lee, I. M., Hamer, M., & Stamatakis, E. (2017). Association of "weekend warrior" and other leisure time physical activity patterns with risks for all-cause, cardiovascular disease, and cancer mortality. *JAMA Internal Medicine, 177*(3), 335–342. https://doi.org/10.1001/jamainternmed.2016.8014.

Olfson, M., Gerhard, T., Huang, C., Crystal, S., & Stroup, T. S. (2015). Premature mortality among adults with schizophrenia in the United States. *JAMA Psychiatry*, 1–10. https://doi.org/10.1001/jamapsychiatry.2015.1737.

Ortega, F. B., Silventoinen, K., Tynelius, P., & Rasmussen, F. (2012). Muscular strength in male adolescents and premature death: Cohort study of one million participants. *BMJ, 345*, e7279. https://doi.org/10.1136/bmj.e7279.

Petzold, M. B., Bischoff, S., Rogoll, J., Plag, J., Teran, C., Brand, R., et al. (2017). Physical activity in outpatients with mental disorders: Status, measurement and social cognitive determinants of health behavior change. *European Archives of Psychiatry and Clinical Neuroscience, 267*(7), 639–650. https://doi.org/10.1007/s00406-017-0772-3.

Rosenbaum, S., Ward, P. B., & International Working Group. (2016). The simple physical activity questionnaire. *Lancet Psychiatry, 3*(1), e1. https://doi.org/10.1016/S2215-0366(15)00496-4.

Ross, R., Blair, S. N., Arena, R., Church, T. S., Despres, J. P., Franklin, B. A., et al. (2016). Importance of assessing cardiorespiratory fitness in clinical practice: A case for fitness as a clinical vital sign: A scientific statement from the American Heart Association. *Circulation, 134*(24), e653–e699. https://doi.org/10.1161/CIR.0000000000000461.

Sharpe, J. K., Stedman, T. J., Byrne, N. M., Wishart, C., & Hills, A. P. (2006). Energy expenditure and physical activity in clozapine use: Implications for weight management. *Australian and New Zealand Journal of Psychiatry, 40*(9), 810–814. https://doi.org/10.1080/j.1440-1614.2006.01888.x.

Stubbs, B., Firth, J., Berry, A., Schuch, F. B., Rosenbaum, S., Gaughran, F., et al. (2016). How much physical activity do people with schizophrenia engage in? A systematic review, comparative meta-analysis and meta-regression. *Schizophrenia Research, 176*(2), 431–440.

Subramaniapillai, M., Arbour-Nicitopoulos, K., Duncan, M., McIntyre, R. S., Mansur, R. B., Remington, G., et al. (2016). Physical activity preferences of individuals diagnosed with schizophrenia or bipolar disorder. *BMC Research Notes, 9*, 340. https://doi.org/10.1186/s13104-016-2151-y.

Suetani, S., Rosenbaum, S., Scott, J. G., Curtis, J., & Ward, P. B. (2016). Bridging the gap: What have we done and what more can we do to reduce the burden of avoidable death in people with psychotic illness? *Epidemiology and Psychiatric Sciences, 25*(3), 205–210. https://doi.org/10.1017/S2045796015001043.

Suetani, S., Saha, S., Milad, A., Eakin, E., Scott, J. G., & McGrath, J. J. (2017). Common mental disorders and recent physical activity status: Findings from a National Community Survey. *Social Psychiatry and Psychiatric Epidemiology, 52*(7), 795–802. https://doi.org/10.1007/s00127-016-1307-3.

Suetani, S., Scott, J. G., & McGrath, J. J. (2017). The importance of the physical health needs of people with psychotic disorders. *Australian and New Zealand Journal of Psychiatry, 51*(1), 94–95. https://doi.org/10.1177/0004867416662151.

Suetani, S., Waterreus, A., Morgan, V., Foley, D. L., Galletly, C., Badcock, J. C., et al. (2016). Correlates of physical activity in people living with psychotic illness. *Acta Psychiatrica Scandinavica, 134*(2), 129–137. https://doi.org/10.1111/acps.12594.

Ussher, M., Stanbury, L., Cheeseman, V., & Faulkner, G. (2007). Physical activity preferences and perceived barriers to activity among persons with severe mental illness in the United Kingdom. *Psychiatric Services, 58*(3), 405–408. https://doi.org/10.1176/ps.2007.58.3.405.

Vallance, J. K., Winkler, E. A., Gardiner, P. A., Healy, G. N., Lynch, B. M., & Owen, N. (2011). Associations of objectively-assessed physical activity and sedentary time with depression: NHANES (2005–2006). *Preventive Medicine, 53*(4–5), 284–288. https://doi.org/10.1016/j.ypmed.2011.07.013.

Vancampfort, D., De Hert, M., Myin-Germeys, I., Rosenbaum, S., Stubbs, B., Van Damme, T., et al. (2017). Validity and correlates of the International Physical Activity Questionnaire in first-episode psychosis. *Early Intervention in Psychiatry*. https://doi.org/10.1111/eip.12521.

Vancampfort, D., Knapen, J., Probst, M., Scheewe, T., Remans, S., & De Hert, M. (2012). A systematic review of correlates of physical activity in patients with schizophrenia. *Acta Psychiatrica Scandinavica, 125*(5), 352–362. https://doi.org/10.1111/j.1600-0447.2011.01814.x.

Vancampfort, D., Knapen, J., Probst, M., van Winkel, R., Deckx, S., Maurissen, K., et al. (2010). Considering a frame of reference for physical activity research related to the cardiometabolic risk profile in schizophrenia. *Psychiatry Research, 177*(3), 271–279. https://doi.org/10.1016/j.psychres.2010.03.011.

Vancampfort, D., Rosenbaum, S., Probst, M., Soundy, A., Mitchell, A. J., De Hert, M., et al. (2015). Promotion of cardiorespiratory fitness in schizophrenia: A clinical overview and meta-analysis. *Acta Psychiatrica Scandinavica, 132*(2), 131–143. https://doi.org/10.1111/acps.12407.

Vancampfort, D., Rosenbaum, S., Schuch, F. B., Ward, P. B., Probst, M., & Stubbs, B. (2016). Prevalence and predictors of treatment dropout from physical activity interventions in schizophrenia: A meta-analysis. *General Hospital Psychiatry, 39*, 15–23. https://doi.org/10.1016/j.genhosppsych.2015.11.008.

Vancampfort, D., Rosenbaum, S., Schuch, F., Ward, P. B., Richards, J., Mugisha, J., et al. (2017). Cardiorespiratory fitness in severe mental illness: A systematic review and meta-analysis. *Sports Medicine, 47*(2), 343–352. https://doi.org/10.1007/s40279-016-0574-1.

Vancampfort, D., Rosenbaum, S., Ward, P. B., & Stubbs, B. (2015). Exercise improves cardiorespiratory fitness in people with schizophrenia: A systematic review and meta-analysis. *Schizophrenia Research, 169*(1–3), 453–457. https://doi.org/10.1016/j.schres.2015.09.029.

WHO. (2010). *Global recommendations on physical activity for health.* Geneva, Switzerland: WHO.

Definition of Key Terms

Body mass index A commonly used indicator of anthropometric height to weight characteristics in adults. The body mass index is calculated as an individual's weight in kilograms divided by the square of the individual's height in metres (kg/m^2).

Cardiorespiratory fitness The ability of the circulatory, respiratory, and muscular systems to supply oxygen during sustained physical activity.

Exercise A subtype of physical activity that is planned, repetitive, and structured, and it has a specific intention of improving or maintaining fitness.

Metabolic syndrome A cluster of risk factors comprising of elevated waist circumference, elevated triglyceride concentration, reduced high-density lipid concentration, elevated blood pressure, and elevated fasting glucose concentration. The presence of three or more of the risk factors is diagnostic of the metabolic syndrome.

Physical activity Any bodily movement produced by skeletal muscles that results in energy expenditure.

CHAPTER 13

Screening and Assessment of Substance Use Disorder in Psychosis

Kim T. Mueser
Center for Psychiatric Rehabilitation, Departments of Occupational Therapy, Psychological and Brain Sciences, and Psychiatry, Boston University, Boston, MA, United States

Key Learning Objectives

- To appreciate the significance of co-occurring substance use disorders in people with psychosis
- To understand the need for routine enquiry about substance use disorders in clients with psychosis
- To learn about the process of screening and assessment for substance use disorders

Substance use disorders are common in people with psychotic disorders such as schizophrenia, schizoaffective disorder, and schizophreniform disorder, as well as in disorders that frequently include psychotic features, such as bipolar disorder and major depression (Hartz et al., 2014). Substance use disorders have a major effect on worsening the course of psychotic disorder, including treatment nonadherence, increased rates of re-hospitalisation, worse health outcomes, greater involvement in the criminal justice system, more severe symptoms, and increased risk of both aggression and suicide (Large, Mullin, Gupta, Harris, & Nielssen, 2014). There is a growing research literature demonstrating the effectiveness of integrating mental health and substance use disorder treatment for people with co-occurring disorders (see Chapter 22). However, in routine practice, substance use disorders are often missed by clinicians, resulting in underdiagnosis and undertreatment of the co-occurring disorder. Because effective treatment begins with detection of the disorder, having accurate and

A Clinical Introduction to Psychosis. https://doi.org/10.1016/B978-0-12-815012-2.00013-4

Routine enquiry about substance use disorders is invaluable for clients with psychosis.

sensitive measures for the assessment of substance use disorders in persons with a psychotic disorder is of critical importance.

The present chapter provides clinical guidance for the assessment of co-occurring substance use disorders in people with a psychotic disorder. It begins with a brief review of the epidemiology of substance use disorders in persons with a psychotic disorder, followed by an overview of the assessment process. The remainder of the chapter is devoted to describing a four-stage process for organising and conducting the assessment, including detection, classification, functional assessment, and functional analysis. The final stage of assessment is then used for treatment planning.

EPIDEMIOLOGY

In this chapter, the term *alcohol use disorder* refers to the persistent use of alcohol resulting in significant health, psychosocial, and/or physical problems consistent with a psychiatric diagnosis according to a diagnostic system such as the *Diagnostic and Statistical Manual* (DSM) or *International Classification of Diseases* (ICD) series. We use the term *drug use disorder* to refer to a similar pattern of problematic use of other licit or illicit substances (e.g. cannabis, cocaine, hallucinogens, heroin), or the misuse of prescription or over-the-counter medications, whereas the term *substance use disorder* (and substances) refers to problematic use of either alcohol or drugs.

Prevalence

Substance use is widespread among people with psychotic disorders.

There is significant variation across most countries in the prevalence of drug disorders, with somewhat less variation in the prevalence of alcohol use disorder (Somers, Goldner, Waraich, & Hsu, 2007). The lifetime prevalence of substance use disorders in people with a psychotic disorder is approximately 50%, compared to only 10%–20% in the general population (Merikangas & McClair, 2012). The prevalence of current or recent substance use disorder over the past year is approximately 25%–35% in people with a psychotic disorder, compared to 5%–10% in the general population.

Examination of the prevalence of substance use disorder in specific severe mental illnesses indicates rates of over 50% for both schizophrenia and bipolar disorder, with rates of 25%–35% for depressive and anxiety disorders (Kessler, Chiu, Demler, & Walters, 2005; Merikangas et al., 1998; Morgan et al., 2014; Regier et al., 1990). However, there is evidence that people with more severe course of major depression, as indicated by history of psychiatric hospitalisation, have similarly high rates of substance use disorder (about 50%) to individuals with schizophrenia or bipolar disorder (Mueser et al., 2000; Mueser, Yarnold, & Bellack, 1992), suggesting that the severity of the psychiatric disorder contributes to the increased comorbidity with substance use disorder, and not the presence of psychotic symptoms per se.

Specific Types and Patterns of Substance Use Disorder

The specific types of substances used by individuals with substance use disorder are primarily determined by access to the substances, with alcohol use disorder typically most common, followed by cannabis use disorder, and then by other drug use disorders. When certain market forces prevail or laws restrict access to substances for some individuals, differences in the most commonly used substance and the prevalence of specific substance use disorders may ensue.

Ease of access is a key factor driving the *type* of substances used.

For example, in the early 1980s, the most common illicit substance used in Philadelphia, United States, was cannabis, which was replaced in the mid-1980s by crack cocaine. Examination of substance use disorders of individuals with schizophrenia admitted to a psychiatric hospital during this period indicated a shift in the most common type of drug use disorder, with cannabis use disorder most common in the early 1980s (Mueser et al., 1990), which was then replaced by cocaine use disorder in the mid-1980s (Mueser et al., 1992). For another example, in a recent study of a large cohort of individuals entering treatment for a first episode of psychosis, the most common substance used by individuals under age 21 was cannabis, whereas after age 21 alcohol was the most commonly used substance (Brunette et al., 2018). The shift in most commonly used substance by older individuals reflects the effects of the legal age for using alcohol (21 years old) in most states in the United States, and suggests that although cannabis was illegal, it was more readily obtained than alcohol for individuals under the age of 21.

Polysubstance use is common in people with psychotic disorders, with significant numbers of individuals having problems related to two or more substances (Brunette et al., 2018; Stefamis et al., 2014). People with a psychotic disorders have increased prevalence of a broad range of commonly misused substances, including alcohol, cannabis, stimulants, sedatives, and hallucinogens. However, rates of opiate addiction in persons with a psychotic disorder do not appear to be significantly elevated compared to the general population (Chiapelli, Chen, Hackman, & Hong, 2018).

Use of multiple substances is common in people with psychotic disorder.

Onset and Course

Substance use disorders typically have an onset in people with psychotic disorder that parallels individuals in the general population, with the disorder usually beginning in adolescence between the ages of 14 and 20 years old. The onset of substance use disorders tends to precede the onset of psychotic disorders, although in many cases both disorders develop within a relatively brief period of time, making it difficult to determine 'which came first' (Silver & Abboud, 1994). Substance use, especially drug use, is associated with an earlier onset of psychosis (Mueser et al., 1990; Salyers & Mueser, 2001; Stefamis et al., 2014; Veen et al., 2004).

The course of co-occurring substance use disorders in people with a psychosis is variable, with some people becoming sober soon after developing a psychotic disorder, but many others experiencing a more chronic and relapsing course of illness (Harrison et al., 2008; Weibell et al., 2017). Among individuals who have a co-occurring substance use disorder, estimates are that with integrated treatment between 10% and 20% achieved stable remission per year (Drake et al., 2006; Drake et al., 2016).

Substance use complicates the course of illness in people with psychosis.

Demographic and Clinical Correlates

Most of the demographic correlates of substance use disorder in persons with a co-occurring psychosis are similar to those found in the primary addiction population (Kavanagh et al., 2004; Large et al., 2014; Mueser et al., 1990; Mueser et al., 1992; Mueser et al., 2000). Male gender, younger age, single marital status, and lower educational levels are all associated with higher rates of substance use disorder, as is a family history of substance use disorder. Race and ethnicity tend to not be related to substance use disorder, although they may reflect differences in types of substances used within specific socio-cultural groups or geographic regions.

With respect to clinical correlates of substance use disorder, cannabis use, especially before the age of 15, has been linked to an increased risk of developing schizophrenia across several large birth cohort studies (Andréasson, Allebeck, Engström, & Rydberg, 1987; Arseneault, Cannon, Witton, & Murray, 2004; Hambrecht & Häfner, 2000). Whether this association reflects the effects of cannabis on precipitating a psychotic disorder or the possible effects of the prodrome of psychosis is uncertain.

As in the general population, a history of conduct disorder in childhood and antisocial personality disorder in adulthood are associated with an increased risk of substance use disorder in persons with a psychosis (Mueser et al., 1999). Furthermore, among individuals with the co-occurring substance use disorder, those who also have antisocial personality disorder tend to have a more severe course of their disorder, including an earlier onset of their substance use disorder, and more medical, legal, social, and employment problems (Mueser et al., 1997; Mueser et al., 2006; Mueser et al., 2012).

Childhood conduct disorder is a significant risk factor for substance use disorder in psychosis.

However, there are two clinically relevant correlates of substance use disorder in persons with a psychosis that differ from the general population. First, individuals with the psychotic disorder who have a co-occurring substance use disorder often have had *better* premorbid social functioning than similar persons without a substance use disorder. In multiepisode patients, this association tends to be strongest for cannabis use disorder (Cohen & Klein, 1970; Compton, Broussard, Ramsay, & Stewart, 2011; Salyers & Mueser, 2001). Second, people with a co-occurring substance use disorder tend to have better cognitive functioning than individuals with only a psychotic disorder. In multiepisode patients, this association is strongest for cannabis use disorder in countries where cannabis use is common (Potvin, Joyal, Pelletier, & Stip, 2008), whereas in first-episode patients it is been shown for both cannabis and alcohol use disorder (Brunette et al., 2018). These associations likely reflect the fact that individuals with better premorbid social and cognitive functioning are more likely to be introduced to substances through their social connections, and to develop substance use disorders compared to people who are more socially withdrawn and have fewer social relationships (Cohen & Klein, 1970). Indeed, in countries where cannabis use is less normative such as Norway, cannabis use is associated with worse premorbid social functioning and greater neurocognitive impairment (Ringen et al., 2008; Ringen et al., 2010).

OVERVIEW OF ASSESSMENT

The assessment of substance use disorders in persons with a psychotic disorder can be conceptualised as involving a series of five interacting stages or steps (Mueser, Noordsy, Drake, & Fox, 2003). The process begins with *detection*, or the identification of individuals who may be experiencing problems related to their drug or alcohol use. Following detection of possible substance use problems, the next stage is *classification*, where the goal is to determine whether the individual is in fact experiencing significant substance use problems, and meets criteria for a substance use disorder according to an established diagnostic system such as the DSM or ICD series. Following the verification of a substance use disorder, a *functional assessment* is conducted in order to develop a thorough understanding of the person's substance use behaviour, and to place it within the broader context of the person's psychosocial functioning. Following the functional assessment, a *functional* (or *contextual*) *analysis* is conducted to evaluate the role that substance use plays in the individual's life, and to identify critical factors that may influence the person's use of substances. This functional analysis provides critical information that informs the last stage of the assessment process, *treatment planning*.

DETECTION

The purpose of the detection (or screening) stage is identify individuals who *may* be experiencing problems related to their use of substances. Because the consequences of substance use disorders are so dire in people with a psychotic disorder, there is a much greater cost to missing an individual who has a substance use disorder than in incorrectly identifying someone as having such a disorder when in fact they do not. Therefore, the goal at the detection stage is to 'cast a wide net' in identifying people who may have a substance use disorder, and to expect to rule out some of these individuals in the classification stage who are found not to have a disorder.

Screening can help identify clients who may benefit from fuller assessment of substance use problems.

A variety of strategies are useful for detecting people who have a possible substance use disorder. When working with anyone with the psychotic disorder, it is desirable to have a high overall index of suspicion about who may have a substance use disorder, considering that the prevalence of these disorders is approximately 50% in this population. In fact, one of the most potent predictors of current substance use disorder is a history of substance use problems in the past (Barry et al., 1995). In addition, being aware of which individuals are most likely to have substance use problems (e.g. young men who live alone or with parents, history of conduct disorder, antisocial personality disorder), awareness of the clinical and psychosocial consequences of substance use (e.g. relapses and rehospitalisations, housing instability, family conflict, money problems, involvement with the criminal justice system, significant depression) can further increase the clinician's ability to detect substance use disorder in their clients.

Clear, direct, nonjudgemental questioning helps ensure that substance use is not missed.

There is abundant evidence that substance use disorders are underdetected in routine treatment of people with psychotic disorders (Bahorik, Newhill, Queen, & Eack, 2014; Barbee, Clark, Craqanzano, Heintz, & Kehoe, 1989; Haddock et al., 2009). While there is no single reason for the high rate of underdetection, one of the most important reasons is that clinicians often fail to ask their clients about their substance use habits. Therefore, direct, frank questioning about use of substances is of critical importance.

Simply asking an individual about their substance use often provides honest and direct answers. It is important to inquire about the person's use of substances in a direct, matter-of-fact, nonblaming way. Clinicians who feel self-conscious about raising the topic can let the client know that they routinely talk with their clients about their use of substances. Questions about substance use should be initially focused on the person's recent substance use, such as over the past month, and inquire about both alcohol and drug use. For example:

- 'I'd like to ask you a few questions that I ask everybody who I work with. Can you tell me about your alcohol use?'
- 'About how many days in the past month did you drink alcohol?'
- 'On how many of those days over the past month did you drink enough so you felt tipsy, intoxicated, or drunk?'
- 'Do you sometimes smoke pot or hash?'
- 'Over the past month, on how many days did you get high smoking?'

While direct questioning about substance use often reveals useful information, it cannot be relied upon as the only source of information for detecting a substance use disorder. A number of brief screening measures have been shown to have acceptable reliability and validity for identifying substance use disorders in people with psychosis. Some of these measures are extremely brief and require only a few minutes to complete, while others are somewhat longer, but generally do not require more than 10–15 min to complete. Some of these measures have been developed specifically for people with a psychotic disorder or another severe mental illness (e.g. the Dartmouth Assessment of Lifestyle Inventory; Rosenberg et al., 1998), while others were developed for the general population but have acceptable sensitivity for detecting substance use disorders in people with major psychiatric disorders (e.g. the Alcohol Use Disorder Identification Test; Babor, Higgins-Biddle, Saunders, & Monteiro, 2001). Table 13.1 provides

Table 13.1 **Screening Instruments for Substance Use Disorder in People With Psychosis**

Instrument	Substance	Number of items
Alcohol Use Disorder Identification Test (AUDIT) (Babor et al., 2001)	Alcohol	10
Cut Down-Annoyed-Guilt-Eye opener (CAGE-AID) (Brown & Rounds, 1995)	Alcohol and drugs	4
Drug Abuse Screening Test (DAST) (Skinner, 1982)	Drugs	10
DrugCheck Problem List (PL) (Kavanagh et al., 2011)	Drugs	12
Drug Use Disorders Identification Test (DUDIT) (Berman, Bergmanb, Palmstiernac, & Schlyter, 2005)	Drugs	11
Dartmouth Assessment of Lifestyle Inventory (DALI) (Rosenberg et al., 1998)	Alcohol and drugs	17
Michigan Alcoholism Screening Test (MAST) (Selzer, 1971)	Alcohol	24

a summary of some screening instruments for detecting substance use disorders in people with psychosis.

In addition to the use of screening instruments, biological measures such as urinalysis for alcohol detection and hair analysis for drug detection can provide useful information about substance use in people with a psychotic disorder (Haddock et al., 2009; McPhillips et al., 1997; Swartz, Swanson, & Hannon, 2003). While urine analysis can only detect alcohol use within the past several hours, hair analysis can detect drug use ranging back weeks or even months, depending on the length of hair. However, although the use of these and other biological measures of substance use can provide an objective measure of substance use, they do not provide information about the possible consequences of substance use. In addition, implementation of these biological screening measures in routine treatment settings for psychosis can be challenging, as staff members are often uncomfortable about using them, and clients may as well, especially those with no significant history of substance use.

CLASSIFICATION

Once an individual has been identified as having a possible substance use disorder, the focus of assessment shifts to evaluating whether the person meets criteria for a substance use disorder.

Diagnostic Criteria for Substance Use Disorders

The specific diagnostic criteria for substance use disorder have changed in recent years, most specifically from DSM-IV (American Psychiatric Association, 1994) to DSM-5 (American Psychiatric Association, 2013). However, diagnosis of substance use disorders in both the ICD and DSM series is generally based on the presence of three types of problems. These problems pertain to the impact of substance use on functioning, physical dependence on substances, and psychological dependence. Common problems related to substance use are summarised in Table 13.2 and described below.

IMPACT OF SUBSTANCE USE ON FUNCTIONING

Substance use can lead to major negative consequences in the realms of psychosocial (role, social, self-care and independent living skills), medical, or psychological functioning. When these effects are repeated or sustained over a significant period of time (e.g. 1 month or more), diagnostic criteria for negative consequences of substance use are met. Substance use often causes strains in social relationships with family members and intimate partners, and is a major contributing factor to domestic violence. Because many people with psychotic disorders live at home or depend on family members for assistance in managing their disorders and their lives, their relationships with close relatives are often strained and a source of major conflict (Kashner et al., 1991; Niv, Lopez, Glynn, & Mueser, 2007; Salyers & Mueser, 2001).

People with comorbid substance use disorders are vulnerable to poor social, work, and health outcomes.

The use of alcohol or drugs can contribute to problems at work or school, leading to job loss or school dropout, and interfere with participation in vocational rehabilitation programs such as supported employment. Substance use can lead to problems in the ability to care for one's basic living needs, such as personal hygiene, nutrition, apartment or home maintenance, and stable housing. Use of substances can also worsen preexisting medical conditions (e.g. diabetes, ulcers) and contribute to the development of new medical problems (e.g. liver problems). Substance use can lead to other problematic social behaviours such as 'drunk and disorderly' conduct, driving while intoxicated or high, and getting into fights, which can have legal consequences of their own aside from consequences related to the use of illegal drugs. Furthermore, these consequences of substance use, as well as the direct impact of substances themselves, can pose threats to psychological functioning, leading to problems such as depression, anxiety, and suicidal ideation.

PHYSICAL DEPENDENCE

Physical dependence is defined in terms of the development of tolerance to the effects of the substance, thereby requiring the person to consume increasing amounts of the substance to achieve desired effects, and withdrawal symptoms following the reduction or cessation of substance use. Physical dependence on a substance results in a cycle of increasing use that has both physical and psychosocial consequences. As people use greater amounts of a substance, they become at increased risk for negative physical consequences (such as cirrhosis of the liver due to alcohol use, or precipitation of psychotic symptoms due to stimulant use), as well as overdose. Furthermore, increased efforts to obtain substances can lead to a range of problematic social behaviours (e.g. lying and stealing from family, robbery, exchanging sex for drugs, drug dealing). Although physical dependence on substances is a major concern for people with a psychotic

Table 13.2 Problems Used to Define Substance Use Disorders

Problem	Description
Negative consequences of use	■ Recurrent use of substances leading to failure to meet obligations at work, school, or home ■ Continued substance use despite persistent or recurrent social or interpersonal problems caused or worsened by use of the substance ■ Important social, work, or recreational activities given up or reduced because of substance use ■ Recurrent substance use in physically hazardous situations ■ Continued substance use despite knowledge of having recurrent or persistent physical problem like to have been caused or worsened by alcohol use
Physical dependence	■ Tolerance to the effects of substances, as indicated by: – Need to use more substance to attain desired effect or intoxication – Marked reduction in effect with continued use of same amount of substance ■ Withdrawal effects
Psychological dependence	■ Using more substance or for a longer period than was intended ■ Persistent desire or unsuccessful efforts to cut down or control substance use ■ A great deal of time spent obtaining substances, using them, or recovering from them ■ Cravings or a strong desire to use substance

disorder, in general the rates of physical dependence are somewhat lower for these individuals than in the primary addiction population (Mueser, Drake, & Wallach, 1998; Mueser, Kavanagh, & Brunette, 2007).

PSYCHOLOGICAL DEPENDENCE

Psychological dependence is defined in terms of the impact and dominance of the person's use of substances on their day-to-day lives and their psychological well-being. Common indicators of psychological addiction include spending inordinate amounts of time using substances, making repeated efforts to cut down, and using greater amounts of substances than intended. These psychological consequences often replace other drives or motivations that individuals typically have that organise and give purpose to their lives, such as the desire to work or complete school, to establish and maintain close and loving relationships, to sustain independent living, and to have enjoyable recreational pursuits. Psychological dependence on substances is especially important for people with a psychotic disorder. Given the often-marginal level of functioning of people with psychosis in these life domains, evaluating psychological dependence has implications for understanding the motives underlying substance use (Addington & Duchak, 1997), as addressed in the later section of this chapter on 'Functional Assessment'.

Measures

The classification of substance use disorders is optimally conducted with the use of a structured clinical interview. Extensive research has shown that structured clinical interviews resulted in more reliable and valid psychiatric diagnoses, across the range of psychiatric disorders, including addiction. A variety of different structured clinical interviews have been developed, which cover a broad range of psychiatric disorders, including addiction. Examples of such widely used instruments include the *Structured Clinical Interview for DSM-5* for which several versions are available (First, Williams, Karg, & Spitzer, 2015a, 2015b), the *Mini-International Neuropsychiatric Interview* (Sheehan et al., 1998), and the *World Mental Health Composite International Diagnostic Interview* (Kessler & Ustün, 2004).

Clinician training is essential to achieve reliable assessment of substance use disorders.

Although structured diagnostic interviews are the sine qua non of assessment, they require significant training to administer, and time to complete. However, there are viable alternatives to these interviews that can lead to reliable and valid diagnoses in routine clinical practice when their implementation is accompanied by appropriate training. One such approach is the use clinician rating scales.

Two such clinician rating skills are the Alcohol Use Scale (AUS) and the Drug Use Scale (DUS) (Mueser, Noordsy, Drake, & Fox, 2003). These measures were designed to evaluate the presence of a substance use disorder over the past 6 months. Focusing on the person's use of substances over the past 6 months has greatest relevance for treatment planning as it provides an indication of the most recent problems related to substance use. In addition, the 6-month time-frame covered by these measures makes them suitable for administering on a routine basis every 6 months in order to evaluate treatment response and to inform further treatment planning.

The AUS and DUS require clinicians to evaluate the consequences of substance use disorder based on the broad range of available data, including client self-reports supplemented with interview questions, reports of significant others such as family members, the treatment team, and medical records, including the results of any substance use toxicology tests. The use of multiple sources of information to establish a diagnosis of substance use disorder is preferred over reliance on a single source (Desmarais, Van Dorn, Sellers, Young, & Swartz, 2013). This information is then consolidated into a rating on a five-point scale regarding the consequences of the client's use of substances during the worst 1-month period over the past 6 months. Box 13.1 summarises the anchors for the five-point rating scales used in the AUS and DUS, revised for DSM-5.

The clinician rating scales for alcohol and drug use disorder require some training of clinical staff (Mueser et al., 1995). The general recommendation is to conduct a 2- to 3-h initial training in which the diagnostic criteria for substance use disorders are first covered, the clinician rating scales (AUS, DUS) and instructions for its use are reviewed, and practice cases are rated and discussed with the leader. It is useful if this introductory session is followed by several 1-h

Box 13.1 Anchors for Clinician Ratings of Substance Use on the Clinician Alcohol Use Scale and Drug Use Scale-Revised for DSM-5

Ratings pertain to the worst 1 month period over the past 6 months. See Table 13.2 for list of problems related to substance use.

1 = ABSTINENT: No alcohol/drug use over the past 6 months

2 = USE WITHOUT IMPAIRMENT: Client used alcohol/drugs during this time period but experienced 0 or only 1 problem

3 = MILD SUBSTANCE USE DISORDER: Client used alcohol/drugs during this time interval and during the worst month experienced 2–3 problems

4 = MODERATE SUBSTANCE USE DISORDER: Client used alcohol/drugs during this time interval and during the worst month experienced 4–5 problems

5 = SEVERE SUBSTANCE USE DISORDER: Client used alcohol/drugs during this time interval and during the worst month experienced 6 or more problems

trainings in which clinicians provide and discuss additional ratings on practice cases, as well as present cases of their own that were rated, and any questions and challenges they experienced. Conducting at least annual reliability trainings is important to ensure that clinician ratings remain accurate over the long term. Research shows that when routine training is provided to clinicians on the use of the AUS and DUS valid and reliable ratings of substance use disorder can be obtained (Drake, Mueser, & McHugo, 1996; Møller & Linaker, 2010).

Functional Assessment

The functional assessment stage is focused on individuals who have been identified as having a current or recent substance use disorder, with the aim of developing a more thorough understanding of the nature of their substance use problems in order to inform treatment planning. A comprehensive assessment at this stage involves obtaining detailed information about the specific circumstances in which substances are used and their consequences, as well as evaluating potential motives that may underline the person's use of substances. Additional information is required in order to understand the individual's psychosocial functioning across the broad range of life domains, including both areas of challenge as well as strengths and social supports.

A functional assessment helps to pin down the motives, circumstances, and consequences of substance use.

In the following sections, methods for evaluating patterns of substance use are first reviewed, followed by the assessment of consequences of substance use, and then motives and reasons. The final section addresses a comprehensive assessment of the broad range of psychosocial life domains.

Patterns of Substance Use

Both the frequency and intensity of substance use guides treatment planning.

Information about the frequency and intensity of an individual's use of substances over time can provide valuable information that informs treatment planning. Some individuals with psychotic disorders use relatively low or moderate amounts of substances on a regular basis, such as drinking one or two drinks per day or on most days, or smoking modest amounts of cannabis several times per week. Despite the relatively low amounts of substances these individuals use, such use can have negative consequences because of the increased sensitivity to substance effects associated with psychotic disorders (D'Souza et al., 2005; D'Souza et al., 2006; Mueser et al., 1998). Other individuals may have a less self-regulated pattern of substance use, with use characterised by periods of intensive use often accompanied by drastic consequences (e.g. homelessness, symptom relapses, unsafe sexual behaviours, aggression, legal problems), interspersed with periods of abstinence, which are sometimes related to those consequences (e.g. psychiatric hospitalisation or incarceration).

One useful instrument for evaluating an individual's pattern of substance use is the Time-line Follow-Back Calendar (TFBC) (Mueser, Noordsy, Drake, & Fox, 2003; Sacks, Drake, Williams, Banks, & Herrell, 2003). The TFBC is an interview-based assessment in which the clinician reviews with the client his or her daily use of different substances over a 6-month period, using a calendar and identifying important events to the client that occurred during this period as reference points. Information is obtained regarding the person's daily use of specific substances over the period, with an emphasis on the pattern of use (e.g. types of substances, frequency of use, regularity) rather strict accuracy in terms of amount of use. The TFBC was first developed and validated for use with people with alcohol use disorders (Sobell & Sobell, 1992), but since then was expanded to include drugs, and for use in people with comorbid psychiatric disorders (Carey, Carey, Maisto, & Henson, 2004; DeMarce, Burden, Lash, Stephens, & Grambow, 2007; Mueser, Noordsy, Drake, & Fox, 2003).

Consequences of Substance Use

As previously noted, information regarding the consequences of an individual's use of substances should be obtained through multiple sources of information (e.g. self-report, collateral reports, medical records) rather than a single source. The consequences of substance use are far-reaching, and therefore assessment must review the broad range of areas of functioning. One of the most established measures for evaluating the consequences of substance use is the Addiction Severity Index (ASI), currently in its sixth edition (Cacciola, Alterman, Habing, & McLellan, 2011; Denis, Cacciola, & Alterman, 2013; McLellan, Cacciola, Alterman, Rikoon, & Carise, 2006). The ASI is a semistructured interview designed to evaluate the impact of substance use on seven different areas of functioning, including medical, social, employment/school, family/social, legal, and psychiatric. The assessment includes information about both objective (e.g. specific problems with family members or the law) and subjective (e.g. how distressed the person was) aspects of substance use consequences, with a focus on the past 30 days, past 6 months, and lifetime problems.

The ASI has been used successfully in persons with psychotic disorders (Corse, Hirschinger, & Zanis, 1995), although the severity index scores for different domains tend to be lower than in primary addiction populations. An alternative measure to the ASI that was specifically designed to evaluate the consequences of substance use in people with a psychotic disorder is the Substance Use Event Survey for Severe Mental Illness (SUESS) (Bennett, Bellack, & Gearon, 2006). The SUESS is a briefer (20–30 min) interview shown to be well tolerated by persons with severe psychiatric disorders, with good evidence supporting its reliability and validity.

Psychosocial Functioning

The final step in the functional assessment is to evaluate the individual's functioning across the range of life domains. This assessment will be informed by the results of the assessment of substance use consequences, but goes beyond that evaluation by developing an understanding of the individual's adjustment in each life domain, as well as their satisfaction and motivation to make changes in each area. Substance use may or may not be having an impact on areas of functioning that are affected by the mental illness. For example, the substance use of one client who had a circle of friends with whom he used substances led to conflict with his parents, money problems, and exacerbations of his psychotic symptoms. However, he got along with his friends, and although he wanted to have a girlfriend, his social relationships were not worsened by his substance use.

The evaluation of psychosocial adjustment and motivation to change should cover the domains of social functioning (friends, intimate relationships), family relationships, role functioning (work or school), finances and money management, illness management (including symptoms, relapses, re-hospitalisations), well-being, leisure and recreation, independent living and self-care skills, health and wellness, and religion and spirituality. For each domain, the clinician should seek to understand the quality of the person's functioning, their satisfaction or dissatisfaction with that area, and their desire to make changes in the area. Identifying areas of psychosocial functioning that the individual wants to change is critical for treatment planning. Collaboration with the client on making changes in desired areas forms the basis for the therapeutic alliance between the clinician and client, and maximises retention in treatment. In addition, work on desired areas of change often leads to an increased awareness of the client about the negative effects of substance use on achieving their goals, which can harness motivation to work on reducing or stopping their substance use (i.e. motivational interviewing).

Shared decision making enhances the efficacy of treatment of substance use disorders.

The assessment of psychosocial adjustment can be conducted through the use of informal interview methods, and may extend over several sessions. The clinician should demonstrate genuine interest and concern about the quality of the client's functioning across the different domains, and make efforts to ensure that the client feels comfortable with the process. Other potentially useful resources for conducting the psychosocial assessment include the Functional Assessment

Interview (Mueser, Noordsy, Drake, & Fox, 2003) and the Recovery Strategies module of the Illness Management and Recovery program (Gingerich & Mueser, 2010; Gingerich & Mueser, 2011).

Reasons and Motives for Substance Use

An understanding of the primary motives or reasons for using substances can be invaluable to treatment planning. The extent to which an individual's substance use is related to, or driven by, specific needs or desires can point to the importance of targeting those areas in order for treatment to be maximally effective (Mueser, Noordsy, Drake, & Fox, 2003). For example, individuals who use substances as a strategy for coping with distressing symptoms (e.g. 'self-medication') can benefit from learning alternative and more effective coping strategies.

Motives for substance use are often similar in people with or without psychosis.

There are many different reasons people use substances, both in the general population and among persons with a psychotic disorder. Research on motives or reasons for using substance have identified three common motives, including socialisation, coping with negative feelings, and pleasure enhancement. Abundant research has shown that these same motives are also important in people with a psychotic disorder (Addington & Duchak, 1997; Laudet, Magura, Vogel, & Knight, 2004; Mueser, Nishith, Tracy, DeGirolamo, & Molinaro, 1995; O'Hare & Sherrer, 2012; Warner et al., 1994), for several reasons. First, people with psychotic disorders frequently have poor social functioning, and thus substance use with others can facilitate social connection, friendship, and intimacy. Second, psychiatric symptoms are often a cause of significant distress, and substances may be used to escape or counteract the effects of those symptoms (Khantzian, 1985; Khantzian, 1997). Third, people with psychotic disorders frequently lack a broad range of leisure and recreational activities, and thus the pleasurable effects of substance use are often appealing.

While these are common reasons for using substances in both the general population and among people with SMI, there are many other reasons that are more unique to persons with psychotic disorders. For example, many people with a psychotic disorder lack involvement in meaningful activities such as work, school, or family responsibilities, and substance use may be partly the result of not having any to do with one's time. It is established that substance use increases in the general population when people have more free time on their hands, such as following the loss of a job or retirement. For another example, substance use may reflect an attempt to escape the demoralising effects of being diagnosed with a serious psychiatric disorder. Box 13.2 provides a list of common reasons for substance use in people with a psychotic disorder.

There are several approaches to assessing motives or reasons for substance use. First, over the course of conducting the comprehensive assessment and learning about the circumstances in which the client uses substances, the clinician should be alert to clues regarding possible motives and explore them as appropriate. For example, clients who frequently use substances with others, questions can be asked to more fully understand the role of substance use in those relationships

Box 13.2 Common Reasons and Motives for Using Substances in Persons With a Psychotic Disorder

- Something to do with old friends
- A way to meet new people
- Reduces social anxiety
- Feels good
- Get 'high'
- Nothing to do
- Escape from psychiatric diagnosis and stigma
- Forget about one's troubles/worries
- Reduction of hallucinations
- Escape from depression
- Reduction in posttraumatic stress disorder (PTSD) symptoms
- Get to sleep/pass out
- Relaxation
- Stress reduction

(e.g. Does the client use with old friends as a way of spending time together? Does the client report that using substances make her feel more comfortable interacting with other people? Has the client developed relationships with others by using substances together and sharing personal resources such as money or their apartment to facilitate substance use?)

Second, directly asking the client about the reasons for using substances or their perceived benefits of use may reveal motives that are not otherwise apparent. Normalising substance use as a common human behaviour, and explaining that everyone has reasons for using substances, can reduce defensiveness and facilitate a more open discussion of some of the reasons the person uses substances. Third, standard measures of reasons for using substances can be administered, such as the Drinking Motives Measure (Cooper, Russell, Skinner, & Windle, 1992), which has also been adapted to evaluate motives for using drugs, and found to be reliable and valid in persons with a psychotic disorder (Mueser, Nishith, et al., 1995).

Insight and Motivation to Change

The final area of assessment is the client's insight into his or her substance use problems and motivation to change their substance use habits. Denial and minimisation of the effects of substance use on one's life are common in people with addiction and should be expected. Nevertheless, most individuals have at least some insight into their substance use problems. Understanding the individual's insight and motivation to change has important implications for treatment planning, and the extent to which the reduction of substance use is a shared goal between the clinician and client. The client's insight and motivation to change may become evident over the course of conducting the assessment. For example, when discussing some of the consequences of substance use, the client may spontaneously talk about his or her desire to cut down or stop using substances. However, in the absence of clear evidence, the best approach to evaluating

Motivation for change can be influenced by a clinician's style of interaction.

insight and motivation is to have direct discussions with the client that incorporate the clinician's frank observations based on the assessment completed thus far.

For example, to evaluate insight, the clinician could say, 'We've spent some time talking about your substance use, and some of its effects on your life. For example, we talked about how using substances has created a lot of tension with your family, and may have contributed to relapses of your symptoms. What do you think about all this? Do you think you have a substance use problems? How serious do you think this problem is?' Most clients have at least some insight into having substance use problems, but significant minimisation of the problems is common.

The question of motivation to change is only relevant for clients who have some insight into their problems. A similarly direct approach can be used to explore this motivation. Although stated desire by the client to change substance use habits is desirable, words alone can tell only so much about the person's motivation to change. It has been argued the true motivation to change is characterised by a pattern in which efforts to change are reflected in behaviours consistent with the verbal intentions (Miller & Rollnick, 2012), such as repeated efforts to cut down or stop using substances, or actual success in substance use reduction. In line with this more behavioural approach to defining motivation, the Stages of Treatment Rating Scale was developed to assess clients' motivational stage (Drake et al., 1996; Mueser, Noordsy, Drake, & Fox, 2003), based on the trans-theoretical model of the stages of change with respect to treatment of a co-occurring substance use disorder (DiClemente & Prochaska, 1998; Kofoed, Kania, Walsh, & Atkinson, 1986). Four different stages of treatment are distinguished on the scale, with each stage including an early and late level, resulting in an eight-point scale. The *engagement stage* corresponds to prior to when the client has established a working relationship with the clinician, which is defined as seeing the clinician on a regular basis. The *persuasion stage* corresponds to when a therapeutic relationship has been established with the clinician treating the co-occurring disorder and discussion has begun to address the client's substance use, but there has been no sustained effort to cut down or stop using substances. The *active treatment stage* corresponds to when, in the context of this therapeutic relationship, the client has begun to reduce substance use or has made repeated attempts to cut down for at least 1 month or more. The *relapse prevention stage* corresponds to when the client's substance use disorder has been in remission for at least 6 months, and the focus of treatment shifts to relapse prevention and extending the recovery other areas of functioning.

FUNCTIONAL ANALYSIS

The functional analysis (or contextual analysis) component of assessment is aimed at reaching a formulation of the person's substance use behaviour that will serve to inform treatment planning. Specifically, based on the information collected during the assessment thus far, the clinician seeks to identify which factors contribute most strongly to the individual's continued substance use, as well as what areas of functioning potentially affected by substance use might the client most want to work on changing.

Theoretical Basis for the Functional Analysis

The theoretical rationale underlying the functional analysis is that all behaviour is the product of the consequences of the behaviour vs the alternative to the behaviour (Bijou & Peterson, 1971; Goldiamond, 1974). The working assumption of this analysis is that the positive consequences (i.e. reinforcement) of a behaviour (e.g. substance use) and the negative consequences of the alternative behaviours (e.g. abstinence) together outweigh the combined negative consequences of the behaviour and positive consequences of the alternative behaviour. Based on this assumption, a behaviour (such as substance use) can be changed by modifying one (or more) of the four contingencies maintaining the behaviour: (1) reducing the positive consequences of the behaviour, (2) increasing the negative consequences of the behaviour, (3) increasing the positive consequences of the alternative behaviour, or (4) decreasing the negative consequences of the alternative behaviour. One tool for facilitating the identification of critical factors maintaining substance use in people with a psychotic disorder is the 'Pay-Off Matrix', which guides clinicians in systematically organising information based on a comprehensive assessment in order to select those factors that have the greatest promise for changing in treatment (Mueser, Noordsy, Fox, & Wolfe, 2003).

A pay-off matrix can help clients focus on the pros and cons of changing their substance use.

Treatment Planning Based on the Functional Analysis

From the perspective of treatment planning, the identification of key factors that maintain the client's substance use can lead to interventions designed to reduce or increase the impact of any of the four contingencies. However, in practice, it is difficult to modify two of the factors. Specifically, it is difficult to increase the negative consequences of substance use, which are already very negative, although technically disulfirim can be used for this purpose (Mueser, Noordsy, Fox, & Wolfe, 2003). It is also practically difficult to reduce the positive consequences of using substances, although naltrexone and other addiction medications technically may serve this purpose (Green, Noordsy, Brunette, & O'Keefe, 2008). However, the other two contingencies are more readily modifiable and lend themselves to targeting in treatment, including reducing the negative consequences of not using substances, and increasing the positive consequences of abstinence.

As discussed in the previous section on 'Reasons and Motives' for substance use, the primary reasons people with a psychotic disorder use substances fall into three broad categories, including facilitating socialisation, coping with symptoms, and the pleasurable effects of substances. Therefore, without addressing the underlying motives for using substances, attempts to reduce clients' substance use may meet with resistance as individuals are reluctant to give up their friendships, their strategies for coping with symptoms, and some of the few sources of pleasure and relaxation in their lives. However, the specific reasons for using substances can be targeted in treatment, and people can be helped to develop skills and opportunities for having rewarding relationships with others (e.g. social skills training), effective coping strategies, and leisure and recreational activities that do not rely on the use of substances. To the extent that treatment is effective at selectively targeting critical motives underlying substance use, the negative consequences of abstinence will be reduced, shifting the person towards substance use reduction and abstinence.

Similar to how treatment can target the reduction of negative consequences of not using substances, it can also target increases in the benefits of not using substances. Some substance use interventions do this explicitly, such as contingent reinforcement for abstinence (Bellack, Bennet, Gearon, Brown, & Yang, 2006; Sigmon & Higgins, 2006). However, another approach is to focus on increasing the perceived benefits of not using substances by identifying personally meaningful changes that the person wants to make, and actively pursuing and making those changes as a major focus of collaborative work between the client and clinician. By establishing these desired changes and goals, and supporting the client's sense of hope and self-efficacy that they can be achieved, and beginning to take practical steps towards achieving the goals, the advantages of abstinence are in effect increased, and with it motivation to cut down or stop using substances. (Miller & Rollnick, 2012; Mueser, Noordsy, Drake, & Fox, 2003).

Examples of changes in psychosocial functioning desired by clients that can become treatment goals and lead to motivation for abstinence include a young woman who wants to be a better mother role model for her two young children, a young man who wants to return to college to compete his degree, a man who want to get a job so he will have money to spend on his girlfriend, and a woman who wants to reconnect with her church group and friends after many years of absence.

The critical information for conducting a functional analysis is a comprehensive assessment of the individual's substance use behaviour and its consequences, as well as an understanding of the person psychosocial adjustment and desire for change. The identification of which factors are most critical in maintaining the person's use of substances, and the most malleable factors that have the potential to redirect the person towards cutting down use of substances and abstinence, is a matter of clinical judgement. Thus, the functional analysis, and the specific factors thought to be maintaining substance use behaviour should be conceptualised as a working hypothesis that guides treatment planning, with the accuracy of the hypothesis reflected by the success to which changes in the identified behaviours lead to changes in the outcome, or continued use of substances vs. cutting down or abstinence (Hayes & Nelson, 1986). In order to maximise changing some of the critical factors maintaining substance use, Mueser, Noordsy, Drake, and Fox (2003) recommend that treatment plans for people with co-occurring disorders include at least one intervention targeting reduction of the negative consequences of not using substances (e.g. increasing strategies for coping with symptoms, improving social skills for relationships with people who do not use substances), and at least one intervention aimed at increasing the perceived positive consequences of not using substances (e.g. working on functional goals such as close relationships, work, or school).

SUMMARY AND CONCLUSIONS

Substance use disorders are common in persons with a psychotic disorder, and contribute to worse course of illness. The accurate identification of people with co-occurring disorders is of fundamental importance to its treatment. The goals and methods of assessment can be divided into four phases, including: (1) *detection*, aimed at identifying people who have a possible substance use disorder, (2) *classification*, aimed at determining whether a client has a substance use disorder according to a diagnostic system, (3) *functional assessment*, aimed at developing a comprehensive understanding of the context in which the individual's substance use occurs, and (4) *functional analysis*, aimed at identifying which factors are most critical to maintaining substance use and preventing changes to less destructive behaviours in order to inform treatment planning. Clinicians have a broad range of tools at their disposal to assist in conducting a rigorous assessment of substance use disorders in persons with a psychotic disorder, and developing treatment plans that have promise for reducing the untoward effects of substance use on their lives.

References

Addington, J., & Duchak, V. (1997). Reasons for substance use in schizophrenia. *Acta Psychiatrica Scandinavica, 96*, 329–333.

American Psychiatric Association (1994). *Diagnostic and statistical manual of mental disorders (DSM-IV)* (4th ed.). Washington, DC: American Psychiatric Association.

American Psychiatric Association (2013). *Diagnostic and statistical manual of mental disorders (DSM-5)* (5th ed.). Washington, DC: American Psychiatric Association.

Andréasson, S., Allebeck, P., Engström, A., & Rydberg, U. (1987). Cannabis and schizophrenia: A longitudinal study of Swedish conscripts. *Lancet, 2*, 1483–1486.

Arseneault, L., Cannon, M., Witton, J., & Murray, R. M. (2004). Causal association between cannabis and psychosis: Examination of the evidence. *British Journal of Psychiatry, 184*, 110–117.

Babor, T. F., Higgins-Biddle, J. C., Saunders, J. B., & Monteiro, M. G. (2001). *AUDIT: The alcohol use disorders identification test: Guidelines for use in primary care* (2nd ed.). Geneva: World Health Organization, Department of Mental Health and Substance Dependence.

Bahorik, A. L., Newhill, C. E., Queen, C. C., & Eack, S. M. (2014). Underreporting of drug use among individuals with schizophrenia: Prevalence and predictors. *Psychological Medicine, 44*, 61–69.

Barbee, J. G., Clark, P. D., Craqanzano, M. S., Heintz, G. C., & Kehoe, C. E. (1989). Alcohol and substance abuse among schizophrenic patients presenting to an emergency service. *Journal of Nervous and Mental Disease, 177*, 400–407.

Barry, K. L., Fleming, M. F., Greenley, J. R., Widlak, P. A., Kropp, S., & McKee, D. (1995). Assessment of alcohol and other drug disorders in the seriously mentally ill. *Schizophrenia Bulletin, 21*, 313–321.

Bellack, A. S., Bennet, M. E., Gearon, J. S., Brown, C. H., & Yang, Y. (2006). A randomized clinical trial of a new behavioral treatment for drug abuse in people with severe and persistent mental illness. *Archives of General Psychiatry, 63*, 426–432.

Bennett, M. E., Bellack, A. S., & Gearon, J. S. (2006). Development of a comprehensive measure to assess clinical issues in dual diagnosis patients: The Substance Use Event Survey for Severe Mental Illness. *Addictive Behaviors, 31*, 2249–2267.

Berman, A. H., Bergmanb, H., Palmstiernac, T., & Schlyter, F. (2005). Evaluation of the Drug Use Disorders Identification Test (DUDIT) in criminal justice and detoxification settings and in a Swedish population sample. *European Addiction Research, 11*, 22–32.

Bijou, S. W., & Peterson, R. F. (1971). Functional analysis in the assessment of children. P. McReynolds (Ed.), *Vol. 2 Advances in psychological assessment* (pp. 63–78). Palo Alto, CA: Science and Behavior Books.

Brown, R. L., & Rounds, L. A. (1995). Conjoint screening questionnaires for alcohol and other drug abuse: Criterion validity in a primary care practice. *Wisconsin Medical Journal, 94*, 135–140.

Brunette, M. F., Mueser, K. T., Babbin, S., Meyer-Kalos, P., Rosenheck, R., Correll, C. U., et al. (2018). Demographic and clinical correlates of substance use disorders in first episode psychosis. *Schizophrenia Research, 194*, 4–12.

Cacciola, J. S., Alterman, A., Habing, B., & McLellan, A. T. (2011). Recent status scores for version 6 of the Addiction Severity Index (ASI-6). *Addiction, 106*, 1588–1602.

Carey, K. B., Carey, M. P., Maisto, S. A., & Henson, J. M. (2004). Temporal stability of the Timeline Followback Interview for alcohol and drug use with psychiatric outpatients. *Journal of Studies on Alcohol, 65*, 774–781.

Chiapelli, J., Chen, S., Hackman, A., & Hong, I. E. (2018). Evidence for differential opioid use disorder in schizophrenia in an addiction treatment population. *Schizophrenia Research, 194*, 26–31.

Cohen, M., & Klein, D. F. (1970). Drug abuse in a young psychiatric population. *American Journal of Orthopsychiatry, 40*, 448–455.

Compton, M., T., Broussard, B., ., Ramsay, C. E., & Stewart, T. (2011). Pre-illness cannabis use and the early course of nonaffective psychotic disorders: Associations with premorbid functioning, the prodrome, and mode of onset of psychosis. Schizophrenia Research, 126, 71–76.

Cooper, M. L., Russell, M., Skinner, J. B., & Windle, M. (1992). Development and validation of a three-dimensional measure of drinking motives. *Psychological Assessment, 4*, 123–132.

Corse, S. J., Hirschinger, N. B., & Zanis, D. (1995). The use of the Addiction Severity Index with people with severe mental illness. *Psychiatric Rehabilitation Journal, 19*, 9–18.

DeMarce, J. M., Burden, J. L., Lash, S. J., Stephens, R. S., & Grambow, S. C. (2007). Convergent validity of the Timeline Followback for persons with comorbid psychiatric disorders engaged in residential substance use treatment. *Addictive Behaviors, 32*, 1582–1592.

Denis, C. M., Cacciola, J. S., & Alterman, A. I. (2013). Addiction Severity Index (ASI) summary scores: Comparison of the Recent Status Scores of the ASI-6 and the Composite Scores of the ASI-5. *Journal of Substance Abuse Treatment, 45*, 444–450.

Desmarais, S. L., Van Dorn, R., Sellers, B. G., Young, M. S., & Swartz, M. S. (2013). Accuracy of self-report, biological tests, collateral reports and clinician ratings in identifying substance use disorders among adults with schizophrenia. *Psychology of Addictive Disorders, 27*, 774–787.

DiClemente, C. C., & Prochaska, J. O. (1998). Toward a comprehensive, transtheoretical model of change: Stages of change and addictive behaviors. In W. R. Miller, & N. Heather (Eds.), *Treating addictive behaviors* (2nd ed., pp. 3–24). New York: Plenum Press.

Drake, R. E., Luciano, A., Mueser, K. T., Covell, N. H., Essock, S. M., Xie, H., et al. (2016). Longitudinal course of clients with co-occurring schizophrenia-spectrum and substance use disorders in urban mental health centers: A seven-year prospective study. *Schizophrenia Bulletin, 42*, 202–211.

Drake, R. E., McHugo, G. J., Xie, H., Fox, M., Packard, J., & Helmstetter, B. (2006). Ten-year recovery outcomes for clients with co-occurring schizophrenia and substance use disorders. *Schizophrenia Bulletin, 32*, 464–473.

Drake, R. E., Mueser, K. T., & McHugo, G. J. (1996). Clinician rating scales: Alcohol Use Scale (AUS), Drug Use Scale (DUS), and Substance Abuse Treatment Scale (SATS). In L. I. Sederer, & B. Dickey (Eds.), *Outcomes assessment in clinical practice* (pp. 113–116). Baltimore, MD: Williams & Wilkins.

D'Souza, D. C., Abi-Saab, W. M., Madonick, S., Forselius-Bielen, K., Doersch, A., Braley, G., et al. (2005). Delta-9-tetrahydrocannabinol effects in schizophrenia: Implications for cognition, psychosis, and addiction. *Biological Psychiatry, 57*, 594–608.

D'Souza, D. C., Gil, R. B., Madonick, S., Perry, E. B., Forselius-Bielen, K., Braley, G., et al. (2006). Enhanced sensitivity to the euphoric effects of alcohol in schizophrenia. *Neuropsychopharmacology, 31*, 2767–2775.

First, M. B., Williams, J. B. W., Karg, R. S., & Spitzer, R. L. (2015a). *Structured clinical interview for DSM-5 disorders: Clinician version*. Washington, DC: American Psychiatric Press.

First, M. B., Williams, J. B. W., Karg, R. S., & Spitzer, R. L. (2015b). *Structured clinical interview for DSM-5 disorders: Research version (SCID-5-RV)*. Washington, DC: American Psychiatric Press.

Gingerich, S., & Mueser, K. T. (2010). *Illness management and recovery implementation resource kit*. (revised ed.) Rockville, MD: Center for Mental Health Services, Substance Abuse and Mental Health Services Administration.

Gingerich, S., & Mueser, K. T. (2011). *Illness management and recovery: Personalized skills and strategies for those with mental illness* (3rd ed.). Center City, MN: Hazelden.

Goldiamond, I. (1974). Toward a constructional approach to social problems: Ethical and constitutional problems raised by applied behavioral analysis. *Behavior, 2*, 1–85.

Green, A. I., Noordsy, D. L., Brunette, M. F., & O'Keefe, C. D. (2008). Substance abuse and schizophrenia: Pharmacotherapeutic intervention. *Journal of Substance Abuse Treatment, 34*, 61–71.

Haddock, G., Cross, Z., Beardmore, R., Tarrier, N., Moring, J., & Barrowclough, C. (2009). Assessing illicit substance use in schizophrenia: The relationship between self report and detection by hair analysis. *Schizophrenia Research, 114*, 180–181.

Hambrecht, M., & Häfner, H. (2000). Cannabis, vulnerability, and the onset of schizophrenia: An epidemiological perspective. *Australian and New Zealand Journal of Psychiatry, 34*, 468–475.

Harrison, I., Joyce, E. M., Mutsatsa, S. H., Hutton, S. B., Huddy, V., Kapasi, M., et al. (2008). Naturalistic follow-up of co-morbid substance use in schizophrenia: The West London first-episode study. *Psychological Medicine, 38*, 79–88.

Hartz, S. M., Pato, C. N., Medeiros, H., Cavazos-Rehg, P., Sobell, J. L., Knowles, J. A., et al. (2014). Comorbidity of severe psychotic disorders with measures of substance use. *JAMA Psychiatry, 71*, 248–254.

Hayes, S. C., & Nelson, R. O. (1986). Assessing the effects of therapeutic interventions. In R. O. Nelson, & S. C. Hayes (Eds.), *Conceptual foundations of behavioral assessment* (pp. 430–460). New York: Guilford Publications.

Kashner, M., Rader, L., Rodell, D., Beck, C., Rodell, L., & Muller, K. (1991). Family characteristics, substance abuse, and hospitalization patterns of patients with schizophrenia. *Hospital and Community Psychiatry, 42*, 195–197.

Kavanagh, D. J., Trembath, M., Shockley, N., Connolly, J., White, A., Isailovic, A., et al. (2011). The DrugCheck Problem List: A new screen for substance use disorders in people with psychosis. *Addictive Behaviors, 36*, 927–932.

Kavanagh, D. J., Waghorn, G., Jenner, L., Chant, D. C., Carr, V., Evans, M., et al. (2004). Demographic and clinical correlates of comorbid substance use disorders in psychosis: Multivariate analyses from an epidemiological sample. *Schizophrenia Research, 66*, 115–124.

Kessler, R. C., Chiu, W. T., Demler, O., & Walters, E. E. (2005). Prevalence, severity, and comorbidity of 12-month DSM-IV disorders in the National Comorbidity Survey Replication. *Archives of General Psychiatry, 62*, 617–627.

Kessler, R. C., & Ustün, T. B. (2004). The World Mental Health (WMH) survey initiative version of the World Health Organization (WHO) Composite International Diagnostic Interview (CIDI). *International Journal of Methods in Psychiatric Research, 13*, 93–121.

Khantzian, E. (1985). The self-medication hypothesis of addictive disorders: Focus on heroin and cocaine dependence. *American Journal of Psychiatry, 142*, 1259–1264.

Khantzian, E. J. (1997). The self-medication hypothesis of substance use disorders: A reconsideration and recent applications. *Harvard Review of Psychiatry, 4*, 231–244.

Kofoed, L., Kania, J., Walsh, T., & Atkinson, R. (1986). Outpatient treatment of patients with substance abuse and coexisting psychiatric disorders. *American Journal of Psychiatry, 143*, 867–872.

Large, M., Mullin, K., Gupta, P., Harris, A., & Nielssen, O. (2014). Systematic meta-analysis of outcomes associated with psychosis and co-morbid substance use. *Australian and New Zealand Journal of Psychiatry, 48*, 418–432.

Laudet, A. B., Magura, S., Vogel, H. S., & Knight, E. L. (2004). Perceived reasons for substance misuse among persons with a psychiatric disorder. *American Journal of Orthopsychiatry, 74*, 365–375.

McLellan, A. T., Cacciola, J. C., Alterman, A. I., Rikoon, S. H., & Carise, D. (2006). The Addiction Severity Index at 25: Origins, contributions and transitions. *American Journal on Addictions, 15*, 113–124.

McPhillips, M. A., Kelly, F. J., Barnes, T. R. E., Kuke, P. J., Gene-Cos, N., & Clark, K. (1997). Detecting comorbid substance misuse among people with schizophrenia in the community: A study comparing the results of questionnaires with analysis of hair and urine. *Schizophrenia Research, 25*, 141–148.

Merikangas, K. R., & McClair, V. L. (2012). Epidemiology of substance use disorders. *Human Genetics, 131*, 779–789.

Merikangas, K. R., Mehta, R. L., Molnar, B. E., Walters, E. E., Swendsen, J. D., Aguilar-Gaziola, S., et al. (1998). Comorbidity of substance use disorders with mood and anxiety disorders: Results of the International Consortium in Psychiatric Epidemiology. *Addictive Behaviors, 23*, 893–907.

Miller, W. R., & Rollnick, S. (2012). *Motivational interviewing: Preparing people for change. In* (3rd ed.). New York: Guilford Press.

Møller, T., & Linaker, O. M. (2010). Using brief self-reports and clinician scales to screen for substance use disorders in psychotic patients. *Nordic Journal of Psychiatry, 64*, 130–135.

Morgan, V., McGrath, J. J., Jablensky, A., Badcock, J. C., Waterreus, A., Bush, R., et al. (2014). Psychosis prevalence and physical, metabolic and cognitive co-morbidity: Data from the second Australian national survey of psychosis. *Psychological Medicine, 44*, 2163–2176.

Mueser, K. T., Crocker, A. G., Frisman, L. B., Drake, R. E., Covell, N. H., & Essock, S. M. (2006). Conduct disorder and antisocial personality disorder in persons with severe psychiatric and substance use disorders. *Schizophrenia Bulletin, 32*, 626–636.

Mueser, K. T., Drake, R. E., Ackerson, T. H., Alterman, A. I., Miles, K. M., & Noordsy, D. L. (1997). Antisocial personality disorder, conduct disorder, and substance abuse in schizophrenia. *Journal of Abnormal Psychology, 106*, 473–477.

Mueser, K. T., Drake, R. E., Clark, R. E., McHugo, G. J., Mercer-McFadden, C., & Ackerson, T. (1995). *Toolkit for evaluating substance abuse in persons with severe mental illness*. Cambridge, MA: Evaluation Center at HSRI.

Mueser, K. T., Drake, R. E., & Wallach, M. A. (1998). Dual diagnosis: A review of etiological theories. *Addictive Behaviors, 23*, 717–734.

Mueser, K. T., Gottlieb, J. D., Cather, C., Glynn, S. M., Zarate, R., Smith, L. F., et al. (2012). Antisocial personality disorder in people with co-occurring severe mental illness and substance use disorders: Clinical, functional, and family relationship correlates. *Psychosis, 4*, 52–62.

Mueser, K. T., Kavanagh, D. J., & Brunette, M. F. (2007). Implications of research on comorbidity for the nature and management of substance misuse. In P. M. Miller, & D. J. Kavanagh (Eds.), *Translation of addictions science into practice* (pp. 277–320). Amsterdam: Elsevier.

Mueser, K. T., Nishith, P., Tracy, J. I., DeGirolamo, J., & Molinaro, M. (1995). Expectations and motives for substance use in schizophrenia. *Schizophrenia Bulletin, 21*, 367–378.

Mueser, K. T., Noordsy, D. L., Drake, R. E., & Fox, M. L. (2003). *Integrated treatment for dual disorders: A guide to effective practice.* New York: Guilford Press.

Mueser, K. T., Noordsy, D. L., Fox, L., & Wolfe, R. (2003). Disulfiram treatment for alcoholism in severe mental illness. *American Journal on Addictions, 12,* 242–252.

Mueser, K. T., Rosenberg, S. D., Drake, R. E., Miles, K. M., Wolford, G., Vidaver, R., et al. (1999). Conduct disorder, antisocial personality disorder, and substance use disorders in schizophrenia and major affective disorders. *Journal of Studies on Alcohol, 60,* 278–284.

Mueser, K. T., Yarnold, P. R., & Bellack, A. S. (1992). Diagnostic and demographic correlates of substance abuse in schizophrenia and major affective disorder. *Acta Psychiatrica Scandinavica, 85,* 48–55.

Mueser, K. T., Yarnold, P. R., Levinson, D. F., Singh, H., Bellack, A. S., Kee, K., et al. (1990). Prevalence of substance abuse in schizophrenia: Demographic and clinical correlates. *Schizophrenia Bulletin, 16,* 31–56.

Mueser, K. T., Yarnold, P. R., Rosenberg, S. D., Swett, C., Miles, K. M., & Hill, D. (2000). Substance use disorder in hospitalized severely mentally ill psychiatric patients: Prevalence, correlates, and subgroups. *Schizophrenia Bulletin, 26,* 179–192.

Niv, N., Lopez, S. R., Glynn, S. M., & Mueser, K. T. (2007). The role of substance use in families, attributions and affective reactions to their relative with severe mental illness. *Journal of Nervous and Mental Disease, 195,* 307–314.

O'Hare, T., & Sherrer, M. (2012). Substance use motives in people with severe mental illness: Comparisons among four diagnostic groups. *Journal of Social Work Practice in the Addictions, 12,* 370–390.

Potvin, S., Joyal, C. C., Pelletier, J., & Stip, E. (2008). Contradictory cognitive capacities among substance-abusing patients with schizophrenia: A meta-analysis. *Schizophrenia Research, 100,* 242–251.

Regier, D. A., Farmer, M. E., Rae, D. S., Locke, B. Z., Keith, S. J., Judd, L. L., et al. (1990). Comorbidity of mental disorders with alcohol and other drug abuse: Results from the Epidemiologic Catchment Area (ECA) study. *Journal of the American Medical Association, 264,* 2511–2518.

Ringen, P. A., Melle, I., Birkenaes, A. B., Engh, J. A., Faerden, A., Vaskinn, A., et al. (2008). The level of illicit drug use is related to symptoms and premorbid functioning in severe mental illness. *Acta Psychiatrica Scandinavica, 118,* 297–304.

Ringen, P. A., Vaskinn, A., Sundet, K., Engh, J. A., Jónsdóttir, H., Simonsen, C., et al. (2010). Opposite relationships between cannabis use and neurocognitive functioning in bipolar disorder and schizophrenia. *Psychological Medicine, 40,* 1337–1347.

Rosenberg, S. D., Drake, R. E., Wolford, G. L., Mueser, K. T., Oxman, T. E., Vidaver, R. M., et al. (1998). The Dartmouth Assessment of Lifestyle Instrument (DALI): A substance use disorder screen for people with severe mental illness. *American Journal of Psychiatry, 155,* 232–238.

Sacks, J. A., Drake, R. E., Williams, V. F., Banks, S. M., & Herrell, J. M. (2003). Utility of the Time-Line Follow-Back to assess substance use among homeless adults. *Journal of Nervous and Mental Disease, 191,* 145–153.

Salyers, M. P., & Mueser, K. T. (2001). Social functioning, psychopathology, and medication side effects in relation to substance use and abuse in schizophrenia. *Schizophrenia Research, 48,* 109–123.

Selzer, M. L. (1971). The Michigan Alcoholism Screening Test: The quest for a new diagnostic instrument. *American Journal of Psychiatry, 127,* 1653–1658.

Sheehan, D. V., Lecrubier, Y., Sheehan, K. H., Amorim, P., Janavis, J., Weiller, E., et al. (1998). The Mini-International Neuropsychiatric Interview (M.I.N.I): The development and validation of a structured diagnostic psychiatric interview for DSM-IV and ICD 10. *Journal of Clinical Psychiatry, 59,* 22–33.

Sigmon, S. C., & Higgins, S. T. (2006). Voucher-based contingent reinforcement of marijuana abstinence among individuals with serious mental illness. *Journal of Substance Abuse Treatment, 30*, 291–295.

Silver, H., & Abboud, E. (1994). Drug abuse in schizophrenia: Comparison of patients who began drug abuse before their first admission with those who began abusing drugs after their first admission. *Schizophrenia Research, 13*, 57–63.

Skinner, H. A. (1982). The Drug Abuse Screening Test. *Addictive Behaviors, 7*, 363–371.

Sobell, L. C., & Sobell, M. B. (1992). Timeline Follow-Back: A technique for assessing self-reported alcohol consumption. In R. Z. Litten, & J. Allen (Eds.), *Measuring alcohol consumption: Psychosocial and biological methods* (pp. 41–72). Totowa, NJ: Humana Press.

Somers, J. M., Goldner, E. M., Waraich, P., & Hsu, L. (2007). Prevalence studies of substance-related disorders: A systematic review of the literature. *Canadian Journal of Psychiatry, 49*, 373–384.

Stefamis, N. C., Dragovic, M., Power, B. D., Jablensky, A., Castle, D., & Morgan, V. A. (2014). The effect of drug use on the age at onset of psychotic disorders in an Australian cohort. *Schizophrenia Research, 156*, 211–216.

Swartz, M., Swanson, J. W., & Hannon, M. J. (2003). Detection of illicit substance use among persons with schizophrenia by radioimmunoassay of hair. *Psychiatric Services, 54*, 891–895.

Veen, N. D., Selten, J.-P., van der Tweel, I., Feller, W. G., Hoek, H. W., & Kahn, R. S. (2004). Cannabis use and age at onset of schizophrenia. *American Journal of Psychiatry, 161*, 501–506.

Warner, R., Taylor, D., Wright, J., Sloat, A., Springett, G., Amold, S., et al. (1994). Substance use among the mentally ill: Prevalence, reasons for use and effects on illness. *American Journal of Orthopsychiatry, 64*, 30–39.

Weibell, M. A., Hegelstad, W. T. V., Auestad, B., Bramness, J., Evensen, J., Haahr, U., et al. (2017). The effect of substance use on 10-year outcome in first-episode psychosis. *Schizophrenia Bulletin, 43*, 843–851.

Definition of Key Terms

Alcohol use disorder Refers to the persistent use of alcohol resulting in significant health, psychosocial, and/or physical problems.

Drug use disorder Refers to the problematic use of licit or illicit substances other than alcohol (e.g. cannabis, cocaine, hallucinogens, heroin), or the misuse of prescription or over-the-counter medications.

Substance use disorder Refers to problematic use of either alcohol or drugs.

SECTION 3
Linking Assessment to Treatment

CHAPTER 14
Clinical Case Formulation

Katherine Berry*,†, Gillian Haddock*,†, Georgie Paulik‡,§
*Division of Psychology and Mental Health, School of Health Sciences, University of Manchester, Manchester, United Kingdom, †Greater Manchester Mental Health Foundation Trust, Manchester Academic Health Sciences Centre, Manchester, United Kingdom, ‡Perth Voices Clinic, Murdoch, WA, Australia, §University of Western Australia, Perth, WA, Australia

Key Learning Objectives

- Understand the role of a formulation-based approach to working with people with psychosis.
- Awareness of the importance of considering issues of reliability and validity in relation to formulation.
- Key information to consider and include in formulations for people with psychosis.
- Introduce a cognitive-behavioural interpersonal model of formulation, incorporating ideas about how problems interact with the responses of significant others.
- The importance of the collaborative nature of the process of developing formulations with clients and significant others.
- The key factors to consider when using a formulation to make decisions about which evidence-based treatment strategies to select and in which order.

INTRODUCTION

What Is Formulation?

Case conceptualisation, also known as **case formulation**, provides a framework for bringing together biological, societal, cultural, and psychological factors that might be responsible for the development and maintenance of psychological problems and thus facilitates planning and implementing the most appropriate intervention (Kinderman, 2005; Tarrier & Calam, 2002).

Case formulation is a theory-driven conceptualisation of information gathered during a clinical assessment. It generates hypotheses about the cause(s) and maintenance of client problems.

Formulation may have a potential advantage over diagnosis of psychosis in being more amenable to being developed as part of a collaborative process, in incorporating strengths, and in considering personal meaning (see example in Box 14.1). This may be helpful in engaging the person in a process of understanding their experiences. There is a paucity of systematic research comparing the traditional practice of psychiatric diagnosis alone with psychological formulation. Nonetheless, formulation may be especially useful when diagnosis has been

A Clinical Introduction to Psychosis. https://doi.org/10.1016/B978-0-12-815012-2.00014-6

Box 14.1 Hypothetical Example: Case Formulation[a]

Adam is 27 years old and has recently been admitted to an inpatient mental health ward. Adam's diagnosis is 'psychosis' or 'schizophrenia', which gives us clues about the types of symptoms that he might be experiencing, such as hallucinations, delusions, and possibly thought disorder and impairment in functioning. In contrast, a formulation shared and developed with Adam and people involved in his care over a few weeks or months might look like this:

Background information gathered from the assessment

Adam grew up with his mother and younger brother. His parents separated when he was 2 years old. Adam had not seen his dad since the separation and his whereabouts were unknown. Following the separation, Adam's mother was in a long-term relationship with a man who was physically and emotionally abusive towards her in front of Adam and his brother. This relationship ended several years ago and around this time Adam started to spend long periods of time on his own playing video games and smoking cannabis. Adam's mother and brother became increasingly concerned about his mental health. He stopped going to college and eventually stopped going out the house altogether. He was also heard shouting very loudly by his family and neighbours throughout the night threatening to kill people if they did not leave him alone. Adam's mother became increasingly concerned about Adam when she found knives in his room which he explained were necessary to keep the family safe.

Adam refused to seek help from any services, but his GP contacted the mental health team in response to his mother's worries. The team experienced difficulties in engaging with Adam and became increasingly concerned about his wellbeing. He was becoming more agitated in response to possible hallucinatory voices and had talked to his mother about wanting to kill people who he believed were trying to harm the family. Eventually, he was sectioned under the Mental Health Act and the police had to use force and handcuffs to get him into the police van and then onto the ward. When Adam was first admitted, he told ward staff that he was being admitted as part of a government conspiracy and he did not feel that he needed to be in hospital. Adam appeared to be reluctant to engage with the staff on the ward and spent long periods of time on his own in his room.

Formulation

In terms of the formulation, it could be hypothesised that earlier relationships, including the absence of Adam's father and his mother's experience of abuse, resulted in him experiencing a limited sense of control over his experiences (see Chapter 10 in this volume on the role of trauma in psychosis). As a child, in particular, he may have lacked the capacity to protect his mother. It could further be hypothesised that Adam's beliefs around conspiracy might be functional for him, as within this delusional system he is the powerful protector of others. For example, such beliefs may enhance his self-esteem and give him a feeling of control. It is possible that if Adam still held any beliefs about a conspiracy and his role in saving the world, he may be motivated to maintain this belief system and be resistant to any attempts to challenge it, including from mental health staff. Although functional in some respects, it could be hypothesised that Adam's psychosis may prevent him from investing in, and consequently achieving, 'normal' social goals (see Chapter 9 in this volume). In a vicious cycle, lack of achievement in relation to 'normal' social goals, such as going to college and developing relationships with others may result in a loss of self-esteem and therefore increase his investment in delusional thinking. Adam might also compare himself to his peers who have achieved potentially valued goals, further lowering his self-confidence.

The possible role of substance use, such as cannabis, in maintaining Adam's difficulties with motivation and any psychotic symptoms he may be experiencing is important to consider. Possible reasons why Adam might use cannabis include the fact that he might not see this behaviour as a problem if he doesn't have other activities to stimulate him or fill his time. Adam might also use cannabis to help him cope with difficult emotions if he hasn't learned other ways to successfully regulate affect when growing up. Furthermore, it is possible that the distressing experiences of being forcibly admitted to hospital by the police might have led him to view the psychiatric systems and staff as controlling and abusive. Such perceptions of mental health services might be an additional reason why Adam finds it difficult to trust staff.

Implications for treatment

On the basis of the formulation, it would be important to try to engage Adam in activities that give him feelings of self-confidence and control, so that he would not have to rely on delusional beliefs to experience these feelings. As Adam's delusional beliefs may be very functional for him, starting to challenge these beliefs may result in significant distress and resistance. It may therefore be first important to help him to develop alternative ways of coping with difficult feelings. Given Adam's difficulty in acknowledging his mental health needs, helpful interventions might also involve normalising mental health problems and the effects of stress. For example, talking to Adam about examples of successful people who have developed mental health problems and the high incidence of mental health problems in the population. In order to help Adam develop skills in recognising his emotional needs and communicating these to others, it would be helpful to reflect back and empathise with any emotional reactions he was able to describe. The formulation would suggest that Adam may initially find these conversations difficult and back off, so the therapist should progress gently, but persist.

[a] Adapted from Berry, K., & Lobban, F. (2015). Formulating collaboratively with carers. In N. Tarrier & J. Johnson (Eds.), *Case formulations in cognitive behaviour therapy* (2nd ed.). London: Routledge.

experienced as disempowering (Honos-Webb & Leitner, 2001). There is also emerging evidence that it may help significant others' understand client's problems and hold more optimism about treatment (Berry et al., 2009).

Case conceptualisation is a fundamental process in most schools of psychotherapy. It is a core competency for clinical psychologists at all levels of training, is key to individualised treatment planning, and has been recognised as a clinical skill in its own right (Beck, 1985; Dudley et al., 2010). Case formulation is a process within psychological assessment and therapy that is recommended worldwide. It is important for psychologists to research what theoretical models are most commonly used in their country and if there are any specific national guidelines. In the United Kingdom, for example, formulation appears in the regulatory requirements for counselling, health, and forensic psychologists (Health Professions Council, 2009) and is consistent with evidence-based practice in psychology as adopted by the American Psychological Association (Anderson, 2006). Outside the psychology profession, it is also recognised within the psychiatry curriculum (Royal College of Psychiatrists, 2017) and is included in the current Core Mental Health Skills Education and Training Framework, which applies to all mental health and related professions in England.

According to Johnstone and Dallos (2013), formulations across different therapeutic schools, and across countries, differ in terms of the factors viewed as most relevant, the explanatory concepts they use, the emphasis given to the role of the clinician's own experiences in influencing explanations that are generated, the extent to which an expert versus collaborative stance is adopted, their position in relation to psychiatric diagnosis, and the way in which the formulation is developed, shared, and used within therapy. However, irrespective of the approach adopted, a case conceptualisation initially involves the clinician deciding on a theoretical perspective and developing a hypothesis about the factors that cause and maintain a client's problems to then guide a personally meaningful intervention, test the hypothesis, and revise the intervention accordingly

(Johnstone & Dallos, 2013; Persons, Beckner, & Tompkins, 2013). Case conceptualisation is particularly suited to working with complex presentations or when standard, problem-specific conceptualisations and interventions are ineffective (Davidson, 2008).

Brief Overview of Key Models of Formulation and Evidence Base

Researchers have investigated the clinical effectiveness of a case conceptualisation approach to psychotherapy using various therapeutic modalities (e.g. cognitive behavioural therapy, psychodynamic psychotherapy, interpersonal therapy) and across different clinical groups. However, despite the fact that case formulation is considered such a core professional competency, review studies have shown mixed evidence regarding the approach (Bucci et al., 2016). From a clinical perspective, the quality of case conceptualisation is largely dependent on the quality of the clinician's assessment and the information derived from it (Johnstone et al., 2011). Specific training and ongoing clinical supervision in formulation are integral to the process of developing meaningful and theoretically sound formulations (Page et al., 2008). Recognition of variations in the quality of conceptualisation has led to the development of more robust methods for assessing the quality of case conceptualisations, specifically in terms of reliability and validity. Whereas **reliability** studies of the quality of a generated case conceptualisation focus on how reliably a conceptualisation can be replicated by another therapist, **validity** studies largely focus on how well a case formulation predicts psychotherapy outcomes.

Reliability of case formulation: the degree to which a conceptualisation can be replicated by another therapist.

Validity of case formulation: how well a case formulation predicts psychotherapy outcomes.

Whether or not therapists agree on case conceptualisations for individual clients has been a notable problem for some time, with past research tending to evaluate the quality of case conceptualisations within psychoanalytic and psychodynamic traditions. For example, Seitz's (1966) study illustrated that independent conceptualisations of psychoanalytic process of five analysts resulted in zero consensus. Building on this early work, Luborsky (1977) developed the Core Conflictual Relationship Theme (CCRT) method to more reliably capture the psychodynamic narrative and overcome the problems inherent in reliably and validly measuring the quality of case conceptualisations. Since that time, other researchers (e.g. Caston, 1993; Horowitz, Rosenberg, Ureno, Kalehzan, & O'Halloran, 1989) have carried out empirical studies investigating the complexities of measuring the quality of case conceptualisations, with evidence, in some cases, of excellent levels of agreement regarding the key elements of conceptualisation (mean of 0.92; Horowitz & Rosenberg, 1994). It is, however, noteworthy that these research studies have not focused on clients with psychosis.

However, such positive findings are not consistent across the literature. Research shows that while there is good reliability for the descriptive elements of cognitive models of case conceptualisation, the explanatory or mechanistic elements of conceptualisation are less reliable (Bieling & Kuyken, 2003; Fothergill & Kuyken, 2002; Persons, Mooney, & Padesky, 1995). For example, Fothergill and Kukyen (2002) found increased reliability on some, but not all, inferential aspects of cognitive case formulation, and more experienced therapists were not consistently more reliable than less experienced raters using a systematically described cognitive case formulation method. Using an atheoretical model of case conceptualisation, Eells, Kendjelic and Lucas (1998) found similar results, in that there was good support for the descriptive, but not the inferential aspects of formulation.

There are also mixed findings in terms of validity and utility of case formulation for clients themselves. These findings have been explored by three studies focusing specifically on Cognitive Behavioural Therapy (CBT) for psychosis. Chadwick et al. (2003) examined the effect of case formulation in CBT for psychosis on the perception of the **therapeutic alliance**, strength of delusional beliefs, and self-evaluative beliefs across a number of different study designs.

Therapeutic alliance: The degree to which therapists and clients agree on the tasks and goals of therapeutic work in addition to the degree of emotional bond between the pair.

Contrary to hypotheses, the authors found no evidence that formulation-driven CBT for psychosis improves clients' perceptions of therapeutic alliance, reduces conviction in core beliefs, or eases distress. Furthermore, in semistructured interviews, clients reported mixed reactions to formulation. Nine clients reported increased understanding of their problems, and six reported positive emotional reactions to case formulation. Six clients also reported negative emotional responses to formulation—a possibility also highlighted by other clinical groups (Butler, 1998). In contrast, for therapists, case formulation was found to have a significant impact on perception of therapeutic alliance, to increase both optimism about therapy and understanding of clients' problems, and to enhance theory–practice links.

Exploring a similar issue, a later study by Pain et al. (2008) used content analysis methodology to assess clients' experience of the case formulation process in CBT for psychosis. In addition, therapists ranked seven documented benefits for them of case formulation. The authors found that formulation triggered multiple cognitive, emotional, and behavioural reactions in most participants. Reactions also varied among clients and over time within the same clients. Overall, clients were equally as positive as they were negative about the formulation process. For therapists, the most useful aspects of case formulation were found to be increased understanding of clients, a clear sense of direction, and enhancement of the therapeutic relationship.

More recently, Spencer et al. (2018) used principal stratification to explore the process variables that modified treatment effects from CBTp for individuals with schizophrenia who chose not to take antipsychotic medication. The authors noted that those who received a longitudinal formulation had poorer treatment outcomes than those who did not. However, the findings fell short of reaching statistical significance and the study was limited to a small sample size.

From a practical perspective, the research on case formulation highlights a number of issues to consider. First, it is important to develop methods of assessing the reliability and validity of case formulations (Bucci et al., 2016). The assessment of reliability would most likely involve using standardised tools or assessment methods which determine the extent to which the formulations of novice therapists or those in training are in line with the formulations of more experienced clinicians. The assessment of validity would most likely involve assessing the extent to which the use and quality of formulations are valued by clients and predict therapy outcomes. Second, the existing research also highlights that it is important for therapists to be mindful of clients' possible negative reactions to case formulation, including a reduced sense of hope in relation to future change. It is, however, noteworthy that previous studies of clients' perceptions of case formulation have had small sample sizes, highlighting the need to carry out more research on this topic, including factors, which determine the nature of people's reactions to the formulation process.

What Information to Include in Your Formulation

Person's (1989) book *Cognitive Therapy in Practice: A Case Formulation Approach* provided one of the first guidebooks on case formulation. She described the case formulation as having six parts: (a) developing a problem list; (b) outlining the proposed underlying mechanisms; (c) explaining the way in which the proposed mechanism leads to the problems on the problem list; (d) highlighting the precipitants of current problems; (e) describing the origins of the mechanisms in the client's life; and (f) hypothesising obstacles to treatment. As highlighted earlier, the quality of a formulation is determined largely by the quality of the available information. As such the formulation may draw on a range of information as outlined in the assessment chapters, including potential mechanisms proposed in the development of psychotic symptoms. This includes information about hypothesised interaction between symptoms, and other factors likely to impact on symptom expression and coping, such as cognitive impairment, physical health, and social functioning.

When working with people with psychosis, it is particularly important not only to include symptoms in the formulation but also the person's beliefs about and emotional response to symptoms and diagnosis. For example, psychosis can have a significant impact on the person's sense of self-worth and result in feelings of low mood, hopelessness, and suicidal ideation (Bucci & Tarrier, 2016). Bucci and Tarrier (2016) describe a clinical model of psychosis, which provides a framework for cognitive behavioural formulation and treatment. The model assumes that the experience of psychotic symptoms results from the interaction of internal factors such as genetics, the development of maladaptive beliefs or deficits in cognitive flexibility, and external factors, such as trauma and overly demanding interpersonal environment. Processing biases (see Chapter 8 of this volume), such as in source monitoring in the case of hallucinations and probabilistic reasoning in the case of delusions, in conjunction with difficulties in affect regulation result in disturbances in perception and related psychotic experiences. According to the model, once a psychotic experience is activated, the individual appraises or gives meaning to the experiences which determine the nature of emotional and behavioural consequences. The important aspect of this model is that the appraisal and consequent reaction serves to maintain the psychotic experience. For example, anxiety in response to paranoid beliefs will elevate arousal and increase the likelihood of further information processing biases. Similarly, social avoidance in response to paranoia may result in confirmatory rumination and limited opportunity to disconfirm beliefs. Thus, providing the client with some psychoeducation around these processes, with delivery altered according to their level of insight and cognitive abilities, may be helpful during formulation.

Other common models of formulation for psychosis also draw on key Cognitive Therapy concepts (Beck, 1976) relating to appraisals of, or beliefs about, experiences and the role of behavioural and emotional factors in maintaining problems (Chadwick & Birchwood, 1994; Garety, Kuipers, Fowler, Freeman, & Bebbington, 2001; Morrison, 2001). The idea central to these cognitive models is that appraisals, or the way that people interpret experiences, determine associated distress and functioning, and that these appraisals result from schemas that develop in the context of their life. The models differ slightly in terms of the emphasis that they place on specific types of appraisals. For example, Chadwick and Birchwood (1994) emphasise the role of beliefs about voices' power and malevolence in leading to distress, whereas Garety et al. (2001) highlight the role of appraisals of emotional and cognitive phenomena being as external to the self (Garety et al., 2001), and Morrison (2001) emphasises appraisals of experiences as being uncontrollable, dangerous, and unacceptable to the individual's culture (Morrison, 2001; also see Morrison et al., 2004 for a practical 'cognitive therapy' approach to formulation). Hardy (2017) also proposes a formulation model, which is specifically to aid formulation of clients with psychosis who have significant past trauma (see Chapters 10 and 19 for more on trauma and psychosis).

One particularly important issue to consider in formulation for people with psychosis—who often have multiple and complex interacting problems—is which symptoms or experiences are primary and should therefore be addressed first. For example, in some circumstances, threatening voices may be hypothesised to be fuelling paranoid delusions, so the focus of therapy would be on reducing the perceived power and veracity of the voices. In the case of Adam described here, a historical sense of powerlessness and beliefs about lack of personal control and poor self-efficacy are hypothesised to underlie paranoid and grandiose delusions, so tackling these in therapy may reduce Adam's investment in delusions without having to directly challenge delusional thinking. In fact, using self-esteem enhancing interventions to address grandiose delusions associated with an underlying low sense of self-esteem is a common therapeutic strategy in CBT for psychosis (Knowles et al., 2011).

Factors that are also particularly crucial to highlight in the context of formulation for psychosis are the possible role of trauma and abuse. There is a large and growing body of research that indicates a causal role for these events in many or most mental health presentations and psychosis in particular (Read & Bentall, 2012;

Varese, Smeets, et al., 2012) and a trauma-informed formulation can be a powerful way of integrating this knowledge into interventions. A further factor is the possible role of mental health treatment and services in exacerbating the person's difficulties. This perspective recognises that services may not only be unhelpful but re-traumatising through disempowering and coercive practices (Berry et al., 2013; Berry, Ford et al., 2015; Hardy, 2017). An equally important factor to also draw attention to is an awareness of the wider societal context and the impact of sociocultural factors, including stigma on the development, expression, and understanding of mental distress (see Chapter 3 of this volume).

Although these three issues can readily be incorporated into existing cognitive-behavioural models of psychosis, we would argue that the mechanisms via which they influence psychosis have not been as well articulated. For example, traumatic experiences either resulting from earlier abuse, abusive practices in mental health services or experiences of stigma or bullying may not only increase vulnerability to future psychosis via beliefs systems, but also through mental processes such as dissociation. Dissociation is often defined as the 'lack of normal integration of thoughts, feelings and experiences into the stream of consciousness and memory' (Bernstein & Putnam, 1986, p. 727). Although it can be experienced in the absence of a history of trauma, dissociation is frequently observed in the immediate aftermath of traumatic events, and trauma survivors can sometimes experience a heightened predisposition to dissociative many years after the original traumatic event (e.g. Dalenberg et al., 2012). In line with others, we have recently proposed that psychotic symptoms such as hallucinatory voices can be understood as dissociated components of the self or 'compartmentalised' trauma-related intrusive memories (Berry, Varese, and Bucci, 2017). In some predisposed individuals, these internal states and cognitive events are experienced and/or interpreted as external and current rather than internal and memory-based, possibly as a result of biased source monitoring processes that have also been shown to underpin hallucination proneness in numerous studies (e.g. Badcock and Hugdahl, 2012; Varese, Barkus, et al., 2012; Varese, Smeets, et al., 2012). In such instances, working on treating dissociation in therapy may help to reduce hallucinatory experiences.

One further criticism of the aforementioned formulation models of psychosis is that they place relatively less emphasis on the role of systemic factors in the maintenance of distress. We have developed a cognitive-interpersonal formulation of psychosis (Berry & Lobban, 2015; Berry, Ford, et al., 2015; Berry, Haddock, et al., 2015) that draws on the key principles of cognitive-behavioural models of psychosis highlighted here but also specifically emphasises how significant others within the person's environment might be drawn into maintaining the person's difficulties. For example, people who withdraw socially in response to psychosis are often harder to engage and may both overtly and covertly 'push' other people away, thus maintaining their avoidance and meaning that their needs get missed. Conversely, people who are sensitive to rejection from others, and consequently hypervigilant to indications that significant others cannot support them, may be overly dependent in relationships. In turn, this dependence may lead others to 'burn out' and consequently lack capacity to offer support, thus fuelling the person's underlying beliefs. In Fig. 14.1, we present an example of this model based on the client Adam.

Sharing and Collaboratively Developing Formulations

Rather than providing service users with a formulation prepared by the therapist in advance, a collaborative nonexpert approach should be taken in clinical practice. By this means, the service users bring their own understanding of their experiences and the psychological therapists brings together information about psychological processes and evidence-based interventions. In other words, the process of case formulation should be collaborative rather than imposed, taking into account the client's views and beliefs about their problems (see Box 14.2). This is important, as in addition to deriving interventions, an important element of shared formulation is generating a more compassionate understanding of the service user's current behaviours; thus, the formulation is an intervention in itself. In this respect, although formulation is often described as if it is an event, it is actually a process or a shared exploration that has no definite end point. Indeed, the constantly changing nature of service users' circumstances and understanding of problems necessitates that formulations are frequently reviewed and updated. However, there are times and purposes for which a summary—a formulation-as-an-event—may be useful, such as at the start and end of contact with mental health services (Johnstone et al., 2011).

Kinderman and Lobban (2000) present a method of developing formulations with clients with psychosis through an evolutionary process. Early in the therapeutic process, simple formulations involving straightforward theoretical models are presented, which are systematically elaborated as therapy proceeds. For instance, initial 'mini-formulations' could be as simple as introducing a single concept such as the effects of hypervigilance or of avoidance. This process involves developing, collaboratively with clients, successive layers of formulation. Each of these layers builds on and incorporates the previous one, yet involves an incremental increase in complexity, depth and informational content.

Work by our research group has also shown that **sharing case formulations** with both formal and informal carers can be helpful in terms of promoting more positive relationships between people with psychosis and people around them (Berry & Lobban, 2015). The process of developing shared formulations provides richer conceptualisations of the service users' social context and leads to more creative treatment strategies, which draw on wider resources. It helps ensure a more consistent way of working with service users' problems over time, and across family or staff members. Furthermore, developing formulations with carers can be useful when service users themselves are unable or unwilling to actively engage in therapy. Importantly, the process of formulating may also provide an opportunity for carers to reflect on and receive emotional support in relation to difficulties that arise in their day-to-day interactions with service users.

Sharing case formulations with family members, carers, and clinical staff can be beneficial in promoting positive relationships between people with psychosis and those around them.

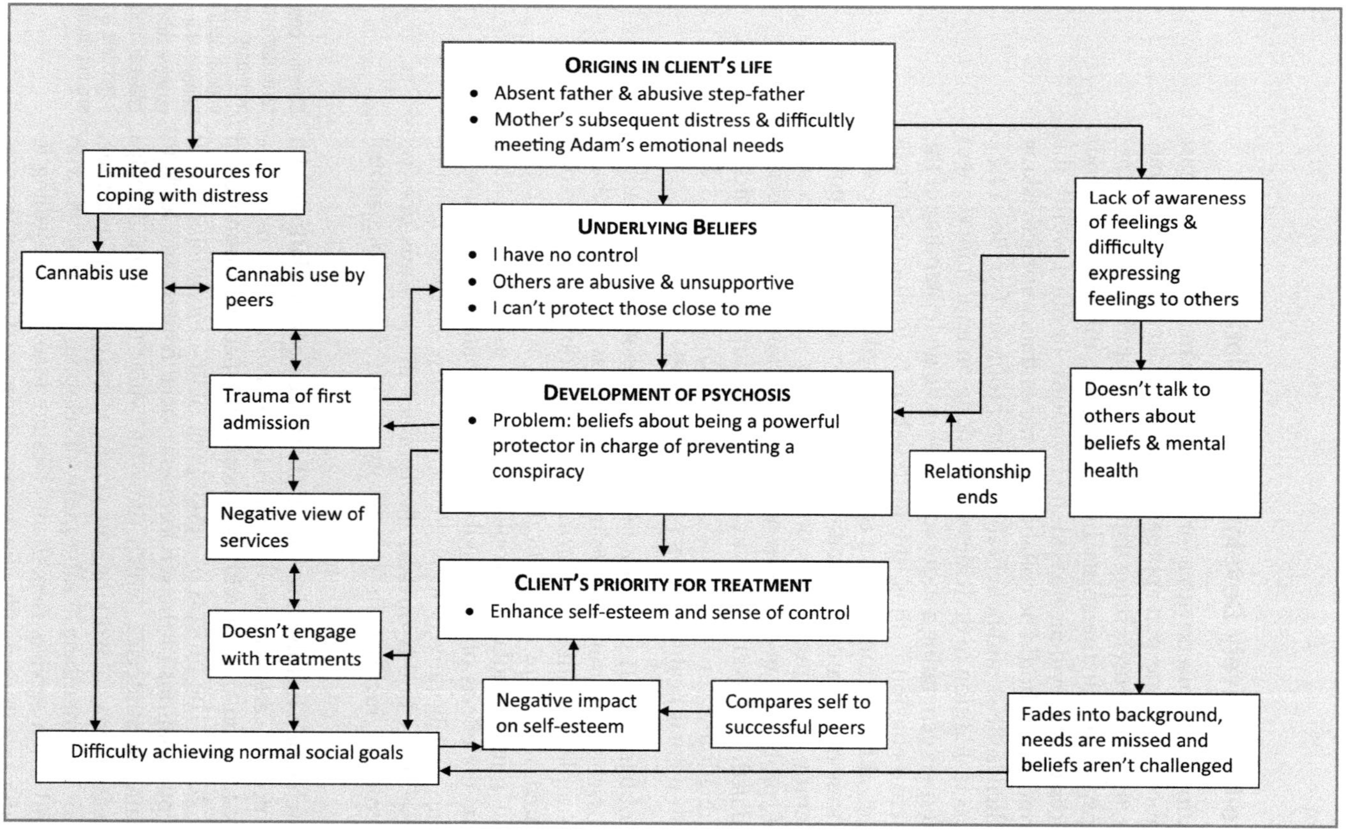

FIG. 14.1

Example of cognitive behavioural interpersonal model of formulation. Reproduced and adapted with permission from Berry, K., & Lobban, F. (2015). Formulating collaboratively with carers. In N. Tarrier & J. Johnson (Eds.), *Case formulations in cognitive behaviour therapy* (2nd ed.). London: Routledge.

Box 14.2 Hypothetical Example: Sharing the Formulation

In the case of Adam described, the therapist might start by developing 'mini' and relatively nonthreatening formulations, which help him to see possible links between thoughts of danger and harm, emotional responses associated with threat and behavioural reactions such as avoidance and arming himself for protection. Such mini-formulations may be used to socialise him to the idea underlying CBT that thoughts rather than situations themselves drive emotional responses and instigate conversations about the role of past experiences, including the role of earlier trauma in determining later beliefs about threat from others and the need to seek safety. Within these conversations, it would be important to emphasise the functional nature of these underlying beliefs given the reality of the threat when growing up, whilst sensitively communicating the idea that former adaptive beliefs can be less helpful in later 'safer' environments.

Once Adam feels secure within the therapy relationship, listened to and understood, it may also be helpful to explore further with him his self-image and the impact that earlier experiences and the experiences of psychosis have had on how he might see himself. These conversations would provide a rationale for self-esteem enhancing interventions, which ultimately might reduce the value and investment he may have in maintaining delusional beliefs.

Developing shared conceptualisations with carers is a key component of family interventions for people with a diagnosis of schizophrenia (e.g. Barrowclough and Tarrier, 1992; Stanbridge and Burbach, 2007) and using simple case conceptualisation has been proposed as a useful way of helping relatives to understand the experiences of people with mental health problems (Charlesworth and Reichelt, 2004). The British Psychological Society advocate the use of **team formulation** to promote a more psychosocial perspective to team thinking and there has been a growth in the practice over recent years (British Psychological Society, Division of Clinical Psychology, 2011). Many different models of team formulation have been described in the literature with different client groups, including psychiatric rehabilitation (Berry, Haddock, et al., 2015; Davenport, 2002; Hewitt, 2008; Meaden and Hacker, 2011; Summers, 2006), acute inpatient wards (Kennedy, 2009), learning disability (Ingham, 2011), and dementia care homes (James, 2011). Nonetheless, there is limited evidence for the effectiveness of team formulation. Evaluations of this work have primarily involved qualitative interviews or service evaluation of the team members' experiences. These studies largely suggest that mental health professionals value shared formulation in terms of bringing together staff with different viewpoints and encouraging more creative thinking, but they suggest that for formulations to impact on patient outcomes, there needs to be clear links to patient care planning (Hewitt, 2008; Kennedy et al., 2003; Summers, 2006). There is also some preliminary evidence from case studies and pre- and postmeasure designed studies that shared formulation can change staff attributions and attitudes towards service users (Berry and Haddock, 2008; Janes and Shirley, 2008; Meaden and Hacker, 2011) and reduce challenging behaviours (Ingham, 2011; Janes and Shirley, 2008; Newman Taylor & Sambrook, 2012). The lack of evidence base for formulation might help explain the findings of a recent study by Christofides et al. (2012). In this study, psychologists working in both inpatient

Team formulations may be an effective way of promoting a psychosocial perspective in clinical services but have yet to be rigorously evaluated.

and community settings were interviewed about their use of formulations with multidisciplinary teams. Psychologists reported that formulations were shared mostly through informal means, such as ideas during a team discussion, and that they were often wary of formalising formulation processes with staff due to concerns about staff viewing them as unwelcome experts.

We recently conducted an intervention study that looked at the impact of shared formulation developed using the cognitive-behavioural interpersonal model of psychosis described here. We present specific information that might be elicited in relation to each aspect of the model in Table 14.1, and as such can be used to guide the shared formulation process.

Table 14.1 Cognitive Interpersonal Model of Team Formulation

Needs	The therapist explains that the purpose of the meeting is to help develop a better understanding of the service user and his or her need. The therapist then elicits staff members' views about the patients' needs.
Strengths and resources	The therapist elicits the service user's strengths and resources, including both personal and environmental resources.
Goals and values	The therapist elicits the service user's goals and values.
Significant life events	The therapist elicits key events (both positive and negative) in the service user's life, which can be supplemented with information recorded from the medical notes or the therapist's own interviews with the service user.
Beliefs	The therapist explains that life experiences can influence beliefs about self, others, world in general and the future and provides examples for those unfamiliar with the cognitive model. (e.g. *if you have frequently been the victim of violence you may believe you are vulnerable, other people are aggressive, and the world is a dangerous place*). Using Socratic dialogue, the therapist then asks the group to generate possible positive and negative beliefs the service user may have about himself, other people (including team) and the world in general.
Ways of coping	Using Socratic dialogue, the therapist asks the group to think about how the hypothesised beliefs are likely to affect how the service user interacts with others (including team) and copes with stress and life in general (e.g. *if a person believes that other people can't be trusted, he is likely to avoid putting trust in people, may avoid close relationships with others or may be hostile towards others*). The therapist emphasises that strategies may be short-term solutions to managing distress, or they might have been useful at a different stage of the person's life.
Consequences	Using Socratic dialogue, the therapist asks the group how to think about the possible impact of the service user's interactional styles and methods of coping. The therapist focuses on how the styles are likely to maintain the service user's problems (e.g. *if a person avoids close relationships, he will be deprived of opportunities to learn that people can be trusted*). The therapist emphasises how the person makes the team feel, think, and respond (e.g. *an aggressive patient may lead staff to back off and disengage*).

Table 14.1	Cognitive Interpersonal Model of Team Formulation—cont'd
Implications for support planning	Using Socratic dialogue, the therapist asks the group to think about ways of engaging the service user and interventions that might help break maintenance cycles. It is also useful to think about the service user's goals and values as a way of motivating them, and what has worked well for them in the past

Taken from Berry, K., Haddock, G., Kellett, S., Awenat, Y., Szpak, K., & Barrowclough, C. (2017). Understanding outcomes in a randomized controlled trial of a ward-based intervention on psychiatric inpatient wards: A qualitative analysis of staff and patient experiences. *Journal of Clinical Psychology*, *73*(10), 1211–1225.

In our study, we recruited a total of 85 staff and 51 patients across 10 psychiatric rehabilitation units in Greater Manchester, UK (Berry, Ford, et al., 2015; Berry, Haddock, et al., 2015; Berry et al., 2017). We used a cluster randomised design with five of the units receiving the intervention over 24 weekly one-hour sessions and the other five units receiving treatment as usual. We developed a shared formulation for all patients on the unit and depending on the number of patients in the service these were reviewed more than once. An average of five members of staff (range: 1–12) attended each formulation meeting and staff attended a median of four meetings (range: 0–11) over the course of the intervention. We assessed several outcomes including staff-patient relationships, patient symptoms and functioning, and staff burnout at baseline, posttreatment and six-month follow-up. Compared with treatment as usual, patients in the intervention arm felt less criticised by their key workers and reported improvements in ward atmosphere following the intervention. Staff in the intervention arm also reported lower levels of depersonalisation postintervention. This study was a pilot study and as such was not large enough to detect statistically significant improvements in longer-term patient outcome, but differences in patient outcomes were in the direction suggesting a more positive change for those on wards receiving the intervention. More in-depth interviews suggested that staff valued the intervention in terms of improving understanding of patients' needs and developing new ways of working with patients. Patients also described changes in staff members' behaviour towards them, with staff members being more proactive in approaching patients. Key barriers included competing demands on staff members' time and staff anxieties about or resistance towards their practice being challenged by a psychologist, which are consistent with previous research (Berry and Haddock, 2008). Key facilitators were managerial support, including ring fencing time for the intervention and promoting staff attendance, and the fact that the intervention focused on drawing out the team members' own strengths in working with service users.

Using Formulations to Select Intervention Strategies

A key challenge to formulations is how and when to select appropriate treatment techniques (Tarrier & Johnson, 2016). As individual formulations take into account a large number of unique characteristics across a variety of personal and environmental variables, it is very difficult to know how to select the most effective treatment strategy.

First and foremost, it is important to ensure that the formulation is used to generate ideas about evidence-based interventions such as those outlined in the treatment guidelines in Chapter 1. With the importance of evidence-based interventions in mind, it is helpful to also consider literature outlined in Chapter 15 on how to judge emerging interventions in terms of efficacy. Once the therapist has specified the range of possible evidence-based treatments, they should then use the formulation to guide treatment choices within those specified treatments.

Efficacy: the capacity for producing a desired result or effect (i.e. the desired treatment outcome).

To facilitate this process, Nezu and Nezu (1989) suggest that treatment strategies should be linked to each identified problem and provide a general approach to how the problem will be resolved. For example, such as decreasing threat appraisals in the context of paranoia or using a behavioural experiment to challenge perceived power of voices in the context of command hallucinations. As indicated here, it may be particularly important to consider which symptoms are primary and therefore important to address first. Decisions about what to focus on first may also be influenced by the severity of problems. For example, in the context of many problems, it may be helpful to choose to work on the problem hypothesised to be most amenable to change to give the client a 'quick win', in order to enhance motivation to work on more entrenched 'harder to treat' problems. Similarly, the client's goals are equally important to consider. For example, although it might be hypothesised that substance misuse underlies the client's difficulties with psychosis, the client may not see substances as a problem and only be willing to engage on more secondary problems. In such instances, the therapist should work on the problems that are most pertinent to the client to facilitate engagement with a view to addressing underlying problems once the therapeutic relationship is more established.

This overall approach to selecting treatment methods assumes that the formulation is a way of generating hypotheses that are tested through the implementation of treatments, and thus whether the formulation is useful or not will depend on whether or not the problem is resolved. In this respect, it is important to continually monitor process towards goals in therapy through the regular use of standardised outcome measures. Lack of progress should then be interpreted in terms of the formulation, bearing in mind the possible need to redevelop the formulation in light of new information.

CONCLUSIONS

The advantage of the case formulation approach is that it allows a flexible and uniquely tailored understanding of each person's problems irrespective of diagnosis. Whilst a formulation can be an intervention, to improve understanding and demonstrate empathy, it is also generally accepted that case formulations are most helpful when they generate ideas about evidence-based interventions that support and maximise opportunities for recovery. Formulation can be particularly helpful in working with complex cases that do not conform to standard systems of categories of clinical problems.

Of course, there is no guarantee that a formulation will always be received well by the client, or is a safe guard against pathologising, excluding social contexts, or imposing a perspective with which the client disagrees (Johnstone, 2017). Like any intervention, it depends largely on how it is done. As such, the UK, Division of Clinical Psychology *Good Practice Guidelines* (2011) specify a number of principles in formulating, including that the process should be collaborative, respectful of service users' views about accuracy and helpfulness, expressed in ordinary and accessible language, culturally sensitive, nonjudgemental, and inclusive of strengths and achievements. Psychologists are also encouraged to take a reflective stance that reduces the risk of using formulation in insensitive, nonconsenting, or disempowering ways (DCP, 2011).

ADDITIONAL SELF-DIRECTED READING

Berry, K., Haddock, G., Kellett, S., Roberts, C., Drake, R., & Barrowclough, C. (2015). Feasibility of a ward-based psychological intervention to improve staff and patient relationships in psychiatric rehabilitation settings. *British Journal of Clinical Psychology, 55*(3), 236–252.

Johnstone, L., & Dallos, R. (2013). *Formulation in psychology and psychotherapy: Making sense of people's problems* (2nd ed.). New York: Routledge.

Mumma, G. (2011). Validity issues in cognitive-behavioral therapy case formulation. *European Journal of Psychological Assessment, 27*(1), 29–49.

Rento, J. C., Dunn, H., Williams, S., & Bentall, R. P. (2004). *Cognitive therapy for psychosis: A formulation based approach.* London: Routledge.

See the formulation chapter from: Page, A.C., & Stritzke, W.G. (2015). *Clinical psychology for trainees* (2nd ed.). United Kingdom: Cambridge University Press. Morrison, A. P.

Tarrier, N., & Johnson, J. (2016). *Case formulation in cognitive behaviour therapy.* London and New York: Routledge.

References

Anderson, N. B. (2006). Evidence-based practice in psychology. *American Psychologist, 61*(4), 271–285.

Badcock, J. C., & Hugdahl, K. (2012). Cognitive mechanisms of auditory verbal hallucinations in psychotic and non-psychotic groups. *Neuroscience and Biobehavioral Reviews, 36*, 431–438.

Barrowclough, C., & Tarrier, N. (1992). *Families of schizophrenic patients: Cognitive behavioural intervention.* Boca Raton, FL: Chapman and Hall/CRC.

Beck, A. T. (1976). Cognitive Therapy and the Emotional Disorder. Oxford: International Universities Press.

Beck, A. T. (1985). Cognitive therapy, behaviour therapy, psychoanalysis and pharmacotherapy: A cognitive continuum. In M. J. Mahoney, et al.(Eds.), *Cognition and psychotherapy.* New York: Plenum Press.

Bernstein, E. M., & Putnam, F. W. (1986). Development, reliability, and validity of a dissociation scale. *The Journal of Nervous and Mental Disease, 174*(12), 727–735.

Berry, K., Barrowclough, C., & Wearden, A. (2009). A pilot study investigating the use of psychological formulations to modify psychiatric staff perceptions of service users with psychosis. *Behavioural and Cognitive Psychotherapy, 37*(1), 39–48.

Berry, K., Ford, S., Jellicoe-Jones, & Haddock, G. (2013). PTSD symptoms associated with the experiences of psychosis and hospitalisation. A review of the literature. *Clinical Psychology Review, 33*, 526–538.

Berry, K., Ford, S., Jellicoe-Jones, L., & Haddock, G. (2015). Trauma in relation to psychosis and hospital experiences: The role of past trauma and attachment. *Psychology and Psychotherapy: Theory, Research and Practice, 88*, 227–239.

Berry, K., & Haddock, G. (2008). The implementation of the NICE guidelines for schizophrenia: Barriers to the implementation of psychological interventions and recommendations for the future. *Psychology and Psychotherapy: Theory, Research and Practice, 81*(4), 419–436.

Berry, K., Haddock, G., Kellett, S., Awenat, Y., Szpak, K., & Barrowclough, C. (2017). Understanding outcomes in a randomized controlled trial of a ward-based intervention on psychiatric inpatient wards: a qualitative analysis of staff and patient experiences. *Journal of Clinical Psychology, 73*(10), 1211–1225.

Berry, K., Haddock, G., Kellett, S., Roberts, C., Drake, R., & Barrowclough, C. (2015). Feasibility of a ward-based psychological intervention to improve staff and patient relationships in psychiatric rehabilitation settings. *British Journal of Clinical Psychology, 55*(3), 236–252.

Berry, K., & Lobban, F. (2015). Formulating collaboratively with significant others. In N. Tarrier, & J. Johnson (Eds.), *Case formulation in cognitive behaviour therapy: The treatment of challenging and complex cases* (2nd ed., pp. 304–321). London: Taylor & Francis.

Berry, K., Varese, F., & Bucci, S. (2017). Cognitive attachment model of voices: Evidence base and future implications. *Frontiers in Psychiatry, 8*, 1–13.

Bieling, P. J., & Kuyken, W. (2003). Is cognitive case formulation science or science fiction? *Clinical Psychology: Science and Practice, 10*(1), 52–69.

British Psychological Society, Division of Clinical Psychology. (2011). *Good practice guidelines on the use of psychological formulation.* Leicester.

Bucci, S., French, L., & Berry, K. (2016). Measures assessing the quality of case conceptualization: A systematic review. *Journal of Clinical Psychology, 72*(6), 513–632.

Bucci, S., & Tarrier, N. (2016). A cognitive behavioural case formulation approach to the treatment of psychosis. In N. Tarrier, & J. Johnson (Eds.), *Case formulation in cognitive behaviour therapy* (pp. 166–187). London and New York: Routledge.

Butler, G. (1998). Clinical formulation. In A. S. Bellack & M. Hersen (Eds.), *Comprehensive clinical psychology*. Oxford: Pergamon.

Caston, J. (1993). Can analysts agree? The problems of consensus and the psychoanalytic mannequin: I. A proposed solution. *Journal of the American Psychoanalytic Association, 41*(2), 493–511.

Chadwick, P., & Birchwood, M. (1994). The omnipotence of voices: A cognitive approach to auditory hallucinations. *British Journal of Psychiatry, 164*(2), 190–201.

Chadwick, P., Williams, C., & Mackenzie, J. (2003). Impact of case formulation in cognitive behavior therapy for psychosis. *Behavior Research and Therapy, 41*(6), 671–680.

Charlesworth, G. M., & Reichelt, K. F. (2004). Keeping conceptualizations simple: Examples with family carers of people with dementia. *Behavioural and Cognitive Psychotherapy, 32*(4), 401–409.

Christofides, S., Johnstone, L., & Musa, M. (2012). Chipping in: Clinical psychologists' descriptions of their use of formulation in multi-disciplinary team working. *Psychology and Psychotherapy: Theory, Research and Practice, 85*(4), 424–435.

Dalenberg, C. J., Brand, B. L., Gleaves, D. H., Dorahy, M. J., Loewenstein, R. J., Cardeña, E., et al. (2012). Evaluation of the evidence for the trauma and fantasy models of dissociation. *Psychological Bulletin, 138*(3), 550–588.

Davenport, S. (2002). Acute wards: Problems and solutions. A rehabilitation approach to in-patient care. *Psychiatric Bulletin, 26*, 385–388.

Davidson, K. M. (2008). Cognitive-behavioural therapy for personality disorders. *Psychiatry, 7*(3), 117–120.

Division of Clinical Psychology. (2011). *Good practice guidelines on the use of psychological formulation.* Leicester, England: British Psychological Society.

Dudley, R., Park, I., James, I., & Dodgson, G. (2010). Rate of agreement between clinicians on the content of a cognitive formulation of delusional beliefs: The effect of qualifications and experience. *Behavioural and Cognitive Psychotherapy, 38*(2), 185–200.

Eells, T. D., Kendjelic, E. M., & Lucas, C. P. (1998). What's in a case formulation?: Development and use of a content coding manual. *The Journal of Psychotherapy Practice and Research, 7*(2), 144–153.

Fothergill, C. D., & Kuyken, W. (2002). *The quality of cognitive case formulation rating scale* [unpublished manuscript]. UK: University of Exeter.

Garety, P. A., Kuipers, E., Fowler, D., Freeman, D., & Bebbington, P. E. (2001). A cognitive model of the positive symptoms of psychosis. *Psychological Medicine, 31*(2), 189–195.

Hardy, A. (2017). Pathways from trauma to psychotic experiences: a theoretically informed model of posttraumatic stress in psychosis. *Frontiers in Psychology, 8*, 697.

Health Professions Council. (2009). *Standards of proficiency: Practitioner psychologists.* London, England: Author.

Hewitt, J. (2008). Dangerousness and mental health policy. *Journal of Psychiatric and Mental Health Nursing, 15*(3), 186–194.

Honos-Webb, L., & Leitner, L. M. (2001). How using the DSM causes damage: A client's report. *Journal of Humanistic Psychology, 41*(4), 36–56.

Horowitz, L., & Rosenberg, S. (1994). The consensual response psychodynamic formulation: part 1. Method and research results. *Psychotherapy Research, 4*(3–4), 222–233.

Horowitz, L. M., Rosenberg, S. E., Ureño, G., Kalehzan, B. M., & O'Halloran, P. (1989). Psychodynamic formulation, consensual response method, and interpersonal problems. *Journal of Consulting and Clinical Psychology, 57*(5), 599–606.

Ingham, B. (2011). Collaborative psychosocial case formulation development workshops: A case study with direct care staff. *Advances in Mental Health and Intellectual Disabilities, 5*(2), 9–15.

James, I. A. (2011). *Understanding behaviour in dementia that challenges: A guide to assessment and treatment.* London and Philadelphia: Jessica Kingsley.

Janes, E., & Shirley, L. (2008). Acknowledging the man, not the behaviour. *Journal of Dementia Care, 16*(1), 20–25.

Johnstone, L. (2017). Psychological formulation as an alternative to psychiatric diagnosis. *Journal of Humanistic Psychology, 58*(1), 30–46.

Johnstone, L., & Dallos, R. (2013). *Formulation in psychology and psychotherapy: Making sense of people's problems* (2nd ed.). New York: Routledge.

Johnstone, L., Whomsley, S., Cole, S., & Oliver, N. (2011). *Good practice guidelines on the use of psychological formulation.* Leicester: British Psychological Society.

Kennedy, F. (2009). The use of formulation in inpatient settings. In I. Clarke, & H. Wilson (Eds.), *Cognitive behaviour therapy for acute inpatient mental health units: Working with clients, staff and the milieu.* Hove: Routledge.

Kennedy, F., Smalley, M., & Harris, T. (2003). Clinical psychology for inpatient settings: Principles for development and practice. *Clinical Psychology Forum, 30*, 21–24.

Kinderman, P. (2005). A psychological model of mental disorder. *Harvard Review of Psychiatry, 12*(4), 206–217.

Kinderman, P., & Lobban, F. (2000). Evolving formulations: Sharing complex information with clients. *Behavioural and Cognitive Psychotherapy, 28*(3), 307–310.

Knowles, R., McCarthy-Jones, S., & Rowse, G. (2011). Grandiose delusions: A review and theoretical integration of cognitive and affective perspectives. *Clinical Psychology Review, 31*, 684–696.

Luborsky, L. (1977). Measuring a pervasive psychic structure in psychotherapy: The core conflictual relationship theme. In N. Freedman, & S. Grand (Eds.), *Communicative structures and psychic structures* (pp. 367–395). New York: Springer.

Meaden, A., & Hacker, D. (2011). *Problematic and risk behaviours in psychosis: A shared formulation approach.* London and New York: Routledge.

Morrison, A. P. (2001). The interpretation of intrusions in psychosis: An integrative cognitive approach to hallucinations and delusions. *Behavioral and Cognitive Psychotherapy, 29*(3), 257–276.

Morrison, A. P., Rento, J. C., Dunn, H., Williams, S., & Bentall, R. P. (2004). *Cognitive therapy for psychosis: A formulation based approach.* London: Routledge.

Newman Taylor, K., & Sambrook, S. (2012). CBT for culture change: Formulating teams to improve patient care. *Behavioural and Cognitive Psychotherapy, 40*, 496–503.

Nezu, A. M., & Nezu, C. M. (1989). Clinical decision making in the practice of behavior therapy. In A. M. Nezu, & C. M. Nezu (Eds.), *Clinical decision making in behavior therapy: A problem-solving perspective* (pp. 57–113). Champaign, IL: Research Press.

Page, A. C., Stritzke, W. G. K., & McLean, N. J. (2008). Toward science-informed supervision of clinical case formulation: A training model and supervision method. *Australian Psychologist, 43*(2), 88–95.

Pain, C. M., Chadwick, P., & Abba, N. (2008). Clients' experience of case formulation in cognitive behaviour therapy for psychosis. *British Journal of Clinical Psychology, 47*(2), 127–138.

Persons, J. B. (1989). *Cognitive therapy in practice: A case formulation approach.* New York: Norton.

Persons, J. B., Beckner, V. L., & Tompkins, M. A. (2013). Testing case formulation hypotheses in psychotherapy: Two case examples. *Cognitive and Behavioral Practice, 20*(4), 399–409.

Persons, J. B., Mooney, K. A., & Padesky, C. A. (1995). Interrater relability of cognitive-behavioral case formulations. *Cognitive Therapy and Research, 19*(1), 21–34.

Read, J., & Bentall, R. P. (2012). Negative childhood experiences and mental health: Theoretical, clinical and primary prevention implications. *The British Journal of Psychiatry, 200*(2), 89–91.

Royal College of Psychiatrists. (2017). *Using formulation in general psychiatric care: Good practice.* London: Royal College of Psychiatrists.

Seitz, P. F. (1966). The consensus problem in psychoanalytic research. In L. A. Gottschalk, & A. H. Auerbach (Eds.), *Methods of research in psychotherapy* (pp. 209–225). New York: Springer.

Spencer, H. M., McMenamin, M., Emsley, R., Turkington, D., Dunn, G., Morrison, A. P., et al. (2018). Cognitive behavioral therapy for antipsychotic-free schizophrenia spectrum disorders: does therapy dose influence outcome. *Schizophrenia Research, 202*, 385–386.

Stanbridge, R., & Burbach, F. (2007). Developing family-inclusive mainstream mental health services. *Journal of Family Therapy, 29*(1), 21–43.

Summers, A. (2006). Psychological formulations in psychiatric care: Staff views on their impact. *Psychiatric Bulletin, 30*, 341–343.

Tarrier, N., & Calam, R. (2002). New developments in cognitive-behavioural case formulation. Epidemiological, systemic and social context: an integrative approach. *Behavioural and Cognitive Psychotherapy, 30*(3), 311–328.

Tarrier, N., & Johnson, J. (2016). *Case formulation in cognitive behaviour therapy.* London and New York: Routledge.

Varese, F., Barkus, E., & Bentall, R. P. (2012). Dissociation mediates the relationship between childhood trauma and hallucination-proneness. *Psychological Medicine, 42*(05), 1025–1036.

Varese, F., Smeets, F., Drukker, M., Lieverse, R., Lataster, T., Viechtbauer, W., et al. (2012). Childhood adversities increase the risk of psychosis: a meta-analysis of patient-control, prospective-and cross-sectional cohort studies. *Schizophrenia Bulletin, 38*, 661–671.

Definition OF Key Terms

Efficacy The capacity for producing a desired result or effect (i.e. the desired treatment outcome).

Formulation A framework for bringing together biological, societal, cultural, and psychological factors that might be responsible for the development and maintenance of problems, which can then be used to guide decisions about evidence-based treatments.

Reliability of formulation How closely a conceptualisation can be replicated by another therapist.

Therapeutic alliance The degree to which therapists and clients agree on the tasks and goals of therapeutic work in addition to the degree of emotional bond between the pair.

Validity of formulation How well a case formulation predicts outcomes (including outcomes in therapy).

SECTION 4
Therapies

CHAPTER 15
Cognitive Behavioural Therapies for Psychosis

Louise Johns*,†, Louise Isham‡,§, Rachel Manser§
*Oxford Health NHS Foundation Trust, Oxford, United Kingdom, †Department of Psychiatry, University of Oxford, Oxford, United Kingdom, ‡Oxford Cognitive Approaches to Psychosis (O-CAP), University of Oxford, Oxford, United Kingdom, §Oxford Cognitive Therapy Centre, Oxford Health NHS Foundation Trust, Oxford, United Kingdom

Key Learning Objectives

- Describe the key principles of using CBT with people with psychosis
- Outline the different components of CBT for psychosis
- Review the current evidence base and recommendations
- Identify facilitators and barriers to the delivery of CBT for psychosis in practice

INTRODUCTION

Therapy Overview

Cognitive Behaviour Therapy for Psychosis (CBTp) is an adaptation of CBT for anxiety and depression to the problems of psychosis. It is informed by research into the psychological mechanisms underpinning psychotic experiences, and tailored to accommodate the difficulties of people with psychosis. Cognitive models of psychotic experiences indicate that it is not unusual experiences per se that cause distress, but the appraisal of these experiences as external, personally significant, and threatening (Bentall, Fernyhough, Morrison, Lewis, & Corcoran, 2007; Birchwood & Chadwick, 1997; Byrne, Birchwood, Trower, & Meaden, 2006; Freeman, Garety, Kuipers, Fowler, & Bebbington, 2002; Garety, Bebbington, Fowler, Freeman, & Kuipers, 2007; Garety, Kuipers, Fowler, Freeman, & Bebbington, 2001; Morrison, 2001). Unhelpful coping and safety-seeking behaviours maintain distress and disability by preventing disconfirmation of negative appraisals (Brett et al., 2007; Gaynor, Ward, Garety, & Peters, 2013; Heriot-Maitland, Knight, & Peters, 2012). CBTp aims to break these

Cognitive Behaviour Therapy for Psychosis (CBTp) is an adaptation of CBT for emotional disorders to the problems of psychosis.

A Clinical Introduction to Psychosis. https://doi.org/10.1016/B978-0-12-815012-2.00015-8

maintenance cycles by helping people to make sense of their psychotic experiences in a way that promotes effective coping, and counters negative appraisals of self and illness.

Key Principles of CBTp (Therapy Approach)

Core elements of CBTp interventions include agreed goals, a warm and respectful therapeutic style, collaborative partnership, individual case conceptualisation, and change strategies implemented during and between sessions (Morrison & Barratt, 2010). Client and therapist work together to reduce the client's distress, enhance coping, and achieve specific therapy goals. The approach is like CBT for any other disorder: individualised, matched to the client, and collaborative (Fowler, Garety, & Kuipers, 1995) and guided by the case formulation (see Chapter 14 for more on case-formulations). CBTp differs, however, in that it requires the therapist to have a greater focus on engagement; be more flexible in approach; and take care not to over arouse clients and exacerbate psychotic experiences.

Individual CBTp sessions typically take place weekly to fortnightly over 6–9 months, with follow-up appointments post therapy. Some experts advocate a more intensive approach (e.g. Freeman & Waite, 2017), and our clinical experience suggests that between-session phone calls, text messages, or emails can be extremely helpful in generating and maintaining hope and momentum between sessions. Sessions follow CBT structure, beginning with agenda setting and concluding with feedback. Session length and pacing is flexible: therapists need to adapt to the complexity and heterogeneity of clients' presentations, their emotional sensitivity, cognitive difficulties, and changes in mental state. Therapeutic style is collaborative and nondidactic, and two-way feedback is emphasised throughout the session. Interventions follow a line of least resistance. Therapists focus on what clients are ready to work with, explicitly checking this out (*'How does that sound?', 'What do you think?', 'Might that help?'*). Socratic questioning may be used less, with more 'floating' ideas instead. Open mindedness and genuine curiosity towards clients' beliefs, and empathy with their difficulties, are essential within CBTp, together with a normalising and culturally informed approach to psychotic experiences and processes. Postsession ratings of therapist empathy and understanding are useful (Burns & Nolen-Hoeksema, 1992).

CBTp therapeutic approach: Open mindedness and genuine curiosity towards clients' experiences and beliefs are essential.

Normalising: using information about unusual experiences in the population to reduce fear or shame.

CBTp requires collaborative therapy goals. However, these do not require 'insight' and the therapist can work using the person's frame of reference, for example, 'help to manage current difficulties with other people' rather than 'help with paranoia'. It is important to discuss the pros and cons of working on a particular problem, so the client can make an informed choice about whether to proceed. If it is difficult to establish a focus at the beginning of therapy, let the person tell their story in their own way. Then, once you have an overview of their difficulties and their 'model of understanding', you can develop a problem and goal list. Remain open about therapy priorities, which may not necessarily be psychotic symptoms. It is worth stating explicitly that the aim of CBTp is not to get rid of psychotic symptoms, nor is it about 'challenging' the client's

Aims of CBTp: to achieve client-generated behavioural goals rather than 'getting rid' of psychotic symptoms.

delusional beliefs to increase insight, nor a way of improving compliance with medication. The aim of therapy is to work towards achieving client-generated behavioural goals that improve functioning and social inclusion.

CBTp involves making changes in appraisals and behaviour, through new learning and in the context of a good therapeutic relationship. The focus on appraisals helps clients to make sense of unusual experiences and events, to take a different perspective and/or react in new ways. Homework maximises new learning and setting homework (between-session tasks) is associated with improved outcome and greater satisfaction in CBTp, even though clients may need additional therapist support to complete assignments (Dunn, Morrison, & Bentall, 2006; Glaser, Kazantzis, Deane, & Oades, 2000; Miles, Peters, & Kuipers, 2007; Rector & Health, 2007). In our clinical experience, clients are more likely to engage in a homework task if (a) it is practised within therapy first, and (b) we make between session contact (phone/text/email) to review progress with the task and troubleshoot as necessary.

Format and Elements of CBTp

CBTp progresses through the following phases:

- Engagement and development of a therapeutic relationship
- Assessment
- Establish shared problem and goal list
- Formulation
- Interventions derived from formulation
- Relapse management

These stages overlap in practice, and engagement, assessment, and formulation remain key parts of the work throughout therapy. Stages of CBTp are described, with reference to an illustrative case example (see Box 15.1).

ENGAGEMENT AND ASSESSMENT

A noncolluding, nonconfrontative therapeutic style is required, using the client's own terminology. Use words like 'experienced' and 'knew' early on in therapy, to avoid minimising or dismissing the client's report, changing to 'felt' and 'thought' only if and when this matches the client's understanding.

> **Example:** 'Can I just check I've understood you correctly? You were walking past somebody and you saw her get out her mobile phone. You knew immediately that she was doing this to film you and was intending to put it on the internet. Have I got that right?'

Clients should feel heard and understood, with you viewing them as reasonable and their concerns and reactions as understandable, for example: *'I can understand why you feel constantly on the alert with all this going on'*; *'I can see why you choose to stay inside as much as possible'*. It is important to validate clients' explanation of their experiences, for example: *'It's really understandable, given what you*

Box 15.1 Case Example

John[a] reports that he is being filmed without his consent and that these films are being placed on the internet as part of a conspiracy to persuade people to harm him. He hears voices commenting on his actions (for example, saying 'he's taking the next left, don't lose him') and describes seeing CCTV cameras and people on their mobile phones 'everywhere', which he appraises as evidence of the filming. He believes this started when a neighbor spread 'lies and rumors' about him after they had fallen out. John feels anxious and avoids going out whenever possible. If he does leave the house he makes an effort to disguise his appearance, tries to vary the route he takes so that he is less 'predictable', and carefully looks out for signs of being filmed. He spends most of his time at home and spends a lot of time worrying about the filming and how people might harm him. He finds it hard to get to sleep, and has noticed that lack of sleep tends to make the voices and his anxiety about the situation worse. He reports feeling depressed saying that he doesn't feel he is able to do the things he'd like to do.

[a]A hybrid of anonymised cases.

went through in the past with people bullying you, why you would have concerns about people wanting to harm you'; 'So the voices started soon after you fell out with your neighbour. It makes sense why at the time you assumed he was doing this in retaliation'. It is important to empathise frequently and to use explicit empathic comments, for example: *"I'm sorry to hear that ... that sounds really difficult for you ... it sounds like you've been through a tough time'*, since clients with psychosis may misinterpret or not pick up subtle nonverbal cues.

To facilitate engagement, use the client's own words and model of understanding, and avoid contradicting the person's beliefs.

It is unhelpful to contradict clients' strongly held beliefs and their understanding of unusual experiences. Aim for a stance that is open, neutral, tentative, and respectful.

Example:

John: 'My friend tells me nothing is going on, it's just my imagination, and that none of this is happening. You believe me, don't you?'

Therapist: 'I certainly believe that you are noticing a lot of CCTV cameras and people on their mobile phones. I guess it's hard for me to know for certain whether they are filming you on every occasion or whether there could sometimes be another explanation. Maybe we can look at that together in therapy'.

Specific reassurance is helpful for fears arising from delusional ideas or about being crazy, for example, if a client asks if you think they are mad, answer directly with *'No, I don't think so at all'*. This can be followed up with a normalising comment like, *'It seems like you are going through a really difficult time at the moment, trying to understand and cope with a lot of distressing experiences'*, and exploring the client's understanding of being 'mad' or 'crazy'.

It is important during sessions to check for, and deal collaboratively with, any counter-therapeutic or delusional beliefs about the therapist, and any misinterpretations of the therapist's intentions and meaning. For example, John may misinterpret the therapist's behaviour if he sees them using a mobile phone, and require specific feedback about their intentions when this occurs.

Voices may impede engagement by distracting clients, increasing anxiety, and telling them not to trust you. Additional engagement strategies include using a symbolic pause button to increase clients' control over the session (Meaden, Keen, Aston, Barton, & Bucci, 2013), seeking permission to ask difficult questions, and talking briefly about nontherapy topics as an agreed distraction strategy. It is helpful to preempt difficulties, for example, discussing coping strategies in case voices worsen temporarily after sessions. Avoid setting yourself in opposition to the voices, as this can place clients in an uncomfortable 'mediating' position. Passing a message to the voice can be helpful, for example *'I wonder if it would be helpful for you to tell the voices that our meetings are not to get rid of them but to help with your distress'*. Similarly, you can ask clients what concerns their voices have about sessions and then discuss these concerns with the client.

Assessment begins with general questions to get an overview, followed by specific questions to build up a maintenance formulation (what happened, how did you make sense of it, how did you feel, how did you respond/what did you do to cope, what impact did that have?). Key to CBTp assessment is clarifying experience-appraisal links, and asking what the person notices that leads to the appraisals. The 'intrusion' may be an internal feeling or emotion, a hallucinatory experience, or an external event (that may also have anomalous perceptual qualities). The assessment process also elucidates the key processes and behaviours that are maintaining the experiences and distressing appraisals (see Box 15.2).

During assessment, focus on appraisals and behaviours preventing the person reaching their goal.

Box 15.2 Case Example

Therapist (T): ...would it be okay to talk me through what happened the last time you tried to go out?

John (J): Yeah...it was a couple of days ago. I tried to go to the corner shop to get cigarettes, but they were filming me.

T: Oh gosh – that sounds really difficult. Could you tell me a bit more about what happened?

J: I waited till pretty late because I thought there wouldn't be so many people around. I was really anxious, but I got so close and I thought I might just make it this time. But then I turned the corner next to the shop and there was a man stood outside talking into his mobile.

T: Okay. And so when you saw him, what sense did you make of that?

J: Well he obviously knew I'd be there and had his phone out ready to film me.

T: Okay. How quickly did you realise that? Was that as soon as you saw him or...?

J: Yeah. Straight away.

T: Oh gosh. That must've been really hard. So when you saw him and you realised that, how did you feel?

J: Really anxious. I don't want them watching me.

T: That's completely understandable. So what did you do?

J: I got out of there. Ran home.

T: That sounds like it was a really horrible experience.

Continued

BOX 15.2 Case Example—cont'd

J: Yeah. I tried going a different route back but other people were filming me too.

T: How did you know? Did you see other people with phones?

J: No. I just knew. I could feel it. In my gut. I have really good gut instincts for things.

T: What does that feel like – the gut instinct?

J: I can just feel their eyes on me – my skin feels hot. And my stomach churns. And I just feel really pumped – full of adrenaline.

T: Okay. And when you notice those feelings, what goes through your mind?

J: Obviously that they are watching me.

T: That sounds awful. Okay. So what happened once you got home?

J: Well, I was relieved to get back… but still pretty anxious.

T: Okay.. and so once you got home what did you do?

J: I tried watching TV but I couldn't stop thinking about it all. I was just trying to work out what to do. But what if next time they try and follow me into the house? I think I'm going to have to go out in disguise or something.

GOAL SETTING

Goals are important to orientate therapy, as the key problems to work on are those that are preventing the client from achieving their goals. It is most productive to develop 'SMART' goals (specific, measurable, achievable, relevant, and time sensitive), which are best framed in terms of things the person would like to do rather than how they will feel. Useful goal-setting questions include: 'What would you like to be different? If you weren't so bothered by people watching you, what would you be able to do that you can't do now?'

FORMULATION

The formulation emphasises the understandability of the client's position, typically bringing together their vulnerability factors, life events, affect, past and current unusual experiences, appraisals, cognitive biases, and behaviour. It provides an idiosyncratic understanding of the factors that are maintaining distress and preventing the client reaching their goals. There are many models to draw on to aid formulation. Earlier models of psychosis (e.g. Garety et al., 2001; Morrison, 2001) provide helpful generic frameworks for formulating positive psychotic symptoms. More recently, results from factor analytic and genetic studies demonstrating the independence of specific psychotic experiences have resulted in a move towards experience-specific models and translational treatments (Ronald et al., 2014; Zavos et al., 2014). For example, Freeman (2016) and Freeman et al. (2002) provide an evidence-based model of persecutory delusions, which highlights the role of key psychological processes, including excessive worry, low self-confidence, anomalous experiences, sleep dysfunction, reasoning biases, and safety-seeking behaviours, in maintaining persecutory beliefs. Byrne et al. (2006) and Birchwood et al. (2018) provide an experience-specific model of command hallucinations, which highlights the importance of the perceived power of voices in influencing compliance with harmful commands. Gumley and Schwannauer's (2006) model of relapse emphasises the role of catastrophic interpretations of attenuated symptoms as a sign of impending relapse in driving negative emotions and safety-seeking behaviours, which can then worsen the psychotic symptoms.

Where a relevant evidence-based experience-specific model exists, the clinician should draw on this to guide their assessment, formulation, and intervention, as these models identify specific mechanisms that are likely to be relevant for the client. However, formulation should always be idiosyncractic and therefore if a mechanism identified by a model is not found (or an additional one is identified) the formulation should reflect this.

Formulation alone, particularly complex, developmental formulation, whilst useful for therapists, can be perceived as unhelpful by clients (Morberg Pain et al., 2008). That said, for clients whose goal is to gain a better understanding of their experiences (particularly clients with trauma histories), developmental formulations may be very helpful (Longden, Corstens, Escher, & Romme, 2012; Morrison, 2017). Developing a shared formulation needs to be done accessibly, linking the formulation to the client's goals and identifying strategies for change. During assessment, eliciting recent, typical examples of the client's problem in terms of specific triggers, cognitions, emotional and behavioural responses will provide more useful information for CBTp than discussions about general patterns. Drawing simple free-hand diagrams of these examples in the sessions helps the client to understand the cognitive-behavioural model, see how the different factors interact and maintain their problems, as well as showing how these vicious cycles can be broken. You can check the links (lines) and causality (direction of the arrows) with clients to understand the mechanisms maintaining their appraisals and distress, for example, use of safety behaviours, attentional biases, which are used to plan treatment and identify strategies for change.

Formulation should start with maintenance loops relevant to the client's problems and goals.

Figs 15.1–15.6 show examples of maintenance formulations for John. Fig. 15.1 shows an 'ABC'-style formulation, which aims to capture the key information (triggers, appraisals, responses) in one summary diagram. This type of formulation is useful for the therapist as it brings together a lot of information in one place, showing all the different processes that have been identified as maintaining the difficulties. However, formulations such as this may not be so helpful for clients if they do not clearly demonstrate *how* each maintenance cycle works. Therefore, Figs 15.2–15.6 show some examples of simple shared maintenance loops that might be developed in therapy (this is not intended to be comprehensive, and more examples could be developed). Such formulations can be built upon as therapy progresses (Kinderman & Lobban, 2000), and may start with just a single cycle.

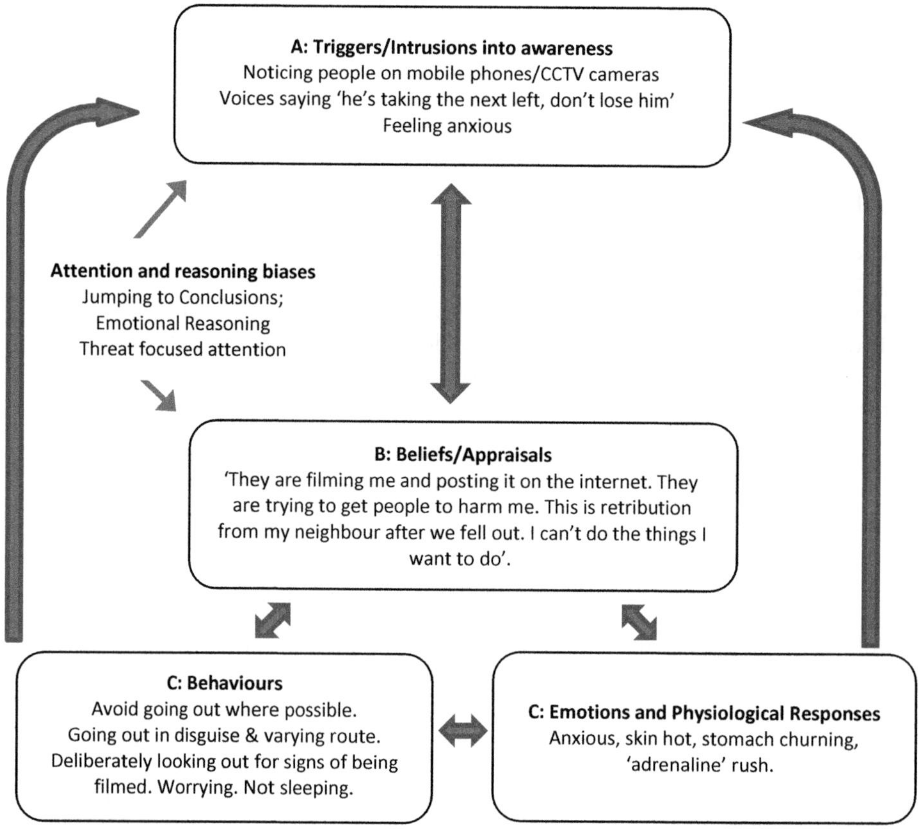

FIG. 15.1
ABC maintenance formulation for John (In an ABC model, the A refers to an Antecedent (here this is the 'trigger' or 'Intrusion into awareness' box), the B refers to the Belief (or appraisal) and the C represents the Consequences (here divided into two boxes to capture separately the affective and physiological responses, and the behavioural consequences).

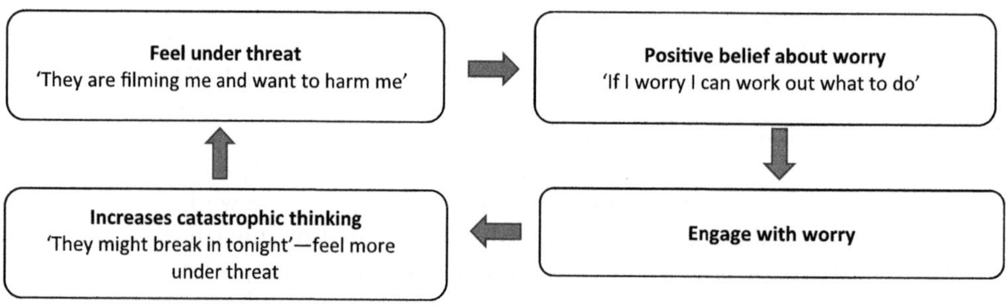

FIG. 15.2
Maintenance loop: Worry (Worry has been identified as a key causal and maintenance mechanism for persecutory delusions, and targeting worry results in significant improvements in the delusional belief. For more information, the reader can refer to Freeman, Dunn, et al., 2015).

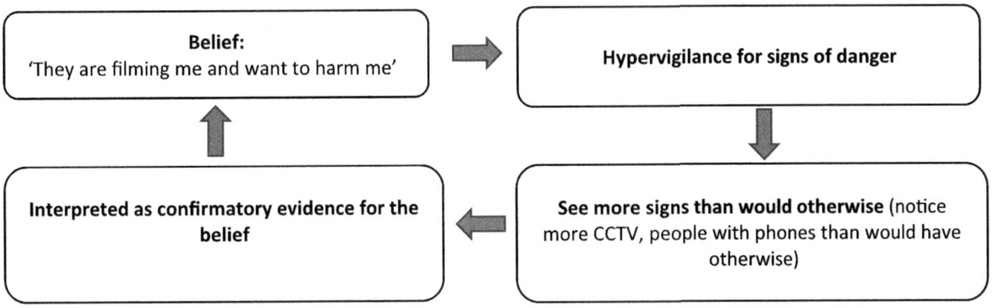

FIG. 15.3
Maintenance loop: Hypervigilance.

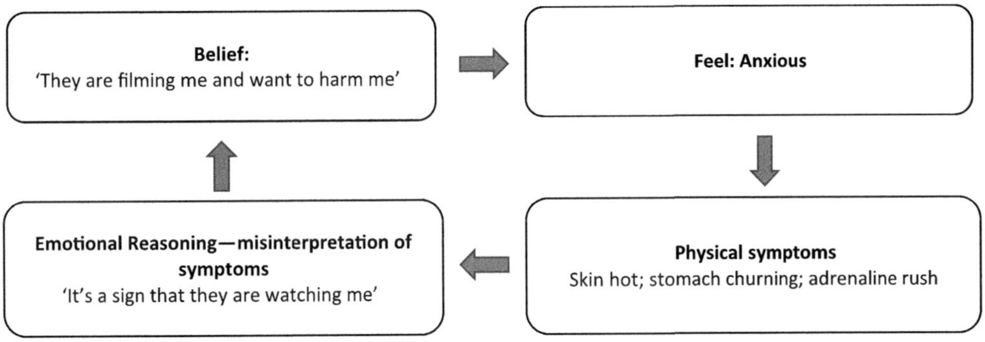

FIG. 15.4
Maintenance loop: Emotional Reasoning.

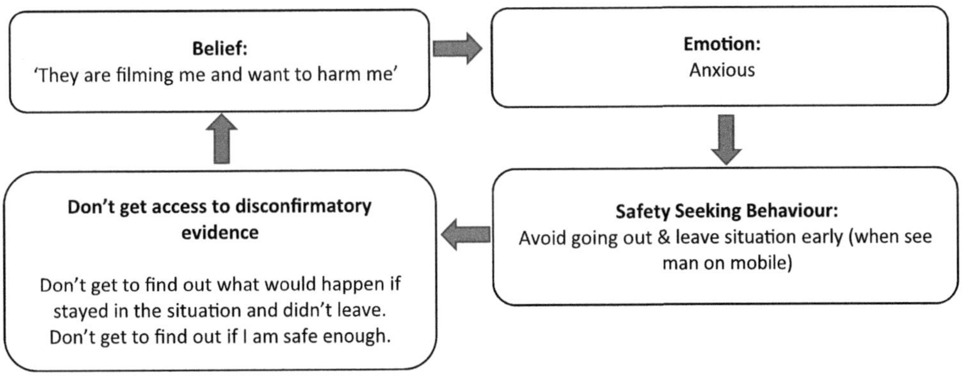

FIG. 15.5
Safety Seeking Behaviour—avoidance & leaving situation early (A number of other safety behaviours were also evident in the case described (e.g. going out in disguise; varying the route taken home). These could be formulated in a very similar way).

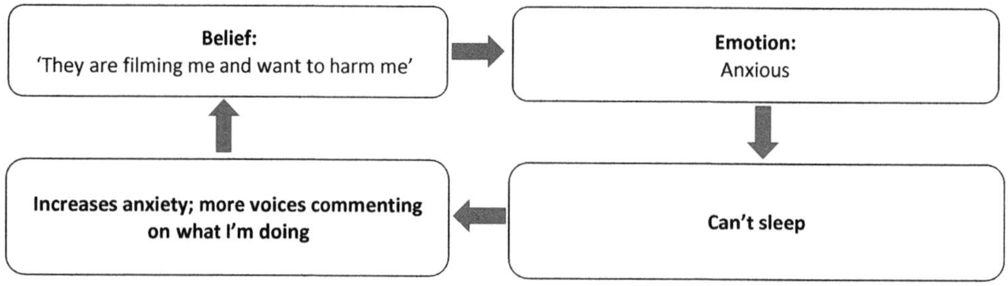

FIG. 15.6
Sleep difficulties and voices.

INTERVENTIONS

There are specific interventions for working with hallucinations, delusional beliefs, reasoning biases, and negative symptoms. As well as working with psychotic symptoms, you are likely to work directly with emotional distress and also with trauma in some cases.

Self-Regulation of Psychotic Symptoms (Enhancing Coping Strategies)

Initial intervention strategies focus on the behaviours in the maintenance formulation, to identify alternative strategies for coping with distressing symptoms and for the client to try these during and between sessions. It can be helpful to ask clients to complete diaries between sessions to identify factors that impact on specific symptoms, with the aim of managing situations and behaviours that worsen symptoms and building on behaviours that improve them. You can suggest strategies for particular symptoms, for example, humming for voices (Farhall, Greenwood, & Jackson, 2007), and many strategies can be borrowed from affect work, for example, relaxation, distraction, mindfulness. It is important that these are derived from the formulation, and are not inadvertent safety behaviours. For John, coping could include humming when out, paying attention to something else rather than CCTV cameras and mobile phones, reducing the time spent worrying, thinking about, and doing other things during the day.

Clients usually initiate some coping strategies, but have often not tried them systematically. Coping Strategy Enhancement (CSE) (Tarrier, 2002; Tarrier, Harwood, Yusopoff, Beckett, & Baker, 1990) is a structured intervention that involves building on the client's existing repertoire of coping strategies, and brief CSE can help clients with distressing voices (see Chapter 26). Troubleshoot coping strategies before the client tries them, and then tweak them if they do not work. Although coping may only provide short-term relief from symptoms, it can increase the client's sense of control. You can set up behavioural experiments to evaluate the impact of using a specified strategy, for example, on mood, or unusual experiences, or beliefs. When reviewing the effect of coping strategies, you can reflect on the mechanism and incorporate positive outcomes into the client's appraisals, as appropriate. A change in experiences, for example, noticing fewer instances of people talking, that is contingent on the client's behaviour can be used to question their appraisals, particularly beliefs about power and control over their experiences. For example: *'You noticed that you heard fewer people talking to you when you started humming to yourself…what does that say about your ability to have some control over them?…and what does that say about the power of them in relation to you?'*

Specific Belief Change

Delusional appraisals of experiences in psychosis are usually external, personal, and threatening (physical or psychological harm). The emphasis in CBTp is on reducing distress and preoccupation, increasing the client's sense of control and hope, and improving functioning, rather than requiring major belief change. There are four levels of belief change (Johns, Jolley, Keen, & Peters, 2014):

Belief change work: CBTp focuses primarily on reducing distress and preoccupation rather than conviction.

(1) No change. Therapy focuses on improving the client's mood and coping, and different ways of reacting (i.e. working 'within the delusion'). The aim is to increase clients' understanding of how their current coping strategies might be exacerbating their difficulties (as shown in Figs 15.2 and 15.3, for example), and suggest alternative behavioural and cognitive strategies.

(2) Change implications of the belief and impact on functioning—beliefs about what the client can do despite the belief. For example, *'They are filming me and I might be harmed, but I can still go and visit my family anyway'*.

(3) Change one or more aspect of the belief, for example, the harassment is less widespread than originally thought, or voices are less powerful or not always truthful (i.e. increasing belief flexibility).

(4) Fully change conviction in the belief—the client no longer believes it to be the case or, even, does not believe it was ever true.

Change at any level can be helpful, and you are not necessarily aiming for level 4. A shift, for example, 'it is not as unsafe as I thought' can permit sufficient behaviour change to allow the client to meet their goals. Preparatory work is needed beforehand, including assessing the implications of belief change. Some delusional beliefs serve a protective function, and it is important not to pursue change that might lower the person's mood or self-esteem. You can find an acceptable narrative for change with the client, for example, 'They aren't filming me as much as they used to, they must have got bored and moved on. I'm safer now'.

Novice therapists can sometimes rush in with challenging delusional beliefs while still assessing them. This can jeopardise the therapeutic alliance, invalidate the client's experience, and increase the client's anxiety and need to defend their explanations of events. Instead, use the formulation to make sense of the experiences that have led to delusions, highlighting links between delusional appraisals and distress, and enhance motivation to consider alternatives by linking these to less distress.

> **Example:** 'When you notice people using their mobile phones and think they are filming you, that makes you feel scared and you try to keep safe. How would you feel… if it turned out that on some of those occasions, there was another reason for them to be using their phone that wasn't related to you?'

Cognitive change is facilitated by puzzling together about possible exceptions for specific situations ('Was *everybody* using their mobile trying to film you when you went out? Was there any other reason why that particular person might have used their mobile on that occasion?'). Alternative explanations for particular instances can be identified, considering with the client whether there is any possibility at all that a single event could be due to something else, such as chance, bad luck, or things to do with the other person (i.e. not threatening and not personal to the client). It can be helpful to normalise the client's original conclusion before asking whether, in retrospect, there could be another explanation, for example: *'of course it's completely understandable, given your experience of being filmed in the past, that when you saw the CCTV camera you'd think 'it's happening again'. I'm just wondering though… is there any possibility at all that on this occasion there could have been another reason for the camera to be there'*. The generation of acceptable alternative beliefs, rather than simply creating doubt, is crucial, since doubt in the absence of plausible alternatives is associated with lower self-esteem (Freeman et al., 2004). Be prepared to suggest or 'float' some ideas, as clients may not be able to generate alternatives themselves (Freeman et al., 2004). Suggest alternatives as 'possibilities' without taking personal ownership of them, which makes it easier to back down without damaging the therapeutic relationship. The accumulation of alternative explanations for numerous instances can be used as evidence against a delusional belief and to test out beliefs using behavioural experiments. Any new alternative belief needs to be explanatory, acceptable, and credible to the client. A detailed formulation of the client's experiences can often provide an alternative nondelusional explanation.

Normalising Unusual or Anomalous Experiences

A normalising approach is central to CBT for psychosis. By normalising, we mean making psychotic experiences understandable by normal psychological processes (such as dissociation, thinking biases, predictive processing) and the impact of adverse life events. Normalisation also refers to the continuum of psychotic experiences in the general population (van Os, Linscott, Myin-Germeys, Delespaul, & Krabbendam, 2009), and knowledge that these experiences are part of normal human experience and valued in some cultural groups (Larøi et al., 2014; Peters et al., 2016; Powers, Corlett, & Ross, 2018). A normalising approach is helpful when trying to understand and re-appraise distressing psychotic experiences with clients. Psycho-education about the prevalence of these experiences worldwide (Johns et al., 2004; Mcgrath et al., 2015), and in situations of extreme stress, bereavement or sleep/sensory deprivation (Freeman et al., 2017; Kamp &

Due, 2018; Mason & Brady, 2009; Reeve, Emsley, Sheaves, & Freeman, 2018; Sheaves et al., 2016) can help to normalise the experience, together with making links with the client's personal history, especially past experiences of trauma and victimisation, in order to understand why the person might be having these symptoms.

Normalisation is also important when clients fear they are 'mad' or 'crazy', and have problematic appraisals such as being abnormal, fear of losing control, or low expectations of recovery. Personal accounts from people with similar experiences (with or without a need for care) can be illuminating for clients. Key messages for clients include 'you're not crazy', 'you're not alone', and 'you can live a fulfilling life'. It is important to share the information sensitively, so as not to not minimise the client's experiences or distress, and to get feedback about what the client concludes.

Cognitive Biases

Clients with psychosis can show a range of cognitive biases (distortions in the way they process information), for example:

- Emotional reasoning
  Cl: 'everyone was staring at me'.
  Th: 'how did you know?'
  Cl: 'I felt it, in my gut. I felt hot, my cheeks were burning, and I felt so anxious... so I knew they were staring at me'
- Jumping to conclusions
  Th: 'so when you first heard the voice what did you think?'
  Cl: 'it was my neighbour'.
  Th: 'did you know that straight away or were you unsure at first? Trying to figure out...'
  Cl: 'No. I knew the second I heard it that it was him'.

Some of these biases are particularly associated with psychotic symptoms (van der Gaag et al., 2013), including memory bias (not remembering the source of information), co-variation bias (overestimating causality and underestimating chance), jumping to conclusions (making hasty decisions on the basis of limited information), and confirmation bias (bias against disconfirmatory evidence). Others are less specific to psychosis, such as emotional reasoning (reaching conclusions on the basis of feelings) and perceptual bias (selective attention for information).

Ways of working with these biases in therapy include increasing awareness and labelling them (normalising), and introducing techniques to compensate for them, such as deliberately considering other information, slowing down decision making. Specific metacognitive training packages for clients with schizophrenia have been found to reduce cognitive biases, delusional conviction, and distress (Moritz et al., 2011; Waller et al., 2015; Waller, Freeman, Jolley, Dunn, & Garety, 2011), although the results are varied (van Oosterhout et al., 2016). These materials can be incorporated into individual CBTp sessions (see resources).

Another approach to metacognition focuses on clients' tendency to overthink (worry or ruminate) or attempt to control their thinking (Parker, Wells, & Morrison, 2014). Intervention includes collaborative understanding of the client's goal of dwelling on certain thoughts, often indicated by metacognitive beliefs in the formulation, then practising strategies to interrupt control strategies (worry postponement) and let thoughts go (detached mindfulness). These metacognitive interventions often form part of the initial work on coping strategies. They are further indicated in CBTp when the content of the client's beliefs could suggest that belief change work is contra-indicated, such as longstanding and complex delusional systems, concerns about the consequences of evaluating beliefs, or psychological reactance due to the person not feeling believed. Worry is highly prevalent in people with persecutory delusions and it is a key causal and maintenance factor (Freeman et al., 2012; Freeman & Garety, 1999; Startup, Freeman, & Garety, 2007). Targeting worry directly in therapy significantly reduces worry, persecutory delusions, and delusional distress (Freeman, Dunn, et al., 2015; Freeman, Waite, et al., 2015).

CBTp involves working directly with thought processes as well as content.

Working With Emotion

Anxiety and depression work is an integral part of CBTp. The prevalence of these problems in clients with psychosis is higher than it is in the general population (Achim et al., 2011) and affective processes are central to the development and maintenance of psychotic symptoms (Birchwood, 2003; Fowler et al., 2012; Freeman & Garety, 2003; Paulik & Badcock, 2010). It is often easier to engage clients initially by assessing and formulating affective disturbance, which can be framed as caused by the presenting problem. Affect work with John could target, for example, his anxiety about people filming him, or depression caused by staying at home and avoiding activities. Strategies for working with affect include standard CB approaches for anxiety and depression, but usually adapted to take account of the presence of anomalous experiences and strongly held beliefs.

Use of avoidance and other safety behaviours to reduce anxiety is common in people with voices and paranoia, and play a key role in maintaining threatening appraisals and delusional beliefs (Freeman et al., 2007; Gaynor et al., 2013; Hacker, Birchwood, Tudway, Meaden, & Amphlett, 2008; Nothard, Morrison, & Wells, 2008). These avoidant behaviours can also maintain negative beliefs about oneself following a psychotic episode and fear of adverse outcomes (failure, rejection, relapse), relevant to both social anxiety (Birchwood et al., 2007) and negative symptoms (Rector, Beck, & Stolar, 2005). Graded exposure can be used to target anxious avoidance of situations, and to test out particular (delusional) thoughts and beliefs. Clients develop an idiosyncratic hierarchy of feared situations, working towards a values-based goal, and approach each situation with the therapist's support (including accompanying the client or being available by phone). In addition to learning that feared outcomes do not occur as predicted, and some habituation of the anxiety, key learning following exposure is an increased sense of perceived control (Mineka & Thomas, 1999).

In CBTp, you typically approach exposure more slowly than in CBT for anxiety, to avoid overarousing the client and potentially exacerbating psychotic symptoms. Also, some clients' fears are so terrifying, for example, believing 100% that they will be killed, that graded exposure seems very risky (or implies that you don't take their fears seriously). In these cases, it is important to do plenty of preparatory work on the client's thoughts and beliefs beforehand. The client will often use coping strategies initially, which may be formulated as safety behaviours. These enable the client to start achieving their goals, and can gradually be dropped. A client may choose to retain some safety behaviours, which, although will prevent them fully testing their beliefs, may not matter if the client is able to achieve their goals.

Depression is a common reaction to psychosis, and is associated with appraisals of shame, entrapment, loss and self-blame (Birchwood, Iqbal, & Upthegrove, 2005). Clients with negative symptoms also express depressive cognitions regarding failure and lack of hope for improvement (Grant & Beck, 2009). CBTp incorporates behavioural and cognitive strategies for both depression and negative symptoms. Behavioural activation reduces depression by helping clients to increase levels of rewarding activity (Mazzucchelli, Kane, & Rees, 2009), and can be used to reduce depression and negative symptoms in this client group (Mairs, Lovell, Campbell, & Keeley, 2011; Waller et al., 2013, 2018). You can include positive imagery to increase anticipatory success and pleasure, and hence clients' motivation to engage in activities. Cognitive techniques for depression, as described by Beck, Rush, Shaw, and Emery (1979) can be used with clients with psychosis, questioning the accuracy of negative thoughts, testing out (negative) predictions, and working with cognitive biases and schema (Padesky, 1994).

Working with affect is an integral part of CBTp.

Negative Symptoms

Cognitive behavioural techniques used for depression are helpful for amotivational negative symptoms, which involve low expectancies of success and pleasure (Rector et al., 2005). Interventions to help clients achieve valued goals can target their negative predictions about future performance and expectancy of pleasure, addressing the difference between what is anticipated and what is likely to be experienced. Compassion-focused approaches can also activate positive affect, reduce defeatist thoughts, and increase hope (White, Laithwaite, & Gilbert, 2012). Intervention strategies are outlined in Box 15.3, using an illustrative case example.

Relapse Management

Towards the end of therapy, whilst acknowledging any concerns about ending, we may start to taper sessions to give clients greater opportunities to practise skills. As part of normalising, it is important to explain that anomalous experiences, belief conviction, and mood can fluctuate across time. In the relapse management plan, we also normalise and plan for setbacks in the future. Plans include potential triggers, early and later warning signs of relapse, and actions the client can take (using skills learned in therapy and accessing support from

Box 15.3 Case Example

Frank[b] has a diagnosis of schizophrenia and no current positive symptoms. He lacks motivation and energy to do things, and says he does not feel interested in life. He does very little during the day, mainly staying at home watching television. He manages to shop and cook, and to look after his daughter at the weekend. He talks to his sister on the phone when she calls him, about once a month. He often thinks 'there's no point in doing things', 'they won't lead to anything', 'I can't be bothered'. He also feels self-conscious when he goes out and worries about what others think of him. Frank's therapy goal is to have a more satisfying life, including seeing family members, getting exercise during the day, and doing interesting activities with his daughter.

Treatment approach:

- Formulating examples of his difficulties (events, thoughts, feelings, behaviours)
- Linking his goals with underlying values (connecting with others, staying healthy, doing different things, being a good father). Taking small actions towards his goals (the values are the reasons why, the 'what's the point?')
- Planning the steps involved in detail and problem solving potential obstacles
- Using imagery to visualise doing an activity, to enhance expected pleasure and success
- Questioning negative thoughts, looking for evidence for and against them, testing them out, considering alternatives, and being more open-minded rather than dismissive (e.g. 'I never know until I try, change takes time' rather than 'It will never get better')
- For self-consciousness, noticing that all sorts of people do things, e.g. go to the gym, reducing self-focus, behavioural experiments to test feared outcomes
- Compassion-focused exercises, e.g. imagery, loving kindness meditation
- Planning a maintenance strategy

[b] A hybrid of anonymised cases.

others). Services can inadvertently catastrophise the meaning of hallucinations or delusional beliefs returning or increasing in frequency or intensity (Gumley & Schwannauer, 2006), and services and families can be risk averse, which can hamper clients' progress and confidence. Towards the end of therapy, it can be worth addressing fears about relapse with clients, their families, and other professionals involved. It can be useful at this point to discuss sharing the relapse plan more widely.

As with all forms of CBT, the therapist aims to guide the client to become their own therapist and become more equipped to deal with difficulties that might arise. To support this, the therapist completes a therapy blueprint and plan for the future with the client, which helps to consolidate the learning achieved during therapy. This blueprint usually starts with a review of the presenting problems, therapy goals, and what has been accomplished in therapy. Here, if clients feel any shame about their previous beliefs, it is worth emphasising that their difficulties were understandable at the time. For example, John might include in his blueprint, 'It's understandable I kept noticing people with their phones because I had become very anxious and on high alert after falling out with my neighbour'. The ending can be a time to celebrate what the client has achieved, and to reinforce that progress is attributed to their efforts and commitment. Throughout the course of CBT, it is helpful to draw attention to the generalisability of skills gained. For example, John might have on his blueprint a reminder: 'Whenever I realise I'm jumping to conclusions about something, remember to stop and think of what else might be going on'. The blueprint 'document' is developed in a way that is most accessible for the client, which might be a written handout, notes, or messages on a mobile phone, or an audio recording.

Efficacy and Effectiveness of CBTp

To date, there have been at least 20 metaanalyses reviewing up to 55 CBTp treatment trials, with varying trial selection criteria, contradictory interpretations of the findings, and ongoing debate regarding the efficacy of CBTp. The results of these metaanalyses, however, are generally consistent. For the primary outcome (usually an overall symptom measure), the average effect size (ES) is in the small-to-moderate range (for example, 0.33, Jauhar et al., 2014; 0.47, Pfammatter, Junghan, & Brenner, 2006; 0.40, Wykes, Steel, Everitt, & Tarrier, 2008; 0.37, Zimmermann, Favrod, Trieu, & Pomini, 2005), with smaller effects in more methodologically rigorous trials (Jauhar et al., 2014; Wykes et al., 2008). The strongest RCT evidence is for positive symptoms of psychosis (Bighelli et al., 2018; Turner, Van der Gaag, Karyotaki, & Cuijpers, 2014), although this is partly because most trials have positive symptoms as their primary outcome. There is good evidence for the effectiveness of CBTp for people with persisting symptoms despite medication (Burns, Erickson, & Brenner, 2014), although in a recent trial of CBT for clients with clozapine-resistant schizophrenia, improvements in psychiatric symptoms posttreatment were not maintained at follow-up (Morrison et al., 2018). CBT is helpful for both hallucinations (Thomas et al., 2014) and delusions (Mehl, Werner, & Lincoln, 2015), there is currently slightly better evidence for hallucinations (Van der Gaag, Valmaggia, & Smit, 2014), and the effects are larger for therapies that target specific maintenance factors (Lincoln & Peters, 2018; discussed below). Trials comparing CBTp with other types of psychological interventions have not shown a convincing advantage (Jones, Hacker, Cormac, Meaden, & Irving, 2012; Kennedy & Xyrichis, 2017; Lynch, Laws, & McKenna, 2010; Mehl et al., 2015; Turner et al., 2014), and there is a need to strengthen the evidence base for CBTp compared to an alternative therapy. The evidence for CBTp so far is almost exclusively as an adjunct to medication. However, a recent pilot RCT comparing antipsychotic medication versus CBTp versus antipsychotics plus CBTp found that CBTp could potentially help patients who choose not to take medication (Morrison et al., 2018).

In addition to its effect on positive symptoms, CBTp has been found to alleviate negative symptoms (Grant, Huh, Perivoliotis, Stolar, & Beck, 2012; Klingberg et al., 2011; Staring, ter Huurne, & van der Gaag, 2013), reduce depression (Peters et al., 2010), and improve social functioning and recovery (Fowler et al., 2018). However, a recent metaanalysis found only small benefits of CBTp on functioning and distress and no impact on quality of life (Laws, Darlington, Kondel, Mckenna, & Jauhar, 2018). The evidence for CBTp helping to prevent relapse is mixed (Garety et al., 2008; Gumley et al., 2003). Similarly, there is mixed evidence for acute psychosis and early psychosis, as clients are improving anyway (Bird et al., 2010; Drury, Birchwood, & Cochrane, 2000; Marshall & Rathbone, 2011; Ruggeri et al., 2015).

FACTORS AFFECTING OUTCOMES

Around half of those offered CBTp engage with therapy, and various factors mediate therapy outcomes. Engagement is related to the person's views of their problems (Freeman et al., 2013) and outcome is influenced by symptom severity and duration, cognitive flexibility, social support, preexisting coping skills and functioning, but not IQ or cognitive impairment (Garety et al., 2008; Morrison et al., 2012; O'Keeffe, Conway, & McGuire, 2017; Perivoliotis et al., 2010; Premkumar et al., 2011; Tarrier & Wykes, 2004). Good therapeutic alliance is associated with better outcomes (Goldsmith, Lewis, Dunn, & Bentall, 2015; Jung, Wiesjahn, & Lincoln, 2014), and high-quality training and delivery of CBTp-specific interventions are necessary to achieve positive outcomes (Dunn et al., 2012; Steel, Tarrier, Stahl, & Wykes, 2012). Outcome is also related to therapy duration (National Institute for Health and Care Excellence, 2009, 2014; (Sarin, Wallin, & Widerlöv, 2011), and entrenched symptoms might need a longer course of therapy, similar to the continued use of medication (Morrison, Pyle, et al., 2018).

Specific training and supervision is a vital element in the effective practice of CBTp.

CULTURAL ADAPTATION

Evidence suggests that there is an increased risk of schizophrenia in individuals from migrant or ethnic minority populations (Cantor-Graae & Selten, 2005; Fearon et al., 2006). However, whether CBTp is effective in these groups is unclear, since ethnic minorities are often underrepresented in clinical trials (Degnan et al., 2018). There is evidence of higher dropout rates and poorer outcomes from CBT in some black and minority ethnic groups (specifically African-Caribbean and Black African groups) compared to a White population within the UK (Rathod, Kingdon, Smith, & Turkington, 2005), which highlights a need to develop and evaluate culturally adapted approaches. Some work has begun in this area, and outcomes from early RCTs comparing culturally adapted CBTp against treatment as usual have been encouraging. These studies have typically found a positive impact on overall symptomatology, positive symptoms, and negative symptoms (Habib, Dawood, Kingdon, & Naeem, 2015; Kumar et al., 2010; Naeem et al., 2015; Rathod et al., 2013; So et al., 2015). However, further methodologically rigorous trials are required, testing culturally adapted CBTp versus traditional CBT formats or other control interventions, and collecting follow-up data.

What factors should clinicians hold in mind then when working with different cultural groups? A recent review of culturally adapted psychosocial interventions considered what constituted 'cultural adaptation' (Degnan et al., 2018). Themes describing the type of adaptations made were identified using qualitative analysis. These included: using native language, incorporating alternative illness models, understanding expectations about the role of family members, integrating culturally appropriate coping mechanisms, and addressing any culturally specific barriers to accessing sessions and developing a therapeutic alliance. Hence, there are a number of factors to hold in mind when considering culture, although all within the CBT therapist's usual practice of tailoring the therapy to make it accessible and acceptable to the client.

SYMPTOM-SPECIFIC APPROACHES

The modest research evidence for the efficacy of CBTp is due partly to the research designs. RCTs tend to evaluate composite CBT approaches for heterogeneous samples of patients, while measuring multiple outcomes. This approach is necessary given the selection of participants for most trials by broad diagnostic group rather than for particular problems, but it can limit any assessment of what works for whom, and potentially masks what is, and what is not, being dealt with effectively in therapy (Jolley & Garety, 2011; Thomas, 2015).

A limitation of testing generic CBTp is that it includes a variety of intervention methods used in various combinations according to the person's presenting problems and therapy goals. Furthermore, the therapeutic targets are not easily captured by a single primary outcome measure. As described in the formulation section, current developments in CBTp involve evaluating discrete intervention components for specific psychotic symptoms, taking a 'causal-interventionist approach' (Freeman, 2011). Studies have examined the cognitive, emotional, and behavioural processes involved in triggering and maintaining these symptoms (see Formulation section). These studies have the advantage of being able to demonstrate specific outcomes in a more homogeneous client group with respect to the target problem, and to evaluate prescribed interventions and their mechanisms of change. There is good empirical evidence for targeted studies on delusions and hallucinations (Lincoln & Peters, 2018; Mehl et al., 2015), with medium-to-large effects. Positive effects have been reported for reducing persecutory delusions by targeting worry (Freeman, Dunn, et al., 2015; Freeman, Waite, et al., 2015), and for reducing compliance with command hallucinations by targeting power beliefs (Birchwood et al., 2014; Trower et al., 2004). These symptom-focused approaches are potentially more efficient, and modular stand-alone interventions can be combined into a more comprehensive therapy (Freeman, 2016).

Delivery of CBTp and Challenges to Implementation

FUNDAMENTAL PRINCIPLES OF CBTp

Clients' experiences of CBTp, ascertained from qualitative interviews, group into common themes that overlap with the core elements of CBTp. They include experiencing CBTp as: a respectful relationship, a process of person-centred engagement, an education process, helping to improve personal understanding, an active process of structured learning, hard work, a healing process, and related to recovery and outcomes (Kilbride et al., 2013; Messari & Hallam, 2003). Syntheses of qualitative research into experiences of CBTp (Berry & Hayward, 2011; Holding, Gregg, & Haddock, 2016; Wood, Burke, & Morrison, 2015) draw together the ingredients of CBTp valued by clients, together with challenging aspects of the therapy. CBTp helps through formulating and understanding psychotic experiences, including illustrating maintenance loops and making links between current and past experiences. Normalisation and acceptance of psychotic experiences is also helpful, appreciating that leading a meaningful life is possible while psychotic experiences continue. The collaborative therapeutic relationship is vital, with client and therapist working together. A challenge of CBTp is talking about difficult experiences and managing the associated emotions, which reinforces the need for appropriate pacing and ongoing two-way feedback during sessions.

Core competences for work with people with psychosis have been developed (see www.ucl.ac.uk/CORE/), and (Brabban, Byrne, Longden, & Morrison, 2016) provide ten tips for the delivery of ethical and recovery-orientated CBTp (see resources). Regular supervision of therapists helps to ensure fidelity to CBTp treatment protocols, particularly reviewing audio- or video recordings of therapy sessions. Therapist competence and adherence can be assessed using rating scales such as the Cognitive Therapy Scale—Revised (CTS-R) (Blackburn et al., 2001; Young & Beck, 1980), the Assessment of Core CBT Skills (ACCS; Muse, McManus, Rakovshik, & Thwaites, 2017), and the Revised-Cognitive Therapy for Psychosis Adherence Scale (R-CTPAS) (Rollinson et al., 2008; Startup, Jackson, & Pearce, 2002).

IMPLEMENTATION IN ROUTINE PRACTICE

Based on the research evidence, international clinical guidelines recommend that CBTp should be offered to all clients with a psychotic disorder (Kreyenbuhl, Buchanan, Dickerson, & Dixon, 2010; National Institute for Health and Care Excellence, 2009, 2014; Royal Australian and New Zealand College of Psychiatrists, 2005). Effectiveness studies in routine services have also shown that CBTp leads to improvements in symptoms and functioning (Jolley et al., 2015; Kråkvik, Gråwe, Hagen, & Stiles, 2013; Lincoln et al., 2012; Morrison et al., 2004; Peters et al., 2015). However, despite the evidence base and clarity of the guidelines, delivery of CBTp in routine services is low (Colling et al., 2017; The Schizophrenia Commission, 2012). The limited availability of CBTp can be explained by a number of factors, including lack of trained staff, lack of protected time to deliver the therapy and receive supervision, and conflicts between service priorities and therapy not seen as priority intervention (Haddock et al., 2014; Ince, Haddock, & Tai, 2016; Prytys, Garety, Jolley, Onwumere, & Craig, 2011; Shafran et al., 2009). In some countries, lack of appropriate health insurance (Chamberlin, 2004), and poor access to basic psychological health facilities (World Health Organization, 2014) may be a further barrier to accessing therapy.

The use of brief targeted therapies has been suggested as a means to improve access to CBTp (Hazell, Hayward, Cavanagh, & Strauss, 2016; Naeem et al., 2016). However, modular targeted interventions that are applied one after another can add up to lengthy therapies (like generic CBTp), and this may similarly restrict their implementation in busy services with limited numbers of staff trained to deliver these interventions. Where CBT therapists work in teams, the CBT therapist can develop the individually tailored case formulation with the client, and the case manager or an assistant psychologist can deliver parts of the therapy, such as coping strategy enhancement (van der Gaag, 2014).

The United Kingdom Improving Access to Psychological Therapies for people with Severe Mental Illness (IAPT-SMI) initiative showed that it is possible to enhance the delivery of CBTp at scale within existing services. The key facilitators were appropriate service structure, including established referral pathways and expert supervision arrangements, ring-fenced funding, and the recruitment of well-trained, or trainable, therapists into specialist therapy posts (Johns et al., 2019; Jolley et al., 2015). This framework is replicable in other services, and new investment can translate readily into efficient and effective therapy delivery when the facilitators of implementation are in place (Jolley, 2018).

Widening access to CBTp requires roles that are dedicated, at least in part, to therapy delivery.

CONCLUSION AND FUTURE DIRECTIONS

CBTp is a recommended treatment for schizophrenia and psychosis, and treatment trials show small-to-moderate effects on psychotic symptoms, mood, and functioning. Generic CBTp includes various change strategies that are used flexibly according to the person's presenting problems and therapy goals. The therapy is individualised, collaborative, and matched to the client. It is guided by the case formulation and emphasises a warm and respectful therapeutic relationship. Overall therapy gains within a heterogeneous client group, with different problems and goals, can be hard to capture. Current developments in CBTp involve evaluating discrete intervention components for specific psychotic symptoms and their maintenance factors. Studies of these therapies, which use measures of the intervention targets, have shown large treatment effects. Delivery of CBTp in routine practice remains a challenge, but access to therapy can be improved using specific service initiatives.

QUIZ QUESTIONS

(1) Which of the following is a SMART goal?
   (a) To feel less anxious when going out
   (b) To cope better with the voices
   (c) To go to the gym twice a week
   (d) To feel more confident

(2) Which of the following CBT interventions would you tend to start with in CBTp?
   (a) Verbal exploration of beliefs to search for any disconfirmatory evidence

   (b) Behavioural experiments
   (c) Working with cognitive biases
   (d) Enhancing coping strategies
(3) Which of the following is not supported by the current evidence base?
   (a) CBTp improves negative symptoms
   (b) CBTp works for people regardless of the quality of the therapeutic alliance
   (c) CBTp alleviates distressing voices and paranoid beliefs
   (d) CBTp helps people with longstanding psychosis
(4) Which of the following presents the greatest current challenge to implementing CBTp?
   (a) Too few adequately trained therapists
   (b) Clients do not choose a talking therapy when it is offered
   (c) Not enough clients engage with therapy
   (d) It is too difficult to form a trusting therapeutic relationship with this client group

ANSWERS TO QUIZ QUESTIONS:

1. (c)
2. (d)
3. (b)
4. (a)

RECOMMENDED READINGS

Brabban, A., Byrne, R., Longden, E., & Morrison, A. P. (2016). The importance of human relationships, ethics and recovery-orientated values in the delivery of CBT for people with psychosis. *Psychosis: Psychological, Social and Integrative Approaches*, 9(2), 157–166. https://doi.org/10.1080/17522439.2016.1259648.

Johns, L., Jolley, S., Keen, N., & Peters, E. (2014). CBT for people with psychosis. In *How to Become a More Effective CBT Therapist: Mastering Metacompetence in Clinical Practice* (pp. 191–207). Chichester: Wiley.

Morrison, A. P. (2017). Psychosis Psychological, Social and Integrative Approaches A manualised treatment protocol to guide delivery of evidence- based cognitive therapy for people with distressing psychosis: Learning from clinical trials Rationale for following a protocolised m. *Psychosis*, 9(3), 271–281. https://doi.org/10.1080/17522439.2017.1295098.

LINKS TO RESOURCES (TABLE 15.1)

Psychosis Research Unit website: http://www.psychosisresearch.com/cbt

Metacognitive Training for Psychosis: https://clinical-neuropsychology.de/metacognitive_training-psychosis/

Accounts of lived experience of psychosis http://healthtalk.org/peoples-experiences/mental-health/experiences-psychosis/topics

Table 15.1 Therapy Manuals

Authors (year of publication)	Book title
CBT for Psychosis/Schizophrenia	
Kingdon and Turkington (1994)	CBT of Schizophrenia
Fowler et al. (1995)	CBT for Psychosis: Theory and Practice
Nelson (1997)	CBT with Schizophrenia. A Practice Manual
Kingdon and Turkington (2002)	The Case-Study Guide to CBT of Psychosis
Morrison (2002)	A Casebook of Cognitive Therapy for Psychosis
Morrison, Renton, Dunn, Williams, and Bentall (2003)	Cognitive Therapy for Psychosis: A Formulation-Based Approach
Kingdon and Turkington (2008)	Cognitive Therapy of Schizophrenia. 2nd Ed.
Nelson (2005)	Cognitive-Behavioural Therapy with Delusions and Hallucinations. A Practice Manual.
Beck, Rector, Stolar, and Grant (2009)	Schizophrenia: Cognitive Theory, Research, and Therapy
Wright, Kingdon, Turkington, and Ramirez Basco (2009)	Cognitive Therapy for Severe Mental Illness
Hagen, Turkington, Berge, and Gråwe (2010)	CBT for psychosis: A symptom-based approach
Steel (2013)	CBT for Schizophrenia: Evidence-based Interventions and Future Directions
Lecomte, Leclerc, and Wykes (2016)	Group CBT for Psychosis: A Guidebook for Clinicians.
Cupitt (2018)	CBT for Psychosis
CBT for Particular Psychotic Symptoms or Phases of Psychosis	
Chadwick, Birchwood, and Trower (1996)	Cognitive Therapy for Delusions, Voices, and Paranoia
French and Morrison (2004)	Early detection and Cognitive Therapy for people at high risk of developing psychosis
Byrne et al. (2006)	A Casebook of CBT for Command Hallucinations: A Social Rank Theory Approach
Larkin and Morrison (2006)	Trauma and Psychosis: New Directions for Theory and Therapy
Gumley and Schwannauer (2006)	Staying Well after Psychosis: A Cognitive Interpersonal Approach to Recovery and Relapse Prevention
Freeman, Bentall, and Garety (2008)	Persecutory Delusions: Assessment, Theory, and Treatment
Meaden et al. (2013)	Cognitive Therapy for Command Hallucinations. An Advanced Practical Companion
van der Gaag et al. (2013)	CBT for Those at Risk of First Episode Psychosis
Williams (2013)	A CBT Approach to Mental Health Problems in Psychosis
Waters, Ree, and Chiu (2017)	Delivering CBT for Insomnia in Psychosis
Self-Help Guides	
Freeman, Freeman, and Garety (2016)	Overcoming Paranoid and Suspicious Thoughts
Morrison, Renton, French, and Bentall (2008)	Think You're Crazy, Think Again: A Resource Book for Cognitive Therapy for Psychosis
Turkington et al. (2009)	Back to Life, Back to Normality: Cognitive Therapy, Recovery and Psychosis
Hayward, Kingdon, and Strauss (2018)	Overcoming Distressing Voices
Hayward, Hazell, Kingdon, and Strauss (2018)	An Introduction to Self-Help for Distressing Voices

References

Achim, A. M., Maziade, M., Raymond, E., Olivier, D., Merette, C., & Roy, M.-A. (2011). How prevalent are anxiety disorders in schizophrenia? A meta-analysis and critical review on a significant association. *Schizophrenia Bulletin, 37*(4), 811–821. https://doi.org/10.1093/schbul/sbp148.

Beck, A. T., Rector, N. A., Stolar, N., & Grant, P. (2009). *Schizophrenia: Cognitive theory, research, and therapy*. New York: Guilford Press.

Beck, A. T., Rush, A. J., Shaw, B. F., & Emery, G. (1979). *Cognitive therapy of depression (the Guilford clinical psychology and psychopathology series)*. New York: Guilford.

Bentall, R. P., Fernyhough, C., Morrison, A. P., Lewis, S., & Corcoran, R. (2007). Prospects for a cognitive-developmental account of psychotic experiences. *The British Journal of Clinical Psychology*. https://doi.org/10.1348/014466506X123011.

Berry, C., & Hayward, M. (2011). What can qualitative research tell us about service user perspectives of CBT for psychosis? A synthesis of current evidence. *Behavioural and Cognitive Psychotherapy, 39*(04), 487–494. https://doi.org/10.1017/S1352465811000154.

Bighelli, I., Salanti, G., Huhn, M., Schneider-Thoma, J., Krause, M., Reitmeir, C., et al. (2018). Psychological interventions to reduce positive symptoms in schizophrenia: Systematic review and network meta-analysis. *World Psychiatry, 17*(3), 316–329. https://doi.org/10.1002/wps.20577.

Birchwood, M. (2003). Pathways to emotional dysfunction in first-episode psychosis. *British Journal of Psychiatry, 182*(May), 373–375. https://doi.org/10.1192/bjp.182.5.373.

Birchwood, M., & Chadwick, P. (1997). The omnipotence of voices: Testing the validity of a cognitive model. *Psychological Medicine*. https://doi.org/10.1017/S0033291797005552.

Birchwood, M., Dunn, G., Meaden, A., Tarrier, N., Lewis, S., Wykes, T., et al. (2018). The COMMAND trial of cognitive therapy to prevent harmful compliance with command hallucinations. *Psychological Medicine, 48*(12), 1966–1974. https://doi.org/10.1017/S0033291717003488.

Birchwood, M., Iqbal, Z., & Upthegrove, R. (2005). Psychological pathways to depression in schizophrenia: studies in acute psychosis, post psychotic depression and auditory hallucinations. *European Archives of Psychiatry and Clinical Neuroscience, 255*(3), 202–212. https://doi.org/10.1007/s00406-005-0588-4.

Birchwood, M., Michail, M., Meaden, A., Tarrier, N., Lewis, S., Wykes, T., et al. (2014). Cognitive behaviour therapy to prevent harmful compliance with command hallucinations (COMMAND): A randomised controlled trial. *The Lancet Psychiatry, 1*(1), 23–33. https://doi.org/10.1016/S2215-0366(14)70247-0.

Birchwood, M., Trower, P., Brunet, K., Gilbert, P., Iqbal, Z., & Jackson, C. (2007). Social anxiety and the shame of psychosis: a study in first episode psychosis. *Behaviour Research and Therapy, 45*(5), 1025–1037. https://doi.org/10.1016/J.BRAT.2006.07.011.

Bird, V., Premkumar, P., Kendall, T., Whittington, C., Mitchell, J., & Kuipers, E. (2010). Early intervention services, cognitive–behavioural therapy and family intervention in early psychosis: Systematic review. *British Journal of Psychiatry, 197*(05), 350–356. https://doi.org/10.1192/bjp.bp.109.074526.

Blackburn, I.-M., James, I. A., Milne, D. L., Baker, C., Standart, S., Garland, A., et al. (2001). The revised cognitive therapy scale (CTS-R): Psychometric properties. *Behavioural and Cognitive Psychotherapy, 29*(04), 431–446. https://doi.org/10.1017/S1352465801004040.

Brabban, A., Byrne, R., Longden, E., & Morrison, A. P. (2016). The importance of human relationships, ethics and recovery-orientated values in the delivery of CBT for people with psychosis. *Psychosis: Psychological, Social and Integrative Approaches, 9*(2), 157–166. https://doi.org/10.1080/17522439.2016.1259648.

Brett, C. M. C., Peters, E. R., Johns, L. C., Tabraham, P., Valmaggia, L. R., & McGuire, P. (2007). Appraisals of anomalous experiences interview (AANEX): A multidimensional measure of psychological responses to anomalies associated with psychosis. *The British Journal of Psychiatry. Supplement, 51*, s23–s30. https://doi.org/10.1192/bjp.191.51.s23.

Burns, A. M. N., Erickson, D. H., & Brenner, C. A. (2014). Cognitive-behavioral therapy for medication-resistant psychosis: A meta-analytic review. *Psychiatric Services, 65*(7), 874–880. https://doi.org/10.1176/appi.ps.201300213.

Burns, D. D., & Nolen-Hoeksema, S. (1992). Therapeutic empathy and recovery from depression in cognitive-behavioral therapy: A structural equation model. *Journal of Consulting and Clinical Psychology*. https://doi.org/10.1037/0022-006X.60.3.441.

Byrne, S., Birchwood, M., Trower, P., & Meaden, A. (2006). *A casebook of cognitive behaviour therapy for command hallucinations: A social rank theory approach*. Hove: Routledge.

Cantor-Graae, E., & Selten, J.-P. P. (2005). Schizophrenia and migration: A meta-analysis and review. *American Journal of Psychiatry, 162*(1), 12–24. https://doi.org/10.1176/appi.ajp.162.1.12.

Chadwick, P., Birchwood, M., & Trower, P. (1996). *Cognitive therapy for delusions, voices and paranoia*. Chichester: Wiley.

Chamberlin, J. (2004). Survey says: More Americans are seeking mental health treatment. *Monitor on Psychology, 35*, Retrieved from https://www.apa.org/monitor/julaug04/survey.aspx.

Colling, C., Evans, L., Broadbent, M., Chandran, D., Craig, T. J., Kolliakou, A., et al. (2017). Identification of the delivery of cognitive behavioural therapy for psychosis (CBTp) using a cross-sectional sample from electronic health records and open-text information in a large UK-based mental health case register. *BMJ Open, 7*(7), 1–10. https://doi.org/10.1136/bmjopen-2016-015297.

Cupitt, C. (Ed.). (2018). *CBT for psychosis: Process orientated therapies and the third wave*. London: Routledge.

Degnan, A., Baker, S., Edge, D., Nottidge, W., Noke, M., Press, C. J., et al. (2018). The nature and efficacy of culturally-adapted psychosocial interventions for schizophrenia: A systematic review and meta-analysis. *Psychological Medicine, 48*, 714–727. https://doi.org/10.1017/S0033291717002264.

Drury, V., Birchwood, M., & Cochrane, R. (2000). Cognitive therapy and recovery from acute psychosis: A controlled trial. 3. Five-year follow-up. *The British Journal of Psychiatry, 177*, 8–14.

Dunn, G., Fowler, D., Rollinson, R., Freeman, D., Kuipers, E., Smith, B., et al. (2012). Effective elements of cognitive behaviour therapy for psychosis: Results of a novel type of subgroup analysis based on principal stratification. *Psychological Medicine, 42*(05), 1057–1068. https://doi.org/10.1017/S0033291711001954.

Dunn, H., Morrison, A. P., & Bentall, R. P. (2006). The relationship between patient suitability, therapeutic alliance, homework compliance and outcome in cognitive therapy for psychosis. *Clinical Psychology & Psychotherapy*. https://doi.org/10.1002/cpp.481.

Farhall, J., Greenwood, K. M., & Jackson, H. J. (2007). Coping with hallucinated voices in schizophrenia: A review of self-initiated strategies and therapeutic interventions. *Clinical Psychology Review*. https://doi.org/10.1016/j.cpr.2006.12.002.

Fearon, P., Kirkbride, J. B., Morgan, C., Dazzan, P., Morgan, K., Lloyd, T., et al. (2006). Incidence of schizophrenia and other psychoses in ethnic minority groups: Results from the MRC AESOP study. *Psychological Medicine, 36*(11), 1541–1550. https://doi.org/10.1017/S0033291706008774.

Fowler, D., Garety, P. A., & Kuipers, E. (1995). *Cognitive behaviour therapy for psychosis: Theory and practice*. John Wiley Sons.

Fowler, D., Hodgekins, J., French, P., Marshall, M., Freemantle, N., McCrone, P., et al. (2018). Social recovery therapy in combination with early intervention services for enhancement of social recovery in patients with first-episode psychosis (SUPEREDEN3): A single-blind, randomised controlled trial. *The Lancet Psychiatry, 5*(1), 41–50. https://doi.org/10.1016/S2215-0366(17)30476-5.

Fowler, D., Hodgekins, J., Garety, P., Freeman, D., Kuipers, E., Dunn, G., et al. (2012). Negative cognition, depressed mood, and paranoia: a longitudinal pathway analysis using structural equation modeling. *Schizophrenia Bulletin, 38*(5), 1063–1073. https://doi.org/10.1093/schbul/sbr019.

Freeman, D. (2011). Improving cognitive treatments for delusions. *Schizophrenia Research, 132*(2–3), 135–139. https://doi.org/10.1016/J.SCHRES.2011.08.012.

Freeman, D. (2016). Persecutory delusions: a cognitive perspective on understanding and treatment. *The Lancet Psychiatry, 3*(7), 685–692. https://doi.org/10.1016/S2215-0366(16)00066-3.

Freeman, D., Bentall, R., & Garety, P. (2008). *Persecutory delusions: Assessment, theory, and treatment.* New York: Oxford University Press.

Freeman, D., Dunn, G., Garety, P., Weinman, J., Kuipers, E., Fowler, D., et al. (2013). Patients' beliefs about the causes, persistence and control of psychotic experiences predict take-up of effective cognitive behaviour therapy for psychosis. *Psychological Medicine, 43*(2), 269–277. https://doi.org/10.1017/S0033291712001225.

Freeman, D., Dunn, G., Startup, H., Pugh, K., Cordwell, J., Mander, H., et al. (2015). Effects of cognitive behaviour therapy for worry on persecutory delusions in patients with psychosis (WIT): A parallel, single-blind, randomised controlled trial with a mediation analysis. *The Lancet Psychiatry, 2*(4), 305–313. https://doi.org/10.1016/S2215-0366(15)00039-5.

Freeman, D., Freeman, J., & Garety, P. (2016). *Overcoming paranoid and suspicious thoughts: A self-help guide using cognitive behavioural techniques* (2nd ed.). London: Robinson.

Freeman, D., & Garety, P. A. (1999). Worry, worry processes & dimensions of delusions: An exploratory investigation of a role for anxiety processes in the maintenance of delusional distress. *Behavioural and Cognitive Psychotherapy, 27*, 47–52.

Freeman, D., & Garety, P. A. (2003). Connecting neurosis and psychosis: the direct influence of emotion on delusions and hallucinations. *Behaviour Research and Therapy, 41*(8), 923–947. https://doi.org/10.1016/S0005-7967(02)00104-3.

Freeman, D., Garety, P. A., Fowler, D., Kuipers, E., Bebbington, P. E., & Dunn, G. (2004). Why do people with delusions fail to choose more realistic explanations for their experiences? An empirical investigation. *Journal of Consulting and Clinical Psychology, 72*(4), 671–680. https://doi.org/10.1037/0022-006X.72.4.671.

Freeman, D., Garety, P. A., Kuipers, E., Fowler, D., & Bebbington, P. E. (2002). A cognitive model of persecutory delusions. *British Journal of Clinical Psychology, 41*(Pt 4), 331–347.

Freeman, D., Garety, P. A., Kuipers, E., Fowler, D., Bebbington, P. E., & Dunn, G. (2007). Acting on persecutory delusions: the importance of safety seeking. *Behaviour Research and Therapy, 45*(1), 89–99. https://doi.org/10.1016/J.BRAT.2006.01.014.

Freeman, D., Sheaves, B., Goodwin, G. M., Yu, L.-M., Nickless, A., Harrison, P. J., et al. (2017). The effects of improving sleep on mental health (OASIS): A randomised controlled trial with mediation analysis. *The Lancet Psychiatry, 4*(10), 749–758. https://doi.org/10.1016/S2215-0366(17)30328-0.

Freeman, D., Stahl, D., McManus, S., Meltzer, H., Brugha, T., Wiles, N., et al. (2012). Insomnia, worry, anxiety and depression as predictors of the occurrence and persistence of paranoid thinking. *Social Psychiatry and Psychiatric Epidemiology, 47*(8), 1195–1203. https://doi.org/10.1007/s00127-011-0433-1.

Freeman, D., & Waite, F. (2017). Persistent persecutory delusions: The spirit, style and content of targeted treatment. *World Psychiatry, 16*(2), 208–209. https://doi.org/10.1002/wps.20425.

Freeman, D., Waite, F., Startup, H., Myers, E., Lister, R., McInerney, J., et al. (2015). Efficacy of cognitive behavioural therapy for sleep improvement in patients with persistent delusions and hallucinations (BEST): A prospective, assessor-blind, randomised controlled pilot trial. *The Lancet Psychiatry, 2*(11), 975–983.

French, P., & Morrison, A. P. (2004). *Early detection and cognitive therapy for people at high risk of developing psychosis.* John Wiley & Sons Ltd.

Garety, P. A., Bebbington, P. E., Fowler, D., Freeman, D., & Kuipers, E. (2007). Implications for neurobiological research of cognitive models of psychosis: A theoretical paper. *Psychological Medicine, 37*(10), 1377–1391. https://doi.org/10.1017/S003329170700013X.

Garety, P. A., Fowler, D., Freeman, D., Bebbington, P. E., Dunn, G., & Kuipers, E. (2008). Cognitive-behavioural therapy and family intervention for relapse prevention and symptom reduction in psychosis: randomised controlled trial. *British Journal of Psychiatry, 192*(6), 412–423. https://doi.org/10.1192/bjp.bp.107.043570.

Garety, P. A., Kuipers, E., Fowler, D., Freeman, D., & Bebbington, P. E. (2001). A cognitive model of the positive symptoms of psychosis. *Psychological Medicine, 31*(2), 189–195. https://doi.org/10.1017/S0033291701003312.

Gaynor, K., Ward, T., Garety, P. A., & Peters, E. R. (2013). The role of safety-seeking behaviours in maintaining threat appraisals in psychosis. *Behaviour Research and Therapy, 51*(2), 75–81. https://doi.org/10.1016/j.brat.2012.10.008.

Glaser, N. M., Kazantzis, N., Deane, F. P., & Oades, L. G. (2000). Critical issues in using homework assignments within cognitive-behavioral therapy for schizophrenia. *Journal of Rational-Emotive & Cognitive-Behavior Therapy, 18*(4), 247–261. https://doi.org/10.1023/A:1007888615752.

Goldsmith, L. P., Lewis, S. W., Dunn, G., & Bentall, R. P. (2015). Psychological treatments for early psychosis can be beneficial or harmful, depending on the therapeutic alliance: An instrumental variable analysis. *Psychological Medicine, 45*(11), 2365–2373. https://doi.org/10.1017/S003329171500032X.

Grant, P. M., & Beck, A. T. (2009). Defeatist beliefs as a mediator of cognitive impairment, negative symptoms, and functioning in schizophrenia. *Schizophrenia Bulletin, 35*(4), 798–806. https://doi.org/10.1093/schbul/sbn008.

Grant, P. M., Huh, G. A., Perivoliotis, D., Stolar, N. M., & Beck, A. T. (2012). Randomized trial to evaluate the efficacy of cognitive therapy for low-functioning patients with schizophrenia. *Archives of General Psychiatry, 69*(2), 121–127. https://doi.org/10.1001/archgenpsychiatry.2011.129.

Gumley, A., O'Grady, M., McNay, L., Reilly, J., Power, K., & Norrie, J. (2003). Early intervention for relapse in schizophrenia: Results of a 12-month randomized controlled trial of cognitive behavioural therapy. *Psychological Medicine, 33*(3), 419–431. https://doi.org/10.1017/S0033291703007323.

Gumley, A., & Schwannauer, M. (2006). *Staying well after psychosis.* John Wiley Sonshttps://doi.org/10.1002/9780470713303.

Habib, N., Dawood, S., Kingdon, D., & Naeem, F. (2015). Preliminary evaluation of culturally adapted CBT for psychosis (CA-CBTp): Findings from developing culturally-sensitive CBT project (DCCP). *Behavioural and Cognitive Psychotherapy, 43*(2), 200–208. https://doi.org/10.1017/S1352465813000829.

Hacker, D., Birchwood, M., Tudway, J., Meaden, A., & Amphlett, C. (2008). Acting on voices: Omnipotence, sources of threat, and safety-seeking behaviours. *British Journal of Clinical Psychology, 47*(2), 201–213. https://doi.org/10.1348/014466507X249093.

Haddock, G., Eisner, E., Boone, C., Davies, G., Coogan, C., & Barrowclough, C. (2014). An investigation of the implementation of NICE-recommended CBT interventions for people with schizophrenia. *Journal of Mental Health, 23*(4), 162–165. https://doi.org/10.3109/09638237.2013.869571.

Hagen, R., Turkington, D., Berge, T., & Gråwe, R. W. (2010). *CBT for psychosis: A symptom-based approach.* London: Routledge.

Hayward, M., Hazell, C., Kingdon, D., & Strauss, C. (2018). *An introduction to self-help for distressing voices.* London: Robinson.

Hayward, M., Kingdon, D., & Strauss, C. (2018). *Overcoming distressing voices* (2nd ed.). London: Robinson.

Hazell, C. M., Hayward, M., Cavanagh, K., & Strauss, C. (2016). A systematic review and meta-analysis of low intensity CBT for psychosis. *Clinical Psychology Review, 45*, 183–192. https://doi.org/10.1016/J.CPR.2016.03.004.

Heriot-Maitland, C., Knight, M., & Peters, E. R. (2012). A qualitative comparison of psychotic-like phenomena in clinical and non-clinical populations. *The British Journal of Clinical Psychology, 51*(1), 37–53. https://doi.org/10.1111/j.2044-8260.2011.02011.x.

Holding, J. C., Gregg, L., & Haddock, G. (2016). Individuals' experiences and opinions of psychological therapies for psychosis: A narrative synthesis. *Clinical Psychology Review, 43*, 142–161. https://doi.org/10.1016/J.CPR.2015.10.004.

Ince, P., Haddock, G., & Tai, S. (2016). A systematic review of the implementation of recommended psychological interventions for schizophrenia: Rates, barriers, and improvement strategies. *Psychology and Psychotherapy: Theory, Research and Practice, 89*(3), 324–350. https://doi.org/10.1111/papt.12084.

Jauhar, S., Mckenna, P. J., Radua, J., Fung, E., Salvador, R., & Laws, K. R. (2014). Cognitive-behavioural therapy for the symptoms of schizophrenia: Systematic review and meta-analysis with examination of potential bias. *British Journal of Psychiatry, 204*(1), 20–29. https://doi.org/10.1192/bjp.bp.112.116285.

Johns, L., Jolley, S., Garety, P., Khondoker, M., Fornells-Ambrojo, M., Onwumere, J., et al. (2019). Improving Access to psychological therapies for people with severe mental illness (IAPT-SMI): Lessons from the South London and Maudsley psychosis demonstration site. *Behaviour Research and Therapy, 116*, 104–110. https://doi.org/10.1016/j.brat.2019.03.002.

Johns, L., Jolley, S., Keen, N., & Peters, E. (2014). CBT for people with psychosis. In *How to become a more effective CBT therapist: Mastering metacompetence in clinical practice* (pp. 191–207). Chichester: Wiley.

Johns, L. C., Cannon, M., Singleton, N., Murray, R. M., Farrell, M., Brugha, T., et al. (2004). Prevalence and correlates of self-reported psychotic symptoms in the British population. *British Journal of Psychiatry, 185*(oct.), 298–305. https://doi.org/10.1192/bjp.185.4.298.

Jolley, S. (2018). Implementing cognitive-behavioral therapy for people with psychosis: Local and national initiatives in the United Kingdom. *Psychiatric Services, 69*(9), 952–955. https://doi.org/10.1176/appi.ps.201800131.

Jolley, S., & Garety, P. A. (2011). Cognitive-behavioural interventions. In *Schizophrenia: Current science and clinical practice* (pp. 185–215). Chichester, UK: John Wiley & Sons, Ltd. https://doi.org/10.1002/9780470978672.ch7.

Jolley, S., Garety, P. A., Peters, E. R., Fornells-Ambrojo, M., Onwumere, J., Harris, V., et al. (2015). Opportunities and challenges in improving access to psychological therapies for people with severe mental illness (IAPT-SMI): Evaluating the first operational year of the South London and Maudsley (SLaM) demonstration site for psychosis. *Behaviour Research and Therapy, 64*, 24–30. https://doi.org/10.1016/j.brat.2014.11.006.

Jones, C., Hacker, D., Cormac, I., Meaden, A., & Irving, C. B. (2012). Cognitive behaviour therapy versus other psychosocial treatments for schizophrenia. *The Cochrane Database of Systematic Reviews, 4*(4). https://doi.org/10.1002/14651858.CD008712.pub2.

Jung, E., Wiesjahn, M., & Lincoln, T. M. (2014). Negative, not positive symptoms predict the early therapeutic alliance in cognitive behavioral therapy for psychosis. *Psychotherapy Research, 24*(2), 171–183. https://doi.org/10.1080/10503307.2013.851425.

Kamp, K. S., & Due, H. (2018). How many bereaved people hallucinate about their loved one? A systematic review and meta-analysis of bereavement hallucinations. *Journal of Affective Disorders*. https://doi.org/10.1016/J.JAD.2018.09.039.

Kennedy, L., & Xyrichis, A. (2017). Cognitive behavioral therapy compared with non-specialized therapy for alleviating the effect of auditory hallucinations in people with reoccurring schizophrenia: A systematic review and meta-analysis. *Community Mental Health Journal, 53*(2), 127–133. https://doi.org/10.1007/s10597-016-0030-6.

Kilbride, M., Byrne, R., Price, J., Wood, L., Barratt, S., Welford, M., et al. (2013). Exploring service users' perceptions of cognitive behavioural therapy for psychosis: A user led study. *Behavioural and Cognitive Psychotherapy, 41*(01), 89–102. https://doi.org/10.1017/S1352465812000495.

Kinderman, P., & Lobban, F. (2000). Evolving formulations: Sharing complex information with clients. *Behavioural and Cognitive Psychotherapy*. https://doi.org/10.1017/S1352465800003118.

Kingdon, D. G., & Turkington, D. (1994). *Cognitive behavioural therapy of schizophrenia*. New York: Guilford Press.

Kingdon, D. G., & Turkington, D. (2002). *The case study guide to cognitive behaviour therapy of psychosis*. Chichester: John Wiley and Sons.

Kingdon, D. G., & Turkington, D. (2008). *Cognitive therapy of schizophrenia* (2nd ed.). New York: Guilford Press.

Klingberg, S., Wölwer, W., Engel, C., Wittorf, A., Herrlich, J., Meisner, C., et al. (2011). Negative symptoms of schizophrenia as primary target of cognitive behavioral therapy: Results of the randomized clinical TONES study. *Schizophrenia Bulletin, 37*(Suppl 2), S98–110. https://doi.org/10.1093/schbul/sbr073.

Kråkvik, B., Gråwe, R. W., Hagen, R., & Stiles, T. C. (2013). Cognitive behaviour therapy for psychotic symptoms: A randomized controlled effectiveness trial. *Behavioural and Cognitive Psychotherapy, 41*, 511–524. https://doi.org/10.1017/S1352465813000258.

Kreyenbuhl, J., Buchanan, R. W., Dickerson, F. B., & Dixon, L. B. (2010). The schizophrenia patient outcomes research team (PORT): Updated treatment recommendations 2009. *Schizophrenia Bulletin, 36*, 94–103. https://doi.org/10.1093/schbul/sbp130.

Kumar, D., Zia Ul Haq, M., Dubey, I., Dotivala, K. N., Veqar Siddiqui, S., Prakash, R., et al. (2010). Effect of meta-cognitive training in the reduction of positive symptoms in schizophrenia. *European Journal of Psychotherapy & Counselling, 12*(2), 149–158. https://doi.org/10.1080/13642537.2010.488875.

Larkin, W., & Morrison, A. P. (2006). *Trauma and psychosis: New directions for theory and therapy*. Hove: Routledge.

Larøi, F., Luhrmann, T. M., Bell, V., Christian, W. A., Deshpande, S., Fernyhough, C., et al. (2014). Culture and hallucinations: Overview and future directions. *Schizophrenia Bulletin, 40*(Suppl. 4), S213–S220. https://doi.org/10.1093/schbul/sbu012.

Laws, K. R., Darlington, N., Kondel, T. K., Mckenna, P. J., & Jauhar, S. (2018). Cognitive behavioural therapy for schizophrenia-outcomes for functioning, distress and quality of life: A meta-analysis. *BMC Psychology, 6*(32), 1–10. https://doi.org/10.1186/s40359-018-0243-2.

Lecomte, T., Leclerc, C., & Wykes, T. (2016). *Group CBT for psychosis: A guidebook for clinicians*. New York: Oxford University Press.

Lincoln, T. M., & Peters, E. R. (2018). A systematic review and discussion of symptom specific cognitive behavioural approaches to delusions and hallucinations. *Schizophrenia Research, 203*, 66–79. https://doi.org/10.1016/j.schres.2017.12.014.

Lincoln, T. M., Ziegler, M., Mehl, S., Kesting, M.-L., Lüllmann, E., Westermann, S., et al. (2012). Moving from efficacy to effectiveness in cognitive behavioral therapy for psychosis: A randomized clinical practice trial. *Journal of Consulting and Clinical Psychology, 80*(4), 674–686. https://doi.org/10.1037/a0028665.

Longden, E., Corstens, D., Escher, S., & Romme, M. (2012). Voice hearing in a biographical context: A model for formulating the relationship between voices and life history. *Psychosis: Psychological, Social and Integrative Approaches, 4*(3), 224–234. https://doi.org/10.1080/17522439.2011.596566.

Lynch, D., Laws, K. R., & McKenna, P. J. (2010). Cognitive behavioural therapy for major psychiatric disorder: Does it really work? A meta-analytical review of well-controlled trials. *Psychological Medicine, 40*(1), 9. https://doi.org/10.1017/S003329170900590X.

Mairs, H., Lovell, K., Campbell, M., & Keeley, P. (2011). Development and pilot investigation of behavioral activation for negative symptoms. *Behavior Modification, 35*(5), 486–506. https://doi.org/10.1177/0145445511411706.

Marshall, M., & Rathbone, J. (2011). Early intervention for psychosis. *Cochrane Database of Systematic Reviews, 6*. https://doi.org/10.1002/14651858.CD004718.pub3.

Mason, O. J., & Brady, F. (2009). The psychotomimetic effects of short-term sensory deprivation. *The Journal of Nervous and Mental Disease, 197*(10), 783–785. https://doi.org/10.1097/NMD.0b013e3181b9760b.

Mazzucchelli, T., Kane, R., & Rees, C. (2009). Behavioral activation treatments for depression in adults: A meta-analysis and review. *Clinical Psychology: Science and Practice, 16*(4), 383–411. https://doi.org/10.1111/j.1468-2850.2009.01178.x.

Mcgrath, J. J., Saha, S., Al-Hamzawi, A., Alonso, J., Bromet, E. J., Bruffaerts, R., et al. (2015). Psychotic experiences in the general population: A cross-national analysis based on 31,261 respondents from 18 countries. *JAMA Psychiatry, 72*(7), 697–705. https://doi.org/10.1016/S2214-109X(16)30265-0.Cost-effectiveness.

Meaden, A., Keen, N., Aston, R., Barton, K., & Bucci, S. (2013). *Cognitive therapy for command hallucinations: An advanced practical companion.* London: Routledge.

Mehl, S., Werner, D., & Lincoln, T. M. (2015). Does cognitive behavior therapy for psychosis (CBTp) show a sustainable effect on delusions? A meta-analysis. *Frontiers in Psychology, 6*, 1450. https://doi.org/10.3389/fpsyg.2015.01450.

Messari, S., & Hallam, R. (2003). CBT for psychosis: A qualitative analysis of clients' experiences. *British Journal of Clinical Psychology, 42*(2), 171–188. https://doi.org/10.1348/014466503321903580.

Miles, H., Peters, E., & Kuipers, E. (2007). Service-user satisfaction with CBT for psychosis. *Behavioural and Cognitive Psychotherapy, 35*(1), 109–116. https://doi.org/10.1017/S1352465806003158.

Mineka, S., & Thomas, C. (1999). *Mechanisms of change in exposure therapy for anxiety disorders.* John Wiley & Sons.

Morberg Pain, C., Chadwick, P., Abba, N., Pain, C. M., Chadwick, P., & Abba, N. (2008). Clients' experience of case formulation in cognitive behaviour therapy for psychosis. *The British Journal of Clinical Psychology, 47*(2), 127–138. https://doi.org/10.1348/014466507X235962.

Moritz, S., Kerstan, A., Veckenstedt, R., Randjbar, S., Vitzthum, F., Schmidt, C., et al. (2011). Further evidence for the efficacy of a metacognitive group training in schizophrenia. *Behaviour Research and Therapy, 49*(3), 151–157. https://doi.org/10.1016/j.brat.2010.11.010.

Morrison, A. P. (2001). The interpretation of intrusions in psychosis: An integrative cognitive approach to hallucinations and delusions. *Behavioural and Cognitive Psychotherapy, 29*(3), 257–276. https://doi.org/10.1017/S1352465801003010.

Morrison, A. P. (Ed.). (2002). *A casebook of cognitive therapy for psychosis.* Hove: Brunner-Routledge.

Morrison, A. P. (2017). A manualised treatment protocol to guide delivery of evidence-based cognitive therapy for people with distressing psychosis: Learning from clinical trials. *Psychosis: Psychosis Psychological, Social and Integrative Approaches, 9*(3), 271–281. https://doi.org/10.1080/17522439.2017.1295098.

Morrison, A. P., & Barratt, S. (2010). What are the components of CBT for psychosis? A Delphi study. *Schizophrenia Bulletin, 36*(1), 136–142. https://doi.org/10.1093/schbul/sbp118.

Morrison, A. P., Law, H., Carter, L., Sellers, R., Emsley, R., Pyle, M., et al. (2018). Antipsychotic drugs versus cognitive behavioural therapy versus a combination of both in people with psychosis: A randomised controlled pilot and feasibility study. *The Lancet Psychiatry, 5*(5), 411–423. https://doi.org/10.1016/S2215-0366(18)30096-8.

Morrison, A. P., Pyle, M., Gumley, A., Schwannauer, M., Turkington, D., MacLennan, G., et al. (2018). Cognitive behavioural therapy in clozapine-resistant schizophrenia (FOCUS): An assessor-blinded, randomised controlled trial. *The Lancet Psychiatry, 5*(8), 633–643. https://doi.org/10.1016/S2215-0366(18)30184-6.

Morrison, A., Renton, J., Dunn, H., Williams, S., & Bentall, R. (2003). *Cognitive therapy for psychosis: A formulation-based approach.* London: Routledge.

Morrison, A. P., Renton, J. C., French, P., & Bentall, R. P. (2008). *Think you're crazy, think again: A resource book for cognitive therapy for psychosis*. London: Routledge.

Morrison, A. P., Renton, J. C., Williams, S., Dunn, H., Knight, A., Kreutz, M., et al. (2004). Delivering cognitive therapy to people with psychosis in a community mental health setting: An effectiveness study. *Acta Psychiatrica Scandinavica*, *110*(1), 36–44. https://doi.org/10.1111/j.1600-0447.2004.00299.x.

Morrison, A. P., Turkington, D., Wardle, M., Spencer, H., Barratt, S., Dudley, R., Brabban, A., & Hutton, P. (2012). A preliminary exploration of predictors of outcome and cognitive mechanisms of change in cognitive behaviour therapy for psychosis in people not taking antipsychotic medication. *Behaviour Research and Therapy*, *50*(2), 163–167. https://doi.org/10.1016/j.brat.2011.12.001.

Muse, K., McManus, F., Rakovshik, S., & Thwaites, R. (2017). Development and psychometric evaluation of the assessment of core CBT skills (ACCS): An observation-based tool for assessing cognitive behavioural therapy competence. *Psychological Assessment*, *29*(5), 542–555.

Naeem, F., Khoury, B., Munshi, T., Ayub, M., Lecomte, T., Kingdon, D., et al. (2016). Brief cognitive behavioral therapy for psychosis (CBTp) for schizophrenia: Literature review and meta-analysis. *International Journal of Cognitive Therapy*, *9*(1), 73–86. https://doi.org/10.1521/ijct_2016_09_04.

Naeem, F., Saeed, S., Irfan, M., Kiran, T., Mehmood, N., Gul, M., et al. (2015). Brief culturally adapted CBT for psychosis (CaCBTp): A randomized controlled trial from a low income country. *Schizophrenia Research*, *164*(1–3), 143–148. https://doi.org/10.1016/j.schres.2015.02.015.

National Institute for Health and Care Excellence. (2009). *Schizophrenia: Core interventions in the treatment and management of schizophrenia in primary and secondary care (update)*. London: Gaskell.

National Institute for Health and Care Excellence. (2014). *Psychosis and schizophrenia in adults: Treatment and management (CG178)*. London: National Institute for Health and Care Excellence.

Nelson, H. (1997). *Cognitive behavioural therapy with schizophrenia: A practice manual*. Cheltenham: Nelson Thornes Ltd.

Nelson, H. E. (2005). *Cognitive-behavioural therapy with delusions and hallucinations. A practice manual* (2nd ed.). Cheltenham: Nelson Thornes Ltd.

Nothard, S., Morrison, A. P., & Wells, A. (2008). Identifying specific interpretations and exploring the nature of safety behaviours for people who hear voices: An exploratory study. *Behavioural and Cognitive Psychotherapy*, *36*(3), 353–357. https://doi.org/10.1017/S1352465808004372.

O'Keeffe, J., Conway, R., & McGuire, B. (2017). A systematic review examining factors predicting favourable outcome in cognitive behavioural interventions for psychosis. *Schizophrenia Research*, *183*, 22–30. https://doi.org/10.1016/j.schres.2016.11.021.

Padesky, C. A. (1994). Schema change processes in cognitive therapy. *Clinical Psychology & Psychotherapy*, *1*(5), 267–278. Retrieved from www.padesky.com.

Parker, S., Wells, A., & Morrison, A. P. (2014). Metacognitive change as a predictor of outcome in cognitive therapy for psychosis. *The Israel Journal of Psychiatry and Related Sciences*, *51*, 8–16.

Paulik, G., & Badcock, J. C. (2010). The roles of negative affect in auditory hallucinations. In M. S. Payne (Ed.), *Hallucinations: Types, stages and treatments*. New York: Nova Science Publishers.

Perivoliotis, D., Grant, P. M., Peters, E. R., Ison, R., Kuipers, E., & Beck, A. T. (2010). Cognitive insight predicts favorable outcome in cognitive behavioral therapy for psychosis. *Psychosis-Psychological Social and Integrative Approaches*, *2*(1), 23–33. https://doi.org/10.1080/17522430903147520.

Peters, E., Landau, S., McCrone, P., Cooke, M., Fisher, P., Steel, C., et al. (2010). A randomised controlled trial of cognitive behaviour therapy for psychosis in a routine clinical service. *Acta Psychiatrica Scandinavica*, *122*(4), 302–318. https://doi.org/10.1111/j.1600-0447.2010.01572.x.

Peters, E. R., Crombie, T., Agbedjro, D., Johns, L. C., Stahl, D., Greenwood, K., et al. (2015). The long-term effectiveness of cognitive behavior therapy for psychosis within a routine psychological therapies service. *Frontiers in Psychology*, *6*, 1658. https://doi.org/10.3389/fpsyg.2015.01658.

Peters, E. R., Ward, T., Jackson, M., Morgan, C., Charalambides, M., McGuire, P., et al. (2016). Clinical, socio-demographic and psychological characteristics in individuals with persistent psychotic experiences with and without a "need for care". *World Psychiatry, 15*(1), 41–52. https://doi.org/10.1002/wps.20301.

Pfammatter, M., Junghan, U. M., & Brenner, H. D. (2006). Efficacy of psychological therapy in schizophrenia: Conclusions from meta-analyses. *Schizophrenia Bulletin, 32*(Suppl 1), S64–S80. https://doi.org/10.1093/schbul/sbl030.

Powers, A. R., Corlett, P. R., & Ross, D. A. (2018). Guided by voices: Hallucinations and the psychosis spectrum. *Biological Psychiatry, 84*(6), e43–e45. https://doi.org/10.1016/j.biopsych.2018.07.015.

Premkumar, P., Peters, E. R., Fannon, D., Anilkumar, A. P., Kuipers, E., & Kumari, V. (2011). Coping styles predict responsiveness to cognitive behaviour therapy in psychosis. *Psychiatry Research, 187*(3), 354–362. https://doi.org/10.1016/j.psychres.2010.12.029.

Prytys, M., Garety, P. A., Jolley, S., Onwumere, J., & Craig, T. (2011). Implementing the NICE guideline for schizophrenia recommendations for psychological therapies: A qualitative analysis of the attitudes of CMHT staff. *Clinical Psychology & Psychotherapy, 18*(1), 48–59. https://doi.org/10.1002/cpp.691.

Rathod, S., Kingdon, D., Smith, P., & Turkington, D. (2005). Insight into schizophrenia: The effects of cognitive behavioural therapy on the components of insight and association with sociodemographics—data on a previously published randomised controlled trial. *Schizophrenia Research, 74*(2–3), 211–219. https://doi.org/10.1016/j.schres.2004.07.003.

Rathod, S., Phiri, P., Harris, S., Underwood, C., Thagadur, M., Padmanabi, U., et al. (2013). Cognitive behaviour therapy for psychosis can be adapted for minority ethnic groups: A randomised controlled trial. *Schizophrenia Research, 143*(2–3), 319–326. https://doi.org/10.1016/j.schres.2012.11.007.

Rector, N. A., Beck, A. T., & Stolar, N. (2005). The negative symptoms of schizophrenia: A cognitive perspective. *Canadian Journal of Psychiatry, 50*(5), 247–257. https://doi.org/10.1016/j.ahj.2005.01.046.

Rector, N. A., & Health, M. (2007). Homework use in cognitive therapy for psychosis: A case formulation approach. *Cognitive and Behavioral Practice, 14*, 303–316.

Reeve, S., Emsley, R., Sheaves, B., & Freeman, D. (2018). Disrupting sleep: The effects of sleep loss on psychotic experiences tested in an experimental study with mediation analysis. *Schizophrenia Bulletin*. https://doi.org/10.1093/schbul/sbx103.

Rollinson, R., Smith, B., Steel, C., Jolley, S., Onwumere, J., Garety, P. A., et al. (2008). Measuring adherence in CBT for psychosis: A psychometric analysis of an adherence scale. *Behavioural and Cognitive Psychotherapy, 36*(2), 163–178. https://doi.org/10.1017/S1352465807003980.

Ronald, A., Sieradzka, D., Cardno, A. G., Haworth, C. M. A., McGuire, P., & Freeman, D. (2014). Characterization of psychotic experiences in adolescence using the specific psychotic experiences questionnaire: Findings from a study of 5000 16-year-old twins. *Schizophrenia Bulletin, 40*(4), 868–877. https://doi.org/10.1093/schbul/sbt106.

Royal Australian and New Zealand College of Psychiatrists. (2005). Royal Australian and New Zealand College of Psychiatrists clinical practice guidelines for the treatment of schizophrenia and related disorders. *Australian and New Zealand Journal of Psychiatry, 39*(1–2), 1–30. https://doi.org/10.1111/j.1440-1614.2005.01516.x.

Ruggeri, M., Bonetto, C., Lasalvia, A., Fioritti, A., de Girolamo, G., Santonastaso, P., et al. (2015). Feasibility and effectiveness of a multi-element psychosocial intervention for first-episode psychosis: Results from the cluster-randomized controlled GET UP PIANO trial in a catchment area of 10 million inhabitants. *Schizophrenia Bulletin, 41*(5), 1192–1203. https://doi.org/10.1093/schbul/sbv058.

Sarin, F., Wallin, L., & Widerlöv, B. (2011). Cognitive behavior therapy for schizophrenia: a meta-analytical review of randomized controlled trials. *Nordic Journal of Psychiatry, 65*(3), 162–174. https://doi.org/10.3109/08039488.2011.577188.

Shafran, R., Clark, D. M., Fairburn, C. G., Arntz, A., Barlow, D. H., Ehlers, A., et al. (2009). Mind the gap: Improving the dissemination of CBT. *Behaviour Research and Therapy, 47*(11), 902–909. https://doi.org/10.1016/j.brat.2009.07.003.

Sheaves, B., Bebbington, P. E., Goodwin, G. M., Harrison, P. J., Espie, C. A., Foster, R. G., et al. (2016). Insomnia and hallucinations in the general population: findings from the 2000 and 2007 British psychiatric morbidity surveys. *Psychiatry Research, 241*, 141–146. https://doi.org/10.1016/j.psychres.2016.03.055.

So, S. H.-W., Chan, A. P., Chong, C. S.-Y., Wong, M. H.-M., Lo, W. T.-L., Chung, D. W.-S., et al. (2015). Metacognitive training for delusions (MCTd): Effectiveness on data-gathering and belief flexibility in a Chinese sample. *Frontiers in Psychology, 6*, 730. https://doi.org/10.3389/fpsyg.2015.00730.

Staring, A. B. P., ter Huurne, M.-A. B., & van der Gaag, M. (2013). Cognitive behavioral therapy for negative symptoms (CBT-n) in psychotic disorders: A pilot study. *Journal of Behavior Therapy and Experimental Psychiatry, 44*(3), 300–306. https://doi.org/10.1016/J.JBTEP.2013.01.004.

Startup, H., Freeman, D., & Garety, P. A. (2007). Persecutory delusions and catastrophic worry in psychosis: Developing the understanding of delusion distress and persistence. *Behaviour Research and Therapy, 45*, 523–537. https://doi.org/10.1016/j.brat.2006.04.006.

Startup, M., Jackson, M., & Pearce, E. (2002). Assessing therapist adherence to cognitive-behaviour therapy for psychosis. *Behavioural and Cognitive Psychotherapy, 30*(03), 329–339. https://doi.org/10.1017/S1352465802003077.

Steel, C. (Ed.). (2013). *CBT for schizophrenia: Evidence-based interventions and future directions*. Ltd: John Wiley & Sons.

Steel, C., Tarrier, N., Stahl, D., & Wykes, T. (2012). Cognitive behaviour therapy for psychosis: The impact of therapist training and supervision. *Psychotherapy and Psychosomatics, 81*(3), 194–195. https://doi.org/10.1159/000334250.

Tarrier, N. (2002). The use of coping strategies and self-regulation in the treatment of psychosis. In A. P. Morrison (Ed.), *A casebook of cognitive therapy for psychosis* (p. 308). Hove: Brunner-Routledge.

Tarrier, N., Harwood, S., Yusopoff, L., Beckett, R., & Baker, A. (1990). Coping strategy enhancement (CSE): A method of treating residual schizophrenic symptoms. *Behavioural Psychotherapy, 18*(04), 283. https://doi.org/10.1017/S0141347300010387.

Tarrier, N., & Wykes, T. (2004). Is there evidence that cognitive behaviour therapy is an effective treatment for schizophrenia? A cautious or cautionary tale? *Behaviour Research and Therapy, 42*(12), 1377–1401. https://doi.org/10.1016/j.brat.2004.06.020.

The Schizophrenia Commission (2012). *The abandoned illness: A report from the schizophrenia commission*. London: Rethink Mental Illness.

Thomas, N. (2015). What's really wrong with cognitive behavioral therapy for psychosis? *Frontiers in Psychology, 6*, 323. https://doi.org/10.3389/fpsyg.2015.00323.

Thomas, N., Hayward, M., Peters, E., Van Der Gaag, M., Bentall, R. P., Jenner, J., et al. (2014). Psychological therapies for auditory hallucinations (voices): Current status and key directions for future research. *Schizophrenia Bulletin, 40*(Suppl. 4). https://doi.org/10.1093/schbul/sbu037.

Trower, P., Birchwood, M., Meaden, A., Byrne, S., Nelson, A., & Ross, K. (2004). Cognitive therapy for command hallucinations: randomised controlled trial. *British Journal of Psychiatry, 184*(Apr.), 312–320. https://doi.org/10.1192/bjp.184.4.312.

Turkington, D., Kingdon, D., Rathod, S., Wilcock, S. K. J., Brabban, A., Cromarty, P., et al. (2009). *Back to life, back to normality: Cognitive therapy, recovery and psychosis*. Cambridge University Press.

Turner, D. T., Van der Gaag, M., Karyotaki, E., & Cuijpers, P. (2014). Psychological interventions for psychosis: A meta-analysis of comparative outcome studies. *The American Journal of Psychiatry, 171*(5), 523–538. https://doi.org/10.1176/appi.ajp.2013.13081159.

van der Gaag, M. (2014). The efficacy of CBT for severe mental illness and the challenge of dissemination in routine care. *World Psychiatry, 13*(3), 257–258. https://doi.org/10.1002/wps.20162.

van der Gaag, M., Schütz, C., ten Napel, A., Landa, Y., Delespaul, P., Bak, M., et al. (2013). Development of the Davos assessment of cognitive biases scale (DACOBS). *Schizophrenia Research, 144*(1–3), 63–71. https://doi.org/10.1016/j.schres.2012.12.010.

Van der Gaag, M., Valmaggia, L. R., & Smit, F. (2014). The effects of individually tailored formulation-based cognitive behavioural therapy in auditory hallucinations and delusions: A meta-analysis. *Schizophrenia Research, 156*(1), 30–37. https://doi.org/10.1016/j.schres.2014.03.016.

van Oosterhout, B., Smit, F., Krabbendam, L., Castelein, S., Staring, A. B. P., & van der Gaag, M. (2016). Metacognitive training for schizophrenia spectrum patients: A meta-analysis on outcome studies. *Psychological Medicine, 46*(01), 47–57. https://doi.org/10.1017/S0033291715001105.

van Os, J., Linscott, R. J., Myin-Germeys, I., Delespaul, P., & Krabbendam, L. (2009). A systematic review and meta-analysis of the psychosis continuum: Evidence for a psychosis proneness–persistence–impairment model of psychotic disorder. *Psychological Medicine, 39*(02), 179. https://doi.org/10.1017/S0033291708003814.

Waller, H., Emsley, R., Freeman, D., Bebbington, P. E., Dunn, G., Fowler, D., et al. (2015). Thinking well: A randomised controlled feasibility study of a new CBT therapy targeting reasoning biases in people with distressing persecutory delusional beliefs. *Journal of Behavior Therapy and Experimental Psychiatry, 48*, 82–89. https://doi.org/10.1016/j.jbtep.2015.02.007.

Waller, H., Freeman, D., Jolley, S., Dunn, G., & Garety, P. A. (2011). Targeting reasoning biases in delusions: A pilot study of the Maudsley review training programme for individuals with persistent, high conviction delusions. *Journal of Behavior Therapy and Experimental Psychiatry, 42*(3), 414–421. https://doi.org/10.1016/j.jbtep.2011.03.001.

Waller, H., Garety, P. A., Jolley, S., Fornells-Ambrojo, M., Kuipers, E., Onwumere, J., et al. (2013). Low intensity cognitive behavioural therapy for psychosis: A pilot study. *Journal of Behavior Therapy and Experimental Psychiatry, 44*(1), 98–104. https://doi.org/10.1016/j.jbtep.2012.07.013.

Waller, H., Landau, S., Fornells-Ambrojo, M., Jolley, S., McCrone, P., Halkoree, R., et al. (2018). Improving implementation of evidence based practice for people with psychosis through training the wider workforce: Results of the GOALS feasibility randomised controlled trial. *Journal of Behavior Therapy and Experimental Psychiatry, 59*, 121–128. https://doi.org/10.1016/j.jbtep.2017.12.004.

Waters, F., Ree, M. J., & Chiu, V. (2017). *Delivering CBT for insomnia in psychosis.* UK: Routledge.

White, R., Laithwaite, H., & Gilbert, P. (2012). The role of social defeat in the emergence and persistence of negative symptoms in psychosis. In A. Gumley, A. Gillham, K. Taylor, & M. Schwannauer (Eds.), *Psychosis and emotion: The role of emotions in understanding psychosis, therapy and recovery.* Routledge.

Williams, E. (2013). *A CBT approach to mental health problems in psychosis.* London: Routledge.

Wood, L., Burke, E., & Morrison, A. P. (2015). Individual cognitive behavioural therapy for psychosis (CBTp): A systematic review of qualitative literature. *Behavioural and Cognitive Psychotherapy, 43*(03), 285–297. https://doi.org/10.1017/S1352465813000970.

World Health Organization. (2014). *Schizophrenia.* World Health Organization. Retrieved from http://www.who.int/mental_health/management/schizophrenia/en/.

Wright, J. H., Kingdon, D., Turkington, D., & Ramirez Basco, M. (2009). *Cognitive therapy for severe mental illness.* American Psychiatric Publishing, Inc.

Wykes, T., Steel, C., Everitt, B., & Tarrier, N. (2008). Cognitive behavior therapy for schizophrenia: Effect sizes, clinical models, and methodological rigor. *Schizophrenia Bulletin, 34*(3), 523–537. https://doi.org/10.1093/schbul/sbm114.

Young, J., & Beck, A. T. (1980). *Cognitive therapy scale: Rating manual.* 36th: Unpublished manuscript.

Zavos, H. M. S., Freeman, D., Haworth, C. M. A., McGuire, P., Plomin, R., Cardno, A. G., et al. (2014). Consistent etiology of severe, frequent psychotic experiences and milder, less frequent manifestations: A twin study of specific psychotic experiences in adolescence. *JAMA Psychiatry*, *71*(9), 1049–1057. https://doi.org/10.1001/jamapsychiatry.2014.994.

Zimmermann, G., Favrod, J., Trieu, V. H., & Pomini, V. (2005). The effect of cognitive behavioral treatment on the positive symptoms of schizophrenia spectrum disorders: A meta-analysis. *Schizophrenia Research*, *77*(1), 1–9. https://doi.org/10.1016/j.schres.2005.02.018.

Definition of Key Terms

Behavioural experiment is a planned experience or observation conducted during or between therapy sessions to test predictions and gain new information relevant to problematic cognitions or behaviours. The aim is to update cognitions through new learning.

Cognitive Behaviour Therapy for Psychosis (CBTp) is an adaptation of CBT for emotional disorders, tailored to the needs of people with psychosis. CBTp targets behaviours and cognitive appraisals of psychosis-related experiences that may be contributing to symptom maintenance and related distress and functional impairment.

Cognitive biases are errors or skewed ways of thinking usually based upon mental shortcuts. These may affect how we process information (reasoning biases), what we take notice of (attentional biases), or what we recall (memory biases). Biased thinking processes can lead to and maintain a distressing belief or appraisal.

Graded exposure is a behavioural technique involving systematically and gradually increasing exposure, progressing towards being present in the most feared situation without the use of safety behaviours.

Homework is important to maximise learning and application in daily life. Homework is an agreed and planned task that is completed between therapy sessions to enhance learning during therapy. It may include recording information, practising a technique learnt in the session, or carrying out a behavioural experiment.

Normalising is a key part of CBTp and involves using information about the prevalence of anomalous experiences in the general population and about psychological mechanisms to assist people in making sense of and reducing fear or shame about their experiences.

CHAPTER 16

Third-Wave CBT Interventions for Psychosis

Lyn Ellett, Jessica Kingston
Department of Psychology, Royal Holloway University of London, Egham, United Kingdom

Key Learning Objectives

- To introduce Third-Wave CBT interventions for psychosis, including Person-Based Cognitive Therapy, Metacognitive Therapy, Acceptance and Commitment Therapy, and Compassion Focused Therapy.
- Discuss the ways in which these interventions have been adapted for people with psychosis.
- Provide an overview of the evidence base for each therapy.
- Consider the limitations in the evidence base for each therapeutic approach.

INTRODUCTION

Historically, psychosis was viewed and treated from a predominantly psychiatric perspective whereby treatments focused on symptom reduction through medical intervention. However, increasing recognition for the role of psychological, social, and environmental factors gave rise to psychological interventions for psychosis. The First Wave of Interventions applied behavioural principles to modify behavioural problems and de-emphasised cognition. In the 1980s, with the advent of Cognitive Behaviour Therapy (CBT), the Second Wave of Interventions aimed to reduce distress by recognising and modifying unhelpful beliefs about distressing experiences (Mander & Kingdon, 2015). Cognitive Behaviour Therapy for psychosis (CBTp) is now recommended as a front-line treatment for psychosis, internationally. However, despite the many benefits of CBTp, it is by no means a panacea. CBTp has been criticised for straying from the theoretical routes of CBT, de-emphasising emotion and overemphasising symptom change, and failing to focus sufficiently on mechanisms of change (e.g. Birchwood & Trower, 2006). Furthermore, metaanalyses (e.g. Jauhar et al., 2014; Laws, Darlington, Kondel, McKenna, & Jauhar, 2018; Wykes, Steel, Everitt, & Tarrier, 2008) have indicated that CBTp achieves small treatment effects for positive

A Clinical Introduction to Psychosis. https://doi.org/10.1016/B978-0-12-815012-2.00016-X

and total symptoms with a recent metaanalysis suggesting that effects were not maintained over time and that effects were nonsignificant when adjusting for possible publication bias (Laws et al., 2018). Together, these criticisms and limitations have given rise to Third-Wave CBT approaches, which use mindfulness and acceptance to alter the way in which individuals relate to their psychotic experiences. This chapter will discuss the following third wave CBT therapies and how they have been developed/adapted for psychosis: Person-Based Cognitive Therapy (PBCT), Metacognitive Therapy (MCT), Acceptance and Commitment Therapy (ACT), and Compassion-Focused Therapy (CFT). The chapter will first summarise each of the therapies and associated adaptations for this client group, followed by reviewing the emerging evidence base and summarising the limitations, for each intervention in turn.

PERSON-BASED COGNITIVE THERAPY

Person-Based Cognitive Therapy was specifically developed to alleviate the distress experienced by people with psychosis.

Core Beliefs are fixed beliefs about the self, which can be either positive or negative.

Person-Based Cognitive Therapy (PBCT, Chadwick, 2006) combines Cognitive Behaviour Therapy for Psychosis (CBTp), and mindfulness practice. It was specifically developed for individuals with psychosis and addresses three key areas that are known to maintain distress: (1) persecutory delusions and beliefs about voices; (2) individuals' responses to psychotic symptoms that maintain distress, such as avoidance, rumination and worry, and fighting or struggling with voices; and (3) core beliefs (schema), which define the self as fixed and negative. The focus in PBCT is on experiential therapeutic techniques, which includes traditional CBTp techniques (such as guided discovery and behavioural experiments), mindfulness practice, working with positive and negative schematic beliefs (using the two-chair technique—see Chadwick, 2003), and a focus on positive behaviour change. PBCT is typically delivered in a group format (though it can be delivered individually), and usually consists of 12 weekly sessions lasting 90 min each. 10-min mindfulness practice occurs in each session, and individuals are invited to practice mindfulness daily between sessions.

Adaptations of Mindfulness Practice for Psychosis

Mindfulness is a technique used to increase awareness of ourselves and the world around us.

In PBCT, the same mindfulness practice is used throughout. To date, three main adaptations to mindfulness practice have been suggested (Chadwick, 2006). First, each practice is a maximum of 10 min in length—this is typically the most that individuals with psychosis can manage. Second, guidance during practice occurs every 30–60 s, thereby avoiding any extended silences. This is essential in aiding decentring from psychotic experiences (e.g. voices) and (unhelpful) responses to them (e.g. rumination and struggle), and facilitates focus on present moment experience with clearer awareness. Psychotic sensations are also explicitly referred to during a practice—promoting normalising of distressing psychotic experience and thereby giving them equal status with any other sensations that arise during a practice. Experiences noticed and reactions to them are explored and elaborated in the enquiry that follows a practice. Third, individuals are invited and encouraged to practice mindfulness between therapy sessions, and are provided with a 10-min audio-guided meditation to facilitate this. However, practice outside sessions is not an essential requirement.

Evidence Base

There is increasing evidence showing the potential benefits of PBCT for individuals with a diagnosis of Schizophrenia who experience auditory hallucinations (voices). An initial uncontrolled study found significant prepost improvement in clinical functioning amongst 10 patients with Schizophrenia following a group mindfulness intervention; secondary analyses also indicated improvement in mindfulness skills (Chadwick, Taylor, & Abba, 2005). An uncontrolled study of 9 PBCT groups involving 62 individuals with distressing voices found significant improvements in psychological health, voice distress, and voice control, which were maintained at 1-month follow up (Dannahy et al., 2011). In a randomised feasibility trial (Chadwick, Hughes, Russell, Russell, & Dagnan, 2009), 22 individuals with distressing voices were randomly allocated to either group-based mindfulness therapy or a waitlist control, and significant improvement in clinical functioning (measured using the CORE questionnaire) and mindfulness skills was found following the mindfulness intervention. In another study, individuals with Schizophrenia randomised to an 8-week mindfulness intervention showed significantly more improvements in mindfulness than those randomised to waitlist control (Langer, Cangas, Salcedo, & Fuentes, 2012). In the first full RCT of group PBCT for people with distressing voices (Chadwick et al., 2016), 108 individuals were randomised to either group PBCT or treatment as usual. Results showed significant between-group post intervention benefits in voice-related distress, perceived controllability of voices and recovery. Participants in the PBCT group also reported lower post treatment levels of depression, which was maintained at 6-month follow up.

Currently, the evidence base for persecutory delusions is much more limited. To date, there are only two published case studies showing the benefits of 6 sessions of weekly mindfulness practice in reducing conviction and distress associated with paranoid beliefs, depression and anxiety (Ellett, 2013). Our group is currently running the first pilot RCT evaluating group PBCT specifically for individuals with persecutory delusions.

A recent metaanalysis (10 RCTs included) found a small but significant effect of third-wave interventions on positive symptoms (Hedges $g=0.29$) compared with control post intervention (Louise, Fitzpatrick, Strauss, Rossell, & Thomas, 2018). Mindfulness-based interventions delivered in a group format resulted in larger effects ($g=0.46$) than those delivered in an individual format. Moderate effects were also found for depressive symptoms ($g=0.39$) and mindfulness ($g=0.56$).

Qualitative research has also examined mechanisms of change in mindfulness for psychosis. Potential mechanisms identified have included allowing voices, thoughts, and images to come and go without reacting or struggle, and reclaiming power through acceptance of psychosis and the self (Abba, Chadwick, & Stevenson, 2008). Collectively, these studies attest to the benefits of group-based mindfulness therapy for individuals who experience distressing voices, and suggest potential change mechanisms.

Limitations

The effectiveness of PBCT for psychotic symptoms is promising for voices but more research is needed for persecutory delusions.

There are a number of limitations with the evidence base to date that warrant consideration. At present, there is more evidence for the effectiveness of group PBCT with individuals experiencing distressing voices; there has been much less research focus on effectiveness for individuals with persecutory delusions. To date, only one full RCT comparing PBCT with treatment as usual has been undertaken, and there are no published studies that have compared PBCT with an active control group. Although comparison to treatment as usual is appropriate to initially test effectiveness (Chadwick et al., 2016), it is not possible to rule out any placebo effects or effects due to nonspecific group factors. Furthermore, studies are still needed to examine factors that might mediate clinical change, such as changes in mindfulness skills, acceptance of psychosis and self, or metacognitive insights explored following practice. Additionally, the majority of studies to date have been conducted by experienced clinicians with specific skills and expertise in delivering mindfulness, psychological therapy, and working with individuals with psychosis—translation of effects into wider clinical practice still needs to be determined. Finally, longer-term effects of PBCT are yet to be established.

Research into the effectiveness of PBCT could also be strengthened in a number of key areas, including use of independent raters to assess adherence to therapy and more robust assessments of mindfulness practice between sessions, neither of which were systematically undertaken in the full voices RCT. The latter is particularly important as self-report of mindfulness practice is subject to reporting bias. However, it should be noted that self-report is commonly used in mindfulness-based research trials and is therefore not a specific limitation solely associated with research with individuals with psychosis.

METACOGNITIVE THERAPY (MCT)

Metacognitive therapy focuses on understanding and modifying cognitive biases associated with the symptoms of psychosis.

Cognitive Biases are thinking errors that affect the decisions and judgements that people make.

Metacognitive therapy draws on the literature about cognitive biases in information processing. A key aim of metacognitive therapy is to increase knowledge and understanding of the impact and dysfunctional nature of cognitive biases associated with specific symptoms (see Chapter 8). This is achieved through use of a number of structured experiential exercises that specifically target key cognitive biases. Metacognitive exercises are combined with other therapy techniques, including CBT and third-wave approaches, including 'detached mindfulness'. A psychological model of the aetiology and maintenance of individuals' symptoms is developed during therapy, which is focused on common cognitive biases experienced, and how they result in the experience of psychological symptoms.

Adaptations for Individuals With Psychosis

MCT was first introduced for individuals with Schizophrenia by Moritz and Woodward (2007). It can be delivered in both an individual and group format, and typically consists of 8 sessions each lasting 45–60 min. There are eight 'training modules' that target specific cognitive biases in Schizophrenia, including:

attribution bias (making external personal attributions for negative events—1 module); jumping to conclusions (tendency to gather less data/evidence before making a decision—2 modules); belief inflexibility (bias against disconfirmatory evidence—1 module); theory of mind (difficulty in representing beliefs and thoughts of others—2 modules); overconfidence in errors (1 module) and mood and self esteem (1 module). The same basic structure is followed for each of the training modules: (a) a range of experiential exercises introduce the individual to the specific cognitive bias; (b) there is a focus on the link between the bias and psychotic symptoms experienced, (c) there is an emphasis on the impact of generalisation to daily life, and (d) alternative strategies are also explored. The modules can be downloaded free of charge from the following website: http://www.uke.de/mct.

Evidence Base

To date, there has been one narrative review (Moritz, Andreou, Schneider, Wittekind, et al., 2014), one systematic review (Jiang, Zhang, Zhu, et al., 2015), and two metaanalyses (Eichner & Berna, 2016; Van Oosterhouth, Smit, Krabbendam, Castelein, et al., 2016) of the evidence base of MCT for Schizophrenia. One metaanalysis (Van Oosterhouth et al., 2016) included 11 studies, all of which included an MCT condition, which was compared against either treatment as usual (8 studies), neurocognitive training (Cogpack) (2 studies) or supportive counselling (1 study), and focused on three specific outcomes—positive symptoms, delusions, and data gathering bias. Effect sizes were calculated using Hedges g, and were reported as 0.26 for positive symptoms, 0.22 for delusions, and 0.31 for data gathering; all were found to be nonsignificant. Another metaanalysis was conducted, which included 3 additional studies (Aghotor, Pfueller, Moritz, Weisbrod, & Roesch-Ely, 2010; Erawati, Keliat, Helena, & Hamid, 2014; Moritz et al., 2011) that weren't included in the van Oosterhout et al. review due to the exclusion criteria implemented. Effect sizes (Hedge's g) were reported for positive symptoms ($g = -0.34$; note negative sign favours MCT), delusions ($g = -0.41$), and acceptance of the intervention ($g = -0.84$); all were found to be significant. Overall, the metaanalyses show small-medium effect sizes of MCT on a range of clinical outcomes including positive symptoms, delusions, data gathering, and acceptance of the intervention.

Limitations

There are a number of limitations with the evidence base to date that warrant consideration. It is difficult to draw any definitive conclusions about the effectiveness of MCT given the contrasting recommendations of the two metaanalyses conducted so far—one concluding that the evidence does not support the dissemination of MCT in routine care (Van Oosterhouth et al., 2016) and one concluding that the evidence does support dissemination (Eichner & Berna, 2016). In addition, few studies to date have examined maintenance of intervention effects by including a follow-up phase, such that the long-term effects of MCT

The effectiveness of MCT for psychotic symptoms is still under debate, due to conflicting conclusions derived from recent metaanalyses.

are yet to be clearly established. However, data are encouraging as two studies report significant effects for positive symptoms and delusions assessed at 6–36 months following an MCT intervention (Favrod et al., 2014; Moritz, Andreou, et al., 2014; Moritz, Veckenstedt, et al., 2014). MCT specifically addresses cognitive biases in Schizophrenia, particularly in relation to delusions; therefore, applicability to other psychotic symptoms such as auditory hallucinations (hearing voices) is less clear, and the therapeutic focus is not on working with delusional beliefs directly. Furthermore, the clinical relevance of MCT in relation to its impact on daily life and social functioning is yet to be determined—future studies would usefully include measures of both global and social functioning. Finally, a number of the studies evaluating MCT have excluded people with severe psychosis, and studies to date have focused mainly on assessing clinical outcomes; therefore, future research might usually examine mechanisms of change of this therapeutic approach.

ACCEPTANCE AND COMMITMENT THERAPY (ACT)

The overarching aim of ACT is to use acceptance and mindfulness-based strategies to reduce the extent to which unwanted psychological events (e.g. difficult thoughts, feelings, images, memories) dominate experience and behaviour, and to increase the extent to which an individual's personal values inform and guide behaviour (Hayes, Strosahl, & Wilson, 1999). Unlike traditional CBT, ACT focuses on changing one's relationship with difficult internal experiences. ACT adopts the perspective that individuals are typically embroiled in a battle against unwanted psychological events; a battle in which they invest great time and energy in attempting to control, suppress, and eliminate those unwanted events ('experiential avoidance'). ACT proposes, and aims to provide, a range of opportunities for the individual to engage with unwanted psychological events in a new context, characterised by openness and acceptance ('psychological flexibility'). From this perspective, psychological events are simply events of the mind that rise and then pass.

Acceptance and Commitment Therapy uses acceptance and mindfulness-based strategies to help change the individual's relationship with difficult internal experiences and promote behaviours that are consistent with the individual's values.

ACT uses six core psychological processes that aim to increase psychological flexibility: acceptance (being in psychological contact with difficult psychological experiences without attempts to suppress or alter those experiences), cognitive defusion (reducing the extent to which thoughts are viewed as literal truths), mindfulness (being centred in the present moment), self-as-context (experiencing the self with moment to moment awareness, rather than through a self-narrative), values (clarifying and defining meaningful life directions), and committed action (committing to behaviours that are governed by values).

Adaptations for Individuals With Psychosis

The transdiagnostic nature of ACT means that the application of ACT to different types of disorders is not inherently different. However, using ACT with individuals who are experiencing symptoms of psychosis requires some modifications (see Thomas, Morris, Shawyer, & Farhall, 2013 for fuller consideration). ACT aims to disrupt the extent to which the individual uses psychological events as a guide for action, by fundamentally shifting their relationship with psychological events. In this way, individuals are invited to reconsider some core aspects of how they understand themselves and their experiences. Given that this is an area that individuals with psychosis often have preexisting difficulties with, the ACT clinician needs to proceed gently, adjusting their rate to the needs of the individual, and eliciting regular feedback in order to gauge responses to, experience of, and engagement with, therapeutic techniques. In keeping with adaptations for mindfulness in PBCT, it is also recommended that mindfulness practices are no longer than 10 min with short periods of silence (no longer than 10 s) so as not to overwhelm (Butler et al., 2016). Furthermore, home practice of mindfulness is recommended, but with an accepting stance towards noncompliance (Butler et al., 2016).

Some content adaptations have also been recommended (Bach & Hayes, 2002; Thomas et al., 2013). ACT utilises a range of metaphors to engage individuals in the aforementioned processes of change. To accommodate the cognitive difficulties that some individuals with psychosis may present with (e.g. difficulties in abstract thinking and memory), the use of short, simple, visual and/or active metaphors is recommended. For example, a number of short cartoons have been developed for metaphors such as 'tug-of-war with a monster'. Similarly, metaphors such as 'passengers on the bus' can be acted out to enhance engagement and recall, as well as using a small number of common metaphors throughout therapy sessions (Butler et al., 2016). In addition to these ACT-specific content adaptations, it can also be useful to incorporate information on the continuum between psychotic experiences and those experiences of the nonpsychotic population, which can help to normalise and gently disrupt existing (unhelpful) relationships with psychotic experiences.

Evidence Base

There have been a number of studies evaluating the effectiveness of ACT for psychotic symptoms. A small number of RCTs have evidenced promising effects of ACT for acute psychosis when compared to treatment as usual (TAU). In an inpatient setting, Bach and Hayes (2002) randomised individuals ($N=80$) with positive symptoms to either treatment as usual (TAU) or TAU plus 4 sessions of ACT. They reported that the addition of ACT to TAU significantly reduced rehospitalisation over a 4-month and 1-year (Bach, Hayes, & Gallop, 2012) follow-up period. Subsequently, Gaudiano and Herbert (2006) conducted a smaller RCT ($N=40$), randomising inpatients with a diagnosis of schizophrenia to either enhanced TAU or enhanced TAU plus ACT (approximately three 1-h sessions). Individuals receiving ACT reported significantly less distress related to hallucinations and less social impairment as compared to the control group. However, there were no between-group differences for hallucination frequency, believability, total psychiatric symptoms or thought disorder. At 4-month follow-up, rehospitalisation was lower in the ACT group, but not significantly so. Assessors and staff were not blind to condition, and at times the therapist collected

The evidence base for the **effectiveness of ACT for psychotic symptoms** is in its infancy: some positive and some nonsignificant treatment effects have been reported.

posttreatment measures, both of which are important study limitations. More recently, Tyrberg, Calbring, and Lundgren (2016) conducted an RCT in a Swedish inpatient setting, in which individuals with psychosis ($N=22$) were randomised to TAU or TAU plus an average of 2 ACT sessions. Authors reported lower rehospitalisation rates at 4-month follow-up in the ACT plus TAU group, but this difference was not statistically significant. Again, assessors were not blind to group allocation, which may have biased the findings.

There is also some evidence to suggest that ACT is beneficial for outpatients with symptoms of psychosis. Shawyer et al. (2017) recently compared ACT to a befriending intervention ($N=47$) for individuals with psychosis and command hallucinations. Both interventions were manualised, and consisted of eight 50-min sessions. The authors reported no significant differences for the primary outcome measure, overall mental state (including positive negative and general symptoms), postintervention. However, those in the ACT group had significantly greater improvements in positive symptoms at 6-month follow-up and significantly less voice-related distress. Rehospitalisation rates at follow-up were comparable across conditions. Spidel, Lecomte, Kealy, and Daigneauly (2017) examined the effects of ACT for individuals with psychosis and a history of childhood trauma ($N=50$) to either a 10-session ACT group or TAU. Attending ACT was associated with decreased symptoms and an increase in acceptance. Assessing acceptability and feasibility of ACT groups for outpatients with psychosis ($N=69$), Johns et al. (2016) conducted an uncontrolled trial and reported high levels of acceptability and group satisfaction, as well as prepost improvement in mood and psychological functioning.

Two RCTs have piloted ACT for emotional difficulties following psychosis. White et al. (2011) conducted a feasibility RCT comparing ACT (10 sessions) plus TAU to TAU for emotional dysfunction following psychosis ($N=24$). Those in the ACT plus TAU condition were significantly more likely to have passed the cut-off from depressed to not depressed at 5-month follow up compared to those in the TAU condition. Furthermore, those in the ACT group had significantly fewer crises and showed a significant reduction in negative symptoms. Subsequently, Gumley et al. (2017) examined the effects of ACT for depression following psychosis, randomising individuals with Schizophrenia plus Major Depression ($N=29$) to ACT (average of 15 sessions) plus TAU versus TAU. Depression was assessed at 5-and 10-month follow-up, but there were no between-group differences, as measured using the clinician-administered Calgory Depression Scale for Schizophrenia. Using the Beck Depression Inventory, a significant effect in favour of ACT (large effect size) at 5-month follow-up was found.

Limitations

Despite some promising preliminary findings, the research on ACT for psychosis is still in its infancy. The trials are limited to small sample sizes and, in several cases, assessors have not been blind to group allocation. Significant differences have not been reported on some primary outcome measures; however, the pilot nature of these studies means that lack of statistical differences could be attributable to them being underpowered. The use of active control groups further compounds the issue of power, because between-group effect sizes are typically smaller when comparing two active groups. In a recent review of mindfulness and acceptance-based interventions for psychosis, Louise et al. (2018) included four ACT RCTs and concluded that ACT showed 'negligible, nonsignificant treatment effects' (Hedges $g=0.08$) when evaluating the extent to which ACT reduced psychotic symptoms. Three of the four RCTs compared ACT to an active control. In a separate systematic review of ACT for psychosis, Wakefield, Roebuck, and Boyden (2018) reported that ACT appears to be a useful intervention for individuals experiencing psychosis, but that the lack of scientific rigour, and the potential for bias, means that current findings must be interpreted with caution.

COMPASSION-FOCUSED THERAPY (CFT)

The overarching aim of CFT is to develop skills in compassion towards the self and others, as a means of improving affect regulation (Gilbert, 2009). Compassion describes a sensitivity to suffering (one's own suffering or the suffering of others) and a commitment to try to alleviate and prevent it. CFT emerged from the observation that individuals with psychological difficulties often have marked difficulties in experiencing warmth and kindness towards themselves, whilst showing high levels of shame and self-criticism. Based on neurophysiological research, Gilbert describes three systems that are thought to have evolved to regulate affect: The *Threat and Protection System* detects threats in one's environment, activating emotional responses that are designed to protect the individual (e.g. fight or flight); The *Drive and Excitement System* orientates one towards positive rewards in the environment and is involved in the regulation of positive emotions such as excitement and pleasure; The *Contentment, Soothing and Social Safeness System* regulates a sense of contentment and safety and is thought to develop through an attuned, responsive, and caring style of parenting. CFT proposes that these systems interact in complex ways and that psychological difficulties arise when these systems become 'unbalanced' (e.g. over activation of the threat system and under activation of the soothing system). CFT aims to understand the functioning and interaction of these three systems and to readdress the balance. The key principles in CFT are to enhance the individual's sensitivity towards their own well-being, needs, and experiences of distress, and to help individuals to respond to their difficult experiences with kindness, compassion, and warmth.

Compassion is defined as a sensitivity to suffering—be that one's own suffering or the suffering of others—and a commitment to try to alleviate and prevent it.

Adaptations for Individuals With Psychosis

Several authors have proposed that a CFT approach is well suited to the needs of individuals with psychosis (e.g. see Braehler et al., 2013). There is considerable evidence that processing and regulating threat, especially social threat, is a core difficulty for these individuals, as they have often experienced difficult early attachments and/or experiences of bullying and humiliation, as well as high levels of shame and self-criticism. Although research in applying CFT to those with psychosis is in its infancy (see section later), a few adaptations have been suggested. Both Mayhew and Gilbert (2008) and Laithwaite, O'Hanlon, Collins, and Doyle (2009) reported that individuals with psychosis found it difficult to relate to personal experiences of compassion, and therefore found it challenging to generate compassionate imagery, with some reporting feeling fearful towards their compassionate image. Given this, individuals suggested allocating more therapy time for generating compassionate images, and more input from clinicians in facilitating this. Furthermore, in Laithwait et al.'s study, group facilitators helped to generate a group compassionate image, as well as suggesting to group members that they could think of a place or nonhuman object that generated feelings of warmth and safety. A cartoon illustration of using CFT with clients who hear voices has been developed by Dr. Charlie Heriot-Maitland from the Department of Psychology at King's College (https://www.youtube.com/watch?v=VRqI4lxuXAw).

Evidence Base

To date, only a small number of studies have investigated the application of compassion focused therapy to individuals with psychosis (Martins, Castilho, Santos, & Gumley, 2017). These studies are limited to a small number of case studies (Kennedy & Ellerby, 2016; Mayhew & Gilbert, 2008), uncontrolled pre-post pilot studies (Johnson et al., 2011; Laithwaite et al., 2009), and a feasibility randomised control trial (Braehler et al., 2013).

Mayhew and Gilbert (2008) conducted a small case series ($N=3$) using 12 1-h individual compassionate mind training therapy sessions with voice hearers. All participants reported a reduction in frequency of positive symptoms and a reduction in the extent to which voices were experienced as malevolent and persecuting and an increase in reassuring voices. One individual experienced less benefits as they felt that they did not deserve compassion. Laithwaite et al. (2009) conducted an uncontrolled trial ($N=18$) piloting group CFT in a maximum-security hospital. The authors reported significant improvements in depression, self-esteem, and general psychopathology, which were maintained at 6-week follow-up. Johnson et al. (2011) examined the effectiveness of a loving kindness meditation with outpatients (N=18) with persistent negative symptoms. Individuals received six 1-h group sessions and reported decreased negative symptoms and increased positive emotions and psychological recovery. Finally, Braehler et al. (2013) conducted a prospective randomised trial in which adults with a Schizophrenia-spectrum disorder were randomised to CFT (16 sessions of group therapy) plus TAU ($N=22$) versus TAU (N=18). Compared to TAU, those in the CFT group had significantly higher rates of clinical improvement postintervention. Increases in compassion were significantly associated with reductions in depression and perceived marginalisation.

Limitations

Overall, research to date has supported the feasibility and acceptability of compassion focused therapy for psychosis. However, the research is very much in its infancy and there are a number of limitations with the evidence base to date that warrant consideration. To date, outcomes are limited to small and predominantly self-selected samples, with most studies being uncontrolled trials in which researchers are not blind to the intervention received. Only one study has implemented randomisation procedures and compared CFT to TAU. Although this level of methodological rigour is suitable for initial examination of CFT for this group, it means that the impact of CFT specific components, as opposed to nonspecific therapy factors (e.g. attending a group, therapist time) cannot be estimated. Furthermore, research to date has used highly experienced practitioners, which means it is possible that therapist expertise, as opposed to treatment techniques, accounts for improvements. Given these limitations, there is a clear need for the current findings to be replicated using more rigorous research trials (Martins et al., 2017). Future research could benefit from implementing more rigorous experimental designs, such as by randomising individuals to CFT versus an active alternative, using assessors that are blind to group allocation, measuring adherence to CFT procedures, measuring processes of change, and recruiting larger samples.

The evidence base for the **effectiveness of CFT for psychotic symptoms** is limited: robust randomised controlled trials are needed to provide more convincing support for this therapy.

CONCLUDING REMARKS

In this chapter, we have reviewed third-wave interventions for psychosis, which has focused on four main approaches: PBCT, MCT, ACT, and CFT. An overview of each approach is provided, alongside key adaptations for individuals with psychosis, and an overview of the evidence base for each approach, including discussion of limitations. Collectively, the evidence suggests that third-wave interventions, which (to a varied extent) integrate mindfulness with more traditional CBT techniques, hold promise for individuals with psychosis. However, it is clear that more rigorous research is required in order to examine the specific impact of each therapy. The level of scientific rigour with which these therapies have been examined to date is reasonable and appropriate given that many of the approaches are at an early stage of development and adaptation for individuals with psychosis. Future research is needed to investigate therapeutic outcomes using well controlled designs and attending to key quality variables such as allegiance bias. Moving forward, it would be important to replicate effects in different settings and across different research teams. Future research is also required to examine key mechanisms of change associated with each therapeutic approach. There are a range of other new generation CBTp therapies currently in development (for example, Relating Therapy and AVATAR therapy), which have not been covered here, though some of which are covered elsewhere in the textbook (Section 4).

QUIZ QUESTIONS

1. What adaptations to mindfulness practice have been suggested within the PBCT approach?
   (a) Limit practice time to 10 min
   (b) Avoid extended silences
   (c) Practice outside sessions is not essential but is encouraged
   (d) All of the above
2. What combinations of cognitive biases are targeted in Metacognitive Therapy for Schizophrenia?
   (a) Jumping to conclusions, attribution bias, and overestimation of errors
   (b) Belief inflexibility and Theory of Mind bias
   (c) Jumping to conclusions, Theory of Mind, and belief inflexibility
   (d) Jumping to conclusions, belief inflexibility, theory of mind, attribution bias, and overestimation of errors
3. What are the core aims of ACT?
   (a) To help clients focus on positive experiences
   (b) To help clients be more rational in response to difficult thoughts and feelings and to use these more rational cognitions to guide behaviour
   (c) To reduce the extent to which difficult thoughts and feelings guide behaviour and increase the extent to which values guide behaviour
   (d) To get rid of difficult thoughts and feelings
4. The evidence base on CFT for Psychosis is:
   (a) Strongly supportive of using CFT with this client group
   (b) Limited to small and predominantly self-selected samples, with most studies being uncontrolled trials
   (c) Limited to clients of a specific culture and therefore may not generalise
   (d) Mixed, with one metaanalysis supporting the application of CFT to clients with psychosis and the other suggesting that we need to proceed with caution.

ANSWERS TO QUIZ QUESTIONS:

1. (d)
2. (d)
3. (c)
4. (b)

SELF-DIRECTED LEARNING

Braehler, C., Gumley, A., Harper, J., Wallace, S., Norrie, J., & Gilbert, P. (2013). Exploring change processes in compassion focused therapy: Results of a feasibility randomised controlled trial. *British Journal of Clinical Psychology, 52*, 199–214.

Chadwick, P. (2006). *Person based cognitive therapy for distressing psychosis*. Wiley.

Moritz, S., & Woodward, T.S. (2007b). Metacognitive training in Schizophrenia: From basic research to knowledge translation and intervention. *Current Opinion in Psychiatry 20*, 619–625.

O'Donoghue, E., Morris, E., Oliver, J., Johns, L., & Hayes, S. (2018). *ACT for psychosis recovery*. New Harbinger.

Wells, A., & Matthews, G. (1994). *Attention and emotion: A clinical perspective*. Hove (UK): Erlbaum.

References

Abba, N., Chadwick, P. D. J., & Stevenson, C. (2008). Responding mindfully to distressing psychosis: A grounded theory analysis. *Psychotherapy Research, 18*, 77–87.

Aghotor, J., Pfueller, U., Moritz, S., Weisbrod, M., & Roesch-Ely, D. (2010). Metacognitive training for patients with schizophrenia (MCT): Feasibility and preliminary evidence for its efficacy. *Journal of Behavior Therapy and Experimental Psychiatry, 41*, 207–211.

Bach, P., & Hayes, S. (2002). The use of acceptance and commitment therapy to prevent the rehospitalization of psychotic patients: A randomized controlled trial. *Journal of Consulting and Clinical Psychology, 70*, 1129–1139.

Bach, P., Hayes, S., & Gallop, R. (2012). Long-term effects of brief acceptance and commitment therapy for psychosis. *Behavior Modification, 36*(2), 165–181.

Birchwood, M., & Trower, P. (2006). The future of CBT for psychosis: not a quasi-neuroleptic. *British Journal of Psychiatry, 188*, 107–108.

Braehler, C., Gumley, A., Harper, J., Wallace, S., Norrie, J., & Gilbert, P. (2013). Exploring change processes in compassion focused therapy in psychosis: Results of a feasibility randomized controlled trial. *British Journal of Clinical Psychology, 52*(2), 199–214.

Butler, L., Johns, L., Byrne, M., Joseph, C., O'Donoghue, E., Jolley, S., et al. (2016). Running acceptance and commitment therapy groups for psychosis in community settings. *Journal of Contextual Behavioral Science, 5*, 33–38.

Chadwick, P. (2003). Two chairs, self-schemata and a person based approach to psychosis. *Behavioural and Cognitive Psychotherapy, 31*(4), 439–449.

Chadwick, P. (2006). *Person-based cognitive therapy for distressing psychosis.* Chichester: Wiley.

Chadwick, P., Hughes, S., Russell, D., Russell, I., & Dagnan, D. (2009). Mindfulness groups for distressing voices and paranoia: A replication and randomized feasibility trial. *Behavioural and Cognitive Psychotherapy, 37*(4), 403–412.

Chadwick, P., Strauss, C., Jones, A. M., Kingdon, D., Ellett, L., Dannahy, L., et al. (2016). Group mindfulness-based intervention for distressing voices: A pragmatic randomised controlled trial. *Schizophrenia Research, 175*, 168–173.

Chadwick, P., Taylor, K. N., & Abba, N. (2005). Mindfulness groups for people with psychosis. *Behavioural and Cognitive Psychotherapy, 33*(3), 351–359.

Dannahy, L., Hayward, M., Strauss, C., Turton, W., Harding, E., et al. (2011). Group person-based cognitive therapy for distressing voices: Pilot data from nine groups. *Journal of Behavior Therapy and Experimental Psychiatry, 42*(1), 111–116.

Eichner, C., & Berna, F. (2016). Acceptance and efficacy of metacognitive training (MCT) on positive symptoms and delusions in patients with schizophrenia: A meta-analysis taking into account important moderators. *Schizophrenia Bulletin, 42*(4), 952–962.

Ellett, L. (2013). Mindfulness for paranoid beliefs: Evidence from two case studies. *Behavioural and Cognitive Psychotherapy, 41*(2), 238–242.

Erawati, E., Keliat, B. A., Helena, N., & Hamid, A. (2014). The influence of metacognitive training on delusion severity and metacognitive ability in schizophrenia. *Journal of Psychiatric and Mental Health Nursing, 21*, 841–847.

Favrod, J., Rexhaj, S., Bardy, S., Ferrari, P., Hayoz, C., Moritz, S., et al. (2014). Sustained antipsychotic effect of metacognitive training in psychosis: A randomized controlled study. *European Psychiatry, 29*, 275–281.

Gaudiano, B. A., & Herbert, J. D. (2006). Acute treatment of inpatients with psychotic symptoms using acceptance and commitment therapy. *Behaviour Research and Therapy, 44*, 415–437.

Gilbert, P. (2009). Introducing compassion-focused therapy. *Advances in Psychiatric Treatment, 15*, 199–208.

Gumley, A., White, R., Briggs, A., Ford, I., Barry, S., Stewart, C., et al. (2017). A parallel group randomised open blinded evaluation of acceptance and commitment therapy for depression after psychosis: Pilot trial outcomes (ADAPT). *Schizophrenia Research, 183*, 143–150.

Hayes, S., Strosahl, K., & Wilson, K. (1999). *Acceptance and commitment therapy: An experiential approach to behaviour change.* New York: Guilford Press.

Jauhar, S., McKenna, P. J., Radua, J., Fung, E., Salvador, R., & Laws, K. R. (2014). Cognitive-behavioural therapy for the symptoms of schizophrenia: Systematic review and meta-analysis with examination of potential bias. *British Journal of Psychiatry, 204*, 20–29.

Jiang, J., Zhang, L., Zhu, Z., et al. (2015). Metacognitive training for schizophrenia: A systematic review. *Shanghai Archives of Psychiatry, 27*(3), 149–157.

Johns, L., Oliver, J., Khondoker, M., Byrne, M., Jolley, S., Wykes, T., et al. (2016). The feasibility and acceptability of a brief Acceptance and Commitment Therapy (ACT) group intervention for people with psychosis: The 'ACT for life' study. *Journal of Behavior Therapy and Experimental Psychiatry, 50*, 257–263.

Johnson, D., Penn, D. L., Fredrickson, B. L., Kring, A. M., Meyer, P. S., Catalino, L. I., et al. (2011). A pilot study of loving-kindness meditation for the negative symptoms of schizophrenia. *Schizophrenia Research, 129*(2–3), 137–140.

Kennedy, A., & Ellerby, M. (2016). A compassion-focused approach to working with someone diagnosed with schizophrenia. *Journal of Clinical Psychology, 72*(2), 123–131.

Laithwaite, H., O'Hanlon, M., Collins, P., & Doyle, P. (2009). Recovery after psychosis (RAP): A compassion focused programme for individuals residing in high security settings. *Behavioural and Cognitive Psychotherapy, 37*, 511–526.

Langer, A. I., Cangas, A. J., Salcedo, E., & Fuentes, B. (2012). Applying mindfulness therapy in a group of psychotic individuals: a controlled study. *Behavioural and Cognitive Psychotherapy, 40*(1), 105–111.

Laws, K., Darlington, N., Kondel, T., McKenna, P., & Jauhar, S. (2018). Cognitive behavioural therapy for schizophrenia—Outcomes for functioning, distress and quality of life: A meta-analysis. *BMC Psychology, 6*, 32.

Louise, S., Fitzpatrick, M., Strauss, C., Rossell, S. L., & Thomas, N. (2018). Mindfulness- and acceptance-based interventions for psychosis: Our current understanding and a meta-analysis. *Schizophrenia Research, 192*, 57–63.

Mander, H., & Kingdon, D. (2015). The evolution of CBT for psychosis. *Psychology Research and Behavior Management, 8*, 63–69.

Martins, M., Castilho, P., Santos, V., & Gumley, A. (2017). Schizophrenia: An exploration of an acceptance, mindfulness, and compassion-based group intervention. *Australian Psychologist, 52*, 514–523.

Mayhew, S., & Gilbert, P. (2008). Compassionate mind training with people who hear malevolent voices: A case series report. *Clinical Psychology & Psychotherapy, 15*(2), 113–138.

Moritz, S., Andreou, C., Schneider, B. C., Wittekind, C. E., Menon, M., Balzan, R. P., et al. (2014). Sowing the seeds of doubt: A narrative review on metacognitive training in schizophrenia. *Clinical Psychology Review, 34*, 358–366.

Moritz, S., Kerstan, A., Veckenstedt, R., Randjbar, S., Vitzthum, F., Schmidt, C., et al. (2011). Further evidence for the efficacy of a metacognitive group training in schizophrenia. *Behaviour Research and Therapy, 49*, 151–157.

Moritz, S., Veckenstedt, R., Andreou, C., Bohn, F., Hottenrott, B., Leighton, L., et al. (2014). Sustained and "sleeper" effects of group metacognitive training for schizophrenia: A randomized clinical trial. *JAMA Psychiatry, 71*, 1103–1111.

Moritz, S., & Woodward, T. S. (2007). Metacognitive training in schizophrenia: From basic research to knowledge translation and intervention. *Current Opinion in Psychiatry, 20*, 619–625.

Shawyer, F., Farhall, J., Thomas, N., Hayes, S. C., Gallop, R., Copolov, D., et al. (2017). Acceptance and commitment therapy for psychosis: Randomised controlled trial. *British Journal of Psychiatry, 210*, 140–148.

Spidel, A., Lecomte, L., Kealy, D., & Daigneauly, I. (2017). Acceptance and commitment therapy for psychosis and trauma: Improvement in psychiatric symptoms, emotion regulation, and treatment compliance following a brief group intervention. *Psychology and Psychotherapy: Theory, Research and Practice, 91*, 248–261.

Thomas, N., Morris, E., Shawyer, F., & Farhall, J. (2013). Acceptance and commitment therapy for voices. In E. M. J. Morris, L. C. Johns, & J. E. Oliver (Eds.), *Acceptance and commitment therapy and mindfulness for psychosis* (pp. 95–111). Wiley-Blackwell.

Tyrberg, M., Calbring, P., & Lundgren, T. (2016). Brief acceptance and commitment therapy for psychotic inpatients: a randomized controlled feasibility trial in Sweden. *Nordic Psychology, 69*, 110–125.

Van Oosterhouth, B., Smit, F., Krabbendam, S., Castelein, S., et al. (2016). Metacognitive training for schizophrenia spectrum patients: A meta-analysis on outcome studies. *Psychological Medicine, 46*, 47–57.

Wakefield, S., Roebuck, S., & Boyden, P. (2018). The evidence base of acceptance and commitment therapy (ACT) in psychosis: A systematic review. *Journal of Contextual Behavioral Science, 10*, 1–13.

White, R. G., Gumley, A. I., McTaggart, J., Rattrie, L., McConville, D., Cleare, S., et al. (2011). A feasibility study of acceptance and commitment therapy for emotional dysfunction following psychosis. *Behaviour Research and Therapy, 49*, 901–907.

Wykes, T., Steel, C., Everitt, B., & Tarrier, N. (2008). Cognitive behaviour therapy for schizophrenia: Effect sizes, clinical models, and methodological rigor. *Schizophrenia Bulletin, 34*, 523–537.

Definition of Key Terms

Acceptance describes the process of turning towards and experiencing difficult experiences (e.g. thoughts, feelings, situations).

Acceptance and Commitment Therapy (ACT) uses acceptance and mindfulness-based strategies to help change the individual's relationship with difficult internal experiences and to promote behaviours that are consistent with the individual's values.

Cognitive Biases are thinking errors that affect the decisions and judgements that people make.

Compassion describes sensitivity to suffering—be that one's own suffering or the suffering of others—and a commitment to try to alleviate and prevent it.

Compassion-focused therapy uses cognitive behavioural strategies to help individuals develop compassion towards the self and others, as a means of improving well-being and recovery from mental health difficulties.

Core Beliefs are fixed beliefs about the self that can be either positive or negative.

Metacognitive therapy focuses on understanding and modifying cognitive biases associated with the symptoms of psychosis.

Mindfulness is a technique used to increase awareness of ourselves and the world around us.

Person-Based Cognitive Therapy (PBCT) integrates cognitive behaviour therapy with mindfulness practice, with an additional focus of working with positive and negative beliefs about the self.

CHAPTER 17

Cognitive Remediation to Improve Functional Outcome

Alice Medalia, Alice Saperstein
College of Physicians and Surgeons, Columbia University Irving Medical Center, New York, NY, United States

Key Learning Objectives

- To introduce cognitive remediation as a treatment for the cognitive dysfunction associated with schizophrenia spectrum disorders
- To learn how cognitive remediation impacts cognition and community functioning
- To learn about factors that impact effectiveness of cognitive remediation
- To introduce some common approaches to conducting cognitive remediation
- To appreciate the challenges and opportunities when treating cognition

INTRODUCTION

Cognitive Impairment in Schizophrenia: Cognitive deficits are a prominent, stable feature of schizophrenia from the time of first episode throughout the course of illness. Cognitive deficits also exist in people at high risk for developing psychosis and contribute to their functional decline (Carrión et al., 2011). Deficits are evident in a variety of neurocognitive domains, including attention, processing speed, working memory, verbal learning and memory, and problem solving, on the order of 1 to 2 standard deviations below the normative mean (Kurtz, 2005). In addition, deficits in social cognition include impairments in facial affect recognition, in perceiving and interpreting social cues, and theory of mind. Even when a person scores in the normal range on cognitive tests, they likely have deficits relative to how they would have scored before they became ill. Virtually 100% of people with schizophrenia experience cognitive impairment, if measured against their preillness ability, and about 80% score significantly lower than an age-matched healthy population (Kurtz, Donato, & Rose, 2011; Wilk et al., 2005).

Current pharmacologic treatments provide little benefit for cognitive deficits.

Cognitive deficits are largely unresponsive to current pharmacologic treatment and add significantly to illness burden by imposing limitations on functioning, such as on the ability to adhere to pharmacotherapy, to participate in and benefit from psychosocial rehabilitation programs, and to perform in the social,

A Clinical Introduction to Psychosis. https://doi.org/10.1016/B978-0-12-815012-2.00017-1

vocational, and educational roles integral to community integration (Bowie, Reichenberg, Patterson, Heaton, & Harvey, 2006; Green, Kern, & Heaton, 2004). Cognition is thus a key intervention target because cognitive skills are needed to help people with schizophrenia achieve their recovery goals—to work, go to school, live independently, and socialise.

What is it like to have cognitive deficits? Imagine what it is like to constantly forget things you used to be able to easily remember, or to struggle to pay attention and follow what someone is saying. Cognition can be difficult to talk about because most people do not share a vocabulary about neuropsychological functions. A question like, 'How is your cognitive functioning?' is not likely to elicit information, because cognition means different things to different people. Rather, questions phrased to include common cognitive terms such as, 'Have you been finding it difficult to pay attention?' are more likely to invite commentary. Similarly, a strengths-based approach would be to ask, 'Do you think that if you could pay attention better it would be helpful at school/work/when you talk with friends?' Because attention is a skill that is easily understood and is a frequent cognitive complaint (Medalia & Thysen, 2008), questions about attention are a good place to start when asking about perception of cognitive difficulties (Box 17.1).

Cognitive deficits are not visible, and many people do not appreciate that they are a common symptom of psychosis, so others do not readily understand why someone forgot an appointment or to do the agreed-upon errands. Forgetfulness may be misinterpreted by others as lack of motivation, and inattentiveness may be seen as a sign of disinterest. Patients feel shame as they attempt to do tasks they previously did easily, and they fear criticism or ridicule if they ask for help. Anticipation of failure leads to increasing withdrawal from activities, which in turn deprives them of opportunities to develop their cognitive skills (Medalia, Herlands, Saperstein, & Revheim, 2017). Unless cognitive health is addressed, community functioning will continue to suffer.

Cognitive deficits and daily functioning: Performance on tests of neuropsychological functions predicts whether a person with schizophrenia will be able to meet functional goals (Green, 1996), and thus continues to be an abundant and critical area of continued research. The cognitive symptoms most frequently

Box 17.1 First-Person Account[a]

Chris is a 24-year-old high school graduate who always wanted to be a computer technician but has struggled to find work since becoming ill. He told his doctor, "I just can't focus. I used to be good at reading but now it is hard. When people talk to me sometimes, it is like the information is coming so fast."

[a] First-person accounts and descriptions of cases are based on real cases, but are systematically disguised to protect confidentiality.

cited as impacting functional outcome in people with schizophrenia are captured by the acronym **S**MART: **s**peed of processing, **m**emory, **a**ttention, **r**easoning, **t**act/social cognition. Studies examining how cognitive impairments impact functioning indicate that relationships are multivariate, direct, and indirect (Joseph et al., 2017; Thomas et al., 2017). First, cognitive abilities such as quickly and accurately processing information, focusing, and paying attention directly impact how well one is able to perform at work, communicate effectively, and function independently in the community (Green, 1996). Second, these and additional cognitive abilities, such as reasoning and remembering verbal information, impact the acquisition of social, work, and independent living skills (Bowie & Harvey, 2006). The goal of many psychosocial rehabilitation programs is to develop such skill competencies for use in everyday life (Bowie et al., 2006; Bowie et al., 2008). Third, skill learning and deployment in real-world situations are further impacted by symptom severity, perceived self-competency, as well as resources and opportunity (Bowie et al., 2008; Cardenas et al., 2013; Holshausen, Bowie, Mausbach, Patterson, & Harvey, 2014). Given the complexity of these relationships, cognitive approaches to improving functional outcome must be integrative and comprehensive.

Key cognitive processes to improve daily functioning:
Speed of information processing
Memory
Attention
Reasoning
Tact/social cognition

What is cognitive remediation: Cognitive Remediation (CR) is an evidence-based, recovery-oriented behavioural intervention, which focuses on reducing cognitive deficits in order to enhance life skills in people with psychiatric illness. Different from Cognitive Behavioural Therapy approaches that focus on the content and form of thoughts and beliefs, CR targets the neuropsychological skills that underlie thinking.

Cognitive remediation targets the neuropsychological skills that underlie thinking.

While a broad range of neuropsychological and social cognitive deficits may be targeted, CR for schizophrenia is increasingly focused on targeting those deficits, which contribute most to social dysfunction and community outcome. Table 17.1 illustrates how CR targets 'SMART' skills to improve both cognitive and functional outcomes.

CR programs are grounded in theory and empirical evidence. Psychiatric rehabilitation forms the foundation; rehabilitation models aim to decrease level of disability, promote adaptation, and thereby improve psychosocial functioning. Specific methods of treating cognition in schizophrenia are based on cognitive psychology, neuroscience, and neuropsychology. Further, CR is informed by methods of learning enhancement, drawing upon theories from the fields of educational and clinical psychology. The influence of these theoretical foundations is evident in the clinical techniques that have been incorporated in evidence-based CR approaches, as will be discussed later in this chapter.

Cognitive remediation draws on multiple approaches, from neuropsychology to rehabilitation psychology.

While all approaches to CR are learning-based, they vary depending on the extent to which they use restorative and/or compensatory techniques to improve cognitive ability. In practice, the remediation methods employed will depend on the population, setting, and resources available. Restorative techniques use repeated task practice on exercises designed to activate the neural networks associated with

Remediation methods will vary based on clients' needs, recovery goals, and service setting.

Table 17.1 SMART Goals to Improve Functioning

Cognitive target	Cognitive goals	Functional goals (examples)
Speed of Processing	Practice responding quickly and accurately to visual and/or auditory stimuli	Attending and responding to environmental cues both accurately and quickly support all aspects of daily living, school, and work
Memory	Perform mental tasks using visual or verbal information held in mind; practice strategies to facilitate encoding and recall for information heard or read	Retention and recall for verbal content are needed to follow instructions, learn class material, and recall details of a conversation or book. Visual memory helps to find objects and navigate routes.
Attention	Practice focusing on task-relevant visual and/or auditory information for increasing periods of time; identify common distractions and develop strategies to remain focused on the task at hand	Concentrating on task-relevant information while filtering irrelevant stimuli is important for work or school tasks, effective communication, and for efficiently completing activities of daily living
Reasoning	Practice working through problems of increasing complexity and performing tasks that have multiple steps and more distal goals in a logical and organised fashion	Logic and problem-solving skills are needed to organise and plan, manage time, increase independence, complete tasks for school/work, socialise, set reasonable goals and work steadily toward desired outcomes
Tact/ Social Cognition	Learn elements of social perception to recognise social cues and make judgments about emotions, thoughts, beliefs, and intentions of others	Improving accuracy of emotion and social cue perception and interpretation will facilitate appropriate interaction with others

cognitive domains and harness mechanisms underlying neuroplasticity to improve cognitive processing (Vinogradov, Fisher, & de Villers-Sidani, 2012). Restorative approaches can be described as Bottom Up or Top Down, which refers to the progression or focus of exercises on lower- or higher-order cognitive skills. Titration of task difficulty is a central element of repeated cognitive practice, which ensures that learning remains novel and challenging, while rewarding success. Compensatory techniques teach skills and strategies to enhance information processing or circumvent cognitive impairment to enhance behavioural adaptation. Skills and strategies learned in-session are practiced and strengthened to the point of habit, so as to allow for their routine use in everyday life. Cognitive remediation may employ computerised exercises, therapist-guided instruction, or combine computer exercises with verbal discussion and group-based activities to link training exercises to everyday life. In social cognitive approaches, complex social cognitive processes are broken down into component skills, which are practiced, taught and learned using rehearsal, modelling, and role-play with corrective feedback (Box 17.2).

Box 17.2 Definitions of Core Cognitive Remediation Components

Restorative Exercises: Drill and practice on exercises that target a specific cognitive skill or set of skills, usually done on a computer by accessing web-based programs.

Example: A computer activity simulates a restaurant, and the user enters as the waiter and earns more tips by remembering the orders and names of customers.

Bottom Up/Top Down: Scaffolding the presentation of restorative tasks with the more basic cognitive exercises first is called Bottom Up, which differs from the Top-Down model that starts remediation with complex tasks, assuming the component cognitive skills will be exercised.

Example: Bottom up starts with processing speed, attention, and working memory, and proceeds to verbal memory and problem solving. Top-Down remediation may start with problem-solving exercises.

Task Titration: A motivational enhancement design applied to exercises, so that the difficulty level adapts to the user's skill level, assuring they are correct about 80% of the time and thus stay challenged but do not become discouraged.

Example: A target tracker task used to improve attention reduces the visibility of the target as the user becomes more proficient at tracking.

Compensatory Strategies: Strategies are offered to compensate for a cognitive weakness by drawing on cognitive strengths or using environmental supports.

Example: Use of sticky notes, organisational strategies, and electronic aids are taught to help people remember better.

Bridging Groups: Discussion groups link the restorative cognitive exercises to the use of cognitive skills in everyday life.

Example: After working on tasks to improve attention and memory, there is a discussion of how those skills are used when visiting the doctor, or taking a class, or completing a project at the job site.

Strategy Coaching: providing individually tailored suggestions to aid information processing and efficient completion of cognitive tasks during CR.

Example: Teaching the use of verbal associations to remember a list of words.

People with schizophrenia must believe that their actions can lead to positive outcomes or else they may have little incentive to take on challenging treatment tasks. This has been demonstrated not only in the context of CR, but also in the context of utilising learned psychosocial skills to carry out daily life tasks (Cardenas et al., 2013). Two specific components of many CR programs, which are designed to enhance engagement and learning, are strategy coaching and Bridging. Strategy coaching involves providing individually tailored suggestions to aid information processing and efficient completion of cognitive tasks during CR. Examples of strategies are forming associations, verbal mediation, using visual cues, and dividing complex tasks into smaller components. Whether prompted by the therapist or the exercise program itself, participants learn to identify how best to approach a task, monitor outcomes of strategy selection, and incorporate feedback to generate alternative approaches or reinforce and expand the use of strategies to further promote task success. This process not only develops the skill of metacognition, being able to think about one's own thinking (Reeder et al., 2017; Tsapekos, Taylor, & Cella, 2017), but through enhancing performance, supports perceived competency, which in turn supports

Strategy coaching promotes the transfer of cognitive gains to daily life.

engagement, persistence, and therefore learning. Further, when strategies are practiced in, or are discussed with respect to ecologically relevant contexts, their use is more likely to generalise to real-world activities integral to functioning.

Bridging is the therapeutic process that fosters behaviour change following cognitive remediation by linking cognitive skills and strategies to recovery goals and real-world functioning. The goal is to speed the transfer of cognitive gains from the clinical setting to everyday life by increasing motivation to learn, improving metacognition, reinforcing skill learning to promote success and competency, and by providing opportunities for skills to be practiced in a supportive therapeutic context. Three types of Bridging techniques have been identified (Bowie & Medalia, 2016). The first involves training the participant to monitor and document their activities and progress in CR. This enhances awareness of what is being practiced in-session and facilitates greater metacognition for real-world application, particularly with respect to personal goals. Second, therapist-led verbal discussions further aim to help participants understand how those cognitive skills being trained are linked to everyday behaviours. Enhancing the saliency of cognitive skills in relation to concrete goals and real-world functioning promotes engagement and motivation, which are integral to maintenance of learning and transfer. Third, role plays and simulations of real-world environments have the advantage of providing practice of skills and strategies in a safe, supportive context with ample opportunity for repetition, corrective feedback, and praise. Opportunities for successful skill implementation facilitate skill acquisition and increase self-competency for cognitive performance. When relevant cues from the simulation are replicated outside of the treatment session, acquired skills are more likely to be employed in real-world contexts.

CR Implementation: With the growing awareness that cognitive skills can be improved with cognitive remediation and that this translates into better real-world functioning, there is increasing interest in making CR more readily available to people with severe mental illness.

Agencies that are considering how to provide CR as an evidence-based practice have questions as to what is involved in implementing CR in systems of care. Common questions include: What exactly is CR and what happens in a CR session?; Are there different CR approaches and, if so, how does one choose?; Who should be eligible to receive the service?; Does it work for everyone?; Is it covered by insurance plans?; Who would provide it?; How do we implement it? Increasingly the answers to these questions are being addressed in the literature (Medalia, Saperstein, Erlich, & Sederer, 2018) and we address here some of these issues.

CR is indicated when a person has cognitive deficits impacting their functioning, even after other treatment approaches have been tried. Once medication and environmental adjustments have been applied, if a person continues to struggle cognitively they may be a good candidate for CR. Let's return to Chris, the young man who wanted to finish his studies to be a computer technician but kept dropping out of classes. His psychiatrist was able to help him feel more alert in the morning by adjusting the timing of his medications, and his family connected him to a wake-up service, but he was still unable to focus during class. Chris attended CR and was able to improve his attention and processing speed and finish his class.

In clinical settings, CR can be found on long-term residential or inpatient services, and in outpatient clinics that offer psychosocial rehabilitation programming. Cognitive remediation is increasingly being paired with vocational training, supportive education, social skills, and independent living skills training, therefore providing a broader rehabilitation context for improving cognition. Cognitive remediation is conducted by mental health clinicians who receive specific training to do this intervention. When clinicians study how schizophrenia impacts cognition, and the various techniques to improve cognitive skills, they are more effective at promoting positive cognitive outcomes (Medalia & Richardson, 2005). The website www.teachrecovery.com provides an example of a cognitive remediation training venue for clinicians.

EMPIRICAL SUPPORT FOR CR

The literature supporting CR efficacy for schizophrenia spectrum disorders has been reported in numerous randomised controlled trials, summarised by metaanalytic studies. There is a solid empirical base indicating moderate outcomes for proximal intervention targets, neurocognitive or social cognitive (McGurk, Twamley, Sitzer, McHugo, & Mueser, 2007; Wykes, Huddy, Cellard, McGurk, & Czobor, 2011). The 2011 metaanalysis, which represents an aggregate of research with over 2000 participants, indicates that the findings of moderate effect on global cognition are not significantly affected by the quality of trial methodology (Wykes et al., 2011). In a subset of the metaanalytic studies that examined durability, treatment gains were reported up to 8-months post-treatment. CR is also reported to increase self-esteem and is linked to improvement in quality of life (Garrido et al., 2013). In complement, learning benefits reported by CR participants include gains in specific cognitive domains as well as in strategy use and skills to aid social abilities and everyday functioning (Contreras, Lee, Tan, Castle, & Rossell, 2016; Medalia, Erlich, Soumet-Leman, & Saperstein, 2017; Medalia, Herlands, et al., 2017). Further, the social experience of participating in CR in a group setting, as well as the positive, motivating influence of the therapist have been reported as impacting self-efficacy as well as learning outcomes (Cella, Reeder, & Wykes, 2015; Contreras et al., 2016; Reeder et al., 2015).

CR can effectively and sustainably improve cognition and functioning in people with schizophrenia spectrum disorders.

When examining the collective CR outcomes research, no participant variables have emerged as significantly impacting the effect sizes associated with CR (Wykes et al., 2011). However, individual studies have reported significant moderating effects of a number of baseline factors. Some research has found a significant effect of age and education, with greater cognitive benefit in younger participants and those with higher education (Kontis, Huddy, Reeder,

Landau, & Wykes, 2013; Lindenmayer et al., 2017; McGurk et al., 2007; Vita et al., 2013). There may be an advantage for those with better pretreatment cognitive ability, particularly in the domains of attention and working memory (Fiszdon, Cardenas, Bryson, & Bell, 2005; Kurtz, Seltzer, Fujimoto, Shagan, & Wexler, 2009; Lindenmayer et al., 2017; Medalia & Richardson, 2005). There is a wealth of research that has delineated the role of motivation in facilitating learning, and an accumulating literature on the role of intrinsic motivation in cognitive learning in people with schizophrenia (Saperstein & Medalia, 2016). Intrinsic motivation refers to the motivation to engage in an activity because of its intrinsic value or interest, and differs from extrinsic motivation, which refers to motivation to engage in behaviour because rewards extrinsic to the activity itself may ensue. Clinical perspectives informed by Self Determination Theory (Deci & Ryan, 1985) and Expectancy Value Theory (Eccles & Wigfield, 2002) have informed CR research, with evidence indicating roles for perceptions of competency, program interest, and perceived program value as contributing to cognitive improvement (Bryce et al., 2018; Choi, Fiszdon, & Medalia, 2010).

Variability in the impact of CR on functional outcome has led to a research focus on the issue of generalisation by examining clinical approaches that enhance cognition and promote transfer to real-world functioning. The remainder of this chapter will summarise the extant knowledge base and most promising avenues for further research to yield an optimal cognitive remediation treatment model that enhances the potential for generalisation. We start with a patient's perspective on how CR can impact daily functioning, which is provided in Box 17.3.

Box 17.3 First-Person Account of the CR Experience

I have to admit when I first stepped into the computer lab for my first session of cognitive remediation I was sceptical. How could a bunch of computer games help me reach my ultimate goal of getting sharper and quicker with my thinking? My goal was to get back to work with a better head on my shoulders and to be able to think quicker on my feet for the purpose of interviewing. Also, I wanted to have the ability to become more focused on work tasks. While I was not sure how to get to my goals, cognitive remediation had never been something I thought would be useful.

Now I have been in the program over a month I realise I could not have been more wrong in my thinking. All the computer activities acted as a vehicle for improving my cognitive skills. The first thing I noticed that started to recover and 'grow' was my memory. I got better at the tasks on the computer, but also at home and in the job application process. For the first time, I was taking the skills from the computer lab into real life.

Another program helped with my attention to detail and processing speed. Each session lasts an hour and builds upon the previous session. I noticed that the practice had a profound effect on me when I was listening to people. I could hear more clearly and gather the information they were telling me with ease. In essence, it made me a better listener.

MEASUREMENT OF FUNCTIONAL OUTCOME

An understanding of how functional outcomes are assessed is crucial when evaluating research on the efficacy of CR for schizophrenia. Functional outcomes are assessed with respect to competency and capacity. Functional competence refers to the attainment of a sustained level of functioning in a real-world setting, for example educational attainment, vocational status, and degree of independent living. In studies of the impact of social cognition interventions, social competence is measured as current levels of social autonomy and social activity. However, given the practical challenges of direct observation or self-report, rating behaviours in real-world settings can be difficult to do. Furthermore, attainment of goals is not just the result of cognitive skill—it is the end result of a complex interaction of person-related (e.g. motivation) and environmental (e.g. resource availability) factors. Functional improvement requires time and opportunities to practice new skill sets.

Functional capacity is different—it assesses skill performance in a controlled setting, in reference to functionally relevant domains. Assessment of capacity may be preferred because the measures are indicative of a person's *potential* to function, all other person and environmental obstacles aside. In many CR studies, functional capacity is assessed through role play tests of social skill, knowledge, and use of skills for finance management, medication management, self-care, and independent living. Performance-based measures are reliable, correlated highly with cognition, and have criterion validity with respect to real-world functioning (Mausbach, Moore, Bowie, Cardenas, & Patterson, 2009). Still, performance-based measures have limitations: they become outdated as technology changes the way people function, cultural differences in functioning may be hard to capture, and little is known about how performance-based capacity measures predict more nuanced areas of functioning (e.g. work quality) or skills that relate more specifically to personal goals. An emerging trend is to therefore look at personal goal attainment, which may reflect adaptive skill acquisition en route to vocational, educational, social, or independent living goal attainment (Medalia & Bowie, 2016). This allows for CR to be paired with other meaningful skills-based interventions and for functional outcome to be measured as it pertains to achievement of personally relevant functional goals.

Functional capacity assesses skill performance in controlled rather than 'real-world' settings.

WHAT IS THE IMPACT OF CR ON FUNCTIONAL OUTCOME?

The Wykes et al. (2011) metaanalysis of randomised controlled trials with schizophrenia spectrum patients found a significant medium size effect on functional outcomes at posttreatment (0.42) with evidence for durability of functional gains at follow-up assessment (0.37). Effect sizes for functional outcome were similar for trials of good (0.39) and poor (0.44) methodological quality. Significantly stronger effects were found in studies that provided adjunctive psychiatric rehabilitation (0.59) compared with studies that examined patients treated with cognitive remediation alone (0.28), replicating the pattern of results (see Fig. 17.1) reported in the metaanalysis by McGurk et al. (2007). A second independent metaanalysis specific to social cognitive interventions reviewed 19 studies consisting of 692 subjects, the majority of whom had schizophrenia or schizoaffective disorder (Kurtz & Richardson, 2012). Cognitive remediation for social cognition in schizophrenia had a medium effect size for improving overall psychiatric symptoms (0.68) and a large effect (0.78) on measures of functional capacity, and observer-rated community and institutional functioning. Thus, the literature supports CR as a treatment for schizophrenia that yields significant, durable improvements in daily functioning with evidence indicating that cognitive gains translate to improvements in social and community functioning as well as psychiatric symptoms.

Since the publication of these metaanalytic studies, additional research has examined CR approaches to enhance the impact of CR on functional outcome. The data continue to show that there are significant functional benefits when CR is combined, either sequentially or concomitantly, with skills training. An important study from Bowie, McGurk, Mausbach, Patterson, and Harvey (2012) provides a direct examination of this approach. This randomised controlled trial examined the effect of combining functional skills training with CR that used computer-based restorative cognitive exercise and strategy coaching. While CR administered alone resulted in cognitive gains, and skills training alone was effective for improving the functional skills taught, the combined treatment yielded greater effects on performance-based measures of adaptive

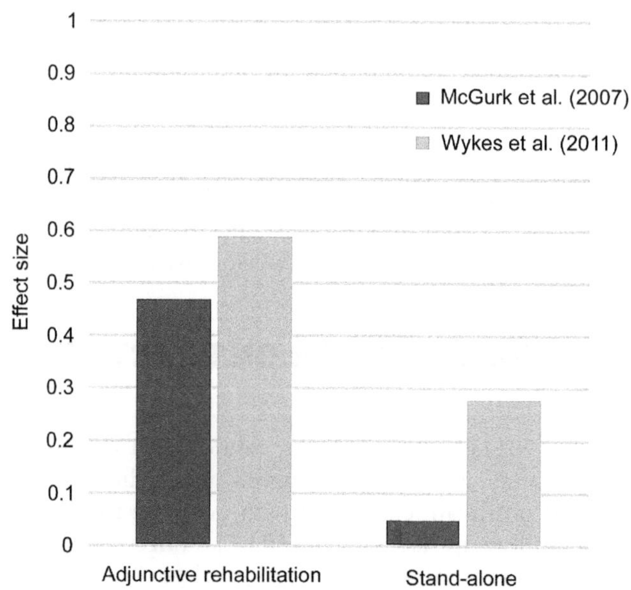

FIG. 17.1
Effects of CR on functioning: Stand-alone versus provided with adjunctive rehabilitation.

skills, real-world community or household responsibilities, and in work, relative to either treatment administered alone (Bowie et al., 2012). These results show the value of combining cognitive and functional skill learning so that skills transfer more readily to everyday life.

Integrating CR with skills training boosts treatment gains in everyday life.

Other approaches combine neuro- and social cognitive training to improve functional outcome. Integrative programs have been found to improve neurocognition, social cognition, and social adjustment in chronically ill (Hogarty, Greenwald, & Eack, 2006) and early course patients with schizophrenia (Eack et al., 2009) or schizoaffective disorder (Lewandowski, Eack, Hogarty, Greenwald, & Keshavan, 2011). Importantly, the results of mediation analyses investigating the mechanism of treatment effect suggest that improvement in both social cognition and neurocognition may be needed to achieve an optimal functional response (Eack, Pogue-Geile, Greenwald, Hogarty, & Keshavan, 2011). Parallel evidence suggests that social cognition is a key mediator between neurocognition and functional outcome, indicating that improving social cognition may be particularly important for generalisation to occur (Schmidt, Mueller, & Roder, 2011). How cognitive remediation and social cognitive interventions should be combined to optimally enhance functional recovery remains an empirical question.

While more effective than providing cognitive training as a stand-alone treatment, implementation of sequentially combined skills training or integrated cognitive remediation approaches may be hampered by resource limitations such as cost, time, and training capacity when deployed in routine care settings. A more efficient approach may be to embed CR within everyday treatment programs. Supported employment (SE) is an evidence-based treatment that provides intensive and continuous vocational coaching and support to individuals with serious mental illness. McGurk et al. (2015) demonstrated that the addition of CR, which integrated computer-based cognitive exercise and strategy coaching, increased the likelihood of employment, resulted in more weeks worked and in better income compared to SE alone. The findings are striking given that in this study, the comparison SE condition was enhanced by including provision of cognitive strategy training by the employment specialist, and that the sample was composed of prior SE nonresponders. Further, the resulting employment gains were sustained at 1-year follow up (McGurk et al., 2015). These outcomes are clinically significant because employment is considered by multiple stakeholders as a benchmark of functional recovery.

Education also plays an important role for individuals with serious mental illness. In a preliminary feasibility trial, Kidd, Kaur-Bajwa, and Haji-Khamneh (2012) reported that CR conducted in the context of a supported education program resulted in improved learning, concentration, executive functioning, and psychiatric symptoms (Kidd et al., 2012). In a later effectiveness trial (Kidd et al., 2014), supported education was compared to supported education with CR, which entailed 20 50-min sessions of computer-based learning exercises with 10 weekly 50-min group discussion sessions of cognitive skills and compensatory strategies. While both treatment groups demonstrated improvements in cognitive functioning, rates of academic completion and teacher-rated academic functioning favoured adjunctive CR. The combination also proved more beneficial for self-esteem rated posttreatment and at 4-month follow-up.

A different approach to directly address issues of generalisation is to build simulated real-world tasks and role-plays into the CR session. Bowie and colleagues report on a trial comparing the efficacy and effectiveness of action-based cognitive remediation (ABCR) to traditional computer-based CR (tCR). Both consisted of a 10-week group, including 2-h, twice weekly sessions of computer-based cognitive exercises with strategy monitoring and therapist coaching. Both involved detailed therapeutic elements to enhance transfer with a focus on work, but tCR used a discussion-based platform while ABCR used props to simulate work settings and tasks, and role-plays matched to computer-based exercises to make explicit links between cognitive practice and specific real-world applications. At posttreatment and at 10-week follow-up, ABCR participants demonstrated greater independent and community living skills, greater self-confidence to engage with cognitively challenging tasks, and a trend toward higher rates of employment (Bowie, Grossman, Gupta, Holshausen, & Best, 2017).

The significant benefits of providing CR in combination with other skills-based and recovery-oriented interventions are well represented by recent research as reported here (Bowie et al., 2012; Kidd et al., 2014; McGurk et al., 2015) as well as by the multitude of studies that preceded them (see McGurk et al., 2007; Medalia & Saperstein, 2013; Wykes et al., 2011). The study by Bowie et al. (2017) further showcases the significant role of an active therapist in CR to foster generalisation, and particularly the importance of creating a psychotherapeutic environment in which cognitive and real-life skills are conceptualised and are practiced as being inextricably linked. While the corpus of research supports a holistic approach to CR, implementation in real-world clinic settings must consider resource availability and cost. If disability reduction and better community integration results from approaches with high therapist involvement, the benefits may outweigh the costs. It will be important for future research to further evaluate the relative benefits of CR that is primarily technology based, which may be more portable and remotely delivered, yet may be clinically appropriate for only a subset of people with schizophrenia.

MAXIMISING THE IMPACT OF CR ON FUNCTIONAL OUTCOME

People with schizophrenia spectrum disorders typically have a long history of disability and withdrawal from vocational, educational, and social pursuits. Thus, even when cognitive gains are made, self-competency beliefs, intrinsic motivation, an autonomy supportive environment, and opportunity are some of the factors that affect transfer of cognitive skills (Cardenas et al., 2013; Holshausen et al., 2014; Medalia & Choi, 2009). Evidence gathered across clinical and experimental research studies calls attention to two general treatment approaches to maximise therapeutic outcome. Techniques to (1) enhance generalisation and (2) personalise treatment, guide current empirically informed applications of CR in the clinical community and continue to be a focus of research to develop new empirically based approaches that augment learning for people with schizophrenia.

TECHNIQUES TO ENHANCE GENERALISATION OF COGNITIVE GAINS

1. Practice cognitive skills in multiple contexts: While repeated practice on one task may allow for transfer of cognitive skills to new tasks with similar properties, practice of the same skill on an array of tasks or in different modalities facilitates transfer of training to a broader array of novel tasks and contexts (Bowie et al., 2017; Fuchs, Fuchs, & Prentice, 2003; Rougier, Noelle, Braver, Cohen, & O'Reilly, 2005). Thus, CR participants should be encouraged to practice cognitive skills on a variety of tasks.
2. Strategy coaching: Drill-and-practice exercises should be employed with strategy coaching to encourage self-monitoring, verbalisation, and the development of compensatory techniques to successfully approach new cognitive challenges.
3. Bridging groups: Weekly or biweekly Bridging groups promote metacognitive processing, which fosters the integration of lower- and higher-order cognitive functions, and provide a social learning context to reinforce the link between cognitive learning, everyday life, and rehabilitation goals (Box 17.4).
4. Provide CR in the context of recovery interventions that foster community functioning: Cognitive training is more likely to generalise to psychosocial outcomes when placed in a therapeutic context that teaches vocational skills, skills needed to succeed in academic and social settings, healthy/wellness behaviours, and symptom management.

Box 17.4 First-Person Account of the Bridging Group Experience

Taylor, a 28year-old diagnosed with schizoaffective disorder, is enrolled in the Thinking Well group, the cognitive remediation service at her outpatient clinic. Taylor wrote: Last month in Bridging group, our clinician taught us about learning styles—some people are big picture learners and others are detail oriented. I am a morning learner, while one of my peers says he learns better at night. We talked about having our style and the problems that arise when our style does not fit the situation. Like when I go to study group at school and can't keep up with the flow of ideas during the study sessions. We talked about how some of this is my processing speed and I am working on computer exercises to improve that. I also think best in the morning and this group is at night when I am so tired I can't think straight. Someone suggested I see if my study group could ever meet during the day, to see whether that helps. I did and turns out sometimes we could meet in the day. It's such a simple change, but wow what a difference! Thanks, Thinking Well.

APPROACHES TO PERSONALISE TREATMENT

1. Address individual cognitive needs: CR programs personalise treatment by tailoring the treatment plan to suit the specific needs (and priorities) of the individual. After measuring baseline cognitive skill level, training activities may be selected to target specific cognitive abilities or areas of functioning in the context of an individual's personal strengths, weaknesses, and unique rehabilitation goals. Research suggests that creating a personalised program of CR tailored to a person's baseline cognitive profile may lead to better outcomes (Medalia, Saperstein, Hansen, & Lee, 2016; Murthy et al., 2012) than giving every person the same palette of cognitive exercises.
2. Address psychological barriers: Depressed mood, anxiety, low motivation, and doubts about self-efficacy are prevalent in schizophrenia spectrum disorders and impact cognitive functioning and cognitive remediation outcomes (Fiszdon, Kurtz, Choi, Bell, & Martino, 2016; Medalia & Richardson, 2005; Tas, Brown, Esen-Danaci, Lysaker, & Brune, 2012; Ventura et al., 2014). Treatment is more effective when it personalises CR by optimising motivation to learn and addresses the cognitive thinking errors that impact cognitive activity (Brett, McGovern, Choi, & Fiszdon, 2018; Choi et al., 2010; Choi & Medalia, 2010). The systematic identification of the mechanisms within individual clients that are working to motivate and demotivate may lead to stronger personalisation of instructional interventions during CR. Motivation and learning are enhanced when cognitive learning employs instructional techniques that provide an enjoyable learning environment, contextualise learning activities in reference to real-world scenarios and personal goals, and provide opportunities for choice, emphasising personal control and supporting self-efficacy, motivation (Choi & Medalia, 2010; Cordova & Lepper, 1996). Cognitive-behavioural strategies can be provided one-on-one or during Bridging groups to change negative self-appraisals or doubts about self-competency and promote 'success' beliefs. For example, catastrophising may lead someone to think that if they made one error they will fail the cognitive exercise. CBT approaches to address thinking errors in the CR session can promote greater self-confidence and motivation (Best & Bowie, 2017).
3. Address biological variables: An emerging approach to personalising treatment attends to genetic variability, psychophysical profile, medication response, and the tailoring of adjuvant treatments to enhance neuroplasticity among those who may be less likely to benefit (Medalia et al., 2016). Personalisation may include the careful selection of atypical antipsychotic medications to support the neural mechanisms underlying learning and/or the concurrent use of interventions such as repetitive transcranial magnetic stimulation (Levkovitz, Rabany, Harel, & Zangen, 2011; Ziemann, 2005) or transcranial direct current stimulation (Mondino, Haesebaert, Poulet, Suaud-Chagny, & Brunelin, 2015) to enhance cortical plasticity.

FUTURE DIRECTIONS: CHALLENGES AND OPPORTUNITIES

There are a number of practical challenges when providing cognitive remediation for people with psychotic symptoms and disorders as well as opportunities for future research.

Challenge 1: Integration of Neuroscience Informed Approaches to Personalise Treatment

Mounting evidence indicates that the cognitive deficits of schizophrenia stem from maladaptive plasticity within neural circuits (Keshavan, Mehta, Padmanabhan, & Shah, 2015). Abnormal neuroplasticity in schizophrenia is hypothesised to be in part the result of neurochemical alterations in several neurotransmitter and neuromodulatory systems (Forsyth & Lewis, 2017). Efforts are underway to improve cognition using drugs targeting the neurotransmitter and neuromodulatory systems in schizophrenia that promote neuroplasticity. As neuroscience-informed approaches to measuring and enhancing neuroplasticity become refined, there will be an opportunity to personalise CR and enhance treatment effectiveness.

Neuroplasticity refers to the functional and structural adaptations of the brain to an ever-changing environment.

Challenge 2: Integration of New Technologies

With the boom in new technologically based interventions for people with psychosis comes an opportunity to refine CR and address issues like adherence and stigma (Ben-Zeev, Kaiser, & Krzos, 2014). CR requires on average 32 sessions and the logistical demands of attending clinics 2–4 times a week can be a deterrent to adherence. New technologies like mobile apps potentially offer greater ease of use and accessibility (Biagianti et al., 2017). Because computer-based exercises are constantly being developed and improved, evaluation of available products by clinicians is a continuous process (Herlands & Medalia, 2016). If a CR service is to stay current and take advantage of the latest developments in technology, the clinician needs to devote time on a regular basis to consider whether newly available exercises, programs, and learning platforms should be purchased.

Challenge 3: Integration of CR With Other Recovery-Oriented Treatments

While research supports combining CR with other recovery-oriented treatments to better impact functional outcome, it does not provide a nuanced understanding of the optimal sequencing and dosing or even the range of recovery interventions with which CR can be combined. Furthermore, CR is only one way to address cognitive problems. There is no 'one size fits all' approach to improving cognitive skills and everyday functioning, rather, there are multiple strategies that can be integrated in a treatment plan. How cognitive health is addressed will be informed by assessments of cognitive functioning, client interest in addressing cognitive health, and an evaluation of the available resources. Through the process of shared decision making, the approach that may best help each individual meet his/her needs can be determined.

Challenge 4: Improve Personalisation of CR

Despite positive group results for the use of CR interventions, there are substantial individual differences in response to treatment. Personalisation through the use of tailoring variables has the potential to improve CR delivery to maximise treatment outcomes. As research identifies the cognitive, psychological, and biological markers that inform treatment response, clinicians will be better able to customise CR to the individual recipient. The broader mission of personalisation is to find and utilise tailoring variables that capture individual characteristics, needs, and preferences in order to positively impact all stages of care, including prevention, diagnosis, treatment, and follow-up.

Challenge 5: Identify How CR Can Be Most Effective for First-Episode Psychosis

Already at first episode, most people with schizophrenia have cognitive impairments that significantly contribute to poor functioning at school and work. When cognition is left untreated, the resultant low level of functioning during the first years following the onset of psychosis predicts long-term outcome (Harrison et al., 2001). Research indicates that those who receive CR at a younger age (Wykes et al., 2009) and earlier stage of schizophrenia (Breitborde et al., 2015; Eack et al., 2009) have greater functional, social, and cognitive gains than older populations with the illness (Bowie, Grossman, Gupta, Oyewumi, & Harvey, 2014). The course of psychotic illness may be improved if timely evidence-based care is provided (Kane et al., 2016; Nordentoft, Rasmussen, Melau, Hjorthøj, & Thorup, 2014), arguing for addressing cognitive health early in the course of illness to reduce the cognitive deficit and its subsequent impact on quality of life and on recovery.

While evidence suggests that provision of CR to people in the early stage of schizophrenia, and in the context of rehabilitation services, results in both cognitive and functional gains, it is unclear whether CR can enhance the cognitive and functional outcomes for people with first-episode psychosis receiving treatment in Coordinated Specialty Care (CSC). CSC builds on considerable, global evidence for team-based early psychosis treatment that offers a range of services including evidence-based psychopharmacology, health and wellness education and primary care coordination, psychoeducation, cognitive behavioural psychotherapy, case management, peer support services, employment and education supports, family engagement and supports, behavioural activation, social skills training, substance use treatment, and coping skills training. It remains to be determined if and how CR should be integrated with these comprehensive programs.

Challenge 6: Implementation in Large and Small Systems of Care

An increased focus on cognitive health and the implementation of evidence-based CR complements care practices that address physical and mental health in routine practice settings. CR programs are scalable, making them cost effective in addition to being efficacious (Patel et al., 2010) and well received (Soumet-Lehman, Erlich, & Medalia, 2018). It is feasible to implement CR in a large, geographically, culturally, and linguistically diverse system of care (Amado & Sederer, 2016; Ikezawa et al., 2011; Medalia, Erlich, et al., 2017). Still, multiple factors can impact whether the CR environment is supportive enough to sustain the program. Dynamic leadership is key, as is having a culture where cognitive health is recognised by providers. Adequate staffing to run the CR program is obviously needed, but the effects of staffing in complementary services are also impactful. Implementation of CR in mental healthcare systems requires operationalising training for CR clinicians. They require foundational knowledge about cognitive skills and CR, they require training in the use of cognitive exercises and compensatory techniques, and in the teaching techniques that promote motivation to learn. Technology support is essential to ensure consistent access to the web-based cognitive exercises. Finally, ongoing program evaluation is critical for fidelity and program sustainability.

CONCLUSION

Cognitive remediation is an effective, well-received behavioural treatment that can benefit cognition with positive impact on role functioning in the community. There are internet- and print-based resources available to facilitate implementation in both small and large systems of care (see reading and resource sections). The growing presence of cognitive remediation programs in North America, Europe, Asia, and Australia speaks to its utility in geographically, culturally, and linguistically diverse clinical care systems.

ADDITIONAL SELF-DIRECTED READING

Medalia, A., & Bowie, C.R. (2016). *Cognitive remediation to improve functional outcomes*. New York, NY: Oxford University Press.

Medalia, A., Herlands, T., Saperstein, A., & Revheim, N. (2017). *Cognitive remediation for psychological disorders*. New York, NY: Oxford University Press.

Medalia, A., Saperstein, A.M., Erlich, M.D., & Sederer, L.I. (2018). Cognitive remediation in large systems of psychiatric care. *CNS Spectrums, 2*, 1–11.

Roberts, D.L., Penn D. L., & Combs D.R. (2015). *Social cognition and interaction training (SCIT)*. New York, NY: Oxford University Press.

Wykes, T., Huddy, V., Cellard, C., McGurk, S.R., & Czobor, P. (2011). A meta-analysis of cognitive remediation for schizophrenia: Methodology and effect sizes. *American Journal of Psychiatry, 168*(5), 472–485.

LINKS TO RESOURCES

Lectures about Cognitive Remediation: www.teachrecovery.com

Handbook for Families about Cognitive Dysfunction and Cognitive Remediation in the Psychiatric Disorders: https://www.omh.ny.gov/omhweb/cogdys_manual/cogdyshndbk.pdf

Cognitive Remediation in Psychiatry. Annual conference held early June, New York City: www.cognitive-remediation.org

QUIZ QUESTIONS

1. Which of the following statements about Cognitive Remediation is false?
   (a) Behavioural approaches to treating cognitive impairment must be accompanied by pharmacological intervention in order for neuroplastic changes in the brain to occur
   (b) Changes in brain structure have been documented with changes in cognitive function following cognitive training
   (c) Cognitive skill improvement reflects brain mechanisms associated with learning
   (d) Pharmacological intervention with behavioural intervention may act synergistically to enhance cognitive outcomes
2. Which of the following is true regarding the inclusion of verbal discussion groups in Cognitive Remediation practice?
   (a) Verbal discussion is most important during the initial stages of treatment engagement to build motivation for participating in Cognitive Remediation
   (b) Verbal discussion is most important when Cognitive Remediation is integrated with Vocational Rehabilitation so that work skills may be practiced and reinforced
   (c) Verbal discussion plays a role throughout Cognitive Remediation by reinforcing the links between cognitive skills and strategy use in everyday life
   (d) Verbal discussion is used in place of computer-based cognitive exercises in routine Cognitive Remediation practice
3. Research shows that which of the following is true about Cognitive Remediation outcomes?
   (a) Cognitive remediation is more effective for younger than older patients
   (b) Cognitive remediation is equally effective for psychiatric symptom improvement as for neurocognition
   (c) Effect sizes for neurocognition are moderate when conducted 2-3 times per week but large when conducted more frequently
   (d) Functional outcomes are enhanced when Cognitive Remediation is embedded within a broader program of psychiatric rehabilitation

4. With respect to Cognitive Remediation practice, scalability means which of the following?
   (a) Cognitive programs can be purchased for a large number of clients at low cost
   (b) Cognitive Remediation can serve a large number of clients in varied settings with equal effectiveness
   (c) Cognitive Remediation can be provided one-on-one within a public psychiatry setting
   (d) Cognitive Remediation is provided if other psychosocial intervention services (e.g. work therapy, social skills training) are also received

ANSWERS TO QUIZ QUESTIONS:

1. (a)
2. (c)
3. (d)
4. (b)

References

Amado, I., & Sederer, L. I. (2016). Implementing cognitive remediation programs in France: The "secret sauce". *Psychiatric Services, 67*(7), 707–709.

Ben-Zeev, D., Kaiser, S., & Krzos, I. (2014). Remote "hovering" with individuals with psychotic disorders and substance use: Feasibility, engagement, and therapeutic alliance with a text-messaging mobile interventionist. *Journal of Dual Diagnosis, 10*(4), 197–203.

Best, M. W., & Bowie, C. R. (2017). A review of cognitive remediation approaches for schizophrenia: From top-down to bottom-up, brain training to psychotherapy. *Expert Review of Neurotherapeutics, 17*(7), 713–723.

Biagianti, B., Fisher, M., Howard, L., Rowlands, A., Vinogradov, S., & Woolley, J. (2017). Feasibility and preliminary efficacy of remotely delivering cognitive training to people with schizophrenia using tablets. *Schizophrenia Research: Cognition, 10*, 7–14.

Bowie, C. R., Grossman, M., Gupta, M., Holshausen, K., & Best, M. W. (2017). Action-based cognitive remediation for individuals with serious mental illnesses: Effects of real-world simulations and goal setting on functional and vocational outcomes. *Psychiatric Rehabilitation Journal, 40*(1), 53–60.

Bowie, C. R., Grossman, M., Gupta, M., Oyewumi, L. K., & Harvey, P. D. (2014). Cognitive remediation in schizophrenia: Efficacy and effectiveness in patients with early versus long term course of illness. *Early Intervention in Psychiatry, 8*(1), 32–38.

Bowie, C. R., & Harvey, P. D. (2006). Cognitive deficits and functional outcome in schizophrenia. *Neuropsychiatric Disease and Treatment, 2*(4), 531–536.

Bowie, C. R., Leung, W. W., Reichenberg, A., McClure, M. M., Patterson, T. L., Heaton, R. K., et al. (2008). Predicting schizophrenia patients' real-world behavior with specific neuropsychological and functional capacity measures. *Biological Psychiatry, 63*(5), 505–511.

Bowie, C. R., McGurk, S. R., Mausbach, B., Patterson, T. L., & Harvey, P. D. (2012). Combined cognitive remediation and functional skills training for schizophrenia: effects on cognition, functional competence, and real-world behavior. *The American Journal of Psychiatry, 169*, 710–718.

Bowie, C. R., & Medalia, A. (2016). Bridging groups. In A. Medalia, & C. R. Bowie (Eds.), *Cognitive remediation to improve functional outcomes* (pp. 66–87). New York, NY: Oxford University Press.

Bowie, C. R., Reichenberg, A., Patterson, T. L., Heaton, R. K., & Harvey, P. D. (2006). Determinants of real-world functional performance in schizophrenia subjects: Correlations with cognition, functional capacity, and symptoms. *American Journal of Psychiatry, 163*(3), 418–425.

Breitborde, N. J., Bell, E. K., Dawley, D., Woolverton, C., Ceaser, A., Waters, A. C., et al. (2015). The Early Psychosis Intervention Center (EPICENTER): Development and six-month outcomes of an American first-episode psychosis clinical service. *BMC Psychiatry, 15*, 266.

Brett, B. L., McGovern, J. E., Choi, J., & Fiszdon, J. M. (2018). Improving treatment motivation in individuals with psychosis: predictors of response to motivational enhancement. *Psychiatry Research, 266*, 36–39.

Bryce, S. D., Lee, S. J., Ponsford, J. L., Lawrence, R. J., Tan, E. J., & Rossell, S. L. (2018). The impact of intrinsic motivation on session attendance and reliable cognitive improvement in cognitive remediation in schizophrenia. *Schizophrenia Research, 202*, 354–360.

Cardenas, V., Abel, S., Bowie, C. R., Tiznado, D., Depp, C. A., Patterson, T. L., et al. (2013). When functional capacity and real-world functioning converge: The role of self-efficacy. *Schizophrenia Bulletin, 39*(4), 908–916.

Carrión, R. E., Goldberg, T. E., McLaughlin, D., Auther, A. M., Correll, C. U., & Cornblatt, B. A. (2011). Impact of neurocognition on social and role functioning in individuals at clinical high risk for psychosis. *American Journal of Psychiatry, 168*(8), 806–813.

Cella, M., Reeder, C., & Wykes, T. (2015). Group cognitive remediation for schizophrenia: exploring the role of therapist support and metacognition. *Psychology and Psychotherapy: Theory, Research and Practice, 89*, 1–14.

Choi, J., Fiszdon, J. M., & Medalia, A. (2010). Expectancy-value theory in persistence of learning effects in schizophrenia: Role of task value and perceived competency. *Schizophrenia Bulletin, 36*(5), 957–965.

Choi, J., & Medalia, A. (2010). Intrinsic motivation and learning in a schizophrenia spectrum sample. *Schizophrenia Research, 118*(1–3), 12–19.

Contreras, N. A., Lee, S., Tan, E. J., Castle, D. J., & Rossell, S. L. (2016). How is cognitive remediation training perceived by people with schizophrenia? A qualitative study examining personal experiences. *Journal of Mental Health, 25*(3), 260–266.

Cordova, D. J., & Lepper, M. R. (1996). Intrinsic motivation and the process of learning: Beneficial effects of contextualization, personalization, and choice. *Journal of Educational Psychology, 88*, 715–730.

Deci, E. L., & Ryan, R. M. (1985). *Intrinsic motivation and self-determination in human behavior*. New York, NY: Plenum Press.

Eack, S. M., Greenwald, D. P., Hogarty, S. S., Cooley, S. J., DiBarry, A. L., Montrose, D. M., et al. (2009). Cognitive enhancement therapy for early-course schizophrenia: Effects of a two-year randomized controlled trial. *Psychiatric Services, 60*(11), 1468–1476.

Eack, S. M., Pogue-Geile, M. F., Greenwald, D. P., Hogarty, S. S., & Keshavan, M. S. (2011). Mechanisms of functional improvement in a 2-year trial of cognitive enhancement therapy for early schizophrenia. *Psychological Medicine, 41*(6), 1253–1261.

Eccles, J. S., & Wigfield, A. (2002). Motivational beliefs, values, and goals. *Annual Review of Psychology, 53*, 109–132.

Fiszdon, J. M., Cardenas, A. S., Bryson, G. J., & Bell, M. D. (2005). Predictors of remediation success on a trained memory task. *Journal of Nervous and Mental Disease, 193*(9), 602–608.

Fiszdon, J. M., Kurtz, M. M., Choi, J., Bell, M. D., & Martino, S. (2016). Motivational interviewing to increase cognitive rehabilitation adherence in schizophrenia. *Schizophrenia Bulletin, 42*, 327–334.

Forsyth, J. K., & Lewis, D. A. (2017). Mapping the consequences of impaired synaptic plasticity in schizophrenia through development: An integrative model for diverse clinical features. *Trends in Cognitive Science, 21*(10), 760–778.

Fuchs, L. S., Fuchs, D., & Prentice, K. (2003). Explicitly teaching for transfer: Effects on third grade students' mathematical problem solving. *Journal of Educational Psychology, 95*, 293–305.

Garrido, G., Barrios, M., Penadés, R., Enríquez, M., Garolera, M., Aragay, N., et al. (2013). Computer-assisted cognitive remediation therapy: Cognition, self-esteem and quality of life in schizophrenia. *Schizophrenia Research, 150*(2–3), 563–569.

Green, M. F. (1996). What are the functional consequences of neurocognitive deficits in schizophrenia? *American Journal of Psychiatry, 153*(3), 321–330.

Green, M. F., Kern, R. S., & Heaton, R. K. (2004). Longitudinal studies of cognition and functional outcome in schizophrenia: Implications for MATRICS. *Schizophrenia Research, 72*(1), 41–51.

Harrison, G., Hopper, K., Craig, T., Laska, E., Siegel, C., Wanderling, J., et al. (2001). Recovery from psychotic illness: A 15-and 25-year international follow-up study. *British Journal of Psychiatry, 178*, 506–517.

Herlands, T., & Medalia, A. (2016). How to assess and choose computerized cognitive exercises. In A. Medalia, & C. R. Bowie (Eds.), *Cognitive remediation to improve functional outcomes* (pp. 155–175). New York, NY: Oxford University Press.

Hogarty, G. E., Greenwald, D. P., & Eack, S. M. (2006). Durability and mechanism of effects of cognitive enhancement therapy. *Psychiatric Services, 57*(12), 1751–1757.

Holshausen, K., Bowie, C. R., Mausbach, B. T., Patterson, T. L., & Harvey, P. D. (2014). Neurocognition, functional capacity, and functional outcomes: The cost of inexperience. *Schizophrenia Research, 152*(2–3), 430–434.

Ikezawa, S., Mogami, T., Hayami, Y., Sato, I., Kato, T., Kimura, I., et al. (2011). The pilot study of a neuropsychological educational approach to cognitive remediation for patients with schizophrenia in Japan. *Psychiatry Research, 195*(3), 107–110.

Joseph, J., Kremen, W. S., Franz, C. E., Glatt, S. J., van de Leemput, J., Chandler, S. D., et al. (2017). Predictors of current functioning and functional decline in schizophrenia. *Schizophrenia Research, 188*, 158–164.

Kane, J. M., Robinson, D. G., Schooler, N. R., Mueser, K. T., Penn, D. L., Rosenheck, R. A., et al. (2016). Comprehensive versus usual community care for first-episode psychosis: 2-Year outcomes from the NIMH RAISE early treatment program. *American Journal of Psychiatry, 173*(4), 362–372.

Keshavan, M. S., Mehta, U. M., Padmanabhan, J. L., & Shah, J. L. (2015). Dysplasticity, metaplasticity, and schizophrenia: Implications for risk, illness, and novel interventions. *Development and Psychopathology, 27*(2), 615–635.

Kidd, S. A., Kaur, J., Virdee, G., George, T. P., McKenzie, K., & Herman, Y. (2014). Cognitive remediation for individuals with psychosis in a supported education setting: A randomized controlled trial. *Schizophrenia Research, 157*(1–3), 90–98.

Kidd, S. A., Kaur-Bajwa, J., & Haji-Khamneh, B. (2012). Cognitive remediation in a supported education setting. *Psychiatric Services, 63*(5), 508–509.

Kontis, D., Huddy, V., Reeder, C., Landau, S., & Wykes, T. (2013). Effects of age and cognitive reserve on cognitive remediation therapy outcome in patients with schizophrenia. *American Journal of Geriatric Psychiatry, 21*(3), 218–230.

Kurtz, M. M. (2005). Neurocognitive impairment across the lifespan in schizophrenia: An update. *Schizophrenia Research, 74*(1), 15–26.

Kurtz, M. M., Donato, J., & Rose, J. (2011). Crystallized verbal skills in schizophrenia: relationship to neurocognition, symptoms, and functional status. *Neuropsychology, 25*(6), 784–791.

Kurtz, M. M., & Richardson, C. L. (2012). Social cognitive training for schizophrenia: A meta-analytic investigation of controlled research. *Schizophrenia Bulletin, 38*(5), 1092–1104.

Kurtz, M. M., Seltzer, J. C., Fujimoto, M., Shagan, D. S., & Wexler, B. E. (2009). Predictors of change in life skills in schizophrenia after cognitive remediation. *Schizophrenia Research, 107*(2–3), 267–274.

Levkovitz, Y., Rabany, L., Harel, E. V., & Zangen, A. (2011). Deep transcranial magnetic stimulation add-on for treatment of negative symptoms and cognitive deficits of schizophrenia: A feasibility study. *International Journal of Neuropsychopharmacology, 14*(7), 991–996.

Lewandowski, K. E., Eack, S. M., Hogarty, S. S., Greenwald, D. P., & Keshavan, M. S. (2011). Is cognitive enhancement therapy equally effective for patients with schizophrenia and schizoaffective disorder? *Schizophrenia Research, 125*(2–3), 291–294.

Lindenmayer, J. P., Ozog, V. A., Khan, A., Ljuri, I., Fregenti, S., & McGurk, S. R. (2017). Predictors of response to cognitive remediation in service recipients with severe mental illness. *Psychiatric Rehabilitation Journal, 40*(1), 61–69.

Mausbach, B. T., Moore, R., Bowie, C., Cardenas, V., & Patterson, T. L. (2009). A review of instruments for measuring functional recovery in those diagnosed with psychosis. *Schizophrenia Bulletin, 35*(2), 307–318.

McGurk, S. R., Mueser, K. T., Xie, H., Welsh, J., Kaiser, S., Drake, R. E., et al. (2015). Cognitive enhancement treatment for people with mental illness who do not respond to supported employment: A randomized controlled trial. *American Journal of Psychiatry, 172*(9), 852–861.

McGurk, S. R., Twamley, E. W., Sitzer, D. I., McHugo, G. J., & Mueser, K. T. (2007). A meta-analysis of cognitive remediation in schizophrenia. *American Journal of Psychiatry, 164*(12), 1791–1802.

Medalia, A., & Bowie, C. R. (2016). *Cognitive remediation to improve functional outcomes*. New York: NY: Oxford University Press.

Medalia, A., & Choi, J. (2009). Cognitive remediation in schizophrenia. *Neuropsychology Review, 19*(3), 353–364.

Medalia, A., Erlich, M. D., Soumet-Leman, C., & Saperstein, A. M. (2017). Translating cognitive behavioral interventions from bench to bedside: the feasibility and acceptability of cognitive remediation in research as compared to clinical settings. *Schizophrenia Research, 203*, 49–54.

Medalia, A., Herlands, T., Saperstein, A., & Revheim, N. (2017). *Cognitive remediation for psychological disorders*. New York: NY: Oxford University Press.

Medalia, A., & Richardson, R. (2005). What predicts a good response to cognitive remediation interventions? *Schizophrenia Bulletin, 31*(4), 942–953.

Medalia, A., & Saperstein, A. M. (2013). Does cognitive remediation for schizophrenia improve functional outcomes? *Current Opinion in Psychiatry, 26*(2), 151–157.

Medalia, A., Saperstein, A. M., Erlich, M. D., & Sederer, L. I. (2018). Cognitive remediation in large systems of psychiatric care. *CNS Spectrums, 2*, 1–11.

Medalia, A., Saperstein, A. M., Hansen, M. C., & Lee, S. (2016). Personalised treatment for cognitive dysfunction in individuals with schizophrenia spectrum disorders. *Neuropsychological Rehabilitation, 28*(4), 602–613.

Medalia, A., & Thysen, J. (2008). Insight into neurocognitive dysfunction in schizophrenia. *Schizophrenia Bulletin, 34*(6), 1221–1230.

Mondino, M., Haesebaert, F., Poulet, E., Suaud-Chagny, M. F., & Brunelin, J. (2015). Fronto-temporal transcranial direct current stimulation (tDCS) reduces source-monitoring deficits and auditory hallucinations in patients with schizophrenia. *Schizophrenia Research, 161*(2–3), 515–516.

Murthy, N. V., Mahncke, H., Wexler, B. E., Maruff, P., Inamdar, A., Zucchetto, M., et al. (2012). Computerized cognitive remediation training for schizophrenia: An open label, multi-site, multinational methodology study. *Schizophrenia Research, 139*(1–3), 87–91.

Nordentoft, M., Rasmussen, J. O., Melau, M., Hjorthøj, C. R., & Thorup, A. A. (2014). How successful are first episode programs? A review of the evidence for specialized assertive early intervention. *Current Opinion in Psychiatry, 27*(3), 167–172.

Patel, A., Knapp, M., Romeo, R., Reeder, C., Matthiasson, P., Everitt, B., et al. (2010). Cognitive remediation therapy in schizophrenia: Cost-effectiveness analysis. *Schizophrenia Research, 120*, 217–224.

Reeder, C., Huddy, V., Cella, M., Taylor, R., Greenwood, K., Landau, S., et al. (2017). A new generation computerised metacognitive cognitive remediation programme for schizophrenia (CIRCuiTS): A randomised controlled trial. *Psychological Medicine, 4*, 1–11.

Reeder, C., Pile, V., Crawford, P., Cella, M., Rose, D., Wykes, T., et al. (2015). The feasibility and acceptability to service users of CIRCuiTS, a computerized cognitive remediation therapy programme for schizophrenia. *Behavioural and Cognitive Psychotherapy, 25*, 1–18.

Rougier, N. P., Noelle, D. C., Braver, T. S., Cohen, J. D., & O'Reilly, R. C. (2005). Prefrontal cortex and flexible cognitive control: Rules without symbols. *Proceedings of the National Academy of Sciences of the United States of America, 102*, 7338–7343.

Saperstein, A. M., & Medalia, A. (2016). The role of motivation in cognitive remediation for people with schizophrenia. *Current Topics in Behavioral Neurosciences, 27*, 533–546.

Schmidt, S. J., Mueller, D. R., & Roder, V. (2011). Social cognition as a mediator variable between neurocognition and functional outcome in schizophrenia: Empirical review and new results by structural equation modeling. *Schizophrenia Bulletin, 37*(Suppl. 2), S41–S54.

Soumet-Lehman, C., Erlich, M., & Medalia, A. (2018). Acceptability and perceived effectiveness of cognitive remediation in real-world clinical practice. *Psychiatric Services, 69*, 493–494.

Tas, C., Brown, E. C., Esen-Danaci, A., Lysaker, P. H., & Brune, M. (2012). Intrinsic motivation and metacognition as predictors of learning potential in patients with remitted schizophrenia. *Journal of Psychiatric Research, 46*(8), 1086–1092.

Thomas, M. L., Green, M. F., Hellemann, G., Sugar, C. A., Tarasenko, M., Calkins, M. E., et al. (2017). Modeling deficits from early auditory information processing to psychosocial functioning in schizophrenia. *JAMA Psychiatry, 74*(1), 37–46.

Tsapekos, D., Taylor, R., & Cella, M. (2017). Feasibility and acceptability of a brief cognitive remediation targeting metacognition in acute inpatients with psychosis: A case series. *Neuropsychological Rehabilitation, 20*, 1–15.

Ventura, J., Subotnik, K. L., Ered, A., Gretchen-Doorly, D., Hellemann, G. S., Vaskinn, A., et al. (2014). The relationship of attitudinal beliefs to negative symptoms, neurocognition, and daily functioning in recent-onset schizophrenia. *Schizophrenia Bulletin, 40*(6), 1308–1318.

Vinogradov, S., Fisher, M., & de Villers-Sidani, E. (2012). Cognitive training for impaired neural systems in neuropsychiatric illness. *Neuropsychopharmacology, 37*, 43–76.

Vita, A., Deste, G., De Peri, L., Barlati, S., Poli, R., Cesana, B. M., et al. (2013). Predictors of cognitive and functional improvement and normalization after cognitive remediation in patients with schizophrenia. *Schizophrenia Research, 150*(1), 51–57.

Wilk, C. M., Gold, J. M., McMahon, R. P., Humber, K., Iannone, V. N., & Buchanan, R. W. (2005). No, it is not possible to be schizophrenic yet neuropsychologically normal. *Neuropsychology, 19* (6), 778–786.

Wykes, T., Huddy, V., Cellard, C., McGurk, S. R., & Czobor, P. (2011). A meta-analysis of cognitive remediation for schizophrenia: Methodology and effect sizes. *American Journal of Psychiatry, 168*(5), 472–485.

Wykes, T., Reeder, C., Landau, S., Matthiasson, P., Haworth, E., & Hutchinson, C. (2009). Does age matter? Effects of cognitive rehabilitation across the age span. *Schizophrenia Research, 113*(2–3), 252–258.

Ziemann, U. (2005). Improving disability in stroke with RTMS. *Lancet Neurology, 4*(8), 454–455.

Definition of Key Terms

Bridging groups Bridging groups are verbal discussion groups composed of the clients who are taking part in cognitive remediation. The content of these groups, which can be broadly divided into metacognitive and skill building, is intended to bridge the work on restorative cognitive exercises to cognitive activity as applied in real world settings. In addition to providing a different, social context for cognitive skill building, bridging group discussion offers opportunities for clients to exchange ideas and build social supports.

Cognitive deficits A reduction or loss in basic perceptual and cognitive processes compared to the population norm or premorbid state.

Cognitive remediation 'Cognitive remediation is a behavioral training intervention targeting cognitive deficit (attention, memory, executive function, social cognition, or metacognition), using scientific principles of learning, with the ultimate goal of improving functional outcomes. Its effectiveness is enhanced when provided in a context (formal or informal) that provides support and opportunity for extending to everyday functioning' (Defined by the Cognitive Remediation Expert Working Group, 2012).

Functional outcome Functional outcome distinguishes itself from clinical outcome, with a focus on an individual's recovery in areas such as vocational, educational, and social functioning rather than symptom resolution.

Generalisation Generalisation is the process of transferring skills from one setting to another. In cognitive remediation, generalisation occurs when a cognitive skill or strategy practiced in-session is applied to a real-world task.

CHAPTER 18

Promoting Psychosocial Functioning and Recovery in Schizophrenia Spectrum and Other Psychotic Disorders

Olga Santesteban-Echarri*, Simon Rice[†,‡], César González-Blanch[§], Mario Alvarez-Jimenez[†,‡]

*Hotchkiss Brain Institute, Mathison Centre for Mental Health Research & Education, University of Calgary, Calgary, AB, Canada, [†]Centre for Youth Mental Health, University of Melbourne, Melbourne, VIC, Australia, [‡]Orygen, The National Centre of Excellence in Youth Mental Health, Parkville, VIC, Australia, [§]University Hospital Marqués de Valdecilla-IDIVAL, Santander, Spain

Key Learning Objectives

- Learn about the primary components and effectiveness of psychosocial interventions for psychosis.
- Become familiar with specific adaptations of social skills training for youth with psychosis.
- Increase awareness of interventions that integrate new technologies to maximise social recovery.
- Critically evaluate studies of psychosocial interventions targeting different stage of illness.

INTRODUCTION

Although the positive (i.e. delusions and hallucinations), negative (i.e. anhedonia or avolition) and disorganised symptoms (i.e. bizarre thinking) are distinct features of schizophrenia and related psychotic disorders, a decline in everyday functioning and quality of life is one of the core deficits of the illness (Harvey, Heaton, et al., 2012; Harvey, McClure, et al., 2012; Harvey & Strassnig, 2012; see Box 18.1 for a case example). Social functioning comprises essential skills required to successfully live in society, such as independent living (e.g. cleaning,

Decline in social functioning is a core difficulty observed in people with schizophrenia spectrum disorders.

A Clinical Introduction to Psychosis. https://doi.org/10.1016/B978-0-12-815012-2.00018-3

Box 18.1 Case Study: TJ[a]

TJ is a Caucasian 21-year-old male. *Role functioning*: TJ started his second year at college in September, studying a major in economics and minor in Spanish. Throughout the previous year, TJ had A's and B+ grades on average. However, TJ reports that he recently commenced smoking cannabis often and playing video games all night with his roommate. With his sleeping pattern inversed, he spent most of the day sleeping. Accordingly, he missed several assignments and his grades starting dropping. He felt his mood was very low and did not want to interact with classmates or lecturers to follow up with the assignments. TJ stated, 'I felt as though I lost all my motivation'. TJ was employed 1 day a week in the university sports center helping with the gear rental. In February, he began a leave of absence from work because 'it was too stressful and I had to deal with too many students'.

Social functioning: TJ reports having several friends at the beginning of the year (around 10 close friends and multiple acquaintances). TJ was living on a dorm, where he shared a room with a friend. TJ was also part of a fraternity and the soccer team, seeing his friends out of college multiple times a week. TJ had been in a relationship with his girlfriend for nearly 2 years. However, TJ felt that due to his low mood, he began to push people away. He stated that he went from having a large group of friends to one close friend, his roommate, with whom he smoked cannabis on a daily basis. Because friends insisted in trying to hang out with him, TJ had some significant conflict with them. Moreover, TJ stated that his friendship with his roommate drifted after a fight regarding personal space and TJ's suspiciousness regarding his belief of hidden cameras in the room. TJ also shared that he had problems with his girlfriend, as he believed that she had been unfaithful. As such, things became 'rocky', and conflict increased between TJ and his partner. He reports that those months were very stressful, and now TJ and his partner are currently on a break. TJ explains that he feels he has lost interest in dating.

After progressive isolation, growing loneliness, and withdrawal from studies and work, TJ moved back to his family home. Now he lives with his parents, although these relationships are also difficult. TJ reports that they forced him to leave college as a means to control him and spy on him, as his bedroom 'is not exactly as it used to be'. He is sure that his parents have installed cameras in the room, and he tries to avoid contact with his parents as much as possible. TJ currently spends most of his time alone playing video games, rarely leaving his room.

[a]This is a hypothetical example.

hygiene, cooking, etc.), engaging in social relationships (e.g. social skills), and abilities in education and work (Lecomte, Corbière, & Briand, 2008). The impairment of day-to-day functioning accompanying psychotic illness accounts for much of the social, personal, and economic burden (Trautmann, Rehm, & Wittchen, 2016). Societal costs of poor psychosocial outcome in schizophrenia are estimated in billions per year, signalling a pressing public health concern (Trautmann et al., 2016; Wu et al., 2005). It is critical to understand the mechanisms that lead to poor functional recovery.

Poor psychosocial functioning may be a cause, correlate, or consequence of illness in people with psychosis.

There are several hypothesised pathways to poor psychosocial functioning in schizophrenia, which are not mutually exclusive. One model states that poor psychosocial functioning may be an early indicator of a neurodevelopmental and chronic illness—probably of genetic origin (Harvey, Heaton, et al., 2012; Harvey, McClure, et al., 2012). Because psychosocial impairment is usually observed before the onset of illness, this would support the theory. An alternative explanation is that psychosocial functioning could be the consequence of factors related to the onset of illness (i.e. anxiety, depression, stigma, substance use, and a decrease in socialisation; Killackey & Yung, 2007). There is evidence supporting this view, as psychosocial functioning deteriorates at the same time as symptoms of psychosis develop (from hereon we will use the term psychosis to comprise schizophrenia and schizophrenia spectrum disorders). Poor functioning is also observed accompanying subthreshold symptoms in the prodromal phase of psychosis, with youth at clinical high risk for psychosis showing poorer social functioning than healthy controls (Addington et al., 2011). Accordingly, psychosocial functioning could be improved after treating these associated symptoms. Cornblatt et al. (2003) suggested a neurodevelopmental model proposing that the well-known vulnerability for psychosis comprises deficits in four—necessary but not sufficient—domains: Cognitive-Affective-Social-Isolation-School/work problems (referred to as the 'CASIS' cluster). From this view, deficits in these domains are a precondition for the development of psychotic disorders, particularly schizophrenia, and positive symptoms are an independent process that would progress to a chronic course of illness (i.e. schizophrenia) in the presence of deficits in CASIS.

The stability of poor functioning over the course of illness remains a critical clinical concern. Although the majority of first-episode psychosis (FEP) individuals (around 75%) achieve remission of their positive symptoms after antipsychotic medication (Cassidy, Norman, Manchanda, Schmitz, & Malla, 2010), functional recovery does not occur in the same way. One of the frequent consequences of the onset of psychosis is a downward spiral of loneliness and disconnection from the community and peers, interruption of hobbies and school, and difficulties in work-related activities directly affecting long-term well-being (Penn, Waldheter, Perkins, Mueser, & Lieberman, 2005). FEP youth may remain isolated with poor social functioning (Lieberman et al., 1993). Specifically, FEP youth have smaller support systems (Macdonald, Hayes, & Baglioni, 2000), social networks (i.e. youth are 5–9 times less likely to have close friends compared with their healthy controls counterparts; Morgan et al., 2008), and they report feeling lonely 35% of the time (Sündermann, Onwumere, Kane, Morgan, & Kuipers, 2014).

Loneliness and social isolation are common in people with, or at increased risk for, psychotic disorders.

Symptom remission helps short-term functional recovery, but it is not enough, nor necessary (Alvarez-Jimenez et al., 2012). Because functional recovery is not usually achieved with symptom remission after antipsychotic medication, poor functioning often remains stable from illness onset (Cornblatt et al., 2003). In fact, less than 15% of individuals with psychosis show adequate functioning 5 years after the first episode of illness (Patterson, Moscona, McKibbin, Davidson, & Jeste, 2001). For example, the majority of individuals with schizophrenia do not achieve normative milestones in self-care, work, and social functioning such as marriage or stable relationships (Harvey & Bellack, 2009); most have markedly reduced social networks (Patterson et al., 1997), and limited socially oriented activities. Moreover, competence in social skills is usually impaired in individuals with schizophrenia (Patterson et al., 2001). Additionally, a feature of poor functioning comprises socially disruptive behaviour (i.e. intrusive requests, inappropriate questions and comments, impairment in the tone or volume of voice, speech deficits, and impaired judgement of interpersonal distance; Harvey, Heaton, et al., 2012; Harvey, McClure, et al., 2012). Furthermore, not only the quality and quantity of interactions are reduced, the motivation to interact (i.e. social motivation) is also greatly diminished.

PSYCHOSOCIAL INTERVENTIONS FOR IMPROVING FUNCTIONING IN PSYCHOSIS AND SCHIZOPHRENIA SPECTRUM DISORDERS

In general, while pharmacological interventions are effective in reducing positive symptoms, these are not considered the first-line treatment for enhancing social functioning in individuals with psychosis (Alvarez-Jimenez et al., 2016). Moreover, randomised controlled trials (RCTs) of antipsychotic drugs have usually neglected to report on social functioning outcomes (i.e. social performance, social interaction, and interpersonal skills). Out of the few pharmacological studies reporting on functioning, results are contradictory. One study found that an 8-week intervention for individuals with schizophrenia treated with both quetiapine and risperidone resulted in a medium-to-large improvement of social functioning (Harvey, Patterson, Potter, Zhong, & Brecher, 2006). Nevertheless, another RCT reported that the use of both risperidone and clozapine only marginally improved social functioning (Bellack et al., 2004). Given this, psychosocial interventions are indicated for addressing functioning deficits as a complementary intervention to medication.

Social skills training is based in learning theory and typically implemented in groups.

The development of psychological interventions to improve social functioning began in the 1970s in the context of deinstitutionalisation. Interventions known as social skills training (SST) were implemented. The term 'skills'—compared to the term 'abilities'—indicates that these interventions are primarily grounded in learning experiences. Therefore, SST uses behaviour therapy and learning theory principles for teaching individuals to improve their communication skills. These theories postulate that acquisition of new behaviours is easier when observing others. Therefore, these interventions focused on interpersonal difficulties and comprised several behavioural techniques (i.e. modelling, role playing, instructions, coaching, and feedback of social abilities) illustrated in more detail in Table 18.1 and Fig. 18.1. SST usually follows a group format, where techniques are learned and practiced throughout the sessions. Learning theory posits that only successful utilisation of social skills in real life will strengthen the individual's social competence. Thus, as an indirect result of the training and mastering of social skills, there can be an improvement in self-esteem, self-efficacy, mood, optimism, and self-confidence (Kopelowicz, Liberman, & Zarate, 2006). Although initial reviews of SST interventions available until the 1980s concluded that social anxiety was improved in individuals with schizophrenia, social functioning was not as improved and one of the limitations attributed to these interventions was the lack of generalisation to real-life circumstances (Wallace et al., 1980).

Table 18.1 Common Social Skills Training Techniques

Skill	Procedure
Problem identification	To recognise and determine barriers and obstacles that are preventing the individual from achieving personal goals.
Goal setting	To produce a list of short-term objectives, which will help to achieve the principal goal. Specific steps (i.e. behaviours) need to be specified for successful achievement of the short-term objective.
Role playing	Also known as 'behavioural rehearsal'. To learn, demonstrate, and improve nonverbal, verbal, and paralinguistic skills (i.e. gestures, body language, facial expressions, tone and pitch of voice) through a social interaction.
Positive/ corrective feedback	Feedback focusing on the quality rather on the quantity of the behaviours shown.
Social modelling	The therapists (or other individuals from the group) show the interpersonal behaviour chosen and the individual learns it vicariously (i.e. learning behaviours through observation of reward and negative feedback to others, rather than through direct experience).
Behavioural practice	To repeat the skills until the conversation and the interaction with others reaches a quality level similar to that needed for a successful interaction in the real-world situation.
Positive reinforcement/ problem solving	Employed at the end of the session based on the performance of the individual during the session. Reinforcement of the behaviours increases the likelihood to be initiated and repeated in the future, with communication skills will increasing over time.
Positive social reinforcement	The therapist and other group members praise all the skills that demonstrated an improvement. The praise is always contingent to the behaviour.
Homework assignments	To rehearse the learned skills in real-life situations. This serves as a motivation and as practice to implement the communication skills to achieve the personal goals.
General steps on social skills training:	STEP 1 • RATIONALE • Why is important to learn it STEP 2 • STEPS • Create smaller objectives/steps STEP 3 • DEMONSTRATION • The terapists models the skill STEP 4 • ROLE-PLAY • Practice the skill with other group members STEP 5 • FEEDBACK • Praise and suggestions for improvement STEP 6 • PRACTICE • Use the skills in real-life situations

Adapted from Kopelowicz, A., Liberman, R. P., & Zarate, R. (2006). Recent advances in social skills training for schizophrenia. *Schizophrenia Bulletin, 32*(Suppl. 1) S12–S23.

A systematic review and metaanalysis of generic or traditional SST programs for schizophrenia performed by the Cochrane Database of Systematic Reviews team (Almerie et al., 2015) included 13 RCTs ($n = 975$ participants). The review concluded that individuals allocated to a SST program had better social functioning and quality of life than those allocated to standard care. However, when

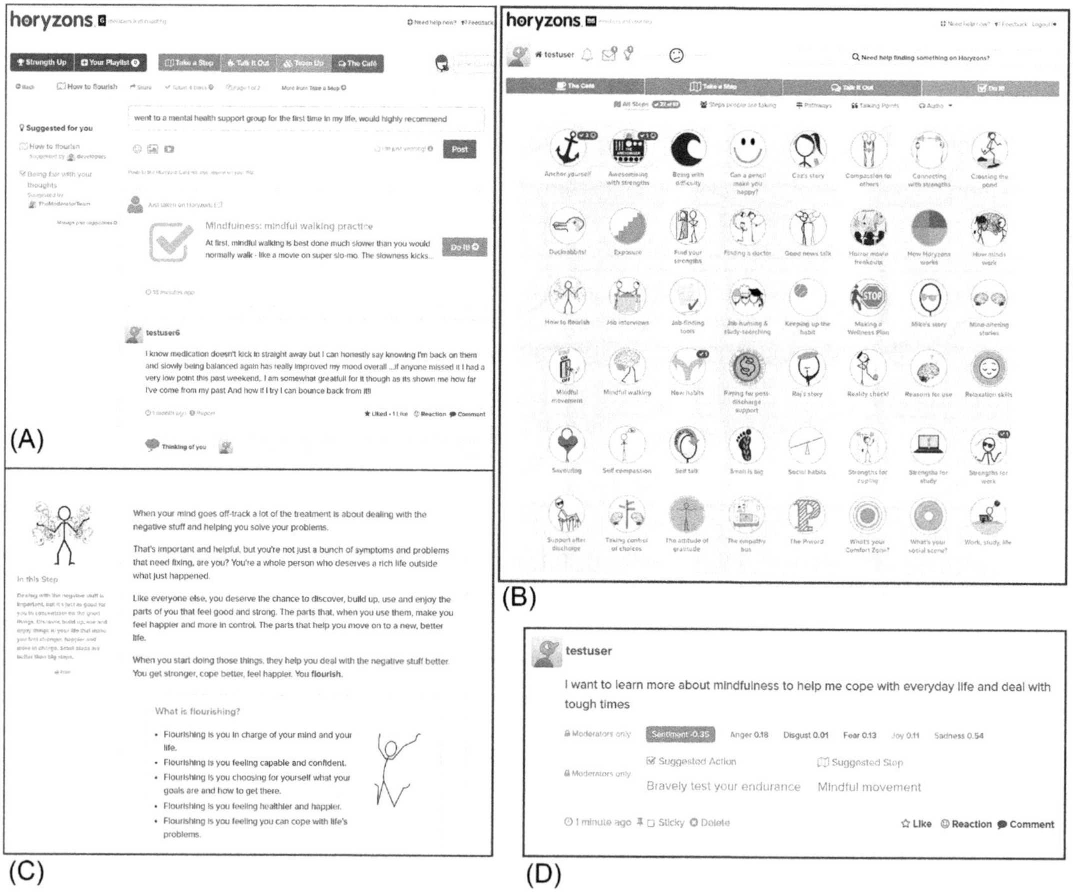

FIG. 18.1

HORYZON's examples. (A) HORYZON's main page, The Café newsfeed; (B) the Steps page, where users can browse steps; (C) example of a part of a step, 'How to Flourish'; and (D) example of a suggested Step based on a comment. Adapted from Santesteban-Echarri, O., Álvarez-Jiménez, M., Gleeson, J., & Rice, S. M. (2018). Social media interventions for adolescents and young people with depression and psychosis. In M. A. Moreno & A. Radovic (Eds.), *Technology and adolescent mental health* (pp. 187–205). Cham, Switzerland: Springer International Publishing.

compared to a nonspecific social intervention (i.e. a discussion group), there was no evidence that SST programs were superior for either social functioning or quality of life. Although SST seemed to improve social functioning, evidence was limited, and data quality was rated as low.

Contemporary social recovery interventions encompass social cognitive-perceptual processes.

Since the original SST conceptualisation, a broader range of interventions can be included within the umbrella of a more contemporary definition of SST (i.e. including social cognition; Horan et al., 2009), from now on termed *social recovery interventions* (SRI). Contrasting with the techniques employed by cognitive remediation, which focus on improving neuropsychological factors (i.e. executive functioning, attention, or memory), SRI focuses on social perception and social cognition processes (Horan et al., 2009). Furthermore, SRI may include some cognitive-behavioural therapy (CBT) techniques (Granholm, Holden, Link, & McQuaid, 2014) adapted to the group format (i.e. cognitive restructuring), as well as life skills management, psychoeducation, and relapse prevention plans (Patterson et al., 2006; Xiang et al., 2007). The latest metaanalytic review of SRI comprised SST and related interventions for psychosis (Turner et al., 2017) including 27 RCTs ($n = 1437$ participants). The authors developed a SST subtyping with a description of four types of SST based on the available evidence. Table 18.2 summarises the types of SRI intervention and presents the studies included in each one.

Effect sizes for current social recovery interventions are small to nonsignificant.

The main results of the metaanalysis on social performance outcome (Turner et al., 2017) showed that when combining all comparator therapies (i.e. CBT, psychoeducation, supportive counselling, befriending, and occupational therapy), there was a positive significant small effect of SRI on improving social functioning (Hedge's g between 0.33 and 0.37). This effect, however, lost significance as power decreased and risk of bias increased. Moreover, SRI was not superior to treatment as usual (TAU) or active control conditions (AC), and significant

Statistical power is a measure of the likelihood of finding statistical significance in a sample if the effect exists in the full population.

Table 18.2 Types of Contemporary Social Skill Training Interventions for Schizophrenia

Type of social recovery intervention
■ **Generic social skills training (SST)**: The SST interventions are consistent with the original SST models from the 1980s. Based on social learning theories and behaviourally oriented, therapists engage individuals with schizophrenia in interpersonal training group sessions. Through modelling, practice, and group feedback, skills trained comprise verbal and nonverbal communication, assertiveness, learning appropriate responses to social situations, and stress reduction skills.
■ **Cognitive-behavioural skills training (CBSST):** These interventions integrate generic SST with CBT techniques (i.e. behavioural experiments, cognitive restructuring, or challenging negative thoughts) through three modules (i.e. social skills, problem solving, and CBT).
■ **Social-cognitive skills training (SCST):** These interventions are therapy-led behavioural or reflective interventions, which focus on social cognitive processes (different from cognitive remediation). These interventions may include videos or computer programs to enhance social responses learning and may follow a drill-and-repeat skill practice, heuristic rehearsal, skills practice, and homework assignments.
■ **University of California Los Angeles—Functional adaptive skills training based (UCLA-FAST):** These interventions integrate generic SST with relapse prevention, psychoeducation, and daily self-management activities (i.e. independent travelling or medication management) to generalise the skills learnt to real-life circumstances throughout a more practical skill-based training.

Adapted from Turner, D. T., McGlanaghy, E., Cuijpers, P., Van Der Gaag, M., Karyotaki, E., & MacBeth, A. (2017). A meta-analysis of social skills training and related interventions for psychosis. *Schizophrenia Bulletin, 44*(3), 475–491.

heterogeneity was noted across studies. Nevertheless, SRI demonstrated better effects than any pooled comparator, TAU, and AC for negative symptoms.

Furthermore, other combinations of multiple treatment approaches have attempted to enhance SRI results and functional outcome. Integrated Psychological Therapy (IPT) comprises social skills and problem solving training, social cognition, and neurocognitive remediation with the ultimate goal of achieving a successful psychosocial rehabilitation and social competence in schizophrenia (Roder, Brenner, & Kienzle, 2002; Roder, Brenner, Kienzle, & Hodel, 1988). IPT is manualised and follows five sequential programs, namely: (1) neurocognition (e.g. memory, attention, or cognitive flexibility) where individuals learn alternative strategies through repetitive training and practice of group interactive exercises (Krabbendam & Aleman, 2003); (2) social cognition (e.g. emotional expression, and emotional and social perception); (3) interpersonal communication (e.g. executive functioning or verbal fluency); (4) interpersonal skills (e.g. role play); and (5) problem solving. An Individual's difficulties and strengths shape the target goals of each subprogram (Roder et al., 2002). IPT, originally developed in Germany has since been translated into 10 languages, and it has been broadly disseminated over Europe (Roder, Mueller, Mueser, & Brenner, 2006).

A metaanalytic review of IPT for schizophrenia (Roder et al., 2006) included 30 studies ($n=1393$ participants). IPT was more effective in improving psychosocial functioning ($d=0.34$), symptoms ($d=0.31$), and neurocognition ($d=0.40$) than the control comparison, showing a small but significant effect size for each domain. Importantly, these effect sizes, favouring IPT, were maintained over an average period of 8 months at follow-up. Results were similar across different settings (outpatient or inpatient; community or research), phases of illness (chronic or acute), and type of assessment (self-report or expert rating). A subsample of seven high-quality studies ($n=362$ participants) confirmed the results for each domain suggesting that IPT could be an effective SRI to improve social recovery for people with schizophrenia.

The review by Turner et al. (2017) concluded that SRI should be used in routine mental health care for negative symptoms. However, future research should disentangle these mechanisms of action to provide greater insight into the pathways involved between negative symptoms and social functioning.

EARLY INTERVENTION AND PSYCHOLOGICAL INTERVENTIONS FOR IMPROVING FUNCTIONING IN FIRST-EPISODE PSYCHOSIS

The interventions described here focus on individuals with established schizophrenia and psychotic-related disorders. However, difficulties with social functioning start early, often at the onset of illness and even earlier, at the prodromal phase of the illness (i.e. clinical high-risk for psychosis, CHR), where social functioning deficits are pervasive (Addington, Penn, Woods,

Addington, & Perkins, 2008). Moreover, social functioning deficits are a strong predictor of transition to psychosis (Fusar-Poli et al., 2010), and lead to poor long-term outcomes (Lieberman et al., 1993; Penn et al., 2005). Despite this evidence, only a few studies have developed interventions to target social functioning as the main treatment outcome for people in FEP or CHR. Due to the focus of the chapter examining schizophrenia spectrum and psychotic disorders, we will only cover the evidence related to the former.

Social functioning deficits significantly predict transition to psychosis.

Following the Cognitive Behavioural Social Skills Training (CBSST) model (see Table 18.2), a pilot study ($n = 22$; mean age: 25) adapted social skills training in combination with CBT for younger, FEP youth to test the feasibility of CBSST for this population (Herman, Shireen, Bromley, Yiu, & Granholm, 2016). Audiovisual information (i.e. from popular TV shows such as *The Big Bang Theory*), behavioural examples, and activities were youth-centred. Modules were completed only once to prevent boredom in youth (i.e. individuals with schizophrenia often need repetition due to greater cognitive impairments). Themes covered in depth were stigma and demoralisation. Modular rolling admissions permitted youth to start the group at the beginning of any module. Other than that, the structure remained the same as the original CBSST with three modules (i.e. social skills, problem solving, and CBT) and 18 sessions. Social functioning was the primary outcome (i.e. appearance, hygiene, food preparation, transportation, money management, leisure activities, job seeking and maintenance, and social relationships) measured with the Independent Living Skills Survey (ILSS; Wallace, Liberman, Tauber, & Wallace, 2000). Other outcomes assessed were adaptive functioning, with the Multnomah Community Ability Scale (MCAS; Barker, Barron, McFarland, & Bigelow, 1994), a global level of role and social functioning with the Global Assessment of Functioning Scale (GAF; American Psychiatric Association, 2000), and the setting of operationalised goals with the Goal Attainment Scaling (GAS; Hurn, Kneebone, & Cropley, 2006). The study was feasible and accepted by participants and providers, who referred to enjoyment and change in social functioning because of the group. Participants were able to identify goals to work on and learned to modify unhelpful beliefs, which perpetuate poor functioning. After the intervention, scores on independent living skills, adaptive functioning, global functioning, and goal setting improved significantly (medium-to-large effect size $d = 0.70$), and gains were maintained at 3-month follow-up. Youths learned communication skills directly related to their goals, which, in turn, may enhance the motivation to put in practice the learned skills.

A recently published high-quality RCT addressed the treatment outcome gap in early intervention services with the primary goal of enhancing social recovery by including specialised social recovery therapy in the services provided (Fowler et al., 2018). All the participants received care from the early intervention services (i.e. intensive and oriented case management, peer support, supported employment, group intervention, psychiatric medication management, CBT for psychosis and family work). The study randomised 155 participants to social recovery therapy (SRT) + early intervention services (EIS) ($n = 75$; mean age: 24.15) or EIS alone ($n=79$; mean age: 24.84). SRT is a manualised therapy (Fowler et al., 2009; Fowler, French, & Hodgekins, 2013) implemented by accredited CBT therapists delivered in three stages. A minimum of six therapy sessions is needed, to consider it a sufficient therapy dose. The six sessions included the assessment and at least two individual sessions for the formulation of the case and the behavioural experiments. Table 18.3 summarises the content discussed in each stage of the SRT + EIS.

The primary outcome was time spent on social activities such as education, work or voluntary work, sports, leisure, childcare and chores over the past month, measured with an adapted version of the Time Use Survey (Hodgekins et al., 2014). Social functioning was compared to averages of nonclinical groups (i.e. youth aged 16–36 usually engage in 63.5 h/week of structured activities; poor social functioning is considered when engaging in activities less than 30 h/week; Hodgekins et al., 2014). Participants received an average 16.49 sessions of SRT + EIS over 9 months, and there was a large significant increase in structured activities of 8.1 h compared with EIS alone. Clinical benefits (i.e. positive and negative symptoms, depressive and social anxiety symptoms) were also observed. However, a precise interpretation of maintenance of treatment effects was not possible at 15 months due to high attrition of participants, and low statistical power of estimations. Despite the limitations, this is one of the first RCTs reporting improvements in social functioning in a FEP cohort adopting a rigorous study design and methodology. Therefore, provision of high-quality, intensive, and active early intervention services may be the most appropriate model to

Table 18.3 Stages of Social Recovery Therapy in Early Intervention Services

Stage	Therapeutic procedures
Stage 1: Engagement and formulation of the case	▪ Identification of a list of problems. ▪ Assessment of motivation (i.e. previous hopes, goals, and expectations). ▪ Development of day-to day achievable steps.
Stage 2: New activities	▪ Referral to services (i.e. education or community provider, vocational agencies, and sports and social activities) ▪ Cognitive work (i.e. addressing negative beliefs, stigma, and hopelessness). ▪ Behavioural experiments (i.e. management of symptoms).
Stage 3: Social activities	▪ New social activities. ▪ Cognitive work (i.e. enhancing feelings of agency and mastery). ▪ Behavioural experiments are more specific to problems encountered in the social activities. ▪ Therapists visit the youth in the community and social places.

Adapted from Fowler, D., Hodgekins, J., French, P., Marshall, M., Freemantle, N., McCrone, P., ... Birchwood, M. (2018). Social recovery therapy in combination with early intervention services for enhancement of social recovery in patients with first-episode psychosis (SUPEREDEN3): A single-blind, randomised controlled trial. *The Lancet Psychiatry, 5*(1), 41–50.

follow to improve social functioning in the early stages of illness (National Institute for Health and Care Excellence (NICE), 2014).

The new focus on social recovery is also compatible with novel psychological models proposing that targeting positive emotions (Garland et al., 2010) and self-efficacy (Browne et al., 2017; Vaskinn, Ventura, Andreassen, Melle, & Sundet, 2015) improves social functioning in psychosis and FEP. Browne and colleagues proposed an Individual Resiliency Training (IRT) program (based in the NAVIGATE multicomponent intervention; Mueser et al., 2015), which focuses on enhancing resilience and personal strengths in all aspects of treatment to foment well-being and augment self-determination. The primary target of the IRT is to improve quality of life, promote resiliency and client's accomplishment of personal goals through 14 standard main modules and tailored modules. Specifically, modules comprise topics such as strengths and resiliency, and assess goal setting and satisfaction with several life areas. Twenty-four character strengths organised by virtue are assessed with the 24-item Brief Strengths Test (Peterson & Seligman, 2004). The study examined the associations between character strengths and changes in functional recovery outcomes after 6 months of treatment in FEP youth ($n = 105$; mean age: 23.6). Those who viewed themselves as capable of being loved, kind, or socially intelligent had better improvements in well-being. Moreover, greater improvement in interpersonal relationships was noted among those who viewed themselves as a leader, fair person, and a citizen. It seems that early intervention programs, which focus in enhancing the personal strengths of FEP youth and utilise integrative psychosocial therapies (comprising SRI and CBT at least) for functional recovery, may help to increase the number of structured activities and improve subsequent communication skills, interpersonal relationships, independent living skills, and global functioning.

ONLINE, SOCIAL MEDIA, AND MOBILE-BASED TECHNOLOGIES TO MAXIMISE SOCIAL RECOVERY

More recently, novel interventions that combine online, social media, and mobile-based technology integrated with evidence-based interventions have arisen with the primary goal of targeting social functioning and maximising social recovery.

Consistent with the moderated online social therapy (MOST) model (Lederman, Wadley, Gleeson, Bendall, & Alvarez-Jimenez, 2014; Wadley, Lederman, Gleeson, & Alvarez-Jimenez, 2013), the HORYZONS study (developed by our group in Melbourne, Australia; see Alvarez-Jimenez et al., 2013, 2019; Gleeson et al., 2014; Lederman et al., 2014) has been designed to improve long-term outcomes in FEP youth. Following participatory design principles (Schuler & Namioka, 1993), HORYZONS was developed iteratively through a process of testing and systematic feedback with focus groups of FEP individuals and clinicians. HORYZONS comprises (1) individually personalised interactive therapeutic content, (2) peer-to-peer social networking, and (3) peer and professional moderation through positive psychology principles (Seligman, Rashid, & Parks, 2006), self-determination theory principles (Ryan & Deci, 2000), and the supportive accountability model (Mohr, Cuijpers, & Lehman, 2011). Over a 1-month pilot study ($n = 20$; age: 15–25), the HORYZONS intervention was found to be feasible, acceptable, safe, and engaging among FEP youth. Seventy percent of users used the system for at least 3 weeks, and 95% engaged in the social networking (SN) features and reported feeling more socially connected. Moreover, results of the study indicated a significant reduction in depression symptoms at 1-month follow-up, explicitly in those with a more frequent utilisation of the website (Alvarez-Jimenez et al., 2013). It is important to note that online environments sometimes may intensify symptoms such as suspiciousness that characterise youth with FEP (Nitzan, Shoshan, Lev-ran, & Fennig, 2011). However, youth reported feeling safe, and there was no inappropriate use of the platform or adverse events reported during the study. This highlights the importance of safety measures due to the vulnerability of youth recovering from psychosis. First, the online SN was password protected. Second, the moderation by expert clinicians, who offered close monitoring and intervention for any signs of deterioration, was the primary reason youth gave for feeling safe within the HORYZONS platform (Gleeson et al., 2014).

Safety measures are an important feature of online or mobile interventions for social recovery.

As described in an example in Santesteban-Echarri, Álvarez-Jiménez, Gleeson, and Rice (2018), in HORYZONS there is Facebook-style newsfeed Café page that serves as each user's main page, where users can share experiences, write posts, react to posts from other users, give and obtain support, and gain different viewpoints and validation (see Fig. 18.1A). Another important feature of the platform is the therapy content, where suggestions are made by the moderators in addition to posts promoting 'popular' therapy content taken by other users appearing in the newsfeed. Therapy content is ordered in Steps (i.e. interactive therapy modules with increased difficulty designed to exercise and develop a range of psychological skills, as shown in Fig. 18.1B). For instance, Fig. 18.1C illustrates one Step 'How to Flourish'. Users can read the content, apply the knowledge learned in their lives, or interact with the content and contribute to a 'mini-newsfeed' by commenting on a Talking Point. Once the Step is completed, users can feed back into The Café by sharing a link to the Step or rating the Step and sharing this rating with a message. Finally, based on previous steps and comments from users, the system suggests other relevant Steps the user might like to try (see Fig. 18.1D; D'Alfonso et al., 2017).

The use of an integrated SN with peer support, expert moderation, and therapy content may enhance empowerment and social connectedness in FEP youth. The question remains however as to whether increased online social interaction may facilitate social functioning in other domains. While promising, the findings from the pilot study need to be confirmed. A major 5-year RCT of the HORYZONS platform has currently finalised at Orygen, The National Centre of Excellence in Youth Mental Health, Australia (protocol available, see Alvarez-Jimenez et al., 2019). The HORYZONS RCT is an 18-month single-blind, parallel groups

Key issue: The ecological validity of online and mobile psychosocial interventions is not yet established.

study with 170 FEP youth (age: 16–27) allocated to early intervention services (EIS) or EIS + HORYZONS. After a 40-month recruitment and 18-month intervention phase, recruitment was finalised in January 2017. The primary outcome at 18-month follow-up is social functioning assessed by the Personal and Social Performance Scale (PSP; Nasrallah, Morosini, & Gagnon, 2008) and the First Episode Social Functioning Scale (FESFS; Lecomte et al., 2014). Furthermore, to obtain a dynamic picture of youth's social functioning, the study incorporates a cutting-edge Smartphone Ecological Momentary Assessment (SEMA) application (Gleeson et al., 2017). SEMA delivers random surveys every 90 min over a 12-h period for 7 days after each assessment time point (i.e. baseline, 6-, 12-, and 18-months). The application tracks nearly real-time responses regarding social interaction (e.g. 'How much time have you spent interacting with others, since the last survey?'), social isolation (e.g. 'At the moment, how lonely do you feel?'), perceived social efficacy, critical comments, and social rank. There were some feasibility issues identified in the pilot study (i.e. difficulty to measure psychotic relapse with the PANSS via phone or Skype-based assessments) addressed in the RCT by choosing other secondary outcomes. HORYZONS is the first RCT to test an online-based intervention to foster long-term social functioning in FEP, having the potential to augment the benefits of the actual early intervention services for FEP.

VIRTUAL REALITY TECHNOLOGY TO MAXIMISE SOCIAL RECOVERY

One of the key components of any SRI is the practice and application of new skills that would facilitate generalisation of the social behaviours learned. However, opportunities for implementation of new social skills in daily life can be difficult for individuals with psychotic disorders, being one of the most significant limitations of SRI (Kopelowicz et al., 2006). Therefore, to overcome the low generalisation of skills to the day-to-day activities, and lower the costs that would be associated if a clinician tried a naturalistic observation of the skills, researchers have employed new technologies such as virtual reality (VR). VR aims to integrate computer graphics, sound, and sensory outputs in real time to simulate the real world through computer-generated scenarios with which the person can interact (Gregg & Tarrier, 2007). Initial studies using VR in schizophrenia focused on clinical outcomes and positive symptoms (Fornells-Ambrojo et al., 2008; Freeman et al., 2003). Only a few studies have explored the utility of VR for improving other functional outcomes on schizophrenia such as medication management skills (Kurtz, Baker, Pearlson, & Astur, 2007), communication and conversational skills (Ku et al., 2007; Park et al., 2009, 2011), and VR-SST (Rus-Calafell, Gutiérrez-Maldonado, & Ribas-Sabaté, 2014).

Generalisation of social functioning gains from the clinic to everyday life is often limited.

Park et al. (2011) developed a VR program for SST for individuals with schizophrenia and tested it in a RCT ($n=91$; aged 18–45) by comparing VR role playing (SST-VR; $n=46$) to the traditional role playing (SST-TR; $n=45$). SST was administered through 10 bi-weekly 90-min sessions over 5 weeks covering:

(1) conversational skills training (e.g. start, end, and maintain a conversation); (2) assertiveness skills training (e.g. make or reject a request); and (3) emotional expression skills training (e.g. express positive and negative emotions). Both SST groups had four to five members. Homework to practice the skills between sessions was encouraged, and techniques such as therapist modelling, role playing, and feedback were employed in both SST modalities. The only difference between SST modalities was the role playing, with SST-TR using picture, video, modelling and written materials; while the SST-VR employed virtual interactive scenarios and avatars (i.e. the individual can move around with a joystick and 'talk' by choosing multiple-choice answers) and the rest of the group participants observed the interaction through a television monitor. Feedback was provided by the therapist, in both modalities. Social skills were measured in an unstructured role play with 10 scenarios (see Fig. 18.2). Nonverbal behaviours (i.e. voice quality, gesture and position, and conversational properties) were measured with Trower's Social Behavior Scales (SBS; Trower, Bryant, & Argyle, 1978). Assertiveness was measured with the Rathus Assertiveness Schedule (RAS; Rathus, 1973). Interpersonal relationship skills were evaluated with the Relationship Change Scale (RCS; Schlein & Guerney, 1977) and individuals' responses to problem-solving situations were measured with the Social Problem Solving Inventory Revised (SPSI-R; D'Zurilla, Nezu, & Maydeu-Olivares, 2002). Results showed that participants in the SST-VR had higher motivation and

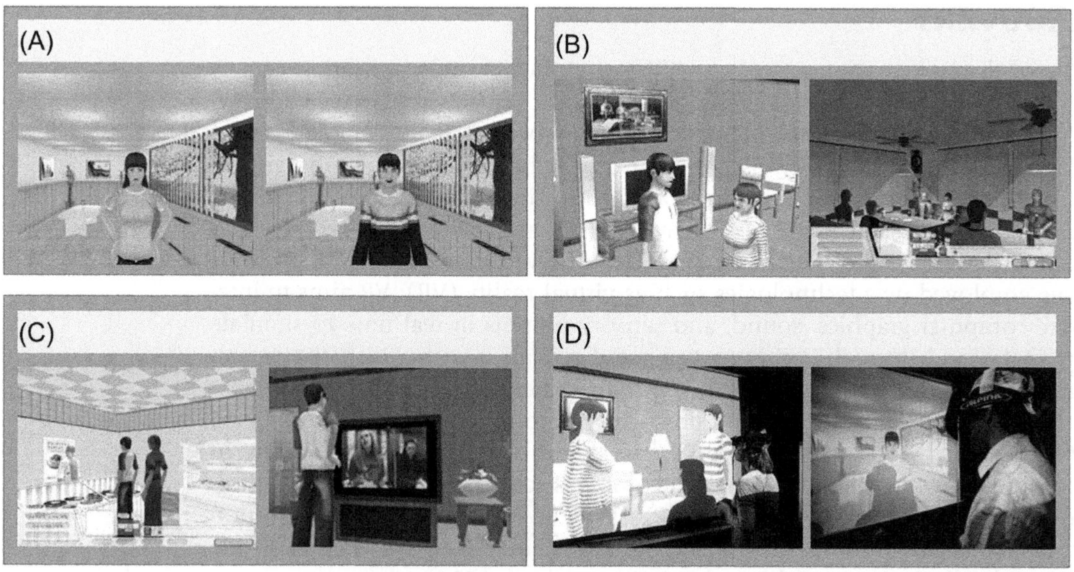

FIG. 18.2

Examples of SST with VR role plays. (A) Conversation skills training, (B) assertiveness skills training, (C) emotion expression skills training, and (D) examples of training sessions. From Park, K. M., Ku, J., Choi, S. H., Jang, H. J., Park, J. Y., Kim, S. I., et al. (2011). A virtual reality application in role-plays of social skills training for schizophrenia: A randomized, controlled trial. *Psychiatry Research, 189*(2), 166–172.

participation rates than those in the SST-TR modality. There were no differences between modalities in overall social skills as both groups improved significantly postintervention. However, conversational skills (i.e. use of social reinforcements, response length, and turn taking) were better in the SST-VR group, whereas nonverbal skills (i.e. posture, proximity, and gaze) were better in the SST-TR group. Importantly, providing feedback to the SST-VR group regarding their nonverbal skills was difficult for therapists due to the head-mounted display (HMD) that participants were wearing. Participants of the SST-VR group scored higher in assertiveness and reported feeling less anxious and with more control and power when interacting with avatars instead of a real person.

Rus-Calafell et al. (2014) developed a VR integrated program *Soskitrain* (see Fig. 18.3) to train social skills and improve generalisation of learned behaviours in the real world in individuals with a diagnosis of schizophrenia or schizoaffective disorder ($n=12$; age: 18–55). After four preliminary sessions (i.e. orientation, familiarisation with the program, demo projection, and program instructions), the program followed 16 individual 1-h sessions twice a week with a manual for at-home practice. Each session was divided into 30 min of skills

FIG. 18.3
Examples of *Soskitrain* scenarios. From Rus-Calafell, M., Gutiérrez-Maldonado, J., & Ribas-Sabaté, J. (2014). A virtual reality-integrated program for improving social skills in patients with schizophrenia: A pilot study. *Journal of Behavior Therapy and Experimental Psychiatry, 45*(1), 81–89.

content, and 30 min of VR practice. Seven target skills with increased difficulty (Kopelowicz et al., 2006) were trained: (1) social perception; (2) processing social information; (3) responding and sending skills; (4) affiliative skills; (5) assertive communication; (6) instrumental role skills; and (7) conversational skills. Participants could interact with virtual avatars and received positive or negative feedback. The clinician had access to the number of errors, time employed in a conversation, and percentage of accurate assertive behaviours. Outcomes of interest were social performance and anxiety, measured with the Assertion Inventory (AI; Gambrill & Richey, 1975), the Simulated Social Interaction Test (SSIT; Curran, 1982), and the Social Avoidance and Distress Scale (SADS; Watson & Friend, 1969); and social functioning, measured with the Social Functioning Scale (SFS; Birchwood, Smith, Cochrane, Wetton, & Copestake, 1990). Results showed a decrease in social avoidance and an improvement in social skills (i.e. withdrawal, interpersonal communication, prosocial activities, and recreation) after the VR-SST, and these improvements were maintained at 4-month follow-up. Although social anxiety and social discomfort improved after the VR-SST, the improvement was not maintained at 4-month follow-up. Finally, a pattern of learning in assertive behaviours and emotion perception was observed.

Some common limitations of these novel studies using VR technology are the small sample size, lack of blinded raters, and with some exceptions (i.e. Park et al., 2011), there is still a scarcity of controlled designs. VR seems to motivate individuals with schizophrenia, and due to its less anxiety-provoking virtual environment, it can be a good starting point to engage individuals in a more extended SRI. However, VR is not refined enough to improve some important social skills yet (i.e. nonverbal behaviours). Moreover, VR technology is still expensive, and scenarios are not as flexible as face-to-face role plays from SRI. Although we cannot conclude that VR could replace SRI, it seems a promising and useful additional therapeutic tool for improving social functioning in individuals with schizophrenia.

Another novel approach improving social functioning recovery in individuals with schizophrenia could be through games played consistently in therapy time (i.e. in a day-hospital). Although there are some games available for prompting conversations for individuals with schizophrenia, these are not current anymore, and only focus on a very specific skill of an SRI (Favrod, Aillon, & Bardoit, 1995; Liberman, 1972). The game *The Train* (Torres, Mendez, Merino, & Moran, 2002) is a program of rehabilitation, which reproduces a railway trip in which participants run into unanticipated problems that need to be solved when the train reaches each station. Participants play in four teams of two to four participants. The therapist can adapt the game according to the capabilities and deficits of each participant to make it a means of rehabilitation. Through its appealing design, the game combines skills learning through amusement with the primary aim to increase participants' motivation and engagement in the skills acquisition process. Specifically, The Train (60–90 min) comprises 60 modules of SST (main focus), 17 modules of problem solving, 13 modules of coping techniques,

17 modules of psychoeducation, 20 modules of social areas, and 236 problems (i.e. cognitive remediation techniques to improve learning deficits such as questions about memory, calculus, attention, polysemy, construction of sentences, conceptual rankings, and abstract reasoning). Preliminary results ($n=49$; aged 18–50) of the effectiveness of The Train (Torres et al., 2002) have shown good skill acquisition, durability, and generalisation of the learned skills. Participants were randomly assigned to Group 1 ($n=19$; The Train, SST, psychomotor skills training, and occupational therapy), Group 2 ($n=16$; SST, psychomotor skills training, and occupational therapy), or Group 3 ($n=14$; occupational therapy). The main outcome was social functioning measured with the SFS (Birchwood et al., 1990). After 6 months of intervention, the Group 1 improved significantly in social withdrawal, interpersonal functioning, recreational activities, and work. The Group 2 improved significantly in independence, withdrawal, and work; while those from Group 3 improved in work and prosocial activities. It seems that receiving positive feedback from participation in an easy and structured game with clear norms provided greater enhancement in interpersonal functioning. The Train could be a promising motivational tool to be added to other social rehabilitation packages.

FUTURE DIRECTIONS FOR SOCIAL RECOVERY INTERVENTIONS AND SOCIAL FUNCTIONING IMPROVEMENT

Despite social recovery interventions, specifically SST, emerging in the 1980s, these interventions remain in a development phase. New adapted forms of SST, SRI as components of integrated therapies and comprehensive services for new populations of patients, implementing a wide variety of new technologies and in new clinical settings have started to arise. Although SRI seem feasible and acceptable, there remain gaps between theory, practice, and the real-life situations that need to be revisited. Future directions for SRI are indicated here.

Generalisation

One of the major limitations of SRI is the generalisation of skills to the day-to-day of the individuals. Social rehabilitation should integrate factors available in the environment of the individuals (i.e. peer support and community help). However, this movement and shift from the professional to the consumer and community needs to be facilitated by mental health providers (Kopelowicz et al., 2006). One way to make help more available in the community could be by the utilisation of communication technologies. Rather than using technology as a means to provide face-to-face interventions in a digital environment, we can use the best of clinical psychology enhanced by the latest technologies to develop completely new ways of therapy delivery. We have seen some promising examples of the integration of new technologies for the improvement of functional recovery. The potential remains to use chat rooms, the Internet, VR, and mobile-based applications for consultation with professionals, enhancement of social networking, education, and generalisation of skills to the community. Thus, in the following years, researchers and clinicians will likely work in improving the synergy of therapy and technology for the generalisation of social functioning and SRI to enhance personal long-term goals such as enhanced independent living, employment/education, and friendships/dating (Davidson, 2003).

Empowerment and Self-Efficacy

Self-directed recovery of social functioning enhances empowerment and self-efficacy.

We have reviewed examples of highly specialised youth-centred early intervention services, which integrate the patient in the decision-making process of the treatment (Alvarez-Jimenez et al., 2013; Fowler et al., 2018). These intervention services follow an interactive process of decision making and self-directed recovery plan between therapists and individuals with FEP, which seem to work. This would be the ideal therapy process, as it provides the individuals the self-efficacy, empowerment, and self-responsibility regarding their recovery process, in conjunction with professional guidance (Adams & Drake, 2006). However, this is often not the case in centres providing treatment for individuals in a later stage of the illness (i.e. individuals with schizophrenia). It is essential to promote informed decision making among *all* clients. Therefore, one of the traditional SST modules, which covers being proactive and assertive in the interaction with the mental health provider, should be a benchmark of functional recovery interventions systematically implemented (Eckman, Liberman, Phipps, & Blair, 1990).

Integration of Programs

Integrated programs may be best for promoting psychosocial recovery, and require more investigation.

While medication improves symptoms of psychosis, social anxiety and depression are almost always present in psychosis as comorbid disorders. Most of the time, these symptoms are also addressed with medication. However, CBT approaches are usually first-line evidence-based treatments for these symptoms, showing more efficacy than other forms of psychotherapy (Cape, Whittington, Buszewicz, Wallace, & Underwood, 2010; Hofmann & Otto, 2018) and medication (Cuijpers, Andersson, Donker, & Van Straten, 2011). Moreover, although CBT for psychosis focuses on symptoms for the most part, it has been highlighted that the behavioural assignments (i.e. experiments) should be focused on practice and developing social skills (Lecomte & Lecomte, 2002). Therefore, integrative programs (i.e. medication, CBT, IPT, and SST), adapted for specific phases of the illness, seem to be the best approach to improve the broad conjunction of clinical and psychosocial difficulties and augment the efficacy of single-programs in the treatment of psychosis (Herbert et al., 2005; Van Brunt, 2000). An intensive combination of case management and multisystem outreach (i.e. visiting the youth and accompanying and engaging them with services) is essential to boost social recovery; whereas CBT-based interventions are needed to encourage and maintain engagement, and reduce concomitant symptoms, especially among those who have not previously responded to standard treatment (Fowler et al., 2018).

Fidelity of Treatment Delivery and Dissemination

In the US, there has been a slow but important dissemination effort of SRI to therapists since the 1980s. The international dissemination of some SRI modalities has been considerable, including translation into more than 23 languages (i.e. modules of the University of California Los Angeles—UCLA; Liberman et al., 1993). Moreover, SRI seems to be increasingly widely implemented by therapists. As we have reviewed, there are several RCTs focusing on SRI for psychosis exclusively (Liberman, 2007). However, the main difficulty relies on adopting a consensus method of delivery and maintaining a high-fidelity standard to the original interventions, which should be a focus and a goal of future research.

Treatment fidelity: the degree to which an intervention is implemented *as planned*, for all clients, over time.

Identification of Risk Factors of Poor Functional Recovery

Identifying variables associated with poor long-term functioning may help to identify vulnerable individuals who are more likely to have worse functional outcomes. Moreover, this could inform the development of innovative-targeted interventions designed to tackle such mechanisms and therefore, improve functional recovery. Our team examined predictors of functioning in FEP ($n=55$ studies; Santesteban-Echarri et al., 2017). Sociodemographic, clinical, neuroimaging, and physical variables had little impact on long-term functioning. Conversely, duration of untreated psychosis, most cognitive variables, and concurrent remission of positive and negative symptoms were independently related to functional recovery. Because the first 3–5 years after the onset of illness may constitute a critical period in affecting long-term outcome in psychosis (Birchwood, Todd, & Jackson, 1998; Crumlish et al., 2009), it is critical that integrative therapeutic programs focus on enhancing these factors.

CONCLUSIONS

Functional recovery has traditionally been tackled with psychosocial interventions, specifically those focusing on social recovery interventions. SRI seems to have a positive significant effect on improving social functioning, although there is a wide heterogeneity of SRI components. Integration programs combining SRI and CBT, and especially other intensive integrated interventions (IPT or SRI + early intervention services) seem to be more effective overall in improving global functioning than those programs that focus exclusively on social skills training. Specifically, one of the primary limitations of these interventions has been the lack of generalisation of results to the broader day-to-day experience of individuals. The latest research trends, focusing on online, mobile-based, and virtual reality technology to promote functional recovery, have tried to improve generalisation of the skills learned. However, while promising, these interventions require highly specialised multidisciplinary teams to develop the tools, and are still expensive. There is a need for further identification of components of treatment that can be effectively translated to broader (i.e. nonresearch) environments to maximise the generalisation to the real-life lived experience of individuals with psychosis. Finally, new models and well-established theories need to be integrated with the latest technologies to develop novel interventions, which will likely transform the social recovery field.

QUIZ QUESTIONS

1. What is the most common step order in a social skills training (SST) intervention?
   (a) Steps, rationale, role play, demonstration, feedback, and practice.
   (b) Rationale, steps, demonstration, role play, feedback, and practice.
   (c) Demonstration, rationale, steps, role play, practice, and feedback.
   (d) Rationale, steps, demonstration, practice, feedback, and role play.
2. What are the modules of the CBSST program proposed by Granhold et al.?
   (a) Introduction Module, Social Skills module, Problem-Solving Skills Module, and Cognitive Skills Module.
   (b) Behavioural Module, Social Skills Module, Feedback Module, and Cognitive Skills Module.
   (c) Social Skills Module, Cognitive Rehabilitation Module, and Behavioural Module.
   (d) Social Skills Module, Behavioural Module, and Problem-Solving Module.
3. What is one of the major limitations of the social skills training (SST) programs? Choose the most correct.
   (a) There are no randomised control designs of SST programs available.
   (b) All the SRI interventions have been designed only for individuals with diagnosis of schizophrenia.
   (c) One of the biggest limitations of the SST programs is the lack of generalisation of the skills learnt in-group to participants' environments and real life.
   (d) There are no pure SST programs because all the interventions use an integrated design to enhance clinical benefits.

ANSWERS TO QUIZ QUESTIONS:

1. (b)
2. (d)
3. (c)

RECOMMENDED READINGS

Almerie, M., Al Marhi, M. O., Jawoosh, M., Alsabbagh, M., Matar, H., Maayan, N., et al. (2015). Social skills programmes for schizophrenia. *Cochrane Database of Systematic Reviews*, (6). (Review).

Bellack, A. S., Mueser, K. T., Gingerich, S., & Agresta, J. (2013). *Social skills training for schizophrenia, second edition: A step-by-step guide* (2nd ed.). Guildford Publications.

Grandholm, E., McQuaid, L., John, R., & Holden, J. L. (2016). *Cognitive-behavioral social skills training for schizophrenia. A practice treatment guide.* New York, NY: Guilford Press.

Turner, D. T., McGlanaghy, E., Cuijpers, P., Van Der Gaag, M., Karyotaki, E., & MacBeth, A. (2017). A metaanalysis of social skills training and related interventions for psychosis. *Schizophrenia Bulletin, 44*(3), 475–491.

References

Adams, J., & Drake, R. (2006). Shared decision-making and evidence-based practice. *Community Mental Health Journal, 42*, 87–105.

Addington, J., Cornblatt, B. A., Cadenhead, K. S., Cannon, T. D., McGlashan, T. H., Perkins, D. O., et al. (2011). At clinical high risk for psychosis: Outcome for nonconverters. *American Journal of Psychiatry, 168*, 800–805.

Addington, J., Penn, D., Woods, S. W., Addington, D., & Perkins, D. O. (2008). Social functioning in individuals at clinical high risk for psychosis. *Schizophrenia Research, 99*(1–3), 119–124. https://doi.org/10.1016/j.schres.2007.10.001.

Almerie, M., Al Marhi, M. O., Jawoosh, M., Alsabbagh, M., Matar, H., Maayan, N., et al. (2015). Social skills programmes for schizophrenia. *Cochrane Database of Systematic Reviews*,(6) [Review], Article No.: CD009006(2015). https://doi.org/10.1002/14651858.CD009006.pub2.

Alvarez-Jimenez, M., Bendall, S., Koval, P., Rice, S., Cagliarini, D., Valentine, L., et al. (2019). The HORYZONS trial: Protocol for a randomised controlled trial of a Moderated Social Therapy to maintain treatment effects from first episode psychosis services. *BMJ Open, 9*, e24104.

Alvarez-Jimenez, M., Bendall, S., Lederman, R., Wadley, G., Chinnery, G., Vargas, S., et al. (2013). On the HORYZON: Moderated online social therapy for long-term recovery in first episode psychosis. *Schizophrenia Research, 143*(1), 143–149.

Alvarez-Jimenez, M., Gleeson, J. F., Henry, L. P., Harrigan, S. M., Harris, M. G., Killackey, E., et al. (2012). Road to full recovery: Longitudinal relationship between symptomatic remission and psychosocial recovery in first-episode psychosis over 7.5 years. *Psychological Medicine, 42*(3), 595–606.

Alvarez-Jimenez, M., O'Donoghue, B., Thompson, A., Gleeson, J. F., Bendall, S., Gonzalez-Blanch, C., et al. (2016). Beyond clinical remission in first episode psychosis: Thoughts on antipsychotic maintenance vs. guided discontinuation in the functional recovery era. *CNS Drugs, 30*(5), 357–368.

American Psychiatric Association. (2000). *Diagnostic and statistical manual of mental disorders DSM-IV-TR* (4th ed.). Washington, DC: American Psychiatric Association.

Barker, S., Barron, N., McFarland, B., & Bigelow, D. (1994). A community ability scale for chronically ill consumers: Part 1. Reliability and validity. *Community Mental Health Journal, 30*, 363–383.

Bellack, A. S., Schooler, N. R., Marder, S. R., Kane, J. M., Brown, C. H., & Yang, Y. (2004). Do clozapine and risperidone affect social competence and problem solving? *American Journal of Psychiatry, 161*, 364–367.

Birchwood, M., Smith, J. O., Cochrane, R., Wetton, S., & Copestake, S. (1990). The Social Functioning Scale. The development and validation of a new scale of social adjustment for use in family intervention programmes with schizophrenic patients. *The British Journal of Psychiatry, 157*(6), 853–859.

Birchwood, M., Todd, P., & Jackson, C. (1998). Early intervention in psychosis. The critical period hypothesis. *The British Journal of Psychiatry, 172*(33), 53–59.

Browne, J., Estroff, S. E., Ludwig, K., Merritt, C., Meyer-Kalos, P., Mueser, K. T., et al. (2017). Character strengths of individuals with first episode psychosis in Individual Resiliency Training. *Schizophrenia Research, 195*, 448–454.

Cape, J., Whittington, C., Buszewicz, M., Wallace, P., & Underwood, L. (2010). Brief psychological therapies for anxiety and depression in primary care: Metaanalysis and meta-regression. *BMC Medicine, 8*, 38–51.

Cassidy, C. M., Norman, R., Manchanda, R., Schmitz, N., & Malla, A. (2010). Testing definitions of symptom remission in first-episode psychosis for prediction of functional outcome at 2 years. *Schizophrenia Bulletin, 36*(5), 1001–1008.

Cornblatt, B., Lencz, T., Smith, C., Correll, C., Auther, A., & Nakayama, E. (2003). The schizophrenia prodrome revisited: A neuro-developmental perspective. *Schizophrenia Bulletin, 29*, 633–651.

Crumlish, N., Whitty, P., Clarke, M., Browne, S., Kamali, M., Gervin, M., et al. (2009). Beyond the critical period: Longitudinal study of 8-year outcome in first-episode non-affective psychosis. *British Journal of Psychiatry, 194*(1), 18–24.

Cuijpers, P., Andersson, G., Donker, T., & Van Straten, A. (2011). Psychological treatment of depression: Results of a series of meta-analyses. *Nordic Journal of Psychiatry, 65*(4), 354–364.

Curran, J. P. (1982). A procedure for the assessment of social skills: The simulated social interactions test. In J. P. Curran, & P. M. Monti (Eds.), *Social skills training: A practical handbook for assessment and treatment* (pp. 313–347). New York, NY: Guilford Press.

D'Alfonso, S., Santesteban-Echarri, O., Rice, S., Wadley, G., Lederman, R., Miles, C., et al. (2017). Artificial intelligence-assisted online social therapy for youth mental health. *Frontiers in Psychology, 8*(796), 1–13.

D'Zurilla, T. J., Nezu, A. M., & Maydeu-Olivares, A. (2002). *Social problem-solving inventory-revised (SPSI-R): Technical manual.* New York, NY: Multi-Health Systems, Inc.

Davidson, L. (2003). *Living outside mental illness: Qualitative studies of recovery in schizophrenia.* New York, NY: York University Press.

Eckman, T., Liberman, R., Phipps, C., & Blair, K. (1990). Teaching medication management skills to schizophrenic patients. *Journal of Clinical Psychopharmacology, 10*, 33–38.

Favrod, J., Aillon, N., & Bardoit, G. (1995). "Competence" un chevel de Troy dans les soins [A Trojan horse in health care]. *Cahiers Psychiatriques Genevois, 18*, 47–53.

Fornells-Ambrojo, M., Barker, C., Swapp, D., Slater, M., Antley, A., & Freeman, D. (2008). Virtual reality and persecutory delusions: Safety and feasibility. *Schizophrenia Research, 104*(1–3), 228–236. https://doi.org/10.1016/j.schres.2008.05.013.

Fowler, D., French, P., & Hodgekins, J. (2013). CBT to address and prevent social disability in early and emerging psychosis. In C. Steel (Ed.), *CBT for schizophrenia: Evidence based interventions and future directions* (pp. 143–167). Oxford: John Wiley & Sons.

Fowler, D., Hodgekins, J., French, P., Marshall, M., Freemantle, N., McCrone, P., et al. (2018). Social recovery therapy in combination with early intervention services for enhancement of social recovery in patients with first-episode psychosis (SUPEREDEN3): A single-blind, randomised controlled trial. *The Lancet Psychiatry, 5*(1), 41–50.

Fowler, D., Hodgekins, J., Painter, M., Reilly, T., Crane, C., MacMillan, I., et al. (2009). Cognitive behaviour therapy for improving social recovery in psychosis: A report from the ISREP MRC trial platform study (improving social recovery in early psychosis). *Psychological Medicine, 39*(10), 1627–1636.

Freeman, D., Slater, M., Bebbington, P. E., Garety, P. A., Kuipers, E., Fowler, D., et al. (2003). Can virtual reality be used to investigate persecutory ideation? *Journal of Nervous and Mental Disease, 191*(8), 509–514.

Fusar-Poli, P., Byrne, M., Valmaggia, L., Day, F., Tabraham, P., Johns, L., et al. (2010). Social dysfunction predicts two years clinical outcome in people at ultra high risk for psychosis. *Journal of Psychiatric Research, 44*(5), 294–301.

Gambrill, E. D., & Richey, C. A. (1975). An assertion inventory for use in assessment and research. *Behavior Therapy, 6*(4), 550–561.

Garland, E. L., Fredrickson, B., Kring, A. M., Johnson, D. P., Meyer, P. S., & Penn, D. L. (2010). Upward spirals of positive emotions counter downward spirals of negativity: Insights from the broaden-and-build theory and affective neuroscience on the treatment of emotion dysfunctions and deficits in psychopathology. *Clinical Psychology Review, 30*(7), 849–864.

Gleeson, J., Lederman, R., Koval, P., Wadley, G., Bendall, S., Cotton, S., et al. (2017). Moderated online social therapy: A model for reducing stress in carers of young people diagnosed with mental health disorders. *Frontiers in Psychology, 8*, 1–8.

Gleeson, J. F., Lederman, R., Wadley, G., Bendall, S., McGorry, P. D., & Álvarez-Jiménez, M. (2014). Safety and privacy outcomes from a people with first-episode psychosis safety and privacy outcomes from a moderated online social therapy for young people with first-episode psychosis. *Psychiatric Services, 65*(4), 546–550.

Granholm, E., Holden, J., Link, P. C., & McQuaid, J. R. (2014). Randomized clinical trial of cognitive behavioral social skills training for schizophrenia: Improvement in functioning and experiential negative symptoms. *Journal of Consulting and Clinical Psychology, 82*(6), 1173–1185.

Gregg, L., & Tarrier, N. (2007). Virtual reality in mental health. A review of the literature. *Social Psychiatry and Psychiatric Epidemiology, 42*(5), 343–354.

Harvey, P. D., & Bellack, A. S. (2009). Toward a terminology for functional recovery in schizophrenia: Is functional remission a viable concept? *Schizophrenia Bulletin, 35*(2), 300–306.

Harvey, P. D., & Strassnig, M. (2012). Predicting the severity of everyday functional disability in people with schizophrenia: Cognitive deficits, functional capacity, symptoms, and health status. *World Psychiatry, 11*, 73–79.

Harvey, P. D., Heaton, R. K., Carpenter, W. T., Green, M. F., Gold, J. M., & Schoenbaum, M. (2012). Functional impairment in people with schizophrenia: Focus on employability and eligibility for disability compensation. *Schizophrenia Research, 140*(1–3), 1–8.

Harvey, P. D., McClure, M. M., Patterson, T. L., McGrath, J. A., Pulver, A. E., Bowie, C. R., et al. (2012). Impairment in functional capacity as an endophenotype candidate in severe mental illness. *Schizophrenia Bulletin, 38*(6), 1318–1326.

Harvey, P. D., Patterson, T. L., Potter, L. S., Zhong, K., & Brecher, M. (2006). Improvement in social competence with short-term atypical antipsychotic treatment: A randomized, double-blind comparison of quetiapine versus risperidone for social competence, social cognition, and neuropsychological functioning. *The American Journal of Psychiatry, 163*(11), 1918–1925.

Herbert, J., Gaudiano, B., Rheingold, A., Myers, V., Dalrymple, K., & Nolan, E. (2005). Social skills training augments the effectiveness of cognitive behavioral group therapy for social anxiety disorder. *Behaviour Therapy, 36*, 125–138.

Herman, Y., Shireen, H., Bromley, S., Yiu, N., & Granholm, E. (2016). Cognitive-behavioural social skills training for first-episode psychosis: A feasibility study. *Early Intervention in Psychiatry*, 15–17.

Hodgekins, J., French, P., Birchwood, M., Mugford, M., Christopher, R., Marshall, M., et al. (2014). Comparing time use in individuals at different stages of psychosis and a non-clinical comparison group. *Schizophrenia Research, 161*(2), 188–193.

Hofmann, S. G., & Otto, M. W. (2018). *Cognitive behavioral therapy for social anxiety disorder. Evidence-based and disorder-specific treatment techniques* (2nd ed.). New York, NY: Routledge.

Horan, W. P., Kern, R. S., Shokat-Fadai, K., Sergi, M. J., Wynn, J. K., & Green, M. F. (2009). Social cognitive skills training in schizophrenia: An initial efficacy study of stabilized outpatients. *Schizophrenia Research, 107*(1), 47–54.

Hurn, J., Kneebone, I., & Cropley, M. (2006). Goal setting as an outcome measure: A systematic review. *Clinical Rehabilitation, 20*, 756–772.

Killackey, E., & Yung, A. R. (2007). Effectiveness of early intervention in psychosis. *Current Opinion in Psychiatry, 20*(2), 121–125.

Kopelowicz, A., Liberman, R. P., & Zarate, R. (2006). Recent advances in social skills training for schizophrenia. *Schizophrenia Bulletin, 32*(Suppl. 1), S12–S23.

Krabbendam, L., & Aleman, A. (2003). Cognitive rehabilitation in schizophrenia: A quantitative analysis of controlled studies. *Psychopharmacology, 169*, 376–382.

Ku, J., Han, K., Lee, H. R., Jang, H. J., Kim, K. U., Park, S. H., et al. (2007). VR-based conversation training program for patients with schizophrenia: A preliminary clinical trial. *Cyberpsychology & Behavior, 10*(4), 567–574.

Kurtz, M. M., Baker, E., Pearlson, G. D., & Astur, R. S. (2007). A virtual reality apartment as a measure of medication management skills in patients with schizophrenia: A pilot study. *Schizophrenia Bulletin, 33*(5), 1162–1170.

Lecomte, T., Corbière, M., & Briand, C. (2008). Psychosocial functioning assessment. In K. T. Mueser, & D. P. Jeste (Eds.), *The clinical handbook of schizophrenia*. New York, NY: Guilford Press.

Lecomte, T., Corbière, M., Ehmann, T., Addington, J., Abdel-Baki, A., & MacEwan, B. (2014). Development and preliminary validation of the First Episode Social Functioning Scale for early psychosis. *Psychiatry Research, 216*(3), 412–417.

Lecomte, T., & Lecomte, C. (2002). Towards uncovering robust principles of change inherent in cognitive-behavioral therapy for psychosis. *The American Journal of Orthopsychiatry, 72*, 50–57.

Lederman, R., Wadley, G., Gleeson, J. F., Bendall, S., & Alvarez-Jimenez, M. (2014). Moderated online social therapy: Designing and evaluating technology for mental health. *ACM Transactions on Computer-Human Interaction, 2*(1), 1–27.

Liberman, R. (1972). Reinforcement of social in- teraction in a group of chronic schizophrenics. In R. Rubin, C. Franks, & H. Fensterheim (Eds.), *Vol. 3 Advances in behavior therapy*. New York, NY: Academic Press.

Liberman, R. (2007). Dissemination and adoption of social skills training: Social validation of an evidence-based treatment for the mentally disabled. *Journal of Mental Health, 16*(5), 595–623.

Liberman, R., Wallace, C., Blackwell, G., Eckman, T., Vaccaro, J., & Kuehnel, T. (1993). Innovations in skills training for the seriously mentally ill. *Innovations & Research, 2*, 43–60.

Lieberman, J., Jody, D., Geisler, S., Alvir, J., Loebel, A., Szymanski, S., et al. (1993). Time course and biologic correlates of treatment response in first-episode schizophrenia. *Archives of General Psychiatry, 50*, 369–376.

Macdonald, E. M., Hayes, R. L., & Baglioni, A. J. (2000). The quantity and quality of the social networks of young people with early psychosis compared with closely matched controls. *Schizophrenia Research, 46*(1), 25–30.

Mohr, D. C., Cuijpers, P., & Lehman, K. (2011). Supportive accountability: A model for providing human support to enhance adherence to eHealth interventions. *Journal of Medical Internet Research, 13*(1), e30.

Morgan, C., Kirkbride, J., Hutchinson, G., Craig, T., Morgan, K., Dazzan, P., et al. (2008). Cumulative social disadvantage, ethnicity and first-episode psychosis: A case-control study. *Psychological Medicine, 38*(12), 1701–1715.

Mueser, K. T., Penn, D. L., Addington, J., Brunette, M. F., Gingerich, S., Glynn, S. M., et al. (2015). The NAVIGATE program for first-episode psychosis: Rationale, overview, and description of psychosocial components. *Psychiatric Services, 66*(7), 680–690.

Nasrallah, H., Morosini, P., & Gagnon, D. D. (2008). Reliability, validity and ability to detect change of the Personal and Social Performance scale in patients with stable schizophrenia. *Psychiatry Research, 161*(2), 213–224.

National Institute for Health and Care Excellence (NICE). (2014). *Psychosis and schizophrenia in adults: Treatment and management*. London, England: Nice Clinical Guideline 178.

Nitzan, U., Shoshan, E., Lev-ran, S., & Fennig, S. (2011). Internet-related psychosis—A sign of the times? *Israel Journal of Psychiatry and Related Sciences, 48*(3), 207–211.

Park, K. M., Ku, J., Choi, S. H., Jang, H. J., Park, J. Y., Kim, S. I., et al. (2011). A virtual reality application in role-plays of social skills training for schizophrenia: A randomized, controlled trial. *Psychiatry Research, 189*(2), 166–172.

Park, K. M., Ku, J., Park, I. H., Park, J. I., Kim, S. I., & Kim, J. J. (2009). Improvement in social competence in patients with schizophrenia: A pilot study using a performance-based measure using virtual reality. *Human Psychopharmacology, 24*, 619–627.

Patterson, T. L., Mausbach, B. T., McKibbin, C., Goldman, S., Bucardo, J., & Jeste, D. V. (2006). Functional Adaptation Skills Training (FAST): A randomized trial of a psychosocial intervention for middle-aged and older patients with chronic psychotic disorders. *Schizophrenia Research, 86*(1–3), 291–299.

Patterson, T., Moscona, S., McKibbin, C., Davidson, K., & Jeste, D. (2001). Social skills performance assessment among older patients with schizophrenia. *Schizophrenia Research, 48*, 351–360.

Patterson, T., Semple, S., Shaw, W., Halpain, M., Moscona, S., Grant, I., et al. (1997). Self-reported social functioning among older patients with schizophrenia. *Schizophrenia Research, 27*, 199–210.

Penn, D. L., Waldheter, E. J., Perkins, D. O., Mueser, K. T., & Lieberman, J. A. (2005). Psychosocial treatment for first-episode psychosis: A research update. *American Journal of Psychiatry, 162*(12), 2220–2232.

Peterson, C., & Seligman, M. E. P. (2004). In American Psychological Association (Ed.), *Character strengths and virtues: A handbook and classification*. Wasington, DC: Oxford University Press.

Rathus, S. A. (1973). A 30-item schedule for assessing assertive behavior. *Behavior Therapy, 4*, 398–406.

Roder, V., Brenner, H., & Kienzle, N. (2002). *Integriertes Psychologisches Therapieprogramm für schizophren Erkrankte (IPT)*. Weinheim, Germany: Berarbeitete Auflage.

Roder, V., Brenner, H., Kienzle, N., & Hodel, B. (1988). *Integriertes Psychologisches Therapieprogramm (IPT) für schizophrene patienten: Psychologie*. München Weinheim, Germany: Verlags Union.

Roder, V., Mueller, D. R., Mueser, K. T., & Brenner, H. D. (2006). Integrated psychological therapy (IPT) for schizophrenia: Is it effective? *Schizophrenia Bulletin, 32*(Suppl. 1), S81–S93.

Rus-Calafell, M., Gutiérrez-Maldonado, J., & Ribas-Sabaté, J. (2014). A virtual reality-integrated program for improving social skills in patients with schizophrenia: A pilot study. *Journal of Behavior Therapy and Experimental Psychiatry, 45*(1), 81–89.

Ryan, R., & Deci, E. (2000). Self-determination theory and the facilitation of intrinsic motivation, social development, and well-being. *The American Psychologist, 55*(1), 68–78.

Santesteban-Echarri, O., Álvarez-Jiménez, M., Gleeson, J., & Rice, S. M. (2018). Social media interventions for adolescents and young people with depression and psychosis. In M. A. Moreno, & A. Radovic (Eds.), *Technology and adolescent mental health* (pp. 187–205). Cham, Switzerland: Springer International Publishing.

Santesteban-Echarri, O., Paino, M., Rice, S., González-Blanch, C., McGorry, P., Gleeson, J., et al. (2017). Predictors of functional recovery in first-episode psychosis: A systematic review and meta-analysis of longitudinal studies. *Clinical Psychology Review, 58*. https://doi.org/10.1016/j.cpr.2017.09.007.

Schlein, G., & Guerney, B. (1977). Relationship change scale. In B. G. Guerney (Ed.), *Relationship enhancement: Skill-training program for therapy, problem prevention, and enrichment*. San Francisco, CA: Jossey-Bass.

Schuler, D., & Namioka, A. (1993). *Participatory design: Principles and practices*. Hillsdale, NJ: Routledge, Taylor & Francis group.

Seligman, M. E. P., Rashid, T., & Parks, A. C. (2006). Positive psychotherapy. *American Psychologist, 61*(8), 774–788.

Sündermann, O., Onwumere, J., Kane, F., Morgan, C., & Kuipers, E. (2014). Social networks and support in first-episode psychosis: Exploring the role of loneliness and anxiety. *Social Psychiatry and Psychiatric Epidemiology, 49*(3), 359–366.

Torres, A., Mendez, L. P., Merino, H., & Moran, E. A. (2002). Improving social functioning in schizophrenia by playing the train game. *Psychiatric Services, 53*(7), 799–801.

Trautmann, S., Rehm, J., & Wittchen, H. (2016). The economic costs of mental disorders. *EMBO Reports, 17*, 1245–1249.

Trower, P., Bryant, B., & Argyle, M. (1978). *Social skill and mental health*. Pittsburgh, PA: University of Pittsburgh Press.

Turner, D. T., McGlanaghy, E., Cuijpers, P., Van Der Gaag, M., Karyotaki, E., & MacBeth, A. (2017). A meta-analysis of social skills training and related interventions for psychosis. *Schizophrenia Bulletin, 44*(3), 475–491.

Van Brunt, D. (2000). Modular cognitive-behavioral therapy: Dismantling validated treatment programs into self-standing treatment plan objectives. *Cognitive and Behavioral Practice, 7*, 156–165.

Vaskinn, A., Ventura, J., Andreassen, O., Melle, I., & Sundet, K. (2015). A social path to functioning in schizophrenia: From social self-efficacy through negative symptoms to social functional capacity. *Psychiatry Research, 228*(3), 803–807.

Wadley, G., Lederman, R., Gleeson, J., & Alvarez-Jimenez, M. (2013). Participatory design of an online therapy for youth mental health. In: *OZCHI'13*.

Wallace, C., Liberman, R., Tauber, R., & Wallace, J. (2000). The Independent Living Skills Survey: A comprehensive measure of the community functioning of severely and persistently mentally ill individuals. *Schizophrenia Bulletin, 26*, 631–658.

Wallace, C. J., Nelson, C. . J., Liberman, R. P., Aitchison, R. A., Lukoff, D., John, E. P., et al. (1980). A review and critique of social skills training with schizophrenic patients. *Schizophrenia Bulletin, 6*, 42–63.

Watson, D., & Friend, R. (1969). Measurement of social evaluative anxiety. *Journal of Consulting and Clinical Psychology, 33*, 448–457.

Wu, E. Q., Birnbaum, H. G., Shi, L., Ball, D. E., Kessler, R. C., Moulis, M., et al. (2005). The economic burden of schizophrenia in the United States in 2002. *Journal of Clinical Psychiatry, 66*(9), 1122–1129.

Xiang, Y. T., Weng, Y. Z., Li, W. Y., Gao, L., Chen, G. L., Xie, L., et al. (2007). Efficacy of the community re-entry module for patients with schizophrenia in Beijing, China: Outcome at 2-year follow-up. *British Journal of Psychiatry, 190*, 49–56.

Definition of Key Terms

Early intervention Early intervention of psychosis (EIP) comprises: (1) early detection and treatment of first episode of psychosis; (2) maintained treatment during the 'critical period' (i.e. the first 3–5 years after onset of illness); and (3) early detection and treatment of relapses.

First-episode psychosis First-episode psychosis (FEP) refers to a first experience of psychotic symptoms or a psychotic episode. Although the term FEP was initially used as a synonym for schizophrenia, it is now a distinct concept and not indicative of a specific diagnosis, instead a feature of the broad spectrum of psychotic illnesses. FEP can include other disorders such as schizoaffective psychosis or schizophreniform disorder. This broad symptom-led approach is useful in reducing stigma and treating psychosis as early as possible.

Online intervention Psychosocial intervention delivered through a device with Internet connectivity (i.e. mobile-based interventions, computer-based interventions). Online interventions have advantages such as anonymity, easy access independent of time and location, cost effectiveness for large populations, and the potential of such interventions to be perceived as less stigmatising.

Psychosis A mental disorder in which cognition, affective response, ability to recognise reality and ability to communicate and relate to others is significantly impaired. The most common presentation is as a syndrome involving positive symptoms (i.e. hallucinations, delusions, and illusions), which are usually accompanied by negative symptoms (i.e. mood disturbances) and functioning impairment.

Psychosocial interventions Nonmedication therapies for individuals experiencing mental illness and/or their families. Therapies include psychotherapy, coping skills, training and supported employment, and education services.

Schizophrenia spectrum disorder The spectrum of psychotic disorders, including schizophrenia, schizoaffective disorder, delusional disorder, schizotypal personality disorder, schizophreniform disorder, brief psychotic disorder, as well as psychosis associated with substance use or medical conditions.

Social functioning A global term used to refer to several areas of functioning (i.e. school and work activities, leisure activities, living skills, and forming peer and family relationships).

Social skills Socially acceptable learned behaviours that facilitate communication and interactivity with others (both verbally and nonverbally, through gestures, body language, and personal appearance) to elicit positive responses and assist in avoiding negative responses.

Virtual reality Technology integrating immersive real-time computer graphics, sounds, and other sensory input to create a computer-generated world within which the user can interact. The virtual environment is presented through a head-mounted display (HMD) (i.e. a helmet or goggles containing screens along with stereo earphones). The user can explore and navigate the virtual world by motion tracking devices attached to the HMD, enabling the computer to adapt the field of view to the user's movements.

CHAPTER 19

Trauma Therapies in Psychosis

447

David van den Berg*,†, Irene van de Giessen‡, Amy Hardy§,¶

*Parnassia Psychiatric Institute, The Hague, The Netherlands, †VU University, Amsterdam, The Netherlands, ‡Director of Non-Profit Organization, Foundation for Recovery Talent, Koudekerke, The Netherlands, §Department of Psychology, Institute of Psychiatry, Psychology and Neuroscience, King's College London, London, United Kingdom, ¶South London and Maudsley NHS Foundation Trust, London, United Kingdom

Key Learning Objectives

- Know what the current evidence base is for trauma-focused therapies in psychosis
- Understand the rationale and basics of these therapies, and how they are delivered in psychosis
- Be informed about a way of conceptualising trauma therapy in psychosis

INTRODUCTION

We've learned from Chapter 10 that traumatic experiences, particularly multiple victimisation, and posttraumatic stress reactions are common in psychosis compared to the general population, and associated with worse clinical and functional outcomes. Trauma appears to play a causal role in psychosis, at least for a subgroup of people, and psychological factors, including emotion regulation, event memories, and beliefs appear to underlie this association. Despite these findings, in clinical practice, both traumatic experiences and PTSD are often not assessed in psychosis services, meaning it is rare for people to be offered specialist interventions (de Bont et al., 2015). Thus, many people with a combination of trauma, psychosis, and posttraumatic stress symptoms end up being stuck in a vicious cycle that is exacerbated by the lack of access to effective therapies. A change is however occurring, as evidence accrues that people with posttraumatic stress and psychosis are willing and able to engage in trauma-focused therapies, and that therapy is safe and effective. Several international guidelines recommend screening for both trauma and PTSD in people with psychosis and

A Clinical Introduction to Psychosis. https://doi.org/10.1016/B978-0-12-815012-2.00019-5

to offer trauma-focused treatment when indicated (e.g. Galletly et al., 2016; NICE, 2014). In clinical practice, we need to balance these new scientific findings, with the needs and preferences of service users, and the service context in which they are seen. In Box 19.1, Irene describes her experiences of what helped and hindered her recovery. This chapter aims to support this process by giving an overview of the evidence base for different trauma-focused therapies, and by providing some clinical guidance for how to treat posttraumatic stress in psychosis (PTSp) based on the model that we presented in Chapter 10. We suggest you read Chapter 10 before this chapter.

Box 19.1 Finding My Sheep Paths

Mind the sheep. They keep on walking, and always the same path. That way sheep paths are formed. Paths that make areas difficult to enter, slowly accessible. It seems nothing and insignificant, but as so often in life, seemingly insignificant things, with hindsight turn out to be much more important than you had expected. Looking back, I can say that making a difficult to enter area accessible is just what I did in my recovery process. The jungle of emotions that traumatisation in early youth had created in my head, I slowly turned into an area I feel at home in and do not get lost in, due to the sheep paths I formed.

My voices brought me into contact with psychiatry. A psychiatrist told me I suffered from schizophrenia. I would have to use medication permanently, I would not be able to have a relationship, I would not be able to finish my education and I would only live in protected surroundings. The idea that because of my 'illness' I could not be part of my own solution resulted in long-term feelings of humiliation and reduction to just my problem. My behaviour was judged and treated as a symptom, not as the understandable effect of trauma and this kept my psychiatrist from seeing the possibility that my behaviour was my way of dealing with misery, anger and physical and emotional pain.

At times my voices were downright dangerous in the tasks they gave me. Through a simple assignment I discovered that the voices were nothing without me. I ordered them to clean my room without help. They were unable to do this and so the first doubts about their power over me had risen. I realised that the only power they had was the power I gave them. They needed me to perform certain tasks and talk to certain people; without me they were powerless. Only then was I able to make demands about the way and the moment they could talk to me. A real sheep path was created! By setting limits to my voices I gained more and more control over my own behaviour. Because I gained more control and the sheep paths in the jungle of my emotions kept broadening, it became possible to explore the relation between my voices and my life history. A significant step was to part from the voices and recognise the meaning of functioning without them. Work and everything that implies, making friends and 'living' my life made a great difference.

A fundamental change only broke through when, I learned to put into a wider perspective the feelings of deficit that arose in crisis and the range of reactions this provoked. I learned to observe with benevolent attention. I kept being friendly towards myself, even if I noticed things I myself or others condemned. Standing up for myself was important. I grew increasingly conscious of the fact that I had a choice and need not be a slave of my emotions. I was now deliberately creating my own sheep paths. I now have to look after its maintenance! Without awareness the jungle of emotions will go its own way again. My recovery did not follow a line of a protocolled process. It was rock-hard work and walking these seemingly insignificant paths over and over again, in order to make that hard to enter space of my emotions a bit more accessible. It was worth it!

TRAUMA-INFORMED AND TRAUMA-FOCUSED THERAPIES

Broadly speaking, there are two ways of managing the impact of trauma in psychosis. First, there are *trauma-informed therapies* for psychosis, most predominantly formulation-based CBT for psychosis (CBTp; Chapters 14 and 15), in which trauma and its consequences are included in the formulation of the problems that someone is experiencing (e.g. how trauma shapes intrusive experiences, the meaning that is given to these experiences, and the emotional and behavioural responses) (e.g. Morrison, 2017). Trauma-informed CBT interventions mainly focus on helping individuals understand what led to the development and maintenance of their current difficulties, on collaboratively investigating beliefs to develop alternative, more helpful ideas, and trying out and evaluating different strategies.

Second, there are trauma-focused therapies (TFTs). These are individually delivered psychotherapeutic treatments for PTSD that mainly utilise trauma-focused cognitive and/or behavioural techniques (Watts et al., 2013). Eye movement desensitisation and reprocessing (EMDR) therapy is also considered to be a trauma-focused treatment (Diehle, Schmitt, Daams, Boer, & Lindauer, 2014; Lee et al., 2016). TFTs focus mainly on decreasing the frequency and intensity of intrusive memories and associated beliefs, and on reducing avoidance behaviours that maintain problems. This then generally improves other PTSD symptoms, such as hyperarousal and sleep difficulties. Several types of TFT have been found to be effective, and although there are clear differences, there are also many commonalities (Schnyder et al., 2015). We will briefly review the most important TFTs.

Trauma-focused therapies address trauma memories/stimuli, associated beliefs and emotions, and aim to improve functioning.

Prolonged exposure therapy (PE) is an experiential form of CBT and the most studied TFT (Foa, Hembree, & Rothbaum, 2007). In PE, both imaginal exposure (i.e. using imagination to relive the traumatic memory with support from the therapist) and in vivo exposure (i.e. exposing oneself to stimuli that were previously avoided out of fear of triggering traumatic intrusions) are used. The working mechanisms are under debate, but it appears they may be attributable to habituation (exposure leading to a weakening of associations between trauma stimuli and negative emotions), inhibition (exposure resulting in new associations between trauma stimuli and neutral or positive reactions, which have a retrieval advantage over original trauma stimuli and response associations), and falsification of negative expectations (e.g. experiencing that you don't go mad when you expose yourself to your traumatic memories and that you can actually tolerate it).

Prolong exposure: A form of CBT where both imaginal and in vivo exposure are used.

Several variants of prolonged exposure have been developed and tested. Narrative Exposure Therapy (NET) is a form of exposure that was designed for refugees who survived trauma (Stenmark, Catani, Neuner, Elbert, & Holen, 2013). In NET the therapist helps the person to chronologically construct a life story with a time-line that contains both traumatic and positive experiences.

Narrative Exposure Therapy: A form of exposure therapy that entails the construction of a timeline of events and narrative exposure.

During narration, the person is encouraged to connect with their sensory-perceptual experiences during trauma, whilst describing it as a past event and attending to differences between then and now. Imagery rescripting is another variant of exposure in which restructuring is induced during the imaginal reliving of the traumatic event (Smucker, 1995). The focus during exposure is to change distressing meanings associated with images, through imaginal modification. The modification can involve perceptual transformations (e.g. putting a barrier between the person and their attacker) or may have a relational focus (e.g. addressing unmet developmental needs such as not being cared for or feeling safe, through the person relating differently to others or others relating differently to them) (Arntz & Weertman, 1999).

Imagery rescripting is another variant of exposure in which restructuring is induced during the imaginal reliving of the traumatic event.

Cognitive restructuring *(CR) or cognitive processing therapies* are also a form of CBT, but with a focus on using cognitive evaluation to modify trauma-related beliefs and associated cognitive biases related to events and their consequences (e.g. addressing beliefs that 'the abuse was my fault', 'I can't trust anyone', and 'I'm going mad'). Several different protocols have been developed, some also including an element of exposure (Resick & Schnicke, 1992).

Cognitive Restructuring uses cognitive evaluation to modify trauma-related beliefs and associated cognitive biases.

Trauma-focused cognitive therapy for PTSD is a CBT protocol that includes both behavioural and cognitive techniques, mainly reliving with restructuring, in vivo exposure, reducing safety behaviours and stimulus discrimination (attending to stimuli in the here and now that were not present during the trauma and can therefore reduce the sense of threat) (Ehlers & Wild, 2015).

Eye-movement desensitisation and reprocessing therapy (EMDR) is a psychotherapeutic approach in which memory representations of traumatic life experiences are 'reprocessed' with an 8-phase protocol (Shapiro, 2001). The most important element is the fact that the person is asked to focus on the currently most distressing image of a traumatic memory together with its associated meaning and bodily sensations, whilst concentrating on a distracting stimulus (generally following the fingers of the therapist, which are moving side to side, with their eyes). Intermittently, the person is asked to briefly describe what came to mind before continuing with the reprocessing. This can be sufficient to support the memory in become less distressing, if not the therapist can introduce cognitive and imaginal interventions to modify the image (called 'cognitive interweaves'). The working mechanism is still under debate, but there appears to be strongest support for the working memory account, since it has been repeatedly found that performing a dual task that taxes working memory capacity whilst retrieving an emotional memory, reduces the vividness and emotionality of memories (van den Hout, Bartelski, & Engelhard, 2012).

Eye-movement desensitisation and reprocessing focuses on imaginally processing trauma memory and associated meanings, whilst concentrating on a distracting stimulus.

To recap, we have defined CBTp as a trauma-informed therapy, given that it considers the role of trauma during formulation and intervention through targeting its impact on intrusions, beliefs, and coping responses. In contrast, the main approach in trauma-focused therapies is to directly target intrusive trauma memories, although beliefs and coping responses are also addressed. Given the overlap between them, we view CBTp and TFT as complementary and recommend their integration (trauma-focused CBT for psychosis, tf-CBTp) to support the delivery of effective psychological therapies for PTSp. CBTp provides the overarching framework (see Morrison, 2017) but, importantly, its principles and techniques are augmented by the memory reprocessing approaches from TFT. As we will see from trial therapy evidence to date, there are preliminary indications that reprocessing memories may be beneficial for psychosis.

RESEARCH FINDINGS

The evidence base for trauma-informed CBTp is covered elsewhere in this book (Chapter 15), so here we will focus on research findings concerning TFT in psychosis. We emphasise that this is a fairly new area of research, and there have been few robust trials. Of the TFTs described in the previous section, to date only PE, EMDR, and CR have been tested in high-quality studies. Replication of findings is necessary, including head-to-head comparisons of different TFTs in psychosis, and to examine the effects of TFTs on outcomes other than PTSD. Disentangling the effects of different TFTs may be difficult, however, as they all contain overlapping and distinct elements and target several different processes. All include at least some form of exposure to traumatic events, target negative beliefs associated with the trauma, give emotional support, provide psychoeducation, and assist emotion regulation. In other words, although the emphasis in these different therapies is on different elements of traumatic stress, there is much overlap and we still know little about what elements are responsible for the observed treatment effects (Cooper, Clifton, & Feeny, 2017).

The mechanisms underlying trauma focused therapies for psychosis are still unclear.

Trauma-Focused Therapies in Psychosis, What Do We Know Now?

In the last decade, several pilot studies reported positive effects on PTSD for PE or EMDR in psychosis (de Bont, van Minnen, & de Jongh, 2013; Frueh et al., 2009; Grubaugh et al., 2016; van den Berg & van der Gaag, 2012). These effects were confirmed in a large randomised controlled trial ($n = 155$) in which participants with both psychosis and PTSD were randomly assigned to receive either 8 sessions of PE, 8 sessions of EMDR, or waiting list for trauma-focused therapy (WL). The latter group received their therapy of choice after 6 months. All participants received treatment-as-usual for psychosis. Compared to WL, both PE and EMDR significantly decreased clinician-rated PTSD symptoms (severity scores almost halved), presence of PTSD diagnosis (PTSD came in remission in almost 60% of the participants), self-rated PTSD symptoms, and negative posttraumatic cognitions (van den Berg et al., 2015). In this trial, standard PE and EMDR protocols were used, and therapy was not preceded by stabilising psychotherapeutic interventions. In the first session, the therapist delivered psychoeducation about PTSD and together with the participant developed a hierarchy of the most relevant trauma memories based on subjective units of distress scores (SUD) and frequencies of intrusions. Trauma memories were reprocessed with PE or EMDR from sessions 2 to 8, and therapists started with the highest-ranking trauma on the hierarchy and worked their way down in the consecutive sessions. It's important to note that as this trial was conducted in the Netherlands all participants received reasonably high-quality treatment-as-usual for psychosis in flexible assertive outreach teams. The Netherlands is also a high-income country with one of the best social support systems in the world. These are important contextual factors, since these may have a stabilising effect on people and a beneficial impact on engagement with therapy. Still, the fact that these treatments were shown to be so effective in people with psychosis is highly promising.

To date, three RCTs have tested the effectiveness of a 12–16 session cognitive restructuring protocol (Mueser, Rosenberg, Jankowski, Hamblen, & Monica, 2004) that is an adapted version of Cognitive Processing Therapy for people with complex needs (e.g. learning difficulties, substance use or psychosis; Mueser et al., 2015, 2008; Steel et al., 2016). The most important adaptation of the protocol is the exclusion of exposure and behavioural experiments, based on the assumption that people would be more likely to engage in therapy if it was less emotionally demanding, and it would be less likely to have a detrimental impact on them. It's important to note however, that in the two Mueser et al. trials, only a minority of the participants had a primary diagnosis of psychotic disorder (15.7% and 33.3%, respectively). In both these trials, the adapted cognitive restructuring protocol was found to effectively reduce PTSD symptoms at posttreatment in the participants with severe mental illness; these results are in line with the pilot study that this same research group performed before their first RCT (Rosenberg, Mueser, Jankowski, Salyers, & Acker, 2004). However, for the subgroup of participants with psychosis, no statistically significant differences were observed in any of the outcomes between CR and the control groups (i.e. treatment-as-usual or three sessions of breathing retraining and psychoeducation) (Sin & Spain, 2016). A third RCT using the same protocol in a UK sample with psychosis ($n=61$) found no beneficial effects of the adapted CR protocol on PTSD, compared to routine clinical services for psychosis (Steel et al., 2016). In this trial, both the experimental and control group showed modest improvements in PTSD symptoms. An important limitation of this study is, however, that the entry criteria were broadened (DSM-IV-TR PTSD criteria C and D were omitted) due to lower-than-anticipated recruitment rates. As a result, only 34 of the 61 participants met the full criteria for PTSD and the mean baseline CAPS severity score was lower compared to other trials.

In summary, for PTSD symptoms, there is some evidence to support the effectiveness of standard PE and EMDR protocols in people with psychosis. Moreover, the adapted cognitive restructuring protocol by Mueser et al. (2004) appears to have merit in treating PTSD in patients with nonpsychotic severe mental health problems. However, the available data do not yet support its efficacy in individuals with psychosis, although a more methodologically robust trial is currently underway (Hardy & van den Berg, 2017; Sin & Spain, 2016).

Data supporting the efficacy of cognitive restructuring for PTSD in psychosis are still lacking.

In relation to outcomes other than PTSD, a recent review found TFTs to have neutral to positive side-effects on symptoms of psychosis, depression, and anxiety (Brand, McEnery, Rossell, Bendall, & Thomas, 2017). The positive effects on psychosis in this review were especially strong in the TFTs with direct memory reprocessing (i.e. PE and EMDR). PE and EMDR reduced paranoia and resulted in more remission from psychosis. PE also reduced depression. However, at a group level, neither PE nor EMDR had a significant effect on auditory verbal hallucinations and social functioning (de Bont et al., 2016). These findings are in line with findings observed in TFT trials in general PTSD samples, TFT has neutral to positive side-effects on many other problems, like depression (Aderka, Foa, Applebaum, Shafran, & Gilboa-Schechtman, 2011; Ronconi, Shiner, & Watts, 2015; van Minnen, Zoellner, Harned, & Mills, 2015), whilst there is little evidence for the reverse (i.e. that treating depression or psychosis reduces PTSD). This tentatively suggests that PTSD symptoms or their underlying mechanisms may have a powerful role in maintaining PTSp. As a result, effectively treating PTSD may be a sensible first step, as generalisation to other problems may be expected (van Minnen et al., 2015).

Are Trauma-Focused Therapies Safe in Psychosis?

Most clinicians are reluctant to use trauma-focused therapy for psychosis (Becker, Zayfert, & Anderson, 2004; Frueh, Cusack, Grubaugh, Sauvageot, & Wells, 2006; Meyer, Farrell, Kemp, Blakey, & Deacon, 2014; Salyers, Evans, Bond, & Meyer, 2004). They fear it will be too stressful for clients and exacerbate difficulties, and that this may result in adverse events, e.g. symptom worsening, self-harm, suicide attempts, crisis contacts, or suicide attempts. Contrary to the expectation of these clinicians, TFT was found to be feasible and to reduce the odds of symptom exacerbation, adverse events, and revictimisation compared to waiting list for PTSD (van den Berg et al., 2016). This is confirmed by the fact that none of the TFT studies on psychosis that have been published to date reported an increase in adverse events or high rates of exacerbation of PTSD symptoms. In addition, in the studies with participants with psychosis, dropout rates of around 20% for PE and EMDR and around 30% for CR were observed, which is in the range of rates found in general PTSD samples (Hembree et al., 2003).

Current data suggest trauma-focused therapies for psychosis are feasible, acceptable, and safe.

The foregoing suggests that although TFT can definitely be emotionally burdensome, it is generally sufficiently safe. Importantly, people with traumatic stress generally have positive attitudes towards evidence-based TFTs, would choose to undergo TFT again, would recommend TFT to loved ones and view it as preferable to medication (Becker, Darius, & Schaumberg, 2007; Feeny, Zoellner, Mavissakalian, & Roy-Byrne, 2009; Kehle-Forbes, Polusny, Erbes, & Gerould,

2014; Reger et al., 2013). In essence, facing up to traumatic memories is not pleasurable and it can be demanding. Yet one of the defining features of traumatic stress is that trauma memories keep intruding into awareness. People are constantly reliving their traumas involuntarily - assisting them in reprocessing their traumatic memories in a supportive, safe context is not the 'cruellest of cures' (Olatunji, Deacon, & Abramowitz, 2009). It's actually a sensible strategy. We know that the key sustaining factor in anxiety is avoidance. In this sense, PTSD can be viewed as a kind of phobia of traumatic memories, resulting in constant attempts to suppress these memories and to avoid stimuli that may trigger them. A sensible approach in supporting someone with PTSD, even if they have psychosis, is to break these vicious cycles of avoidance by helping them actively expose themselves to the memories and potential triggers, and to help them experience that their negative expectations (e.g. 'I won't be able to cope and will go totally crazy or die') do not happen and that they actually become less distressed.

TREATING POSTTRAUMATIC STRESS IN PSYCHOSIS

In Chapter 10, we outlined our PTSp model, a theoretically informed transdiagnostic heuristic for how to conceptualise the key psychological mechanisms that contribute to common difficulties in people with posttraumatic stress and psychosis. The central premise is that past experiences stored in event memories interact with beliefs, survival strategies, and emotion regulation to create a vulnerability for having problematic experiences, explanations, and responses in the present, which then maintain each other. Earlier in this chapter, we described how we believe that CBTp and TFT should be combined when intervening with PTSp. Based on our model, we have developed a phased trauma-focused cognitive-behaviour therapy for psychosis (tf-CBTp) approach. In this section, we describe the phased therapy and provide some clinical guidance for how to do this work, building on the overview of assessment and formulation in Chapter 10. Please note that the aim is to provide a concise guide for delivering therapy, and so it does not comprehensively reflect the complexity of people's problems or resilience factors in real life. Further, it is important to hold in mind that complexity is the norm in working with trauma in psychosis, and hypotheses about difficulties and their relationship to trauma are always probabilistic. Clinical decision making should be guided by the evidence, clinical experience, and the person's preference. It can be very difficult to balance these factors and shared decision making should be the norm. People must provide informed consent and not be coerced to do things they do not want to do, but similarly the therapist must ensure not to collude with their own or their client's avoidance of the emotionally burdensome task of facing up to trauma. The therapeutic relationship, particularly in relation to issues of trust and control, is fundamental to this work and provides an opportunity for the person to have corrective emotional experiences, which are different from how they were treated in the past.

Shared decision making forms the ground work when treating posttraumatic stress in psychosis.

TRAUMA-FOCUSED COGNITIVE-BEHAVIOUR THERAPY FOR PTSp: A PHASED APPROACH

We will return to Janet (see Chapter 10 and Fig. 10.1 for a description of Janet's problems) to illustrate how the therapy can be used in practice. The phases can be applied somewhat flexibly, depending on the formulation and client preferences. As the therapeutic techniques and approaches are described extensively elsewhere (see the references to CBTp and TFT protocols earlier in this chapter), we will not explain them in detail here, but rather give an overview of how to apply them to PTSp. In brief, the focus is on modifying difficulties in the present, informed by an understanding of how vulnerability factors from the past context may be driving them. A therapeutic priority is to reprocess problematic memories, which may involve: contextualising reexperienced memories so they are less likely to intrude; directly modifying memory content to change associated distressing beliefs; or forming more helpful memories by adopting new cognitive, behavioural, or interpersonal strategies, which can then compete with trauma-related memories and give rise to more positive experiences, explanations, and responses in the present (Brewin, 2006). A key dilemma concerns in what order problems should be addressed and what techniques should be used. Most of the available research has focused on either reprocessing decontextualised memories (as in trauma-focused therapies for PTSD) or on modifying beliefs and emotional regulation strategies (as in CBTp). There is however little evidence about how to combine them. Based on the available literature and our clinical experience, three phases are outlined.

Reprocessing problematic memories is a key priority when treating posttraumatic stress in psychosis.

Phase One: Assessment, Formulation, Goal Setting, and Psychoeducation

The assessment and formulation of trauma and posttraumatic stress problems is described in Chapter 10. In the context of therapy, developing a shared formulation and setting goals and hopes for the therapy is a useful way to begin your collaboration. It helps the person feel in control and supported to start the intervention phase of the work, based on an informed understanding of what you are going to work on, in what order you are going to do it, and with what interventions. You agree to work together as a team to monitor progress and treatment goals.

During this phase, therapists can also validate and normalise difficulties. This may encourage reflection on beliefs (e.g. 'it was my fault') and explanations ('I am going crazy') that play a role in maintaining distress, and increase motivation to engage in change strategies. Psychoeducation should be integrated and metaphors can be useful for supporting the person's understanding of how trauma has contributed to their vulnerability factors in the past and shaped their current difficulties. A comparison of trauma (Greek for wound) leaving a physical wound can be an accessible metaphor. It illustrates how we all experience wounds, and that, in time, most will heal. But that some wounds are so deep or complex, or occur in a context that negatively influences the natural healing process (e.g. dirt in a physical wound or loved ones that did not respond adequately to the adverse experience in psychotrauma) that they don't heal properly and can continue to cause pain (reexperiencing). And that it is our natural tendency to want to avoid pain, which actually prevents healing. Therefore, we must face up to and take care of our wounds in order to recover. Like cleaning and stitching a large and dirty wound that will not heal by itself, reprocessing traumas is not pleasurable and it is likely to hurt, but it is not harmful and can help. Like physical scars, scars from trauma will always be visible. People don't forget what happened, but they can be more able to let go of the traumatic experiences so they have less of a detrimental impact on life. It is important to adopt such a recovery-oriented attitude, to instil hope that the person can reclaim or build a valued life. As with any therapeutic intervention, it is important to ensure the person is willing and able to provide informed consent to undergo the therapeutic interventions, and that this is actively reviewed during therapy. Informed consent includes understanding the rationale, accepting that it may be burdensome, and having realistic hopes regarding outcome.

Adopting a recovery-oriented approach to therapy helps to instil hope and positive expectations.

The normalising information and the development of a shared formulation helps many individuals to understand better what happened to them and how this still affects them in the present. These insights can have a significant impact on the distress that people experience. Feeling unsafe is, for instance, suddenly less associated with present dangers and more with dangers that lie in the past. And the formulation yields factors that can be targeted with psychotherapeutic interventions, which gives hope that change is possible (see Box 19.2).

Phase Two: Memory Work (Contextualising and Elaborating Memories)

As highlighted earlier, trauma memory work is at the core of our tf-CBTp framework, and we tentatively suggest that reprocessing memories associated with reexperiencing should be the main priority for intervention. As we have seen earlier, reexperiencing can safely and effectively be reduced in people with psychosis with EMDR and PE, which have also been shown to reduce paranoia (Brand et al., 2017; van den Berg et al., 2015, 2016). In addition, we believe that Imagery

Box 19.2 JANET: Formulation and Psychoeducation

Janet had never related the taste of semen or voices telling her that she was bad to her history of sexual abuse. Developing the case formulation and receiving psychoeducation helped her understand that part of what she experienced in the here and now, were actually shadows from the past. She also felt strengthened by the idea that her wounds could be healed, and that there was a way to leave her past behind her and stop it from intruding in the present. This increased her motivation for phase 2.

Rescripting (IR) and EMDR can be useful in targeting memories associated with distressing beliefs and psychotic experiences (Arntz & Weertman, 1999; Smucker, 1995). These imaginal approaches can be very potent in reducing distressing emotions associated with beliefs, although to date there has been little investigation of their impact in the context of psychosis. An alternative approach, tested in people with psychosis, is Competitive Memory Training (COMET), which may be used to as an additional intervention to increase the chance that positive memory representations will be activated instead of memories linked to negative views of the self (van der Gaag, van Oosterhout, Daalman, Sommer, & Korrelboom, 2012).

The simple wound metaphor highlights a key principle in doing memory exposure work, the importance of exposure to traumatic psychic injuries. As a therapist, your role is to adopt the stance of a supportive clinician: the memory work will be challenging, though it is recommended and there is substantiated hope that it will be beneficial. There is an ongoing, unresolved debate about the utility of psychotherapeutic stabilisation (i.e. emotional and interpersonal regulation) to prepare for memory work in TFT. One view is that it is essential for safety and engagement with exposure, particularly for people who have difficulty managing emotions and relationships (Cloitre et al., 2012). The alternative view is that it colludes with avoidance, does not improve outcomes, and may actually postpone treatment gains (De Jongh et al., 2016). We believe it is important to strike a balance. The emphasis should be on progressing the reprocessing work, alongside supporting emotional regulation as much as needed, but as little as possible. A secure therapeutic relationship, involvement with the person's support network, and a comprehensive safety/risk management plan are the foundation of this. It may also be helpful to incorporate strategies for managing hyperarousal and dissociation.

The need for psychotherapeutic stabilisation prior to trauma-focused therapy is still under debate.

A complexity in applying memory exposure work in psychosis is that most people have experienced multiple events. It is not possible or necessary to reprocess all of these. Instead, target memories can be selected by collaboratively developing a hierarchical list of the reexperienced or intrusive memories that are hindering the person most or are most associated with their negative beliefs. We recommend targeting the worst event first, where possible, to help the person learn that they can tolerate exposure. An alternative approach is to develop a timeline and focus on reprocessing the first, worst, typical, and last events, as this may support the organisation of autobiographical memory. *Drawing on the PTSp model, there are three main ways in which directly targeting event memories with therapeutic techniques can be useful and may potentially improve a range of difficulties:*

- First, they are useful in reducing the frequency, vividness, and distress associated with trauma memory intrusions. They may elaborate decontextualised memories (including those related to both reexperiencing and hallucinatory intrusions) within a broader narrative of the event, and as a result stop them from intruding as sensory perceptions in the here and now. This may also reduce arousal and dissociative detachment, and improve sleep.

- Second, they involve changing the unhelpful survival strategy of avoiding memories and memory triggers. This supports people in learning that they can handle their own memories, and increases their distress tolerance and emotional regulation skills.
- Third, they may support people in seeing the complete or broader meanings of their traumatic memories. This may help people modify negative beliefs that influence difficulties in the present, and develop more helpful ideas (see Box 19.3).

Phase Three: Work on Beliefs, Appraisals, Responses, Survival Strategies, Emotion Regulation, and Triggers

Phase three of the tf-CBTp model is the broadest phase and the content is highly dependent on the specific remaining problems. This phase may be particularly relevant when memory work is either not indicated or not effective, or when people are not yet willing or able to engage in memory exposure. For people who have completed memory work, the focus is on addressing residual difficulties or problems, which are linked to their therapy goals. Standard second- and third-wave cognitive and behavioural techniques can be used to work on beliefs, emotion regulation strategies, psychotic experiences, and triggers. This may often involve reviewing the formulation of these difficulties. Therapists should support learning of new strategies in sessions, use cognitive and behavioural experiments, and collaboratively plan how to generalise useful techniques to the person's daily life. Problem solving should be used as needed (see Box 19.4).

Box 19.3 JANET: Memory Work

Janet initially received prolonged exposure, countering her avoidance and dissociation, and reprocessed eight trauma memories; four concerned the sexual abuse (including a memory of an incident in which she got semen in her mouth), two the physical abuse, and two the bullying.

Janet's abuse memories became more contextualised and she was able to start making sense of her experiences of being bullied and abused. She learnt that her memories were not dangerous and that she could have control over them. She was also able to consider that the abuse was probably not her fault and that she was not bad and weak, although she struggled to emotionally connect to this and still felt ashamed. EMDR was then used to further target her self-blame connected to the memories of abuse, and she was able to experience how, being a small child, she was actually innocent and good enough, which reduced the intensity of her distress.

At the end of the memory work, the intensity of reexperiencing and hallucinations of tasting semen reduced and she had less intrusions of the bullying. Importantly, when her memories were triggered she no longer suppressed them. Janet was less aroused and slept better.

Box 19.4 JANET: Coping and Reclaiming Life

For Janet, this phase involved experimenting with going out and being around people whilst letting down her guard. To support her in approaching these emotionally charged situations, she learnt to regulate her breathing when anxious, ground herself when dissociated, and use compassionate imagery when negative thoughts about herself arose. She started to worry less about what others thought of her and stand up more to the voice when it criticised her. Using several cognitive techniques helped Janet to understand that the voice was probably not the devil, but a reflection of negative interactions in the past combined with self-blame. By the end of therapy, she believed that she was a good enough person and she was able to ignore the voice. As a result, the voice frequency decreased and Janet felt sufficiently safe and self-assured around others to be able to achieve her therapy goal of joining a choir.

CONCLUSION

This chapter has highlighted that, in contrast to concerns about using trauma-focused therapies in psychosis, the emerging evidence base indicates that these interventions can be safe and effective in people with psychosis and PTSD, suggesting that they should be implemented in frontline services. We also presented a phased approach to tf-CBTp to help guide formulation and intervention for the broader range of PTSp difficulties. Avenues for future research include improving our understanding of how trauma and psychosis are associated and how targeting trauma memories may impact on psychosis. We hope that the phased tf-CBTp framework presented here will assist you in working collaboratively with people to target their problems and to support them in living a valued life.

Acknowledgements

We are grateful to Dr. Rachel Brand and Dr. Neil Thomas for their comments on an earlier version of this chapter.

References

Aderka, I. M., Foa, E. B., Applebaum, E., Shafran, N., & Gilboa-Schechtman, E. (2011). Direction of influence between posttraumatic and depressive symptoms during prolonged exposure therapy among children and adolescents. *Journal of Consulting and Clinical Psychology, 79*(3), 421–425. https://doi.org/10.1037/a0023318.

Arntz, A., & Weertman, A. (1999). Treatment of childhood memories: Theory and practice. *Behaviour Research and Therapy, 37*(8), 715–740.

Becker, C. B., Darius, E., & Schaumberg, K. (2007). An analog study of patient preferences for exposure versus alternative treatments for posttraumatic stress disorder. *Behaviour Research and Therapy, 45*(12), 2861–2873. https://doi.org/10.1016/j.brat.2007.05.006.

Becker, C. B., Zayfert, C., & Anderson, E. (2004). A survey of psychologists' attitudes towards and utilization of exposure therapy for PTSD. *Behaviour Research and Therapy, 42*(3), 277–292. https://doi.org/10.1016/s0005-7967(03)00138-4.

Brand, R. M., McEnery, C., Rossell, S., Bendall, S., & Thomas, N. (2017). Do trauma-focussed psychological interventions have an effect on psychotic symptoms? A systematic review and meta-analysis. *Schizophrenia Research*. https://doi.org/10.1016/j.schres.2017.08.037.

Brewin, C. R. (2006). Understanding cognitive behaviour therapy: A retrieval competition account. *Behaviour Research and Therapy*, *44*(6), 765–784. https://doi.org/10.1016/j.brat.2006.02.005.

Cloitre, M., Courtois, C. A., Ford, J. D., Green, B. L., Alexander, P., Briere, J., et al. (2012). *The ISTSS expert consensus treatment guidelines for complex PTSD in adults*: (p. 21). Retrieved November 5 from:(2012). http://www.istss.org/AM/Template.cfm?Section=ISTSS_Complex_PTSD_Treatment_Guidelines&Template=/CM/ContentDisplay.cfm&ContentID=5185.

Cooper, A. A., Clifton, E. G., & Feeny, N. C. (2017). An empirical review of potential mediators and mechanisms of prolonged exposure therapy. *Clinical Psychology Review*, *56*, 106–121. https://doi.org/10.1016/j.cpr.2017.07.003.

de Bont, P. A., van den Berg, D. P., van der Vleugel, B. M., de Roos, C., de Jongh, A., van der Gaag, M., et al. (2015). Predictive validity of the trauma screening questionnaire in detecting post-traumatic stress disorder in patients with psychotic disorders. *The British Journal of Psychiatry: The Journal of Mental Science*, *206*(5), 408–416. https://doi.org/10.1192/bjp.bp.114.148486.

de Bont, P. A., van den Berg, D. P., van der Vleugel, B. M., de Roos, C., de Jongh, A., van der Gaag, M., et al. (2016). Prolonged exposure and EMDR for PTSD v. A PTSD waiting-list condition: Effects on symptoms of psychosis, depression and social functioning in patients with chronic psychotic disorders. *Psychological Medicine*, 1–11. https://doi.org/10.1017/S0033291716001094.

de Bont, P. A., van Minnen, A., & de Jongh, A. (2013). Treating PTSD in patients with psychosis: A within-group controlled feasibility study examining the efficacy and safety of evidence-based PE and EMDR protocols. *Behavior Therapy*, *44*, 717–730. https://doi.org/10.1016/j.beth.2013.07.002.

De Jongh, A., Resick, P. A., Zoellner, L. A., van Minnen, A., Lee, C. W., Monson, C. M., et al. (2016). Critical analysis of the current treatment guidelines for complex PTSD in adults. *Depression and Anxiety*. https://doi.org/10.1002/da.22469.

Diehle, J., Schmitt, K., Daams, J. G., Boer, F., & Lindauer, R. J. (2014). Effects of psychotherapy on trauma-related cognitions in posttraumatic stress disorder: A meta-analysis. *Journal of Traumatic Stress*, *27*(3), 257–264. https://doi.org/10.1002/jts.21924.

Ehlers, A., & Wild, J. (2015). Cognitive therapy for PTSD: Updating memories and meanings of trauma. In U. Schnyder, & M. Cloitre (Eds.), *Evidence based treatments for trauma-related psychological disorders* (pp. 161–187). Cham: Springer.

Feeny, N. C., Zoellner, L. A., Mavissakalian, M. R., & Roy-Byrne, P. P. (2009). What would you choose? Sertraline or prolonged exposure in community and PTSD treatment seeking women. *Depression and Anxiety*, *26*(8), 724–731. https://doi.org/10.1002/da.20588.

Foa, E. B., Hembree, E. A., & Rothbaum, B. O. (2007). *Prolonged exposure therapy for PTSD: Emotional processing of traumatic experiences: Therapist guide*. Oxford: Oxford University Press [Retrieved from LOC].

Frueh, B. C., Cusack, K. J., Grubaugh, A. L., Sauvageot, J. A., & Wells, C. (2006). Clinicians' perspectives on cognitive-behavioral treatment for PTSD among persons with severe mental illness. *Psychiatric Services (Washington, DC)*, *57*(7), 1027–1031. https://doi.org/10.1176/appi.ps.57.7.1027.

Frueh, B. C., Grubaugh, A. L., Cusack, K. J., Kimble, M. O., Elhai, J. D., & Knapp, R. G. (2009). Exposure-based cognitive-behavioral treatment of PTSD in adults with schizophrenia or schizoaffective disorder: A pilot study. *Journal of Anxiety Disorders*, *23*(5), 665–675. https://doi.org/10.1016/j.janxdis.2009.02.005.

Galletly, C., Castle, D., Dark, F., et al. (2016). Royal Australian and New Zealand College of Psychiatrists clinical practice guidelines for the management of schizophrenia and related disorders. *Australian and New Zealand Journal of Psychiatry*, *50*, 410–472.

Grubaugh, A. L., Clapp, J. D., Frueh, B. C., Tuerk, P. W., Knapp, R. G., & Egede, L. E. (2016). Open trial of exposure therapy for PTSD among patients with severe and persistent mental illness. *Behaviour Research and Therapy*, *78*, 1–12. https://doi.org/10.1016/j.brat.2015.12.006.

Hardy, A., & van den Berg, D. (2017). Healing traumatic memories in psychosis: A response to sin and Spain (2016). *Psychosis*, *9*(1), 95–96. https://doi.org/10.1080/17522439.2016.1264993.

Hembree, E. A., Foa, E. B., Dorfan, N. M., Street, G. P., Kowalski, J., & Tu, X. (2003). Do patients drop out prematurely from exposure therapy for PTSD? *Journal of Traumatic Stress*, *16*(6), 555–562. https://doi.org/10.1023/B:JOTS.0000004078.93012.7d.

Kehle-Forbes, S. M., Polusny, M. A., Erbes, C. R., & Gerould, H. (2014). Acceptability of prolonged exposure therapy among U.S. Iraq war veterans with PTSD symptomology. *Journal of Traumatic Stress*, *27*(4), 483–487. https://doi.org/10.1002/jts.21935.

Lee, D. J., Schnitzlein, C. W., Wolf, J. P., Vythilingam, M., Rasmusson, A. M., & Hoge, C. W. (2016). Psychotherapy versus pharmacotherapy for posttraumatic stress disorder: Systemic review and meta-analyses to determine first-line treatments. *Depression and Anxiety*. https://doi.org/10.1002/da.22511.

Meyer, J. M., Farrell, N. R., Kemp, J. J., Blakey, S. M., & Deacon, B. J. (2014). Why do clinicians exclude anxious clients from exposure therapy? *Behaviour Research and Therapy*, *54*, 49–53. https://doi.org/10.1016/j.brat.2014.01.004.

Morrison, A. P. (2017). A manualised treatment protocol to guide delivery of evidence-based cognitive therapy for people with distressing psychosis: Learning from clinical trials. *Psychosis*. https://doi.org/10.1080/17522439.2017.1295098.

Mueser, K. T., Gottlieb, J. D., Xie, H., Lu, W., Yanos, P. T., Rosenberg, S. D., et al. (2015). Evaluation of cognitive restructuring for post-traumatic stress disorder in people with severe mental illness. *The British Journal of Psychiatry: The Journal of Mental Science*. https://doi.org/10.1192/bjp.bp.114.147926.

Mueser, K. T., Rosenberg, S. D., Jankowski, M. K., Hamblen, J. L., & Monica, D. (2004). A cognitive-behavioral treatment program for posttraumatic stress disorder in persons with severe mental illness. *American Journal of Psychiatric Rehabilitation*, *7*(2), 107–146 [Retrieved from Google Scholar].

Mueser, K. T., Rosenberg, S. D., Xie, H., Jankowski, M. K., Bolton, E. E., Lu, W., et al. (2008). A randomized controlled trial of cognitive-behavioral treatment for posttraumatic stress disorder in severe mental illness. *Journal of Consulting and Clinical Psychology*, *76*(2), 259–271. https://doi.org/10.1037/0022-006X.76.2.259.

NICE. (2014). Psychosis and schizophrenia in adults: Prevention and management. https://www.nice.org.uk/guidance/cg178.

Olatunji, B. O., Deacon, B. J., & Abramowitz, J. S. (2009). The cruelest cure? Ethical issues in the implementation of exposure-based treatments. *Cognitive and Behavioral Practice*, *16*(2), 172–180 [Retrieved from Google Scholar].

Reger, G. M., Durham, T. L., Tarantino, K. A., Luxton, D. D., Holloway, K. M., & Lee, J. A. (2013). Deployed soldiers' reactions to exposure and medication treatments for PTSD. *Psychological Trauma: Theory, Research, Practice and Policy*, *5*(4), 309–316. https://doi.org/10.1037/a0028409.

Resick, P. A., & Schnicke, M. K. (1992). Cognitive processing therapy for sexual assault victims. *Journal of Consulting and Clinical Psychology*, *60*(5), 748–756 [Retrieved from Google Scholar].

Ronconi, J. M., Shiner, B., & Watts, B. V. (2015). A meta-analysis of depressive symptom outcomes in randomized, controlled trials for PTSD. *The Journal of Nervous and Mental Disease*, *203*(7), 522–529. https://doi.org/10.1097/NMD.0000000000000322.

Rosenberg, S. D., Mueser, K. T., Jankowski, M. K., Salyers, M. P., & Acker, K. (2004). Cognitive-behavioral treatment of PTSD in severe mental illness: Results of a pilot study. *American Journal of Psychiatric Rehabilitation*, *7*(2), 171–186. https://doi.org/10.1080/15487760490476200.

Salyers, M. P., Evans, L. J., Bond, G. R., & Meyer, P. S. (2004). Barriers to assessment and treatment of posttraumatic stress disorder and other trauma-related problems in people with severe mental illness: Clinician perspectives. *Community Mental Health Journal*, *40*(1), 17–31.

Schnyder, U., Ehlers, A., Elbert, T., Foa, E. B., Gersons, B. P., Resick, P. A., et al. (2015). Psychotherapies for PTSD: What do they have in common? *European Journal of Psychotraumatology*, *6*, [Retrieved from Google Scholar].

Shapiro, F. (2001). *Eye movement desensitization and reprocessing: Basic principles, protocols, and procedures*. New York: Guilford Press.

Sin, J., & Spain, D. (2016). Psychological interventions for trauma in individuals who have psychosis: A systematic review and meta-analysis. *Psychosis*, 1–15. https://doi.org/10.1080/17522439.2016.1167946.

Smucker, M. R. (1995). Imagery rescripting: A new treatment for survivors of childhood sexual abuse suffering from posttraumatic stress. *Journal of Cognitive Psychotherapy*, *9*(1), 3–17 (Retrieved from Google Scholar).

Steel, C., Hardy, A., Smith, B., Wykes, T., Rose, S., Enright, S., et al. (2016). Cognitive-behaviour therapy for post-traumatic stress in schizophrenia. A randomized controlled trial. *Psychological Medicine*, 1–9. https://doi.org/10.1017/S0033291716002117.

Stenmark, H., Catani, C., Neuner, F., Elbert, T., & Holen, A. (2013). Treating PTSD in refugees and asylum seekers within the general health care system. A randomized controlled multicenter study. *Behaviour Research and Therapy*, *51*(10), 641–647. https://doi.org/10.1016/j.brat.2013.07.002.

van den Berg, D. P., de Bont, P. A., van der Vleugel, B. M., de Roos, C., de Jongh, A., Van Minnen, A., et al. (2015). Prolonged exposure vs eye movement desensitization and reprocessing vs waiting list for posttraumatic stress disorder in patients with a psychotic disorder: A randomized clinical trial. *JAMA Psychiatry*, *72*(3), 259–267. https://doi.org/10.1001/jamapsychiatry.2014.2637.

van den Berg, D. P., de Bont, P. A., van der Vleugel, B. M., de Roos, C., de Jongh, A., van Minnen, A., et al. (2016). Trauma-focused treatment in PTSD patients with psychosis: Symptom exacerbation, adverse events, and revictimization. *Schizophrenia Bulletin*, *42*(3), 693–702. https://doi.org/10.1093/schbul/sbv172.

van den Berg, D. P., & van der Gaag, M. (2012). Treating trauma in psychosis with EMDR: A pilot study. *Journal of Behavior Therapy and Experimental Psychiatry*, *43*(1), 664–671. https://doi.org/10.1016/j.jbtep.2011.09.011.

van den Hout, M. A., Bartelski, N., & Engelhard, I. M. (2012). On EMDR: Eye movements during retrieval reduce subjective vividness and objective memory accessibility during future recall. *Cognition and Emotion*, *27*(1), 177–183. https://doi.org/10.1080/02699931.2012.691087.

van der Gaag, M., van Oosterhout, B., Daalman, K., Sommer, I. E., & Korrelboom, K. (2012). Initial evaluation of the effects of competitive memory training (COMET) on depression in schizophrenia-spectrum patients with persistent auditory verbal hallucinations: A randomized controlled trial. *The British Journal of Clinical Psychology/the British Psychological Society*, *51*(2), 158–171. https://doi.org/10.1111/j.2044-8260.2011.02025.x.

van Minnen, A., Zoellner, L. A., Harned, M. S., & Mills, K. (2015). Changes in comorbid conditions after prolonged exposure for PTSD: A literature review. *Current Psychiatry Reports*, *17*(3), 549. https://doi.org/10.1007/s11920-015-0549-1.

Watts, B. V., Schnurr, P. P., Mayo, L., Young-Xu, Y., Weeks, W. B., & Friedman, M. J. (2013). Meta-analysis of the efficacy of treatments for posttraumatic stress disorder. *The Journal of Clinical Psychiatry*, *74*(6), e541–e550. https://doi.org/10.4088/JCP.12r08225.

Definitions of Key Terms

Trauma explanation: Trauma can be defined as any event(s) that a person interprets as representing a significant physical or psychological threat to the self, including those that they witness in others.

Posttraumatic stress (PTS) The range of mental health difficulties people can experience following trauma, reflecting a transdiagnostic approach.

Posttraumatic stress disorder (PTSD) A disorder of posttraumatic stress with core symptoms of reexperiencing, avoidance, negative changes in cognitions and mood, and hyperarousal, with a complex subtype also including self-disturbances (self-concept, interpersonal relating, and emotional regulation.

Posttraumatic stress in psychosis (PTSp) The range of posttraumatic stress difficulties that people with psychosis may experience following trauma, reflecting a transdiagnostic approach.

Trauma-focused therapies (TFT) A family of therapies that share common mechanisms, including exposure to trauma memories and stimuli, modifying trauma-related beliefs, managing emotions and reclaiming life.

CHAPTER 20

Better Sleep: Evidence-Based Interventions

Felicity Waite*,†, Bryony Sheaves*,†,‡

*Oxford Cognitive Approaches to Psychosis, Department of Psychiatry, University of Oxford, Oxford, United Kingdom, †Oxford Health NHS Foundation Trust, Oxford, United Kingdom, ‡Nuffield Department of Clinical Neurosciences, Sleep and Circadian Neuroscience Institute, University of Oxford, Oxford, United Kingdom

Key Learning Objectives

- To recognise that sleep problems are pervasive and their treatment may result in improvements in psychotic experiences and wellbeing.
- To learn from patient accounts that psychological interventions for sleep problems are valued.
- To be aware of the current evidence base for brief, targeted, cognitive-behavioural treatments for improving sleep in patients with psychosis.
- To understand the key mechanisms hypothesised to underpin sleep, and its disruption, and apply this in a targeted psychological intervention.
- To apply sleep science and core CBT principles in order to adapt specific treatment techniques in response to the individualised formulation.

INTRODUCTION

When I'm tired, everything is worse

Waite, Evans, et al. (2016, p. 186)

Over recent years, there has been increasing awareness of the importance of sleep to mental health (Freeman et al., 2017). Historically, sleep problems have been understood as a symptom of the psychiatric disorder or as a nonspecific epiphenomenon. Yet recent research has turned this traditional view on its head and instead shown that sleep disruption is one causal factor in the occurrence of paranoia, hallucinatory experiences, and mood state (Freeman et al., 2017; Harvey et al., 2015; Reeve, Emsley, Sheaves, & Freeman, 2018). Patients and staff

Research clearly indicates a causal role of sleep disturbance in psychotic symptoms.

A Clinical Introduction to Psychosis. https://doi.org/10.1016/B978-0-12-815012-2.00020-1

Box 20.1 Sleep Apnea

Obstructive sleep apnea (OSA) is a sleep-related breathing disorder in which airflow is reduced due to blocking of the upper airway during sleep. OSA is treated using a Continuous Positive Airway Pressure (CPAP) device, which ensures adequate airflow throughout sleep.

- Estimates of prevalence indicate rates of approximately 24% in patients with schizophrenia (Annamalai, Palmese, Chwastiak, Srihari, & Tek, 2015).
- Given the high prevalence, prior to undertaking psychological sleep work, clinicians should screen and seek onward referral for those at high risk.
- The STOP-BANG Sleep Apnea Questionnaire (Chung, Abdullah, & Liao, 2016) can be used to screen patients.
- Diagnosis and treatment requires a full assessment at a respiratory sleep medicine clinic. Further details on the assessment of OSA are provided in Chapter 11.

recognise the need for effective interventions, yet sleep problems are often overlooked and treatment is rarely provided (Rehman et al., 2017).

Nightmares are a common sleep problem in people with psychotic disorders.

In patients with psychosis sleep disruption is common, complex, and pervasive. However, sleep disruption is an umbrella term and it is only by assessing the underlying sleep disorder(s) that appropriate treatments can be identified. The majority of patients with psychosis meet diagnostic criteria for at least one sleep disorder and in fact comorbidity is the norm (Reeve, Sheaves, & Freeman, 2018). Insomnia (50%) and nightmare disorder (48%) are the most common disorders (Reeve, Sheaves, et al., 2018), and both are amenable to psychological interventions. There are also high rates of sleep apnea, which requires a respiratory intervention (see Box 20.1). This chapter will outline psychological approaches to improving sleep in patients with psychosis and bipolar affective disorder, with a particular focus on insomnia and nightmares.

EVIDENCE-BASED PSYCHOLOGICAL INTERVENTIONS FOR DISRUPTED SLEEP IN PATIENTS WITH PSYCHOSIS

> It sorted out my sleep and I am a better person for it
>
> **Waite, Evans, et al. (2016, p. 187)**

Cognitive behavioural therapy (CBT) interventions have an established evidence base for the treatment of insomnia (Irwin, Cole, & Nicassio, 2006; Mitchell, Gehrman, Perlis, & Umscheid, 2012; Riemann & Perlis, 2009) and nightmare disorder (Casement & Swanson, 2012; Hansen, Höfling, Kröner-Borowik, Stangier, & Steil, 2013) and are recommended in clinical treatment guidelines (Aurora et al., 2010; National Institute for Health and Care Excellence (NICE), 2015; Qaseem et al., 2016). However, these guidelines are based on trials which have typically excluded patients with psychosis and bipolar affective disorder.

A series of clinical studies have evaluated the effect of CBT for insomnia (CBT-I) across the spectrum of severity of psychotic experiences (Bradley et al., 2017; Freeman et al., 2017; Freeman, Waite, et al., 2015; Sheaves et al., 2017). The largest was a randomised controlled trial (RCT) of digital CBT-I, which recruited 3755 university students across the United Kingdom, all of whom had insomnia (Freeman et al., 2017). The intervention was highly effective for treating insomnia (Cohen's d effect size = 1.11) and also led to small but highly significant improvements in hallucinatory experiences (d = 0.24) and paranoid thoughts (d = 0.19). Importantly, changes in sleep mediated around two-thirds of the change in paranoia and just under half of the change in hallucinatory experiences. This provides the most robust evidence that insomnia is a mechanism fuelling psychotic experiences. However, the sample was recruited based on insomnia alone and therefore the majority were not in touch with mental health services.

In clinical samples, trials of adapted CBT-I have shown that large effect size improvements in insomnia can be achieved in those at ultra-high risk for psychosis (UHR) (Bradley et al., 2017), with persistent psychotic symptoms (Freeman, Waite, et al., 2015) and during an acute episode (Sheaves et al., 2017). In addition to the clinical benefits, a health economic evaluation of the Better Sleep Trial (Freeman, Waite, et al., 2015) indicated that the sleep intervention may also be cost effective (Tsiachristas, Waite, Freeman, & Luengo-Fernandez, 2018). Importantly, these interventions are popular with patients: in these trials therapy uptake was between 89% and 100%. The treatment of sleep disturbance may be delivered as an effective stand-alone module. It is also currently being evaluated as one component of a longer-term psychological therapy for persecutory delusions (Freeman et al., 2016).

Interventions to improve sleep give significant benefit to clients and are potentially cost-effective for services.

Treatments to improve sleep are a priority for clients with psychosis, and uptake is often high.

In these trials, each intervention had key adaptations to meet the needs of that group. In the UHR group, particular consideration was given to a shift in circadian timing (to become more of an 'evening type'), which is a typical part of adolescent development. In patients with persistent psychotic experiences, particular attention was given to the sleep environment, the use of sleep as an escape from distressing psychotic experiences, and the impact of medication (Waite, Myers, et al., 2016). The acute phase intervention was delivered in 2 weeks in order that patients received a full dose of therapy prior to discharge. Enhanced light exposure (increasing daytime exposure to light and fostering a dark evening environment) was used to mitigate the effects of low light levels in hospital, which can disrupt circadian rhythms (Sheaves et al., 2018).

The current evidence has evaluated treatments delivered on an individual basis. The effects of group interventions have not yet been tested.

To treat nightmares, clinical guidelines recommend imagery rehearsal (IR) training (a particular CBT technique) (Aurora et al., 2010). Whilst different IR protocols exist, the basic elements include a psychoeducation phase, rescripting a change of ending to the nightmare, and daily imaginal rehearsal of the new dream narrative (Casement & Swanson, 2012). Metaanalytic data show that IR leads to moderate reductions in nightmare frequency, in patients without a diagnosis of psychosis (Casement & Swanson, 2012). Recently, a brief CBT for

Despite patients and clinicians recognising the problem of hypersomnia, excessive or oversleeping, there has been little research addressing this issue.

nightmares protocol was tested in a pilot RCT with patients experiencing persecutory delusions. Large effect size reductions in both nightmare severity and insomnia were found when compared with standard care alone (Sheaves et al., 2019). This encouraging pilot result merits testing in a larger trial.

The key treatment techniques and adaptations from these trials are outlined below.

OVERVIEW OF TREATMENT

What Drives Healthy Sleep? How Can We Use This to Successfully Treat Sleep Disturbance?

Sleep comprises distinct phases or cycles, which repeat throughout the night (see Box 20.2). It is widely understood that two biological processes govern sleep: homeostatic sleep pressure (process S) and circadian rhythm (process C) (Borbély, 1982) (see Chapter 11). Process S is the need, or propensity, for sleep, which increases as a result of time awake. Process C is the body's natural 24-h circadian rhythm or 'body clock', which dictates the timing of sleep. These two processes interact such that the peak need for sleep coincides with the circadian timing, which initiates sleep. However, there is a third psychological factor, which can disrupt these processes: hyperarousal. Hyperarousal refers to heightened physiological alertness and increased responsiveness to stimuli, typically driven by anxiety. This alerting system can disrupt sleep, despite high sleep pressure and aligned circadian timing (Harvey, 2002). Therefore, all three factors require consideration to successfully treat sleep problems.

Principles of the Treatment Approach

> It's an active, 'doing' therapy
>
> **Waite, Evans, et al. (2016, p. 189)**

Although described as a 'talking therapy', the therapy sessions are active and change strategies are initiated in the first session. Whenever possible, sessions include

Box 20.2 Sleep Architecture

Polysomnography (an integrated assessment of neural activity, oxygen levels, heart rate, breathing, and movement during sleep) indicates distinct phases of sleep. Broadly these are split into nonrapid eye movement sleep (NREM) and rapid eye movement sleep (REM). These phases of sleep occur to a different degree across the sleep window, appearing as cycles on a hypnogram (see Chapter 11). For example, the majority of deep sleep (NREM stage 3) is achieved early in the sleep window. A greater degree of REM sleep (dreaming sleep) occurs later in the sleep period. Brief awakenings between sleep cycles are a normal part of human sleep, but they are so brief that we are not usually aware of them.

experiential learning, for example going for a walk in the session to reduce sleepiness, boost energy, and exposure to daylight. Outpatient interventions are delivered in between 4 (nightmares) to 8 (insomnia) weekly sessions; however, inpatient treatment is better suited to an intensive (14-day) therapy window. Contact between sessions by text message, email, or telephone calls supports the implementation of strategies. Patients will often have multiple, interacting difficulties (e.g. paranoia, voices, low mood), of which sleep disruption is only one. The brevity and targeted nature of this sleep intervention gives permission to both the patient and therapist to focus on the specific sleep-related treatment goals.

Promoting Engagement and Motivation

> I didn't think it would work at first
>
> **Waite et al. (2018, p. 4)**

Medication can have a significant impact on sleep (see Box 20.3).

Despite wanting treatment for sleep problems, many patients describe negative expectations about the likely effectiveness of psychological therapy to improve sleep (Faulkner & Bee, 2017; Waite et al., 2018). Providing concise, easy-to-understand summaries of the evidence base promotes hope and facilitates initial engagement. The language used to describe the rationale for treatment strategies can influence engagement and implementation of strategies. Examples of phrases you could use in therapy are provided in Table 20.1. Sleep problems cause significant daytime impairment (Kyle, Espie, & Morgan, 2010). Feeling exhausted, struggling to concentrate, as well as distressing psychotic experiences, can undermine engagement and learning during therapy sessions. Therefore, the therapist acknowledges and monitors these common difficulties and adjusts the session. For example, timing sessions to when the patient is most alert, incorporating breaks, and being active in the session to combat sleepiness.

Assessment, Formulation, and Goal Setting

> It sort of opened my eyes as such, it gave me a wider understanding of what actually affects my sleep
>
> **Waite et al. (2018, p. 4)**

A brief assessment focused specifically on sleep problems, their history, and the current factors disrupting sleep is conducted. The assessment includes gathering an example of a recent, typical 24-h period of sleep problems, including wake time, rise time, bedtime, and time of sleep onset. Information about medication, including recent changes, is collected due to the potential effects on sleep and fatigue (see Box 20.3). For insomnia, tick lists of common maintenance factors for sleep disruption, for example 'I don't have a regular bedtime and wake-up time'; 'I hear voices that stop me sleeping'; 'I don't do much in the day, so am not tired enough to sleep well' allow swift assessment and collaborative discussion about which factors to target in therapy. Table 20.1 provides an example of

Table 20.1 Key Assessment Items, Intervention Strategies, and Descriptive Phrases Used in Treatment

Sleep process	Example assessment items	Core treatment strategies	Descriptions used in therapy
Circadian rhythm alignment	*'I don't have a regular bedtime and wake-up time'* *'I sleep during the day'.* *'My room is too light at night time'*	Setting regular bed and wake times, using daily activity points, setting regular meal times, managing exposure to light/dark, and utilising other social zeitgebers.	*'We live in a world of rhythms, for example night follows day, and we need to get your rhythms back in sync'.* *'How much sleep do you need each night? Let's match this sleep window to your natural body clock'*
Sleep pressure	*'I don't do much in the day, so am not tired enough to sleep well'* *'I lie-in in the mornings and can't sleep the following night'* *'I nap in the day, which decreases my 'sleep pressure' at night'* *'I go to bed early which decreases my 'sleep pressure''*	Increase sleep pressure by increasing daytime activity, ensuring rise time is early enough, reduce naps, and ensure bedtime is late enough.	*'A 24 hour problem requires a 24 hour solution'.* *'It might sound odd, but going to bed later actually means getting to sleep faster and at the time that you want'.* *'The 24-hour body clock ensures that peak alertness and performance occurs in the day and a good block of sleep occurs at night'.*
Presleep hyperarousal	*'I hear voices that stop me sleeping'* *'Thoughts go through my head and keep me awake'.* *'I have a lot of worries which keep me awake'.* *'I feel anxious when I am trying to sleep'.* *'I worry about other people harming me'.* *'I feel too upset to sleep'.*	Worry reduction strategies, cognitive restructuring techniques, and night-time relaxation. Stimulus control to relearn the association between bed and sleep, rather than distressing voices and fears.	*'Worry takes us to the worst-case-scenario in our mind, this triggers anxiety and our body reacts by being on 'high-alert'. This is the opposite to the relaxed, calm feelings we need in order to sleep. We need to feel safe to fall asleep'* *'Bed equals sleep. When we have difficulty sleeping, bed can become associated with wakefulness, anxiety, paranoia or a place where we hear voices. To get sleep back on track, we need to boost the connection between bed and sleep'.*

Table 20.1 Key Assessment Items, Intervention Strategies, and Descriptive Phrases Used in Treatment—cont'd

Sleep process	Example assessment items	Core treatment strategies	Descriptions used in therapy
	'I don't have a regular pre-bed routine that helps me unwind'		
Nightmares	*'I wake from frightening dreams'* *'I have nightmares'*	Imagery rehearsal training, reducing periods of oversleeping (if present), grounding techniques, switching attentional focus (from voices/worries), relaxation.	*'Whilst your current nightmare(s) have been played many times, we'll work together to create a director's cut, with a new ending that you prefer'*.
Sleep promoting environment and behaviours	*'I have a lot of caffeine (coffee, tea, coke, chocolate)'* *'I smoke before I go to bed'.* *'My bed is uncomfortable'.*	Promote sleep hygiene to facilitate sleep.	*'Setting the scene for good sleep'* *'Becoming a sleep expert'* *'Stacking the odds in favour of sleep'*

Box 20.3 Sleep and Medication

Prescribed medication can have a range of side effects, including sedation, fatigue, anxiety, and nightmares. Some medications directly disrupt sleep, for example a known side effect of some antidepressants is nightmares. Sedating side effects can make it difficult to get up in the morning and fatigue may prompt patients to head to bed before the start of their planned sleep window. Medication should be reviewed in collaboration with the prescriber. Reviewing a timeline of medication changes and symptom onset can help to identify any correlations.

Psychological strategies can also be of benefit in managing medication side effects, for example scheduling pleasant morning activities as part of a rise-up routine is particularly important for people who report a 'hangover' effect from medication. In this example, behavioural experiments can be used to test beliefs about the production and use of energy.

how each factor can be targeted with a specific treatment technique. Further example assessment lists are available in Sheaves et al. (2018) and Myers, Startup, and Freeman (2013).

When nightmares are present, information is gathered about their frequency, when they occur in the sleep period (e.g. 3 am or 9 am), beliefs about what the nightmare might mean and whether the content relates to daytime symptoms (e.g. worries, persecutory beliefs, or threats from voices). Assessment of nightmare content is brief (a bullet point account) and only conducted if the person feels able to share the content. The therapists' aim is to learn enough detail to allow for the image to be rescripted, but not so much as to re-expose the patient to highly distressing content.

Ensure sleep treatment goals are specific, measurable, achievable, realistic, and time-limited.

Treatment goals should be sleep focused, for example the ideal timing and quality of sleep, or daytime energy levels. It is important to ensure goals are specific, measurable, achievable, realistic, and time limited. Measures to assess progress are set in this initial session. Often this includes a sleep diary a standard component in CBT-I (see Carney et al., 2012), self-report measures, for example the Insomnia Severity Index (Bastien, Vallières, & Morin, 2001), Sleep Condition Indicator (Espie et al., 2014), or Disturbing Dreams and Nightmare Severity Index (Krakow, 2006), and potentially objective estimates of sleep for example actigraphy devices. Actigraphy is the measurement of movement via a small accelerometer device. It is a validated measure and frequently used in sleep research. Commercially available fitness trackers are also widely accessible, though most are not validated. Both can be used to estimate sleep via periods of inactivity. *For a full description of assessment tools see* Chapter 11.

The formulation is focused explicitly on sleep disruption and the key factors currently maintaining the sleep problem, rather than a complex or longitudinal formulation of the multiple problems patients' experience. However, co-morbid symptoms feature if they contribute to the sleep problem, for example hearing voices at night which prevents sleep onset or depression causing difficulties with energy and motivation to get up in the morning. As in all CBT, the formulation evolves collaboratively throughout the intervention; however, the therapists' goal is to produce a formulation, which is advanced enough by the end of the first session to enable intervention strategies to be implemented immediately. An example formulation can be seen in Fig. 20.1.

Intervention Strategies

Repertoire of skills

Waite et al. (2018, p. 4)

Insomnia

CBT techniques can be used to precisely target the key mechanisms, which regulate or disrupt sleep: circadian rhythm (process C), homeostatic sleep pressure (process S), and hyperarousal:

1. To target circadian rhythm alignment, which dictates the timing of sleep, exposure to light or dark, which is the key zeitgeber, or time cue, can be used to promote wakefulness or sleep. Circadian rhythms can also be

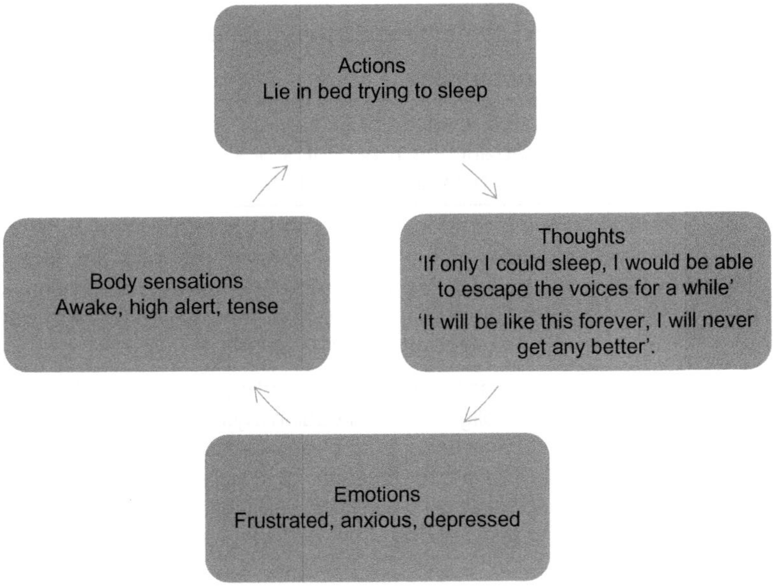

FIG. 20.1
Example maintenance cycle formulation of sleep difficulties.

established by setting consistent bed and wake times, daily activity points, regular meal times, and other social zeitgebers.

2. To target sleep pressure, which increases as a function of time awake and dictates the propensity to sleep, it is important to enable patients to rise early enough, reduce naps, and head to bed late enough to ensure that sleep pressure is optimally high at the desired bed time. This typically involves increasing daytime activity to combat fatigue. The motivational benefits of fitness trackers or wearable devices can support this work.
3. To target presleep hyperarousal, which can disrupt sleep despite circadian entrainment and high sleep pressure, worry reduction strategies, cognitive restructuring techniques, and night-time relaxation are used. Stimulus control enables patients to relearn the association between bed and sleep and interrupt voices and paranoid concerns, which often take hold in bed when there are few distractions. Specific strategies to address hyperarousal related to psychotic experiences, such as listening to the radio or using cue cards, may be incorporated in the treatment.

Table 20.2 provides descriptions of the standard CBT-I techniques. The core treatment technique should target the underlying mechanism that is driving the sleep disruption. Additional strategies should be used as needed to boost the effectiveness of the intervention. Psychotic experiences directly (e.g. voices causing hyperarousal at night which prevents sleep onset) and indirectly (e.g. reduced activity due to paranoid fears, (over)using sleep as a coping strategy

Table 20.2 Descriptions of Standard CBT for Insomnia Intervention Strategies

Technique	Description of strategy
Psychoeducation	Psychoeducation involves providing key information regarding the process of sleep and the impact of poor sleep. For example, using a hypnogram to explain the different stages and cycles of sleep.
Sleep hygiene	Sleep hygiene is a specific psychoeducational intervention. It focuses on addressing a number of environmental (e.g. lack of suitable bed, noise at night, bedroom too hot/cold) and behavioural (e.g. excess caffeine, using TV or computer screens at night) factors that may reduce sleep quality and quantity.
Setting the sleep window (adapted sleep restriction)	Regular bed and rise times are set according to goal sleep duration. The sleep windows is aligned with circadian rhythm and at the time of peak sleep pressure. This helps to stabilise sleep and promote a consistent sleep pattern. Key anchor times to set include wake time, bedtime, meal times and scheduling activities, i.e. energising activities (with light) in the morning and relaxing activities (with dark) in the evening. We cannot directly control the onset of sleep; therefore, we need to manipulate the process we have control over: wakefulness. This means to delay the sleep phase we need to promote wakefulness in the evening and to advance the sleep phase we need to trigger waking in the morning. If the timing of the sleep window requires adjusting to the natural light/dark cycle, increments of between 15 and 60 min are made at a time. After approximately 1 week, once the sleep pattern has re-established within the adjusted window, the sleep times can be altered by another increment. The exact scale of the increments should be agreed with the individual as this strategy can result in a reduction of the total sleep time (i.e. a form of sleep restriction).
Stimulus control	Stimulus control enables patients to relearn the association between bed and good quality sleep. This is achieved by limiting the time in bed not sleeping. Therefore, the bed is only used for sleep and sexual activity. One is instructed to only go to bed when feeling sleepy (after following a wind-down routine to prepare the mind and body for sleep). The 15-minute rule is one component of stimulus control. This strategy is used if one is not asleep within approximately 15 min, one gets out of bed, engages in relaxing activities in a different room, and returns to bed only when feeling 'sleep'-tired.
Wind-down routine	A wind-down routine is crucial for preparing the mind and body for sleep. This transitional phase promotes a shift from an alert daytime state to a relaxed and sleepy night-time state preceding sleep. Typically, this takes 60–90 min and includes relaxing activities, reducing use of screens (which emit blue light which inhibits the release of melatonin, the sleep inducing hormone), and 'putting the day to rest' to conclude thoughts reviewing the day and planning for the next (Espie, 2006).

Table 20.2 Descriptions of Standard CBT for Insomnia Intervention Strategies—cont'd

Technique	Description of strategy
Rise-up routine	A rise-up routine includes waking at a set time and incorporates light and activity to enable one to overcome sleep inertia (the commonly occurring tired, groggy feeling on waking).
Cognitive strategies	Cognitive restructuring and behavioural experiments may be used to test out specific beliefs related to disrupted sleep and daytime fatigue. Cognitive strategies, for example a worry period, might be used to reduce the impact of worry on sleep.
Relaxation	To reduce physiological and emotional arousal, relaxation techniques (including breathing exercises and progressive muscle relaxation) can be used to facilitate sleep.

Box 20.4 Sleep Restriction

Sleep restriction aims to increase sleep pressure and improve sleep efficiency (the percentage of time asleep whilst in bed). This is achieved by restricting the sleep window to the current total sleep time (e.g. if the sleep diary indicates 6 h of sleep, the opportunity for sleep is 6 h). This sleep window is then gradually increased so that it is in line with the goal sleep duration. It should be noted that, despite being regarded as an effective treatment technique, formal sleep restriction is not used in this protocol. This is because it leads to short-term sleep deprivation, sleepiness, and fatigue and may therefore exacerbate psychiatric symptoms or lead to disengagement from therapy. Therefore, for patients with psychosis, the principles are followed but adapted: we set a consistent sleep window without restricting below the target duration (typically 7–8 h).

leading to disrupted circadian rhythm and reduced sleep pressure) disrupt sleep and its treatment. Therefore CBT-I techniques may require adaptation and CBTp techniques (e.g. distraction and attentional switching skills to cope with voices) may be added to the treatment. Throughout the sleep treatment, important learning and reappraisal of psychotic experiences may occur (e.g. 'I can switch my attention from voices, therefore the voices are not as powerful as I thought') although this is not the primary target. Examples of adaptations, including sleep restriction procedures (see Box 20.4), are provided in the case examples.

Nightmares

The key technique used is IR; however, in order to boost efficacy and reduce reliance on a single treatment strategy, novel cognitive-behavioural treatment techniques are used, based on targets identified through a large general population survey (Rek, Sheaves, & Freeman, 2017). These include targeting presleep worry and reducing oversleeping. Specific psychoeducation information about how the brain functions during REM (dreaming) sleep targets beliefs about nightmares (e.g. 'they are a sign of the future') and offers an alternative explanation for the bizarre, yet perceptually real and emotionally intense experience.

Review of Outcome

> So, the therapist would give me a technique and then I'd come back and say: 'This worked for me; this didn't work for me,' and then we could kind of work around that
>
> **Waite et al. (2018, p. 4)**

Progress towards goals is assessed as a standard feature of each session. For example, when targeting nightmares, progress is monitored by asking the client 'Over the past week how much of a problem have your nightmares been?', which is rated from 0 (no problem) to 6 (extremely severe) each session. This information directs the course of therapy: to continue with a particular technique or to implement a new strategy. Measurement and feedback can promote hope and motivation, which is especially important given the difficulty of implementing the intervention techniques.

Future Implementation

> Every time that I try to implement some of those strategies, there is a definite benefit, but it's quite difficult to maintain
>
> **Waite et al. (2018, p. 4)**

Key messages (e.g. the main strategy or idea learnt during the session) are identified and noted each session. This results in a concise *therapy blueprint* (record of learning, key strategies, and ways to overcome challenges) developed as part of the therapy process. This can be used to identify future goals, potential barriers to implementation, and sources of support to promote good sleep for the long term.

CASE STUDIES

To demonstrate the intervention approach, five illustrative case studies are presented. In line with the evidence base, the primary target of these interventions is insomnia and nightmares. Information about hypnotic medication is provided in Box 20.5. Given the high levels of comorbidity, the case studies highlight the adaptations needed to treat insomnia in the context of other comorbid sleep problems. The case examples include adaptations for different types and severity of psychotic experiences, for example adjustments to treatment for young people at ultra-high risk of psychosis and providing interventions on an inpatient ward.

Box 20.5 Reducing Hypnotic Medication

Hypnotics are often prescribed for brief insomnia (2–4 weeks). When insomnia persists, CBT-I is the recommend treatment. Tolerance and rebound effects of hypnotics are well established: this includes the (re) emergence of insomnia symptoms as a result of discontinuing the medication. For patients with psychosis, any tapering and stopping of hypnotics needs to be considered in the context of neuroleptic and other medication. Psychoeducation regarding rebound effects helps manage expectations and gives a clear rationale for tapering. This should include consideration of rebound effects exacerbating psychotic experiences. Tapering should be conducted in partnership with the prescriber as part of a CBT-I intervention.

INSOMNIA

> I used to stay in bed trying to get some sleep for hours, things going through my mind. I used to wake up in the middle of the night and I used to get up very early in the morning as well
>
> Trying to sleep and the voices distract me and they keep me awake.
>
> **Waite et al. (2015, p. 185)**

Insomnia is defined as a difficulty initiating or maintaining sleep or nonrestorative sleep despite adequate time and opportunity to sleep. This results in impaired daytime functioning, such as poor concentration, mood disturbance, and daytime tiredness (NICE, 2015). It is the most commonly reported sleep problem. Insomnia has been identified throughout the spectrum of severity of psychotic experiences, including in people at UHR (Poe et al., 2017), those experiencing a first episode (Reeve, Sheaves, et al., 2018), alongside persistent symptoms (Freeman, Waite, et al., 2015), and during an acute episode (Haynes, Parthasarathy, Kersh, & Bootzin, 2011) (Box 20.6).

Box 20.6 Client Example: 'Mitul'[a]

For years Mitul experienced difficulties getting to sleep, staying asleep, and waking too early, which left him feeling exhausted, on edge, and struggling to cope with distressing voices. During a typical circadian period, Mitul would go to bed at 9pm, but would not fall asleep until approximately 3am. Whilst lying in bed, he would hear voices, worry about his safety, and this would result in feelings of hopelessness and suicidal thoughts. In the night, he would wake 2–3 times before waking for the day at 7am. Feeling exhausted, he would try to relax in bed until 11am and avoid any activities to conserve energy. Later during the day, he would retreat to bed to escape distressing voices and low mood. He would spend around 18h in bed, yet was sleeping for only 4 h.

[a]Hypothetical case.

The key treatment targets for Mitul were:

(1) Increasing sleep pressure (increasing daytime activity, aligning bedtime with his circadian rhythm);
(2) Reducing presleep hyperarousal (using a wind-down routine, switching attentional focus, and using relaxation strategies);
(3) Implementing stimulus control (re-associating bed with sleep).

Stimulus Control: Bed Equals Sleep

In order to re-associate bed with sleep, rather than distressing wakefulness characterised by hearing voices, paranoid fears, and frustration at lack of sleep, Mitul needed to reduce the time spent in bed not sleeping. In other words, to *only use bed for sleep*. For Mitul this meant firstly, delaying bedtime to reduce sleep onset latency (time taken to fall asleep) and time spent listening to voices. Secondly, developing alternative strategies to cope with psychotic experiences instead of retreating to bed during the daytime. Thirdly, implementing the '15-minute rule' to prevent long periods in bed at night *trying* to sleep whilst experiencing distressing worries and voices.

Setting the Sleep Window

Planning an appropriate bedtime, matched to the individual's circadian rhythm can increase the chances of sleep at the desired time and hence reduce time spent attending to voices or worries. In order for Mitul to delay bedtime, a list of potential activities was generated and incorporated into an extended wind-down routine (e.g. selecting a TV series or podcast). Loneliness is often experienced in the evening and night period; therefore, for Mitul, it was agreed that bedtime would be delayed until midnight, but not later.

Reducing Presleep Hyperarousal

Worries, voices, and negative affect contribute to hyperarousal. Therefore, strategies to switch attentional focus are used to reduce arousal. For some clients this may involve planning a worry period (Freeman, Dunn, et al., 2015) in order to postpone worries that come to mind in bed. For Mitul switching attention away from voices to a calming auditory input (such as a premade music play list, or specific radio station), or using a relaxation audio prior to sleep was particularly helpful.

Increasing Daytime Activity

As a circadian cue to distinguish daytime/night time and support stimulus control (by preventing the use of bed during the day), a schedule of activities was developed. This included the 'Five ways to wellbeing': give, connect, be active, take notice, and keep learning (Foresight Mental Capital and Wellbeing Project, 2008). However, paranoid thoughts that others would physically attack him made Mitul fearful about leaving the house. Therefore, a range of activities, which could be completed at home, for example learning new art techniques from online resources or following an exercise video, was initiated. Gradually engaging in activities outside the house was promoted by going for walks in session. This allowed Mitul to directly increase his activity and discover that it was possible he was safe enough to engage in everyday activities.

INSOMNIA AND CIRCADIAN RHYTHM DISRUPTION

> I could be like staying up to about two, three o'clock in the morning and then going to sleep, and then I'd be napping for like an hour or two during the day, and then staying up all night because I'd slept during the day.
>
> **Waite et al. (2018, p. 3)**

Circadian rhythm disruption (CRD) refers to misalignment in the timing of sleep. This is conceptualised as disruption to process C in the two-process model of sleep (Borbély, 1982). There are many forms of circadian misalignment, including advanced/delayed cycles, non-24-h cycle lengths, and highly irregular and fragmented sleep patterns. Disruptions in sleep timing are commonly reported by patients with psychosis (Reeve, Sheaves, et al., 2018; Waite et al., 2018), yet exact prevalence rates have not yet been established (Cosgrave, Wulff, & Gehrman, 2018). Importantly, disrupted sleep timing may be the result of other sleep problems, for example insomnia may delay sleep onset, as described in the previous case study.

Adolescence is the peak age of onset of psychosis. Developmental changes during adolescence include a delayed sleep phase. Sleep disturbance and CRD in young people at ultra-high risk of psychosis is widespread (Poe et al., 2017), and associated with poor outcomes, persistence of psychotic experiences, and transition to psychosis (Lunsford-Avery et al., 2017). Sleep disruption is often the first marker of deterioration noticed by patients and families. Addressing sleep disturbance at this time may prevent mental health difficulties (Bradley et al., 2017; Freeman et al., 2017) (Box 20.7).

Box 20.7 Client Example: 'Rebecca'[a]

Over the last year, 18-year-old Rebecca had been struggling to attend college, especially in the morning. She found it hard to wake before 11am as her sleep onset was often after 2am: she simply didn't feel tired earlier. But the timing of her sleep was causing difficulties in her day-to-day functioning: arguments at home and concerns raised at college had become the norm. Rebecca noticed that her energy increased later in the day and often spent hours late at night trying to do college work and connecting online with friends. To combat fatigue throughout the day, Rebecca would use 'energy drinks' with high caffeine content.

[a]Hypothetical case.

The key treatment techniques for Rebecca were:

(1) Circadian entrainment (setting the sleep window, using light/dark exposure, boosting social zeitgebers, for example meal and activity times);
(2) Establishing the environmental and lifestyle context for sleep;
(3) Psychoeducation regarding sleep architecture and timing during adolescence.

Understanding Sleep

Engaging the wider system (family, friends, partners, educational staff, and other members of the care team) in treatment shares knowledge and facilitates the implementation of strategies.

During adolescence sleep architecture changes. Melatonin (a marker of circadian rhythm) is released later causing a delay in sleepiness. Homeostatic sleep drive is also reduced, and hence sleep onset is delayed (Blake, Sheeber, Youssef, Raniti, Allen, 2017). A 'sleep team', including Rebecca's family and college tutor, was formed to ensure the wider system had the necessary information to understand sleep problems, set realistic expectations for change, and support the implementation of intervention strategies.

Setting the Sleep Window

At the start of treatment, Rebecca's sleep window was from approximately 2 am–11 am. Her goal window was 12 midnight–8 am, in order to attend college classes in the morning. To achieve this, it was necessary to adjust the sleep window. To advance the sleep phase, the wake time needed to be gradually moved earlier. Given the delayed phase, it was agreed to start the realignment process by waking at 10.45 am and going to bed at 1.45 am. Light is the most important factor governing our circadian system. Natural daylight has over 10,000 lx (the measure of intensity of illumination). In comparison, artificial light in an average room has 50–500 lx. Therefore, light and energising activities, including firstly opening the curtains and then getting outside, were scheduled as part of Rebecca's rise-up routine.

Circadian Entrainment: Light and Technology

Rebecca would often spend hours at night on her phone and laptop. These devices emit blue light, which stimulates the circadian system and promotes wakefulness. Many devices now offer a blue light filter, which can be used in the evening. Yet, reducing the night-time use of technology remains an important treatment target as the content, as well as the light, can be stimulating and thus disrupt the preparation for sleep. However, Rebecca feared social exclusion if she reduced time online. A sleep diary (on her phone) was used to compare 1 week of using technology as usual with 1 week of reduced use of technology at night. From this experiment, Rebecca learnt that she could reduce technology use at night, without any negative social consequences, and she could fall asleep earlier.

Setting the Scene for Sleep

Although one cannot directly control the onset of sleep, we can stack the odds in favour of falling asleep by ensuring the right environment. Sleep hygiene can often feel like a long list of do's and don'ts. Therefore, targeting specific factors with a clear rationale can promote engagement and experimentation. For Rebecca, drinking energy drinks throughout the day and using tech in bed were clear targets for change.

INSOMNIA, OVERSLEEPING AND DAYTIME FATIGUE

> I would just sleep through the day and that put a massive strain on my social life, mood, and mental health. It turned my life the other way round, so I would be up at night and then I wouldn't be up in the day, wouldn't go out and see people because I was sleeping. I think it was very unhealthy.
>
> **Waite et al. (2018, p. 4)**

Given the detrimental impact on day-to-day functioning, oversleeping is recognised as an important issue by patients (Waite et al., 2018; Waite, Evans, et al., 2016) and healthcare professionals (Rehman et al., 2017). However, there has been a lack of research on excessive sleeping. There are multiple potential causes of excessive sleep: it may be secondary to insomnia (i.e. a means of catching up on lost sleep), a strategy to cope with distressing psychotic experiences, or a separate disorder. Daytime fatigue may be a result of too little or too much sleep, side effects of medication, or the impact of depression. At the present time, we do not know the mechanisms underpinning oversleeping. However, it is a common complaint, which requires further research (Box 20.8).

Box 20.8 Client Example 'Linda'[a]

Linda experienced low mood and critical voices. She would often feel very lethargic and lacking energy, especially after waking. As she did not have any regular activities, she would often doze in bed, drifting in and out of sleep. Her sleep pattern alternated between extended sleep periods (e.g. 9 pm until 12 midday) and periods of insomnia due to lack of sleep pressure and hyperarousal from voices.

[a]Hypothetical case.

The key treatment techniques for Linda were:

(1) Stabilising the sleep window;
(2) Increasing daytime activity to increase sleep pressure, distract from distressing voices, and enhance mood;
(3) Boosting daytime energy (using energy experiments).

Stabilising the Sleep Window: Reducing Oversleeping and Increasing Daytime Activity

Psychoeducation about sleep inertia, the tired, groggy feeling after waking, can help normalise fatigue on waking. A rise-up routine can be used to stabilise the sleep window and initiate an increase in daytime activity. This can be particularly important in the context of depression and psychotic experiences. As part of the rationale for establishing a consistent sleep routine, Linda's sleep pattern was described as a 'pendulum swinging from too much to too little sleep'. Regular activities every morning helped to regulate both sleep and mood. Cue cards with motivational statements, for example 'get up and get going to feel good', were used to remind Linda of the strategy and boost motivation despite low mood and fatigue.

Daytime Fatigue

To address daytime fatigue, energy experiments can be used to discover that activity rather than additional sleep generates more energy. Energy experiments involve rating energy levels (and mood when depression is present) before and after engaging in an activity, for example, 30 s of jogging on the spot (for further examples, see Waters, Ree, & Chiu, 2017). For Linda, scheduling energy-giving activities (e.g. listening to a particular music playlist, exercise, time outdoors) for soon after the planned rise time and at usual nap times was particularly useful. An activity tracker was used to measure this increase in activity, which boosted motivation. A review of the timing and dose of medication may be needed as medication side effects can include fatigue (see Box 20.3).

INSOMNIA IN THE CONTEXT OF REDUCED NEED FOR SLEEP

> I remember sleeping for about 4 ½ hours a night. I wasn't aware that it had a negative impact on my psychological wellbeing. I was very much elated, which was acting upon the sleep. But sleep was a benchmark, a sign that things weren't as they should be, because I was sleeping too little.
>
> **Sheaves et al. (2018)**

During an acute episode of mania, the majority of patients experience a reduced need for sleep (Harvey, 2008). Patients report a reduced total sleep time, but do not miss the sleep they lose. In fact, rather than having a slight drop in mood, which is typical with restricted sleep time, patients experience elevated levels of positive affect and excess energy. For many, the restricted sleep eventually triggers a period of oversleeping, which subsequently reduces the likelihood of nocturnal sleep, maintaining insomnia. CBT-I leads to positive improvements in insomnia and bipolar symptoms (Harvey et al., 2015), and the intervention has recently been adapted for those in an acute episode (Sheaves et al., 2017).

It is a feasible psychological intervention irrespective of the patient's level of insight into their elevated mood.

During an episode of reduced need for sleep, hyperarousal delays sleep onset. However rather than being driven by anxiety, the hyperarousal is fuelled by positive affect and/or irritability. There is an excess of energy in the presleep period and the typical response is to take advantage of this by doing stimulating activities (e.g. exercise, online shopping or work), rather than winding down for sleep. Circadian dysregulation may also underpin reduced need for sleep due to a hypersensitivity to light, which inhibits melatonin production (a bio-marker of circadian rhythmicity) (Harvey, 2008). This can leave sleep out of sync with the environmental light–dark cycle. Following a pilot trial of dark therapy with promising improvements on manic symptoms (Barbini et al., 2005), particular attention to light exposure may be warranted for this group (Box 20.9).

Box 20.9 Client Example 'Tim'[a]

Tim was on an acute psychiatric ward after being admitted due to risk of suicide. At the start of his admission, he was severely depressed. This subsequently switched to hypomania. Tim had become more active and chatty, had worked throughout the night on a new project, and as a consequence his mood was 'loads better'. Tim's goal at the start of therapy was to overcome fatigue related to depression. Tim thought that he had met this and therefore didn't need further therapy. The goal was therefore reviewed and a new goal was set: to increase the chances of sleep at night in order to boost his thinking skills for his new work project.

[a]Hypothetical case.

The key treatment targets for Tim were:

(1) Reducing hyperarousal to promote sleep onset.
(2) Stabilising total sleep time across nights.
(3) Reducing light exposure at night.

In order to allow these to be targeted, active strategies to optimise engagement were crucial.

Optimising Engagement in Therapy

Mood and sleep can fluctuate rapidly, particularly in an acute setting. The therapist is therefore required to be responsive to this and tailor the session to the current sleep presentation. For Tim, this meant agreeing new goals to ensure therapy still felt relevant to him. Tim viewed his sleep loss as helpful for increasing his productivity. Therefore, psychoeducation about the link between optimal sleep, cognitive ability, and productivity was shared. As a result, Tim agreed to work on stabilising his sleep across nights as a tool to boost his work productivity.

Whilst Tim's mood was elevated shorter 30-min sessions were used, with breaks to facilitate attention. Tim's therapy was delivered in an intensive format

(9 sessions over 2 weeks), which ensured that his sleep plan could be rapidly tested and optimised before the next night of sleep. In session, Tim and his therapist agreed to limit his activity in the evening to wind down for sleep. This was facilitated by use of a health tracker (wearable tech device), to agree a between session limit of his evening step count. Tim was instantly able to see if he was on track to meet his target by looking at the step count in the evening. The inpatient ward team facilitated engagement by checking his progress in the evening.

Reducing Hyperarousal Though a Graded Wind-Down Routine

Typical wind-down activities (e.g. relaxation audios) can be so incongruent with manic hyperarousal that they are experienced as irritating or boring. The response can therefore be to disengage from the activity or become more aroused due to irritation. A longer and graded wind-down, which incorporates interests, can facilitate engagement. Tim's evening gradually worked towards listening to short relaxation audios in his room. He watched the heart rate monitor on his fitness tracker to focus his attention and found it rewarding to see his heart rate drop as a result of relaxation. The feedback from wearable tech devices is very popular with patients.

Reducing Light Exposure at Night

A dark evening environment is emphasised to cue the circadian system for nighttime (and therefore sleep). Tim used a dimmer switch during his wind-down routine and added a temporary blackout blind to the window. This is an accessible technique for patients experiencing an acute manic episode, and the implementation can easily be supported by family, friends, or staff.

Measuring Progress

As Tim's sleep stabilised, his mood also dropped from being elevated to euthymic. It was important to frame this decrease in mood as a success, in order to sustain active sleep and mood management in the longer term. Outputs from wearable devices provide data, which can be summarised in graphs, entered into the end of therapy letter, and shared with the wider system (with consent).

NIGHTMARES

> Having nightmares is really hard, because it affects my anxiety really badly. It's almost like having dreams that are going to happen. I'm always worried and on guard. It can be draining and hard to cope sometimes because the nightmares can be horrific.

Nightmares play out highly distressing imagery, which disrupts restorative sleep and sets a negative emotional tone for the day ahead. They typically occur in late night REM sleep. Nightmares have been associated cross-sectionally with paranoia and hallucinations (Sheaves et al., 2016), even whilst controlling for negative affect and stressful life experiences (Rek et al., 2017). Unsurprisingly, there are very high levels of comorbidity between nightmares and insomnia; nightmares both directly disrupt sleep and can trigger a fear of sleep, delaying sleep onset. Patients develop a range of behaviours, which are intended as a means of coping with nightmares, but further disrupt sleep (e.g. using alcohol or substances prior to sleep, avoiding going to bed, or setting alarms to break up sleep as a means of avoiding REM sleep) (Box 20.10).

Box 20.10 Client Example 'John'[a]

John is a 30-year-old man who has experienced nightmares since he was a child. He has a persecutory belief that he will be physically attacked and humiliated by a group of teenagers. This is played out in his nightmares, in which he is attacked, though the exact details vary from night to night. He is scared of sleeping and it therefore takes him around 3h to get to sleep. He believes that his nightmares are a warning of what may happen in the daytime and hence feels very anxious the subsequent day. He keeps his curtains closed, stays inside, and on particularly bad days considers taking his own life. He has noticed that many of his nightmares happen in the early hours of the morning, so he sets an early alarm to avoid them. However, he is typically so tired that he struggles to get up at that time. He falls back to sleep and often wakes late morning after another nightmare.

[a]Hypothetical case.

The key treatment techniques for John were:

(1) Providing an alternative explanation for the occurrence of nightmares through psychoeducation.
(2) Reducing the impact of distressing imagery and related appraisals.
(3) Targeting his fear of nightmares by increasing skills to manage the distress.
(4) Monitoring and managing risk

Psychoeducation

Whilst the content of nightmares may draw on daytime experiences, the perceptual experience can be distorted and bizarre and trigger a search for meaning (Freeman, Garety, Kuipers, Fowler, & Bebbington, 2002). Patients interpret their nightmares as meaning something about the future, like John ('they are a warning of what will happen in the daytime'), or about themselves ('They mean I'm a bad person'), or others ('It's my persecutor implanting them into my mind at night') and these interpretations fuel distress. Describing how the brain functions during dreaming sleep can offer an explanation for the bizarre, yet perceptually real and emotionally intense experience, which may alleviate the distress. The therapist informs the patient that whilst some areas of the brain are very active during dreaming sleep (areas that serve visual, auditory, motor, emotion, and memory functions), areas that serve logic and planning are less active (particularly areas of the prefrontal cortex). This means that dreams can seem very real and emotionally intense, yet are often bizarre, illogical experiences and we do not necessarily act in them as we would when awake. John found that seeing his nightmares from this 'scientific perspective' made them seem less scary.

IR

A brief overview of the nightmare narrative is established. The most distressing point is identified and the associated meaning elicited ('what makes that the worst part?'). In some cases, the meaning driving distress is directly related to the events within the nightmare ('I can't do anything to stop him') and in other cases distress is fuelled by what that moment in the nightmare means about the person or others ('it's the devil trying to break me'). The change of ending of the nightmare restructures the meaning that is driving distress, see Fig. 20.2 for examples.

Once the new ending is planned, guided imagery is used to elaborate the narrative in rich sensory detail. The therapist prompts for these details, and in some cases, where distress is very high, prompts the participant to move onto the next element in the planned rescript. For John, the worst moment in his nightmare was his thought 'I can't do anything to stop them'. He therefore changed the ending by asking his favourite cartoon character to help him fight off his attackers and escape to a meadow where he felt safe. He immediately found the imagery both empowering and calming and reported a reduction in intensity of his nightmares (they seemed more 'watered down').

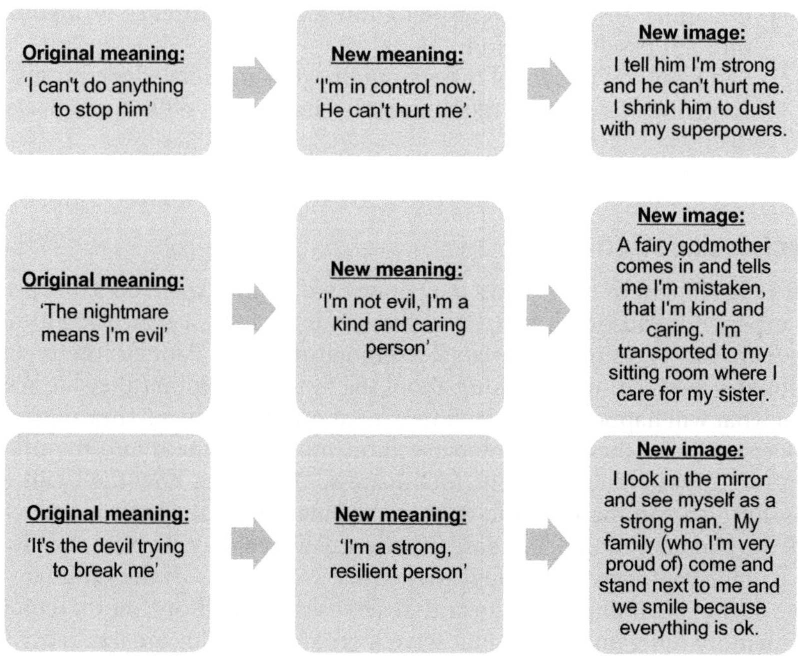

FIG. 20.2
Examples of rescripting appraisals and images in nightmares.

Reducing Presleep Hyperarousal

Worries and distressing voices prior to sleep provide negative content for dreams and heighten negative affect, which increases the chances of a nightmare. John used a worry period in the early evening (Freeman, Dunn, et al., 2015), followed by relaxation to reduce anxiety. In bed, he practiced switching attention away from worries.

Managing Night-Time Distress

Nightmares trigger acute distress in the middle of the night. This heightened distress fuels a fear of nightmares, which increases the chances of them occurring. John felt terrified when he woke from a nightmare, which made it hard for him to return to sleep. He therefore wrote a 'compassionate message from my daytime self'. This included a comforting message and a reminder of the strategies he could use such as grounding techniques, and the 15-minute rule. This approach interrupted rumination about the nightmare, and fostered feelings of calm to hasten sleep onset and encourage better quality sleep.

Strategies the Next Day

Following a nightmare, people often feel tired, low, and anxious and therefore find it more difficult to get up. This can result in returning to sleep and oversleeping. Longer sleep duration is associated with the occurrence of nightmares, likely owing to the greater amount of REM sleep the longer one has slept (Rek et al., 2017). John found psychoeducation helpful for seeing the cycles of REM sleep (on a hypnogram), and this helped him understand why his dreams occurred at the same time each night. This set the rationale for reducing periods of oversleeping.

Monitoring and Managing Risk

Longitudinal studies show that frequent nightmares are associated with eight times greater odds of later suicidal ideation (Li, Lam, Chan, Yu, & Wing, 2012) suicide attempts (Li, Lam, Yu, Zhang, & Wing, 2010), and 57% greater risk of later death by suicide (Tanskanen et al., 2001). Whether nightmares are an epiphenomenon or causally related to suicidal ideation is yet to be established. However, suicidal ideation is very common in patients experiencing nightmares and psychosis (Sheaves et al., 2019). Close team liaison and active monitoring of suicidal ideation from the outset of therapy is recommended (Box 20.11).

Nightmares are associated with an increase in suicidal ideation.

SUMMARY

> If I sleep, I can do everything better
>
> **Waite, Evans, et al. (2016, p. 188)**

Sleep problems in patients with psychosis are complex and pervasive. Sleep disturbance is one causal mechanism underpinning psychotic experiences and

Box 20.11 Questions for Adapted CBT-I Self-Supervision

Assessment

- What are the specific sleep-related goals?
- Have the key factors disrupting sleep been identified?
- Are the exact times for going to bed, lights out, waking and getting out of bed known?

Formulation

- Is the formulation of factors disrupting sleep clear?
- Is the formulation focused on sleep problems?

Intervention

- Has a consistent sleep window (regular bed and wake times) been set?
- Is the sleep window achievable?
- Is the sleep window aligned with the circadian rhythm?
- Has a presleep wind-down routine been established?
- Is a rise-up routine in place?
- Is there sufficient daytime activity?
- Have energy experiments been used to address fatigue?
- Is there sufficient light in the morning and darkness in the evening?
- Has night-time worry been addressed?
- Are there strategies in place to cope with psychotic experiences at night-time?
- Does the environment need adapting to promote sleep?
- Could the sessions be made more active?
- Has the focus remained on sleep?
- Is there anything you can do to boost engagement and motivation?
- Have each of the sleep disrupting factors been addressed?

Review of outcome

- Do the measures allow us to track progress towards the therapy goals?

Future implementation

- Have potential barriers to a future with good sleep been identified and addressed?
- Has a 'sleep team' been established to support long-term implementation?

therefore requires treatment. Brief, targeted, cognitive-behavioural interventions can be effective for improving sleep in patients with psychotic symptoms and disorders. However, comorbidity of sleep problems is the norm rather than the exception. Therefore, treatment needs to be formulation led and target the key mechanisms disrupting sleep for the individual. Given the findings from clinical trials, the descriptions from patients, and reflections from therapists, there is cause for hope and optimism regarding the potential for positive outcomes when treating sleep problems in patients with psychosis.

QUIZ QUESTIONS

1. What are the two factors hypothesised to govern the biological process of sleep?
   (a) Sleep pressure & Circadian rhythm
   (b) Relaxation & Fatigue
   (c) Body clock & Hyperarousal
2. Current perspectives, informed by recent evidence, conceptualise sleep disruption as:
   (a) A symptom of psychiatric illness, in this case, psychosis

(b) A nonspecific epiphenomenon (or secondary effect of psychosis)
(c) A contributory causal factor in the onset of psychotic experiences

3. Treatment guidelines suggest the first-line treatment for persistent insomnia should be:
(a) Hypnotic medication
(b) Cognitive behavioural therapy interventions
(c) Neuroleptic medication

ANSWERS TO QUIZ QUESTIONS:

1. (a) Process C, circadian rhythm, and Process S, homeostatic sleep pressure, have been identified as regulating sleep (Borbély, 1982). However, a third important factor, which can disrupt sleep is hyperarousal. All three should be considered when assessing, formulating, and intervening to improve disrupted sleep.

2. (c) Historically sleep problems had been understood as a symptom of the psychiatric disorder or a nonspecific epiphenomenon. Yet recent research has turned this traditional view on its head and instead shown that sleep disruption is one causal factor in the occurrence of paranoia, hallucinatory experiences, and mood state in bipolar disorder (Freeman et al., 2017; Harvey et al., 2015; Reeve, Emsley, et al., 2018).

3. (b) International clinical guidelines recommend CBT as the first-line treatment for persistent insomnia (duration of >4 weeks) (National Institute for Health and Care Excellence, 2015; Qaseem et al., 2016). CBT interventions have an established evidence base for the treatment of insomnia (Irwin et al., 2006; Mitchell et al., 2012; Riemann & Perlis, 2009) and have been successfully adapted for patients with psychotic experiences (e.g. Freeman, Waite, et al., 2015; Sheaves et al., 2017).

ADDITIONAL RESOURCES FOR SELF-DIRECTED LEARNING

Espie, C. A., 2006. Overcoming insomnia and sleep problems: A self help guide using cognitive behavioural techniques. London: Constable and Robinson.

Harvey, A. G., Buysse, D. J., 2018. Treating sleep problems: A transdiagnostic approach. New York: Guildford Press.

Sheaves, B., Isham, L., Bradley, J., Espie, C., Barrera, A., Waite, F., … Freeman, D., 2018. Adapted CBT to stabilize sleep on psychiatric wards: A transdiagnostic treatment approach. Behavioural and Cognitive Psychotherapy.

Waite, F., Myers, E., Harvey, A. G., Espie, C. A., Startup, H., Sheaves, B., Freeman, D., 2016. Treating sleep problems in patients with schizophrenia. *Behavioural and Cognitive Psychotherapy, 44*, 273–287.

Waters, F., Ree, M. J., Chiu, V., 2017. Delivering CBT for insomnia in psychosis. New York: Routledge.

Video produced by the Sleep and Circadian Neuroscience Institute (University of Oxford) explaining circadian rhythms: https://youtu.be/2BoLqqNuqwA.

'10 Top Tips' for improving sleep: https://www.ndcn.ox.ac.uk/research/sleep-circadian-neuroscience-institute/training-and-dissemination/having-trouble-with-your-sleep.

References

Annamalai, A., Palmese, L. B., Chwastiak, L. A., Srihari, V. H., & Tek, C. (2015). High rates of obstructive sleep apnea symptoms among patients with schizophrenia. *Psychosomatics, 56*, 59–66.

Aurora, R. N., Zak, R. S., Auerbach, S. H., Casey, K. R., Chowdhuri, S., Karippot, A., et al. (2010). Best practice guide for the treatment of nightmare disorder in adults. *Journal of Clinical Sleep Medicine, 6*, 389–401.

Barbini, B., Benedetti, F., Colombo, C., Dotoli, D., Bernasconi, A., Cigala-Fulgosi, M., et al. (2005). Dark therapy for mania: A pilot study. *Bipolar Disorders, 7*, 98–101.

Bastien, C. H., Vallières, A., & Morin, C. M. (2001). Validation of the insomnia severity index as an outcome measure for insomnia research. *Sleep Medicine, 2*, 297–307.

Blake, M. J., Sheeber, L. B., Youssef, G. J., Raniti, M. B., & Allen, N. B. (2017). Systematic review and meta-analysis of adolescent cognitive–behavioral sleep interventions. *Clinical Child and Family Psychology Review, 20*, 227–249. https://doi.org/10.1007/s10567-017-0234-5.

Borbély, A. A. (1982). A two process model of sleep regulation. *Human Neurobiology, 1*, 195–204.

Bradley, J., Freeman, D., Chadwick, E., Harvey, A. G., Mullins, B., Johns, L., et al. (2017). Treating sleep problems in young people at ultra-high risk of psychosis: A feasibility case series. *Behavioural and Cognitive Psychotherapy, 46*, 276–291.

Carney, C. E., Buysse, D. J., Ancoli-Israel, S., Edinger, J. D., Krystal, A. D., Lichstein, K. L., et al. (2012). The consensus sleep diary: Standardizing prospective sleep self-monitoring. *Sleep, 35*, 287–302.

Casement, M. D., & Swanson, L. M. (2012). A meta-analysis of imagery rehearsal for post-trauma nightmares: Effects on nightmare frequency, sleep quality, and posttraumatic stress. *Clinical Psychology Review, 32*, 566–574.

Chung, F., Abdullah, H. R., & Liao, P. (2016). STOP-bang questionnaire a practical approach to screen for obstructive sleep apnea. *Chest.* https://doi.org/10.1378/chest.15-0903.

Cosgrave, J., Wulff, K., & Gehrman, P. (2018). Sleep, circadian rhythms, and schizophrenia: Where we are and where we need to go. *Current Opinion in Psychiatry, 31*, 176–182.

Espie, C. A. (2006). *Overcoming insomnia and sleep problems: A self help guide using cognitive behavioural techniques.* London, UK: Constable and Robinson.

Espie, C. A., Kyle, S. D., Hames, P., Gardani, M., Fleming, L., & Cape, J. (2014). The sleep condition Indicator: A clinical screening tool to evaluate insomnia disorder. *BMJ Open, 4*.

Faulkner, S., & Bee, P. (2017). Experiences, perspectives and priorities of people with schizophrenia spectrum disorders regarding sleep disturbance and its treatment: A qualitative study. *BMC Psychiatry, 17*, 1–17.

Foresight Mental Capital and Wellbeing Project. (2008). *Foresight mental capital and wellbeing project final project report—Executive summary.* London: The Government Office for Science.

Freeman, D., Dunn, G., Startup, H., Pugh, K., Cordwell, J., Mander, H., et al. (2015). Effects of cognitive behaviour therapy for worry on persecutory delusions in patients with psychosis (WIT): A parallel , single-blind, randomised controlled trial with a mediation analysis. *Lancet Psychiatry, 2*, 305–313.

Freeman, D., Garety, P. A., Kuipers, E., Fowler, D., & Bebbington, P. E. (2002). A cognitive model of persecutory delusions. *The British Journal of Clinical Psychology, 41*, 331–347.

Freeman, D., Sheaves, B., Goodwin, G. M., Yu, L.-M., Nickless, A., Harrison, P. J., et al. (2017). The effects of improving sleep on mental health (OASIS): A randomised controlled trial with mediation analysis. *The Lancet Psychiatry, 4*, 749–758.

Freeman, D., Waite, F., Emsley, R., Kingdon, D., Davies, L., Fitzpatrick, R., et al. (2016). The efficacy of a new translational treatment for persecutory delusions: Study protocol for a randomised controlled trial (The Feeling Safe Study). *Trials, 17*, 134–142.

Freeman, D., Waite, F., Startup, H., Myers, E., Lister, R., McInerney, J., et al. (2015). Efficacy of cognitive behavioural therapy for sleep improvement in patients with persistent delusions and hallucinations (BEST): A prospective, assessor-blind, randomised controlled pilot trial. *The Lancet Psychiatry, 2*, 975–983.

Hansen, K., Höfling, V., Kröner-Borowik, T., Stangier, U., & Steil, R. (2013). Efficacy of psychological interventions aiming to reduce chronic nightmares: A meta-analysis. *Clinical Psychology Review, 33*, 146–155.

Harvey, A. G. (2002). A cognitive model of insomnia. *Behaviour Research and Therapy, 40*(8), 869–893. Retrieved from http://www.ncbi.nlm.nih.gov/pubmed/12186352.

Harvey, A. G. (2008). Sleep and circadian rhythms in bipolar disorder: Seeking synchrony, harmony, and regulation. *The American Journal of Psychiatry, 165*, 820–829.

Harvey, A. G., Soehner, A. M., Kaplan, K. A., Hein, K., Lee, J., Kanady, J., et al. (2015). Treating insomnia improves mood state, sleep, and functioning in bipolar disorder: A pilot randomized controlled trial. *Journal of Consulting and Clinical Psychology, 83*, 564–577.

Haynes, P. L., Parthasarathy, S., Kersh, B., & Bootzin, R. R. (2011). Examination of insomnia and insomnia treatment in psychiatric inpatients. *International Journal of Mental Health Nursing, 20*, 130–136.

Irwin, M. R., Cole, J. C., & Nicassio, P. M. (2006). Comparative meta-analysis of behavioral interventions for insomnia and their efficacy in middle-aged adults and in older adults 55+ years of age. *Health Psychology, 25*, 3–14.

Krakow, B. (2006). Nightmare complaints in treatment-seeking patients in clinical sleep medicine settings: Diagnostic and treatment implications. *Sleep, 29*, 1313–1319.

Kyle, S. D., Espie, C. A., & Morgan, K. (2010). "...Not just a minor thing, it is something major, which stops you from functioning daily": Quality of life and daytime functioning in insomnia. *Behavioral Sleep Medicine, 8*, 123–140.

Li, S. X., Lam, S. P., Chan, J. W. Y., Yu, M. W. M., & Wing, Y.-K. (2012). Residual sleep disturbances in patients remitted from major depressive disorder: A 4-year naturalistic follow-up study. *Sleep, 35*, 1153–1161.

Li, S. X., Lam, S. P., Yu, M. W. M., Zhang, J., & Wing, Y. K. (2010). Nocturnal sleep disturbances as a predictor of suicide attempts among psychiatric outpatients: A clinical, epidemiologic, prospective study. *The Journal of Clinical Psychiatry, 71*, 1440–1446.

Lunsford-Avery, J. R., Gonçalves, B. d. S. B., Brietzke, E., Bressan, R. A., Gadelha, A., Auerbach, R. P., et al. (2017). Adolescents at clinical-high risk for psychosis: Circadian rhythm disturbances predict worsened prognosis at 1-year follow-up. *Schizophrenia Research, 189*, 37–42.

Mitchell, M. D., Gehrman, P., Perlis, M., & Umscheid, C. A. (2012). Comparative effectiveness of cognitive behavioral therapy for insomnia: A systematic review. *BMC Family Practice, 13*, 40.

Myers, E., Startup, H., & Freeman, D. (2013). Improving sleep, improving delusions: CBT for insomnia in individuals with persecutory delusions. In C. Steel (Ed.), *CBT for schizophrenia: Evidence-based interventions and future directions* (pp. 213–233). Chichester: John Wiley & Sons.

National Institute for Health and Care Excellence. (2015). *Managing long term insomnia (>4 weeks) [WWW Document]*. NICE Clinical Knowledge Summaries.

Poe, S. L., Brucato, G., Bruno, N., Arndt, L. Y., Ben-David, S., Gill, K. E., et al. (2017). Sleep disturbances in individuals at clinical high risk for psychosis. *Psychiatry Research, 249*, 240–243.

Qaseem, A., Kansagara, D., Forciea, M. A., Cooke, M., Denberg, T. D., Barry, M. J., et al. (2016). Management of chronic insomnia disorder in adults: A clinical practice guideline from the American College of Physicians. *Annals of Internal Medicine, 165*, 125–133.

Reeve, S., Emsley, R., Sheaves, B., & Freeman, D. (2018). Disrupting sleep: The effects of sleep loss on psychotic experiences tested in an experimental study with mediation analysis. *Schizophrenia Bulletin, 44*, 662–671.

Reeve, S., Sheaves, B., & Freeman, D. (2018). Sleep disorders in early psychosis: Incidence, severity, and association with clinical symptoms. *Schizophrenia Bulletin*.

Rehman, A., Waite, F., Sheaves, B., Biello, S., Freeman, D., & Gumley, A. (2017). Clinician perceptions of sleep problems, and their treatment, in patients with non-affective psychosis. *Psychosis, 9*, 129–139.

Rek, S., Sheaves, B., & Freeman, D. (2017). Nightmares in the general population: Identifying potential causal factors. *Social Psychiatry and Psychiatric Epidemiology, 52*, 1123–1133.

Riemann, D., & Perlis, M. L. (2009). The treatments of chronic insomnia: A review of benzodiazepine receptor agonists and psychological and behavioral therapies. *Sleep Medicine Reviews, 13*, 205–214.

Sheaves, B., Freeman, D., Isham, L., McInerney, J., Nickless, A., Yu, L.-M., et al. (2017). Stabilising sleep for patients admitted at acute crisis to a psychiatric hospital (OWLS): An assessor-blind, pilot randomised controlled trial. *Psychological Medicine*, 1–11.

Sheaves, B., Isham, L., Bradley, J., Espie, C., Barrera, A., Waite, F., et al. (2018). Adapted CBT to stabilize sleep on psychiatric wards: A transdiagnostic treatment approach. *Behavioural and Cognitive Psychotherapy, 46*, 661–675.

Sheaves, B., Porcheret, K., Tsanas, A., Espie, C. A., Foster, R. G., Freeman, D., et al. (2016). Insomnia, nightmares, and chronotype as markers of risk for severe mental illness: Results from a student population. *Sleep, 39*, 173–181.

Sheaves, B., Holmes, E. A., Rek, S., Taylor, K. M., Nickless, A., Waite, F., ... Freeman, D. (2019). Cognitive behavioural therapy for nightmares for patients with persecutory delusions (Nites): An assessor-blind, pilot randomized controlled trial. *The Canadian Journal of Psychiatry*. https://doi.org/10.1177/0706743719847422.

Tanskanen, A., Tuomilehto, J., Viinamäki, H., Vartiainen, E., Lehtonen, J., & Puska, P. (2001). Nightmares as predictors of suicide. *Sleep, 24*, 844–847.

Tsiachristas, A., Waite, F., Freeman, D., & Luengo-Fernandez, R. (2018). Cost-effectiveness of cognitive–behavioural therapy for sleep disorder added to usual care in patients with schizophrenia: The BEST study. *BJPsych Open, 4*, 126–135.

Waite, F., Bradley, J., Chadwick, E., Reeve, S., Bird, J. C., & Freeman, D. (2018). The experience of sleep problems and their treatment in young people at ultra-high risk of psychosis: A thematic analysis. *Frontiers in Psychiatry, 9*, 375.

Waite, F., Evans, N., Myers, E., Startup, H., Lister, R., Harvey, A. G., et al. (2016). The patient experience of sleep problems and their treatment in the context of current delusions and hallucinations. *Psychology and Psychotherapy: Theory, Research and Practice, 89*, 181–193.

Waite, F., Myers, E., Harvey, A. G., Espie, C. A., Startup, H., Sheaves, B., et al. (2016). Treating sleep problems in patients with schizophirenia. *Behavioural and Cognitive Psychotherapy, 44*, 273–287.

Waters, F., Ree, M. J., & Chiu, V. (2017). *Delivering CBT for insomnia in psychosis*. New York: Routledge.

Definition of Key Terms

CBT-I Cognitive behavioural therapy for insomnia.

Insomnia Difficulty initiating or maintaining sleep or nonrestorative sleep despite adequate time and opportunity to sleep.

Ciracadian rhythm The body clock, a natural 24-h pattern that dictates the timing of sleep.

Circadian rhythm disruption (CRD) Misalignment between the timing of sleep and the environmental light–dark cycle.

Sleep pressure The need or drive for sleep, which increases as a result of time awake.

Hyperarousal Heightened physiological alertness and increased responsiveness to stimuli, typically driven by anxiety.

Actigraphy The measurement of movement via an accelerometer device to infer periods of sleep.

Sleep window The time allocated for sleep each night.

Sleep inertia The tired, groggy feeling after waking.

CHAPTER 21

Get Moving: Physical Activity and Exercise for Mental Health

Hamish Fibbins[*,†], **Oscar Lederman**[*,‡], **Simon Rosenbaum**[†,§]
[*]Keeping the Body in Mind Program, South Eastern Sydney Local Health District, Sydney, NSW, Australia, [†]School of Psychiatry, University of New South Wales, Sydney, NSW, Australia, [‡]School of Medical Sciences, University of New South Wales, Sydney, NSW, Australia, [§]Black Dog Institute, Randwick, NSW, Australia

Key Learning Objectives

- Identify the psychological, cognitive, and physical health benefits of physical activity.
- Understand current approaches to increasing exercise in people with psychosis.
- Define the role of exercise specialists in mental healthcare settings.
- Describe common motivators and barriers to implementing interventions to increase physical activity in mental health populations.

INTRODUCTION

Chapter 12 outlined the international physical activity guidelines to complement mental health treatment and identified the barriers and facilitators in meeting these recommendations for people living with mental illness. Drawing on the current evidence base, this chapter (see Box 21.1) details practical recommendations for exercise prescription in real-world settings and provides key educational points to support individuals living with mental illness to be more active. We will look at various types of physical activity that can be prescribed and discuss the role of other health professionals in supporting physical activity promotion. Barriers and contraindications to physical activity will be explored as well as the impact of staff culture in mental health settings and how it influences patient outcomes.

People living with mental illness, ranging from high prevalence disorders such as depression through to those with schizophrenia spectrum disorders, can experience a range of benefits from engaging in regular physical activity.

A Clinical Introduction to Psychosis. https://doi.org/10.1016/B978-0-12-815012-2.00021-3

Box 21.1 Summary of Key Issues

- Physical activity and exercise improve a range of health-related outcomes for people living with mental illness including; cardiometabolic risk factors, muscular strength, cardiorespiratory fitness, cognition, positive and negative symptoms and sleep quality.
- Multiple barriers exist for people living with mental illness preventing engagement in regular exercise. Mental health clinicians are in a unique position to identify these barriers and utilise goal setting and evidence-based strategies to increase motivation.
- Exercise professionals specialising in mental health, including exercise physiologists and physiotherapists, are well placed to work with people living with mental illness to assist in improving exercise habits.
- Creating a culture within mental health settings that supports the integration of physical health care including a focus on physical activity may help to improve health outcomes for people living with mental illness.

Beneficial effects include a clinically significant reduction in cardiometabolic risk, including increased cardiorespiratory fitness, lowered blood pressure, and improvements in glucose metabolism, contributing to closing the identified mortality gap in this vulnerable population (Firth, Cotter, Elliott, French, & Yung, 2015; Vancampfort et al., 2017; Vancampfort, Rosenbaum, Ward, & Stubbs, 2015). The reduction in cardiometabolic risk (defined as the ability to reduce risk by 15% and mortality by 20%), through improvements to cardiorespiratory fitness, can occur in as little as 8 weeks (Firth et al., 2015).

Exercise may impact on neurogenesis and increase hippocampal volume in people with schizophrenia.

Improvements in cognitive function, mood, and psychiatric symptomology can also occur in response to regular physical activity (Dauwan, Begemann, Heringa, & Sommer, 2016; Firth et al., 2016). For people living with schizophrenia, significant clinical improvements in psychiatric symptomology, neurocognition, functioning, and co-morbidities can occur with as little as 90 min of moderate-to-vigorous physical activity each week (Firth et al., 2015). Regarding the changes to psychotic symptoms, clinically significant improvements are seen in both positive (SMD = −0.54, 95% CI: −0.95 to −0.13) and negative (SMD = −0.44, (95% CI −0.78 to −0.09) symptoms. Exercise has also been shown to impact neurogenesis with increased physical fitness correlated to increases in brain volume (Pajonk et al., 2010; Scheewe et al., 2013). For conditions such as mild-to-moderate depression, exercise improves symptoms with similar effects to medications and psychotherapy (Cleare et al., 2015). For more serious mental illnesses such as major depressive disorder and schizophrenia, exercise is recommended as an adjunct to usual care (Yung & Firth, 2017). These studies suggest that no singular type of exercise is superior to another in improving mental health symptoms, so long as exercise intensity is moderate-high.

It should be noted that while the benefits of exercise for people with mental illness are wide ranging, there is substantial difficulty in engaging this population to perform regular physical activity (Ashdown-Franks et al., 2018). Education is an effective tool to motivate those who are contemplating beginning or returning to physical activity. Key conceptual, empirical, and educational points for supporting physical activity engagement for patients with mental illness, including patients with a psychotic disorder, are discussed below. The role of mental health exercise specialists in facilitating engagement in exercise for people living with mental illness is discussed later in this chapter.

PHYSICAL ACTIVITY VS. EXERCISE—WHAT'S THE DIFFERENCE?

'Physical activity' and 'exercise' are terms that are used to describe similar but separable concepts (Caspersen, Powell, & Christenson, 1985). While these terms are sometimes used interchangeably, it is important to understand their correct definition. *Physical activity* can be thought of as an umbrella term that encompasses any movement of the body that requires energy expenditure. Standing in a queue, walking up stairs, and running for the bus are all examples of being physically active. *Exercise* is a structured and planned subset of physical activity that is generally repetitive in nature and performed for purposes relating to improvements in physical fitness and health (see Box 21.1). *Physical fitness* refers to the ability of the body to perform physical activity and exercise and has direct implications for health. For example, cardiorespiratory fitness is associated with cardiovascular health, whilst muscular strength is associated with functional capacity (performing daily tasks) and bone mineral density. Aspects of fitness can be measured through validated testing procedures and are usually conducted by a qualified exercise professional (Box 21.2) (see Chapter 12).

Exercise is a structured and planned subset of physical activity.

Physical fitness is the body's capacity to perform physical activity and exercise.

Another form of physical activity, which is often overlooked, is *incidental activity*. Incidental activity is generally unplanned and low impact in nature (e.g. housework); however, it could include higher-intensity activities such as physical labour. Examples of typical incidental activity include carrying shopping bags, gardening, and dog walking. Incidental activity is encouraged in international recommendations on physical activity to be performed daily and 'as much as

Box 21.2 Types of Exercise

Aerobic exercise: any type of sustained activity performed that results in increased heart rate and respiratory (breathing) rate. Running, cycling, swimming, and walking are common forms of aerobic exercise.

- International guidelines suggest we engage in aerobic activity at least five times each week for 30 min duration (although it can be completed in smaller doses of 5–15 min throughout the day) (Garber et al., 2011).
- Physiological adaptations such as improved heart, circulatory and lung function, promotion of weight management, and improvements in functional capacity can occur in response to aerobic exercise.
- Of particular relevance for people living with psychotic disorders, regular aerobic exercise also improves cognitive functioning (Firth et al., 2017) and negative symptoms (Ventura & McEwen, 2017).

Resistance exercise: involves movements against a resistance or force. Weights-based equipment or body-weight training (calisthenics) are two common examples of resistance exercise.

Continued

Box 21.2 Types of Exercise—cont'd

- Recommendations for the general population are to perform resistance exercise targeting all the major muscle groups (compound exercises) for at least two times each week (Garber et al., 2011; Vancampfort et al., 2017).
- Benefits of resistance exercise include increased muscle size and strength, increased bone mineral density and metabolic benefits, including decreased blood glucose levels, and improved insulin sensitivity (Winett & Carpinelli, 2001).
- Similar to aerobic exercise, these benefits extend to mental health symptoms with reductions in depressive symptoms (Gordon et al., 2018) regardless of health status as well as anxiety symptoms (Gordon, McDowell, Lyons, & Herring, 2017) in healthy people and those with an established mental illness.

Sedentary behaviour is associated with risk of cardiometabolic problems in people with psychosis.

possible' to reduce time spent being sedentary (which is strongly associated with cardiometabolic complications particularly in mental health populations (Vancampfort et al., 2017)). *Stretching/flexibility* is a form of physical activity where muscle groups are stretched to improve their elasticity with benefits, including reduced risk of injury and increased range of motion. *Mind-body exercises*, including yoga, tai-chi, and qigong, are also evidence-based complementary physical activity treatments for mental disorders with physical and mental health benefits well documented (Klatte, Pabst, Beelmann, & Rosendahl, 2016; Price, 2017; Rosenbaum, Tiedemann, & Ward, 2014).

'F.I.T.T' Principles

Key principles for individualised exercise: **F**requency **I**ntensity**T**ime/duration**T**ype

The F.I.T.T principles of exercise can be used to help tailor an individualised program and appropriately provide exercise recommendations for people living with mental illness (Medicine, 2013). The principles specify that the exercise being performed should consider the Frequency (F), Intensity (I), Time/Duration (T), and Type (T) that is most appropriate for the person, taking into account their individual circumstance, including exercise history, comorbid physical health conditions, and available resources.

Fitness vs. Fatness

Exercise alone may not be effective in achieving weight loss.

Increasing fitness can reduce the risk of morbidity and mortality independent of changes in weight.

While increasing exercise and minimising time spent being sedentary is something that clinicians should encourage of their clients, it is important to recognise the relatively small impact that exercise has on achieving clinically relevant weight loss. Research tells us that in the absence of dietary change, exercise alone isn't particularly effective in achieving weight loss (Firth et al., 2015), i.e. 'you can't out-run a bad diet' (Malhotra, Noakes, & Phinney, 2015). For overweight or obese individuals in the general population, achieving weight loss to a desired BMI category ($<25\,kg/m^2$) can be difficult, with as little as one in 210 males and one in 124 females achieving this without surgery (Fildes et al., 2015). The good news is that exercise and physical activity that improves fitness (in particular cardiorespiratory/aerobic fitness) can be protective against cardiometabolic diseases, independent of any changes in weight (Firth et al., 2015; Jae et al., 2016; Van Citters et al., 2010). Therefore, clinicians encouraging mental health clients to engage in any form of physical activity can be beneficial, irrespective of their body mass index. Clients often benefit from learning that engagement in exercise can lead to improvements in mental health and wellbeing independent of weight loss (Brand et al., 2018; Stanton, Reaburn, & Happell, 2016).

Sleep and Exercise: A Bidirectional Relationship

Sleep is imperative for human health. When sleep is impaired, it can lead to a cascade of physical and mental health issues (see Chapters 11 and 20). For example, insufficient sleep is associated with weight gain, leading to obesity as well as metabolic abnormalities, including metabolic syndrome. Additionally, abnormal sleep is a known risk factor for the development and exacerbation of psychiatric symptoms and is one of the most commonly reported symptoms in patients at risk of developing psychosis, i.e. those with at-risk mental states (ARMS). Given sleep disturbances and sleep disorders (e.g. insomnia) are highly comorbid with mental illness, addressing such behaviours and improving 'sleep hygiene' is imperative to aid mental health treatment and reduce cardiometabolic risk (Lederman et al., 2018). Exercise programs can lead to beneficial effects on improving sleep quality (whilst also directly improving physical and mental health outcomes) in patients with mental illness and should therefore be considered a key factor when addressing holistic health (Lederman et al., 2018).

Exercise has direct beneficial effects on sleep quality in people with mental illness.

BARRIERS TO EXERCISE IN A MENTAL HEALTH SETTING

The low rates of engagement in physical activity by the general population can be attributed to several variables, including lack of motivation, the perception of 'not having time to exercise', poor confidence, and knowledge surrounding exercise, financial and social factors, or lack of enjoyment (Stutts, 2002). In addition to these common barriers, people living with mental illness are presented with further unique challenges preventing engagement in physical activity.

A recent systematic review (Firth et al., 2016) highlighted three broad barriers people with severe mental illness face to engaging in regular exercise:

Physical, psychological, and socioeconomic barriers to exercise are common for people with severe mental illness.

1. *Physical Health Barriers:* given the higher rates of comorbid chronic physical health conditions, e.g. cardiovascular disease, diabetes, musculoskeletal disorders and pain, it is reasonable to expect physical health can act as a major barrier to exercising. A low cardiorespiratory fitness (commonly present in individuals with severe mental illness) affects individual ability to perform aerobic activities particularly for periods

of longer duration. Studies have also reported that people with severe mental illness are more likely to experience fatigue or low energy, particularly because of psychotropic medication side effects.

2. *Psychological barriers*: Low mood, lack of motivation, mental stress, and depression are all commonly reported as barriers to exercise in people with psychosis. This is exacerbated by acute psychotic symptoms, including hallucinations, persecutory thoughts, and delusions. Other psychological barriers, including disinterest in exercise, feeling unsafe when exercising, and fears of injury, have also been noted.
3. *Socio-ecological barriers:* Social support is a known facilitator of physical activity. Individuals experiencing psychosis are more likely to experience social isolation than the general population, acting as a barrier to engagement in physical activity. Lack of a partner to exercise with and lack of time to exercise are also commonly cited reasons for inactivity. Economic barriers, including the cost of services as well as lack of access to resources, also impede participation in many physical activity programs.

Similarly, when trying to facilitate uptake and engagement in physical activity in the general community, there are steps that can be taken to support people living with mental illness to increase physical activity levels. Mental health clinicians can support their patients by encouraging them to focus on motivating factors to participate in exercise.

A focus should be placed on additional motivating factors to exercise participation, including social participation, creating routine, improvement of psychological symptoms, sleep quality, and self-esteem. Encouraging individualised support from a specialist such as an exercise physiologist, or other networks, including friends or family members, can assist in more successful uptake of long-term engagement of physical activity (Lederman et al., 2017).

Contraindications to Exercise

In the absence of severe physical issues, low-to-moderate intensity physical activity is a safe and effective adjunctive treatment approach. As such, mental health clinicians should begin by encouraging their clients to engage in activities that are light in nature, such as walking and promoting incidental activity. Before beginning vigorous exercise or higher-intensity activities, clients should see their doctor or general practitioner for a physical examination to be medically cleared to exercise. There are prescreening tools available to identify potential contraindicated conditions that most exercise specialists will employ prior to working with a client and can be used by other health professionals when screening a client prior to engaging in vigorous exercise. While a mental health-specific tool is not currently available, a commonly utilised questionnaire is the Physical Activity Readiness Questionnaire (Australia, 2011) (PARQ). The PARQ includes a short series of questions to identify 'red flags' or absolute contraindications to exercise and preclude safe participation in exercise. Exercise is typically low risk for most people living with mental illness and while there are no specific contraindications to exercise for clients with mental illness, certainly there are some special considerations that need to be accounted for.

Exercise is typically low risk for most people living with mental illness and should be strongly encouraged.

In Iieu of the regular exercise contraindicated conditions (e.g. uncontrolled hypertension, unstable angina, and recent cardiovascular complications), mental health-specific precautions may include:

(i) *Lethargy, tiredness, and fatigue*: medication side effects, sleep disturbances, and negative symptoms may lead to higher rates of lethargy and lack of concentration. Tailoring programs to suit individuals' level of tiredness/wakefulness can increase the likelihood of safe exercise participation.
(ii) *Social phobias*: this type of anxiety disorder may act as a major barrier to client participation in exercise. Initially avoiding exercise as part of a group is important as well as encouraging the same exercise trainer or partner to attend sessions, for regularity. Setting small goals, establishing routine, and gradual progression can help with a sense of achievement and familiarity in a gym setting.
(iii) *Medication side-effects*: pharmacological treatments can affect a patient's capacity to perform exercise. Increased tiredness is most common in addition to balance issues, hypersalivation, dry mouth, increased sweating, and visual disturbances may need to be considered. Explaining this to the patient as well as close monitoring (ideally under the supervision and guidance of an accredited exercise specialist, e.g. exercise physiologists and physiotherapists) is recommended.
(iv) *Intellectual disabilities:* clients who may be experiencing cognitive and intellectual barriers, including processing delays and behavioural concerns, may need further support and instruction when beginning exercising. Providing clear instructions and demonstration about the activity, for example, use of cue/picture cards, in addition to incorporating game play can be effective.
(v) *Acute Psychotic Symptoms:* Acute psychotic symptoms can present as a barrier to performing exercise safely; however, they are not a contraindication to exercise. Avoiding higher-intensity exercises or avoiding exercises that require a high level of precision/concentration should be considered. Choosing activities such as mind-body exercises, light walking, and resistance exercise using body weight and light stretching can be beneficial. In the case of mania and other positive symptoms of psychosis, removing distractions such as loud music and other people exercising in the area can be helpful to keeping focused.

For further reading on specific barriers to physical activity for people living with psychosis, please consider: Fogarty and Happell (2005), Newberry, Dean, Sayyah, and Mittal (2018), and Yung and Firth (2017).

MOTIVATION TO EXERCISE

Evidence suggests that adults often do not get the recommended amount of daily physical activity.

The strong evidence linking exercise and improved physical and mental health outcomes highlights the need for long-term adherence to physical activity for people experiencing mental illness. Given the little research showing that interventions can be effective in changing physical activity and sedentary behaviour in this population (Ashdown-Franks et al., 2018), identifying what motivates people to exercise is of interest to support long term behaviour change. In Australia, only slightly more than half of all adults meet the recommended guidelines for physical activity—150 min of moderate exercise or 75 min of vigorous exercise weekly (Statistics, 2015). Rates of nonengagement are similar in Europe where approximately 60% of adults are not engaging in the recommended physical activity levels (Oja, Bull, Fogelholm, & Martin, 2010). Likewise, in the United States, less than half of the population meet physical active guidelines (Carlson, Fulton, Pratt, Yang, & Adams, 2015). The rates of people staying engaged in a program once they commence are not high, with only half of those who commence exercise programs remaining regularly active 6 months later (Linke, Gallo, & Norman, 2011). Considering that it is difficult for the general population to meet the recommended guidelines and that people living with mental illness face additional barriers, extra support may be required to assist people with psychosis to sustain a higher level of physical activity. Some research, for instance, indicates that negative symptoms in people with schizophrenia are associated with lower levels of motivation towards exercise (Vancampfort et al., 2015).

Lack of motivation could be attributed to individual interests and priorities, the stigma associated with structured exercise and negative past experiences. Other competing factors may limit participation in an exercise program, including work and education demands, family commitments, and insufficient access to resources (Ussher, Stanbury, Cheeseman, & Faulkner, 2007). Another strong factor is a feeling of insufficient competency or experience to perform specific exercises. Lack of education around how to exercise can lead to reduced confidence and affect participation. Evidence suggests that externally driven forces of motivation can lead to short-term engagement in exercise programs. For examples, many people engage in exercise and attend gyms based on 'controlled' feelings of motivation, where they feel they 'should' participate rather than having true feelings of *wanting* to engage. Lack of volition in exercise is typically associated with external motivators such as promises of rewards or a focus on change in appearance. As such, the importance of clinicians discussing these issues during case formulation with mental health consumers should be considered, so that their preferences and priorities are well known.

So, what motivates to people to engage in regular exercise and more importantly, how can clinicians help to facilitate increased participation of their mental health clients in physical activity?

Self-Determination Theory (Deci & Ryan, 2008) is commonly used by exercise specialists to determine individual motivation and help facilitate client engagement and enjoyment in long-term physical activity. This theory focuses on the human motivation that underlies certain behaviours and can be applied with an exercise focus to determine one's motivation to exercise. Self-Determination Theory can also be applied to people with psychosis to understand motivation deficits (Gard et al., 2014) and to assist with wellbeing and recovery (Breitborde, Kleinlein, & Srihari, 2012). Generally, Self-Determination Theory can be used to identify extrinsic (external) and intrinsic (internal) forms of motivation. Feelings of accomplishment, improving a skill, and overcoming a challenge can all be experienced following participation in an exercise program. These are all examples of intrinsic motivators and are more likely to support long-term adherence to exercise. The Self-Determination Theory adopts three basic needs that nurtures motivation in an activity and is relevant particularly in a physical activity setting. These three basic psychological needs include: a sense of autonomy, competence, and relatedness of a form of exercise. If these needs are met, there is largely an automatic and internal drive of motivation to encourage exercise. For people living with schizophrenia, their level of self-determination can play an important role in adopting, and long-term engagement in, physical activity (Vancampfort, Stubbs, Venigalla, & Probst, 2015).

Self-Determination Theory is concerned with supporting our intrinsic tendencies to behave in effective and healthy ways.

Motivational interventions have been shown to be effective in producing statistically significant improvements to engagement in physical activity groups and increases to physical activity levels for people living with schizophrenia (Beebe et al., 2011).

Motivational interviewing is effective when assisting people in improving attitudes to exercise and identifying internal motivators to help them in continuing engagement. In doing so, adopting the transtheoretical model to determine the individuals 'stage of change' can be effective in guiding education and exercise prescription. Stages of change and its application to exercise education/prescription are described.

(i) *Precontemplation*: this time should be used to provide education and encourage the person to begin to start thinking about physical activity and learn about the benefits of regular engagement. Using articles or videos can be an effective way of starting a conversation, as well as listing benefits that may occur because of exercising, and asking about the level of importance of these benefits currently to the client.

(ii) *Contemplation*: clients during this stage can be encouraged to start engaging in some form of physical activity. Clinicians should provide information and challenge current beliefs. Barriers should be addressed as well as tactics to overcome them (see next section for specifics). Broad goals should be made as well as a plan to commit to adhere to these goals.

(iii) *Preparation*: regular physical activity should be facilitated during this period. Strategies that can be used to help adherence to regular exercise include encouragement to exercise with a partner, recording activity performed weekly, and monitoring activity with a smartphone application or activity tracker. It is also important to acknowledge past experiences, vicarious experiences, social persuasion and physiological/affective states.

(iv) *Action*: Clients should be encouraged to be working towards maintaining their current activity over a long period of time. Medium-to-long-term goals should be set such as participating in inspirational activities. Obstacles to engagement should be well established with goals to overcome them.

(v) *Maintenance*: individuals should be prepared to continue independently with their exercise routine and be able to identify personal intrinsic motivators to exercise. Trying new activities can be helpful in this stage as well as strategies to get back on track if there is a lapse in exercise.

Listening to client's needs and goals can help to determine a more recovery-focused approach to exercise prescription.

Key features of discussion when facilitating motivational interviewing include providing basic, as well as specialised, advice, which is where a specialist such as an exercise physiologist can be helpful to provide exercise prescription. Identifying and reducing barriers to engaging in exercise can help clients in making more informed choices and heightening levels of intrinsic motivation. Rolling with resistance, reflective listening, and practicing empathy to improve the quality of discussion can help to determine a more individualised and recovery-focused session. Finally, clear goals should be established to assist the client in adherence to the program.

EXERCISE PROFESSIONALS IN MENTAL HEALTH SETTINGS

Mounting evidence has shown that physical activity programs are acceptable and feasible for people living with mental illness; however, specialised support is required for this population to overcome barriers to participation and maintain long-term adherence to physical activity. Healthcare professionals that specialise in physical activity with mental health experience can prescribe tailored interventions, which can also ease the burden of providing such interventions by other mental health staff (Furness, Hewavasam, Barnfield, McKenna, & Joseph, 2018; Stanton, Rosenbaum, Lederman, & Happell, 2018).

Accredited Exercise Physiologists have specific training and expertise in prescribing and increasing adherence of exercise for people with mental illness.

Australia provides one of the world's most robust referral systems to exercise services for people with a mental illness. One example is the chronic disease management plan, which supports referral to exercise specialists, such as Accredited Exercise Physiologists (AEPs) (Government, 2018). AEPs are university-qualified health professionals who are trained and ideally placed to prescribe and deliver exercise interventions for people with complex and chronic medical conditions (Lederman et al., 2016). AEPs promote evidence-based exercise across varying population groups, including cardiometabolic, neurological, musculoskeletal, cancer, pulmonary, and more recently mental healthcare settings. Exercise and Sports Science Australia (ESSA) is the peak body representing the profession, and under the accreditation scheme, AEPs are becoming well recognised as important members within mental health treatment facilities. AEPs combine theoretical behaviour change techniques, including goal setting and motivational interviewing, to establish recovery-focused physical activity programs for mental health clients.

AEPs work across many mental healthcare settings ranging from acute inpatient wards, community health care centres, residential settings, private practice organisations, and nongovernment organisations (Lederman et al., 2017). They may be embedded as part of a multidisciplinary healthcare team or in private settings, which are accessible through government-supported referral schemes. AEPs work in not only providing effective and highly acceptable services to clients but also upskilling mental health clinicians to provide physical health and exercise-based interventions (Stanton, Donohue, Garnon, & Happell, 2016; Wynaden, Barr, Omari, & Fulton, 2012).

There are several pathways to care that prescribers can utilise when referring clients to AEP services.

(i) A general-practitioner (GP) initiated referral can be performed through the Australian universal healthcare system, Medicare, which allows people with chronic health conditions including mental illness to access allied health services for up to five consultations a year with much of the consultation fee being able to be claimed as a rebate. Access to AEP services is also achievable through Department of Veterans Affairs (DVA) funding, which can be initiated through a GP referral (Government, 2018).

(ii) Mental health clinicians based in hospital settings can refer through discharge plans to AEPs in community settings, e.g. in general-practice or nongovernmental organisations.

(iii) AEP services are also available through self-referral and may be eligible for a rebate service through private healthcare.

Other international organisations have been established in response to the expanding field of physical activity specialists in mental health settings. The International Organisation of Physical Therapists in Mental Health (IOPTMH) consists of physical therapists throughout Europe who are interested and working in mental health. IOPTMH states that physiotherapists are physical health experts who are integral to the multidisciplinary health team in promoting good health to people living with mental illness (Stubbs et al., 2014).

CREATING A CULTURE THAT PROMOTES POSITIVE PHYSICAL HEALTH

The overwhelming evidence highlighting the physical inequities of people living with mental illness has prompted calls for high-quality physical healthcare to be incorporated as part of mental health services (Stewart, 2015). The Australian Mental Health Commission has labelled the mortality gap a 'national disgrace' (Commission, 2014) and UK publications state that the inaction occurring is a form of 'lethal discrimination' (Thornicroft, 2011). As a result, work has been initiated to enshrine 'key principles, processes and standards' in internationally recommended guidelines—Healthy Active Lives (HeAL) declaration, which outlines key targets and instructions to achieve good health for people living with mental illness (Shiers & Curtis, 2014).

Despite this, there remains significant challenges in how to practically implement these principles within mental health services, which have not traditionally included physical health and lifestyle interventions in their treatment programs.

Health professionals who engage in healthy behaviours are more likely to promote such behaviours to their clients.

Calls for novel interventions to help convert research findings into practice within mental health services have been made and, recently, addressing staff culture regarding physical health services has been identified as a way of bridging the mental and physical divide (Rosenbaum et al., 2015). Health professionals who engage in healthy behaviours are more likely to have positive conversations about healthy lifestyle with their clients and are more likely to refer them to exercise specialists (Fibbins, 2018; Stanton, Happell, & Reaburn, 2015). Hence, providing targeted physical health interventions to mental health clinicians may be an effective method of outcomes for patients (Fie, Norman, & While, 2012). While the majority of the research conducted so far has been performed in general health settings, a 2018 systematic review of exercise interventions for staff members in mental health settings found that such programs were feasible and acceptable with limited dropouts (Fibbins, Ward, Watkins, Curtis, & Rosenbaum, 2018). See Box 21.3 for an example of a real-world physical health intervention targeting mental health staff.

Programs in health services internationally have indicated that such interventions do not negatively impact productivity of staff performing clinical duties and that job satisfaction, morale, and workforce capacity can improve (Forsberg, Björkman, Sandman, & Sandlund, 2008; Hjorth, Davidsen, Kilian, Jensen, & Munk-Jorgensen, 2016; Tucker et al., 2016). This conclusion is supported by research in acute psychiatric settings that highlights the important role of exercise in reducing barriers often faced by mental health clinicians when prescribing exercise (Stanton et al., 2015).

Box 21.3 A Real-World Physical Health Intervention for Mental Health Staff

Setting: Keeping the Body in Mind (KBIM) are multidisciplinary health teams working within the mental health service of South Eastern Sydney Local Health District, Australia. KBIM include a Clinical Nurse Consultant (CNC), Exercise Physiologist (EP), Dietitian, and Peer Worker.

Methods and Goals: Evidence-based lifestyle interventions are delivered to mental health clients for the prevention and treatment of metabolic syndrome in consumers with severe mental illness. Throughout 2015 and 2016, KBIM delivered a comprehensive 16-week lifestyle intervention targeting *staff members* of the local mental health service. Staff included in the intervention were from varying disciplines, including administration services, psychiatrists, nurses, allied health, psychologists, and executive management. Labelled the 'Keeping our Staff in Mind' (KoSiM) program, the aim of the intervention was to improve staff understanding of cardiometabolic health and needs of their clients living with mental illness, as well as the important role of the different KBIM clinicians in addressing these needs. A secondary aim was to improve staff knowledge and confidence in physical health, monitoring, and interventions, improve their own physical health, and move towards a culture that was inclusive of physical health.

Outcomes: The program had significant positive effects with marked increases to staff knowledge and confidence in delivering physical health interventions. Improvements to staff anthropometry, physical activity levels, and nutritional quality were also evident (Poole, Rossimel, & Fibbins, 2018).

CONCLUSION

Physical activity and exercise can improve physical and mental health for people living with mental illness. Dedicated physical activity practitioners, including exercise physiologists, sports psychologists, and physiotherapists, can deliver evidence-based programs to help overcome barriers and facilitate motivation of mental health clients. Facilitating culture change and ensuring mental health staff themselves value physical activity and exercise is integral in motivating clients and improving health outcomes in this vulnerable population.

QUIZ QUESTIONS

1. What are the recommended weekly physical activity levels for an individual?
2. List five barriers that someone with a mental illness may face when engaging in physical activity.
3. True or false: Exercise is sufficient by itself to achieve clinically significant weight loss in people living with a mental illness.

ANSWERS TO QUIZ QUESTIONS:

1. 150 min of moderate-intensity exercise or 75 min of vigorous intensity exercise.
2.
   - Physical health barriers (increased rates of CVD, diabetes, musculoskeletal conditions, lower cardiorespiratory fitness, fatigue, low energy)
   - Psychological barriers (low mood, mow motivation, mental stress, depression, psychotic symptoms, anxiety)
   - Socio-economic barriers (social isolation, lack of time, cost of and access to services)
3. False. Without dietary changes, it is extremely difficult for people living with a mental illness to achieve clinically significant weight loss.

SELF-DIRECTED LEARNING RESOURCES

Textbook: Stubbs, B., & Rosenbaum, S. (2018). *Exercise-based Interventions for mental illness: Physical activity as part of clinical treatment*. Academic Press.

South Eastern Sydney Local Health District's Keeping the Body in Mind Training Videos. https://www.seslhd.health.nsw.gov.au/keeping-body-mind

Website: International Physical Health in Youth Stream (iphYs). https://www.iphys.org.au/

Website: Exercise and Sports Science Australia (ESSA) https://www.essa.org.au/

References

Ashdown-Franks, G., Williams, J., Vancampfort, D., Firth, J., Schuch, F., Hubbard, K., et al. (2018). Is it possible for people with severe mental illness to sit less and move more? A systematic review of interventions to increase physical activity or reduce sedentary behaviour. *Schizophrenia Research, 202*, 3–16. https://doi.org/10.1016/j.schres.2018.06.058.

Australia, E. A. S. S. (2011). *Adult pre-exercise screening system.* Retrieved from https://www.essa.org.au/wp-content/uploads/2011/09/Screen-tool-version-v1.1.pdf.

Beebe, L. H., Smith, K., Burk, R., McIntyre, K., Dessieux, O., Tavakoli, A., et al. (2011). Effect of a motivational intervention on exercise behavior in persons with schizophrenia spectrum disorders. *Community Mental Health Journal, 47*(6), 628–636.

Brand, S., Colledge, F., Ludyga, S., Emmenegger, R., Kalak, N., Sadeghi Bahmani, D., et al. (2018). Acute bouts of exercising improved mood, rumination and social interaction in inpatients with mental disorders. *Frontiers in Psychology, 9*, 249. https://doi.org/10.3389/fpsyg.2018.00249.

Breitborde, N. J. K., Kleinlein, P., & Srihari, V. H. (2012). Self-determination and first-episode psychosis: associations with symptomatology, social and vocational functioning, and quality of life. *Schizophrenia Research, 137*(1–3), 132–136. https://doi.org/10.1016/j.schres.2012.02.026.

Carlson, S. A., Fulton, J. E., Pratt, M., Yang, Z., & Adams, E. K. (2015). Inadequate physical activity and health care expenditures in the United States. *Progress in Cardiovascular Diseases, 57*(4), 315–323. https://doi.org/10.1016/j.pcad.2014.08.002.

Caspersen, C. J., Powell, K. E., & Christenson, G. M. (1985). Physical activity, exercise, and physical fitness: Definitions and distinctions for health-related research. *Public Health Reports, 100*(2), 126.

Cleare, A., Pariante, C. M., Young, A. H., Anderson, I. M., Christmas, D., Cowen, P. J., et al. (2015). Evidence-based guidelines for treating depressive disorders with antidepressants: A revision of the 2008 British association for psychopharmacology guidelines. *Journal of Psychopharmacology, 29*(5), 459–525.

Commission, N. M. H (2014). *The national review of mental health programmes and services* (p. 67). Sydney: NMHC.

Dauwan, M., Begemann, M. J., Heringa, S. M., & Sommer, I. E. (2016). Exercise improves clinical symptoms, quality of life, global functioning, and depression in schizophrenia: A systematic review and meta-analysis. *Schizophrenia Bulletin, 42*(3), 588–599. https://doi.org/10.1093/schbul/sbv164.

Deci, E. L., & Ryan, R. M. (2008). Self-determination theory: A macrotheory of human motivation, development, and health. *Canadian Psychology/Psychologie Canadienne, 49*(3), 182.

Fibbins, H. (2018). Self-reported physical activity levels of the 2017 Royal Australian and New Zealand college of psychiatrists (RANZCP) conference delegates and their exercise referral practices. *Journal of Mental Health*, 1–8. https://doi.org/10.1080/09638237.2018.1521935.

Fibbins, H., Ward, P. B., Watkins, A., Curtis, J., & Rosenbaum, S. (2018). Improving the health of mental health staff through exercise interventions: A systematic review. *Journal of Mental Health, 27*(2), 184–191. https://doi.org/10.1080/09638237.2018.1437614.

Fie, S., Norman, I. J., & While, A. E. (2012). The relationship between physicians' and nurses' personal physical activity habits and their health-promotion practice: A systematic review. *Health Education Journal, 72*(1), 102–119. https://doi.org/10.1177/0017896911430763.

Fildes, A., Charlton, J., Rudisill, C., Littlejohns, P., Prevost, A. T., & Gulliford, M. C. (2015). Probability of an obese person attaining normal body weight: Cohort study using electronic health records. *American Journal of Public Health, 105*(9), e54–e59. https://doi.org/10.2105/ajph.2015.302773.

Firth, J., Cotter, J., Elliott, R., French, P., & Yung, A. R. (2015). A systematic review and meta-analysis of exercise interventions in schizophrenia patients. *Psychological Medicine, 45*(7), 1343–1361. https://doi.org/10.1017/S0033291714003110.

Firth, J., Rosenbaum, S., Stubbs, B., Gorczynski, P., Yung, A. R., & Vancampfort, D. (2016). Motivating factors and barriers towards exercise in severe mental illness: A systematic review and meta-analysis. *Psychological Medicine, 46*(14), 2869–2881. https://doi.org/10.1017/S0033291716001732.

Firth, J., Stubbs, B., Rosenbaum, S., Vancampfort, D., Malchow, B., Schuch, F., et al. (2017). Aerobic exercise improves cognitive functioning in people with schizophrenia: A systematic review and meta-analysis. *Schizophrenia Bulletin, 43*(3), 546–556. https://doi.org/10.1093/schbul/sbw115.

Firth, J. S. B., Rosenbaum, S., Vancampfort, D., Malchow, B., Schuch, F., Elliot, R., et al. (2016). Aerobic exercise improves cognitive functioning in people with schizophrenia: A systematic review and meta-analysis. *Schizophrenia Bulletin, 43*(3), 546–556. https://doi.org/10.1093/schbul/sbw115.

Fogarty, M., & Happell, B. (2005). Exploring the benefits of an exercise program for people with schizophrenia: A qualitative study. *Issues in Mental Health Nursing, 26*(3), 341–351. https://doi.org/10.1080/01612840590915711.

Forsberg, K. A., Björkman, T., Sandman, P. O., & Sandlund, M. (2008). Physical health—A cluster randomized controlled lifestyle intervention among persons with a psychiatric disability and their staff. *Nordic Journal of Psychiatry, 62*(6), 486–495. https://doi.org/10.1080/08039480801985179.

Furness, T., Hewavasam, J., Barnfield, J., McKenna, B., & Joseph, C. (2018). Adding an accredited exercise physiologist role to a new model of care at a secure extended care mental health service: A qualitative study. *Journal of Mental Health, 27*(2), 120–126. https://doi.org/10.1080/09638237.2017.1294744.

Garber, C. E., Blissmer, B., Deschenes, M. R., Franklin, B. A., Lamonte, M. J., Lee, I. M., et al. (2011). American college of sports medicine position stand. Quantity and quality of exercise for developing and maintaining cardiorespiratory, musculoskeletal, and neuromotor fitness in apparently healthy adults: guidance for prescribing exercise. *Medicine and Science in Sports and Exercise, 43*(7), 1334–1359. https://doi.org/10.1249/MSS.0b013e318213fefb.

Gard, D. E., Sanchez, A. H., Starr, J., Cooper, S., Fisher, M., Rowlands, A., et al. (2014). Using self-determination theory to understand motivation deficits in schizophrenia: The 'why' of motivated behavior. *Schizophrenia Research, 156*(2–3), 217–222. https://doi.org/10.1016/j.schres.2014.04.027.

Gordon, B. R., McDowell, C. P., Hallgren, M., Meyer, J. D., Lyons, M., & Herring, M. P. (2018). Association of efficacy of resistance exercise training with depressive symptoms: Meta-analysis and meta-regression analysis of randomized clinical trials. *JAMA Psychiatry, 75*(6), 566–576. https://doi.org/10.1001/jamapsychiatry.2018.0572.

Gordon, B. R., McDowell, C. P., Lyons, M., & Herring, M. P. (2017). The effects of resistance exercise training on anxiety: A meta-analysis and meta-regression analysis of randomized controlled trials. *Sports Medicine, 47*(12), 2521–2532. https://doi.org/10.1007/s40279-017-0769-0.

Government, A. (2018). *Medicare Benefits Schedule—Item 10953*. Retrieved from www9.health.gov.au/mbs/fullDisplay.cfm?type=item&qt=ItemID&q=10953.

Hjorth, P., Davidsen, A. S., Kilian, R., Jensen, S. O., & Munk-Jorgensen, P. (2016). Intervention to promote physical health in staff within mental health facilities and the impact on patients' physical health. *Nordic Journal of Psychiatry, 70*(1), 62–71.

Jae, S. Y., Franklin, B. A., Choo, J., Yoon, E. S., Choi, Y.-H., & Park, W. H. (2016). Fitness, body habitus, and the risk of incident Type 2 diabetes mellitus in korean men. *American Journal of Cardiology, 117*(4), 585–589. https://doi.org/10.1016/j.amjcard.2015.11.046.

Klatte, R., Pabst, S., Beelmann, A., & Rosendahl, J. (2016). The efficacy of body-oriented Yoga in mental disorders: A systematic review and meta-analysis. *Deutsches Ärzteblatt International, 113*(12), 195–202. https://doi.org/10.3238/arztebl.2016.0195.

Lederman, O., Grainger, K., Stanton, R., Douglas, A., Gould, K., Perram, A., et al. (2016). Consensus statement on the role of accredited exercise physiologists within the treatment of mental disorders: A guide for mental health professionals. *Australasian Psychiatry, 24*(4), 347–351. https://doi.org/10.1177/1039856216632400.

Lederman, O., Suetani, S., Stanton, R., Chapman, J., Korman, N., Rosenbaum, S., et al. (2017). Embedding exercise interventions as routine mental health care: Implementation strategies in residential, inpatient and community settings. *Australasian Psychiatry, 25*(5), 451–455. https://doi.org/10.1177/1039856217711054.

Lederman, O., Ward, P. B., Firth, J., Maloney, C., Carney, R., Vancampfort, D., et al. (2018). Does exercise improve sleep quality in individuals with mental illness? A systematic review and meta-analysis. *Journal of Psychiatric Research, 109*, 96–106.

Linke, S. E., Gallo, L. C., & Norman, G. J. (2011). Attrition and adherence rates of sustained vs. Intermittent exercise interventions. *Annals of Behavioral Medicine, 42*(2), 197–209. https://doi.org/10.1007/s12160-011-9279-8.

Malhotra, A., Noakes, T., & Phinney, S. (2015). It is time to bust the myth of physical inactivity and obesity: you cannot outrun a bad diet. *British Journal of Sports Medicine, 49*(15), 967.

Medicine, A. C. O. S. (2013). *ACSM's guidelines for exercise testing and prescription*. Lippincott Williams & Wilkins.

Newberry, R. E., Dean, D. J., Sayyah, M. D., & Mittal, V. A. (2018). What prevents youth at clinical high risk for psychosis from engaging in physical activity? An examination of the barriers to physical activity. *Schizophrenia Research*, https://doi.org/10.1016/j.schres.2018.06.011.

Oja, P., Bull, F. C., Fogelholm, M., & Martin, B. W. (2010). Physical activity recommendations for health: What should Europe do? *BMC Public Health, 10*(1), 10. https://doi.org/10.1186/1471-2458-10-10.

Pajonk, F.-G., Wobrock, T., Gruber, O., Scherk, H., Berner, D., Kaizl, I., et al. (2010). Hippocampal plasticity in response to exercise in schizophrenia. *Archives of General Psychiatry, 67*(2), 133–143.

Poole, J., Rossimel, E., & Fibbins, H. (2018). Making the link between staff and service-user health. *Mental Health Practice, 21*(7).

Price, C. A. (2017). *Tai Chi/Qi Gong in mental health treatment and prevention: A review of meta-analytic evidence and an analysis of evidence congruence with training practices*. Undergraduate Thesis-University of Vermont.

Rosenbaum, S., Tiedemann, A., & Ward, P. B. (2014). Meta-analysis physical activity interventions for people with mental illness: A systematic review and meta-analysis. *Journal of Clinical Psychiatry, 75*, 1–11.

Rosenbaum, S., Watkins, A., Ward, P. B., Pearce, D., Fitzpatrick, K., & Curtis, J. (2015). Psychiatry HeAL thyself!. *Australian and New Zealand Journal of Psychiatry, 50*(6), 600. https://doi.org/10.1177/0004867415620023.

Scheewe, T. W., van Haren, N. E., Sarkisyan, G., Schnack, H. G., Brouwer, R. M., de Glint, M., et al. (2013). Exercise therapy, cardiorespiratory fitness and their effect on brain volumes: A randomised controlled trial in patients with schizophrenia and healthy controls. *European Neuropsychopharmacology, 23*(7), 675–685.

Shiers, D., & Curtis, J. (2014). Cardiometabolic health in young people with psychosis. *The Lancet Psychiatry, 1*(7), 492–494.

Stanton, R., Donohue, T., Garnon, M., & Happell, B. (2016). Participation in and satisfaction with an exercise program for inpatient mental health consumers. *Perspectives in Psychiatric Care, 52*(1), 62–67. https://doi.org/10.1111/ppc.12108.

Stanton, R., Happell, B., & Reaburn, P. (2015). Investigating the exercise-prescription practices of nurses working in inpatient mental health settings. *International Journal of Mental Health Nursing, 24*(2), 112–120. https://doi.org/10.1111/inm.12125.

Stanton, R., Reaburn, P., & Happell, B. (2016). The effect of acute exercise on affect and Arousal in inpatient mental health consumers. *Journal of Nervous and Mental Disease, 204*(9), 658–664. https://doi.org/10.1097/nmd.0000000000000510.

Stanton, R., Rosenbaum, S., Lederman, O., & Happell, B. (2018). Implementation in action: How Australian exercise physiologists approach exercise prescription for people with mental illness. *Journal of Mental Health, 27*(2), 150–156. https://doi.org/10.1080/09638237.2017.1340627.

Statistics, A. B. O. (2015). *4364.0.55.004 - Australian Health Survey: Physical Activity, 2011–12*. Retrieved from http://www.abs.gov.au/ausstats/abs@.nsf/lookup/D4495467B7F7EB01CA257BAC0015F593?opendocument.

Stewart, R. (2015). Mental disorders and mortality: So many publications, so little change. *Acta Psychiatrica Scandinavica, 132*(5), 410–411. https://doi.org/10.1111/acps.12476.

Stubbs, B., Soundy, A., Probst, M., De Hert, M., De Herdt, A., & Vancampfort, D. (2014). Understanding the role of physiotherapists in schizophrenia: An international perspective from members of the international organisation of physical therapists in mental health (IOPTMH). *Journal of Mental Health, 23*(3), 125–129.

Stutts, W. C. (2002). Physical activity determinants in adults: Perceived benefits, barriers, and self efficacy. *AAOHN Journal, 50*(11), 499–507. https://doi.org/10.1177/216507990205001106.

Thornicroft, G. (2011). Physical health disparities and mental illness: The scandal of premature mortality. *The British Journal of Psychiatry, 199*(6), 441–442. https://doi.org/10.1192/bjp.bp.111.092718.

Tucker, S., Farrington, M., Lanningham-Foster, L. M., Clark, M. K., Dawson, C., Quinn, G. J., et al. (2016). Worksite physical activity intervention for ambulatory clinic nursing staff. *Workplace Health & Safety, 64*(7), 313–325. https://doi.org/10.1177/2165079916633225.

Ussher, M., Stanbury, L., Cheeseman, V., & Faulkner, G. (2007). Physical activity preferences and perceived barriers to activity among persons with severe mental illness in the United Kingdom. *Psychiatric Services, 58*(3), 405–408.

Van Citters, A. D., Pratt, S. I., Jue, K., Williams, G., Miller, P. T., Xie, H., et al. (2010). A pilot evaluation of the in SHAPE individualized health promotion intervention for adults with mental illness. *Community Mental Health Journal, 46*(6), 540–552. https://doi.org/10.1007/s10597-009-9272-x.

Vancampfort, D., De Hert, M., Stubbs, B., Ward, P. B., Rosenbaum, S., Soundy, A., et al. (2015). Negative symptoms are associated with lower autonomous motivation towards physical activity in people with schizophrenia. *Comprehensive Psychiatry, 56*, 128–132. https://doi.org/10.1016/j.comppsych.2014.10.007.

Vancampfort, D., Firth, J., Schuch, F. B., Rosenbaum, S., Mugisha, J., Hallgren, M., et al. (2017). Sedentary behavior and physical activity levels in people with schizophrenia, bipolar disorder and major depressive disorder: A global systematic review and meta-analysis. *World Psychiatry, 16*(3), 308–315. https://doi.org/10.1002/wps.20458.

Vancampfort, D., Rosenbaum, S., Ward, P. B., & Stubbs, B. (2015). Exercise improves cardiorespiratory fitness in people with schizophrenia: A systematic review and meta-analysis. *Schizophrenia Research, 169*(1–3), 453–457.

Vancampfort, D., Stubbs, B., Venigalla, S. K., & Probst, M. (2015). Adopting and maintaining physical activity behaviours in people with severe mental illness: The importance of autonomous motivation. *Preventive Medicine, 81*, 216–220.

Ventura, J., & McEwen, S. (2017). 97. Adding aerobic exercise to cognitive training improves negative symptoms and social functioning in first-episode schizophrenia: an initial RCT. *Schizophrenia Bulletin, 43*(Suppl 1), S52. https://doi.org/10.1093/schbul/sbx021.135.

Winett, R. A., & Carpinelli, R. N. (2001). Potential health-related benefits of resistance training. *Preventive Medicine, 33*(5), 503–513. https://doi.org/10.1006/pmed.2001.0909.

Wynaden, D., Barr, L., Omari, O., & Fulton, A. (2012). Evaluation of service users' experiences of participating in an exercise programme at the Western Australian state forensic mental health services. *International Journal of Mental Health Nursing, 21*(3), 229–235. https://doi.org/10.1111/j.1447-0349.2011.00787.x.

Yung, A. R., & Firth, J. (2017). How should physical exercise be used in schizophrenia treatment? *Expert Review of Neurotherapeutics, 17*(3), 213–214. https://doi.org/10.1080/14737175.2017.1275571.

Definition of Key Terms

Aerobic exercise Sustained activity that results in increased heart rate and respiratory rate.

Cardiorespiratory fitness The ability of the respiratory and circulatory systems to deliver oxygen to skeletal muscles throughout physical activity.

Exercise A structured and planned subset of physical activity that is generally repetitive in nature and performed for purposes relating to improvements in fitness and health.

Exercise Physiologist A university educated health professional who is trained and ideally placed to prescribe and deliver exercise interventions for people with complex and chronic medical conditions.

F.I.T.T principles 'Frequency', 'Intensity', 'Time/duration', 'Type'. Principles of exercise that can be used to tailor an exercise program for an individual.

Incidental activity Generally unplanned and low impact physical activity.

Physical activity Any movement of the body that requires energy expenditure.

Resistance exercise Activity that involves movements against a resistance of force.

CHAPTER 22

Treating Comorbid Substance Use and Psychosis

Amanda L. Baker, Alexandra M.J. Denham, Sonja Pohlman, Kristen McCarter
School of Medicine and Public Health, University of Newcastle, Newcastle, NSW, Australia

Key Learning Objectives

- To understand that tobacco, alcohol, caffeine, and illicit drug use can be successfully treated among people with psychosis
- To encourage a long-term perspective with consideration of tiered interventions over time for substance use and other health behaviours
- To monitor mental health and substance use over time to track progress and step interventions up or down
- To tailor interventions using information from assessment and an interactive case formulation

INTRODUCTION

As described in Chapter 13 by Mueser and colleagues, smoking, alcohol, and other drug use are highly prevalent among people diagnosed with psychosis. Assessment instruments and procedures were described in that chapter and we will return to the utility of these in this chapter, especially in terms of understanding reasons for use and collaboratively monitoring progress. Chapter 14 covered case formulation and psychological interventions to reduce substance use among people with a psychotic disorder. This chapter builds on Chapters 13 and 14 by considering how best to tailor interventions, using information obtained during the assessment and working on a collaborative case formulation to inform treatment.

The high co-occurrence of substance use and psychosis can present a challenge for treatment. Integrated treatment refers to the treatment for two or more conditions concurrently in the same setting. It has been found to be superior compared to separate treatment of individual disorders among people with severe mental illness (SMI; including people with psychosis) (Drake, Mueser,

Integrated treatment for psychosis and substance use leads to better outcomes

A Clinical Introduction to Psychosis. https://doi.org/10.1016/B978-0-12-815012-2.00022-5

Brunette, & McHugo, 2004; Mueser & Gingerich, 2013). This approach aids consistent treatment with common objectives and reduces burden on the individual consumer (Deady et al., 2015).

A note on a few general principles of therapy. Following assessment and case formulation, there is no 'one size fits all' treatment. Firstly, a range of interventions will likely be required. Many people living with psychosis may use substances occasionally and nonproblematically. Psychoeducation and monitoring of substance use may be all that is required. However, as hazardous use or substance use disorders are common, brief to more intensive interventions will be called for. Many people use substances hazardously or problematically on an intermittent basis, so monitoring and stepping up and down intensity of intervention is likely to be beneficial. Taking a long-term perspective and encouraging healthy lifestyle, vocational and social activities are likely to be helpful (Lubman & Sundram, 2003). Secondly, as in any counselling, the goals of treatment will be determined by the individual. Many people choose to work towards reducing substance use before abstaining. Others may abstain for a while and start using again, and formulate a goal of regaining abstinence. Again, monitoring use regularly will inform your interactions with the person and together you can help work on various goals over time. Thirdly, optimism about treatment is important. Convey an optimistic attitude that change is possible and that you are there to help. Even if substance use is not reduced, it is important for clinicians to work on improving functioning in people with co-existing disorders, and not to assume that continued substance use prevents them from benefitting from other psychosocial interventions (Cather et al., 2018). A fourth principle of therapy is to assume that polydrug use is the norm and the person may select to work on one or more or all substance use at a time. Orford (2001) has pointed out that motivational and self-control strategies can often be employed to reduce use of numerous substances.

Hazardous use, and substance use disorders are common in psychosis.

Optimism about treatment is important.

We will provide a brief overview about the effectiveness of psychological treatments for substance use in, and guidelines for, people with psychosis. Based on your assessment and case formulation, you will be able to tailor treatment informed by the evidence. Intervening for substance use in psychosis can be helped enormously by a team approach to the issue, so we will be covering that too. Firstly, though, a few words about the term 'recovery', which has been a little controversial especially in relation to reducing substance use.

CONVERGENCE IN 'RECOVERY'

Recently, in the treatment of psychosis and also in substance use treatment, there has been a shift in how recovery is viewed. Whereas recovery may have once been viewed as an absence of psychotic symptomatology or abstinence from substance use, there is a new emphasis on wellness and quality of life. Recovery has been defined as 'a deeply personal, unique process of changing one's attitudes, values, feelings, goals, skills, and/or roles' and 'a way of living a satisfying, hopeful, and contributing life…' (Anthony, 1993). At the same time, in treating psychosis and substance use disorder, there has been recognition that continuing care, across treatment settings (e.g. from inpatient to outpatient), within treatment teams and over time, is likely to be of benefit (McLellan, McKay, Forman, Cacciola, & Kemp, 2005). In this context, a case formulation-driven approach can assist the person to link their substance use with their values, goals, and hopes for the future and monitor convergence in terms of recovery from psychosis and also from substance use that is at odds with values, goals, and hopes for the future.

Continuing care, across treatment settings (e.g. from inpatient to outpatient), within treatment teams and over time, is likely to be helpful.

REASONS FOR SUBSTANCE USE AMONG PEOPLE WITH PSYCHOSIS

Previous research suggests that for efforts to reduce substance use to be successful, it is necessary to understand the antecedents of use (Gregg, Barrowclough, & Haddock, 2007; Kuntsche, Knibbe, Gmel, & Engels, 2006; Thornton, Baker, Johnson, Kay-Lambkin, & Lewin, 2012). Substance use motives have been theorised as the final common pathway to use (Cooper, 1994; Cox & Klinger, 1988). Research has investigated motives for substance use in people with psychosis (Lobbana et al., 2010; Mueser, Nishith, Tracy, DeGirolamo, & Molinaro, 1995; Spencer, Castle, & Michie, 2002). Studies into substance use reduction interventions in comorbid populations have shown differential efficacy based on specific substance use (Baker, Turner, Kay-Lambkin, & Lewin, 2009). Gaining a clearer understanding of reasons for substance use gives insight to design more targeted interventions, which can hopefully prevent a transition to more sustained hazardous or dependent levels of use and treat existing substance use disorders. For example, using a specifically modified motives questionnaire based on that of Cooper, Russell, Skinner, and Windle (1992), Thornton et al. (2012) found that among substance users with psychosis, people smoked tobacco primarily for coping motives, consumed alcohol for social motives, and cannabis for pleasure enhancement. It is important to remember that motives and patterns of substance use are idiosyncratic and, as with the general population, it cannot be assumed that all substance use will be problematic for people with psychosis. Careful assessment is required, which helps the client and therapist develop a shared understanding of the function and impact of each used substance and its relationship with their mental and physical health.

Interventions need to consider both the motives for, and types of, substance use.

In the following content, we overview the effectiveness of interventions for different substances among people with psychosis, followed by a table summarising suggested approaches. Except for tobacco, available evidence suggests usual treatment is at least partly effective for substance use in people with psychosis (e.g. Petersen et al., 2007). Unless specifically addressed with combination behavioural and pharmacotherapy, smoking appears to remain stable. In addition to improvements with usual treatment, there is accumulating evidence that psychological interventions are consistently associated with better outcomes compared to comparison conditions for alcohol, cannabis, or psychostimulant use among people being treated for psychosis. We summarise key findings from reviews of the literature, and other research, here.

OVERVIEW OF PSYCHOLOGICAL MANAGEMENT OF SUBSTANCE USE PROBLEMS AMONG PEOPLE WITH PSYCHOSIS

Psychostimulants

As described in Chapter 13, stimulant use is almost universal among people with psychosis. Stimulant drugs include legal drugs like tobacco and caffeine, and illegal drugs like cocaine and methamphetamine. It is thought that stimulant use relates to the negative symptoms associated with psychosis itself and the sedative effects of medications. However, stimulant use is widespread across society and as stated earlier, an understanding of reasons for use is important in each individual.

Tobacco

Rates of smoking and tobacco related illness remain high in people with psychosis.

People with psychotic disorders typically die 20 years earlier than the general population, largely due to smoking-related diseases such as cardiovascular disease and cancer (Callaghan et al., 2014). Smokers with psychosis are an increasing proportion of all smokers (Lasser, Boyd, & Woolhandler, 2002), because smoking is not showing the same rate of decline among people living with psychosis as among the general population (Lê Cook et al., 2014). In addition to increased mortality, smoking in people with psychosis has also been associated with more psychiatric symptoms, increased hospitalisations, and higher required psychiatric medication dosages (Prochaska, 2011) because components of tobacco smoke accelerate the metabolism of some antidepressant and antipsychotic medications (Banham & Gilbody, 2010).

The majority of people with psychosis want to quit to smoking.

People with SMI are about as likely to want to quit as those in the general population (Siru, Hulse, & Tait, 2009). Smoking cessation benefits mental health as well as physical health. A recent metaanalysis of primarily noncontrolled trials found that quitting smoking is associated with improved quality of life and reduced depression, anxiety, and stress. Effect sizes for these differences were as large in people with SMI as in the general population, and equal to or larger than those of antidepressant treatment for mood and anxiety disorders (Taylor et al., 2014). Further, sustained reductions in smoking have important financial benefits and may increase the chance of future cessation (Banham & Gilbody, 2010).

Combined psychological and pharmacological interventions are recommended for smoking cessation.

Reviews of the smoking cessation literature among people with schizophrenia (Hitsman, Moss, Montoya, & George, 2009; Tidey & Miller, 2015) are supportive of repeated longer-term psychological (usually a combination of motivational interviewing and cognitive behaviour therapy, CBT) and pharmacological interventions. In addition, the recent Evaluating Adverse Events in a Global Smoking

Cessation Study (EAGLES) randomised controlled trial (RCT) found no significant increase in neuropsychiatric adverse events attributable to varenicline or bupropion relative to nicotine patch or placebo (Anthenelli et al., 2016). If using nicotine replacement therapy, combination therapy (patch plus lozenge, spray, gum, or inhalator etc.) is recommended over single formulations (Cahill, Stevens, Perera, & Lancaster, 2013). Better session attendance is associated with higher quit rates and rewards for attendance may assist smoking cessation efforts (Hitsman et al., 2009; Tidey & Miller, 2015). The reviews (Hitsman et al., 2009; Tidey & Miller, 2015) also suggest that intermediate treatment goals, such as smoking reduction, may be helpful in shoring up motivation, self-efficacy and making financial gains and that electronic cigarettes may also assist in achieving abstinence from cigarettes. Although contentious, electronic cigarettes have a growing evidence base to support their use in smoking cessation (McNeil et al., 2015).

Having emphasised the utility of a long-term approach, it remains to be said that even brief interventions for smoking can be helpful among people with psychosis. Steinberg, Williams, Stahl, Budsock, and Cooperman (2016) found that compared to interactive education, motivational interviewing with feedback significantly increased quit attempts. Similarly, less intensive interventions, involving nicotine replacement therapy and monitoring of symptoms, medications and interactions between medications and smoking reduction, delivered in person (Williams et al., 2010) or by telephone (Baker et al., 2017), have been found to be as effective as more intensive interventions.

Brief and low intensive interventions for smoking can be effective.

Caffeine

Although caffeine is one of the most commonly consumed stimulants, it has received little treatment attention. Its use is widespread among people with psychosis and has been reviewed by Williams and Gandhi (2008) in schizophrenia and Kunitake et al. (2017) in bipolar disorder. Caffeine increases arousal and may exacerbate the course of bipolar disorder (Kunitake et al., 2017) and may interfere with the clearance of some psychotropic drugs (Kunitake et al., 2017; Williams & Gandhi, 2008). In the paper by Kunitake et al. (2017), advice to limit caffeine intake (from 13 to 20 cups to no more than 10 cups per day) was associated with increased blood levels of lithium and amelioration of psychiatric symptoms in a patient with bipolar disorder.

Excessive caffeine use can have a negative impact on symptoms in bipolar disorder.

Cocaine and Methamphetamine

Few studies have solely focussed on psychostimulant use (cocaine, methamphetamine) reduction among people with psychosis. McDonell et al. (2013) conducted an RCT of 3 months of contingency management for stimulant abstinence plus treatment as usual or treatment as usual with reinforcement for study participation only, among people attending community mental health centres (39% schizoaffective spectrum disorder, 33% bipolar disorder, 29%

major depressive disorder). The stimulant contingent condition experienced significantly fewer days of stimulant drug use, lower levels of injection drug use and alcohol use, and fewer psychiatric symptoms and psychiatric hospital admissions.

Two of our studies reported on subsamples of people with SMI (Baker et al., 2002, 2006) using methamphetamine. In the Baker et al. (2002) study, inpatients were assigned to either motivational interviewing or a self-help booklet control, with both conditions showing reductions in methamphetamine use at 12-month follow-up. There was also a significant reduction in mental health symptomatology over time. People with SMI living in the community showed benefits of CBT (Baker et al., 2006). Compared to treatment as usual, Baker et al. (2006) found that 10 sessions of CBT were associated with a large reduction in methamphetamine use and benefits in terms of lower depression scores and better global functioning.

Motivational interviewing, CBT, and contingency management on an outpatient basis can be helpful in reducing methamphetamine or cocaine use.

In summary, legal and illegal stimulants always need to be assessed among people with psychosis. Simple advice can be helpful in reducing caffeine use. Admission to psychiatric hospital is itself often associated with sustained reductions in psychostimulant use. Motivational interviewing, CBT, and contingency management on an outpatient basis can be helpful. Contingency management, rewarding people for healthy behaviours, shows promise among people with psychosis and is considered further here.

Alcohol

Alcohol is commonly consumed at hazardous or harmful levels by people with psychosis (see Chapter 13). In a review of psychological interventions for excessive alcohol consumption among people with psychotic disorders (Baker, Hiles, Thornton, Hides, & Lubman, 2012), the results of seven RCTs indicated that assessment interviews, brief motivational interventions, and longer CBT interventions have all been associated with reductions in alcohol consumption, including inpatients. However, longer interventions provided additional benefits in reducing depression and better functioning and alcohol outcomes. They recommended that psychological interventions be integrated with standard care for people with psychosis.

Excessive alcohol use in psychosis is responsive to psychological interventions.

Another review (Sawicka & Tracy, 2017) has focussed on the efficacy of naltrexone, an opioid antagonist postulated to reduce alcohol craving, in treating alcohol use disorder in individuals with comorbid psychosis. Sawicka and Tracy (2017) point out that there is a modest evidence base for naltrexone use among people with alcohol use disorder and psychosis, but it appears to be safe and effective. They also point to guidelines recommending psychosocial before pharmacological interventions. On balance, they state that the use of naltrexone can be supported, but issues such as adherence and the possibility of exacerbated dysphoria need to be considered.

Cannabis

Recent reviews of the literature (Baker, Thornton, Hides, & Dunlop, 2012; Baker, Hides, & Lubman, 2010; McLoughlin et al., 2014; Hjorthoj, Baker, Fohlmann, & Nordentoft, 2014) have reported that motivational interviewing and/or CBT for cannabis use appears to be moderately effective on quantity of use. Positive symptoms have also been shown to improve with intervention (Hjorthoj et al., 2014), along with global functioning (Baker et al., 2009, 2010). Longer interventions appear to be more effective than shorter interventions (Baker et al., 2012; Hjorthoj et al., 2014).

Motivational interviewing and/or CBT for cannabis use appears to be moderately effective.

Although cannabis and other substance use may improve as people enter treatment, and atypical antipsychotics may be effective in reducing psychotic symptoms, there is no evidence that atypical antipsychotics impact significantly in reducing substance use (Baker, Thornton, et al., 2012). As stated, agonist approaches are an important component of nicotine dependence treatment and cannabidiol (CBD), a nonpsychoactive cannabinoid has been proposed as a potential medication for psychotic symptoms and as an agonist medication for cannabis use (Baker, Thornton, et al., 2012; McLoughlin et al., 2014). Current evidence is insufficient regarding the utility of CBD in psychosis treatment or in the treatment of cannabis use (McLoughlin et al., 2014).

REVIEWS OF MIXED SUBSTANCE MISUSE STUDIES

In addition to reviews of treatments for specific substance use types among people with psychosis, others have reviewed mixed substance misuse treatment studies among subgroups of people with psychosis such as first-episode psychosis (Wisdom, Manuel, & Drake, 2011); schizophrenia (De Witte, Crunelle, Sabbe, Moggi, & Dom, 2014; Wobrock & Soyka, 2008); bipolar disorder (Gregory, 2011; Salloum & Brown, 2017; Secades-Álvarez & Fernández-Rodríguez, 2017; Vaz & Crockford, 2017); or samples of people with SMI (e.g. Horsfall, Cleary, Hunt, & Walter, 2009; Hunt, Siegfried, Morley, Sitharthan, & Cleary, 2013; Kelly, Daley, & Douaihy, 2012; Rebgetz, Kavanagh, & Hides, 2015; Temmingh, Williams, Siegfried, & Stein, 2018). Similar to the conclusions noted, these reviews found that many people reduce their substance use after an episode of psychosis (e.g. Wisdom et al., 2011); second-generation antipsychotics are more effective than first-generation antipsychotics in treating schizophrenia and comorbid substance abuse but are limited in their effectiveness (Kelly et al., 2012); motivational interviewing, CBT, contingency management, relapse prevention, case management, and skills training are effective (Horsfall et al., 2009); and family interventions show promise with regards to improving client and family functioning (De Witte et al., 2014). Among people with bipolar disorder and substance misuse, quetiapine and valproate have shown superiority on psychiatric symptomatology and reduced alcohol consumption, respectively (Secades-Álvarez & Fernández-Rodríguez, 2017). Group interventions with

Including family in interventions can improve client and family functioning.

education, relapse prevention, and family inclusion have also been associated with reductions in symptomatology and alcohol and drug use (Gregory, 2011; Secades-Álvarez & Fernández-Rodríguez, 2017). Reviews noted methodological limitations of the available literature, with the need for more homogeneous samples, including relating interventions to expected outcomes, such as type of substance use (De Witte et al., 2014) (like those reviewed earlier), the need for more experimental trials (Gregory, 2011), and larger sample sizes (Wisdom et al., 2011).

GUIDELINES FOR CO-EXISTING PSYCHOSIS AND SUBSTANCE MISUSE

A number of guidelines on the treatment of psychosis and substance misuse are available (see Table 22.1). The guideline by Crockford and Addington (2017) is very practical and could be adapted to various clinical settings. However, since its publication, there has been further evidence on the safety of varenicline for smoking among people with mental ill-health (Anthenelli et al., 2016). Guidelines for clinicians may focus on the context, structure, and content of interventions (Royal Australian and New Zealand College of Psychiatrists, 2016), improving access to ongoing support services (NICE, 2016), and acceptable information provision and delivery (Early Psychosis Guidelines Writing Group and EPPIC National Support Program, 2016) as part of a multicomponent treatment plan. By following the most recent guidelines, clinicians are provided the tools to deliver up-to-date, acceptable, and evidence-based treatment strategies to assist people with comorbid substance use and psychosis, and in turn increase their health and wellbeing.

COMMON ELEMENTS ACROSS THE GUIDELINES

Across the guidelines, there is a strong theme of understanding the unique and complex clinical challenges of treating people who have psychotic disorders with co-existing substance use disorders. These guidelines proposed recommendations for treatment and practice, which can help clinicians to: (1) assess the treatment needs of this population; (2) engage individuals in evidence-based and acceptable treatment; (3) support patient agency in treatment decision-making; and (4) provide ongoing services and programs, which can support significant improvements in health and well-being. Some guidelines also offer specialised recommendations for priority settings and strategies for those who are at clinical high risk states of psychosis (NSW Department of Health, 2009; Schmidt et al., 2015) and guidance on multidisciplinary service providers such as social work services to provide ongoing and tailored long-term support (Perron et al., 2010; National Institute for Health and Care Excellence (NICE), 2011; National Institute for Health and Care

Table 22.1 Guidelines on the Treatment of Psychosis and Substance Misuse

Guidelines	Aim	Areas focussed on
Early Psychosis Guidelines Writing Group (2010), Early Psychosis Guidelines Writing Group (2016) Australian Clinical Guidelines for Early Psychosis, 2nd edition	To assist health practitioners make appropriate decisions (i.e. based on good evidence and/or the consensus of a panel of experts) in service provision to those with early onset psychosis	1. Access to care 2. Assessment 3. Treatment for early psychosis 4. Early psychosis treatment across all phases 5. Sexual health 6. Case management 7. Treatment within the least restrictive environment 8. Family involvement 9. Goals as guides to treatment 10. Group programs 11. Psychoeducation 12. Suicide prevention 13. Vocational and educational services 14. Substance use (including cigarette use) 15. Treatment of psychiatric comorbidity 16. Consumer participation 17. Carer participation 18. Information about specific populations
NICE (2011) Coexisting severe mental illness (psychosis) and substance misuse assessment and management in healthcare settings	This guideline covers the assessment and management of adults and young people (aged 14 years and older) who have a clinical diagnosis of psychosis with coexisting substance misuse	1. Guidance 2. Principles of care 3. Recognition of psychosis with coexisting substance misuse 4. Primary care 5. Secondary care mental health services 6. Substance misuse services 7. Inpatient mental health services 8. Staffed accommodation 9. Specific issues for young people with psychosis and coexisting substance misuse

Continued

Table 22.1 Guidelines on the Treatment of Psychosis and Substance Misuse—cont'd

Guidelines	Aim	Areas focussed on
NICE (2016) Coexisting severe mental illness and substance misuse: Community health and social care services	How to improve services for people aged 14 and above who have been diagnosed as having coexisting severe mental illness and substance misuse. The aim is to provide a range of coordinated services that address people's wider health and social care needs, as well as other issues such as employment and housing These guidelines are for: ▪ Commissioners and providers, including those working in primary care ▪ Staff working in all services who come into contact with this group ▪ The criminal justice system ▪ Voluntary and community sector organisations ▪ People aged 14 and above diagnosed as having coexisting severe mental illness and substance misuse and who live in the community, their families, and carers	1. First contact with services 2. Referral to secondary care mental health services 3. The care plan: multiagency approach to address physical health, social care, housing and other support needs 4. Partnership working between specialist services, health, social care, and other support services and commissioners 5. Improving service delivery 6. Maintaining contact between services and people with co-existing severe mental illness and substance misuse who use them
NSW Department of Health (2009) NSW clinical guidelines for the care of persons with comorbid mental illness and substance use disorders in acute care settings	These guidelines have been written for practitioners working in the drug and alcohol and/or mental health sectors who provide care for people with comorbid mental health and substance use disorders and who work in the following environments: ▪ Acute ▪ Nonacute ▪ Community settings ▪ Hospitals ▪ Government ▪ Nongovernment	1. Focus on workforce planning and development 2. Improved infrastructure and systems development 3. Improved response in priority settings for priority clients 4. Improved promotion, prevention and early intervention strategies

Table 22.1 Guidelines on the Treatment of Psychosis and Substance Misuse—cont'd

Guidelines	Aim	Areas focussed on
	It is acknowledged that these guidelines will be useful for those practitioners providing care to people with comorbid mental health and substance use disorders in a variety of other clinical settings, including emergency departments, justice health, general wards, and general practice. Information specifically relevant to each of these clinical settings has been included within the guidelines	
Perron, Bunger, Bender, Vaughn, and Howard (2010) Treatment guidelines for substance use disorders and serious mental illnesses: Do they address co-occurring disorders	Practice guidelines are important tools for improving the delivery of evidence-based practices and reducing inappropriate variation in current treatment approaches	1. Recommendations for co-occurring disorders 2. Multidisciplinary guidelines 3. Treatment outcomes
Royal Australian and New Zealand College of Psychiatrists (2016) clinical practice guidelines for the management of schizophrenia and related disorders	This guideline provides recommendations for the clinical management of schizophrenia and related disorders for health professionals working in Australia and New Zealand	1. The stages of schizophrenia: a framework for clinical care 2. Comorbid substance use 3. Treatment: context, structure, and content of interventions 4. Physical health
Schmidt et al. (2015) EPA guidance on the early detection of clinical high-risk states of psychoses	This guidance paper from the European Psychiatric Association (EPA) aims to provide evidence-based recommendations on early intervention in clinical high-risk (CHR) states of psychosis, assessed according to the EPA guidance on early detection	Provided seven recommendations based on literature review and metaanalysis
American Psychiatric Association Practice Guidelines for Psychiatric Assessment of Adults (2016)	In the context of an initial psychiatric evaluation, a major goal of these guidelines is to improve the identification of psychiatric signs and symptoms, psychiatric disorders (including substance use disorders), other medical conditions (that could affect the accuracy of a	1. Review of psychiatric symptoms, trauma history, and psychiatric treatment history 2. Substance use assessment 3. Assessment of suicide risk

Continued

Table 22.1 Guidelines on the Treatment of Psychosis and Substance Misuse—cont'd

Guidelines	Aim	Areas focussed on
	psychiatric diagnosis), and patients who are at increased risk for suicidal or aggressive behaviours	4. Assessment of risk for aggressive behaviours 5. Assessment of cultural factors 6. Assessment of medical health 7. Quantitative assessment 8. Involvement of the patient in treatment decision making 9. Documentation of the psychiatric evaluation
Crockford and Addington (2017) Canadian schizophrenia guidelines: Schizophrenia and other psychotic disorders with coexisting substance use disorders	The objectives of this review were to identify evidence-based practices best practices that improve outcomes for individuals with schizophrenia and substance used disorders	Provided 43 recommendations based on literature review and metaanalysis of clinical guidelines

Excellence (NICE), 2016; Early Psychosis Guidelines Writing Group, 2010; Early Psychosis Guidelines Writing Group, 2016). These resources can be used by clinicians to inform practice and provide treatments, interventions and services to people who have psychotic disorders with co-existing substance use disorders.

TREATMENT MANUALS

Treatment manuals are guides used to inform clinicians of best practice models of treatment for a particular population (Wilson, 1997). Various treatment manuals and clinical handbooks exist for individuals who are diagnosed with comorbid substance use and psychosis (Baker & Velleman, 2007; Graham, 2004; Graham, Copello, Birchwood, & Griffith, 2016; Marel et al., 2016; Mueser, 2003; Teesson, 2004; Weiss & Connery, 2011). Other tools and resources to assist patients in managing their mental health in addition to their substance misuse can be helpful, such as the mental health and smoking tools and resources developed by Quit Victoria (Quit Victoria, 2018). Treatment manuals can be used flexibly to personalise treatment for an individual with comorbid substance use and psychosis.

ADOPTING A TIERED HEALTH PROMOTION INTERVENTION

On the basis of the existing evidence, using assessment and case formulation approaches as described in previous chapters, standard treatment might involve a tiered intervention along the lines that that we have previously described as implemented in a service for young people at ultra high risk for psychosis and in early psychosis (Bucci et al., 2010). It is important that the intervention is non-stigmatising and appealing. Given the rise in obesity, diabetes, and cardiovascular disease among people with psychosis, a health promotion approach, praising people for healthy behaviours (e.g. not using substances) and stepping up intervention for unhealthy behaviours, is acceptable and appealing to service users. Table 22.2 outlines this approach, building on knowledge of stages of change and employing motivational interviewing.

Tiered interventions are adapted to the severity of substance use.

Table 22.2 A Tiered 'Health Promotion' Approach

1. Seek permission to screen and assess health behaviours, linking these with better mental and physical health.
2. Start with questions about activity (e.g. walking, leisure screen time) and diet (e.g. number of fruit and vegetables per day, soft drink consumption, take-away meals), then move to smoking, alcohol, cannabis, other drug use.
3. Praise for healthy behaviours (e.g. not smoking) and provide brief advice regarding potential benefits (health, interactions with antipsychotics and other medications).
4. Ask about concerns in each domain (activity, diet, substance use), e.g. what concerns you about your drinking like you do?
   What concerns you the most about that?
5. Assess stage of change using a readiness ruler (e.g. 'On a scale of 0–10, how important is it for you to reduce your drinking?')
6. Use decisional balance (Good things/Less good things about health behaviours, e.g. drinking)
7. Ask about possible links between the health behaviours to presenting mental or physical health symptoms, e.g. how does the drinking affect your mood? And what about your weight?
8. Seek permission to provide information.
9. Assess confidence to improve health behaviours ('On a scale of 0–10, how confident are you that you can reduce your drinking?')
10. Discuss options for changing each behaviour (including family involvement).
11. Collaborate on a change plan: 'What's the next step?'
12. Monitor improvement and maintenance of change, mental health symptoms, physical health issues of concern and substance use and other health behaviours
13. Step up CBT, family and other interventions, from brief to more intensive (using telephone, face-to-face, or group modalities).
14. Refer for specialised treatment if agreed with client (e.g. Quitline) and also for maintenance support (e.g. SMART Recovery, mutual aid group based on CBT principles)

STAGES OF CHANGE

The stages of change model may help inform one's approach to raising the issue and addressing a range of health behaviours, including substance use. DiClemente (2017) describes how the stages of change (precontemplation [no current interest in change], contemplation, preparation, action, and maintenance) are practically helpful in counselling people with psychotic disorders when psychotic symptoms are managed. Each stage is associated with specific tasks and goals (DiClemente, 2017), summarised in Box 22.1.

MOTIVATIONAL INTERVIEWING

As described in Chapter 13 with assessment, a nonjudgemental and empathic approach to management is important to better outcomes. In addition, employing motivational interviewing techniques (Miller & Rollnick, 2012) enhances the likelihood of change. Facilitate goal setting by identifying stage of change using a 'readiness ruler' (Rollnick, Mason, & Butler, 1999), 'On a scale from 1-10, how important is it for you to reduce your drinking?' If a low number, engage the person in a motivational interviewing decisional balance exercise 'What are the good things about drinking? And what are the less good things about drinking?' Sometimes it may also be helpful to ask 'What would it take to move you up to an '8' for importance?' Link drinking to the presenting mental and physical health symptoms by asking, for example, 'How does the drinking affect your mood/ your weight, etc.?' Seek permission to provide information on the possible relationship with the person's presenting symptomatology (referring back to any information from screening instruments) and seek their feedback 'How does that sound to you?' If the person rated importance quite highly, move on to assess confidence (Rollnick et al., 1999) by asking 'How confident are you that you can reduce your drinking'? If confidence is high, ask the person what ideas they have about how to go about change. If quite a low number is given, seek

Box 22.1 Stages of Change Model (DiClemente, 2017)

Precontemplation: With a goal of serious consideration of change, tasks include (i) increasing awareness of the need for substance use reduction, (ii) concern about current level of use and (iii) imagining the possibility of change.

Contemplation: The goal is for the person to reach a decision to change, through tasks of (i) considering the good and not so good aspects of the current level of use and (ii) the potential for change.

Preparation: Here the goal is to form a feasible action plan through (i) increasing commitment and (ii) making an acceptable, accessible, and likely effective change plan.

Action: Successful action is taken to reduce substance use through (i) implementing strategies for change, (ii) revising the plan, and (iii) sustaining commitment.

Maintenance: Long-term change is achieved via (i) sustaining multiple changes and integrating them into lifestyle and (ii) avoiding slips.

permission to give information about possible helpful strategies, 'I wonder if you would be interested to hear what others have found helpful in this situation?' Discuss a change plan for drinking by asking something like 'So, what's the next step?' If the person is not ready to reduce their alcohol intake to nonhazardous levels, keep working with them on a harm minimisation goal, keeping the door open to future change.

CASE STUDY: RENEE (A HYPOTHETICAL CASE PRESENTATION)

Initial Presentation

'Renee' is a 31-year-old woman diagnosed with schizoaffective disorder. She was referred by her General Practitioner (GP) for assistance with managing her depression. Renee described that she had experienced delusions of persecution and reference, thinking that a childhood friend was 'out to get her' and was trying to have her arrested. She was distrustful and said that she would hear a voice, which told her she was worthless and deserved this. These symptoms are generally well controlled by antipsychotic medication. However, Renee said she has struggled with continued low mood.

Assessment

Renee reported that she finds it hard to get out of bed in the morning and can feel overwhelmed by negative thoughts. She says on some days it can be hard to differentiate between the voice and her own negative thoughts. Further in the assessment, Renee admits that she has been using methamphetamine and cannabis for about 10 years but has been uncomfortable sharing this with her GP. Her substance use started socially, and she stopped while she was pregnant with her daughter who is now 5 years old. Renee said she started to use methamphetamine again 4 years ago as she finds it gives her energy to keep up with household tasks and her child. She said that she also finds smoking a few cones each night helps her to calm down and get to sleep, especially if she has used methamphetamine recently. Renee is separated from her partner and has limited social support from her family and friends. Although she takes her prescribed medication, Renee admits that she sometimes forgets, especially if her mood is low or she has been feeling good while using methamphetamine. She smokes 10–15 cigarettes a day and noted her smoking time is 'break time for myself'. Renee does not drink alcohol as she saw the effect of heavy alcohol use on her father and 'doesn't want my daughter to go through that'.

Presenting Problems

When asked about goals, Renee identified that she would like assistance with cutting down her tobacco use and in improving her mood. She says she doesn't see a problem with cannabis use as 'it's natural' and although she finds the methamphetamine use is helpful, she doesn't like the crash and that it is illegal.

Intervention

Assessment of readiness to change for each substance identified that Renee was precontemplative about her cannabis use and contemplative about her methamphetamine and nicotine use. Motivational interviewing was used to nonjudgementally explore Renee's patterns of substance use. This information was then used to develop a comprehensive formulation, which allowed Renee to see the functional nature of her substance use and its relationship to her mental health symptoms. Renee was then able to recognise the role of her methamphetamine and cannabis use in coping with both low mood and parenting. She decided she wished to reduce her use of methamphetamine. To support this, structured problem solving was used to help develop options for practical and emotional supports. Behavioural activation was used to identify and schedule pleasant events. Cognitive therapy was used to help build awareness of thoughts and challenge negative attributions of events. Renee was able to engage with a parent group where she formed some new friendships and developed increased self-efficacy around her ability to parent effectively. Sleep hygiene and relaxation training were used to offer alternatives to cannabis to assist with sleep, and Renee found as she reduced her methamphetamine use she didn't feel the same drive to smoke cannabis. Renee felt more confident to discuss her substance use with her GP and this assisted in better management of her medication. In her final sessions, Renee reflected on changes made in therapy and developed a relapse prevention plan, which outlined strategies to manage high-risk situations for psychosis and substance use. She reported feeling more in control and positive about managing the future for her daughter and herself.

BARRIERS AND FACILITATORS

Treatment in routine clinical settings of those with comorbid substance use and psychosis may be influenced by numerous barriers and facilitators, occurring at multiple levels. Organisational barriers include the silo structure and poor system integration of treatment services (Mental Health and Drug and Alcohol Office, 2015). Clinician barriers can include lack of knowledge, time constraints within busy clinical settings (Ross et al., 2015), and clinician attitudes and comfort in working with people presenting with either psychosis or substance use (Ziedonis et al., 2005). Patient barriers to treatment include socioeconomic factors, mental health symptoms (which may reduce capacity to attend appointments in routine clinical settings), and stigma (Livingston, Milne, Fang, & Amari, 2012; Orygen Youth Health, 2018).

Facilitators of treatment in routine clinical settings for those with comorbid psychosis and substance use also span the organisational, clinician, and patient spheres. At the organisational level, implementing minimum standards for clinician knowledge of assessment and integration of treatments has been shown to improve treatment (Early Psychosis Guidelines Writing Group and EPPIC National Support Program, 2016). Training (Brunette et al., 2008), active collaboration with drug treatment services, and clinician access to specialist substance use treatment supervision for those working in mental health settings may serve to address knowledge and confidence barriers to providing treatment for clients with comorbid substance use and psychosis (Early Psychosis Guidelines Writing Group and EPPIC National Support Program, 2016). The inclusion of psychoeducation for families of those with co-occurring substance use and psychosis may also facilitate treatment in routine clinical settings (Early Psychosis Guidelines Writing Group and EPPIC National Support Program, 2016).

CLINICIAN ATTITUDES TO WORKING WITH CLIENTS WITH SUBSTANCE USE DISORDERS

Although people with substance use disorders present in multiple routine clinical settings, clinicians are not often well versed in this area of practice. This can increase the likelihood of negative reactions towards clients with substance use disorders, with many health professionals having been found to have lower regard, decreased motivation, and less satisfaction when working with this client group (Van Boekel, Brouwers, Van Weeghel, & Garretsen, 2013). These views can be related to the clinician's perception of the control someone has over their substance use (e.g. 'poor willpower') and perceived fault in developing the condition (Spiehs & Conner, 2018). Families of persons with co-occurring schizophrenia and substance use disorder have been found to be more likely to blame their relative for his/her symptoms than relatives of persons with schizophrenia alone (Niv, Lopez, Glynn, & Mueser, 2007).

Perceived stigma can lead to poorer client outcomes as those who feel stigmatised are less likely to seek out and access treatment services, or have been reported to drop out of care earlier (Brener, Hippel, Kippax, & Preacher, 2010). A study of clinical psychology trainees found that students endorsed more negative emotional reactions towards clients with substance use disorders than those with major depressive disorder (Mundon, Anderson, & Najavits, 2015). These reactions were improved with training and supervision, an effect, which is mirrored in the mental health workforce (Van Boekel et al., 2013). Supervision can assist clinicians to identify and unpack any implicit biases they may hold towards specific areas of client work or client groups.

The language that clinicians use can help to reduce stigma associated with both substance use and mental health disorders. In a study which compared attitudes towards two fictional health service clients (one described as a 'substance abuser' and the other as having a 'substance use disorder'), participants responded that those described as 'substance abusers' were less likely to benefit from treatment but more likely to benefit from punishment, more at risk of being socially threatening, more responsible for their substance related issues, and better able to control their substance use without help, than if the same person was described as 'having a substance use disorder' (Kelly & Westerhoff, 2010). Using person-first language (i.e. 'diagnosed with an alcohol use disorder' vs. 'an alcoholic') reinforces that a behavioural health diagnosis is not the defining characteristic of a person. Finally, organisational understanding and commitment to reduce the factors which create stigma can help to improve both clinician satisfaction and client outcomes.

QUIZ QUESTIONS

1. For people living with psychosis who use substances, intensive intervention is always required.
   (a) True
   (b) False
2. When a person is considering the 'good and not so good' things about their current use of a substance, they are likely to be in the _____ stage of change:
   (a) action
   (b) contemplation
   (c) preparation
   (d) precontemplation
3. Can a person living with psychosis change multiple health behaviours?
   (a) Yes
   (b) No
4. People living with psychosis use substances primarily to cope with their mental health symptoms.
   (a) True
   (b) False
5. Which of the following have been associated with reductions in alcohol consumption among people with psychosis?
   (a) longer CBT interventions
   (b) assessment interviews
   (c) brief motivational interventions
   (d) all of the above

ANSWERS TO QUIZ QUESTIONS:

1. False. A range of interventions may be appropriate based on the level of use and its impact including psychoeducation, monitoring, brief or more intensive interventions.
2. (d) contemplation
3. Yes. Collaborative goal setting is fundamental to a good treatment outcome and many people chose to work on more than one goal at once (e.g. reducing alcohol consumption whilst cutting down on smoking).
4. False. While coping with mental health symptoms may be one reason people living with psychosis identify as a reason for substance use, there may be a range of reasons and these can differ based on the substance used. It is important to assess the functional nature of use of each substance independently.
5. All of the above. Evidence from several randomised controlled trials suggests that psychological interventions should be integrated with standard care for people with psychosis.

END-OF-CHAPTER SELF-DIRECTED LEARNING

Current Controversies

There have been criticisms of the transtheoretical model of stage of change with regards to the validity of stage progression equating ultimately to behaviour change (Davidson, 1992, 1998). However, we think it remains a clinically useful tool to help address change with a person when they present with substance use issues.

The efficacy of electronic cigarettes is currently receiving research attention, yet they are widely available in some countries. There is debate about their wide availability and also whether they might be considered an alternative source of NRT among heavily dependent smokers.

The goal of moderation of substance use is accepted in many countries but less so in others (El-Guebaly, 2015; Room, 2015). Reducing substance use and harms associated with use may be pragmatic goals for clients.

Websites and Online Resources

The following websites and online resources provide useful information for clinicians working with people with comorbid mental illness and substance use (Table 22.3).

Table 22.3 Websites and Online Resources

Resource	Website	Content
Effective models of care for comorbid mental illness and illicit substance use: An Evidence Check review brokered by the Sax Institute for the NSW Mental Health and Drug and Alcohol Office.	https://www.saxinstitute.org.au/wp-content/uploads/Comorbid-mental-illness-and-illicit-substance-use.pdf	▪ Review of different types and efficacy of models of care for adults with comorbid mental illness and substance use
Motivational Interviewing Network of Trainers (MINT).	https://motivationalinterviewing.org	▪ List of international training events in motivational interviewing (online and face-to-face) ▪ Collection of publications, including instructional videos and clinical practice manuals
National Drug and Alcohol Research Centre (2018)	https://ndarc.med.unsw.edu.au/	▪ Extensive list of treatment-related resources ▪ Specific resources on comorbidity, including self-help material for people who use substance and experience psychosis

Continued

Table 22.3 Websites and Online Resources—cont'd

Resource	Website	Content
NHMRC Centre of Research Excellence in Mental Health and Substance Abuse.	https://comorbidity.edu.au/training/webinars	▪ Access to mental health and substance use focussed webinars ▪ Comorbidity resources for the public, professionals, and researchers
Orygen Youth Health	https://www.orygen.org.au/	▪ Access to online training modules in working with clients experiencing psychosis, including substance use and early psychosis ▪ Clinical practice resources and fact sheets
Quit Victoria	https://www.quit.org.au/resources/mental-health/tools-and-resources/	▪ Mental health and smoking client resources ▪ Clinical guide to supporting smoking cessation

RECOMMENDED READINGS

Baker, A. L., Hides, L., & Lubman, D. I. (2010). Treatment of cannabis use among people with psychotic or depressive disorder: A systematic review. *The Journal of Clinical Psychiatry, 71*(3):247–54. https://doi.org/10.4088/JCP.09r05119gry

Baker, A., Hiles, S., Thornton, L., Hides, L., & Lubman, D. (2012). A systematic review of psychological interventions for excessive alcohol consumption among people with psychotic disorders. *Acta Psychiatrica Scandinavica, 126*(4), 243–255.

Baker, A., & Velleman, R. (Eds.). (2007). *Clinical handbook of co-existing mental health and drug and alcohol problems.* East Sussex: Routledge.

Lubman, D. I., King, J. A., & Castle, D. J. (2010). Treating comorbid substance use disorders in schizophrenia. *International Review of Psychiatry, 22*(2), 191–201. https://doi.org/10.3109/09540261003689958

Miller, W.R., & Rollnick, S. (2012). *Motivational interviewing: Helping people change* (3rd ed.). New York: Guilford Press.

Tidey, J. W., & Miller, M. E. (2015). Smoking cessation and reduction in people with chronic mental illness. *BMJ, 351*(10.1136).

State of Queensland, Queensland Health. (2010). *Dual diagnosis clinical guidelines: Co-occuring mental health and alcohol and other drug problems.* Drug and Alcohol Treatment Strategy Unit and Mental Health Alcohol and Other Drugs Directorate, Queensland Health.

References

Anthenelli, R. M., Benowitz, N. L., West, R., St Aubin, L., McRae, T., Lawrence, D., et al. (2016). Neuropsychiatric safety and efficacy of varenicline, bupropion, and nicotine patch in smokers with and without psychiatric disorders (EAGLES): A double-blind, randomised, placebo-controlled clinical trial. *The Lancet, 387*(10037), 2507–2520.

Anthony, W. A. (1993). Recovery from mental illness: The guiding vision of the mental health service system in the 1990s. *Psychosocial Rehabilitation Journal, 16*(4), 11.

APA Work Group on Psychiatric Evaluation (2016). *The American Psychiatric Association practice guidelines for the psychiatric evaluation of adults* (3rd ed.). Retrieved from https://psychiatryonline.org/doi/pdf/10.1176/appi.books.9780890426760.

Baker, A. L., Bucci, S., Lewin, T. J., Kay-Lambkin, F., Carr, V. J., & Constable, P. (2006). Cognitive-behavioural therapy for substance use disorders in people with psychotic disorders: Randomised controlled trial. *British Journal of Psychiatry, 188*(5), 439–448. https://doi.org/10.1192/bjp.188.5.439.

Baker, A. L., Hiles, S., Thornton, L., Hides, L., & Lubman, D. (2012). A systematic review of psychological interventions for excessive alcohol consumption among people with psychotic disorders. *Acta Psychiatrica Scandinavica, 126*(4), 243–255.

Baker, A. L., Lewin, T., Reichler, H., Clancy, R., Carr, V., Garrett, R., et al. (2002). Evaluation of a motivational interview for substance use within psychiatric in-patient services. *Addiction, 97*(10), 1329–1337.

Baker, A. L., Thornton, L., Hides, L., & Dunlop, A. (2012). Treatment of cannabis use among people with psychotic disorders: A critical review of randomised controlled trials. *Current Pharmaceutical Design, 18*(32), 4923–4937.

Baker, A. L., Turner, A., Kay-Lambkin, F. J., & Lewin, T. (2009). The long and the short of treatments for alcohol or cannabis misuse among people with severe mental disorders. *Addictive Behaviors, 34*(10), 852–858.

Baker, A. L., & Velleman, R. (Eds.), (2007). *Clinical handbook of co-existing mental health and drug and alcohol problems*. East Sussex: Routledge.

Baker, A. L., Hides, L., & Lubman, D. I. (2010). Treatment of cannabis use among people with psychotic or depressive disorder: A systematic review. *The Journal of Clinical Psychiatry, 71*(3), 247–254. https://doi.org/10.4088/JCP.09r05119gry.

Baker, A. L., Richmond, R., Kay-Lambkin, F. J., Filia, S. L., Castle, D., Williams, J. M., et al. (2017). Randomised controlled trial of a healthy lifestyle intervention among smokers with psychotic disorders: Outcomes to 36 months. *The Australian and New Zealand Journal of Psychiatry, 52*(3), 239–252.

Banham, L., & Gilbody, S. (2010). Smoking cessation in severe mental illness: What works? *Addiction, 105*(7), 1176–1189.

Brener, L., Hippel, W. V., Kippax, S., & Preacher, K. J. (2010). The role of physician and nurse attitudes in the health care of injecting drug users. *Substance Use & Misuse, 45*(7–8), 1007–1018.

Brunette, M. F., Asher, D., Whitley, R., Lutz, W. J., Wieder, B. L., Jones, A. M., et al. (2008). Implementation of integrated dual disorders treatment: A qualitative analysis of facilitators and barriers. *Psychiatric Services, 59*(9), 989–995.

Bucci, S., Baker, A., Halpin, S. A., Hides, L., Lewin, T. J., Carr, V. J., et al. (2010). Intervention for cannabis use in young people at ultra high risk for psychosis and in early psychosis. *Mental Health and Substance Use: Dual Diagnosis, 3*(1), 66–73.

Cahill, K., Stevens, S., Perera, R., & Lancaster, T. (2013). Pharmacological interventions for smoking cessation: An overview of reviews. *Cochrane Database of Systematic Reviews, 5*. CD009329, https://doi.org/10.1002/14651858.CD009329.pub2.

Callaghan, R. C., Veldhuizen, S., Jeysingh, T., Orlan, C., Graham, C., Kakouris, G., et al. (2014). Patterns of tobacco-related mortality among individuals diagnosed with schizophrenia, bipolar disorder, or depression. *Journal of Psychiatric Research, 48*(1), 102–110.

Cather, C., Brunette, M. F., Mueser, K. T., Babbin, S. F., Rosenheck, R., Correll, C. U., et al. (2018). Impact of comprehensive treatment for first episode psychosis on substance use outcomes: A randomized controlled trial. *Psychiatry Research, 268*, 303–311.

Cooper, M. L. (1994). Motivations for alcohol use among adolescents: Development and validation of a four-factor model. *Psychological Assessment, 6*(2), 117.

Cooper, M. L., Russell, M., Skinner, J. B., & Windle, M. (1992). Development and validation of a three-dimensional measure of drinking motives. *Psychological Assessment, 4*(2), 123.

Cox, W. M., & Klinger, E. (1988). A motivational model of alcohol use. *Journal of Abnormal Psychology, 97*(2), 168.

Crockford, D., & Addington, D. (2017). Canadian schizophrenia guidelines: Schizophrenia and other psychotic disorders with coexisting substance use disorders. *The Canadian Journal of Psychiatry, 62*(9), 624–634.

Davidson, R. (1992). Prochaska and DiClemente's model of change: A case study? *British Journal of Addiction, 87*, 821–822.

Davidson, R. (1998). The transtheoretical model: A critical overview. In W. R. Miller, & N. Heather (Eds.), *Treating addictive behaviors*. (2nd ed., pp. 25–38). New York: Plenum.

De Witte, N. A., Crunelle, C. L., Sabbe, B., Moggi, F., & Dom, G. (2014). Treatment for outpatients with comorbid schizophrenia and substance use disorders: A review. *European Addiction Research, 20*(3), 105–114.

Deady, M., Barrett, E. L., Mills, K. L., Kay-Lambkin, F., Haber, P., Shand, F., et al. (2015). *Effective models of care for comorbid mental illness and illicit substance use*. Retrieved from https://www.saxinstitute.org.au/wp-content/uploads/Comorbid-mental-illness-and-illicit-substance-use.pdf.

DiClemente, C. C. (2017). *Addiction and change second edition: How addictions develop and addicted people recover*. New York: Guilford Press.

Drake, R. E., Mueser, K. T., Brunette, M. F., & McHugo, G. J. (2004). A review of treatments for people with severe mental illnesses and co-occurring substance use disorders. *Psychiatric Rehabilitation Journal, 27*(4), 360.

Early Psychosis Guidelines Writing Group and EPPIC National Support Program (2010). *Australian clinical guidelines for early psychosis: A brief summary for practitioners* (2nd ed.). Melbourne: Orygen, The National Centre of Excellence in Youth Mental Health.

Early Psychosis Guidelines Writing Group and EPPIC National Support Program (2016). *Australian clinical guidelines for early psychosis* (2nd ed.). Melbourne: Orygen, The National Centre of Excellence in Youth Mental Health.

El-Guebaly, N. (2015). *Cross-cultural aspects of addiction. In M. Galanter, H. Kleber, & K. T. Brady (Eds.), The American Psychiatric Publishing textbook of substance abuse treatment*(5th ed.). Retrieved from https://psychiatryonline.org/doi/full/10.1176/appi.books.9781615370030.mg04.

Graham, H. L. (2004). *Cognitive-behavioural integrated treatment (C-BIT): A treatment manual for substance misuse in people with severe mental health problems*. John Wiley & Sons.

Graham, H. L., Copello, A., Birchwood, M. J., & Griffith, E. (2016). *Brief integrated motivational intervention: A treatment manual for co-occuring mental health and substance use problems*. John Wiley & Sons.

Gregg, L., Barrowclough, C., & Haddock, G. (2007). Reasons for increased substance use in psychosis. *Clinical Psychology Review, 27*(4), 494–510.

Gregory, V. L. (2011). Cognitive-behavioral therapy for comorbid bipolar and substance use disorders: A systematic review of controlled trials. *Mental Health and Substance Use, 4*(4), 302–313.

Hitsman, B., Moss, T. G., Montoya, I. D., & George, T. P. (2009). Treatment of tobacco dependence in mental health and addictive disorders. *The Canadian Journal of Psychiatry, 54*(6), 368–378.

Hjorthoj, C. R., Baker, A., Fohlmann, A., & Nordentoft, M. (2014). Intervention efficacy in trials targeting cannabis use disorders in patients with comorbid psychosis systematic review and meta-analysis. *Current Pharmaceutical Design, 20*(13), 2205–2211.

Horsfall, J., Cleary, M., Hunt, G. E., & Walter, G. (2009). Psychosocial treatments for people with co-occurring severe mental illnesses and substance use disorders (dual diagnosis): A review of empirical evidence. *Harvard Review of Psychiatry, 17*(1), 24–34.

Hunt, G. E., Siegfried, N., Morley, K., Sitharthan, T., & Cleary, M. (2013). Psychosocial interventions for people with both severe mental illness and substance misuse. *Schizophrenia Bulletin, 40*(1), 18–20.

Kelly, J. F., & Westerhoff, C. M. (2010). Does it matter how we refer to individuals with substance-related conditions? A randomized study of two commonly used terms. *International Journal of Drug Policy, 21*(3), 202–207.

Kelly, T. M., Daley, D. C., & Douaihy, A. B. (2012). Treatment of substance abusing patients with comorbid psychiatric disorders. *Addictive Behaviors, 37*(1), 11–24.

Kunitake, Y., Mizoguchi, Y., Sogawa, R., Matsushima, J., Kato, T. A., Kawashima, T., et al. (2017). Effect of excessive coffee consumption on the clinical course of a patient with bipolar disorder: A case report and literature review. *Clinical Neuropharmacology, 40*(4), 160–162.

Kuntsche, E., Knibbe, R., Gmel, G., & Engels, R. (2006). Who drinks and why? A review of socio-demographic, personality, and contextual issues behind the drinking motives in young people. *Addictive Behaviors, 31*(10), 1844–1857.

Lasser, K., Boyd, J., & Woolhandler, S. (2002). Smoking and mental illness: A population-based prevalence study. *Year Book of Psychiatry and Applied Mental Health, 2002*(1), 179–180.

Lê Cook, B., Wayne, G. F., Kafali, E. N., Liu, Z., Shu, C., & Flores, M. (2014). Trends in smoking among adults with mental illness and association between mental health treatment and smoking cessation. *JAMA, 311*(2), 172–182.

Livingston, J. D., Milne, T., Fang, M. L., & Amari, E. (2012). The effectiveness of interventions for reducing stigma related to substance use disorders: A systematic review. *Addiction, 107*(1), 39–50.

Lobbana, F., Barrowclough, C., Jeffery, S., Bucci, S., Taylor, K., Mallinson, S., et al. (2010). Understanding factors influencing substance use in people with recent onset psychosis: A qualitative study. *Social Science & Medicine, 70*(8), 1141–1147.

Lubman, D. I., & Sundram, S. (2003). Substance misuse in patients with schizophrenia: A primary care guide. *Medical Journal of Australia, 178*(9), S71.

Marel, C., Mills, K. L., Kingston, R., Gournay, K., Deady, M., Kay-Lambkin, F., et al. (2016). *Guidelines on the management of co-occurring alcohol and other drug and mental health conditions in alcohol and other drug treatment settings* (2nd ed.). Sydney, Australia: Centre of Research Excellence in Mental Health and Substance Use, National Drug and Alcohol Research Centre, University of New South Wales.

McDonell, M. G., Srebnik, D., Angelo, F., McPherson, S., Lowe, J. M., Sugar, A., et al. (2013). Randomized controlled trial of contingency management for stimulant use in community mental health patients with serious mental illness. *American Journal of Psychiatry, 170*(1), 94–101.

McLellan, A. T., McKay, J. R., Forman, R., Cacciola, J., & Kemp, J. (2005). Reconsidering the evaluation of addiction treatment: From retrospective follow-up to concurrent recovery monitoring. *Addiction, 100*(4), 447–458.

McLoughlin, B. C., Pushpa-Rajah, J. A., Gillies, D., Rathbone, J., Variend, H., Kalakouti, E., et al. (2014). Cannabis and schizophrenia. *Cochrane Database of Systematic Reviews, 10*. https://doi.org/10.1002/14651858.CD004837.pub3.

McNeil, A., Brose, L., Calder, R., Hitchman, S., Hajek, P., & McRobbie, H. (2015). *E-cigarettes: An evidence update: A report commissioned by Public Health England*. Crown Copyright. 111p.

Mental Health and Drug and Alcohol Office (2015). *Effective models of care for comorbid mental illness and illicit substance use: Evidence check review.* Retrieved from NSW Ministry of Health http://www.health.nsw.gov.au/mentalhealth/publications/Publications/comorbid-mental-care-review.pdf.

Miller, W. R., & Rollnick, S. (2012). *Motivational interviewing: Helping people change* (3rd ed.). New York: Guilford Press.

Mueser, K. T. (2003). *Integrated treatment for dual disorders: A guide to effective practice.* New York: Guilford Press.

Mueser, K. T., & Gingerich, S. (2013). Treatment of co-occurring psychotic and substance use disorders. *Social Work in Public Health, 28*(3–4), 424–439.

Mueser, K. T., Nishith, P., Tracy, J. I., DeGirolamo, J., & Molinaro, M. (1995). Expectations and motives for substance use in schizophrenia. *Schizophrenia Bulletin, 21*(3), 367–378.

Mundon, C. R., Anderson, M. L., & Najavits, L. M. (2015). Attitudes toward substance abuse clients: An empirical study of clinical psychology trainees. *Journal of Psychoactive Drugs, 47*(4), 293–300.

National Drug & Alcohol Research Centre. (2018). *National Drug & Alcohol Research Centre—Home.* Retrieved from https://ndarc.med.unsw.edu.au/.

National Institute for Health and Care Excellence (NICE). (2011). *Coexisting severe mental illness (psychosis) and substance misuse assessment and management in healthcare settings.* Retrieved from https://www.nice.org.uk/guidance/cg120.

NICE. (2016). *Coexisting severe mental illness and substance misuse: Community health and social care services.* Retrieved from https://www.nice.org.uk/guidance/ng58.

Niv, N., Lopez, S. R., Glynn, S. M., & Mueser, K. (2007). The role of substance use in families' attributions and affective reactions to their relative with severe mental illness. *The Journal of Nervous and Mental Disease, 195*(4), 307–314.

NSW Department of Health (2009). *NSW clinical guidelines for the care of persons with comorbid mental illness and substance use disorders in acute care settings.* Retrieved from http://www.health.nsw.gov.au/mentalhealth/programs/mh/Publications/comorbidity-report.pdf.

Orford, J. (2001). Addiction as excessive appetite. *Addiction, 96*(1), 15–31.

Orygen Youth Health. (2018). *Orygen youth health—Principles.* Retrieved from https://oyh.org.au/about-us/principles.

Perron, B. E., Bunger, A., Bender, K., Vaughn, M. G., & Howard, M. O. (2010). Treatment guidelines for substance use disorders and serious mental illnesses: Do they address co-occurring disorders? *Substance Use & Misuse, 45*(7–8), 1262–1278.

Petersen, L., Jeppesen, P., Thorup, A., Øhlenschlæger, J., Krarup, G., Østergård, T., et al. (2007). Substance abuse and first-episode schizophrenia-spectrum disorders. The Danish OPUS trial. *Early Intervention in Psychiatry, 1*(1), 88–96.

Prochaska, J. J. (2011). Smoking and mental illness—breaking the link. *New England Journal of Medicine, 365*(3), 196–198.

Quit Victoria. (2018). Mental health and smoking: Tools and resources. Retrieved from: https://www.quit.org.au/resources/mental-health/tools-and-resources/.

Rebgetz, S., Kavanagh, D. J., & Hides, L. (2015). Can exploring natural recovery from substance misuse in psychosis assist with treatment? A review of current research. *Addictive Behaviors, 46*, 106–112.

Rollnick, S., Mason, P., & Butler, C. (1999). *Health behavior change: A guide for practitioners.* Edinburgh, Scotland: Churchill Livingston.

Room, R. (2015). Cultural aspects and responses to addiction. In *Textbook of addiction treatment: International perspectives* (pp. 107–114). Springer.

Ross, L. E., Vigod, S., Wishart, J., Waese, M., Spence, J. D., Oliver, J., et al. (2015). Barriers and facilitators to primary care for people with mental health and/or substance use issues: A qualitative study. *BMC Family Practice, 16*(1), 135.

Royal Australian and New Zealand College of Psychiatrists (2016). Clinical practice guidelines for the treatment of schizophrenia and related disorders. *Australian and New Zealand Journal of Psychiatry, 39*(1–2), 1–30.

Salloum, I. M., & Brown, E. S. (2017). Management of comorbid bipolar disorder and substance use disorders. *The American Journal of Drug and Alcohol Abuse, 43*(4), 366–376.

Sawicka, M., & Tracy, D. K. (2017). Naltrexone efficacy in treating alcohol-use disorder in individuals with comorbid psychosis: A systematic review. *Therapeutic Advances in Psychopharmacology, 7*(8–9), 211–224.

Schmidt, S. J., Schultze-Lutter, F., Schimmelmann, B. G., Maric, N. P., Salokangas, R. K. R., Riecher-Rössler, A., et al. (2015). EPA guidance on the early intervention in clinical high risk states of psychoses. *European Psychiatry, 30*(3), 388–404. https://doi.org/10.1016/j.eurpsy.2015.01.013.

Secades-Álvarez, A., & Fernández-Rodríguez, C. (2017). Review of the efficacy of treatments for bipolar disorder and substance abuse. *Revista de Psiquiatría y Salud Mental (English Edition), 10*(2), 113–124.

Siru, R., Hulse, G. K., & Tait, R. J. (2009). Assessing motivation to quit smoking in people with mental illness: A review. *Addiction, 104*(5), 719–733.

Spencer, C., Castle, D., & Michie, P. T. (2002). Motivations that maintain substance use among individuals with psychotic disorders. *Schizophrenia Bulletin, 28*(2), 233–247.

Spiehs, J., & Conner, S. (2018). Considerations for substance-use disorder language: Cultivating a shift from 'addicts in recovery' to 'people who thrive'. *Journal of Public Health Policy, 39*(3), 372–378.

Steinberg, M. L., Williams, J. M., Stahl, N. F., Budsock, P. D., & Cooperman, N. A. (2016). An adaptation of motivational interviewing increases quit attempts in smokers with serious mental illness. *Nicotine & Tobacco Research, 18*(3), 243–250. https://doi.org/10.1093/ntr/ntv043.

Taylor, G., McNeill, A., Girling, A., Farley, A., Lindson-Hawley, N., & Aveyard, P. (2014). Change in mental health after smoking cessation: Systematic review and meta-analysis. *BMJ, 348*, g1151.

Teesson, M. (2004). *Comorbid mental disorders and substance use disorders: Epidemiology, prevention and treatment.* Sydney, Australia: National Drug and Alcohol Research Centre. University of New South Wales.

Temmingh, H. S., Williams, T., Siegfried, N., & Stein, D. J. (2018). Risperidone versus other antipsychotics for people with severe mental illness and co-occurring substance misuse. *Cochrane Database of Systematic Reviews. 2018*(1). https://doi.org/10.1002/14651858.CD011057.pub2.

Thornton, L. K., Baker, A. L., Johnson, M. P., Kay-Lambkin, F., & Lewin, T. J. (2012). Reasons for substance use among people with psychotic disorders: Method triangulation approach. *Psychology of Addictive Behaviors, 26*(2), 279.

Tidey, J. W., & Miller, M. E. (2015). Smoking cessation and reduction in people with chronic mental illness. *BMJ, 351*. h4065, https://doi.org/10.1136/bmj.h4065.

Van Boekel, L. C., Brouwers, E. P., Van Weeghel, J., & Garretsen, H. F. (2013). Stigma among health professionals towards patients with substance use disorders and its consequences for healthcare delivery: Systematic review. *Drug and Alcohol Dependence, 131*(1–2), 23–35.

Vaz, G., & Crockford, D. (2017). The diagnosis and treatment of comorbid bipolar and substance use disorders. *Canadian Journal of Addiction, 8*(2), 13–16.

Weiss, R. D., & Connery, H. S. (2011). *Integrated group therapy for bipolar disorder and substance abuse.* New York: Guilford Press.

Williams, J. M., & Gandhi, K. K. (2008). Use of caffeine and nicotine in people with schizophrenia. *Current Drug Abuse Reviews*, *1*(2), 155–161.

Williams, J. M., Steinberg, M. L., Zimmermann, M. H., Gandhi, K. K., Stipelman, B., Budsock, P. D., et al. (2010). Comparison of two intensities of tobacco dependence counseling in schizophrenia and schizoaffective disorder. *Journal of Substance Abuse Treatment*, *38*(4), 384–393.

Wilson, G. T. (1997). Treatment manuals in clinical practice. *Behaviour Research and Therapy*, *35*(3), 205–210. https://doi.org/10.1016/S0005-7967(96)00091-5.

Wisdom, J. P., Manuel, J. I., & Drake, R. E. (2011). Substance use disorder among people with first-episode psychosis: A systematic review of course and treatment. *Psychiatric Services*, *62*(9), 1007–1012.

Wobrock, T., & Soyka, M. (2008). Pharmacotherapy of schizophrenia with comorbid substance use disorder—Reviewing the evidence and clinical recommendations. *Progress in Neuro-Psychopharmacology and Biological Psychiatry*, *32*(6), 1375–1385.

Ziedonis, D. M., Smelson, D., Rosenthal, R. N., Batki, S. L., Green, A. I., Henry, R. J., et al. (2005). Improving the care of individuals with schizophrenia and substance use disorders: Consensus recommendations. *Journal of Psychiatric Practice*, *11*(5), 315.

Definition of Key Terms

Cannabidiol (CBD) A nonpsychoactive cannabinoid.

Comorbidity Co-occurrence of two or more health conditions.

Integrated treatment Treatment for two or more conditions concurrently in the same setting.

Recovery A personally unique process of changing one's attitudes, values, feelings, goals, skills, and/or roles and living a satisfying, hopeful, and contributing life.

CHAPTER 23

A Brief Guide to Medications for Psychosis

537

Anthony Harris

Discipline of Psychiatry, Sydney Medical School, University of Sydney, Sydney, NSW, Australia; Brain Dynamics Centre, The Westmead Institute for Medical Research, Sydney, NSW, Australia

Key Learning Objectives

- Understand the role of the dopaminergic system in controlling psychotic symptoms
- Describe common adverse effects that limit the use of antipsychotic medication
- Understand the role of clozapine in the treatment of schizophrenia
- Describe the use of lithium and anticonvulsant medications in bipolar disorder
- Critically evaluate the advantages as against disadvantages of antipsychotic medication prescription for psychotic disorders

INTRODUCTION

This chapter will introduce the reader to the evidence for the use of medications, in particular antipsychotic medications, for the treatment of psychosis. Antipsychotics are a diverse group of medications that have been variously described as neuroleptics, major tranquillisers, typical or atypical antipsychotics, and more recently first-, second-, and third-generation antipsychotics. This final nomenclature—First Generation Antipsychotics (FGA), Second Generation Antipsychotics (SGA), and Third Generation Antipsychotics (TGA)—will be used in this chapter recognising that it has only a loose relationship to underlying chemical structure or receptor affinity and reflects as much the chronology of their introduction. It is hoped that this nomenclature will be replaced by one based on pharmacological action such as the Neuroscience-based Nomenclature (NbN) for psychotropic drugs (Caraci et al., 2017); however, common use refers to FGA, etc. Although they are a cornerstone for the treatment of psychotic disorders such as schizophrenia, they are also used in a wide range of other psychiatric disorders reflecting their broad range of actions, so their description as antipsychotics is misleading.

Neuroscience-based nomenclature uses the best available pharmacological evidence to guide drug selection.

A Clinical Introduction to Psychosis. https://doi.org/10.1016/B978-0-12-815012-2.00023-7

Chlorpromazine is a first-generation antipsychotic: it acts on dopaminergic, muscarinic, and histaminic receptors.

Antipsychotics were serendipitously discovered and introduced into practice in 1952 after the original development of chlorpromazine as an anaesthetic agent. Its ability to calm patients was noted and its use in the treatment of psychotic patients proved to be transformative in the care of people with schizophrenia (Porter, 1997). Understanding the mode of action of antipsychotics, as well as their many adverse effects, has provided much information in developing an understanding of the illness, schizophrenia, and neuroscience more generally (Baumeister & Francis, 2002).

Mode of Action

The common action of antipsychotic medications is their ability to block Dopamine D_2 receptors (Seeman, 1992). Their antipsychotic effect is correlated with their affinity for this receptor (Seeman & Lee, 1975) and requires at least a 65%–70% receptor occupancy (Kapur, Zipursky, Jones, Remington, & Houle, 2000). However, exceeding that threshold, i.e. > 80% blockade, is associated with an increased risk of extrapyramidal side effects (EPSE) an adverse effect of antipsychotic medications (Kapur et al., 2000). Although antipsychotics block postsynaptic receptors, the site of increased dopaminergic activity in schizophrenia appears to be presynaptic, suggesting that antipsychotics are not addressing the underlying cause of the imbalance in dopaminergic function (Abi-Dargham & Rodenhiser, 2000; Howes et al., 2012).

Extrapyramidal side effects can include rigidity, tremor, and slowed movements (bradykinesia). These abnormal movements can become chronic or tardive.

In addition to their dopaminergic effects, antipsychotic medications have a broad range of other receptor actions that differ from medication to medication and are responsible for the different profiles of these medications. For example, the binding affinity of many of the SGAs for the $5HT_{2A}$ (serotonin) receptor has been proposed as one of the key mechanisms by which SGAs minimise EPSE. Sedation, weight gain, postural hypotension, and hyperprolactinaemia are related in turn to drug activity at histaminic, muscarinic, alpha 1 adrenergic, and dopaminergic receptors.

Pharmacokinetics of Medication

All medication needs to be absorbed into the body, transported to the site of its action, and then removed. Pharmacokinetics describes this process of absorption, distribution through the body, metabolism, and excretion. It interacts with individual patient factors such as their genetics, age, other diseases, and environmental factors, e.g. smoking. This complex interaction leads to considerable interindividual variability in the effect of any medication (see Table 23.1).

Bioavailability refers to the fraction of a drug that enters circulation, and so is able to have an effect.

The bioavailability of a medication is a measure of the proportion of the administered drug that is absorbed into the body and makes its way to the site of action. While most antipsychotic medications are absorbed in the gastrointestinal system, a few are significantly affected by food. Asenapine cannot survive being swallowed but is absorbed through the buccal mucosa and is administered as a sublingual wafer. Both ziprasidone and lurasidone require food to increase their bioavailability and should always be taken with food.

Table 23.1 Basic Pharmacodynamic Information About the Absorption and Metabolism of Commonly Available Antipsychotic Medications

	Bioavailability	$t_{1/2}$ (hrs)	Metabolism	Renal/Hepatic
amisulpride	? Food effect	12	Renal excretion	Renal
aripiprazole	–	75–146	2D6, 3A4	–
asenapine	Oral absorption	24	1A4, 1A2	hepatic
brexpiprazole	–	91	3A4, 2D6	Renal & hepatic
chlorpromazine	Smoking effect	8–35	2D6, 1A2	hepatic
clozapine	Smoking effect	12	1A2	?
haloperidol	Smoking effect	14–26	2D6, multiple pathways	–
lurasidone	Food effect	18	3A4	Renal & hepatic
olanzapine	Smoking effect	30	1A2	–
paliperidone	–	18	Renal/faecal excretion	Renal
quetiapine	–	6	3A4	Hepatic
risperidone	–	3/20[a]	2D6	Renal & Hepatic
trifluoperazine	–	10–20	1A2	Hepatic
ziprasidone	Food effect	7	Aldehyde oxidase	No
zuclopenthixol		20	2D6, 3A4	Hepatic

Bioavailability warns if there is an effect for smoking (Desai, Seabolt, & Jann, 2001) or if the drug needs to be taken with food. Renal/hepatic warns if caution is required if the patient has renal or hepatic compromise. $t_{1/2}$ = half-life in hours.
Desai, H. D., Seabolt, J., & Jann, M. W. (2001). Smoking in patients receiving psychotropic medications. *CNS Drugs, 15*(6), 469–494. https://doi.org/10.2165/00023210-200115060-00005.
[a] Active metabolite.

Once absorbed, the medication is transported to the site of action across the blood brain barrier. This is affected by the metabolism and excretion of the drug, which is measured by the medication's half-life or the time needed to clear 50% of the drug. The half-life gives an indication as to how frequently the medication needs to be administered. Medications with a short half-life require administration on a twice-daily basis at a minimum. It is difficult to remember to take a medication twice daily, so slow-release compounds have been developed for medications with short half-lives such as quetiapine and paliperidone. A different approach to increasing half-life and improving treatment adherence is to give the medication as a long-acting injection (LAI), sometimes known as a depot injection. These formulations slowly release the active drug over 2–13 weeks depending upon the formulation. This approach improves the steady delivery of the medication but has to be carefully tailored to the individual as the adverse effects that are experienced can take a long time to resolve. Not all antipsychotics have LAI formulations available.

Depot injections, or long-acting injections, are slow-release, longer-acting forms of antipsychotics.

Once the medication is absorbed, it is metabolised and excreted. The majority of antipsychotic medications are metabolised, mostly via oxidation and then conjugation, by the cytochrome P450 system (Preskorn, 2012a). This complex system is under genetic control and can be induced or inhibited, accelerated or slowed, by the co-administration of other medications (e.g. carbamazepine) or substances. An example of this is the induction of the CYP 1A2 enzyme by cigarette smoking, which increases the metabolism of olanzapine and clozapine (Desai et al., 2001; Rostami-Hodjegan et al., 2004). This can cause issues as patients stabilised in hospital, which is usually a nonsmoking environment, experience a decrease in the levels of these medications on discharge when they resume smoking. This is another reason to provide smoking cessation/reduction therapies with people with psychotic illnesses, quite apart from the other physical health benefits of smoking cessation.

Finally, the excretion of the metabolites via the gut or kidneys can be affected by the presence of renal or hepatic disease. This can cause significant increases in the concentration of the medication, requiring either a lowering of the dose or the selection of a different medication. For example, both amisulpride and paliperidone have extensive renal excretion and are not recommended for people with kidney disease. Similarly, asenapine and lurasidone are affected by moderate-to-severe hepatic disease and should be used with especial care in people with significant liver disease (Preskorn, 2012b).

TREATMENT OF FIRST-EPISODE PSYCHOSIS

The initial pharmacological treatment of a person presenting with their first episode of psychosis is decided upon by balancing a number of important clinical factors (Early Psychosis Guidelines Writing Group and EPPIC National Support Program, 2016). The clinical team must build rapport and understanding in difficult circumstances with a person whose symptoms are often barriers to this, particularly persecutory ideas or distressing auditory hallucinations. The setting of care may vary from the supportive surroundings of home with family helping to reality base the individual with the psychotic illness, to the alienating surrounding of an acute psychiatric inpatient unit with all of its turmoil and activation. These differences feed back into treatment choices.

The treatment setting can have a powerful effect on building rapport.

Diagnosis is important at this stage of treatment. The diagnosis of an affective psychosis such as mania would direct treatment towards a mood stabiliser such as lithium or sodium valproate (Malhi et al., 2015), whereas the diagnosis of an organic psychotic disorder (e.g. anti-NMDA encephalitis) would indicate the need for treatment of the underlying cause. Individuals with a psychotic mood disorder or an organic psychotic disorder may still require treatment with antipsychotic medication, but this will be in addition to other treatment strategies.

A number of antipsychotic medications—amisulpride, aripiprazole, quetiapine, risperidone, and ziprasidone—have an evidence base as effective treatments at this early stage of treatment (see Fig. 23.1). The initial medication chosen needs to balance the profile of symptoms and the burden of adverse effects. Recent practice has suggested that the second- and third-generation antipsychotic medications have an advantage to first-generation antipsychotic medications because of their greater tolerability; however, this is only relative as the majority of individuals find taking antipsychotic medication problematic.

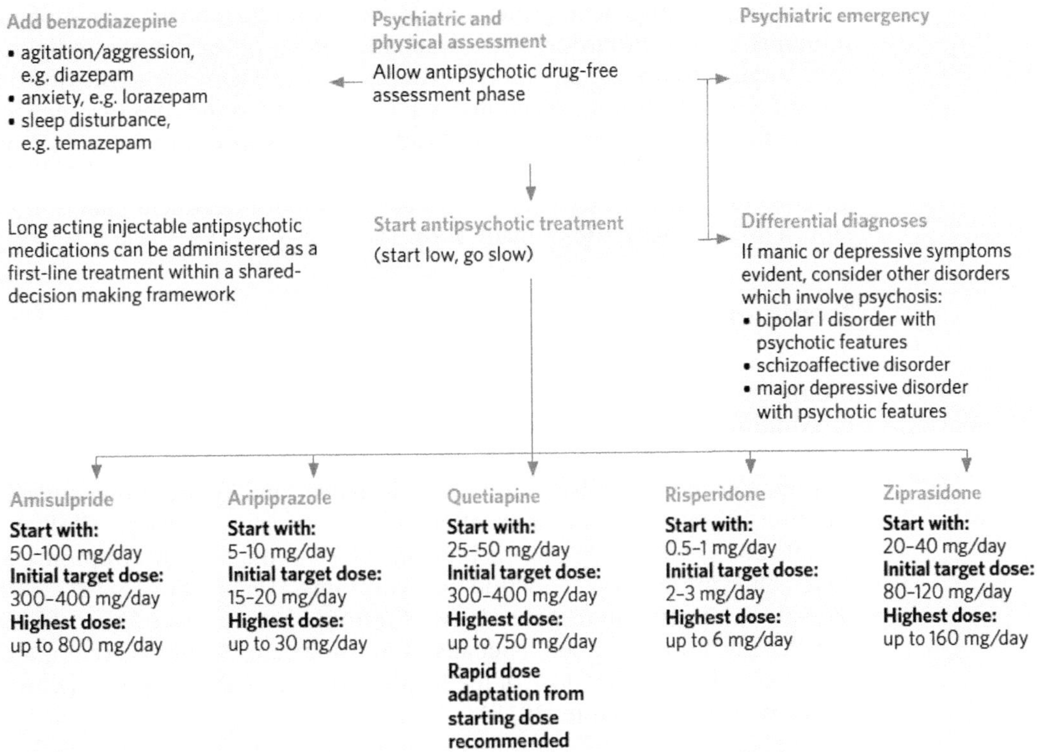

FIG. 23.1
Initial pharmacological treatment of first episode nonaffective psychosis (Early Psychosis Guidelines Writing Group and EPPIC National Support Program, 2016).

A second general principle is to attempt to keep the dose of medication as low as possible and to only increase this dose gradually—the so called 'go low, go slow' approach. Treatment response at low doses of medication is commonly observed at this early stage of illness (Emsley, Rabinowitz, & Medori, 2006). Emsley and colleagues (Emsley et al., 2006) observed treatment response in 46% of a cohort of young people in the first 1–2 weeks of treatment in a large randomised controlled trial of antipsychotic medication at doses below the general target dose. The greatest improvement on a week-to-week basis is usually seen in the initial two weeks of treatment (Leucht, Busch, Hamann, Kissling, & Kane, 2005). Conversely, early treatment nonresponse is a predictor of longer-term nonresponse and can indicate the need to change medication (Samara et al., 2015).

Prescribing guidelines for first-episode psychosis aim for the lowest possible dose of antipsychotics.

Many people with a psychotic illness are troubled by sleeplessness and agitation in the acute phase. This can be addressed with either an antipsychotic medication with sedative properties or by the addition of a benzodiazepine such as diazepam (5–10 mg) or lorazepam (1–2 mg). The use of a benzodiazepine allows for a targeted reduction in sedating medication when the acute phase of the illness has passed.

A third important general principle is to work with the patient to identify and minimise adverse effects such as movement disorders or weight gain. Individuals who are antipsychotic medication naïve appear to have a greater sensitivity to the adverse effects of these medications, so it is important to start this treatment alliance at the time of first prescription. As adverse effects are one of the main drivers of treatment nonadherence (Verdoux et al., 2000), the acknowledgement of adverse effects and the development of a collaborative treatment plan is important to the long-term use of medication.

Treatment Response

There is a very good chance of treatment response to antipsychotic medication during the first episode of schizophrenia, with 81.3% having a 20% reduction in symptoms and 51.9% having a 50% reduction in symptoms (Zhu et al., 2017). Response is predicted by being female, older, with a shorter duration of undiagnosed psychosis, antipsychotic naïve, and being more unwell at baseline. Treatment response after relapse lessens (Emsley, Chiliza, & Asmal, 2013) with only 53% achieving a 20% reduction in symptoms and 23% achieving a 50% reduction in symptoms (Leucht et al., 2017). This reduction in treatment response is evident from after the first relapse of illness (Emsley, Oosthuizen, Koen, Niehaus, & Martinez, 2013) and is accompanied by the need for a higher dose of medication to achieve that response (Bowtell, McGorry, & O'Donoghue, 2018).

Although improvement with treatment can continue for many weeks or months, the largest percentage change in symptoms occurs in the first 1–2 weeks after commencing medication (Agid, Kapur, Arenovich, & Zipursky, 2003). Of the trials that have then examined systematically changing or maintaining individuals on medication, some (Kinon et al., 2010; Lieberman et al., 2005; Louwerens & van der Meij, 2000), though not all (Kahn et al., 2018; Kinon, Kane, Johns, & Al, 1993), have found a small advantage for changing to a medication with a substantially different receptor profile.

There has been considerable debate about whether any one antipsychotic medication is more effective. The introduction of Second-Generation Antipsychotics (SGAs) was accompanied by a degree of hyperbole that did not eventuate in significantly improved patient outcomes (Geddes, Freemantle, Harrison, & Bebbington, 2000; Heres et al., 2006; Leucht, Kissling, & Davis, 2009). However, recent trials and metaanalyses have helped to better delineate the advantages and disadvantages of different medications in treatment. Clozapine (see later) remains the most effective antipsychotic for positive symptoms (Leucht et al., 2009; Leucht et al., 2013; Siskind, Siskind, & Kisely, 2017; Tiihonen et al., 2006), an advantage that is clearer after initial treatment. However, its adverse effects have relegated it to a third-line treatment. Metaanalysis shows a diverse group of antipsychotics (amisulpride, olanzapine, and risperidone) that appear to have a small advantage over other antipsychotic medications (Leucht et al., 2009; Leucht et al., 2013). These advantages are slight and need to be balanced by concerns about the adverse effect profile of these medications and their cost when compared to First-Generation Antipsychotics (FGAs) such as haloperidol. Although all antipsychotics have an effect upon negative symptoms, these effects are not large, and no antipsychotic medication is more efficacious than any other in their treatment (Fusar-Poli et al., 2014; Leucht, Corves, et al., 2009).

Antipsychotic medication is also significantly better than placebo in preventing relapse over 12 months, with an estimated difference in relapse rates of 27% as against 64% (Number Needed to Treat = 3 CI: 2–3) (Leucht et al., 2012). This difference holds true for rehospitalisation (10% vs 26% Number Needed To Benefit =5 CI: 4–9) and improved quality of life. This is at the cost of increased weight, movement disorders, and sedation. There is some evidence that SGAs have a small advantage over first-generation antipsychotics in decreasing relapse and rehospitalisation (Kishimoto et al., 2013). This effect is increased if the medication is given in long-acting injectable (LAI) form. The superiority of LAI medications in reducing relapse rates is strongest in mirror design trials in which individuals are compared to themselves off and then on LAIs (Kishimoto, Nitta, Borenstein, Kane, & Correll, 2013) and in population-based observational studies where they are superior to their oral equivalents (Tiihonen, Mittendorfer-Rutz, Majak, et al., 2017). However, this superiority is not as evident in randomised controlled trials (Kishimoto et al., 2012; Leucht et al., 2012).

Number Needed to Treat calculates the number of patients needed to be treated with one therapy versus another for one patient to improve in a specific way over a defined period.

When Can You Stop Antipsychotic Medication?

One of the most vexed questions in the field of treatment of psychosis, and schizophrenia in particular, is how and when to stop antipsychotic medication. Recommendations for antipsychotic medication cessation vary widely, from as little as 6 months to as long as 2 years after the first episode of psychosis (Gaebel, Weinmann, Sartorius, Rutz, & McIntyre, 2005). Recognition of the burden of adverse effects and the natural reluctance of many patients to continue treatment ad infinitum has led to a number of different approaches to lowering the total burden of antipsychotic medication via medication 'holidays' or with planned treatment cessation.

Planned treatment cessation after FES has a high rate of relapse, from 41% to 79% after 12 months (Zipursky, Menezes, & Streiner, 2014). Despite this, it is preferable to sudden cessation, which is associated with early relapse and discontinuation effects (Viguera, Baldessarini, Hegarty, van Kammen, & Tohen, 1997). These high rates of relapse are consistent with relapse rates observed in longitudinal studies of first episode (Álvarez-Jiménez, Parker, Hetrick, McGorry, & Gleeson, 2011; Robinson et al., 1999) or chronic schizophrenia (Takeuchi et al., 2017). Planned treatment cessation remains controversial with the advantages in long-term functioning for at least some patients who discontinue medication (Chan, Hui, Chang, Lee, & Chen, 2019; Wunderink, Nieboer, Wiersma, Sytema, & Nienhuis, 2013) being contested by others in the field (Goff et al., 2017).

TREATMENT-RESISTANT SCHIZOPHRENIA (TRS)

The concept of treatment resistance is not congruent with recent concepts of Recovery.

Incomplete recovery is also known as treatment resistance and is unfortunately common in the management of schizophrenia (Pantelis & Lambert, 2003). It is important to understand that treatment resistance does not preclude other management strategies and that it is not caused by any resistance by the person with schizophrenia to treatment per se. Careful consideration should be given to the language employed when discussing this with individuals as their own perception of their situation may be very different to this terminology. They may see their situation as part way along a personal recovery journey or transformation that is orthogonal to the clinical definition of treatment resistance. This way of regarding their situation is likely to be far more fruitful than a more narrow, clinical definition.

For research purposes, treatment resistance is defined (Howes et al., 2017) as a state of persistent symptoms of at least moderate severity, for >12 weeks' duration and accompanied by a functional impairment. People should have had two or more trials of antipsychotic medication, at a dose of >600 mg chlorpromazine equivalents (Andreasen, Pressler, Nopoulos, Miller, & Ho, 2010) each treatment trial being for a minimum of at least 6 weeks.

Unfortunately, treatment resistance occurs in approximately 20% of cases from first presentation (Demjaha et al., 2017). With each relapse, there is a risk of the development of treatment nonresponse, partial response or the progression to an illness with more prominent negative symptoms (Wiersma, Nienhuis, Slooff, & Giel, 1998). In addition to the risk of incomplete recovery, with each relapse, treatment response takes longer and requires a higher dose of medication to achieve (Bowtell et al., 2018; Emsley, Oosthuizen, et al., 2013).

Clozapine

Agranulocytosis—is the loss of neutrophils, an important class of infection fighting white blood cells. It is associated with clozapine but which can occur rarely with other medications.

Metabolic syndrome comprises central obesity, hypertension, dyslipidaemia, and glucose intolerance or insulin resistance. There is a high rate of diabetes mellitus type 2 and coronary heart disease.

The treatment of TRS was altered for the better with the reintroduction of clozapine after the seminal trial of Kane and colleagues found that 30% of patients with TRS responded to clozapine (Kane, Honigfeld, Singer, Meltzer, & Clozaril Collaborative Study, 1988). Clozapine had been withdrawn from use because of its propensity to cause agranulocytosis, a potentially fatal reduction in neutrophils, however, its effectiveness, along with the introduction of a rigorous monitoring system, has seen its widespread use. Clozapine is the most effective of the antipsychotic medications for the positive symptoms of psychosis (Leucht et al., 2013; Siskind, McCartney, Goldschlager, & Kisely, 2016). Subsequent systematic review has estimated that nearer 40% of TRS will respond to a trial of clozapine, with a reduction in symptoms of at least 20% (Siskind et al., 2017). Clozapine also has the advantage of causing little or no movement disorders (Leucht et al., 2013; Lieberman, Saltz, & Johns, 1991) and reducing the rate of completed suicide (Hennen & Baldessarini, 2005) in people with schizophrenia. These advantages come at a high price of potential adverse effects, including weight gain, metabolic syndrome, sedation, hypersalivation, constipation, seizures, and myocarditis in addition to the 1%–2% rate of agranulocytosis (King & Wager, 1998; Leucht et al., 2013).

Part of the advantage of clozapine may be the effective and rigorous monitoring that establishes close and continued care for a group of patients who are frequently marginalised. The combination of effectiveness and close monitoring has meant that it is one of the most effective antipsychotic medication in reducing re-hospitalisation (Tiihonen, Mittendorfer-Rutz, Majak, et al., 2017).

Other Pharmacological Strategies for Treatment-Resistant Schizophrenia

Unfortunately, somewhere between 12% and 20% of individuals with schizophrenia will not respond even after being treated with clozapine (Siskind et al., 2017) and many others will only have a partial response at best. This has led to the trial of numerous augmentation strategies that have combined antipsychotic medications and a wide range of agents, including other antipsychotics, antidepressants, anticonvulsants, oestrogen, lithium, nutraceuticals, and antiinflammatory agents (Correll et al., 2017). Although these approaches can help, they need to be closely monitored as the burden of taking multiple medications, known as polypharmacy, increases the risk of adverse effects and mortality (Fleischhacker & Uchida, 2014).

Nutraceuticals describe a group of vitamins or minerals that have nutritional value and are used to treat dietary deficiency or for their antiinflammatory or antioxidant properties.

Negative symptoms have been targeted using antidepressants. This requires the careful delineation of negative symptoms with its amotivation, affective blunting and anhedonia from depression, as depression in schizophrenia is itself a target of successful pharmaceutical treatment using antidepressants (Gregory, Mallikarjun, & Upthegrove, 2017). On metaanalysis, a small-to-moderate effect on negative symptoms has been found with a NNT = 15 (Fusar-Poli et al., 2014; Singh, Singh, Kar, & Chan, 2010).

Dietary, vitamin, and mineral supplementation strategies are also commonly used by people with psychosis. These are trialled with the rationale of addressing dietary deficiencies or for their antioxidant and antiinflammatory properties. The studies examining these treatments are small and highly heterogeneous; nonetheless a small advantage has been found on metaanalysis for the use of the vitamin B group, especially if provided early in the course of the illness. No effect was found for other vitamins or minerals (Vitamins C, D, E, zinc, or chromium) (Firth et al., 2017). Polyunsaturated fatty acids (omega-3 and -6 fatty acids) have also been trialled unsuccessfully for the treatment of the At-Risk Mental State (McGorry et al., 2017) and with mixed results for chronic schizophrenia (Chen, Chibnall, & Nasrallah, 2015). *N*-acetyl cysteine, which is a strong antioxidant, has been shown to be effective for negative symptoms in a number of small studies (Chen, Chibnall, & Nasrallah, 2016).

A number of trials have found small effects using nonsteroidal antiinflammatory medications such as aspirin, celecoxib (Zheng et al., 2017), or antibiotics such as minocycline (Khandaker et al., 2015). It is hoped that these medications address an underlying inflammatory process that might contribute to or even cause psychosis (Khandaker et al., 2015). Although the studies are significant, the effect size is small and of limited clinical importance (Nitta et al., 2013). More specific targeting of inflammatory mechanisms in individuals with autoimmune encephalitis (Scott et al., 2018) or treatment early in the course of the illness may improve results.

Treatment trials that have targeted N-Methyl D-Aspartate (NMDA) neurotransmission with glutamatergic agents, glycine, or glutamate transporters have failed to demonstrate any consistent benefit (Fusar-Poli et al., 2014). This is also true for similar treatments aimed at improving cognition in schizophrenia using comparable pharmacological agents (Keefe et al., 2011; Sinkeviciute et al., 2018).

Medication in the At-Risk Mental State

Although it is clear that the treatment of choice for young people in an At-Risk Mental State for psychosis (ARMS) is cognitive behavioural therapy (Early Psychosis Guidelines Writing Group and EPPIC National Support Program, 2016), a number of medications have been trialled in this context. Firstly, antipsychotic medications have been found to significantly delay the transition to psychosis (McGorry et al., 2002) but at the cost of significant adverse effects (McGlashan et al., 2006), and as the great majority of people in the ARMS do not transition to psychosis, the risk benefit ratio does not favour the use of antipsychotic medications. There is also a possibility that exposure to an antipsychotic may *increase* the likelihood of transition in some individuals (Fusar-Poli et al., 2015). Antidepressants have also decreased the transition to psychosis; however, the evidence for this is only observational (Cornblatt et al., 2007; Fusar-Poli et al., 2015). And finally, the earlier promise of omega-3 fatty acids for the treatment of the ARMS (Amminger et al., 2010) has not been borne out by a further, more methodologically rigorous, study (McGorry et al., 2017). Targeted treatment of insomnia, agitation, or mood disturbance in young people in an at-risk mental state may be required, but the use of antipsychotic medication should probably be reserved for those with high levels of distress or psychotic symptoms (Early Psychosis Guidelines Writing Group and EPPIC National Support Program, 2016).

MEDICATION FOR AFFECTIVE PSYCHOSES

The psychoses can include both psychotic depression and mania. Indeed phenomenologically, mania can be indistinguishable from acute schizophrenia at its peak, with accurate diagnosis requiring a longitudinal history (Carlson & Goodwin, 1973). The diagnosis of mania is important from a therapeutic point of view as it indicates the usefulness of a mood stabiliser—lithium or sodium valproate (Cipriani, Reid, Young, Macritchie, & Geddes, 2013; Malhi et al., 2015). Both these agents have been used for the treatment of acute mania and for its prophylaxis. Lithium also decreases the rate of completed suicide over time

(Cipriani, Hawton, Stockton, & Geddes, 2013). Both lithium and sodium valproate have significant adverse effects and require careful management. In particular, lithium can cause thyroid and renal adverse effects (Malhi, Tanious, & Das, 2012). Sodium valproate is sedating, increases weight, causes polycystic ovary syndrome, and rarely can cause hepatotoxicity. Both lithium and sodium valproate are teratogenic (Chisolm & Payne, 2016). However, many people with mania are treated with an antipsychotic medication either as monotherapy or in combination with a mood stabiliser, both for the initial psychotic episode (Cipriani et al., 2011) and for longer-term prophylaxis (Malhi et al., 2015). In addition to their effect upon psychotic symptoms, antipsychotics, along with the use of benzodiazepines, can also improve agitation, arousal, and insomnia.

Teratogenic agents can cause birth malformations.

Psychotic depression is a severe form of depression characterised by a severe disturbance of mood, somatic symptoms of depression such as early morning wakening and weight loss, and delusions and hallucinations that take up mood-congruent themes of loss and guilt experienced by the individual. Treatment with both an antipsychotic and an antidepressant is superior to either agent alone (Wijkstra et al., 2015), but because of the high risk of the illness to the individual and lower rates of response, electroconvulsive therapy may be indicated (Malhi et al., 2015; UK ECT Review Group, 2003).

ADVERSE EFFECTS OF ANTIPSYCHOTIC MEDICATIONS

Antipsychotic medications have a high burden of adverse or side effects (see Table 23.2). These adverse effects impinge upon the quality of life of people who are taking them and are associated with poor treatment adherence (Higashi et al., 2013). The acknowledgement of these adverse effects and the active targeting to reduce them is an important part of a joint treatment plan. General principles in the reduction of adverse effects include the use of medication with the least burden of adverse effects, the use of the lowest possible dose of medication, and the avoidance of polypharmacy.

The agreement of the individual being treated to take medication as prescribed has been variously called compliance, adherence or concordance, each word connoting a different emphasis in terms of the relative involvement of the patient or consumer and their treating physician in treatment decisions (Fawcett, 1995). Poor treatment adherence is one of the most common reasons for relapse (Higashi et al., 2013; Robinson et al., 1999) and reflects the burden of adverse effects, reluctance to continue taking medication (Higashi et al., 2013) and confusion over the required duration of treatment with medication (Gaebel et al., 2005). Important differences are evident between different antipsychotic medications in the range and severity of adverse effects. These differences should have considerable effect upon choice of medication and should form an important part of the conversation between patient and treating physician. However, because of the significant consequences of poor medication compliance, treatment adherence is a whole of treating team responsibility. Specific therapies such

Table 23.2 Relative Likelihood of Antipsychotic Medication to Cause Common Adverse Effects

Generic	Sedation	Weight gain	EPSE	Anticholinergic	↑ Prolactin
amisulpride	+	+	++	–	+++
aripiprazole	+	+	–	–	–
asenapine	++	++	+	–	+/–
brexpiprazole	+	+	–	–	–
chlorpromazine	+++	+++	++	+++	+++
clozapine	++++	+++	O	XXX	–
haloperidol	+	++	+++	+	+++
lurasidone	++	+	++	–	+/–
olanzapine	+++	+++	–	++	+
paliperidone	+	++	+	–	+++
quetiapine	++	++	+	+	+
risperidone	+	++	++	–	+++
trifluoperazine	+	++	+++	+	+++
ziprasidone	+	+/–	+	–	–
zuclopenthixol	+	++	+++	+	+++

–=not caused; O=less than placebo; +/–=negligible; +=small; ++=moderate; +++=marked; ++++=severe; XXX=paradoxical increase in salivation, highly anticholinergic.

as adherence therapy may have a limited effect upon improving medication adherence; however, their role over and above good assertive care is still unclear (Gray et al., 2016).

Movement Disorders

There are four broad types of movement disorders induced by antipsychotic medication—parkinsonism, dystonia, akathisia, and tardive dyskinesias. They are thought to occur because of the blockade of D_2 receptors in the basal ganglia by antipsychotic medication (Kapur et al., 2000) and are more common with high-potency antipsychotics such as haloperidol (Leucht et al., 2013).

Parkinsonism is similar to idiopathic Parkinson's Disease, with a low-frequency tremor, most obvious in the hands, slowed movements or bradykinesia, increased rigidity, which can be seen in a decrease in the expressive capacity of the face, a loss of normal arm swing, and a lead-pipe or cogwheel rigidity of the arms when examined. Other features can include sialorrhea (i.e. hypersalivation) and a loss of vocal range and power.

Dystonia is the contraction of a voluntary muscle. It is often sudden, painful, and distressing, and frequently starts in people who have little exposure to antipsychotics, are young or have diagnoses other than schizophrenia. Any muscle group can be affected but can include muscles in the tongue, neck (torticollis), extraocular muscles of the eyes (oculogyric crisis), the laryngeal and pharyngeal muscles, the arms, legs, or back. These muscle contractions can become long term or tardive.

Akathisia is an inner sense of restlessness that is frequently, though not always, combined with objective signs of restlessness such as pacing, rocking, tapping, marching, or moving of the feet. Akathisia can continue at night interfering with sleep and is often described as being very unpleasant, leading to poor treatment adherence and even suicidal ideation (Gibb & Lees, 1986). It too can become tardive or chronic in form. The objective motor signs of akathisia can be misinterpreted as agitation or anxiety and be treated with more antipsychotic medication leading to a vicious spiral of increased medication dose and worsening symptoms.

Tardive dyskinesia (TD) is a repetitive hyperkinetic movement disorder that includes combinations of tics, choreiform, and dystonic movements. They are most common in the tongue and orobuccal muscles but can and frequently do include muscles throughout the body. TD commences in the context of long-term antipsychotic use but can become manifest with dose reductions or cessation. It is predisposed to by high dose, FGA, increasing age, being female, and having another neurological illness, e.g. dementia (Correll, Leucht, & Kane, 2004).

Metabolic Adverse Effects

The metabolic effects of antipsychotic medications include obesity, dyslipidaemia, and diabetes mellitus. The combination of these adverse effects along with the negative environmental factors associated with schizophrenia, including poverty, poor diet, reduced exercise, and substance abuse (Brown, Birtwistle, Roe, & Thompson, 1999; Galletly et al., 2012), explains much of the increasing mortality gap between the general community and people with schizophrenia (Lawrence, Hancock, & Kisely, 2013; Nielsen, Uggerby, Jensen, & McGrath, 2013).

Weight gain is early and rapid in young people exposed to antipsychotics for the first time (Álvarez-Jiménez et al., 2008). This adverse effect is more prominent with olanzapine, clozapine, and chlorpromazine and least with haloperidol, lurasidone, and ziprasidone (Leucht et al., 2013); however, most antipsychotics cause significant weight gain over time (Álvarez-Jiménez et al., 2008). Olanzapine and clozapine are the most likely to cause dyslipidaemia (De Hert, Detraux, van Winkel, Yu, & Correll, 2012), followed by quetiapine and risperidone. And again, clozapine and olanzapine have a significantly deleterious effect on insulin resistance, glucose metabolism dysregulation (Newcomer, 2002), and diabetes (Yood et al., 2009). Aripiprazole, ziprasidone, and lurasidone are less likely to cause this.

The focus on physical health in people with severe mental illness (see Chapters 12 and 21), whether it be in young or older people, has led to the development of clear guidelines for the prevention and management of metabolic adverse effects (Early Psychosis Guidelines Writing Group and EPPIC National Support Program, 2016; Galletly et al., 2016; Lambert, Chapman, & Consensus Working, 2004). These include the selection of antipsychotic medications less likely to cause metabolic adverse effects, the early institution of exercise and healthy lifestyle programs (Vancampfort et al., 2015), and the early use of medication such as metformin to help with weight and glucose control (Newall et al., 2012).

Raised Prolactin

Prolactin is a hormone that stimulates lactation and a number of other reproductive functions (Freeman, Kanyicska, Lerant, & Nagy, 2000). It is secreted by the anterior pituitary under the control of dopamine D_2 receptors and has actions in the breast, liver, ovaries, testes, and prostate. D_2 receptor blockade by antipsychotic medications causes an increase in prolactin levels, which, in turn, inhibits sex hormone secretion and leads to breast enlargement, galactorrhoea, sexual dysfunction and acne in both men and women; menstrual changes and hirsutism in women; and gynaecomastia in men. In the long run, hyperprolactinaemia can cause osteoporosis and bone fracture (Howard, Kirkwood, & Leese, 2007; Inder & Castle, 2011). FGAs and a number of SGAs (e.g. amisulpride, risperidone, and paliperidone) (Grigg et al., 2017; Leucht et al., 2013) cause a significant increase in prolactin. Management of hyperprolactinaemia includes regular measurement of prolactin levels, changing to antipsychotics that do not cause hyperprolactinaemia, using hormone treatment or the oral contraceptive pill according to age (Grigg et al., 2017).

Other Adverse Effects

There are a range of other adverse events of importance. A number of antipsychotic medications, e.g. amisulpride and ziprasidone (Leucht et al., 2013), increase the risk of developing a cardiac arrhythmia such as torsades de pointes, which can lead to sudden death (Glassman & Bigger, 2001). The risk can be estimated by measuring the length of the QT interval from an electrocardiogram (ECG). This risk can become an issue especially when problematic medications are prescribed in combination with other medications that prolong the QTc interval—the QT interval corrected for heart rate (Isbister, 2015). Use of an alternate antipsychotic medication may be warranted.

Anticholinergic effects such as a dry mouth, blurred vision, bladder instability or retention, constipation and cognitive deficits are caused by antipsychotics with a high burden of anticholinergic adverse effects such as clozapine, chlorpromazine, and olanzapine (Chew et al., 2008). Treatment is by lowering the dose or changing medication.

Clozapine inflicts a heavy burden of adverse effects beyond what has already been described. Blood dyscrasias, such as agranulocytosis, is the target of a compulsory monitoring program (Winckel & Siskind, 2017). Although well described as an adverse effect of clozapine, blood dyscrasias are also found with other antipsychotic or psychotropic medications (Stüber et al., 2004). Myocarditis, due to clozapine, can cause sudden death or cardiomyopathy and requires careful monitoring (Haas et al., 2007; Mental Health and Drug and Alcohol Office, 2012; Winckel & Siskind, 2017). Severe constipation is relatively common in people prescribed clozapine and has led to death due to bowel perforation (Palmer, McLean, Ellis, & Harrison-Woolrych, 2008).

Other Neurological Adverse Effects

Other than movement disorders, antipsychotics are associated with an increased risk of seizures particularly chlorpromazine (Itil & Soldatos, 1980) and clozapine (Williams & Park, 2015). This risk is related to a prior diagnosis of epilepsy, high dose of medication, and rapid rate of dose escalation. Treatment can include decreasing the dose of antipsychotic, adding an anticonvulsant medication or changing to a less proconvulsant medication. Neuroleptic Malignant Syndrome (NMS) is a potentially life-threatening syndrome of fever, muscle rigidity, altered level of consciousness, and autonomic disturbance (Pope, Keck, & McElroy, 1986). Key laboratory findings include a greatly elevated creatine phosphokinase (CPK), reflecting muscle breakdown, and an elevated white cell count. Treatment is a medical emergency and includes stopping treatment with antipsychotics, using bromocriptine to reverse dopaminergic blockade and/or dantrolene to stabilise the syndrome in more severe cases (Strawn, Keck, & Caroff, 2007). Electroconvulsive therapy has been used successfully as a second-line treatment if the patient does not respond to other treatments or if a differential diagnosis of malignant catatonia is possible (Troller & Sachdev, 1999).

CONCLUSIONS

Medications are an effective method of treating psychotic symptoms across a range of diagnoses. Many individuals cannot function or be free of distressing symptoms without antipsychotic medications; however, this is at the cost of significant adverse effects. The effect of antipsychotic medications is centred upon their ability to decrease and sometimes stop positive psychotic symptoms such as auditory hallucinations and delusions; however, they are less efficacious in the treatment of other symptoms domains such as negative symptoms and ineffective for the treatment of cognitive symptoms. Although there is evidence for differing levels of effectiveness for different antipsychotic medications, much of the evidence has been produced by the pharmaceutical industry and requires independent verification (Heres et al., 2006). A range of other agents have been trialled with lesser degrees of success, the exception being the role of mood stabilisers in the treatment of affective psychoses. Further improvement in the pharmacological treatment of psychosis awaits a significant aetiological advance that will unlock new ways of treating these disorders.

DISCLOSURES

Dr. Harris has received consultancy fees from Janssen Australia and Lundbeck Australia. He has been on an advisory board for Sumitomo Dainippon Pharma. He has received payments for educational sessions run for Janssen Australia and Lundbeck Australia. He has developed educational material for Servier. He is also the recipient of an investigator initiated grant from Takeda Pharmaceutical Company. He is the chair of One Door Mental Health.

ADDITIONAL SELF-DIRECTED READING

Taylor, D. M., Barnes, T. R. E., & Young, A. H. (2018). *The Maudsley Prescribing Guidelines in Psychiatry* (13th ed.). Wiley-Blackwell. ISBN: 978-1-119-44260-8.

Early Psychosis Guidelines Writing Group and EPPIC National Support Program. (2016). *Australian Clinical Guidleines for Early Psychosis*. Melbourne: Orygen, The National Centre of Excellence in Youth Mental Health.

LINKS TO RESOURCES

- Neuroscience-based nomenclature http://www.nbn2.com/
- https://www.orygen.org.au/Education-Training/Resources-Training/Resources/Free/Clinical-Practice/Australian-Clinical-Guidelines-for-Early-Psychosis
- https://www.ranzcp.org/Files/Resources/Publications/CPG/Clinician/CPG_Clinician_Full_Schizophrenia-pdf.aspx
- https://www.nice.org.uk/guidance/cg178

References

Abi-Dargham, A., & Rodenhiser, J. (2000). From the cover: Increased baseline occupancy of D2 receptors by dopamine in schizophrenia. *Proceedings of the National Academy of Sciences of the United States of America, 97*, 7673–7675.

Agid, O., Kapur, S., Arenovich, T., & Zipursky, R. B. (2003). Delayed-onset hypothesis of antipsychotic action. A hypothesis tested and rejected. *Archives of General Psychiatry, 60*, 1228–1235.

Álvarez-Jiménez, M., González-Blanch, C., Crespo-Facorro, B., Hetrick, S. E., Rodríguez-Sánchez, J. M., Pérez-Iglesias, R., et al. (2008). Antipsychotic-induced weight gain in chronic and first episode psychotic disorders. A systematic critical reappraisal. *CNS Drugs, 22*(7), 547–562.

Álvarez-Jiménez, M., Parker, A. G., Hetrick, S. E., McGorry, P. D., & Gleeson, J. F. (2011). Preventing the second episode: A systematic review and meta-analysis of psychosocial and pharmacological trials in first-episode psychosis. *Schizophrenia Bulletin, 37*(3), 619–630. https://doi.org/10.1093/schbul/sbp129.

Amminger, G. P., Schäfer, M. R., Papageorgiou, K., Klier, C. M., Cotton, S. M., Harrigan, S. M., et al. (2010). Long-chain omega-3 fatty acids for indicated prevention of psychotic disorders. *Archives of General Psychiatry, 67*, 146–154.

Andreasen, N. C., Pressler, M., Nopoulos, P., Miller, D., & Ho, B. C. (2010). Antipsychotic dose equivalents and dose-years: A standardized method for comparing exposure to different drugs. *Biological Psychiatry, 67*, 255–262.

Baumeister, A. A., & Francis, J. L. (2002). Historical development of the dopamine hypothesis of schizophrenia. *Journal of the History of the Neurosciences, 11*(3), 265–277.

Bowtell, M., McGorry, P., & O'Donoghue, B. (2018). Is a higher dose of antipsychotic medication required to treat a relapse following discontinuation in first episode psychosis? *Schizophrenia Research, 204*, 407–408. https://doi.org/10.1016/j.schres.2018.07.032.

Brown, S., Birtwistle, J., Roe, L., & Thompson, C. (1999). The unhealthy lifestyle of people with schizophrenia. *Psychological Medicine, 29*, 697–701.

Caraci, F., Enna, S. J., Zohar, J., Racagni, G., Zalsman, G., Brink, W., et al. (2017). A new nomenclature for classifying psychotropic drugs. *British Journal of Clinical Pharmacology, 83*(8), 1614–1616. https://doi.org/10.1111/bcp.13302.

Carlson, G. A., & Goodwin, F. K. (1973). The stages of mania. A longitudinal analysis of the manic episode. *Archives of General Psychiatry, 28*, 221–228.

Chan, S. K. W., Hui, C. L. M., Chang, W. C., Lee, E. H. M., & Chen, E. Y. H. (2019). Ten-year follow up of patients with first-episode schizophrenia spectrum disorder from an early intervention service: Predictors of clinical remission and functional recovery. *Schizophrenia Research, 204*, 65–71. https://doi.org/10.1016/j.schres.2018.08.022.

Chen, A. T., Chibnall, J. T., & Nasrallah, H. A. (2015). A meta-analysis of placebo-controlled trials of omega-3 fatty acid augmentation in schizophrenia: Possible stage-specific effects. *Annals of Clinical Psychiatry, 27*(4), 289–296.

Chen, A. T., Chibnall, J. T., & Nasrallah, H. A. (2016). Placebo-controlled augmentation trials of the antioxidant NAC in schizophrenia: A review. *Annals of Clinical Psychiatry, 28*(3), 190–196.

Chew, M. L., Mulsant, B. H., Pollock, B. G., Lehman, M. E., Greenspan, A., Mahmoud, R. A., et al. (2008). Anticholinergic activity of 107 medications commonly used by older adults. *Journal of the American Geriatrics Society, 56*(7), 1333–1341. https://doi.org/10.1111/j.1532-5415.2008.01737.x.

Chisolm, M. S., & Payne, J. L. (2016). Management of psychotropic drugs during pregnancy. *BMJ, 352*, h5918. https://doi.org/10.1136/bmj.h5918.

Cipriani, A., Barbui, C., Salanti, G., Rendell, J., Brown, R., Stockton, S., et al. (2011). Comparative efficiency and acceptability of antimanic drugs in acute mania: A multiple treatments meta-analysis. *Lancet, 378*(9799), 1306–1315.

Cipriani, A., Hawton, K., Stockton, S., & Geddes, J. R. (2013). Lithium in the prevention of suicide in mood disorders: Updated systematic review and meta-analysis. *BMJ, 346*, 136–146. https://doi.org/10.1136/bmj.f3646.

Cipriani, A., Reid, K., Young, A. H., Macritchie, K., & Geddes, J. (2013). Valproic acid, valproate and divalproex in the maintenance treatment of bipolar disorder. *Cochrane Database of Systematic Reviews*, (10), Cd003196. https://doi.org/10.1002/14651858.CD003196.pub2.

Cornblatt, B. A., Lencz, T., Smith, C. W., Olsen, R., Auther, A. M., Nakayama, E., et al. (2007). Can antidepressants be used to treat the schizophrenia prodrome? Results of a prospective, naturalistic treatment study of adolescents. *The Journal of Clinical Psychiatry, 68*(4), 546–557. https://doi.org/10.4088/JCP.v68n0410.

Correll, C. U., Leucht, S., & Kane, J. M. (2004). Lower risk for tardive dyskinesia associated with second-generation antipsychotics: A systematic review of 1-year studies. *American Journal of Psychiatry, 161*(3), 414–425.

Correll, C. U., Rubio, J. M., Inczedy-Farkas, G., Birnbaum, M. L., Kane, J. M., & Leucht, S. (2017). Efficacy of 42 pharmacologic cotreatment strategies added to antipsychotic monotherapy in schizophrenia: Systematic overview and quality appraisal of the meta-analytic evidence. *JAMA Psychiatry, 74*(7), 675–684. https://doi.org/10.1001/jamapsychiatry.2017.0624.

De Hert, M., Detraux, J., van Winkel, R., Yu, W., & Correll, C. U. (2012). Metabolic and cardiovascular adverse effects associated with antipsychotic drugs. *Nature Reviews. Endocrinology, 8*(2), 114–126.

Demjaha, A., Lappin, J. M., Stahl, D., Patel, M. X., MacCabe, J. H., Howes, O. D., et al. (2017). Antipsychotic treatment resistance in first-episode psychosis: Prevalence, subtypes and predictors. *Psychological Medicine, 47*, 1981–1989. https://doi.org/10.1017/S0033291717000435.

Desai, H. D., Seabolt, J., & Jann, M. W. (2001). Smoking in patients receiving psychotropic medications. *CNS Drugs, 15*(6), 469–494. https://doi.org/10.2165/00023210-200115060-00005.

Early Psychosis Guidelines Writing Group and EPPIC National Support Program. (2016). *Australian clinical guidelines for early psychosis*. Melbourne: Orygen, The National Centre of Excellence in Youth Mental Health.

Emsley, R., Chiliza, B., & Asmal, L. (2013). The evidence for illness progression after relapse in schizophrenia. *Schizophrenia Research, 148*(1), 117–121. https://doi.org/10.1016/j.schres.2013.05.016.

Emsley, R., Oosthuizen, P., Koen, L., Niehaus, D., & Martinez, L. (2013). Comparison of treatment response in second-episode versus first-episode schizophrenia. *Journal of Clinical Psychopharmacology, 33*(1), 80–83. https://doi.org/10.1097/JCP.0b013e31827bfcc1.

Emsley, R., Rabinowitz, J., & Medori, R. (2006). Time course for antipsychotic treatment response in first-episode schizophrenia. *The American Journal of Psychiatry, 163*(4), 743–745. https://doi.org/10.1176/appi.ajp.163.4.743.

Fawcett, J. (1995). Compliance: Definitions and key issues. *Journal of Clinical Psychiatry, 56*, 4–8.

Firth, J., Stubbs, B., Sarris, J., Rosenbaum, S., Teasdale, S., Berk, M., et al. (2017). The effects of vitamin and mineral supplementation on symptoms of schizophrenia: A systematic review and meta-analysis. *Psychological Medicine, 47*(9), 1515–1527. https://doi.org/10.1017/S0033291717000022.

Fleischhacker, W. W., & Uchida, H. (2014). Critical review of antipsychotic polypharmacy in the treatment of schizophrenia. *The International Journal of Neuropsychopharmacology, 17*(07), 1083–1093. https://doi.org/10.1017/S1461145712000399.

Freeman, M. E., Kanyicska, B., Lerant, A., & Nagy, G. (2000). Prolactin: Structure, function, and regulation of secretion. *Physiological Reviews, 80*(4), 1523–1631. https://doi.org/10.1152/physrev.2000.80.4.1523.

Fusar-Poli, P., Frascarelli, M., Valmaggia, L., Byrne, M., Stahl, D., Rocchetti, M., et al. (2015). Antidepressant, antipsychotic and psychological interventions in subjects at high clinical risk for psychosis: OASIS 6-year naturalistic study. *Psychological Medicine, 45*(6), 1327–1339. https://doi.org/10.1017/S003329171400244X.

Fusar-Poli, P., Papanastasiou, E., Stahl, D., Rocchetti, M., Carpenter, W., Shergill, S., et al. (2014). Treatments of negative symptoms in schizophrenia: Meta-analysis of 168 randomized placebo-controlled trials. *Schizophrenia Bulletin, 41*, 892–899. https://doi.org/10.1093/schbul/sbu170.

Gaebel, W., Weinmann, S., Sartorius, N., Rutz, W., & McIntyre, J. S. (2005). Schizophrenia practice guidelines: International survey and comparison. *British Journal of Psychiatry, 187*(3), 248–255. https://doi.org/10.1192/bjp.187.3.248.

Galletly, C., Castle, D., Dark, F., Humberstone, V., Jablensky, A., Killackey, E., et al. (2016). Royal Australian and New Zealand College of Psychiatrists clinical practice guidelines for the management of schizophrenia and related disorders. *Australian and New Zealand Journal of Psychiatry, 50*(5), 410–472. https://doi.org/10.1177/0004867416641195.

Galletly, C. A., Foley, D. L., Waterreus, A., Watts, G. F., Castle, D. J., McGrath, J. J., et al. (2012). Cardiometabolic risk factors in people with psychotic disorders: The second Australian national survey of psychosis. *Australian & New Zealand Journal of Psychiatry, 46*(8), 753–761. https://doi.org/10.1177/0004867412453089.

Geddes, J., Freemantle, N., Harrison, P., & Bebbington, P. (2000). Atypical antipsychotics in the treatment of schizophrenia: Systematic overview and meta-regression analysis. *British Medical Journal, 321*, 1371–1376.

Gibb, W., & Lees, A. (1986). The clinical phenomenon of akathisia. *Journal of Neurology, Neurosurgery and Psychiatry, 49*, 861–866.

Glassman, A. H., & Bigger, J. T. J. (2001). Antipsychotic drugs: Prolonged QTc interval, torsade de pointes, and sudden death. *American Journal of Psychiatry, 158*, 1774–1782.

Goff, D. C., Falkai, P., Fleischhacker, W. W., Girgis, R. R., Kahn, R. S., Uchida, H., et al. (2017). The long-term effects of antipsychotic medication on clinical course in schizophrenia. *American Journal of Psychiatry, 174*(9), 840–849. https://doi.org/10.1176/appi.ajp.2017.16091016.

Gray, R., Bressington, D., Ivanecka, A., Hardy, S., Jones, M., Schulz, M., et al. (2016). Is adherence therapy an effective adjunct treatment for patients with schizophrenia spectrum disorders? A systematic review and meta-analysis. *BMC Psychiatry, 16*(1), 90. https://doi.org/10.1186/s12888-016-0801-1.

Gregory, A., Mallikarjun, P., & Upthegrove, R. (2017). Treatment of depression in schizophrenia: Systematic review and meta-analysis. *British Journal of Psychiatry, 211*(4), 198–204. https://doi.org/10.1192/bjp.bp.116.190520.

Grigg, J., Worsley, R., Thew, C., Gurvich, C., Thomas, N., & Kulkarni, J. (2017). Antipsychotic-induced hyperprolactinemia: Synthesis of world-wide guidelines and integrated recommendations for assessment, management and future research. *Psychopharmacology, 234*(22), 3279–3297. https://doi.org/10.1007/s00213-017-4730-6.

Haas, S., Hill, R., Krum, H., Liew, D., Tonkin, A., Demos, L. L., et al. (2007). Clozapine-associated myocarditis. A review of 116 cases of suspected myocarditis associated with the use of clozapine in Australia during 1993–2003. *Drug Safety, 30*(1), 47–57.

Hennen, J., & Baldessarini, R. J. (2005). Suicide risk during treatment with clozapine: A meta-analysis. *Schizophrenia Research, 73*, 139–145.

Heres, S., Davis, J. M., Maino, K., Jetzinger, E., Kissling, W., & Leucht, S. (2006). Why olanzapine beats risperidone, risperdione beats quetiapine and quetiapine beats olanzapine: An exploratory analysis of head-to-head comparison studies of second-generation anntipsychotics. *American Journal of Psychiatry, 163*, 185–194.

Higashi, K., Medic, G., Littlewood, K. J., Diez, T., Granström, O., & De Hert, M. (2013). Medication adherence in schizophrenia: Factors influencing adherence and consequences of nonadherence, a systematic literature review. *Therapeutic Advances in Psychopharmacology, 3*(4), 200–218. https://doi.org/10.1177/2045125312474019.

Howard, L., Kirkwood, G., & Leese, M. (2007). Risk of hip fracture in patients with a history of schizophrenia. *British Journal of Psychiatry, 190*, 127–134.

Howes, O. D., Kambeitz, J., Kim, E., Stahl, D., Slifstein, M., Abi-Dargham, A., et al. (2012). The nature of dopamine dysfunction in schizophrenia and what this means for treatment: Meta-analysis of imaging studies. *Archives of General Psychiatry, 69*(8), 776–786. https://doi.org/10.1001/archgenpsychiatry.2012.169.

Howes, O. D., McCutcheon, R., Agid, O., de Bartolomeis, A., van Beveren, N. J. M., Birnbaum, M. L., et al. (2017). Treatment-resistant schizophrenia: Treatment response and resistance in psychosis (TRRIP) Working group Consensus guidelines on diagnosis and terminology. *American Journal of Psychiatry, 174*(3), 216–229. https://doi.org/10.1176/appi.ajp.2016.16050503.

Inder, W. J., & Castle, D. (2011). Antipsychotic-induced hyperprolactinaemia. *Australian and New Zealand Journal of Psychiatry, 45*(10), 830–837. https://doi.org/10.3109/00048674.2011.589044.

Isbister, G. K. (2015). Risk assessment of drug-induced QT prolongation. *Australian Prescriber, 38*, 20–24.

Itil, T., & Soldatos, C. (1980). Epiletogenic side effects of psychotrophic drugs. *Journal of the American Medical Association, 244*, 1460–1463.

Kahn, R. S. P., Winter van Rossum, I. P., Leucht, S. P., McGuire, P. P., Lewis, S. W. P., Leboyer, M. P., et al. (2018). Amisulpride and olanzapine followed by open-label treatment with clozapine in first-episode schizophrenia and schizophreniform disorder (OPTiMiSE): A three-phase switching study. *The Lancet Psychiatry*, (18), 30252–30259. https://doi.org/10.1016/S2215-0366.

Kane, J. M., Honigfeld, G., Singer, J., & Meltzer, H. Y. Clozaril Collaborative Study, G. (1988). Clozapine for the treatment-resistant schizophrenic: A double blind comparison with chlorpromazine. *Archives of General Psychiatry, 45*, 789–796.

Kapur, S., Zipursky, R., Jones, C., Remington, G., & Houle, S. (2000). Relationship between dopamine D(2) occupancy, clinical response, and side effects: A double-blind PET study of first-episode schizophrenia. *American Journal of Psychiatry, 157*, 514–520.

Keefe, R. S. E., Buchanan, R. W., Marder, S. R., Schooler, N. R., Dugar, A., Zivkov, M., et al. (2011). Clinical trials of potential cognitive-enhancing drugs in schizophrenia: What have we learned so far? *Schizophrenia Bulletin, 39*(2), 417–435. https://doi.org/10.1093/schbul/sbr153.

Khandaker, G. M., Cousins, L., Deakin, J., Lennox, B. R., Yolken, R., & Jones, P. B. (2015). Inflammation and immunity in schizophrenia: Implications for pathophysiology and treatment. *Lancet Psychiatry, 2*(3), 258–270. https://doi.org/10.1016/s2215-0366(14)00122-9.

King, D. J., & Wager, E. (1998). Haematological safety of antipsychotic drugs. *Journal of Psychopharmacology, 12*(3), 283–288. https://doi.org/10.1177/026988119801200309.

Kinon, B. J., Chen, L., Ascher-Svanum, H., Stauffer, V. L., Kollack-Walker, S., Zhou, W., et al. (2010). Early response to antipsychotic drug therapy as a clinical marker of subsequent response to the treatment of schizophrenia. *Neuropsychopharmacology, 35*(2), 581–590.

Kinon, B. J., Kane, J. M., Johns, C., & Al, E. (1993). Treatment of neuroleptic-resistant schizophrenic relapse. *Psychopharmacology Bulletin, 29*(2), 309–314.

Kishimoto, T., Agarwal, V., Kishi, T., Leucht, S., Kane, J. M., & Correll, C. U. (2013). Relapse prevention in schizophrenia: A systematic review and meta-analysis of second-generation antipsychotics versus first-generation antipsychotics. *Molecular Psychiatry, 18*(1), 53–66. (2013). http://www.nature.com/mp/journal/v18/n1/suppinfo/mp2011143s1.html.

Kishimoto, T., Nitta, M., Borenstein, M., Kane, J. M., & Correll, C. U. (2013). Long-acting injectable versus oral antipsychotics in schizophrenia: A systematic review and meta-analysis of mirror-image studies. *Journal of Clinical Psychiatry, 74*(10), 957–965. https://doi.org/10.4088/JCP.13r08440.

Kishimoto, T., Robenzadeh, A., Leucht, C., Leucht, S., Watanabe, K., Mimura, M., et al. (2012). Long-acting injectable vs oral antipsychotics for relapse prevention in schizophrenia: A meta-analysis of randomized trials. *Schizophrenia Bulletin, 40*, 192–213. https://doi.org/10.1093/schbul/sbs150.

Lambert, T. J. R., Chapman, L. H., & Consensus Working, P. (2004). Diabetes, psychotic disorders and antipsychotic therapy: A consensus statement. *Medical Journal of Australia, 181*, 544–548.

Lawrence, D., Hancock, K. J., & Kisely, S. (2013). The gap in life expectancy from preventable physical illness in psychiatric patients in Western Australia: Retrospective analysis of population based registers. *BMJ, 346*, f2539. https://doi.org/10.1136/bmj.f2539.

Leucht, S., Busch, R., Hamann, J., Kissling, W., & Kane, J. M. (2005). Early onset hypothesis of antipsychotic drug action: A hypothesis tested, confirmed and extended. *Biological Psychiatry, 57*, 1543–1549.

Leucht, S., Cipriani, A., Spineli, L., Mavridis, D., Örey, D., Richter, F., et al. (2013). Comparative efficacy and tolerability of 15 antipsychotic drugs in schizophrenia: A multiple-treatments meta-analysis. *The Lancet, 382*(9896), 951–962. https://doi.org/10.1016/S0140-6736(13)60733-3.

Leucht, S., Cipriani, A., Spineli, L., Mavridis, D., Orey, D., Richter, F., et al. (2017). 60 years of placebo-controlled antipsychotic drug trials in acute schizophrenia: Systematic review, Bayesian meta-analysis and meta-regression of efficacy predictors. *American Journal of Psychiatry, 174*, 927–942. https://doi.org/10.1176/appi.ajp.2017.16121358.

Leucht, S., Corves, C., Arbter, D., Engel, R. R., Li, C., & Davis, J. M. (2009). Second-generation versus first-generation antipsychotic drugs for schizophrenia: A meta-analysis. *Lancet, 373*, 31–41.

Leucht, S., Kissling, W., & Davis, J. M. (2009). Second-generation antipsychotics for schizophrenia: Can we resolve the conflict? *Psychological Medicine, 39*(10), 1591–1602. https://doi.org/10.1017/S0033291709005455.

Leucht, S., Komossa, K., Rummel-Kluge, C., Corves, C., Hunger, H., Schmid, F., et al. (2009). A meta-analysis of head-to-head comparisons of second-generation antipsychotics in the treatment of schizophrenia. *American Journal of Psychiatry, 166*, 152–163.

Leucht, S., Tardy, M., Komossa, K., Kissling, W., Salanti, G., & Davis, J. M. (2012). Antipsychotic drugs versus placebo for relapse prevention in schizophrenia: A systematic review and meta-analysis. *Lancet, 379*, 2063–2071.

Lieberman, J. A., Saltz, B. L., & Johns, C. A. (1991). The effects of clozapine on tardive dyskinesia. *British Journal of Psychiatry, 158*, 503–510.

Lieberman, J. A., Stroup, T. S., McEvoy, J. P., Swartz, M. S., Rosenheck, R. A., Perkins, D. O., et al. (2005). Effectiveness of Antipsychotic Drugs in Patients with Chronic Schizophrenia. *The New England Journal of Medicine, 353*(12), 1209–1223.

Louwerens, J. W., & van der Meij, A. P. M. (2000). Therapy resistance: The effectiveness of the second antipsychotic drug, a multicentric double-blind comparative study ("switch study"). *Schizophrenia Research, 41*, 183–184.

Malhi, G. S., Bassett, D., Boyce, P., Bryant, R., Fitzgerald, P. B., Fritz, K., et al. (2015). Royal Australian and New Zealand college of psychiatrists clinical practice guidelines for mood disorders. *Australian and New Zealand Journal of Psychiatry, 49*(12), 1087–1206. https://doi.org/10.1177/0004867415617657.

Malhi, G. S., Tanious, M., & Das, P. (2012). The science and practice of lithium therapy. *Australian and New Zealand Journal of Psychiatry, 46*, 192–211.

McGlashan, T. H., Zipursky, R. B., Perkins, D., Addington, J., Miller, T., Woods, S. W., et al. (2006). Randomized, double-blind trial of olanzapine versus placebo in patients prodromally symptomatic for psychosis. *The American Journal of Psychiatry, 163*(5), 790–799. https://doi.org/10.1176/ajp.2006.163.5.790.

McGorry, P. D., Nelson, B., Markulev, C., Yuen, H. P., Schafer, M. R., Mossaheb, N., et al. (2017). Effect of omega-3 polyunsaturated fatty acids in young people at ultrahigh risk for psychotic disorders: The NEURAPRO Randomized Clinical Trial. *JAMA Psychiatry, 74*(1), 19–27.

McGorry, P. D., Yung, A. R., Phillips, L. J., Yuen, H. P., Francey, S., Cosgrave, E., et al. (2002). Randomized controlled trial of interventions designed to reduce the risk of progression to first-episode psychosis in a clinical sample with subthreshold symptoms. *Archives of General Psychiatry, 59*, 921–928.

Mental Health and Drug and Alcohol Office. (2012). *Clozapine-induced myocarditis—Monitoring protocol. (PD2012_005)*. North Sydney, Australia: New South Wales Government.

Newall, H., Myles, N., Ward, P. B., Samaras, K., Shiers, D., & Curtis, J. (2012). Efficacy of metformin for prevention of weight gain in psychiatric populations: A review. *International Clinical Psychopharmacology, 27*, 69–75.

Newcomer, J. W. (2002). Abnormalities in glucose regulation during antipsychotic treatment of schizophrenia. *Archives of General Psychiatry, 59*, 337–345.

Nielsen, R. E., Uggerby, A. S., Jensen, S. O. W., & McGrath, J. J. (2013). Increasing mortality gap for patients diagnosed with schizophrenia over the last three decades—A Danish nationwide study from 1980 to 2010. *Schizophrenia Research, 146*, 22–27.

Nitta, M., Kishimoto, T., Muller, N., Weiser, M., Davidson, M., Kane, J. M., et al. (2013). Adjunctive use of nonsteroidal anti-inflammatory drugs for schizophrenia: A meta-analytic investigation of randomized controlled trials. *Schizophrenia Bulletin, 39*(6), 1230–1241. https://doi.org/10.1093/schbul/sbt070.

Palmer, S. E., McLean, R. M., Ellis, P. M., & Harrison-Woolrych, M. (2008). Life-threatening clozapine-induced gastrointestinal hypomotility: An analysis of 102 cases. *Journal of Clinical Psychiatry, 69*(5), 759–768.

Pantelis, C., & Lambert, T. J. R. (2003). Managing patients with "treatment-resistant" schizophrenia. *Medical Journal of Australia, 178*, S62–S66.

Pope, H. G., Keck, P. E., & McElroy, S. L. (1986). Frequency and presentation of neuroleptic malignant syndrome in a large psychiatric hospital. *American Journal of Psychiatry, 143*, 1227–1233.

Porter, R. (1997). *The greatest benefit to mankind*. London: Harper Collins.

Preskorn, S. H. (2012a). Clinically important differences in the pharmacokinetics of the ten newer "atypical" antipsychotics: Part 2. Metabolism and elimination. *Journal of Psychiatric Practice, 18*, 361–368.

Preskorn, S. H. (2012b). Clinically important differences in the pharmacokinetics of the ten newer "atypical" antipsychotics: Part 3. Effects of renal and hepatic impairment. *Journal of Psychiatric Practice, 18*, 430–437.

Robinson, D., Woerner, M. G., Alvir, J. M., Bilder, R., Goldman, R., Geisler, S., et al. (1999). Predictors of relapse following response from a first episode of schizophrenia or schizoaffective disorder. *Archives of General Psychiatry, 56*, 241–247.

Rostami-Hodjegan, A., Amin, A. M., Spencer, E. P., Lennard, M. S., Tucker, G. T., & Flanagan, R. J. (2004). Influence of dose, cigarette smoking, age, sex, and metabolic activity on plasma clozapine concentrations: A predictive model and nomograms to aid clozapine dose adjustment and to assess compliance in individual patients. *Journal of Clinical Psychopharmacology, 24*, 70–78.

Samara, M. T., Leucht, C., Leeflang, M. M., Anghelescu, I. G., Chung, Y. C., Crespo-Facorro, B., et al. (2015). Early improvement as a predictor of later response to antipsychotics in schizophrenia: A diagnostic test review. *The American Journal of Psychiatry, 172*(7), 617–629. https://doi.org/10.1176/appi.ajp.2015.14101329.

Scott, J. G., Gillis, D., Ryan, A. E., Hargovan, H., Gundarpi, N., McKeon, G., et al. (2018). The prevalence and treatment outcomes of antineuronal antibody-positive patients admitted with first episode of psychosis. *BJPsych Open, 4*(2), 69–74. https://doi.org/10.1192/bjo.2018.8.

Seeman, P. (1992). Dopamine receptor sequences: Therapeutic levels of neuroleptics occupy D2 receptors, clozapine occupies D4. *Neuropsychopharmacology, 7*, 261–284.

Seeman, P., & Lee, T. (1975). Antipsychotic drugs: Direct correlation between clinical potency and presynaptic action on dopamine neurons. *Science, 188*(4194), 1217–1219.

Singh, S. P., Singh, V., Kar, N., & Chan, K. (2010). Efficacy of antidepressants in treating the negative symptoms of chronic schizophrenia. *British Journal of Psychiatry, 197*, 174–179.

Sinkeviciute, I., Begemann, M., Prikken, M., Oranje, B., Johnsen, E., Lei, W. U., et al. (2018). Efficacy of different types of cognitive enhancers for patients with schizophrenia: A meta-analysis. *NPJ Schizophrenia, 4*(1), 22. https://doi.org/10.1038/s41537-018-0064-6.

Siskind, D., McCartney, L., Goldschlager, R., & Kisely, S. (2016). Clozapine v. first- and second-generation antipsychotics in treatment-refractory schizophrenia: Systematic review and meta-analysis. *British Journal of Psychiatry, 209*, 385–392. https://doi.org/10.1192/bjp.bp.115.177261.

Siskind, D., Siskind, V., & Kisely, S. (2017). Clozapine response rates among people with treatment-resistant schizophrenia: Data from a systematic review and meta-analysis. *The Canadian Journal of Psychiatry, 62*(11), 772–777. https://doi.org/10.1177/0706743717718167.

Strawn, J. R., Keck, J. P. E., & Caroff, S. N. (2007). Neuroleptic Malignant Syndrome. *American Journal of Psychiatry, 164*(6), 870–876. https://doi.org/10.1176/ajp.2007.164.6.870.

Stüber, S., Grohmann, R., Engel, R., Bandelow, B., Ludwig, W.-D., Müller-Oerlinghausen, B., et al. (2004). Blood dyscasias induced by psychotropic medication. *Pharmacopsychiatry, 37*(Suppl 1), S70–S78.

Takeuchi, H., Kantor, N., Sanches, M., Fervaha, G., Agid, O., & Remington, G. (2017). One-year symptom trajectories in patients with stable schizophrenia maintained on antipsychotics versus placebo: Meta-analysis. *The British Journal of Psychiatry, 211*(3), 137–143. https://doi.org/10.1192/bjp.bp.116.186007.

Tiihonen, J., Mittendorfer-Rutz, E., Majak, M., et al. (2017). Real-world effectiveness of antipsychotic treatments in a nationwide cohort of 29 823 patients with schizophrenia. *JAMA Psychiatry, 74*(7), 686–693. https://doi.org/10.1001/jamapsychiatry.2017.1322.

Tiihonen, J., Wahlbeck, K., Lînnqvist, J., Klaukka, T., Ioannidis, J. P. A., Volavka, J., et al. (2006). Effectiveness of antipsychotic treatments in a nationwide cohort of patients in community care after first hospitalisation due to schizophrenia and schizoaffective disorder: Observational follow-up study. *British Medical Journal, 333*, 224. https://doi.org/10.1136/bmj.38881.382755.382752F.

Troller, J. N., & Sachdev, P. S. (1999). Electroconvulsive treatment of neuroleptic malignant syndrome: A review and report of cases. *Australian and New Zealand Journal of Psychiatry, 33*, 650–659.

UK ECT Review Group. (2003). Efficacy and safety of electroconvulsive therapy in depressive disorders: A systematic review and meta-analysis. *The Lancet, 361*(9360), 799–808. https://doi.org/10.1016/S0140-6736(03)12705-5.

Vancampfort, D., Rosenbaum, S., Probst, M., Soundy, A., Mitchell, A. J., De Hert, M., et al. (2015). Promotion of cardiorespiratory fitness in schizophrenia: A clinical overview and meta-analysis. *Acta Psychiatrica Scandinavica, 132*(2), 131–143. https://doi.org/10.1111/acps.12407.

Verdoux, H., Lengronne, J., Liraud, F., Gonzales, B., Assens, F., Abalan, F., et al. (2000). Medication adherence in psychosis: Predictors and impact on outcome. A 2-year follow-up of first-admitted subjects. *Acta Psychiatrica Scandinavica, 102*, 203–210.

Viguera, A. C., Baldessarini, R. J., Hegarty, J. D., van Kammen, D. P., & Tohen, M. (1997). Clinical risk following abrupt and gradual withdrawal of maintenance neuroleptic treatment. *Archives of General Psychiatry, 54*, 49–55.

Wiersma, D., Nienhuis, F. J., Slooff, C. J., & Giel, R. (1998). Natural course of schizophrenic disorders: A 15-year follow-up of a Dutch incidence cohort. *Schizophrenia Bulletin, 24*, 75–85.

Wijkstra, J., Lijmer, J., Burger, H., Cipriani, A., Geddes, J., & Nolen, W. A. (2015). Pharmacological treatment for psychotic depression. *Cochrane Database of Systematic Reviews*, (7), CD004044. https://doi.org/10.1002/14651858.CD004044.pub4.

Williams, A. M., & Park, S. H. (2015). Seizure associated with clozapine: Incidence, etiology, and management. *CNS Drugs, 29*, 101–111.

Winckel, K., & Siskind, D. (2017). Clozapine in primary care. *Australian Prescriber, 40*(6), 231–236. https://doi.org/10.18773/austprescr.2017.067.

Wunderink, L., Nieboer, R. M., Wiersma, D., Sytema, S., & Nienhuis, F. J. (2013). Recovery in remitted first-episode psychosis at 7 years of follow-up of an early dose reduction/discontinuation or maintenance treatment strategy: Long-term follow-up of a 2-year randomized clinical trial. *JAMA Psychiatry, 70*(9), 913–920. https://doi.org/10.1001/jamapsychiatry.2013.19.

Yood, M. U., DeLorenze, G., Quesenberry, C. P., Jr., Oliveria, S. A., Tsai, A. L., Willey, V. J., et al. (2009). The incidence of diabetes in atypical antipsychotic users differs according to agent—Results from a multisite epidemiologic study. *Pharmacoepidemiology and Drug Safety, 18*, 791–799. https://doi.org/10.1002/pds.1781.

Zheng, W., Cai, D. B., Yang, X. H., Ungvari, G. S., Ng, C. H., Muller, N., et al. (2017). Adjunctive celecoxib for schizophrenia: A meta-analysis of randomized, double-blind, placebo-controlled trials. *Journal of Psychiatric Research, 92*, 139–146. https://doi.org/10.1016/j.jpsychires.2017.04.004.

Zhu, Y., Li, C., Huhn, M., Rothe, P., Krause, M., Bighelli, I., et al. (2017). How well do patients with a first episode of schizophrenia respond to antipsychotics: A systematic review and meta-analysis. *European Neuropsychopharmacology, 27*(9), 835–844. https://doi.org/10.1016/j.euroneuro.2017.06.011.

Zipursky, R. B., Menezes, N. M., & Streiner, D. L. (2014). Risk of symptom recurrence with medication discontinuation in first-episode psychosis: A systematic review. *Schizophrenia Research, 152*(2–3), 408–414. https://doi.org/10.1016/j.schres.2013.08.001.

Definition of Key Terms

Agranulocytosis Is the loss of neutrophils, an important class of infection-fighting white blood cells. It is associated with clozapine but which can occur rarely with other medications.

Akathisia A movement disorder characterised by a subjective sense of inner restlessness and increased restlessness and purposeless movement.

Bioavailability The proportion of the administered drug that is absorbed into the body and makes its way to the site of action.

Bradykinesia A slowing of movement seen in Parkinsonism, a form of extra-pyramidal side effects.

Cytochrome P450 system A system of liver enzymes that are responsible for much of the metabolism of antipsychotic and other medications.

Dystonia An involuntary spasm or contraction of a muscle group. Can happen spontaneously but is also an adverse effect of antipsychotic medication.

Extrapyramidal symptoms Movement disorders that are caused by the blockade of dopaminergic receptors in the nigrostriatal system.

Half-life The time needed to clear 50% of a drug from the body.

Long-acting injection Also known as a depot medication. A means of giving medication in an injection from which the medication is slowly released, typically over a 2–4 week period.

Metabolic syndrome Is a syndrome of central obesity, hypertension, dyslipidaemia, and glucose intolerance or insulin resistance. There is a high rate of diabetes mellitus type 2. It is accompanied by an increased rate of morbidity and premature mortality usually due to cardiovascular disease.

Neuroleptic Malignant Syndrome (NMS) Is a potentially life-threatening syndrome of fever, muscle rigidity, altered level of consciousness, and autonomic disturbance.

Tardive dyskinesia A long-term movement disorder caused by blockade of dopamine receptors that is characterised by involuntary oro-buccal movements, and constant twisting and writhing movements of hands, feet, and other body parts.

CHAPTER 24

Getting in Early: Early Intervention Services for Psychosis

Jesse Gates[*,†], **Eóin Killackey**[*,‡]

[*]Orygen, The National Centre of Excellence in Youth Mental Health, Parkville, VIC, Australia, [†]La Trobe University, Melbourne, VIC, Australia, [‡]Centre for Youth Mental Health, The University of Melbourne, Melbourne, VIC, Australia

Key Learning Objectives

- Develop an awareness of the clinical staging model and rationale for early intervention in psychosis.
- Understand the various consensus statements and guidelines that address issues and complexity in the treat of early psychosis intervention and service delivery.
- Become familiar with evidence-based treatments for early psychosis.
- Understanding complexity in early psychosis and how psychologists and neuropsychologists can use their skills to provide assessment and treatment.

INTRODUCTION

In any other area of healthcare, the idea that you should intervene at the earliest moment of illness is accepted as common sense. In many cases, having evidence of an illness in progress, or risk for an illness, and not acting would be seen to be negligent. Not intervening early would be likely to cause distress if avoidable outcomes are later experienced, or more invasive interventions are required later on. However, it is only relatively recently that the same common sense became apparent in mental health care. There are many reasons for this, including underfunding, stigma and discrimination, low belief in the effectiveness of treatments, and a pervasive belief that decline rather than recovery was inevitable. This was especially so in the psychoses.

However, over the last 30 years, there has been increasing evidence that this way of thinking was not correct. Provided with comprehensive and sustained early

A Clinical Introduction to Psychosis. https://doi.org/10.1016/B978-0-12-815012-2.00024-9

Early intervention for psychosis aims for rapid detection and treatment of emerging symptoms.

intervention, people with psychosis can make recoveries. Additionally, where it was previously thought that the development of psychosis could only be discerned in retrospect, we now know that it is possible to identify a proportion of people at high risk of developing psychosis and intervene to reduce the likelihood of a psychotic disorder occurring or progressing.

This chapter will discuss a number of areas related to early intervention in psychosis: the clinical staging model; consensus statements and guidelines for treatment; identification and intervention for those at risk of psychosis; evidence for the effectiveness of early intervention; issues around the establishment of early intervention programs; the inclusion of families and carers in treatment planning; and the distinct contribution that psychologists make to early intervention teams.

CLINICAL STAGING MODELS AND EARLY INTERVENTION IN PSYCHOSIS

The psychosis prodrome refers to early signs or symptoms that precede definitive diagnosis of a psychotic disorder.

For most of the history of 20th century psychiatry, mental illness and in particular psychotic illness was considered dichotomously—either an individual had an illness, or they did not. The prodrome—a period of decline in functioning before crossing the diagnostic threshold of a psychotic illness—was recognised only in retrospect and there was little consideration given to either identifying an individual in this phase or to providing intervention at this point. Although as early as the 1920s there had been suggestion of earlier intervention in psychotic illness (Sullivan, 1927), there was very little practical response to these calls until the 1990s. In 1992 the Early Psychosis Prevention and Intervention Centre commenced operation in Melbourne with an approach of providing comprehensive, sustained treatment to those experiencing a first episode of psychosis (McGorry, Edwards, Mihalopoulos, Harrigan, & Jackson, 1996). This was a radical departure, both from the earlier asylum era, and the existing community mental health services, which, at that time, largely, managed those with multiple episodes of illness.

A next logical step in this development was pushing the window of intervention to the period prior to the first episode (Yung & McGorry, 1996). This was an area of active research and eventual clinical practice. The research resulted in an increased capacity to screen and identify young people at risk of psychosis (Yung et al., 1998, 2003). A number of trials since have shown that intervention in this phase can reduce the rate of transition to psychosis (van der Gaag et al., 2013).

The fact that any episodes of psychosis can be prevented if intervention occurs in the high-risk phase, suggests that rather than psychotic illness being a dichotomous state, it is possible that there is a more dynamic process of illness developing. This further suggests that if the stages of illness could be delineated, treatments most appropriate to the stage at which an individual presented could be developed and applied. This idea is borrowed from many areas of physical medicine in which pathology is known to develop through a series of stages. Illness that is identified at an earlier stage can be treated with a less invasive or disruptive treatment than that which presents in later stages.

Table 24.1 The Staging Model for Psychosis (Orygen Youth Health Research Centre, 2010)

Stage	Definition
0	Increased risk of psychotic disorder—no symptoms currently
1a	Mild or nonspecific symptoms of psychosis, including neurocognitive deficits. Mild functional change or decline
1b	Ultra-high risk of psychosis: Moderate but subthreshold symptoms, with moderate neurocognitive changes and functional decline to caseness or chronic poor functioning ($\geq$30% drop in SOFAS in previous 12 months OR $<$ 50 for previous 12 months)
2	First episode of psychotic disorder: Full threshold disorder with moderate–severe symptoms, neurocognitive deficits, and functional decline (GAF 30–50) includes acute and early recovery periods
3a	Incomplete remission from first episode of care
3b	Recurrence or relapse of psychotic disorder, which stabilises with treatment but at a level of GAF, residual symptoms, or neurocognition below the best level achieved following remission from first episode
3c	Multiple relapses, with objective worsening in clinical extent and impact of illness
4	Severe, persistent OR unremitting illness as judged by symptoms, neurocognition, and disability criteria

The application of a staging model to mental illness was proposed in 2006 (McGorry, Hickie, Yung, Pantelis, & Jackson, 2006). The rationale for this proposition was in response to the observation that diagnosis on the basis of defined disorders in mental illness was a less accurate guide both to treatment and prognosis than it should be (McGorry et al., 2006). It was suggested that a staging model would be a 'more refined form of diagnosis' (p. 617) (McGorry et al., 2006) allowing for a more nuanced selection of treatments and giving a narrower range of potential outcomes. Further, a staging model was suggested as a means to organise the growing range of biological findings around mental illness. The potential here was to eventually be able to identify biological markers of stage of illness. Finally, conceptualising mental illness as a series of disorders that require more intense and potentially invasive treatment at later stages would promote early intervention, preservation of ability, and minimisation of functional and social disability (McGorry et al., 2006). In the 2006 staging model for psychosis, 5 stages of mental illness were articulated. These range from stage 0 where there is a heightened risk perhaps because of family history but no symptoms, through stage 4, which is severe, persistent unremitting illness (see Table 24.1).

GUIDELINES AND CONSENSUS STATEMENTS ON EARLY PSYCHOSIS

As mentioned, the first early psychosis service opened in 1992. This was followed soon after in various locations around the world, from the United Kingdom to Europe, North America, and Asia (McGorry, Killackey, & Yung, 2008). However, it was not until 2005 that an International Consensus Statement—the 'Early

Psychosis Declaration' (EPD)—outlining recommendations for early intervention (EI) for young people with early psychosis was published (Bertolote & McGorry, 2005). This statement was published in collaboration with the World Health Organisation and the International Early Psychosis Association. Development of the consensus statement proceeded through consultation with experts within the field of early psychosis, and was published in conjunction with International Clinical Practice Guidelines (ICPG) (International Early Psychosis Association Writing Group, 2005).

Currently, too few people with, or at high risk for, psychosis have timely access to optimal treatment.

Consensus statements and international declarations are intended to articulate values, goals, and standards that have been recognised as important ingredients to enhance the care of individuals across a range of areas in medicine. Despite the knowledge and availability of interventions that have the potential to limit progression through more disabling stages of illness, and to reduce likelihood of relapse, it was—and still is—acknowledged that many individuals with early psychosis do not receive timely or sustained care that is consistent with current evidence (International Early Psychosis Association Writing Group, 2005). Furthermore, the consensus statement sought to clarify and recommend treatment that not only addressed symptoms of the disorder, but recognised the overall impact or burden of disease and outlined a means forward. The EPD emphasises the need for comprehensive programs that address the multiple and complex needs of treatment in early psychosis through 'supporting recovery, independence, equity and self-sufficiency and of facilitating the uptake of social, educational and employment opportunities' (Bertolote & McGorry, 2005).

The consensus statement outlines 10 strategic recommendations (see Box 24.1), along with 5-year outcomes that a comprehensive and effective program would deliver to people with early psychosis and their families. Inherent in these recommendations is the recognition of the wide-ranging impacts of psychosis,

Box 24.1 Ten Recommendations From the International Consensus Statement

1. Provide treatment in primary care: early detection and access to comprehensive community-based mental health services
2. Make psychotropic and psychosocial interventions available
3. Provide care in the community: move towards least restrictive and coercive service approaches
4. Educate the public: raise community awareness about the importance and the opportunities for earlier detection and improved management of psychosis
5. Involve communities, families, and consumers
6. Establish national policies, programs, and legislation
7. Develop human resources
8. Link with other sectors to facilitate the increasingly regarded concept of recovery
9. Monitor community mental health: relevant indicators of early psychosis
10. Support more research

i.e. that it not only affects the individual, but also the individual's wider family and community.

Where the EPD acts as an overall guide to the values and goals of early psychosis services, the ICPG synthesise the vast body of evidence surrounding treatment for early psychosis into practice-based recommendations that can be used by clinicians. The EPD and ICPG have served as the foundation for a number of national guidelines that address the specific context of services in countries like Australia and New Zealand (Couroupis, Francey, Gregory, & Stavely, 2016; Galletly et al., 2016), Canada (Ehmann, Hanson, Yager, Dolazell, & Gilbert, 2010), Italy (De Masi et al., 2008), Japan (Mizuno, 2017), and the United Kingdom (Baird et al., 2012) and regions within the United States (Blea, Hayden-Lewis, Penkin, & Roberts, 2013; Heinssen, Goldstein, & Azrin, 2014).

While there is some variation across guidelines about specific recommendations, there are key elements recognised as essential for effective treatment programmes in early psychosis outlined by the ICPG. Since local guidelines are developed to address unique service provision within areas, the ICPG recommendations will be the focus of this outline.

Duration of untreated psychosis is defined as the time from the first symptom of psychosis to the start of treatment.

The very notion of early intervention is founded on the fact that the duration of untreated psychosis (DUP) is related to worse outcomes. Therefore, *access* to services is seen as critical in reducing DUP. Access refers to a range of areas, including promoting community awareness about how to obtain help, and that primary healthcare professionals should be competent in recognising the early clinical features of psychosis (Bertolote & McGorry, 2005). Other initiatives to improve access that have been recommended include development of close links between primary and specialist mental health services, while developing undergraduate and postgraduate education. Vitally, when someone is identified as experiencing symptoms of psychosis, mental health services should provide timely and flexible assessment, with treatment preferably commencing prior to the development of crisis. A key element of enhancing access also rests in the acknowledgement that family are indispensable in engagement in this process of assessment and early treatment, but also have needs of their own.

International guidelines acknowledge that the period of recovery from 6 to 18 months, and up to 5 years—defined as the 'critical period'—is speculative. While people with first-episode psychosis (FEP) appear at greatest risk of relapse during this period, timeline for remission and subsequent relapse of symptoms is variable. Still, during this period, there are a number of key interventions that have been shown to reduce the risk of relapse.

Guidelines recommend that the first-line treatment for early psychosis is low-dose antipsychotic medication, preferably atypical antipsychotics, using the principle of 'start low, go slow' due to the risk of side effects (Galletly et al., 2016; International Early Psychosis Association Writing Group, 2005). Assessment and treatment should be provided as early as possible in order to reduce DUP.

The early commencement of antipsychotic medication has been effective at reducing risk of subsequent relapse and managing acute distress associated with early psychosis; however, adequate consideration should be given to the adverse side effects of antipsychotic medication. Effective treatment for FEP requires much greater breadth than only treatment of the symptoms of psychosis. Guidelines recommend broad psychosocial interventions be made available, including cognitive behaviour therapy (CBT) not only for symptoms of psychosis but also comorbid depression and anxiety. Programmes should include a variety of support options to develop social skills in order to facilitate recovery, such as groups and social skills training. Vocational interventions are an essential component of effective early intervention services, given the high levels of unemployment for people with early psychosis and challenges returning to the workplace.

Comprehensive early intervention approaches place an equal focus on functional as well as symptomatic recovery.

More recently, consensus statements have been developed that address the complexity arising from the development of psychosis and subsequent treatment. Recent guidelines have been published that outline the best evidence base for treatment of trauma in psychosis (Cragin, Straus, Blacker, Tully, & Niendam, 2017). Some examples of other consensus statements include the Meaningful Lives consensus statement that seeks to set goals for employment and educational outcomes for young people with FEP (International First Episode Vocational Recovery (iFEVR) group, 2010). This is important, as 40%–50% of young people with FEP are unemployed at first contact with services, and this rises dramatically over the first 3 years of illness to 75%–95% (Rinaldi et al., 2010); while 20% of people with FEP have never worked (Killackey, Jackson, & McGorry, 2008; Killackey, Jackson, Gleeson, Hickie, & McGorry, 2006). Lack of education and employment leads to not only significant financial burden but has also been associated with loss of social capital, exacerbation of stressors, and lack of a socially valued role (International First Episode Vocational Recovery (iFEVR) group, 2010). The Meaningful Lives statement outlines goals—along with processes to enable achievement of these goals—to improve education and employment outcomes for people with FEP.

Physical health is another area of great concern, as individuals diagnosed with a psychotic disorder experience expected life spans of 10–25 years less than the general population (Laursen, Munk-Olsen, & Vestergaard, 2012). Contributing factors include antipsychotic medication (De Hert et al., 2011), inequalities in healthcare (Foley & Morley, 2011), and cardiovascular disease risk factors such as lack of exercise, poor diet, weight gain, and high rates of smoking (Parks, Svendsen, Singer, & Foti, 2006). Much of the physical health deterioration occurs soon after initial treatment with antipsychotic medication (Alvarez-Jimenez et al., 2008), and comprehensive treatment programs for early psychosis should aim to address physical health concurrently with mental health concerns in order to prevent weight gain and promote healthy lifestyles (Gates, Killackey, Phillips, & Alvarez-Jimenez, 2015). Similar to the Meaningful Lives consensus statement, in 2013 the International Physical Health in Youth Working Group published the *Healthy Active Lives: Keeping the Body in Mind in Youth with Psychosis* consensus statement addressing the issue of physical health in psychosis along with goals and principles to guide treatment (iphYs Writing Group, 2014).

IDENTIFYING AND TREATING PEOPLE AT RISK OF DEVELOPING PSYCHOSIS

How Are People at High Risk of Psychosis Identified?

Over the years, a number of approaches have been used to try to identify those at increased risk of developing psychosis. An early approach was the so called 'high-risk' approach. In this approach, a number of studies followed cohorts of children who had family members with psychotic illness (Orygen Youth Health Research Centre, 2010). These cohorts were often followed for very long periods. However, because the risk conferred by genetic association is small, the rate of transition to psychotic illness of the cohort members was also small. While this is an approach that is interesting from an epidemiological and phenomenological point of view, it is not a feasible approach for identification and early intervention. This is for two key reasons. Firstly, it will not identify the majority of people who will develop psychotic illness. Secondly, the time frame over which people need to be followed (often up to 30 years) is not practical. Additionally, there are ethical problems about the potential labelling of people as being at risk when most are unlikely to develop a psychotic illness.

In order to modify this approach further, subsequent studies focused in on those who were adolescent and young adult offspring of people with psychotic illness. The reason for this is that the peak age of onset of psychotic illness is from the middle of adolescence through to the late 20s. Thus, this cohort is enhanced for transition to illness within a much shorter timeframe. One such study was the Edinburgh High Risk Study, which followed 163 people at high risk who came into the cohort with a mean age of 21. Over 2.5 years of follow up, 20 (12.2%) of these people developed a psychotic disorder (Johnstone, Ebmeier, Miller, Owens, & Lawrie, 2005). While this approach reduced the window in which a cohort needed to be followed, with 87% of the cohort not developing psychosis it does not concentrate risk sufficiently to reduce false positives and make this a feasible screening method for clinical prevention. In order to identify a feasible cohort for prevention and early intervention, there is a need to more accurately identify the prodrome prospectively rather than retrospectively.

Three approaches to this have been developed: psychosis proneness, basic symptoms, and ultra-high risk.

Psychosis Proneness

This was a concept pioneered by Chapman and Chapman (Chapman & Chapman, 1987; Chapman, Chapman, Kwapil, Eckblad, & Zinser, 1994). The idea of psychosis proneness was that those who experienced attenuated psychotic symptoms or who experienced infrequent isolated symptoms, as well as those who experienced social and physical anhedonia or who were impulsive were more likely to experience psychosis. In an early report, they noted that of 162 people followed over 2.5 years 3 had developed psychosis (Chapman &

Chapman, 1987). In their larger research, they followed 508 people over 10 years and found that those who had scored higher on perceptual abnormalities and magical thinking were more likely to have developed psychosis (Chapman et al., 1994). However, the actual number who developed illness was only 14 out of the 508 (2.8%). In part, this was because the research recruited college students. It is now well known from other research that psychotic-like experiences (e.g. hearing voices or noises that others don't hear) without experiencing psychosis is not uncommon in general community samples (Johns et al., 2014). This dilutes the utility of using general population groups to identify people at clinical risk, even with the addition of anhedonia. Thus, because of the low rate of true positives, the psychosis proneness approach is not sufficient to base early intervention or prevention approaches on.

Basic Symptoms

Basic symptoms are subtle, subjective disturbances in mental processes experienced in all stages of psychotic disorder.

The Basic Symptoms approach was developed in German-speaking countries (Frauke Schultze-Lutter & Theodoridou, 2017). Basic symptoms are subjectively experienced abnormalities in areas such as cognition, perception, and attention. A tool was developed to measure the basic symptoms called the Schizophrenia Prediction Instrument Adult version (SPI-A) (Schultze-Lutter, Addington, Ruhrmann, & Klosterkoetter, 2007). In order to capture the developmental aspects for younger people, a second tool, the Schizophrenia Prediction Instrument for Children and Youth (SPI-CY) (Schulze-Lutter, Marshall, & Koch, 2012) was developed. Basic symptoms approaches show a transition rate to psychosis over 9.6 years of 49% and over 1 year of 24% (Klosterkotter, Hellmich, Steinmeyer, & Schultze-Lutter, 2001). It is important to note that the subjectively experienced element of these symptoms is very important. Many of these experiences would not be observable at their earliest stages to other people. In this way, the basic symptoms differ from some of the observable phenomena such as reduced functioning that form the ultra-high risk criteria. These criteria are used to identify people at risk of developing psychosis in a number of, mainly, German speaking countries (Fusar-Poli et al., 2013).

Ultra-High Risk

The ultra-high risk (UHR) approach seeks to identify people at high risk of developing psychosis over the next 12 months. This timeframe indicates a need for intervention but requires a high risk to be both feasible and ethical. UHR approaches acknowledge that there are a number of pathways to developing risk for psychosis and so seek to develop categories of risk and determine membership of a risk group based on a combination of state and trait risk factors. This concept was originally developed by Alison Yung and others in Melbourne (Fusar-Poli et al., 2013); it builds on the idea of multiple types of risk and combines elements such as genetic risk, with observable symptoms such as decline in functioning. This variability led to a number of categories of people who could meet criteria for being at ultra-high risk (see Box 24.2).

Box 24.2 Ultra-High-Risk Criteria Groups

1. Experiencing subthreshold positive symptoms that are not severe or persistent enough to be regarded as evidence of sustained psychosis and which would not be sufficient to meet a diagnostic threshold for disorder.
2. Brief Limited Intermittent Psychotic Symptoms (BLIPS). BLIPS are episodes of psychosis that resolve spontaneously within 7 days.
3. Those who have a first- or second-degree relative with any psychotic disorder and who themselves have experienced a 30% decline in functioning over the last 12 months (as measured on scales such as the Social and Occupational Functioning Assessment Scale; SOFAS).

A number of scales have been developed to assess UHR status. These include the Comprehensive Assessment of At Risk Mental State (CAARMS) (Yung et al., 2005), the Structured Interview for Prodromal Syndromes (SIPS) and the Scale of Prodromal Symptoms (SOPS) (Miller et al., 2003), and the Basel Screening Instrument for Psychosis (BSIPS) (Riecher-Rossler et al., 2007). Initial use of the UHR criteria found 12-month transition rates of 34.6% (Yung, Phillips, Yuen, & McGorry, 2004). More recent research has seen lower transition rates, but a large metaanalyses found that independent of the measurement tool used, membership of the UHR group conferred a risk of transition to psychosis of 18% by 6 months, 22% by 12 months, 29% by 2 years, and 36% by 3 years (Fusar-Poli et al., 2012). While still not perfect, the UHR paradigm allows for the identification of a group who have an indicated need for intervention. While there have been some criticisms of the UHR concept (Castle, 2012), other concepts that are accepted in physical medicine have a much lower rate of transition to illness. For example, the prediabetes risk state will result in only 5%–10% of people developing diabetes in a 12-month period (Tabak, Herder, Rathmann, Brunner, & Kivimaki, 2012). Further the threshold for action in physical medicine is lower too. In cardiovascular medicine with only a 7.5% risk of heart attack in a 10-year period, current guidelines recommend the initiation of statin treatment to manage high cholesterol (Stone et al., 2014). With a 22%, 12-month transition rate, UHR criteria are more than the equal of identifying a high-risk group in other areas of medicine. The question that then remains is how to treat this group to manage the risk. In the next section, we will look at the kind of interventions provided for the UHR group.

How Are People at High Risk of Psychosis Treated and What Have Been the Results?

There have been three main approaches to the treatment of those in the UHR group. These have been psychological interventions, interventions that involve antipsychotic medication, and interventions that involve novel agents such as omega-3 polyunsaturated fatty acid (PUFA).

Omega-3 PUFA, found in fish oil, is a dietary supplement that has been used to treat a number of medical conditions. A promising trial conducted in Vienna found that among 81 participants who were assessed as being at ultra-high risk for psychosis, those randomised to a condition in which they were treated with fish oil ($n = 41$) for 12 weeks had a significantly lower rate of transition to psychosis over 12 months than those who received a placebo ($n = 40$) (Amminger, Schäfer, Papageorgiou, et al., 2010). In the fish oil group, 2 people transitioned to psychosis compared to 11 people in the placebo group. This study indicated that a low-risk biological intervention might be able to prevent transition to psychosis. The same group followed up the participants of their original trial after 6.7 years. In the interim, a further 2 people in the fish oil group had developed psychosis compared to a further 5 people in the placebo group (Amminger, Schäfer, Schlögelhofer, Klier, & McGorry, 2015). Further, the fish oil group was functioning better and had less other psychopathology than the placebo group (Amminger et al., 2015). However, attempts to replicate this study in larger samples have not shown benefits for fish oil (McGorry, Nelson, Markulev, et al., 2017). There is a need for further research to understand if fish oil or other novel agents might be able to help prevent the transition to psychosis. The attraction of such agents is that they are easy to administer, tend to have high acceptability to clients, are nonstigmatised and widely available. If they are shown to be effective, research showing how they prevent transition to psychosis may be able to shed light on the process of illness onset.

Antipsychotic medication has also been used to prevent transition to psychosis in research (Deas et al., 2016; van der Gaag et al., 2013). These studies have used a range of second-generation antipsychotic medications. In general, these studies have found that there is a decreased rate of transition to psychosis in the groups that have been prescribed medication compared to those in control groups (van der Gaag et al., 2013). However, there are also a number of issues with the use of antipsychotic medication in this population that should be considered. For example, side effects of these medications are common and can be distressing for those taking them. In the context of a group in which best prediction indicates only ¼ to 1/3 are likely to transition to a psychotic disorder, the ethics of exposing people who may have never developed the illness to these medications needs to be considered. Network metaanalyses in which different treatments can be compared to each other show that there is no advantage of medication above psychological treatments (Davies et al., 2018), which raises further the ethical questions about prescription of antipsychotic medication before the onset of threshold psychotic disorder.

Finally, psychological interventions have been used to treat people at high risk of psychosis, which tend to take a cognitive behavioural approach. These interventions include elements familiar to any practitioner of Cognitive Behavioural Therapy (CBT)—engagement, formulation development, goal setting, identifying, judging, and evaluating core beliefs and behavioural experiments (Morrison et al., 2004). Some have, in addition, included psychoeducation about some of the biological processes of psychotic illness as well as specific modules targeting the development of paranoid thinking (van der Gaag et al., 2012). CBT interventions have shown to be effective in repeated studies and metaanalyses (van der Gaag et al., 2013), and are a lower risk intervention than medication. There may also be wider benefit in that many people who are at high risk and who would not in any case have developed psychosis, do present with other mental health problems such as depression or anxiety. The formulation-driven approach of CBT is ideal for addressing these other presenting problems. However, there may be some stigma attached to receiving CBT as it is usually administered in a mental health setting and is not seen as a general health intervention in the way that a supplement such as fish oil may be.

Overall there is evidence for the ability of early intervention services to prevent transition to psychosis in some cases. While there are now a number of clinics set up to provide these services in many countries, there is still a need to refine our knowledge around both more accurate identification of those at risk and understanding which intervention will work best for which individual.

IS EARLY INTERVENTION IN PSYCHOSIS EFFECTIVE?

Guidelines make specific recommendations about treatments and interventions that should be implemented for early psychosis, and generally these are made because those interventions have been found to be effective at reducing, eliminating, or minimising the harm that accrues from either withholding or not having access to treatment. However, an important question needs to be asked—how is treatment determined to be 'effective', and by who? A purely medical, symptom-focused approach may evaluate symptom alleviation or reduced hospitalisation as outcomes of effectiveness in treatment. A broader client-centred approach might encompass aspects of recovery and functional recovery. The recovery framework is a peer-led movement, by and for people with mental illness that grew in the early 1990s (see Chapter 5). The guiding principles of recovery-oriented care emphasise 'gaining and retaining hope, understanding of ones abilities and limitations, engagement in an active life, personal autonomy, social identity, meaning and purpose in life, and a positive sense of self' (Department of Health and Ageing, 2013) (p. 10). When taking these broader concepts into account, evaluation of effectiveness might be more elusive. Maybe a starting point for effectiveness then is whether programs for early psychosis address the goals and concerns of consumers of these services, and people with psychosis more broadly. When asked about their priorities, young people with psychosis list in order of preference that what they would like out of treatment is employment, education, relationships, housing, and health (Ramsay et al., 2011). Any analysis of effectiveness should therefore consider both 'medical' and 'functional' recovery outcomes as important, along with interactions between the two.

The latest Cochrane review published in 2014 evaluated the effectiveness of various components of early intervention services (Marshall & Rathbone, 2014). It identified a total of 18 randomised controlled trials (RCTs) of sufficient quality to include in the review. However, metaanalyses were inappropriate due to the heterogeneity of studies included. The authors identified that overall, phase-specific treatments for people with FEP may help with employment outcomes through individual placement support, and that family therapy is an important component of treatment (Marshall & Rathbone, 2014). A further systematic review and metaanalysis by Alvarez-Jimenez, Parker, Hetrick, McGorry, and Gleeson (2011) examined whether specialised early intervention services were able to limit relapse of a second episode. They found evidence that compared to treatment as usual, specialised services were effective at preventing relapse in the first 2 years after psychosis onset.

Two landmark studies of early intervention services include the Lambeth Early Onset (LEO) Team in London, and OPUS Trial from Scandinavia. In 2004, the LEO team reported an RCT of 144 people with FEP (nonaffective) who were randomised to either specialised care with assertive outreach and evidence-based biopsychosocial interventions, or standard care delivered by community mental health teams (Craig et al., 2004). Compared to standard care, those receiving specialised care were less likely to relapse, had fewer hospital admissions, and were less likely to drop out of the study, although relapse was no longer significant when controlling for sex, previous psychotic episodes, and ethnicity. The OPUS trial is the largest RCT to date ($N = 547$) investigating whether specialised treatment for first-episode schizophrenia was more effective than standard treatment, with psychotic symptoms the primary outcome measure. At 1- and 2-year follow up, specialised early intervention services led to improved positive and negative symptoms of psychosis compared to standard treatment, but also reported lower substance use, better treatment adherence, and more satisfaction with treatment (Petersen et al., 2005). However, although these were both important studies showing short-term benefits of early intervention services, they both found that long-term follow-up at 5 years indicated no benefit in relation to readmission rates or length of hospital admission (Gafoor et al., 2010) or for psychotic symptoms (Bertelsen et al., 2008). A recent metaanalysis also indicated that specialised early intervention services did *not* substantially improve the odds ratio for experiencing a relapse compared to standard care at any of 9-months, 24-months, or 10-years (Fusar-Poli, McGorry, & Kane, 2017).

These findings call into question whether or not early intervention services fulfil their remit. As discussed, the model rests on the assumptions that prevention of progression through stages of psychosis is possible through specialised services that provide effective biopsychosocial intervention, and that reduction in DUP is predictive of better outcomes (Killackey & Yung, 2007). While there appears to be good evidence that DUP is related to poorer long-term outcomes in schizophrenia (Penttila, Jaaskelainen, Hirvonen, Isohanni, & Miettunen, 2014), it has been questioned if reduced DUP is related to reduced relapse (Alvarez-Jimenez et al., 2012) and functional outcomes (Bosanac, Patton, & Castle, 2010), and recently whether early intervention services are even able to reduce DUP (Oliver et al., 2018). There does not yet appear to be sufficient evidence that early intervention services lead to better long-term outcomes compared to standard care based on above evidence. However, this is likely not because the concept of early intervention is flawed, but because most early intervention services (and those evaluated earlier), are only provided for approximately 2 years after entry into those services. It is likely that for benefits to persist, early intervention services need to be provided for up to 5 years, given this appears to be the 'critical' period where risk of relapse is greatest (Fusar-Poli et al., 2017).

While a purely medical and symptom focused approach indicates it is questionable that 2-year treatment is sufficient to reduce risk of relapse, functional outcomes are also important. A recent systematic review of the literature examining specialised early intervention services found that importantly these services are related to greater patient satisfaction (Petersen et al., 2005) and improved personal well-being, including sense of purpose, motivation, curiosity, and emotional engagements (Kane et al., 2016). Vitally, these improvements also led to better quality of life, involvement in school and work, and reduced burden to family. These findings lend evidence to early intervention services as actually addressing the needs that young people with psychosis identify as being important, while also being consistent with recovery principles.

Despite antipsychotic medication being the first-line treatment for psychosis, questions remain regarding the potential iatrogenic effects of ongoing antipsychotic treatment after an initial episode. While there is good evidence that early discontinuation increases the risk of subsequent relapse of psychosis compared to continued treatment (Alvarez-Jimenez, Priede, et al., 2012), a Dutch study (Wunderink, Nieboer, Wiersma, Sytema, & Nienhuis, 2013) led by Lex Wunderink suggests that early discontinuation may be related to improved functional outcomes in the long term. Given the most important outcomes identified by consumers of early intervention services include functional outcomes related to education and employment, whether antipsychotic medication administered beyond the point of remission actually aids or hinders functional outcomes is vital to establishing effectiveness. The Wunderink study found that for inpatients who were assigned to an early discontinuation condition, despite increased relapse at 2-year follow-up, at 7 years they experienced twice the 'recovery' and 'functional' remission of those in maintenance treatment, defined as >6-months symptomatic and functional remission at 7-year follow up. Functional remission implies proper social functioning in the domains of everyday life and this was evaluated using the social functioning scale.

IMPLEMENTING EARLY PSYCHOSIS SERVICES: 3 CASE STUDIES

Australia

Australia was a pioneer of early intervention in psychosis (Killackey, Nelson, & Yung, 2008) with the establishment of the EPPIC service in 1992 following on from earlier work dating back to the mid 1980s (Killackey, Nelson, et al., 2008). Despite this, and while there have been a number of stand-alone early psychosis services, it took 25 years for the emergence of a national early psychosis program providing a consistent model of care across the country.

Box 24.3 Components of Care in the Australian National Early Psychosis Model

1. Community Education and Awareness
2. Easy Access to Service
3. Home-based Care and Assessment
4. Continuing Care Case Management
5. Medical Treatments
6. Psychological Interventions
7. Functional Recovery
8. Mobile Outreach
9. Group Programs
10. Family Program and Family Peer Support
11. Youth Participation and Peer Support Program
12. Partnerships
13. Workforce Development
14. Ultra-High-Risk Detection and Care

In 2010 the National Advisory Council on Mental Health commissioned a feasibility report on an Australian early psychosis system. The ensuing report (Orygen Youth Health Research Centre, 2011) recommended a comprehensive early psychosis service, with one service per million population (20 services at that time) providing care for up to 5 years.

Significant public advocacy and support (e.g. see https://youtu.be/ne19036MyKU) led the Federal Government to commit $244 Million dollars to establish a 16-centre national system in partnership with States that would have to provide matched funding. Agreement with the states was not able to be reached and in 2013 the federal government directly funded 9 services. Currently 6 of those services are established and have a current caseload (September 2018) of nearly 2500 young people. These services are still building their case load.

A specific model (Hughes et al., 2014; Stavely, Hughes, Pennell, Mcgorry, & Purcell, 2013) is prescribed for these services in which they provide 14 components of care. These are shown in Box 24.3. Two further components of care (Access to streamed youth-friendly inpatient care, and, Access to youth-friendly subacute beds) are not funded through the model and are in some places provided through partnerships with state-based inpatient services. As a consequence of having a defined model, a fidelity scale has also been developed (Killackey, 2014, 2016), which has aided implementation and consistency of service offering across the country.

England

Following the Australian example, a number of early psychosis services were developed in parts of England in the mid-1990s. Following a change in government in 1997, an increasing evidence base and public advocacy by organisations such as Rethink, early intervention became a policy priority (McDaid, Park, Iemmi, Adelaja, & Knapp, 2016). In an initial funding commitment, 32 early psychosis services were established across England. Following further evidence development, advocacy and demand, more funding was committed, and the eventual number of services developed across England grew to 150. Services are provided to over 10,000 people with early psychosis each year (Rethink Mental Illness, 2014). English early psychosis services typically provide medical, psychological, and social treatment, with an increasing number also being cognisant of the physical health needs of young people presenting with psychosis.

A number of other policy changes have impacted on the provision of early psychosis services in England. Firstly, early psychosis intervention was included in the National Institute for Health and Care Excellence (NICE) guidelines for the treatment of psychosis and schizophrenia (National Collaborating Centre for Mental Health, 2014). The NICE guidelines across all medical conditions indicate treatment that should be provided for certain conditions through the NHS. On-the-ground-reports, however, suggest that funding is not always provided to enable services to meet their commitments to provide care in concordance with NICE guidelines (Gilburt, 2018; Rethink Mental Illness, 2014). In response to the disparity between physical and mental healthcare, a policy called Parity of Esteem was adopted. This sets out the expectation that people with mental illness receive timely access to evidence-based interventions in the same way that people with physical health do. Reports about progress towards implementing this policy indicate that there is a way to go before it can be said to have been achieved (Gilburt, 2018). One of the limiting factors is the creation of a skilled workforce to meet demand.

A further threat to early psychosis services in England has been a lack of ring-fenced funding for the services. In other words, the local authority that commissions health services through the NHS has the discretion about how to spend money. Consequently, many services have reducing or fluctuating funding (Rethink Mental Illness, 2014), while some services have closed or been absorbed into general community mental health teams (McDaid et al., 2016). Despite these challenges, England has arguably the largest early psychosis program in the world.

United States

As opposed to England and Australia, the United States has a very different health system, and prior to the Affordable Care Act in 2009 obtaining health insurance was difficult for many people with mental health conditions (Dixon, Goldman, Srihari, & Kane, 2018). With some exceptions such as Oregon Early Assessment and Support Alliance (EASA), most early psychosis services in the United States have been associated with University Clinics, or directly funded by research, even though services are provided to the community. More recently following the NIMH-funded Recovery After an Initial Episode of Schizophrenia (RAISE) studies (Dixon et al., 2015; Kane et al., 2015, 2016) there has been a great development of community-based services for people with first-episode psychosis developing. There has also been some allocation of federal funding that has encouraged the growth of early intervention services (Dixon et al., 2018), but there is a need for more local and state funding to assist these services to further develop. Some states such as Oregon and New York have invested in disseminating the model and it is to be hoped that as success is seen in these areas, pressure will come on other states to support the development of their own local early psychosis programs based on the models developed through the RAISE projects and other international evidence.

Challenges in Implementing Early Intervention Services

The three case studies illustrate a number of common challenges. The first is funding. Many adult mental health systems internationally are underfunded and have adapted to manage acuity where they don't have the resources to focus on recovery. Early intervention is a completely recovery-oriented model and requires engagement with those with psychosis for a prolonged period. Despite many analyses that show this is actually more economic than alternate models of care provision (McDaid et al., 2016; Mihalopoulos et al., 2012; Mihalopoulos, Harris, Henry, Harrigan, & McGorry, 2009), including in the American context (Rosenheck et al., 2016), many policy makers continue to preference the provision of beds over community-based, recovery-oriented care. It is also possible that the same discrimination towards mental ill health that led to the need for policies, such as parity of esteem in the United Kingdom, underpin the lack of engagement with evidence-based funding in mental health.

A further challenge raised in all three situations is work force. The challenge around work force is twofold. Firstly, if a new sector is created in a service system, there is a need for more psychologists, social workers, nurses, OTs, psychiatrists, and other disciplines to staff it. Growth in these workforces requires support and takes time. The second workforce challenge is for workers to come to services with an optimistic, recovery-oriented mind-set. Workers from traditional mental health settings may have (unconsciously) taken on the often pessimistic belief in the inevitability of decline that is found in many underresourced services that only focus on the management of acuity and relapse.

A great opportunity revealed in the case studies is the recruitment of the public as allies in the demand for reform of mental health and a focus on early intervention and recovery. In both the English and Australian examples, public advocacy was crucial to achieving policy outcomes. Mental health has often been removed from the community, even though broadly it touches nearly everyone. Workers in mental health as well as being clinicians and researchers might also wish to advocate for mental health, whether the opportunity is with friends and neighbours, or with politicians and policy makers.

A final issue to consider is that there is benefit in having a model to establish a service with. This allows for services in different areas of a region/state/country to provide similar levels of care, as well as allowing those developing a service to measure which areas of service they have done well and in which areas they should focus improvement. The International Early Psychosis Service has recently looked at international fidelity scales to support service development (Addington et al., 2018).

FAMILY AND CARERS

Involvement of family and carers is a key component of treatment in early intervention services. The Early Psychosis Declaration notes that early intervention services with high-level resources should provide family and key supports of people with early psychosis with services appropriate to their needs, and that early engagement of families and close friends is a determinant of effectiveness (Bertolote & McGorry, 2005). Guidelines invariably recommend family intervention as receiving some of the highest-level evidence and support (Galletly et al., 2016; Orygen Youth Health Research Centre, 2010). Within the Australian context, 'family' is considered to be a broad term that includes parents, siblings, partners, carers, extended family members, and close friends. The involvement of family should occur, where possible, from the beginning of assessment and into treatment.

Engaging family should be prioritised during assessment both for their own sake, but also because they can be partners in care (Orygen Youth Health Research Centre, 2010). Involving family for their own sake is vital to managing family responses to a relative developing psychosis. Having a family member experience FEP and subsequently accessing treatment can be traumatic not just for the individual, but also for family members. Partnering with families can serve to minimise trauma and develop shared understanding of what is happening. It should also be emphasised that family interventions for early psychosis might be quite different than for people with chronic schizophrenia (Askey, Gamble, & Gray, 2007). Family may experience a sense of loss and grief associated with relative developing early psychosis most often during early adulthood, interrupting developmental and occupational trajectories (Day, Starbuck, & Petrakis, 2017). Furthermore, family members can experience stigma, embarrassment, isolation, loss of mastery and control, decreased self-worth, and also have their own vocational trajectories disrupted (Bibou-Nakou, Dikaiou, & Bairactaris, 1997).

Family work during the assessment phase typically includes psychoeducation regarding psychosis, its treatment and prognosis, alongside developing a shared understanding of the family explanatory models for psychosis. Assessment with family might also include examination of the impact of psychosis on individual family members, establishing family strengths and coping strategies, and reviewing how they manage stress. Australian guidelines recommend that all families should be provided with a family peer support worker who can assist in providing information and emotional support, especially where the consumer does not want family involvement in their treatment (ORYGEN Youth Health, 2010). Another important aspect of family assessment includes a review of the patterns of communication, as families high in expressed emotion—particularly critical comments—have been associated with increased rates of relapse (Alvarez-Jimenez et al., 2012).

Various specific forms of family interventions have been developed for treatment. These have included therapies that focus on psychoeducation only—either individually or in multifamily groups—and more varied interventions, including relapse prevention and early warning signs monitoring, stress management, communication skills training (primarily to address high expressed emotion), problem solving skills and affect regulation. More structured programs have included CBT for relapse prevention (Gleeson et al., 2010). This particular program, for example, included five phases of therapy, including assessment and engagement, assessment of family communication, burden and coping, psychoeducation regarding relapse risk, and review of early warning signs and documentation of relapse prevention planning.

While family interventions in chronic schizophrenia have a well-established evidence base, findings for early psychosis interventions have been more equivocal (Onwumere, Bebbington, & Kuijper, 2011). A widely cited study by Linszen and colleagues (Linszen et al., 1996) found that for families already low in expressed emotion, interventions that target expressed emotion may in fact make outcomes worse. Alvarez-Jiménez et al. conducted a systematic review and metaanalysis of psychosocial interventions in early psychosis to prevent the second episode, with family intervention included in their analysis (Alvarez-Jimenez et al., 2011). They noted that pooled treatment effects of 2 trials indicated that family interventions were not significantly effective for preventing relapse in young FEP patients. However, it was also noted that there was very limited research in the area and contrasting results. Given the robust evidence in later phases, the authors note it was both surprising there has been a lack of RCTs for early psychosis, but also that there is good theoretical potential for these interventions to prevent relapse. It may be that longer family interventions are needed for clinical benefits in FEP patients. Similarly, an alternate systematic review and metaanalysis noted that although family interventions were effective at reducing risk of relapse or hospital admission compared to standard care at the end of treatment, this was not evident at 2-year follow-up(Bird et al., 2010).

A more recent study found that an intensive family intervention was associated with greater improvements (over 12 months) in family burden and caregiving experience, reduced severity of psychotic symptoms, and duration of re-hospitalisation (Chien, Thompson, Lubman, & McCann, 2016). Similarly, Gleeson et al. (2010) found that compared to treatment as usual, families randomised to relapse prevention therapy reported less stress associated with negative symptoms of their relatives, and increased opportunities to make a positive contribution to their care. However, they did not find any significant differences in expressed emotion or critical comments between groups. There is certainly more need for studies examining the effectiveness of family interventions both in preventing relapse and in determining whether they address the specific needs of the family.

EARLY INTERVENTION SERVICE TEAMS AND THE PLACE OF PSYCHOLOGISTS

Individuals with early psychosis require complex assessment, treatment, and intervention approaches to effectively reduce the distress and disability that can accrue. As such, treatment centres will typically provide assertive case management, medication, individual or group psychotherapy, supported employment and education services, and family intervention as support (Heinssen et al., 2014). A comprehensive biopsychosocial evidence-based approach to treating a young person with FEP requires a treating team with capacity to address distressing symptoms, and maintain/regain educational, vocational, and social development. Typically, the primary treating teams comprise a case manager with a background in clinical psychology, social work, occupation therapy, or mental health nursing. The case manager works with a psychiatrist or psychiatric registrar who is under the supervision of a consultant psychiatrist (Hughes et al., 2014). The case manager acts as the primary contact for the young person and their family to provide individually tailored treatment designed to match the stage of illness. Case managers provide support with psychoeducation, relapse prevention, CBT for psychosis and comorbidity, along with linking to other specialist services for housing, drug and alcohol, educational, vocational, financial, and legal assistance.

Working alongside the primary treating team in a comprehensive early psychosis service could also be a variety of other specialists. Guidelines recommend that individual placement and vocational support is provided (Galletly et al., 2016). Furthermore, early psychosis services should address not just the mental health and vocational needs of individuals with psychosis, but also physical health (Gates et al., 2015; iphYs Writing Group, 2014). For example, following the pioneering work of the Bondi Early Psychosis Service in Sydney, the Early Psychosis Prevention and Intervention Centre (EPPIC) in Melbourne provides young people with access to dieticians and exercise physiologists. EPPIC also provides consumers with the opportunity to attend group programs to reduce social isolation and improve confidence, self-esteem, anxiety, and symptom management (Hughes et al., 2014). While family intervention might be conducted by case managers themselves, specific family workers also assist where complex family presentations exist. In addition, family peer support workers who have a lived experience of a young person treated for early psychosis provide a key role in supporting families (Hughes et al., 2014).

With such a diverse range of expertise and experience in multidisciplinary teams, what then is the role of a clinical psychologist and neuropsychologist as a research-practitioner? Clinically, cognitive deficits are a common experience that can start well before onset of FEP. Psychologists and neuropsychologists have unique capacity to administer cognitive assessments that can be useful for diagnostic clarification in the assessment phase, but also in developing a more nuanced formulation of a young person's skills and deficits that can aid in treatment (Galletly et al., 2016). In fact, EPPIC has recently employed a neuropsychologist to conduct cognitive assessments for more complex and specialised cases.

From a treatment perspective, clinical psychologists generally receive in-depth training in therapies such as CBT. CBT is one of the key evidence-based therapeutic approaches in working with young people with psychosis that has been used to effectively manage distress and severity of psychotic symptoms (Bird et al., 2010). CBT is also an effective treatment for common comorbid disorders like anxiety, depression, and sleep disturbances in early psychosis. However, one study of CBT for psychosis that focused on psychoeducation, addressing positive symptoms and comorbidities, indicated that an extra degree of expertise may be required when working with people with psychosis compared to other populations (Farhall, Freeman, Shawyer, & Trauer, 2009). The strong foundation of CBT provided in postgraduate training programs for psychologists provides a solid basis for further development of CBT provision in early psychosis.

Early intervention services in many places around the world have grown out of their infancy and are now well established as an essential service for young people experiencing an FEP. Despite this, there are still a range of questions that remain to be answered about the most effective components of treatment. Research is a vital means of developing evidence-based practice. While early intervention services have been effective in the short term at reducing relapse and hospitalisation, further research is required to explore unique methods of prolonging these benefits in the longer term. CBT and family interventions have some evidence for effectiveness, but they are still equivocal at this stage. Training in evaluation of research methods and evidence in clinical psychology and neuropsychology professional training programs is essential to be able to weed out those spurious findings from the meaningful and continue building the body of evidence for effective treatments in early intervention for psychosis.

CONCLUSION

Over the better part of three decades now, early intervention in psychosis services have developed from a small base, to being implemented as standard care for those experiencing the onset of psychosis in a number of countries. A number of elements make this approach to mental health stand out. From the outset, early intervention for psychosis has developed as a clinical-research paradigm in which new findings are translated into practice. This is evident in the development of fidelity scales alongside the expansion of services. Further, early intervention services build on an evidence base towards the goal of symptomatic and functional recovery for young people experiencing psychosis. As such, the valuing and use of specific disciplinary skills is important within an early psychosis model. Clinicians who are most likely to successfully contribute to this field are those who come with an appreciation of the scientist–practitioner approach. Another key difference is that early intervention has always been an area in which advocacy, alongside those with lived experience, for better, more accessible, more evidence-based care, is a key part of early intervention. Again, this requires a skill set of being able to summarise and articulate research, integrate it with clinical and lived experience, and present it to myriad audiences in a convincing way. Finally, early intervention is the application of common sense to an area of severe mental illness. No one should have to wait until they have achieved chronicity and developed disability to get appropriate care.

SELF-DIRECTED LEARNING

Books

Jackson, H. J., & McGorry, P. D. (Eds.). (2009). *The recognition and management of early psychosis: A preventive approach* (2nd ed.). Cambridge: Cambridge University Press.

Fowler, D. F., Garety, P. A., & Kuipers L. (1995). *Cognitive behaviour therapy for psychosis: Theory and practice*. London: Wiley.

Guidelines

NICE Psychosis and Schizophrenia in Adults: Prevention and Management Clinical Guidelines https://www.nice.org.uk/guidance/cg178.

Brief version of Australian Clinical Practice Guidelines for First Episode Psychosis https://www.ranzcp.org/Files/Resources/Publications/CPG/Clinical-Guidelines-for-Early-Psychosis_A-Summary.aspx.

NICE: Implementing the Early Intervention in Psychosis Access and Waiting Time Standard: Guidance https://www.england.nhs.uk/mentalhealth/wp-content/uploads/sites/29/2016/04/eip-guidance.pdf.

First person accounts of psychosis

Trips & Journeys: Personal Accounts of Early Psychosis.

An important collection that symbolises the courage of young people who have directly experienced early psychosis. Available (for a price) here https://www.orygen.org.au/Education-Training/Resources-Training/Resources/Paid/General/Trips-Journeys.

QUIZ QUESTIONS

(1) What are the three groups that describe people at ultra-high-risk?
(2) Are early intervention services effective at reducing the risk of relapse for young people with FEP? How might early intervention services improve these outcomes?
(3) List 3 reasons for including family in treatment for early intervention.
(4) Which of the following (may be more than one) is the best first-line treatment for a young person with ultra-high risk?
  (a) CBT alone
  (b) Antipsychotic medication
  (c) A combination of A & B
  (d) CBT and medication for other disorders as indicated
(5) True or False: Young people with psychosis are at least, if not more, interested in educational and employment outcomes than about their health outcomes?

ANSWERS TO QUIZ QUESTIONS:

1. 1. People with family history and significant functional decline. 2. Those with brief limited intermittent psychotic symptoms. 3. Those experiencing subthreshold symptoms.

2. In the short term (~2 years), two large RCTs have shown that early intervention services are effective at improving psychotic symptoms, substance use, treatment adherence, and treatment satisfaction than standard treatment, but these differences are not maintained at long-term follow-up. Providing early

intervention for up to 5 years of the 'critical period' may improve clinical outcomes.

3. Reasons may include providing family support in response to trauma from psychosis, developing shared understanding of psychosis, providing support for loss and grief, addressing stigma, gaining collateral, supporting families to develop more effective communication, and better clinical outcomes.
4. Both (a) and (d) would be correct.
5. True

References

Addington, D., Birchwood, M., Jones, P., Killackey, E., McDaid, D., Melau, M., et al. (2018). Fidelity scales and performance measures to support implementation and quality assurance for first episode psychosis services. *Early Intervention in Psychiatry*. https://doi.org/10.1111/eip.12684.

Alvarez-Jimenez, M., Gleeson, J. F., Henry, L. P., Harrigan, S. M., Harris, M. G., Killackey, E., et al. (2012). Road to full recovery: Longitudinal relationship between symptomatic remission and psychosocial recovery in first-episode psychosis over 7.5 years. *Psychological Medicine, 42*(3), 595–606. https://doi.org/10.1017/S0033291711001504.

Alvarez-Jimenez, M., Gonzalez-Blanch, C., Crespo-Facorro, B., Hetrick, S., Rodriguez-Sanchez, J. M., Perez-Iglesias, R., et al. (2008). Antipsychotic-induced weight gain in chronic and first-episode psychotic disorders: A systematic critical reappraisal. *CNS Drugs, 22*(7), 547–562.

Alvarez-Jimenez, M., Parker, A. G., Hetrick, S. E., McGorry, P. D., & Gleeson, J. F. (2011). Preventing the second episode: A systematic review and meta-analysis of psychosocial and pharmacological trials in first-episode psychosis. *Schizophrenia Bulletin, 37*(3), 619–630.

Alvarez-Jimenez, M., Priede, A., Hetrick, S., Bendall, S., Killackey, E., Parker, A., et al. (2012). Risk factors for relapse following treatment for first episode psychosis: A systematic review and meta-analysis of longitudinal studie. *Schizophrenia Research, 139*(1), 116–128.

Amminger, G., Schäfer, M. R., Papageorgiou, K., et al. (2010). Long-chain ω-3 fatty acids for indicated prevention of psychotic disorders: A randomized, placebo-controlled trial. *Archives of General Psychiatry, 67*(2), 146–154. https://doi.org/10.1001/archgenpsychiatry.2009.192.

Amminger, G. P., Schäfer, M. R., Schlögelhofer, M., Klier, C. M., & McGorry, P. D. (2015). Longer-term outcome in the prevention of psychotic disorders by the Vienna omega-3 study. *Nature Communications, 6*. https://doi.org/10.1038/ncomms8934.

Askey, R., Gamble, C., & Gray, R. (2007). Family work in first-onset psychosis: A literature review. *Journal of Psychiatric and Mental Health Nursing, 14*(4), 356–365. https://doi.org/10.1111/j.1365-2850.2007.01093.x.

Baird, J., Bell, S., Brabban, A., Burbach, F., Campbell, A., Dodgson, G., … Zoetti, M. (2012). *IRIS guidelines: Early intervention in psychosis iris guidelines update (September)*. Retrieved from https://protect-au.mimecast.com/s/QaN4C91ZVBSnR2Z1soQQ3V?domain=eprints.worc.ac.uk.

Bertelsen, M., Jeppesen, P., Petersen, L., Thorup, A., Ohlenschlaeger, J., le Quach, P., et al. (2008). Five-year follow-up of a randomized multicenter trial of intensive early intervention vs standard treatment for patients with a first episode of psychotic illness: The OPUS trial. *Archives of General Psychiatry, 65*(7), 762–771. https://doi.org/10.1001/archpsyc.65.7.762.

Bertolote, J., & McGorry, P. (2005). Early intervention and recovery for young people with early psychosis: Consensus statement. *British Journal of Psychiatry, 187*(S48), s116–s119. https://doi.org/10.1192/bjp.187.48.s116.

Bibou-Nakou, I., Dikaiou, M., & Bairactaris, C. (1997). Psychosocial dimensions of family burden among two groups of carers looking after psychiatric patients. *Social Psychiatry and Psychiatric Epidemiology, 32*(2), 104–108. https://doi.org/10.1007/bf00788928.

Bird, V., Premkumar, P., Kendall, T., Whittington, C., Mitchell, J., & Kuipers, E. (2010). Early intervention services, cognitive-behavioural therapy and family intervention in early psychosis: Systematic review. *The British Journal of Psychiatry: The Journal of Mental Science, 197*(5), 350–356. https://doi.org/10.1192/bjp.bp.109.074526.

Blea, P., Hayden-Lewis, K. A., Penkin, A., & Roberts, M. (2013). *Practice guidelines for Oregon Early Assessment and Support Alliance (EASA)*. Oregon: EASA.

Bosanac, P., Patton, G. C., & Castle, D. J. (2010). Early intervention in psychotic disorders: Faith before facts? *Psychological Medicine, 40*(3), 353–358.

Castle, D. J. (2012). Is it appropriate to treat people at high-risk of psychosis before first onset?—No. *Medical Journal of Australia, 196*(9), 557. https://doi.org/10.5694/mja12.10669.

Chapman, L. J., & Chapman, J. P. (1987). The search for symptoms predictive of schizophrenia. *Schizophrenia Bulletin, 13*(3), 497–503.

Chapman, L. J., Chapman, J. P., Kwapil, T. R., Eckblad, M., & Zinser, M. C. (1994). Putatively psychosis-prone subjects 10 years later. *Journal of Abnormal Psychology, 103*(2), 171–183.

Chien, W. T., Thompson, D. R., Lubman, D. I., & McCann, T. (2016). A randomized controlled trial of clinician-supported problem-solving bibliotherapy for family caregivers of people with first-episode psychosis. *Schizophrenia Bulletin, 42*(6), 1457–1466.

Couroupis, A., Francey, S., Gregory, K., & Stavely, H. (2016). *Australian clinical guidelines for early psychosis* (2nd ed.). Melbourne: Orygen, National Centre of Excellence in Youth Mental Health.

Cragin, C. A., Straus, M. B., Blacker, D., Tully, L. M., & Niendam, T. A. (2017). Early psychosis and trauma-related disorders: Clinical practice guidelines and future directions. *Frontiers in Psychiatry, 8*. https://doi.org/10.3389/fpsyt.2017.00033.

Craig, T. K., Garety, P., Power, P., Rahaman, N., Colbert, S., Fornells-Ambrojo, M., et al. (2004). The Lambeth Early Onset (LEO) Team: Randomised controlled trial of the effectiveness of specialised care for early psychosis. *British Medical Journal, 329*(7474), 1067.

Davies, C., Cipriani, A., Ioannidis, J. P. A., Radua, J., Stahl, D., Provenzani, U., et al. (2018). Lack of evidence to favor specific preventive interventions in psychosis: A network meta-analysis. *World Psychiatry: Official Journal of the World Psychiatric Association, 17*, 196–209.

Day, K., Starbuck, R., & Petrakis, M. (2017). Family group interventions in an early psychosis program: A re-evaluation of practice after 10 years of service delivery. *The International Journal of Social Psychiatry, 63*(5), 433–438. https://doi.org/10.1177/0020764017710301.

De Hert, M., Correll, C., Bobes, J., Cetkovich-Bakmas, M., Cohen, D., Asai, I., et al. (2011). Physical illness in patients with severe mental disorders. I. Prevalence, impact of medications and disparities in health care. *World Psychiatry: Official Journal of the World Psychiatric Association, 10*(1), 52–77.

De Masi, S., Sampaolo, L., Mele, A., Morciano, C., Cappello, S., Meneghelli, A., & de Girolamo, G. (2008). The Italian guidelines for early intervention in schizophrenia: Development and conclusions. *Early Intervention in Psychiatry, 2*(4), 291–302. https://doi.org/10.1111/j.1751-7893.2008.00091.x.

Deas, G., Kelly, C., Hadjinicolaou, A. V., Holt, C., Agius, M., & Zaman, R. (2016). An update on: Meta-analysis of medical and non-medical treatments of the prodromal phase of psychotic illness in at risk mental states. *Psychiatria Danubina, 28*(Suppl. 1), 31–38.

Department of Health and Ageing. (2013). *A national framework for recovery-oriented mental health services: Guide for practitioners and providers*. Canberra: Common Wealth of Australia.

Dixon, L. B., Goldman, H. H., Bennett, M. E., Wang, Y., McNamara, K. A., Mendon, S. J., et al. (2015). Implementing coordinated specialty care for early psychosis: The RAISE connection program. *Psychiatric Services, 66*(7), 691–698. https://doi.org/10.1176/appi.ps.201400281.

Dixon, L. B., Goldman, H. H., Srihari, V. H., & Kane, J. M. (2018). Transforming the treatment of Schizophrenia in the United States: The RAISE initiative. *Annual Review of Clinical Psychology, 14*, 237–258. https://doi.org/10.1146/annurev-clinpsy-050817-084934.

Ehmann, T., Hanson, L., Yager, J., Dolazell, K., & Gilbert, M. (2010). *Standards and guidelines for early psychosis intervention (EPI) programs.* Vancouver: Province of British Columbia, Ministry of Health Services.

Farhall, J., Freeman, N. C., Shawyer, F., & Trauer, T. (2009). An effectiveness trial of cognitive behaviour therapy in a representative sample of outpatients with psychosis. *The British Journal of Clinical Psychology, 48*(1), 47–62. https://doi.org/10.1111/j.2044-8260.2009.tb00456.x.

Foley, D., & Morley, K. (2011). Systematic review of early cardiometabolic outcomes of the first treated episode of psychosis. *Archiives of General Psychiatry, 68,* 609–616.

Fusar-Poli, P., Bonoldi, I., Yung, A. R., Borgwardt, S., Kempton, M. J., Valmaggia, L., et al. (2012). Predicting psychosis: Meta-analysis of transition outcomes in individuals at high clinical risk. *Archives of General Psychiatry, 69*(3), 220–229. https://doi.org/10.1001/archgenpsychiatry.2011.1472.

Fusar-Poli, P., Borgwardt, S., Bechdolf, A., Addington, J., Riecher-Rössler, A., Schultze-Lutter, F., et al. (2013). The psychosis high-risk state: A comprehensive state-of-the-art review. *JAMA Psychiatry, 70*(1), 107–120. https://doi.org/10.1001/jamapsychiatry.2013.269.

Fusar-Poli, P., McGorry, P. D., & Kane, J. M. (2017). Improving outcomes of first-episode psychosis: An overview. *World Psychiatry: Official Journal of the World Psychiatric Association, 16*(3), 251–265. https://doi.org/10.1002/wps.20446.

Gafoor, R., Nitsch, D., McCrone, P., Craig, T. K., Garety, P. A., Power, P., et al. (2010). Effect of early intervention on 5-year outcome in non-affective psychosis. *The British Journal of Psychiatry: The Journal of Mental Science, 196*(5), 372–376. https://doi.org/10.1192/bjp.bp.109.066050.

Galletly, C., Castle, D., Dark, F., Humberstone, V., Jablensky, A., Killackey, E., et al. (2016). Royal Australian and New Zealand college of Psychiatrists clinical practice guidelines for the management of schizophrenia and related disorders. *Australian and New Zealand Journal of Psychiatry, 50*(5), 410–472. https://doi.org/10.1177/0004867416641195.

Gates, J., Killackey, E., Phillips, L., & Alvarez-Jimenez, M. (2015). Mental health starts with physical health: Current status and future directions of non-pharmacological interventions to improve physical health in first episode psychosis. *Lancet: Psychiatry, 2*(8), 726–742.

Gilburt, H. (2018). *Funding and staffing of NHS mental health providers: Still waiting for parity.* Retrieved from: https://www.kingsfund.org.uk/publications/funding-staffing-mental-health-providers#conclusion.

Gleeson, J. F., Cotton, S. M., Alvarez-Jimenez, M., Wade, D., Crisp, K., Newman, B., et al. (2010). Family outcomes from a randomized control trial of relapse prevention therapy in first-episode psychosis. *The Journal of Clinical Psychiatry, 71*(4), 475–483. https://doi.org/10.4088/JCP.08m04672yel.

Heinssen, R. K., Goldstein, A. B., & Azrin, S. T. (2014). *Evidence-based treatments for first episode psychosis: Components of coordinated specialty care (NIMH white paper).* Bethesda, MD: National Institute of Mental Health.

Hughes, F., Stavely, H., Simpson, R., Goldstone, S., Pennell, K., & McGorry, P. (2014). At the heart of an early psychosis centre: The core components of the 2014 early psychosis prevention and intervention centre model for Australian communities. *Australasian Psychiatry, 22*(3), 228–234. https://doi.org/10.1177/1039856214530479.

International Early Psychosis Association Writing Group. (2005). International clinical practice guidelines for early psychosis. *British Journal of Psychiatry, 187*(S48), s120–s124. https://doi.org/10.1192/bjp.187.48.s120.

International First Episode Vocational Recovery (iFEVR) group. (2010). Meaningful lives: Supporting young people with psychosis in education, training and employment: An international consensus statement. *Early Intervention in Psychiatry, 4*(4), 323–326.

iphYs Writing Group. (2014). *Healthy active lives: Keeping the body in mind in youth with psychosis.* Bondi: International Physical Health in Youth Stream.

Johns, L. C., Kompus, K., Connell, M., Humpston, C., Lincoln, T. M., Longden, E., et al. (2014). Auditory verbal hallucinations in persons with and without a need for care. *Schizophrenia Bulletin, 40*(Suppl. 4), S255–S264. https://doi.org/10.1093/schbul/sbu005.

Johnstone, E. C., Ebmeier, K. P., Miller, P., Owens, D. G., & Lawrie, S. M. (2005). Predicting schizophrenia: Findings from the Edinburgh high-risk study. *The British Journal of Psychiatry: The Journal of Mental Science, 186*, 18–25. https://doi.org/10.1192/bjp.186.1.18.

Kane, J. M., Robinson, D. G., Schooler, N. R., Mueser, K. T., Penn, D. L., Rosenheck, R. A., et al. (2016). Comprehensive versus usual community care for first-episode psychosis: 2-Year outcomes from the NIMH RAISE early treatment program. *The American Journal of Psychiatry, 173*(4), 362–372. https://doi.org/10.1176/appi.ajp.2015.15050632.

Kane, J. M., Schooler, N. R., Marcy, P., Correll, C. U., Brunette, M. F., Mueser, K. T., et al. (2015). The RAISE early treatment program for first-episode psychosis: Background, rationale, and study design. *The Journal of Clinical Psychiatry, 76*(3), 240–246. https://doi.org/10.4088/JCP.14m09289.

Killackey, E. (2014). *Staying true: A plan to measure fidelity in the delivery of early psychosis services in Australia.* Melbourne: Orygen, The National Centre of Excellence in Youth Mental Health.

Killackey, E. (2016). *The EPPIC model integrity tool.* Parkville, Australia: Orygen, The National Centre of Excellence in Youth Mental Health.

Killackey, E., Jackson, H. J., & McGorry, P. D. (2008). Vocational intervention in first-episode psychosis: Individual placement and support v. treatment as usual. *The British Journal of Psychiatry: The Journal of Mental Science, 193*(2), 114–120. https://doi.org/10.1192/bjp.bp.107.043109.

Killackey, E., Nelson, B., & Yung, A. (2008). Early detection and intervention in psychosis in Australia: History, progress and potential. *Clinical Neuropsychiatry, 5*(6), 279–285.

Killackey, E., & Yung, A. R. (2007). Effectiveness of early intervention in psychosis. *Current Opinion in Psychiatry, 20*(2), 121–125. https://doi.org/10.1097/YCO.0b013e328017f67d.

Killackey, E. J., Jackson, H. J., Gleeson, J., Hickie, I. B., & McGorry, P. D. (2006). Exciting career opportunity beckons! Early intervention and vocational rehabilitation in first-episode psychosis: Employing cautious optimism. *The Australian and New Zealand Journal of Psychiatry, 40* (11 – 12), 951–962. https://doi.org/10.1111/j.1440-1614.2006.01918.x.

Klosterkotter, J., Hellmich, M., Steinmeyer, E. M., & Schultze-Lutter, F. (2001). Diagnosing schizophrenia in the initial prodromal phase. *Archives of General Psychiatry, 58*(2), 158–164.

Laursen, T. M., Munk-Olsen, T., & Vestergaard, M. (2012). Life expectancy and cardiovascular mortality in persons with schizophrenia. *Current Opinion in Psychiatry, 25*(2), 83–88. https://doi.org/10.1097/YCO.0b013e32835035ca.

Linszen, D., Dingemans, P., Van der Does, J. W., Nugter, A., Scholte, P., Lenior, R., et al. (1996). Treatment, expressed emotion and relapse in recent onset schizophrenic disorders. *Psychological Medicine, 26*(2), 333–342.

Marshall, M., & Rathbone, J. (2014). Early intervention for psychosis. *Cochrane Database of Systematic Reviews, 6*(6). https://doi.org/10.1002/14651858.CD004718.pub3.

McDaid, D., Park, A.-L., Iemmi, V., Adelaja, B., & Knapp, M. (2016). *Growth in the use of early intervention for psychosis services: An opportunity to promote recovery amid concerns on health care sustainability.* London: Personal Social Services Research Unit/School of Economics and Political Science.

McGorry, P., Edwards, J., Mihalopoulos, C., Harrigan, S. M., & Jackson, H. J. (1996). EPPIC: An evolving system of early detection and optimal management. *Schizophrenia Bulletin, 22*(2), 305–326.

McGorry, P. D., Hickie, I. B., Yung, A. R., Pantelis, C., & Jackson, H. J. (2006). Clinical staging of psychiatric disorders: A heuristic framework for choosing earlier, safer and more effective interventions. *Australian and New Zealand Journal of Psychiatry, 40*(8), 616–622.

McGorry, P. D., Killackey, E., & Yung, A. (2008). Early intervention in psychosis: Concepts, evidence and future directions. *World Psychiatry: Official Journal of the World Psychiatric Association, 7*(3), 148–156.

McGorry, P. D., Nelson, B., Markulev, C., et al. (2017). Effect of ω-3 polyunsaturated fatty acids in young people at ultrahigh risk for psychotic disorders: The neurapro randomized clinical trial. *JAMA Psychiatry, 74*(1), 19–27. https://doi.org/10.1001/jamapsychiatry.2016.2902.

Mihalopoulos, C., Harris, M., Henry, L., Harrigan, S., & McGorry, P. (2009). Is early intervention in psychosis cost-effective over the long term? *Schizophrenia Bulletin*, *35*(5), 909–918. https://doi.org/10.1093/schbul/sbp054.

Mihalopoulos, C., McCrone, P., Knapp, M., Johannessen, J. O., Malla, A., & McGorry, P. (2012). The costs of early intervention in psychosis: Restoring the balance. *The Australian and New Zealand Journal of Psychiatry*, *46*(9), 808–811. https://doi.org/10.1177/0004867412457999.

Miller, T. J., McGlashan, T. H., Rosen, J. L., Cadenhead, K., Cannon, T., Ventura, J., et al. (2003). Prodromal assessment with the structured interview for prodromal syndromes and the scale of prodromal symptoms: Predictive validity, interrater reliability, and training to reliability. *Schizophrenia Bulletin*, *29*(4), 703–715.

Mizuno, M. (2017). *Treatment plans and implementation for early psychosis: Preliminary guidance 2017.* Tokyo: Japanese Society for Early Intervention in Psychosis. http://www.jseip.jp/doc/早期精神病ガイダンス2017.pdf.

Morrison, A. P., French, P., Walford, L., Lewis, S. W., Kilcommons, A., Green, J., et al. (2004). Cognitive therapy for the prevention of psychosis in people at ultra-high risk: Randomised controlled trial. *British Journal of Psychiatry*, *185*, 291–297.

National Collaborating Centre for Mental Health. (2014). *Psychosis and Schizophrenia in adults: The NICE guideline on treatment and management. Updated edition* (p. 2014). London: National Institute for Health and Care Excellence.

Oliver, D., Davies, C., Crossland, G., Lim, S., Gifford, G., McGuire, P., et al. (2018). Can we reduce the duration of untreated psychosis? A systematic review and meta-analysis of controlled interventional studies. *Schizophrenia Bulletin*, *44*(6), 1362–1372. https://doi.org/10.1093/schbul/sbx166.

Onwumere, J., Bebbington, P., & Kuijper, E. (2011). Family interventions in early psychosis: Specificity and effectiveness. *Epidemiology and Psychiatric Sciences*, *20*(2), 113–119. https://doi.org/10.1017/S2045796011000187.

ORYGEN Youth Health. (2010). *The Australian clinical guidelines for early psychosis.* Melbourne: ORYGEN Youth Health Research Centre.

Orygen Youth Health Research Centre (2010). In P. D. McGorry, S. Dodd, R. Purcell, A. Yung, A. Thompson, S. Goldstone, & E. Killackey (Eds.), *Australian clinical guidelines for early psychosis* (2nd ed.). Parkville: Orygen Youth Health Research Centre.

Orygen Youth Health Research Centre. (2011). *Early psychosis feasibility study report. For the National Advisory Council on Mental Health.* Retrieved from: http://www.health.gov.au/internet/main/publishing.nsf/content/C1A49DEC3BC514E5CA25792B00781998/$File/earlypsy.pdf.

Parks, J., Svendsen, D., Singer, P. A., & Foti, M. E. (2006). *Morbidity and mortality in people with serious mental illness (13th technical report).* Alexandria, VA: National Association of State Mental Health Program Directors.

Penttila, M., Jaaskelainen, E., Hirvonen, N., Isohanni, M., & Miettunen, J. (2014). Duration of untreated psychosis as predictor of long-term outcome in schizophrenia: Systematic review and meta-analysis. *The British Journal of Psychiatry: The Journal of Mental Science*, *205*(2), 88–94. https://doi.org/10.1192/bjp.bp.113.127753.

Petersen, L., Jeppesen, P., Thorup, A., Abel, M. B., Ohlenschlaeger, J., Christensen, T. O., et al. (2005). A randomised multicentre trial of integrated versus standard treatment for patients with a first episode of psychotic illness. *BMJ*, *331*(7517), 602. https://doi.org/10.1136/bmj.38565.415000.E01.

Ramsay, C. E., Broussard, B., Goulding, S. M., Cristofaro, S., Hall, D., Kaslow, N. J., et al. (2011). Life and treatment goals of individuals hospitalized for first-episode nonaffective psychosis. *Psychiatry Research, 189*(3), 344–348. pii: S0165-1781(11)00436-7. https://doi.org/10.1016/j.psychres.2011.05.039.

Rethink Mental Illness. (2014). *Lost generation: Why young people with psychosis are being left behind, and what needs to change.* Retrieved from London https://www.rethink.org/media/973932/LOST%20GENERATION%20-%20Rethink%20Mental%20Illness%20report.pdf.

Riecher-Rossler, A., Gschwandtner, U., Aston, J., Borgwardt, S., Drewe, M., Fuhr, P., et al. (2007). The basel early-detection-of-psychosis (FEPSY)-study—Design and preliminary results. *Acta Psychiatrica Scandinavica, 115*(2), 114–125. https://doi.org/10.1111/j.1600-0447.2006.00854.x.

Rinaldi, M., Killackey, E., Smith, J., Shepherd, G., Singh, S. P., & Craig, T. (2010). First episode psychosis and employment: A review. *International Review of Psychiatry, 22*(2), 148–162. https://doi.org/10.3109/09540261003661825.

Rosenheck, R., Leslie, D., Sint, K., Lin, H., Robinson, D. G., Schooler, N. R., et al. (2016). Cost-effectiveness of comprehensive, integrated care for first episode psychosis in the NIMH RAISE early treatment program. *Schizophrenia Bulletin, 42*(4), 896–906. https://doi.org/10.1093/schbul/sbv224.

Schultze-Lutter, F., Addington, J., Ruhrmann, S., & Klosterkoetter, J. (2007). *Schizophrenia proneness instrument, adult version (SPI-A).* Rome: Giovanni Fiorito Editore.

Schultze-Lutter, F., & Theodoridou, A. (2017). The concept of basic symptoms: Its scientific and clinical relevance. *World Psychiatry: Official Journal of the World Psychiatric Association, 16*(1), 104–105. https://doi.org/10.1002/wps.20404.

Schulze-Lutter, F., Marshall, M., & Koch, H. (2012). *Schizophrenia proneness instrument, child and youth version (SPI-CY).* Rome: Giovanni Fiorito Editore.

Stavely, H., Hughes, F., Pennell, K., Mcgorry, P. D., & Purcell, R. (2013). *EPPIC model and service implementation guide.* Melbourne: Oryugen Youth Health Research Centre.

Stone, N. J., Robinson, J. G., Lichtenstein, A. H., Bairey Merz, C. N., Blum, C. B., Eckel, R. H., et al. (2014). 2013 ACC/AHA guideline on the treatment of blood cholesterol to reduce atherosclerotic cardiovascular risk in adults: A report of the American College of Cardiology/American Heart Association Task Force on Practice Guidelines. *Journal of the American College of Cardiology, 63*(25 Pt B), 2889–2934. https://doi.org/10.1016/j.jacc.2013.11.002.

Sullivan, H. (1927). The onset of schizophrenia. *American Journal of Psychiatry, 6*, 105–134.

Tabak, A. G., Herder, C., Rathmann, W., Brunner, E. J., & Kivimaki, M. (2012). Prediabetes: A high-risk state for diabetes development. *Lancet, 379*(9833), 2279–2290. https://doi.org/10.1016/s0140-6736(12)60283-9.

van der Gaag, M., Nieman, D. H., Rietdijk, J., Dragt, S., Ising, H. K., Klaassen, R. M. C., et al. (2012). Cognitive behavioral therapy for subjects at ultrahigh risk for developing psychosis: A randomized controlled clinical trial. *Schizophrenia Bulletin, 38*(6), 1180–1188 [1745–1701 (Electronic)].

van der Gaag, M., Smit, F., Bechdolf, A., French, P., Linszen, D. H., Yung, A. R., et al. (2013). Preventing a first episode of psychosis: Meta-analysis of randomized controlled prevention trials of 12-month and longer-term follow-ups. *Schizophrenia Research, 149*(1–3), 56–62. https://doi.org/10.1016/j.schres.2013.07.004.

Wunderink, L., Nieboer, R. M., Wiersma, D., Sytema, S., & Nienhuis, F. J. (2013). Recovery in remitted first-episode psychosis at 7 years of follow-up of an early dose reduction/discontinuation or maintenance treatment strategy: Long-term follow-up of a 2-year randomized clinical trial. *JAMA Psychiatry, 70*(9), 913–920. https://doi.org/10.1001/jamapsychiatry.2013.19.

Yung, A., & McGorry, P. D. (1996). The prodromal phase of first-episode psychosis: Past and current conceptualizations. *Schizophrenia Bulletin*, *22*(2), 353–370.

Yung, A., Phillips, L. J., McGorry, P. D., McFarlane, C. A., Francey, S., Harrigan, S., et al. (1998). Prediction of psychosis. A step towards indicated prevention of schizophrenia. *British Journal of Psychiatry—Supplementum*, *172*(33), 14–20.

Yung, A., Phillips, L. J., Yuen, H. P., Francey, S. M., McFarlane, C. A., Hallgren, M., et al. (2003). Psychosis prediction: 12-Month follow up of a high-risk ("prodromal") group. *Schizophrenia Research*, *60*(1), 21–32.

Yung, A. R., Phillips, L. J., Yuen, H. P., & McGorry, P. D. (2004). Risk factors for psychosis in an ultra high-risk group: Psychopathology and clinical features. *Schizophrenia Research*, *67*(2–3), 131–142.

Yung, A. R., Yuen, H. P., McGorry, P. D., Phillips, L. J., Kelly, D., Dell'Olio, M., et al. (2005). Mapping the onset of psychosis: The comprehensive assessment of at-risk mental states. *The Australian and New Zealand Journal of Psychiatry*, *39*(11–12), 964–971. https://doi.org/10.1111/j.1440-1614.2005.01714.x.

Definition of Key Terms

Prodrome A period, generally recognised in retrospect, of decline in functioning before crossing the diagnostic threshold of a psychotic illness. The prodrome often includes some experience of non-specific symptoms or low-level psychotic experiences.

Ultra-high risk A term used to describe those who meet one of three criteria indicating that they may be at high risk of transitioning to psychosis within a short (6–12 month) timeframe.

First-episode psychosis The first episode of a psychotic illness in which a diagnostic threshold has been met.

Early warning signs Idiosyncratic behaviours and symptoms that indicate that a psychotic episode may be about to occur.

Functional recovery Recovery that is focused more on the individual's capacity to function—i.e. engage in age-appropriate functional behaviours such as attend school or work, participate in their communities, have friendships and relationships, and have secure housing at a level of independence that they are happy with.

SECTION 5
New Directions in Research and Practice

CHAPTER 25

Beyond Belief—New Approaches to the Treatment of Paranoia

Philippa Anne Garety*,†, Thomas Ward*,†, Mar Rus-Calafell‡,§
*Department of Psychology, King's College London, Institute of Psychiatry, Psychology & Neuroscience, London, United Kingdom, †South London and Maudsley NHS Foundation Trust, London, United Kingdom, ‡Department of Psychiatry, Oxford University, Oxford, United Kingdom, §Oxford Health NHS Foundation Trust, Oxford, United Kingdom

Key Learning Objectives

- To introduce ways of thinking about 'paranoia' and 'delusions'
- To learn about paranoia as a lived experience
- To enable learning of methods of engagement, assessment, and treatment for therapy
- To learn about digital innovations in psychological assessment and treatment of paranoia
- To introduce SlowMo, a novel blended digital therapy for fears of harm from others

INTRODUCTION

What Is Paranoia?—Some Lived Experiences

> It's fear. I'm fearing people. I would feel humiliated and that adds to the fear. I fear violence. But physical harm heals quickly. The humiliation can take longer - I've got some scars on me from 35 or 40 years... like a wound, a visible wound. Walking down the street is like walking barefoot on glass - you don't want anyone to see you but people are seeing you and knowing you. You can't concentrate. You are feeling invisible pain come from everywhere . . . but when I turn round no-one is there. I'm lost in this world of mine . . . I sometimes think that people could see things inside me . . .

A Clinical Introduction to Psychosis. https://doi.org/10.1016/B978-0-12-815012-2.00025-0

> things I didn't want people to know, things I was ashamed of . . . I don't know if you can imagine it . . . it's like you are screaming, screaming for rest . . . for peace. It's like it's a warzone every moment of the day.
>
> **(Anthony, 54-year-old Black Chinese British)**

> When I'm walking down the road I'm always looking out for this person following me. If I hear screaming or people outside, I think my son is in danger. You feel like everyone is against you. You don't trust no-one, even friends and family. It puts you in a shell.
>
> **(Alex, 30 years old, Black British Caribbean man)**

> I worry about people every day . . . whether people are gonna harm me or shout at me. Being on my own is terrifying sometimes. Sometimes I'll sit in the flat and not go out. [If I do go out] I can't hang around anywhere, I gotta go in, gotta get back. I think people are looking at me and judge me all the time . . . because I have an illness.
>
> **(Joanne, 36 years old, White British)**

> When it was really bad, it was more triggers like body language, eye contacts, things people would say that would relate to the day or week that I'm having . . . and I was thinking . . . how could they know . . . obviously there's some sort of . . . conspiracy? People know what's going on in my life, whether it be there's cameras or somehow someone knows what's inside my head
>
> **(James, 42 years, White British)**

What Is Paranoia?—Common Defining Features on a Continuum

Paranoia refers to the fear that other people intend to cause you harm.

Anthony, Alex, Joanne and James, four service users, are describing here their lived experience of 'paranoia'. As individuals from diverse social and cultural backgrounds, each person's experiences are unique, but they also share some common features. They all experience concerns and worries for their own safety—Anthony tellingly says 'It's like it's a warzone every moment of the day'. There is a strong emphasis on 'fear' regarding harm from others, whether it may be physical harm to themselves or loved ones, or harm to their social well-being or standing. Two of this group (James and Anthony) report an unsettling sense that others can know what is going on in their heads. An added layer of distress comes from the sense that others are *intending* to cause harm. These features—a fear of harm that is intentional—conform to a widely used formal definition of persecutory ideation (Freeman & Garety, 2000). This is our focus in this chapter.

Paranoia is a common symptom of psychosis, but paranoid thinking also occurs in milder forms in the general population.

Fear of harm from others is common in the general population—which of us has not sometimes had 'paranoid' or suspicious thoughts about others, whether known to us or strangers, thinking they might do us some wrong? Research has shown that mild forms of paranoia are present in 20%–30% of an epidemiologically sampled general population: these concerns included 'worries over social inferiority, worries about criticism by others, concerns about being used or hurt and a reluctance to reveal too much in case people used it in adverse ways' (Bebbington et al., 2013). The same researchers found that 10% of the population spend a lot of time wondering whether they could trust their friends or work colleagues, and that 2% thought that some group was plotting to cause them serious harm or injury. Thus, we can think of paranoia as being on a continuum with everyday worries about others—with many people experiencing some concerns and a few having very serious fears, which might be especially strongly held, preoccupying and impacting negatively on everyday life: these serious fears would be likely to meet the criteria for '**persecutory delusions**' (Freeman & Garety, 2000). In the Box 25.1, we consider service users' views of these key terms, 'paranoia' and 'delusion'.

Box 25.1 A Word About Language: the p-word and the d-word

As clinical psychologists, we often face choices about the words we use in the clinic. Are 'paranoia' and 'delusion' helpful words to use? These are terms that some might find stigmatising, unacceptable or inaccurate. We, instead, use the person's own preferred language in the clinic and, for wider audiences, such as in our current research trial where we need a generally acceptable and clear set of terms, we have adopted 'fears of (deliberate) harm from others'. We asked some service users what they think about the words 'paranoia' and 'delusions'. This is what they told us.

> [Paranoia]- When I heard the word I thought "that's a bit much… It doesn't describe me. Now I can kind of accept paranoia as a word - it can sometimes help people to understand. But if people don't understand what it means it can be a painful experience.
> [Delusions] The word is used like an insult. The first time it is used against you it wounds you and then it continues and it stays in the same place wounding you each time.
>
> Anthony

> I think paranoia is a kinder word than delusions. It is more professional than saying "you are thinking things that ain't happening", that is a bit more aggressive. [Delusions] sounds a bit rude, like "you don't understand where a man is coming from". I don't like it. My spirit don't take to it. You need to break it down a bit.
>
> Alex

> The 'paranoia' word scares me sometimes. Because I know that's what it is and what it means…. I don't like it. I didn't understand it at first I would have preferred if I'd been explained to me. Actually I think I looked it up . . . [on the] . . . internet.
>
> Joanne

> Delusions I've heard quite often. As long as the patient is aware of their true meaning then, I don't know if it's helpful, but I think it has a less negative impact . . . it puts some explanation as to what's going on in their mind. Right this is what it is, I can find ways of dealing with and getting through this situation.
>
> James

It is noteworthy that these four service users generally find both the terms paranoia and delusions potentially problematic, and question their use and meanings, though Anthony says 'paranoia' 'can sometimes help people to understand', and James sees that 'delusion' does put 'some explanation as to what is going on in the mind'. Naturally others with lived experienced may have different opinions. However, in our experience, almost all would agree with the key tip for professionals from the same service users (Section 6) to 'Get your attitude right - be thoughtful and respectful'.

Conceptualising Paranoia or 'Fears of Harm From Others'

We all have to consider from time to time whether people might be untrustworthy or hostile to us in some way. Given that fears about others are common, paranoid thoughts can be seen as an understandable response to threat but one which can, in particular circumstances, become excessive and negatively affect a person's life, in the same way as anxious thoughts. Cognitive models offer a framework for understanding these phenomena and pointers to which factors might contribute to the occurrence of clinically relevant distressing paranoid thoughts (or 'delusions'), as opposed to more everyday concerns (Freeman, Garety, Kuipers, Fowler, & Bebbington, 2002; Garety & Freeman, 2013; Garety & Hardy, 2017). These cognitive models in general accept the importance of biological and social levels of explanation, but highlight the particular contribution of psychological mechanisms to the development and persistence of paranoia, involving both emotional and reasoning processes.

Cognitive models of paranoia provide psychological mechanisms linking causal and maintenance factors to subjective experiences and resulting paranoid thoughts.

In these models, it is proposed that subjective experiences, like hearing voices, facilitate certain distressing appraisals when combined with specific reasoning and information processing biases (such as a 'fast thinking' reasoning style); schematic beliefs about the self (e.g. 'I am weak and vulnerable') and others (e.g. 'Other people are hostile and dangerous'); current emotional disturbance (e.g. anxiety or depression); and social factors (e.g. isolation and adversity). For example, a person who is stressed, and has a history of being bullied, together with other biopsychosocial vulnerabilities, may conclude that the meaning of the snatches of speech, which they keep hearing, is that neighbours are sending hostile messages through the wall with the goal of upsetting them. Or, a stranger we notice glancing at us in the street may be appraised as 'someone following me in order to cause me harm'. A key point here is that it is not the experiences in themselves, such as hearing fragmentary voices, or noticing a person looking at us, but the way in which we appraise, or make sense of, them that determines their clinical relevance and provides the key focus of psychological therapy; depending on the appraisal, these experiences may come to be viewed as benign (even life-enhancing in the case of some experiences) or alternatively result in beliefs, which are distressing and affect quality of life (Garety & Hardy, 2017; Peters et al., 2016).

How everyday experiences are appraised (or made sense of) contributes to the level of distress associated with paranoia.

A second and important feature of cognitive conceptualisations of 'delusions' is their multidimensionality. Studies of 'delusional beliefs' reveal a range of characteristics, which vary in degree: factor analyses typically identify conviction, distress, preoccupation, and impact on everyday life as key dimensions (Garety & Hemsley, 1987; Haddock, McCarron, Tarrier, & Faragher, 1999; Peters, Joseph, Day, & Garety, 2004).

Are 'Persecutory Delusions' or 'Fears of Harm From Others' Beliefs?

A contested issue is whether the (persecutory) delusion is 'a fixed false belief' (as the psychiatric definitions state). Indeed is it a belief? Cognitive models focus on appraisals of experience, but some have questioned the traditional view of appraisal as a belief about a specific experience, arguing that the appraisals exist before the experience and contribute to determining the experience itself, as so-called 'priors' in a Bayesian view of cognition (Fletcher & Frith, 2009; Woods & Wilkinson, 2017). The attentive reader might have noted that in the foregoing text we have used a variety of terms—concerns, fears, worries, thoughts, beliefs, appraisals. Importantly the service users we discussed this with talked instead of fears, anxieties, worries. This terminology represents our view that these phenomena are frequently not rigidly fixed, the 'fixed firm belief held with 100% conviction' of traditional psychiatric diagnoses. Rather they are dynamic processes of sense-making and 'modes of being in the world' (Woods & Wilkinson, 2017), incorporating preexisting expectations, which may change, to a greater or lesser extent, with circumstances, recent events, mood, moment-by-moment affective state, dynamically shifting self-conceptualisations and with the application of differing reasoning styles. It is important to note that these individual processes of sense making occur within a social and cultural context where experiences of deprivation, discrimination, and exclusion (among other social factors) can have cascading effects. Similarly, past trauma may also play a role in the interplay between experience and appraisal in a range of ways: meanings encoded in memories shape the present moment; direct re-experiencing of events; highly fragmentary intrusive memories that may, for some, contribute to anomalous experiences such as voices; and emotional regulation strategies such as dissociation and hyperarousal (Hardy, 2017; see also Chapter 10 in this volume, for a detailed discussion on this issue). Research using Experience Sampling Methodology, which asks people to self-rate their persecutory thoughts at random time points during the day, amply demonstrates within-day variations in self ratings of paranoid thoughts—with changing levels of occurrence, conviction, and distress (Ben-Zeev, Morris, Swendsen, & Granholm, 2012; So, Peters, Swendsen, Garety, & Kapur, 2014; Thewissen, Bentall, Lecomte, van Os, & Myin-Germeys, 2008). These different terms also emphasise the multidimensionality of delusions referred to earlier. From an experiential or phenomenological viewpoint, the person might be aware of and seek help for worries, a state of ruminative emotional distress; or for fears, laden with anxiety and avoidance of the feared situation or people; for problems in performing everyday activities, such as not being able to go out with the life-changing impact of isolation; or for strong beliefs, characterised by fierce conviction and searching out confirmatory evidence. These are examples, which map onto the dimensions of preoccupation, distress, impact and conviction listed here.

ASSESSMENT AND ENGAGEMENT FOR THERAPY

Elsewhere in this book, there is guidance on assessment. So here we highlight some particular issues relevant to assessing fears of deliberate harm from others.

Case formulations, which incorporate individuals' experiences and perspectives, aim to address the many causal factors likely to be involved.

Firstly, as suggested, these fears (or beliefs or thoughts or worries) are complex, multidimensional, and not fixed; thus, the assessment must assume variation and, as in any thorough formulation-based assessment, be conducted within a framework, which considers a range of background and triggering factors. In addition to detailed assessment of psychological factors (such as appraisal, reasoning, and safety behaviours), the role of the social and cultural context needs to be carefully considered throughout assessment and intervention. Worries about harm from others are fundamentally social appraisals. Possible variations in the cultural norms governing social interaction are important to consider, including (but not limited to) the meaning of body language, use of direct or indirect speech, attitudes towards expressed criticism, and culturally sanctioned social boundaries (for example, the involvement of family and extended communities in the individuals life). Within our South-East London clinic, we work with people from diverse social and cultural backgrounds, many of whom have experienced significant social deprivation and exclusion. Fears of being attacked (and the attendant hypervigilance to danger) may be influenced by direct experience of, or indirect exposure to, street violence, gang activity, knife crime, and violent robbery. Similarly, fears of negative evaluation from others can be influenced by the previous experiences of discrimination, racism, and social stigma that are commonly reported to us in the clinic. Our advice is to be mindful of this broader context but do not assume that two people from (superficially) similar backgrounds will experience the world in the same way. The key is to ask open questions, which provide an opportunity for the person to explore the potential role of social and cultural factors in their current worries.

An empathic attitude towards your client's problems and achievements helps to develop a good collaborative relationship.

Secondly, in all good psychological assessment, the importance of empathy and engaging with the person's own perspective and experiences is paramount. But with these types of concerns, this is absolutely essential. People with fears about harm from others are accustomed to having their fears minimised or not understood, and they commonly find trusting others difficult in the context of often difficult relational histories. Conveying empathic understanding and acceptance is central—and is best achieved by adopting a genuine spirit of enquiry, seeking fully to understand what has led the person to hold these fears, how they view them now, how they impact on their everyday lives, and what the person would like to be different in the future.

Furthermore, given our conceptualisation, in order to develop a full understanding, as well as clarifying the current concerns, the variation along key dimensions, the triggers and consequences, and social and cultural factors, we assess *the way* the person is thinking or appraising events and experiences.

Cognitive models point to a number of factors, but research suggests that particularly important for the development and persistence of fears about others intending harm are fast- and slow-thinking styles and emotional processes. Specifically, research has documented the over use of 'fast thinking', or 'jumping to conclusions' on the basis of limited evidence; and underactivation of slow, reflective thinking, generating and considering a range of alternative ideas (see Ward & Garety, 2017); as well as disturbance in key emotional processes, including worry and self-representation (see Freeman & Garety, 2014 for a review).

Dual process models of reasoning—termed 'fast' and 'slow' thinking—provide a useful framework to address the thinking styles, which contribute to fears about others intending harm.

When assessing the way a person is thinking about their worry, we aim for an open and questioning style—not being afraid to explore, circling around the beliefs where helpful and eliciting valued ideas. We are interested in understanding *how* the person holds this belief or concern—is it questioned, what might be alternative ideas or explanations for what has been happening, might the person consider *at all* being mistaken; in brief, exploring the flexibility of the person's thinking. There are also more formal tools for such assessments, such as the Maudsley Assessment of Delusions schedule (Wessely et al., 1993), and the Explanations of Experiences (EoE) interview assessing Alternative Explanations (Freeman et al., 2004). In Box 25.2, some key questions used, together with a transcript of an assessment of 'belief flexibility' is given as an example for assessing the way a person thinks about their fears—the example also shows, as emphasised earlier, how we can remain alive to important social experiences (in this case of racism) at the same time as we assess individual reasoning.

CURRENT RESEARCH FINDINGS POINTING TO NEW TREATMENT APPROACHES

In the past decade, following the emergence of a range of cognitive psychological therapies for psychosis, trials and metaanalyses of trial results have demonstrated their effectiveness for psychosis in general and for delusions in particular (Turner, van der Gaag, Karyotaki, & Cuijpers, 2014; van der Gaag, Valmaggia, & Smit, 2014; Wykes, Steel, Everitt, & Tarrier, 2008). However, most of these reviews and metaanalyses suggest that the effects are small-moderate, especially with regard to paranoia and 'delusions'. One way forward, it has been argued, is to adopt a 'causal-interventionist' approach to improving therapy effectiveness, which involves developing tailored interventions to target the specific mechanisms that research has shown to play a causal role in the problem to be treated (Freeman, 2011; Freeman, Waite, et al., 2016; Mehl, Werner, & Lincoln, 2015). Recent years have seen the development of a number of 'single-symptom' treatments, which target both specific outcomes and key hypothesised causal mechanisms. For example, the Command CBT trial, a treatment aimed specifically at reducing compliance to distressing command

A causal interventionist approach aims to improve therapy effectiveness by targeting hypothesised causal mechanisms and examining the effect on the symptom or problem being treated.

hallucinations, targets the single mechanism of the power dimension of voice appraisal (Birchwood et al., 2014; Birchwood et al., 2017), while the Worry Intervention Trial aims to reduce persecutory delusions by specifically targeting worry as a causal mechanism for paranoia (Freeman et al., 2015). Our own current research focusses on fast and slow thinking as contributing to fears about harm from others, and the SlowMo trial (Garety et al., 2017) therefore targets thinking habits in order to reduce these fears.

Another key issue is that despite the innovations in psychological therapy for psychosis over the past two decades, and the widespread recommendations in treatment guidelines (such as NICE, 2014) that evidence-based therapies, including CBT for psychosis, should be made available, there is a severe implementation challenge (Haddock et al., 2014; Thomas, 2015; van der Gaag, 2014). Estimates suggest that even in well-established national health services such as

Box 25.2 Assessing Belief Flexibility

Belief flexibility is defined as the metacognitive capacity of reflecting on one's own beliefs, changing them in the light of reflection and evidence, and generating and considering alternatives (Garety et al., 2005). Importantly, belief flexibility has been shown to predict response to psychological treatment (see, for example Garety et al., 1997). We offer here two excerpts from much longer assessments where the focus is on the flexibility of thinking about the fear. Both people have had very high conviction levels. One person, Prateep, does not countenance any alternative ways of thinking, whereas the other person, Gill, does have some other ideas about what might be happening, including the possible role of anxiety in influencing the way she thinks.

HOW IS IT ASSESSED?

1: Prateep- Main worry: My neighbour is harassing and abusing me

I=Interviewer; P: Prateep

I: Prateep, I can hear that this is a very difficult situation. Can I ask you what makes you realise that your neighbour is doing this? **[Sensitive exploration of evidence for the belief]**

P: Well, it started out with him shouting out the window, swearing and racist stuff and banging on the wall. Maybe he thought I was making too much noise but he told people to harass me and it's been nasty ever since. Now he has started firing a beam of insults into my room ...I feel a kind of heat on my face and then I hear the same swear words over and over like he's firing them directly into my mind [**Evidence includes external evidence (shouting and banging) as well as internal evidence (including compelling anomalous experiences)**]

I: Ok Prateep, thank you. You also told me about the racism you experienced at school and how this affected you - I can hear how difficult this has been to be experiencing this again **[sensitive linking to past experiences].** So just to recap you have heard him shouting and recently this experience of heat on your face and hearing a beam of insults. I wanted to ask if you thought there could be any other explanation for these things even if you thought it was really unlikely? [**Assessing Alternative Explanations (AEs) for the evidence**]

P: It sounds bizarre I know, but I know it's real, it's actually happening, I just know. It's going on all day and all night. [**Use of fast thinking, 'I just know', in the absence of AE**]

I: And when you think about it now, is it at all possible you're mistaken about this? [**Assessing Possibility of being Mistaken**]

Participant: No, I'm sure I'm not mistaken. It made me ill because it went on 24/7. [**No possibility of being mistaken**]

2: Gill- Main worry: People are plotting to attack and harm me.

I=Interviewer; G: Gill

I: I can hear that this is a very difficult situation. Can I ask - what makes you realise that this is happening? [**Sensitive exploration of evidence for the belief**]

G: ...other people talking on their phones or hearing someone screaming and shouting and feeling like it's me they're talking about me . . . Say when I feel anxious and I look around and I catch someone's eye . . . I just know this person was looking at me already...it feels like they can see through my mind . . . [**Compelling internal subjective evidence, including reference and anomalous experience**]

I: Ok Gill, so there are a few things that make you sure of what is going on . . . [. . . summary of evidence]. I was wondering if you think there could be any other explanation for those things, even if you thought it was really unlikely? [**Alternative Explanations question**]

G: when it's that intense I can't think of any other reason . . . but speaking now I'm calmer . . . I can tell myself that it's just the way I was thinking . . . but you see when it's happening it's as real as can be [**Possible AE- 'How my mind was working at the time, when anxious'**]

in the UK, only 10%–20% of people routinely access psychological therapy (Colling et al., 2017; Haddock et al., 2014; Schizophrenia Commission, 2012). Implementation science lists many barriers to the uptake of treatment: these include not only the effectiveness of the treatment but also its accessibility, appeal, and extent to which the treatment is delivered with fidelity. Innovations in inclusive design and the use of digital technologies are now being tested to address some of these barriers to implementation.

DIGITAL APPROACHES: VIRTUAL REALITY, APPS, AND BLENDED THERAPY

In this era of digital revolution, there has consequently been a rapid increase in the use of technology directed at both efficacy and implementation of psychological interventions for paranoia. Digital technology offers new opportunities for improving well-established cognitive and behavioural techniques in an engaging and tailored way, as well as providing novel therapeutic contexts within which core psychological processes can be targeted in real time with immediate feedback.

One of the more promising technologies is Virtual Reality (VR). VR can be defined as technology that integrates real-time computer graphics, sounds, and other sensory input to create a computer-generated world with which the user can interact (Gregg & Tarrier, 2007). The ecological validity of this approach is strengthened by the sense of presence (the psychological sensation of 'being

Advantages of VR are that it offers observation of real-time interactions and behaviours, and also manipulation of the environment, enabling testing out of new responses in a controlled and safe setting.

there') that individuals can experience in virtual environments (Slater, 2003). Key advantages of VR are that it offers researchers and clinicians the possibility not only of observing the user's real-time behaviour when interacting with virtual agents, but also of controlling and modifying the environment and the responses of the avatars or simulated stimuli and tasks (Rizzo, Schulteis, & Rothbaum, 2003). Immersive VR (most commonly delivered in a Head-Mounted Display, HMD) is typically the choice for applications where a controlled stimulus environment is desirable for driving a user's perceptual experience within a specific programmed world (Rizzo & Koenig, 2017). However, there is also a more basic form of VR, the nonimmersive VR, where the content is presented on a flat-screen computer monitor and the user interacts with a three-dimensional computer graphic using a joystick, a mouse, or a gamepad. VR should be clearly differentiated from Augmented Reality (AR) applications, which refers to an interface that allows the user to interact with information and virtual elements inserted in the real environment (Carmigniani & Furth, 2011).

Disadvantages of VR may include cybersickness, limitations in usability for people with visual or other impairments and environments lacking socio-cultural relevance for diverse user populations.

The main disadvantages of the use of VR concern equipment usability in certain populations, for example people with visual impairment or needing vision correction beyond the fine-tuning available, and cybersickness, which occurs when exposure to VR causes symptoms that are similar to motion sickness symptoms (e.g. general discomfort, headache, or nausea). System developers are introducing new software and hardware solutions to diminish the likelihood of cybersickness, such as slow forward speed, giving people at least some control over their movement, and having users seated. There is also an increased awareness of the need for a socio-cultural perspective when developing and implementing virtual environments: specific attention and care is being put into populating culturally rich virtual environments with virtual agents behaving in line with socio-cultural behavioural patterns, to provide users with an engaging and realistic experience. This becomes a challenge when researchers and clinicians from diverse cultures and heritage aim to share environments to deliver therapy, as these environments may include artefacts and virtual humans that are relevant for the population they were created for but not for other people with different cultural backgrounds.

In the context of paranoia, the particular value of VR rests on the assumption that by programming an environment in which the degree of hostility that the virtual characters display can be manipulated (for example to be neutral, benign, or hostile) it allows a more valid assessment of paranoia than self-report methods, where it is not known whether the hostile intent reported as experienced by the patient is accurate or not (Freeman et al., 2005). VR offers innovative possibilities of modifying and controlling avatars' behaviour as well as enabling introduction of environmental factors, such as number and appearance of people present or amount of eye contact, which may elicit paranoia and help to identify factors associated in everyday life with persecutory thoughts (Freeman et al., 2008). This controllability and environment manipulation also offers novel treatment possibilities: for example, the person may be given the opportunity to test out how it feels to drop key safety behaviours in a controlled and predictable setting (see Freeman, Bradley, et al., 2016 and Pot-Kolder et al., 2018 for interventional studies of immersive virtual reality for paranoia). Crucially VR environments allow 'embodied' cognitive processes to be targeted 'in action', potentially matching the dynamic conceptualisation of appraisals outlined here with the ultimate aim that improvements made in VR environments will generalise to real-life contexts. A recent systematic review has shown that VR is a well-accepted, safe, and efficient method to assess and treat paranoia (Rus-Calafell, Garety, Sason, Craig, & Valmaggia, 2018).

The evidence shows that VR is a well-accepted, safe, and efficient tool for both the assessment and treatment of paranoia, with the potential to facilitate new learning of emotional and behavioural responses to feared situations.

There is also a growing body of work and research exploring the potential of smartphone technologies to enhance therapy outcomes, improve medication adherence, and to promote self-management for people with psychosis, including people with fears of harm from others. Mobile software applications ('apps'), sometimes combined with wearable devices (a wrist band, watch, or clothes connected to the phone gathering physiological information for extended periods), are the most common form of smartphone technology, also known as mHealth (or mobile Health). Smartphone technology has the potential to significantly improve mental healthcare, through extending the reach of services and providing adjunctive support to existing psychosocial interventions (Firth et al., 2016). A recent metaanalysis showed that >65% of people with psychosis own a smartphone, with an increase up to 81% in the last decade, and that the majority of users are in favour of using mobile phones (>60%) to track or monitor their mental health (Firth et al., 2016).

Mobile apps can help users to assess and monitor their thoughts, keep track of their subjective mood and anxiety levels in a personalised, digital, and visual way. Both the clinician and individual can track different parameters over time to characterise treatment outcomes (Luxton, McCann, Bush, Mishkind, & Reger, 2011). One of the main advantages of mobile apps is that they provide a new form of the classic structured diary techniques in the form of momentary assessments, such as the Experience Sampling Method (ESM; Myin-Germeys et al., 2009) or Ecological Momentary Assessment (EMA; Heron & Smyth, 2010), defined as naturalistic methods to distribute surveys that individuals complete in the context of everyday life. Additionally, these methods have the advantage that the information is collected digitally and in real time, using the person's own device, and can also be shared with the authorised clinician's web-based dashboard (Ben-Zeev et al., 2014). These forms of assessment can contribute to identifying the person's individual risk factors or symptom patterns and identify treatment goals (Myin-Germeys, Birchwood, & Kwapil, 2011; Reininghaus, Depp, & Myin-Germeys, 2016). Feedback on change in real time may then facilitate behavioural changes and improve therapy generalisation into the person's daily life.

One potential disadvantage of smartphone applications for paranoia is that some users may present some mistrust around how the information is used (i.e. data protection and person's privacy) or an increased fear that they could be tracked by their phone. Another disadvantage often discussed is the accessibility to mobile technologies from people living in low-income and middle-income countries. In a recent review, Naslund and colleagues (Naslund et al., 2017) showed that phone subscriptions exceed 80% of the population in many middle- and low-income countries in Africa, Central America, and South Asia, and concluded that mobile technologies could in reality overcome barriers by offering access to supportive resources, as individuals in these countries may not have access to mental healthcare, but most of them have access to a mobile phone (Naslund et al., 2017).

Blended therapy refers to any combination of web-, mobile-, or technology-based application with face-to-face therapy.

A further step in the use of technology as a tool for psychological interventions is the hybrid treatment format of blended interventions. Blended therapy can be considered as any combination of web-, mobile-, or technology-based application with face-to-face therapy. Its main goal is to combine the advantages of face-to-face therapy and online (or mobile) interventions, by having the 'best of both worlds' (Wentzel, van der Vaart, Bohlmeijer, & van Gemert-Pijnen, 2016). SlowMo is the first blended digital therapy targeting fear of harm from others (Garety et al., 2017), which we now describe in more detail.

SlowMo: A BLENDED DIGITAL THERAPY FOR FEARS OF HARM FROM OTHERS

SlowMo therapy is a novel digital approach, which employs innovative use of digital technology to target the fast thinking habits (also known as emotional or 'gut-based' reasoning) that have been associated with fears of harm from others. SlowMo has been developed in collaboration between service users, designers, researchers, and clinicians, adopting a user-centred design approach (Hardy et al., 2018) ensuring accessibility and usability for people regardless of background or experience with technology. The therapy consists of eight individual, face-to-face sessions, delivered by trained therapists, assisted by a webapp with interactive personal accounts and scenarios. A specially designed smartphone app helps the person embed strategies into everyday life. As such SlowMo is an example of a **blended therapy** approach attempting to combine the best of existing talking therapies with novel digital technology to increase engagement, effectiveness, and generalisation to everyday life.

SlowMo Face-to-Face Sessions Supported by Webapp

The first two sessions involve building the metacognitive skill of noticing thoughts (visualised on the webapp as spinning bubbles) and thinking habits such as fast thinking. Personalised session content includes a visual formulation screen (see Fig. 25.1) created by the person, which displays the worry bubbles alongside key triggers and the impact of worries on the person's life. Throughout, there is an emphasis on delivering normalising messages regarding how common fast thinking and worries about others are in the general population. Key interactive features involve three characters (Sam, Nadia, and James) who are introduced in Session 1 and followed thereafter as they discuss their own worries about others and their attempts to **Slow** down for a **Mo**ment. Another important interactive feature takes

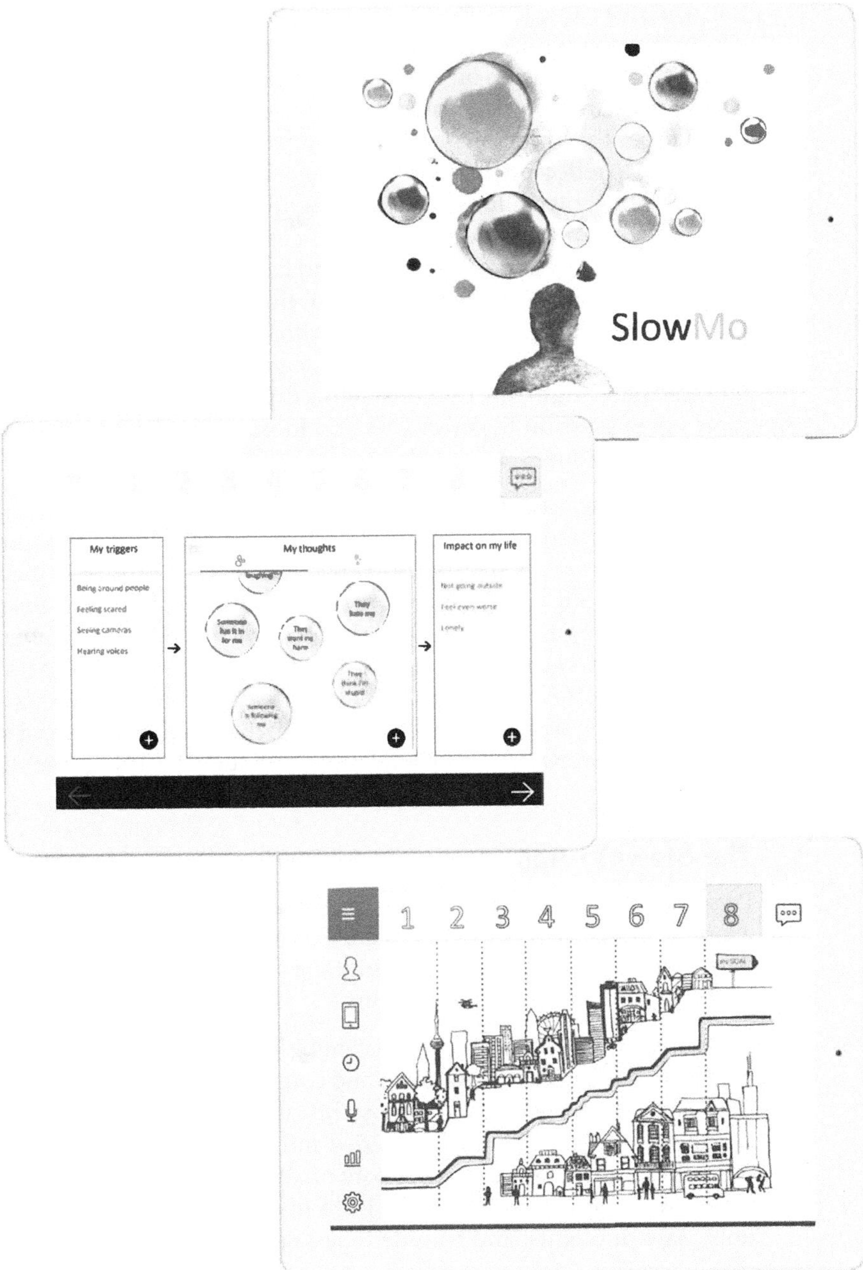

FIG. 25.1

The SlowMo digital webapp to support face to face sessions—*top* to *bottom*: SlowMo Home screen, personalised formulation and overall therapy journey. Copyright retained by the authors, published in modified form in Garety, P. A., Ward, T., Freeman, D., Fowler, D., Emsley, R., Dunn, G., … Hardy, A. (2017). SlowMo, a digital therapy targeting reasoning in paranoia, versus treatment as usual in the treatment of people who fear harm from others: Study protocol for a randomised controlled trial. *Trials*, *18*(1), 510. https://doi.org/10.1186/s13063-017-2242-7.

the form of a game (Session 3) in which people are asked to judge 'What is happening?' in two ambiguous scenarios with options to 'slow down and take another look' or make a decision on what is seen. The game is designed to demonstrate the nature of fast thinking (jumping to conclusions) and promote the idea of slowing down to see the bigger picture. These interactive features act as a springboard for the person to reflect on their own experiences, placing the person in control of how they share their own information. This blended approach reduces the potential for people feeling 'put on the spot' when asked about their own experiences, which can be reported by some during standard face-to-face therapy. Over the sessions, people learn that everyone thinks fast at times and this can be useful; however, thinking slow can be helpful in dealing with stress and worries about other people. From Session 4 onwards, a range of strategies are introduced, which support the process of slowing down, e.g. considering the impact of mood (Session 5) and past experiences (Session 6) on worries and looking for alternative explanations for stressful situations.

Each strategy acts as an invitation to slow down for a moment and reflect. Common thinking 'traps' are introduced, for example the human tendency to assume that situations are about us personally (Session 4) or only noticing information that confirms our fears (confirmation bias) and missing other possibly helpful clues (Session 7). Each session ends by focusing on applying the strategies during the following week using the SlowMo mobile phone app. The person records a key learning point and a message for the week in either audio or text form. These messages can be accessed by the person from the mobile phone and also form the basis of a review and consolidation conducted during the final session (Session 8).

The SlowMo App

Personalised session content from the webapp (see earlier) is synchronised with a mobile app, which has been designed to support the person to slow down for a moment in situations where fast thinking is triggered and they feel under threat in daily life. The app includes a range of features (see storyboard in Fig. 25.2).

For example, people are able to select bubbles when they notice fast thinking and use the key strategies to slow down and consider safer alternatives. Slowing down to consider the bigger picture is most difficult when we feel anxious, so the app is designed to act as a kind of 'extended mind' resource (Ward & Garety, 2017), providing ready access to a repository of alternative safety ideas, previously generated in therapy sessions (in the form of easily accessible alternative explanations, safer thoughts, and recorded messages).

A key principle of the SlowMo approach is that assessment and intervention should include working with the person in real-life environments where fears of others are triggered (e.g. public transport or crowded markets). As discussed in the assessment section, this allows the fear of harm from others to be understood within a broader social and cultural context, which may include experiences of social deprivation, discrimination, and exclusion. Consider, for

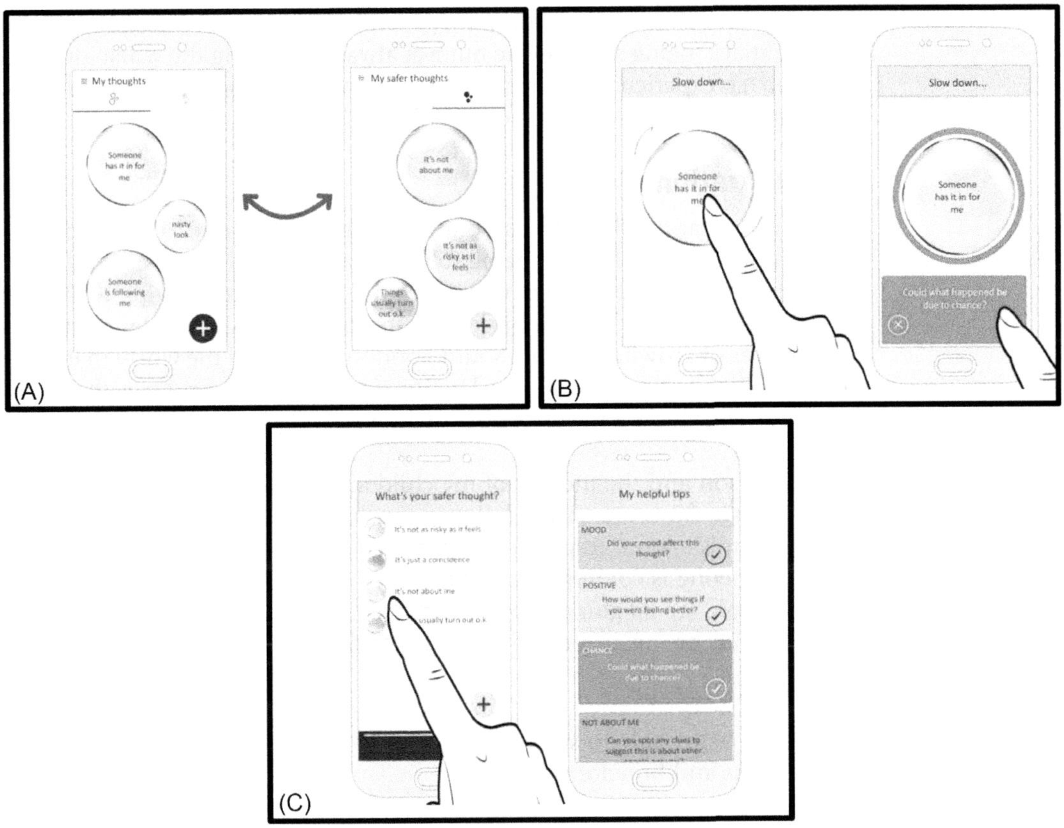

FIG. 25.2
Key SlowMo app functionality: (A) Screens for noticing 'worry bubbles' and 'safer thoughts'; (B) Cue to 'slow down for a moment' followed by a tip to support generating safer alternative thoughts; (C) Easy-access to personalised safer thoughts and 'key tips' from face-to-face sessions. Copyright retained by the authors, submitted for publication in modified form to *Journal of Internet Medical Research*. https://doi.org/10.2196/11222.

example, an individual living in an area with higher-than-average rates of violence and crime, who has perhaps experienced an acid attack or recently had police cordon off their street due to a fatal stabbing. While fast thinking (and attendant safety behaviours) are likely to be key factors maintaining current distress, a narrow focus on reasoning may risk the therapist being experienced as someone who simply does not 'get' the lived experience of the person. Likewise, for someone whose fears of negative social evaluation occur in the context of experiences of racism, an exclusive focus on the 'jumping to conclusions', which does not include sensitive consideration of prior experience, may result in the person inferring that 'slowing down for a moment' might be helpful for others but not 'someone like me'. In such cases, a sensitive understanding of context may allow for a therapeutic common ground to emerge, for example the person fearing attack 'being street aware but not always expecting the worst' or the person who has experienced racism considering that 'I've experienced people at their worst in the past but not everyone is like this'.

An Illustration

Alex is a 30-year-old Black British Caribbean man who came to SlowMo therapy reporting significant fears of being followed and that his son was in danger of being harmed. These worries were affecting Alex's relationships with friends and family and holding him back from important life goals. Alex spoke of his experiences of growing up on a South London estate and the worry that looking at someone 'the wrong way' can lead to significant danger. Over the first few meetings, Alex built a picture of his main worries using thought bubbles:

- 'My son and the mother of my child are in danger'
- 'A man from my past is following me'
- 'Friends are out to get me'
- 'Someone is coming into my house'
- 'People are laughing at me'
- 'People are against me (including my family)'

Key identified triggers:

- Not being able to see my son
- Stress and boredom
- Overhearing conversations and laughter on the street (particularly 'street-wise' people)
- Seeing a dark-skinned man in a car
- Things seeming troubled in the flat, e.g. missing cigarettes or sugar
- Hearing screams of women or children (e.g. on TV, play-station, or noise from the street)

Using the phone and the SlowMo strategies, Alex developed an ability to react differently when worries were triggered. For example, if he heard a scream on the computer or laughter/ noise outside the window, he used the phone to slow down and consider safer thoughts like 'this is just crowd noise on a computer game' or 'the screaming is just kids being loud on their way home from school'. During session 4, he spoke of a situation when he became suspicious that his bin lid was on the floor and fast thinking was telling him 'people have come into my home'. By slowing down, he worked out that the lid could easily have been knocked off by his friend's dog who had been in the flat the day before, i.e. a safer alternative explanation. This was used as a good example of how worries can make us focus our attention on things that we would usually not even notice and build them up in our minds. With regards to fears that people were stealing sugar and cigarettes, he realised that it would be unusual if someone did break in and only take a few spoons of sugar rather than other more expensive items. Finally, he started to question the worry that a man was following him in a car with his son. He started to realise that his son would certainly not have been able to keep this a secret (he would have been too excited to have seen his dad!). Following are some of the key safer thoughts and audio messages Alex added to his phone for use in daily life:

- Slow down when you are thinking fast. Don't overreact to your thoughts.
- Think—It could be a coincidence.
- Pay more attention to what you are doing with your day.
- Try to think positive thoughts.
- Don't overthink—relax and think over
- Remember—it is never too late to make changes in your life.

Alex's engagement with SlowMo therapy supported him to notice and counteract the effects of fast thinking and (over time) develop an ability to slow down and consider alternative explanations (see discussion on belief flexibility). In the final session, he described how he was no longer allowing 'inklings' of threat to become 'full-blown reacting' and was no longer seeing thoughts and worries as truth. In his own words, **'I slow down. .. I think different, act different, and feel different'** [see Box 25.3 for Alex's view on using the SlowMo smartphone app].

Box 25.3 Service User Experiences of SlowMo

This is what Alex said about the SlowMo therapy:

> I've done what I set out to do. I have learned to deal with my worries and temper. I've stopped thinking people are following me and out to get me - it is just a little inkling every now and again, but everyone has little inklings. The fears are not so intense and I can deal with them with the phone. You know like constantly being on the phone, tapping it in, and following the routine kind of like makes you notice what is going on, and when you use the phone, slow down your thinking and look at the whole situation....when you jam it into your head it almost comes like automatic, instead of always tapping it in your phone I can now do it in my head, like if I'm playing on my play-station and hearing the screams I can say 'don't worry it is just the scream of the crowd on the computer, no-one is in danger

And this is the experience of another person who tried SlowMo:

> [SlowMo was] very effective . . .
> It was helpful in that I could relate it to my everyday life and get through. I was given the opportunity, which I'm very thankful for, to changing my aspect of thinking and try looking at things in a different way and pop the bubble. Especially say 'right put it all in there' [i.e. using the worry bubbles and slowing down steps on phone], 'right let's concentrate on that', 'get rid of that that's gone', yeah very good. I'm still actually using that (the phone).

CONCLUSIONS

Our focus here has been on paranoia, or fears of harm from others. We have highlighted how language and terminology are both important and highly contested in this area, and the service users we asked about this, generally told us that 'delusions' is not acceptable to them, seen as being disrespectful or opaque, though one person thought the term could provide an explanation for what is going on in the mind. 'Fear' is what they often describe and a term, which some preferentially use. But we have noted too the variety of terms, the complexity of conceptualisations, the dynamic interplay, and fluctuations in experience, and that these fears are on a continuum with every day concerns, and multidimensional. Much has changed in the understanding of paranoia or fears of harm from others. There is a changing landscape of psychological treatment too. In attempts to improve both efficacy and implementation, new 'causal interventionist' approaches to treatment are being developed and tested. These identify and target mechanisms, such as thinking habits, worry, and appraisals of voices, and offer more intensive focussed treatments. In a rapidly changing digital world, technology is also being incorporated into treatment. We critically examined an example of these trends, SlowMo, a novel blended digital therapy, which targets the mechanism of fast and slow thinking to reduce fears of harm from others and described the therapy and service user experiences of this approach.

AND FINALLY...

The same service users who commented at the beginning of this chapter on our use of terms like 'paranoia' and 'delusions' offered this advice for us mental health professionals about language and how best to communicate. Here are some key pointers:

- Get your attitude right—be thoughtful and respectful.
- Treat people with kindness and understanding.
- Try to be someone the person can reach out to.
- Make time for people—Sit down with them and make the effort to listen and explain things to people
- Treat people as individuals.
- Let people know they are not alone but don't compare them with other people.
- Engage in a conversation—don't just ask questions.
- Don't give up. If the person cancels meetings, keep trying.

RESOURCES—OPEN ACCESS

(1) Our SlowMo therapy website: http://slowmotherapy.co.uk/

(2) Follow SlowMo on twitter: @SlowMotherapy

(3) Two talks by Professor Daniel Freeman, Oxford UK: 'Paranoia: Developments in Understanding and Treatment':

https://www.youtube.com/watch?reload=9&v=6ijwEaOABIk

https://www.youtube.com/watch?v=Dw9nM8O29ek

(4) Psychosis Research Unit, Manchester UK: 'CBT for Psychosis: Discussing the advantages and disadvantages of paranoia':
https://www.youtube.com/watch?v=N2RxUfmj1KY
http://www.psychosisresearch.com/

(5) Orygen Youth Health in Melbourne, Australia produce a range of factsheets on mental health including psychosis:
https://oyh.org.au/our-services/training-resources/free-downloads-youth-mental-health-resources/fact-sheets

(6) Myth busting information for young people, friends and families on unusual experiences, paranoia and early psychosis:
https://www.isanyoneelselikeme.org.uk/

Acknowledgements

The authors would like to acknowledge Anthony, Alex, Joanne, and James for sharing their insight and experiences throughout the sections on service user perspectives. We would also like to thank Amy Hardy, Ujala Ilyas, Elâ Örücü, and Sue Barwick for their assistance in preparing this chapter.

PAG, TW, and MRC acknowledge funding for the SlowMo project from the Efficacy and Mechanism Evaluation (EME) Programme, an MRC and NIHR partnership Project, ref. 15/48/21.

The EME Programme is funded by the MRC and NIHR, with contributions from the CSO in Scotland and NISCHR in Wales and the HSC R&D Division, Public Health Agency in Northern Ireland. PAG acknowledges support from the National Institute for Health Research (NIHR) Biomedical Research Centre of the South London and Maudsley NHS Foundation Trust and King's College London. TW acknowledges support by the NIHR collaboration for Leadership in Applied Health Research and Care South London at King's College Hospital NHS Foundation Trust. The views expressed in this publication are those of the author(s) and not necessarily those of the MRC, NHS, NIHR, or the Department of Health.

References

Bebbington, P. E., McBride, O., Steel, C., Kuipers, E., Radovanovic, M., Brugha, T., et al. (2013). The structure of paranoia in the general population. *The British Journal of Psychiatry, 202*, 419–427. https://doi.org/10.1192/bjp.bp.112.119032.

Ben-Zeev, D., Brenner, C. J., Begale, M., Duffecy, J., Mohr, D. C., & Mueser, K. T. (2014). Feasibility, acceptability, and preliminary efficacy of a smartphone intervention for schizophrenia. *Schizophrenia Bulletin, 40*(6), 1244–1253. https://doi.org/10.1093/schbul/sbu033.

Ben-Zeev, D., Morris, S., Swendsen, J., & Granholm, E. (2012). Predicting the occurrence, conviction, distress, and disruption of different delusional experiences in the daily life of people with schizophrenia. *Schizophrenia Bulletin, 38*(4), 826–837. https://doi.org/10.1093/schbul/sbq167.

Birchwood, M., Dunn, G., Meaden, A., Tarrier, N., Lewis, S., Wykes, T., et al. (2017). The COMMAND trial of cognitive therapy to prevent harmful compliance with command hallucinations: Predictors of outcome and mediators of change. *Psychological Medicine*, 1–9. https://doi.org/10.1017/S0033291717003488.

Birchwood, M., Michail, M., Meaden, A., Tarrier, N., Lewis, S., Wykes, T., et al. (2014). Cognitive behaviour therapy to prevent harmful compliance with command hallucinations (COMMAND): A randomised controlled trial. *Lancet Psychiatry, 1*(1), 23–33. https://doi.org/10.1016/S2215-0366(14)70247-0.

Carmigniani, J., & Furth, B. (2011). Augmented reality: An overview. In B. Furth (Ed.), *Handbook of augmented reality* (pp. 3–46). New York: Springer.

Colling, C., Evans, L., Broadbent, M., Chandran, D., Craig, T. J., Kolliakou, A., et al. (2017). Identification of the delivery of cognitive behavioural therapy for psychosis (CBTp) using a cross-sectional sample from electronic health records and open-text information in a large UK-based mental health case register. *BMJ Open*. *7*(7), https://doi.org/10.1136/bmjopen-2016-015297.

Firth, J., Cotter, J., Torous, J., Bucci, S., Firth, J. A., & Yung, A. R. (2016). Mobile phone ownership and endorsement of "mHealth" among people with psychosis: A meta-analysis of cross-sectional studies. *Schizophrenia Bulletin*, *42*(2), 448–455. https://doi.org/10.1093/schbul/sbv132.

Fletcher, P. C., & Frith, C. D. (2009). Perceiving is believing: A Bayesian approach to explaining the positive symptoms of schizophrenia. *Nature Reviews. Neuroscience*, *10*(1), 48–58. https://doi.org/10.1038/nrn2536.

Freeman, D. (2011). Improving cognitive treatments for delusions. *Schizophrenia Research*, *132*(2–3), 135–139. https://doi.org/10.1016/j.schres.2011.08.012.

Freeman, D., Bradley, J., Antley, A., Bourke, E., DeWeever, N., Evans, N., et al. (2016). Virtual reality in the treatment of persecutory delusions: randomised controlled experimental study testing how to reduce delusional conviction. *The British Journal of Psychiatry*, *209*(1), 62–67. https://doi.org/10.1192/bjp.bp.115.176438.

Freeman, D., Dunn, G., Startup, H., Pugh, K., Cordwell, J., Mander, H., et al. (2015). Effects of cognitive behaviour therapy for worry on persecutory delusions in patients with psychosis (WIT): A parallel, single-blind, randomised controlled trial with a mediation analysis. *Lancet Psychiatry*, *2*(4), 305–313. https://doi.org/10.1016/S2215-0366(15)00039-5.

Freeman, D., & Garety, P. (2014). Advances in understanding and treating persecutory delusions: A review. *Social Psychiatry and Psychiatric Epidemiology*, *49*(8), 1179–1189. https://doi.org/10.1007/s00127-014-0928-7.

Freeman, D., & Garety, P. A. (2000). Comments on the content of persecutory delusions: Does the definition need clarification? *The British Journal of Clinical Psychology*, *39*(Pt 4), 407–414.

Freeman, D., Garety, P. A., Bebbington, P. E., Slater, M., Kuipers, E., Fowler, D., et al. (2005). The psychology of persecutory ideation II: A virtual reality experimental study. *The Journal of Nervous and Mental Disease*, *193*(5), 309–315.

Freeman, D., Garety, P. A., Fowler, D., Kuipers, E., Bebbington, P. E., & Dunn, G. (2004). Why do people with delusions fail to choose more realistic explanations for their experiences? An empirical investigation. *Journal of Consulting and Clinical Psychology*, *72*(4), 671–680. https://doi.org/10.1037/0022-006X.72.4.671.

Freeman, D., Garety, P. A., Kuipers, E., Fowler, D., & Bebbington, P. E. (2002). A cognitive model of persecutory delusions. *The British Journal of Clinical Psychology*, *41*(Pt 4), 331–347.

Freeman, D., Pugh, K., Antley, A., Slater, M., Bebbington, P., Gittins, M., et al. (2008). Virtual reality study of paranoid thinking in the general population. *The British Journal of Psychiatry*, *192*(4), 258–263.

Freeman, D., Waite, F., Emsley, R., Kingdon, D., Davies, L., Fitzpatrick, R., et al. (2016). The efficacy of a new translational treatment for persecutory delusions: study protocol for a randomised controlled trial (the feeling safe study). *Trials*, *17*(1), 134. https://doi.org/10.1186/s13063-016-1245-0.

Garety, P., Fowler, D., Kuipers, E., Freeman, D., Dunn, G., Bebbington, P., et al. (1997). London-East Anglia randomised controlled trial of cognitive-behavioural therapy for psychosis. II: predictors of outcome. *The British Journal of Psychiatry*, *171*, 420–426.

Garety, P. A., & Freeman, D. (2013). The past and future of delusions research: From the inexplicable to the treatable. *The British Journal of Psychiatry*, *203*(5), 327–333. https://doi.org/10.1192/bjp.bp.113.126953.

Garety, P. A., Freeman, D., Jolley, S., Dunn, G., Bebbington, P. E., Fowler, D. G., et al. (2005). Reasoning, emotions, and delusional conviction in psychosis. *Journal of Abnormal Psychology*, *114*(3), 373–384. https://doi.org/10.1037/0021-843X.114.3.373.

Garety, P. A., & Hardy, A. (2017). The clinical relevance of appraisals of psychotic experiences. *World Psychiatry, 16*(2), 140–141. https://doi.org/10.1002/wps.20408.

Garety, P. A., & Hemsley, D. R. (1987). Characteristics of delusional experience. *European Archives of Psychiatry and Neurological Sciences, 236*(5), 294–298.

Garety, P. A., Ward, T., Freeman, D., Fowler, D., Emsley, R., Dunn, G., et al. (2017). SlowMo, a digital therapy targeting reasoning in paranoia, versus treatment as usual in the treatment of people who fear harm from others: Study protocol for a randomised controlled trial. *Trials, 18*(1), 510. https://doi.org/10.1186/s13063-017-2242-7.

Gregg, L., & Tarrier, N. (2007). Virtual reality in mental health: A review of the literature. *Social Psychiatry and Psychiatric Epidemiology, 42*(5), 343–354. https://doi.org/10.1007/s00127-007-0173-4.

Haddock, G., Eisner, E., Boone, C., Davies, G., Coogan, C., & Barrowclough, C. (2014). An investigation of the implementation of NICE-recommended CBT interventions for people with schizophrenia. *Journal of Mental Health, 23*(4), 162–165. https://doi.org/10.3109/09638237.2013.869571.

Haddock, G., McCarron, J., Tarrier, N., & Faragher, E. B. (1999). Scales to measure dimensions of hallucinations and delusions: The psychotic symptom rating scales (PSYRATS). *Psychological Medicine, 29*(4), 879–889.

Hardy, A. (2017). Pathways from trauma to psychotic experiences: A theoretically informed model of posttraumatic stress in psychosis. *Frontiers in Psychology, 8*. https://doi.org/10.3389/fpsyg.2017.00697.

Hardy, A., Wojdecka, A., West, J., Matthews, E., Golby, C. K., Ward, T., et al. (2018). How inclusive, user-centred design research can improve psychological therapies for psychosis. The development of SlowMo. *Journal of Medical Internet Research: JMIR, 5*(4), https://doi.org/10.2196/preprints.11222.

Heron, K. E., & Smyth, J. M. (2010). Ecological momentary interventions: incorporating mobile technology into psychosocial and health behaviour treatments. *British Journal of Health Psychology, 15*(Pt 1), 1–39. https://doi.org/10.1348/135910709X466063.

Luxton, D. D., McCann, R. A., Bush, N. E., Mishkind, M. C., & Reger, G. M. (2011). mHealth for mental health: Integrating smartphone technology in behavioral healthcare. *Professional Psychology: Research and Practice, 42*, 505–512. https://doi.org/10.1037/a0024485.

Mehl, S., Werner, D., & Lincoln, T. M. (2015). Does cognitive behavior therapy for psychosis (CBTp) show a sustainable effect on delusions? A meta-analysis. *Frontiers in Psychology, 6*. https://doi.org/10.3389/fpsyg.2015.01450.

Myin-Germeys, I., Birchwood, M., & Kwapil, T. (2011). From environment to therapy in psychosis: A real-world momentary assessment approach. *Schizophrenia Bulletin, 37*(2), 244–247. https://doi.org/10.1093/schbul/sbq164.

Myin-Germeys, I., Oorschot, M., Collip, D., Lataster, J., Delespaul, P., & van Os, J. (2009). Experience sampling research in psychopathology: Opening the black box of daily life. *Psychological Medicine, 39*(9), 1533–1547. https://doi.org/10.1017/S0033291708004947.

Naslund, J. A., Aschbrenner, K. A., Araya, R., Marsch, L. A., Unutzer, J., Patel, V., et al. (2017). Digital technology for treating and preventing mental disorders in low-income and middle-income countries: a narrative review of the literature. *Lancet Psychiatry, 4*(6), 486–500. https://doi.org/10.1016/S2215-0366(17)30096-2.

NICE. (2014). *Psychosis and schizophrenia in adults: Prevention and management*. Retrieved from https://www.nice.org.uk/guidance/CG178.

Peters, E., Joseph, S., Day, S., & Garety, P. (2004). Measuring delusional ideation: the 21-item Peters et al. delusions inventory (PDI). *Schizophrenia Bulletin, 30*(4), 1005–1022.

Peters, E., Ward, T., Jackson, M., Morgan, C., Charalambides, M., McGuire, P., et al. (2016). Clinical, socio-demographic and psychological characteristics in individuals with persistent psychotic experiences with and without a "need for care". *World Psychiatry, 15*(1), 41–52. https://doi.org/10.1002/wps.20301.

Pot-Kolder, R., Geraets, C. N. W., Veling, W., van Beilen, M., Staring, A. B. P., Gijsman, H. J., et al. (2018). Virtual-reality-based cognitive behavioural therapy versus waiting list control for paranoid ideation and social avoidance in patients with psychotic disorders: A single-blind randomised controlled trial. *Lancet Psychiatry, 5*(3), 217–226. https://doi.org/10.1016/S2215-0366(18)30053-1.

Reininghaus, U., Depp, C. A., & Myin-Germeys, I. (2016). Ecological interventionist causal models in psychosis: Targeting psychological mechanisms in daily life. *Schizophrenia Bulletin, 42*(2), 264–269. https://doi.org/10.1093/schbul/sbv193.

Rizzo, A., Schulteis, M. T., & Rothbaum, B. O. (2003). Ethical issues for the use of virtual reality in the psychological sciences. In S. S. Bush, & M. L. Drexler (Eds.), *Ethical issues in clinical neuropsychology* (pp. 243–280). Amsterdam: Swets & Zeitlinger Publishers.

Rizzo, A. S., & Koenig, S. T. (2017). Is clinical virtual reality ready for primetime? *Neuropsychology, 31*(8), 877–899. https://doi.org/10.1037/neu0000405.

Rus-Calafell, M., Garety, P., Sason, E., Craig, T. J. K., & Valmaggia, L. R. (2018). Virtual reality in the assessment and treatment of psychosis: A systematic review of its utility, acceptability and effectiveness. *Psychological Medicine, 48*(3), 362–391. https://doi.org/10.1017/S0033291717001945.

Schizophrenia Commission. (2012). *The abandoned illness: A report from the schizophrenia comission.* London: Rethink Mental Illness.

Slater, M. (2003). A note on presence terminology. *Presence Connect, 3*, 3.

So, S. H., Peters, E. R., Swendsen, J., Garety, P. A., & Kapur, S. (2014). Changes in delusions in the early phase of antipsychotic treatment—An experience sampling study. *Psychiatry Research, 215*(3), 568–573. https://doi.org/10.1016/j.psychres.2013.12.033.

Thewissen, V., Bentall, R. P., Lecomte, T., van Os, J., & Myin-Germeys, I. (2008). Fluctuations in self-esteem and paranoia in the context of daily life. *Journal of Abnormal Psychology, 117*(1), 143–153. https://doi.org/10.1037/0021-843X.117.1.143.

Thomas, N. (2015). What's really wrong with cognitive behavioral therapy for psychosis? *Frontiers in Psychology, 6*. https://doi.org/10.3389/fpsyg.2015.00323.

Turner, D. T., van der Gaag, M., Karyotaki, E., & Cuijpers, P. (2014). Psychological interventions for psychosis: A meta-analysis of comparative outcome studies. *The American Journal of Psychiatry, 171*(5), 523–538. https://doi.org/10.1176/appi.ajp.2013.13081159.

van der Gaag, M. (2014). The efficacy of CBT for severe mental illness and the challenge of dissemination in routine care. *World Psychiatry, 13*(3), 257–258. https://doi.org/10.1002/wps.20162.

van der Gaag, M., Valmaggia, L. R., & Smit, F. (2014). The effects of individually tailored formulation-based cognitive behavioural therapy in auditory hallucinations and delusions: A meta-analysis. *Schizophrenia Research, 156*(1), 30–37. https://doi.org/10.1016/j.schres.2014.03.016.

Ward, T., & Garety, P. A. (2017). Fast and slow thinking in distressing delusions: A review of the literature and implications for targeted therapy. *Schizophrenia Research*. https://doi.org/10.1016/j.schres.2017.08.045.

Wentzel, J., van der Vaart, R., Bohlmeijer, E. T., & van Gemert-Pijnen, J. E. (2016). Mixing online and face-to-face therapy: How to benefit from blended care in mental health care. *JMIR Mental Health, 3*(1), e9. https://doi.org/10.2196/mental.4534.

Wessely, S., Buchanan, A., Reed, A., Cutting, J., Everitt, B., Garety, P., et al. (1993). Acting on delusions. I: PREVALENCE. *The British Journal of Psychiatry, 163*, 69–76.

Woods, A., & Wilkinson, S. (2017). Appraising appraisals: Role of belief in psychotic experiences. *Lancet Psychiatry, 4*(12), 891–892. https://doi.org/10.1016/S2215-0366(17)30434-0.

Wykes, T., Steel, C., Everitt, B., & Tarrier, N. (2008). Cognitive behavior therapy for schizophrenia: effect sizes, clinical models, and methodological rigor. *Schizophrenia Bulletin, 34*(3), 523–537. https://doi.org/10.1093/schbul/sbm114.

Definition of Key Terms

Appraisal The cognitive evaluation and interpretation of an experience or event.

Belief flexibility The metacognitive capacity of reflecting on one's own beliefs, changing them in the light of reflection and evidence, and generating and considering alternatives.

Blended therapy Any combination of web-, mobile- or technology-based application with face-to-face therapy.

Fast thinking Rapid or immediate judgement, jumping to conclusions, emotional, gut-based reasoning.

Paranoia The fear that other people intend to cause you harm.

Persecutory delusions Beliefs or thoughts held with high intensity that others are persecuting you or intend to cause you harm.

SlowMo Slow down for a moment, a blended therapy for fears of harm from others, targeting fast and slow thinking.

Slow thinking Analytical, rational, considered reasoning.

CHAPTER 26

Being a Scientist–Practitioner in the Field of Psychosis: Experiences From Voices Clinics

Georgie Paulik*†, Neil Thomas‡,§, Evie Glasshouse¶, Mark Hayward‖,#
*Perth Voices Clinic, Murdoch, WA, Australia, †University of Western Australia, Perth, WA, Australia, ‡Centre for Mental Health, Swinburne University of Technology, Hawthorn, VIC, Australia, §Alfred Health, Melbourne, VIC, Australia, ¶School of Psychology and Exercise Science, Murdoch University, Murdoch, WA, Australia, ‖University of Sussex, Brighton, United Kingdom, #Sussex Partnership NHS Foundation Trust, Worthing, United Kingdom

Key Learning Objectives

- To learn about voices clinics and how they address the needs of clients, clinicians, and students.
- To introduce the scientist–practitioner model and its application for people with psychosis.
- To understand the challenges and limitations when translating basic research findings into clinical services
- To consider ways of integrating lived experience perspectives into service delivery and new research agendas.

INTRODUCTION

Since the 1950s, there has been a major move in high-income countries from services treating psychotic disorders primarily in inpatient settings ('asylums'), to seeing these clients in the community. This transition in mental health services has had numerous benefits, including seeing the client and their experiences in their own real-world context, allowing the client to retain their current level of functioning (i.e. working, seeing friends and family, engaging in leisure and coping activities, etc.), better protection of human rights, reducing stigma, and increasing client satisfaction and treatment adherence (Thornicroft & Tansella, 2002).

A Clinical Introduction to Psychosis. https://doi.org/10.1016/B978-0-12-815012-2.00026-2

Similarly, there has been a recent shift from clinician's choosing treatments based on diagnosis, to selecting interventions, which target specific experiences or symptoms causing distress and functional impairment. For instance, as reviewed in Chapter 15, Cognitive Behaviour Therapy for psychosis (CBTp) comprises a wide variety of topics and skills to cover the diversity of different symptoms that may be present in people with psychosis, and is typically oriented to the chosen goal of the client. More recently, CBTp and other third-wave CBT interventions (see Chapter 16) have started to target specific symptoms, such as delusions or hallucinations, so that more time is spent in therapy on the most relevant experiences for an individual in the hope that such targeted interventions may generate better outcomes (e.g. Freeman & Garety, 2006; Hayward, Edgecumbe, Jones, Berry, & Strauss, 2017; Hayward, Jones, Bogen-Johnston, Thomas, & Strauss, 2017; Shawyer et al., 2012; Strauss, Thomas, & Hayward, 2015; Trower et al., 2004). This symptom-focussed approach also helps to reduce the influence of a diagnosis upon treatment choices, which may be helpful when seeing client's whose diagnosis has been shown to have modest-poor interrater reliability and stability, such as delusional disorder, transient/brief psychotic disorder, and psychosis not-otherwise-specified (Fusar-Poli et al., 2016). A particular advantage of this shift in treatment focus is that some of the symptoms common to psychosis—such as voice hearing—also occur in other clinical populations, as well as in the 'healthy' population. Thus, targeting specific symptoms focusses attention on developing treatments that specifically address their underlying causal mechanisms.

Hallucination: an experience involving the apparent perception of something not present.

Hallucinations are a ubiquitous example of a 'symptom' that can be experienced trans-diagnostically. A hallucination refers to a perception that cannot be explained by stimuli in the physical environment, such that a person hears (*auditory hallucinations*), sees (*visual hallucinations*), feels (*tactile hallucinations*, or *somatic hallucinations* when the sensation occurs within the body), smells (*olfactory hallucinations*), or tastes (*gustatory hallucinations*) something that no one else within their environment can detect. The most well-known type of hallucination is auditory, typically in the form of 'hearing voices' (as the experience will be named hereafter). Large population studies have found that a significant proportion of people (2.5%) hear voices at some stage of their lives (not due to a condition such as drug intoxication or fever), and often in the absence of diagnosable mental disorder or other psychotic symptoms (e.g. McGrath, Saha, Al-Hamzawi, et al., 2015). Somewhat of a surprise to many is that most people who hear voices will be given a diagnosis other than a psychotic disorder, or no diagnosis at all (Johns et al., 2014). The other most common diagnostic groups in which hallucinations present include Posttraumatic Stress Disorder (PTSD), other anxiety disorders, mood disorders, personality disorders, and eating disorders (Alsawy, Wood, Taylor, & Morrison, 2015; Waters, Blom, Jardri, Hugdahl, & Sommer, 2017), as well as a range of neurological conditions, such as Alzheimer's Disorder and Parkinson's Disease (El Haj, Jardri, Larøi, & Antoine, 2016; Pagonabarraga et al., 2016). In addition, hallucinatory experiences are relatively common in 'healthy' younger (Maijer, Palmen, & Sommer, 2017) and older adults, including those recently bereaved (Badcock, Dehon, & Larøi, 2017).

This new trend in targeting interventions at specific symptoms, irrespective of diagnosis, is emerging in transdiagnostic voices clinics around the world. These include clinics in Melbourne (Australia), Sussex (UK), Perth (Australia), and until recently Utrecht (Netherlands). Additionally, child and adolescent clinics (not covered in this chapter) have also opened in Lille (France), Groningen (Netherlands) and Perth (Australia—a second site of Perth Voices Clinic). These clinics have been set up to meet the need for (1) individual and group psychological therapies for people who experience distressing voices or other related perceptual experiences, (2) training of current and future psychologists and other mental health clinicians, and (3) conducting further research in this field. Fig. 26.1 illustrates the basic structure and activities at three adult voices clinics, with the allocation of time spent across these activities shown in Fig. 26.2.

Voices clinics provide dedicated out-patient services for people distressed by voices that others cannot hear.

The scientist–practitioner model (also called the Boulder Model or the research–practitioner model) provides a fundamental basis for the practice of clinical psychology and clinical neuropsychology. It is a graduate training approach for professional psychologists that encourages clinicians in the field to utilise empirical research to influence their applied practice, while simultaneously allowing their applied practice to shape the direction of their future research (Corrie & Callanan, 2001). There is a continuum of perspectives on what it means to be a scientist–practitioner, with one end of the continuum occupied by clinicians who keep up to date with the latest advances in evidence-based practices and evaluate their own clients' progress only, through to the other end, occupied by clinician-researchers conducting translational research. The scientist–practitioner model is the program most commonly used to train psychologists in Australia, United Kingdom, United States, and Canada. Translational research can be simply conceptualised as 'the translation from basic

A core principle of the **scientist–practitioner model** is that research and practice are inherently intertwined.

Translational research applies findings from basic research to enhance clinical practice and policy.

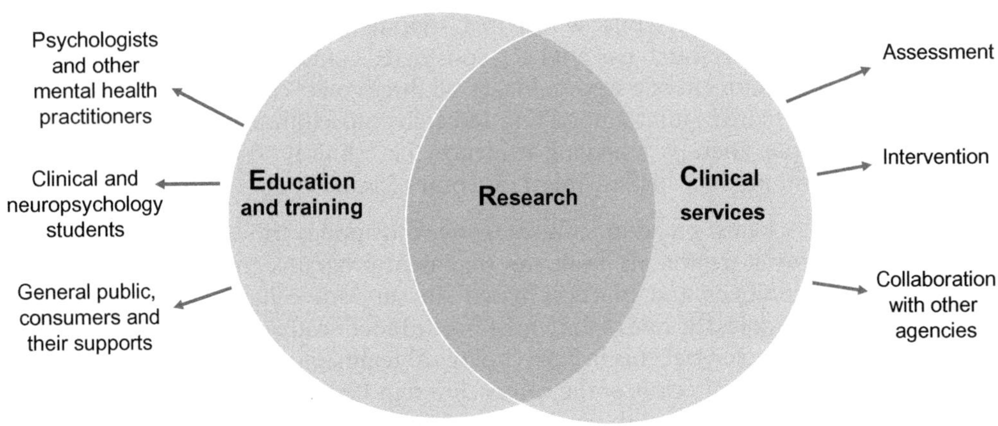

FIG. 26.1
The three principal pillars of activity in the Melbourne, Sussex, and Perth voices clinics.

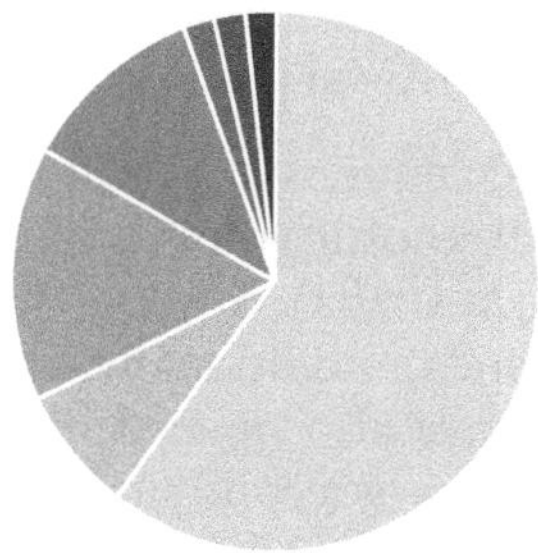

FIG. 26.2
Estimated division of service activities at the voices clinics.

research to new clinical interventions that can be used to improve human health', with the most successful translational research transferring 'results from empirical research into health practice and policy' (Werner-Seidler, Perry, & Christensen, 2016, p. 1). This chapter will help to illustrate the benefits and challenges of this process in real clinical settings.

Despite its strengths, however, there have been several criticisms of the scientist–practitioner model (Long & Hollin, 1997). For instance, it has been argued that the roles and skills of the scientist and practitioner are incompatible—an argument that has not been substantiated. Another is that the reality of clinical settings is not conducive to research. Indeed, putting research into practice is rarely simple, due to a range of structural, organisational, and funding barriers, including low prioritisation of research roles for professional psychologists (Smith & Thew, 2017). Thus, whilst this argument may seem compelling, it is often because research has not been considered—and thus built-in—during the initial development of a service. In fact, all three voices clinics are good examples of the alternative—that embedding research into clinical practice is viable. Furthermore, there is emerging evidence that clinical services that have a research arm produce better clinical outcomes (Smith & Thew, 2017).

'A scientist-practitioner is someone who applies critical thought to practice, uses proven treatments, evaluates treatment programs and procedures, and applies techniques and practices based on supportive literature. As such, one who embodies the role of a scientist-practitioner neatly integrates science and practice to best serve clients in a psychological realm' (Jones & Mehr, 2007, p. 770). The Clinical Directors of the voices clinics in Perth (GP), Melbourne (NT), and Sussex (MH) regard themselves as scientist–practitioners—with their research and clinical work in the field of voice hearing mutually informing one another. Here, we use these three examples to illustrate how a scientist–practitioner could establish and run a voices clinic, embed translational research, and incorporate a teaching agenda. Complementing these viewpoints, each subsection will be summarised and critiqued from a research-consumer perspective (author EV).

THE DEVELOPMENT OF THE MELBOURNE, SUSSEX, AND PERTH VOICES CLINICS

Table 26.1 provides a summary of the operating models of the voices clinics in Melbourne (Australia; MVC), Sussex (UK; SVC), and Perth (Australia; PVC). There are significant overlaps between the three clinics, which are mostly intentional, as the clinics have worked together and supported one another's development and refinement to ensure the best treatments, training, and research are being provided. There are also several differences between the clinics, related to different funding models, needs of the local communities, and research expertise of the Directors—that also illustrates the flexibility of these services.

Table 26.1 A Comparison of Models of Operation of the Three Voices Clinics

	Melbourne voices clinic	Sussex voices clinic	Perth voices clinic
Timeline	Opened in 2006.	Opened May 2014, with the support of MVC.	Opened May 2016, with the support of SVC and MVC.
Current objectives	(1) Provide assessment and consultation (2) Specialist provision of current best-practice psychological intervention for voices (3) Provide training to postgraduate clinical psychology students (4) Conduct research to expand the evidence-base for psychological approaches to hearing voices, including trials of new intervention approaches	(1) Provide assessment and evidence-based interventions to voice hearers (2) Train and supervise mental health practitioners in the delivery of evidence-based interventions to voice hearers (3) Conduct clinical and other research into voice hearing (4) Provide other education and support to consumers and their carers (i.e. through forums, website, events)	(1) Provide assessment and evidence-based interventions to voice hearers (2) Provide training and supervision to postgraduate psychology students (3) Train mental health practitioners to work effectively with voice hearers (4) Establish a research registry and conduct research on hearing voices across age groups

Continued

Table 26.1 A Comparison of Models of Operation of the Three Voices Clinics—cont'd

	Melbourne voices clinic	Sussex voices clinic	Perth voices clinic
	(5) Support the local Hearing Voices Network		(5) Provide education and advocacy (e.g. stigma reduction) in the community
Location	Based in a research centre with joint affiliations to university and hospital.	Based within community mental health teams and early intervention in psychosis services across the National Health Service, in Sussex. This location serves the aim of increasing access to therapy by enabling and supporting members of the existing mental health workforce.	Based at Murdoch University. This location helps to facilitate research collaborations and training of future psychologists. PVC has recently opened a youth site (ages 12–25) at the request of Headspace, a youth mental health service.
Treatments	Formulation-based CBT for voices, based on coping strategy enhancement (CSE; Tarrier, Harwood, Yusopoff, Beckett, & Baker, 1990) and cognitive therapy (Chadwick & Birchwood, 1994; Morrison, Haddock, & Tarrier, 1995). Other approaches (e.g. third wave, trauma-focused) may be drawn on when justified by individual formulation. Novel interventions are offered via research trials. All intervention is one-to-one. The clinic refers clients to peer support groups run by local Hearing Voices Network.	CBT-informed interventions: CSE over four individual sessions (Hayward, Edgecumbe, et al., 2017); Guided CBT for voices (GiVE; Hazell, Hayward, Cavanagh, Jones, & Strauss, 2017; Hazell, Hayward, Cavanagh, Jones, & Strauss, 2018) over 8 individual sessions; Relating Therapy (Hayward, Jones, et al., 2017) over 16 individual session; and Mindfulness-based Therapy (Chadwick et al., 2016) offered over 12 group sessions. Patients are typically offered a combination of therapies that begins with CSE.	CBT for voices is standard individual intervention. The behavioural section is CSE therapy and the cognitive section is taken from GiVE. PVC also offers Imagery Rescripting (Hagenaars & Arntz, 2012) for voice hearers with PTSD. Both approaches are 10 sessions, including the initial assessment session.
Funding model	The Clinic operates as an arm of a hallucinations research program,	Funded by the NHS as part of routine clinical care.	Bulk billing of clients (no payments received from client) through the

Table 26.1 A Comparison of Models of Operation of the Three Voices Clinics—cont'd

	Melbourne voices clinic	Sussex voices clinic	Perth voices clinic
	supported by space within a research centre, with therapy provision via students on placement. Previous models have included Medicare bulk-billing.		Australian national public health scheme, Medicare. This covers the costs of 10 sessions per calendar year.
Outcomes measures	Measures vary according to treatment, usually including PSYRATS-AH. Ecological momentary assessment also used in recent trials. Voice Impact Scale recently introduced.	Hamilton Program for Schizophrenia Voices Questionnaire; Patient Health Questionnaire; Generalised Anxiety Disorder Assessment; Five Factor Mindfulness Questionnaire; Beliefs About Voices Questionnaires—Revised; Rosenberg Self Esteem Scale; Choice of Outcome In CBT for psychosEs questionnaire; Short Warwick-Edinburgh Mental Well-being Scale.	PSYRATS-AH; Beliefs About Voices Questionnaires—Revised Depression Anxiety and Stress Scale; Rosenberg Self Esteem Scale; Self Compassion Scale; PTSD Symptom Scale Social and Occupational Functioning Scale
Addressing community needs and consultation with people with lived experience	Strong relationship with local Hearing Voices Network, including collaborative research. Lived Experience Advisory Panel embedded in associated research team.	Works closely with local organisations, including the Hearing Voices Network and universities, to help shape and promote the service. SVC is also advised by a group of people with lived experience. A website has been developed to facilitate the sharing of resources and lessons learnt.	Works closely with the Hearing Voices Network (WA) and other local mental health services, to help shape and promote the service. PVC adopts a 'codesign' approach to service and research, and includes people with lived experience on its Research Advisory Committee. Website offers resource pages for consumers, carers, and clinicians, plus on-line, moderated, peer support forums

Notes: *PSYRATS-AH*, Psychotic Symptoms Rating Scale—Auditory Hallucinations.

Melbourne's Voices Clinic: Initial Implementation of an Evidence-Based Model

Since its inception, the core aim of MVC has been to increase access to empirically supported psychological interventions for people with persisting and distressing voices. To base practice on best evidence, therapy choices were initially influenced by prevailing trial evidence and clinical practice guidelines (e.g. National Institute for Clinical Excellence, 2014) on psychological interventions for psychosis. In line with this, the principle treatment chosen was Cognitive Behavioural Therapy for psychosis (CBTp; Thomas, Rossell, Farhall, Shawyer, & Castle, 2011). CBTp is an individual, formulation-based, psychological therapy approach, which draws from the broad repertoire of cognitive behavioural methods according to individual need (see Chapter 15). CBTp provided a model that was well suited to being offered in a specialist clinic setting: strongly grounded in best practice, yet having much flexibility for individual tailoring to accommodate complexity.

Yet, as CBTp is quite a broad model, to inform our therapeutic approach at the clinic we found benefit in more specific operationalisations of practice suited to seeing a critical mass of people with the specific experience of voices. In considering the available CBTp literature, the *coping strategy enhancement* (CSE) approach described by Tarrier et al. (1990) and Tarrier (1992) for residual psychotic symptoms, proved useful as an initial organising framework. This approach involves a collaborative process of developing an individualised functional analysis of voices, which is used to inform development, implementation, and fine-tuning of more effective coping. The functional analysis considers variables that predict variation in the occurrence of voices (e.g. stress, sleep, environmental noise, activity, specific triggers) and how the person responds to them (e.g. interacting with voices, emotional responses, conscious coping strategies). The use of functional analysis also provided a formulation framework suited to incorporating empirical research on antecedents of voices (e.g. from experience sampling research) and potential helpfulness versus unhelpfulness of different coping responses. Hence, this approach enabled practice to be based upon a synthesis of (a) a randomised trial-validated therapeutic framework, (b) broad behavioural principles, (c) empirical research on potential triggering and maintaining cycles for distress in relation to voices, and (d) the client's own observations of patterns in their experiences.

Whilst relatively uniform in our initial use of coping enhancement for clients seen at MVC, subsequent sessions would become more flexible and formulation driven, drawing on multiple models and methods reported in the literature. Most typically, the cognitive part of CBTp was influenced by the cognitive models of Chadwick, Birchwood, and others (Birchwood, Meaden, Trower, Gilbert, & Plaistow, 2000; Chadwick & Birchwood, 1994; Gilbert et al., 2001; Trower et al., 2004) and Morrison and colleagues (Morrison, 1998, 2001), which explicitly incorporate the role of appraisals and beliefs about voices in mediating the associated distress. In this way, our therapeutic work with people who hear voices broadly conformed to a CBTp approach (e.g. Fowler, Garety, & Kuipers, 1995), with behavioural formulation (functional analysis) and work (coping, modifying responses to voices) in earlier stages, and cognitive restructuring being used, as indicated, in the individual case as therapy progresses.

In determining the duration of therapy, MVC was influenced by the Medicare funding model available in Australia, which funded 12 sessions per year (now reduced to 10). Although trials of CBTp have often offered longer courses of 16–20 sessions, there were pragmatic reasons for trialling a briefer intervention (concerning sustainability and funding), and in fact we found 12 sessions provided sufficient treatment time for most people when we were working on the specific target of voices. Those clients who had need for further work were invited to consider re-referral as an option for further intervention. Finally, whilst most assessments and interventions were initially delivered by the Clinical Director (NT), the majority are now delivered by postgraduate clinical psychology students on placement at MVC. This shift in operations has the advantage of freeing up the Clinical Director's time to apply for research grants and provide advanced training to psychology students and upskilling other healthcare professionals.

Melbourne's Voices Clinic: As a Specialist Clinic and Centre for Research

As the MVC progressed and developed an increasing level of specialist practice-based expertise, we have examined ways to develop innovations in practice. This has included both published advancements to conducting therapy for voices and application of therapeutic methods within the context of research trials, which has aligned well with PhD students working with the clinic to examine a particular approach. This enabled the clinic to move from a model of implementing evidence-based practise into one where practise begins to inform evidence. For example, work at the clinic has supported the development of ways to adapt acceptance and commitment therapy (Thomas, Morris, Shawyer, & Farhall, 2013) and mindfulness training (Louise, Rossell, & Thomas, in press) for voices; using smartphones to support coping (Bell et al., 2018); peer work for voices (Dent-Pearce, Daya, Karagounis, & Thomas, 2015); and trauma-focused therapy (Brand, Rossell, Bendall, & Thomas, 2017). These have enabled the clinic to make contributions to the international literature ranging from conceptual contributions, small case series, and pilot and feasibility trials conducted at the clinic (e.g. Bell et al., 2018; Louise et al., in press) to larger grant-funded trials for people with psychosis conducted as part of collaborations with broader research teams and local mental health services (e.g. Shawyer et al., 2017; Thomas et al., 2016).

A challenge we have faced in doing this is how to offer a specific intervention to people coming to the clinic in place of an individually tailored therapy as the standard option. We have navigated this issue by offering clients the opportunity to receive either current 'best practice' therapy or a trial of a 'new way of working'. As participation with a trial is often readily available, it can be feasible for people to do a course of a new therapy whilst on a waiting list for best practice therapy afterwards, or vice versa. This is complemented by focused recruitment from local networks directly into intervention studies. This testing of new ways of working creates a spirit of collaboration with clients of the clinic, who are able to provide feedback on new therapeutic methods that can be captured systematically via qualitative research. Alongside this, the nonintervention based research stream is supported by colocation with other hallucination researchers. Clinic clients can opt in to a register to be contacted about current research studies, which supports recruitment to parallel studies. As well as conducting questionnaire-based and experimental research on psychological processes related to therapies, this program has included studies of hallucination phenomenology, and mechanisms of hallucinations using neurocognitive and imaging methods.

Sussex Voices Clinic: Increasing Access to Evidence-Based Interventions (for Clients and Clinicians)

The scientist–practitioner model is also operational at SVC in the evidence-based therapies chosen and delivered. The interventions offered by SVC follow a similar approach to MVC—as the accessible and behavioural approach of CSE is offered initially, followed by a more explicit cognitive focus on beliefs about voices and self. However, rather than behavioural and cognitive work being blended, a stepped approach is offered. All clients are offered four sessions of CSE at 'Level 1' to facilitate engagement, stabilisation, and some early gains. This intervention can be offered by frontline practitioners with brief training and ongoing supervision. A range of locally developed and evaluated therapies are available within the second step for clients who want and need further therapy. The interventions at 'Level 2' were all developed and evaluated within SVC and vary in length (4–16 sessions), modality (group or individual), content (with some containing 'third-wave' elements such as mindfulness practices and the development of assertive relating) and the therapist skill required to deliver them (some requiring delivery by expert therapists, and others by frontline practitioners). The choice of intervention at Level 2 is informed by both the needs of the client and the availability of appropriately trained therapists within the client's clinical team.

A core principle of SVC is the robust collection of data by Clinic Assistants (who are not involved in the delivery of the interventions). This commitment to data collection is allowing large datasets to be accumulated, and the analysis of this data allows us to evaluate the clinical and cost effectiveness of these evidence-based interventions within the 'real world' of routine clinical practice. Lessons learnt from these evaluations influence subsequent practice within SVC and are also made available more widely through publication (e.g. Hayward, Edgecumbe, et al., 2017). Analysis of our data also allows us to explore other important issues, such as engagement/drop-out and predictors of outcome

(Paulik, Jones, & Hayward, 2018) and effectiveness within nonpsychosis populations. So again, allowing research to inform practise, and in turn practise to be written up as clinical research, with this feedback cycle continuing with the aim of refining and improving interventions.

Sussex Voices Clinic: As a Centre for Research

Clients within SVC are routinely offered opportunities to participate in high quality research studies. Studies focus upon client experiences of receiving therapy (McHale, Hayward, & Jones, 2018), the assessment of clinician attitudes towards voice hearing (e.g. Bogen-Johnston, de Visser, Strauss, Berry, & Hayward, 2017), and the ability of nonexpert therapists to deliver CBT interventions (ISRCTN 16166070 https://doi.org/10.1186/ISRCTN16166070).

In addition to the evaluations described, SVC also offers its patients opportunities to participate in high-quality national, multisite studies that are exploring various aspects of the care and treatment of patients with severe mental health problems. SVC has also developed and led the delivery of studies that have evaluated the development of novel interventions and measures, but always does so in collaboration with other clinical services and sites.

Perth Voices Clinic: A Specialist Service in Development

As with the other two voices clinics, PVC operates within the scientist–practitioner model by following the 'utilise', 'evaluate', and 'produce' aspects of the scientist–practitioner model, as follows: (1) *Using empirically supported treatments*: the primary intervention offered (CBT) was chosen because it (a) has well-established efficacy, (b) is recommended in treatment guidelines for psychosis (see Chapter 1), and (c) has been the main approach used in the other two voices clinics, with good outcomes (Hayward, Edgecumbe, et al., 2017; Hayward, Jones, et al., 2017; Paulik et al., 2018; Thomas et al., 2011); (2) *Evaluating and modifying treatments*: PVC routinely evaluates the effectiveness of its interventions through the administration of standard outcomes measures for all clients at the beginning, middle, and end of therapy and uses these outcomes to make improvements to practice, when indicated (e.g. due to limited gains on measures of self-esteem and daily functioning more time is now spent during the CSE therapy phase on improving activities, which give the client a sense of achievement); (3) *Contributing to the evidence base*: PVC encourages experiences learnt through client assessment and therapy to drive new research directions, i.e. practice-driven research. For example, due to the high rates of repeat childhood trauma reported by PVC clients (and in the research literature), PVC is currently piloting an intervention for PTSD in voice hearers named Imagery Rescripting. PVC plans to apply for funding to conduct a randomised controlled trial (RCT) on this approach if the pilot has positive outcomes, so that effectiveness can be established, and ultimately to inform health practice and policy.

Perth Voices Clinic: As a Centre for Education and Training

As shown in Table 26.1, PVC places a large emphasis on education and training. It is part of our mission statement to help upskill future and current psychologists and allied health workers in the fields of psychosis and voice hearing. Our goal for this educational component is to dispel common myths around voice hearing, and to help eradicate stigma. Our training and advocacy work includes providing advanced training to postgraduate student psychologists at local universities, and having students on placement at PVC. From a teaching and training perspective, embedding students within PVC means that future clinical psychologists are gaining the knowledge, skills, and confidence to deliver psychological therapies for people hearing voices or with other hallucinatory experiences across a range of diagnoses. Our trainees report valuing the opportunity to work with clients in a structured and supportive environment, and that it has helped them to erase the stigma and anxiety around discussing these symptoms with clients (see Box 26.1).

Our broader educational initiatives include providing (1) free 1-h presentations on voice hearing to local government and nongovernment mental health services, (2) workshops delivered to local mental health organisations on

Box 26.1 A Student Perspective on Working in a Voices Clinic

Caitlin Reddyhough

I undertook placement at PVC during the first year of my Masters in Applied Psychology (Clinical Psychology) at Murdoch University. There was a consistent emphasis throughout all of my studies in psychology, on the necessity of integrating research into practise, in line with the scientist–practitioner model. However, I often found little clear direction on how to practically achieve this. My placement at PVC gave me a clear framework of how to integrate research with practise, and also the first-hand evidence of the benefits of this approach. I found that the structured administration of assessment measures during the CBT for voices program served not only as a useful way for me to track my client's progress, but also as a useful reflection tool throughout therapy. At the beginning of my placement, I felt some ambivalence about getting one of my colleagues to invite my clients to join the PVC research registry. However, I was surprised to find that clients were more often than not eager to be given the opportunity to contribute to research, and at times gained a sense of accomplishment by doing so.

My placement at PVC opened my mind to the wide range of possible presentations of voice hearers. Naturally this led to some uncertainty as to whether they would all be able to equally benefit from the same treatment program. However, I actually found that following the empirically supported framework of CBT for voices allowed for greater room to individually tailor therapy to meet my clients' individual needs and preferences. While I followed the same treatment framework, therapy looked very different for each of my clients. Working with the diverse range of clients at PVC ignited my passion for research in the area of voice hearing. Following placement at PVC, I have articulated in to the Doctorate in Psychology, which provides a greater opportunity for translational research. My research is focussing on reducing healthcare professionals' stigma towards people who hear voices. I am particularly grateful for having undertaken a placement at PVC at the outset of my training, and can see how this experience has shaped my approach to clinical practice and research.

assessment and evidence-based interventions for voice hearers, (3) hosting international guest presenters at open workshops on voice hearing, and (4) speaking at local community events relating to voice hearing (i.e. information sessions held by the local Hearing Voices Network, at mental health conferences, and at special events, such as World Hearing Voices Day). Education of the general community, including people with lived experience and expertise in hearing voices and their family and friends, is also essential. Finally, we have developed a website and Facebook page and contribute pieces to Australian newspapers and magazines to help disseminate accurate information on voice hearing in an easily accessibly way.

Perth Voices Clinic: As a Centre for Research

PVC has a Research Director, Prof. Johanna C. Badcock, with particular expertise in the field of cognition and voices/hallucinations in clinical and nonclinical groups. Having both a Clinical and Research Director has enabled both the separation and integration of these two activities—both of which have been important at different stages of service development. To get research activity happening, willing participants need to be accessible. We cannot put the cart before the horse. As such, since its inception in 2016 PVC dedicated much of its time to setting up the clinical and student training components of the clinic, and establishing a network of local, national, and international research collaborators. In this time, PVC has also received ethics approval to routinely evaluate the clinical service and publish on these findings, and to develop a research registry for both youth and adults (both of which require participant consent). The research registry comprises a list of names of people who hear voices who are willing to be contacted (a consent-to-contact list) by researchers recruiting into their projects on voices or related experiences. PVC has also set up a Research Advisory Committee, which meets every 6 months, and membership is held by a range of clinicians (from the nongovernment and government mental health sectors), researchers, academics, and people with lived experience. This committee governs the use of the registry and helps guide research being conducted at PVC in other ways, including helping ensure research is translational where possible. The Clinical Director has continued her research interests in developing novel clinical interventions for voices, while The Research Director has expanded her research program on the causal mechanisms of hallucinations to include studies examining the role of socioemotional factors in the onset of hallucinations. Both directors continue to supervise student research investigating voices relating to several topics, including stigma, self-compassion, and hallucinations in older adults. One of the broader research goals of PVC is to widen the scope of topics being explored and the age range being investigated, within the field of voices research. To this end, PVC encourages researchers and consumers with divergent areas of interest and expertise to engage in cross- or interdisciplinary collaborations and cosupervision of students.

CONSUMER PERSPECTIVE ON VOICES CLINICS

Historically, mental health treatment has been derived from a top-down, paternalistic medical model in which the client has little to no say in their treatment options (Bellack, 2006). In recent times, consumers have advocated for a more client-centred and heterogeneous model in the treatment of mental health concerns. Consumers of mental health services should be considered the experts of their personal journey as well as evaluating the services rendered to them, with their individual experience being an important part of shaping future therapy approaches (Bennetts, Pinches, Paluch, & Fossey, 2013). Where possible, it is in the best interests of their clients if clinics consider both: (1) the client outcomes of their treatment approaches on a regular basis and shape treatment style to the individual: and (2) seek input from consumers about the clinic's treatment approaches.

The three voices clinics described do this by incorporating the council of an advisory team of individuals with lived experience, which helps guide clinics and practitioners to a model of treatment, which values the individual needs of the client, as well as creating a stronger therapeutic alliance between practitioner and client. Consumers of specialist clinics such as voices clinics may have exhausted other treatment options available to them and come seeking the service for an immediate need. While research is an integral part of the scientist–practitioner model, it may not be a client's primary concern. Therefore, a blended approach such as those taken by these three voices clinics highlights how clients can still have their primary needs met, as well as informing future research of the effectiveness of the clinic's practices.

Summary

The three voices clinics each uphold the principles of the scientist–practitioner model in their own ways. The first established clinic, MVC, is CTBp focused, which lends itself to an evidence-based practice approach that can be tailored to suit the individual needs of clients seeking help to cope with the challenges they face. However, it has been highlighted that this approach could also be too broad and lead to ineffective implementation. MVC also has the resources to conduct research trials on promising therapies in conjunction with the regular CBTp practices offered. SVC only offers proven therapies based on empirical evidence and conducts regular evaluations of clinical outcomes and the cost effectiveness of treatments. PVC has followed suit in this way, and also benefits from having both a Research and Clinical director, which enables the clinic to conduct both treatment and research in a parsimonious fashion. All clinics seek the input of consumers with lived experience of voices to continually evolve the clinic's practices. There is no 'right' way to implement the scientist–practitioner model, as seen here. Constricted by funding, availability of trained practitioners, and the needs of the client base, voices clinics should operate in a manner, which is able to offer the best treatment available as indicated by evidence, as well as being open to tailoring their approaches to the individual client in a method, which is an effective use of their resources.

CHALLENGES FOR THE VOICES CLINICS

Ethics of Combining Research and Practice

Conducting clinical research trials within a clinical service presents ethical issues. It is critical that any interventions that have not yet shown to be effective are not presented to clients as though efficacy has already been established, and clients must be given the choice to participate in the trial *or* the evidence-based treatment delivered as standard practice at that clinic. In keeping with ethical and responsible conduct of research, there must also not be any persuasion on behalf of the clinician as to which treatment the client choses to do. The clinics' procedures for managing this issue have been to carefully delineate the dual roles of researchers and those offering treatment, with consent to any research study being conducted by a researcher separate from the study team.

Balancing Empirically Supported Treatment With Innovations in Practice

Evidence-based practice involves the therapist making decisions about which therapy to deliver based on three guiding factors: (1) the best-available research evidence bearing on which treatments work best and why, (2) clinical judgement and experience in assessment and formulation of a client's presenting problems, and (3) client preferences and values. Working as a scientist–practitioner can involve weighing up how to balance between the implementation of empirically supported treatments and the use of more innovative therapy techniques, particularly in centres developing their own expertise. The NICE (2014) guidelines for psychotic disorders, for instance, recommend implementing therapy based on a manual that has been used in randomised controlled trials (RCTs). Yet, recent literature on interventions for voices has taken findings from the largest trials in new directions (Thomas et al., 2014). In practice, this can mean choosing between following with fidelity a well-established therapy manual that is over 20 years old (e.g. Fowler et al., 1995; Kingdon & Turkington, 1994), or using emerging therapeutic methods that have promising, but ultimately, limited data available for their effectiveness.

Empirically supported treatments refer to treatments that have met a minimum standard of research evidence.

This challenge is, in part, offset by the strongest evidence being for CBTp, which is an overtly formulation-based therapy that does not constrain delivery to a set series of methods. Many therapeutic methods such as competitive memory training (van der Gaag, van Oosterhout, Daalman, Sommer, & Korrelboom, 2012) and relating-based therapies (Hayward, Jones, et al., 2017; Paulik, Hayward, & Birchwood, 2013) have been trialled as discrete interventions, but it is feasible to incorporate elements from these approaches into formulation-driven CBTp. In turn, this provides opportunities for creative applications of therapeutic methods to voices, which may be scaled up into research trials.

We should remind ourselves, also, that most RCTs have involved comparisons with treatment-as-usual, which only demonstrates that seeing a therapist per se is more helpful than not seeing a therapist at all—leaving us to question the added value of the specific techniques of the intervention (Thomas, 2015). In practice, the field in psychological interventions is less black-and-white than in clinical drug trials: interventions delivered are often individually tailored, they include a range of intended and unintended therapeutic elements, and target outcomes that rely on subjective ratings. Hence, in our field, operating as a scientist–practitioner often requires consideration and integration of incomplete and complex data across therapy trails, and careful attention to information about the client's own experiences.

Consumer Perspective

For the individual client, hearing voices, like many symptoms of mental illness, may not have a single trajectory of progression nor be generated by similar factors (Allott et al., 2011). Individuals should not be treated with a 'one size fits all' approach, but rather a 'best fit' for each individual. However, the finite resources of clinics mean that a compromise of the chosen approaches may be necessary. One issue is that the lack of research on individual differences between voice hearers makes it challenging to choose best practices, with most evidence coming from psychosis research that may not translate perfectly in the context of voice hearing. The approach taken by a clinic should be to use the best available practice while considering the needs of their clientele. If resources permit, steps should be taken to both add to the existing body of knowledge about the effectiveness (or lack thereof) of the chosen treatment by the use of outcome measures, and implement other evidence-based treatments that may be effective for certain client's needs.

WHERE TO FROM HERE

The Final Stage of 'Translational' Research

As discussed in the previous two sections, all three clinics are conducting research into the effectiveness of novel or adapted interventions for voice hearers. Although conducting RCTs is considered by most as the last stage of translational research, Westfall, Mold, and Fagnan (2007) found that only 14% of interventions considered 'evidence based' are used in day-to-day clinical practice. Thus, in all areas of clinical research, including voice hearing, time and energy must be dedicated to ensuring that the very final stage of translational research is being achieved—that is, the outcomes of RCTs are being effectively integrated into policy and practise. This is more likely to be achieved when conducting 'context sensitive science', whereby the research is developed and conducted within the context in which it is intended for use (Werner-Seidler et al., 2016). Increasing stakeholder involvement and transdisciplinary collaboration throughout the research process is also likely to be instrumental to achieving these goals. All three Voices Clinics aspire to be influenced by the needs and views of their stakeholders and will continue to actively develop their practice in the light of lessons learnt within the 'real world'.

ADDITIONAL SUGGESTED READING ON THE SCIENTIST–PRACTITIONER MODEL

Lane, D. A., & Corrie, S. (2015). *The modern scientist-practitioner: A guide to practice in psychology*. US: Routledge.

Page, A., & Stritzke W. G. K. (2015). *Clinical psychology for trainees: Foundations of science-informed practice* (2nd ed.). UK: Cambridge University Press.

Sayette, M. A., Mayne, T. J., & Norcross, J. C. (2004). *Insider's guide to graduate programs in clinical and counseling psychology*. New York: Guilford.

References

Allott, K., Alvarez-Jimenez, M., Killackey, E. J., Bendall, S., McGorry, P. D., & Jackson, H. J. (2011). Patient predictors of symptom and functional outcome following cognitive behaviour therapy or befriending in first-episode psychosis. *Schizophrenia Research, 132*, 125–130. https://doi.org/10.1016/j.schres.2011.08.011.

Alsawy, S., Wood, L., Taylor, P., & Morrison, A. (2015). Psychotic experiences and PTSD: Exploring associations in a population survey. *Psychological Medicine, 45*(13), 2849–2859. https://doi.org/10.1017/S003329171500080X.

Badcock, J. C., Dehon, H., & Larøi, F. (2017). Hallucinations in healthy older adults: An overview of the literature and perspectives for future research. *Frontiers in Psychology, 8*, 1134. https://doi.org/10.3389/fpsyg.2017.01134.

Bell, I. H., Fielding-Smith, S. F., Hayward, M., Rossell, S. L., Lim, M. H., Farhall, J., & Thomas, N. (2018). Smartphone-based ecological momentary assessment and intervention in a blended coping-focused therapy for distressing voices: Development and case illustration. *Internet Interventions, 14*, 18–25.

Bellack, A. S. (2006). Scientific and consumer models of recovery in schizophrenia: Concordance, contrasts, and implications. *Schizophrenia Bulletin, 32*, 432–442. https://doi.org/10.1093/schbul/sbj044.

Bennetts, W., Pinches, A., Paluch, T., & Fossey, E. (2013). Real lives, real jobs: Sustaining consumer perspective work in the mental health sector. *Advances in Mental Health, 11*, 313–325. https://doi.org/10.5172/jamh.2013.11.3.313.

Birchwood, M., Meaden, A., Trower, P., Gilbert, P., & Plaistow, J. (2000). The power and omnipotence of voices: Subordination and entrapment by voices and significant others. *Psychological Medicine, 30*, 337–344.

Bogen-Johnston, L., de Visser, R., Strauss, C., Berry, K., & Hayward, M. (2017). "That little doorway where I could suddenly start shouting out": Barriers and enablers to the disclosure of distressing voices. *Journal of Health Psychology*. https://doi.org/10.1177/1359105317745965 [First published online 22nd December 2017].

Brand, R., Rossell, S. L., Bendall, S., & Thomas, N. (2017). Can we use an interventionist-causal paradigm to untangle the relationship between trauma, PTSD and psychosis? *Frontiers in Psychology, 8*. https://doi.org/10.3389/fpsyg.2017.00306.

Chadwick, P., & Birchwood, M. (1994). The omnipotence of voices. A cognitive approach to auditory hallucinations. *British Journal of Psychiatry, 164*, 190–201.

Chadwick, P., Strauss, C., Jones, A.-M., Kingdon, D., Ellett, L., Dannahy, L., & Hayward, M. (2016). Group mindfulness-based intervention for distressing voices: A pragmatic randomised controlled trial. *Schizophrenia Research, 175*(1), 168–173. https://doi.org/10.1016/j.schres.2016.04.001.

Corrie, S., & Callanan, M. M. (2001). Therapists' beliefs about research and the scientist-practitioner model in an evidence-based health care climate: A qualitative study. *British Journal of Medical Psychology, 74*, 135–149. https://doi.org/10.1348/000711201160858.

Dent-Pearce, L., Daya, I., Karagounis, J., & Thomas, N. (2015). Integrating peer work with a specific therapeutic target: Experiences from the Voice Exchange program. In K. Kellehear, A. Lane, M. Cassaniti, B. Tooth, C. Chapman, & S. Robertson, et al. (Eds.), *Proceedings of the 24th TheMHS mental health services conference 2014 ("what we share makes us strong")*. Balmain, Australia: TheMHS.

El Haj, M., Jardri, R., Larøi, F., & Antoine, P. (2016). Hallucinations, loneliness, and social isolation in Alzheimer's disease. *Cognitive Neuropsychiatry, 21*, 1–13. https://doi.org/10.1080/13546805.2015.1121139.

Fowler, D., Garety, P., & Kuipers, E. (1995). *Cognitive behaviour therapy for psychosis: Theory and practice*. Chichester, England: Wiley.

Freeman, D., & Garety, P. (2006). Helping patients with paranoid and suspicious thoughts: A cognitive–behavioural approach. *Advances in Psychiatric Treatment, 12*(6), 404–415.

Fusar-Poli, P., Cappucciati, M., Rutigliano, G., Heslin, M., Stahl, D., Brittenden, Z., et al. (2016). Diagnostic stability of ICD/DSM first episode psychosis diagnoses: Meta-analysis. *Schizophrenia Bulletin, 42*, 1395–1406.

Gilbert, P., Birchwood, M., Gilbert, J., Trower, P., Hay, J., Murray, B., et al. (2001). An exploration of evolved mental mechanisms for dominant and subordinate behaviour in relation to auditory hallucinations in schizophrenia and critical thoughts in depression. *Psychological Medicine, 31*, 1117–1127.

Hagenaars, M. A., & Arntz, A. (2012). Reduced intrusion development after post-trauma imagery rescripting; an experimental study. *Journal of Behavior Therapy and Experimental Psychiatry, 43*, 808–814.

Hayward, M., Edgecumbe, R., Jones, A., Berry, C., & Strauss, C. (2017). Brief coping strategy enhancement for distressing voices: An evaluation in routine clinical practice. *Behavioural and Cognitive Psychotherapy*, 1–12. https://doi.org/10.1017/S1352465817000388.

Hayward, M., Jones, A., Bogen-Johnston, L., Thomas, N., & Strauss, C. (2017). Relating therapy for distressing auditory hallucinations: A pilot randomized controlled trial. *Schizophrenia Research, 183*, 137–142.

Hazell, C. M., Hayward, M., Cavanagh, K., Jones, A.-M., & Strauss, C. (2017). Guided self-help cognitive behavioral intervention for VoicEs (GiVE): Study protocol for a pilot randomized controlled trial. *Trials, 17*(351). https://doi.org/10.1186/s13063-016-1494-y.

Hazell, C. M., Hayward, M., Cavanagh, K., Jones, A. M., & Strauss, C. (2018). Guided self-help cognitive-behaviour Intervention for VoicEs (GiVE): Results from a pilot randomised controlled trial in a transdiagnostic sample. *Schizophrenia Research, 195*, 441–447.

Johns, L. C., Kompus, K., Connell, M., Humpston, C., Lincoln, T. M., Longden, E., et al. (2014). Auditory verbal hallucinations in persons with and without a need for care. *Schizophrenia Bulletin, 40*, S255–S264. https://doi.org/10.1093/schbul/sbu005.

Jones, J. L., & Mehr, S. L. (2007). Foundations and assumptions of the scientist-practitioner model. *American Behavioral Scientist, 50*, 766–771. https://doi.org/10.1177/0002764206296454.

Kingdon, D. G., & Turkington, D. (1994). *Cognitive-behavioral therapy of schizophrenia*. New York, NY: Guilford Press.

Long, C. G., & Hollin, C. R. (1997). The scientist-practitioner model in clinical psychology: A critique. *Clinical Psychology & Psychotherapy*, *4*(2), 75–83.

Louise S., Rossell S.L. and Thomas N., Acceptability, feasibility and preliminary outcomes of an individual mindfulness intervention for hearing voices, *Behavioural and Cognitive Psychotherapy* (in press).

Maijer, K., Palmen, S. J. M. C., & Sommer, I. E. C. (2017). Children seeking help for auditory verbal hallucinations; who are they? *Schizophrenia Research*, *183*, 31–35. https://doi.org/10.1016/j.schres.2016.10.033.

McGrath, J. J., Saha, S., Al-Hamzawi, A., et al. (2015). Psychotic experiences in the general population: A cross-national analysis based on 31 261 respondents from 18 countries. *JAMA Psychiatry*, *72*, 697–705. https://doi.org/10.1001/jamapsychiatry.2015.0575.

McHale, C., Hayward, M., & Jones, F. W. (2018). Building a grounded theory of engagement in mindfulness-based group therapy for distressing voices. *Qualitative Health Research*, *28*, 2169–2182.

Morrison, A. (1998). A cognitive analysis of the maintenance of auditory hallucinations: Are voices to schizophrenia what bodily sensations are to panic? *Behavioural and Cognitive Psychotherapy*, *26*(4), 289–302.

Morrison, A. P. (2001). The interpretation of intrusions in psychosis: An integrative cognitive approach to hallucinations and delusions. *Behavioural and Cognitive Psychotherapy*, *29*, 257–276.

Morrison, A., Haddock, G., & Tarrier, N. (1995). Intrusive thoughts and auditory hallucinations: A cognitive approach. *Behavioural and Cognitive Psychotherapy*, *23*(3), 265–280. https://doi.org/10.1017/S1352465800015873.

National Institute for Clinical Excellence. (2014). *Psychosis and schizophrenia in adults: Prevention and management (Clinical guideline CG178)*. https://www.nice.org.uk/guidance/cg178.

Pagonabarraga, J., Martinez-Horta, S., Fernandez de Bobadilla, R., Perez, J., Ribosa-Nogue, R., Marin, J., et al. (2016). Minor hallucinations occur in drug naive Parkinson's disease patients, even from the premotor phase. *Movement Disorders*, *31*, 45–52. https://doi.org/10.1002/mds.26432.

Paulik, G., Jones, A.-M., & Hayward, M. (2018). Brief coping strategy enhancement for distressing voices: Predictors of engagement and outcome in routine clinical practice. *Clinical Psychology & Psychotherapy*, *25*, 634–640.

Paulik, G., Hayward, M., & Birchwood, M. (2013). Cognitive behavioural relating therapy (CBRT) for voice hearers: A case study. *Behavioural and Cognitive Psychotherapy*, *41*(5), 626–631. https://doi.org/10.1017/S1352465812001014.

Shawyer, F., Farhall, J., Mackinnon, A., Trauer, T., Sims, E., Ratcliff, K., et al. (2012). A randomised controlled trial of acceptance-based cognitive behavioural therapy for command hallucinations in psychotic disorders. *Behaviour Research and Therapy*, *50*(2), 110–121.

Shawyer, F., Farhall, J., Thomas, N., Hayes, S. C., Gallop, B., Copolov, D., et al. (2017). A randomised controlled trial of acceptance and commitment therapy for psychosis. *British Journal of Psychiatry*, *210*, 140–148. https://doi.org/10.1192/bjp.bp.116.182865.

Smith, K. V., & Thew, G. R. (2017). Conducting research in clinical psychology practice: Barriers, facilitators, and recommendations. *The British Journal of Clinical Psychology*, *56*(3), 347–356. https://doi.org/10.1111/bjc.12142.

Strauss, C., Thomas, N., & Hayward, M. (2015). Can we respond mindfully to distressing voices? A systematic review of evidence for engagement, acceptability, effectiveness and mechanisms of change for mindfulness-based interventions for people distressed by hearing voices. *Frontiers in Psychology*, *6*, 1154.

Tarrier, N. (1992). Management and modification of residual positive psychotic symptoms. In M. J. Birchwood & N. Tarrier (Eds.), *Innovations in the psychological management of schizophrenia: Assessment, treatment and services* (pp. 147–169). Chichester, England: Wiley.

Tarrier, N. T., Harwood, S., Yusopoff, L., Beckett, R., & Baker, A. (1990). Coping strategy enhancement (CSE): A method of treating residual schizophrenic symptoms. *Behavioural Psychotherapy, 18*, 283–293.

Thomas, N. (2015). What's really wrong with cognitive behavioural therapy for psychosis? *Frontiers in Psychology, 6*, e323. https://doi.org/10.3389/fpsyg.2015.00323.

Thomas, N., Farhall, J., Foley, F., Rossell, S. L., Castle, D., Ladd, E., et al. (2016). Randomised controlled trial of a digitally assisted low intensity intervention to promote personal recovery in persisting psychosis: SMART-therapy study protocol. *BMC Psychiatry, 16*, e312. https://doi.org/10.1186/s12888-016-1024-1.

Thomas, N., Hayward, M., Peters, E., van der Gaag, M., Bentall, R. P., Jenner, J. M., et al. (2014). Psychological therapies for auditory hallucinations (voices): Current status and key research directions. *Schizophrenia Bulletin, 40*(suppl. 4), s202–s212. https://doi.org/10.1093/schbul/sbu037.

Thomas, N., Morris, E. M. J., Shawyer, F., & Farhall, J. (2013). Acceptance and commitment therapy for voices. In E. M. J. Morris, L. C. Johns, & J. E. Oliver (Eds.), *Acceptance and commitment therapy and mindfulness for psychosis* (pp. 95–111). Chichester, England: Wiley-Blackwell. https://doi.org/10.1002/9781118499184.ch7.

Thomas, N., Rossell, S., Farhall, J., Shawyer, F., & Castle, D. (2011). Cognitive behavioural therapy for auditory hallucinations: Effectiveness and predictors of outcome in a specialist clinic. *Behavioural and Cognitive Psychotherapy, 39*, 129–138. https://doi.org/10.1017/S1352465810000548.

Thornicroft, G., & Tansella, M. (2002). Balancing community-based and hospital-based mental health care. *World Psychiatry, 1*(2), 84–90.

Trower, P., Birchwood, M., Meaden, A., Byrne, S., Nelson, A., & Ross, K. (2004). Cognitive therapy for command hallucinations: Randomised controlled trial. *The British Journal of Psychiatry, 184*(4), 312–320.

van der Gaag, M., van Oosterhout, B., Daalman, K., Sommer, I. E., & Korrelboom, K. (2012). Initial evaluation of the effects of competitive memory training (COMET) on depression in schizophrenia-spectrum patients with persistent auditory verbal hallucinations: A randomized controlled trial. *British Journal of Clinical Psychology, 51*, 158–171.

Waters, F., Blom, J., Jardri, R., Hugdahl, K., & Sommer, I. (2017). Auditory hallucinations, not necessarily a hallmark of psychotic disorder. *Psychological Medicine*, 1–8. https://doi.org/10.1017/S0033291717002203.

Werner-Seidler, A., Perry, Y., & Christensen, H. (2016). An Australian example of translating psychological research into practice and policy: Where we are and where we need to go. *Frontiers in Psychology, 7*, 200. https://doi.org/10.3389/fpsyg.2016.00200.

Westfall, J. M., Mold, J., & Fagnan, L. (2007). Practice-based research-"blue highways" on the NIH roadmap. *Journal of the American Medical Association, 297*, 403–406. https://doi.org/10.1001/jama.297.4.403.

Definitions of Key Terms

Hallucination A perception that cannot be explained by stimuli in the physical environment, such that a person hears (*auditory hallucinations*, also called *'hearing voices'*), sees (*visual hallucinations*), feels (*tactile hallucinations*, or *somatic hallucinations* when the sensation occurs within the body), smells (*olfactory hallucinations*), or tastes (*gustatory hallucinations*) something that no one else within their environment can detect.

Scientist–practitioner model A graduate training approach in psychology that encourages clinicians to utilise, critically evaluate, and produce new research findings (also called the Boulder Model or the research–practitioner model).

Translational research Translation from basic scientific research findings to new clinical interventions and practises, with the aim to inform health practice and policy.

Voices clinics Out-patient clinics, which target hallucination-type experiences, the most common of which are auditory (hence the title 'voices' clinic).

Evidence-based practice Clinical practice that integrates the best available research evidence with clinical judgement and client preferences and values.

Empirically supported treatment Describes treatments that meet a minimum standard of empirical support.

CHAPTER 27

The Therapeutic Use of Digital Technologies in Psychosis

Imogen H. Bell*,†, Michelle H. Lim*,‡, Neil Thomas*,†

*Centre for Mental Health, School of Health Sciences, Swinburne University of Technology, Hawthorn, VIC, Australia, †Alfred Health, Melbourne, VIC, Australia, ‡Iverson Health Innovation Research Institute, Swinburne University of Technology, Hawthorn, VIC, Australia

Key Learning Objectives

- Understand ways in which digital technology can be used in the clinical care of people experiencing psychosis.
- Develop a critical appreciation of the evidence base involving the use of digital technology in psychosis.
- Understand barriers and issues associated with using digital technology for treatment of psychosis, including relevant ethical considerations.

INTRODUCTION

Digital technology is advancing at an exponential rate. Within the field of mental health, this expansion has led to the development of digital tools and applications capable of improving current available treatments. For people with persisting and recurring mental health conditions such as psychosis, evidence suggests that these technologies may offer opportunities to enhance these treatments and support self-management in daily life (O'Hanlon et al., 2016; Treisman et al., 2016). Despite stereotypes that people with psychosis typically do not use digital technologies (Williams, Fossey, Farhall, Foley, & Thomas, 2018), current evidence suggests this population is interested in using them for mental health (Firth et al., 2015; Thomas, Foley, Lindblom, & Lee, 2017). Although these developments are promising, there remain barriers to successful implementation of digital technology in the field of mental health, and questions regarding how to select and use applications across different clinical populations remain to be answered.

The evidence shows that people with psychosis are interested in using technology for their mental health.

This chapter provides an overview of potential applications of digital technology in the psychological treatment of psychotic conditions, including a summary of currently available and potential future technologies. State-of-the-art research is

A Clinical Introduction to Psychosis. https://doi.org/10.1016/B978-0-12-815012-2.00027-4

reviewed, along side discussion of the current evidence base, and barriers and issues related to the use of technology in this clinical population.

TYPES OF DIGITAL TECHNOLOGIES

The use of technology in the context of mental health care and research is referred to as **digital mental health** or **e-mental health**.

Digital technology is an umbrella term referring to electronic devices or applications capable of recording, storing, and processing information in digital form, including computers, mobile devices, and the internet. The use of these technologies in the context of mental healthcare and research is often referred to broadly as *digital mental health or e-mental health* (Lal & Adair, 2014). A list of major technologies with accompanying definitions and an example use in psychosis is detailed in Table 27.1.

Table 27.1 Types, Definitions, and Potential Uses of Digital Technologies in Psychosis

Technology type	Definition	Potential use
Smartphones	Hand-held personal computer capable of running applications and connecting to the internet	Coping strategy reminders sent via specialised application (*app*)
Tablets	Large touch screen personal computer	Tool for sharing multimedia-based psychoeducation material
SMS and text messaging	The use of mobile devices to send and receive short text, image, or audio messages	Daily text message reminders of goals and therapeutic strategies
Email	Asynchronous method of transmitting text-based communication between computers	Weekly emails to people completing an online self-help program for psychosis to promote engagement and discuss progress
Blogs and podcasts	Regularly updated webpage or audio recordings sharing information in an informal format	Weekly podcast by a person with lived experience sharing stories of recovery
Computer-based applications	Software programs run on personal computers such as PC or MacBook	Software program delivering computer-based cognitive behavioural therapy for psychosis on a personal computer
Websites	Online 'pages' viewed via the internet	Remote access to information about a mental health condition
Wearables and sensors	Devices worn on the person, which passively record physiological data	Smartwatch, which passively monitors the level of activity in someone experiencing negative symptoms to monitor the outcomes of a behavioural activation treatment
Virtual reality	An immersive and interactive virtual environment involving three-dimensional simulation	Exposure therapy involving increasing levels of social interactions within virtual environments to treat paranoia
Augmented reality	Superimposing computer-generated images on to real-world environments	The use of visual cues within a real-world environment to prompt adaptive behavioural responses

Table 27.1 Types, Definitions, and Potential Uses of Digital Technologies in Psychosis—cont'd

Technology type	Definition	Potential use
Avatars	Visual representation of a person or entity	Creation of avatars to represent the identity of an individual's voice hearing experiences
Telehealth	Provision of healthcare remotely via telecommunication	Providing supportive counselling via the telephone
Videoconferencing	Remote simultaneous communication via audio and video streaming	Providing face-to-face counselling to a geographically isolated person
Social media and forums	Communication and sharing of information with others via online communities	Social media page for members who hear voices to share advice, experiences and provide support for one another
Online chat and instant messaging	A form of immediate text-based online communication	24-h chat service providing supportive counselling or advice for people in crisis

USE OF DIGITAL TECHNOLOGY AMONGST PEOPLE WITH PSYCHOSIS

There is growing research showing that people diagnosed with a psychotic disorder are able to use digital technology for their mental healthcare and many find them helpful for this purpose (Ainsworth et al., 2013; Alvarez-Jimenez et al., 2013, 2014; Batra et al., 2017; Berry et al., 2016; World Health Organisation, 2010). Further, at the time of writing, the estimate of smartphone ownership is around 80% amongst people with psychosis, with the vast majority using technology such as this on a daily basis (Firth et al., 2015; Gay, Torous, Joseph, Pandya, & Duckworth, 2016).

Research shows that most people with a psychotic disorder own a smartphone and use technology on a daily basis for their mental health.

These findings challenge early presumptions that people with severe mental illness are unable to benefit from advances in digital mental health, although barriers to technology adoption exist (Communities and Local Government, 2008) and there remains a significant minority still yet to fully engage (Robotham, Satkunanathan, Doughty, & Wykes, 2016).

BENEFITS AND USE OF TECHNOLOGY IN PSYCHOSIS POPULATIONS

Whilst psychological interventions for psychosis such as cognitive behavioural therapy (CBT) can be effective, there remain a number of key challenges in meeting need. First, effect sizes for CBT for psychosis suggest it provides relatively modest incremental improvements to recovery (Jauhar et al., 2014; van der Gaag, Valmaggia, & Smit, 2014) and alternative intervention modalities have shown a similar range of effects (e.g. Brand, McEnery, Rossell, Bendall, &

Benefits of digital technology include increasing access to mental health care, fostering self-management, supporting generalisation of therapeutic strategies to daily life, and enhancing intervention exposure.

Thomas, 2017; Louise, Fitzpatrick, Strauss, Rossell, & Thomas, 2017). To improve the effectiveness of psychological therapy, there may be benefits in capitalising on opportunities to increase the potency of interventions via supportive use of digital technologies. As reviewed later, these technologies have been used successfully in people with psychosis and show promise for improving clinical outcomes and recovery.

Second, the availability of therapists to provide psychological therapies to persons with psychosis is limited (Kohn, Saxena, Levav, & Saraceno, 2004; Kreyenbuhl, Nossel, & Dixon, 2009), so there are benefits in developing ways of enabling a larger number of people to access them beyond standard face-to-face delivery formats (Thomas, 2015). As well as including fully self-guided interventions, this might include blending independent digital resource use with face-to-face therapy to maximise intervention exposure.

Due to growing recognition of the role of digital technology in healthcare delivery, it is likely that service users as well as providers will grow to use new technologies more and more in routine treatment. Understanding how digital technology can be used in routine clinical care is likely to soon form a fundamental part of training in mental health fields and be established as an ongoing professional responsibility (Torous, Chan, Luo, Boland, & Hilty, 2018). To aid in this, the following section provides a brief overview of current digital technologies which have been investigated and hold potential in the treatment of psychotic conditions, with relevant examples provided where possible to illustrate their varying applications.

SPECIFIC USES OF DIGITAL TECHNOLOGY FOR PSYCHOSIS TREATMENT AND MANAGEMENT

Clinical Assessment

Digital technology can be used to administer, score, and assist with interpreting clinical assessments.

Assessment plays an important role in all areas of psychological practice, from initial case conceptualisations to monitoring the outcomes of treatment. Digital technology has unique capabilities, which may improve the quality and extend the benefit of assessment during treatment.

DIGITAL TOOLS FOR ASSESSMENT IN SESSION

Tablets and computer-based tools can provide a digital platform to administer and score psychometric tests and assessments in session. This may offer a more user-friendly and convenient way of conducting assessments for both clinician and client, and can reduce the likelihood of scoring errors through automated report summaries. Engaging and stimulating designs may also enhance user experience to promote richer and more reliable data. For example, researchers have developed an assessment tool in the form of a mobile app for children, which uses a customisable avatar character with developmentally appropriate language to help identify and characterise hallucinatory experiences across different sensory modalities and differentiate them from more typical imaginary experiences (Demeulemeester et al., 2015).

Smartphone apps and computer-based tools can be used to assist with screening for psychotic disorders and identifying evidence-based treatments using automatic algorithms. One example is the freely available OPCRIT+ computer-based program (Rucker et al., 2011), which has been used primarily as a research tool, offering checklists of symptoms pertaining to psychiatric conditions with automatic diagnostic algorithms. The system is now being used within services of the National Health Service in the United Kingdom, and has shown good diagnostic reliability and validity (Brittain, Stahl, Rucker, Kawadler, & Schumann, 2013). These technologies have broad applications beyond psychosis; however, they may be particularly beneficial in complex presentations where accurate diagnosis is challenging.

REAL-TIME, REAL-WORLD ASSESSMENT

Ecological momentary assessment (EMA), also known as *experience sampling methodology* (ESM), has been a major development in the e-mental health field with important clinical utility in psychosis (Shiffman, Stone, & Hufford, 2008; Trull & Ebner-Priemer, 2009).

Ecological momentary assessment involves real-time assessment in the person's natural environments.

EMA involves the repeated real-time measurement of variables such as symptoms, thoughts, behaviours, and context, in their natural environment. Typically, this occurs through specialist smartphone apps, which deliver several alerts per day over several days requesting the user to complete identical surveys asking about current or very recent experiences. Survey responses are usually uploaded to a secure online server that can be accessed remotely by the researcher or clinician.

EMA has been used as a research tool in psychosis for decades (Oorschot, Kwapil, Delespaul, & Myin-Germeys, 2009); however, more recently, its clinical utility has been recognised (Bell, Lim, Rossell, & Thomas, 2017; Myin-Germeys et al., 2009; Trull & Ebner-Priemer, 2009). This includes the ability to capture and measure phenomena more accurately in natural environments and in real time, which can overcome recall bias and increase the reliability of the data collected (Piasecki, Hufford, Solhan, & Trull, 2007; Stone et al., 1998). This is particularly important in psychosis where memory impairments are common and heightened emotional reactivity can shape retrospective self-report (Ben-Zeev, McHugo, Xie, Dobbins, & Young, 2012; Jacobsen et al., 2018; Myin-Germeys, van Os, Schwartz, Stone, & Delespaul, 2001). EMA data can also capture phenomena in their natural environment, affording greater ecological validity, and sensitivity to the relationship between clinical variables and the context in which they occur. Finally, as EMA involves repeat measurement over several days, it is possible to examine how variables interact not only in the moment but also over time.

Because a large amount of information is captured for a single person, EMA has been used to examine dynamic patterns in symptoms on an individual basis (Oorschot, Lataster, Thewissen, Bentall, et al., 2012; Oorschot, Lataster, Thewissen, Wichers, & Myin-Germeys, 2012). Fig. 27.1 shows how EMA can be used to track nuanced relationships between clinical variables, in this case

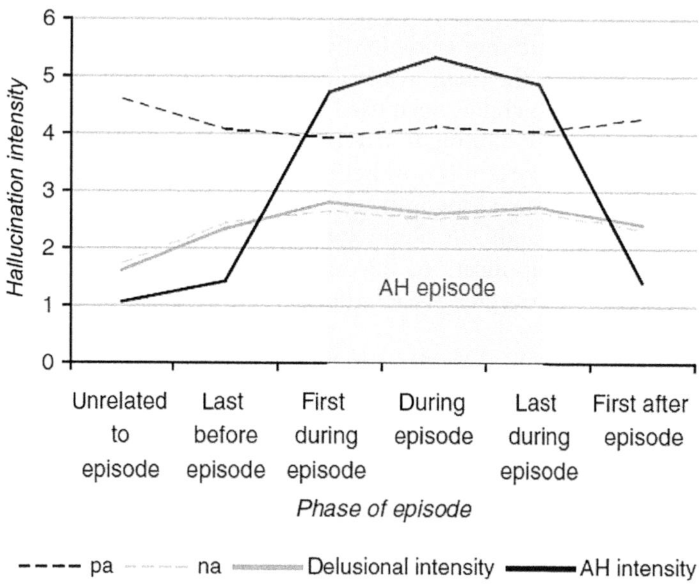

FIG. 27.1

Dynamic patterns in the relationship between hallucinations and delusions measured over time using ecological momentary assessment (Oorschot, Lataster, Thewissen, Bentall, et al., 2012). [*Note*: *pa*, positive affect, *na*, negative affect].

delusions and hallucinations (Oorschot, Lataster, Thewissen, Bentall, et al., 2012). As these relationships tend to differ between people, the use of EMA to develop more individualised formulations could inform more tailored interventions.

EMA has also been used to inform functional analysis, which is a formulation method examining how symptoms are maintained by understanding their antecedents and consequences. In research conducted by the authors (Bell et al., 2018), EMA has been feasible for self-monitoring voice hearing experiences and other variables such as mood and coping responses. Our protocol has involved conducting monitoring over a 6-day period, after which an individual client's data are analysed statistically to identify predictors of fluctuations in the intensity of their voices over time. A summary of this information is then taken by the therapist to the following session with the client, and used as part of a collaborative discussion about patterns in their voices. This source of data is discussed along-side the client's own observations, and the therapist's knowledge of common patterns for other people who hear voices. A functional analysis of the client's voices is built, leading to the selection of specific coping strategies (in line with traditional methods described by Tarrier, 1992). To encourage successful use of these strategies, personalised reminders were sent to the person via the app between remaining sessions. This is referred to as an *ecological momentary intervention*, discussed later in this chapter. Box 27.1 provides an example of this use of EMA with a hypothetical client experiencing distressing voices.

Box 27.1 Ecological Momentary Assessment to Assist in Functional Analysis of Voices

Sally[a] experienced critical and commanding voices throughout the day, which seemed to come out of nowhere and made it hard to concentrate when she was at work. To help understand more about what was contributing to the voices, Sally's psychologist asked if she would be willing to complete some monitoring using a smartphone app. The therapist explained that by monitoring when the voices happened and some other things that might be happening at the same time, they might think of some better ways of managing them.

Sally agreed to the monitoring and after some help learning how to use the app, she answered 10 short surveys each day for 6 days outside of her therapy sessions. During this monitoring, Sally started to notice some patterns in her voices. They were much worse when she was on the way to work and seemed to be more critical when she was around other people. In the next session, Sally's therapist had some feedback from the monitoring which seemed to fit with her own experience. The feedback showed that her voices tended to be worse in the mornings and when she was around other people. The feedback also showed that when she responded to the voices by doing what they told her to do, they tended to become worse later on and she felt more anxious. When discussing this with her therapist, it became clearer that her voices seemed to be reflecting her feelings of insecurity around her workmates, which was particularly bad in the mornings when she would worry about how her work performance might be judged during the day. Sally realised that by avoiding going near other people because the voices told her to, she was making herself more anxious.

Sally and her therapist came up with some ways of managing her anxiety better using breathing techniques and worked on improving Sally's confidence at work by engaging more with her workmates and recognising her achievements.

[a]Hypothetical client example.

Our observations have been that providing feedback of EMA data promoted awareness and learning both during and outside of session. These fit with findings that the use of EMA is feasible and acceptable amongst people with psychotic experiences and can be used in a clinical setting (Granholm, Loh, & Swendsen, 2008; Johnson et al., 2009; Kimhy et al., 2006; Palmier-Claus et al., 2012, 2013). Such tools can be informative for eliciting fruitful discussion about experiences; however, clinicians should be cautious of the potential for over interpreting data obtained from a limited sample of experiences. This underlines the importance of using such tools as part of a collaborative discussion about experiences.

EMA monitoring of psychotic experiences appears to be feasible and acceptable; however, clinical interpretation of the data requires caution.

PASSIVE SENSORS FOR ASSESSMENT

It is also possible to collect data in real time using mobile sensors, which can track changes in physiological or environmental states passively, that is, without the person's awareness, using *ambulatory assessment* technologies such as smart watches. For example, Ben-Zeev et al. (2017) created an app to collect a combination of both active (EMA surveys three times per week) and passive (multimodal behavioural sensing such as physical activity, device use, and speech) data from users to identify predictors of hospitalisation. A small trial with five

Ambulatory assessment uses passive sensors to capture real-time data.

participants who were hospitalised whilst using the system over 12 months found unique patterns within the data, which varied between individuals, highlighting the utility of mobile technology for identifying clinically significant changes on a person-by-person basis.

DIGITAL TECHNOLOGY TO BETTER CHARACTERISE PSYCHOTIC PHENOMENA

Amid dissatisfaction with traditional diagnostic schemes such as DSM-5 (American Psychiatric Association, 2013) in characterising the heterogeneous and overlapping landscape of mental health experiences, digital technology has been proposed as an alternative means of characterising individual differences in mental health based on more personalised, contextually sensitive information (Torous, Onnela, & Keshavan, 2017; Van Os, Delespaul, Wigman, Myin-Germeys, & Wichers, 2013). For example, Torous, Kiang, Lorme, and Onnela (2016) designed an app to collect a wide variety of active and passive momentary data, with an individualised *digital phenotype* of the user then presented visually on a web-based system, including patterns in symptoms and related information. In the near future, clinicians might utilise apps such as this to record data of individual clients to better characterise their experiences, inform more personalised treatments, and monitor changes in illness states.

A **digital phenotype** refers to unique patterns of individual momentary assessment data collected from digital devices in natural environments.

Symptom Monitoring and Relapse Prevention

Digital technology can be used to monitor symptoms and other clinically relevant information, which can provide a basis for illness self-management, clinician tracking of individual treatment response, and identifying potential need for escalated intervention.

DIGITAL DAIRIES

In psychosis treatment, diaries can be a useful tool to promote reflection on experiences in the moment (Cohen, Edmunds, Brodman, Benjamin, & Kendall, 2013) and allow recording of important information that may not be readily recalled in sessions. However, amongst people with psychosis, completing homework tasks such as diaries can be challenging (Dunn, Morrison, & Bentall, 2002). Digital diaries may offer a means of overcoming this through automated reminders to complete diary entries on the device, allowing more accurate, quicker, and secure recordings (Dale & Hagen, 2007).

General mood diary apps are at a more advanced phase of development compared to technologies specific for psychosis. Many of these apps have additional integrated functions like visualisations of mood diary entries, space for text-based journal entries, and suggestions for coping with emotions. In the general population, the use of these apps has been associated with improvements in mood, potentially through a mechanism involving increased emotional self-awareness (Bakker & Rickard, 2018). A simpler alternative could be the use of local smartphone apps such as calendars, notes, and reminders to record experiences.

MONITORING SIGNS OF RELAPSE

A common role of psychologists is to assess, monitor, and respond to signs of risk. However, in traditional services where clients are usually seen weekly at a maximum, changes in risk are difficult to detect and often missed. Through remote capturing of risk-related information via digital devices, the clinician and client can better identify and respond to early warning signs.

Mobile devices can be used to track and respond to early warning signs of relapse or risk.

Researchers have developed specific apps to monitor and track early warning signs of relapse. One example is an app that was developed in collaboration with service users, carers, and clinicians, which allows the user to monitor their mental health status and communicate signs of relapse to their treatment team. The team employed a stepped intervention approach, whereby minor worsening in illness-related variables triggers therapeutic messages designed to reduce relapse risk, and more severe changes leads to alerting of key clinicians and a nominated carer. The app is currently undergoing pilot evaluation, with no published findings at this time. A more automated system of monitoring early warning signs was developed by Španiel et al. (2012), involving remote monitoring of symptoms, with automated alerts sent to psychiatrists to increase medication in those deemed at risk. Although the system reduced hospitalisation rates, concerns were raised by psychiatrists who felt a more personalised approach to intervention involving medication was needed. Further, information regarding user experiences in this study was not recorded, which is important given the ethical implications of collecting personal data from patients regarding their mental health.

Symptom Self-Management

There has been growing emphasis on more user-led, empowering approaches to mental health treatment, with digital technology at the forefront of new developments in this area. This has been largely led by consumer movements that have argued for more person-centred, recovery-focused models of care, and there is evidence supporting the clinical benefit of shifting to such models.

WEBSITES AND SELF-DIRECTED PROGRAMS

There are now countless websites targeting mental health, many of which are specifically relevant for psychosis. These platforms vary from basic text-based information pages to forums allowing the sharing of information between users. Certain information kiosks are now being placed at services to allow immediate access to health information via digital devices such as tablet computers within clinical waiting rooms. These devices can also be used to collect basic information to streamline processes and reduce wait times.

Self-directed programs provide a means of delivering structured interventions over the internet or using computers. Gottlieb, Romeo, Penn, Mueser, and Chiko (2013) developed a computerised skills-based CBT program targeting improved coping with hearing voices. The program uses text, video, audio, and interactive exercises to deliver materials on self-monitoring, coping enhancement, cognitive therapy skills, and relapse prevention. Findings from two small studies (Gottlieb et al., 2013, 2017) indicated good engagement and satisfaction with the program, which was accessed on computers at a local service. Improved clinical outcomes indicated that users of the program enhanced social functioning, although a larger trial is needed.

Other technologies involve the provision of information via the internet, which might be used autonomously or as a service aid, such as the Australian Department of Health *Head to Health* website (https://headtohealth.gov.au/), which provides a directory of digital resources and services relating to mental health. Websites run by peers offer some particularly well-developed sites at this time. In Australia, probably the most widely used moderated forums for severe mental illness include SANE Australia's online forum, which contain a number of active peer communities. For more specific issues in psychosis, for example those who report voice hearing experiences, the Intervoice website (http://www.intervoiceonline.org/) and local Hearing Voices Network websites may be useful. These digital platforms aim to empower people with lived experience of hearing voices through sharing information and facilitating peer-to-peer support.

Specialised smartphone apps can also provide information and deliver interventions on-demand, facilitating independent self-management of mental health. A review by Firth and Torous (2015) identified five smartphone apps for psychosis, with broad aims from symptom monitoring or self-management, to increasing physical activity amongst people with psychiatric disorders, including schizophrenia (Aschbrenner et al., 2015; Ben-Zeev et al., 2014; Macias et al., 2015; Naslund, Aschbrenner, Barre, & Bartels, 2015; Palmier-Claus et al., 2012). Firth and Torous (2015) concluded that overall people with psychosis are willing and able to use apps safely to achieve specific aims.

MOMENTARY INTERVENTIONS

A particular area of development for smartphone apps has been extending the application of the regular prompting used in ecological momentary assessment to deliver therapeutic interventions, termed *ecological momentary intervention* (EMI; Heron & Smyth, 2010). EMI prompts may be simple, such as the scheduled medication reminders, or complex depending on certain contexts or responses to preceding items. For example, someone who reports that they are hearing voices may be presented with a different EMI prompt (e.g. a coping statement) versus if they are not hearing voices (e.g. a motivational statement).

Ecological momentary intervention involves the real-time delivery of therapeutic prompts or reminders in daily life via mobile devices.

The use of EMI has been subject to some research in psychosis, with support for feasibility, acceptability, and potential for improving clinical outcomes (Bell et al., 2017). Ben-Zeev et al. (2014) developed an app that involves individual tailoring of intervention components with different therapeutic targets. Participants select intervention domains, with targeted EMI prompts based on CBT principles sent to them daily depending on if they reported experiencing symptoms or related concerns. Feedback from users was largely positive, with reports that the app helped them feel supported and was easy to use. Researchers have also developed and evaluated an EMI-based smartphone app for early psychosis (Bucci et al., 2018). The app delivers theory-driven therapeutic material, which can be accessed on-demand, in addition to EMI prompts using branching logic depending on if the person is experiencing symptoms. Participants complete questions a few times per day, with EMI prompts focusing on cognitive appraisals, belief conviction, emotions, and associated behaviours. A preliminary evaluation suggested that young people with early psychosis were highly satisfied with the app and there were clinical benefits over and above simple monitoring of symptoms, though a larger trial will more definitively determine clinical benefits.

Using Technology to Enhance Standard Interventions

Digital technology can also be used in conjunction with standard psychological therapy, either as the primary therapeutic modality or as a tool to enhance the treatment. One example discussed earlier involved the provision of feedback of EMA data to inform functional analysis in-session (Bell et al., 2018).

VIDEO MATERIAL

Another example is the use of multimedia material (e.g. videos) to enhance communication of information to people with psychosis during session. Video may have potential advantages of providing engaging material and promoting discussion about topics that may be difficult to elicit via Socratic dialogue alone. In promoting recovery, use of videos of people with lived experience sharing their stories of recovery can provide material that it would not be possible for the therapist to present themselves. These sorts of videos can be popular. The TED Talk by Eleanor Longden called 'The Voices in My Head', for example, has had several million views. Thomas et al. (2016) have found that multimedia material using people with lived experience of psychosis has been a feasible and acceptable way to prompt discussion about recovery, with clients feeling that these enhanced their sessions with their workers. Furthermore, results from a qualitative study indicated that people often felt that videos of others discussing their own recovery made them feel less alone, and more inspired and hopeful about their own recovery (Williams et al., 2018).

AUGMENTED AND VIRTUAL REALITY

The use of augmented reality (AR) and virtual reality (VR) is a promising area of development, which have received some attention in psychosis treatment. The most common use of VR in mental health has been in exposure therapy, with VR enabling clients to enter anxiety-provoking environments in a controlled way to promote habituation (Freeman et al., 2017). In psychosis, VR has had particular applications to paranoia, with avatars being used within virtual environments to represent threatening or rejecting others (Freeman et al., 2016). A review of the literature on VR for psychosis conducted by Rus-Calafell, Garety, Sason, Craig, and Valmaggia (2018) found that it has been used broadly for assessment of cognition (e.g. Sorkin, Weinshall, Modai, & Peled, 2006), cognitive remediation (e.g. Chan, Ngai, Leung, & Wong, 2010), exposure therapy (e.g. Pot-Kolder et al., 2018), and skills training (e.g. Park et al., 2011). Across these studies, VR was found to be safe and acceptable for people with psychosis, and RCTs have shown that the technology can lead to improved outcomes such as reducing paranoia through graded exposure in virtual environments (Freeman et al., 2016; Pot-Kolder et al., 2018). A particular advantage of this technology is enabling people to engage in exposure tasks efficiently and whilst in a safe environment, which can be more tolerable than real-life exposure, and appears to lead to larger reductions in anxiety compared to nonexposure-based therapies (Freeman et al., 2017).

Another application has been the use of avatars for the treatment of psychosis, such as for hearing voices (Craig et al., 2018; Leff, Williams, Huckvale, Arbuthnot, & Leff, 2013). One study involved the creation of a digital character representing a client's persecutory voices. The therapist then personifies the voice of the character, facilitating dialogue between the client and their voice, whilst at the same time guiding them in seeking more adaptive, assertive interactions, which grow more effective over time. Findings from an RCT of this novel intervention found it was safe, feasible, and acceptable, with widespread improvements in outcomes related to voices compared with supportive counselling; however, these were not maintained at 6 months follow up.

Improving Cognition and Supporting Daily Functioning

A major area of development has been the use of digital technology for enhancing cognition or compensating for cognitive deficits. Many of the more complex technologies have been adapted from the literature on cognitive remediation in schizophrenia, which offer computer-based platforms for delivering traditional treatment components. This was one of the first uses of digital technology, and metaanalysis has supported some benefit in psychosis, particularly for improving social cognition (Grynszpan et al., 2011).

Other studies have examined the independent use of digital technologies targeting cognition or functioning in psychosis. Schlosser et al. (2018) evaluated an app that was designed to enhance motivation, reinforce goal achievement, and provide social networking. Findings from an RCT indicated that participants were overall very satisfied with the app and had a good level of engagement. Clinical outcomes were also positive, showing improvements in depression, defeatist beliefs, self-efficacy and motivation, which were maintained at 3 months follow up.

Facilitating Social Relationships

Social networking, from shared interest groups to dating sites, is already common place within the general population (Lee, Noh, & Koo, 2013) and has been used extensively in those with problematic anxiety and depression (Seabrook, Kern, & Rickard, 2016). Individuals with psychosis presentations demonstrate difficulties with social anhedonia and social cognition (Couture, Penn, & Roberts, 2006; Kwapil, 1998), report more impoverished social networks and lower social support (Gayer-Anderson & Morgan, 2013; MacDonald, Sauer, Howie, & Albiston, 2005), and are vulnerable to experiencing distressing levels of loneliness (Lim, Gleeson, Alvarez-Jimenez, & Penn, 2018). However, even in those with impoverished social networks, digital interventions can be used to connect like-minded people, promote social confidence, and facilitate peer support. A digital intervention that can allow young people to access evidence-based health information and also provide a safe online environment, which allows them to interact with their peers, would therefore be highly valuable (Alvarez-Jimenez et al., 2014).

IMMEDIATE USES OF TECHNOLOGY IN PSYCHOSIS TREATMENT

Although research is at an early stage, some digital technologies are available now for clinicians interested in using them with their clients experiencing psychosis. These include:

- Use of basic smartphone functions, e.g. electronic notes as a means of recording experiences, calendar scheduling or reminders for daily activities, or support
- SMS or phone support outside of session
- Secure video-conferencing systems for remote access to therapy
- Stress management, relaxation, or mindfulness apps
- Websites for information on psychosis and accessing services or supports
- Forums and social media to promote peer interaction

The following sections highlight some of the issues for consideration in terms of the overall quality of evidence and the use of these technologies with individuals with psychosis.

CLINICAL ISSUES AND CAUTIONS

Evidence Base of Current Digital Technologies

The literature to date on digital technology for mental health is in its infancy, with limited investigations undertaken to establish effectiveness and safety. This research is currently dominated by pilot studies with small sample sizes, limiting inferences beyond the immediate research. Nonetheless, findings from these studies do suggest that digital technologies hold the potential to benefit people with psychosis, though further research is clearly needed before firm conclusions can be drawn.

Although it is likely that more validated technologies will become more widely available, there remain challenges ahead. For example, little is known about how to best integrate digital technology within current clinical care models. It is not simply about how digital technology can benefit the individual with psychosis, but also how it can be used and delivered by the services in which these individuals are embedded (Lim & Penn, 2018). This is particularly relevant for complex or highly novel digital interventions, such as the promising avatar-based intervention for voices (Craig et al., 2018; Leff et al., 2013), where the potential for so called *digital placebo effect* has been proposed (Torous & Firth, 2016), and implementation in standard practice may present challenges (Mohr, Lyon, Lattie, Reddy, & Schueller, 2017). Client confidence and the competency of the practitioner delivering these interventions are also likely to influence treatment response. As such, it is important to develop appropriate models of training to establish and maintain the professional competency of those delivering services involving technology (e.g. Torous, Chan, Luo, et al., 2018). Furthermore, it is important to understand more about the attitudes of mental health workers to using these technologies in their clinical work; a factor, which will certainly influence the uptake and emphasis placed on using them within current treatment models. Research has shown that whilst clinicians are optimistic about the potential for technology in mental health care, they are also understandably cautious for a variety of reasons, including the limited evidence base of current technologies and the importance of these complementing, not replacing, traditional roles (Berry, Bucci, & Lobban, 2017).

Currently little is known about how best to implement digital technologies within mental health services.

There is also a need for further research to better understand the limitations of particular types of digital technologies and their use in psychosis. For example, the collection of ecological momentary assessment data to inform digital phenotypes, remotely monitor risk, and aid in formulation is clearly promising; however, questions remain as to what information needs to be collected, via what means, and how best to interpret it. Other limitations include the reliability of information from digital resources, such as websites and information-based apps. A demonstration of this caution was highlighted by Larsen, Nicholas, and Christensen (2016), who systematically reviewed available apps targeting suicide prevention, finding that very few adhered to evidence-based guidelines, and some even provided dangerous recommendations such as taking drugs to cope with suicidal ideation. Finally, it is important to further examine the preferences and perspectives of different clinical populations in using these technologies. In doing so, there would be benefit in conducting collaborative research that involves key stakeholders, particularly those with lived experience, in the development and ongoing evaluation process (Brett et al., 2014).

Barriers to Technology Adoption for Psychosis

Barriers to technology adoption by persons with psychosis include both illness-related factors (e.g. negative symptoms) and social factors related to living with disability (e.g. lacking sufficient income to afford a data plan). A summary of these, based on analyses by Community and Local Governments (2008) and Rotondi, Spring, Hanusa, Eack, and Haas (2017), and empirical data from Villagonzalo, Arnold, Farhall, Rossell, and Thomas (2019), is presented in Table 27.2. There will be significant individual differences in these variables

Table 27.2 Barriers and Facilitators to Engagement With Digital Technology in Psychosis

Variable	Potential barrier	Potential strategies
Social		
Older age	Cohort effect of less familiarity with computers, leading to less confidence and skill development.	Coaching in basic internet use for mental health. Linkages with courses.
Extended unemployment Fewer years of education	Lower prior opportunity for skill development via daily use of technology.	Coaching in internet use for mental health. Linkages with courses.
Income (lower)	Difficulties affording devices and data plans.	Identify WIFI hotspots in neighbourhood and wifi availability in services.
Lack of access to computer/internet at home	Use inconvenient.	Consider mobile phone use. Identify locations to access computers.
Poor reading literacy	Difficulties understanding written content.	Consider use of video streaming sites.
Poor English language	Difficulties understanding English language content.	Coaching in finding resources in native language and/or use of translation functions.
Clinical		
Negative symptoms	Reduced self-initiation of use.	Link usage to daily routines. Use of automated prompts. Include the passive capabilities to reduce need for active input.
Cognitive impairments Disorganisation symptoms	Difficulties sustaining and focusing attention.	Identify simple sites. Declutter and organise smartphone home-screen and computer desktop. Use simple mode available on some smartphones.
Ideas of reference and paranoia	Internet material seen as salient to paranoid ideas.	Coach in evaluating robustness and trustworthiness of internet sites and information.
Disagreement with or unawareness of having mental health problems	Not relating to, or feeling invalidated by, illness-focused content.	Identification of sites and resources with nonothering/nonmedical language.

indicating their importance as considerations in an individualised treatment plan, most of which can be overcome with support.

Despite the apparent interest amongst those with psychosis in using digital technologies for daily mental healthcare, research shows that generally engagement and ongoing use with these technologies is low. A naturalistic study by Torous, Staples, et al. (2017) examined usage rates amongst 622 people who downloaded a publicly available smartphone app for schizophrenia. They found a

Long-term engagement with digital technologies is low amongst people with psychosis.

small subset of individuals continued to use the app regularly; however, the vast majority of users did not continue to engage beyond a few times. This study is important as most of the current research on engagement has been conducted in the context of clinical trials, which tend to show higher levels of engagement than is observed in naturalistic settings (Fleming et al., 2018).

A review of engagement with mental health smartphone apps was conducted by Torous, Nicholas, Larsen, Firth, and Christensen (2018). The authors highlight the low rate of engagement across different mental and physical health conditions and suggest this may be due to several factors, including apps not being user-friendly or designed specifically for users, having no guarantees for privacy or security, being unhelpful in crisis situations, and people perceiving them to be untrustworthy or unreliable. These factors reflect the early stage of this research area, where the evidence regarding user preferences and appropriate designs is still being established, and there is a lack of oversight to protect users from unsavoury commercial practices. Furthermore, little is known about the various cultural factors that might affect engagement with these technologies, with the majority of current research being conducted in Western countries. These factors are likely to vary depending on the individual, making it a challenge to develop technologies that suit every need.

Ethical Issues

Although the underlying principles remain the same, the ethical landscape of clinical practice changes with the introduction of digital technology. Issues related to data security and privacy, technological issues, responding to remote indicators of risk, ownership of data collected through commercial apps, and dealing with inequality regarding access and costs of the technology, are all relevant considerations for clinicians. Further, clinicians have a professional responsibility to ensure the information and services provided to their clients are evidence-based, which is clearly an ongoing issue in the field e-mental health. A thorough review of these issues is provided by Bauer et al. (2017), with major areas of caution highlighted below.

SECURITY, PRIVACY, AND CONFIDENTIALITY

Digital technologies are a relatively new frontier for healthcare. As such, various regulatory bodies remain behind in dealing with the issues they present for maintaining appropriate standards. Amongst users, one of the primary concerns has been around maintaining privacy, which has been substantiated by research. A study by Sunyaev, Dehling, Taylor, and Mandl (2014) identified 35,000 health-related apps, amongst which only 30.5% of the most frequently rated had a form of privacy policy, and the majority of these were poorly worded and insufficiently transparent.

Another related issue is that of data security. Devices such as smartphones or smartwatches are often lost or stolen, leaving the user's data exposed. Although such risks can be minimised by training clients to take appropriate security measures, such as passcode protections and secure handling of devices outside the home, it is difficult to ensure these cautions are being enacted. Furthermore, even the most secure of databases have been subject to hacking or use by third parties for questionable practices. As such, it is not possible to ensure total security with a high degree of certainty, although the better technologies do provide some assurances, which are typically detailed when signing up to use the product.

Before digital technologies are widely implemented in clinical settings, it is critical that sufficient measures are established to protect users. This has been the topic of a number of review articles, which reflect some movement towards the regulation of health-related technologies (Armontrout, Torous, Fisher, Drogin, & Gutheil, 2016; Kotz, Gunter, Kumar, & Weiner, 2016; Torous, Andersson, et al., 2019). Consistent standards and independent regulation would assist clinicians in their decision making and ultimately protect the consumer; however, until these further developments occur, it is still largely up to the resourceful clinician to decide which technologies are safe, effective, and meet professional standards.

DECISION MAKING

Not all individuals will readily adopt and engage with digital interventions. As with all decisions regarding appropriate treatment, a thorough assessment and formulation should inform the choice of whether to involve digital technology in the treatment of people with psychosis. This should be in line with the client's own goals for treatments and take in to account available options, their evidence base, and client's capabilities (e.g. technological competency, risk issues). Clinicians should also work flexibly and respectfully with their clients when raising the possibility of using digital technology during treatment. Put simply, technology should be offered, not prescribed, to clients and discussed in terms of their concerns, potential benefits, and reasons for its use. Clinicians should ensure that adequate consent and assistance is provided in the use of any technology in the provision of treatment, and engagement should be monitored with appropriate adaptation or discontinuation where necessary. Box 27.2 provides an example of how this may be undertaken for a trainee psychologist who is working with an older man diagnosed with schizophrenia.

To assist clinicians in the evaluation and selection of smartphone apps for clinical treatment, the American Psychiatric Association (APA) developed the App Evaluation Model (see Torous, Chan, Gipson, et al., 2018; Torous, Nicholas, et al., 2018). The model uses a hierarchical framework of factors to consider when discussing and making decisions about the use of specific apps in mental health treatment. At this time, the model provides a useful heuristic for decision making, however as this area evolves, research may give rise to new resources and novel solutions. Further guidance for clinicians on strategies for evaluating and selecting health-related apps is provided in Boudreaux et al. (2014).

In addition to relevant research literature, one of the best resources for clinicians to refer to are the relevant ethical guidelines under which they practice, many of which have developed specific resources for the use of technology in

Box 27.2 Working Ethically With Digital Technology

Harry[a] was a 68-year-old man who had a long-standing history of psychotic episodes, which regularly resulted in hospitalisation. He sought help from a clinical psychologist to find better ways of managing his symptoms and stay out of hospital.

In the first session, his psychologist suggested using a smartphone app, which helped to monitor his symptoms and had the option of sending alerts to his key clinician if his condition worsened. Harry was very concerned about this device monitoring him and immediately rejected the idea. He also wasn't very confident using apps, though he did own a basic smartphone. The psychologist seemed genuinely interested in some of the reasons for Harry's concerns, so Harry explained that he did not want to be taken to hospital at any moment if he wasn't feeling well. After talking this through, the psychologist explained that Harry could choose whether or not he wanted his key clinician to be alerted about how he was doing. The psychologist showed Harry the app and explained how it worked, highlighting different places where he could customise it to do what he wanted. Harry particularly liked the part which sent him encouraging messages. The psychologist also told Harry about how other people had found the app helpful for keeping track of how they were doing, but she also said that not all people have found it useful. Harry and his psychologist decided to give it a go for a week to see if it was helpful and discuss whether to keep using it in the next session. Harry felt reassured that he could stop using it at any time and that he could choose when and how he used it.

In the next session, Harry explained to the psychologist that he had used the app for a couple of days but after that it became annoying to him. Harry was surprised when his psychologist didn't challenge him to keep using the app and instead they talked about some other ways to achieve his goals. This made Harry feel respected and in control of his treatment decisions, which made him feel more motivated and supported.

[a]Hypothetical client example.

psychological practice. For example, guidelines on the use of digital mental health technologies have been produced by national representative bodies, including the Australian Psychological Society (2011), American Psychological Association (2013), and The British Psychological Society (2009). Specialist professional development initiatives are also available, many of which are offered for free online (e.g. eMHprac http://www.emhprac.org.au/training/).

FUTURE DIRECTIONS

Digital technology will continue to advance and grow increasingly more involved in mental healthcare. For people with psychosis, this offers opportunities to access new avenues of treatment, which may ultimately improve their lives. As early career psychologists continue to develop their clinical skills and learn new ways of working with their clients, it would benefit them to maintain awareness of how digital technology might be used to enhance their clinical practice. This will involve maintaining familiarity with new developments and their evidence base as they arise, as well as an understanding of the evolving practical and ethical issues relevant to this unique client group.

FURTHER READING

Bauer, M., Glenn, T., Monteith, S., Bauer, R., Whybrow, P. C., & Geddes, J. (2017). Ethical perspectives on recommending digital technology for patients with mental illness. *International Journal of Bipolar Disorders, 5*(1), 6.

O'Hanlon, P., Aref-Adib, G., Fonseca, A., Lloyd-Evans, B., Osborn, D., & Johnson, S. (2016). Tomorrow's world: Current developments in the therapeutic use of technology for psychosis. *British Journal of Psychiatry Advances, 22*(5), 301–310.

Treisman, G. J., Jayaram, G., Margolis, R. L., Pearlson, G. D., Schmidt, C. W., Mihelish, G. L., ... & Misiuta, I. E. (2016). Perspectives on the use of eHealth in the management of patients with schizophrenia. *The Journal of Nervous and Mental Disease, 204*(8), 620.

Torous, J. B., Chan, S. R., Gipson, S. Y. M. T., Kim, J. W., Nguyen, T. Q., Luo, J., & Wang, P. (2018). A hierarchical framework for evaluation and informed decision making regarding smartphone apps for clinical care. *Psychiatric Services, 69*(5), 498–500.

QUIZ QUESTIONS

1. There is sufficient evidence to start using mobile apps in the clinical care of people with psychosis
   a. True
   b. False
   c. There is some evidence, but more research is needed
   d. There is sufficient evidence, but their use should be considered on a case-by-case basis
2. People diagnosed with a psychotic condition are likely to:
   a. Own a smartphone
   b. Not own a smartphone
   c. Use the internet regularly
   d. A and C
3. Clinicians should be cautious of using digital technology in their treatment of clients with psychosis because:
   a. Clients may feel uncomfortable or unfamiliar with technology
   b. The evidence base is still developing
   c. There are unique ethical issues involved
   d. All of the above
4. When introducing the idea of using a particular technology with clients who experiences psychosis, (it is important to first):
   a. Check that the technology has been sufficiently researched in this population
   b. Critically evaluate the technology and use it yourself
   c. Make them download and try it
   d. A and B
5. The majority of the apps available for mental healthcare have sufficient evidence base and targeted evaluations in psychosis
   a. True
   b. False

ANSWERS TO QUIZ QUESTIONS:

1. (c)
2. (d)
3. (d)
4. (d)
5. (b)

References

Ainsworth, J., Palmier-Claus, J., Machin, M., Barrowclough, C., Dunn, G., Rogers, A., et al. (2013). A comparison of two delivery modalities of a mobile phone-based assessment for serious mental illness: Native smartphone application vs text-messaging only implementations. *Journal of Medical Internet Research, 15*(4).

Alvarez-Jimenez, M., Alcazar-Corcoles, M., Gonzalez-Blanch, C., Bendall, S., McGorry, P., & Gleeson, J. (2014). Online, social media and mobile technologies for psychosis treatment: A systematic review on novel user-led interventions. *Schizophrenia Research, 156*(1), 96–106. https://doi.org/10.1016/j.schres.2014.03.021.

Alvarez-Jimenez, M., Bendall, S., Lederman, R., Wadley, G., Chinnery, G., Vargas, S., et al. (2013). On the HORYZON: Moderated online social therapy for long-term recovery in first episode psychosis. *Schizophrenia Research, 143*(1), 143–149. https://doi.org/10.1016/j.schres.2012.10.009.

American Psychiatric Association. (2013). *Diagnostic and statistical manual of mental disorders* (5th ed.). Washington, DC: American Psychiatric Pub.

American Psychological Association. (2013). *Guidelines for the practice of telepsychology.* Retrieved from: http://www.apapracticecentral.org/ce/guidelines/telepsychology-guidelines.pdf.

Armontrout, J., Torous, J., Fisher, M., Drogin, E., & Gutheil, T. (2016). Mobile mental health: Navigating new rules and regulations for digital tools. *Current Psychiatry Reports, 18*(10), 1–7.

Aschbrenner, K. A., Naslund, J. A., Barre, L. K., Mueser, K. T., Kinney, A., & Bartels, S. J. (2015). Peer health coaching for overweight and obese individuals with serious mental illness: Intervention development and initial feasibility study. *Translational Behavioral Medicine, 5*(3), 277–284.

Australian Psychological Society. (2011). *Ethical guidelines for providing psychological services and products using the internet and telecommunications technologies.* Retrieved from: https://www.psychology.org.au/APS/media/pdfs/Legacy/EG-Internet.pdf.

Bakker, D., & Rickard, N. (2018). Engagement in mobile phone app for self-monitoring of emotional wellbeing predicts changes in mental health: MoodPrism. *Journal of Affective Disorders, 227*, 432–442.

Batra, S., Baker, R. A., Wang, T., Forma, F., Di Biasi, F., & Peters-Strickland, T. (2017). Digital health technology use in patients with serious mental illness: A systematic review of the literature. *Medical Devices: Evidence and Research, 10*, 237–251.

Bauer, M., Glenn, T., Monteith, S., Bauer, R., Whybrow, P. C., & Geddes, J. (2017). Ethical perspectives on recommending digital technology for patients with mental illness. *International Journal of Bipolar Disorders, 5*(1), 6.

Bell, I. H., Fielding-Smith, S. F., Hayward, M., Rossell, S. L., Lim, M. H., Farhall, J., et al. (2018). Smartphone-based ecological momentary assessment and intervention in a coping-focused intervention for hearing voices (SAVVy): Study protocol for a pilot randomised controlled trial. *Trials, 19*(1), 262. https://doi.org/10.1186/s13063-018-2607-6.

Bell, I. H., Lim, M. H., Rossell, S. L., & Thomas, N. (2017). Ecological momentary assessment and intervention in the treatment of psychotic disorders: A systematic review. *Psychiatric Services.* https://doi.org/10.1176/appi.ps.201600523.

Ben-Zeev, D., Brenner, C., Begale, M., Duffecy, J., Mohr, D., & Mueser, K. (2014). Feasibility, acceptability, and preliminary efficacy of a smartphone intervention for schizophrenia. *Schizophrenia Bulletin, 40(6)*, 1244–1253. sbu033.

Ben-Zeev, D., Brian, R., Wang, R., Wang, W., Campbell, A. T., Aung, M. S., et al. (2017). CrossCheck: Integrating self-report, behavioral sensing, and smartphone use to identify digital indicators of psychotic relapse. *Psychiatric Rehabilitation Journal, 40*(3), 266.

Ben-Zeev, D., McHugo, G., Xie, H., Dobbins, K., & Young, M. (2012). Comparing retrospective reports to real-time/real-place mobile assessments in individuals with schizophrenia and a nonclinical comparison group. *Schizophrenia Bulletin, 38*(3), 396–404.

Berry, N., Bucci, S., & Lobban, F. (2017). Use of the internet and mobile phones for self-management of severe mental health problems: Qualitative study of staff views. *JMIR Mental Health, 4*(4).

Berry, N., Lobban, F., Emsley, R., et al. (2016). Acceptability of interventions delivered online and through mobile phones for people who experience severe mental health problems: A systematic review. *Journal of Medical Internet Research, 18*.

Boudreaux, E. D., Waring, M. E., Hayes, R. B., Sadasivam, R. S., Mullen, S., & Pagoto, S. (2014). Evaluating and selecting mobile health apps: Strategies for healthcare providers and healthcare organizations. *Translational Behavioral Medicine, 4*(4), 363–371.

Brand, R. M., McEnery, C., Rossell, S., Bendall, S., & Thomas, N. (2017). Do trauma-focussed psychological interventions have an effect on psychotic symptoms? A systematic review and meta-analysis. *Schizophrenia Research, 195*, 13–22.

Brett, J., Staniszewska, S., Mockford, C., Herron-Marx, S., Hughes, J., Tysall, C., et al. (2014). Mapping the impact of patient and public involvement on health and social care research: A systematic review. *Health Expectations, 17*(5), 637–650.

Brittain, P. J., Stahl, D., Rucker, J., Kawadler, J., & Schumann, G. (2013). A review of the reliability and validity of OPCRIT in relation to its use for the routine clinical assessment of mental health patients. *International Journal of Methods in Psychiatric Research, 22*(2), 110–137.

Bucci, S., Barrowclough, C., Ainsworth, J., Machin, M., Morris, R., Berry, K., et al. (2018). Actissist: Proof-of-concept trial of a theory-driven digital intervention for psychosis. *Schizophrenia Bulletin, 44*, 1070–1080.

Chan, C. L., Ngai, E. K., Leung, P. K., & Wong, S. (2010). Effect of the adapted virtual reality cognitive training program among Chinese older adults with chronic schizophrenia: A pilot study. *International Journal of Geriatric Psychiatry, 25*(6), 643–649.

Cohen, J. S., Edmunds, J. M., Brodman, D. M., Benjamin, C. L., & Kendall, P. C. (2013). Using self-monitoring: Implementation of collaborative empiricism in cognitive-behavioral therapy. *Cognitive and Behavioral Practice, 20*(4), 419–428.

Communities and Local Government. (2008). *Digital exclusion profiling of vulnerable groups: Adults with mental health problems: A profile*. London: Communities and Local Government.

Couture, S. M., Penn, D. L., & Roberts, D. L. (2006). The functional significance of social cognition in schizophrenia: A review. *Schizophrenia Bulletin, 32*(1), S44–S63. https://doi.org/10.1093/schbul/sbl029.

Craig, T. K., Rus-Calafell, M., Ward, T., Leff, J. P., Huckvale, M., Howarth, E., et al. (2018). AVATAR therapy for auditory verbal hallucinations in people with psychosis: A single-blind, randomised controlled trial. *The Lancet Psychiatry, 5*(1), 31–40.

Dale, O., & Hagen, K. B. (2007). Despite technical problems personal digital assistants outperform pen and paper when collecting patient diary data. *Journal of Clinical Epidemiology, 60*(1), 8–17.

Demeulemeester, M., Kochman, F., Fligans, B., Tabet, A. J., Thomas, P., & Jardri, R. (2015). Assessing early-onset hallucinations in the touch-screen generation. *The British Journal of Psychiatry, 206*(3), 181–183.

Dunn, H., Morrison, A. P., & Bentall, R. P. (2002). Patients' experiences of homework tasks in cognitive behavioural therapy for psychosis: A qualitative analysis. *Clinical Psychology & Psychotherapy, 9*(5), 361–369.

Firth, J., Cotter, J., Torous, J., Bucci, S., Firth, J. A., & Yung, A. R. (2015). Mobile phone ownership and endorsement of "mHealth" among people with psychosis: A meta-analysis of cross-sectional studies. *Schizophrenia Bulletin, 42*(2), 448–455.

Firth, J., & Torous, J. (2015). Smartphone apps for schizophrenia: A systematic review. *JMIR mHealth and uHealth, 3*(4), e102.

Fleming, T., Bavin, L., Lucassen, M., Stasiak, K., Hopkins, S., & Merry, S. (2018). Beyond the trial: Systematic review of real-world uptake and engagement with digital self-help interventions for depression, low mood, or anxiety. *Journal of Medical Internet Research, 20*(6), e199.

Freeman, D., Bradley, J., Antley, A., Bourke, E., DeWeever, N., Evans, N., et al. (2016). Virtual reality in the treatment of persecutory delusions: Randomised controlled experimental study testing how to reduce delusional conviction. *The British Journal of Psychiatry, 209*, 62–67 [bjp. bp. 115.176438].

Freeman, D., Reeve, S., Robinson, A., Ehlers, A., Clark, D., Spanlang, B., et al. (2017). Virtual reality in the assessment, understanding, and treatment of mental health disorders. *Psychological Medicine, 47*(14), 2393–2400.

Gay, K., Torous, J., Joseph, A., Pandya, A., & Duckworth, K. (2016). Digital technology use among individuals with schizophrenia: Results of an online survey. *JMIR Mental Health, 3*(2).

Gayer-Anderson, C., & Morgan, C. (2013). Social networks, support and early psychosis: A systematic review. *Epidemiology and Psychiatric Sciences, 22*(2), 131–146. https://doi.org/10.1017/s2045796012000406.

Gottlieb, J., Romeo, K., Penn, D., Mueser, K., & Chiko, B. (2013). Web-based cognitive–behavioral therapy for auditory hallucinations in persons with psychosis: A pilot study. *Schizophrenia Research, 145*(1), 82–87.

Gottlieb, J. D., Gidugu, V., Maru, M., Tepper, M. C., Davis, M. J., Greenwold, J., et al. (2017). Randomized controlled trial of an internet cognitive behavioral skills-based program for auditory hallucinations in persons with psychosis. *Psychiatric Rehabilitation Journal, 40*(3), 283.

Granholm, E., Loh, C., & Swendsen, J. (2008). Feasibility and validity of computerized ecological momentary assessment in schizophrenia. *Schizophrenia Bulletin, 34*(3), 507–514.

Grynszpan, O., Perbal, S., Pelissolo, A., Fossati, P., Jouvent, R., Dubal, S., et al. (2011). Efficacy and specificity of computer-assisted cognitive remediation in schizophrenia: A meta-analytical study. *Psychological Medicine, 41*(1), 163–173.

Heron, K., & Smyth, J. (2010). Ecological momentary interventions: Incorporating mobile technology into psychosocial and health behaviour treatments. *British Journal of Health Psychology, 15*(1), 1–39.

Jacobsen, P., Peters, E., Ward, T., Garety, P. A., Jackson, M., & Chadwick, P. (2018). Overgeneral autobiographical memory bias in clinical and non-clinical voice hearers. *Psychological Medicine, 49*, 113–120.

Jauhar, S., McKenna, P., Radua, J., Fung, E., Salvador, R., & Laws, K. (2014). Cognitive-behavioural therapy for the symptoms of schizophrenia: Systematic review and meta-analysis with examination of potential bias. *The British Journal of Psychiatry, 204*(1), 20–29.

Johnson, E. I., Grondin, O., Barrault, M., Faytout, M., Helbig, S., Husky, M., et al. (2009). Computerized ambulatory monitoring in psychiatry: A multi-site collaborative study of acceptability, compliance, and reactivity. *International Journal of Methods in Psychiatric Research, 18*(1), 48–57.

Kimhy, D., Delespaul, P., Corcoran, C., Ahn, H., Yale, S., & Malaspina, D. (2006). Computerized experience sampling method (ESMc): Assessing feasibility and validity among individuals with schizophrenia. *Journal of Psychiatric Research, 40*(3), 221–230.

Kohn, R., Saxena, S., Levav, I., & Saraceno, B. (2004). The treatment gap in mental health care. *Bulletin of the World Health Organization, 82*(11), 858–866.

Kotz, D., Gunter, C. A., Kumar, S., & Weiner, J. P. (2016). Privacy and security in mobile health: A research agenda. *Computer, 49*(6), 22.

Kreyenbuhl, J., Nossel, I. R., & Dixon, L. B. (2009). Disengagement from mental health treatment among individuals with schizophrenia and strategies for facilitating connections to care: A review of the literature. *Schizophrenia Bulletin, 35*(4), 696–703.

Kwapil, T. R. (1998). Social anhedonia as a predictor of the development of schizophrenia-spectrum disorders. *Journal of Abnormal Psychology, 107*(4), 558–565.

Lal, S., & Adair, C. E. (2014). E-mental health: A rapid review of the literature. *Psychiatric Services, 65*(1), 24–32.

Larsen, M. E., Nicholas, J., & Christensen, H. (2016). A systematic assessment of smartphone tools for suicide prevention. *PLoS One, 11*(4).

Lee, K.-T., Noh, M.-J., & Koo, D.-M. (2013). Lonely people are no longer lonely on social networking sites: The mediating role of self-disclosure and social support. *Cyberpsychology, Behavior and Social Networking, 16*(6), 413–418.

Leff, J., Williams, G., Huckvale, M., Arbuthnot, M., & Leff, A. (2013). Computer-assisted therapy for medication-resistant auditory hallucinations: Proof-of-concept study. *The British Journal of Psychiatry, 202*(6), 428–433.

Lim, M. H., Gleeson, J. F. M., Alvarez-Jimenez, M., & Penn, D. L. (2018). Loneliness in psychosis: A systematic review. *Social Psychiatry and Psychiatric Epidemiology, 53*(3), 221–238. https://doi.org/10.1007/s00127-018-1482-5.

Lim, M. H., & Penn, D. L. (2018). Using digital technology in the treatment of schizophrenia. *Schizophrenia Bulletin*. https://doi.org/10.1093/schbul/sby081.

Louise, S., Fitzpatrick, M., Strauss, C., Rossell, S. L., & Thomas, N. (2017). Mindfulness-and acceptance-based interventions for psychosis: Our current understanding and a meta-analysis. *Schizophrenia Research, 192*, 57–63.

MacDonald, E., Sauer, K., Howie, L., & Albiston, D. (2005). What happens to social relationships in early psychosis? A phenomenological study of young people's experiences. *Journal of Mental Health, 14*(2), 129–143. https://doi.org/10.1080/09638230500060052.

Macias, C., Panch, T., Hicks, Y. M., Scolnick, J. S., Weene, D. L., Öngür, D., et al. (2015). Using smartphone apps to promote psychiatric and physical well-being. *Psychiatric Quarterly, 86*(4), 505–519.

Mohr, D. C., Lyon, A. R., Lattie, E. G., Reddy, M., & Schueller, S. M. (2017). Accelerating digital mental health research from early design and creation to successful implementation and sustainment. *Journal of medical Internet research, 19*(5), e153.

Myin-Germeys, I., Oorschot, M., Collip, D., Lataster, J., Delespaul, P., & van Os, J. (2009). Experience sampling research in psychopathology: Opening the black box of daily life. *Psychological Medicine, 39*(09), 1533–1547.

Myin-Germeys, I., van Os, J., Schwartz, J., Stone, A., & Delespaul, P. (2001). Emotional reactivity to daily life stress in psychosis. *Archives of General Psychiatry, 58*(12), 1137–1144.

Naslund, J. A., Aschbrenner, K. A., Barre, L. K., & Bartels, S. J. (2015). Feasibility of popular m-health technologies for activity tracking among individuals with serious mental illness. *Telemedicine and e-Health, 21*(3), 213–216.

O'Hanlon, P., Aref-Adib, G., Fonseca, A., Lloyd-Evans, B., Osborn, D., & Johnson, S. (2016). Tomorrow's world: Current developments in the therapeutic use of technology for psychosis. *BJPsych Advances, 22*(5), 301–310.

Oorschot, M., Kwapil, T., Delespaul, P., & Myin-Germeys, I. (2009). Momentary assessment research in psychosis. *Psychological Assessment, 21*(4), 498.

Oorschot, M., Lataster, T., Thewissen, V., Bentall, R., Delespaul, P., & Myin-Germeys, I. (2012). Temporal dynamics of visual and auditory hallucinations in psychosis. *Schizophrenia Research, 140*(1), 77–82.

Oorschot, M., Lataster, T., Thewissen, V., Wichers, M., & Myin-Germeys, I. (2012). Mobile assessment in schizophrenia: A data-driven momentary approach. *Schizophrenia Bulletin, 38*(3), 405–413.

Palmier-Claus, J. E., Ainsworth, J., Machin, M., Barrowclough, C., Dunn, G., Barkus, E., et al. (2012). The feasibility and validity of ambulatory self-report of psychotic symptoms using a smartphone software application. *BMC Psychiatry, 12*(1), 172. https://doi.org/10.1186/1471-244X-12-172.

Palmier-Claus, J. E., Rogers, A., Ainsworth, J., Machin, M., Barrowclough, C., Laverty, L., et al. (2013). Integrating mobile-phone based assessment for psychosis into people's everyday lives and clinical care: A qualitative study. *BMC Psychiatry, 13*(1), 34.

Park, K.-M., Ku, J., Choi, S.-H., Jang, H.-J., Park, J.-Y., Kim, S. I., et al. (2011). A virtual reality application in role-plays of social skills training for schizophrenia: A randomized, controlled trial. *Psychiatry Research, 189*(2), 166–172.

Piasecki, T. M., Hufford, M. R., Solhan, M., & Trull, T. J. (2007). Assessing clients in their natural environments with electronic diaries: Rationale, benefits, limitations, and barriers. *Psychological Assessment, 19*(1), 25.

Pot-Kolder, R. M., Geraets, C. N., Veling, W., van Beilen, M., Staring, A. B., Gijsman, H. J., et al. (2018). Virtual-reality-based cognitive behavioural therapy versus waiting list control for paranoid ideation and social avoidance in patients with psychotic disorders: A single-blind randomised controlled trial. *The Lancet Psychiatry, 5*(3), 217–226.

Robotham, D., Satkunanathan, S., Doughty, L., & Wykes, T. (2016). Do we still have a digital divide in mental health? A five-year survey follow-up. *Journal of Medical Internet Research, 18*(11).

Rotondi, A. J., Spring, M. R., Hanusa, B. H., Eack, S. M., & Haas, G. L. (2017). Designing eHealth applications to reduce cognitive effort for persons with severe mental illness: Page complexity, navigation simplicity, and comprehensibility. *JMIR Human Factors, 4*(1).

Rucker, J., Newman, S., Gray, J., Gunasinghe, C., Broadbent, M., Brittain, P., et al. (2011). OPCRIT+: An electronic system for psychiatric diagnosis and data collection in clinical and research settings. *The British Journal of Psychiatry, 199*(2), 151–155.

Rus-Calafell, M., Garety, P., Sason, E., Craig, T., & Valmaggia, L. (2018). Virtual reality in the assessment and treatment of psychosis: A systematic review of its utility, acceptability and effectiveness. *Psychological Medicine, 48*(3), 362–391.

Schlosser, D. A., Campellone, T. R., Truong, B., Etter, K., Vergani, S., Komaiko, K., et al. (2018). Efficacy of PRIME, a mobile app intervention designed to improve motivation in young people with schizophrenia. *Schizophrenia Bulletin, 44*(5), 1010–1020.

Seabrook, E. M., Kern, M. L., & Rickard, N. S. (2016). Social networking sites, depression, and anxiety: A systematic review. *JMIR Mental Health, 3*(4), e50. https://doi.org/10.2196/mental.5842.

Shiffman, S., Stone, A., & Hufford, M. (2008). Ecological momentary assessment. *Annual Review of Clinical Psychology, 4*, 1–32.

Sorkin, A., Weinshall, D., Modai, I., & Peled, A. (2006). Improving the accuracy of the diagnosis of schizophrenia by means of virtual reality. *American Journal of Psychiatry, 163*(3), 512–520.

Španiel, F., Hrdlicka, J., Novak, T., Kozeny, J., Hoeschl, C., Mohr, P., et al. (2012). Effectiveness of the information technology-aided program of relapse prevention in schizophrenia (ITAREPS): A randomized, controlled, double-blind study. *Journal of Psychiatric Practice, 18*(4), 269–280.

Stone, A., Schwartz, J., Neale, J., Shiffman, S., Marco, C., Hickcox, M., et al. (1998). A comparison of coping assessed by ecological momentary assessment and retrospective recall. *Journal of Personality and Social Psychology, 74*(6), 1670.

Sunyaev, A., Dehling, T., Taylor, P. L., & Mandl, K. D. (2014). Availability and quality of mobile health app privacy policies. *Journal of the American Medical Informatics Association, 22*(e1), e28–e33.

Tarrier, N. (1992). Management and modification of residual positive psychotic symptoms. In M. Birchwood, & N. Tarrier (Eds.), *Innovations in the psychological management of schizophrenia: Assessment, treatment and services* (pp. 147–169). Wiley Series in Clinical Psychology.

The British Psychological Society. (2009). *The provision of psychological services via the internet and other non-direct means.* Retrieved from: https://www1.bps.org.uk/system/files/Public%20files/psychological_services_over_the_internet.pdf.

Thomas, N. (2015). What's really wrong with cognitive behavioral therapy for psychosis? *Frontiers in Psychology, 6*, 323.

Thomas, N., Farhall, J., Foley, F., Leitan, N. D., Villagonzalo, K.-A., Ladd, E., et al. (2016). Promoting personal recovery in people with persisting psychotic disorders: Development and pilot study of a novel digital intervention. *Frontiers in Psychiatry, 7*, 196.

Thomas, N., Foley, F., Lindblom, K., & Lee, S. (2017). Are people with severe mental illness ready for online interventions? Access and use of the internet in Australian mental health service users. *Australasian Psychiatry, 25*, 257–261.

Torous, J., Andersson, G., Bertagnoli, A., Christensen, H., Cuijpers, P., Firth, J., et al. (2019). Towards a consensus around standards for smartphone apps and digital mental health. *World Psychiatry, 18*(1), 97.

Torous, J., Chan, S., Luo, J., Boland, R., & Hilty, D. (2018). Clinical informatics in psychiatric training: Preparing today's trainees for the already present future. *Academic Psychiatry, 42*(5), 694–697.

Torous, J., & Firth, J. (2016). The digital placebo effect: Mobile mental health meets clinical psychiatry. *The Lancet Psychiatry, 3*(2), 100–102.

Torous, J., Kiang, M. V., Lorme, J., & Onnela, J.-P. (2016). New tools for new research in psychiatry: A scalable and customizable platform to empower data driven smartphone research. *JMIR Mental Health, 3*(2).

Torous, J., Nicholas, J., Larsen, M. E., Firth, J., & Christensen, H. (2018). Clinical review of user engagement with mental health smartphone apps: Evidence, theory and improvements. *Evidence-Based Mental Health, 21*(3), 116–119.

Torous, J., Onnela, J., & Keshavan, M. (2017). New dimensions and new tools to realize the potential of RDoC: Digital phenotyping via smartphones and connected devices. *Translational Psychiatry, 7*(3).

Torous, J., Staples, P., Slaters, L., Adams, J., Sandoval, L., Onnela, J. P., et al. (2017). Characterizing smartphone engagement for schizophrenia: Results of a naturalist mobile health study. *Clinical Schizophrenia & Related Psychoses, (2017)*. https://doi.org/10.3371/CSRP.JTPS.071317[Epub ahead of print].

Torous, J. B., Chan, S. R., Gipson, S. Y.-M. T., Kim, J. W., Nguyen, T.-Q., Luo, J., et al. (2018). A hierarchical framework for evaluation and informed decision making regarding smartphone apps for clinical care. *Psychiatric Services, 69*(5), 498–500.

Treisman, G. J., Jayaram, G., Margolis, R. L., Pearlson, G. D., Schmidt, C. W., Mihelish, G. L., et al. (2016). Perspectives on the use of eHealth in the management of patients with schizophrenia. *The Journal of Nervous and Mental Disease, 204*(8), 620.

Trull, T., & Ebner-Priemer, U. (2009). Using experience sampling methods/ecological momentary assessment (ESM/EMA) in clinical assessment and clinical research: Introduction to the special section. *Psychological Assessment, 21*(4), 457–462.

van der Gaag, M., Valmaggia, L. R., & Smit, F. (2014). The effects of individually tailored formulation-based cognitive behavioural therapy in auditory hallucinations and delusions: A meta-analysis. *Schizophrenia Research, 156*(1), 30–37.

Van Os, J., Delespaul, P., Wigman, J., Myin-Germeys, I., & Wichers, M. (2013). Psychiatry beyond labels: Introducing contextual precision diagnosis across stages of psychopathology. *Psychological Medicine, 43*(7), 1563–1567.

Villagonzalo, K. A., Arnold, C., Farhall, J., Rossell, S. L., Foley, F., & Thomas, N. (2019). Predictors of overall and mental health-related internet use in adults with psychosis. *Psychiatry Research, 278*, 12–18.

Williams, A., Fossey, E., Farhall, J., Foley, F., & Thomas, N. (2018). Recovery after psychosis: Qualitative study of service user experiences of lived experience videos on a recovery-oriented website. *JMIR Mental Health*, *5*(2), e37. https://doi.org/10.2196/mental.9934.

World Health Organisation. (2010). *WHO releases mhGAP intervention guide app*. Retrieved from: http://www.who.int/mental_health/mhgap/e_mhgap/en/.

Definition of Key Terms

Digital Mental Health or eMental Health Refers to the use of technology in the context of mental healthcare and research.

Ecological momentary assessment, or experience sampling Involves the use of mobile devices to assess phenomena in real-time, in daily life.

Ecological momentary intervention Involves the real-time delivery of therapeutic prompts or reminders within daily life via mobile devices.

Ambulatory assessment Uses passive sensors to capture real-time data

Digital phenotype Is a term referring to unique patterns of individual data collected from digital sources.

Digital placebo effect Refers to the influence of expectation on the therapeutic benefits of digital technology, rather than the technology itself.

CHAPTER 28

Tracking Language in Real Time in Psychosis

Terje B. Holmlund*, Taylor L. Fedechko†, Brita Elvevåg*,‡, Alex S. Cohen†
*Department of Clinical Medicine, UiT The Arctic University of Norway, Tromsø, Norway, †Department of Psychology, Louisiana State University, Baton Rouge, LA, United States, ‡Norwegian Centre for eHealth Research, University Hospital of North Norway, Tromsø, Norway

Key Learning Objectives

- To learn about the strengths and weaknesses of currently used clinical and performance-based measures of language functions.
- To learn about objective language assessments for measuring language functions in patients with serious mental illnesses.
- To gain an appreciation of using objective language assessments to track language dysfunctions in 'real time'.
- To identify potential obstacles that challenge attempts to move beyond 'proof of concept,' as well as solutions that may address these.

INTRODUCTION

> An individual with psychosis is asked to describe how it felt to meet a close relative.[1]
> Interviewer: "How good did it feel, on a scale of 0 to 10?"
> Patient with psychosis: "It was about like a scream opposite… about half of a scream opposite."

This striking example illustrates how language can be disrupted in individuals with psychosis. In this response, the patient employs commonly used words and largely adheres to the grammatical and syntactical norms of natural speech. However, the meaning of the language is lost and hence, the patient's speech is largely ineffective as a means of answering the interviewer's question. This type of language disturbance is but one of many that are commonly seen in psychosis, such as schizophrenia, and reflects one of several different symptoms. The

[1] Context altered slightly for privacy reasons.

A Clinical Introduction to Psychosis. https://doi.org/10.1016/B978-0-12-815012-2.00028-6

present chapter will discuss the clinical utility of measuring language to track symptoms of psychosis and will describe:

1. How language has and is being used to understand and track various aspects of psychosis.
2. How automated and objective methods of language analysis can be used to understand and track psychosis.
3. How automated and objective methodologies could be implemented for understanding and tracking psychosis in 'real time'.

DEFINING LANGUAGE AND ITS RELEVANCE TO PSYCHOSIS

Language, defined broadly as a system of communication, is an important human ability that is intimately tied to a broad range of critical social, occupational, and recreational functions. Language can be expressed through a variety of media (i.e. writing, signing, scripted speech, emojis) and contains both linguistic (i.e. verbal content of language) and paralinguistic features (i.e. nonverbal language characteristics) (Warren, 2012; Whitehorn & Zipf, 1943). There are many mutually interdependent 'components' of language, occurring across lexical (i.e. concerning individual words), syntactical (i.e. concerning how words are structurally organised together), coherence (i.e. concerning the linearity and logical flow of the ideas being expressed), and semantic (i.e. the symbolic meaning of language) domains. Functionally speaking, language is potentially dependent on a broad range of psychological, physiological, and psychomotor, attentional, memory, personality, social, and cultural factors (Kita, 2003), and reflects input from an impressively diverse set of neurobiological systems (Poeppel, Idsardi, & Van Wassenhove, 2008). For these reasons, analysing and tracking the language of individuals with psychosis can provide information about a diverse set of psychological, psychophysiological, and socio-cultural functions. From the dawn of psychology, language was seen as a 'window' into an individual's internal experience (Pennebaker, Mehl, & Niederhoffer, 2003; Pinker, 2003).

Key components of language:
Lexical (words)
Syntactic (structure)
Coherence (consistency, clarity)**Semantic** (meaning)

Language is also a critical medium through which psychosis can be understood and tracked. In part, this is because the cognitive, affective, motivational, and social factors underlying language are of central importance in psychosis (American Psychiatric Association, 2013; World Health Organization, 2018). Clinically speaking, language is one of the primary mediums by which patients communicate information about their symptoms and experiences, and hence, by which clinicians diagnose their patients (Awad & Voruganti, 2000). Language, in both form and function, is also a primary target of mental status exams, neuropsychological status exams, structured clinical interviews, and is informally assessed in virtually all in vivo psychiatric and psychological assessments (Harvey, Earle-Boyer, & Wielgus, 1984; Rush, First, & Blacker, 2008). Language functions can be disrupted in a number of ways in psychosis, for example, in ineffectual or inappropriate lexical choice (e.g. neologisms, echolalia), incoherent and illogical semantics, unusually 'flat' and sparse prosodic vocalisations, or patently bizarre or improbable content. With respect to the cardinal symptoms of psychosis, these can reflect delusions (e.g. perseveration with delusional content), disorganisation (e.g. ineffectual semantics and coherence), alogia (e.g. decreased speech production), blunted affect (e.g. aprosodic speech), social anhedonia (e.g. reduced responsivity and interpersonal 'accommodation'), mania (e.g. pressured speech), depression (e.g. reduced use of positively valenced emotion words), and a myriad of other basic cognitive and affective features (American Psychiatric Association, 2013; Andreasen & Grove, 1986; World Health Organization, 2018).

Multiple components of language may be disrupted in people with psychosis.

UNDERSTANDING AND TRACKING PSYCHOSIS THROUGH LANGUAGE: PAST AND PRESENT

Clinical Ratings and Self-Report Approaches

Measuring language has been essential for understanding psychosis since the early conceptualisations of psychosis in neurology, psychiatry, and psychology. For example, disturbances in the ability to express logical and semantically coherent ideas (i.e. thought disorder, loose associations) and emotion through speech (i.e. blunted affect) were included in some of the first descriptions of schizophrenia (Bleuler, 1950; Kraepelin, 1919). Language remains central to the diagnostic criteria of schizophrenia-spectrum disorders, as components of language are included both in the *Diagnostic and Statistical Manual of Mental Disorders* 5 (American Psychiatric Association, 2013) and the *International Statistical Classification of Diseases and Related Health Problems*-11 (World Health Organization, 2018). Also, in standard medical note taking from clinical evaluations, it is important to describe patients' language usage with a nomenclature that is as precise and objective as possible. Indeed, well-written clinical notes have been, and remain, a core method to document and communicate language aberrations in patients.

Prior to the 1970s, the primary means of evaluating language in clinical settings mainly involved clinician impression, linguistic analysis of language procured from projective tests, and some clinician-based rating scales (Cancro, 1969; Harrow & Quinlan, 1985). Beginning in the 1970s, clinical rating scales and semi-structured clinical interviews became more commonplace. Psychometric evaluation of these scales revealed that with appropriate training and monitoring, they demonstrate adequate interrater reliability and face, concurrent, and predictive validity for a number of critical clinical functions. Although it is unclear to what degree these ratings were and are actually employed in clinical practice, they have become the 'gold standard' for formally evaluating language within the context of psychosis. Examples include the Scale for the Assessment of Thought, Language, and Communication (TLC), a clinical rating system for operationalising and quantifying various aspects of speech (Andreasen, 1986), the Scale for the Assessment of Positive Symptoms (SAPS; Andreasen, 1984), the Scale for the Assessment of Negative Symptoms (SANS; Andreasen, 1983), the Positive and Negative Syndrome Scale for schizophrenia (PANSS; Kay, Fiszbein, & Opler, 1987), and the Brief Psychiatric Rating Scale (BPRS; Lukoff, Liberman, & Nuechterlein, 1986). These tools generally have a scope wider than language assessment and aim for a more general description of psychiatric state/status (e.g. the BPRS and PANSS). In these cases, the language component may comprise only part of a compound score. Even so, the inclusion of a language component in these assessments highlights the importance of language aberrations, and the importance of recording such findings in mental status and general psychiatric assessments.

Reliable and accurate documentation of language usage is a core skill for clinicians.

Generally speaking, clinical rating scales involve a clinician integrating information from various behavioural, self-report, historical, and collateral sources. An ordinal-based scoring rubric, generally comprised between four and seven points, is used to help quantify the level of language dysfunction. The time scale of these measures varies, as they can involve retrospective evaluation of language during an epoch of weeks or focus on evaluating language solely observed during a brief interview. A common feature, and often notable challenge, for these rating scale systems involves paring down the complex and dynamic information present in various aspects of language, to a single ordinal-based value. Clinical rating scales generally require considerable time and personnel resources to ensure reliable administration. The importance of clinical rating scales cannot be understated, as they have provided tools for defining, organising, and quantifying language dysfunctions in both clinical treatment and research settings (Andreasen, 1986; see McKenna & Oh, 2005 for a historical review). Beyond their use for diagnosis, clinical rating scales have allowed for tracking language functions over time. This function has been critical to a wide range of clinical and research applications, such as in forensic and clinical decision making, pharmaceutical, psychosocial development and efficacy studies, and for understanding neurodevelopmental trajectories of psychosis over time.

Self-report measures of language functions have also been employed to understand various aspects of the psychosis-spectrum. Although self-report scales are limited to one source of information, namely an individual's self-perception, this type of measure is attractive in that it can be administered to large populations and scored without the need for trained experts. They can also be administered repeatedly to individual patients, and hence, reflect a potentially efficient means of tracking them over time. An example of a self-report measure is the Schizotypal Personality Questionnaire (SPQ), which (amongst other things) asks individuals to extent to which they 'wander off topic' and 'use words in unusual ways' (Raine, 1991). Widely used and validated multidimensional psychopathology measures, such as the Personality Assessment Inventory (PAI) and the various versions of the Minnesota Multiphasic Personality Inventories (MMPI-2, MMPI-2-RF), contain subscales and items broadly measuring positive and disorganised symptoms (Ben-Porath & Tellegen, 2008; Morey, 1991; Tellegen & Ben-Porath, 2011). Even shorter self-report questionnaires, such as the Prodromal Questionnaire—Brief version (PQ-B), assess disorganised speech (Loewy, Pearson, Vinogradov, Bearden, & Cannon, 2011). While an important complement to language assessment in psychosis, the use of self-report measures should be balanced in light of the potential self-report based confounds and biases (see Cohen & Elvevåg, 2014; Podsakoff, MacKenzie, Lee, & Podsakoff, 2003).

Psycholinguistic Approaches

Psycholinguistics, as a scientific discipline devoted to understanding language, has also been used to understand psychosis (e.g. Fromkin, Rodman, & Hyams, 2007). While clinical rating scales are developed and scaled to measure various hierarchically defined gradations of *impairment* in language related functions, psycholinguistic sciences tend to conceptualise language as a *continuous* function in the population. Thus, measures adopted from psycholinguistic sciences are scaled to evaluate a broad range of maladaptive and adaptive functioning, and generally produce data that are more normally distributed, and hence, are more compatible with the Research Domain Criteria (RDoC) recently proposed by the United States' National Institute of Mental Health (Insel et al., 2010). For example, rather than focusing on circumstantial or tangential speech, linguistic sciences might focus on coherence, speech 'typicality', or effectiveness (Elvevåg, Foltz, Weinberger, & Goldberg, 2007; Hoffman, Kirstein, Stopek, & Cicchetti, 1982). This approach can be used to identify genetic and neural mechanisms that give rise to and maintain psychotic language. Exemplars of various types of disordered speech from individuals with psychosis are included in Table 28.1.

Psycholinguistic-based conceptualisations operationalise language as a continuum ranging from maladaptive to adaptive functioning.

Table 28.1 Exemplars of Various Types of Disordered Speech From Individuals With Psychosis, and the Linguistic Concept That Captures the Disorder

Case study example	Linguistic concept
(describing worries) 'I would like to be a good person. Stand on my own two feet. But the only time I stood all day at five o'clock in the morning till five o'clock at night was in the back-yard shooting guns more than six years ago'.	Semantic-level deviation: Concreteness
Interviewer: Are you currently experiencing loss of pleasure or interest in activities you used to enjoy? *Patient: 'I don't want to go down the wrong road. I want to keep my head up high and be alive and not worry too much about what it brings'.*	Semantic-level deviation: Tangent
(describing auditory hallucinations) 'Uh I have to catch a grip now. I have to think. It was like uh it was really like something that been in my brain to uh make me think of something that was true and happening. It was something on that point, it was like you could take that terminology and put it in the blank what it means maybe you, you would uh know what I was talking about. There was a certainty'.	Semantic- and lexical-level deviation: Neologism Quantity-level deviation: Paucity of content of speech
'I would torture myself up to earning everything I desire, if I wouldn't get tortured I would do it if I wouldn't get tortured up to earning everything I desire and everything [Patient first name] would be getting and could get'.	Semantic-level deviation: Perseveration Syntactical deviation

There are many psycholinguistic-based systems that have been used to understand psychosis. Though a comprehensive exploration of these systems is beyond the present chapter, a few particularly salient examples are worth mentioning. The Communication Disturbances Index (CDI) involves behaviourally coding transcribed language for specific types of 'referential failures' thought to be central to schizophrenia, mania, and depression-spectrum pathology (Docherty, DeRosa, & Andreasen, 1996). The CDI has greatly improved sensitivity over clinical rating scales, and hence, has been used to understand subtle changes in language as a result of affective and cognitive experimental manipulations. This provides important information about potential mechanisms underlying language disturbances in psychosis (Docherty, 2012). Other approaches, capitalising on automated and computerised analysis of language extracted from text, audio, natural language, and social media sources, have been used in psychosis research. Measures such as the type-token ratio (see also Covington & McFall, 2010), and Computerised Propositional Idea Density Rater (Brown, Snodgrass, Kemper, Herman, & Covington, 2008) provide various metrics quantifying the complexity of language and the number of semantic concepts being communicated. Word embedding approaches, such as Latent Semantic Analysis (Foltz, Kintsch, & Landauer, 1998), quantify relationships between words within natural language, based on comparison to large linguistic corpuses (available in many languages). In this manner, semantic linearity, typicality, and coherence can be statistically derived. Lexical analysis, for example, using the Linguistic Inquiry and Word Count (Pennebaker et al., 2003) can help evaluate delusional themes based on automated text searches for, for example, paranoid or grandiose content (Junghaenel, Smyth, & Santner, 2008; Strous et al., 2009). Computerised acoustic analysis, for example using the Computerised assessment of Affect from Natural Speech, has shown promise for measuring alogia and blunted vocal affect in psychosis (Cohen, Alpert, Nienow, Dinzeo, & Docherty, 2008; Cohen, Kim, & Najolia, 2013; Cohen, Mitchell, Docherty, & Horan, 2016). Moreover, using these technologies, specific fluctuations in voice volume have been shown to predict hostility feelings in patients with serious mental illness (Cowan et al., 2018). Despite demonstrated 'proof of concept' for clinical use of these various systems, to our knowledge, none have been employed in clinical practice on any meaningful scale.

Referential failures involve the use of a referent (e.g. he, she, it) that is ambiguous, undefined, or otherwise confusing.

Psycholinguistic tools for language analysis are not yet routinely used in clinical practice.

LANGUAGE AND PSYCHOSIS AS DYNAMIC PHENOMENA

Psychosis is not a static phenomenon. Rather, it varies considerably within people, over time (e.g. minutes, hours and days), and as a function of stress levels, use of licit and illicit substances, sleep quality, and other environmental conditions. Being able to track fluctuations in psychosis is critical for monitoring patients, matching them to the most effective and least restrictive psychosocial or pharmacological interventions, and for reducing healthcare and emergency expenditures

(Insel, 2010, 2017). Language is similarly dynamic, and the present chapter assumes that tracking language as a dynamic function can reveal important information about psychosis. Such an endeavour requires that measures of language functions are sufficiently sensitive to both the subtle and not-so-subtle changes that psychosis potentially shows over various, user-defined, temporal epochs.

Accurate assessment of language requires careful consideration of context.

A critical factor for understanding language dynamics involves 'context'. Context includes the physical and social factors in the environment, and the cognitive, affective, and motivational resources needed for meeting the demands of the language task at hand. Language produced in response to a friend in a relaxed setting will vary considerably compared to language produced in response to a mental health professional in a forensic setting while being video recorded. Within the confines of traditional language assessment, attempts to reduce the potential impact of context are commonplace, for example, by 'standardising' the data collection environment, the language task instruction, and potential stimuli used to elicit speech. Projective tests, involving the use of abstract, ambiguous, or emotionally valenced stimuli, reflect one attempt to collect language samples under a controlled context. Projective measures such as the Rorschach inkblot test (Rorschach, 1942) and the Thematic Apperception Test (TAT; Murray, 1943) reflect such measures that are still used in some research and clinical settings—though they tend to require considerable resources to administer and have questionable validity for many purposes (Wood, Lilienfeld, Garb, & Nezworski, 2000). Language procured from these tests is quantified using a variety of systems (Liddle et al., 2002; Linscott, 2005; Solovay et al., 1986; Wynne & Singer, 1963). Another context for procuring language involves sentence completion tasks. The Cloze test, for example, requires people to provide responses to missing words in larger verbal statement (Taylor, 1953). Responses are evaluated for 'communicability' and predictability (Ragin & Oltmanns, 1987; Rutter, Wishner, Kopytynska, & Button, 1978). Traditional neuropsychological-based measures of expressive language ability, such as verbal fluency tests, are also commonly used in psychosis research. Verbal fluency tests involve having individuals produce as many words as they can within a relatively brief period of time that fit predefined parameters, for example, beginning with a specific letter, fitting a semantic profile (e.g. animals), or possessing a certain quality (e.g. words that refer to things deemed unpleasant).

Even within the same assessment, language that seems odd in one context may appear conventional in the next. Consider the person who produced the semantic *nonsequitur* demonstrated at the beginning of this chapter 'about half of a scream opposite'. Within several minutes, this patient also produced rather linear and typical responses. For example, the patient's response to the question 'Have you ever felt irritable or angry for days on end?' was 'it's not days on end, it's probably once every two days'. This individual also produced other examples of coherent language, including an answer to the questions 'Is anyone going out of their way to give you a hard time or trying to hurt you? Do you feel in danger?' by reporting 'I feel like somebody was trying to hurt me, but I didn't feel like I was in danger'. However, later during the interview, when asked about a bizarre belief endorsed by the patient (i.e. being the main G-d in his religion), the following language, which shows relatively extreme linguistic disturbances, was provided:

> Uh you see uh same one [Patient's first name] doing lately with his spaced out after the last contingency starting with pre- be it afterwards starting with extra added in with the spaced out for yourself don't do the bad one, do the nice one. If you do the bad one, you're usually transformed spaced out, the spaced out afterwards, and so on afterwards. Save that one, save the spaced out after ones, after one for yourself, save that one work for yourself, the spaced out after one and you'll become high enough to do anything on Earth. Girl for the girl, guy for the guy.

All of the language examples from this individual occurred in close temporal proximity to each other (i.e. within a few hours), but occurred in different contexts (i.e. in response to different questions). This illustrates the importance of considering context when evaluating and tracking psychosis, even over short temporal epochs.

Recent technological and computational advances have allowed for tracking language both within traditional clinical settings procedures and beyond. The latter, which involves understanding psychosis through acoustic, lexical, and semantic analysis extracted from natural speech, has been integrated into various mobile/ambulatory recording methods (e.g. ecological momentary assessment, experiential sampling) (e.g. see Holmlund, Foltz, et al., 2019). These methods provide for a potentially more comprehensive assessment across contexts in real time as individuals navigate their daily routines. From the extant research literature using these technologies, it is clear that individuals with serious mental illness have the capacity to use such technology in the context of research studies for at least short periods of time (e.g. weeks in Granholm, Ben-Zeev, Fulford, & Swendsen, 2013; Granholm, Loh, & Swendsen, 2007). Feasibility of using these technologies has been demonstrated using passive (i.e. continuous or intermittent recording of the individual and their environment; Minor, Davis, Marggraf, Luther, & Robbins, 2018; Wang et al., 2016) and active (e.g. recorded only when the patient is engaged in phone, social media, or other communications) (Cohen et al., 2019) recording approaches. Additionally, semantic analysis of online social media has been conducted (e.g. Joseph et al., 2015). These ambulatory technologies can potentially be used in conjunction with other types of objective and ambulatory assessment (e.g. electrophysiological, actigraphy, and reaction time) that are becoming increasingly employed to understand various aspects of psychosis (Raugh, Chapman, Bartolomeo, Gonzalez, & Strauss, 2019).

TRACKING PSYCHOSIS THROUGH LANGUAGE: FUTURE DIRECTIONS

Towards 'Real Time' Assessment

From an assessment perspective, many components of language are not well represented in general clinical tests (i.e. unless one is specifically assessing speech and language disorders). Furthermore, many existing language tests were designed in an era where the available technology consisted of a stopwatch, pen, and paper; thus, the metrics generated were easily counted surface-phenomena that were considered static. By contrast, modern technologies allow for the automated and precise measurement of language, combined with computerised analyses of aspects such as acoustic and semantic properties (see, e.g. Elvevåg et al., 2016). Along with improved precision comes the challenge of having extremely sensitive assays that require calibration to intra- and interindividual differences; hence, their specificity remains necessary to establish, likely via consortium-level efforts (Foltz, Rosenstein, & Elvevåg, 2016). Nonetheless, a foreseeable future includes these diverse metrics being combined via algorithms and tested in randomised clinical trials of clinical decision systems in a manner akin to the current use of diagnostic systems (e.g. DSM 5, ICD 11). Such technology has the potential to make precision medicine possible by leveraging the probability weightings in such a manner that these metrics act as digital phenotypes and enable accurate prognosis and suitable treatment action (e.g. Insel, 2010, 2017).

Modern technologies allow for the automated and precise measurement of language.

To illustrate the types of speech data that could comprise this language digital phenotype, descriptions are presented of four traditionally, and commonly collected, types of language data of differing complexity (i.e. verbal fluency task data, Stroop task data, verbal memory recall task data, and clinical interview data). Although these tasks differ in scope to the more clinically oriented language assessment measures, they come with numerous benefits such as being easily normed, and having minimal privacy and clinical concerns. These benefits have contributed to them being commonly and widely employed. Hence, these are some of the technologies that are likely to be the first to be validated for widespread clinical use. Furthermore, the use of well-established and constrained tasks can have a benefit in clinical settings, as low complexity tasks can be utilised with patients displaying more severe symptomatology. Establishing the utility of these tasks can serve as important building blocks for more advanced methods of language assessment in psychosis.

First, consider the simple verbal fluency task. Evaluating patients' verbal fluency by counting the number of unique nouns (e.g. animals) produced in a short period (e.g. 1–3 min) is one of the most widely employed language tests in psychiatric research. By leveraging modern computational language technology, new methods to analyse verbal fluency output enable two things, namely (i) moving beyond simple word counts to chart the actual temporal dynamics of speech itself, and (ii) the objective quantification of the semantic relationship of the word utterances (Holmlund, Cheng, Foltz, Cohen, & Elvevåg, 2019; see Fig. 28.1, Panel A). The availability of high precision timestamping of word utterances (on the order of $\pm$10 ms) allows examination of the temporal dynamics of the individual words in spontaneous speech. This opens the floodgates for the reconceptualisation of many traditional research tools that employ speech as the medium through which behaviour is assayed. However, given the novelty of this work, it is imperative that magnitudes more data are collected to establish

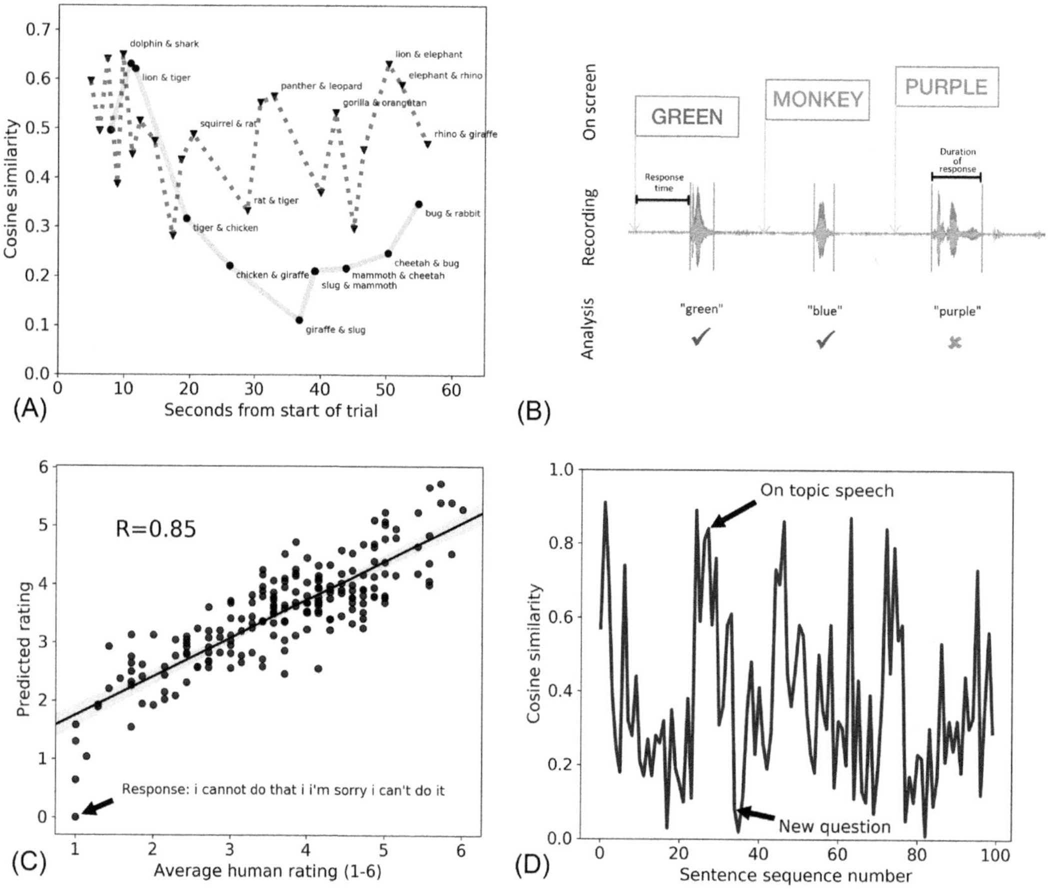

FIG. 28.1
Examples of how digital tools can be used for analysis of language expressions.

the robustness and stability of these metrics, and explore to what extent they might be affected by subtle nuances of different natural language approaches and computational platforms. Nonetheless, these new analytic approaches and metrics promise to be a useful addition to the current clinical research toolkit and they will likely contribute towards refinements of clinical theories regarding the nature of putative language differences in patients.

Second, consider the Stroop task, which requires focused attention to name the ink colour of a printed word (MacLeod, 1991), while ignoring the potentially conflicting meaning of the word itself (e.g. naming the red ink that the word **BLUE** is written in). Although traditionally, performance on the entire task has been timed as a whole (i.e. on the order of 45 s, which is viable with a stopwatch), readily available technology, such as smart devices, makes it equally possible to collect detailed reaction time data per response. Recent advances in speech technology (Automatic Speech Recognition specifically) enable (i) automated machine transcriptions of the recordings in people with serious mental illnesses[2]; (ii) precise timestamping of voice response onsets; and (iii) measurements of the duration of vocal responses (i.e. how long a word is uttered) (Holmlund, Cheng, Foltz, Cohen, Bernstein, et al., 2019; see Fig. 28.1, Panel B). Furthermore, beyond simple accuracy and time-stamping measurements, it is now technologically feasible to assay expression of affective states using prosodic elements of speech such as sound pressure and pitch. Indeed, affect measures derived from the acoustic properties in a person's utterance of a simple colour word in the Stroop task can provide a surprising amount of clinically relevant information (Cheng et al., 2018). The fact that these vital clues can be obtained in a nonthreatening manner is a large benefit in the assessment of patients with psychosis, in that confrontation of potentially arousing topics can be avoided.

Third, consider a verbal memory recall task such as story memory, or prose recall, which is employed in tests such as the Logical Memory part of the Wechsler Memory Scale (Wechsler, 1945). These tests measure verbal episodic memory as scored by human listeners who count linguistic forms in a spoken response. Natural language processing approaches can go beyond (i) simple counting of linguistic units and/or themes (Dunn, Almeida, Barclay, Waterreus, & Flicker, 2002; Rosenstein, Diaz-Asper, Foltz, & Elvevåg, 2014) to deeper semantic themes, and (ii) Automatic Speech Recognition provides a promising approach to speed the transcription process and allow measures to be instantly applied to analyse recall performance. In combination, this potentially provides more sensitive and diagnostic methods along with enabling realistic applications of such speech methods in ambulatory settings (see Holmlund, Foltz, et al., 2019). A recent study examining story memory over multiple days in patients with psychosis via a self-administered smartphone-based application automatically analysed recalls using multiple natural language processing techniques. The results indicated that automated scoring techniques, including transcripts generated via Automatic Speech Recognition methods, closely matched trained human scores and ratings of spoken narrative recalls (see Fig. 28.1, Panel C), thus strongly suggesting that automated approaches to speech can provide reliable assessment of memory recall (Chandler et al., 2019).

The three aforementioned examples are based upon tasks that produce stimulus-elicited speech, and such speech may differ from speech in dialogue. A whole new set of factors are introduced, though, when another individual, such as an interviewer, is present as s/he inevitably steers the conversation. At first glance, the automatic analysis of a clinical interview might be considered an ultimate goal; however, there are at least two reasons why this might

[2] In a recent study, the word error rate was calculated at 6.26%, which is considered highly accurate (Holmlund, Cheng, Foltz, Cohen, Bernstein, et al., 2019).

not be a useful research direction. First, although it is technically possible to use the aforementioned methods with dialogue, the clinical interview itself is an interaction in which the direction and topic is constrained by the interviewer. Therefore, an automated approach that compares the semantic similarity (i.e. the content and meanings) of what the interviewer says in a clinical interview to what the patient thus responds would look something like Fig. 28.1, Panel D, in which the coherence between interviewer and patient is computed (using latent semantic analysis) throughout the conversation. At points where the coherence between the two speakers is low, this could either be the introduction of a new question or the patient responds tangentially.[3] As conceptualised in this figure, dialogue would not be well suited to be fully automated in terms of language analysis. Second, there has been a strong movement in clinical research in mental health away from reliance on human-made DSM categories and moving to embracing the NIMH RDoC framework (Insel et al., 2010) that encourages the collection of behavioural data (Catts & O'Toole, 2017; Cohen, Le, Fedechko, & Elvevåg, 2017; Elvevåg et al., 2017). In other words, the new NIMH RDoC framework necessitates different forms of data collection, and in terms of the language domain, uninterrupted speech samples for natural language processing are superior to dialogue from clinical interviews (Elvevåg et al., 2016).

Automatic analysis of natural speech from a clinical interview is a challenging endeavour.

In sum, analysing spontaneous speech in individuals with psychosis can reveal theory-relevant information and is potentially clinically useful in terms of providing information on state, fluctuations, risk of relapse/illness development, and prognosis (Bedi et al., 2015; Corcoran et al., 2018; Elvevåg, Foltz, Rosenstein, & DeLisi, 2010; Hirschberg, Hjalmarsson, & Elhadad, 2010; Rosenstein, Foltz, DeLisi, & Elvevåg, 2015). Remarkably, even in just the sounds of patients' voices, there are clues that are extremely valuable clinically. For example, a lack of vocal modulation across changing state is a potential indicator of a worsening clinical state. Thus, vocal recordings of these acoustic signals can be a critical component of monitoring in serious mental illness if these dynamic vocal signals are tracked over time with state-related variables (Cohen et al., 2019). However, in order to translate the 'potential' of spontaneous speech analysis into widely employed tools, considered core to the clinical process, full-scale randomised controlled trials are needed. These studies must compare newer speech assessment techniques to traditional methods. More critically, though, the numerous novel assays can be evaluated in terms of both specificity and sensitivity (i.e. calibrated), and their relationship to other data types (e.g. nonlanguage behavioural data, other medical data) can be modelled. These models will employ algorithms to 'weight' the different measurements so as to guide treatment choices by being a core component of a clinical decision support system to assist in risk evaluation and treatment prioritisation. Only at this point will the promise of these novel language metrics truly have clinical translation

[3] A challenge with any test that generates lots of information is to reduce this to summary values. The trained ear in some sense 'smooths' through such spoken speech and finds a meaningful average or prototype, so when leveraging technology we have to make such processes explicit by employing moving averages or something similar so as to smooth out noise.

value. To achieve large-scale implementation, careful consideration about practical, legal, and technical challenges in implementation of these speech tools is required (for further discussion, see Holmlund, Foltz, et al., 2019). Fig. 28.2 illustrates how such data can be collected (Fig. 28.2, Panel A); analysed (Fig. 28.2, Panel B); and then conveyed to clinicians and patients in a useful manner (Fig. 28.2, Panel C).

Towards 'Real-Time' Objective Assessment of Speech in Psychosis: The Requirements

COLLECTION

The steady progress of natural language processing tools holds great promise, increasing the possibility of implementing the methods currently being developed. However, there are requirements to the infrastructure that are needed to leverage such gains (for further details, see Holmlund, Foltz, et al., 2019). Recording and processing speech in a clinical or ambulatory setting will always necessitate great care, particularly in the context of patients with psychiatric disorders. A predictable environment with trust between patients and clinicians is vital to any diagnostic or therapeutic process. Therefore, any covert introduction of speech processing technology could have severely detrimental consequences to this trust. If introducing speech recording as a practical solution, it will be imperative to gain consent from the patient prior to any attempt to implement these new methods. As with any other novel research or clinical endeavour, care must be taken to explain this methodology to patients regarding the methods used for recording and processing of their voice, the right to refuse participation, and the right to withdraw consent and have their data deleted at any time. These patient rights' regarding the control and availability of their speech data are a nontrivial challenge to the current infrastructure of employing technology for speech assessment purposes.

After consent is obtained, capturing speech in a digital format starts with microphones. Equipping clinical facilities with high-quality microphones can be straightforward, but capturing real-time language use in individuals experiencing varied symptoms necessitates sophisticated methodology. Ambulatory assessment is a methodology being increasingly used to measure human experience in real-world settings, where personal mobile devices can be used for interactive testing and high-quality speech recordings. Generating records of clinically relevant behaviour outside of the controlled environment of institutions or laboratories can risk unpredictable situations, in particular with patients in the psychosis spectrum. Consider a hypothetical scenario with a spoken Stroop task, which only solicits naming the colour of ink (e.g. GREEN or RED) that the words are written in. However, just because that is the task specified does not prevent a participant from talking about other topics that will be also recorded, namely ones that could be highly sensitive or clinically very relevant (e.g. 'I feel like I want to kill myself right now!'). Thus this seemingly innocuous task has now resulted in highly sensitive data that requires real-time processing such that timely clinical intervention is possible. The automatic analysis of such data from

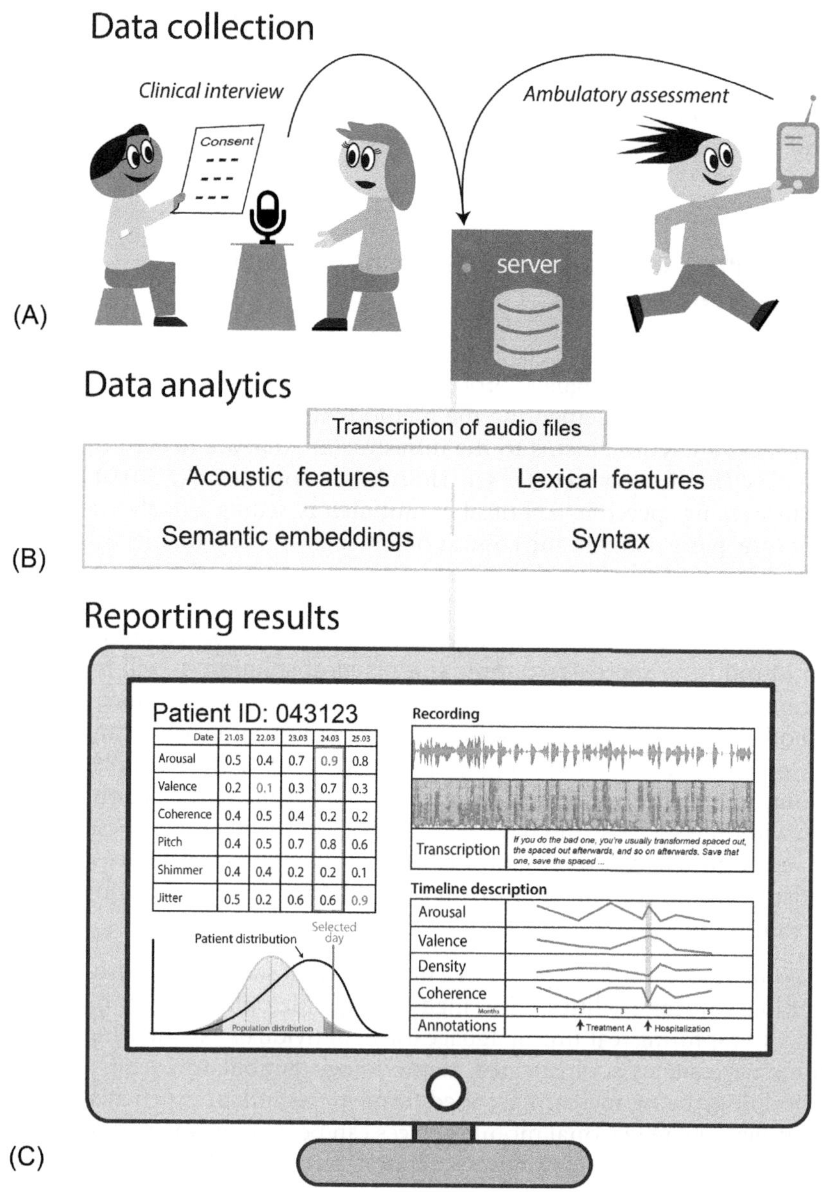

FIG. 28.2

Moving towards real time objective assessment of speech in psychosis requires collecting, analysing and reporting on speech data in a safe and useful manner.

Even seemingly innocuous audio recordings of patients can contain clinically sensitive information.

an analytic perspective is not straightforward as clearly the response has violated the task requirement (of naming ink colours).

The security of transferring, storing, and processing speech recordings with highly sensitive information is complex (Holmlund, Foltz, et al., 2019). Moving data across networks, in particular when using remote and internet-connected devices, requires carefully crafted procedures using encryption, strict access control, and a solid legal framework of contracts protecting the privacy of the users. Even so, there is no ready-made, permanent solution that can promise long-term safety from breaches, particularly across nations that have different standards, laws, and technologies. This is a continuous process that small research groups or clinics can be ill-equipped to handle over a long period of time without dedicated personnel. Beyond the available technical measures, it is essential that any such system is robust against problematic user behaviour. In short, it should not be possible for a patient to (either intentionally or unintentionally) misuse these speech assessment tools in a way that sensitive information is transferred somewhere inappropriate, or not to the clinician or researcher.

ANALYTICS

There has been rapid progress in the development of semantic analysis tools, in part, borne from private sector computer industries.

Computational methods for analysing speech are continuously evolving and providing increased precision and sophistication. To enable these methods, the raw data from microphones must be converted into digital format suited for quantitative analysis of relevant acoustic features, and speech must be transcribed into words for lexical, syntactical, and semantic analysis. While transcription traditionally has been a very labour intensive, the continuous efforts from both academic and commercial enterprises are encouraging, as many challenges that have been intractable now hold promise of fast and easily deployable solutions. For example, consider how companies such as Google have seemingly automated large-scale speech recognition, and made leveraging these tools fast and relatively easy via their internet connected services. This kind of progress, courtesy of the needs of the computer industry, has also been seen in the development of semantic analysis tools, borne out of efforts to understand the semantic relationships between words across languages, for improvement of translation tasks for computers. For the assessment of psychosis, these tools for quantifying semantic relationships are of particular importance, as they can be leveraged to measure the degree of speech that is off-topic or the degree to which a patient moves from topic to topic during discourse. Several aspects still need to be addressed, such as individual and cultural differences in the use of language. Acoustic analyses of the basic prosodic features of recordings (e.g. fundamental frequency, jitter, shimmer) provide valuable information about speaker arousal and emotional valence (Cohen et al., 2019; Cohen, Renshaw, Mitchell, Kim, 2016). The content and organisation of speech further provides information on semantics, lexical surface features, syntax, prosody, and quantity. Importantly, this technology has not been systematically evaluated in clinical populations; therefore, its clinical utility remains to be established. Individual and cultural differences in the language of individuals with psychosis remain a critical, and largely unexplored frontier of language research.

REPORTING

After data processing, the next crucial step to tracking language will be to provide real-time, clinically valuable feedback to both patients and clinicians. Depending on the clinical situation, a large array of measures described in this chapter may be relevant to track in patients with psychosis, taking care to not create a situation of information overflow and lack of utility for the clinician. This is a difficult balance to strike, and one where the understanding of best practice will continuously evolve based on the experience of researchers and clinicians along with the opportunities that technology and new analytic frameworks has to offer. This is particularly true if feedback is provided directly to patients—individuals who likely have limited formal training in psychometrics. While there are a variety of creative ways such information can be conveyed, it may be advisable to introduce new data in formats familiar to the clinicians: via tables and simple charts (see Fig. 28.2, Panel C). These formats will allow for a lower threshold of entry for incorporation of the novel language metrics into clinical workflows, but will put the onus on the developers of these methods to display the most relevant information. Current computer architecture is such that feedback variables can be provided in real time, to potentially save and enhance lives, translating the medical benefit of research 'bench to bedside' in a matter of minutes. However, to be able to provide individual and immediate feedback for research and clinical purposes, it is necessary to develop computer architectures, systems, algorithms, and network protocols to acquire, store, and analyse speech data. It will also be necessary to incorporate legal frameworks on data privacy and strike a good balance between protecting the individual's right to own data and society's need to access such data for research (for further discussion, see Holmlund, Foltz, et al., 2019). Once this secure infrastructure is in place, the research focus can be on establishing the methodology in clinical research to efficiently make use of such tools.

CONCLUSION

Language is a clinically useful medium for understanding a broad range of psychosis-related symptoms. Language is undeniably a core behavioural variable for understanding mental health and for measuring treatment responsiveness. Technology affords new methods to assist in the process of quantifying and thus tracking language behaviour, but these new tools must be empirically understood so as to be correctly interpreted. However, evaluations in clinical scenarios are based on observing combinations of both language and nonlanguage human behavior. Put differently, to correctly 'model the context' within which any behaviour occurs, we must also acknowledge that there are multiple data streams, which are clinically valuable (e.g. lexical, acoustic, semantic aspects of language). Any machine attempt to leverage technology for clinical purposes must thus also collate these multiple data streams. This is a remarkably complex statistical and computational requirement, and necessitates longitudinal research data in order to correctly 'weight' and interpret the data streams correctly for the different clinical conditions. The promise of personalised medicine must necessarily use both population norms and personalised norms. However, with continuous monitoring and the sheer volume of data that is possible, there is the unprecedented opportunity to add the temporal component to any personalised norm. In other words, mental and cognitive life is dynamic and thus baselines fluctuate massively. Finding a sensible way to establish clinical meaningful norms when the quantity of data available has exploded is no minor task, and it undoubtedly will be an exciting area of research. By solving these problems, we can envisage a day in the foreseeable future when for example we are capturing some signs of agitation (from the patient's verbal content and manner of speaking), and this is evident in real time on our futuristic desktop (see Fig. 28.2, Panel C). A skilled clinician who is familiar with these particular patients will naturally adjust the threshold of clinical intervention when judging the state of agitation. However, a future clinical decision support system could also provide such guidance but do so in combination (i.e. in context) with behavioural (and other) metrics to enable a tailored thresholding that matches both population statistics and an individualised threshold for that patient (i.e. a personalised medicine approach). This is of course a hypothetical example, but it is **the future** we envisage. Research is necessary to produce the longitudinal data that can confirm or disconfirm this type of conjecture, and thus inform the algorithms that will differentially 'weight' data types—including language—in any clinical decision support system.

QUIZ QUESTIONS

1. Which components of speech are often affected in individuals with psychosis (select all that apply)?
   a. Syntax
   b. Semantic-level information
   c. Lexical-level information
   d. Prosody
2. Spontaneous speech and its deviations in individuals with psychosis are:
   a. Trait-like and static
   b. State-like, dynamic, and context dependent
   c. Best measured only as a means to get information reported about symptoms and experiences (i.e. what someone says)
   d. Best measured as a behaviour that gives us information about how someone speaks in addition to information about symptoms conveyed in the content of the speech (i.e. what someone says)
3. What is Natural Language Processing?
   a. Comprehension of language by individuals with psychosis as it occurs in real time
   b. Using measures like the TLC to rate spontaneous speech deviations
   c. A broad method of leveraging computational power and technological advances to assess, understand, and model language
   d. Rating an individual's spontaneous speech sample for comprehensibility
4. What methods have been used to measure the real-time fluctuations in spontaneous speech in individuals with psychosis?
   a. Self-report questionnaires (e.g. MMPI, SPQ, PQ-B)
   b. Clinical ratings (e.g. TLC)
   c. Linguistic ratings (e.g. CDI)

5. Why is modelling real-time language in individuals with psychosis so difficult?
   a. Language is dynamic and context dependent
   b. There is a lot of information in spontaneous speech and we are only just beginning to be able to measure all of it
   c. Language greatly differs between individuals

ANSWERS TO QUIZ QUESTIONS:

1. (a, b, c, d)
2. (b, d)
3. (c)
4. None of the above
5. (a, b, c)

END-OF-CHAPTER SELF-DIRECTED LEARNING

1. If you are interested in learning more about natural language processing and latent semantic analysis in particular, visit http://lsa.colorado.edu/ and see how latent semantic analysis can be conducted.
2. Elvevåg, B., Cohen, A. S., Wolters, M. K., Whalley, H. C., Gountouna, V.-E., Kuznetsova, K. A., ... Nicodemus, K. K. (2016). An examination of the language construct in NIMH's research domain criteria: Time for reconceptualization! *American Journal of Medical Genetics Part B: Neuropsychiatric Genetics, 171*(6), 904–919. https://doi.org/10.1002/ajmg.b.32438.
3. Holmlund, T.B., Foltz, P.W., Cohen, A.S., Johansen, H.D., Sigurdsen, R., Fugelli, P., ... Elvevåg, B. (2018). Moving psychological assessment out of the controlled laboratory setting and into the hands of the individual: Practical challenges. *Psychological Assessment* (in press).

Acknowledgments

We are grateful for useful discussions with numerous collaborators, notably Drs. Peter W. Foltz, Jared Bernstein, and Jian Cheng.
Funding: This project was funded, in part, by grant #231395 from the Research Council of Norway awarded to Brita Elvevåg.

References

American Psychiatric Association. (2013). *Diagnostic and statistical manual of mental disorders (DSM-5)*. Arlington, VA: American Psychiatric Publishing.

Andreasen, N. C. (1983). *The scale for the assessment of negative symptoms (SANS)*. Iowa City, IA: The University of Iowa.

Andreasen, N. C. (1984). *Scale for the assessment of positive symptoms (SAPS)*. Iowa City, IA: The University of Iowa.

Andreasen, N. C. (1986). Scale for the assessment of thought, language, and communication (TLC). *Schizophrenia Bulletin, 12*(3), 473–482. https://doi.org/10.1093/schbul/12.3.473.

Andreasen, N. C., & Grove, W. M. (1986). Thought, language, and communication in schizophrenia: Diagnosis and prognosis. *Schizophrenia Bulletin, 12*(3), 348–359. https://doi.org/10.1093/schbul/12.3.348.

Awad, A. G., & Voruganti, L. N. P. (2000). Intervention research in psychosis: Issues related to the assessment of quality of life 1. *Schizophrenia Bulletin, 26*(3), 557–564. https://doi.org/10.1093/oxfordjournals.schbul.a033477.

Bedi, G., Carrillo, F., Cecchi, G. A., Slezak, D. F., Sigman, M., Mota, N. B., et al. (2015). Automated analysis of free speech predicts psychosis onset in high-risk youths. *NPJ Schizophrenia, 1*, 15030. https://doi.org/10.1038/npjschz.2015.30.

Ben-Porath, Y. S., & Tellegen, A. (2008). *MMPI-2 RF: Minnesota multiphasic personality inventory-2 restructured form: Hand scoring starter kit with 5 softcover test booklets.* Minneapolis, MN: University of Minnesota Press.

Bleuler, E. (1950). *Dementia praecox or the group of schizophrenias.* Oxford, England: International Universities Press.

Brown, C., Snodgrass, T., Kemper, S. J., Herman, R., & Covington, M. A. (2008). Automatic measurement of propositional idea density from part-of-speech tagging. *Behavior Research Methods, 40*(2), 540–545. https://doi.org/10.3758/BRM.40.2.540.

Cancro, R. (1969). Prospective prediction of hospital stay in schizophrenia. *Archives of General Psychiatry, 20*(5), 541–546. https://doi.org/10.1001/archpsyc.1969.01740170045006.

Catts, S. V., & O'Toole, B. (2017). Raising the standard of care in the treatment of schizophrenia: Yes we can! *Australian and New Zealand Journal of Psychiatry, 51*(515), 438–440. https://doi.org/10.1177/0004867417700278.

Chandler, C., Foltz, P. W., Cheng, J., Bernstein, J. C., Rosenfeld, E. P., Cohen, A. S., et al. (2019). Overcoming the bottleneck in traditional assessments of verbal memory: Modeling human ratings and classifying clinical group membership. In K. Niederhoffer, K. Hollingshead, P. Resnik, R. Resnik, & K. Loveys (Eds.), *Proceedings of the sixth workshop on computational linguistics and clinical psychology. Minneapolis, MN, USA, June,* (pp. 137–147). https://www.aclweb.org/anthology/W19-3016.

Cheng, J., Bernstein, J., Rosenfeld, E., Foltz, P. W., Cohen, A. S., Holmlund, T. B., et al. (2018). Modeling self-reported and observed affect from speech. In *Proceedings Interspeech 2018, Hyderabad, India, September 2018* (pp. 3653–3657). https://doi.org/10.21437/Interspeech.2018-2222.

Cohen, A. S., Alpert, M., Nienow, T. M., Dinzeo, T. J., & Docherty, N. M. (2008). Computerized measurement of negative symptoms in schizophrenia. *Journal of Psychiatric Research, 42*(10), 827–836. https://doi.org/10.1016/j.jpsychires.2007.08.008.

Cohen, A. S., & Elvevåg, B. (2014). Automated computerized analysis of speech in psychiatric disorders. *Current Opinion in Psychiatry, 27*(3), 203–209. https://doi.org/10.1097/YCO.0000000000000056.

Cohen, A. S., Fedechko, T. L., Schwartz, E. K., et al. (2019). Ambulatory vocal acoustics, temporal dynamics, and serious mental illness. *Journal of Abnormal Psychology, 128*(2), 97–105. https://doi.org/10.1037/abn0000397.

Cohen, A. S., Kim, Y., & Najolia, G. M. (2013). Psychiatric symptom versus neurocognitive correlates of diminished expressivity in schizophrenia and mood disorders. *Schizophrenia Research, 146* (1–3), 249–253. https://doi.org/10.1016/j.schres.2013.02.002.

Cohen, A. S., Le, T. P., Fedechko, T. L., & Elvevåg, B. (2017). Can RDoC help find order in thought disorder? *Schizophrenia Bulletin, 43*(3), 503–508. https://doi.org/10.1093/schbul/sbx030.

Cohen, A. S., Mitchell, K. R., Docherty, N. M., & Horan, W. P. (2016). Vocal expression in schizophrenia: Less than meets the ear. *Journal of Abnormal Psychology, 125*(2), 299–309. https://doi.org/10.1037/abn0000136.

Cohen, A. S., Renshaw, T. L., Mitchell, K. R., & Kim, Y. (2016). A psychometric investigation of "macroscopic" speech measures for clinical and psychological science. *Behavior Research and Methods, 48*(2), 475–486. https://doi.org/10.3758/s13428-015-0584-1.

Corcoran, C. M., Carrillo, F., Fernández-Slezak, D., Bedi, G., Klim, C., Javitt, D. C., et al. (2018). Prediction of psychosis across protocols and risk cohorts using automated language analysis. *World Psychiatry, 17*(1), 67–75. https://doi.org/10.1002/wps.20491.

Covington, M. A., & McFall, J. D. (2010). Cutting the Gordian knot: The moving-average type–token ratio (MATTR). *Journal of Quantitative Linguistics, 17*(2), 94–100. https://doi.org/10.1080/09296171003643098.

Cowan, T., Le, T. P., Elvevåg, B., Foltz, P. W., Tucker, R. P., Holmlund, T. B., et al. (2018). Comparing static and dynamic predictors of risk for hostility in serious mental illness: Preliminary findings. *Schizophrenia Research, 204*, 432–433. https://doi.org/10.1016/j.schres.2018.08.030.

Docherty, N. M. (2012). On identifying the processes underlying schizophrenic speech disorder. *Schizophrenia Bulletin, 38*(6), 1327–1335. https://doi.org/10.1093/schbul/sbr048.

Docherty, N. M., DeRosa, M., & Andreasen, N. C. (1996). Communication disturbances in schizophrenia and mania. *Archives of General Psychiatry, 53*(4), 358–364. https://doi.org/10.1001/archpsyc.1996.01830040094014.

Dunn, J., Almeida, O., Barclay, L., Waterreus, A., & Flicker, L. (2002). Latent semantic analysis: A new method to measure prose recall. *Journal of Clinical and Experimental Neuropsychology, 24*(1), 26–35. https://doi.org/10.1076/jcen.24.1.26.965.

Elvevåg, B., Cohen, A. S., Wolters, M. K., Whalley, H. C., Gountouna, V.-E., Kuznetsova, K. A., et al. (2016). An examination of the language construct in NIMH's research domain criteria: Time for reconceptualization! *American Journal of Medical Genetics Part B: Neuropsychiatric Genetics, 171*(6), 904–919. https://doi.org/10.1002/ajmg.b.32438.

Elvevåg, B., Foltz, P. W., Rosenstein, M., & DeLisi, L. E. (2010). An automated method to analyze language use in patients with schizophrenia and their first-degree relatives. *Journal of Neurolinguistics, 23*(3), 270–284. https://doi.org/10.1016/j.jneuroling.2009.05.002.

Elvevåg, B., Foltz, P. W., Rosenstein, M., Ferrer-i-Cancho, R., De Deyne, S., Mizraji, E., et al. (2017). Thoughts about disordered thinking: Measuring and quantifying the laws of order and disorder. *Schizophrenia Bulletin, 43*(3), 509–513. https://doi.org/10.1093/schbul/sbx040.

Elvevåg, B., Foltz, P. W., Weinberger, D. R., & Goldberg, T. E. (2007). Quantifying incoherence in speech: An automated methodology and novel application to schizophrenia. *Schizophrenia Research, 93*(1–3), 304–316. https://doi.org/10.1016/j.schres.2007.03.001.

Foltz, P. W., Kintsch, W., & Landauer, T. K. (1998). The measurement of textual coherence with latent semantic analysis. *Discourse Processes, 25*(2–3), 285–307. https://doi.org/10.1080/01638539809545029.

Foltz, P. W., Rosenstein, M., & Elvevåg, B. (2016). Detecting clinically significant events through automated language analysis: Quo imus? *NPJ Schizophrenia, 2*(1), 15054. https://doi.org/10.1038/npjschz.2015.54.

Fromkin, V. A., Rodman, R., & Hyams, N. (2007). *An introduction to language* (8th ed.). Boston, MA: Thomson Wadsworth.

Granholm, E., Ben-Zeev, D., Fulford, D., & Swendsen, J. (2013). Ecological momentary assessment of social functioning in schizophrenia: Impact of performance appraisals and affect on social interactions. *Schizophrenia Research, 145*(1–3), 120–124. https://doi.org/10.1016/J.SCHRES.2013.01.005.

Granholm, E., Loh, C., & Swendsen, J. (2007). Feasibility and validity of computerized ecological momentary assessment in schizophrenia. *Schizophrenia Bulletin, 34*(3), 507–514. https://doi.org/10.1093/schbul/sbm113.

Harrow, M., & Quinlan, D. M. (1985). *Disordered thinking and schizophrenic psychopathology*. New York, NY: Gardner Press.

Harvey, P. D., Earle-Boyer, E. A., & Wielgus, M. S. (1984). The consistency of thought disorder in mania and schizophrenia: An assessment of acute psychotics. *The Journal of Nervous and Mental Disease, 172*(8), 458–463. https://doi.org/10.1097/00005053-198408000-00003.

Hirschberg, J., Hjalmarsson, A., & Elhadad, N. (2010). "You're as sick as you sound": Using computational approaches for modeling speaker state to gauge illness and recovery. In *Advances in speech recognition: Mobile environments, call centers and clinics* (pp. 305–322). Boston, MA: Springer.

Hoffman, R. E., Kirstein, L., Stopek, S., & Cicchetti, D. V. (1982). Apprehending schizophrenic discourse: A structural analysis of the Listener's task. *Brain and Language, 15*(2), 207–233. https://doi.org/10.1016/0093-934X(82)90057-8.

Holmlund, T. B., Cheng, J., Foltz, P. W., Cohen, A. S., Bernstein, J., Rosenfeld, E., et al. (2019). Automated analysis of speech in a remotely administered Stroop test. Manuscript submitted for publication.

Holmlund, T. B., Cheng, J., Foltz, P. W., Cohen, A. S., & Elvevåg, B. (2019). Updating verbal fluency analysis for the 21st century: Applications for psychiatry. *Psychiatry Research, 273*, 767–769. https://doi.org/10.1016/j.psychres.2019.02.014.

Holmlund, T. B., Foltz, P. W., Cohen, A. S., Johansen, H., Sigurdsen, R., Fugelli, P., et al. (2019). Moving psychological assessment out of the controlled laboratory setting: Practical challenges. *Psychological Assessment, 31*(3), 292–303. https://doi.org/10.1037/pas0000647.

Insel, T. R. (2010). Rethinking schizophrenia. *Nature, 468*(7321), 187–193. https://doi.org/10.1038/nature09552.

Insel, T. R. (2017). Digital phenotyping: Technology for a new science of behavior. *JAMA: The Journal of the American Medical Association, 318*(13), 1215–1216. https://doi.org/10.1001/jama.2017.11295.

Insel, T. R., Cuthbert, B., Garvey, M., Heinssen, R., Pine, D. S., Quinn, K., et al. (2010). Research domain criteria (RDoC): Toward a new classification framework for research on mental disorders. *American Journal of Psychiatry, 167*, 748–751. https://doi.org/10.1176/appi.ajp.2010.09091379.

Joseph, A. J., Tandon, N., Yang, L. H., Duckworth, K., Torous, J., Seidman, L. J., et al. (2015). #Schizophrenia: Use and misuse on Twitter. *Schizophrenia Research, 165*(2–3), 111–115. https://doi.org/10.1016/J.SCHRES.2015.04.009.

Junghaenel, D., Smyth, J., & Santner, L. (2008). Linguistic dimensions of psychopathology: A quantitative analysis. *Journal of Social and Clinical Psychology, 27*(1), 36–55. https://doi.org/10.1521/jscp.2008.27.1.36.

Kay, S. R., Fiszbein, A., & Opler, L. A. (1987). The positive and negative syndrome scale (PANSS) for schizophrenia. *Schizophrenia Bulletin, 13*(2), 261–276. https://doi.org/10.1093/schbul/13.2.261.

Kita, S. (Ed.)., (2003). *Pointing: Where language, culture, and cognition meet.* New York, NY: Psychology Press.

Kraepelin, E. (1919). *Dementia praecox and paraphrenia.* Chicago, IL: Chicago Medical Book.

Liddle, P. F., Ngan, E. T., Caissie, S. L., Anderson, C. M., Bates, A. T., Quested, D. J., et al. (2002). Thought and language index: An instrument for assessing thought and language in schizophrenia. *British Journal of Psychiatry, 181*, 326–330.

Linscott, R. J. (2005). Thought disorder, pragmatic language impairment, and generalized cognitive decline in schizophrenia. *Schizophrenia Research, 75*(2), 225–232. https://doi.org/10.1016/J.SCHRES.2004.10.007.

Loewy, R. L., Pearson, R., Vinogradov, S., Bearden, C. E., & Cannon, T. D. (2011). Psychosis risk screening with the prodromal questionnaire-brief version (PQ-B). *Schizophrenia Research, 129*(1), 42–46. https://doi.org/10.1016/j.schres.2011.03.029.

Lukoff, D., Liberman, R. P., & Nuechterlein, K. H. (1986). Symptom monitoring in the rehabilitation of schizophrenic patients. *Schizophrenia Bulletin, 12*(4), 578–602. https://doi.org/10.1093/schbul/12.4.578.

MacLeod, C. M. (1991). Half a century of research on the Stroop effect: An integrative review. *Psychological Bulletin, 109*(2), 163–203. https://doi.org/10.1037/0033-2909.109.2.163.

McKenna, P. J., & Oh, T. M. (2005). *Schizophrenic speech: Making sense of bathroots and ponds that fall in doorways.* Cambridge, UK: Cambridge University Press.

Minor, K. S., Davis, B. J., Marggraf, M. P., Luther, L., & Robbins, M. L. (2018). Words matter: Implementing the electronically activated recorder in schizotypy. *Personality Disorders, Theory, Research, and Treatment, 9*(2), 133–143. https://doi.org/10.1037/per0000266.

Morey, L. C. (1991). *Personality assessment inventory.* Odessa, FL: Psychological Assessment Resources. Retrieved from: http://www4.parinc.com/WebUploads/samplerpts/PAI32.pdf.

Murray, H. A. (1943). *The thematic apperception test manual.* Cambridge, MA: Harvard University Press.

Pennebaker, J. W., Mehl, M. R., & Niederhoffer, K. G. (2003). Psychological aspects of natural language use: Our words, our selves. *Annual Review of Psychology, 54*(1), 547–577. https://doi.org/10.1146/annurev.psych.54.101601.145041.

Pinker, S. (2003). *The language instinct.* London, UK: Penguin.

Podsakoff, P. M., MacKenzie, S. B., Lee, J.-Y., & Podsakoff, N. P. (2003). Common method biases in behavioral research: A critical review of the literature and recommended remedies. *The Journal of Applied Psychology, 88*(5), 879–903. https://doi.org/10.1037/0021-9010.88.5.879.

Poeppel, D., Idsardi, W. J., & Van Wassenhove, V. (2008). Speech perception at the interface of neurobiology and linguistics. *Philosophical Transactions of the Royal Society of London B: Biological Sciences, 363*(1493), 1071–1086. https://doi.org/10.1098/rstb.2007.2160.

Ragin, A. B., & Oltmanns, T. F. (1987). Communicability and thought disorder in schizophrenics and other diagnostic groups: A follow-up study. *The British Journal of Psychiatry, 150*(4), 494–500. https://doi.org/10.1192/BJP.150.4.494.

Raine, A. (1991). The SPQ: A scale for the assessment of schizotypal personality based on DSM-III-R criteria. *Schizophrenia Bulletin, 17*(4), 555–564. https://doi.org/10.1093/schbul/17.4.555.

Raugh, I. M., Chapman, H. C., Bartolomeo, L. A., Gonzalez, C., & Strauss, G. P. (2019). A comprehensive review of psychophysiological applications for ecological momentary assessment in psychiatric populations. *Psychological Assessment 31*(3), 304.

Rorschach, H. (1942). *Psychodiagnostics.* Oxford, England: Grune and Stratton.

Rosenstein, M., Diaz-Asper, C., Foltz, P. W., & Elvevåg, B. (2014). A computational language approach to modeling prose recall in schizophrenia. *Cortex, 55,* 148–166. https://doi.org/10.1016/j.cortex.2014.01.021.

Rosenstein, M., Foltz, P. W., DeLisi, L. E., & Elvevåg, B. (2015). Language as a biomarker in those at high-risk for psychosis. *Schizophrenia Research, 165*(2), 249–250. https://doi.org/10.1016/j.schres.2015.04.023.

Rush, A., First, M., & Blacker, D. (2008). *Handbook of psychiatric measures* (2nd ed.). Washington, DC: American Psychiatric Association Publishing.

Rutter, D. R., Wishner, J., Kopytynska, H., & Button, M. (1978). The predictability of speech in schizophrenic patients. *The British Journal of Psychiatry, 132*(3), 228–232. https://doi.org/10.1192/S000712500028327X.

Solovay, M. R., Shenton, M. E., Gasperetti, C., Coleman, M., Kestnbaum, E., Carpenter, J. T., et al. (1986). Scoring manual for the thought disorder index. *Schizophrenia Bulletin, 12*(3), 483–496. https://doi.org/10.1093/schbul/12.3.483.

Strous, R., Koppel, M., Fine, J., Nachliel, S., Shaked, G., & Zivotofsky, A. (2009). Automated characterization and identification of schizophrenia in writing. *Journal of Nervous and Mental Disease, 197*(8), 585–588. https://doi.org/10.1097/NMD.0b013e3181b09068.

Taylor, W. L. (1953). "Cloze procedure": A new tool for measuring readability. *Journalism Bulletin, 30*(4), 415–433. https://doi.org/10.1177/107769905303000401.

Tellegen, A., & Ben-Porath, Y. S. (2011). *MMPI-2-RF: Minnesota multiphasic personality inventory-2 restructured form: Technical manual.* Minneapolis, MN: University of Minnesota Press.

Wang, R., Aung, M. S., Abdullah, S., Brian, R., Campbell, A. T., Choudhury, T., et al. (2016). CrossCheck: Toward passive sensing and detection of mental health changes in people with schizophrenia. In *ACM International Joint Conference on Pervasive and Ubiquitous Computing, Heidelberg, Germany, September 2016* (pp. 886–897). https://doi.org/10.1145/2971648.2971740.

Warren, P. (2012). *Introducing psycholinguistics.* Cambridge, UK: Cambridge University Press.

Wechsler, D. (1945). *Wechsler memory scale.* San Antonio, TX: Psychological Corporation.

Whitehorn, J. C., & Zipf, G. K. (1943). Schizophrenic language. *Archives of Neurology and Psychiatry, 49* (6), 831–851. https://doi.org/10.1001/archneurpsyc.1943.02290180055006.

Wood, J. M., Lilienfeld, S. O., Garb, H. N., & Nezworski, M. T. (2000). The Rorschach test in clinical diagnosis: A critical review, with a backward look at Garfield (1947). *Journal of Clinical Psychology, 56*(3), 395–430. https://doi.org/10.1002/(SICI)1097-4679(200003)56:3<395::AID-JCLP15>3.0.CO;2-O.

World Health Organization. (2018). *The ICD-11 classification of mental and behavioural disorders: Clinical descriptions and diagnostic guidelines.* Geneva, Switzerland: World Health Organization.

Wynne, L. C., & Singer, M. T. (1963). Thought disorder and family relations of schizophrenics: II. A classification of forms of thinking. *Archives of General Psychiatry, 9*(3), 199–206. https://doi.org/10.1001/archpsyc.1963.01720150009002.

Definition of Key Terms

ALOGIA A CLINICAL SYMPTOM ASSOCIATED WITH REDUCED SPEECH PRODUCTION.

Actigraphy Digital measurement of an individual's physical activity, such as through recording of geolocation, motor activity, or movement using a sensor.

Anhedonia A clinical symptom characterised by a deficit in the ability to experience, recall, process, or report pleasurable experiences.

Coherence A linguistic quality characterised by consistency and clarity.

Digital phenotyping A methodology measuring individual differences of various psychologically relevant phenomenon using objective data derived from interactions with digital technology, such as computationally derived linguistic indices.

Echolalia A clinical symptom characterised by repetition of sounds or linguistic qualities of vocalisations made by other speakers.

Language A system of symbolic communication for use between organisms.

Lexical A linguistic quality focused on word-level units.

Neologisms A clinical symptom characterised by the use of 'new' words created by the speaker that are confusing to the listener.

Pressured speech A clinical symptom characterised by inappropriately rapid speech production.

Psycholinguistics The study of the psychological utility and development of language.

Research Domain Criteria (RDoC) An initiative by the United States' National Institute of Mental Health, focused on explicating mental disorders across levels of complexity within the central nervous system (i.e. from genes to behaviour).

Schizotypy A set of genetically and environmentally mediated traits associated with the latent, yet often unexpressed, risk for developing schizophrenia-spectrum disorders.

Syntax A quality of language associated with the arrangement of words and phrases.

Semantics A quality of language focused on its symbolic meaning.

CHAPTER 29

Integrating Lived Experience Perspectives Into Clinical Practice

Catherine van Zelst[*,†,‡]

[*]Department of Psychiatry and Neuropsychology, User Research Centre, Maastricht University, Maastricht, The Netherlands, [†]Institute for Mental Health Care Eindhoven (GGzE), Eindhoven, The Netherlands, [‡]Mental Health First Aid (MHFA), Eindhoven, The Netherlands

Key Learning Objectives

- To learn more about the implications of lived experience perspectives in clinical care.
- To learn about peer support and ways of implementation.
- To learn about incorporating both consumer and provider perspectives into practice.
- To learn from participatory research on mental health and psychosis.

INTRODUCTION

This chapter highlights the benefits of turning personal experience with psychosis into something valuable for peers, their significant others, and mental health professionals. We will look at the characteristics and consequences of optimal implementation of lived experiences and peer support for clinical practice. Findings apply to people with mental illness in general, and people with psychosis in particular. The chapter starts with describing developments in mental health, hereby focusing on the consumer movement and the recovery movement. The power of first-person accounts and reports of lived experience are described for peer support. Elements of peer support are explained and examples of peer support initiatives are given. The use of participatory research, a driving force to emancipate the consumer and recovery movement, is described. At the end of the chapter, recommendations for mental health professionals are offered for optimising destigmatising and recovery-oriented practice and treatment for people with psychosis. We also look at the disclosure dilemma of mental health professionals with respect to their own lived experience.

A Clinical Introduction to Psychosis. https://doi.org/10.1016/B978-0-12-815012-2.00029-8

HISTORICAL BACKGROUND OF A MOVEMENT

'Nothing About Us Without Us'[1]

Various mental health movements around the world precede recent advances focusing on recovery and recovery-oriented care, as advocated by the recovery movement.

For example, Gumber and Stein (2013) describe four major mental health movements in the United States: the deinstitutionalisation movement of the early 1960s, the community support movement of the 1970s, the consumer/survivor movement of the 1980s, and the current recovery movement. These four mental health reform movements developed as a response to the social, economic, and political environment of their time in history (Gumber & Stein, 2013).

The ongoing gap between the individual's needs and mental health services motivates the recovery movement.

In the 1980s, people on the receiving end of mental health and psychiatric services began to be seen as 'consumers', giving them the right to make choices and be involved in the kind of services that are offered. Because of the gap between needs and services, some people began to present themselves as 'survivors' of psychiatry, of specific services, or of the distress related to the illness itself (Wallcraft & Nettle, 2009).

Peer support workers have their own wealth of experience with mental illness.

Gumber and Stein (2013), examining 69 published first-person accounts written by adults with schizophrenia from 1979 to 2010 within the historical context of the four major mental health movements mentioned, found a lack of significant differences in the themes of first-person accounts over the years. They concluded that this seemed to indicate that social barriers and treatment obstacles for people who cope with schizophrenia had not substantially changed over these three decades, and that this indicated a failure of the successive mental health movements to meaningfully address challenges faced by people diagnosed with schizophrenia (Gumber & Stein, 2013). Implementing lived experience in mental health care, e.g. by means of peer support, may address such challenges and create opportunities for destigmatisation and recovery-oriented care. Moreover, there are numerous examples of programs designed to reduce stigma, which involve people with lived experience. The voices of people with lived experience can have the power to stimulate mental health services to be more aware and supportive of dignity in mental health (Ziedonis, Larkin, & Appasani, 2016).

WHAT IS IMPORTANT (AND WHY?)

Lived Experience, Language, and Concepts

LIVED EXPERIENCE

Adults involved in the mental health system over many years of their lives can be viewed as informal historians of community mental health care (Stein et al., 2015).

[1]This slogan advocates the idea that no policy should be decided by any representative without the full and direct participation of members of the group(s) affected by that policy (Wikipedia).

First-person accounts on the topic of mental health and illness can be used as valuable insights for mental health professionals. The attention to lived experience of people with psychosis is growing. Knowledge about lived experience of psychotic symptoms gives insight into subjective and at the same time invisible or concealable experiences. For most people, it is difficult to imagine what it is like to experience paranoia, while experiences of hearing voices or other hallucinations may be difficult to grasp. However, psychotic experiences are basic human experiences that can occur in the 'general population'.

LANGUAGE

The framing of 'schizophrenia' (or serious mental illness in general) as a pervasive handicap of which recovery is impossible, leads to mental health professionals who are alienated from what people with these illnesses experience. In mental health care, diagnosing people is most often part of 'treatment as usual'. Therefore, it is of high importance to acknowledge that whether we talk about people with schizophrenia spectrum disorder as 'having symptoms' or as 'persons with psychotic experiences' or, stigmatising, as 'schizophrenics' can make a huge difference: terms that have stigmatising connotations can be hurtful, while adjusting language use to the person can positively contribute to the therapeutic relationship and quality of treatment in general. Emphasising the roles that are, or have been, significant for the individual in his or her daily life can be normalising and empowering; attention to both new roles (e.g. a new job or other daily activities after an episode of psychosis) or roles one already had (e.g. being a relative) is clearly needed. Emphasising roles can also contribute to destigmatisation, because the focus of an individual changes accordingly with illness or psychotic experiences starting to be a smaller part of their perceived identity.

Language is powerful: being mindful of what we say can promote a positive approach to psychosis.

Another aspect in language use is the influence of bias. The bias that occurs in mental health professionals may also occur in peer supporters and any other person. As Deegan notes (2017), '...We need to always be learning about our biases and preconceptions so that we can bracket or suspend them rather than imposing them on our peers. As peer supporters, we care deeply about the lived experience of our peers. We use their words and strive to see the world through their eyes. This allows us to enter into deep dialogue and connection.' (Deegan, 2017).

Furthermore, individuals can have difficulty conveying what they are experiencing, which is problematic for relationships, in general, but is especially evident in interactions with providers of health care. Individuals with schizophrenia are at risk of feeling disempowered and misunderstood and, therefore, not helped (Walsh, Hochbrueckner, Corcoran, & Spence, 2016).

'Each Narrative Counts'

Narratives on mental health give direct insight into experiences of psychopathology, and on how to cope with these.

At the same time, thousands of first-person accounts of recovery resound with courage, resilience, and achievement. The belief that recovery is possible for everyone does significantly contribute to hope by the individual. The most critical channel for the development of a recovery paradigm is provided by the writings and activism of psychiatric 'survivors', e.g. Chamberlin (1978), Deegan (1988, 1992), Fisher (1994); O'Hagan (1991) (see Piat & Sabetti, 2009).

CONCEPTS

Peer Support

Davidson, Chinman, Sells, and Rowe (2006) conceptualised peer support as involving one or more persons who have a history of mental illness and who have experienced significant improvements in their psychiatric condition offering services and/or supports to other people with serious mental illness who are considered to be not as far along in their own recovery process. Peer support is based on the belief that people with experience of adversity (having faced, endured, and overcome this) can offer useful support, encouragement, hope, and perhaps mentorship to others facing similar situations (Davidson et al., 2006). Peer support may be an important asset in modern mental health care. Three types of peer support services for individuals with serious mental illness are distinguished: (1) Peers added to traditional services; (2) Peers in existing clinical roles; and (3) Peers delivering structured curricula (Chinman et al., 2014). Repper et al. (2013) explain core principles of peer support. It is important for peer support to be mutual, reciprocal, nondirective, recovery focused, strengths based, progressive, and safe. Over the last years, interventions delivered by peer support workers have gained popularity and have been included in policy guidance (Stubbs, Williams, Shannon, Gaughran, & Craig, 2016). However, despite the promotion and uptake of peer support internationally, there is little evidence from current trials about the effectiveness of peer support for people with severe mental illness (Lloyd-Evans et al., 2014). Whilst a metaanalysis by Lloyd-Evans et al. (2014) indicated there is negligible support for the effectiveness of peer support, there is some encouraging evidence that peer support has small effects on constructs related to internalised stigma (Pyle, Pilling, Machin, Allende-Cullen, & Morrison, 2018).

From another perspective, peer-to-peer interactions may have positive effects in specific contexts. Individuals with psychotic disorders can value and benefit from digital interventions that include moderated peer-to-peer interactions. Incorporating peer-to-peer communication into digital interventions may increase compliance with other evidence-based therapies by producing more acceptable and engaging online environments (Biagianti, Quraishi, & Schlosser, 2018).

In any type of peer support, it is important to address challenges of working as a peer-support provider, including role conflict, boundaries, disclosure of peer status, role ambiguity, low compensation, and limited hours of work (Miyamoto & Sono, 2012).

Recovery

Recovery is not a linear process.

When thinking about recovery, it is important to note that recovery is not a linear process; e.g. although people may relapse to, or stabilise in, a certain phase of their recovery process, they can progress after this as well. In a study with experts by experience aimed to establish consensus about the meaning of recovery among individuals with experience of psychosis, regarding definitions of recovery, the highest level of consensus was reached for 'recovery is the achievement of a personally acceptable quality of life' and 'recovery is feeling better about yourself'. Notably, participants did not feel that factors such as reduced hospitalisation or relapses were essential for demonstrating recovery (Law & Morrison, 2014).

Moreover, in recovery processes, the concept of hope is of the utmost importance. Results from a study of Hasson-Ohayon, Kravetz, Meir, and Rozencwaig (2009) suggest that increasing the hope of persons with schizophrenia may directly and positively increase both their quality of life and the usefulness of their insight into their illness. On the other hand, it is important for practitioners to be able to acknowledge hopelessness among patients and to work with them from their existing situation (Hayes, Herrman, Castle, & Harvey, 2017).

Hope bolsters the recovery process for mental illness.

Empowerment

Empowerment refers to the level of choice, influence, and control that users of mental health services can exercise over events (or experiences) in their lives (User empowerment in mental health—A statement by the WHO Regional Office for Europe, 2010). Empowerment can be individual and collective. Individual or personal empowerment can be considered as the opposite of self-stigma (internalised stigma) (Corrigan & Lundin, 2001). In the domain of mental health, empowerment can be seen as a process of the individual with mental health complaints, but also as a process of relatives or other significant others who may be subject to stigma by association (Ostman & Kjellin, 2002). Importantly, to 'be empowered', a person or group requires an environment that provides options and ascribes authority to the person to choose. Moreover, empowerment is affected by the subjective reality of the person, e.g. a person could have many options, but their *perception* of the options may be much more limited (Rapp & Goscha, 2006, p. 27).

Experiential Knowledge and Experiential Expertise

Experts by experience and peer support workers implement experiential knowledge in daily life in order to help others with similar experiences. Experiential knowledge includes experiences of mental health problems, the meaning people give to their problems and strategies developed to handle these. All individual stories together form collective experiential knowledge: knowledge about how it is to live with mental vulnerability and its consequences. Being capable of passing on this knowledge to others in any form points to experiential expertise (Boevink, 2017, p. 95). This has become an increasingly valued element of service design and delivery by mental health service providers (Oates, Drey, & Jones, 2017).

Everyone with mental illness develops experiential knowledge.

Dignity and Respect

Obviously, dignity is at the core of psychological well-being, social connection, and humanity. Both in clinical practice and research, mental health interventions that explicitly promote and preserve dignity for people experiencing mental distress are growing. Advocating for dignity for people with mental distress and isolation requires a redoubling of effort to engage someone who may feel disconnected, to communicate even when someone seems uncomprehending, and to connect when someone's perceptions and understanding are different from one's own (Ziedonis et al., 2016). Attention for sensitivity and respect for each individual's values, beliefs, and culture, such as in recovery-oriented mental health practice, is also needed: it challenges discrimination and stigma wherever it exists (National standards for mental health services 2010. Principles of recovery oriented mental health practice, 2010).

Social Inclusion

Promoting social inclusion can diminish stigma as a 'second disease'.

A socially inclusive approach includes recovery-oriented practice, an emphasis on social outcomes and participation, and also attention to the rights of people with mental ill health, as well as to citizenship, equality, and justice, and the problems of stigma and discrimination (Royal College of Psychiatrists. Position statement. Mental health and social inclusion. Making psychiatry and mental health services fit for the 21st century, 2009).

Self-Determination

Self-determination requires individuals' rights to control the direction of their lives and their treatment free from undue external influence. Of course, this includes the right to exercise control in the planning of services and supports (Tondora, Miller, Slade, & Davidson, 2014).

The Individual's Choice and Shared Decision Making

Shared Decision Making (SDM) in mental health care involves clinicians and service users working together to make decisions. Slade notes that it is worth addressing the complex issues relating to power, control, expertise, and valued knowledge, because SDM has the potential to contribute to supporting people to live as well as possible in communities of their own choosing (Slade, 2017).

The Purpose

'A VOICE AND A CHOICE'

Lived experience, experiential knowledge, and experiential expertise can contribute to the field of mental health.

The concepts explained here point to the purpose of the movement and represent current trends. Lived experience, experiential knowledge, and experiential expertise can contribute to self-help; to making sure that clinical and recovery-oriented care reflect consumer goals; to making a change in the mental health system; and to making a change in society. All these elements can add significantly to the quality of life of people with psychotic experiences and their significant others as well.

The Need for Involving People With Lived Experience

Historically, service users have not been given meaningful roles in research and change efforts related to the services they use. This is changing as scholars and a growing number of funding bodies now call for greater consumer involvement in mental health services research and improvement (Case et al., 2014). The primary purposes of involvement of people with first-hand experience in mental health research are improving the quality, relevance, and utility of research, and impacting on the lives of service users (Davidson, Ridgway, Schmutte, & O'Connell, 2009).

Transformation can occur in the exchange of and combining of different knowledge bases. The development of local knowledge using participatory processes to understand the different lived experience perspectives of clinicians, consumers, and carers provides the key to service development in recovery-oriented care (Kidd, Kenny, & McKinstry, 2015).

HOW CAN THIS BE REALISED?

Peer Support Work

One of the routes in which lived experience and experiential knowledge can contribute to goals of the movement is via the work of peer workers. Peer workers offer different types of support, including emotional support (empathy and camaraderie); informational support (connections to information and referrals to community resources that support health and wellness); instrumental support (concrete supports such as housing or employment); affiliational support (connections to community supports, activities, and events) (SAMHSA Infographic. Peers supporting recovery from mental health conditions, 2017); being there, being present, being an individual with your own lived experiences (independent of certification or job / job description); normalisation; being a model both for people with psychotic experiences and professionals; advocacy; destigmatisation; increasing resilience; and emphasising civil rights.

Peer workers may offer many different types of support.

According to Mahlke, Kramer, Becker, and Bock (2014), crucial issues for implementation include the clarification of role and job description of peer support workers and nonpeer staff, organisational support strategies, training and adequate supervision. This does not mean that people without, e.g. clarification of role and job description can't do meaningful work supported by their experiential expertise. In any case, in a world of perceived categories (also in the domain of peer support), simply being there for each other, listening, connectedness, belonging, and addressing humanity are of the utmost importance. The effects of receiving peer support are broad and include not only clinical effects, such as improved quality of life or decreased hospitalisation rate, but also personal and emotional effects, such as feelings of understanding or trust (Miyamoto & Sono, 2012). Using peers to provide support to consumers at this stage of their recovery seems highly effective as an adjunct to mainstream mental health services, since it has personal benefit to consumers and peers, substantial savings to systems, as well as much potential for encouraging mental health service culture and practice towards a greater recovery focus and improved collaboration with general practitioners (Lawn, Smith, & Hunter, 2008).

Participatory Research

Lived experience can be addressed in peer support work, participatory research, advocacy, and political action.

An essential core value of any research about peer working is that it is grounded in and co-designed by people with lived experience (Pyle et al., 2018). Participatory approaches support the inclusion of perspectives of lived experience (Kidd et al., 2015). The differences between consumers and researchers in priorities for research and outcome measurement are one of the reasons why consumers should be involved in all phases of research. Consumer involvement is already especially critical at the beginning phases of research, when priorities are set and outcome measures are selected, although involvement at the analysis phase is also necessary to ensure consistency of interpretations with consumer experience (Del vecchio & Blyler, 2009). A participatory research project undertaken by people with schizophrenia under the guidance of a university researcher is described by Schneider et al. (2004). The results indicate that good communication with professionals is essential to people with schizophrenia; it helped them accept the fact that they are ill and learn to live with the illness. The research offered a transformative experience to group members and is contributing to change in the practice of health care for people with severe mental illnesses. Participatory research involves the members of the research group in meaningful participation in all stages of the research process, including developing the research question, gathering the data, analysing the data, and disseminating and using the results (Schneider et al., 2004). Benefits and challenges of involving service users in research are described by Faulkner (2009). Note that, in participatory research, it is important to avoid bias (e.g. when blinding is not possible) and tokenism.

Both benefits and challenges should be acknowledged in working with people with lived experience.

According to Russo and Stastny (2009), some of the necessary conditions and suggestions for roles that we could all take in moving towards true research partnerships are: (1) Start from scratch instead of pretending equality exists; (2) Create standards of collaboration; and (3) Position users/survivor researchers strategically in funding agencies, institution review/ethics boards, and grant review committees, rather than merely engaging them as consultants, data collectors, or co-investigators (Russo & Stastny, 2009).

Advocacy and Political Action

Mental health advocacy involves actions to improve relevant social, community, and service systems to reduce stigma and discrimination. It has been led by people with mental disorders and carers, but also involves the cooperation of providers of health services as well as members of the broader community (Gee & McGarty, 2013). Note that user involvement is often introduced into policy and practice as something, which intrinsically reduces the inequalities between service users and professionals, while, if inequalities are not addressed as part of the process, involvement itself can perpetuate injustice, reinforcing lack of respect, lack of power, and lack of resources. It can cause isolation of service users, instead of provision of opportunities for their mutual support and empowerment. Equal user involvement in strategic decision making requires going beyond creating arenas of participation. It is important to ensure that service users' structural disadvantages are addressed in order to enable their equal participation in the decisions that affect their lives (McDaid, 2009).

INCORPORATING CONSUMER AND PROVIDER PERSPECTIVES INTO PRACTICE

The question may rise how to incorporate all relevant knowledge and expertise, from both consumer and provider perspectives, into practice. In the following, an overview is given of incorporating consumer priorities and values, and addressing power imbalances, stigma, and self-disclosure among professionals.

Incorporating Consumer Priorities

Neglecting consumers' views of priorities in treatment can hinder recovery.

Clinicians and patients may differ concerning the goals of treatment. Clinicians should carefully take into consideration patients' preferences, e.g. because neglect of consumers' views may compromise outcome and adherence to treatment (Moritz, Berna, Jaeger, Westermann, & Nagel, 2017). In a study by Moritz et al. (2017), participants with schizophrenia considered the treatment of affective and cognitive problems as more important than the treatment of positive symptoms. Remarkably, this was also true for those with elevated positive symptoms. In ideal situations, treatment is evidence-based and takes into consideration service users' preferences. Clinicians often face the dilemma that what is effective, such as antipsychotics, is not always liked, and what is liked, such as Art Therapy, does not always yield strong effects (Moritz et al., 2017).

Insight into preferences, satisfaction, and treatment goals of patients is important for reaching treatment alliance and may increase the success of initiated treatment. In a study by Sterk, Winter van Rossum, Muis, and De Haan (2013), respondents ranked their treatment *preferences* regarding treatment content. Items ranked most important were 'prompt assistance, preferably in own environment', 'attention for medication', 'appropriate attitude of the professional caregiver'. Following this, psychiatric services should pay great attention to early outpatient intervention with supportive counselling and an appropriate attitude of the caregiver with attention for medication use. Also, improvement is warranted for practical assistance, help in regaining autonomy, and help with physical health (Sterk et al., 2013).

Values and a Scientist–Practitioner-Based Profession

By combining aspects of the recovery policy with evidence from the science of positive psychology there are increasing attempts to include strengths and values work with mental health staff and consumers. Oades and Anderson (2012) describe how the collaborative recovery model (CRM), with its emphasis on strengths and values, draws on the emerging evidence based on positive psychology.

Essential life goals of people with psychotic experiences may not differ from those without these experiences.

Not every mental health professional realises that people receiving mental health services want essentially the same things out of life that practitioners do—a home, family, faith, a sense of purpose, health, and other such things. However, 'recovery' for mental health service users should involve pretty much the same things that mental health service practitioners see as being a part of their own well-being and quality of life. Recovery-oriented and person-centred care is about getting past this 'us/them' dynamic to truly partner with people in recovery in their efforts to attain their personally defined and valued goals (Tondora et al., 2014, p. 4).

Mental health professionals have to be aware of the role they have in the eyes of their service users.

Outcomes for people with mental illness need to include the expectations and aspirations shared by all humans instead of just lower-order thresholds or standards commonly valued in the human service system, such as stability, compliance, and satisfaction with services. Valued, enduring relationships, opportunities for community membership, and economic security are reasonable expectations for everyone, no matter how severe or disabling a condition one may have (Tondora et al., 2014).

Addressing Power Imbalances

> We all need to take a deep breath and look to our personal and collective strengths without putting down others in the process
>
> **Epstein (2013)**

Power can be seen as part authority and part confidence or perception of authority. A person can have the formal authority to make a choice or decision but may perceive they do not have that authority or they do not have the confidence to select. The perception or subjective reality of many clients, however, is that the authority is vested in mental health personnel (Rapp & Goscha, 2006, p. 27)—a topic which, in relevant situations, can be addressed in treatment and care.

Stigma and Disclosure Among Professionals

Both service users and mental health professionals may have to deal with disclosure decisions.

Moreover, mental health professionals are not free from stigma (as discussed in Chapter 3). Becoming more aware of own prejudice can help in the therapeutic relationship in clinical care and can also contribute to recovery-oriented care. Furthermore, mental health professionals who are not labelled with a diagnosis, and therefore, are not marginalised in the same way, might be able to influence inequities to support consumers (Happell & Scholz, 2018).

When mental health professionals do have (a diagnosis of) mental health problems, the topic of self-disclosure may arise. All practicing clinical and neuropsychologists (and other mental health professionals) need to be familiar with, and follow the relevant regulatory guidelines on self-disclosure in their place of work. Various theoretical orientations have different perspectives on the appropriateness of therapist self-disclosure (Knox & Hill, 2003). Knox and Hill (2003) give suggestions with respect to self-disclosure, such as Use therapist self-disclosure because it is a helpful intervention, but use it infrequently and judiciously;

Box 29.1 Reflective Questions for Mental Health Professionals

A colleague tells you about his or her own prior lived experience with psychosis and suggests that telling this to patients with psychotic experiences may have positive consequences in the domain of treatment.

- Does it matter whether your colleague's experiences are with psychosis or another mental illness (burn-out, anxiety, depression)?
- How do you feel about people with lived experience participating in mental health care (as a peer support worker or other mental health professional)?
- Are there any enabling or hindering factors in your work environment that you perceive (and are these changing for the worse/better)?
- What are the professional and/or regulatory requirements in your workplace in relation to notification of mental health problems?

Use appropriate content in therapist self-disclosures; Use appropriate levels of intimacy in therapist self-disclosures; Fit the disclosure to the particular client's needs and preferences; Have appropriate reasons for self-disclosing; and Return the focus to the client after therapist self-disclosure (Knox & Hill, 2003).

A study by Miller and McNaught (2018) explored how experienced cognitive behaviour therapy (CBT) practitioners make decisions around therapist self-disclosure. There were two overarching themes in terms of how they made decisions to self-disclose: (A) the *rules* for therapist self-disclosure (TSD) use (subthemes: (a) it must have a clear purpose, (b) it must fit, (c) the therapist must maintain boundaries, and (d) the therapist must always reflect on his/her use of TSD) and (B) *how* they use TSD (subthemes: (a) using it as a tool for change and (b) using it to manage the therapeutic relationship).

In terms of deciding what information to self-disclose, research suggest the decision is influenced by ethical considerations, personal comfort with self-disclosure, previous experiences of TSD either as therapist or client, the norms of colleagues, and the therapist's theoretical orientation (Miller & McNaught, 2018). Some reflective questions on disclosure are listed in Box 29.1.

WHAT ARE GOOD EXAMPLES OF PEER SUPPORT?

Disclosure Decisions: Honest, Open, Proud

Honest, Open, Proud (HOP) is a peer-led group program that supports participants with mental illness in their disclosure decisions (Coming Out Proud Program, 2011–2012; Mulfinger et al., 2018). As disclosure decisions depend on the setting and are very individual, HOP discusses levels of disclosure, settings of disclosure, and how to choose persons to disclose to. Importantly, it is not HOP's aim to push participants towards disclosure, but to empower them to make their own decision (Mulfinger et al., 2018). There is, indeed, a range of strategic approaches to disclosure (see Corrigan & Lundin, 2001).

Preferred approach of disclosure can vary with context.

Peer Support Groups

Peer support groups are a valuable service and resource that brings together people affected by a similar concern so that they are able to explore solutions to overcome shared challenges and feel supported by others who have had similar experiences (Creating peer support groups in mental health and related areas. WHO QualityRights training to act, unite and empower for mental health, 2017). Castelein et al. (2008) showed that guided peer support groups are a useful intervention for people suffering from psychosis by enabling and strengthening mutual relationships.

Peer support groups can provide an opportunity to reduce isolation and enhance the process of personal recovery; it encourages people to express their thoughts, feelings, and personal concerns in a peer-to-peer learning environment. While the evidence base is promising, the field could benefit from more rigorous, pragmatic trials with follow-up measurements to establish a solid evidence base (Castelein, Bruggeman, Davidson, & van der Gaag, 2015). Stubbs et al. (2016) concluded that there is inconsistent evidence to support the use of peer support workers to improve the physical health and promote lifestyle change among people with serious mental illness, noting that the small sample sizes, heterogeneity of interventions, outcome measures, and lack of clarity about the unique contribution of PSW means no definitive conclusions can be made about the benefits of PSW and physical health in SMI.

It is important to know what interventions are effective for individuals, subgroups, or all people with psychosis.

Hearing voices peer support groups can offer a powerful alternative to mainstream psychiatric approaches for understanding and coping with states typically diagnosed as 'hallucination' in a similar way (Dillon & Hornstein, 2013). A study by Beavan, De Jager, and Dos Santos (2017) on peer-support groups for voice hearers contributes to the small but growing literature on peer-supported interventions for psychosis and psychotic-like experiences.

Wellness Recovery Action Planning: WRAP

WRAP explores key values of recovery, such as hope, personal responsibility, education, self-advocacy, and support, and provides a structured process for developing individualised WRAP plans (Copeland, 2002 in Pratt, MacGregor, Reid, & Given, 2013). Pratt et al. (2013) studied the WRAP (Wellness Recovery Action Planning) approach, which was found to be very relevant and appeared to have a positive impact on many of the participants (Pratt et al., 2013).

DISCUSSION AND CONCLUSION: WHAT IS THE FUTURE?

Lived experience with psychosis can be valuable for consumers, their significant others, and mental health professionals. For consumers, feeling understood and connected with other people can improve by addressing experiential knowledge. For significant others, experiences of consumers can point the way on how to treat and approach people with similar mental health complaints in their daily life. In both significant others and mental health professionals, knowledge of and insight into mental health complaints in general, and psychotic experiences specifically, may increase. Experiential expertise can also be incorporated by presence of peers and initiatives of peer support in and outside mental health organisations.

While it may seem like the narratives of people with psychosis are more useful for gaining understanding in schizophrenia spectrum disorder than narratives of people with other symptoms, there are also many things that these narratives on mental illness can share: People with any mental illness all hope that they can recover, many want to feel connected or feel that they belong, do useful activities in their daily life, etc. Including people with lived experience in mental health care and participatory research can be empowering by itself and has multiple other advantages, including increasing understanding of phenomena treated or studied and setting better priorities. Mental health professionals can collaborate with people with lived experience to optimise treatment.

In this chapter, we discussed narratives, peer support, participatory research, and advocacy and political action. The implementation of these and of experiential expertise per se will likely continue to grow in the future. While there is not one way of implementing experiential expertise, there are certain issues that have to be considered, like degree of implementation of expertise (what is needed and what can be offered?), and timing and appropriateness of self-disclosure by mental health professionals.

Looking into ways of collaborating with each other is very important for optimising care. If there are barriers in the working environment, ways should be found to diminish these. When we want to include lived experience perspectives into care, a first goal to achieve is making the working environment as destigmatising and open as possible. Looking at one's own prejudice (it seems likely that everyone is prejudiced to a certain degree) can help in increasing awareness of these and changing possible stigmatising behaviour and reducing the chance of iatrogenic stigma.

To implement lived experience perspectives, we have to diminish stigma and taboo of mental illness.

Foremost, collaboration between people with lived experience and mental health professionals can increase our understanding of what psychotic experiences (and psychosis) and the best treatment approaches are.

RECOMMENDED READINGS

(1) Corrigan, P., & Lundin, R. (2001). *Don't call me nuts! coping with the stigma of mental illness.* USA: Recovery Press.

(2) Tondora, J., Miller, R., Slade, M., & Davidson, L. (2014). *Partnering for recovery in mental health. A practical guide to person-centered planning.* UK: John Wiley & Sons.

(3) Peterson, D., & Gordon, S. (2009). *Stepping out of the shadows. Insights into self-stigma and madness.* New Zealand: Pindar NZ.

(4) Wikipedia. n.d. Nothing about us without us. Retrieved from: https://en.wikipedia.org/wiki/Nothing_About_Us_Without_Us

References

Beavan, V., De Jager, A., & Dos Santos, B. (2017). Do peer-support groups for voice-hearers work? A small scale study of Hearing Voices Network support groups in Australia. *Psychosis, 9*(1), 57–66.

Biagianti, B., Quraishi, S. H., & Schlosser, D. A. (2018). Potential benefits of incorporating peer-to-peer interactions into digital interventions for psychotic disorders: A systematic review. *Psychiatric Services, 69*(4), 377–388. https://doi.org/10.1176/appi.ps.201700283.

Boevink, W. (2017). *Planting a tree. On recovery, empowerment and experiential expertise.* (PhD thesis), Utrecht. Retrieved from: https://assets.trimbos.nl/docs/c5077090-73e0-4c2e-b329-84921ce5ff32.pdf.

Case, A. D., Byrd, R., Claggett, E., DeVeaux, S., Perkins, R., Huang, C., et al. (2014). Stakeholders' perspectives on community-based participatory research to enhance mental health services. *American Journal of Community Psychology, 54*(3–4), 397–408. https://doi.org/10.1007/s10464-014-9677-8.

Castelein, S., Bruggeman, R., Davidson, L., & van der Gaag, M. (2015). Creating a supportive environment: Peer support groups for psychotic disorders. *Schizophrenia Bulletin, 41*(6), 1211–1213. https://doi.org/10.1093/schbul/sbv113.

Castelein, S., Bruggeman, R., van Busschbach, J. T., van der Gaag, M., Stant, A. D., Knegtering, H., et al. (2008). The effectiveness of peer support groups in psychosis: A randomized controlled trial. *Acta Psychiatrica Scandinavica, 118*, 64–72.

Chamberlin, J. (1978). *On our own: Patient-controlled alternatives in the mental health system.* New York: Hawthorn Books.

Chinman, M., George, P., Dougherty, R. H., Daniels, A. S., Ghose, S. S., Swift, A., et al. (2014). Peer support services for individuals with serious mental illnesses: Assessing the evidence. *Psychiatric Services, 65*(4), 429–441. https://doi.org/10.1176/appi.ps.201300244.

Coming Out Proud Program (2011–2012). Retrieved from: http://comingoutproudprogram.org/.

Copeland, M. E. (2002). Overview of WRAP: Wellness recovery action plan. *Mental Health Recovery Newsletter, 3*, 1–9.

Corrigan, P., & Lundin, R. (2001). *Don't call me nuts! Coping with the stigma of mental illness.* USA: Recovery Press.

Creating peer support groups in mental health and related areas. WHO QualityRights training to act, unite and empower for mental health (2017). Retrieved from: http://apps.who.int/iris/bitstream/handle/10665/254813/WHO-MSD-MHP-17.13-eng.pdf;jsessionid=1EDCD71C8D238F3B5F4E89F4994581BE?sequence=1.

Davidson, L., Chinman, M., Sells, D., & Rowe, M. (2006). Peer support among adults with serious mental illness: A report from the field. *Schizophrenia Bulletin, 32*(3), 443–450. https://doi.org/10.1093/schbul/sbj043.

Davidson, L., Ridgway, P., Schmutte, T., & O'Connell, M. (2009). Purposes and goals. In J. Wallcraft, B. Schrank, & M. Amering (Eds.), *Handbook of service user involvement in mental health research* (pp. 87–98). UK: John Wiley & Sons.

Deegan, P. (2017). *The roots of lived experience and peer support.* Retrieved from: https://www.patdeegan.com/blog/posts/roots-lived-experience-and-peer-support.

Deegan, P. E. (1988). Recovery: The lived experience of rehabilitation. *Psychiatric Rehabilitation Journal, 11*(4), 11–19.

Deegan, P. E. (1992). The independent living movement and people with psychiatric disabilities. Taking back control over our own lives. *Psychiatric Rehabilitation Journal, 15*, 5–19.

Del vecchio, P., & Blyler, C. R. (2009). Topics. In J. Wallcraft, B. Schrank, & M. Amering (Eds.), *Handbook of service user involvement in mental health research* (pp. 99–112). UK: John Wiley & Sons.

Dillon, J., & Hornstein, G. A. (2013). Hearing voices peer support groups: A powerful alternative for people in distress. *Psychosis, 5*(3), 286–295.

Epstein, M. (2013). *The consumer movement in Australia: A memoir of an old campaigner.* Melbourne, Our Consumer Place. Retrieved from: www:ourcommunity.com.au/files/OCP/HistoryOfConsumerMovement.pdf.

Faulkner, A. (2009). Principles and motives for service user involvement in mental health research. In J. Wallcraft, B. Schrank, & M. Amering (Eds.), *Handbook of service user involvement in mental health research* (pp. 13–24). UK: John Wiley & Sons.

Fisher, D. B. (1994). A new vision of healing as constructed by people with psychiatric disabilities working as mental health providers. *Psychiatric Rehabilitation Journal, 17*(3), 67–81.

Gee, A., & McGarty, C. (2013). Aspirations for a cooperative community and support for mental health advocacy: A shared orientation through opinion-based group membership. *Journal of Applied Social Psychology, 43*, E426–E441.

Gumber, S., & Stein, C. H. (2013). Consumer perspectives and mental health reform movements in the United States: 30 years of first-person accounts. *Psychiatric Rehabilitation Journal, 36*(3), 187–194. https://doi.org/10.1037/prj0000003.

Happell, B., & Scholz, B. (2018). Doing what we can, but knowing our place: Being an ally to promote consumer leadership in mental health. *International Journal of Mental Health Nursing, 27*(1), 440–447. https://doi.org/10.1111/inm.12404.

Hasson-Ohayon, I., Kravetz, S., Meir, T., & Rozencwaig, S. (2009). Insight into severe mental illness, hope, and quality of life of persons with schizophrenia and schizoaffective disorders. *Psychiatry Research, 167*(3), 231–238. https://doi.org/10.1016/j.psychres.2008.04.019.

Hayes, L., Herrman, H., Castle, D., & Harvey, C. (2017). Hope, recovery and symptoms: The importance of hope for people living with severe mental illness. *Australasian Psychiatry, 25*(6), 583–587. https://doi.org/10.1177/1039856217726693.

Kidd, S., Kenny, A., & McKinstry, C. (2015). The meaning of recovery in a regional mental health service: An action research study. *Journal of Advanced Nursing, 71*(1), 181–192. https://doi.org/10.1111/jan.12472.

Knox, S., & Hill, C. E. (2003). Therapist self-disclosure: Research-based suggestions for practitioners. *Journal of Clinical Psychology: In Session, 59*, 529–539.

Law, H., & Morrison, A. P. (2014). Recovery in psychosis: A Delphi study with experts by experience. *Schizophrenia Bulletin, 40*(6), 1347–1355.

Lawn, S., Smith, A., & Hunter, K. (2008). Mental health peer support for hospital avoidance and early discharge: An Australian example of consumer driven and operated service. *Journal of Mental Health, 17*(5), 498–508.

Lloyd-Evans, B., Mayo-Wilson, E., Harrison, B., Istead, H., Brown, E., Pilling, S., et al. (2014). A systematic review and meta-analysis of randomised controlled trials of peer support for people with severe mental illness. *BMC Psychiatry, 14*, 39. https://doi.org/10.1186/1471-244X-14-39.

Mahlke, C. I., Kramer, U. M., Becker, T., & Bock, T. (2014). Peer support in mental health services. *Current Opinion in Psychiatry, 27*(4), 276–281. https://doi.org/10.1097/YCO.0000000000000074.

McDaid, S. (2009). An equality of condition framework for user involvement in mental health policy and planning: Evidence from participatory action research. *Disability & Society, 24*(4), 461–474.

Miller, E., & McNaught, A. (2018). Exploring decision making around therapist self-disclosure in cognitive behavioural therapy. *Australian Psychologist, 53*, 33–39.

Miyamoto, Y., & Sono, T. (2012). Lessons from peer support among individuals with mental health difficulties: A review of the literature. *Clinical Practice and Epidemiology in Mental Health, 8*, 22–29.

Moritz, S., Berna, F., Jaeger, S., Westermann, S., & Nagel, M. (2017). The customer is always right? Subjective target symptoms and treatment preferences in patients with psychosis. *European Archives of Psychiatry and Clinical Neuroscience, 267*(4), 335–339.

Mulfinger, N., Muller, S., Boge, I., Sakar, V., Corrigan, P. W., Evans-Lacko, S., et al. (2018). Honest, open, proud for adolescents with mental illness: Pilot randomized controlled trial. *Journal of Child Psychology and Psychiatry, 59*(6), 684–691. https://doi.org/10.1111/jcpp.12853.

National standards for mental health services 2010. Principles of recovery oriented mental health practice. (2010). Retrieved from: http://www.health.gov.au/internet/publications/publishing.nsf/Content/mental-pubs-n-servst10-toc~mental-pubs-n-servst10-pri.

Oades, L. G., & Anderson, J. (2012). Recovery in Australia: Marshalling strengths and living values. *International Review of Psychiatry, 24*(1), 5–10. https://doi.org/10.3109/09540261.2012.660623.

Oates, J., Drey, N., & Jones, J. (2017). 'Your experiences were your tools'. How personal experience of mental health problems informs mental health nursing practice. *Journal of Psychiatric and Mental Health Nursing, 24*(7), 471–479. https://doi.org/10.1111/jpm.12376.

O'Hagan, M. (1991). *Stopovers on my way home from Mars.* Auckland, NZ: New Moon Press.

Ostman, M., & Kjellin, L. (2002). Stigma by association: Psychological factors in relatives of people with mental illness. *The British Journal of Psychiatry, 181*, 494–498.

Piat, M., & Sabetti, J. (2009). The development of a recovery-oriented mental health system in Canada: What the experience of commonwealth countries tells us. *Canadian Journal of Community Mental Health, 28*(2), 17–33. https://doi.org/10.7870/cjcmh-2009-0020.

Pratt, R., MacGregor, A., Reid, S., & Given, L. (2013). Experience of wellness recovery action planning in self-help and mutual support groups for people with lived experience of mental health difficulties. *ScientificWorldJournal, 2013*. https://doi.org/10.1155/2013/180587.

Pyle, M., Pilling, S., Machin, K., Allende-Cullen, G., & Morrison, A. P. (2018). Peer support for internalised stigma experienced by people with psychosis: Rationale and recommendations. *Psychosis, 10*(2), 146–152.

Rapp, C. A., & Goscha, R. J. (2006). *The strengths model. Case management with people with psychiatric disabilities* (2nd ed.). New York: Oxford University Press.

Repper, J., Aldridge, B., Gilfoyle, S., Gillard, S., Perkins, R., & Rennison, J. (2013). *Peer support workers: Theory and practice.* London: Implementing Recovery Through Organisational Change.

Royal College of Psychiatrists. Position statement. Mental health and social inclusion. Making psychiatry and mental health services fit for the 21st century (2009). Retrieved from: https://www.rcpsych.ac.uk/pdf/social%20inclusion%20position%20statement09.pdf.

Russo, J., & Stastny, P. (2009). Beyond involvement: Looking for a common perspective on roles in research. In J. Wallcraft, B. Schrank, & M. Amering (Eds.), *Handbook of service user involvement in mental health research* (pp. 61–72). UK: John Wiley & Sons.

SAMHSA Infographic. Peers supporting recovery from mental health conditions (2017). Retrieved from: https://www.samhsa.gov/sites/default/files/programs_campaigns/brss_tacs/peers-supporting-recovery-mental-health-conditions-2017.pdf.

Schneider, B., Scissons, H., Arney, L., Benson, G., Derry, J., Lucas, K., et al. (2004). Communication between people with schizophrenia and their medical professionals: A participatory research project. *Qualitative Health Research, 14*(4), 562–577. https://doi.org/10.1177/1049732303262423.

Slade, M. (2017). Implementing shared decision making in routine mental health care. *World Psychiatry, 16*(2), 146–153. https://doi.org/10.1002/wps.20412.

Stein, C. H., Leith, J. E., Osborn, L. A., Greenberg, S., Petrowski, C. E., Jesse, S., et al. (2015). Mental health system historians: Adults with schizophrenia describe changes in community mental health care over time. *The Psychiatric Quarterly, 86*(1), 33–48. https://doi.org/10.1007/s11126-014-9325-3.

Sterk, B., Winter van Rossum, I., Muis, M., & De Haan, L. (2013). Priorities, satisfaction and treatment goals in psychosis patients: An online consumer's survey. *Pharmacopsychiatry, 46*(3), 88–93. https://doi.org/10.1055/s-0032-1327732.

Stubbs, B., Williams, J., Shannon, J., Gaughran, F., & Craig, T. (2016). Peer support interventions seeking to improve physical health and lifestyle behaviours among people with serious mental illness: A systematic review. *International Journal of Mental Health Nursing, 25*(6), 484–495. https://doi.org/10.1111/inm.12256.

Tondora, J., Miller, R., Slade, M., & Davidson, L. (2014). *Partnering for recovery in mental health. A practical guide to person-centered planning.* UK: John Wiley & Sons.

User empowerment in mental health—A statement by the WHO Regional Office for Europe (2010). Retrieved from: http://www.euro.who.int/__data/assets/pdf_file/0020/113834/E93430.pdf.

Wallcraft, J., & Nettle, M. (2009). History, context and language. In J. Wallcraft, B. Schrank, & M. Amering (Eds.), *Handbook of service user involvement in mental health research* (pp. 1–11). UK: John Wiley & Sons.

Walsh, J., Hochbrueckner, R., Corcoran, J., & Spence, R. (2016). The lived experience of schizophrenia: A systematic review and meta-synthesis. *Social Work in Mental Health, 14*(6), 607–624.

Ziedonis, D., Larkin, C., & Appasani, R. (2016). Dignity in mental health practice & research: Time to unite on innovation, outreach & education. *The Indian Journal of Medical Research, 144*(4), 491–495. https://doi.org/10.4103/0971-5916.200885.

Definition of Key Terms

Lived experience in the domain of mental health consists of the individual's experiences with mental health and illness and recovery, as well as the experiences of their significant others.

Participatory research involves planning and conducting research with people whose experiences are under study.

Peer support consists of different types of support and services one or more persons with past or present experiences with mental illness offer to others with mental health problems.

Consumer movement refers to an association of individuals with experience with mental health problems and mental health services.

Self-disclosure is communication with respect to revealing information about yourself to another person or group of persons.

Index

Note: Page numbers followed by *f* indicate figures and *t* indicate tables.

D

E

F

L

M

N

T

9780128150122